CW01667100

Ibbs and Tillett: The Rise and Fall of a Musical Empire

For my mother

and in memory of my father,

who always enjoyed a good long read

Ibbs and Tillett: The Rise and Fall of a Musical Empire

CHRISTOPHER FIFIELD

ASHGATE

© Christopher Fifield, 2005

All rights reserved. No part of this publication may be reproduced, stored in a retrieval system, or transmitted in any form or by any means, electronic, mechanical, photocopying, recording or otherwise, without the prior permission of the publisher.

Christopher Fifield has asserted his moral right under the Copyright, Designs and Patents Act, 1988, to be identified as the author of this work.

Published by
Ashgate Publishing Limited
Gower House
Croft Road
Aldershot
Hants GU11 3HR
England

Ashgate Publishing Company
Suite 420
101 Cherry Street
Burlington, VT 05401-4405
USA

Ashgate website: http://www.ashgate.com

British Library Cataloguing in Publication Data

Fifield, Christopher
Ibbs and Tillett : the rise and fall of a musical empire
1. Ibbs and Tillett (Firm) – History 2. Concert agents – Great Britain – History
I. Title
338.7'6178

Library of Congress Cataloging-in-Publication Data

Fifield, Christopher.
Ibbs and Tillett : the rise and fall of a musical empire / Christopher Fifield.
p. cm.
Includes bibliographical references (p.) and index.
ISBN 1-84014-290-1 (alk. paper)
1. Ibbs and Tillett. 2. Concert agents – England – Biography. I. Title.

ML406.I23F54 2004
780'.92'2–dc22 2004001823

ISBN 1 84014 290 1

Printed on acid-free paper

Typeset in Garamond by Express Typesetters Ltd, Farnham, Surrey
Printed and bound in Great Britain by TJ International, Padstow, Cornwall

Contents

Appendices

Plates

Preface

During the course of selecting photographs for my biography of the conductor Hans Richter (*True Artist and True Friend*, Clarendon Press, 1993), I was advised to contact the late Wilfred Stiff, former Managing Director of Ibbs and Tillett. He invited me to his home in the summer of 1990 and showed me boxes of papers, brochures, letters and photographs, which he had kept safe from loss and damage as the agency made two moves during its final years from its long-established premises at 124 Wigmore Street. Ibbs and Tillett had ceased its operations just three years earlier (by which time Wilfred was no longer in charge), and while its reputation as Britain's best known concert agency was still fresh, a decade later, as we approach the centenary of its founding, a new generation of musicians has never heard of it. Ibbs remains rather overshadowed because it was a Tillett (Emmie) who continued to head the firm for a further half century after his death. Having unearthed a splendid photograph of the seated Richter holding a score of *Die Meistersinger*, Wilfred then proceeded to show me the rest of the archive in more detail, and informed me of more material stored in tea chests in a warehouse on the outskirts of London. He also revealed his intention of writing this history, but sadly death intervened in 1996, and so the task fell to me as a result of a commission from the Tillett Trust. Fortunately half the name of Ibbs and Tillett lives on with the Tillett Trust, a charitable organization dedicated to helping young musicians. It was founded with a generous gift from Emmie Tillett, and offers modest one-off grants to young professional classical musicians in the early stages of their performing careers, and goes a small way towards filling the financial gap when educational bursaries have stopped and professional fees are only intermittently forthcoming. Typical projects which attract funding are short-term performing courses, specialist coaching prior to performance of new repertoire, or travel costs to participate in international competitions, while funds are specifically not available for educational courses, purchase of instruments, commissioning of new works or commercial recordings.

The Tillett archive contains fascinating material, and will be of interest to scholars of many aspects of the music profession, in particular its performance practice and social context in the last years of the nineteenth century and throughout the whole of the twentieth. Letters lie at the heart of the material, but there are also three unique audition books recording the successes and (largely) failures of aspiring singers and a few instrumentalists, cumbersome ledgers recording the minutiae of fees and details of engagements, annually issued artist brochures (an incomplete run, but starting in 1906), photographs, contracts, programmes, newspaper cuttings and various ephemera, all of it in variable condition and extremely haphazard in terms of its consistency. There are large gaps, and the nearer one gets to the last years so the amount of extant material disappointingly decreases, sometimes limiting itself to the tax affairs of visiting foreign artists or detailed correspondence between the agency and its foreign counterparts regarding overseas tours and concerts by British artists. Something for everyone would therefore appear to be a precise summary of the content of the archive, and at the time of writing, its final location has yet to be decided.

The structure of the book is chronological. Starting with the concert agent Narciso Vert (Tillett's uncle and Richter's manager, hence the request for the photograph) it traces the fortunes of the agency which was created after his unexpected death in 1905, and proceeds in blocks of years per chapter covering artists, events and letters, depending upon the quantity of available material. For reasons of length, the formal greeting and signing-off of each letter has generally been topped and tailed, spelling and grammar has been tweaked here and there, although in the case of those from foreigners (complete with their quaint, charming and sometimes colourful English) they have been left in their original form with no editorial [*sic*] to interrupt the flow. All letters originally written in foreign languages have been translated by the author. Pedro Tillett's unpublished memoir is a rough and ready, somewhat disjointed manuscript, but hopefully judicious editing has produced some interesting results. There are many appendices containing a variety of material, such as letters from Edward Elgar, Sergei Rachmaninov, Myra Hess and Kathleen Ferrier which proved too numerous to appear in the body of the main text. Others contain selected artists' brochures (two or three per decade) reproducing their haphazard, non-alphabetical listing, while the rest contain miscellaneous contracts and programmes to illustrate the agency's working method. There is also Emmie Tillett's five-year diary 1965–69, her only diary to survive and which, as it happens, records five fascinating if turbulent years for Ibbs and Tillett. The decline and fall of the Roman empire took from the reign of the Emperor Augustus in AD 31 to the fall of Constantinople in 1453, some 1500 years, but for Ibbs and Tillett, which bestrode the music profession like a Colossus, it took just 84 years to rise and fall.

Acknowledgements

My thanks go first and foremost to the Chairman of the Tillett Trust, Paul Strang, for a vast amount of help and information, wise advice and a guiding hand through potentially choppy waters; also to the Trust's extremely efficient Secretary Katie Avey, always willing and able to gently move the project along just when a prod was needed. I also gratefully acknowledge Jeanne Strang's laborious efforts on my behalf in obtaining permission from copyright owners, a thankless task, in some cases obtaining no response but generally rewarded with favourable replies, so a few refusals were hard to understand. Though only very distantly related to either Robert Leigh Ibbs or John Tillett, the Revd Selwyn Tillett and Peter Hendy-Ibbs threw themselves enthusiastically into the task of tracing the genealogy of both men for me with admirable dedication and dogged persistence, and I am truly grateful to them for undertaking this particular brief. I also thank Renn Wortley in far-away Melbourne for unearthing a wealth of information about Ibbs' tour to Australia in 1907. Photographs were only a problem when it came to the elusive Ibbs, and so I express my gratitude to his godson Haydon Bradshaw and to Reginald Franks (whose father was a close friend of the agent) for providing me with a couple.

Since I began work on this book, I have interviewd, or been in correspondence with, many friends, colleagues, artists, agents, former employees and business associates of Ibbs and Tillett, and to all of them I express my thanks. In purely alphabetical order within the following categories they are: agents Caroline Baird, Martin Campbell-White, Michael Emmerson, Helen Fraser, Terry Harrison, Jasper Parrott, Christa Phelps, Robert Rattray, Andrew Rosner, David Sigall, and Joeske van Walsum; former Ibbs and Tillett employees Richard Apley, Tim Bullamore, Robin Coulson, Andrew Green, Richard Grace, Chrystle Humphries, Christopher Hunt, Sue Martin, Hilary Myerscough, Terry Palmer, Rosemary Pennington, Rosie Pickering, Tom Ponsonby, Callum Ross, Denys Rowlands; to artists Sheila Armstrong, Dame Janet Baker, Lady Evelyn Barbirolli, Una Barry, Malcolm Binns, Charles Corp, Katie Flowers, Sidonie Goossens, Ameral Gunson, Glenville Hargreaves, Ruth Harte, Raimund Herincx, Graham Johnson, Guy Jonson, Peter Katin, Philip Langridge, Ann Murray, Siegmund Nissel, Christine Pembridge, Anna Reynolds, Phyllis Sellick, John Shirley-Quirk, Robert Tear, Marjorie Thomas, Valerie Tryon, Sir David Willcocks; to Gordon Allen (Birmingham Festival Choral Society), Catherine Freeman (Malvern Concert Club), and Howard Greenwood (Richmond Concert Society); to the BBC Written Archives at Caversham, Blackburn Museum and Art Gallery (Rebecca Hill), British Library (Royal Philharmonic Society Archive, Loan 48), IMG, Royal Academy of Music (Kathy Adamson), Royal College of Music (Oliver Davies the omniscient former Keeper of Portraits, and Peter Horton of the Music Library), David Rubin and Partners (John Paylor), Steinway (two former employees Lionel Squibb and Bob Glazebrook), Wigmore Hall Archive; for permission to reproduce letters to copyright owners Laurent Kasper-Ansermet (Ernest Ansermet), Dr Cuillin Bantock (Granville Bantock), Lady Evelyn Barbirolli (Sir John Barbirolli), Jack N. Kirksmith (Harold Bauer), Shirley, Lady Beecham (Sir Thomas Beecham), Robert

Tuggle (Rudolph Bing), Lady Gertrude Bliss (Sir Arthur Bliss), the Frank Bridge Trust (Paul Banks, trustee), the estate of Arnold Bax, Sir Adrian Boult (a member of the family), Britten–Pears Foundation (through Hugh Cobbe); Les Amis d'Emma Calvé (Emma Calvé), Marta Casals-Istomin (Pau Casals), Helen Chaliapin (Boris Chaliapin), Tamara Dewdney (Albert Coates), Jean Cortot (Alfred Cortot), Fritz Curzon (Clifford Curzon), Samuel A. Bowman (Walter Damrosch), Jane Dethick (John Dethick), Sean McGlynn (Ernst von Dohnanyi), Robert Montgomery (Sir Edward Elgar), Julia Falkner (Sir Keith Falkner), David Heather and Richard Robinson (Kathleen Ferrier), Eva Feuermann Lehnsen (Emanuel Feuermann), Edwin Fischer Foundation (Ursula Jones, trustee), Edward German Trust (S.J. Gladwell, trustee), Alexander Glazounov Foundation, Leopold Godowsky III (Leopold Godowsky), Pamela Main (Sir Eugene Goossens), Percy Grainger Estate (Barrie Ould, Administrator), Jan Smaczny (Sir Hamilton Harty), Julian Moyle (Elizabeth Harwood), Nigel and Colin Hess (Myra Hess), Gustav Holst Foundation (Colin Matthews, Executive Administrator), Stephen Isserlis (Julius Isserlis), Lotte Klemperer (Otto Klemperer), Hans Knappertsbusch Gesellschaft (Franz Braun, President), Elisabeth Legge-Schwarzkopf (Walter Legge), the executors of the late Ian Barclay (Sir Alexander Mackenzie), John Count McCormack (his grandfather, John Count McCormack), Ib J. Melchior (Lauritz Melchior), Susanne Baumgartner (Moshe Menuhin), Boris Moiseiwitsch (Benno Moiseiwitsch), Pierre Monteux School (Nancie Monteux-Barendse, President and Administrator), Wendy Pyatt (Gerald Moore), J. Barton Harrison (Eugene Ormandy), SIBA (Selim Palmgren), Jephta Drachman and Joram Piatigorsky (Gregor Piatigorsky), Annette Clement (Gabriel Pierné), Andre Schmidt (Sergei Prokofiev), Alexandre Rachmaninoff, Simon Radford (Robert Radford), Stefan Schnabel, Joy Puritz (Elisabeth Schumann), Emilia Segovia, Alice Wilson of David Higham Associates (Dame Ethel Smyth), Paul Strang (Solomon), Herman E. Muller jnr (Leopold Stokowski), Frau M. Rohla Strauss (Richard Strauss), John M. Kriz (Igor Stravinsky), John G. Teltsch (Georg Szell), Irene Magaloff (Josef Szigeti), Vita Dejmalova (Vaclav Talich), Ursula Vaughan Williams (through Hugh Cobbe), Lady Walton, Maia Studer (Felix Weingartner), Steuart Wilson (a member of the family), Curtis Price (Sir Henry Wood); to John Amis, Felix Aprahamian, John Boyden, Lewis Foreman, Jim Huggon, Joan Ingpen, Norman Lebrecht, Elizabeth Lewis, John Lucas and Simon McVeigh for their help or reminiscences; and finally to those who helped me with their memories but sadly did not live to read the fruits of their contributions, Larry Adler, E. Wulstan Atkins, Beryl Ball, Joseph Cooper, Gwen Cutner, Howard Ferguson, Michal Hambourg, Roy Henderson, Sir Ian Hunter, Norman McCann, Yehudi Menuhin and Rex Stephens. To my publisher Ashgate I extend warm thanks, in particular to Rachel Lynch and Heidi May, and finally to Anna, who guided me patiently through the processes of indexing.

The publishers wish to acknowledge the generous support of the Tillett Trust in the production of this book and their permission to use and reproduce much of their archive.

Narciso Vert, drawn at the Royal Society of Musicians' Festival dinner.
The Illustrated Sporting and Dramatic News, 4 March 1893, page 861

CHAPTER ONE

N. Vert: 'A Veritable Napoleon of Managers'

For most of the twentieth century, from 1906 until 1990, Britain's music profession had its equivalent of Marks and Spencer, Bradford and Bingley or Fortnum and Mason, namely the artists' management agency Ibbs and Tillett, or, as it was affectionately known to many musicians on its books in its last years, 'Fibbs & Toilet'. During the course of its 84-year existence it became the backbone of the music industry throughout the land; every week quartets of singers would be despatched to the myriad numbers of choral societies and music clubs the length and breadth of the country. On a Friday night or Saturday morning, Crewe station on the London, Midland and Scottish Railway became a meeting point where Isobel Baillie, Muriel Brunskill, Heddle Nash and Roy Henderson, on their way to Manchester for a *Messiah*, might meet up with Elsie Suddaby, Mary Jarred, Eric Greene and Keith Falkner on their way to Liverpool for the same work. Rachmaninov might be spotted at Paddington on his way to Cardiff as part of a UK recital tour, while Moiseiwitsch might be seen boarding the boat train at Victoria on his way to Europe for a concert tour. Casals and Piatigorsky could well have passed each other on trains between London and York, Szigeti and Milstein between London and Edinburgh. Such were the lists of artists whose British (and to some extent foreign) careers were in the hands of Ibbs and Tillett.

Though formed in 1906, its connections go back far deeper into the nineteenth century and are rooted in the music publishing company of Chappells, which itself had a varied history. This was founded in 1810 to carry on the 'trade or business of composers of music, music and musical instrument sellers etc. at No.124 Bond Street, London'. Its premises hosted the formation of the Philharmonic Society on 24 January 1813; in 1846 it contracted Mendelssohn to write an opera on Bulwer Lytton's *The Lady of Lyons* but he died the following year. The House of Chappell had great success when it published Charles d'Albert's highly fashionable quadrilles in the 1850s, followed by a remarkably successful series of waltzes and other dance compositions, but probably the most important enterprise of that decade was the opening (on 25 March 1858) of St James's Hall, a project initiated by Chappell & Company. From 1859 to 1901 they (that is, the brothers Tom and Arthur Chappell) managed the famous Popular Concerts on Mondays and Saturdays, immortalized by W.S. Gilbert as 'classical Monday Pops' in *The Mikado*. Whilst they did not promote 'novelties from the pens of living composers', these 1,602 concerts did produce a wealth of chamber music in the instrumental part of the miscellaneous programmes. Among the many distinguished instrumentalists who appeared at them were Clara Schumann, Teresa Carreño, Fanny Davies, Anton Rubinstein, Hans von Bülow, Hallé, Liszt, Saint Saëns, Joachim, Piatti, Wieniawski, Vieuxtemps, Wilhelmj, Eugen d'Albert, Paderewski, Ysaÿe, Busoni, de Pachmann, Harold Bauer and Mark Hambourg. Among the list of eminent singers who took part were Sims Reeves, Santley, Louisa Pyne, Antoinette Sterling, George and Lillian Henschel, Edward Lloyd, Helene Lemmens-Sherrington and Charlotte Sainton-Dolby. In George Eliot's words these concerts were 'our easiest and cheapest pleasures' whilst their Director, Samuel Arthur Chappell, who ran an independent business selling wind instruments at adjoining premises, was eulogized in a sonnet by Robert Browning:

> Thanks, then, to Arthur Chappell, thanks to him,
> Whose every guest henceforth not idly vaunts,
> 'Sense has received the utmost Nature grants,
> My cup is filled with rapture to the brim,
> When, night by night – ah, memory, how it haunts! –
> Music was poured by perfect ministrants,
> By Hallé, Schumann, Piatti, Joachim'

Charlotte Sainton-Dolby, for whom Mendelssohn wrote the contralto part in *Elijah*, had a brother, George Dolby, who operated a Concert and Music Agency from 1858 above the Chappell offices, now at 52 New Bond Street. According to James Henry Mapleson's memoirs, his musical agency, set up in London's Haymarket just two years earlier in 1856, was 'the first established in London'. Dolby, meanwhile, was proposed by Chappells to organize its management of the touring public reading recitals given by Charles Dickens from 1866. One of Dolby's employees was Narciso Vertigliano, referred to in this history as N. Vert just as he himself did, and who took over the Agency when Dolby retired in 1880. He, together with his brothers Fernando, Honorato and Pedro, moved it to 6 Cork Street in 1886. A year later Vert's young nephew, Pedro Tillett, was taken into the firm in a junior position. Narciso Ramon Domingo Vert, of Spanish descent, was born on 8 April 1845 at 402 Euston Road, London. He was a child chorister under Joseph Barnby at St Andrew's Church, Wells Street, then joined Chappells as a clerk before becoming assistant to Dolby. One of his first strokes of luck was his involvement with the management of the Richter concerts from 1880, followed by the concerts given by the Spanish violinist Pablo de Sarasate. Vert also shared the management with Wilhelm Kuhe of some of Adelina Patti's vocal recitals and Anton Rubinstein's piano recitals. His extremely high-quality stable of artists now included some of the most famous and able musicians currently performing, among them the singers Emma Albani, Clara Butt, Ada Crossley, Alice Esty, Suzanne Adams, Muriel Foster, Nellie Melba, and Charles Santley, the pianists Josef Hofmann and Moriz Rosenthal, and the violinists Bronislav Huberman and Jan Kubelik. Many were eager to be taken up by Vert but competition was very tough and the chances of a successful career slim. Among those trying to fashion one was the pianist Walter Bache, then aged 36:

> Like all other miserable pianists, I am very anxious as years go on to get more playing and less teaching engagements. As regards London I must content myself with my annual orchestral concerts and my recital – but I should very much like to try some recitals in the country if you think there would be any reasonable hope of their proving financially successful in the course of a few years.
>
> Do you think I should be doing a very foolish thing if I were to try three or four provincial recitals next autumn, and if you would advise me to make the experiment, would you undertake the management at a fixed salary (or on any other conditions you might suggest)? Of course I should not make a farthing – might possibly lose something. But do you think that the certainty of present failure and loss is so great, and the chance of future success so small as to make the attempt unadvisable? This is where I want your friendly advice. Please to answer as shortly as possible and quite at your own convenience as there is no hurry about the matter. (17 March 1878)

Even the temperamental conductor and brilliant pianist, Hans von Bülow, was forced by changed circumstances to contact Vert and ask for recital work, after he had lost his conducting post in Hanover over a quarrel with the principal tenor:

> I have dismissed last night and very glad that my unbearable slavery as a Königliche Hofkapellmeister [Imperial Court Conductor] is over. Now I am quite free next January, can extend my tournée in England as long as you would judge it advisable and without any haste. Thus you will get less trouble and difficulties in your management of my concerts. Therefore I give you notice at once. I give you full powers for one month and do not object if you were to change even about the date of my coming. With regards in a hurry. (27 October 1879)

Vert had to deal with even more temperamental characters, particularly in the field of recitation, still a popular form of entertainment in the last years of the nineteenth century. F. Bernard Beere was one such artist who had an extremely high opinion of himself, as revealed in this undated postcard: 'Would you care to entertain the idea of a short tour this autumn called 'Mr Bernard Beere's Recitals' associating with me one or two other artists, my name of course being prominent as the star and no other reciter being engaged?', while the actress Ellen Terry took a much more humorous and self-deprecating view of her own talent and marketable qualities in her distinctive scrawled handwriting when she wrote to Vert:

> A young friend staying with me – Signorina Elvira Gambogi – is, I find, anxious to get some engagements for the Promenade Concerts, and it occurs to me that you are the very man to help her (and to help me, for I'm very fond of her). She has a magnificent voice and is a true artist. Last night we gave an "entertainment" here and she roused the people up so, that I'm sure she would shine and become very popular at the P[romenade] C[oncerts]. Let me have a line here (as she remains a few days longer with me) and Miss Gambogi would, if necessary, come to you and sing to you.
>
> I suppose you could not give me an engagement at the "Proms"? I assure you I made a sensation here last night singing in character 'Three Old Maids of Lee'!! Much greater fun than Lady Macbeth! (7 August 1890)

For the next hundred years, Vert and those who came after in this history depended as much upon the recommendations of artists whose opinions he trusted as he did upon his own tried and tested intuition. Nellie Melba demanded 'I want you to look after Miss [Ada] Crossley's interests, so please help her all you can', though she also revealed not only a bullying tone, but also a softer side to her personality in this cause for one struggling female:

> I could sing at Blackpool at the beginning of September but not earlier. I may not be singing at the Opera this season; if I do not, I shall give a concert at the Albert Hall, so mark off a date in June. I cannot arrive in London till the end of May. Please be kind to Miss Mayer. She has a blind mother and two little brothers to keep, and I am afraid she is very poor. (undated, received 1 March 1901)

Sir Hubert Parry, Principal of the Royal College of Music, and the singer Adelina Patti took very different approaches, the former deferential, the latter generous and open-hearted. From Parry:

> One of our students, Miss Buckley by name, asks me for an introduction to you. I don't like to bother you but neither do I like to refuse her. She has a very fine Contralto voice and may be useful in course of time. A pupil of [Manuel] Garcia's! (2 June 1896)

And from Patti:

> I am anxious to introduce to your notice Mlle. Jeanne and Mlle. Marthe Morini, two twin sisters, who have been engaged to sing on my present Concert tour, solos and duets, and who have had a

> very good success. They have charming, sympathetic voices, and I should much like you to hear them, to judge yourself of their merits. They are most anxious to obtain some engagements in England, and as I take a great interest in them, I shall be very pleased if you can see your way to get them any engagements. (1 November 1896)

While, in 1894, the German conductor Felix Mottl based in Karlsruhe had no hesitation in praising the gifted pianist Eduard Risler, who was developing a fine reputation for his recital series of works by one composer, after the example of Hans von Bülow who had died three months earlier:

> Generalmusikdirector Felix Mottl recommends Herr E. Risler as an exceptional, first-class artist, and is convinced that he will celebrate a great triumph in London, as he has in France and Germany. (9 May 1894, translation from German)

By the end of the nineteenth century, anybody who had intentions of becoming an instrumental soloist or an opera singer in Britain was virtually compelled to work with the conductor Hans Richter if they wanted to rise to the top of their profession, because he dominated the musical life of London for 32 years from 1879 and in Manchester as Hallé's successor from 1900 to 1911. The conductor called his London manager 'My dear Mr Vert' and their relationship was always extremely cordial, with Richter's English colourful and quaint at times in these cards and letters to Vert or Pedro Tillett:

> As I do not know Mr Colton, we shall make a trial with Mr A E Matt who played [principal trombone] during the last autumn tour some difficult passages instead of Mr Müller. (24 April 1897)

> "Untrue" in the Telegramme means: it is untrue that I should be prevented from my coming to London in the autumn season. Please send me the printed programmes of the London and tour Concerts. (30 September 1898)

> Would you do me the favour to send somebody to Mr Cameron, the excellent photographer (whose address I cannot remember) and ask him to send to me my photos. It is very urgent, as I intend to distribute some ones to friends at Xmas. (12 December 1898)

> I have written to [conductor Eduard] Colonne that I shall be unable to come to Paris during this season and I will write to him again after my arrival in Vienna. Please do me the favour to send me somebody to Mr Cameron, he may send photographs of mine as soon as possible to Mr Forsyth [Hallé Orchestra], as there is a great demand for. (17 November 1899)

> I noticed the three dates 21, 28 Oct and 4 Nov, which suit me very much. It is a pity that you cannot come to Bayreuth. As for the Vienna Phil. Concert I expected you would say: No! But if their Concerts will not interfere with ours, I shall conduct those with your co-operation and under your direction. (14 July 1901)

> To make the programmes it is necessary for me to know whether we shall have Soloists or Singers in our Concerts and in which. Mr [George] Henschel writes to me of a lady singer, Mrs Myron, but the proposed song will not please me; what will you say about the lady? I shall remain here until the 1st of October, on the 7th or 8th I shall be in London, where we can final the programmes, but I should like to give you at least the programme of the 1st Concert. (20 September 1901)

> Stanford's "Irish" Rhapsodie will not be performed at our Spring Concerts. You will hear about the programme of the 1st Concerts after a few days. (6 April 1902)

Putting up with egos became second nature to Vert, who tolerated it all with apparent good humour and equanimity. Few had greater opinions of themselves than the wife and husband team (note the order) of the contralto Clara Butt and the baritone Kennerley Rumford, the latter's career largely dependent on the fame of his wife. Their concert party tours around Britain formed a vital contribution to the finances of Vert's agency:

> I have meant writing you for sometime to ask you to be sure and make a point of telling all your clients in the different towns where we go on tour to advertise the concerts as Madam Clara Butt's and Mr Kennerley Rumford's, not Miss Clara Butt's alone as it was in many cases last tour. Mr Moon advertised that way and Mr Marshall at Leicester. Please see to this as I shall be very amazed if it happens again, and I'm sure a word in time from you will put matters right. (undated)

Dealing with errors and sorting out misunderstandings, particularly in the matters of concert arrangements, rehearsals and even repertoire, soon became of paramount importance. Some artists spotted such slips in good time, such as the singer David Ffrangcon-Davies, who wrote to Pedro Tillett:

> Thanks for your note in which you say they telegraph that I am to sing in the '*Mass in D minor*'. They doubtless mean the *Mass in B minor* [by Bach]. Would you please cable Vert to retain the Bechstein Hall for me for November 11th 1903, evening. (6 August 1903)

On the matter of commission, it seems at times to have been a movable feast and with some artists dictating their own terms. In 1902 Ben Davies returned from a trip to the United States and told Vert:

> I have just returned from Cincinnati where I was again received with open arms. [Andrew] Black also made a great success. I regret to say that our arrangement of a year ago no longer pays me, so in future I will pay you 10% on all engagements you find me. (19 May 1902)

While another singer, the tenor Edward Lloyd also seems to have held the whip hand in his dealings with his agent:

> You can accept any of the dates for Manchester after Oct. 30th. Do not accept the two dates for Wrexham under fifty guineas August 22nd and 23rd. I was going to call myself today but the day is so hot, I shan't move out till the evening. Come over if you can and we will drink till all's blue, and I will take you out for an evening drink. Send word by Craddock. (undated)

In a weaker bargaining position was the composer and pianist Xaver Scharwenka, who had evidently got himself into financial embarrassment when he asked Vert for more time in settling his debts:

> Forgive me for not being able to send you the balance of my debt at once, for in this financial quarter I have greater payments to make. By the 15th July at the latest you will have the outstanding 18 guineas. (1 July 1879, translation from the German)

Vert was very industrious in planning tours for his artists, but he had to keep a balance regarding who went where and when. Flooding the market could reduce audience numbers, while having celebrated artists in the same town or even too near one another might also affect box office returns. The tenor Edward Lloyd wrote bitterly:

> The business has been dreadful this past week, and everyone is telling me that I am following too quickly after the Butt party. Even the men sharing with me say that in these small towns [Torquay] it is impossible to work Concerts so close together. Now I do feel it very much that my last appearances in these towns should prove a failure, and that you are arranging for Miss Butt to take her Concerts three weeks only before mine (and so taking the wind out of my sails) is a great cause for the empty houses. It is not often I complain, but I think I have a very strong case for complaint in this instance.
>
> I have been asked by several people to sing "Onaway, awake beloved" [from Coleridge-Taylor's *Hiawatha's Wedding Feast*] in Manchester, Liverpool and Birmingham, so please put it in the

programme at these places and cut out "Adelaide". Will you also send off at once to Oxford two copies of the *Preislied* [the so-called Prize Song from Wagner's *Die Meistersinger*] for Tuesday's Concert, as I have promised to sing it as an encore. (undated)

Agents' business dealings with composers were usually more to do with appearances as instrumentalists or conductors rather than in promoting their own compositions, but in the case of Elgar, Vert played a crucial part in his overnight success and is therefore entitled to a particularly unique claim to fame. In 1899 the composer's friend and editor at the music publisher Novello, August Jaeger, sent the score of Elgar's new composition the *Variations on an Original Theme* (*'Enigma'*) (later known as *Enigma Variations*) to Hans Richter through the good offices of Vert:

The parcel with your score came to hand this morning, and I am sending it by tonight's post to Dr Richter together with a letter urging him to perform the work at one of the forthcoming concerts. (22 February 1899)

On 9 March Vert told Elgar:

I have heard from Dr Richter acknowledging the score of your Variations. He is at present travelling in St Petersburg, but on his return he will look through the work, and he says 'that he shall be only too pleased to promote the work of an English artiste'. (Novello archive: 9 March 1899)

On 13 March Elgar wrote to Novello, 'The position regarding the first performance stands thus. I offered the work to Dr Richter (through Mr Vert who sent the score to Vienna)'. A fortnight later the composer contacted Vert again:

I hear from Novello that the score has not yet arrived; it will take some time to produce the copies & I hope the score has started – cd. you find out if Dr Richter has despatched it & if it is delayed on the way. (30 March 1899)

On 31 May, Vert asked for the orchestral parts and the rest is history. Elgar's name was propelled before a far wider public as a result of its premiere on 19 June 1899. That much of this success could be attributed to Vert, who now became Richter's agent for work in Britain, was readily admitted by Elgar two years later to Vert, together with a wry dig at his new admirers:

I had hoped to have seen you before you left Leeds only to say this. The Variations went well &, as you have perhaps seen, were a great triumph for the orchestra & for me: I have to thank you for the introduction to Richter which led to the first performance of the work – you may have forgotten this – but I have not & shd. like you to understand that I am very grateful to you for your kindness when I much needed it. Plenty of people are kind to me now! (13 October 1901)

From about 1916 Elgar loosened his connection with Novello in terms of his conducting activities and placed them more or less entirely in the hands of Ibbs and Tillett; all his letters in the archive are to be found in Appendix 13.

Another composer, but one who earned much of his living as a recitalist was the excellent pianist Edvard Grieg. A diminutive man of extremely frail health, as he got older he became a perpetual risk to schedule as a performer because he often cancelled his trips to Britain due to his very weak heart. He was in London in December 1897 for a recital (his card to Vert is addressed from 47 North Side, Clapham Common, London, the home of the music publisher John Augener), and typically seems to have been anxious to avoid causing problems:

I hope I don't ask too much when I beg you kindly reserve me 5 good seats for the recital the 15th. Tomorrow in the Pops I should be glad if you would be kind enough to manage that the people who wish to see me are permitted to come in the artist room after the concert. (3 December 1897)

The Pops concert on Saturday 4 December and the recital on 15 December featured Grieg's own music in which he played solos, accompanied his wife Nina in some of his songs and Johannes Wolff in one of his violin sonatas. His string quartet Op.27 was also played at both events by Wolff's quartet. Of this ten-concert tour lasting two months Grieg wrote to Julius Röntgen on 19 November 1897: 'The whole thing is crazy. If I get out of this alive I'll surely never do it again.'

Saint Saëns gave Vert the option to select movements from his piano suite, which he intended to include in the second of two concerts he would be giving in London, reported that he had given instructions to the French piano manufacturer Erard to send the piano he had used at the Paris Conservatoire's prize-giving ceremony, and had a query (in English) about the venue for the concerts:

> Au 2me concert j'ai l'intention de jouer ma Suite pour piano (Prélude – Menuet – Gavotte – Gigue) quant aux morceaux d'ensemble vous en déciderez. Il ne m'est plus possible de réserver la question du piano; hier j'ai demandé à la maison Erard de m'envoyer le piano sur lequel j'ai joué à la distribution des prix du Conservatoire. St James's Hall? Queen's Hall? You have said nothing of that to me. (30 October 1901)

Another composer/performer (in this case a conductor) in touch with Vert, but one struggling to make ends meet at the turn of the century was the black musician, Samuel Coleridge-Taylor. His choral trilogy *Hiawatha* had brought him fame (even a Society for him in America) but not in the way that *The Dream of Gerontius* had propelled Elgar's name upwards at about the same time:

> Do you ever have applications for Conductors? If so I wish you would put my name down on your books. I shall have a good deal of time to spend after Christmas and though my two Croydon orchestras will be running till April, I should be glad to entertain anything good in any part of the country. Will you kindly let me know about this? (27 October 1901)

> As you have already heard from me about a proposed visit to the States. The "S.C-T. Society" at Washington want me to conduct three or four concerts for them, and I propose coming over this Autumn. Will you kindly let me know if you can arrange with any other Societies to engage me to conduct *Hiawatha* or any other work of mine? I can put all October, November and the first two weeks of December at your disposal. In the event of you being able to arrange anything, kindly let me know the guaranteed fee they each offer. I also should be pleased to give three or four smaller concerts of my songs, piano and violin pieces if you think it a good idea. An early answer will greatly oblige. (24 January 1904)

> It is now definitely settled that I shall come to the States in November next. I am having $500 for these concerts and would therefore have to charge $200 for a separate concert and rehearsal. If you could also manage six chamber concerts at say Boston, New York, Chicago, Philadelphia and Washington I should be pleased. Could you let me know how the terms would be arranged for these latter. I should want a violinist (Miss Maud Powell if she should be free, as I know her), a soprano or contralto, and a tenor or baritone as the programmes consist chiefly of songs and violin pieces. Please let me have a line as soon as possible. (14 March 1904)

A few years later Coleridge-Taylor was again asking for conducting work, but this time he approached the agency through John Tillett's wife, Hetty Holroyd, the singer Esta d'Argo whom he had married in December 1906. Maybe because he noted the sweetener at the end of the letter to his wife, her husband evidently agreed to act:

> I am writing on a matter of business. Could you kindly ask Mr Tillett to let me know should he hear of anything in the way of a conducting engagement for the summer season anywhere in England. There is one at Colwyn Bay I know, but as I have been asked to recommend someone, I can scarcely apply for it myself. As you would know, I've had any amount of experience in conducting and should love to undertake such an appointment providing it is first class. As for the engagement for Newport (Mon.) in April for *Hiawatha*, I suggested you when I was there last week. I am conducting. (28 December 1908)

> Dear Mr Tillett,
> Thanks for yours of this morning. If you really think it worthwhile writing to Colwyn Bay, I do not mind at all. Perhaps it could be done without mentioning my name at first, just to see if it still remains open? (30 December 1908)

Elgar, on the other hand, was having to fight off the work and seems to have been plagued by requests from music societies throughout the land as a result of his rise to fame. It has always been part of an agent's duty to protect his client from direct approaches from musical organizations or managements, particularly when it comes to the matter of fees. In Elgar's case the society in Bristol seems to have been particularly persistent and Vert received this huffy letter from the composer:

> I have acknowledged the enclosed & have said I have sent it on to you to answer. I am disengaged but I don't see why I shd. go without a fee; if you can arrange anything please do – if not I won't go. You can say I am disengaged. I ought not to go for less than ten guineas. This is what I have said: 'Many thanks for your letter; I have sent it to my agent, Mr Vert, who will tell you of my engagements etc.' (6 November 1901)

Vert evidently sorted the matter out for Elgar, who acknowledged a week later, 'Many thanks; of course I cannot go about the world for nothing. I return the Bristol letter'. [13 November 1901], whereas Sir Julius Benedict had a far harder problem getting money for August Wilhelmj, the leader of his Liverpool Philharmonic Society orchestra, from the organization by which he had been hired:

> I fear that you did not receive the letter of my agent Mr Vert, and shall feel obliged by your kindly sending per return of post the very small fee you agreed to (10 guineas) for Herr Wilhelmj's services on the 9th inst'. (addressee unknown, 23 December 1875)

Most artists were paid directly by the organizations promoting the concert and were then obliged to pay Vert his commission. The American conductor Walter Damrosch reveals how things were rather different in the United States when he wrote from New York:

> Is Miss [Muriel] Foster available for our Sunday afternoon Symphony Concert Jan.8th and on what terms? We pay most of our soloists on a percentage basis of the gross receipts. Then, if they are drawing cash, they make more in proportion. This has proven itself to be a mutually fair and agreeable method'. (6 June 1904)

Nellie Melba, on the other hand, did things her way and Vert, having made a one-off charge for organizing her tours, could only stand by and watch her rake in the takings:

> I am sorry to say I shall be unable to give a concert this year, as I shall not be able to get back from Germany till the 16th and I sail on the 20th for America. We made £1000 in Dublin, which is enormous for such a poor country. I had an enormous reception. I go to Paris on Sunday'. (undated)

Carl Rosa, the experienced opera impresario and conductor, had cause to advise Vert on matters of detail, such as free tickets and programme sales, which had evidently been overlooked after a performance in Scotland:

> I have had a long letter of complaint again from [the agent Gustav] Lewy about the Edinburgh event. I do not mean to particularise but to save appearance against a suspicious nature you better be particular in future as to the free tickets; give strict orders to the agents not to issue any except to the press and tell Lewy before every concert how many you have issued and to whom. Also let the Music Sellers make up their accounts of sales before the doors open and hand Lewy a written statement what the account of advance sale before the doors open is. I am sorry that I should have to press this on you, but I think it is the only way to satisfy them. There is some confusion about the 7th of May having been withdrawn and you must insert something to this effect. The concert for Chamber music advertised for the 7th of May is transferred to the 25th of May and tickets already purchased can be exchanged, however we can talk that over on Wednesday. (9 April 1877)

The German violinist Wilhelmj (leader of the orchestra at the Wagner Festival held in the Royal Albert Hall in the Spring of 1877) had no hesitation in asking for complimentary tickets for a recital given by the visiting Austrian violinist Adolf Rebner:

> Thank you for the Rebner tickets, which will be distributed. Would you have the kindness to send me 2 tickets for Busoni's Chopin recital and much oblige yours very sincerely Prof. Wilhelmj. (8 December 1905)

But the American composer and pianist, Edward Macdowell, touring England in 1903, had good reason for placing an embargo on such free tickets.

> Thank you for your note, and in reply I would say that it might be as well to write to the London House that I will not give one single recital, but if dates can be arranged for the two recitals I will be glad to give them. I expect to return to the city by Wednesday the 1st of April, and will be here should you want to see me about anything. By the way, as Steinway Hall in London is very small, will you please tell the London House that no tickets are to be given away without consulting me. (27 March 1903)

Vert was very involved in the planning and construction of his artists' programmes; he could tell if a work or a song had been overexposed at any particular venue as well as linking his artists to any work intended for performance by any Society or Club. He learnt much from conductors such as Sir Charles Hallé, one of the first major artists with whom he worked, by providing singers and also managing work for him in London as a pianist or for his wife, the violinist Wilma Norman-Neruda.

> When I saw Mme. [Christine] Nilsson last she expressed the desire to sing the *Jewel Song* from *Faust* on account of the Band, and I have therefore included it in the programme instead of the *Ave Maria* which would not do as well. I will send you in a few days the whole programme, somewhat shortened of course from the one you sent me to make room for the Overture and Symphony.
>
> I could accept an engagement at Rochester for Mme. Norman Neruda and myself in February, but the Terms would be fifty Guineas and not thirty-five. I shall return [from Leipzig] to London on the 14th or the 15th inst. (6 October 1875)

The concert, on 28 October 1875, did include the *Ave Maria* after all (with Ludwig Straus playing the violin obbligato,) and not the *Jewel Song*; the Overture was *Egmont*, the symphony Schubert's *Unfinished*.

> I am not sure yet if I can engage Mme. [Edith] Wynne for March 8th; if Mr Chappell can get me the Quartett for the *Liebeslieder*, [Brahms' Waltzes for piano duet and vocal quartet] I shall prefer them and shall know in 2 or 3 days. So if you can keep the date open, please do so. Mr Chappell will be able to tell you if the Quartett can come. (7 February 1877)

Hallé did indeed use the Quartet, who were Thekla Friedländer, Mme H. von Arnim, William Shakespeare and Mr Pyatt. Hans Richter generally gave his manager a choice of programmes (a practice which would be developed by artists in the history of the agency). Some of the following letters (in what can only be described as the Austro-Hungarian conductor's quaint English) are addressed by Richter to Pedro Tillett, who by now was his uncle Vert's office manager:

> The programme of the first and second concert must remain as I have proposed, but the third may be a Wagner night.
>
> Overture : *Tannhäuser*
> Vorspiel und Liebestod : *Tristan und Isolde*
> Overture : *Flying Dutchman*
> Vorspiel : Act III *Meistersinger*
> *Charfreitagszauber* [Good Friday Music: *Parsifal*]
> Beethoven : [Symphony No.3] *Eroica*
>
> I hope that Mme [Ella] Russell and Herr Fröhlich are preparing their pieces. With my best regards to you and Mr Vert, and to all our friends. Letters are always too late on account of the tremendous inundations; they must go by indirect courses. (21 September 1899)
>
> I shall meet Madame [Ellen] Gulbranson, the great Singer of Bayreuth, and if you should intend to invite her for one of our autumn concerts please drop me a line to Bayreuth. I remember that you proposed Mr [Emil] Sauer als [as] Pianist, but not with his own Concerto. But if you decline the cooperation of any Soloist, I send you the programmes of the Concerts including Orchestral works only.
>
> I
>
> Beethoven : Ouverture *Leonora* No.3
> Wagner : Vorspiel *Parsifal*
> Berlioz : a) Love scene, b) Queen Mab from the Symphonie *Romeo and Julia*
> Dvořák : Symphonie *From the New World*
>
> II
>
> Mozart : Symphonie in G minor [No.40 K550]
> Wagner : *Siegfried Idyll*
> Elgar : *Cockaigne* Ouverture (first time at these concerts)
> Smetana : *Vltava* Symphonic Poem
> Tchaikovsky : Suite No.3
>
> III
>
> Wagner : Vorspiel *Meistersinger*, *Charfreitagszauber (Parsifal)*, Eine *Faust* Ouverture, Selection from *Der Ring des Nibelungen*
> Liszt : Hungarian Rhapsody No.1
> Beethoven : 7th Symphonie
>
> I shall arrive on the 8th October. (27 September 1901)

In 1896 Richter became indignant about false press reports about his reputedly failing health, which were coming from Vienna, the city where he resided, and he made a strong request to Vert to ensure that such inaccurate rumours did not reach the English papers. As the years went by these signs of paranoia among artists on how they were perceived by the press became more frequent and of concern to the agency; in some cases litigation ensued. In Richter's case these stories persisted at the time shortly after Hallé's death in October 1895 when he was (correctly) rumoured to be Hallé's successor in Manchester, but even more to the point were those about his uneasy encounter with

Mahler, from 1897 the new Music Director at the Vienna Opera, where Richter had reigned supreme as first Kapellmeister (at his own choice never as Music Director) for nearly a quarter of a century since 1875. The Viennese press had a field day until Richter finally left in 1900, hanging on just long enough to get his optimum pension rights:

> Only these few lines in great haste. A few days ago it was announced in the Viennese newspapers that I was taken ill whilst conducting the last Philharmonic concert, but not a single word of it is true. In case this false report should have found its way into the English newspapers, so please to contradict it at once. Quite in the contrary, I am conducting very often, and am very happy to say in quite good health. The programme for the next season will follow in a few days. (21 February 1896)

Edward Lloyd, while clearly stating his musical intentions when it came to constructing a programme of songs, nevertheless thought it prudent to canvass his agent's opinion and obtain his approval:

> I think the following for the Albert Hall on the 12th :
>
> The Prize Song [Wagner's *Die Meistersinger*]
> *Come Margarita, come* – Sullivan
> *The Holy City* [Alfred Gaul]
>
> I think it would be right of me, out of respect for Sullivan, to sing one of his, and *Come Margarita, come* with orchestra is very beautiful. What do you think? I hope you are better; hoping to see you on Saturday. (undated)

Another singer with whom Vert had a close association in the closing stages of his career was Sir George Henschel, a long-lived artist of great repute as a Lieder and oratorio baritone as well as having a fair reputation as a conductor, for example of the Boston Symphony Orchestra. The following surviving correspondence is both amusing and revealing. He could be gracious, as, for example, when he gave Vert and Edward Lloyd an introduction to a friend in Germany:

> My dear Dr Forchheimer, you will be delighted to make the acquaintance of Mr Edward Lloyd and his, as well as my, friend and adviser Mr N. Vert. You know the beauties of your city so well and also how to make strangers acquainted with them, that I am sure the pleasure of this new triple acquaintance will be a hearty and mutual one. (April 1888)

But years later, after his announced retirement, Henschel had need of writing a rather sharp note to Vert:

> I thought I had written you that I shall not sing any more in public. So please cancel Maidstone and Manchester. (7 December 1901)

Henschel was an incredibly versatile musician, who accompanied himself in Lieder recitals and on recordings, and was even known to sing the first clarinet part of a symphony during a performance he was conducting with the Scottish Orchestra when the player was taken ill. Amazingly, 27 years later, long after Vert's death and in the heyday of Ibbs and Tillett, there was a further encounter with the singer, by now 78 years old (he died aged 84 in 1934). The first letter came from the Westdeutsche Konzertdirektion, Cologne to Ibbs and Tillett, who forwarded it to Georg [*sic*] Henschel:

> Dear Sirs,
> In reply to your letter of the 18th inst., we don't believe that the Westdeutsche Rundfunk realises that the Georg Henschel they wish to engage is the same who sang in Cologne 56 years ago, but the song of this artist pleased the Directors of the Rundfunk who have heard him in the London Broadcasting. We beg to draw your attention to the fact that the Westdeutsche Rundfunk concert will be no public one and Mr Henschel would be required to sing twice or three times. Please let us know as soon as possible the artist's fee. (20 April 1928)

Reply from Henschel to Ibbs and Tillett:

> Gentlemen,
> I have received yours of yesterday re Cologne Rundfunk engagement, and here is my answer. To sing only Schubert is quite out of the question (in German I would say "ausgeschlossen"). I should be prepared to sing a) *Der Leiermann*, b) *Das Wandern* – Schubert, Cruyantino's Song from *Claudine von Villabella* – Beethoven, *The Grenadiers* – Schumann, *The Erlking* – Löwe, and perhaps *Lied eines Schmiedes* – Schumann, of course being reassured that there is no visible audience. My fee would be one hundred and fifty guineas.
>
> If by any chance, through circumstances over which I have no control (illness, indisposition or so), I should not be able, after having arrived there, to sing, the Rundfunk would agree to pay me a fee of twenty five guineas for expenses, loss of time etc. I should also like to know the date on which that broadcasting is to take place.
>
> Please let the people know that I play my own accompaniments. (24 April 1928)

Vert's primary source of artists was the singing profession, not only for the opera companies, but also for the numerous oratorio performances which took place weekly throughout the land. Whenever a singer was in London for Carl Rosa's Opera Company, the Italian seasons which ran at Covent Garden from the autumn to late spring or the German Opera season in the early summer, he would make contact with all the visiting celebrities. The English tenor Joseph Maas, at the time preoccupied with preparing the title role of England's first *Rienzi*, wrote:

> My dates up to January are filled up as I am on the Tour with [Carl] Rosa. I have been limited to accept Concert engagements and have had to refuse a great many owing to my Operatic engagements. With regard to the Rochester Philharmonic Society, at present I can give you no promise of singing there. (30 August 1879)

The French bass Pol Plançon had concerns about the identity of his accompanist for a forthcoming concert at the Royal Albert Hall on 11 June 1902:

> Voulez-vous avoir la bonté de me dire qui m'accompagnera au piano le 11 juin à l'Albert Hall et si des morceaux d'opéras servient mieux que d'autres. (24 May 1902)

The American soprano Alwina Valleria, on the other hand, had to postpone an invitation to discuss a collaboration.

> I have received your letter on my arrival in town today, and as I am leaving again this evening for a week I cannot avail myself of your kind offer to call on me just now. I should be very pleased to see you on my return, for although I have nearly concluded an engagement for the autumn and winter, I should like to speak with you to see what arrangements could be made for the future. (13 August 1879)

The autumn engagement in question proved to be her Metropolitan Opera debut as Marguerite in Gounod's *Faust*. She had a London operatic career from 1882 until she virtually retired from the opera stage four years later. Vert was able to obtain her first oratorio work with a *Messiah* in Manchester on Boxing Day 1882, and appearances at the Handel and Leeds Festivals in the following year.

CHAPTER TWO

An American Venture and the Death of Vert: 1902–5

On 1 July 1902, Narciso Vert and his nephew Pedro Tillett, now a partner in the firm, drew up articles of partnership with Pedro's younger brother John Hudson Tillett (with the agency since 1887) to establish and manage a branch of the agency in New York. Premises were rented from Boosey and Company at 9 East 17th Street at $500 per annum. The starting capital was £500, half put in by Vert and Pedro, the other by John who was entitled to an initial salary of £5 per week. Part of the contract stated that 'all rent, salaries and other expenses of the business shall be paid out of the capital until the profits shall be sufficient for the purpose', an assumption that was to prove crucial to the success of the venture. Vert had already had dealings with America, such as securing a contract for the soprano Margaret Macintyre to sing at the Cincinnati Musical Festival in 1898.

> Below is the contract between Cincinnati Musical Festival Association and Margaret Macintyre
>
> IT IS HEREBY AGREED between the Cincinnati Musical Festival Association, a corporation under the laws of Ohio and Miss Macintyre, that she will sing in five concerts at the Music Festival to be given by said Association during the week commencing May 23rd 1898, that she will be present at Cincinnati for rehearsals commencing Friday evening May 20th 1898, and that prior to said Festival she will not sing, or be advertised to sing in public in the city of Cincinnati, except at said Festival, nor at any point within two hundred miles of said city. She shall sing Berlioz's *Damnation of Faust*, Beethoven's *Missa Solemnis*, in selections from Wagner's works, and also other solos and concerted music in two other concerts, the selections to be agreed upon between her and the Music Director [Theodore Thomas].
>
> In consideration whereof and of the faithful performance of this agreement on her part, said association agrees to pay her at the close of the Festival the sum of Six hundred pounds (£600).
>
> Witness the corporate title and seal of said Association hereunto affixed by Wm N. Hobart, its President, thereunto duly authorized by its Board of Directors, this 27th day of January 1898, and the signature of said Miss Macintyre.

Cincinnati had tried in vain to tempt conductor Hans Richter to succeed Arthur Nikisch in 1893 as the city orchestra's Music Director (and again two years later when the man appointed, Emil Paur, proved inadequate). Richter hated sea journeys – even a crossing of the English Channel tested the limit of his endurance – and in fact he never went to America, although even in 1905 he was clearly reconsidering the idea of a visit in part of a letter to Vert.

> I will not say: No! The time you mentioned in your letter is rather convenient, especially if it would be possible to move forward the time of the Festival one or two weeks. Either at the end of January or at the beginning of February I shall be in London and we could discuss the matter. The programme book you have sent to me is also very tempting to go to America, because it shows that the Cincinnati Festival stands on the highest artistic standard and the co-operating artists are the best ones one can find. If we can combine the America trip and the Covent Garden Opera, I think I shall cross the Atlantic Ocean. (15 January 1905)

In much the same way that Ibbs and Tillett would come to dominate the infrastructure of the performance of music in Britain as the twentieth century progressed, in America the scene was largely controlled by the Wolfsohn Bureau at the time John Tillett was trying to establish a branch of Vert's agency in New York. In 1879 August Wilhelmj arrived in America for a concert tour but found conditions there very different from Europe, where he was a renowned violinist. In America his name was hardly known, publicity and advertising were scant and he found himself in a managerial wilderness, where there was no country-wide organization nor any individual to run one. Undeterred, Wilhelmj set forth and by his superlative performances began to make his mark. In Chicago he met the dynamic Henry Wolfsohn, then 32, owner of a music conservatory in Louisville, Kentucky, and already beginning to make a name for himself as someone familiar with conditions in America for promoting concerts. Wolfsohn took Wilhelmj's tour in hand, began sending telegrams ahead to his contacts in scores of cities and towns throughout the continent and generally transformed a modest success into a triumph. Wilhelmj, himself not without influence, sang the young man's praises, for he had made more money on this tour than ever before, while Wolfsohn, encouraged by his own success, sold his music school and moved to New York.

In the summer of 1881, Wolfsohn presented a series of evening Promenade Concerts in the Metropolitan Concert Hall on the site of which the Broadway Theatre now stands. After its success, the piano firm Steinway invited him to undertake the management of a tour for the brilliant pianist Rafael Joseffy (a parallel here with Dolby's emergence from the London firm of Chappell & Company to work for Charles Dickens). Despite a series of obstacles, including serious attacks of stage-fright before Joseffy gave his recitals, Wolfsohn had a personal success which brought him to the attention of Clara Louise Kellogg, the American soprano who ran her own touring concert company. Wolfsohn hired Carl Strakosch (who later became Kellogg's husband) as an advance agent whom he sent ahead of the touring group to secure arrangements for accommodation and performances. Three years later, in 1884, the Wolfsohn Musical Bureau was formally launched from premises at 331 East 14th Street, New York. For ten years its principal business was with the big opera stars, who followed the current custom to reserve the right to arrange such concert appearances as they chose, turning to the bureau to provide the service of running the event. Instrumentalists were only gradually absorbed into the activities of the bureau, mainly on the back of promotion by Steinway. A further personal triumph for Wolfsohn was a festival in Madison Square Garden for the soprano Adelina Patti in the autumn of 1881, for which he set seat prices at a mere $1.50 and attracted an audience of thousands whilst Patti was guaranteed $5000 for her appearance.

Gradually Wolfsohn built up his stable of artists, mainly to service the field of opera, but there were also music festivals in places such as Cincinnati, Worcester, Springfield and St Louis. His lists make formidable reading, and included such singers as Lilli Lehmann, Italo Campanini, Marianne Brandt, Paul Kalisch, Sofia Scalchi, Antonio Galassi, Emma Juch, Clementine de Vere, Theodore Reichmann, Maria Ritter-Goetze, Minnie Hauk, Giuseppe del Puente, Albert Niemann and Anton Schott. To these he added Amalie Materna, Emil Fischer, Max Alvary and Anton van Rooy as recitalists and promoted such instrumentalists as the pianists Adele aus der Ohe and Franz Rummel, and the violinists Franz Wilcek and Maud Powell. Many of them appeared at a testimonial gala for the conductor Max Maretzek at the Metropolitan Opera on 12 February 1889 conducted by Theodore Thomas, Anton Seidl and Walter Damrosch, influential men whose conducting activities would generate even more business for the ever-expanding Wolfsohn Musical Bureau. Astutely he widened awareness of the Bureau's name by putting on a series of free concerts in Castle Garden in 1891 at which artists, orchestras and conductors alike gave their services with support from public spirited (i.e. wealthy) citizens to defray the expenses.

Wolfsohn's lists were predominantly made up of European artists but gradually he began to explore indigenous talent in America, Maud Powell being one of his first successes. Like Vert in Britain, he came to respect the opinions of artists already on his books, for example the tenor William Rieger had nothing but praise for a young contralto he had heard called Olive Fremstad. Wolfsohn had already reacted with indifference to an approach made on her behalf by her singing teacher, Frederick Bristol, but now granted her an audition following Rieger's recommendation. After placing her with Lilli Lehmann for a few final singing lessons, Fremstad began a career which would win her worldwide fame. He also worked hard on behalf of Ernestine Schumann-Heink, who he discovered in 1892 as a house contralto at the Hamburg Opera, and enticed to New York to join the Met, first on a salary of $75 a week, but soon advancing to the level of an opera star where she could command $500 for an appearance on one of Wolfsohn's concert tours. Also from overseas came the violinist Fritz Kreisler, the pianist Josef Hofmann (playing in knickerbockers at ten years old when he appeared in 1887), the Belgian violinist César Thomson (the first artist imported directly by Wolfsohn from abroad), the oratorio singers Lillian Blauvelt, Ben Davies, Evan Williams, David Ffrangcon-Davies, George and Lillian Henschel, Muriel Foster and the ubiquitous Clara Butt. He had great success with a tour by the eminent French organist Alexandre Guilmant and followed it with an even more adventurous one by an impressive trio consisting of Josef Hofmann, Fritz Kreisler and Jean Gérardy. By the turn of the century Raoul Pugno, Ernst von Dohnányi, Alexander Siloti, Hugo Becker, Josef Hollman, Blanche Marchesi, Pablo Casals, Franz Ondricek, Jacques Thibaud, Charles Gilibert and Mischa Elman had been managed by Wolfsohn, who by May 1902 had even extended his activities to promoting artists such as Kreisler in London when he made his debut there under Hans Richter. For the 1903–04 season, the Philharmonic Society of New York turned to Wolfsohn for their guest conductors and he supplied men of the calibre of Edouard Colonne, Sir Henry Wood, Felix Weingartner, Fritz Steinbach, Emil Paur and Richard Strauss. Further highlights included tours by Caruso at the end of the 1907–08 season and one by Rachmaninov in 1909–10, while plans were laid for Sousa's Band to tour a couple of years later. Wolfsohn did not live to see this for he died in 1909 and was succeeded by A.F. Adams and Thomas Quinlan, though after a year Adams acquired sole rights.

A flourishing, competitive music agency thus awaited John Tillett when he arrived in July 1902 to establish a branch office in New York for his uncle Narciso Vert. For two years he struggled against Wolfsohn's intensely fierce and dominating stranglehold on America's musical affairs until, by March 1904, he was all for giving up:

> My dear Uncle,
>
> I have been on the point of writing you again and again on a very important question, as I think you will agree, but have deferred doing so until now, hoping that matters might improve considerably

and that there would be no necessity for this letter, which I know will be disappointing reading to you, containing as it does anything but good news. The question I have been turning over in my mind for some time past is whether any money can be made out of an American Musical Agency run on our lines at this late day. I am persuaded to say "No" after viewing the ground as I have done these last eighteen months or more. Perhaps I am rather hasty in my conviction, but I cannot help feeling terribly discouraged at the result of my strenuous efforts (pardon the Americanism) since I arrived in this country. It may be that we haven't had the right artists to handle and have struck bad times. In any case it is my duty to report to you at once the state of affairs and leave it to you and Pedro to decide whether it will be wise to venture on another season. Mind you, I am perfectly willing to remain out here and work for all I know, if you should decide so, but the question is whether you are disposed to put up the necessary finance, unless you see some pretty sure sign of a return in the near future, or whether you consider that my services are more valuable and can be better employed at home. Somehow I cannot help thinking the latter to be the case, but you and Pedro will know best on this point.

It seems almost impossible for me to fully explain matters by letter as there is much to be told and much to be argued. One thing sure is that the musical field is not improving in this country and that European artists find it more difficult now than in the past to make big money. One reads a tremendous lot of the fabulous sums carried away by different artists, but with one or two rare exceptions such is not the case. The competition is terrible and as I have already mentioned, I am afraid there is not much chance for an Agency run on our straightforward and honest lines. All the leading American artists like [David] Bispham, [Ellison] van Hoose, [Herbert] Witherspoon etc., much as they dislike Wolfsohn, are afraid to leave him, who, as they say, holds the reins almost everywhere, which I have to own is no exaggeration. Unless we are prepared to guarantee a whole lot of artists for a season or two, I am quite sure it will be impossible to get in touch with the Societies and concert givers. This is the true state of affairs, only there is a lot more agony to pile on, which can be left over for the present.

Although I dare not tell the artists, I know for certain of two or three instances where Henry Wolfsohn has prevented people engaging [Theodor] Lierhammer, William Green and Muriel Foster, as was the case last year over Ben Davies of course, by unfair means, but no more of these distressing admissions. I have said enough for you to judge for yourselves whether we are to continue our business over here, and I shall await with much anxiety the result of your decision. Whatever you may settle, I think you will see the necessity of my coming over to London at the end of the present season, which will be towards the latter part of May, but before starting I must hear from you in order to leave things as they should be. Enclosed is the balance sheet for our first year, 1902-3; it has been passed by Maxwell [George Maxwell of Boosey & Co, music publishers at the same premises], so all is in order. As regards our second year now drawing to a close, I hope to be able to pull through without calling on you for more money but it will be a close shave.

Pending your answer I shall take no definite steps in regard to Marie Hall etc., but I will try and speak with Ellis of Boston re their concerts. The London Trio would, I am positive, have no success here and for the few engagements that might be secured I am sure nothing like the fee they would require to cover their necessary heavy expenses could be secured. I am afraid they couldn't get any piano house to back them as the pianist herself is not a big enough card. I am of your opinion regarding the lecture tour on Roman Catholic music, which I am sure the general public doesn't care a rap about, but perhaps one of the educational bureaux might be interested in the scheme and I will see what can be done with them. I will also make enquiries if Savage is looking for any new artists for his company next season. This refers to Miss Alexander and Miss Booth. He may intend visiting London soon, in which case you could arrange for them both to sing for him.

[Lillian] Nordica is a very difficult lady to get hold of as she is travelling so much. I think I had better write her on the question of doing work for her in England next winter. According to newspaper reports she is to return here for the Metropolitan Opera season, but this may not be true. She has been doing big business lately with her Wagner concerts, in which she was associated with Walter Damrosch. I have written Uncle Fernando by this mail re [Ludwig] Wüllner. Do you really think he would be successful here? I have not heard him myself, but from what people tell me I think it very doubtful if the American public would appreciate him. In any case the guarantee he asks is impossible; ten concerts per month, terms $500 per concert, travelling and hotel in addition for himself, accompanist and servant. I dare say he would take less, but I would be afraid to run him at half that figure.

If reports are true again, we are to have three big opera "stars" in the field next winter with their own Concert companies, Melba, Calvé and Eames and in the virtuoso line Ysaÿe, de Pachmann and Hofmann, so somebody will get hit pretty hard, for I don't think the country will stand for so much in one season. It will be a short one I fancy on account of the Presidential election when, they tell me, everything is at a standstill in the musical line. The successes of this season have been *Parsifal*, Caruso, Reisenauer and of course Melba's tour, but she is no stranger. Regarding Thibaud, opinions differ. The press did not treat him well here [New York], but I understand in the other cities he made good. Busoni, Arbos and others tell me he went away very dissatisfied with his manager, but I suppose he will be out here again under the same auspices. The press wouldn't look at [the English pianist Gertrude] Peppercorn and with one exception (*The Sun*) I don't think they troubled to criticise her playing. The notice in the paper mentioned was terrible. Virgo will have told you all about the Patti tour, which came suddenly to a conclusion last week. I only wonder it didn't bust up sooner. The supporting artists have been treated shabbily, one Anton Hegner by name being dropped a few thousand miles away from this city in the middle of the tour. He has a lot to say, as you may well imagine. Steinway's are dropping money over the Richard Strauss Festival, although it is given out that the houses are all money.

I have taken a very bad cold, but I am taking good care of myself and shall soon be myself again. There is an awful lot of sickness about owing to the terribly severe changes in the weather. It is warm and wet one day and the next we find ourselves walking home in a blizzard with winds that go clean through you. Everyone is praying for spring and I must say that I shall be glad to welcome it. I need not say I am very glad to hear that all are well at home and trust you are keeping in good health yourself. With love and kind remembrances to all friends, believe me your affectionate nephew Jack. (14 March 1904)

As it happens, a small number of letters, three from the spring of 1904 and one from the same period in the following year, written by mezzo soprano Muriel Foster have survived in the archive. They are addressed to 'Mr Tillett', though whether to Pedro or John is unclear:

I am surprised to hear that Mr Wolfsohn has given it out that he is to control my business in the States next year. He certainly has suggested it to me, but nothing was arranged. I now write to say definitely that I wish you to manage all my affairs in the States. I hope to arrive about Dec 31st [19]05 and will have six weeks and possibly 9 or 10 at your disposal. (17 April 1904)

Thank you very much for your good wishes. It is sad to think that there are to be no more American tours, but I shall always have the pleasantest of recollections of the work we did together. (24 August 1904)

I was so pleased to get your letter this morning with such satisfactory news. I was getting anxious but did not want to bother you by writing and worrying. It is splendid, I think. I should not book anything more under $350 now, as we are so well advanced I think we can afford to be firm, don't you? I will let you have photos etc. next week. Please tell Mr [conductor Wilhelm] Gericke at once that I propose singing 'O attritone' from *Odysseus* Max Bruch and 'Furibondo' (a florid air) Handel, and I hope he will agree to these. If not, 'Allmacht' Schubert instead of Bruch aria. Many thanks for enquiries re maid. I have had an excellent holiday and am splendidly well, and had a great success at Gloucester (cuttings follow). I wonder how much has been spent on advertisements. Don't you think we might cut these down now, as perhaps it is hardly necessary to advertise much when we are nearly booked up, as I must be in England by March 7th, and the money could be saved for say the following year. I think this is all at present. Many thanks for the work you have done. (14 September ?1904)

Thank you for your letter. I am very sorry you will be unable to continue managing my work for me in USA as I felt so confident leaving it in your hands. I have written Mr Charlton and will take advantage of your kind offer and come to you for advice when required. I arrive home May 16. (9 May 1905)

Tenor Ben Davies, alluded to in John's report to his uncle, wrote from Boston before moving on to Canada:

> Many thanks for so kindly sending my letters – I received one this morning, I note the contents of yours last week re rehearsal at Toronto, also as to "Onaway" at Montreal. I leave here tomorrow (Wed:) evening for Toronto and hope to be in N. York on Saturday night 10 o'clock – or 10.30. Shall go to the Earlington [Hotel]. I note rehearsal on Sunday. You will be glad to hear that I got on splendidly here – was in fine voice, and Gericke was very kind. He never said anything to me about being late – he begs of me to return next season, but we can talk that over when we meet – the papers were good here except Philip Hales – he dislikes me I believe. Never mind – he'll get over it.
>
> Give my best regards to Geo[rge Maxwell?] and tell him I hope to see him well and jolly on Sunday. Kindest regards, hoping you are A.1.
>
> P.S. Have had a lovely time here – enjoyed myself. (14 April 1903)

A few months later, Davies wrote from Sheringham in Norfolk to John Tillett, who had come over from America to London to report to his uncle:

> I too am very sorry not to be at home – should have liked to have seen you muchly. If you can come down here for a few days we shall be glad to see you. Have a little room vacant – send me a card if you can come. (24 September 1903)

After Narciso Vert's death in 1905 the trustees of his estate tried to lay claim on John Tillett for monies owing from the American venture and its losses. Eventually they thought fit to withdraw their claim after enough evidence had been supplied to them by Vert's brother, Fernando, and by the lawyer, George Maxwell, both of them requested by John Tillett to back his counter-assertion that Vert had readily agreed to bear the losses incurred. Tillett kept some notes on the affair:

> Maxwell's first interview with the Governor [Narciso Vert], June 1903, when he told him that the business would require fresh capital by August to carry things through. My inability to find any further money, the Governor's willingness to send out the necessary money (£300 was cabled in August or September). Cable also received announcing [Edward] Lloyd's inability to come to America. My trip to London during September 1903 re [Muriel] Foster tour. My interview with the Governor, when it was personally understood I had no more money to put into the business. My letter of March 1904 giving my views of the situation of affairs and advice to close the agency. My visit to London in June to settle matters when it was decided after interviews with Maxwell and between ourselves that it would be advisable to close the agency for good. The arrangement being that I was to return to New York to look after Muriel Foster's tour (January–February 1905), which had already been entered into, at the end of which I was to return to London. The Governor was to send out the necessary money for the expenses (£50 being given to me before sailing and a further £50 and £20 cabled out afterwards). The understanding that there would be a loss as the expenses incurred would be greater than the commission realised on the Foster tour, but this [was] considered more advisable than to break faith with Miss Foster. Maxwell's offer, and which was carried out, not to charge any rental at the end of the second year (July 1904), thereby helping the Governor in the matter of expenses with 7 months rental free. The Governor's admission that I had done all in my power to make the agency a success, that he had sent the monies out in order to help me.

Fernando Vert's draft of his affidavit bears out John Tillett's version of events:

> I wish to make the following statement. In the course of a conversation I had with my late brother Narciso Vert shortly before his death regarding the American agency, he told me that he personally was finding all the necessary money to run the business then in existence in New York, and that apart from a certain sum of money which his nephew John Hudson Tillett had embarked in the venture when he first went out to New York, that he was not further responsible in any way and that my brother was bearing the whole expense himself. He further stated that the business had shown no profit and that he had determined at the termination of certain contracts with artists to close the agency altogether and that his nephew John Tillett would return to London.

The trustees decided to withdraw their claim on the grounds that they believed Vert had intended to bear all the losses personally. He died suddenly on 3 June 1905 following a heart attack at his Hampstead home, 28 Elsworthy Road, at the age of 60. On the very day of his death, this report appeared on page five of *The Times* newspaper:

> At Marlborough Street, N VERT, concert agent of Cork Street, Burlington Gardens, W, was summoned before Mr Kennedy for having unlawfully procured on May 15 at Queen's Hall, a child under the age of eleven – namely Vivien Chartres, aged nine, to be on the premises licensed for public entertainment for the purpose of playing at 3pm contrary to the statute. JOHN CHARTRES of Middle Temple Lane was summoned for allowing the child to be on licensed premises for the purpose of playing. Mr H Muskett, solicitor, prosecuted on behalf of the Commissioner of Police, Mr Howard A Lawrance, solicitor, defended. Mr Muskett said that the proceedings were instituted under the Prevention of Cruelty to Children Act. The case came under the section concerning "restrictions". The girl was announced to appear at a concert on the date mentioned. It must have been known there would be difficulties as a representative of Mr Vert called on Sub-divisional Inspector Cutbush at Tottenham Court Road police station apparently to ask what should be done in the circumstances. On May 15 the inspector saw the child's father, but the child appeared at the hall and played several pieces. Inspector Cutbush gave evidence bearing out Mr Muskett's statement, adding that after the interview he called at the Queen's Hall and said that the performance must not take place. Mr Tillett, Mr Vert's representative, said it was too late to stop the performance and that it must go on. Mr Chartres, who was present, told him that he knew the law on the subject, and added, "They are always advertised as young as they are, that's all I can tell you. Her age will be produced at the proper time". Cross examined, [Cutbush said]: He was present at the performance. The child appeared to enjoy her work. Mr Lawrance, in defence, said that the Act was for the prevention of cruelty to children, whereas the child was never perfectly happy without her violin. His clients were only requested to stop the performance at the last moment. Mr Kennedy: I suppose they took the money as usual? Mrs Chartres (the mother of the child) replied that the girl was paid no money for the performance she gave at the Queen's Hall. Medical evidence was called, which showed that while the musical abilities of the girl were abnormal, she was quite healthy and would not suffer in any way by playing several solos. Mr Kennedy said that Mr Vert, an experienced agent, had been warned, but took no notice, and he would have to pay a fine of £25 with £5 costs. Mr Chartres would have to pay a fine of £5 and 2s. costs.

The stress of this incident together with the pressures of winding down the American concern put a heavy strain on his already indifferent health. Placing highly talented youngsters before the public was a fairly common feature of the day. Only a few weeks after Chartres' recital another child violinist, the 11-year-old Franz von Vecsey, played the Beethoven concerto with the London Symphony Orchestra (LSO) under Charles Williams at the same venue. Vert's attitude had been generally recognized as highly responsible in the handling of such young performers, and the Chartres case was generally viewed as a genuine oversight on his part to apply for a licence. In 1887 he had sent the young pianist Josef Hofmann on a recital tour to America in a joint venture with the impresario Henry Abbey, while three years later he drew up a carefully worded contract with the father of the 11-year-old pianist Mark Hambourg.

> Contract made on 2nd August 1887 between Narciso Vert and the impresario Henry Abbey on behalf of the 11-year-old pianist Josef Hofmann for his first tour to the USA in November 1887.
>
> That the said Josef Hofmann shall proceed to New York on or about the 12th November 1887 for the purpose of appearing and performing as a Pianist in 81 concerts to be given by the said Henry Abbey in such of the principal towns in the United States of America as the said Henry Abbey shall think fit.
>
> The first of such concerts shall be given in New York early in the month of December 1887. The remaining concerts shall be given at the rate of four a week during the months of December 1887, January, February, March and April 1888.

The said Josef Hofmann shall give his services at the first of the said concerts without remuneration and the said Henry Abbey shall pay to the said Casimir Hofmann [the boy's father] for the remaining eighty concerts the sum of £5000 by instalments of £250 to be paid per week, the first instalment to be paid immediately after the first week's performances and each subsequent instalment at the end of each succeeding week.

The said Henry Abbey shall pay the first class travelling expenses of the said Josef Hofmann and three other persons who will accompany him from England to New York, and first class travelling and hotel expenses during their stay in the United States, and first class travelling expenses back again to England.

That on or before the 12th October 1887 the said Henry Abbey shall deposit £1000 at the London and County Bank, Hanover Square branch in the name of the said Narciso Vert, and if the said Henry Abbey shall duly perform his part of this agreement, such sum of £1000 shall be taken to be in payment of the last four weekly instalments of £250 but in the breach or non-performance by the said Henry Abbey of this agreement, such £1000 shall be held by the said Narciso Vert to answer the damage which the said Hermann Wolff, Casimir Hofmann and Josef Hofmann or either of them may sustain by reason of such breach or non-performance. In case the said Henry Abbey shall fail to deposit the first sum of £1000 on or before the said 12th October 1887, it shall be lawful for but not obligatory upon the said Narciso Vert as such agent as aforesaid to declare this agreement null and void.

In the event of the said Josef Hofmann being of reason of illness or other inevitable cause unable to perform at all of the said concerts, the said Henry Abbey shall be entitled to deduct a proportionate part of the said weekly instalments in respect of any concert or concerts at which the said Josef Hofmann shall be unable to appear, but shall not be entitled to any other compensation, but if the said Josef Hofmann shall be unable from any cause to appear at any of the said concerts, then the said sum of £1000 shall be returned to the said Henry Abbey.

Contract dated 31st July 1890 between Michel Hambourg and Narciso Vert concerning Max [Mark] Hambourg his 11-year-old son.

To Mr N. Vert, 6 Cork Street, LONDON W

On behalf of my son Max Hambourg I hereby accept your offer of engagement on the terms and conditions hereafter specified, viz:

That the services of the said Max Hambourg are to be at your exclusive disposal for a period of One Year dating from and inclusive of the first day of September 1890, during which time he is to play at such concerts or recitals in Great Britain and Ireland as you may decide to fix, but not more than three times weekly, except in instances specially agreed to by me.

In consideration thereof it is agreed that you are to pay me the sum of Five Hundred pounds (£500.0.0) for the services of the said Max Hambourg for the period mentioned, in four instalments as follows, viz: One hundred and twenty five pounds (£125) on the first of September 1890 and a like sum on the first of December, March and June following respectively, and it is understood that in addition you are to pay the travelling and hotel expenses of Max Hambourg and one other person in connection with any and all engagements that may take place outside London during the term of this contract; it is also understood that I am to receive One Fourth (1/4) of your nett profits of the undertaking.

Furthermore it is agreed that you are to provide the sum of Sixty pounds (£60) over and above the above mentioned amount to defray the cost of transit of the remainder of my family from Moscow to London.

Lastly I concede to you the right of prolonging this engagement for Great Britain and Ireland, the Continent, America and Australia for a period of One, Two or Three Years or any part of the same, upon such terms and conditions as I may consider suitable, and in no case on the conditions and terms of this contract. [signed] Michel Hambourg

Narciso Vert's death was keenly felt in the field of music and its operations. Only three years earlier, on 5 January 1902, and registered as 'Narciso Vert, Citizen and Musician of London', he had been granted the Freedom of the City of London. Several obituaries appeared in the press and many referred to him as the Father of Concert Agents. Another reflected: 'Mr Vert has died with an honourable name, passing away just about the same time as occurs the demolition of St James's Hall [now the site of the Piccadilly Hotel], where we have seen him have some of his best hours. He helped music in England, and was a courteous, sympathetic gentleman, liked by all his clients.' The following substantial piece entitled 'Death of Mr N. Vert' appeared in *The Musical Herald* for 1 July 1905, and regrettably most of the material its author noted in Vert's office (photographs, programmes and letters for example) is no longer extant. The report also deflects responsibility for the Chartres affair on to the police, whose response to an enquiry as to the necessity of procuring a licence for her apparently came too late for anyone to do anything about it. Whether, as it also states, Vert had no longer been 'taking responsibility for office affairs for two or three years' is impossible to corroborate; perhaps this was Pedro Tillett nobly shielding his uncle's posthumous reputation from any scandal.

> Many have been the expressions of regret made during the past month by the very numerous friends of Mr N Vert upon hearing of his death on the 3rd ult. Artists styled him 'the most honest concert agent in London', 'one of the best of men to do business with', and so on. 'I had always found him courteous, civil, kind, and approachable', said a manager to us. He was so long before the public that it is difficult to believe that he was only 61. He made his own way in life. If he did not create the profession of concert agent, he was certainly a pioneer, and became foremost in that line. Flaming advertisement was not his method, although his business was one that would seem to need it above all others. A business so well managed can scarcely lose its position. Mr Vert, in fact, when his health began to fail, put it into the capable hands of his nephew Mr Pedro J. Tillett. Early days are recalled as the representative of the *The Musical Herald* looks round the rooms at 6 Cork Street, W. Photogravures of leading artists look down upon the old concert-goer, and their voices or performances echo through the valley of the years. Rubinstein endorses his portrait apologetically: 'To Mr Narciso Vert in remembrance of much bother, A. Rubinstein, St Petersburg, 12th August, 1886'. Similarly we seem to speak with Bottesini, Patey, Albani, Mascagni, Tamagno, and hosts of others. Here is a letter from Gounod recommending Madame Lucie Palicot. Rubinstein writes from Peterhof, July 23rd, 1881, asking for the favour of an angling outfit, and a postscript (the afterthought must be a disguise) asking if Mr Vert will see the Lord Chamberlain about the possibility of producing Rubinstein's opera *Machabes* at Covent Garden. Liszt writes from Buda Pesth, under date of 31st January, 1883, sending his photograph, always a sign that continuance of friendly relationship is desired. From old letters we turn to bound volumes of old programs [*sic*]. The public history of many of the great departed, as well as of living artists, seems to be enshrined with them. Balfe's Memorial Concert, June 10th 1885, at the Albert Hall, is associated with the name of Mr Vert. So are the Richter Concerts, though at first these bore the name of Mr Hermann Franke, who failed, then Mr Schultz-Curtius put his name on the title-page for a time. Here is the program of the first 'Richter Festival Concert' dated May 5th 1879, at which Mr Georg Henschel sang. These were not the ventures of Herr Richter, as some people have supposed. Others bore the risk and the loss in those tentative days of orchestral concerts. Probably the first series of cheap orchestral concerts was that started in 1890 called 'Young People's Orchestral Concerts', in which Mr Henschel tried to interest the people. It was a fine artistic venture, though a financial failure. To get people to an orchestral concert was a great struggle at that time, and single-handed efforts were risky. The Philharmonic Society must be excepted, but they had a large guarantee fund.
>
> The Patti Concerts were managed by Mr Vert, associated with Mr W. Kuhe and Mr Ambrose Austin. He also managed the Henry Irving and Ellen Terry recital tour, looked after the interests of William Terries and Milward, started George Grossmith on his recitals when he left the Savoy, and had other schemes in hand, apart from the usual musical connection. He began by acting for Charles Dickens in lecture tours. He was associated with Mr George Dolby, brother of Madame Sainton-Dolby. On the failure of that gentleman, Mr Vert took up the business and was agent also for Madame Sainton-

Dolby. Mr Vert's name has been prominent lately in a case of police prosecution for exploiting a prodigy under ten years of age. The newspapers have said that his death was hastened by this business worry, but he knew nothing about it and had not for two or three years past taken the responsibility of affairs at his office. His manager sought police advice as to whether a licence was necessary, but the reply only came two hours before the concert at which the child was to appear, and it was impossible to stop the concert when permission was refused at the last moment.

We ask Mr Tillett whether the public run after prodigies as much as ever. He says that too many prodigies have been brought forward and business has not been great in that line since Hofmann's highly successful appearances under Mr Vert in 1887.

It is curious how orchestral concerts have come to the fore without injuring the best vocal concerts. An orchestral concert used to be quite an event, musically but not financially. Now everybody goes to them, even people who did not go before to the ordinary concert.

'Do the public prefer foreign artists?', we ask. 'It is true', says Mr Tillett, 'that the public still seem to be drawn by a foreign name more than an English one, especially in the instrumental line. But it must be remembered that the foreign names represent the whole of Europe. Isolated cases of specially successful artists can be given in any country, English or foreign. Great artists who are English are perhaps not as plentiful as they might be, but they still create a position for themselves. Leonard Borwick and others might be named as examples, but the fact remains that violinists, cellists, and pianists bearing foreign names and having a Continental reputation are preferred to English artists with an English reputation'.

It is the time of the London season, and Mr Tillett's waiting room is filled with people ready to take their turn to interview him. We must hurry on. A good deal of business is done in arranging for private parties, and many artists make a good income in those circles. Big concerts are in prospect and *débutantes* have their claims. Aspiring vocalists want their voices to be heard. Mr Vert's practice has been to make no charge for hearing singers, but the numbers increase so fast that it may be impossible to continue this service. Yet some idea must be gained of the artist's powers before an agreement can be made, whether it be for the concert agent to take the whole risk of management, to act as agent on payment of expenses to him, to make sharing terms, or to work upon a percentage basis. While it is interesting to get this peep behind the manager's desk, it is sad to think of the vacant chair. Mr Vert was unmarried; his brothers and sisters are living. What a busy life he has led since he was a chorister at St Andrew's, Wells Street. His funeral at Highgate Cemetery, on the 7th ult., was attended by many artists well-known to concert-goers.

At the time of his death, his brothers Fernando and Pedro worked in the firm, the latter as its accountant. The youngest brother Honorato, aged only 35, had died suddenly of pneumonia in Newcastle on 5 May 1893, in the middle of a tour promoted by the agency for Emma Albani, his responsibilities being concert and recital management. It therefore fell to Vert's partner, office manager and elder nephew, Pedro Juan Tillett, to take charge of the agency.

CHAPTER THREE

Memoirs of Pedro Tillett

Some of the events and the musicians mentioned in the two preceding chapters are recalled by Pedro Tillett in somewhat disjointed memoirs written in 1948 at the age of 76. As a 15-year-old apprentice in 1887 he used to walk daily to the Cork Street office by way of Primrose Hill to pick up the bus at the top of Park Street. He used to observe such characters as Dr Goode-Adams ('always well-dressed with an air of affluence') as he drove his pair of fine horses leading the carriage from his home at the junction of Gloucester and Regents Park Roads (on which site Cecil Sharp House stands today), while opposite lived Sir Alexander Mackenzie, then Principal of the Royal Academy of Music.

One of the activities of the office, and a valuable source of revenue, was signing popular sheet music. On behalf of the composers, the agency held rubber stamps with the facsimile of their signatures which had to be impressed upon every copy of their printed music, such as songs, vocal or piano scores. Periodically the publisher would send a curt postcard notifying the agency of the despatch of anything from 500 to 2000 copies of such pieces as 'The Lost Chord' by Sullivan or a vocal score of his *Iolanthe*, 'Goodbye' by Tosti, 'May Morning' by Denza or 'The Devout Lover' by Maude Valerie White. There was an office factotum, known to all as 'Old Scott', whose job it was to rubber stamp each copy. Each morning he would:

> sally forth with an awful old square-shaped leather bag, which he clung to with great tenacity, containing the necessary stamps, and if it was a busy day, he would sign thousands of copies and return late in the afternoon a bit the worse for wear, sit down in the corner and have a doze. Scott was a quaint old character and in addition to his trip to America as valet to Charles Dickens, he had been a dresser to Charles Fechter and Charles Mathews, well-known actors in their day. Then George Dolby took him on and later passed him on to my uncle. He lived in a room over a newsagent's shop in Shaftesbury Avenue and the walls were covered with photos of actors, actresses, playbills and a miscellany of theatrical bits and pieces. I used to go and see him when he was ill and he left me all his junk. When he passed away he must have been over eighty … When we were extra busy, and that was pretty often, Scott used to order grilled chops for us from *The Blue Posts*, a few doors up in Cork Street. My, what beautiful meat, tender as a chicken, and of a delicious flavour. After delivering the chops he would then return to fetch refreshment in the form of a large jug of stout for which this hostelry was noted. *The Blue Posts*, owned by Mrs Schlette and two sons, had a very quiet bar and a very select clientele for lunches, dinners and suppers. Later it became the *Halcyon Club* for women.

There were also the more fashionable restaurants of the day frequented by musicians and artists; Richter favoured Pagani's in Covent Garden but there was also a little restaurant in Mill Street at the back of St George's Church in Hanover Square which became a well-known rendezvous. Owned and run by an Italian named Bellini, 'outside it was unpretentious but very comfy inside, and Bellini used to serve excellent fare', Vert used to entertain Elgar, Edward Lloyd, Foli and Clara Butt there. The Summer Season, however, was the time for At Homes and Soirées given nightly by London's high society, who opened up their London houses:

> In May and June the West End was crowded with beautiful horses and carriages, their occupants being lovely ladies dressed in the most fashionable attire. The shops were filled with beautiful things,

> attractive goods and everywhere was gay with colour. Window boxes were filled with flowers of many hues, which together with freshly painted houses, gave the West End and Mayfair streets a very bright and cheery aspect. Park Lane was most attractive in those days before the huge new hotels and buildings were erected; the Second World War put paid to Bond Street, though the beginning of the end for it was when the omnibus was allowed to use it as a new route to Piccadilly and Victoria, for the street is too narrow for such traffic.

Private engagements, matinees and soirées were very sought after, and among the artists Vert could provide were the singers Melba, Nordica, Caruso, the de Reszke brothers, Plançon and Scotti, but there were also 'Well Known Amateur Musicians', society ladies such as Lady Maud Warrender, Countess Valda Gleichen, the Honourable Rosamond Tufton and Elsie Swinton. The last named mezzo-soprano benefited from this crossover mix of professional and amateur music-making when, despite her high standing in society, she took the unusual step of becoming a professional singer in April 1906, a year after Vert's death. She appears on Ibbs and Tillett's first artists' register as Mrs George Swinton, and on 5 December 1908 was so well established that she was given prime billing over four other artists in a recital at the Bechstein Hall accompanied by Fauré (a friend since 1898). Such private engagements were relatively hard to come by but were well paid, and therefore much sought after by artists:

> Will you accept an "At Home" at [Mrs Harben] 107, Westbourne Terrace, W. on Wednesday next, May 30th at 10pm? Terms twelve guineas (£12.12.0). We asked 20 guineas, but could not get this fee. Will you kindly send us two short groups of songs, not too serious! Mr Liddle will be the accompanist I think. (24 May 1906)

That these events often began late in the evening is confirmed by a card from the London-based Italian composer Ciro Pinsuti to the tenor Edward Lloyd, when he wrote to ask:

> Could you assist a private concert with me on Friday night May 31 at 10.30? I think your terms are 25 guineas, am I right? Kindly send me an early answer. (6 May 1878)

Instrumentalists were also booked; Paderewski, lionized by society, was much in demand and as a result could charge a very high fee, while another pianist, Moriz Rosenthal, once walked out on an important party, reporting (in the third person) to Vert the next morning: 'the people chattered so. He stopped playing until they were quiet, then resumed, but as they began again he got up, closed the piano and departed in a fury. So was his hostess.' Josef Hofmann netted a sum of £1200 in a few weeks at such occasions, while other artists booked included the violinist Johannes Wolff, the cellist Josef Hollman, the song composer and singer Isidore de Lara, the composer and pianist Cecile Chaminade, and the actor and vocalist Maurice Farkoa. Among those who hosted such private concerts was Edgar Cohen, a Director of Harrods, who had a fine house and grounds in Hall Road, St John's Wood and gave Sunday Garden Parties where prominent musicians, actors and actresses foregathered and at which the pianist and composer Tito Mattei was a frequent performer. Another was Mrs Samuel Lewis, wife of the financier, who gave many a soirée or 'At Home' at their beautiful mansion in Grosvenor Square, where her sister, the song writer Hope Temple (married to the composer and conductor André Messager) also entertained with popular ballads. Mrs George Lewis of Portland Place, wife of the renowned solicitor Sir George Lewis had gatherings of popular musicians of the day at her house, while her sister Marie Joshua was one of the most important of these philanthropic hostesses, among her most significant 'catches' being Hans Richter and Edward Elgar, who attended her regular Sunday musical activities at her home in Westbourne Terrace, Hyde Park or at the family's country residence in the Suffolk town of Felixstowe.

As a young clerk, Pedro Tillett was able to observe the good and the great entering and leaving his uncle's office, which also housed a Steinway concert grand piano. Vladimir de Pachmann was a frequent visitor and apparently a 'quaint personality', whose hobby it was to collect precious stones, his wallet always containing uncut diamonds and rubies which he would produce 'with much stealth from an inner pocket of his coat':

> I don't suppose we shall ever have a more beautiful exponent of Chopin's music than when he was in his best period. Latterly his idiosyncrasies became more marked, but around 1898 (when he was about 50) I first noticed the beginnings. Often he would sit down and play a beautiful passage for me, remark on its merits and the delight at his execution together with a curious nasal sniff which became a habit … Another outstanding personality was Hans von Bülow who gave a series of recitals at St James's Hall in 1888 called Historic Recitals of Beethoven's Pianoforte Works. A fussy little man, but a great authority on this composer. Many enthusiasts used to endeavour to reach the Artists' Room with their autograph books but only a few attained their objective. When he was signing a successful applicant's book he always knelt on the floor, putting the book on a chair to sign his name. Once an elderly critic of a musical weekly forced his way into the Artists' Room during an interval, Bülow looked up and, recognising his unwelcome visitor, promptly said "We have no gin this afternoon".

Conductors of the day tended to double as either pianists or composers. Most stayed put in one place (Manns at Crystal Palace, Hallé in Manchester) or at least did not venture abroad. The first to carve an international career as a conductor for himself was Hans Richter, who was active in Bayreuth, Vienna, London and Manchester. Richter was a formidable musician who could play every instrument sufficiently well enough to demonstrate to any orchestral player how to comply with any request he might make, and that alone was sufficient to strike terror into the heart of any weak player. Plucked from the pit of a Viennese theatre to become Wagner's amanuensis at Tribschen on Lake Lucerne, Richter's career developed through the 1860s and 1870s around Wagner's music and culminated at the first Bayreuth Festival when the *Ring* was staged for the first time in 1876. The following year Wagner's London admirers put on a Wagner Festival at the Royal Albert Hall in an attempt to provide the composer with funds towards the losses of 1876, and Richter came as his assistant. The huge orchestra failed to read Wagner's beat, so Richter took over for most of each concert while the composer made a token appearance as conductor in one or two works at the most. He then retired to an armchair and, facing the audience from the platform, glowered at them lest any should dare to look other than contented with what was being played. Meanwhile Richter's conducting was a revelation to orchestras and audiences alike and this event was the start of an association with the United Kingdom which would last for 34 years until the very last concert of his career (at Eastbourne with the LSO on 22 April 1911). One of the leaders of the orchestra at the Wagner Festival in 1877 was Hermann Franke, who later enticed Richter back to London for a series of concerts at St James's Hall in the summer of 1879. Their success was immediate and so began the annual series of Orchestral Festival Concerts in May and June, later to become known as the Richter Concerts. Franke initially collaborated with the impresario Alfred Schultz-Curtius, but the latter soon branched off into the field of opera such as the first

British staging of the *Ring* in 1882 (directed by Angelo Neumann and conducted by Anton Seidl), and brought many famous conductors of Wagner to London including Mottl, Levi, Weingartner, Richard Strauss and the composer's son Siegfried.

Franke's association with Richter was fraught with problems. The former was no businessman, the latter in need of someone to run his business affairs while he concentrated on purely artistic matters. By the mid-1880s, Franke was virtually bankrupt and over-exposing Richter by adding an autumn season to his annual spring visits to London. In November 1886, Richter had decided to put his business affairs into the hands of Chappells (who had already made a secret approach to him a few years earlier through the ubiquitous Marie Joshua), and Arthur Chappell duly placed him in the personal hands of Narciso Vert. His English concert life needed to be reorganized, his programmes were becoming repetitive and stale, and, as if to confirm Franke's unsuitability as a concert manager, he died two years later in a lunatic asylum. In the June and August 1887 issues of the *Musical Times*, reviews of the Richter Concerts included the following observations:

> A new season of these popular concerts began on the 2nd ult., under the sole management of Mr N. Vert, who, not without some trouble and litigation, has made the enterprise, with all its profit (or loss) and its responsibility, his own. Mr Vert is the right man for the place he now fills, proof of which may be seen in the fact that he gave Mr Richter *carte blanche* as to the orchestra, and enabled the conductor both to strengthen and improve its resources.

> This performance (Bach's *Magnificat* and Beethoven's *Choral* symphony) worthily ended the first season under Mr N. Vert's management. Regarding its pecuniary success we know nothing, and are not disposed to indulge in guesses. Our hope is that Mr Vert has made both ends meet, and that, by making the programmes as comprehensive as possible, he will go on to reap a full reward for all his risk and labour.

Vert restricted Richter's appearances in 1887 to the one spring season, but the impact he made upon the conductor's activities in Britain was immediate and positive, for he secured a better orchestra and bigger houses for the conductor, who was well pleased. At last Richter had found the right person to run his English career for him, and Vert performed that function until his death in 1905. Richter's activities in London were very straightforward and largely unchanging in their routine. He would come over from Vienna at the end of the opera season in the spring and conduct a series of concerts in London and the provinces during May and June, then he would take a short holiday before and after the Bayreuth Festival (to which he returned annually from 1888 until 1912). Later his autumn concerts in London, followed by a tour, were revived by Vert. For example in 1895 his itinerary was as follows: Brighton, London, Nottingham, Edinburgh, Glasgow, Manchester, Liverpool, London, Oxford, Birmingham, Sheffield, Bradford and London. When Hallé died in Manchester on the morning of 25 October 1895, Richter was on his way to the city by train from Glasgow, and after the concert he was approached by key members of the board to take the orchestra over. Determined to complete 25 years at the Vienna Opera so that he could benefit from a full pension, Richter only moved to Manchester in January 1900 and remained with the orchestra until 1911. Vert's involvement with Richter lessened once the conductor had moved to England. In June 1904, the new LSO asked him to conduct their inaugural concert, after which he retained a close and regular connection which effectively meant the end of his own Richter Concerts; instead he conducted the LSO both in London and on tour.

From 1903 he conducted an annual season of German opera in the early summer at Covent Garden, but negotiated everything himself with the management.

In the process of organizing the Richter Concerts, usually annually in the summer though in some years he also gave an autumn series, it fell to the agency to put together a choir when required (most often for performances of extracts of Wagner's operas or Beethoven's Ninth Symphony). Pedro Tillett was told to ensure that attendance at rehearsals was satisfactory:

> The Richter Choir, trained by Theodore Frantzen, held their rehearsals at Store Street Hall owned by the pianoforte firm of Wornum & Sons, rather a forlorn place but central, being just off Tottenham Court Road and handy for the male chorus who came on from their business. When they had finished, not having had any dinner, one or two of us used to repair to the Bedford Head Hotel nearby where they specialised in suppers, the favourite ones being tripe and onions and Irish stew washed down with a tankard of Reid's stout, some beer in those days. The Doctor [Richter] used to come for final rehearsals. In the autumns of 1894 and 1895 the Richter Orchestra toured to Brighton, Nottingham, Edinburgh, Glasgow, Manchester, Liverpool, Oxford, Birmingham, Sheffield and Bradford. I accompanied this tour and can vouch for its great success artistically, but although we played to big business, the expenses of travelling an orchestra of about 100 musicians, not to mention other costs, is tremendous and small profit is to be expected, rather a heavy loss.

Pedro Tillett was also sent by his uncle to London concerts at a variety of venues to attend upon his performers. By 1880 the Hanover Square Rooms having disappeared and music having been banished from Exeter Hall by its new owners who placed it at the disposal of the Young Men's Christian Association (YMCA) (the performance of oratorios for amusement being considered improper) St James's Hall, now relatively free of competition, seems to have become an especial favourite with its fine acoustics:

> The seating left much to be desired in parts of the building but the old-fashioned green upholstered Sofa Stalls were comfortable and roomy. The approach to the Hall from the Piccadilly entrance was a marble staircase, somewhat ornate and also trying to the elderly. In the small hall on the ground floor to the left of the same entrance was the home of the Christy Minstrels, and if, when attending recitals I had a few moments to spare or was a trifle surfeited with classical music, I used to pop in to the Minstrels for a change. My first attendance at St James's Hall was at Anton Rubinstein's recital in 1886 and thereafter I used to go to the oratorio concerts of the Novello Choir (such as *Rose of Sharon* and *The Dream of Jubal* (Alexander Mackenzie), *Mors et vita* and *The Redemption* (Gounod), *Stabat Mater* (Dvořák) and Handel's *Messiah* with such artists as Albani, Nordica, Macintyre, Edward Lloyd and Charles Santley). And I distinctly remember Plunket Greene, a handsome young baritone with a fine voice making a first appearance at these concerts, which were generally conducted by Alexander Mackenzie, later by Frederic Cowen.
>
> Nathalia Janotha, a Russian pianist, caused me anxious moments when giving her recitals as she would arrive with several baskets which were carried from her four-wheeler, or growler, by the cabman, linkman or anyone she could enlist for the purpose, up to the Artists' Room, which was quite a climb. With great ceremony they were opened and cats of various kinds appeared. Milk had to be obtained and much fuss made, for she adored them (her mascots as she called them, who always went around with her). While she was playing, I always had to see that the Artists' Room door was shut and the likely roamers put back in their baskets safely. She certainly was a quaint woman and I very much suspect this stunt was not without its advertising aspect, such as the loss of their jewels by prima donnas or violinists mislaying their fiddles. Sophie Menter was also fond of cats but thank goodness she only indulged in one basket of them.
>
> A very interesting event was meeting Edvard Grieg and his wife. My uncle had engaged them for a limited number of recitals in England, including a London one at St James's Hall. The programme consisted of his own compositions for piano and his songs. Madame Grieg's voice was a light one,

> but her rendering of her husband's songs was most agreeable taking into consideration her age, for they were both past their half century. At the end of the engagement my uncle arranged a little dinner party at the Café Royal for the Griegs, my uncle and myself. It was a pleasant occasion as our guests were very simple and easily pleased. I can remember how they enjoyed a bottle of Veuve Cliquot (the sweeter kind) at the end of the dinner, and the ices. Both being petite, they reminded me of two happy children.

The Queen's Hall was opened on 25 November 1893 and with the knowledge that St James's Hall would, in a matter of time, be swept away by plans to build the Piccadilly Hotel on its site, Vert began to hire the new hall for some of his events, particularly those he called National Concerts to mark St George's Day, St Andrew's Day and St Patrick's Day, and on Good Fridays for so-called 'Sacred Concerts'. He linked up with Ascherberg, the music publisher, to give concert performances there of the popular double-bill of *Cavalleria rusticana* and *Pagliacci* on 20 January 1894 featuring Ella Russell, Grace Damian, Edward Lloyd, Ben Davies and Eugene Oudin. Two months later on 2 March, Gounod's *Faust* was presented with Antoinette Trebelli, Edward Lloyd and Charles Santley. Sousa's Band was popular but did not produce financial rewards to the degree expected, though surprisingly an enterprising visit by the Upsala Choir from the University of Oslo did. In 1895 solo recitals were given by the Australian contralto Ada Crossley and Emma Albani, the latter producing a satisfactory profit of £340. In the same year the hall's manager, Robert Newman, began his series of Promenade Concerts with the young conductor Henry Wood and these summer concerts became the principal events there. Nevertheless Vert also went for bigger concerts such as a three-day Bach Choir Festival at Easter 1894 and a performance of Beethoven's Ninth Symphony at a matinee on 20 October 1894 under Richter, two years before his concert series was officially transferred to the Queen's Hall. It was at this evidently momentous performance that the singer Eugene Oudin (Tonio and Alfio in the Mascagni/Leoncavallo double-bill earlier in the year) got so caught up with the enthusiasm of the audience at the end that, while visiting Richter in the artists' room, he suffered a stroke from which he died a fortnight later at the early age of 36.

A few other halls were also used by Vert's artists with Pedro Tillett in attendance:

> Steinway Hall saw me very often during the early period of my career for it was used a great deal by recitalists on account of its size and intimacy, not to mention the cost of a recital there which could be kept to between £20 and £30 according to expenditure on advertising. It also had a most agreeable atmosphere as all the staff, from the managers (Mr Eshelby of the piano firm and John Mackey of the hall) to the attendants, were most willing aids. I can recall being in attendance at recitals given by Sophie Menter, Essipoff, Clotilde Kleeberg, Frederic Lamond, Sapelnikoff, Gabrilowitsch and Teresa Carreño among others.
>
> The Aeolian Hall in New Bond Street was built on the site of the Grosvenor Galleries and much expense was lavished on it by the American company, the Aeolian Co. Ltd., who were interested. The entrance floor was mostly used as a showroom with a richly carpeted passage down the centre lined by comfortable settees leading to the staircase that went up to the hall. This was panelled with dark woodwork throughout giving the whole building a warm effect. The platform was carried out in the same style, while the lighting was alluring with its sconces and electric candles fixed on to the dark panelling. The upper floors contained a number of rooms for music teachers besides piano showrooms.
>
> The last time I spoke to Ellen Terry was in the entrance hall, where I found her seated one day on one of the settees. She was very frail and with her dark spectacles looked old and pathetic, but her voice and manner had all its old charm.

The Bechstein Hall, renamed the Wigmore Hall after the 1914–18 war, was built by the pianoforte house of that name and whose manager in Britain was Max Lindlar, a very astute man. Their pianos became very popular here from the latter part of the 19th century and rightly so for it was a beautiful instrument with mellow tone and highly suitable for recitals, but the Steinway grand came out stronger in concerto work against the background of an orchestra, and many leading pianists preferred it. The Salle Erard was an intimate little hall in the pianoforte galleries of this famous firm in Great Marlborough Street, and was used for recitals when expenses had to be kept low.

CHAPTER FOUR

The First Year: 1906

In the census for the year 1881 there is a London household, which is of particular interest to this history and that is 35 Fitzroy Road, St Pancras (actually Primrose Hill) where two families resided, one named Vert, the other Tillett. The oldest resident was Henrietta Vert, then aged 62 and a widow, and with her lived her daughter Manuella (aged 26), and her sons Narciso (36), Honorato (24), Pedro (22) and Fernando (19), with all four men's occupations described as 'musical agent'. Her other daughter, Henrietta Jeanetta (aged 31), also lived there with her two sons Pedro (aged 7) and John (aged 4), each described as 'scholar'. Their surname was Tillett. Curiously the boys' given ages were both incorrect, for in 1881 Pedro (born 1872) was nine and John (born 1876) five. Henrietta Jeanetta Vert was listed as 'head of the household' and as 'married', but her former husband, or at least the father of her two sons, did not live with his family but is found at 39 Mortimer Street, St Marylebone. His name is John H. Tillet (*sic*), his age 32 and his occupation 'musical agent', though as we shall see, quite what he did in life became something of a movable feast, for at the same address was Elizabeth Tillet (*sic*) aged 23 and listed as 'musical agent's wife'. Pedro and John's parents John and Henrietta had married at All Saints Church, Gordon Square (Euston) on 15 April 1870, at which point John's occupation is described as 'ironmonger of 139 Tottenham Court Road'. He was the son of George Tillett, commission agent (a middle man buying and selling on commission) and Henrietta Jeanetta Teresa Vert of 22 Grafton Street East, daughter of Honorato Vert, inlayer (a craftsman in marquetry). John senior's subsequent occupations were 'commercial traveller' as listed on his son Pedro's birth certificate in 1872, on John junior's birth certificate, four years later, he was described as 'commission agent', while on Pedro's wedding certificate in 1896 he had become a 'Theatrical Manager'.

A brief exploration of the different premises mentioned above shows that 139 Tottenham Court Road, where John Hudson Tillett was living at the time of his marriage, was clearly a large building used as a boarding house. In the 1871 census there are no fewer than 19 residents in several household units, variously described as servants, cashiers, and so on, and although there is no mention of the Tilletts, it may well have been several floors of rooms above a street-front business which was being run quite independently. None of the residents appears to be maintaining a business in their own right, but in the 1882 *Post Office Directory* there is an ironmongery at that address, Geo. Baker & Son, so as this is precisely the occupation stated on his marriage certificate, perhaps he is living over the shop as part-payment. Later in the 1871 census, 14 Tavistock Place (where Pedro was born) looks like another lodging house with no mention of the Tilletts, and 47 Upper Marylebone Street (where John Hudson junior was born) produces much the same information. So it would appear that 62-year-old Henrietta Vert has all four bachelor sons and a daughter living with her as well as her married daughter, who has gone home to mother with her two infants because her own husband has left her. The other name in this history is that of Ibbs, and, according to the Essex Record Office and the 1881 British census, Robert Leigh Ibbs was born on 31 December 1869 in the sub-district of St Peter's in Maldon, Essex, the son of John

Thomas Ibbs (1836–*c*1880), 'a dispensing and family chemist' on Market Hill, and Marion Ibbs (née Budge, born 1842). They had two other children, Percy George Mavon (born 1871, see p. 377, line 17, column 2) and Reginald (born 1879).

After Narciso Vert's death the agency passed to neither of his surviving brothers, Pedro and Fernando, but to his nephew Pedro J. Tillett, who had been taken into partnership from 14 January 1896 after being with his uncle for nine years. However it is unclear why, less than a year after Vert's death, John Tillett then broke away from his brother to form an agency in March 1906 with Robert Leigh Ibbs, another Vert employee who reveals only 'unforeseen circumstances having arisen which led to my severing my connection with Vert's agency' (1 March 1906 to Alfred Granby, see page 33). A postscript to a letter written by John Tillett to Olive Malvery confirms that:

> I have not retired from the Musical business, and shall shortly start an Agency in conjunction with Mr Leigh Ibbs, who was for many years at Cork Street. (7 March 1906)

On the same day John wrote warmly enough to his brother:

> My dear Pedro, since writing to you this morning I have received the accompanying letter and bank notes, value ten pounds, from Miss Olive Malvery, which I hasten to send you.
> Your affectionate brother Jack (7 March 1906)

A day earlier, Ibbs had replied to Pedro that 'the Brighton "return" is in the second drawer of the pedestal desk downstairs, where all the current "returns" are kept', which implies that Pedro was probably in some state of disorganization with the departure of two key members of the agency. Ibbs was a little more forthcoming to William Alfred Dewhirst of Bradford, former chairman of the Subscription Concerts Committee in that city.

> Vert's Agency is still in the hands of Mr Pedro Tillett. It is his brother who has joined forces with me in starting an agency as we were unable to make a suitable arrangement to stay with Mr Pedro Tillett. As I said in my previous letter, we shall be glad if you can see your way to pass some of your engagements through our hands. (8 March 1906)

A postscript to a letter (9 March 1906) to the management of Steinway Hall, booking it on behalf of Misses Pauline and Ethel Hook's Morning Concert on 20 April informs that, 'we shall style ourselves Ibbs and Tillett'. And so the agency came into being, as the *Daily Telegraph* reported in its issue of 10 April 1906:

> A concert and musical agency has been formed by Mr R. Leigh Ibbs in association with Mr John H. Tillett, whose names will be familiar by reason of their having long been prominently connected with the business of the late Mr Vert. As the sole representatives of Madame Clara Butt and Mr Kennerley Rumford, the new agents may be said to make a very promising start. Their offices are at 19 Hanover Square.

Ibbs and Tillett set up the business as tenants of Rooms 9 and 10 at 19–19a Hanover Square on a yearly tenancy at an inclusive annual rent of £100 starting on 25 March 1906. The first thing they had to do was to create a connecting doorway between the two rooms so that the two partners could communicate easily (coincidentally they did the same to 124 Wigmore Street nearly half a century later, when they took over the adjacent No.122 and accommodated the firm of Harold Holt there), after which they had to go out and find themselves some clients. They were fortunate in working for Clara Butt and her husband Kennerley Rumford from the start, for Ibbs was a personal friend, having been a groomsman at their wedding in 1900. Immensely popular as a concert party, Butt would have a varied group of artistes in her group to form 'warm-up acts' to prepare for her entry as the prima donna of the evening. The June edition of the *Musical Times* carried the agency's first advertisement which duly featured Clara Butt:

IBBS & TILLETT
(for sixteen years with the late Mr N. Vert)
MUSICAL AND CONCERT AGENTS,
19, HANOVER SQUARE, LONDON, W,

SOLE REPRESENTATIVES OF

MADAME CLARA BUTT
AND
MR. KENNERLEY RUMFORD

Also included in the advert (though not necessarily all of them associated with a Butt/Rumford concert party) were the tenor Philip Newbury, the baritone Charles Knowles and the American bass Herbert Witherspoon, the violinists Johannes Wolff and Tivadar Nachèz, and the pianist Gertrude Peppercorn. It concluded: 'Engagements negotiated for all the leading artists. Lists of artists especially suitable for Oratorio and Chamber Music concerts sent on application to Ibbs & Tillett.' Their telephone number was given as '3129 Mayfair', its telegraphic address 'Organol, London'.

Another agent active in London at the time, Hugo Görlitz based in New Bond Street, seems to have got wind of the new agency, for his advert was now also appearing regularly in the *Musical Times* and offered 'the greatest facilities for supplying the best English oratorio artists' and undertook, 'when he engages all the artists, to send them fully rehearsed for any works which might be entrusted to them'. By the August issue his advert had been discontinued, while Ibbs and Tillett's appeared randomly throughout the year. In December another one, this time for the National Concert Agency of Victoria Street, was below theirs. Apparently new to London (after 'eight years at Gravesend and four at Reading'), it had been formed 'to meet the requirements of all provincial choral societies' and specialized in vocalists for oratorios and concerts. The year 1906 seems to be the year for such adverts appearing in the *Musical Times*, a practice which none of these agencies continued into 1907, including Ibbs and Tillett. Agents came and went; such adverts had already been in evidence a few years earlier in 1901 when Mr Stedman's Musical Agency (established back in 1877) of 58 Berners Street was offering 'Artists of Opera, Theatre, Oratorio, At Homes, Banquets etc, Choruses, Choir Boys and Girls, singing Lessons and Coaching', while the London Concert & Choir Agency, run by James Bates from a polytechnic in Regent Street, could supply 'Soloists and chorus voices for Festivals, Oratorios, Concerts, Glees and Madrigal Societies'. Further afield there was Swetman's Musical Agency of Chatham Street in Liverpool (established in 1887) who, as their telegraphic address 'Vocalists, Liverpool' indicated, specialized in singers 'for Oratorios, Recitals, Orchestral and Ballad Concerts etc.' To get the new agency up and running, Robert Leigh Ibbs wasted no time in trying to place the Clara Butt party with potential clients. In his letter (already mentioned on page 31) to Alfred Granby of Westcliff-on-Sea in Essex he went on:

> I am now in a position to treat with you for Mme Butt and Mr Kennerley Rumford for an appearance in Southend in September [1906] … Their joint fee for the seaside resorts such as Blackpool, Douglas [Isle of Man] etc is 200 guineas, but in view of the fact that it is a first visit, and that the district is not a very large one, I would make a substantial concession in these terms and ask you 170 guineas for themselves and their accompanist. I could probably arrange to send you a complete concert [party] with them for 180 guineas, which would relieve you of all the bother on that score. (1 March 1906)

A week later Ibbs also offered to negotiate with George Robertson Sinclair (GRS, the eleventh variation in Elgar's *Enigma Variations*) and did everything he could to promote Kennerley Rumford. Sinclair was organist at Hereford Cathedral, one of the venues of the annual Three Choirs Festival, which was regularly supplied with soloists by Narciso Vert and became a favourite with Ibbs and Tillett throughout its existence (Leeds and the Birmingham Triennial Festival were others, though the latter ceased to function after 1912):

> I have today quoted terms for Mme Clara Butt's appearances at your [Hereford] Festival in September next through Vert's Agency. Mrs Rumford wishes me to tell you that should the terms quoted not meet your views, she will be glad to consider any offer you may wish to make her. May I beg you to bear Mr Kennerley Rumford's name in mind. He has been doing a great deal of oratorio work lately, and would, I know, fully justify his inclusion in your Festival. He would be willing to meet you liberally in the question of terms, as he is most anxious to take every opportunity of doing really serious work. I would also strongly bring to your notice a very fine American bass singer, Mr Herbert Witherspoon, whose credentials I send you herewith. He is an extremely gifted artist. (7 March 1906)

Not all went smoothly at first; a Cambridge recital by Kennerley Rumford in the early days of the agency was severely affected by both inclement weather and University college activities, which conspired to reduce audience numbers and the box office revenue. With this recital's origins being pre-March 1906 the income had to be divided between Pedro Tillett, Vert's new owner, and Ibbs and Tillett:

> I send you the returns for last night, which is somewhat of a "facer" [setback], and certainly unexpected. Fate was against us in every possible way. A bitter night with heavy snowstorms, but what killed the booking was the fact that Caius, Selwyn and Trinity all had big social functions on, and the term finals being altered, all the examinations had to start yesterday, so we couldn't have had a worse date. I think we shall have a fair return at Eastbourne. (13 March 1906)

Among those who sent their good wishes and encouragement as the new agency was launched, was the veteran bass-baritone Charles Santley, about to celebrate his golden jubilee as a singer and knighted the following year:

> Dear Ibbs & Tillett,
> I wish you every success in your venture. I don't think any negotiations on my account would bring much grist to your mill, as people do not seem inclined to pay for my services. I have some pupils who I am sure are worth your attention, but I am diffident about troubling you on their account as they would have to depend on their work alone to make their way. At the same time if you require something good, they would be pleased to give you a specimen of their talents. I give a concert at Portman Rooms, May 14th when three will take part, one a Manchester girl of whom I think very highly, who is neglected in her own part of the world as she is not a pupil of the 'Manchester Music School'. I expect also a mezzo soprano who has already appeared in London, a really good artiste. If either of you care to hear them, that would be a good occasion (Durell will accompany), but mind I do not press the matter unless you are at a loose end. I have others quite ready but I cannot put them all into the programme. (10 March 1906)

The Dutch violinist Johannes Wolff, featured in the agency's first advertisements, was eager to be on their artists' list and just as eagerly welcomed by Ibbs:

> Warmest thanks for your good wishes and your extremely kind offer for us to act as your agents. I need hardly say how gladly we accept, and I sincerely hope that our association may be to our mutual advantage. If you are in this neighbourhood tomorrow, we should much like to have a chat with you upon a point which has arisen. (6 March 1906)

Harry Plunket Greene, the baritone and Parry's son-in-law, had tried to mediate in discussions between Pedro Tillett and the breakaway agency in attempt to maintain the status quo, but to no avail. Ibbs then successfully sought permission to place the singer's name on the artists' list:

> In deference to your wishes we have now waited four days to hear if any suggestion has been made to you by the owner of Vert's agency, with a view to our resuming our business relations with him upon a new basis satisfactory to both parties, but as no news has reached us, we find it impossible to wait any longer, and each day's delay militates against us. You know how highly we value the kindliness of heart which has prompted you to use your influence to prevent our severance from 6 Cork Street, but frankly speaking, we do not think that any offer would be made, and even if one is made, that it would be acceptable to us. You can quite understand it is impossible for us to remain inactive any longer, and we have therefore decided to go on with our own arrangements. I presume we shall be at liberty to quote your name on our list of artistes? (6 March 1906)

The Bournemouth-based conductor Dan Godfrey was one of several musicians or concert promoters out in the country to whom Kennerley Rumford was offered by Ibbs in a flurry of letter writing to obtain business:

> Do you think a vocal Recital with Mr Rumford would suit for Bournemouth in Easter week? He has just given these as an experiment at Ryde, Brighton, Cambridge and Eastbourne with very good financial success. I should have suggested one earlier but was stopped by the fact of his appearing at your own Concert. He is assisted by either [the violinists Michael] Zacharewitsch or Tivadar Nachèz, and I should like to know which of these artists you would consider the most useful to you. Liddle is the pianist. Kindly let me hear your views and a possible date. (13 March 1906)

To Dr Alan Gray at Cambridge he wrote:

> I have the pleasure to enclose you notices of the American bass, Mr [Herbert] Witherspoon, and I feel sure you would be more than satisfied should you be able to offer him an engagement. I would also bring to your notice a very excellent light soprano, Miss Esta d'Argo, of whom you have probably heard, and a mezzo-soprano, Miss Maria Yelland, both of whom are meeting with great success and are really good artistes. (13 March 1906)

To J.A. Adamson of Aberdeen:

> I have no definite knowledge of Mr Harrison's plans for next season, except that I believe his first concert will be Paderewski and his last the Queen's Hall Orchestra. For a big vocalist I would suggest Mesdames Suzanne Adams, Ella Russell, Agnes Nicholls, Amy Castles, Susan Strong, Minnie Tracey, Esther Palliser, Alice Esty (sopranos), Muriel Foster, Kirkby Lunn, Marie Brema, Rosa Olitzka, Giulia Ravogli (contraltos). (14 March 1906)

And to J. Aikman Forsyth of the Manchester-based Hallé Concerts Society:

> It is very good of you to have suggested Mons. [Tivadar] Nachèz's name to the Gentlemen's Concerts. As regards lady vocalists, we would suggest Mesdames Suzanne Adams, Susan Strong, Ella Russell, Agnes Nicholls, Minnie Tracey, Emily Squire, Perceval Allen, Gleeson-White (sopranos), Mmes Kirkby Lunn, Rosa Olitzka, Muriel Foster, Marie Brema (contraltos). Your enquiry, however, probably refers to some lesser known but good artistes who might be coming to England next season? We will immediately advise you, should we know of such. Madame [Alwina] Valleria has informed us of her wish to re-enter the Concert world, but I am afraid her name will be unknown to the present generation! [Moriz] Rosenthal has notified us that he hopes to be here for the 1907–8 season, which you may be glad to know. (15 March 1906)

A couple of months later and the pace of work for the agency was clearly increasing. A communication to Miss Cheatham Thompson puts the working expenses of organizing a recital at about £20:

> There is only one afternoon left at the Steinway Hall this month, *viz* Friday June 29th, which has just been given up by someone. It seems to be a very good date, and we have therefore pencilled it hoping that it will suit you. With regard to the expenses for working the recital, we can keep them down to about £20, which sum would include the rent of the hall £6.6.0, management fee £3.3.0, printing about £4 odd, newspaper advertisements £5, delivering bills etc. We have omitted sandwich men, which we do not think really necessary. Kindly let us know if you wish to retain the hall for the date in question as there will be several applications for same, and we shall be asked to give a definite decision. (5 June 1906)

To Frau Gipser in Dresden, who proposed a recital at the more expensive Bechstein Hall in the season of 1907–08, Ibbs and Tillett set out the 'approximate working expenses' in a letter on 25 July 1907 as:

Rent of Hall afternoon	£12.12.0 (evening £13.13.0)
Newspaper advertisements	£10. 0.0.
Printing	£5. 0.0.
Sandwich board men etc	£2. 2.0.
Management fee	£4. 4.0.
Sundries	£1. 0.0.
	£34.18.0.

To Pedro de Zulueta (of Boscombe in Dorset), John Tillett wrote in more detail:

> I much regret that so far we have not been successful in securing you any engagements for next Season, but we are recommending your name whenever the opportunity offers, and have sent copies of your Press notices throughout the Provinces. The Summer Season was certainly not a good one; nearly all the regular "At Home" artists have complained of the scarcity of engagements.
>
> I am very glad to hear of the engagement you have booked at Preston, which I hope may be the means of bringing something else "en route".
>
> With regard to your proposed Recital at the Aeolian Hall, the usual cost for a Recital in the evening is £40, so if you engage an instrumentalist at £5.5.0. and an accompanist at the same figure, you would have to count on your expenses being £50.

Rent of Hall evening	£13.13.0.
Newspaper advertisements	£10. 0.0.
Printing including books of words, say	£5. 0.0.
Sandwich board-men and delivery of bills etc	£2. 2.0.
Management fee	£4. 4.0.
Sundries	£1. 0.0.
Assisting artists	£10.10.0

> Of course you have a good private connection and no doubt could sell enough tickets to cover the above sum. Supposing you sold the Hall out at 10/6, 5/- and 2/6, allowing for the usual Press tickets you could get about £125.0.0. in the Room.

The mutually beneficial 'en route' principle was an inducement to clubs and societies, while at the same time reducing an artist's travelling time and drumming up and maximizing the economic viability of the agency's business. It is exemplified by this letter to Felix Gade of Edinburgh:

Your favour of the 20th inst. duly to hand. We have much pleasure in giving you below a list of the engagements we have so far made for Scotland and the North next Season, that might possibly enable the artists to sing at your Sunday Concerts at special "en route" terms.

Miss Agnes Nicholls

Sunderland	January 22nd
Scarborough	February 4th
Belfast	" 7th
Grimsby	" 14th
Louth	" 17th
Manchester	March 16th
Liverpool	" 24th

Madame Blanche Marchesi

Sheffield	February 11th
Harrogate	" 15th

Miss Esta d'Argo

Keighley	November 19th
Hull	December 6th
Liverpool	" 28th

Miss Louise Dale

Hull	February 10th (in pencil)

Miss Gertrude Lonsdale

Newcastle	November 22nd
Warrington	" 26th

Mr John McCormack

Hull	November 25th
Liverpool	January 28th

Mr Dalton Baker

Liverpool	November 16th/17th

Mr Robert Radford

Hull	November 25th

Mr Plunket Greene

Liverpool	December 9th (pencilled)
Sheffield	February 11th
Harrogate	" 15th

Monsieur Hollman

Sunderland	January 22nd

Herr Leopold Godowsky

Liverpool	January 28th

Miss Agnes Nicholls will be in Scotland on December 11th, 16th and 17th, Mr William Green on February 18th and Mr Dalton Baker on February 1st, 3rd, 5th and 18th, but their engagements will not allow of their accepting any other Concert appearances in Scotland at that time.

We shall be glad to have the opportunity of negotiating with you for the services of any of the above named artists, or for any others you may contemplate engaging for your Concerts next Season, and will be happy to submit terms on hearing from you.

We will also notify you from time to time of any other engagements we may book for the North, and meanwhile thanking you for your communication, we remain yours faithfully Ibbs and Tillett (23 July 1907)

Publicity was a crucial element. Artists who hired the agency to manage their concerts kept a close watch on its effectiveness, and were quite entitled to give (and pay for) specific instructions. William Tilbrook, who would stay with Ibbs and Tillett until the outbreak of the Second World War (by which time he was a Director), was in charge of managing a concert given by pupils of Miss Frances Perkins on 20 July 1907. The following letters were sent by Tilbrook:

We are obliged by your letter, and have noted the alterations in date and place of your concert. We have put the leaflets in hand and hope to let you have them early on Saturday. With regard to the cost of printing, we fear that it will not be possible to complete this for the sum you mention. The printer's estimate is as follows:

25 Posters 10. 6 (50 = 12/6)
100 Circulars 10. 6
100 Cards for enclosure 6. 6
200 Tickets (two kinds, unnumbered) 8. 6 (if numbered 10/6)
and programmes:- 25/- for 250 (4 pages)
21/- " " (2 pages)

Regarding advertisements, we ought to insert at least once in the four dailies *Telegraph*, *Times*, *Standard* and *Morning Post* to secure the likelihood of their sending a critic. The particulars contained in the circular could be condensed to about 10 lines to gain an effective advertisement but could be reduced still further if you so wished.

The cost on this basis would be for the first-named paper 15/- and the others 10/- each.

We shall be glad to hear from you on these points and also which (if any) of the seats you wish to have numbered. (27 June 1907)

Thank you for your letter to hand this morning, and as requested have instructed the printers to send you a 100 more of the circulars. They inform us that the enclosure cards followed the first supply of circulars by the next post, and we trust you duly received them. We note what you say with regard to the advertisement, and will arrange to put the extra notices in the *Morning Post* as you suggest.

With regard to the posting of the bills on the District Railway, we have seen Partingtons, who will undertake in this special instance, to post 25 for two weeks at an inclusive charge of 10/-. If you approve this arrangement, we would suggest that they should be posted at and around Kensington, and we shall be glad to hear if this will be agreeable to you. We will let you have a supply of the tickets directly we receive them from the printers. [1 July 1907)

Miss Perkins evidently prowled the London Underground to reassure herself that her instructions had been followed to the letter, but was not impressed by what she found:

We are in receipt of your post-card, and as requested have the pleasure to enclose you the remainder of the reserved seats with the exception of those which we have kept back for the Press.

We have spoken to Partingtons about the bills, and they assure us that they were posted at the Stations in and around Kensington which you named on Monday last. (10 July 1907)

Miss Perkins had asked for the underground stations at Victoria, Charing Cross, Sloane Square, South Kensington, Gloucester Road, High Street Kensington, Earl's Court, Notting Hill Gate, Queen's Road, Baker Street and Wimbledon to be covered as well as 'two posted at Blackheath Station on the South Eastern Railway, as one of the artistes taking part lives in this district'. This was despite 'being outside the arrangement but if you could possibly manage it we should feel obliged', according to instructions from Tilbrook to Partingtons sent on 3 July 1907. Despite Tilbrook's show of consideration beyond the call of duty, the redoubtable Miss Perkins, who wanted to secure a large audience for the recital by her fledglings, remained dissatisfied and clearly said as much:

> We were sorry to receive your last letter this morning telling us that you had been unable to find any announcements on the District Railway, upon receipt of which we communicated with Partington, who assured us that the bills had been duly posted in accordance with the information supplied by them at the beginning of the week. The writer has this afternoon personally visited Victoria, Sloane Sq[uar]e and South Kensington Stations and found a bill posted at each. At the first-named, on the platform for the trains going Eastward, and at the others on the platform for the trains going Westwards, each were in a good light and in a good position, the two latter being specially so. This being the case it is only fair to assume that the remaining bills have been posted at other Stations and we trust these particulars will be entirely satisfactory to you. We may mention that we have used our influence to post one of your bills in what we consider one of the best positions in the West End, *viz*.- in the centre of Bond Street outside the Aeolian Hall and further we have placed the remaining at the different Music Shops, our only possible medium for gaining publicity without the employment of Sandwich-men, which would of course entail extra expense.
>
> P.S. Will you please let us know the details of the programme at your convenience so that we may put it in hand at the printers; also let us know whether you wish to issue the programme in advance or only at the time of the Concert and oblige. (12 July 1907)
>
> We are obliged by your letter of yesterday enclosing proof of programme which is now in hand. We noted your wishes regarding the two first items and have left out the word "Piano" from the second. We have kept half a dozen tickets here in case they are asked for, and have only sold two stalls up to the present. We have already advised Broadwoods regarding the chairs. (19 July 1907)

After the concert, a couple of letters settling the account followed:

> We thank you for your favour enclosing cheque for £2.2.0. to hand this morning, and as requested send herewith the account of expenses for your pupils Concert on Saturday last.
>
> The only ticket taken at the door was one at 5/- taken by Mrs Care-Orme, Vicarage House, Teddington, who has not favoured us with a remittance, so we think she will probably send direct to you. Messrs Broadwood did not dispose of any tickets in advance. (24 July 1907)
>
> We beg to acknowledge receipt of your cheque value £5.17.0 with many thanks, and enclose herewith the account receipted. (26 July 1907)

The Australian soprano Mary Conly was an artist on Vert's books since early 1903 and with Ibbs and Tillett from 1908 to 1913 before returning to her native land. Here are her solo engagements for the period from late 1906 to early 1907, and she was certainly busy, though they were not largely generated by Ibbs and Tillett:

- 9–12 September 1906: Hereford Three Choirs Festival. *Hymn of Praise* (Mendelssohn). Conductor: Dr G.R. Sinclair.
- 14 October 1906: National Sunday League, Queen's Hall, London. Soloist in *Hymn of Praise* (Mendelssohn), and "I will extol Thee" (from *Eli* by Costa).
- 19 October 1906: Huddersfield Choral Society. *Faust* (Berlioz). Conductor: Dr Henry Coward.
- 20 October 1906: Bradford Permanent Orchestra Concert. Solo vocalist.
- 3 November 1906: Dulwich Philharmonic Society, Crystal Palace, Sydenham. *Hiawatha* (Coleridge-Taylor). Conductor: Arthur Fagge.
- 10 November 1906: Brand Lane Subscription Concert, Free Trade Hall, Manchester. *Samson* (Handel).
- 22 November 1906: Sheffield Musical Union. *Faust* (Berlioz). Conductor: Dr Henry Coward.

6 December 1906: Birmingham Festival Choral Society, Town Hall, Birmingham. *The Golden Legend* (Sullivan). Conductor: Dr G.R. Sinclair.
14 and 15 December 1906: Belfast Philharmonic Society. Two performances of *Messiah* (Handel).
1 January 1907: Edinburgh (Royal) Choral Union, Music Hall, George Street, Edinburgh. *Messiah* (Handel). Conductor: Mr T.H. Collinson.
2 February 1907: Brand Lane Subscription Concert, Free Trade Hall, Manchester. Miscellaneous programme. Conly sang 'Elisabeth's Greeting' (*Tannhäuser*, Wagner), a bracket of three songs: 'How like a flower' (Rubinstein), 'Songs my mother taught me' (Dvořák) and 'If I were a lark' (Clutsam), and the 'Bolero' (*Sicilian Vespers*, Verdi).
6 February 1907: Tramway Men's Concert, St George's Hall, Bradford, Yorkshire.
18 April 1907: Concert of The Strolling Players' Amateur Orchestral Society, Queen's Hall, London. Conductor: Mr Joseph Ivimey. Conly's solos included 'Ernani, Ernani, involami' (*Ernani*, Verdi).

It seems likely that between the two *Messiahs* in Belfast on 14 and 15 December and the one in Edinburgh on New Year's Day 1907 there were other Christmas concert engagements.

Only the stars in the profession, and the agency was doing everything it could to get them onto their books, could set a non-negotiable fee. Conly was not a star, but she was typical of what became the bread-and-butter soloist who swelled the ranks of the agency's artists down the years, and what became known as the General List. In this particular example, and for their one guinea commission, Ibbs and Tillett spent a great deal of time and money on secretarial work, telephone calls, telegrams, letters, postage, a meagre return to service just this one engagement in Bradford on 6 February 1907:

> With regard to the Tramway Men's Concert in Bradford on February 6th next, we are sorry to find that they do not wish to go beyond ten guineas; we have therefore closed the engagement for you at that fee, which you said you would accept. We shall be glad if you will kindly book the date and send us a line in confirmation. The Concert will be given in the St George's Hall. (13 December 1906)

> Thanks for your letter to hand this morning confirming the engagement for February 6th, Bradford. We shall be glad if you will kindly let us have the titles of the songs you propose singing on that occasion, as the Concert promoters wish to prepare the programme. We do not know how many times they wish you to sing, but you might let us have the titles of three songs in case they require you to sing three times during the programme.
>
> Awaiting your early reply. (17 December 1906)

> Will you please let us have your selections for the Concert in Bradford on February 6th, together with the words by return of post, as they are very anxious to issue their programmes without further delay. They ask would you kindly sing the big air from "Ernani".
>
> With kind regards and all good wishes for the New Year. (4 January 1907)

Ibbs and Tillett wrote on 17 December 1906 to H. Palmer at Bradford:

> We duly received your favour of the 14th inst., and wired you on receipt of same to advertise Madame Conly as "The eminent Australian Soprano". We are now in communication with Madame Conly regarding her solos for the Concert on February 6th, and hope to be able to let you have the particulars of same during the course of the next day or two.

According to a further letter from Ibbs and Tillett to him dated 7 January 1907, Conly proposed 'The Moorish Maiden' (Parker), 'Ernani, Ernani, involami' (Verdi) and 'The Rose will blow' (W. King):

> The Bradford people will require you to sing only two songs and they have selected "The Moorish Maiden" for the first part, and "Ernani" for the second part of the programme. They would, however, like you to join Mr Edward Davis, tenor, of the Carl Rosa Opera Co., in the Duet "A

Night in Venice", which we hope will be agreeable to you. For an encore they particularly wish you to sing "Crossing the Bar", which they say will please their audience greatly. We shall be glad if you will kindly let us hear from you by return as our clients are desirous of issuing their programmes this week. (9 January 1907)

Will you kindly let us know tomorrow certain, if you are disengaged on April 18th next, and if so, what your lowest terms would be for a concert at Maidstone (Kent)? (14 January 1907)

In fact Conly was unavailable on 18 April because she was one of the soloists appearing at Queen's Hall (see list of her engagements above).

Enclosed we have pleasure in sending you a copy of the programme for the Concert at Bradford on February the 6th next, which we think you will find all in order. (30 January 1907)

Bradford February the 6th.

Will you kindly note that Mr. Scott the accompanist for the above Concert will be at the Hall at 3 o'clock on the afternoon of the Concert, in order to rehearse your songs with you, and we hope this appointment will suit your convenience.

The encore song "Crossing the Bar" which they suggested some time back is the one by Willeby not Sullivan. You can however please yourself as to what you sing.
Hoping all will pass off satisfactorily. (4 February 1907)

We have just received the enclosed letter from Bradford, which you will no doubt be glad to receive, also the clipping from the *Yorkshire Daily Observer.*

We are very glad to hear that everything passed off so successfully. (12 February 1907)

Such letters also reveal that right from the very start, Ibbs and Tillett's unbending view was that they were running a booking agency and artists provided a service to the client, whether music club, choral society or concert organization, at the lowest possible cost. The baritone Albert Garcia (grandson of the famous tenor Manuel Garcia) received this offer from the agency:

We can secure you an engagement for a concert performance of *Cavalleria Rusticana* at Cleckheaton on March 13th 1907, but the utmost terms we can secure are Six guineas (£6.6.0.). It is a very small and poor Society, and they cannot afford more. Kindly send word by return if you will accept. (11 July 1906)

Mary Conly, too, was warned of the low fee she could expect from Bradford, and, very late in the day, that she would also be asked to bring her own band parts with her:

We understand that you are singing in Huddersfield on Oct 19th next. Will you kindly let us know whether you could sing at Bradford the following night at a Popular Concert, and what your lowest fee would be. They are unable to pay good terms, and as Bradford practically joins Huddersfield, you may be able to quote a really low fee, seeing that your expenses will be so little. (26 April 1906 in the hand of Robert Leigh Ibbs)

We can now definitely offer you the engagement at the Bradford Permanent Orchestra Concert on Saturday October 20th next, terms Ten guineas (£10.10.0) and I shall be glad to know by return of post if we may book you. We believe you mentioned Nov 2nd as a possible date for the Bradford Subs[criptio]n Concert, and if that is the date you have in pencil, we know that another artiste has been engaged by them for that Concert, so that will allow you to accept Oct. 20th. (24 May 1906)

The Secretary of the Bradford Permanent Orchestra has written asking us to inform you that they are relying on your bringing your own band parts (for your 1st and 2nd song) for the concert on October 20th. The rehearsal will be at 2 o'clock. (27 September 1906)

Ibbs and Tillett were also being asked to supply vocalists for the non-standard repertoire to some choral societies, a problem which John Tillett met head on in his reply to Mr J. Hitchen concerning a dramatic cantata by Henry Smart written for the Birmingham Triennial Festival back in 1864:

> Regarding the question of a tenor for your performance of *The Bride of Dunkerron*, I find that as few of the younger tenors are familiar with this work, and as it is always a great help to the conductor to have singers who are quite reliable in every way, I am inclined to recommend your engaging Mr Henry Beaumont for the work in question. He is, as you no doubt know, a very safe artist, and there are very few works he is unacquainted with. (11 June 1906)

Johannes Wolff was close to Grieg (the two men had been a musical partnership of violin and piano since 1889) and he attempted to rekindle an association with the agency going back to Vert years earlier. By now Grieg, always a frail man, was ailing fast with only a year to live, but nevertheless responded with a degree of hope despite politely declining the agency's approach to him to manage a tour to England. He had been in England just a month earlier with two London concerts (at the second he befriended Percy Grainger), played at Buckingham Palace (stopping twice in his attempts to dissuade King Edward VII from talking loudly during the recital) and received an honorary doctorate in music from Oxford University on 29 May 1906. Ibbs and Tillett, aware of the enormous success of these two concerts and of the composer's huge popularity in England, wrote to him at Bergen on his arrival back home in his native Norway:

> Mons. Johannes Wolff, for whom we act as agents in England, has informed us that you might possibly be induced to pay another visit to England in the early autumn, and we beg to say that should you decide to do this, we would feel it a very great honour to be allowed to act as your agents in the matter.
>
> We would be prepared to guarantee you six or eight concerts at least at a nett fee of One Hundred Pounds (£100.0.0) per concert to you, and in addition would defray all your travelling and hotel expenses in England during these concerts, and also those of Madame Grieg, should she decide to accompany you. As you are possibly aware, October is one of the most pleasant months of the English climate and everything should be done to ensure the greatest comfort for you whilst travelling. We are sure you would find the trip a most enjoyable one in every way. The time of the visit we would propose to be from October 11th to about the end of the month. Herr Wolff tells us also that you would like a protegée of yours to be engaged as a vocalist, should you accept the tour. We shall be very glad indeed to meet your wishes in this respect. As this lady is entirely unknown in England, however, we could not do more than pay nominal fees to cover her expenses etc. We would point out, however, that this artiste would have the great advantage of being introduced to the British Public under the most favourable circumstances possible, being associated with so famous an artist as yourself, and therefore we are sure that should the lady make the big success at your concerts to which we may confidently expect, engagements from the principal Societies here would follow in due course. Awaiting the favour of your reply and with best compliments to Madame and yourself, we are yours faithfully, Ibbs & Tillett. (11 June 1906)

The composer replied regretfully:

> Thank you for your kind proposal. I am sorry to say that it will be impossible for me to visit England next autumn. But if I am able to realize my idea of taking a trip to England next year, I should be glad to have the pleasure of making a concert tour under your direction. (26 June 1906)

That was unfortunately not to be, for his last contact with the agency occurred a year later and is referred to in Chapter 5. Another composer/pianist to whom an approach was soon made was the veteran Saint Saëns, then over 70 years of age. In the summer of 1906 he came to England after celebrating the sixtieth anniversary of his first public appearance with a recital at the Salle Erard in Paris on 19 May. He then gave one at the Bechstein Hall in London on 12 July together with the cellist Josef Hollman, including in the programme the first performance in England of the new (1904) cello sonata Op.125. The agency had charge of the practicalities and wrote to the composer's publishers, Durand in Paris:

> We enclose a programme of a recital which Dr Saint Saëns and Monsieur Hollman are to give in London on July 12th next. It is our intention to print an analytical programme for use in the room on the day of the concert, and as your firm are the publishers of Dr Saint Saëns' work, it occurred to us that you might be willing to advertise in same. We can let you have a single page for fifty francs or two pages for seventy-five francs, and in the event of your agreeing to same would undertake not to put any other music publication advertisements in the programme. (26 June 1906)

At the same time the agency was also trying (much as it did with Grieg) to capitalize on the composer's presence (and success) in the country by suggesting further events for the future:

> Another cycle of Musical Festival concerts is being organised in Canada to take place during the Spring of 1908 and Dr Charles Harriss, the founder of the scheme, is now in this country making certain arrangements in connection with same. At the last Festival, which took place in 1903, the programmes were composed entirely of English works and Sir Alexander Mackenzie was engaged as conductor. It is proposed, however, that the programmes of the forthcoming Festival should be devoted to French as well as English compositions; also that an eminent French composer and conductor should be invited as well as an Englishman. Naturally no one would be more welcomed than yourself, if you could be induced to make the trip to Canada.
>
> The tour will probably last one to two months altogether, but it is proposed that you should only participate in the concerts given in the larger cities like Montreal, Toronto, Ottawa and Quebec, and these would necessitate your remaining in the country from two to three weeks or a month at the most. We may mention that there will be a first class orchestra engaged and that there are several excellent choruses in the cities above mentioned, especially Montreal, where Dr Harriss has a trained choir of 500 voices. It is proposed that *Samson & Delilah* should be given, also your other choral work *The Deluge*, as well as your different Symphonies, Overtures etc.
>
> Dr Harriss will be very happy to see you when you come to London to discuss the matter further, but in the meanwhile would like to know whether you are prepared to entertain the proposition, and if so, upon what terms and conditions. We may mention that the French population in the Dominion is very much interested in the Festival, and that Dr Harriss carries important letters on the matter to the British Embassy in Paris from such important men as the Governor General (Earl Grey), Sir Wilfred Laurier, the Prime Minister, who are also interested in the scheme so that you would be appearing in Canada under the very best conditions.
>
> We should mention that the weather in Canada during the Spring is generally very pleasant and warm, so there need be no hesitation in your decision on account of the climate. Will you kindly think the matter over and let us have your answer as soon as possible. (23 June 1906)

The veteran composer, however, took a very gloomy view of his remaining years, would make no plans and in any case was set in his ways, for example wintering in warmer (preferably North African) climes each year, something evidently known to the agency judging by that final paragraph:

> Your proposal is very flattering and I find it very enticing; I see just one obstacle, and that is that in 1908 I shall be 72, and at my age one cannot depend on the future as securely as when one is younger. Be that as it may, when I am next in London I shall be honoured to come and visit you, and we can discuss the matter, which will be very agreeable. Please accept my sincere compliments. (24 June 1906, translation from French)

They made a further request:

> Would you be willing to come to England next Winter to conduct two concerts with the Scottish

> Orchestra, one in Edinburgh and the other in Glasgow on successive evenings? The idea is that you should conduct the entire concert and perform one or more of your works at each. The most suitable dates would be either December 3rd and 4th (1906), January 7th and 8th or 21st & 22nd. In addition to these two Orchestral concerts it might be possible to arrange to give a recital in Edinburgh, all three to come in the same week. Will you kindly let us know if the proposition is an agreeable one to you, and in which case, what would be the lowest fee you would accept for the two Orchestral concerts alone and also for the recital as well. (13 July 1906)

But the composer gave them short shrift in his reply:

> For the past 20 years the state of my health has compelled me to spend the winter in countries in which I am unaffected by the cold, and in December and January I shall be in Egypt. With regrets at being unable to accept your proposals, I beg you to accept my best wishes. (15 July 1906, translation from French)

Ibbs and Tillett made one further attempt to entice him to play, but to no avail even though Saint Saëns had another 18 years to live, until 1924 when he died at the ripe old age of 89:

> For the past 20 years I have spent six months of the winter in warm countries. It is therefore quite pointless to offer me engagements, which, in any case, I no longer accept for any season on account of my advanced age. (15 June 1909, translation from French)

Busoni too was eagerly sought out by the agency, this time by John Tillett, and sure enough his name appeared in the artists' list from 1908:

> I wrote you a week or more ago, but not knowing your private address at the time, sent the letter to Messrs Bechstein's care. Not having had a reply from you, I fear my communication must have gone astray. I sent you a notification of our new Agency, and at the same time enquired if you had made any definite arrangements as regards your future business in this country?
>
> In the event of your not being under contract with anyone, I need not say that we would be most happy to act as your agents and should you see your way to appoint us as such, can assure you that your interests would receive our careful and prompt attention; in fact we would use special efforts on your behalf. Hoping that Madame and yourself are quite well, and with kind regards, believe me sincerely yours, John H Tillett. (20 March 1906)

This was in stark contrast to five years earlier when Busoni had been forced to write from Berlin to Vert:

> In reply to your letter of May 21st, I regret to find you do not offer me even a single engagement, nor any hope for engagements this year. Under these circumstances you will no doubt have no objection to my accepting engagements if they reach me from other sources. This will however not prevent my considering any tour or engagement you may have to offer me in the future. I have asked Messrs Bechstein to remit you the amount of your account. (18 May 1900)

Vying for star billing was sought by certain artists on occasion but (with the initial exception of Clara Butt) not entertained by the agency, who also took precautionary steps to avoid having more than one of their higher profile musicians at a time on a major tour in the country. The pianist Leopold Godowsky, for example, had to be put firmly in his place:

> We note that Mr Godowsky is willing to have us undertake the management of his business affairs in this country, which we need hardly say we shall be very pleased to do and we can promise him that our best endeavours will at all times be devoted in his interests. We note that Mr Godowsky does not wish to bind himself to us for any specified period of time, which we are quite agreeable to, and hope with him that the results of his visits to England will be such that no change in the management of his business will be deemed necessary.

> The stipulation he makes in regard to our giving him an exclusive position in all advertising matter, and that we are to present him as our "star" pianist, and not to place any other pianist above or on equal rank with him is one we do not see that we can fairly entertain as we have already been appointed the English agents for one or two eminent Continental pianists, who are quite willing to place their business in our hands without any such conditions, feeling quite sure that their interests will be properly cared for, as we can assure Mr Godowsky his would be. We may mention that it will be our rule, as far as it is in our power to enforce it, not to arrange to bring to this country more than one "star" pianist at a time, so as to be able to devote all our energies in his behalf.
>
> It is not possible to find sufficient engagements for any pianist to stay longer than two months over here and this fact we hope will convince Mr Godowsky that although we are unable to agree to his stipulation entirely, we shall be able to work in a special way for him and to feature his name in every way with the public, and our clients throughout the provinces. (19 June 1906)

Godowsky was a Pole who had first played in England in the summer of 1890 and had an immediate success, including a command appearance at Court, where, unlike the hapless Grieg and Edward VII, he was more politely received by Queen Victoria. Godowsky then emigrated to America until the turn of the century when he moved to Berlin, but, judging by Ibbs and Tillett's evaluation of his marketable prospects, his name had evidently dropped from public gaze when they corresponded again with his manager Maurice Aronson in the summer of 1906:

> So far we have not received any favourable replies from the Societies in the Provinces, but a great number of the Secretaries are at present away on their holidays and will not be back before the end of the month. The replies we have had are from the Liverpool Philharmonic Society, the Edinburgh Orchestral Society and the Sheffield Subscription Concert Society, all of which have completed their arrangements for next season; also the Liverpool Symphony Concerts. We have also heard from Glasgow (Chamber Society), Newcastle (Chamber Society) who are both contemplating giving one or two concerts and have written to say that they will consider Mr Godowsky's name providing his terms are reasonable. We know it will be useless asking more than forty guineas and very much doubt if they can afford to pay that sum. In any case will you ask Godowsky what his wishes are in regard to the question of terms, that is to say the minimum he will accept.
>
> Unfortunately his name is not sufficiently well known yet in England to command very high terms just at present, but we feel confident that it is only a question of time and the recitals Mr Godowsky is to give in November, March and April next will give the best opportunity to prove what a great artist he is to the Societies in the Provinces and we shall certainly lose no opportunity to acquaint them all of the successes he will meet with, which will be exhibited outside the Bechstein Hall and on the Bechstein board in Regent Street near the Queen's Hall, an excellent position which is noticed by nearly all the people attending the Promenade Concerts, which begin next week and continue nightly until late in October ... We have also been in correspondence with the Manager of the Royal Albert Hall Sunday concerts, a new series of concerts which were organised in London last season, at which nearly all the leading artists appeared. We would like to arrange for Mr Godowsky to play there next season. But all will depend on the question of terms. They are not able to pay full terms. (8 August 1906)

A letter from Godowsky survives in the Tillett archive, written a year or so later, and it makes early mention of a future star cellist (and one who also highly impressed Grieg in the same year), Pablo Casals:

> I just was informed that I could play on the 26th Oct. in London if the date is as favourable as you say, and if we could do something on the days between the 26th and 31st Oct. I leave it to you to decide about it, but I must have the decision at once, as I have to arrange other engagements accordingly. Write to my Berlin address. I think I would prefer not to ask Kreisler to give joint recitals in England. How would Casals do? He is a very great artist. Send me all notices and keep me posted about Meggy's doings [the journalist Gordon Meggy]. Excuse haste! (25 May 1907)

Another future star, but already making a name for himself, was the young German pianist Wilhelm Backhaus, who taught briefly at the Royal Manchester College of Music in 1905, and the following year (when he was only 22 years old) received this offer from Ibbs and Tillett:

> Will you be good enough to let us know whether you can entertain an engagement for 4 concerts on consecutive days in Yorkshire at the end of January 1907, and what your lowest terms would be. The towns are close to each other, and one railway ticket would practically cover the series. The terms will have to be quite reasonable, otherwise my clients would be unable to consider the matter. Please let us hear by return of post. (11 April 1906)

At the other end of the spectrum they were also dealing with unknown singers and instrumentalists, simply putting on their concerts at no risk to themselves. This letter was sent to Thomas Troward, who had high hopes for his daughter:

> We note that you are willing for us to undertake the management of your daughter's recital at the Aeolian Hall on Wednesday afternoon January 23rd (1907) for which date we have now definitely secured the use of the room. We will certainly see that the working expenses do not exceed the sum of £35; in fact we will do our best to keep them as low as possible. The holding capacity of the hall is 400 (320 reserved and 80 unreserved). We would recommend your making the prices of seats 7/6 and 5/- [$37^1/_2$p and 25p] numbered Stalls and 2/- (or 2/6) [10p (or $12^1/_2$p)] for the back area seats.
>
> With regard to the Press, we shall of course send notices and tickets to every critic in the usual way, and although it is impossible to guarantee the presence of every member on account of other concerts which may be given, still we feel sure that the press will be well represented on the occasion of your daughter's debut, and that the principal dailies will all review the recital. We will certainly do all in our power to make the occasion an artistic success. (25 September 1906)

Another was sent to: Lieut. J. Wright, Bandmaster of the Royal Marines at Chatham in response to a request for a cello teacher at the princely salary of 10p an hour:

> We have been thinking on the matter you referred to but regret we do not know a cellist who would be prepared to teach at the Royal Naval School, Chatham at the terms you name (2/- an hour). It would not pay anyone to come down to Chatham specially, at least it appears so to us. We can of course give you a list of several excellent cellists, but they would want higher terms than those mentioned. Would it be any good sending you a few names and addresses? (22 November 1906)

Unknown hopefuls from abroad had also to be dealt with. This reply was sent to Cara Minore Penn in Paris.

> With regard to the prospects for you in this country it is, of course, very difficult for me to say straight away. In any case, it will be necessary for you to make one or more successful appearances in public before any engagements can be counted on. It is somewhat difficult for a new-comer, as you would be, to find immediate recognition here, as the Profession is so overcrowded, and the Societies and Concert-givers are so very conservative in their selection of artists. However there is always room anywhere for a gifted artist provided, of course, they are prepared to wait for the necessary opportunities, and the same applies to Operatic work in this country. (22 August 1907)

Established baritones Robert Radford and Charles Knowles made early appearances with the agency, starting with the choral society in Belfast:

> Owing to the carelessness of the postal authorities our letter with your offer of engagement has only this morning reached Mr Robert Radford's hands, hence the delay in sending you a reply. Mr Radford has just wired from Sheringham (Norfolk), where he is spending his holidays, to say that he is now booked for Bristol on December 15th, so unfortunately will be unable to entertain your offer of engagement for the two *Messiah* performances on December 14th and 15th. We may mention, however, that he is free on February 1st and would be pleased to accept for your miscellaneous concert on that date, if your arrangements are not already completed.
>
> May we have the pleasure of booking the services of another artist in place of Mr Radford for December 14th and 15th? Mr Charles Knowles is still disengaged for both dates, and we believe you know his qualities as a Handelian singer. (16 August 1906)

The agency's association with the mezzo-soprano Muriel Foster went back to Vert's day (she sang the Angel in Elgar's *Dream of Gerontius* at its first performance outside Britain, at Düsseldorf in 1902). Her debut was in 1896 at Bradford in Parry's oratorio *King Saul.* John Tillett's letter to Henry Wolfsohn in New York contained news of her withdrawal from public life. In fact her career was not quite at an end, but limited by illness and she tended to give only recitals in later years:

> Many thanks for your letter to hand this morning regarding Miss Muriel Foster. You will be sorry to learn that this artist will be lost to the musical profession in a very few months. It was only yesterday that her engagement with Mr Ludovic Goetz, a wealthy gentleman, was announced. And she tells me that she will retire into private life at the end of October, so unfortunately the tour we had proposed for her must fall through. Miss Foster is cancelling all her engagements for next season with the exception of the Hereford and Birmingham Festivals and one or two other important concerts. (23 August 1906)

With the advent of the new season 1906–07, Ibbs decided, in September 1906, to try to get newspaper coverage of the forthcoming activities of artists on the agency books. He addressed one such letter to the journalist Morgan Kingston. Those names or facts underlined by Ibbs clarify their significance and importance to the agency:

> I append a few notes in the hope that you may find room for them in your next Musical Column. Mme Clara Butt has completely recovered from her recent severe illness and operation and will make her re-appearance after an absence of eight months at the Royal Albert Hall on the afternoon of Saturday October 13th, when she and her husband, Mr Kennerley Rumford, will give their Annual Concert. The London Symphony Orchestra, Dr Frederic Cowen, Mons. [Josef] Hollman and other eminent artistes have been engaged. Miss Kate Edie will give her first concert on October 29th, when she will have the valued help of Miss Agnes Nicholls, Mrs George Swinton, Miss Muriel Foster (her re-appearance in London), Mr Gervase Elwes, Mr Santley, Mons. Tivadar Nachèz. Godowsky will make his re-appearance in England at a Recital which he will give in the Bechstein Hall on November 5th. He will also return to England for the Spring Season, and will give two further recitals on March 2nd and April 27th. Mr Archy Rosenthal will give a pianoforte Recital at the Aeolian Hall on November 9th, the programme of which will be peculiarly interesting from the fact that it will be compiled exclusively from the compositions of living Pianists. Miss May Elliott (Stavenhagen's most brilliant pupil) will give a pianoforte Recital at the Bechstein Hall on November 15th, when she will have the assistance of the Queen's Hall Orchestra conducted by Mr Henry J Wood. Mr Plunket Greene will give his only London Recital this season on November 30th at the Bechstein Hall. H.M. The King has graciously accepted a copy of Miss Nora Conway's book of poems "My Palace of Thought". Mr Albert Archdeacon has been engaged as principal baritone for the forthcoming Musical Festival at Cape Town, which is to take place in November next under the conductorship of Dr Barlow Dowling. Messrs Ibbs & Tillett have concluded a contract for Mme Clara Butt and Mr Kennerley Rumford to tour throughout Australia, New Zealand and Tasmania during the Winter of 1907–8. They are expected to leave England in August next and to return about Easter 1908.

The Rumfords continued to dominate the activities of, and produce the main income for the agency, with Ibbs having to work noticeably harder on behalf of Kennerley Rumford. The balancing act which the agency was forced to maintain is clear from this letter to Gloucester, where Frederick McCrea was responsible for managing and publicising the touring party's concerts in the area:

> I was sorry not to see you today, but I was engaged endeavouring to pacify Eastbourne! I have discussed the question of Walsall fully with Mr Rumford and we have both come to the conclusion that it would be unwise and unfair to give the Concert on Thursday without Mme Butt. The audience at Walsall is drawn solely by the idea of hearing her, and if we let them get to the Hall, even should they elect to stay rather than make a fruitless journey, it would be obtaining their money under false pretences and this Mme Butt will not consent to. If your local agents will get immediately prominent

bills etc posted over the present bills and in their shop, saying that owing to an attack of influenza Mme Butt is quite unable to sing on Thursday, and that the Concert must therefore be postponed and you also put the announcement in the Birmingham papers on Wednesday and Thursday mornings. I think this will make the fact widely known. Please be very careful, however, to specify that the cause of this disappointment is only influenza as we do not want false rumours flying about. Cheltenham is a vastly different place as there Mr Rumford and Mons. Hollman have a large following and we are taking our risk of a financial failure. Walsall, however, is a totally distinctive audience, and as I say, is drawn by Mme Butt's name alone. You must let me have a statement of your expenses. I greatly regret the inconvenience and trouble caused but as you will understand, we are helpless in such a case. (3 December 1906)

The Rumfords could also show consideration for the 'common' man, however. Even the stationmaster of Bournemouth Central station and his employers, the London and South Western Railway Company, received the following letter of thanks after the Butt concert party had visited the town:

I am desired by Mr & Mrs Rumford to send you their sincere thanks for so kindly enabling them to catch the 5.14 train on Saturday last. They very greatly appreciated your courtesy in detaining the train and hope that your doing so did not cause any inconvenience to your company. Mr & Mrs Rumford are so sorry they had not the opportunity of thanking you personally. (26 November 1906)

As the year 1906 grew to a close, the agency became well established and enjoyed the prospect (alluded to in Ibbs's letter to the press) of an extensive tour by the Butt party of Australia and New Zealand due to begin in the summer of 1907. On a personal level the year ended happily for John Tillett with his marriage on 29 December at St Saviour's Church, Haverstock Hill to Esta d'Argo (mentioned by Ibbs as 'a very excellent light soprano' when selling the agency's artists earlier in the year). Her real name was Hetty Holroyd, and though Yorkshire born, she emigrated to Australia at the age of five. She received her musical education in Sydney (first as a pianist), but made her debut as a singer at its Town Hall in 1897. She then went to Italy before moving to England in 1904 where she sang in Chappell's Ballad Concerts, the Queen's Hall Promenade and Symphony Concerts, the Royal Albert Hall Sunday Concerts as well as appearing in many provincial cities and festivals. She joined the agency at the start and was soon recommended by her fiancé to all from the smallest provincial society to the great Hans Richter, to whom he wrote six weeks before their marriage:

Miss Esta d'Argo has asked me to let you have her concert repertoire, which I have much pleasure in enclosing. I presume Mr Forsyth has informed you that Mrs Swinton is unwell and will be unable to keep the appointment which you kindly arranged for Monday afternoon? (3 November 1906)

Richter generally refused to give recommendations, because he felt that his engagement of an artist was in itself a vote of confidence and should be seen as such by managements. In this instance his antennae were probably alerted to the domestic connection between her and the agency.

You may be persuaded that it is not easy for me to say No! …, but if I should make an exception it would mean great offence to many others who asked me for recommendations, and who are also very good artists. If I should be asked, I would not hesitate to acknowledge the good qualities of Miss d'Argo. The best recommendation is the fact that in a very short period she sang twice in concerts conducted by myself. (19 December 1906)

John Tillett's marriage to Esta d'Argo begs the question of some possible skullduggery when, in his letter of 24 May that year to Mary Conly (reproduced earlier in this chapter), he wrote: 'We believe you mentioned <u>Nov 2nd</u> as a possible date for the

Bradford Subs[criptio]n Concert, and if that is the date you have in pencil, we know that another artiste has been engaged by them for that Concert.' That other artiste was none other than his fiancée.

The agency issued a booklet in 1907 with a bright red cover and the word IMPORTANT at its head. On the inside cover there follows the announcement that, for the season 1907–08:

> Messrs. IBBS & TILLETT have the pleasure to submit the names of the eminent Artistes for whom they act as sole business managers.
>
> All communications respecting these artistes should be addressed to Messrs. Ibbs & Tillett, who are, at the same time, prepared to negotiate for any recognised Artiste.
>
> The entire arrangements for the phenomenally successful "CLARA BUTT-KENNERLEY RUMFORD" tour, 1906–7, as also for Mme. Clara Butt & Mr Kennerley Rumford's approaching AUSTRALASIAN TOUR in 1907–8, have been negotiated by Messrs. Ibbs & Tillett.

There then follows the agency's first list on the next page:

SOLE
Representatives of
Madame CLARA BUTT
and
Mr KENNERLEY RUMFORD

Miss AGNES NICHOLLS
and
Miss ESTA D'ARGO

Madame KIRKBY LUNN
and
Mrs GEORGE SWINTON

Mr WILLIAM GREEN

Mr PLUNKET GREENE
Mr CHARLES KNOWLES
and
Mr DALTON BAKER

Herr LEOPOLD GODOWSKY

Mons. JOHANNES WOLFF
and
Mons. TIVADAR NACHÈZ

Mons. HOLLMAN

The rest of the booklet is taken up with photographs and captions of the artists. The Rumfords stand casually together at the porch of their house, the caption reminding clients of their forthcoming Australasian tour for the 'entire season, 1907–8'. The rest are head-and-shoulder photographs. Agnes Nicholls (Lady Hamilton Harty) is 'the foremost English soprano, prima donna, Covent Garden Opera House', Esta d'Argo, 'the brilliant Australian soprano, of the principal London and Provincial Concerts, Hallé Concerts, Manchester, Bradford, Leeds Choral Union', Kirkby Lunn, 'the eminent contralto, principal contralto of the Covent Garden (London) and Metropolitan Opera House (New York), Mrs George (Elsie) Swinton (no photo but instead a reproduction of John Singer Sargent's drawing of this beautiful woman) is simply 'the new mezzo soprano'. The first of the male singers is William Green, 'the celebrated oratorio tenor, in Australia May–Dec 1907, available Xmas onwards', Plunket Greene is 'the eminent basso', Dalton Baker, 'one of the foremost English baritones, Charles Knowles, 'the well-known baritone of the principal London and provincial concerts', Godowsky was 'the famous Russian [*sic*] pianist "one of the greatest pianists of the day" – *Morning Post*', Johannes Wolff, 'the eminent violinist, Court violinist to the Queen of the Netherlands', Tivadar Nachèz 'the celebrated Hungarian violinist. His new concerto will be performed by him at the London Philharmonic Concert, April 17, 1907', Monsieur Hollman, 'the famous cellist'. A further page advertises both the Capet and Rosé string quartets, the former from Paris, the latter Vienna, for whom Ibbs and Tillett 'have been appointed sole representatives'. Such booklets were issued annually, and so, with sole responsibility for 14 artists (ten singers, a pianist, two violinists and a cellist) and two string quartets, Ibbs and Tillett completed its first year as an agency. That it was a force to be reckoned with may be deduced from an advertisement Pedro Tillett took out in a programme for a concert given by Arthur Fagge's London Choral Society (a performance of *Pompeii* by Benoit Hollander, coincidentally featuring his sister-in-law, the clearly well-connected and ubiquitous Esta d'Argo as Nydia, a blind slave girl) on 4 December 1907 at Queen's Hall. The text for the advertisement read as follows:

N VERT

THE ORIGINAL CONCERT AGENCY

Established 50 Years

Director : PEDRO J TILLETT

ONLY ADDRESS :
6 CORK ST., BURLINGTON GARDENS, W

Telephone : 937 MAYFAIR
Telegrams : VERT'S AGENCY, LONDON

No connection whatever
with any other Agency

CHAPTER FIVE

Clara Butt's Australian Tour: 1907

Clara Butt and Kennerley Rumford gave the impetus for the initial financial success of the agency when, in the summer of 1907, they put the management of a tour to Australia and New Zealand in the hands of Ibbs and Tillett, who in turn linked up with an Australian agency to make arrangements on the ground ahead of the tour party's arrival. This was the firm of J. and N. Tait, consisting of a family of four brothers, headed by Frank (later Sir Frank) Tait. They virtually monopolized concert giving in Australia because they had their finger on the pulse (and purse-strings) of Australian taste, and they loved the Rumfords for their box office appeal. Ibbs sent a few letters of instruction before leaving Britain, to the Australian Press Association in London, and to Tait in Australia. This was sent to the former:

> We should feel greatly obliged if you could see your way to cable out news regarding Madame Clara Butt and Kennerley Rumford's "Farewell" Concert before leaving for Australia, which takes place at the Albert Hall tomorrow afternoon [29 June], and for which we have already sent you tickets, and mention in your cable that Mr and Mrs Rumford have just received a letter from Her Majesty the Queen through her Equerry, the Hon Sidney Greville, saying she regrets she is prevented from being present at the Concert and desiring her Equerry to say that she wishes Mr and Mrs Rumford all success in their tour in the Colonies. All the Agents-General of Australia, New Zealand and Tasmania have accepted invitations to be present at the Concert. We should of course be prepared to bear the cost of such cable if necessary. (28 June 1907)

Having told Tait much the same, a letter from Ibbs continued:

> By the way, it has been suggested that we should give a Concert at Colombo on our way back from Australia, as I understand we spend two days there. You might make a note regarding this, and I could discuss the matter with you when we meet.
>
> We are sorry to hear that the prospects for Madame Albani are not encouraging, but we feared this would be the case. Mr Rumford and I interviewed the P.O. Company on Monday last, and they are evidently doing everything they can to make Mr and Mrs Rumford comfortable during the voyage. They are fixing electric fans etc in all the cabins and are giving a separate table at dinner to them. In mapping out the itinerary of the tour, you will not forget that Mr Rumford would like to give one or two Vocal Recitals apart from the tour Concerts and these I understand you to say would be chiefly in conjunction with Musical Clubs in Melbourne, Sydney etc. I may cable you to give us a few more days rest before commencing operations as Mr and Mrs Rumford think this will [be] necessary. I hope therefore it will not upset your plans to any great extent.
>
> The Recital which Messrs Frank Merrick and Carl Barre gave on Saturday last was a great artistic success, and I think the enclosed [not extant] notices (seeing that they are written by our ultra-clever London critics) are really very good. You will notice that I have edited them pretty freely and you can therefore make very good use of them, as they are all from very important papers here. (28 June 1907)

After the farewell concert, Ibbs reported:

> We are only just recovering from the excitement and enthusiasm of last Saturday at the Albert Hall, which really was an extraordinary sight. I did not cable you, as I had an intimation from Mr Preston that he intended cabling fully regarding the Concert, and also that Her Majesty the Queen had sent Mr and Mrs Rumford a letter expressing her regret that a state engagement prevented her being present at the Concert as she had hoped to be and wishing Mr and Mrs Rumford every success on their tour through the Colonies. By this time you will probably have made very good use of these cables. Many thanks also for your cable saying that you had postponed the opening Concert to

Tuesday September 10th, which suits our plans very much better as Mrs Rumford feels that she should certainly have a longer rest after her voyage.

The reception given by the "Austral" Club duly came off on Wednesday last, and was a very crowded Function. This news also you will probably have had by cable. Mrs Rumford spent a solid hour autographing photographs for enthusiastic members and their friends. The Princess Christian yesterday sent her godson (Master Victor) a very handsome hammered silver bowl and spoon for his birthday, and he is to be taken to pay a state visit to his Royal Godmother at Schonberg House tomorrow morning.

You will be amused to hear that Mrs Rumford's reverence for superstition has decided that under no consideration will she start on this tour on a Friday, and therefore that the whole troupe of us are to go to Tilbury on Thursday the 18th inst., spending the night there, so that we can say that we started on the journey any day but a Friday!! You could possibly work up a little personal paragraph on this.

Another item that would afford good copy was the really extraordinary instance of that terrific thunderstorm raging last Saturday afternoon whilst Mrs Rumford sang "Abide with me" and "Kathleen Mavourneen". The latter was an unique experience as the lightning was playing all around her nearly the whole time, and the crashing of the thunder seem to chime in with the grand chords of the Organ, however this I need not enlarge upon to you!

I saw Miss Murphy and she told me most positively that Melba would not be visiting Australia this Winter but there are persistent notices in all the papers that it is her intention to do so, so I should think it probably means that she will. (5 July 1907)

While John Tillett remained behind in London, Robert Leigh Ibbs set off with the Rumfords on the *SS Mongolia* and arrived in Melbourne on 26 August 1907. Throughout the tour Ibbs sent a series of letters back to London, most of them to Tillett, but some also to his press contacts urging them to write reports of the singers' success and progress. Extracts from the letters provide a vivid account of the high and low points of this strenuous undertaking. The first quoted was written a week after their arrival and was to the journalist E.J. Shellard based in Bristol, where Clara Butt grew up, was educated and where she married:

It may prove of interest to your readers to have a few notes on the voyage etc of Mme Clara Butt and Mr Kennerley Rumford and of their arrival in Australia for their extended tour of the Australian colonies. We left Tilbury on the P & O S.S. "Mongolia" on July 19th in most lovely weather, which continued the whole way to Aden, which we reached on August 4th. There was not a cloud in the sky and scarcely a ripple on the water the whole of this time, so everyone proved to be a splendid sailor! Leaving Aden we ran into a south-west monsoon, and we rolled heavily for four days, which was practically the only bad bit we had the whole voyage. We had the first series of sports between Aden and Colombo, but although we all took a very active part, were none of us among the prize-winners. The night before we reached Colombo (August 9th) Mr and Mrs Rumford gave a concert in aid of the Nautical Charities, which was a great success and realised a large sum. Mr Merrick, Mr Barrie, Mr Godfrey assisted. Mr and Mrs Rumford autographed three programmes which were put up to auction and realised £17, a substantial addition to the Charities.

We spent the next day ashore at Colombo, which is one of the most lovely places imaginable. We sailed that night for Fremantle and for nine days we did not even see another ship! On the Monday we arrived at Fremantle and took on board His Excellency the Governor-General (Lord Northcote), Lady Northcote and staff, also the Governor of Western Australia and Lady Bedford, to all of whom Mr and Mrs Rumford were presented. We arrived at Port Melbourne early on the morning of August 26th, and at 9.30am an influential deputation, headed by the Lord Mayor arrived on board to welcome Mr and Mrs Rumford, bringing great masses of the most lovely flowers. At 11 o'clock we left the ship and took a train to Melbourne, where there was a crowd waiting at the station. Mr and Mrs Rumford drove off in pair-horse carriages to the hotel, where they found their drawing-room a perfect bower of flowers, which kept arriving almost every half hour. The next day the Lord and Lady Mayoress officially welcomed them at the Town Hall at a reception. Some 700 guests were present including the Prime Minister and the wives of nearly all the other ministers. There was a huge crowd in the street, who cheered Mr and Mrs Rumford lustily as they drove along. Wednesday

> brought one of the most charmingly unaffected and sincere of any of the functions, which will be offered Mr and Mrs Rumford. There is to be a Womens' Work Exhibition held here next month on a very large scale, which is being organised by Lady Northcote. An immense choir of 1300 ladies' voices and a full band (also of ladies) has been formed by Mrs Franklin Petersen (wife of the Principal of the University) and trained by her, and the Committee gave a reception to Mr and Mrs Rumford at the Guildhall on Wednesday evening. The Prime Minister and the Lord Mayor were both present. Mr and Mrs Rumford got a tremendous reception on entering the hall, the choir singing the National Anthem. Mrs Petersen made a most charming little speech in which she emphasised the fact that they welcomed and honoured Mrs Rumford, not only as a great artiste but as a woman and a fond mother. The President then asked Mr and Mrs Rumford's acceptance of a magnificent harp of violets etc, bearing the inscription "A welcome to Australia from the Womens' Work Exhibition", and bouquets as well. Then came the most touching event of all. Little girls came forward leading most lovely toys beautifully decorated with flowers, which they begged Mr and Mrs Rumford to accept for their children. Both Mr and Mrs Rumford were almost overcome by this perfectly charming "touch of nature". The Premier of Victoria made a racy speech, saying that he had recently met the King of England, but now he had the honour of meeting the Queen of Song. Mr Rumford replied that the extraordinary warmth and genuine pleasure with which all in Australia had welcomed his wife and himself had touched them more deeply than he could say, and neither of them would ever forget such genuine kindness or regret having undertaken the tour. He warmly praised the wonderful singing of the huge ladies' choir, saying that in England in order to get such splendid results the aid of man had to be sought, but in Australia women were able to achieve such remarkable results unaided. They were pelted with flowers on leaving the hall.

Ibbs's first letter to John Tillett also described the initial events of the tour, but then discussed the matter of other artists, ticket prices and the tour itinerary:

> We got into port about 8am and at 9.30 a large deputation of influential people arrived on board and welcomed the Rs. We went ashore at 11 and up to Melbourne by train, being greeted at the station by a large crowd. Flowers and cards in profusion. Today we have had a tremendous function at the Town Hall, an official reception by the Lord and Lady Mayoress. About 700 present and a huge crowd in the street, who cheered the Rs as they drove away. Tomorrow they are to be received by the "Women of Melbourne" and a choir of 1300 females are to sing a welcome. Friday lunch party at the wealthiest people here, Saturday dinner and theatre party, Sunday luncheon party at Government House with the Governor-General and Lady Northcote, Monday reception by the Philharmonic and Orpheus Societies, then a little rest we hope.
>
> Tait has definitely decided upon 21/-, 10/6 & 5/- [£1.05, 52$^1/_2$p, 25p] for the prices after long and anxious consideration, and we feel he is right as both Paderewski and Melba charged these, and it would never do to place a lower value on the Rs. Melba is due next week, and has it announced that nothing will induce her to sing, but everyone says that she will. [Andrew] Black [Scottish baritone] is in New Zealand, but doing very little. Tait says he is horribly lazy and won't work and doubts if he will ever come back to England. Poor Albani was an awful frost here, and I hear that her best house was under £50!! Isn't it awful? She has been going round to quite small villages and appears to be shockingly badly worked. There was a writ against her here for £125 for printing and an order was obtained to prevent her leaving for New Zealand. Poor old thing, it is too dreadfully sad. The Besses o' the Barn Band are doing extraordinary business still, and they have been here nearly a year.
>
> Keep all the cuttings whilst we are away. I much fear you won't see us back until the end of May. I will send you a suggested tour for 1908/9 as soon as I can. Don't accept any summer engagements definitely, but you can of course do so provisionally. You might advise Boosey and Chappell that the following dates are practically settled. Sydney October 5, 8, 10, 13, 15, 17, 19, Brisbane 26, 29, Toowoomba 30, Melbourne return for the Cup [horse racing] on November 6 & concerts 7, 9. Ballarat 11, Adelaide 13, 16, 19, Perth 26, 28, 30, December 3, Kalgoorlie, Tasmania, Launceston Dec 9, Hobart 13, and back in Sydney for Xmas Day, leaving for New Zealand on January 1st.

Ibbs held his letter to Shellard back until after the first two or three concerts so that he could report on their success:

> It has been simply colossal and an easy case of "Veni, vidi, vici". Both Mr & Mrs Rumford have made the most enormous artistic success, rivalling their social one. The concerts are simply tremendous, each one being larger than the other until last night it was impossible to get another mouse into the hall. The audience on Saturday night simply went delirious with excitement, the whole house standing up and shouting itself hoarse, whilst Mrs Rumford was simply overwhelmed with flowers, some of the trophies being seven or eight feet high. After the first concert Mrs Rumford sent all her flowers to the Melbourne Hospital, and it took two carts to take them.

The popularity of Clara Butt and her party (Ibbs never refers to her other than by her married name) evidently alerted Nellie Melba to make an appearance and remind her fellow countrymen of her own status in Australia. 'Melba arrives tomorrow and has announced that under no considerations whatever will she sing during this stay, but everyone is betting that she will. According to the papers she has maids, chefs, secretaries, valets and motor cars galore with her'. Then the cruellest of luck and the worst nightmare for any singer occurred when both Clara Butt and her husband caught bad colds, probably due to the somewhat treacherous weather they were experiencing (including a hurricane). They took to their beds with nurses and doctors in attendance and arose only on the day of their first concert. Meanwhile the Besses o' the Barn Band continued their 'positively astounding financial success. On Saturday night they actually had an audience of 14,000 people at 2/- and 1/- [10p and 5p in today's money], the receipts being close on £1,000, and this is the 33rd concert they've given in Melbourne alone'. One suspects Ibbs was regretting he was not managing this brass band rather than Clara Butt and her husband. As to future plans and ideas, Ibbs made several suggestions on behalf of himself and his partner to Tait, but received short shrift from his Australian colleague. Tait made no secret of what the country did not want and told Ibbs as much, which he then ruefully passed on to Tillett:

> Tait won't look at [Harry Plunket] Greene or [Josef] Hollman, I'm sorry to say, and thinks Ben Davies will be very ill advised to come out. Music is overdone here, unless you have an absolutely phenomenal attraction. [George] Marshall-Hall [a Melbourne-based conductor who created his own series of symphony concerts] has a big following of all the swagger people here, and finished his season on Saturday, but has had a biggish loss on the season. He only charges 5/-, 3/-, 2/- [25p, 15p, 10p]. There does not appear to be such a thing in Australia as a musical agent, and there certainly does not seem to be any use for one. It seems strange that there are only people like Tait who just speculate in artists. Tait tells me that you wouldn't earn £20 a year obtaining engagements. I hope our typewriter has been worn out in booking artists! I've not come across any semblance of business for us out here so far. I'm known as the private secretary and spoken of as such by the Rumfords!!

William Arundel Orchard was the first conductor of the Sydney Symphony Orchestra, which he created out of the amateur material in the city, and which he gradually turned into a professional body. It also played for singers and instrumentalists brought out by the Tait brothers, including Butt on her 1907 tour; it would appear that of the many artists Orchard and his band accompanied, she was the only one with whom they encountered any problems, as Orchard relates in his memoir *The Distant View*:

> With Dame Clara we were rehearsing "Softly awakes my Heart" [from *Samson and Delilah*]. Towards the end she came in too soon after a few bars rest, so she looked at me and called out in her Amazonian voice, "That's wrong!" "Yes," I said, "you were too soon." "Rubbish," she replied, "I've sung this with the composer [Saint Saëns]. We'll have it again." So we repeated and she was still wrong. "Too soon," I said. "Nonsense, I can't be, " said the Dame. So I turned my stand so she could see the score. The orchestra was getting annoyed. Again the passage was tried and this time as she followed the score things went right; but she was most ungracious about it.

Charles Buttrose wrote of Clara Butt and Kennerley Rumford in his book *Playing for Australia* (1982):

> The duo maintained their grip on Australian audiences for many years. I heard them on their final tour: the once statuesque Dame Clara, getting old, singing most of the concert seated but still with Rumford who, in the chilly Adelaide Town Hall, looked as though he should have been home by the fire with his slippers on, bringing down the house with the duet they made famous, 'The Keys of Heaven'.

So even at this stage of their careers Australians were rapturous in their response – certainly if Ibbs's account of their first concert is anything to go by:

> Well, the die is cast and I think success is assured. Considering their disadvantages Mr & Mrs Rumford sang magnificently and there was little trace of illness about her, but R showed he had a cold towards the end. There was a great crowd to see them arrive and the hall looked splendid. It reached £790, which is considered very good for a first concert. Rumford got a tremendous reception when he went on and was presented with a laurel wreath and a decorated Maori shield after the "Largo". As you may imagine Mrs R had an ovation before she was allowed to commence. After "Divinités du Styx" a perfect furore set in and floral trophies without number almost were handed up in a long stream, the Albert Hall was nothing to it! Each time she appeared more flowers were given up and after "Land of Hope and Glory" the entire audience stood up and shouted at her. Eventually she had to give a third encore and was allowed to leave, dead beat. Melba sent a lovely trophy of white flowers. There was an enormous crowd to see her off and it was quite a picture to see the Rs coming down the main staircase through a huge avenue of flowers, all the attendants lining the stairs carrying the flowers. One bouquet which got rather too near the crowd was snatched out of hand and they fought like cats to get a sprig of it as a souvenir. There is not the slightest doubt the Rs have scored an immense popular success both artistically and socially.

While Ibbs was away news came to him of the death of Grieg. The ailing composer, overworked and already committed to the Leeds Festival, realized in the spring of 1907 that he would not have recovered his strength sufficiently to travel later that year and sent one of his last communications to Ibbs and Tillett four months before his death. He had in fact already made his last public appearance, in the German city of Kiel on 26 April, and subsequently cancelled his visit to England.

> Excuse my not having written earlier. So many alarms have hindered me. Unfortunately I will not be able to appear in the Chappell Ballad Concert the 12th of October as I have to conduct in Leeds the same evening. After Leeds I have still some engagements and, these finished, I am obliged to rest because of my delicate health. That is the reason why I am prevented to accept your kind proposal. (6 May 1907)

Ever the businessman, Ibbs told Tillett from Australia: 'How sad about Grieg's death. It's rather a good thing we had not made any arrangement, or it would have been a big disappointment.'

The Rumfords continued their triumphant conquest of Melbourne with Tait having to lay on extra concerts. From the Australian impresario brothers he learnt a thing or two about the presentation of audience figures to the press, 'the Taits have a system of adding £400 to every house; you can increase the receipts of the concerts to any figure you like as the houses look a great deal more; there are only about 40 guinea seats sold for each concert'. Meanwhile Melba continued her support by appearing among the audience and giving the couple supper parties ('I can't imagine what her game is', wrote Ibbs, 'but there must be something on'). Ibbs was very mindful of the value of publicity and self-publicity. Not only intent on ensuring that the success of the Butt tour in Australia was being reported back in English papers and magazines, he also observed how Australian artists currently working in Europe were receiving the same treatment in Australian papers. Ada Crossley, another contralto, was one such singer. She had made her London debut in 1895 and went on to appear at every great festival in the Empire with such success that she gave no less than five command performances before Queen Victoria in two years. 'Ada Crossley', wrote Ibbs, 'has cables in every paper regarding her colossal success at Gloucester [Three Choirs Festival 1907], also long letters in the Sydney papers as to her "Royal" engagements and the terrific amount she has to refuse! She works things very well.' While acknowledging how well Clara Butt was going down with the Australian public and noting how necessary it was for native Australian artists to keep their names before the public back home, Ibbs was patently disappointed that he was not going to be able to capitalize on Butt's success with other artists from their stable, as he reminded Tillett:

> You must tell Plunket Greene, Nachèz and Hollman that there is no chance here, as Taits will not listen to them, so will you kindly break it to them gently. Greene would be a ghastly failure I'm sure. They won't touch [Vivien] Chartres. The only fiddlers they'll look at are [Jan] Kubelik and [Mischa] Elman, and they are very doubtful about the latter. The Australian people are not musical, although they think they are, but we see the huge difference in enthusiasm when Mrs R sings a German song or 'The Lost Chord'. It is very shocking of course, but painfully true.
>
> Last night [24 September 1907] beat all records. The house was completely sold out by 4pm and over 1000 people were turned away from the doors, apart from the hundreds who were refused tickets during the day. The enthusiasm simply exceeded all bounds and they had hard work to get away from the hall. Melba took 200 stalls and gave Mrs R a big bouquet herself from the front. She's a very clever woman. She gave a big supper at the Grand [Hotel] afterwards to the Rs at which about 40 smart people were present. The floral decorations were beautiful, the initials C. and K.R. being woven all over the place. It wasn't over until about 3am. The receipts were £801, so with tomorrow's final matinée we shall have taken over £5000 here in eight concerts, which isn't bad for a start. We've wanted a bigger hall here for the last four concerts and the police raided us on Saturday and last night, and made us return money to certain people who were standing and send them away. Twenty people even paid 5/- each last night to stand under the platform just to hear, though of course they could see nothing!

Once arrived in Sydney, Ibbs (together with Kennerley Rumford) managed to pursue his love of cricket: 'I saw Master [Victor] Trumper make 89 in 32 minutes at Sydney on Saturday. One over 4.4.6.6.6.6!!!' At the start of the tour they had been made honorary members of Melbourne Cricket Club (Ibbs was proposed by Hugh Trumble) and the MCC out from England were about to commence a series for the Ashes. The Sydney concerts were as successful as those in Melbourne ('a blaze of triumph') and from there the Rumfords gave two in Brisbane. 'A Mr and Mrs Cuzens travelled from the extreme north of Queensland to Brisbane purposely for our two concerts and it took them nearly a week to do it. They had to drive 140 miles and then train for 680 so that the two journeys involved their travelling over 1500 miles. Surely this is a record as regards enthusiasm to hear a concert?' After Adelaide they travelled to Perth when news came that Melba had finally thrown her hat into the ring and set up a rival tour:

> Bribe Kingston or [Ernest] Kuhe to give us a fat "par"[agraph] but failing that get one in "London Day by Day" as we must keep them prominently in the *Daily Telegraph* on account of Melba and Crossley, so please do it at once. Melba gave concerts in Melbourne last Saturday and today, and is to give two big ones at the Exhibition Buildings there at Christmas at cheap prices. Her concerts at Sydney are December 7th and 14th. I knew she wouldn't wait long before making a start, and if we hadn't been the success we are, she would have weighed in with a tour to crush us. This new star of Covent Garden [Luisa Tetrazzini] seems to have hit 'em. She must be a star of the first water,

> but why has she only just shone? How will dear Nellie [Melba] like it? The Bulletin and other rags are already asking this question in their usual coarse way. I fancy she is pretty sick. She had fine concerts here and in Melbourne, but not quite what was expected, and she wasn't in overgood voice in Sydney.

Clara Butt's reception in Perth 'turned up trumps in the end and the third concert went like wildfire', indeed such was the demand that, at a day's notice, a fourth was hastily arranged at Her Majesty's Theatre at popular prices. Booking was opened on the morning of the concert with a queue of 200 people already waiting to buy tickets:

> From 9 o'clock to 12 o'clock the street was almost impassable and by 12 o'clock the entire house was sold out! Dress Circle at 7/6, Stalls 5/- and unreserved at 3/-, over 2500 tickets being issued in three hours. The scene outside the theatre from 6 o'clock to 8 o'clock baffles description. People fought and struggled to get near, and the trams had to be stopped every now and then to prevent people being killed in the streets. Pandemonium reigned both inside and outside the theatre and heaps of ticket holders never even got inside the doors! Ushers and police alike were swept off their feet, and when at last we were able to make a start the house was a wonderful spectacle. The concert lasted nearly three hours instead of two and both Mr and Mrs Rumford had to sing double and triple encores. The enthusiasm and excitement were simply marvellous. We got into very hot water with the authorities, and Tait was to be prevented from leaving Perth without appearing before the magistrates. However they eventually allowed him to go. He has been fined the maximum penalty of £40 and costs.

Tillett was not having much luck getting these events reported in English newspapers despite the pleas from Ibbs, who in turn was evidently being nagged by the Rumfords (probably Mrs) for the lack of coverage. 'I dread the arrival of the beastly paper [*Daily Telegraph*] each week', he wrote. This letter (dated 10 December 1907) contains an example of the coded system concerning financial matters between the two partners which lasted until the end of Emmie Tillett's management of the firm 70 years later. It was known as the *Buckingham* code, each of the ten letters in sequence of the word *Buckingham* given the numbers 1–9 with zero assigned to the final *m* (causing considerable mirth among the firm's employees in later years when a regular fee of 120 guineas was duly recorded as *bum* gns). So Ibbs's report that 'The receipts of this "cheap" concert were *£ign*' signified takings of £576. In a surviving desk diary for 1906 which has sparse entries for Ibbs and Tillett's artists' engagements, it occurs for the first time on 17 February, coincidentally for Kennerley Rumford (*£uc.u.n.* = £23. 2s. 6d. for a vocal recital in Brighton). In later years such a desk diary became a large ledger kept open by Emmie Tillett on her desk. By that time the purpose of the code seemed to be to prevent any artist, who might have had the opportunity to read it, from discovering how much a colleague was being paid.

Preparations began in the New Year of 1908 for the New Zealand leg of the tour. Nevin Tait was asked to:

> arrange for the best possible organ, and if you can get one at low pitch, as at Adelaide, all the better. Should you wish to advertise extra songs for Mrs Rumford, you can use some of the standard encores such as 'Il segreto', 'Caro mio ben', 'My treasure', 'Kathleen' etc. Will you kindly give instructions for the artists' room to be made as comfortable as possible. I suppose we shall have to build a sort of box on the stage, as at Perth, it being a theatre. In that case will you kindly tell them to cover over the top of the box as that is where the dangerous draughts come from in these theatres. Please tell the hotel people to send a carriage and pair with coachmen in livery.

There was some sort of falling out between the Rumfords and Tait at this stage of the tour, with Ibbs caught between the two warring parties. Apparently 'Tait saw Rumford in Melbourne soon after we commenced and suggested that we should do more concerts in the big towns at 50% than some of the smaller ones at 60%'. Because nothing was put into writing, when it came to the reckoning, Clara Butt refused point blank, only to have to back down when Tait insisted on her husband's having made a Gentleman's agreement with him. Despite a great deal of ill-feeling between Tait and the Rumfords, Ibbs felt a lesson had been learned by the whole affair and that in future all such agreements would have to be put into writing. To Tillett he also confided: 'that our commission to date [7 January 1908] amounts to roughly *£imm* [£500], but out of this I have to pay all living expenses, the Rumfords paying all steamship and railway expenses, so that is not all profit to us.'

By the end of this Australian leg of the tour (they returned in March 1908 after visiting New Zealand) Ibbs was becoming agitated at missing out on events occurring back in London. Agencies seemed to be mushrooming businesses at this time:

> I suppose you know that Cyril Streatfield is also starting. He has got some military friend to put up a lot of money, and he announced his intention of making things "hum" in the agency world. I think this tour will see the end of my career as a musical agent! I've had quite enough of it!! I notice that several Saturdays we have had no adverts in the *Daily Telegraph*. Is it want of work or design on your part? I must say I have a sneaking regard for the commercial value of that page on Saturdays, so if you can keep us on it, I would. It looks as though we are going to lose this Test match as well. The last one made us weep. Rank bad captaincy lost it.

Their tour of New Zealand continued in much the same vein of a royal progress, giving concerts in Wellington, Auckland, Christchurch, Dunedin, and then in smaller towns such as Nelson ('the place consists of two sheep only, yet we took *£cbm*' [£310]), Blenheim ('We met our Waterloo there, only taking *£umb* [£201]. We ought never to have gone to such a hole'), Palmerston North ('a disappointment too, only reaching *£uih*' [£258]), Invercargill ('the very last place created. A more dismal, dreary place I have never been in; no hotels or public houses in the place – total prohibition they call it. It was all too ghastly for words') and Napier ('Here we shall have a capital house, but it is the tiniest, filthiest little hovel of a theatre we have ever struck'). By now Ibbs's patience (particularly with Kennerley Rumford) was beginning to wear thin. 'My nerves are very little better, I'm sorry to say, as they are not allowed much rest by the male half of our constellation! In fact I shall be thankful when all is over, and it would take very little to make me throw in the sponge altogether!' They then travelled back to Australia for a series of farewell events in Sydney, Melbourne, Hobart, Launceston, Adelaide and Perth, leaving on 2 May for England where they arrived on 1 June. In his autobiography *Come, Listen to my Song*, the Irish-born impresario Roland Foster, who managed the next Butt tour to Australia, bears out Ibbs's disillusionment with the tour and its travails:

> I learned afterwards that Leigh Ibbs, who had accompanied them on their previous visit to Australia, was not enamoured of that land, or of America, and wished to be excused, being the type of Englishman who is thoroughly unhappy away from Piccadilly, Regent Street and the Queen's Hall 'Proms'.

The importance of reporting events back home in England was also stressed by the composer and pianist Percy Grainger. He was born in Melbourne in 1882 and moved to London in 1901 where he lived until the outbreak of the First World War. He then moved to America, eventually taking citizenship there and died in 1967. During his

London-based years he undertook concert tours of Australia, New Zealand and South Africa, in 1908–9 under Pedro Tillett's management of Vert's agency, and appeared to be on familiar terms with his agent, characterized by a postcard to his mother (20 February 1908, addressed 'to my darling mumlet'), when he wrote from Wakefield during a tour, 'Tillett & I are going to see a Melodrama tonight. It ought to be fun. He's such a nice little chap; nothing coarse about him, I think. Nice & human & kind-thinking', and in a letter to his Danish lover Karen Holten written the same day: 'What do you think I have just done? I and our agent (Tillett; he is a kind man – poor chap, I believe he has had an unhappy life) have been together to the theatre in this little town.' Later that year Grainger wrote this letter to Tillett from Australia.

> We are having a mighty jolly time, though it's starting to be pretty hot. The audiences etc have all been ever so charming to me so far. I did a jolly long walk a few days ago in Gippsland, S.E.Victoria, and enclose a newspaper account of it and a photo taken when some folk were giving me afternoon tea just near the end of the trip eight miles from Sale. If you could use either or both for pars in newspapers or anything, it would be very good. All our lot are always wishing we had you with us on this tour. We miss you very much.
>
> It's hard to say yet when I'll be back in England, but I will let you know later on when I know more. The scenery out here is perfectly gorgeous and gives me the hugest delight. I have introduced lots of stuff quite new to Australian audiences, things of Grieg, Fauré, Debussy, Balfour Gardiner etc., that they have never heard before, and they have taken to them splendidly I am glad to say.
>
> Do be a dear and see my name appears in the papers as often as possible. Are Forsyth and Houghton & Co. advertising me as they promised? I am playing their pieces out here diligently, Gardiner's *Noel* and my *Flower Waltz* Paraphrase (Forsyth) and the *Irish Dances* (Houghton). (6 November 1908)

The influence of the Taits continued to dog Ibbs and Tillett back in England. An attempt to get the soprano Emma Calvé to perform in London in 1910 failed due to an Australian tour she was to undertake for them:

> Mr Tait has written that my debut in Sydney will irrevocably take place on 2 April [1910]. He strongly urges me to leave on the mailboat on 18 February, knowing that I will definitely need eight or ten days of rest to recover from such a long voyage. Bowing to his opinion, I have taken steps to depart on the ship from Marseilles on 18 February. I know from experience that this rest is absolutely necessary, failing which I would be jeopardising my Australian debut, and which would in turn damage the tour.
>
> I am very sorry to be unable to meet your wishes but it is impossible for me to do so. I am singing in Paris from 10–12 February, I could sing for you on the 14th. It's the only date available for London. Please accept my sincere regrets. [undated, possibly end 1909, translation from the French]

CHAPTER SIX

Artists and Auditionees: 1906–12

Vert's agency, whose letterhead read as follows: 'Concert and Musical Agency, established 50 years, Director : Pedro J. Tillett (nephew and only partner of the late N.Vert)' remained at 6 Cork Street, Burlington Gardens, London W and continued to make its approaches to conductors and musical societies. Richter, who remained with the Vert agency, was asked by Pedro:

> Do you think there is any chance for Mr John Harrison, whom of course you know well, at the Opera? He is prepared to sing several parts such as Lohengrin, Siegmund etc, so if you think favourably of the matter, perhaps you could kindly bring it forward. (9 March 1908)

Richter had just conducted the first *Ring* in English at Covent Garden, and a repeat of the cycle was due to take place a year later. His last communication with the agency was from Bayreuth, where he had retired after his departure from Manchester and his final public concert at Eastbourne with the LSO on 22 April 1911. Clearly Ibbs and Tillett did what they could to coax him back for another appearance, but to no avail for the great man sent a card on which he wrote 'I am sorry to say that I cannot accept your offer. With our united best regards' (15 November 1911).

For the first years of its existence therefore, Ibbs and Tillett was in direct competition with Vert's agency, and brother was pitted against brother. John Tillett was establishing his new firm with new schemes, artists and clients. The nature of one such scheme proposed to the singer Gervase Elwes is unclear, but remains an example of John's attempts to widen the activities of the new agency:

> I have thought much over the scheme you spoke to me about and I find the difficulties greater than I at first imagined now that I come to look into the matter. In the first place, as I am probably doing a good deal of provincial work this autumn with [the pianist] Miss Fanny Davies, and might be going again to Germany, I certainly should not have time to devote to such a tour as you suggested before Christmas. Moreover it is now so late in the season that all tours must have been already arranged and therefore all the best dates taken, and we might come in for the remains of audiences everywhere. I am very sorry therefore that I must give up the idea, for at all events this year, as I really should not have time to devote to it. I am sorry as in many ways the scheme seemed a very nice one. (6 March 1907)

The autumn of 1907 was indeed to prove to be a busy one for Elwes, for although his German tour in the spring had been hugely successful, he never returned there again (hopes of doing so were dashed seven years later by the First World War). Instead he had three further recitals with Fanny Davies and also made first appearances at the Three Choirs (Gloucester) and Leeds Festivals.

Building the agency now had to involve taking on newcomers to the profession, as well as enticing away from their current agents those already established. Approaches were sometimes made by the novices themselves, or by their over-ambitious parents. A certain Mrs Parbury went to every imaginable length to convince Ibbs and Tillett of her daughter's artistic talent:

> Thank you for your kind letter. Please do all you can to help my daughter, for she is a brilliant artiste. She has a charming personality and can draw an audience. Lord Curzon and Lord Kitchener were in

> the highest praise of her artistic work, and she has studied in Paris and Italy. The Italians have given her the highest praise and Signor Caruso has promised to sing her compositions. I have heard an audience exclaim "She sings like an angel!" She has those beautiful high notes like Louise Dale. She is tall and graceful with beautiful natural auburn hair and the deportment of a queen.
>
> For she comes of a line of Kings, of which we have the records from the year 800. She is a high type of real old English good breeding. And I think she ought to make a speciality of English music – old Ballads. She is such a perfect lady in mind and manner, that she needs someone to steer for her. I have heard her again and again receive double encores. Her voice is a rich, clear Yorkshire voice.
>
> On my side we have been the Swales of Swaledale, one of the oldest and most honoured Yorkshire families for over 1000 years, and have our pedigree direct from Alfred the Great and Charlemagne. See Debrett under the name of Key, the present baronet is her cousin on her father's side and a cousin of General Gordon who died at Khartoum. Her grandfather, the late Mr George Parbury, was JP for Middlesex, Surrey and Westminster and Deputy Lieutenant of the Tower Hamlets. You will see that her great-grandfather, Sir John Key Bart., was twice Lord Mayor of London, Chamberlain and MP for the City, and it is through the Key family that she is in direct descent from William the Conqueror, Henry I, who married Matilda, daughter of Malcolm King of Scotland, Henry II and King John, whose daughter married Llewellyn Prince of Wales. All Hanover Square, London belonged to her ancestors. I tell you this merely because it is most interesting and proves her pure bred English descent.
>
> I do want you to help her for we have had bad, overwhelming sorrows and trials. Could you make a speciality of her for her English ballads? You could make her a second Jenny Lind or even a Patti, for she is a born genius and a beautiful creature. My husband lost all his inheritance in sport on the turf. He was in the landed gentry and moved in the King's set of friends, and I have had a hard fate to bring up my family of four on my own limited income. One son is in the army. Please try to do something for this dear girl this season, but it must be first class – there is nothing second rate about her and she is as good as she is beautiful. She is out of London just now visiting friends, but the Lyceum Club, Piccadilly will find her. (29 September 1909)

In 1909 the American critic and writer Henry T. Finck wrote a book entitled *Success in music and how it is won*, in which there is a chapter on starting a career with a debut recital, something for which Ibbs and Tillett would become renowned over the years with such events held mainly at London's Wigmore Hall. In Finck's book, agents (or managers as he calls them) get a brief and rather cynical mention, albeit from an American rather than a European point of view. According to Finck, Henry Wolfsohn (with whom John Tillett had competed in trying to promote his uncle Vert's American venture in 1902) was of the opinion that 'only about five percent of those who struggle and aspire can have their ambitions granted'. Finck goes on:

> On returning from Europe, the American who wishes to make a debut usually decides to give a song recital … Managers naturally advise those recitals as they get a share of the $400 or more it costs to give one. They say, quite truly, that they cannot do anything for a novice until they have some newspaper criticisms to circularize as a bait to secure an engagement in or out of town. These criticisms often may not be written after a recital, or, if written, may not be profitable to reprint. Some managers agree, for the sum of two or three thousand dollars, to secure sufficient engagements to launch the beginner successfully; and if the girl happens to be good-looking but penniless, they have the effrontery to suggest dishonourable ways of securing the sum required.
>
> A manager it is not necessary to have. Some agents are honest, some are not; inquiry among musicians is advisable. A good concert agency knows the conditions of the musical market in all cities and towns of the country; he gets demands for artists and sends circulars to inquirers and others. Of course he is, at best, in this business primarily not to help singers or pianists, but to make money. He is interested in the artists entrusted in his care in proportion to the demand for them, and the untried beginner is likely to remain long on the waiting list. Some managers ask a booking fee in advance, others do not.

As their artists' lists demonstrate, Ibbs and Tillett's (and indeed most agencies) activities were, from the outset, largely based on the singer as their principal marketable commodity. It is true that they also had a few instrumentalists (pianists, violinists and cellists) on their books, but the bulk of their artists were vocalists. Aspiring singers had to be heard in audition, and afterwards either Robert Leigh Ibbs or John Tillett would record their observations in a series of books devised expressly for that purpose. Three survive in the archive, dated between 1906 and 1943 (with seven further entries made by Emmie Tillett in early 1950). They are called *Manager's and Conductor's Register, Vocalists and Instrumentalists, compiled and edited by Mr Albert Marchbank and Mr Landon Ronald* (the conductor and husband of the singer Agnes Nicholls), and were published by the Royal Publishing Company in exercise book format with heavy maroon paper covers. At the top of each of the 272 pages is space to enter the name, address, class, age and height of the auditionee. The middle of the page is divided between singers (the entries for which describe 'voice, compass, quality, experience, introduced by and appearance') and instrumentalists ('compass and quality' replaced by 'technique and style'). A few lines are then provided for 'General Remarks' and at the bottom, the page is signed ('examined by') and dated.

Most of the entries, it should be acknowledged, were for would-be hopefuls who probably never proceeded beyond this first audition, but scattered among the pages and over the years are about a dozen names which would become famous and whose careers began with such auditions, initially at such venues as the Salle Erard (a firm of piano makers) or at Ramsden's, a piano merchant in Bond Street. Archibald Ramsden (a Yorkshireman famed for telling funny stories) founded the You-Be-Quiet-Club, whose eminent members included such musicians as Elgar and Richter. For five shillings 'you have the right at anytime that you are passing up Bond Street to enter Mr Ramsden's premises and demand two whiskies with soda', according to the *Referee* (19 May 1901). This social club of 'downright good fellows' had a heraldic shield consisting of two bottles, a cudgel, and a box of cigars. After an evening in Ramsden's company, Richter once observed that 'he has fine paintings, but smells strongly of whisky'.

Nervous auditionees would have been unaware of any of the fine paintings scattered around Ramsden's foyer as they entered his premises with trepidation. According to the audition books, the first one to do so was Margaret Lauder of Sinclair Road in West London on 18 May 1906. She was a contralto, the word 'moderate' written in the class section (which, if it was meant to refer to social status, Ibbs and Tillett completed only once more a month later with the same 'moderate' and then never again), her compass and experience were 'fair', her appearance 'good'. She was introduced by another piano maker, J.B. Challen and was described as being 'available for ballad work'. Lena Elbert of Croydon was less fortunate three days later. Short, of poor appearance and with little experience, she had limited compass (despite a good lower register) and required further study with her teacher (H. Leslie Smith) who had introduced her. On the same day (21 May) a mezzo-soprano called Miss Hickslyne, though short of height and with no experience, nevertheless possessed a big voice of good and sympathetic quality; she had a fair appearance and was also introduced by 'her master', this time Ernest Hodgson. Her programme was listed in General Remarks (a regular place for this detail from now on) and consisted of the aria 'Che faro' (from Gluck's *Orfeo*) and a German song, both of which she sang 'exceedingly well'. She was expected to do well, though she, too, needed to continue with her studies. Age was only entered once (Barton McGuckin's

24-year-old son, the tenor Noel Fleming, in November 1906), instead words such as 'young', 'quite young', 'about 40', 'rather middle age' or even 'uncertain' were euphemisms used on a few occasions. Height was also soon dispensed with.

The violinist Miss Fischer (probably visiting from Prague) had a fair technique and good appearance (though quite what the relevance of appearance was for an instrumentalist, in contrast to a singer who might be destined for the opera stage, is unclear). She was a pupil of the renowned Czech violinist and pedagogue Otakar Ševčík, but, without experience, she was advised 'not to give a recital at present', which only provided her with the age-old dilemma of how to make that initial break into the concert world. Competitions were virtually non-existent at this time, an exception being the International Baritone 100 Guineas Competition held in London in 1896 and won by Charles Tree. The music librarian Alfred Mapleson (whose brother was the more famous impresario James Henry Mapleson) introduced Miss de Lana; quite young and tall, of fair appearance but little experience, she was thought 'more suited for light opera' despite her 'dramatic style'. Mademoiselle Marie Godehaus, sent by Wilhelm Ganz, was a young high-soprano of fairly good quality and moderate appearance. She sang an aria from Massenet's *Manon* and a French song, both very well. 'Says she can sing Oratorio but [I] do not consider her quite suited, her style and production being too French. Excellent for operatic or miscellaneous.' Lally Proska, of Earls Court Road in London, a 'tall but not good looking' mezzo soprano was 'a good artist but nothing remarkable, the voice hollow and unsympathetic. She is going to study oratorio with Alberto Randegger. Made usual promise'. Katherine Barry, on the other hand, was 'a good looking high soprano who sings light French and English songs accompanying herself. Nothing exceptional but pleasing and would suit quite well for At Homes or summer work. She also whistles. Has two sisters, one a reciter and the other a mezzo soprano. Advised her to make a feature of her work with her reciter sister.'

The 'usual promise' given to Lally Proska was clearly the modern equivalent of 'we will let you know if anything comes up', while a promising mezzo-soprano called Norah Barry, stenographer to music publisher William Boosey, was 'advised not to give up her present occupation until prospects are more favourable', a case here of being told not to give up the 'day-job'. Tillett seemed a good judge of voices, he knew what to look out for and recognized both the strengths and the weaknesses of his auditionees. One reads comments such as: 'Voice hard and hollow in parts', 'Dramatic style, good but hard voice', 'A very cultured artist, good voice, and can safely recommend her for any kind of work, especially of a classical character', 'Dramatic voice but rather cold and unsympathetic at times, enunciation if anything exaggerated but this due to her American nationality. Can recommend her for small work at the beginning. Big woman.' Nellie Nutt of Clapham Common: 'has an excellent voice, good compass, especially good in upper register but weak and unsteady in lower. Should do very well and promised to hear her again after further study.' Aubrey Standing's tenor voice had 'not much body or colour'.

On 10 June 1908 the mezzo-soprano Viola Tree, daughter of the actor–manager Sir Herbert Beerbohm Tree, auditioned. She came recommended by 'her master, [Albert] Visetti', and John Tillett was 'very struck with her intelligence, good style, voice which has good possibilities, should do well with further study and experience'. She went on to become an actress rather than a singer, although while still a student at the Royal

College of Music she sang the title role in Gluck's *Iphigenia in Tauris* two years later on 19 February 1910 at His Majesty's Theatre, London. After the pleasure of hearing Miss Tree, it was back to the humdrum of mediocrity with Miss Hamilton (probably from Scotland where her teacher resided) who was 'advised not to think of remaining in London', while Miss Howitt was: 'quite amateurish at present, requiring further study both as regards voice and style. Gave little hope. Has one eye, quite colourless due to an optical operation. Her master, Ernest Hodgson, says this will grow alright in time.' Teachers, however eminent, were not immune from Tillett's tongue-lashing. Percy Rhodes, a tenor from Huddersfield and a pupil of Edouard de Reszke, auditioned with an aria from Handel's *Messiah* followed by 'Che gelida manina' from Puccini's *La Bohème*. He did so with: 'a very powerful middle voice register ([John] Coates quality), upper register quite brilliant but bottom of voice without quality or resonance. A good artist, [who] requires to lose certain vowel defaults brought about by his French master.' On the other hand there was a 'Real bass', Wilfred Platt, whose voice was 'very excellent with a great range and pleasant quality. Promised to speak to Butt of the Palace.' His appearance was 'against him' as he was 'very short'.

Tillett developed a good working relationship with the young Henry Wood, whose Promenade Concerts under Robert Newman's management at the Queen's Hall were already established since 1895. Besides recommending artists to Wood (such as the violinist Tony Maskkof, a pupil of Adolph Brodsky who auditioned with 'an excellent performance of Bruch's concerto' in the summer of 1909), he also heard singers who were coached in oratorio by the conductor. Wood was to remain a celebrated vocal coach throughout his life. Tillett became close to Wood, and, according to the conductor's wife Jessie, became (with the tenor Parry Jones) 'a leading spirit in a movement to mark in a special manner' his golden jubilee as a conductor. A committee formed of many distinguished musicians and administrators was established to organize the Jubilee concert on 5 October 1938, and the event took on a national significance with the celebrated first performance of Vaughan Williams' *Serenade to Music* written especially for 16 solo singers (all of them Ibbs and Tillett artists) whose careers had been helped by Wood.

John Tillett undertook to hear artists again after a further period of study. The contralto Nellie Nutt was one such singer who reappeared after 18 months in December 1908, though she was 'very badly accompanied, she shows much improvement and may recommend her for small work. Tremolo rather noticeable.' Other auditionees came from abroad, the American dramatic contralto Laura Graves, based in Berlin, made a very good impression. She had 'an excellent voice, was an intelligent singer and [he] promised to help her should she return'. Baron Grouvelle from Paris, on the other hand, 'sang French songs, accompanying himself after the style of Maurice Fakon. Quite good and should do well privately.' Occasionally there were vocal ensembles, such as the 'very good and attractive' Mitchell vocal quartet who could be recommended, but the duettist sisters, the Misses Woods of Berners Street, London, who 'sang harmonized songs, [were] very plain, suitable for vaudeville work, voices quite ordinary. Made usual promise.' Not so Laura Evans, 'of fair appearance with a big-ranged dramatic soprano voice and considerable experience'. She sang 'Hear ye Israel' (Mendelssohn's *Elijah*) and 'Goodbye' (Tosti) 'both rather boisterously. Has an excellent voice but sacrifices tonal beauty for volume of voice'; nor the contralto Winifred Ponder who had a 'rather hollow voice and [was] quite uninteresting. Gave no promise.' The latter lady went on to write Clara Butt's biography in 1928.

The soprano Hilda Henson had a problem because her 'enunciation was rather spoiled by prominent upper teeth', whilst Mary Lund's appearance was also 'rather against her'. The pianist Miss de Thael had a 'very good technique and shows every promise but [Tillett] warned her of the difficulties existing and advised her to consider well the step before entering the profession' (18 August 1910). A couple of months later, however, every encouragement was being given to the next hopeful applicant to the agency. He was the first auditionee recorded in the registers who subsequently had a successful professional career, and his name was Norman Allin from Rochdale in Lancashire. His name appears twice, the first time records his audition at the Steinway Hall on 4 October 1910 when he was 26 years old, and had just completed his vocal studies under John Acton and Francis Harford at the Royal Manchester College of Music three months earlier. At his first audition Tillett noted his 'big quality, pure bass voice, good experience and fair appearance. He sang 'Honour and arms', 'Hear, ye winds' and 'Young Dietricht'. Excellent voice, real voice, can safely recommend him'. His second audition took place five years later, on 18 January 1915, having gained 'plenty of experience in the north'. This time he was heard at the Aeolian Hall singing Wotan's Farewell (from Wagner's *Die Walküre*) and a song by Richard Strauss. The comments this time were even more positive. 'A really excellent bass voice, the best after [Robert] Radford. Can safely recommend him for any work, excellent in Wagner.' Tillett sent him to Beecham, with whose Opera Company he subsequently made his operatic debut as the Old Hebrew in Saint Saëns' *Samson and Delilah* a year later in 1916 at the Aldwych Theatre, London. Norman Allin was a member of the Ibbs and Tillett roster for his whole career (which lasted well into his 60s), and included Glyndebourne's first season in 1934 and Henry Wood's Golden Jubilee concert in 1938 when he was one of the 16 soloists in Vaughan Williams' *Serenade to Music*.

On 1 June 1911 John Acton sent another of his pupils to Ibbs and Tillett, this time the tenor John Booth. He was a 31-year-old cotton mill worker at the time, although he had already made his singing debut in his native Bolton ten years earlier. He was heard at Ramsden's premises and sang a ballad followed by 'Total eclipse' (Handel) and the aria 'Il mio tesoro' from Mozart's *Don Giovanni*. 'Excellent voice, good musician and artistic singer, warm voice, can safely recommend him to Gill, Fagge, Mills etc.' Booth's success at his audition can be judged by the fact that it was followed by a debut at the (now Sir) Henry Wood Promenade Concerts that year. Both newcomers, Booth and Allin, were taken on immediately and included in the Ibbs and Tillett Artists' List brochure for the 1911–12 season. Some further good material was heard later in 1911, such as the dramatic contralto Florence Eaton, who had an 'excellent voice, evenly produced and good quality which reminded one of Muriel Foster. Can safely recommend her if she decides to stay here; suggested she should give a recital next May.' Then there was the American bass Thomas Foster Why, whose 'Thus saith the Lord' (from *Messiah* and no doubt followed by 'The trumpet shall sound') revealed a 'most excellent voice, and could safely recommend him. Has offer [from] German Opera Season [Covent Garden], which advised him to accept in spite of the small terms.'

Of the remaining auditionees in the first book, which ends on 2 April 1912, there were a couple of interesting entries. The first was about Joyce Brown, a 16-year-old

Australian violinist and pupil of Ysaÿe and César Thomson. She had won the Gold Medal at the Brussels Conservatoire and played the second movement of Wieniawski's (probably the second) concerto and a piece by Kreisler. It was Ibbs who heard the audition at Ramsden's on 15 February 1912 and placed a reminder to himself in the General Remarks that he had, 'heard her in Melbourne with Rumford in 1908. Should become very good with age and experience.' Joyce Brown was born in 1899, which would have made her 13 years old at the time of her audition with Ibbs and Tillett. She went on later that autumn to make her London debut at the Henry Wood Promenade Concerts at the Queen's Hall on 21 September in August Wilhelmj's arrangement of a Paganini concerto. Although her name is among those listed in Ibbs and Tillett's brochures from the 1912–13 to the 1915–16 editions, she then changed her agent and put her affairs in the hands of the Imperial Concert Agency of Holborn, London. The other entry, worth a mention despite what must have been a grim experience at the time, is for 26 October 1911, when he endured Madame Wilson-Moulder of Nottingham, a soprano with 'worn' quality of voice, and whose appearance is described as 'enormous!' General remarks read 'Elderly, huge, tired voice. Shrieked her top notes, intonation faulty. Sang "A summer night" [Goring Thomas], the "Waltz Song" from *Tom Jones* [Edward German] very badly.' Hitherto details of height had never been completed by either Ibbs or Tillett, but in this particular entry the initial H of 'Height' has been changed to a W and the words '20 stone' added.

Among the singers and instrumentalists, aspiring reciters and entertainers would also audition. Following the tradition of the young Vert's involvement with Charles Dickens's reading recitals, Ibbs and Tillett now carried a fairly long list of reciters in their 1908–09 artists' brochure. Among them was George Grossmith, who, with his son (also called George), had been with Vert. He was a famous comedian and entertainer of his day, including taking leading parts in Gilbert and Sullivan operettas between 1877 and 1889. He was also a forthright character, prepared to complain to Vert at the slightest provocation, as he did while staying at the Grand Hotel in Lowestoft:

> What in the name of Thunder, Hell and Lightning did you send me to this hotel for? It is not in Lowestoft at all; miles from pier, public hall and railway station. I shall be ruined in cabs, to say nothing of the d—— isolation. The *Royal* surely is the best place here. Make a note. This is something between a brand new workhouse, a school board and the *Metropole*, Brighton. Comfortable no doubt, but in the desert of Sahara Boomdeay. P.S. Sims Reeves is singing about this week. (6 September ?)

Another character was the actor Henry Ainley, whose name appears among the reciters in the brochures beginning with 1914–15 until the late 1920s, when Ibbs and Tillett included only entertainers (with or without a piano). At one point Ainley was compelled to write:

> I loathe the idea of reciting at people when they are dining. It is bad enough at any time; please forgive me. Theatre, yes. Concert, yes. But not at people eating. I might recite for £100, not less. (undated)

Three further brief communications survive between Ainley and the agency:

> My dear Tillett, it is good of you to be so tactful. Brown of Eastbourne is a swollen headed pup and a fool. (17 September 1916)

> I shall be glad to recite at Eastbourne on Sunday evening, July 7th at 45%. (22 May 1929)

My next production is at the end of June, and I cannot with safety accept Douglas, IOM [Isle of Man]. I am disappointed because I very much want to go back there, curiously enough they approve of me there. Still, I thank you for the disappointment and I will learn how to be in two places at the same time. Where is Einstein? (28 May 1929)

An important addition to the roster of instrumentalists was Moriz (as he signed himself) Rosenthal. This Polish pianist (by 1906 in his mid-40s) had been a child prodigy at 13, and studied with Liszt for the last nine years of the composer's life. His London debut was on 24 June 1895 at St James's Hall and he quickly won name and fame despite some fierce competition. The pianist Fanny Davies appeared at the same hall in the afternoon together with the renowned clarinettist Richard Mühlfeld – a favourite of Brahms – and the singer Helen Henschel. The very next day Rosenthal could have been completely overshadowed by Paderewski who gave a recital in the same venue, but his playing had been so prodigious and virtuosic that he held his own and made a further appearance on 3 July. A pianist such as Rosenthal (who died in 1946 at the age of 84) was not seen again until Horowitz. Despite evidently having been acquainted with Narciso Vert, Rosenthal was initially reluctant to join Ibbs and Tillett's new venture:

Of course I feel very much inclined to intrust you and Mr Ibbs with the management of my business, but so far I cannot take any immediate decision, being quite uncertain when and under what circumstances I will come to England. It may be I will play in London returning from America in May or June 1907.

Are you still in connection with the Philharmonic Society of Manchester, Liverpool etc. etc.? And could you interest them so far as getting engagements from them for my appearances in the principal concerts? I think this would be very important. I also believe that more advertisement in the papers would be needed as in former years. Who is writing just now at the *Daily Telegraph*, *Times*, *Morning Post*, *Standard* etc.? Is Mr [Joseph] Bennett still at the head of the *Daily Telegraph*? And where are the concerts given since St James's Hall is no more practicabel? Is Queen's Hall very expensif? How about smaller halls? I am no more with Blüthner.

The noble art of self-defence, after the principles of my immortal master Ned Donnelly, I have, alas, neglected. And the Yi-Yitsu seems to me not worthy and dignified enough, so I have to rely upon my little revolver and above all upon my pacific disposition.

You will believe me how sad I felt at the news of the death of my good old friend, your Uncle Vert. (14 March 1906)

John Tillett duly replied that very day:

We are in touch with all the principal Philharmonic Societies such as Liverpool, Manchester, Bradford, Birmingham etc and am glad to say have their confidence, so there would be no difficulty in the matter of our being able to transact engagements with them. As regards the musical critics, Mr Joseph Bennett no longer writes for the *Daily Telegraph*, that is to say the regular notices, but he contributes occasionally an article on musical doings and attends some of the most important concerts. Mr Morgan Kingston is the regular critic of the *Daily Telegraph*, Mr Fuller Maitland still represents the *Times* and Mr Arthur Hervey the *Morning Post*, but Mr Frost of the *Standard* is dead, so is also Mr Balls of the *Daily News* … Now with regard to the question of the halls. We have the Queen's holding close on 3000 people, the Bechstein, with capacity for 600 and the Aeolian, 400 seats. To work a concert well at the Queen's Hall would cost from £90 to £100, and at either the Bechstein or Aeolian say £50. These latter halls are the most popular nowadays with recital artists, the Queen's being considered too expensive and large in most cases, but you would probably decide to go there.

I should mention that there is a restriction at the Bechstein Hall, *viz* that their own piano is used. There has been much talk of late about another hall being built by Steinways, one holding 1500, which would be most popular, but the idea seems to have dropped for the moment. Should this hall be built, as I hope will be the case, there is to be no restriction over the use of the piano.

… I knew you would feel keenly the loss of my respected uncle as you and he were so much together during your visits to this country. (14 March 1906)

Within a few days, an exchange of letters began on the subject of a tour to Australia as Tait was in Britain and discussing the Butt tour:

> Would you be disposed to entertain the idea of a tour in Australia next year beginning about March or April? One of the principal Australian impresarios is now in this country, and we have just arranged with him to take Madame Clara Butt for a tour in the Autumn of 1907. I mentioned that you would be in America this coming Winter, and might be disposed to visit Australia in the spring of 1907, which would be a favourable time for the Colonies. Will you kindly let me hear from you on the matter, and also whether you would accept a sharing arrangement with a certain guarantee per concert, and if so, what your ideas are in this respect. As our client will be returning to Australia shortly, I shall be glad to hear from you by an early post. (23 March 1906)

Rosenthal replied:

> A tour in Australia beginning in the Spring after my American "Tournée" was already proposed to me and the conditions seem to be very good. Therefore and for many other reasons, I could not consider a sharing arrangement whatever and could only accept a fixed engagement. I could begin in May, <u>not earlier</u>.
>
> Should I have the choice of the piano? And how many concerts at least could your client garantee? I should expect at least so much for every concert as I get in America, as the trip is much longer. (26 March 1906)

John Tillett replied:

> I have since seen our client and told him that you would not entertain a sharing arrangement in Australia. He wishes me to ascertain what sum you would require for twenty-five concerts, which is the usual number of engagements guaranteed. Of course you will understand that there are comparatively few big cities in Australia and New Zealand, but if the venture is a great success, these cities can be visited several times, and thus practically double the number of concerts guaranteed.
>
> I do not know upon what conditions you are going to America next Season, but judging by what you have received there before, I must say that I fear no entrepreneur could see his way to engage you for Australia upon the same terms (mind, I may be mistaken in this), at any rate for a first Season. There is big money to be made in the Colonies, but there being practically no Societies as in America, to engage the artist, the recitals have to be run at the entire risk of the entrepreneur. Our client would wish to have the choice of the piano, which would most likely be a Bechstein. Will you kindly consider the matter carefully and let me know at your convenience the guarantee you will require. (4 April 1906)

Rosenthal was unimpressed and stated his demands in more detail:

> It is really very difficult to accept a tour for only 25 concerts in Australia. I may tell you that my last conditions would be : Thousand dollars for each concert and all expenses from Vienna until returning paid. In case I could have the choice of piano (and the benefits arising from it) I would accept 800 dollars per concert. In no case I could accept another piano than a Bechstein, Steinway, Weber, Blüthner or Grotrian. (undated, but April 1906)

Unsurprisingly Tillett, as middle man, became the bearer of bad news from Tait (whom he never names to Rosenthal):

> I have submitted your terms to him, and regret to say that he is not prepared to guarantee anything like the sum you ask, so I am afraid the engagement, as far as he is concerned, must be considered at an end. I take it that you would not be disposed to make any concession in the conditions you have asked? (25 April 1906)

A couple of years later and Rosenthal had joined the agency and began to write what were often rather fussy and highly detailed letters, many of which, from 1908–09 and 1919–21, survive in the archive:

> I agree gladly to appear twice at the concert of March 13th [1909] and to perform 1) the E minor concerto by Chopin, 2) the E flat concerto by Liszt in order to oblige such an artist as Mr [Henry]

> Wood. My only condition is that the piece Mr Wood performs between both concertos should not be too long. A long rest unnerves me badly and I enjoy it to play after a short intermission. I hope there will be no other soloist at the same concert and that I have not to begin, neither to finish the concert. About Eastbourne, Brighton etc. I hope to give you a definite answer before long. Will you have the kindness to remember me to Mr [Edgar] Speyer and to Mr Wood. (31 August 1908)

His programming was typical of the day, four blocks of chronologically arranged music (though nothing of the classical Haydn, Mozart or even Beethoven), ending with a virtuosic flourish, and including a transcription and one of his own compositions:

Programm for London and Edinburgh

1 Air et Variations	Haendel
Passepied	Bach
Gavotte	Padre Martini
Bourrée : Vivace	Scarlatti
2 Carnaval Op.9	Schumann
3 Sonata Op.35 B flat minor	Chopin
Preludes	"
Valse Op.42	"
4 Lindentree	Schubert-Liszt
Papillons	Moriz Rosenthal
Rhapsodie hongroise	Liszt

In the spring of 1909, Rosenthal became embroiled in a dispute with a newspaper which he accused of misrepresenting him after an interview, his English becoming more bizarre, and translating his German thoughts literally as he became more exercised at developments. Unfortunately John Tillett's replies no longer exist and can only be deduced from Rosenthal's subsequent letters sent from Monte Carlo:

> I am implicated in a very disagreeable affair indeed and quite innocently too. There is very much on stake and if necessary I would come over to London in order to facilitate matters. But first let me know if you could not help me out.
>
> The story is shortly this : A representative of the *Evening News* interviewed me when I was in London and published an interview which was entirely false and imaginative in some very important points. He laid the following sentences before my door : The English audiences are not so "madly boisterous" like those of America nor "inclined to be phlegmatic as in Berlin".
>
> Now I pledge my word of honour that I never said such or alike words. I simply characterized American and Berlin audiences as exceedingly enthusiastic and appreciative. When I read the paragraph, I sent a statement to the *Evening News* correcting these words. But no word of my letter was printed.
>
> Worst of all : the *Daily Telegraph*, the *Daily Mail*, the *Birmingham Mail* and a Sheffield paper reproduced the false interview. This story must harm me terribly in America and Berlin, and I have to try the utmost to contradict and to correct it as soon as possible.
>
> Now will you help me in this important affair? Then go to Robin Legge to whom I wrote, or if he declines, to Mr [Joseph] Bennett. Tell them my greetings and my worries and see to it the enclosed lines should be printed. Try the same with the *Daily Mail* and the *Birmingham Mail* and send me as many cuttings as you can if my statement appears.
>
> At the same time take a skillfull lawyer and let him write to the *Evening News* and try to get my Statement in this paper. If not, let him enter process against the *E. News*.
>
> Of course you may count on my gratitude and on a very expressive too. Wire me instantaneously if I must come to London, or if you can pull through matters without my assistance. It is possible Mr Legge has already brought my statement. In this case try it with the other papers and send me 15-20 cuttings from the *D. Telegraph*. But wire me as soon as possible. My adress: Monte Carlo, Hotel Gallia. (31 March 1909)

Rosenthal enclosed the following statement which he wanted to have printed as a rebuttal:

> Permit me to state that the high admiration which I feel for English audiences never interfered with the extraordinary esteem in which I hold the public of Germany and America. The greatest success of my life I experienced in cities like Vienna, Berlin, Paris, London, New York, Boston. It was therefore a most painful surprise to me, when I read in several papers the account of an interview, where I was quoted to call Berlin audiences as "inclined to be phlegmatic" and American audiences as "madly boisterous". Never did I use these expressions and I pledge my word as an artist and gentleman, that I spoke only with the greatest admiration of the deep and enthusiastic appreciation and understanding of the American and Berlin audiences.
>
> By the way : As a matter of fact I never criticize my audiences, I prefer to criticize my own playing and I can only say that by the length of time I derived very much benefit from this habit. You would oblige me infinitely, dear Sir, giving space to this statement in your most esteemed and great paper.
>
> Thanking you most warmly, yours very faithfully
>
> Moriz Rosenthal (31 March 1909)

A few days later and Rosenthal is becoming more incoherent while Tillett must have been wondering if his involvement was not way beyond the call of his profession:

> This morning at 9 o'clock I wired you that Mr Bennett is no more at the *Daily T*, still is the friend of the chief editor and of the owner of this paper, therefore you should see him by all means. Then wired you my thanks for your advising me cabling to America and that I called already.
>
> At 9 o'clock this evening after 12 hours! I got a wire of you, where you say you will try the best to set things right and where you advise me to cable to America. It seems therefore that you did not get my telegramm, as you don't know that I cabled already and you don't refer to Bennett.
>
> I got a letter from Mr Legge. He is wrong in his ideas. He says that my expressions "madly boisterous" is in English language quite clean and polite and does not need retractation. This is of course wrong. One cannot treat the great nation like the American in such a flippant way, and it is too risky to let the matter stand as it is.
>
> I secured a sleeping compartment for Wednesday and will be Thursday at 5 o'clock in London unless you wire me the latest Tuesday that a retractation will appear. If you wire afternoon, it is better to address Hotel Gallia, Monte Carlo as Beausoleil closes the telegraph office at 8 o'clock evening. At day time the telegramm arrives sooner when you address Beausoleil près Monte Carlo (Hotel Gallia).
>
> Am writing at the café with an impossible pen, so I hope you will excuse me. Have you taken already a lawyer against the *Evening News*? (3 April 1909)

A final missive arrived a few days later from the inconsolable Rosenthal:

> I accept the date of October 12th 1909 for London, Queen's Hall.
>
> Thank you ever so much for your kindness. I got yesterday a telegramm from Epstein, who saw Legge. Epstein thinks that I am exaggerating the importance of the interview, but I am sure I am not. Americans are by right very susceptible; it is a great nation, very much greater than one thinks in England and it is terrible when I feel like praising them, I should seem to run them down, especially in England.
>
> Bennett could certainly see to it, the statement should be taken by the *Daily Telegraph*. Would it not be wise I should come over to London, add new interviews to the old one, for instance in the *Morning Post*, or *Times* and set matters right at this occasion? I followed your advice and cabled to my (Weber) Company.
>
> Don't spare your telegramms! They are going on my expense. Thank you ever so much. I will not forget your kind services in this troublesome affair. The Lafayette proofs are moderate. As he refuses complimentary photos I refused the permission to expose or to sell them.
>
> Monte Carlo, April 2nd 1909. There appeared two most wonderful criticisms both from the same date 24 or 27 March (I can not make it out very well) in the *Musical Standard* and in the *Scots Pictorial*. Could you get me 15 to 20 copies of each one? And don't forget to take them up in our criticisms book! (undated, but reply sent 9 April 1909)

The changes in the agency's fortunes which occurred between 1906 and 1908 are remarkable and reflected in the size, format and, above all, content of its brochure. The latter runs to some 32 pages while the earlier 1906 edition was only a 14-page photographic display of each artist. Artists given sole representation were the singers Clara Butt and Kennerley Rumford (still at the head of the list), Agnes Nicholls, Esta d'Argo, Kirkby Lunn, Mrs George (Elsie) Swinton, William Green, Harry Plunket Greene, Herbert Witherspoon, Charles Knowles, and Dalton Baker. The handful of instrumentalists consisted of the pianist Leopold Godowsky, violinists Tivadar Nachèz and Johannes Wolff, cellist Josef Hollman, and the Capet String Quartet. All of them had their photographs placed at various points throughout the publication. John Tillett, as has been noted, did not hesitate to promote the career of his wife, Esta d'Argo (Hetty Holroyd), but as a result he sometimes had to contend with the odd nudge and a wink from acquaintances such as the Liverpool-based choral conductor Harry Evans:

> I shall be glad to know from you as soon as possible as to Kirkby Lunn for Nov. 14th and March 27th. I want to hear Miss Phyllis Lett and shall be in town soon after Easter. The soprano for *Elijah* Dec 19th will be a lady [Esta d'Argo] of your immediate and intimate acquaintance! Can you give me definite news of Ffrangcon-Davies? I hear he is supposed to sing [Granville Bantock's] *Omar Khayyam* on May 25th but Mr Bantock told me on Friday that this arrangement was now altered. Some of our people are anxious to get him, but I am dubious about the advisability of even entering into negotiations. If you can help me by giving some definite information I shall be glad. (12 April 1908)

The rest of the 1908 brochure consists of singers, violinists, cellists, pianists, vocal ensembles, string quartets, accompanists, entertainers, elocutionists, bands (mainly military), song-lectures, and piano recital lectures by Dr Otto Neitzel (see Appendix 1). This was the pattern until the First World War.

Of course the agency also handled the affairs of other musicians on an occasional basis; one such artist was the composer, conductor and teacher Sir Charles Villiers Stanford who wrote:

> I have booked April 24 at Malvern. Apr. 7 at Bournemouth I cannot work; it is the week of the Associated Board exams and I expect Wednesday before Good Friday wd be anything but a good day anywhere! (24 January 1909)
>
> Charles Harriss asked me by wire today to conduct some numbers at the Empire Concert at the Albert Hall on Sat. May 22nd and asked my terms. I wired back that I was free and that he must ask you about terms. I leave the arrangements thereof to you. I shall be back in town tomorrow (Wed.) night. I wish, as he asked for something of mine, that you could get him to have the Sea Songs with H.P.G. [Harry Plunket Greene]. (6 April 1909)

Stanford's opinion was well respected and he would on occasion send students graduating from the Royal College of Music (where he taught for 40 years) or others from elsewhere to be considered by the agency. Two years before his death in 1924 he wrote to John Tillett:

> I send you Mr Wegemann (leader at Monte Carlo), violinist, well-known to S[ain]t Saëns and others as a first rate artist. Perhaps you cd arrange for him to be heard by someone in command? That's what he's here for. Do what you can for him as he was recommended to me by a very old and very musical friend. (1 July 1922)

CHAPTER SEVEN

Artists and Auditionees: 1912–14

The years leading to the outbreak of the First World War were highly productive for the agency. Although military bands were dropped, the loss of entertainers, elocutionists, reciters and lecturers proved to be temporary until the war was in progress. There was a marked increase in the number of singers and instrumentalists, many of whose names (particularly those of foreign artists) were later to become very familiar to the concert-going public. A notable absence from all brochures until the 1960s was that of conductors, many of whom were generally already associated with orchestras, opera houses or, in later years, the BBC. As far as Ibbs and Tillett was concerned the freelance career-conductor evidently became more of a marketable commodity with the growth of air travel, the radio and recordings. But it has to be remembered that the agency's activities were by no means solely limited to those musicians whose names appeared in their publicity, and the year 1910 is a good example. It was a particularly exciting one for London's opera lovers, largely because of the enterprising activities of Thomas Beecham at Covent Garden. He launched his first-ever opera seasons, one in the spring, the other in the autumn and both were notable for including the London premières of two operas by Richard Strauss, first *Elektra* followed later that year by *Salome.* Ibbs and Tillett had plenty of interest in these events. Both sopranos who took the title roles in these Strauss operas had further dealings with Ibbs and Tillett. The American soprano Edyth Walker, who sang the title role of Elektra to great acclaim, took her role as a prima donna and *Kammersängerin* very much to heart in a series of demanding letters written in 1913 from her Swiss home and most of them grandly signed with just her surname, 'Walker':

> I should be pleased to sing at the Leeds Festival but would not care to come for one concert only. My terms are £125 for each concert. (10 February 1913)

> It would hardly be worthwhile to travel from Munich to London [Leeds is meant] and back for one concert. The expenses are much too heavy! You can count it up yourself, fare and hotel for me and my maid, and I need about a week for it all. I will tell you what I will accept as I should be pleased to sing at these well-known Festivals and under Nikisch's wonderful direction! For two concerts £200 clear, that means that the Committee should pay your commission. *Oberon* and *Götterdämmerung* yes, but please only in German! I should also be willing to sing the *Götterdämmerung* Schlussscene [Final Scene] with Nikisch's wonderful reading, or songs by Strauss, although the latter are not so certain before a strange audience – strange for me and I for them. In case you would like me to sing in English, I will gladly do so in case it is an English composition, the translations must and do lose fearfully. I shall be here until Easter but letters will also be forwarded. I hope the Committee will find my offer acceptable. Of course I know Mr [Albert] Coates by name and shall be delighted to sing with him. (13 March 1913)

> Before a definite promise to sing, I must know exactly when the Concerts are to be and the Programmes. My manager here offers me the Gewandhaus [Leipzig] for the 8/9 October and I do not know whether I can accept, as your dates are not fixed. Please let me know at once. (1 April 1913)

> In answer to yours of the 13th V with regard to the programme, I must refer you to yours of the 14 IV containing Herr Nikisch's letter and mentioning three appearances! That is also what I signed for and is definitely:

> 1. Oberon Arie
> 2. *Götterdämmerung* Schlussscene
> 3. *Götterdämmerung* Duett
>
> Should the Committee desire the Strauss songs instead of the Duett, that I will willingly undertake. I should prefer to sing *Götterdämmerung* Schlussscene and Duett in the same Concert. [P.S.] Would a song recital in London in June be successful? Or is it too late now to advertise? What are costs? (15 June 1913)
>
> As I understand [it], I am going to sing Oberon on the October 1st and duet and closing scene *Götterdämmerung* the 3rd. Of course the duet comes first and the scene really closes the evening. I cannot attend a rehearsal on the 25th of September, that means being in London at a hotel six days before the concerts. There was no mention of this when I promised to come, and I find two days before the concerts quite sufficient – more than I have ever given anyone. I have sung Oberon and also Schlussscene with Mr Nikisch (also duet) so that I am sure two days is more than sufficient. With regards to a recital, you seem to think it not quite advisable – I will talk it over with you when I am in London.
>
> Please do secure me room with bath, if possible high up, morning sun and very quiet! (15 August 1913)
>
> Edyth Walker begs Messrs Ibbs and Tillett to secure a room also for my maid very near mine. I hope my room is at least very large otherwise must have two rooms on account of bath failing.
>
> If I hear nothing to the contrary, I shall arrive in Leeds the 28th evening, in case of rehearsal the 29th. [P.S.] Will you send me a score (piano) of the *Oberon* aria in English? If it sounds well to me, I may sing it in English as that is the language in which it was composed. (23 August 1913)
>
> Do pardon me! Will you kindly give the people here [Queen's Hotel, Leeds] their tips – they are all in bed and I shall not see them again.

Waiters 5/-	[25p]
Maid 2/6d	[12½p]
Lift 6d	[2½p]
Porter 2/-	[10p]
[Total] 10/-	[50p]

> Whatever you consider proper. My bill was £8 or £9 in case you go according to that, and I have been here four days. Whatever it is you can reduce from the check! [3 October 1913]

The Finnish soprano Aïno Ackté made her debut at Covent Garden as Elsa in Wagner's *Lohengrin* and Elizabeth in *Tannhäuser* in the German Opera Season of January 1907. In 1910 she was back as Salome, and, according to the *Daily Telegraph*, was 'superb and often seductive'. She became renowned in the role:

> I thank you for your proposition for the Strauss festival in Manchester. My fee to play twice there in *Salome* would be two hundred guineas for the two performances, so long as they do not make extraordinary rehearsals. (22 April 1914)

The American bass-baritone Clarence Whitehill had made his Covent Garden debut under Richter in 1905 as Wotan in Wagner's *Ring* with enormous success, and he became a regular performer at the London opera house, including Richter's famous performances sung in English in 1908 and 1909. In the year under discussion, 1910, Whitehill was also part of Beecham's autumn venture, singing the title role in *Hamlet* by Ambroise Thomas and Jokaanan (or The Prophet as the Lord Chamberlain's office insisted the character be called) in *Salome*. In this letter Whitehill has problems accepting an offer from the Norwich and Norfolk Festival of 1914, although as it happens, this triennial festival was destined for cancellation with the outbreak of hostilities on 1 August of that year, and it would be a further ten years before it was revived:

> Many thanks for your favor of the 19th February, which has reached me after many delays. Our company have just arrived here [Seattle] and we have been on the march since February 1st. I'm afraid it will be impossible for me to be with you as long as November 9th, as my season with the company will begin next year, 1914–15, about November 13th, so you see unless there should be some change, of which I know nothing now, it would be impossible. If there should be anything before the Norwich-Norfolk Festival, at which you probably know I am to sing, you could book me so that it would not interfere with their rehearsals or performances. I shall be in London during May most likely, and shall be happy to see you and discuss these things further. My terms are 60 guineas per performance. (27 March 1914)

In November 1911 another impresario tried his hand at promoting opera in London; this time it was Oscar Hammerstein at his newly built London Opera House in Kingsway, Holborn, and although he had such star singers as Luisa Tetrazzini, Mary Garden, John McCormack and Maurice Renaud on his roster, the public largely stayed away (its most musically interesting event was Josef Holbrooke's *The Children of Don* under Nikisch). One of Hammerstein's singers was the contralto Margarita d'Alvarez, whose plans with Ibbs and Tillett were also disrupted by the outbreak of war:

> I am in receipt of your letter of the 31st [August 1914], and very much regret Mr Brandon Lane has been obliged to abandon his concert at Manchester on October 10th on account of the war, and under the circumstances I can but cancel my engagement for that date though it seems too dreadful. Can you do anything for me in America? I should love to go and have had great successes there. Would you please return my photos if you do not need them. (3 September 1914)

Smarting from his losses of £45000 sustained over the seven months of his operatic experiment, Hammerstein returned to America leaving the field to the Covent Garden Syndicate (their 1912 season, the longest since 1891, lost £15000). A huge discovery in spring 1910 was the 25-year-old tenor Giovanni Martinelli, hailed as a second Caruso after his debut as Cavaradossi in Puccini's *Tosca*. Though Ibbs and Tillett could not engage him, there was a brief exchange of correspondence:

> Ref. your letter asking me to sing in Glasgow and Liverpool, for which I thank you very much, but regret that owing to previous engagements I shall be unable to do so. However I am pleased to introduce to you a friend of the same school as myself, who possesses a beautiful tenor voice and who I can safely say would suit you admirably. I enclose his name and address [Mario Marco, 19 Upper Woburn Place, Holborn, WC] and he will be pleased to give an audition if you write him. (29 May 1913)

The Irish tenor John McCormack made a brief appearance on their lists and left just one letter in the archive directed personally to 'Dear John' from Dublin:

> Thanks so much for both cheques. The weather here is rotten and we all have colds so you can imagine we are in damn bad humour. (9 August 1912)

There is also only one letter from the famous Russian bass Feodor Chaliapin, who was obliged to:

> regret I cannot accept your offer of concerts in Liverpool as per your letter of July 1st. I am engaged during the entire winter from September to March. (3 July 1913)

The Dutch bass-baritone Anton van Rooy had dealings with the agency. He too was part of that glorious operatic year 1910, when he sang Wotan in what transpired to be

Richter's last German Opera Season at Covent Garden in April. His letters, like those of Edyth Walker, concern the 1913 Leeds Festival.

> Having got back from a tour I hurry to reply to yours. I am happy to sing at Leeds. My fee for two Concerts is 160 guineas, 100 for one. Only I must know from you whether we are talking of October 1913 or 1912. As for 1913, I cannot yet undertake anything specific, because I do not know if I am going to America. (19 February 1912, translation from German)

> In response to your letter I wish to inform you that I gladly accept your offer of the Leeds Festival for the first week of October 1913. If I should be going to America, however, I could always sing in England beforehand. (20 September 1912, translation from German)

> Your letter has been sent on to me in Munich. I am quite prepared to accept the two Concerts on 2nd and 4th October in Leeds. Only I think the terms too low for the long stay, which I shall be obliged to undertake due to rehearsals in Leeds. If I do have to attend all these rehearsals, it means I must leave Frankfurt on September 22nd and can only get back there on 6th October. That is almost two weeks during which I can undertake nothing else. I cannot commit myself to such a long time under 200 guineas. Even then there will be practically nothing much left after subtracting your 10% commission and the railway expenses for myself and my servant.
>
> I would like to take this opportunity to recommend to you a wonderful high soprano, Frau Bellwiell from Frankfurt. She sings the Verdi *Requiem* beautifully. Perhaps you could recommend this lady to Leeds. (21 November 1912, translation from German)

> I am more than delighted to hear that Mr Nikisch is conducting and hope I need only arrive on the 27 September and leave on 4 October in the afternoon. I accept the two concerts for 160 guineas [£168], but I ask you to do your utmost to secure one or more engagements either directly before or after the concerts, then the expenses would be spread over the whole and I would also be willing to accept 80 guineas. If more concerts can be arranged so much the better, the higher the terms the higher your commission. Mr [Michael] Balling, who conducts the Hallé concerts in Manchester, is a great friend of mine and I am sure he would let me sing there. I take it for granted that the aforementioned concerts do not have public dress rehearsals, otherwise I must sing with full voice four times instead of twice, a dress rehearsal is like a concert. Please clarify this. Why do the rehearsals not take place directly before the concerts? What do we do on 30 September and 1 October? (28 November 1912, translation from German)

> Please excuse my delayed reply to your letter. It was sent here [Rotterdam] and then on to Frankfurt and then to Leipzig (where I was singing) before back here again. In mid-April I shall talk this delicate subject over with you personally when I am singing at Covent Garden for Mr Nikisch. I quite understand your reasons but I believe it will be alright if I sing in German whilst the chorus sings in English. This was what happened in America, whilst in Switzerland I sang German while the chorus sang in French. The main thing is the music. In any case we shall sort the matter out in London. (23 March 1913, translation from German)

> Would you do me the kindness to send me a printed programme with full text of the Leeds Festival performances. I would like to know exactly what I am to sing from *Parsifal* and *Meistersinger*. I also want to know exactly when I am required in Leeds for the final rehearsals. Naturally I want to leave here as late as possible as I have still many things to do here, and do not wish to be in Leeds any longer than necessary. I must also reserve my room in Leeds. (9 September 1913, translation from German)

> I write to inform you that I am leaving here [Frankfurt] on Saturday 27 September for London, and will be in Leeds on the evening of the 28th. I have had a room reserved there for me and my servant for some time, and have had confirmation of such a reservation of a room at the Queen's Hotel from 29 September. Would you please do me the favour and reserve the room for me from the 28th, however you can cancel the room for my servant as this time I shall not be taking one to Leeds. Therefore I need only one nice room for myself alone from 28 September. The Hotel should be so kind to confirm this.

> Secondly I urgently need to be sent the exact parts of *Parsifal* and *Meistersinger*, so that I know precisely what I am to sing there. If this is not yet ready, what I am to sing from these two operas should be sent to me direct from Leeds. (15 September 1913, translation from German)

Another baritone, Mario Sammarco, was in London for the summer season that year and sang Alec in the revival of *Tess* by Baron D'Erlanger, which had received its English premiere on 14 July 1909 with Destinn and Zenatello also in the cast. Ibbs and Tillett arranged for Sammarco to appear in Scotland:

> In confirmation of your letter of 16 July I agree to accept the engagement for a concert in St Andrew's Hall, Glasgow for Saturday evening October 25th 1913 at an inclusive fee of one hundred guineas [£105] less your 10% commission. For the three items they can choose between
>
> Prologo of *Pagliacci* – Leoncavallo
> Aria *King of Lahore* – Massenet
> Aria 'Largo al factotum' – Rossini
> Aria *Le nozze di Figaro* – Mozart
> Aria *Masked Ball* – Verdi
> Two Tosti songs
>
> Please let me know as soon as possible the choose of the items and send me the contract to sign. Let me know about accompanist, if there is or not. (17 July 1913)

Turning once again to instrumentalists and surveying the period leading to the outbreak of the First World War in August 1914, we find the Czech violinist and pedagogue Otakar Ševčík, who placed the management of a London concert at the Queen's Hall by six of his pupils in the hands of Ibbs and Tillett. The occasion proved to be a particular success for his star pupil, the Australian Daisy Kennedy who played Max Bruch's *Scottish Fantasy* with the Queen's Hall Orchestra under Ševčík. Considered a great discovery, she was immediately taken up by Ibbs and Tillett:

> Thanking you for your kind letter. I am very glad to hear that you are willing to accept the management of my concert and that you have secured the use of the Queen's Hall for December 12th. About the estimate of the working expenses I leave with pleasure matters entirely in the hands of Mrs Henderson and yourselves. (20 May 1911)

The years 1910–14 proved a rich seam during which Ibbs and Tillett began associations with two great composer/pianists, who were extremely popular with the public. The first was Ferruccio Busoni, who had first appeared in London in the autumn of 1897 when he was 31 years old and always held the capital city in great affection. He was an avid reader, particularly of Dickens and, with a penchant for wandering alone through London's streets, took delight in observing people in Dickensian terms. He read Arnold Bennett's *Things that have Interested Me* in 1921, and had been introduced to George Bernard Shaw the previous year. This undated letter was probably written about that time:

> I should wish (for my next "Double" recital) to send invitations to Bernard Shaw, Galsworthy and Arnold Bennett. I know them all a little and they are all interested in music. As I forsee that this Recital will not be "sold out" (as my name as composer is too much on the programme) so this irregularity will not affect the "Box office", and I would gain by a cultured audience. It should be done in time as these gentlemen are mostly engaged with all kinds of duties. Many thanks.
>
> P.S. Perhaps also Chesterton.

Busoni hated so-called Miscellaneous Concerts, which meant long gaps between his several appearances on a programme and a resulting heightening of tension while he paced up and down backstage or in the Green Room:

> I have done a tremendous work during the past five weeks and was obliged to let a good deal of my correspondence unopened, to avoid the crossing of too many difficult subjects in my mind. There was travelling before and between, and much social duty to fulfill. Only yesterday I found the first opportunity to read your kind letters of March 12, 14, 17 and 18.
>
> I remember that we spoke about orchestral concerts and conducting, exclusively of this: I am surprised that your letters contain little or nothing of the kind. I do not see any reason to play at the Philharmonic Society without fee, although I fully consider the honour which results for any artist by the invitation of this historic corporation. Letters before this (of March 12th) have not reached me, so I so know nothing about the Liverpool, Manchester and Bradford engagements mentioned herein.
>
> I spoke with Mr [Egon] Petri about the twin performances; the acceptation of this proposal will depend on the three concerts presented in the last letter. I have decided to decline every concert which bears the label of "Miscellaneous" including the Harrison Tour and the evening at Middlesborough [*sic*]. But before I accept any contract at all I have to avail a final decision about America, to which most probably I will have to sail in the late autumn. (22 March 1914)

Three months later an incomplete letter ends with discussions about a concert in the spring of 1915 with Sir Henry Wood which the intervening outbreak of war once again prevented from happening:

> I still would be inclined to join Sir Wood in the Spring if he likes to. I never promised anything to you and you have no right to let me feel in a way as if I had broken my word. Will you try to arrange something for the Spring? I think I could be able to accept it positively. Anyway if I have caused you trouble excuse me kindly. (14 July 1914)

The second composer/pianist was Sergei Rachmaninov, who had made his London debut in 1899 at the Queen's Hall on 19 April while on a short visit at the invitation of the Philharmonic Society as composer, pianist (his Piano Concerto No.1) and conductor (his orchestral Fantasy *The Rock*). Five years earlier Alexander Siloti had played Rachmaninov's Prelude in C# minor Op.3 and the work immediately became all the rage, making its composer instantly famous, so his visit was greeted with great anticipation and enthusiasm by the English public. At this time (and for about two years) Rachmaninov was prone to severe depression, but this London trip lifted his spirits sufficiently for him to promise Francesco Berger, secretary of the Philharmonic Society, that he would, on his return to Moscow, write a second piano concerto as he did not consider his first good enough. However his depression returned as soon as he was back in Russia. About 1900 he began the new concerto while in the care of a doctor, using suggestion and auto-suggestion, and slowly the composer began his recovery. From 1906–09 he lived in Dresden, from where he toured to Paris and Berlin in 1906. After returning to live in Moscow, he agreed to tour America in the autumn of 1909 in a series of 20 concerts organized by the Wolfsohn Bureau as pianist and conductor. The years 1910–14 were spent in Russia apart from tours undertaken to Germany and England as soloist in his own piano concertos only, and it is during this period that he began his long association with the firm of Ibbs and Tillett. His name appears for the first time in their brochure for the season 1911–12, in the illustrious company of Rosenthal, Godowsky, and Busoni, but separated from the list of 28 other pianists by a telling dividing line (see Appendix 2). The pre-First World War correspondence discusses tours to London and the provinces:

> I have received letter and contract (Liverpool). I shall retain the contract until some details are clarified, such as: How big is the orchestra in Liverpool, and its quality? How much time do the choral numbers take? How long is the rehearsal? Do I get two rehearsals or can I get a third? Who

is going to accompany this concert? Perhaps it can be arranged as follows: I play the third concerto (duration about 40 minutes) and then afterwards conduct the tone poem *Isle of the Dead*, and the rest of the programme consists of the introductory number and the choral work, both of which will be conducted by the conductor who accompanies me? After I receive your reply, I'll send you the signed contract.

Concerning 18 October at Middlesbrough, the programme is as follows: 1) Adagio & Finale from the piano sonata in D minor, 2) Elegie, Prélude, Melodie, Polichinelle Op.3, Barcarolle, Humoresque Op.10 but add that I can substitute the two pieces from the sonata with 6 Preludes from Opp.23 and 32. This programme is for the various piano recitals. I agree to the fee of 60 Guineas – however this is only for an appearance as soloist, and is also subject to the number of engagements I am given.

I can travel to England on the 15th October and stay for three weeks, that is until not later than the 6th or 7th of November, as on 11th November I have a tour beginning in Russia! (4/17 February 1911, translation from German)

In haste I reply to your questions.

1) I accept the piano recitals in Sheffield and Nottingham, but not for less than 70 guineas per concert. Nowhere do I wish to accept less than that sum for piano recitals, which are very strenuous for me.
2) Please let Mr Bechstein know about Messrs Paterson's refusal (which I find incomprehensible). If Bechstein also refuses to provide grand pianos in these cities, I cannot play in them and must sort the matter out personally with Bechstein in Berlin.
3) There's one other matter to clarify. I can no longer undertake engagements where I play and conduct during the same evening. That is beyond my powers, therefore the engagement in Liverpool must be changed. I can either only play or only conduct, preferably play. But I'd like to know immediately who will accompany me in Liverpool. I hope not the same conductor with whom I had to play last year. That would be impossible. [Simon Speelman, known more as a violinist in Manchester and Liverpool orchestras took charge of just the Piano Concerto No.3, while Rachmaninoff himself conducted his own Symphony No.2 in this concert on 24 October 1911. It was to be Hamilton Harty who conducted the Liverpool engagement in January 1914].
4) I agree to play my cello sonata in Bradford.
5) I cannot leave England later than February 15th as I have a 9am rehearsal in Moscow on the 19th. (9 April 1913, translation from German)

For potential clients, Ibbs and Tillett issued *The Bulletin* No.1 in January 1913 of 16 large-size pages to advertise several of their artists (see Appendix 2). Pictured on the cover were the ubiquitous Clara Butt and Kennerley Rumford who were about to begin their 1913–14 world tour in New York on 7 January. All the artists (most with a page, each with a photograph) have extracts from highly favourable press notices from London and provincial newspapers, or countries in the Commonwealth in some cases. Rachmaninov's were limited to five provincial newspaper notices of the Leeds Festival of 1910, but preceding them are a couple of paragraphs, whose author remains unknown. It is entitled 'Rachmaninoff, the great pianist, composer and conductor. Available season 1913–1914':

Rachmaninoff, by common consent, it may be said, occupies the chief place among the Russian composers of the younger generation. Nor are the grounds upon which this distinction is based difficult to determine. If Tschaikowsky voices the passionate, the sombre and tragic, the swift ecstasy of beauty, and if Rimsky-Korsakoff reflects the sunny, the legendary, and the fanciful, Rachmaninoff prefigures the brooding, the sombre reflective state of the soul. Rachmaninoff endures the sight of the darker aspects of Russian life – of all life – but rather as the seer than as the rebel. There is almost a Tolstoyan non-resistance to evil in his attitudes as one feels it through his creations, but there is absolutely nothing of the preacher. He is the painter – the artist only. He looks, and what he sees he depicts; and he looks out on the world of dim distances, of golden lights and shadows, of fateful and steady notion. He records his impressions and presents them to the world without comment. The touch of moderation is over all. The composer is done with the *ignis fatuus* of hyper-exaltation; he is done with the passion of despair. He is disillusioned, yet unembittered. Above all he is a poet.

Russia is to be found in Mons. Rachmaninoff's music, but in a subjective rather than an objective way. There are times when one seems to look deeply through his music into the very background of his race. He is opposed to the ultra-modern through a similar devotion, though by no means a slavish one, to established styles. Rachmaninoff's modernity is to be sought rather in his viewpoint, in his attitude toward music as a means of interpretation, and in the many touches of individuality to be found in his music, than in any attempt at startling harmonic or orchestral effects.

In the autumn of 1913 Rachmaninov undertook a tour of England giving eight concerts, followed by 36 back in Russia. Another one planned for the autumn of the following year got fairly far into the planning stage, but the First World War broke out and all plans had to be shelved: see Appendix 14 for Rachmaninov's correspondence, which was not revived until the summer of 1918, when the possibility of returning to England was proposed by him once again.

The conductor Vassily Safonoff made his first appearance in Britain on 22 February 1906 at the Queen's Hall with the London Symphony Orchestra. Great interest greeted him because, though he conducted without a baton, his music-making impressed, particularly his sense of phrasing. He was also an excellent pianist and teacher, Scriabin and Medtner among his pupils. He conducted at the 1909 Newcastle Festival, but also at Birmingham, Liverpool, Leeds, Edinburgh and Glasgow. His agent was Hermann Wolff of Berlin, but his English concerts were handled by Ibbs and Tillett. Correspondence with the agency survives from the years 1912–14 and he died in Russia in 1918 aged 66. He was an enthusiastic Anglophile (*Who's Who in Music* (1915) lists his club as the English Club in Moscow), a great disciplinarian with an iron fist in a velvet glove, and a highly competent organizer. As one American critic commented (Safonoff was in charge of the Philharmonic Society of New York from 1906–09): 'Russia lost a great general when Safonoff became a conductor.'

In reply to your letters of March 8th and April 9th I'm returning the contract for the Liverpool Philharmonic Society concert on January 21st 1913 signed by me. As you write me, there is usually one chorus item in the programme. I take notice of this and here is my programme for the concert.

1. Beethoven *Leonora* No.3
2. Schumann Piano Concerto (Mr Harold Bauer)
3. Rimsky-Korsakov *The Doom of Oleg* (male chorus and two soloists, a heavy bass and a tenor)
4. Piano solo (Mr Harold Bauer)

Intermission of 10 minutes

5. Tschaikowsky 4th Symphony Op.36, f minor

This programme is possible only when the Schumann piano concerto shall be played, otherwise I must make other combinations.

Material for the Beethoven and Tschaikowsky is mine with my own annotations. The Rimsky-Korsakov item I conducted at the Newcastle-on-Tyne Festival [20 October 1909]. The tenor (I have forgotten the name of the gentleman) [Henry Brearley] was excellent and I should like to have him for the performance, the bass part was sung by Mr Kennerley Rumford … I presume the chorus will be perfectly ready for the first rehearsal, but if this item should be found not desirable, the Committee may put on the programme *The Passing of King Edward* by Mrs [Margaret] Meredith, which I conducted in London with the Leeds chorus [13 January 1911, Queen's Hall]. The material can be procured from the composer, whose address is Woodside, Fleet, Hants. The duration of the programme shall be in both cases about 122 minutes, supposing the piano solos will take about 15 minutes. (12 April 1912)

It's a pity that the Liverpool people want some changes in the programme, especially the 4th Symphony by Tschaikowsky, for the performance of it created a real sensation in London in May

1909, and since then I played it in Newcastle (Festival), Edinburgh, Glasgow, Birmingham, Leeds and London again with tremendous success. A genuine Russian interpretation of this composition would prove a success even if it's played two seasons consecutively in Liverpool. In the whole my programme is combined in a perfect way, regarding the character of the items and even the keys of the items. But I don't intend to cause any disturbance to the Liverpool Committee and will give some suggestions re the programmes.

1) Beethoven *Leonora* No.3
2) Chopin e-minor [Piano] Concerto (Mr Harold Bauer) or Schubert-Liszt *Wanderer* [Fantasy]
3) Meredith *The Passing of King Edward*
4) Piano solo
   Intermission
5) Tschaikowsky 4th Symphony

1) Granville Bantock *The Pierrot of the Minute* Overture
2) Beethoven 4th Piano Concerto G major
3) Meredith *King Edward*
4) Piano solo
   Intermission
5) Tschaikowsky 5th Symphony

1) Beethoven 5th Symphony c-minor
2) Beethoven 4th Piano Concerto G major
   Intermission
3) Meredith *King Edward*
4) Piano solo
   Intermission
5) Tschaikowsky *Francesca da Rimini*

A pure Beethoven programme

1) *Coriolan* Overture
2) *Emperor* Concerto
3) *Leonore* No.3
   Intermission and no piano solos
4) *Choral* Symphony

Please submit these combinations to the Committee and let me know about the matter. (26 April 1912)

Your favour from June 20th to hand. I just wrote a letter to Mr Riley [W.J.Riley, Secretary to the Liverpool Philharmonic Society] about the matters contained in your letter. As the Symphony by Schubert by its character objects to be put at the end of the programme, I don't find my way to meet the wish of the Committee and propose the following programme, giving a short overture for the start.

1) Beethoven *Coriolan* Overture
2) Schubert Symphony
   Intermission
3) Song – Signor [Mario] Sammarco
4) Ippolitoff-Ivanoff *In the Village* [2nd movement from the Caucasian Sketches Op.10] or Glazunoff *Spring*
5) Songs – Signor Sammarco
6) Chorus (directed by Mr Harry Evans)
7) Wagner *Rienzi* Overture or a novelty by Hakon Børresen [1876–1954] *Normannerne*, [*The Normans* Op.16, 1912] a very brilliant overture

I also suggested to Mr Evans to conduct the choral item in the concert of October 28th, whose programme is already definitely settled. Regarding the *Rienzi* Overture, I beg to remember that the Committee have spoken of the 4th Symphony of Tschaikowsky as of a hackneyed piece, but afterwards they did not at all repent to have put it in the programme. Perhaps the same may happen

> also for Wagner's Overture? I hope there will be no further discussion about the programmes. I have important reasons to maintain my original idea and it cannot be done otherwise, without interfering with the artistical value of the programme. (28 June 1913)

Of the 85 auditionees heard by either Ibbs or Tillett at their auditions from May 1912 to the outbreak of war on 1 August 1914, few came up to the required standard. The bass Norman Williams was heard on 8 August 1912 and revealed an 'exceptionally fine voice, real bass yet able to sing most baritone roles, much impressed with him'. Among other things he sang Wotan's Farewell. He was taken on and his name appears in the brochure for 1914–15. No auditions are recorded between 28 August 1912 and 17 January 1913. The contralto Dorothy Webster was heard on 13 March at the Queen's Hall and taken on by the agency, as was Gwladys Renton on 7 May, who sang at the recommendation of John Coates: 'very good voice, sings artistically and with feeling. Quite above the average, very good presence. Think highly of her.' Two weeks later, on 21 May, two singers who were already well established sang to John Tillett at the Queen's Hall: one was the contralto Maud Santley, the other the baritone George Baker. Santley had a 'fine voice and style, very impressed with her. May safely recommend her for any kind of work, especially suited for opera.' Maud Santley had made her debut back in 1899 on a concert tour with Adelina Patti followed by one with Melba. She then sang the title role in Bizet's *Carmen* with the Carl Rosa Opera Company and was taken up by Richter, who had heard her sing in Manchester. She sang in a performance he conducted with the LSO of Bach's *Mass in B minor* on 16 December 1907 at the Queen's Hall, and was then cast as Fricka (*Das Rheingold*) and Waltraute (*Götterdämmerung*) in the English *Ring* of 1908 at Covent Garden, though in the latter, the scene had to be cut when she fell ill at the first performance (she was replaced at the second by Edna Thornton) and she did not participate in its revival the following year. She sang Maddalena to Tetrazzini's Gilda in Verdi's *Rigoletto* as well as other roles. Coincidentally Maud Santley and her fellow auditionee that day, George Baker, had both sung at the Brighton Festival a few months earlier in November 1912, she as Carmen once again, he in Saint Saëns' *Samson and Delilah*. Santley was taken on by Ibbs and Tillett and became a principal contralto in the ill-fated Denhof–Beecham season of opera in the English provinces two months later. For the 1914–15 season she went to the Twentieth Century Opera House in New York as its leading contralto.

George Baker ('very good indeed, excellent voice, can safely recommend him') had also come to his audition with a fair amount of experience and with a recommendation from Landon Ronald. In 1910 he made his first appearance at the Brighton Festival in Saint Saëns' *Samson and Delilah* (which he was to repeat there two years later), sang the part of Siegfried in a centennial performance of Schumann's opera *Genoveva*, and, in 1911, the title role in Cherubini's *The Water Carrier* (*Les Deux Journées*) at His Majesty's Theatre, London. He was a frequent performer at the Queen's Hall Promenade Concerts, Chappell Ballad Concerts, the Crystal Palace, Birmingham Promenade Concerts, and the Liverpool Philharmonic Society. Baker had been an organist and choirmaster in his native north-west England before his vocal studies in Manchester and London with John Acton, Gustave Garcia and Albert Visetti (whose recommendations generally alerted Ibbs and Tillett to hear anyone they proposed). Baker remained on Ibbs and Tillett's books until the Second World War, together with his wife, the soprano Olive Groves, and we shall meet him again briefly in 1953 when Emmie Tillett urged him to press the Committee of the Royal Philharmonic Society (he was then its Chairman), to award its Gold Medal to the dying Kathleen Ferrier.

The general remarks in the audition books, despite their brevity, often reveal a detailed ear and eye on John Tillett's part. He took on the tenor Wilson Thornton as a result of his audition on 12 June 1913. Recommended by Sir Henry Wood, Thornton's voice was 'dramatic and heavy', his appearance 'good, has one queer eye'. He sang from Elgar's *Dream of Gerontius* and 'Winterstürme' from Wagner's *Die Walküre*, the comments noting a 'good voice, [Gervase] Elwes style, warm quality, artistic singer. Consider him suited for Elgar's works, *Gerontius*, *Kingdom* and Bach.' More frequent, however, were dispirited, tired comments reflecting weary days. These include such observations as 'rather uninteresting personality', 'voice not specially good, rather passé', 'appearance fair, wears glasses', 'voice requires more colour and abandon' (this of a tenor from St Paul's Cathedral), 'not young', and the repetitive and well-worn concluding phrase 'made usual promise', which, in the coming age of the telephone, would be a case of 'don't ring us, we'll ring you'.

CHAPTER EIGHT

Concerts and Festivals: 1910–14

Before the darkness of the first of the twentieth century's two world wars was to descend (and both were to have drastic effects upon the fortunes of the agency), a close study of some of the names which appear for the first time in the brochures between 1910 and 1914 makes fascinating reading. Among the instrumentalists there are many whose careers were now beginning, and whose names and reputations would echo down the century. Richter may have been about to retire, but London's public now had a mouth-watering choice of conductors to hear in opera and concert, such as Nikisch, Wood, Beecham, Landon Ronald, Hamilton Harty, Richard Strauss, Safonoff, Mengelberg, Fritz Steinbach and Elgar. The violinists Sarasate and Joachim may have died in 1907, but they were now replaced by Kreisler, Kubelik, Elman, Szigeti, Hubermann, Thibaud, Zimbalist, Daisy Kennedy and May Harrison, all of whom were making their mark in Britain (most of them with their careers already well established in mainland Europe), as well as the cellists Casals and Beatrice Harrison. The late nineteenth-century pianists Hans von Bülow and Anton Rubinstein were dead, but now more than adequately replaced by d'Albert, Busoni, Sapellnikoff, Rosenthal, Paderewski, Sauer, Borwick, Teresa Carreño and Fanny Davies. They in turn were joined by the next generation, including Cortot, Lamond, Scriabin, Dohnányi, Godowsky, Backhaus, Petri, Hambourg, Arthur Rubinstein, Grainger, Merrick, Dawson, and Rachmaninov. Prodigies continued to be presented to the public, among them the boy pianists Solomon (Cutner) and Ernst von Lengyel. The latter was taken up in a big way by Ibbs and Tillett and undertook a tour with Kreisler in 1912, but this highly promising Austrian's career was cut short in 1914, when he died of tuberculosis at the age of 20.

These were exciting and innovative times; in the spring of 1912 the LSO under Arthur Nikisch visited North America and Canada, the first time a European orchestra had toured that continent. Their gruelling schedule comprised 28 concerts (with no soloists) over 20 days including seven days with matinee and evening performances. The idea was the brainchild of the New York agent Howard Pew supported by several American financiers and philanthropists. The year 1912 was also the centenary of the Philharmonic Society and of the Handel Triennial Festival under Frederic Cowen at the Crystal Palace, with Ibbs and Tillett artists Clara Butt, Kennerley Rumford, Esta d'Argo, Perceval Allen, Charles Saunders, Herbert Brown, Ben Davies and Robert Radford the vocal soloists. Upward of three thousand formed the choir and orchestra for *Messiah*, *Israel in Egypt* and excerpts from *Samson* during those heady June days, but the Festival was not to be the last, for it was the Second rather than the First World War which eventually killed it off in 1939. A festival which did not survive the First World War, however, was the Birmingham Triennial Festival. Henry Wood took over from Richter for the 1912 event, a remarkable one in which Elgar conducted his new *Music Makers*, Sibelius his new Fourth Symphony, and among the star instrumentalists sent there by Ibbs and Tillett were Rosenthal and Casals. Bristol had a three-day Musical Festival in October and, as well as its chorus of 450 and orchestra of 105 (de facto the LSO), fielded many soloists from London sent by Ibbs and Tillett. The Festival Director,

George Riseley, conducted Wagner's *Ring* cycle for which the agency provided Agnes Nicholls, Perceval Allen, Edith Clegg, Lloyd Chandos, Morgan Kingston, Robert Radford, and Clarence Whitehill. During the previous month of September, the Three Choirs Festival took place at Hereford under George Sinclair. There were no festivals at Norwich, Sheffield and Leeds that year, having taken place in either 1910 or 1911. William Maitland Strutt, in his poignant *Reminiscences of a Musical Amateur*, written as he lay on his deathbed at the age of 26 in 1911 and published in 1915, summarized in trenchant fashion the status of the 'English provincial festival', now so important in the annual calendar of Ibbs and Tillett's operations:

> The English Provincial Festival is a curious institution. Towns which for the most part have hardly any musical life blossom out every three years or so for the space of a week into an overpowering activity, and then relapse into their torpor until the time for the next festival comes round. In old days, I suppose, the local character of the festival was more accentuated than now, for in modern times it has become customary to secure soloists, orchestra, and as a rule the conductor from external sources; only the chorus remains local, and even in their case a far larger district is drawn on than is generally supposed.

Before leaving William Strutt, his memory of Moriz Rosenthal's appearance on 13 March 1909 with the Queen's Hall Orchestra under Henry Wood is worth reproducing. Rosenthal had not been heard in England for nine years, but his name and reputation alone attracted a large audience. Strutt appears to have been in complete agreement with the reviewer for the *Musical Times* (April 1909) who described Rosenthal as a pianist who 'combines all the virtues and avoids all the vices of pianoforte playing'. From now on Rosenthal's activities in Britain would be managed by Ibbs and Tillett. Strutt considered that:

> Moriz Rosenthal was head and shoulders above any other pianist in the world. On this occasion he played two concerti of widely differing nature. First came Chopin's in E minor (No.1), in my humble opinion an extraordinarily dreary work, but the wonderful perfection of Rosenthal's playing made it seem worth listening to for once. It seemed hardly possible that Chopin's runs should be played with such ease, speed and evenness. At the end of the concert he played Liszt's concerto in E flat ... In this Rosenthal was stupendous. The octave passage towards the end, in which most pianists have to do their damnedest in order to keep up with the most lenient conductor, found him leading the orchestra without a trace of effort and without a single blurred note. At the end the audience was left gasping breathlessly, and too much taken aback to remember to applaud. I went forthwith to purchase a ticket for his recital, which was announced to take place a week or two later, ... at which he not only gave further proof of his astonishing virtuosity, but also showed himself in complete sympathy with all sorts of piano music

The first years of the twentieth century also saw the emergence of two new London orchestras, one of which we have already encountered. The LSO was formed in 1904 as a breakaway by five of Henry Wood's orchestral players for the Promenade Concerts (in a dispute over the system of sending deputy players to rehearsals or performances), while the other orchestra was appropriately called the New Symphony Orchestra (NSO). Elsewhere it has been erroneously reported that this orchestra was the creation of Thomas Beecham, but in fact it was formed in 1905 by three musicians (the flautist Eli Hudson, violinist John Saunders, and the clarinettist Charles Draper, whose name, of the three, has endured to this day), and conducted by Evlyn Howard-Jones at its inaugural concert at the Coronet Theatre, Notting Hill Gate. After a brief tenure in the post by Edward Mason, Beecham became conductor-in-chief but left after two years. It was then (March 1909) that Landon Ronald took up the post, his first concert featuring the Ibbs and Tillett pianist Irene Scharrer in Saint Saëns' G minor Piano Concerto, followed by one in 1910 which introduced Busoni's Piano Concerto with Mark Hambourg as soloist. Sunday afternoons at the Royal Albert Hall became the regular day and venue for concerts by the NSO until 1923, with the orchestra (from 1915) taking the name Royal Albert Hall Orchestra for all occasions when it played at that venue. The year 1912, and the following one, were particularly golden ones for the orchestra as well as contributing invaluably interesting programming in London's concert calendar. The composer Balfour Gardiner devised two series of four choral and orchestral concerts at the Queen's Hall, which presented new works by a large number of contemporary British composers such as Bax, Grainger, Vaughan Williams, Holst, Bantock, Austin, Dale, and Gardiner himself. Other featured composers were Bell, Delius, Poldowski (Lady Dean Paul), O'Neill, Parry, Quilter, Wood, McEwen, Stanford, Scott, and Harty. Two Ibbs and Tillett sopranos, Caroline Hatchard and Carrie Tubb, took part in the first concert of this highly significant series in the annals of twentieth century British music, yet somehow the generosity and largesse of the clear-sighted (and wealthy) Gardiner, an underrated composer in his own right, has been forgotten in the passage of time, during which on the other hand, many of the above mentioned composers secured lasting fame.

E.D. Mackerness, in his book *A Social History of English Music* (1964), underlines the tremendous amount of musical activity from the turn of the century to the First World War and the emergence of, among other things, the concert agent:

> It would be impossible to exaggerate the variety and profusion of English musical life from, say 1897 to 1914. Throughout the country, amateur music-making was extremely vigorous: choirs and small orchestras were numerous ... Two other features of English musical life in this period were the proliferation of concert agencies and the formation of opera companies. The distinction of being the oldest concert agency in the world was claimed by the firm of Vert of Cork Street, London.

As the role played by concert agents grew significantly in the first dozen years of the twentieth century, so too did their image. Ibbs and Tillett supplied not only the great Triennial Festivals (Birmingham, Sheffield, Norwich and Leeds), but increasingly more and more choral societies throughout the land. Rutland Boughton, in his *Death and Resurrection of the Musical Festival* (1913) described the vocal soloists who were brought in for such events as 'heartless mercenaries who slave that they may get a living instead of singing for joy because they have already got it', but he also appreciated the amount of newly commissioned works generated by festivals despite describing their audiences as 'gatherings of such wealthy folk as are too kind, or too lazy, to pot grouse'. Agents too were viewed with wary suspicion in some quarters; L.C. Venables (conductor of the South London Choral Association) in his handbook *Choral and Orchestral Societies* (1886) advocated a method of dealing with agents which sought to place the control of market forces firmly in the hands of the choral society:

> Soloists' terms vary according to circumstances; in other words second-rate professional vocalists get as much as they can. They proceed on the assumption that a society is a flourishing institution, with crowds of members and friends dying to hear them. When a list of artists has been selected, instead of asking them to quote their terms, it is better to offer them *x* guineas, according to their presumed value, and the amount to be expended on the concert. "Concert agents" may sometimes be consulted with advantage, although they mostly have a direct interest in naming large fees for the soloists they represent. As with soloists, they should be asked to furnish names of singers they can provide for a certain sum.

G.F. Sewell, in his *History of the Bradford Festival Choral Society* (1907), also reveals a resentment often felt by organizations in the provinces compelled to apply to the capital for soloists, when he draws attention to a concert given by the Society in the spring of 1883, for which 'there were no "stars" from London at great cost' so local resources were used. This golden jubilee publication lists all the main participants in the concerts from 1856–1906 and the hand of, first, Narciso Vert and then Ibbs and Tillett is clearly seen in the roster of soloists used in all the Bradford Festivals from the mid-1870s. Vert was also the go-between in dealings with Emma Albani, whose husband Ernest Gye was her manager and held out for high fees (such as 500 guineas for six concerts), but the Festival Committee would not back down. A brief diversion back to the first Leeds Musical Festival of 1858 and its committee's view of fees to foreign singers has a resonance even today. The principal 'foreigner' at the 1858 Leeds Festival was the Italian contralto Marietta Alboni, who received £250 for four concerts while the foremost English soprano of the day, Clara Novello, was paid £300 for six appearances, and the emerging Charles Santley received just £42 for five. This extract is from the *History of Leeds Musical Festivals* (1858–89) by Frederick Spark and Joseph Bennett (1892):

> A list of soloists whom it was thought desirable to engage having been drawn up, they were severally asked to state their terms, in the light of a very plain hint that, for sweet charity's sake, the figures should be as small as possible. "In stating your terms," wrote the Hon. Sec., "we would remind you that the surplus funds which may accrue from the Festival will be given to the Leeds General Infirmary, an Institution, which for many years has been in want of pecuniary aid." It does not appear that this suggestive sentence made a very deep impression upon the artists to whom it was addressed; certainly not upon the foreigners, whose demands somewhat astonished and almost nonplussed an unaccustomed committee. We infer this from a passage in a musical publication dated July 3rd 1858: "Owing to the exorbitant demands made for singing by many of the eminent foreign vocalists now in this country, the Leeds Festival Committee have been debating seriously the desirableness of making the Festival exclusively English in order to commence that almost necessary opposition to the rage for 'things foreign' which has so long prevailed in this country. The appreciation of genuine talent, no matter of what country, is nowhere greater than in this town; but Yorkshiremen have strong objections to paying more than a legitimate price for anything, much more for foreign artists to the exclusion of our own country people. We should be delighted to hear that the plan proposed was carried into practice". The writer was doomed to disappointment. However much the committee were disgusted with greed of foreign artists, they could not ignore a general desire to hear them, and some of the most distinguished aliens then available were engaged at considerable cost.

The musical traffic was not entirely one-way nor was the trade confined to solo musicians. As far back as July 1878, Henry Leslie took his unaccompanied choir to the French capital and won first prize with it in an international competition as part of the Paris Exhibition. It proved that if there was one thing the British could produce, it was a fine chorus. As if to prove the point, an adventurous undertaking took place at the beginning of 1906 when the LSO gave two concerts in Paris on the afternoons of Wednesday 10 and Friday 12 January, and took the 292-strong Leeds Festival Chorus along with them. The idea for this visit came from Sir Charles Villiers Stanford (in charge of the Leeds Philharmonic Society from 1897 to 1909 and the city's Triennial Festival Musical Director from 1901 to 1910) and the enterprise was put in the hands of the concert agent L.G. Sharpe of 61 Regent Street, London. Though Sharpe had been involved with concerts since 1886 touring with various artists throughout the world, his agency was relatively new (established in December 1900) and the feather in its cap was the Polish pianist Paderewski. This in turn brought Sharpe to the attention of the fledgling LSO who entrusted their business affairs to him from 1904 until 1923, and again from 1932 until the outbreak of the Second World War in 1939. The 1906 tour to Paris by the LSO and Leeds Festival Chorus was a triumph, despite the overlong programmes (each of two and half hours) ranging from Bach to Stanford himself. The second concert concluded with Beethoven's *Choral* Symphony, for which the soloists (all shortly to become members of the Ibbs and Tillett roster) were Perceval Allen, Marie Brema, John Coates and Francis Braun (Plunket Greene also went along and sang earlier that afternoon instead of Braun in excerpts from Stanford's *Requiem*). Though £1000 had been raised towards touring expenses of the choir, forty of them and all the orchestral players voluntarily paid their own way, while the soloists waived their fees.

An extremely fine and deservedly famous choir trainer in the north of England at the turn of the century was Dr Henry (later Sir Henry) Coward, who, for most of his professional career simultaneously held the posts of chorus master of the Sheffield Musical Union (which he established in 1876 as the Tonic Sol-fa Association until it changed its name in 1892), the Huddersfield Choral Society (from 1901 until 1932), Leeds Choral Union (from 1905), the Newcastle and Gateshead Choral Union (from 1907), and the Choral and Orchestral Union of Glasgow (from 1908), all of them important societies, or, in the case of Leeds and Sheffield, associated with renowned festivals. He too had trenchant views on fees paid to singers and, according to his *Reminiscences* (1919), was evidently no admirer of Narciso Vert, though later in life (he lived until his 95th year in 1944) he did turn to Ibbs and Tillett for his soloists. Planning a concert in November 1879 in Sheffield's Albert Hall, he was shocked at the fees demanded by Vert for five soloists (an anonymous soprano plus the contralto 'Mme [Janet] Patey', tenor 'E[dward] Lloyd', baritone 'C[harles] Santley' and bass 'Signor Foli' – real name Allan James Foley):

> Mr Dawson [Hon. Sec.] received five separate letters, all worded the same and signed N.Vert, stating that he or she would be pleased to sing at the concert for a fee of forty guineas, which made one ask the question "Why this abnormal rise in artists' fees?" I have at hand four circular letters, dated 1861 to 1864, from the secretary of a concert party [of eleven artists] for which the sum quoted was not five times forty guineas, but the almost unbelievable [total] sum of thirty-five guineas ... The contrast in quotation was doubtless largely due to the courteous but 'cute [*sic*] concert agent Mr N. Vert, who practically "cornered" the leading artists and then played off one festival against another, until the fees got to be ridiculously, and for the concert-givers, ruinously high.
>
> ... The great tenor Edward Lloyd sang [Elgar's cantata] *King Olaf* at Barnsley at the close of his farewell tour [29 March 1900]. The principal soprano being indisposed, Mr N.Vert sent as a substitute one of the best known singers [Medora Henson]. We thought we were secure, but just as she was going on to the platform she asked what her fee was going to be. She was told and she said "I must have five guineas more or I will not sing." The secretary, a cool-headed banker, said, "Oh yes you will," and snapped his jaws together. It was a fine contest between a wilful woman and a determined man. Meanwhile Lloyd was waiting to go on, and asked me to ascertain the cause of the delay. I told him and he went to the artists' room for an explanation. The secretary told him that Mr Vert had said the fee was to be *x* guineas, but Madame says she won't sing unless we pay her five guineas more. Lloyd said, "Did Vert say *x* guineas?" "Yes". He turned to Madame, ejaculated, "Come on," and without another word went towards the platform, and the irate lady followed as meekly as a lamb.

In fairness to Vert, a report in the *Musical Times* [January 1901] of Edward Lloyd's farewell concert at the Royal Albert Hall some months later on 12 December 1900 ended most unusually with a tribute to the concert agent. 'A word of hearty congratulation is due to Mr Vert – a veritable Napoleon of managers – who has been

Mr Lloyd's invaluable agent for many years'. Moving on a couple of years to 1902 and Coward was using many of Vert's artists, who would, after their agent's death in 1905, place their musical affairs in the hands of his nephew John Tillett. The 1902 Sheffield Musical Festival was particularly noted for its excellent performance of Elgar's *Dream of Gerontius*. It came hard on the heels of the one at the Three Choirs Festival at Worcester in September with John Coates (replacing William Green who was double booked for the final orchestral rehearsal), Muriel Foster (replacing an indisposed Marie Brema) and Harry Plunket Greene; the two replacements, as it turned out, went on to become very fine exponents of their respective roles. Both events were conducted by Elgar and were to set the work on the road to success in Britain after its woefully inadequate premiere at Birmingham in 1900. Fortunately they could build on its triumph in Düsseldorf under Julius Buths in December 1901 and May 1902. At Sheffield the soloists, Coates, Foster and Ffrangcon-Davies, were in Vert's hands, as were Agnes Nicholls, Ada Crossley, Kirkby Lunn, Ben Davies, William Green, David Bispham and the violinist Ysaÿe, whom he provided for other concerts in the three days of celebrations.

At exactly the time that Ibbs and Tillett were setting up business together in March 1906, Henry Coward was putting together a scheme to take his Sheffield Musical Union on a tour of Germany. It happened at a time when choral societies were venturing more frequently beyond their normal performing habitats and travelling nationally. Not long before, the Leeds Choral Union had sung at London's Royal Albert Hall before the King and Queen, and Henry Wood used them in the capital for Beethoven's *Choral* Symphony at Queen's Hall on 3 March 1906. Yorkshire choruses such as those in Leeds, Sheffield and Huddersfield were beginning to get used to joining up to form huge choirs for events, while at the same time jealously guarding their autonomy. Like the brass bands of the area, every choral organization in the county was fiercely proud. For their March 1906 tour to Germany, the Sheffield chorus numbered just under 300 (but about 60 friends or relatives also went) and, as a political compromise, now included members of other Sheffield choirs. Singers from Leeds, Huddersfield and elsewhere were also added to make up numbers, which, according to *Hazell's Annual*, were 142 from Leeds and 149 from Sheffield. They left on 22 September 1906 in a special train provided by the Great Northern Railway to the Channel, and, while in Europe, were given reserved carriages on normal service trains. They were enthusiastically received in the German cities of Düsseldorf, Cologne and Frankfurt, and scored a huge musical success with their programmes, which consisted of *Messiah*, *Dream of Gerontius*, Thomas Weelkes' madrigal 'As Vesta was from Latmos Hill descending', and choruses by Macfarren, Eaton Faning, Elgar and Parry (the finale to Act One of his oratorio *Judith*). As Julius Buths himself said in the *Düsseldorf Anzeiger*, 'Ensemble, shading, attack, volume, balance, all unapproachable and marvellous. The whole ensemble created envy and astonishment'.

Undaunted by the complexities of organizing such a tour, Coward went on to more ambitious ventures with his choral tours. In 1907 the London-born organist and composer Dr Charles Harriss arrived from Montreal for an engagement on 16 April at London's Queen's Hall, which he had booked together with Coward's Sheffield Choir of 250 voices and the LSO. Harriss had married the wealthy widow of an iron magnate and used his money to promote musical performance and education throughout the British Empire. His Queen's Hall concert was billed 'in honour of the visit to England of the Premiers from the British Dominions beyond the seas' and its lengthy programme involved four conductors, Alexander Mackenzie conducted his *Britannia* overture, Coward took his choir in Bach's motet 'Sing ye to the Lord', Harriss led his own Coronation Mass, *Edward VII*, and Arthur Nikisch concluded the concert with Beethoven's *Choral* Symphony. Sharpe (now on 5 per cent commission on all single engagements for the LSO, half that for tours) organized the concert, but Ibbs and Tillett had their artists in place for the solos, Agnes Nicholls, Alice Lakin, Lloyd Chandos, Ffrangcon Davies and Robert Radford. Harriss was so pleased with the Sheffield Choir that he told Coward, 'here is the instrument that I have been seeking for years to enable me to carry out an educational musical crusade in Canada, in order to set up an exalted standard of choral singing in the Dominion'. Whereupon he invited the 'choralists' (as they were known in the press and elsewhere at the time) to tour Canada in October 1908. In Coward's own summarizing words in his *Reminiscences*, it was 'the greatest musical venture ever undertaken previous to 1908'. They sang before 50000 people, and gave 16 concerts in a dozen venues over a period of as many days. Of the four principal singers who went along, three were to become Ibbs and Tillett artists, Emily Breare (soprano), Henry Brearley (tenor) and Robert Charlesworth (bass).

> Each singer had to undertake nine months' strenuous preparation, to sacrifice four or five weeks salary, to undergo real hard work in the shape of rehearsals and concerts while in Canada, and to run the risks of travel and probable occasional discomforts as well. Every singer, except the principals had to go as an amateur ... each had to pay ten pounds towards the expenses of the adventure. [They came from] the Sheffield Musical Union, with first class auxiliaries from my Leeds, Huddersfield, Newcastle and Southport choirs ... The expenses, though very great, were entirely met, if we except the personal expenses of Dr Harriss. As he was prepared to lose £2000 to carry out his patriotic scheme, he was well satisfied with the loss of, say, £500.

In September 1910 the Sheffield Choir went back to Germany, visiting Aachen, Düsseldorf, Essen, Leipzig and Dresden, and for their varied programmes took Phyllis Lett, Brearley and Charlesworth with them as soloists. The climax to all of Coward's touring activities, however, came in 1911 with a world tour with his Sheffield Choir (plus the usual extras from surrounding Yorkshire towns) leaving Liverpool on 17 March for Canada, then on to parts of America, after which they sailed across the Pacific to Australia, New Zealand and finally to South Africa, arriving back in Plymouth on the last day of September six and a half months later. 'When', wrote R.A. Edwards in his history celebrating the 150th anniversary of the Huddersfield Choral Society (*And the Glory, 1836–1986* (1985)), 'in May 1914, [the] Society received an invitation to send a chorus of 220 to London for a week to sing all the choral music at a Beethoven Festival proposed for April 1915, it was turned down partly due to the inadequacy of the amount offered in payment, but significantly because not enough members were able to spare the necessary time or bear the sacrifice of wages.' It says a lot for the dedication of the Sheffield 'choralists' that, once again, they were able to forego time and money for such an extended period. Nevertheless it turned out to be a gruelling undertaking with strict conditions imposed on all would-be participants, as Coward recalled:

> Each candidate had to pass tests for power, quality and intonation of voice, sight-reading in tune and time, provide a health certificate if necessary, attend 100 sectional and united rehearsals, promise to learn 150 pieces off by heart, practise at least 30 minutes daily and record the time in the special calendar provided at the end of the book of instructions, be prepared to be away from England for 26 weeks, and to sing at six concerts and one matinée when on land. In return for these services

second-class rail, steamboat, and motor carriages would be provided, and good hotel accommodation, together with five pounds for laundry. As it was necessary for each to go as an amateur, no fees would be paid to anyone except to the principals.

The vocal soloists were Jenny Taggart, Maud Wilby, Gertrude Lonsdale, Alice Heeley, Henry Turnpenny, Wilfred Virgo, Robert Charlesworth, Robert Chignell and the Lady Norah Noel, of whom the soprano Jenny Taggart, the tenor Turnpenney and the two baritones/basses were from Ibbs and Tillett. Coward prepared a staggering 18 programmes which consisted of complete performances of *Messiah*, *Dream of Gerontius* and *The Kingdom* (both of which Elgar conducted), Sullivan's *Golden Legend*, Verdi's Requiem, Berlioz's *Damnation of Faust*, Beethoven's *Choral* Symphony, Charles Harriss' own piece *Pan* (which he conducted), a selection from some of these, and finally four miscellaneous collections of shorter works, madrigals, part-songs, glees, some of them unaccompanied others with organ or piano. As they went from country to country and from continent to continent, they hired the local professional orchestras (14 in all) including the Cincinnati Symphony Orchestra (currently conducted by 'Mr Leo Stokovski'), the bizarrely named Gustav Slapoffski Sydney Festival Orchestra, and the more attractively styled Diamond Fields Festival Orchestra based in Kimberley, South Africa. The whole venture went under the description of a 'Musical Festival of the Empire' and furthered Coward's aims of 'Musical Reciprocity around the Empire' to which end he saw himself and his 200 choralists as missionaries for music-making, business-making and Empire-making. Considering that the Boer War had been concluded barely a decade earlier it was remarkable that their reception in South Africa (particularly away from either Johannesburg or 'English' Cape Town) was so cordial. 'The delights of travelling (approximately) 33,850 miles,' he wrote, 'visiting 56 towns in three continents, and singing at 130 concerts before wildly responsive audiences, were such that ... whenever two or three of the worldlings (as they named themselves) meet, they metaphorically fall on each other's necks and revive past raptures.' Coward's was a wonderful achievement, but one never to be repeated because of the intervention of war, and the changes to the fabric of society which that catastrophe brought about over the course of four years.

Henry Coward, as we have seen, had trenchant views on the role of the concert agent and in the years immediately prior to the First World War they became even more virulent, particularly when it came to German musicians and agents (despite the comparatively recent two tours he made with his choir to that country). But England's (and Coward's) debt to Germany could not be denied. Throughout the nineteenth century, it was to there that so many English musicians (among them Sterndale Bennett, Sullivan, and Grove) went to refine their musical education, or their composers came to England either to live and work (Handel for most of his life, Bruch for three years) or to visit (such as Mendelssohn, Liszt, and Wagner). As far as performers were concerned, the traffic was generally one-way. Joachim and Hans von Bülow were frequent visitors, while Hallé, Manns and Richter were conductors who took up residence. Others who moved to London were teachers of the piano such as Pauer, Ganz and Kuhe, Carl Rosa, who became an opera impresario, while critics included Hanslick (who visited) and Franz (anglicized to Francis) Hueffer, who moved to London. While Coward might be accused of ungraciousness and hypocrisy in some of his more colourful comments on German musicians, it should not be forgotten that his reminiscences were written during the First World War:

> I have mentioned previously how by careful "nursing" fees had mounted up enormously. The fact had not escaped the predatory German, always on the lookout for exploitation. He saw in "concert agency" an avenue for "peaceful penetration", or rather purseful plunder, because the craze for anything of the "German brand" was virulent. He therefore found it an easy matter to rush up fees to an absurd pitch, because singers had at their back a gullible set who accepted the estimate of a German agent as gospel. At some festivals we paid one hundred guineas each to instrumentalists for playing a concerto each. Needless to say the performers were not British. I asked the terms of a very young violinist and eighty guineas was named. A Festival Committee sought the services of an *en vogue* German conductor, through his friend, a London musical critic, German of course. He quoted the modest sum of 200 guineas per concert, with the extra stipulation that his friend B. should be engaged to rehearse the orchestra for him. These conditions came "too strong" for even our Germanophiles, proving that even "the worm will turn".

Coward went on to describe how singers had 'waxed fat' in this boom period of high fees until concert promoters and music societies rebelled and the bubble burst:

> I remember a prima donna telling me that a certain Festival Committee would have to pay eighty guineas each concert whether she sang much or little, because "there is no one who can take my place as principal soprano". In this she was mistaken. The answer was "We offer 120 guineas for two concerts, take it or leave it". Her agent, a straight, reliable, level-headed Englishman said, "Take", and she "took".

Fees also had to come down because music education was producing more musicians and with it the supply to the market increased. Besides such august London institutions as the Royal Academy, Royal College, Guildhall School, Trinity College and the London College of Music, there were those in Manchester and Glasgow, as well as burgeoning suburban Conservatoires such as Blackheath, Croydon, Watford or Hampstead. The Associated Board of the Royal Schools of Music (from 1880) and Trinity College of Music set standards with their examination systems, while private teachers proliferated and music clubs and choral societies mushroomed. According to Coward 'there was a decided upward tendency in fees from 1870 to 1900. The palmy days were between 1895 and 1905. Since 1900 fees have declined as a whole, except in the cases of artists with rising reputations, and the days of extravagant demands are now over'. That was not how things were to remain throughout the twentieth century, particularly with the advent of the recording industry which would send conductors' and singers' fees rocketing sky-high.

> In the instrumental world the same influences were in operation. One other fact stands out and hurts, namely the difference in the treatment meted out to British and foreign artists. I will not quote figures, but will pass on with the remark that by aiding, abetting and fostering the colossal conceit of the Teuton, we stimulated that idea of the "superman", the outcome of which has been the present war ... Neglect of home or the homeland exacts a terrible penalty.
>
> As steps in the evolution of fees we find Joachim and Pachmann realized 85 guineas in 1886, Sarasate and Bertha Marx 80 guineas in 1890, Kubelik and Backhaus – the latter a Yorkshireman who contracted "Teutonitis" very severely, which caused the spelling of "house" to change to "haus" because it "paid" £183.15s in 1909. [This is mysterious as Wilhelm Backhaus, if that is who is meant, was born in Leipzig]. Pianists alone figure thus: Saint Saëns £30 in 1895, Hofmann 30 guineas in 1887 and 50 guineas in 1894, d'Albert 60 guineas in 1896, Paderewski 200 guineas in 1898 and forwards. Violinists come out well in the matter of payment, especially during the boom in wonder-children. Thus a young violinist, comet-like appeared, and in October 1893 Kubelik received 200 guineas for appearing at a concert. At such mouth-watering fees it was worth while to produce prodigies so long as they were not "home" products, therefore another meteor in the shape of Vecsey

was forthcoming for 150 guineas an appearance in 1905. But the downward curve appeared to be in evidence, and Mischa Elman, another precocious youngster, had therefore to be content with a paltry £98.14s for about 30 minutes playing in 1907. It was enough to make Joachim, the monarch violinist of his time, turn in his grave [freshly dug in 1907]. Personally I don't think these or even the more modest terms of Miss Marie Hall – 50 guineas in 1904 and 80 guineas in October 1905 – will come again ... At the present time [1918] thoughtful artists and some English agents are keeping an equitable balance between pretensions and "drawing" powers, thus avoiding getting into the "backwash". One of our most popular baritones told me recently that he had protested to his agent against his terms being increased because he preferred "the nimble ninepence to the slow shilling".

CHAPTER NINE

Artists and Auditionees: 1914–18

One of the final high spots of musical life in England before war was declared took place in Canterbury Cathedral on 19 June 1914, when Henry Coward took his Leeds Choral Union there to perform Elgar's *The Apostles* under the composer's direction, with all six solo singers from Ibbs and Tillett – Agnes Nicholls, Muriel Foster, John Coates, Thorpe Bates, Herbert Heyner and Robert Radford. Six weeks later the musical world, like the rest of the country, was having to come to terms with the declaration of war. Concerts were cancelled and musical events, like other forms of entertainment, initially considered inappropriate. Plans for festivals were shelved, artists were unable to travel from or to Germany, ticket receipts were frequently donated to the war effort, and fees to artists were reduced among other attempts to defray concert expenses. Travel was restricted because train services were cut back, the government taxed entertainment and, for reasons of security and energy conservation, street lighting was reduced (which deterred people from venturing out in the evening to rehearsals or concerts); concert halls were commandeered for meetings or requisitioned by the military authorities. The choice of music performed was itself affected by prevailing conditions, German music being the obvious casualty (Coward was a leading advocate of a total boycott of music composed after 1870, which originated from the Fatherland), but the consequence seems to have been a rising popularity of French and Russian music as well as more interest and encouragement for new British compositions.

British musical life, therefore, had to adapt itself to these new conditions. Brighton managed to keep its festival going throughout the war, but most did not. With tourism to continental Europe impossible, those who could afford it went to spas or resorts in Britain, and small instrumental or vocal groups found employment to entertain them in such places during the season, developing what was already a recognized area of musical employment but which was now more competitively sought. As the war developed, and as it was realized that what was predicted to be 'over by Christmas' was going to last a good deal longer, so concert parties were sent across the Channel to entertain the troops on the Western Front; Lena Ashwell, whose Concert Party was one such group and included Ivor Novello and his wartime hit 'Keep the Home Fires Burning', was an entertainer with Ibbs and Tillett from the 1908–9 season. The infrastructure of choirs and orchestras inevitably underwent huge changes, particularly as a consequence of the depletion of their younger male members. Even Henry Coward lost a son killed in action. Some orchestras became entirely made up of women, although such a concept was not unprecedented: the English Ladies Orchestral Society, formed in 1893, was 'believed to be the first Amateur Ladies Orchestra which includes wind as well as stringed instruments' according to its own publicity. It met on Thursday mornings nine months of the year, its members subscribing a guinea. By 1908 its concerts (on average two a year) had raised £2000 for charity and its playing membership stood at 79. On the afternoon of 27 January 1910 the society gave a concert in aid of the Hospital for Crippled and Incurable Children in Leonard Square, Finsbury, London. The orchestra comprised 42 ladies but was conducted by its male musical director, J.S. Liddle.

Just over two years later, on the afternoon of 27 February 1912 the Orchestra Femina gave its inaugural concert at London's Shaftesbury Theatre in aid of the Fresh Air Fund. Put together and conducted by a former viola player in the Queen's Hall Orchestra, Siegfried Wertheim, the band consisted of ladies gathered together from London and elsewhere. *The Standard* previewed the concert five days earlier, its sub-editor's befitting contribution being: 'New excursion into man's field. Striking departure.'

> Another important excursion into man's field of labour is to be made by the other sex in its new-born activities. Thousands of women, it is true, have for years earned their livelihood solely by playing in more or less important permanent institutions up and down the country. But they have always had the humiliating experience of playing second fiddle in every sense of the term to some mere male rival, while among the more complicated, or, rather, less graceful instruments of the orchestra, they have been wholly unrepresented. Lady executants take readily to the violin, and the 'cello, the harp, and, in a lesser degree, the viola are equally designed, when well played, to display as much the charm and grace as the talents of the performer.
>
> Small wonder, therefore, that the higher "strings" of the orchestra have been favoured at the expense of the double bass, the wood wind, the brass, and the percussion. What pretty girl wanted to scrape a giant fiddle bigger than herself; or blow out her cheeks or suck them in for the wind instruments; jerk her arms in and out for the trombone; or swing them about at the kettle-drums? Hence it is that men have had to be engaged to manipulate these unbecoming weapons of music whenever a "ladies'" orchestra was called into being, and consequently the title of the organisation became a misnomer, and anything of a permanency for it was out of the question. But the bassoon and the tympani, the trombone and the horn have yielded their secrets, like the motor car and the aeroplane, to the masterful attainments of the modern lady.
>
> Not a single male will mar the ranks of the Orchestra Femina, and the appearance of a man, Mr Siegfried Wertheim, at the conductor's desk, will only emphasise the fact how little his kind is wanted elsewhere. This organisation makes it first appearance at the Shaftesbury Theatre on Tuesday afternoon next. 'Behind this preliminary appearance', said Mr Wertheim to a *Standard* representative yesterday, 'are months of hard labour in selection and organisation. For the Orchestra Femina is already an established institution, as firmly based on business, law, and order, as the London Symphony Orchestra, the Queen's Hall Orchestra, the New Symphony Orchestra, or any other male corporation. It numbers at present 45 performers, but it will probably reach 60 players before long. The most careful elimination and examination were exercised over the strings, only about one out of fifteen really first-class applicants being chosen. Many well-known recital-givers are to be found among our fiddles, and our 'leader', Miss C.V.King, has played under the great French conductor Eduard Colonne, and won many prizes at the Paris Conservatoire.
>
> Our second leader is Miss Elsie Avrill, and here I may tell you that it is an 'All-British' combine. Every musical camp has been ransacked throughout the country for talent. Only time has prevented our holding actual auditions in every large town, but I had three months of them in London. Can I tell you some of our players? Well, Miss Jessie Bowater and Miss Aldis are among the violas, first 'cello is Miss Bartlett, and first double bass Miss Halfpenny. The trombones and bassoons were, of course, the most difficult to discover. For the former we have Miss Annie Knowles, Mrs Kent and her sister-in-law Miss Hilda Kent, whose sisters, Miss Minnie and Miss Viola, are our two cornet players. We are lucky in having the only lady bassoon players in the country in Miss Lucy Munby and Miss Whitfield. Their possession practically creates a monopoly for the Orchestra Femina. The two oboes, Miss Melliar and Miss Beattie; two clarinets, Miss Walker and Miss Mitton; two flutes, Miss Wild and Miss Woolhouse; and percussion (drums etc) Miss Bolton and Miss Faulcher, complete the usual 'male' section of the orchestra.
>
> Our programme of Tuesday proclaims to a certain extent the seriousness of our endeavours. It includes Beethoven's *Egmont* Overture, *Danse macabre* (Saint Saëns), *Peer Gynt* Suite, and Liszt's second Rhapsodie. But the most interesting item will be a suite selected specially for the occasion by four of England's leading composers [Parry, Cowen, Elgar, Mackenzie]. We have called it the *Knights'* Suite – which is not strictly accurate, for one of the musicians [Parry] is a baronet – on account of each contributor being a 'Sir'. The members of the orchestra will wear a specially designed dress, blue satin and lace, as pretty and graceful a garment as ever adorned a musical comedy star.
>
> The scenery will be in the Adams style, with panels of Rose du Barry, and later on lighting effects

will be introduced to give certain pieces a visual as well as an oral [*sic*] effect. The trade-mark of the Orchestra Femina is the octave F in a big O. A good idea, isn't it?'

In the middle of the First World War the orchestras of London's Stoll Theatres went on strike for more pay, demanding a 50 per cent increase. After a fortnight's stand-off their bluff was met, they lost their posts in October 1916 and were replaced by women instrumentalists in the seven music halls, the Coliseum (where the drummer remained at his post and kept his job, which was a sweet irony because peacetime orchestras were used to having just one woman, the harpist), London Opera House, New Middlesex, and the Empire Theatres at Chiswick, Shepherd's Bush, Hackney and Wood Green. For the 160 vacancies which arose through the sackings, over 2000 women applied. The response by the press to such a turn of events in the musical world makes interesting reading and reflects the problems the agency was dealing with in 'selling' women musicians at this period as well as the prejudices faced by the women musicians themselves.

Oswald Stoll's Musical Director, Alfred Dove, had ten days in which to put together his female orchestras, and for most of them there was one rehearsal on Saturday and a final one on Monday morning preceding the first matinee of the week. The results were rather rough and it took a few days for the bands to settle down and play confidently with secure ensemble. On the matter of a woman's frailty and whether it was either wise or seemly for a delicate girl to play the bassoon or trombone in public, the press was quite vociferous, not to say outrageous, and printed a fair amount of rubbish. Political correctness was unheard of in this, the era of the suffragette, as one such review makes clear:

In the matter of tone, the opinion is almost universal among conductors who have employed women in their orchestras that, while it is generally smaller, it is frequently sweeter and purer than that of the men. It has been rather difficult to form a very definite opinion at the Coliseum, because whereas the orchestra consists normally of a minimum of 28 performers, and is increased to 40 on special occasions, at present Mr Dove has only 23, a number, however, which he intends to increase. It may be taken as beyond dispute, however, that the wind department will always display a certain weakness, and that women have not, as a rule, the lung power of men ... According to [a] well-known conductor, women players of wind instruments are less accurate than men, chiefly, he thinks, because they become nervous and diffident when they have anything like solo playing to do, an especially common occurrence with the woodwind. This, however, is surely a weakness that experience would overcome. And there are certain matters in which practically all conductors agree that women can give points and a beating to men. Mr Dove says that never has he had such an attentive, such a conscientious and such a reliable orchestra under his control and his opinion is shared by many another. And it is the last of these qualities that will carry women very far on their careers as orchestral players should they seriously adopt this means of earning a livelihood.

There ought, undoubtedly, to be a very good opening for women in orchestras all over the country, if the present custom of employing only men were to be abandoned. Every town that deserves the name has at least a theatre and a music hall, and often more than one, while the bigger towns have their half-dozen or so, and it is difficult to see how all these orchestras are to be kept filled with so many men away on active service. The rates of pay vary enormously of course with the size of the town and the class of the theatre. It may be taken, however, that the minimum rate paid is about 32s 6d [£1.52$^1/_2$p] a week, rising to about £2 for the leaders. At the Coliseum, of course, a far higher rate prevails, and there no player is paid less than £2.12s [£2.60p], rising to over £4, the women, be it noted, being paid precisely the same rate as the men were before the change was made. The rates have all been settled long ago by the Amalgamated Musicians' Union, and may be taken as perfectly fair, but it is essential that, if women should enter upon orchestral work, they should not do so at a lower rate than was paid to the men.

Where the supply would come from if a large number of women's orchestras were suddenly

> instituted it is not so easy to see. So far as the strings are concerned, there would doubtless be little difficulty, for though the majority of girls who study the violin or the violoncello do not do so primarily with a view to entering orchestras, they could soon adapt themselves to it. But the woodwind and the brass is another story altogether, and inquiries at the various colleges of music elicited the fact that there are very, very few fair students of the clarinet, the bassoon and the trombone. Indeed it would be strange if there were, for these are not exactly the instruments for the drawing room, and the prospects for girls of making a living as orchestral performers on them have not hitherto been alluring. However Mr Dove says that he has had little difficulty in finding them, even at short notice, so it may be that there are plenty of feminine trombonists blushing unseen, or, rather, blowing unheard, in various parts of the country. It is well known that instruments of this type run in families, so to speak, and it is no uncommon thing to find father and son playing side by side in the same orchestra. Possibly some enthusiasts teach their daughters as well, and these would be ready to step into the peaceful ranks of the orchestra while their men folk are in the more strenuous ranks of the Army. In any case the demand would eventually create the supply, but it takes three years or more to master one of these exacting instruments, so, if there is not a good supply already, a large number of orchestras formed entirely of women must await realisation in the future.
>
> However, that there is no reason why Mr Stoll's experiment should not be successfully imitated by others is sufficiently obvious. I should imagine that those who are not of reasonably robust physique would be well advised to seek work in the theatres rather than in the music halls, for, save on the occasions of the visit of a musical comedy, they will find things less hazardous there. But Mr Dove, who ought to know, tells me that a woman, provided that she is a competent and intelligent player, can be initiated into the trick of accompanying a music hall singer, which one would have thought was none too easy, in an astonishingly brief space of time. He further had no mean opinion of one of the ladies in his orchestra [oboist Dorothy Beattie, later the redoubtable Dorothy Crump, conductor of the Oaks Farm Orchestra in Croydon] to whom at times he entrusts the baton. And, judging by her skilful and sympathetic handling of the orchestra during the pictures and one of the turns on the evening on which I was there, his opinion was justified.

After the dust had settled and the novelty had lost its initial newsworthiness, a short paragraph appeared in *London Opinion* (4 November 1916) which showed that, despite a grudging acknowledgement that no evident drop in musical standards arose as a result of women's orchestras, male prejudice continued to exist:

> As we have heard no more about the women's orchestras at the various Stoll music halls, I suppose it may be taken for granted that they have settled down to their work and are giving satisfaction. I am certain, however, that this will in no wise affect the future composition of the great concert orchestras. Neither Sir Henry Wood, Sir Thomas Beecham, nor Landon Ronald has any objection to lady violinists, violas or cellists playing in the orchestra if, and when, it be found necessary, but I understand that any idea of having lady wind instrument players is out of the question. I am glad myself. I cannot imagine anything more ungraceful or unwomanly than seeing a girl struggling with a huge brass instrument like the trombone, for instance. Women can do much that men can, but they will never be able to sing baritone, become soldiers, or blow wind instruments – unless it be their own trumpets!

There were other ways in which the music profession was affected by the war. There were fewer students entering the music colleges, or taking private lessons and examinations. Music clubs, particularly those giving recitals, reduced their activities, which in turn impacted on Ibbs and Tillett's artists. However large-scale events such as London's Promenade Concerts continued to take place, and other concerts seemed to be unaffected, such as those put on by such established orchestras as the LSO and by organizations like the Royal Philharmonic Society, which was largely kept afloat by Thomas Beecham's money until he was unceremoniously removed at the end of the war in 1918. Opera, however, was badly affected by the war. The golden era went out in a blaze of glory in the summer of 1914, after the first British staging of Wagner's *Parsifal* six months earlier in February (according to Wagner's instructions, it was to remain the preserve of Bayreuth for 30 years after his death – in 1883 – before being staged elsewhere). When *Lohengrin* was performed on 23 May it proved to be the last time for ten years that the German language was heard on stage at Covent Garden. The season closed on 28 July with Verdi's *Aida*, and opera was not staged there again until May 1919. In the meantime it was Beecham (Sir Thomas from 1915), who once again kept opera alive in London with his season of Russian opera at Drury Lane in the summer of 1914. Anti-German feeling not only manifested itself by not singing in the language (instrumental or orchestral music by German composers was not always boycotted), but even the Bechstein Hall in London was removed from the German piano makers, taken over by Debenham's in 1916 and the following year renamed the Wigmore Hall, a venue with which Ibbs and Tillett was to have the closest of associations for years to come.

The Royal family may have changed its Teutonic names from Saxe-Coburg to Windsor and from Battenburg to Mountbatten, but musicians bearing Teutonic-sounding names, such as the Hambourg brothers Mark, Jan and Boris, all three born in South Russia, had to bring a libel case against the *London Mail*, which had cast doubts on their nationality and falsely labelled them Germans. Mark Hambourg, who brought the case in the autumn of 1914, was successful and received £500 in damages. The conductor Basil Cameron, having just changed his name to Hindenburg in 1912 in order to capitalize on preferred foreign-sounding names to further his career, was compelled to make a complete *volte face*, and revert once again to Cameron when war broke out two years later. Publicity for the pianist Archy Rosenthal (not to be confused with Moriz Rosenthal, who was in Europe throughout the war) was compelled to add 'Mr Rosenthal is British, both by birth and parentage' to ensure that he was not boycotted as a foreigner. These were sad times in which artists, who were so often revered in both countries, were now vilified. From Germany Hans Richter and Max Bruch returned their honorary doctorates to English universities, from America the opera singer Elizabeth Schumann-Heink (by now a naturalized citizen of the United States) railed against the English for allegedly preventing thousands of Irish from returning home and fighting with the Germans against the British. Even in January 1919, two months after the end of the war, at his reappearance at the Wigmore Hall, the Scottish pianist Frederic Lamond, who had been trapped in Germany in 1914 and first interned, then sent to Holland, felt compelled to include this 'Important Notice' on the flyer advertising the event:

> Certain malicious rumours implying that Mr Lamond has naturalised or attempted to naturalise as a German subject are entirely without foundation. E A Michell [his London agent] has been authorised to refute absolutely all such libellous reports, and, further, if necessary, institute proceedings against any person spreading these rumours.

In the following season a tenor on Ibbs and Tillett's books, Mischa-Léon, gave a song recital at the Aeolian Hall on 13 March 1920 consisting of German songs sung in the original language, but had to endure an anti-German demonstration in the hall before he could begin.

Early in the war, on 30 September 1914, a meeting was convened by Hubert Bath, musical adviser to the London County Council, at Pagani's restaurant (a famous haunt for musicians) to consider the effect the crisis would have on the musical profession and how to protect the British musician at a time when employment was inevitably going to become harder to obtain. About 100 people attended the meeting, which was presided over by Sir Frederic Cowen. A press release was read out in which it was stated that aliens should no longer be permitted to occupy permanent posts in societies, colleges or schools. Questions needed answering: 'how many alien enemies are still employed in the theatres and music halls as instrumentalists, conductors and choristers … [and what of] touring opera companies and restaurants employing musicians?' Effusive praise was lavished upon English orchestral musicians ('not one of the principal orchestras on the Continent could compare for all-round excellence with our London orchestras', said Landon Ronald) and 'these were hard times for our own instrumentalists, and charity must begin at home' with nothing more than sympathy being offered to any musicians from Britain's allies who might happen to reside in the country. The war, according to the weekly *Musical News* (10 and 24 October 1914):

> has suddenly brought to a head the long-smouldering resentment against foreign dominance in British musical circles … [now is] the chance for the native to assert his proper pre-dominance in the land of his birth … After having their employment prejudicially affected for years past by Germans and Austrians, [orchestral musicians] may be excused if they fail to see how the substitution of French and Belgians is likely to benefit their condition.

A Committee for Music in War-time was formed, consisting of the principals of the four music colleges in London, Sir Alexander Mackenzie, Sir Hubert Parry, Landon Ronald, Sir Frederick Bridge, together with the Director of the Birmingham Institute, Granville Bantock, and with Walter Willson Cobbett as its Honorary Secretary. It met 'to form a register of competent artists requiring work, and willing to accept such fees as either the Committee or the Society engaging them is able to offer. It will collaborate with local musical societies anxious to continue their work, but debarred from doing so by the departure of active helpers, or by lack of sufficient funds to meet expenses.' This decision to encourage the war-time activities of music societies and to act on behalf of the native musical profession was further endorsed by another larger meeting held in the Small Queen's Hall on 13 October again under Cowen's chairmanship. By proposing to act as agents and concert managers, but without taking a percentage commission, this committee was effectively competing with agencies such as Ibbs and Tillett, who meanwhile were doing their bit for the war effort. They sent Clara Butt and Kennerley Rumford to Aberdeen to sing to wounded soldiers at the hospitals there, and supplied two concerts put on by Southport Orchestral Society with two of their artists, the soprano Carrie Tubb and the pianist Alfred Cortot.

In the provinces, the choral societies were adapting to the new circumstances of war and formulating plans for the season accordingly. Bristol Choral Society, for example, cut their season to two choral concerts but planned a series of popular concerts 'at which the choir and one or more well-known principals will sing. These performances are to be of a miscellaneous character and on thoroughly popular lines, and the nett profits of the whole season's concerts will be for the relief of distress caused by the war.' Safonoff appeared in Liverpool for two concerts in the autumn of 1914, the first on 20 October, and aroused mixed feelings by including Brahms and Schumann in a programme which went on with 'items that were more happily chosen. Pierson's fine chorus "Ye Mariners of England" and Elgar's "Sword Song" from *Caractacus*.' The correspondence between Safonoff and Ibbs and Tillett concerning this concert had begun at the end of 1913, and, by the time it concludes nine months later, has had to keep up with ever-developing world events. The original programme ideas change significantly, and the German soloist is forced to withdraw and be replaced by Herbert Brown from the agency:

> Enclosed please find the signed contracts for Liverpool concerts of the Philharmonic Society on October 13th and 27th [1914] with rehearsals on Monday evenings 12th and 26th October at 6pm and 1.30pm on the day of each concert for the sum of one hundred and forty guineas (£147.0.0). (23 December 1913)

> Your letter from December 24th reached me today and I hurry to answer you that October 6th is quite impossible for I am in Norway at this time, but I can manage to give October 20th and November 3rd [1914] for the two concerts in Liverpool. Please let me know as soon as possible if those dates are fixed definitely, for it's of importance for my further dispositions. (29 December 1913)

> To draw up a programme scheme for Liverpool I want to know 1) If there be, outside of my instrumental soloists, vocalists in the programme. 2) What do they sing? What length of items? 3) What length shall be the choral items? I presume Mr Evans shall conduct them. (29 April 1914)

> Can you let me know what Herr [Paul] Knüpfer [German bass] will sing, also the definitive disposition of the 2nd programme of November 3rd, that is if there be a vocalist or a chorus item? (20 June 1914)

After the outbreak of hostilities, Safonoff wrote:

> I don't know if the Liverpool engagements are still valid, but in all cases Mr Beloussoff cannot come, for he has been taken to the war. I presume Mr Knüpfer, as a German, is also unable to come. If the engagements are maintained and the voyage to England should be possible for the middle of October, would the Committee like to engage Miss Vera Brock, who is my soloist for November 9th with the London Symphony (3rd piano concerto G major by [Anton] Rubinstein)? Please let me know as soon as possible (address for telegrams Fonofas, Petrograd). Hurrah for the English army and navy! (16 September 1914)

> The fee is really low but I decided to accept it under the condition that you also would accept a reduction of your fee to 5% on account of the general depression, and I hope you will be willing to do so … I take on the responsibility to reduce the fee for [Vera Brock] to the minimum of 15 guineas as this will be her first appearance in Liverpool … The final version of my programme for October 20th

1)	Schumann	*Manfred* Overture	11 min
2)	Beethoven	2nd symphony	36 min
3)	Mozart	two arias (Herr Knüpfer?)	10 min
	Interval		20 min
4)	Cui	two *a cappella* choruses a) Beauty concealed b) Echo	8 min
5)	Rubinstein	3rd concerto	30 min
6)	Cornelius	aria (Herr Knüpfer)	10 min?
7)	Liszt	*Mephisto* Waltz	12 min
	on and off		10 min
			147 min

> If this is too long we can take a shorter item for the closure instead of Liszt's Waltz, Glinka's brilliant overture from his heroic-phantastic opera *Russlan and Ludmilla*, very brilliant and short, not exceeding 5 minutes so the total will be 142 mins. Material for the Schumann and Rubinstein will be mine, other items c/o Liverpool Philharmonic. N.B. The choruses are edited in England and were performed by me in Newcastle on April 1st this year. In case Herr Knüpfer will not come, may I suggest this (a very nice programme!):

1)	Schumann	*Manfred* Overture	11 min
2)	Beethoven	2nd symphony	36 min
	Interval		20 min

3)	Tschaikowsky	aria from *Jeanne d'Arc* (Miss Esta d'Argo)	10 min
4)	Rubinstein	3rd concerto	30 min
5)	Cui	two *a cappella* choruses a) Beauty concealed b) Echo	8 min
6)	Liszt	*Mephisto* Waltz	12 min
	On and off		10 min
			137 min

November 3rd

1)	Mendelssohn	Symphony A-major [No.4 *Italian*]	28 min
2)	Brahms	Violin concerto (Miss [Isolde] Menges)	44 min
	Interval		20 min
3)	Rubinstein	Three choruses from the *Tower of Babel* with orchestra	9 min
4)	Violin solos		12 min
5)	Tschaikowsky	*Francesca da Rimini*	22 min
	On and off		10min
			145 min

NB: I want one item of great dramatic tension in my programmes. Material for *Francesca* will be mine, other items c/o Liverpool Philharmonic.

I took my information about the present connections with England; it takes more than 6 days, it's terrible! The route goes via Raumo, Stockholm, Christiana, Bergen, Edinburgh. I'm mailing this registered to prevent the loss of this letter as it seems to have been with my letter from the Caucasus. Please answer me as soon as possible 37 Furstatskaïa Street, *Petrograd* (not St Petersburg, we don't want to call our capital in the language of the Prussian snake!) Hip, hip, hip, hurrah for England! (18 September 1914)

A couple of years later Ibbs and Tillett tried to persuade another conductor, Albert Coates, to travel from Russia to conduct in Liverpool during the war but he declined. At the time he was the chief conductor at the Imperial Opera in Petrograd, but his English debut in 1914 at Covent Garden had been a huge success and he was evidently a conductor with a promising future, and a man to watch:

Concerning your kind offer to conduct one or more concerts in Liverpool during the coming season, I am afraid I am unable to absent myself for so long a time as would be necessary during our season here. The journey to England from Petrograd takes 9 days, hence 18 days would go for travelling alone. I could not possibly take, in wartime, so long a leave of absence. Otherwise I should have been delighted to conduct in Liverpool, where I spent nearly all my schooldays. After the war I shall be only too pleased to consider any offers you may be kind enough to make me, but at present I am afraid it is out of the question. (22 September 1916)

Another British conductor beginning to make a name for himself at this time was Hamilton Harty. Richter gave him his big break in 1911, when he conducted his own composition *With the Wild Geese* with the LSO. Like Coates, Harty made his Covent Garden debut just before the First World War (*Tristan and Isolde* and *Carmen* in 1913), appeared in Liverpool in 1914 (with Rachmaninov as soloist, see Chapter 7), and covered the wartime absence in Germany of Michael Balling, Hans Richter's chosen successor with the Hallé at Manchester. Shortly before he joined the Royal Naval Volunteer Reserve for two years from June 1916, Harty went to Bournemouth to guest-conduct Dan Godfrey's orchestra, the engagement negotiated by Ibbs and Tillett. Bournemouth kept its concerts going throughout the war, and two of its string players were killed on active service, theirs and the places of other instrumentalists called up being taken up by Belgian musicians unfit for war service.

I also have had a letter from Godfrey in which he says he would prefer me to go and do the symphony at one of his ordinary Thursday concerts on account of the difficulty of getting rehearsals

> on other days. I have agreed to do this and the question of a concert with Mrs Harty [Agnes Nicholls] had better be left in abeyance, therefore, at least as far as I am concerned. [11 February 1916]

A wartime letter from Edward German to Ibbs and Tillett revealed the diverse interests of John Tillett, who here seems to have become involved in promoting the libretto for a potential operetta, perhaps in the style of the composer's *Merrie England*:

> Quite apart from the merits of the libretto *Allan-a-Dale* which you kindly sent me, I fear I could not set it with success. Receiving it has also made me realise how much work I have on hand to which I am already pledged. I have read the libretto and in returning it speak of it with all respect, and I thank you and Mr James Heard for having allowed me to see it. (29 February 1916)

Artists necessarily made sacrifices of a financial nature during the war years, the pianist Leonard Borwick (with the agency since 1908) offered a reduction.

> In reply to yours of June 10th, I think I may undertake the engagement on 16th November. In regard to terms, my fee for Scottish engagements is ordinarily thirty-five guineas (£36.15.0). Would it be satisfactory to the Society if I quoted special 'war' terms of thirty guineas? (23 June 19?)

Re-establishing contact after his internment (referred to earlier), the pianist Frederic Lamond wrote:

> You will be pleased to hear that I am in Holland, and that I intend taking up my sojourn in Amsterdam for the next few months. I suppose there is nothing in England of any importance as far as concerts or engagements are concerned? I think I have still an account for a concert in Belfast (Philharmonic Society) in February 1914 to pay? (23 April 1917)

As the end of the war became apparent, Rachmaninov began to re-establish his links with England by contacting Ibbs and Tillett once again:

> I send you a telegram today to which I have to add what follows. I'm playing on the 23rd November for the last time in Norwege [Norway], so that I can leave for England in the morning of the 24th, all depends of the English consulate's permission and my getting a steamer leaving at this time. I ask you to undertake all you can to help me to get the permission in question at the consulate in Copenhagen. I, on the other side, will also try to get it.
>
> Now what concerns the honorary. I have not touched the subject because I believe you see by yourself the necessity of raising it, with regard to the dearth and the most expensive travel. Our conditions remain as they have been, 10% from my honorary, so you see it is also in your interest to raise it. I also meant to say some words about my programme. I am able to play 2 piano concertos (the first in a new edition) and three of other composers, Liszt Es dur [E flat major], Tchaikovsky C moll [C minor, but B♭ minor is meant] and [Anton] Rubinstein D moll. (12 July 1918)

Those foreign artists who had been prevented from appearing in Britain during the war, were finding it by no means straightforward to return with their places now occupied by many new British names. A comparison between Ibbs and Tillett's brochures for 1914–15 (printed before the outbreak of war) and that of 1915–16 (both lists are in Appendix 2) makes interesting reading. The later brochure contains no photographs and its title page ends with a euphemistic phrase not only about those artists from the Empire, America and other allied countries who were unable to reach Britain (such as Rachmaninov), but also musicians from hostile Germany and Austria: 'Messrs. Ibbs & Tillett have not included the names of those artists who, according to present arrangements will not be available for this country next season.' The number of solo singers was cut by about a quarter from 184 to 137, sopranos down from 47 to 32, contraltos from 46 to 34, tenors from 46 to 35 and baritones and basses from 45 to 36. Pianists were drastically reduced by about a half, from 61 to 34, violinists from 48 to 36 and cellists from 34 to 25. String quartets (many of them foreign based) fell from 14 to 6, but the number of British entertainers and reciters remained constant. Among those no longer advertised were the singers Aïno Ackté, Maggie Teyte, Julia Culp and John McCormack. There were particularly heavy losses among the instrumentalists, the pianists Rachmaninov, Scriabin, Rosenthal, Busoni, Lamond, Grainger, Backhaus, von Lengyel, Cortot, Dohnányi, Godowsky, Sauer, Siloti and Bauer, the violinists Nachèz, Feuermann, Kreisler, Enesco, Thibaud, Elman, Marteau and Szigeti, the cellists Casals, Gérardy and Carl Fuchs, who, though resident in Manchester, was visiting his mother in Germany when war broke out, and was forced to see the war out there (with Lamond in the ironically named town of Ruhleben, 'peaceful life').

Meanwhile Ibbs and Tillett continued to audition new voices, though albeit more intermittently than before the outbreak of war. The soprano Lilian Stiles-Allen did so on 26 November 1914. 'Fair [but] short and stout in appearance, very good dramatic voice of extensive compass, round and pure quality. Well taught [by] Edward Iles. Very suitable for opera. Safely recommend her.' She was a newcomer added to the brochure for 1915–16. In her subsequent professional career she dropped her Christian name, and later became another of Vaughan Williams' select soloists for his *Serenade to Music*. Norman Allin auditioned a second time on 18 January 1915 (see Chapter 6), though quite why this was deemed necessary is unclear as he had been a featured artist for over four years. The soprano from George Edwardes' musical comedies, Aileen d'Orme, whose appearance was 'good, petite', was recommended by Henry Wood and sang on 16 March 1915: 'a very good natural voice, full and warm quality. Sings operatic music extremely well.' She was taken on, and so was the Yorkshire singer Etty Ferguson three days later, who had a 'very good, rich contralto voice, sings intelligently with plenty of feeling, quite above the average' and could be 'safely recommended'. Plunket Greene sent one of his students at the Royal College of Music to Queen's Hall on 18 June 1915. She was an 18-year-old soprano on a three-year scholarship from Australia, called Madeline Collins: 'an exceptionally good voice, should take a high position' and sure enough she appeared in the 1919–20 brochure with her studies now completed. Another young singer was heard on the same day, the tenor William Heseltine (of 'boyish' appearance), who was taken on because he was 'an exceedingly artistic singer, his interpretations [of arias from Coleridge-Taylor's *Hiawatha's Wedding Feast* and Handel's *Samson*] being those of a very mature artist. Only 22 and should have a very promising future. Quality of voice on the "biggish" side. His teacher wants us to take him up solely.' Brochures for the three years 1916–19 are missing, but Heseltine's name appears in the one for 1919–20 (see Chapter 11 for his second and successful audition). The soprano Lillie Wormald had been on Ibbs and Tillett's books since 1908. She trained at the Royal Manchester College of Music, and was given her first professional date by Richter in Bach's *B minor Mass* at a Hallé concert in the city on 28 November 1901. Her London debut took place four years later singing a Mozart aria under Frederic Cowen at a Philharmonic Society concert on 29 March 1905, in which she shared the platform with the young Pablo Casals making his British debut in Saint Saëns' first cello concerto. She also sang at Henry Wood's Promenade Concerts, so it's hard to understand why she was auditioned on 28 July 1915 at Bechstein Hall. She 'sang the Bell Song from Delibes' *Lakmé* uncommonly well, and 'Songs my Mother [taught me]' by Dvořák. Very good and experienced singer. Think of her for Chappell's concerts.'

This was a strange observation to make of someone who had been known to the agency for seven years. Her name does not reappear on the books.

Another newcomer taken on was the bass-baritone Topliss Green, who had a heavy, dramatic voice, was tall and of good appearance and whose renditions on 19 October 1915 at Bechstein Hall of Verdi's 'Eri tu' from *Un ballo in maschera* and an aria from Coleridge-Taylor's *Hiawatha* were 'somewhat heavy but a very excellent voice and an interesting singer [who] should be good in oratorio and ballads.' In November 1915 the consequences of war were beginning to show even at the auditions. An applicant with a bizarre impediment for a would-be singer was an amateur Belgian baritone called François Veldeman, who tried his hand with a song by the critic and composer George Clutsam ('Myrrah') and a Belgian song. He had a 'very nice and melodious voice [and] with experience might do well. Belgian soldier (Volunteer Grenadiers) fought at Ypres. Wounded in the throat and unfit for further service'. Then there was the baritone Geoffrey Moody: 'dramatic quality, extensive range with an exceptionally good bass-baritone voice, fine range, sang well with great fervour. But for his deformity he should do well.' His appearance was described as 'tall, gentlemanly but one-armed'.

The year 1916 got off to a promising start with the contralto Jeanne Jouve who had a 'dramatic voice with an unusual compass of three octaves'. Introduced to the agents by Henry Wood, she was 'tall and handsome', sang 'Nobil signor', 'The Lute Player', and arias from *Samson and Delilah* and *Martha*. 'Consider her voice one of the most beautiful ever heard, remarkable nuances and quality for an operatic contralto. Should, with ordinary luck, have a big future.' Despite such effusiveness, her name appears only once, in the brochure for 1920–21. Dorothy Moulton (who three years later became the wife of the man who would make his name as an impresario of children's concerts, Sir Robert Mayer) was taken up on 2 May as she had 'a very good, above average, pure voice, if a little lacking in colour. Can safely recommend her. Ready with oratorio, made a big success in "The Singer". Speak to Mills and Mr Boosey.' On 24 May the agency had a remarkable day, only three singers but two of them would prove their worth in the course of time. The first was the 24-year-old Eva Turner, at the time fresh from her debut as a page in Wagner's *Tannhäuser* with the Carl Rosa Opera Company. Her voice was 'extensive' in range, 'dramatic' in quality, her appearance 'nice', and she was proposed to the agency by her teacher Madame Giglia Levy. She sang 'Ritorna vincitor' (*Aida*) and a song entitled 'A Birthday'. Comments recorded were 'good, dramatic voice, warm quality, vibrant. Sings with much fervour and intelligence. A rounder tone would enhance her singing'. She remained with the Carl Rosa Company until 1924, and her name appears for the first time in Ibbs and Tillett's brochure for the 1923–24 season. The next to audition was a young lyric soprano, Dora Labbette, a pupil of Liza Lehmann, of 'charming appearance', who sang a couple of songs by Sullivan, 'Orpheus with his lute' and, from *The Mikado*, 'The sun whose rays'. 'Excellent voice, a pretty singer [who] would do well in musical comedy and ballad concerts.' Her colleague and fellow pupil of Lehmann, the contralto Dorothy Wren, with whom Labbette had given her one and only recital to-date, had a good voice and style, and proved to be an excellent exponent of ballads, so the usual promise for that type of singer was made, that Ibbs and Tillett would recommend her to William Boosey at Chappell's for their Ballad Concerts. Labbette, on the other hand, went on to the books where she remained for many years (and from 1936 to 1940 as Lisa Perli, the stage name for opera which she took in 1935, and for which she also appears to have been with Harold Holt for that side of her new career).

The violinist Marjorie Gunn joined the agency, having auditioned on 7 June 1916 at the Bechstein Hall with a movement from a Beethoven trio and a Hungarian Dance by Brahms. She proved to be 'an excellent player with good broad tone, phrasing good and gives excellent promise.' At an early recital given soon afterwards at the Wigmore Hall she was 'assisted by Myra Hess', a pianist beginning to make her way as we will see in Chapter 10. The baritone George Parker was accepted on the same day having sung from Massenet's *Hérodiade* and Mendelssohn's *Elijah*. 'His only fault, too conscious of production and a lack of intensity. Above the average.' One of Blanche Marchesi's pupils, Megan Thomas, was 'short and countryfied' in appearance and sang 'Spring's awakening' at the Steinway Hall on 30 June 1916, though it was not until the 1923–24 season that her name was found in the brochures. The delay was no doubt due to her youth, but she had 'a very good voice indeed, sang with great facility but requires more style and repose. An artist of great promise.' Interestingly her second audition was barely five months later (24 November) when, despite the 'very charming and youthful voice' she 'must overcome one great fault, i.e. the lack of engaging her audience, at present she sings in a preoccupied, indifferent manner [and] must sing with more animation, and to her audience'. Norah Scott also joined the agency after her second audition on 29 August 1916; she was a 'pure contralto, excellent voice, much improved since last heard [probably two years earlier on 30 July 1914, but the exact date is not entered]. Remember her for oratorio and Irish concerts' (she lived at the time in Belfast). She is entered in the brochure for 1919–20. So is the bass John Buckley, of 'good but slightly lame appearance', another war casualty perhaps, who sang at Steinway Hall on 11 October 1916. Although Pauline Russell does not seem to have been taken on when she sang on 1 November, the fact that a contralto of 'extensive' compass and 'full dramatic' quality could even be considered ready for the professional concert platform at the age of '16–17 years' is surprising, despite her 'remarkably good voice [which] gives unusual promise for her age. She sang a Russian song by Gretchaninoff and a ballad with plenty of confidence and style'.

There was no shortage of singers introduced to the agency by such eminent musicians as Emma Albani, Sir Henry Wood, Landon Ronald and Roger Quilter. The latter, renowned for his generosity in helping his fellow musicians, sent the soprano Eva Hunsdon Brown to be heard on 24 November 1916, when she was accepted as 'a very good voice, sings with authority, dramatic style and fervour' (one of her audition pieces was 'A Secret', a song by her proposer Quilter). Less fortunate aspirants were described with euphemisms such as 'sings with great power and fervour … but fear she is likely to overtax her powers'; 'rather mature in years to start a professional career'; 'certainly made progress both in voice and natural impediment in speech. Advised him to keep to songs of his own composition, at any rate for the present. His present powers not good enough for other work.' 'Appearance nice and lady-like, voice nothing special, very suited for Bach, can safely recommend her for lesser important engagements.' 'Very good and interesting singer, voice somewhat metallic and shrill in high register like many French artists, but otherwise quite good.' 'Poses as an Egyptian, more like a Turk!' (the description of a dramatic mezzo-contralto from Sydenham in south London). 'Sang "Up from Somerset" – makes a feature of West Country songs.' 'The first aria ['Vesti la giubba'] was too big for his limited powers, voice quite tied up, production very bad and unable to sing with any power without producing faulty intonation, quite second rate and difficult to believe that he has sung leading roles with Moody Manners Opera Company. Must have deteriorated.' A French Vicontesse was 'tall, not young', while a Belgian bass was 'big, stout and middle-aged with bad English' and therefore could not be used for concert work in England.

The year 1917 began with a session on 2 February at the newly-named Wigmore Hall, formerly the Bechstein Hall and re-dedicated on 16 January with a recital by the violinist Albert Sammons accompanied by Vassily Safonov. As mentioned earlier, management of the premises had been taken over by Debenham's the previous year and the name changed to deflect anti-German feeling in the middle of the war. When he wrote 'Bigmore Hall', it was clearly force of habit which explained John Tillett's confusion at the start of his General Remarks about the contralto Maud Murray. She was successful that day and taken on by the agency after a rendition of 'O don fatale' (Verdi) and 'Absence' (Easthope Martin) delivered by 'an excellent voice, extensive range and sung with plenty of fervour', an emotional ingredient increasingly favoured if not expected by Tillett. The auspicious start to the day did not continue for long. The 'contralto?' Margaret Kay (the punctuation actually an exclamation mark converted to a question mark) sang 'Dear heart of mine' and 'Robin Adair', and was considered to have 'a freak voice, at times difficult to believe it is a woman singing'. She was dismissed as 'more suitable for the Music Halls where she is at present booked'. More successful contraltos were Gertrude Higgs, who joined the agency after her audition a week later and revealed 'a voice of light quality, but very good and sympathetic, [a] very good artist', and April Pendarvis with her 'very good voice, charming style', who 'sings most artistically', though she had to wait until the 1920–21 season before her name appeared in the agency's brochure. The unlikely-named tenor Enrico Conforti of Balham had no such luck when he auditioned in April.

On 9 May 1917 Dr (later Sir) Edward Bairstow, for many years organist at York Minster, an influential choral conductor at Leeds and Bradford and a highly esteemed singing teacher, accompanied his protegée, the soprano Elsie Suddaby, at her audition at the Wigmore Hall for Ibbs and Tillett. She sang the aria from Brahms's *Requiem* and a song by Parry. 'Excellent voice, good style, think most highly of her' were among comments reported, and she was to remain an Ibbs and Tillett artist throughout her career. Later in the year (1 June) the violinist Evelyn Cooke had success as 'a most promising artist, fine and virile style, broad tone, splendid technique; think highly of her'. Although the tenor Gwynne Jones, who 'sings artistically and has the usual Welsh fervour, should do well', did not make it on to the books, his compatriot Ivor Thomas, 'youthful and fair' of appearance, did, despite the caveat 'good voice, sings with feeling, artistic, has a tendency to sing out of tune, can recommend him for smaller work'. For the second half of 1917 Robert Leigh Ibbs, together with John Tillett's wife Esta d'Argo, ran the auditions and, at the suggestion of Mignon Nevada (a soprano already with the agency), they took on the soprano Lily (later Luella) Paikin on 12 July, of 'pleasing and red bronze hair!', who 'sang very brilliantly and floridly' despite the voice being 'uneven and forced at times', but she 'should become a brilliant artist later on'. A little later it was the turn of Ida Cooper, a soprano who was to stay on the books until the 1930–31 season, and who possessed an 'exceedingly good voice, dramatic with plenty of temperament and expression'. She came recommended by the concert director and musical agent Ethel Robinson, described in *Who's Who in Music* (1915) as 'the first woman to start a concert agency'. South African born, she had established her business way back in 1896 at 7 Wigmore Street, a thoroughfare in London which, some seven years after she sent Ida Cooper for audition, would see Ibbs and Tillett not only as one of her competitors but also as one of her near neighbours.

Before John Tillett resumed officiating at the auditions in October 1918, there are a few undated but colourful entries by Esta d'Argo and Monica Nixon, the latter, together with William Tilbrook, now joining Robert Leigh Ibbs and John Hudson Tillett as one of the four directors of the agency. A Miss Dudley was a soprano 'of uncertain age, quality poor and rather worn, with a very bad tremolo', while Edith Bryce of Clapham Common (despite an introduction by the eminent Ben Davies) sang only ballads, but of the two she sang only one was identified, the other marked by a space on the page. The reason for this omission is probably best explained by the next comment: 'Has rather difficulty to enunciate owing to protrusion of teeth.' The door was left open, however, with the concluding comment 'needs much more study to broaden the voice and secure more finished interpretation, should be heard again later on'. An 'intelligent and expressive rendering of an aria from Gounod's *Irene* and of "Ashes and Roses"' secured a place on the books for the contralto Margaret Norton in the summer of 1918, and she remained with the agency until 1922. She and fellow contraltos Doris Gardner and Elsie Hulme (who were not taken on) were marked down as 'suitable for the State Café at New Year', while Elsie Chambers, a contralto introduced by the pianist Fanny Davies, was also accepted on to the agency's roster on 23 October 1918 because of her 'exceedingly good voice, big rich quality under splendid control, who could be recommended for any kind of work'. This audition session was the last under wartime conditions, for three weeks later the armistice was declared.

CHAPTER TEN

Agencies and Artists: 1918–23

The First World War was to prove as much of a watershed in British musical affairs as it did in so many other walks of life. Wealth, class, social deprivation, work, entertainment, all of these and much else besides underwent change as a result of those four turbulent years. But briefly returning to the company's first two years (1906–08), Ibbs and Tillett had stiff competition from such firms as Daniel Mayer (established in January 1890 at Chatham House, George St, Hanover Square and manager of Erard's piano showrooms in Great Marlborough Street), H. Bernhardt's Philharmonic Concert Direction (Regent Street), Schultz-Curtius (Regent Street), Leslie Hibberd (17 Hanover Square), Ethel L. Robinson (7 Wigmore Street), Chappell's (50 Bond Street), E.A. Michell with Philip Ashbrooke (7a Piccadilly Mansions), Hugo Görlitz (119 New Bond Street), L.G. Sharpe (established in December 1900 at 61 Regent Street), T. Arthur Russell Concert Direction (established 1905 at 13 Sackville Street), Carl Junkermann (122 Regent Street), Clairfeilds Operatic & Concert Direction (1 Langham Place), Lionel Powell, and William Sewell. The names of Fernando Vert (Narciso's brother) and Pedro Tillett (his nephew) were also present among these competitors for a few more years, the former as a partner in Vert and Sinkins, the latter as head of N.Vert.

According to the Public Record Office (PRO BT 31/11218/85658) the London Concert-Direction was founded on 23 August 1905 by Thomas Martin, publisher, and others with a nominal share capital of £1000 at 1000 shares of £1 each as a limited company, with a full memorandum signed by seven, to carry on the business of a concert agency at premises at 41 and 43 Maddox St, London W. By 13 October 1905, Louis Cowen (gentleman) and Laurence Cowen (journalist) were the two directors though not shareholders, and in the same month the agency changed its name to Concert-Direction Limited. In July 1906 it changed its name to Vert & Sinkins Concert-Direction Limited, appointing Farley Sinkins as its Secretary (his 'connection with the business of concert agency dates back from 1867' according to the *Musical Standard* of 19 May 1906) and Laurence Cowen its Managing Director. By May 1907 its Directors were Farley Sinkins, Fernando Vert (in place of Laurence Cowen) and Laurence Rainbow (in place of Louis Cowen). It claimed sole agency in Britain for the Boston Opera Company, Miss Perceval Allen, Mme Lilian Blauvelt, Mme Donalda, Peter Dawson, Mario Guardabassi, Robert Maitland, Harold Bauer, Pablo Casals, Franz von Vecsey, and the St Petersburg String Quartet. Vert and Sinkins were finally dissolved on 26 July 1912.

Another document, PRO BT 31/13448/112794, traces the course of N. Vert Limited between 1910 and 1912. It was registered on 19 November 1910 'to carry on the business of a Concert, Opera, and Musical Agency' and so on. Subscribers are given as J.E. Stevens, and A. Spratt, both clerks, J.J. Edwards & Co its solicitors. Its nominal capital was £3000, that is, 3000 shares at £1, the registered office continued at 6 Cork St, and the original directors were Mme Eileen Russell (concert agent), Edward Michael (journalist), Pedro Juan Tillett (concert agent) with the later additions of Sir Charles McLaren Bart, and Edward Seymour Odell, gentleman. Share distribution was given as Russell with 2498 shares, Odell 250, and Michael 250. In a long agreement dated 6 December 1910 between Eileen Russell and Pedro Juan Tillett, and N. Vert Limited, 'they shall sell to the company sole and exclusive right to name N. Vert, late N. Vert, etc. and all goods and debts' (all from Pedro Tillett). Tillett was to be managing director for a year, full-time to the company, with remuneration a percentage of profits (essentially 20%). By 6 June 1911 Tillett has resigned as director, the agency's capital has increased to £8000 (Lord Aberconway has the additional £5000), and indeed another list of directors confirms that Tillett resigned on 24 May 1911, followed by McLaren on 5 July and Odell on 21 September, with Montague Chester (gentleman) taking the place of Tillett. The decision to wind up the firm voluntarily was taken at a meeting on 27 November 1912, confirmed on 16 December 1912, and on 10 March 1914 it was indeed wound up.

Nevertheless the name of Vert seems to have survived the war as Vert's Concert Agency rather than the terse N. Vert which had adorned posters for so many years from the last two or three decades of the previous century. One event under the name of Vert took place at the Wigmore Hall, a piano recital by Wladimir Cernikoff, assisted by Madame Lavalle (singer) accompanied by Frederick Kiddle, on 27 June 1918. On 5 July a concert arranged by the soprano by Miriam Licette in aid of Princess Alice's Own Troop of BP Scouts was managed by G.E.W. Robinson, whose address is given as 6 Cork St, WC, for so long the home of Vert's agency. A mention of Vert in connection with the Wigmore Hall occurred when Jessie Snow gave a violin recital on 8 April 1919, accompanied by W.H. Reed, together with Astra Desmond accompanied by Anthony Bernard. The billing refers to Vert's Concert Agency (G.W. Robinson) but the address has changed to 18 Burlington St, London W1. Between June and October 1920, Lionel Powell moved into Vert's premises at 6 Cork Street, and by October 1921 the firm was called Lionel Powell & Holt. Concert agencies were evidently drawn to certain streets in central London when they set up their premises, Regent Street, Wigmore Street and Hanover Square being particularly popular. Although the cellist Pablo Casals became an exclusive artist with Ibbs and Tillett from the 1922–23 season, according to a letter written in the Spring of 1920 to Ibbs from New York (where he had spent most of the war), he was clearly still with the firm of Vert for British work:

> I just received your letter and I am sorry that I cannot give you a definite answer to your proposition, as I intend to give in Barcelona my first series of Symphony Concerts from October to December. Would this plan not realise, I would then be able to accept the tour in England. I am leaving for Spain next May and after a short time of being there I shall be in the position of knowing my possibilities.
>
> Please note that in no case I would entertain the idea of playing trio concerts in England and also that Mr Morgan of the Vert Concert Agency is my representative, and that in case of an agreement you would have to make arrangements with him. It would be my pleasure to see you but I am leaving today. (25 March 1920)

By 1920 H.B. Phillips (Orchard Street, Portman Square) and Milgrom's Concert Direction (324 Regent Street) were competitors, and Ethel Robinson's highly active agency had moved to Empire House at 175 Piccadilly. Ibbs and Tillett's association with the Wigmore Hall began to take off after the war. The first concert they promoted there (it was still called the Bechstein Hall at the time) had been a song recital on Thursday 21 June 1906 at 3pm by Herbert Witherspoon accompanied by Conraad von Bos. The second was a song recital on Monday 2 July at 3pm by Violet Morris assisted by Evelyn Suart, Harold Ketelby (violin) accompanied by Louie Heath. When musical activity was necessarily curtailed during the period of the war, between the autumn of 1914 and the summer of 1919 when performances began to pick up again, Ibbs and Tillett promoted 108 events at the hall, but over the next 15 months, between the autumn of 1919 and the end of 1920, they had 101 promotions there. At the end of the war, the London Chamber Concert Society began its musical activities, initially under Phillip Ashbrooke in 1919, but Ibbs and Tillett ran them for the Spring season of ten concerts (five in the afternoon and five in the evening) between February and April 1920. Audience figures do not appear to have satisfied the Directors, for Daniel Mayer's agency was entrusted with them in 1921, though not before a letter to the subscribers had been written in the autumn of 1920 by the Hon. Secretary, Adrian C. Boult:

> The Management will be obliged if intending Subscribers to the Spring Season will at once notify their names addressed to the Organizing Secretary, LONDON CHAMBER CONCERTS, Wigmore Hall, W1. It is a matter of common knowledge that the number of public concerts now taking place in London amount to something over 40 per week – not to mention the innumerable small societies of private persons, who, while paying no rent for Concert Halls and no fees to the advertising columns of the daily papers – are enabled to set up competition against those who have to do both. Under these circumstances and with continued increase in working expenses on all sides, it is of the highest importance to the Directors of these Concerts that they should ascertain in advance what support they may rely on for the spring of 1921.

Flyers and programmes reverted to the use of colour after the austerity of black and white during the conflict, while some changes began to appear in the nature of the recitals themselves. Those given by one artist were relatively uncommon. Normally a solo artist would be featured, but, as we have already seen, to use the terminology of the day, they were 'assisted by' or even 'kindly assisted by' another performer, either a young up-and-coming player or singer, or perhaps one on the descent. The start of the career of the pianist Myra Hess provides a good example. Aged 16, she had first appeared at the Bechstein Hall on 19 July 1906 in a concert given by the Royal Academy of Music's prize-winning pupils of Tobias Matthay, with another appearance the next year on 11 July 1907. Later that year she made her official London debut, which she had to finance herself in time-honoured fashion, at a cost of £87 plus advertising expenses eased by £80 in receipts. It took place under Lionel Powell's management at Queen's Hall on 14 November with the New Symphony Orchestra under Thomas Beecham and she played the Fourth Concertos of Beethoven and Saint Saëns 'with womanly charm and engaging vivacity' according to the *Musical Times* of December 1907. Two months later, on 5 January 1908, she gave her first solo recital at Aeolian Hall, an expensive undertaking at £33, this time managed by Vert's agency, and returned a month later in one solely (and unusually) devoted to a single composer, Beethoven. The next 12 years were tough ones for Hess, who said 'It took me years before I was established. I had a very slow success, my reputation in England was built by giving a recital every season and it took every penny I could save for it' (*Radio Times*, 3 July 1936). She was taken on by Ibbs and Tillett (her name appears from the 1911–12 brochure), but for much of the war years toured with the London String Quartet or another agency pianist, Irene Scharrer, as piano duettist, and also had a personal success in Holland largely due to the help of Dutch friends to make contact with the conductor Willem Mengelberg at the Concertgebouw Orchestra. Usually once a year during the war, she gave a solo recital at her own expense at the Bechstein/Wigmore Hall for which she entrusted the management to Ethel Robinson's agency. It was only after the war that her career took off in Britain and from 1918 became a sole artist with Ibbs and Tillett. She had finally arrived after 'assisting' at recitals by others, such as the one by violinist Marjorie Gunn mentioned in Chapter 9.

Throughout 1921 (but for a summer break of nearly two months from mid-July to mid-September), Ibbs and Tillett gave a total of 77 concerts at the Wigmore Hall, just one fraction of their work elsewhere in London or nationwide throughout Britain. So in this year alone, when they were rebuilding their concert work after the war, they were averaging a couple of promotions each week at one London venue. Here is the list of the agency's promotions at the venue which, in due course, became almost synonymous with their management:

Ruth Brooke (song recital) ass. Charles Phillips (baritone), acc. W. German Reed
Alfred Barker ('the new English violinist'), Minnie Hamblett (piano), acc. Arnold Perry
Edward Isaacs (piano), Helen Anderton (singer)
Adila Fachiri (formerly d'Aranyi) (violin), Ethel Hobday (piano), Adrian C. Boult (conductor)
Jean Waterston (soprano), acc. G. O'Connor-Morris
Gwendolen Mason (harp) with John Coates (tenor), Charles Woodhouse (violin), Ernest Tomlinson (viola), Robert Murchie (flute), Haydn Draper (clarinet), Herbert Kinsey (violin), John Snowden (cello)
Hilda Blake, Harold Williams (vocal recital), acc. Harold Craxton
Fridtjof Backer Gröndahl (piano)
Margaret Tilly (piano)
Rita Sharpe (cello), John Huntington (singer), acc. Cecil Dixon
Brailowsky (piano), Chopin recital
Margaret Costrello (song recital), acc. Phons Dush
Chilton-Griffin (piano)
Irene Scharrer (piano), Chopin recital
Aida Faviell (vocal recital), acc. Hermann Grunebaum
Winifred Griffin (song recital), ass. Charles Phillips (singer), Dorothy Chalmers (violin), acc. W. German Reed
Gladys Clark (violin), acc. G. O'Connor-Morris
Nancy Morgan (harp), ass. John Coates (tenor), Barclay Mason (piano)
Dora Labbette (and Esther Coleman, Hubert Eisdell, Harold Williams), plus horn, timpani, harp and piano
Lauritz Melchior and Holger Hansen (6 April 1921), acc. Harold Craxton
Muriel Hay (violin), acc. F.B. Kiddle
Reimar De Radum (debut of Danish pianist)
Ernest Groom (baritone), ass. Marjorie Hayward (violin), acc. Ethel Attwood
Gabrielle Methot, ass. Carmen Hill, acc. Nem Cooper
Laurance Turner (violin), ass. Harriet Cohen, acc. Harold Craxton
Frank Laffitte (piano)
Edith Marriott (violin), Jessie Bristol (piano)
Lena Kontorovitch (violin), acc. S. Krish, but Eugene Goossens acc. own violin sonata
Giorgio Corrado (baritone), acc. Harold Craxton
Daisy Kennedy (violin), acc. Ella Ivimey (7 May 1921)

Ida Bellerby (piano)
Nora Delmarr (soprano), acc. F. Kiddle
Blanche Pyman, ass. Charles Phillips, acc. W. German Reed
Egerton Tidmarsh (piano)
Beatrice Bellini (piano)
Marjorie Sotham, Catterall Quartet
Hermann Klein, lecture on the art of Patti
Victor Buesst (piano)
Marcia van Dresser, acc. Daisy Bucktrout
Winifred Jenner (Australian mezzo), ass. York Bowen, acc. Lawrance Collingwood
Harriet Cohen (piano)
George Roth (cello), ass. Dorothy Robson (soprano), acc. Ella Ivimey, Charlton Keith
Reginald Werrenrath (singer)
Daisy Kennedy (violin), Benno Moiseiwitsch (piano)
Rosalie Miller (soprano), acc. Bryson Treharne
Monica Scott (singer), ass. Kathleen Cooper, acc. Ethel Attwood
Bruce Simonds (American pianist), July 1921
Jack Karshinsky (piano), Sept 1921
Desiree MacEwan (piano), music for children young and old
Helene Diedrichs
Moriz Rosenthal: seven recitals between Oct and Dec 1921
Myra Hess (piano), 18 October 1921, Bach, Beethoven and Brahms
Rhoda Backhouse (violin), acc. Harold Craxton
Margaret Fairless (violin)
Kathleen Levi (piano)
Philip Wilson (tenor), Gerald Cooper (harpsichord)
Gwladys Naish (soprano), acc. S. Liddle
Roland Hayes (tenor), acc. Lawrence Brown
Walter Rummel, three piano recitals
Reginald Pickering (tenor), acc. Harold Craxton
Gertrude Hall (piano)
Albert Spalding (violin), acc. André Benoist
Edith Bartlett (singer), ass. Ethel Bartlett
Beatrice Harrison (cello), York Bowen (piano)
Olga Lynn (soprano), Désiré Defauw (violin), George Reeves (piano)
Elvira Belmont (song recital), 15 Dec 1921, ass. Beatrice Eveline (cello), Anthony Bernard (piano)

Beyond the Wigmore Hall, Ibbs and Tillett were just as busy placing their artists in London and the provinces. Myra Hess had made inroads into Holland's musical scene, so too had Elgar as a conductor, thanks to his friend Lalla Vandervelde. The Cello Concerto was very new, having just been premiered at the opening concert of the LSO's first post-war season by Felix Salmond and Elgar. The performance turned out to be rather indifferent on the orchestra's part, not Elgar's fault but that of Albert Coates, about to become the orchestra's principal conductor, who had used too much rehearsal time for Scriabin's *Poème d'extase*. Another disappointment was the half-full house.

As I said over the telephone, I have heard nothing from Amsterdam. Would you write and suggest the programme given on the other side; also recommend from me that Mr Felix Salmond shd. be engaged for the new Concerto. Suggested programme:

Overture *Cockaigne*
Symphonic study *Falstaff*
Concerto Violoncello
Variations for orchestra [*Enigma*] (22 October 1919)

Despite such problems, Elgar remained calm and courteous in his thanks to the LSO's directors, which was an entirely different attitude which another composer, Joseph Holbrooke, took in brief dealings with the agency in 1919 and the following year. Permission to reproduce his two letters and two cards has been withheld, but the gist of his first complaint was that, while Ibbs and Tillett advertised certain composers with their names in large capital letters, he was favoured with only small ones, and why were the texts of his songs not reproduced in the programmes, for if the agency cared nothing for his music, he certainly did. He was just as forthright discussing a performance of his own piano concerto, and wrote indignantly to its proposed soloist Myra Hess, while also berating John Tillett. In generally sarcastic tones he debunked his own music as being hopelessly out of date, not having been played since performances by Harold Bauer a decade earlier, and instead proposed to her that she should play the far more critically favoured music of Bax, Delius or Eugene Goossens. Despite excoriating John Tillett, Myra Hess and the London Symphony Orchestra, all were wished a 'Happy New Year!'

An altogether more amiable and less eccentric composer was the Finn, Selim Palmgren, who wanted to visit England:

At the suggestion of Mr J Chester, 11 Great Marlborough Street, I take the liberty of asking you whether you would be able (interested in) to arrange some concerts for me during next season in England (London and other towns) for myself and my wife, the singer Maikki Järnefelt. Mr Chester, who has published many of my works in England, informs me that my compositions are well known in England. In view of this, I think that a concert tour, mainly a Palmgren programme, would be worthwhile. If you can be interested in this, I shall be much obliged if you can let me know immediately. We travel [from Copenhagen] tomorrow to Finland, our address will be Nådendal, Finland. Finally I beg you to excuse my writing in Swedish, but I am not well acquainted with the English language. (2 July 1919, translation from Swedish)

A batch of letters from the pianist Moriz Rosenthal, anxious to restore his connection with England during the immediate aftermath of the war, gives an insight into the plight of such artists:

I might tell you now how happy I am to know that my friends in England are well and spared from this cruel war. Please tell my kindest regards to Mr Simpson and to Mr and Mme Robin Legge, of course also to Mr [Landon] Ronald, Sir Wood and Miss Irene Scharrer. I wish also to state to you that I always remained a Pole, being born in Lemberg, Poland (my father Leo Rosenthal was a Russian, my mother a Pole, and that I never changed the right of domicile, practically staying for many years in Vienna not as Viennese. This enabled me to get my Polish passport. I send you the photo of it in order you may see with your own eyes that I never was your enemy, even in a political way. Please tell about this to all whom it may concern and show them the passport photo … I know you always thought much of my playing, but I can state truthfully that I made gigantic strides in my art and that I will surprise the public and the critics. I did not write English since five years, so please excuse my fantastic style of writing. (30 October 1919)

I am anxious to have your advice, where I should appear in London after so many years of absence. Would a smaller hall injure my name and standing? You don't even mention the old Steinway Hall, does it not exist anymore? I wonder which hall has the best acoustique. Please write me as soon as possible about halls and dates, and I will answer immediately. I would consider to give two or three recitals in London. I would like you to buy a dozen copies of the *Daily Telegraph* (Monday November 24th 1913). Of course I will arrive in time in England for the concerts. (12 May 1920)

The success in Holland was really titanic! I never in my life read such criticisms about myself or any other instrumental or vocal artist. They wrote it was quite as if Paganini and Liszt had appeared from their graves and everything which one read about their playing was realized in my concert. (9 March 1922)

I am desirous to play at the Symphonic concert Queen's Hall, the concerto in G minor by Saint Saëns, then a) Two Etudes Scriabine b) *Rhapsodie espagnole* Liszt-Rosenthal. I would like very much to perform between the Scriabine and the Liszt piece some composition from the pen of an English author. Could you send me some striking work by Bax or Bliss? Would be very thankful to you.

It is a pity my English concerts should be limited to one single performance. I believe that there are now very hard times, but I cannot help to mention to you that Mr [Lionel] Powell has got for Kreisler quite a rich series of engagements, which hold Kreisler busy in England during a whole month. (25 August 1922)

The matter of foreign musicians working in Britain was still a highly sensitive issue, even three years after the war's end. Hamilton Harty was evidently aware of this when he told John Tillett:

If there is a foreign conductor of any sort available, it is probable that the Liverpool Philharmonic won't want me. However my fee would be 50 guineas for a single concert with a reduction for more than one. You might send me any information regarding the fees of the artists I spoke to you about. (25 February 1921)

The situation concerning music and the welfare of artists in Britain in the immediate post-war period is also illustrated by a letter to Ibbs from the composer and pianist Sergei Prokofiev who wanted to visit:

I beg to acknowledge receipt of your favour of March 24th. I am sorry that your London office did not succeed to reach Albert Coates, as it is with him that I should like to make my first appearance, I am sorry too that the London office could not arrange an appearance with the Philharmony. This two failures make me hesitate about the recitals. I suppose, and are you not supposing it too, that one who begins with a recital is only wasting his time and money.

Hoping to hear from you a kind advise and from your London office any news in addition to the negative ones. (25 March 1920)

But the best description of the austerity of the times (in Britain and in the new Soviet Russia) comes from the agency in response to a desperate letter from the cellist Raymond Bööcke writing from Estonia:

Having read in the *Times* your name as a manager, I apply to you intending going to London as an artist. I am a violoncellist, presently professor at the College of Music in Reval [Estonia], where I came in 1917 from Petrograd, leaving that town because of the Bolshevists and the famine. [From] 1908–17 I was soloist and first violoncellist in the orchestra of the Russian Imperial Court at Petrograd, having given many concerts myself and played as soloist in the symphony concerts in Petrograd, Moscow and other towns. I have taken part in concerts arranged by both Empresses, in the intimate soirées of the late Grand Duke Constantine etc.

My repertoire consists of the concertos by Dvořák, Haydn, Lalo, Davidoff, Saint Saëns, Tchaikovsky's *Rococo* variations, *Variations symphoniques* by Boëllmann, Bach etc. and some scores of smaller pieces. Also I dare say to have a large routine in chamber music, having played with many famous artists as Messrs Arensky, Weingartner, Auer, Siloti, Reisemann, Gabrilowitsch and others.

Having lost my fortune by the Bolshevists and Germans, and considering the bad state of the Estonian value, I can't risk to carry my plan out without any financial security. If it were possible to find a sure and proportionate income as soloist and in taking part in chamber music concerts, I would prefer it a great deal, considering this as my real speciality, If not, I am not unwilling to take for some time a situation in some good symphony (not opera) orchestra, as first or second violoncellist, till I succeed in introducing myself to the London public as a soloist and chamber musician.

I am 48 years old, married without family, born in Estonia, descending from Sweden (no German) till 1917 Russian, now Estonian subject. At the College in Reval I am occupied till the beginning of May, but if it were necessary or of importance to be earlier in London, I could arrange affairs and come. Hoping that perhaps you would make me an acceptable offer, I have the honour to be Sir, (16 February 1921)

The reply from Ibbs and Tillett, dated 25 February 1921, was far from encouraging.

We much regret it is quite impossible for us to further your professional interests in this country, and we would strongly advise you not to think of coming to England at the present time, The conditions in the musical world here have been getting steadily worse for some time, and do not show any signs of improving. Until conditions become more normal, and this cannot be whilst the present state of unemployment and industrial unrest continues, it would be quite hopeless for an unknown artist to make it worth his while coming here.

The only method of making oneself known in this country and thereby securing engagements is to give Recitals in London, and this is an extremely costly matter. Even should the artist make a success at these Recitals, it is often a very long time before he can obtain an adequate result.

The musical profession here is most hopelessly overcrowded, and there are literally hundreds of good artists who are unable to find sufficient engagements to repay them for all their hard work and expense incurred.

We regret having to write in this strain, but we think it only fair to tell you there is little or no chance of your being able to succeed here financially unless at any rate you are prepared to spend a considerable amount of money and wait possibly a very long time before the good result came.

A cellist in an altogether different class, Pablo Casals, had no problems resuming his British career after the war. As has been stated earlier, he was still with Vert's firm in 1920, but from the following year had clearly moved to Ibbs and Tillett, who also represented his former lover and fellow cellist Guilhermina Suggia. Casals was finding another outlet for his musicianship, as a conductor, and the letter quoted on page 107 of 25 March 1920 refers to his own creation, the Orquestra Pau Casals in Barcelona (using the Catalan version of his Christian name), which gave its first concert on 13 October that year. In Britain his conducting debut occurred in December 1925, but meanwhile he was still giving recitals and accepting concerto dates, appearing annually in the country between 1921 and 1930:

I shall be very glad to play for my old friends of the Liverpool Philharmonic Society and the Hallé Society of Manchester next season. The epoch of my concerts in England will depend on the arrangements of my orchestral concerts in Barcelona, you will hear from me as soon as possible. The terms from £100 to £120. (5 March 1921)

I received your letter of April 11th and in reply I beg you to note that the date of December 14th is too late for me, as I intend to sail for America about the 10th of December. The fee of 60 guineas for Rochdale is not convenient, the expenses of commission, accompanist etc makes that fee too small. Please tell me how big is the Wigmore Hall [John Tillett's pencilled annotation 600] and which would be the financial result counting with a full Hall and how much the expenses would be [more pencil figures of £150, £200, £75–80].

I hope something can be arranged with the Classical Concert Society. (20 April 1921)

The Classical Concert Society was founded in 1907 by the wealthy Hertfordshire-based German banker and musical patron Edward Speyer for the performance of chamber music and recitals, and for which Casals first played on 20 October 1909 at the Bechstein Hall in a trio with violinist Marie Soldat and pianist Leonard Borwick.

In answer to your letter of the 8th as well as that of June 22nd, I write to say that I accept the list of concerts you have arranged plus the Hallé Concert in Manchester on November 17th, and the one in Rochdale which I accept exceptionally at 60 guineas, Mr Harty playing for me.

Regarding the Royal Philharmonic Society (December 1st), I have accepted the fee of 50 guineas, explaining that I was making with pleasure this reduction for the benefit of the Society.

The fees offered by the Classical Concert Society are insufficient. I am not disposed to accept less than 100 guineas per concert.

I could not arrive in England for any concert before the 15th Nov, but I could stay over Dec 11th, if you can fill the vacant dates. Please inform me about the numbers I must contribute to the Bristol concert.

Please note that I shall play on the 25th of Nov in Paris, 26th in Brussels, 29th with Mrs Casals [the mezzo soprano Susan Metcalfe] in Paris. (14 July 1921)

I am extremely pleased that the great pianist and my good friend Alexander Siloti will partner me on 7 Dec at the Classical Concert. I shall be happy to play Beethoven's A [major Op.69] sonata with him and the one by Grieg, and I agree to play Bach's solo suite in D minor. (Translation from French)

Bristol, 16 Nov.
I intend to play a sonata with Mr Alfred Cortot and the two groups as follows

1. Suite in C major	Bach
2. Sonata	Sammartini – Salmon[d]
Romanze	Friskin
Fileuse (from Pelléas et Mélisande)	Fauré
Allegro appassionato	Saint Saëns

For the second group I hope to have a local accompanist, have you thought of that?

Liverpool 15 Nov.
I propose Haydn's concerto and as solos

Romanze	Friskin
Fileuse (from Pelléas et Mélisande)	Fauré
Allegro appassionato	Saint Saëns

Manchester 17 Nov.

Concerto	Schumann
Solo: Sonata	Sammartini – Salmon[d]

Bradford 18 Nov. Is this a sonata recital with Mr Pouishnoff? I await details.
Queen's Hall Simph. 19 Nov. intend Concerto Haydn; Suite C Bach
Glascow [*sic*] 22 Nov. programme as Liverpool
Rochdale. Chamber music 23 Nov. I would like to decide the programme with Mr Harty. Please ask him to contact me and also to tell me if this is a question of a chamber music concert.
Royal Phil Society 1st Dec. Concerto Schumann; Sonata Sammartini – Salmon[d]

I hope the gap between the 1st and 7th Dec will be filled with other concerts, this is a condition for my accepting the date for the 7th Dec. (2 August 1921)

A batch of letters from Busoni survives from this period. Like pianists Rosenthal, Lamond, Rachmaninov and others outside Britain at the outbreak of war, he was now re-establishing his links with the country. Two years later, however, a downturn in the economic situation was barely capable of sustaining Busoni's fees, and he was in danger of pricing himself out of the market.

About the piano. Steinway has no good instruments outside London. Bechstein is excluded. Erard could only send one for London and not further. So I am contemplating the idea of playing Chappell. If Messrs Chappell were inclined to agree I should expect from them a very generous offer. I hope you will be of the same opinion and [will] please try to arrange. Very busy! Excuse the abrupt shortness. (24 January 1921)

I am afraid I need money again. In fact I am not only afraid, but positively sure about it. Will you help me? Many thanks in advance. (8 February 1921)

Thank you, dear Mr Tillett, for all your kind trouble. The principal answers to your questions are written down in the sheets. There is a project to give a Recital on two pianos with [Egon] Petri, and with chiefly my own things. I would like to use one of the Recital dates for this purpose. Chappell is welcome if he is as good as the last time. But you make a little contract with him to my advantage, if you please. (22 December 1921)

Please help me out of that inconvenience. As much as I remember this is not yet the date contracted for the repetition of the attractive experiment. Moreover I am very busy with my programmes. And I need cash! Please let me know. (received 31 January 1922)

I received the 25 pounds and I thank you for your kindness. Now please do not "over-read" the following. Of course if the grammophon people insist on repeating the records, I will have to do it sometime. But. The one time I did the thing first, I tried my very best; played some of the pieces four times; of some we made two records, on my own suggestion, and altogether I worked with the best conscience and interest. I do not see the probability that the records should improve by repeating; the new ones may prove just as little "satisfactory" as the original ones. And then? Had we to begin over again a third time?

The conditions are most unfavourable. The room, the piano, the chair not inviting, I have to start like a racehorse and to end before four minutes have elapsed. I have to manage the touch and the pedal differently from how I do it usually. What in Heaven's name can be the result of it? Not my own playing, take it for granted! Please consider the objections seriously and put them before Mr Brooks (I think this is the name of the "recording Manager") It is a good rule of the Englishman "not to make a fool of himself". I assure you that we "continentals" have not less our pride and dignity, although we are considered to be only "paid artists". But I hope you think better of me. (1 February 1922)

I am so sorry to worry you again but really I do not feel like playing for Mr Brooks on Monday. I am tired and not well since ten days or more. The new records, under these circumstances, would be a failure again! I have not counted on the possibility of playing for the Columbia when I came to England this time, as I know that April was the date fixed on the paper for that ordeal. The list of pieces (which Mr Brooks insists on having repeated literally) is not ready in my mind and in my hands, and I do not have even the music here to recollect them. I wished Mr Brooks would show you that paper; not because I do not trust him, but in view of the human possibility of a mistake of memory on his side or on mine. (c.10 February 1922)

I wish you would read my letters. In the preceding one I took the liberty of writing to you that I felt

– tired
– ill
– unprepared!
– and was deprived of music for the records.
– That under these circumstances the records would surely prove a repeated failure.

Certainly I could not do anything this Monday. Meanwhile have the kindness of communicating with Mr Brooks and let me know the result of your communication (based on my objections). If I had not the conscience of having tried my best the first time (with no success), I should not feel so hopeless now. (19 February 1922)

I am very glad to be in possession of your kind letter, dated a fortnight ago, and not less glad, indeed (thanks to your efforts) to have a new opportunity of seeing London once more, to visit England again (I read the "Nation" regularly and occasionally the "Manchester Guardian") so that I am able to keep in contact with your country. I am an ignoramus of the worst water and sorry to confess that I never heard before of the town of Rochdale. But I am richly compensated by knowing Bradford in a certain extent. I wonder, which may have been the reason for the "engagement not materialised" in this city, where I was gracefully invited to return … I think now that I will play the last of Mozart's C major concertos [No.25 K503] and the C minor concerto [No.4] by Saint Saëns (both are new for me) but really I do not know which will be my mood half a year later!

I am sorry to say that I was obliged to make arrangements with the Parisian Erard in regard of the instrument. The last Chappell series was not to my satisfaction – As Erard does not "pay", you see that the question is simply an artistic one. I said once: A chapel is not a cathedral (although it may be a worthy construction). I send you programmes later but not too late. (26 July 1922)

I enclose a certificate from my doctor and its translation into English. I feel strongly inclined to fulfill my engagements, but I could not (at present) promise anything definitively. I hope the situation will be cleared before Christmas, when I will be able to give you positive news. Can you wait so long? Probabilities are hopeful. I am sorry to give you so much trouble, but I had a very hard time and am only slowly improving. (27 November 1922)

Ibbs and Tillett's translation of a medical certificate issued by Dr Joseph Cohn of Berlin:

Prof. Ferruccio Busoni has been ill during the months October and November 1922. He was subjected to attack and it took a long time before Busoni could be considered to be in a normal condition again. The next two months (December and January) ought to be spent in complete repose, and the following February and March will still require a great care and economy of efforts. It is indeed necessary that Prof. Busoni should spend this time in the most possible tranquillity. (27 November 1922)

I received your telegram and today I spoke to my doctor. He allows me to begin again public activity with April, and hardly before this time. Consider that I have not been playing (at home) for the last six months! I would not feel comfortable before a London audience, and not prepared and "trained" as the opportunity requires. I am still very weak and not yet fit to perform an extensive Recital programme. I should like to come to London afterwards, perhaps during the Season and to keep my engagements as far as it is possible. What shall we do? Please tell your opinion and try the best. (4 January 1923)

First of all I have to thank you. During that fatal period of illness you have been so very patient and kind, that I highly appreciate your (and Mr R[obert] Newman's) tact and goodness. Yesterday my doctor definitively thought of the possibility of my playing in London on April 28th; he even advises me to do it, and I follow his opinion of conviction. I accept the date and hope fervently that no new obstacle may hinder my intention from being realised. I propose the Piano Concerto in C major by Mozart, which is again a "novelty", I mean the last big one, Koechel 503. And with it my own cadenzas. I will not be able to give recitals, although I regret it. Neither will I be able to finish the Grammophon Records. I beg you to explain the situation to the Grammophon Co. Arrangements on an exclusive scale have been made with Messrs Steinway & Sons, of which I relate to you personally. I am longing to see London again, to live my habitual life. I hope you have transferred to Messrs Chappell my reasons, my regretting and my thanks. For now almost half a century (it sounds!) I am used to continental pianos, all my labour and study have been done on the Steinway, I feel like returning home indeed. And you must understand. (14 February 1923)

Deeply regretting the adversity I am forced to announce you, that (after quite a series of "relapses") the doctor pronounces himself against any travelling in this Spring. Since weeks I have not left the house, every slightest irregularity throws me back again. Our hope is the coming better season, sun and warmth. Under the present circumstances I could impossibly affront the manyfold incidents of a voyage. Please tell this to Mr Newman, to whom I heartily apologise. For the instant I must refuse Mr Brooks' offer. The proposed fee is not satisfactory anyhow. The conditions were in the first case £1000 for 12 records. The desire of renewing the "operations" made me rather expect an increasing of the terms, instead of a reduction of price. I am awaiting Messrs Steinway's contract and hope in many possibilities for the next fall. (17 March 1923)

To make clear the situation to you, as I feel my duty to do, I beg to read these lines. Messrs Steinway & Sons proposed to me a very fair arrangement and expressed at the same time their intention of taking all my business into their hands. I accepted (in principle) the first but objected to the latter, insisting on the point that I could not (nor would) renounce to the enjoying of your kind help and ability in managing my affairs. You are acquainted with my tastes and wishes, I trust you entirely, and I know happily of your friendship to my benefit.

So I told Messrs Steinway (who mean extremely well and show themselves ready to please me in every direction) that I could not find any reason of leaving you abruptly; that your greater experience of my habits and of the habits of English musical societies would only be of help to them and make their task easier. Thus matters stand at present, and I hope for all parts that Mr Trautwetter (to whom this letter is trusted) will succeed in coming to a plain understanding with you, the sooner the better. I agree with you that we may keep our old February dates for England, and I should prefer not to give recitals in general, at least not in the provinces.

More definite arrangements will depend of course on my future state of health, which is slowly but steadily improving, to which improvement the better season (as you sagely remark) will add its beneficial effect. So we hope. Since two months I began again to work. My spirits are in good order, but my body is still weak. Let me hear of you and of the results of the conference which, as it is to expect, will prove more satisfactory than so many previous conferences in the political field. (5 April 1923)

The Steinway affair has been a great disappointment. So we will have to do nothing with these gentlemen. Such a long time you have not written! Did you give me up entirely? Have you anything to propose to me for the coming season, then please let me hear your news. I am longing to be in London again. I have been a "prisoner" for more than one year. Here they are navigating in black waters, everything declining and miserable. It was a hard time, through which I have gone. Now I begin to look forward with more confidence. I hope you are well and still a good friend. (14 August 1923)

I have here your letters and the contracts with me. I am really sorry to hear that the societies have lost their faith and consider my engagement as a risky enterprise. Don't you think that it is always uncertain when you engage an artist for the year afterwards? Everything may happen between on both sides! As it is I beg you to try once more. Two dates are indeed a modest invitation in comparison of the long voyage and my good name. Please address to Paris XXI, 48, rue de Villejust, c/o M. Tauber. (24 September 1923)

Henry Wood continued to use Ibbs and Tillett artists, often reporting back to the management after a concert, and, in time-honoured fashion, frequently sent or recommended potential talent for audition.

Thanks for your letter concerning Mr [Moriz] Rosenthal's appearance with me at the next Brand Lane Concert in Manchester. Please give him my kindest regards and tell him how sorry I am that I am not able to fall in with his wishes to play two concertos, Chopin E minor and Liszt E flat, but with a longish orchestral programme and only two hours Band rehearsal, it is quite impossible for me to rehearse two concertos, so please ask him to play either the Chopin E minor or the Liszt E flat (the public here would much prefer the Liszt) and a nice group of solos, in order to give me a little rest as it is such a fatigue day for me and I must travel back to London all night to be in time for my two Sunday Concerts at Queen's Hall. (19 October 1921)

I understand that Mr Rosenthal will play the *Emperor* Concerto of Beethoven on Saturday, and not the Chopin, and shall take the Band parts to Manchester on the 6.25 from St Pancras on Friday afternoon. If Mr Rosenthal comes straight to the Free Trade Hall from the train arr. Manchester 2.25, it will be all right for Band rehearsal. (24 November 1921)

I was delighted with Miss Molly O'Callaghan, beautiful voice, refined and smooth vocal style, and should certainly make a great success in the Oratorio world. Do ask her to study Bach's *B minor Mass* (B & H edition), *Matthew Passion* and the *Apostles*, and I will certainly see what I can do for her next season. I have already written off to Birmingham about her, and I can't see why Brand Lane can't find a place for her in one of his Choral Concerts when an "All Star" cast is singing.

When you have a few spare moments could you possibly hear a tenor who sang for me at Queen's Hall the other day: Mr Karolek, 8 Leicester Sq. He can bring his own accompanist, Mr Brezinsky, who always plays for him. He has just come from Milan, where he has been two years. I found him a most intelligent singer and an excellent all-round artiste. How beautifully Madame Suggia played last Monday, and what a good ensemble. (22 February 1922)

I will call and see you early next week as I must give you a verbal account of M. Chambys of Nice, as in the whole course of my experience I have never met such a mis-managed concert. (8 May 1927)

CHAPTER ELEVEN

Artists and Auditionees: 1920–29

A comparison of Ibbs and Tillett's brochures available to promoters in the ten years 1911–20 (listed in Appendix 2) makes interesting reading (see the table below). Singers constitute the greatest number, and of the four voice types there is always an even distribution of sopranos, altos, tenors and basses, while among the instrumentalists, pianists prevail over string players. Numbers peak at the start of the First World War, dip noticeably during the course of the war, and rise markedly with the return of peace. The post-war brochure includes four violists for the first time, and a sharp increase in the combined numbers of entertainers (33) and entertainers with piano (30).

	Singers	Pianists	Violinists	Cellists	String quartets	Reciters	Entertainers
1911–12	174	52	46	26	15	–	–
1914–15	184	61	48	34	14	22	46
1915–16	137	34	36	25	14	22	46
1919–20	207	53	40	29	10	27	63

Rispah Goodacre auditioned on 26 March 1919 and impressed with her 'exceptionally fine contralto voice with full mezzo range. Think highly of her, promised to bring her name forward to Chappell, Boosey, Mills.' Her voice had 'wide compass, dramatic and full quality', her appearance 'short [but] good'. She had been recommended to Tillett by Harry Dearth, a baritone already on the roster. Curiously she auditioned again, on 20 February 1924, despite being on the agency's list for the whole 1920s decade. There appeared to be little reason to hear her again, hers was still 'an exceptionally good voice, fine full chest notes and head register, sings with great fervour and may safely recommend her'. Alfred O'Shea was a tenor accepted a month later (16 April 1919) thanks to 'an exceptionally fine voice of the McCormack order, sings most artistically with much fervour, his Italian rendering quite good. Should do well, only apparent faults [are] huskiness and a tendency to open too much'. Another successful tenor was William Heseltine (30 April), 'just returned from active service. Ready with all oratorios, extensive compass and dramatic quality. Made great progress since last audition, should do very well. Voice full and robust, reminds me of Ben Davies at times. Style resembles John Coates. A serious artist.' Nearly four years had elapsed since Heseltine had been heard during the war, on 8 June 1915 (see Chapter 9).

The numbers of auditions then seems to have been considerably reduced by the agency, with Sylvienne d'Albert taken on when she was heard on 14 July 1920. She was a Czech soprano, and, according to the audition book, the daughter-in-law of the composer but it gave no address. She was extremely versatile, with facility in dramatic, lyric and coloratura styles, sang Gounod, Verdi and Mascagni at the Aeolian Hall and revealed 'a most excellent voice, brilliant, dramatic, even throughout register, vivacious. Should have a very good career in opera or concert.' Despite making such a good impression her stay on the books was a brief one, just the 1921–22 season. She had a second audition on 22 October 1921 (an address at Westcliffe-on-Sea in Essex now given). This time she was 'prepared to go into good light opera, and would use the name of Sylvienne Wessely. Excellent voice, improved considerably, animated style, safely recommend her, speak to Percy Pitt, Robert Evett, de Groot, van Noorden', but despite this accolade she was not put on the roster. A week after d'Albert's first audition, on 21 July, Ibbs and Tillett heard the Danish tenor Lauritz Melchior, a singer who had begun his career at the Royal Opera, Copenhagen in 1913 when he was a baritone. In 1918 he made a second debut at the same opera house, this time as a tenor in the title role of Wagner's opera *Tannhäuser*. At the time of his audition with Ibbs and Tillett he was studying the Wagnerian repertoire and went on to appear at Covent Garden on 14 May 1924 as Siegmund in *Die Walküre*. He was represented by Ibbs and Tillett from the 1921–22 until the 1925–26 seasons. His audition report includes the following comments: 'Tenor of extensive compass, robust, operatic quality, tall, imposing for opera. Sang Lohengrin's Narration and Canio's Song (*Pagliacci*) both in Danish. Fine, robust voice, baritone in quality, eminently suited for Wagnerian opera and other dramatic roles.' As listed in Chapter 10, Melchior made an appearance with Holger Hansen in a joint recital accompanied by Harold Craxton at the Wigmore Hall on 6 April 1921 organized by Ibbs and Tillett at the singer's suggestion made the previous autumn.

> As reply your kind letter from 30 October, can I tell you that I am coming to London again from 1 March 1921 and stay for a long time (I am free from my theatre some years), so if you can secure some engagements for me, I shall be glad. If you can arrange the concerts in the Liverpool Philharmonic Society the 1st and 15th March not less than 50 guineas per concert including your commission. (8 November 1920)

Evidently matters went awry when a tour in 1923 to be organized by the impresario Max Mossel had to be cancelled and it was left to Monica Nixon at Ibbs and Tillett, caught in the middle, to pour oil on troubled waters and mollify an irate Melchior. His English (and its spelling) was an immediate victim, and has been left alone, though its meaning remains crystal clear …

> It was a great blow to me to receave your letter telling me that the tour I was engaged for with Mr Mossel is of. I have had much trubbel prosponing my orchestral concert in Berlin with Leo Blech and Blütner Orkester and then suddenly I am standing absolutely without anything to do, please don't tell me that an engagement is in order when it is not so. I think you must do your utmost best to get me something in sted of this, as I have lost a lot of monney and time over it. It is impossible for me to take the engagement to Dublin the 13th of August as you know I am first ariving in England in time for my Douglas concert. Pleace do try to get a concert for me with Rock or somebody else in Dublin in the time I am to your disposal. Tell also Chappells that I am staying on until the end of October. They may want me for one or two Ballad Concerts. I return the contract for the Dublin Concert and hope to get a letter soon from you with something I am able to take. I am working hard for the festivals [Bayreuth] here next year, where I am going to sing *Parsifal* and *Walküre*. (20 July 1923)

From New York there survives one further letter to Monica Nixon written some four years later, by which time the now even busier and more successful Melchior's fee has more than doubled its rate of 1920:

> I have received your kind letter and shall herewith answer it. First of all I am coming to London in the beginning of May and staying until the beginning of June, after that I am going to Denmark and

> from the 15th of June until the end of August I am singing at the 50 years anniversary festivals in Bayreuth. I shall sing five performances in Covent Garden being two *Parsifals*, two *Walküre* and one *Siegfried*, perhaps you can find out the dates of this and then use me for some concerts. I should not mind in the least, but one thing I tell you and that is that my fee as a minimum is £100 and in ordinary cases £150 to £200. (6 March 1927)

> I enclose some clippings [not extant] from my last concert tour, and if you pleace would look up the musical courear from January the 13th, you would find some more. I am after my singing in Bayreuth, staying in Europe for the month September, October, November and December; the first of January 1928 must I again be in New York. I shall have so much work I can overcome abroad singing at the operas and also having a lot of concert work. I should like to make a concert tour in England, Irland and Scotland, if you can bring one together and the pay is deasent. In other cases I shall stay abroad, it is too expensive to go to England without having a known income. Things has gon well for me in this country and my concerts was great successes, so that my booking for the next season is a great success, after the reports from my manager. If you want to have anything in the line of advertising stuf, or know about having me for a tour in England this winther, then write to my privat secretary, he knows about my concert and opera work in Germany and elswere in Europe. I myself shal stay under this adress until the 18th of August, when I leave for Denmark with a Danish boat from her. Hoping to have a word from you and with kind regards for everyboddy and loking forward to seeing you again soon. (6 March 1927)

Casualties among festivals due to the war had included the Three Choirs Festival and most of the larger scale and costlier events, but they were only in abeyance and began to be revived when hostilities ceased. Choral singing had by no means ceased during the war though some changes were implemented, such as afternoon rather than evening performances (for example, some by the Royal Choral Society). Enterprise was by no means at a standstill. New music continued to be heard, such as that by Debussy, Ravel and Stravinsky, not to mention a myriad of new British works by the likes of Bax, Delius, Ireland, Bridge and Bliss. So the shutters did not come down on music in Britain, thanks to such organizations as the Committee of Music in War-time, Broadwood's Camp Concerts, Isidore de Lara's innovative concerts featuring British composers, Thomas Dunhill's Chamber Concerts, and the continuing activities of the Royal Philharmonic Society and Sir Henry Wood's Promenade Concerts in London, Beecham's domination of the Hallé programmes in Manchester, and Dan Godfrey's continuing work at Bournemouth. Only Covent Garden succumbed and remained closed from the summer of 1914 until May 1919, but even here Beecham admirably filled the operatic void at other London venues such as Drury Lane.

Some of the stars of the pre-war years were beginning to wane; signs of this can be discerned in Ibbs and Tillett's brochures. An obvious casualty was the husband and wife partnership of Clara Butt and Kennerley Rumford who were no longer afforded sole representation, and their names disappeared altogether with the 1923–24 brochure. They spent most of the 1920s touring America and Canada, and returned to Australia and New Zealand but this time without Leigh Ibbs who had been with them 20 years before. Who was on the way up and who on the way down the career ladder was also reflected in the order in which artists names appeared, and as they were never alphabetically listed it must be assumed that there was an implied ranking here. Pianists Myra Hess, Benno Moiseiwitsch, Irene Scharrer and William Murdoch joined Rachmaninov and Rosenthal for sole representation in 1920, violinists treated in like manner were all female – Daisy Kennedy, Margaret Fairless and Sybil Eaton – the cellist Josef Hollman was still with the agency but now joined by Felix Salmond and Guilhermina Suggia with sole representation. Among the singers, and still comparing mid-war with immediate post-war times, Alice Wilna, Louise Dale and Laura Evans-Williams (all sopranos) were replaced by Madeline Collins, Donalda, Zoia Rosowsky and Dora Labbette, while the contralto Phyllis Lett was replaced by Astra Desmond and Margaret Balfour. New tenors were Frank Mullings, Arthur Jordan, Mischa-Léon and Webster Millar, while added basses and baritones were Herbert Heyner, Norman Allin and Thorpe Bates.

A curious entry at the end of 1920, in the second of the agency's three extant audition books, is that of a Belgian called Ysaÿe. With the absence of any forename, it can only be speculated whether this might have been Gabriel, one of the three sons of the Belgian virtuoso violinist Eugene Ysaÿe, whose own career was now coming to its end. If it was his son, his style, technique and appearance were 'good' at his audition on 6 October 1920 at which he played a Paganini minuet and two movements from Mendelssohn's Violin Concerto. His playing had 'good tone' and he was deemed to be a 'sympathetic player', who could be 'safely recommended for smaller work'. Lionel Powell had always been the agent for his famous father for work in Britain, however Ysaÿe junior did not make it on to Ibbs and Tillett's roster. The composer Granville Bantock strongly recommended the contralto Denne Parker to Ibbs and Tillett, but she does not appear to have been heard, despite the glowing reference he provided. But she was taken on a few years later and remained on the books from 1926–31, during which time she also created the role of the title role of Bantock's opera *The Sealwoman*. According to *Who's Who in Music* (1949–50) she had by that time become music mistress at St Edward's School, Birmingham, and reading between the lines of Bantock's daughter's biography of her father, was his mistress for a short while in an intense relationship which inspired him to compose during the 1920s:

> There should be no need for me to offer Miss Denne Parker any personal introduction to you. I am however glad to have this opportunity of stating that she created the part of the Shulamite in my new work *The Song of Songs*, of which I conducted the first performance on the 6th inst. at the Gloucester Festival, and that she more than fulfilled my high expectations. She is a singer of real power and temperament – a fine artist – and in the opinion of her many friends will win success and high rank in the musical world. She is likely to be in much demand for future concert and festival work. I shall consider myself fortunate if I can secure Miss Parker's help for any future performances of my works. (8 September 1922)

A singer needing no introduction was John McCormack, who wrote in his usual cheerful Irish way:

> Thank you for your letter. I have written to Mr Harty explaining that for the moment I cannot say if I will be in England in November, and have cabled to America for a postponement of my tour there, and if I am granted the postponement I would be glad to sing with my old friend at the ridiculous fee of 100 guineas in compliment to him. I do hope I will be able to sing with Harty and shall try to do something interesting with him. (5 June 1922)

A couple of notes from Vaughan Williams survive from the 1920s concerning engagements in Kent. In the course of one year he seems to have re-assessed his monetary worth by doubling his fee:

> In reply to your letter of June 15th I shall be happy to conduct one of my works at Margate September next. My fee wd be £5-5-0 and expenses. (30 June 1922)

> With reference to your letter of the 17th, I should not be prepared to conduct a whole concert at Margate. But if the management cared to invite me to conduct one or two of my own compositions

as part of a concert (as I did last year), I should be happy to accept. My fee for this wd be £10.10.0. I am free on September 21st. (23 July 1923)

Another composer (but also a fine pianist) to write to the agency was the Hungarian Ernst von Dohnányi, who had a request to be passed on to Sir Henry Wood:

> Will you kindly inform Sir Henry Wood that I have a newer composition for piano and orchestra entitled *Variations on a Nursery Song* for orchestra with pianoforte obbligato Op.25, which I would prefer to play instead of my concerto in E minor, which is composed now more than twenty years ago. As this work is more an effective orchestra piece than a piano concerto and lasts only 18–20 minutes, in the case Sir Henry agrees to it. I would only play besides another classical concerto, a shorter one for instance Beethoven No.3 or 2, or Schumann, or Liszt E flat, or Mozart G major. Let me know whether this is agreeable to Sir Henry Wood. If not I am willing to play my old concerto too. The variations are a very effective and humorous piece and a novelty too. I am awaiting your reply on my last letter concerning other engagements etc. (7 September 1922)

Dohnányi's request was granted, and Wood duly programmed its first British performance at a Queen's Hall concert on 27 January 1923 with the composer as soloist. The conductor Eugene Goossens was making his mark in Britain after the war, particularly with the first British performance in the concert hall of Stravinsky's controversial ballet music *Sacre du printemps* on 12 December 1921 with his own hand-picked orchestra. He made some trenchant observations of the British and European musical scene to John Tillett:

> Many thanks for your letter re Antwerp. I am glad to have the prospect of conducting there next January, and much appreciate your action in suggesting my name to their committee. I think that Monday 8th of January would suit me quite well for the date of the concert (with rehearsal the previous Sunday). As regards fee, I am a little uncertain as to what they are prepared to pay, but feel that something in the neighbourhood of £400 (minimum) can hardly be called excessive. This works out (at the present rate of exchange) at about 2000 francs; expenses are naturally a fairly heavy item in a trip of this nature and for that reason I don't think the fee excessive. Knowing however that the state of music in Belgium is none too flourishing, I have quoted this figure, but if you think I ought to ask more then by all means go ahead as it's to our mutual benefit to get all we can. I leave the matter in your hands.
>
> By the way, is there any possibility of combining this concert with a few concerts in surrounding cities? I don't think that a concert in Brussels would be very hard to arrange about the same time (particularly as I am well known there through the "Chester" branch as a composer and conductor). There are also Liège and Ghent as very strong musical centres, and there have been several rumours of late that I was to be invited over there, particularly to conduct a Brussels concert. I don't know how far you can probe this matter, but it would certainly be very well worth while to try and arrange (particularly if we could do the trip together!) Paris, I know, is hopeless at the moment, but I'm seriously considering the advisability of giving a couple of concerts in Berlin round about that time (it's the city that really matters, much more so than Vienna at the moment) and even if we gave the concerts ourselves (I should say myself!) it would, at the rate of exchange, not be a very costly item (that is of course if I couldn't get a guest performance). The Berlin trip could follow up the Belgian one. Anyway, let me know what you feel about the matter, perhaps you could get in touch with Berlin right away and find out a few details. As regards the programme for the Antwerp concert, is there any hurry for it and if so, do you know anything about the soloists?
>
> I shall be sending you a cheque shortly in payment of the balance of £130 odd which I owe you over the recent concerts. You might inform Ibbs of this. It's good of you to be so patient, I've had a hell of a time getting the necessary money together. *Entre nous*, there's a scheme afoot for further concerts, this time amply covered by funds, but as yet I've had no definite information. If it matures it'll be a very big thing indeed, no less than a permanent series with my own orchestra (which of course I'd ask you to take charge of as before) and will probably 'put the wind up' musical London. However, *nous verrons*! I'm getting over the 'flu gradually, and am shortly contemplating a mountaineering expedition in the neighbourhood of Snowdon! (6 March 1922)

Two other composers had contact with Ibbs and Tillett during 1923, Gustav Holst and Igor Stravinsky. Surviving communications from Holst consist of a short undated note, which we can assume were written about this time for two reasons. Both sopranos he refers to were currently on the agency's books and his so-called violin songs were already written in 1916–17. It reads:

> I thank you very heartily for consulting me on who should sing my songs. Personally I prefer Dorothy Silk to anyone else. Also Megan Foster sings my violin songs very well indeed. (4 May?)

The other letter concerns a conducting engagement proposed by the agency:

> I have been away from home and regret the delay in answering your letter. I shall be delighted to conduct at the Winter Gardens, Margate, for a fee of ten guineas and first class return fare. With regard to the works to be done, my new Fugal Overture and Fugal Concerto have been put down for first public performance at the Promenade Concerts, Queen's Hall, on October 11th. I suggest that *The Planets* had better not be done unless the orchestra is a big one. On hearing from Mr Saxby I will make some suggestions and should be glad if he would send me a list of the orchestra. (9 July 1923)

The sole surviving communication from Stravinsky also combines his activities as a composer with that of conductor.

> In reply to your letter of 26 January. I would like to come and conduct a concert of my works at the beginning of January 1924 (Saturday 5th, Monday 7th January) on the following conditions.
>
> 1) The programme will consist of the *Firebird* Suite, *Feu d'artifice*, the prelude to the opera *Le Rossignol* with the soprano aria (Rossignol), and the *Pulcinella* Suite to conclude the programme.
> 2) Two preparatory rehearsals will take place before my arrival so that I need only concern myself with the interpretation of these works, for which I would ask a minimum of two rehearsals.
> 3) For the soprano aria in the prelude to *Rossignol* I ask you to engage Madame Vera Janocopulos, an excellent interpreter of my vocal music, already well known to the Belgian public. She would sing some of my songs in the concert, either with orchestral or piano accompaniment, which I would gladly play.
> 4) The Committee would bear the cost of the orchestral material.
> 5) I would ask a fee of seventy pounds for this concert.
>
> Awaiting your favourable reply I ask you, dear Sirs, to accept my sincere greetings. (26 February 1923, translation from French)

The emergence of Myra Hess has already been described, from her first appearance at a Matthay pupils' concert in 1906, through the difficult years of the war, when she had to finance an annual concert at the Wigmore Hall to keep her name before the public, and her country-wide tours with other artists. By the 1920s she was much more established, and after having had her affairs run by several agents, put her career into the hands of Ibbs and Tillett for the rest of her performing life. There were a few artists who were special to the agency, and whose relationships went beyond the boundary of a business relationship to become personal and intimate. Myra Hess was one of them. Apart from Anita Davis Chase, who handled concerts in Boston alone, her American manager was Annie Friedberg (generally referred to as 'Miss F' in Hess' letters to Tillett). She was a forcefully volatile character, but nevertheless competent and tireless on Hess' behalf, and she took 20 per cent commission for her trouble. She could not understand why Hess did not continue to visit America when the Second World War broke out, nor the enormous value in morale to the British public of the wartime National Gallery Concerts which Hess gave instead, and there was considerable friction overshadowing their relationship from her return there in 1946 until Friedberg's death in 1953. Of letters from Hess to Ibbs and Tillett written in the 1920s, many come from her second tour to America in 1923. Her debut there had occurred a year earlier, on 17 January 1922 at the Aeolian Hall, New York after a so-called Intimate Recital, a warm-up, non-reviewed event for invited guests only, at Steinway Hall on 12 January. Only the first of her letters, all of which may be found in Appendix 15, is addressed 'My dear Mr Tillett'; thereafter, and until his death, the greeting became the more familiar 'Dear John'. Hess treated Tillett in a familiar, almost matey fashion, quite unlike anyone else who wrote to him, and was always reproaching him for overworking. A quarter of a century later and there is a striking similarity with singer Kathleen Ferrier, who, after John's death in 1948, developed the same closeness to his second wife Emmie that Hess had had with John. Ferrier too wrote letters from America (although unfortunately we do not have any from Hess's first tour to get her first impressions, as we do with Ferrier), and she, as Hess had done, relied heavily on John Tillett to mould her career through its crucial formative years. But for one letter (1930), for nine years (1926–35) there is no extant correspondence from Myra Hess in the agency's archive, but during those years she was developing into a lynchpin artist for Ibbs and Tillett, especially during the Second World War, as we shall see in due course. For her, the 1920s had been marked by the growing loyalty of her audiences in Holland and by the triumph of her debut in America.

Auditions continued in the 1920s yielding some successes, though one young hopeful was dismissed as 'far too nervous and amateurish, advised her to study further before taking up concert profession. Has had several teachers!!!' But Marion Browne made a success of her audition on 1 June 1921, with her 'charming voice and style' and duly appears from the 1921–22 season, while the ranks of the tenors were increased by the addition of Luigi Simonetta on the same day. A month later the 'much above the average' Scottish contralto Catherine Mentiplay made a good impression, though her soprano duettist Marie Thomson was not so fortunate, despite positive comments about her rendition of the 'Jewel song'. Blanche Marchesi's pupil, the soprano Constance Hardcastle, sang 'with distinction and most artistic, good voice, well taught' on 14 July and was taken on, while a week later the Australian contralto Ivy Philips joined the lists (22 July), and her compatriot Gladys Verona, a *leggiero* soprano with 'most excellent vocal equipment, bird-like quality in upper register, middle unusually warm for voice of her quality, [but] appearance not good, joined two months later on 22 October. The following week saw the appearance of the name Walter Widdop in the audition book (27 October 1921), a tenor destined for greatness. Resident in his native Halifax at the time, Widdop had 'a fine robust voice, warm quality, sings with great fervour, think highly of him. Inclined to give too much voice, quite young, about 25'. In fact he was 29 at the time and, having been taken on at once, made his operatic debut with the British National Opera Company in 1923 in *Aida* (he had sung Radames's aria 'Celeste Aida' at the agency's audition) and then went on to sing several Wagnerian roles at Covent Garden during the 1920s. He was still on Ibbs and Tillett's books in 1949 when he died suddenly on 6 September at the age of 57, a tragedy made all the more poignant because he had sung 'Lohengrin's Farewell' at the Promenade Concert only the night before.

Albert Coates recommended the dramatic soprano Eleanor Paget to the agency and she made a good impression at the same session as Widdop's appearance at the Queen's Hall on 27 October 1921. Though her experience was 'on Music Halls under another name' she sang 'Pleurez mes yeux' and Santuzza's aria from *Cavalleria rusticana*, and revealed an 'excellent dramatic voice, warm round tone, middle register specially good, inclined to take upper notes too much from the chest. Think highly of her, excellent for opera.' Her appearance was 'good, tall and handsome'. John Tillett's understanding of the voice was now becoming more assured and confident. The tenor Oswald Rippon did not succeed because though he 'sings artistically and is a sound musician, he was nothing out of the ordinary. The voice requires lifting and brightening. At present it is produced too far back and lacks a pure tenor ring.'

The next record shows the audition on 11 April 1922 of a cellist, Seth Lancaster, who was taken on. He was a pupil of the Hallé Orchestra's principal cello Carl Fuchs and described as having 'excellent technique. Very pleased with him and can safely recommend him.' Lancaster's name thus appears at the bottom of the list of cellos in the 1922–23 season's brochure amid very distinguished company which includes Pablo Casals, the long-standing Josef Hollman, W.H. Squire, Felix Salmond, Jean Gérardy, while less distinguished, but also one of those listed at the time, was one Giovanni Barbirolli, who was currently earning a living as a back-desk player in the LSO and playing in a string quartet led by Samuel Kutcher. His name had first appeared in the 1919–20 brochure published by the agency (see Appendix 2), but by 1924–25 he has become John Barbirolli and last appears in the publication for 1928–29, by which time his career had changed to that of a conductor.

The soprano Olivia Hilder was also accepted on the day Seth Lancaster auditioned. She sang 'Depuis le jour' 'very well indeed' followed by 'Caro nome'. She possessed an 'excellent voice, clear tone (Melba style), legato and florid singing equally good. Should prove useful to the National Opera Company'. Tillett also advised her to expand her oratorio repertoire. The Russian tenor Max Karolik, sent by Sir Henry Wood, was 'tall and of fine appearance' and had a dramatic voice of extensive compass. His was a 'most excellent voice (in Tchaikovsky and an Italian aria and Romance), warm quality, sings with great fervour. Think most highly of him. Advised him to go to America as there was little opportunity for him here at present' (March 1922). Despite giving such advice, the agency took Karolik on but only for the 1922–23 season. Another tenor, but one who lasted longer, was Albert Lanng who had a 'really fine dramatic voice, ringing Italian quality after Caruso's style'. He was taken on in April 1922. In June (no specific date recorded) they took on an Irish soprano, Lily Meagher, who sang from Handel's *Messiah*, Puccini's *Manon Lescaut*, and two ballads. It was recorded that she possessed a 'most excellent voice, lyric dramatic, true throughout, temperament would do well in opera' though not without the caveat that her appearance was 'good, but has a false eye, which is well disguised'. Despite this, her name is included starting with the 1923–24 artists' list. Later in the year (7 November) the contralto Rose Myrtil (another pupil of Marchesi) revealed an 'excellent voice, of big range and fine timbre' in music by Bizet, Massenet and Hamilton Harty when she auditioned, while the Australian lyric soprano Rosa Alba, heard a month later in Rossini and Fauré at the Queen's Hall, was taken on due to her 'charming voice, light, sings with much grace of style, prepared with oratorio, quite willing to go into light opera. Heard her 2nd time and confirmed previous opinion, very sweet voice' (no record of her first audition with the agency exists in the audition books). Arthur Broadbent was heard to advantage on 10 December 1922 and had 'an exceptionally fine voice, in fact the best heard since Norman Allin. Only 22, should have a fine career. Sings very well, recommend him to Boosey, Newman, Gill, Brooks etc.' Another youngster, the Irish-Canadian lyric soprano Evelyn Tierney (Aeolian Hall, 11 December 1922), was deemed to have an 'excellent voice, great possibilities, requires further tuition, worth watching'. Despite the caution felt about her youthful age 'about 20', Ibbs and Tillett placed her on the list for one season, 1923–24.

The year 1923, the last in which the agency operated from 19 Hanover Square, began with the addition of the Yorkshire soprano Hylda Whipp to the roster after auditioning on 10 January with Aida's aria 'Ritorna vincitor', 'Je suis Tytania' and Solveig's Song (all in English) which revealed 'an excellent and charming voice, bright and telling quality, think highly of her, excellent in every way'. The baritone Ugo Donarelli had a 'fine operatic voice, very dramatic in style, full warm quality, big range. Should be very popular at certain concerts', while the Russian operatic soprano Tatiana Makushina had 'a really fine dramatic voice, full and even throughout. Excellent Lieder singer. Should do very well.' They were both taken on after their auditions which both took place on 2 February 1923. On 12 February they heard the Yorkshire contralto Edna Laidler in Weekes' Music Rooms; she had 'a very good voice, warm quality, sings artistically. Room too small to judge properly as to the full quality of voice, promised to hear her again.' Despite this, she appears for a year in 1923–24, but then no more. The tenor Edward Roberts also auditioned in February 1923 and was deemed an 'artistic singer, good style, voice veiled of the robust type, after [Gervase] Elwes style' and duly accepted. Another contralto, 'charming, young [at] 21 years', Lancashire-based Margaret Milton, was unsuccessful ('nice voice but requires bringing forward, at present not big enough, no carrying power, fear present method not good, made usual promise'), but the final comment 'sings everything from memory' implies perhaps that this was less usual practice at singing auditions than nowadays.

Hetty Tillett (Esta d'Argo) recommended a fellow soprano in April 1923, Phyllis Denmead, who was successful after her Queen's Hall audition and described as a 'very charming, young artist, sweet voice after [Dora] Labbette style, but more versatile'. On 26 April Leah Rusel-Myre, a lyric-dramatic soprano with the British National Opera Company, made it to the artists' list, but only for a year 1923–24, perhaps due to a voice which was considered 'hard in parts due to French production, [but she had a] full middle voice and excellent style'. The last successful artist to audition in 1923 was the Yorkshire lyric soprano Alice Moxon (another recommendation by Hetty Tillett) in May, who had an 'excellent voice, sings with conviction, can safely recommend her'. Audition records were resumed only in February 1924, a month after Ibbs and Tillett had moved from 19 Hanover Square to 124 Wigmore Street where the agency would remain for over half a century, a stone's throw from the hall with which it would so often be associated.

Later in the year the agency held a couple of audition sessions at the Steinway Hall. At the first (2 December) three candidates were taken on: Louise Trenton, a soprano with 'an excellent voice, a good artist far above the average', the contralto Ethel Barker (introduced by the Huddersfield Choral Society), and the 23-year-old bass-baritone Frank Phillips, who sang 'Hear me ye winds and waves', 'Charming Chloe' and 'Why do the nations?', and had a 'good voice, sings with much conviction, artistic', but who achieved greater fame as a news broadcaster for the BBC from 1935. Ten days later, and despite needing 'a little culture and experience', the tenor John Chandler, who 'much impressed [with an] exceedingly good voice, pure tenor quality, [and] warm tone', was accepted. Six months later (10 June 1925) the baritone John Thorne had done well enough to get on to the list for the 1926–27 season, but auditions held at the Steinway Hall on 2 November 1925 were particularly productive for the agency, for it yielded Louise Marshall (a 'tall, handsome mezzo-contralto'), Sophie Wyss ('a soprano with a charming voice, excellent singer suitable for Bach and such works as *Creation*'), Helen Ogilvie (a soprano with an 'excellent voice, full and steady tone, good artist'), and the tenor Heddle Nash ('a very good voice [when] singing upper notes. Sings opera and oratorio equally well. Think highly of him. Audition Mills, Boosey, Wood, BBC'). All were included in the 1926–27 list. Just before Christmas the agency took on three more singers for the following season after a day of auditions (21 December 1925) at the Grotrian Hall. They were the Welsh soprano Nanse Fuller-Mills (recommended by Julius Harrison) and two Yorkshire-based contraltos, Doris Haigh (who had a 'pleasing voice, diction excellent, and sings folksongs with special insight') and Amy King ('good voice, full and warm tone, intelligent singer').

The agency listened to only 16 singers in 1926. Of these (on 11 February) they accepted Andrew Clayton, a tenor recommended by Margaret Balfour, and the soprano Cecil Brown (who was a 'very artistic interpreter, [with] charming platform manner, voice sounds old in parts no doubt due to faulty production') introduced by Harold Samuel and of 'nice, ladylike' appearance. The mezzo-contralto Linda Seymour succeeded on 9 June despite some lukewarm, qualified observations, while on 13 September the Lancashire contralto Annie Broadhurst ('excellent voice, not big but telling and musical quality, sings artistically') and a singer who would have a lengthy relationship with Ibbs and Tillett, the tenor Percy Manchester ('excellent voice, warm quality, has the gift of interpretation, an excellent Lieder singer, might compare him with [Frank] Mullings, [Arthur] Jordan, pupil of Francis Harford and Plunket Greene') made it into the brochure for 1927–28. The songwriter and accompanist Percy Kahn was married to the contralto Olive Kavann ('most excellent voice, full contralto quality yet all the lightness and head notes of a mezzo-soprano, excellent Ballad singer') who auditioned successfully on the same day. At the end of the month (29 September) they were joined by another, but lighter contralto, Betty Bannerman, and the bass Charles Harrison 'a man of 45 years, good voice, big and smooth quality, sings well', and who was also conductor of the Gervase Elwes Choir in Walsall.

Of those who failed their audition there was a bass by the name of Julian Halevy (no mention of whether or not he was related to the composer), recommended by the critic and translator of opera libretti Alfred Kalisch, who failed on non-musical attributes, 'excellent voice of musical and velvety quality, fear his [poor] appearance against him. Looks like an escaped monk, peculiar eye application and restless manner'. Beatrice Wilde, a soprano with 'practically no experience and a voice without distinction if fairly good', was given another chance eight years later in 1934, but failed again although she 'has made good improvement in voice and style, still not first class, voice rather unsympathetic and intonation not good when voice is stressed'.

Only seven singers were heard during June and September 1927, of whom just three, the contraltos Vera Wright and Gwladys Garside were successful and joined the agency from the 1928–29 season, while the soprano Frances Allsom had to wait until the following season, possibly because the aria 'Suicido' from Ponchielli's *La Gioconda* was 'rather too exacting for her vocal powers'. Early in January 1928 the baritone Leyland White, who was taken on from the 1928–29 season, impressed as 'an excellent artist, voice most musical and agreeable. Heard him first at RCM opera performance *Pelléas and Mélisande*, thought him exceptionally good.' On the same day (12 January) the soprano Valentina Aksarova, 'quite a good voice and singer, bright personality', was taken on with White, while the Italian tenor Vittorio Orsini also managed to get on to the list for the same season at his audition on 5 April, because he was 'a very versatile artist, sings equally well in Italian, German, French, and English. Voice at times inclined to be white and nasal, otherwise excellent in every respect'.

In the autumn (11 October 1928) Pedro Tillett sent along the American soprano Ina Souez, who was just beginning to make a name for herself and, a year later, would sing Liù to Eva Turner's Turandot at Covent Garden. She then went on to become one of Glyndebourne's early artists, singing the Mozart repertoire under Fritz Busch in the mid-1930s. At her Grotrian Hall audition she sang an aria from *La Wally* by Catalani and a song by Rimsky-Korsakov, 'very good voice, extensive range, excellent head notes. Safely recommend her. Oratorio, operatic and songs.' A young soprano called Nellie Meyrat ('young and pleasing') sang to the agency just three weeks earlier (24 September 1928) and had 'a good voice, bright and lilting'. Though her name does not subsequently appear on the list for 1929–30, there is the name of a new soprano called Nellie Palliser (and Nellie Meyrat's address is given as Palliser Road in Fulham, west London), which is probably more than coincidental and a case of taking an assumed name for professional purposes. Of the four other singers heard in 1928, the bass-baritone J. Challoner Heaton (recommended by Hamilton Harty) succeeded on 17 October, unlike the 'chubby Yorkshireman' Frank Mercer, a bass with a voice 'much too cathedral in style, smooth but plummy at times and altogether uninspiring. Sang the *Messiah* as a bass but the *St Paul* excerpt [Mendelssohn] more like a throaty tenor.' On the other hand a young tenor called Helmar Fernback, sent from the Royal College of Music by its Principal Sir Hugh Allen, was accepted despite the 'promise to make another appointment'.

The bass baritone Robert Algar (auditioned April 1929) had 'a very good voice, youthful fervour; with experience (hitherto principally in music comedy) should develop into good singer, prone to tighten and whiten head notes, a habit of [his teacher] Thomas Mense'. Sir George Henschel's recommendation of Annie Pimblott, an 'excellent contralto, young, nice appearance, sings well', also led to her success after her audition in May 1929. On 14 May another contralto, Gladys Knight, was taken on (though from the 1930–31 season) because of her 'exceptionally good voice, warm quality even throughout, think highly of her and can safely recommend her – pupil of Dan Price'. The baritone John Morel followed a week later (22 May) 'a singer of distinct style', while on 24 September the tenor Kennedy McKenna and the soprano Thelma Bardsley were taken on, with Gladys Cole ('a really fine dramatic soprano voice, like [Florence] Austral, warm in quality, sang Mozart and Weber arias very well with good phrasing') and the contralto Tessa Richardson following on 17 December to conclude auditions for the decade.

CHAPTER TWELVE

Letters from Artists: 1920–29

In October 1922 a young woman, 26-year-old Emmie Muriel Bass, was recruited by Ibbs and Tillett from Chappell's, where she had worked in the box office since 1916. At the start of her work with the agency she featured very little in the affairs of the company, but gradually her importance grew. Letters began to be addressed to her until, by the 1930s, she was beginning to take personal responsibility for certain artists. The daughter of Arthur and Florence Bass, Emmie was 21 years younger than John Tillett, but over the years their relationship became close until they eventually married two years after the death of John's wife Hetty (Esta d'Argo) in February 1939. Hetty had given up singing in the early 1920s and devoted the rest of her life to teaching. Emmie and John only had a married life of seven years, from their wartime wedding on 10 April 1941 until his death on 20 June 1948. Thereafter Emmie Tillett, a Director of the firm since Robert Leigh Ibbs's retirement in 1937, became Managing Director and ran it until her own retirement in 1978, a total of 56 years in the service of the agency. After withdrawing from the day-to-day running of the agency, she was made its Chairman and died four years later on 16 May 1982 at the age of 85.

Meanwhile the tenancy agreement for 124 Wigmore Street ran from Christmas Day 1923 at an annual rent of £700. Its proximity to the Wigmore Hall was to become more and more significant in the activities of the agency, but the post-war revival of the music festival also produced much work. For example there were the Glasgow Choral and Orchestral Union Concerts, the Handel Festivals, Leeds Triennial Musical Festivals, Norwich Triennial Musical Festivals, and in the field of chamber music, the Bradford Triennial Festival for Chamber Music and the Newcastle Chamber Concerts. Many of the soloists who appeared at these events, whether singers or instrumentalists, were supplied by Ibbs and Tillett, sometimes exclusively so, sometimes specifically requested by the organizers, or in other cases supplied at the suggestion of the agency. To take some of those listed above as examples, the Glasgow Choral and Orchestral Union Concerts were rather unusual because they took place over a longer period, between mid-November and mid-February, and consisted of two weekly concerts, one programme on Tuesday the other on Saturday. The two promoters were respectively the Glasgow Choral Union and the Scottish Orchestra. The concerts were begun in 1898, and, in the first post-war season of 1919–20, there were 13 Tuesday Evening Classical Concerts, two of them choral, and fourteen Popular Concerts, all save one given on Saturday evenings, the exception being given on Thursday 1 January 1920. The orchestra was 70-strong and the venue St Andrew's Hall. The programmes offered subscribers 'an unexampled opportunity of hearing performances of some of the latest compositions by native composers, a considerable number for the first time in Glasgow'. The choir was in the hands of Warren Clemens, and the festival's musical director for that season was Landon Ronald. Ibbs and Tillett provided most of the soloists, who consisted of the singers Olga Haley, Astra Desmond, Gervase Elwes, Robert Radford, Caroline Hatchard, Carmen Hill, John Coates, Flora Woodman, Rosina Buckman, Maurice d'Oisly, Walter Hyde, with the vocal quartet of Agnes Nicholls, Margaret Balfour, John

Coates and Herbert Brown for Handel's *Messiah*, and the concerto soloists Arthur Catterall (Brahms violin), Adela Verne (Schumann piano), Guilhermina Suggia (Saint Saëns No.1 cello), Mark Hambourg (Tchaikovsky piano), Renée Chemet (Saint Saëns No.3 violin), Albert Sammons (Beethoven violin), May Harrison (Mendelssohn violin), Harold Samuel (Grieg piano), Margaret Fairless (Tchaikovsky violin), May Mukle (Tchaikovsky's *Rococo variations*, cello) and Myra Hess, an impressive list, as the prospectus for the series stated, of 'eminent artists [who] have been engaged as vocal and instrumental soloists, and [whose] contributions have been selected to fit into the general Orchestral scheme'. Throughout the 1920s, Ibbs and Tillett continued to provide most of the solo artists, whether singers or instrumentalists, for example in 1921–22 Busoni, Casals, Bratza, Hofmann, Rosenthal, Pouishnoff, Jelly d'Aranyi, Lionel Tertis (now styled 'the Kreisler of the viola') joined the ranks of the instrumentalists provided by the agency, while Ben Davies, Melchior, Henry Brearley and Norman Allin were among the singers. By the end of the decade they had been joined at the Glasgow concerts by artists such as Frederic Lamond, Roy Henderson, Steuart Wilson, Walter Widdop, and Artur Schnabel, who eventually gave his engagements to Ibbs and Tillett as sole agents in 1930. In the case of the baritone Roy Henderson, the agency took him on with effect from New Year 1927. This was their standard letter of the day:

> We hereby undertake to act as your sole representatives for all your professional engagements in Great Britain and Ireland commencing from the above date.
>
> We are to use our best endeavours on your behalf, it being agreed all letters and applications that may be addressed to you shall be referred to us; in fact, that the control of your business in Great Britain and Ireland shall be left in our hands.
>
> Our remuneration to be Ten per cent (10%) of the terms you receive on all engagements during the continuance of this contract. Ibbs and Tillett (1 January 1927)

The Leeds Triennial Musical Festival of 1925 could easily be mistaken for a roster of Ibbs and Tillett artists. They included the singers Florence Austral, Dorothy Silk, Elsie Suddaby, Muriel Brunskill, Margaret Balfour, Walter Hyde, Walter Widdop, Steuart Wilson, Norman Allin, Robert Radford, and Herbert Heyner, while the two solo instrumentalists were Myra Hess and Guilhermina Suggia. The festival consisted of eight concerts, comprising a morning and evening programme on each of four consecutive days in October, the LSO and the Festival Chorus conducted by Albert Coates in the orchestral programmes and by Sir Hugh Allen in the choral works. Three years later Beecham had replaced Coates, while the soloists were still many of those from 1925 as well as others including Dora Labbette, Parry Jones, Keith Falkner, Percy Heming, Dennis Noble, Harold Williams among the singers and Dorothy Hesse, Kathleen Frise-Smith, and May and Beatrice Harrison among the instrumentalists.

The first post-war Norfolk and Norwich Triennial Musical Festival was in 1924, those of 1914, 1917 and 1920 having been abandoned 'on account of the upheaval which affected Norwich and so many other centres of the Kingdom'. Rather than staging a festival in 1923, the committee delayed it by a year to mark the centenary of the very first event in 1824, at which Sir George Smart conducted a chorus of 150 and orchestra of 110. Another postponement by a year had occurred in 1851 to avoid a clash with the Great Exhibition in London's Hyde Park. The next took place in 1854, which not only put it back on track but also avoided that other great autumn Triennial Festival in Birmingham, which, after the Three Choirs Festival, was England's second oldest musical festival until its demise in 1912, placing Norwich as third. The centennial Norwich concerts in October 1924 were conservatively programmed, no Handel, Haydn or Mozart but plenty of Bach, Beethoven and Mendelssohn. The language used in the introduction to the festival programme book was quaintly Victorian and hardly reflected the developing musical world of 1924 with either Schoenberg or Bartók, despite the presence of Stravinsky and his *Firebird* suite. 'The more modern foreign composers laid under contribution are Wagner (with an evening all to himself), Tchaikovsky, Brahms, Berlioz, Strauss, César Franck, Saint Saëns and Stravinsky'. Even more peculiar was the description as being among 'The younger school of English composers' of Elgar (67), Ethel Smyth (66), Delius (62), Vaughan Williams (52), Holst (50) and Frank Bridge (a genuinely younger 45). Ernest Moeran provided the only new work, his second orchestral Rhapsody, which the anonymous author of the Introduction sheepishly acknowledged as 'a rather surprising fact, for in times past Norwich was conspicuous for the enterprise displayed in bringing new works to a first performance'. In fact the next two festivals were to include much more enterprising music than all such past 'memorable' works as Spohr's *Christian Prayer*, Julius Benedict's *Undine* and Arthur Goring Thomas' *Sun Worshippers*, with commissions from the committee to Frank Bridge for his orchestral tone poem *Enter Spring* (1927) and to Arthur Bliss for his oratorio *Morning Heroes* (1930). Sir Henry Wood was conductor of all three four-day festivals (he first appeared there in the festival of 1908), and he took along his Queen's Hall Orchestra to Norwich to join the 270-strong chorus. Meanwhile Ibbs and Tillett supplied all the solo artists, namely the singers Florence Austral, Margaret Balfour, Ethel Bilsland (new to the agency from 1925–26), Muriel Brunskill, Astra Desmond, Edith Furmedge (another newcomer), Phyllis Lett, Dorothy Silk, Maggie Teyte, Carrie Tubb, Norman Allin, John Coates, Tudor Davies, Herbert Heyner, Walter Hyde, Malcolm McEachern, Frank Mullings, Robert Radford, Horace Stevens, Harold Williams, and Archibald Winter. The four instrumental soloists, Cortot, Suggia and the d'Aranyi sisters, also came from the agency.

At the 32nd festival in 1927, Ibbs and Tillett were once again dominant in supplying soloists and even took a full page advert in the illustrated souvenir programme opposite the page listing the participating artists. These were fewer in number, but nevertheless familiar names for the most part with one or two new ones destined for greatness, Florence Austral, Margaret Balfour, Edith Furmedge, Dorothy Silk, Olive Sturgess, Flora Woodman, Arthur Cranmer, Arthur Fear, Arthur Jordan, Roy Henderson, Horace Stevens, Walter Widdop, Harold Williams, Steuart Wilson and Archibald Winter. Pianists Myra Hess, Walter Gieseking, violinist Thibaud, and cellist Suggia were the four instrumentalists. Ibbs and Tillett's advertisement listed forthcoming London Concerts at the Wigmore and Aeolian Halls between September 1927 and May 1928 (including Cortot's only recital at the Palladium in the afternoon of Sunday 11 December 1927). A plethora of talent included Segovia, Elisabeth Schumann (on the books since 1925), the violinist Adolf Busch with pianist Rudolf Serkin, Lamond's recitals, Harold Samuel's Bach week and various string quartets. This advertisement was only placed on the one occasion; by 1930 the only sign of a Tillett advert in the souvenir book is for Tillett's the watchmakers, jewellers and opticians located in the city's St Giles Street. At this festival, apart from the tenor Andrew Clayton, all the soloists came from the agency once again and included some more new names among the regulars. The singers were

Margaret Balfour, Muriel Brunskill, Valetta Iacopi, Jean Kemp, Dora Labbette, Göta Ljungberg, Irene Morden, Dorothy Silk, Elsie Suddaby, Flora Woodman, Arthur Cranmer, Robert Easton, Hubert Eisdell, Roy Henderson, Francis Russell, Horace Stevens, Walter Widdop, and Frederick Woodhouse. Myra Hess, Frederic Lamond, Jelly d'Aranyi and Arturo Bonucci were the instrumental soloists.

Another three-day musical festival, but in June rather than the autumn, was the Triennial Handel Festival held at the Crystal Palace in Sydenham, south London. This huge gathering of singers and orchestra, to say nothing of a vast audience, began in 1862 under Michael Costa (after a trial run in 1857 and the 1859 Handel Commemoration Festival to mark the centenary of the composer's death). In 1883 it was taken on by August Manns until 1900 (when he was aged 75), from 1903 by Frederic Cowen and for the last one in 1926 by Henry Wood (not for the first time Wood conducted a 'last' festival, the other being at Birmingham in 1912). Once again the First World War had brought about cancellation, there was no event between 1912 and 1920. By 1926 the festival had run out of steam, the huge choruses (in 1903 there were 3300) and vast audiences (of anything up to 80000 people in its heyday) were flagging, and it was no longer so popular with the public. By 1926 Bach was a firmly established rival to Handel (and was mercifully never performed by such inflated numbers). London had many more musical venues and concerts were more diverse in programming, with radio and gramophone recording techniques now developed from acoustical to electrical process. Within a decade of the last Handel Festival there would in any case be no more Crystal Palace after the fire, which destroyed it in November 1936. Narciso Vert played his part in providing soloists in the latter years of the nineteenth century and from 1906 Ibbs and Tillett did so too, although in that year the agency was but a few months old. The 1909 Festival also embraced Mendelssohn as it was the centenary of his birth; the 75-year-old Sir Charles Santley, who had sung at every Handel Festival since 1865, was 'the doyen of the soloists' according to the *Musical Times* for July 1909, while others were familiar names from Ibbs and Tillett: Clara Butt, Kennerley Rumford, Ben Davies, Edith Evans, Walter Hyde, Agnes Nicholls, Robert Radford, and Watkin Mills.

It was traditional for the 2500-strong London chorus to be reinforced by contingents of about 800 from the provinces: those from Sheffield, Leeds and Huddersfield were prepared by Henry Coward, others came from Wales. The three concerts in 1912 (on Tuesday, Thursday and Saturday 25–29 June, preceded by an open Grand Rehearsal on Saturday 22 June) featured, as soloists, Pauline Donalda, Esta d'Argo, Perceval Allen, Clara Butt, Ben Davies, Charles Saunders, Kennerley Rumford, Herbert Brown, and Robert Radford, all from the agency. The format remained unchanged after the eight-year gap caused by the war. The main works were *Judas Maccabeus* and *Messiah* for which Agnes Nicholls, Esta D'Argo, Carrie Tubb, Kirkby Lunn, Phyllis Lett, Ben Davies, Walter Hyde, Frank Mullings, Robert Radford, Norman Allin, and Frederick Ranalow were engaged. Cowen's sixth and final festival was in 1923 for which he engaged Agnes Nicholls, Florence Austral, Lilian Stiles-Allen, Phyllis Lett, Edna Thornton, Ben Davies, Walter Hyde, Frank Mullings, Robert Radford, Norman Allin, and Norman Williams for *Israel in Egypt*, a Selection Day (*Samson*, *Jeptha*, *Alexander's Feast*, and a miscellany of other works), and *Messiah*. For Henry Wood's sole festival, the last in 1926, his soloists were Florence Austral, Carrie Tubb, Flora Woodman, Margaret Balfour, Muriel Brunskill, Edith Furmedge, Ben Davies, Joseph Hislop, Walter Widdop, Norman Allin, Robert

Radford, and Horace Stevens. An innovation to the programming by Wood was the inclusion of excerpts from Handel's operas in half of one concert, and with the *Messiah* on 12 June, the Triennial Handel Festivals came to an abrupt end.

By 1922 (when the agency was still at Hanover Square) Ibbs and Tillett were producing a slim brochure entitled *Of special interest to chamber music societies* which, for the 1923–24 season, for example, included seven string quartets with details of their personnel and availability with some critical plaudits, five trios and the London Wind Quintet with their personnel, a list of ten quartets (names only), pianists, string players and vocalists, and finally some 'pre-packed' recitals 'by the following combination of artists' for music clubs and concert societies (see Appendix 3). To promote its artists throughout the land the agency also continued to issue its regular *Bulletins* (first begun in 1913, see Chapter 7), the one for June 1925 reproducing on its front cover Augustus John's famous portrait of Suggia playing her cello. In large format and running to 28 pages, it was entirely devoted to 27 photographs of artists accompanied by extracts from newspaper reviews accumulated world-wide. According to their celebrity status some artists (such as Moiseiwitsch or Myra Hess) were given a whole page to themselves, others (such as Steuart Wilson or Morgan Kingston) had to be content with no photograph, sharing a page with two or three others, and a line or two of notices from the press. Future tours were announced, some of them for the 1925–26 season, together with availability for engagements, and scattered about were boxed advertisements for foreign artists who were not featured in *The Bulletin* (Casals, Rosenthal, Lamond, Dohnányi, Renée Chemet and Suggia). By March 1927, *The Bulletin* (by now bigger at 36 pages and with 44 photographs) did feature foreign artists as well as indigenous ones, with Elisabeth Schumann on its cover. Its back page carried a rather self-conscious photograph of the six members of the English Singers, seated committee-like around a table. By April 1929 it had grown to a 60-page publication with 66 photographs, the duo of Hess and d'Aranyi in action on the cover and an advertisement for His Master's Voice gramophone records featuring 26 Ibbs and Tillett artists (a sign of increased fortune for the agency) now adorning the back page. On the inside of the front cover was a similar advert for Columbia records, although no mention of Ibbs and Tillett here, despite the list of 22 artists represented by the agency. Another sign of these momentous times (which in the mid-1920s included broadcasting, and the BBC taking on the Promenade Concerts in 1927) was, at the end of each artists' newspaper notices, a mention of the gramophone company for which they recorded and, where relevant, the piano they used for recitals or concertos.

Despite the fact that Ibbs and Tillett's lists included no conductors, the agency was active in placing these musicians as guests wherever they could, although Liverpool seems to have been an especial favourite. The composer Gabriel Pierné was offered just such an engagement:

> Please excuse me if I have not replied sooner, but I have been particularly busy this month with concerts and performances of my oratorio *The Children's Crusade*. Taking into account your commission, various other expenses, and having to withdraw from two concerts here in Paris, I could not ask less than eighty-five guineas from the Liverpool Philharmonic Society for two rehearsals and a concert. Please would you keep me informed of the decision of the Liverpool Committee. (28 March 1924, translation from French)

In 1924 the conductor Felix Weingartner was leaving the Vienna Volksoper after a five-year tenure as its Musical Director; a series of letters to John Tillett in connection with Liverpool, Glasgow and London indicate his interest in musical matters in the UK. Weingartner, like Klemperer and Furtwängler, is an example of a conductor who was also very keen for recognition as a composer:

> I am in receipt of your letter enclosing the Liverpool programmes. I consent to them in principle but absolutely cannot do the *Rosenkavalier* selection. It is music I never conduct anywhere, it is not my style and am therefore unable to do so now or ever. Besides, the 7th of Beethoven does not last 38 minutes, but longer, and the second part would therefore be quite long enough. However, I am willing to do so some other short piece instead of the *Rosenkavalier.* (9 July 1924)
>
> I am very disposed to include in the Helensburgh programme Mendelssohn's *Fingals Cave* Op. 26. Also I consent to conduct in the 2nd Liverpool programme the prelude *Tristan* (without the *Liebestod*), what would be too long. Also I am very satisfied to hear, even in a short piece, the celebrated Liverpool choir, conducted by his master. (20 July 1924)
>
> Can you be so kind to ask in Glasgow if perhaps the material of Beethoven's 9th Symphony is regulated after my indications in my book *Advices for performances of Beethoven's symphonies*, Leipzig & London, Breitkopf & Härtel? The most orchestras have accepted this very practicable indications. And if not, can the material be regulated until my arrival in Glasgow? My book is translated in English. (20 September 1924)
>
> The Royal Philharmonic Society was so kind to refuse my new symphony, written as homage to the British public. (2 October 1924)
>
> It is indeed a hard work to fix the Scotch programmes. I will try to answer all the points of Mr Barnes' letter. The Bach concerto (C major edited by Felix Weingartner) is printed by Breitkopf & Härtel. The Handel concerto (D major edited by Gustav Kogel) is printed by Edition Peters, Leipzig. I hope you have received my wire that I consent to the same programme (Beethoven) for Edinburgh and Glasgow. I beg the Committee in Edinburgh to print as follows:
>
> Symphony No.5 in Do [C] minor Weingartner (first performance)
> Programme 25th November: as printed (with *Enigma*)
> Programme 15th November: can be increased by Saint-Saëns *Le Rouet d'Omphale* symphonic poem after the *Symphonic Variations* by Dvořák
> Programme 29th November: Overture *Sakuntala* [Alfano] is much longer than 10 minutes, the three Berlioz pieces longer than 12 minutes and we must count to play twice either the *Ballet des Sylphes* or the *Hungarian March* or both. I never played these pieces without one or two *da capo* [encores]. If we add the Bach concerto the programme is too long (Haydn symphony is surely 30 not 25 minutes). I propose to begin the second part of this programme with the Handel Concerto grosso.
> Programme 6th December: I suppose that Miss Moody [the violinist Alma Moodie] will play the Beethoven concerto, which is much longer than 30 minutes. But we can take instead of Overture *Genoveva*, Overture *Manfred* and *Beschwörung der Alpensee* taken from the music to Byron's *Manfred* by Schumann. You find this music at Breitkopf & Härtel, Leipzig.
> Programme 13th December: Overture *Alceste* is at least 13–14 minutes, Mozart [Symphony No.40] G minor is longer than 23 minutes because I play the repetitions [repeats] in the first part [movement] and Finale. Beethoven *Leonore* is 15 minutes. We must count [assume] that *Invitation to the Waltz* will be played twice. Overture *Rienzi* is longer than 11 minutes. We can begin the 2nd part with two pieces taken from the music to *Le Martyre de Saint Sebastien* by Debussy, but at this moment I cannot say the titles. A short and merry piece is *La fuga di Chioggia*, Scene Veneziane No.III by Mancinelli, publisher Ricordi, Milan. I beg the Committee to choose.
> I will try to give you so soon as possible notices about the pieces you asked. I notice that Dundee approved my suggested programme. I accept Aberdeen programme 19th November, but after Beethoven we must make a little interval, at least 4 minutes. I noticed that the second Aberdeen concert (11th Dec) will be conducted by another conductor.
> Perhaps it is better to omit the remark 'written specially for the British public' on the programmes

[for Weingartner's own Fifth Symphony]. I shall speak with critics and tell them that I gave the first performance of my new symphony to England as a sign of sympathy and that I wrote this work with this intention. (20 October 1924)

My debut here [Glasgow] was indeed a big success. I send you herewith some clippings. The press is of one voice excellent. Mrs Weingartner wrote me that she will send you the Liverpool clippings. When you consent, I shall send you at the end of my engagement here a check about your commission:

10% of £750 Glasgow	£75
" " £157.10 Liverpool	£15.15
	£90.15

I would like to add your expenses in London and beg you kindly to communicate them to me occasionally. (22 November 1924)

I thank you very much for your letter. The Grand Hotel is not comfortable and therefore I stay here [St Enoch Station Hotel owned by the London Midland and Scottish Railway], where I am very well.

The last year you were so kind to offer me a Broadcast Concert. I could extend my stay in London for some days after the 23rd March, when you could arrange me such a concert for a good fee. Then we would have no difficulties with the R[oyal] Philharmonic Society.

Mr Barnes [manager of the Scottish Orchestra] made me the proposition to broadcast my Symphony (the 9th December) to your office and that you could be so friendly to invite London critics to hear it. But I beg you not to do it. The broadcast transmission is not yet absolutely trustworthy. A false impression can happen. But I would be very obliged to you when you could influence some prominent London newspapers to send their critics to here. And – in confidence – it would be much better when these gentlemen came to Glasgow (9th Dec) than to Edinburgh where will be the absolute first performance (8th Dec). The acoustic in the Edinburgh hall is not very good and no work can make there the same impression as in the wonderful St Andrew's Hall in Glasgow.

The Committee here is arranging a public rehearsal of my work the 9th December at 11h 30 to give the occasion to the public to hear it twice. Perhaps this time would be more comfortable for one or another gentleman. (28 November 1924)

Herewith I send you some clippings especially about the sensational performance of the [Beethoven] 9th Symphony. I think you will be satisfied too. Permit me a question in absolute confidence. Are you connected with the L.S.O. [London Symphony Orchestra]? Is it true that this Society is looking for a permanent conductor? I feel so well in England that I could be disposed to accept such a position when the conditions would be sufficiently good. You know that I am not German but Italian. Or must it be an Englishman? When you can answer my questions, it is understood that I keep the answer so confidentially as I ask it for my question. (4 December 1924)

I am so sorry. Since a year I am engaged for the 2nd April to conduct in Mannheim, for the 5th in Berlin and then in some other German cities. Therefore I am not able to accept your kind invitation for the 2/IV. Would it be possible for an earlier date nearer the 23rd March? [pencilled annotation by John Tillett: No, April 2 only date] (4 December 1924)

It is with great pleasure that I come back the next season to Liverpool, when it would be connected with other English engagements. The members of the Committee expressed me often the hope to see me again the next winter. Try to finish this affair together with Liverpool and to adjoin some other towns, chiefly London. I am still free at the same time as this year (November, December).

My Symphony had a splendid reception in Edinburgh and Glasgow. I am sending you some clippings. Please show them occasionally to the Royal Philharmonic Society, which was wrong indeed to refuse this work.

13th–16th I am Liverpool, Adelphi Hotel, then for 10 days Erlenbach bei Zürich. The 28th December Barcelona (Spain), Grand Hotel, 4 Naçiones. Thank you very much for your kind feeling. Miss Bass communicated me about my wife's illness. Thanks God every danger is over. (11 December 1924)

Leopold Stokowski, on the other hand, answered Ibbs and Tillett in a way which illustrates how very different life today has become with jet-setting conductors flying in to rehearse and conduct a concert within less than a week. At the time of writing (1925) Stokowski was in charge of the Philadelphia Orchestra:

> Thank you for your kind suggestions regarding the Royal Philharmonic Society of London and the Liverpool Philharmonic Society. Unfortunately I doubt if I can be in England at that time because probably I am taking my orchestra right across the United States to the Pacific Coast in May 1926, and I would not have time to go to Europe in January as I have only two and a half weeks free then, and that would not give me time to come and go and rehearse and play the concerts.
>
> Hoping I may have the pleasure of conducting these orchestras at some other time, and thanking you for your kind thought of me. (3 February 1925)

Another conductor offered an engagement at Liverpool was Otto Klemperer, though he responded with a request to appear in London first:

> Thank you very much for the kind offer to conduct in Liverpool. I should be very pleased to accept, but think it would be a good thing to arrange a concert in London to introduce me to the English public before the concert in Liverpool. May I ask for an early reply as to whether this might be possible. (24 June 1925, translation from German)

A year later and the correspondence was resumed, this time with Klemperer prepared to delay a London appearance until after he had conducted a concert in Liverpool:

> In response to your last letter, I inform you that I would be pleased to conduct in Liverpool and accept the 2nd November 1926. Perhaps you could arrange a concert for me in London thereafter. From 15th April my address is Wiesbaden, Nordtal 29. (6 April 1926, translation from German)

In the end this project came to nothing and he did not conduct in England until three years later at the Courtauld-Sargent concerts in November 1929. Klemperer's biographer Peter Heyworth describes attempts to get Klemperer to London (by the BBC) in December 1926 and by the Royal Philharmonic Society in 1927, but this proposal from Ibbs and Tillett (apparently unknown to Heyworth) appears to predate both.

The French conductor Pierre Monteux, having flirted briefly with another London agent, came to London in January 1927 to conduct the Royal Philharmonic Orchestra, and had dealings with the agency. His soloist in Mozart and Richard Strauss was Elisabeth Schumann and his programme included the first UK performance of *Hymn to Apollo* by Arthur Bliss. He began and ended his programme with French fare, César Franck's symphonic poem *Psyche* and Berlioz's popular *Symphonie fantastique.*

> I received your letter of the 22nd upon my return from abroad, please excuse me for delaying the answer. Having received some interesting offer from a London agent, I have given him the reclusivity of my contracts for 1925–26. I thank you for your letter, but I am sorry not to be able to give you the satisfactory answer. (28 January 1925)
>
> I received your letter of May 17th and I am happy to tell you that I can accept the engagement with the Royal Philharmonic of London for fifty guineas as I will naturally be passing through London after Liverpool. I thank you very, very much for your work as it is a very good thing for me to conduct an important concert in London. Perhaps at the same time would it be possible for you to arrange a concert with the British Broadcasting Co.? When I conducted a concert last year with that company it was under such terrible conditions that Mr Percy Pitt promised me another concert. I am nearly sure if you speak to him he would be able to give me that concert between January 27th and February 8th when I must leave for Russia. (19 May 1926)
>
> I thank you for your kind letter of the 6th. I surely will let you know in due time when I shall be available for the London [season] 1928–29.

As for Mme Schumann, I will do my best to get her an engagement in Amsterdam following immediately her appearance in The Hague, but I think it would be good at the same time for you to write to Dr Rudolf Mengelberg, who is arranging dates now.

You can refer to my conversation with Mme Schumann and say that I should like to have her sing with the Concertgebouw Orkest in Amsterdam and in The Hague also, where I am sure she will have a great success. (9 May 1927)

I am enclosing the signed copy of my Contract with the Liverpool Philharmonic. I take notice that, even not written in the Contract, it is understood that an additional fee of ten guineas should be paid to me if this concert is broadcast. I hope it will!!! With many thanks, believe me.
Yours sincerely
Pierre Monteux
Will you please take notice of my new address.
(1 August 1928)

The Czech conductor Vaclav Talich made an appearance with the Royal Philharmonic Society in 1928 with his business arrangements in the agency's hands for the event (in the first of three letters on the subject and dated 17 June 1927, he hoped for 60 guineas but was prepared to accept 50). Holst's *Egdon Heath* was played rather than a work by Delius, the soloist in Brahms' Violin Concerto was Joseph Szigeti. The young Czech composer to whom Talich refers was possibly Martinu, then aged 37, whose work *La Bagarre* was given its first performance under Koussevitsky in Boston on 18 November 1927:

... In a few days I shall confirm the programme for the R.P.S. I am awaiting a reply from a young Czech composer, whether he has a second set of performing material of his newest work which Koussevitsky will perform in America next season,. I shall write to you as soon as I have his reply. At present I suggest Berlioz *Carneval Romain*, Delius ? (I would like to play something by Delius but leave the choice of work entirely to the Committee), Brahms Concerto, the new work, Dvořák Symphony No.4 [No.8] in G major. As far as the radio concert is concerned, the 26th February is the only acceptable date for me. Regarding the fee, please suggest it yourself as I am quite ignorant of the possibilities. I can only trust that you will look after our mutual interests. (12 September 1927, translation from German)

The Swiss conductor Ernest Ansermet had made his London debut in 1919, but during the 1920s he became a frequent visitor to the capital and the provinces, and was much involved in the early days of the BBC Symphony Orchestra's activities. After the first letter, in a mix of French and struggling English, he threw caution to the winds and wrote only in English with his programme suggestions to Ibbs and Tillett. A sign of the times is their involvement in contractual arrangements with the new recording companies:

En réponse à votre lettre concernant Birmingham, je vous prier de communiquer au Comité que les Danses du *Prince Igor* et *Firebird* dans le même programme me semblent faire un peu trop de "danses" et que ce serait a little thiring: too much brasses. Je leur propose:

1 Prélude de *Lohengrin*	Wagner
2 Symphony in D [minor]	Franck
3 Introduction et Marche nuptiale du *Coq d'or*	Rimsky-Korsakov
4 *Pastorale d'été*	Honegger
5 *Firebird* Suite	Stravinsky

C'est un peu court, mais difficile. Si *Lohengrin* ne convient pas, on peut mettre le *Prélude des Maîtres Chanteuses*. La deuxième partie pourrait être allongée en mettant à la place de Rimsky-Korsakov: *Cockaigne* ouverture, Elgar, ou *Stenka Razin*, Glazunow, ou *Chansons populaires russes*, Liadov.

Comme je m'embarque pour l'Amèrique du Sud le 3 juin à Cherbourg sur l'*Andes* (R.M.), je vous

prie de demander au Royal Phil[harmonic] de me fixer au plus vite sur mon programme. J'insisterais beaucoup pour y faire le *Faust* Symphonie de Liszt ou une symphonie de Beethoven, l'oeuvre de Walton don't j'ai parlé, Symphonie concertante (en 3 parties), et une œuvre de Debussy, Ravel ou Stravinsky. Veuillez me répondre à Genève, où je serai le 27, sinon avant le 26 ici.
Avec mes meilleurs salutations
(21 May 1927)

Forgive me for being late in my answer about the Birmingham programme and Gramophone dates, but I have preferred to differ my answer till my return here and so I had time to think without haste to the referred questions.

For Birmingham I propose definitely

1 Prélude de *Lohengrin*	Wagner
2 Symphony in D [minor]	Franck
3 Introduction et *Marche nuptiale* du *Coq d'or*	Rimsky-Korsakov
4 *Pastorale d'été*	Honegger
5 *Firebird* Suite (fragments)	Stravinsky

Ronde des Princesses, Danse infernale du Roi Kastcheï, Berceuse et finale

I will bring with me the string parts (or if necessary all the parts) of Franck et Wagner. I may also bring Honegger et Stravinsky parts. But I wish to mention specially that there is an important piano part by Stravinsky, requiring a very good musician and piano player. I will arrive at Birmingham Feb. 21st at the night, Grand Hotel I believe.

I would be glad to settle definitely the arrangement with Columbia. If necessary I would be able to stay in London the 10th and 11th of February, but I would prefer to place this engagement after the 22nd of April. I will be back from Russia at the beginning of April and then I have concerts in Brussels till the 22nd of April, being able to go directly from Brussels to London. With my best thanks for your intervention in the Gramophone affair. (11 January 1928)

Letters from foreign artists, some with charmingly quaint spelling and eccentric turns of phrase, continued to arrive at the agency. These suggestions came from the Russian pianist and agency artist, Nikolai Orloff.

After sending my letter I received your kind letter. I am inclined to play the 2nd concerto of Brahms, but in the second part I would like to execute the concerto No.1 of Czajkowsky [Tchaikovsky] or some solo pieces (Franck, Rachmaninoff, Chopin). I am very anxiosh about the Norwegian concerts. Will you please let me know all the informations about it. The question interest me specially. (undated, received 10 September 1925)

while the American pianist Josef Hofmann, for long an Ibbs and Tillett artist, observed wryly:

May I ask what you mean by saying that I, as a 'Soloist' am supposed to appear three times at Plymouth? A recital composed of three appearances is plenty, and then some! What sort of a performance is it to be at Plymouth, where a soloist is to appear three times? I am rather interested to know before I accept. (28 June 1926)

The soprano Grete Stückgold (English mother/German father) knew exactly what she wanted of Ibbs and Tillett.

It is a long time since you have heard from me; I was so very busey with opera work. Bruno Walter has engaged me for 40 evenings at his opera [Berlin] and is taking me next season to London, for this season everyboddy was engaged. I refused a huge engagement to South America because have not the time for several months. The only month that I could hold open for England is November. I would like to come there and to sing in several towns, because it is impossible for me to come only for two concerts. Inclosed you will find 20 postcards of me. Please let me hear very soon as I have to make all my arrangements. (15 April 1926)

The famous German soprano, Lotte Lehmann, had wonderful expressions translated literally from her native tongue, which endeared her to the agency management and no doubt produced laughter in the office when these were received.

> Just I remark that I have not answered to your kind letter of 11th July. I beg your pardon, I am very silly in settling my correspondence. Please will you be so kind as to give me propositions for a tournée through England in the autumn of 1928, and I hope we will have much pleasure in collaboration. (21 October 1927)

> Dear Mr Ibbs & Tillett,
> Excuse me that I give answer so late; I am ill and in bed since days, had so peine in my had that I could not write. It is very pitty that Broadcasting is not possible in May, but impossible for me to come back again! October 19th is good for me, we can take it for Queen's Hall. (6 May 1929)

The relationship with the cellist Guilhermina Suggia appears to have had its ups and downs; she was clearly a formidable lady, who was quite used to getting her own way, and fully determined in what she would or would not undertake. A common problem for an artist, then and now, either was organizing an engagement herself or accepting a direct approach, and not referring it to the agency. Such situations always led to friction (and no doubt still does) on the matter of commission, and Suggia resolved that Ibbs and Tillett were not entitled to take on any dates they had not secured for her. Like many other artists, however, she was also alert to some of the more parlous financial conditions in some of the smaller music clubs or societies, particularly those away from London, and was always ready to compromise or negotiate in such circumstances, something she felt necessary to point out to the agency.

> I think it ought to be clearly understood that on the next [Max] Mossel tour I only pay you 5% commission on the engagement – it was a purely personal engagement arranged between Mr Mossel and myself, as Mr Mossel will tell you. As regards further engagements in this country, Scotland and Ireland, it must be also quite understood that while I am glad to entertain any engagements you offer, I reserve to myself the right to accept other engagements not coming through your firm. (2 March 1927)

> I have sent you yesterday the two contracts signed for Norwich and Huddersfield, and note that there is an extra town (Ayr, Oct 25th) to add to the Mossel tour.
>
> Regards Australia and New Zealand, I am willing to go but would require a fixed sum of either £200 per concert, a minimum guarantee of twenty-five concerts and all my fares from England to Australia and return, and hotels paid, or a fee of £150 per concert and all fares aller and return from Portugal to Australia and hotel expenses paid for two people – myself and a friend – and please let me know which would be the best time of the year for such a trip.
>
> Regards America, I have also thought that I could undertake a tour there next March and April for a minimum fee of £250 in New York and Boston, and £200 in other towns, and a minimum of twelve concerts in the space of two months including journeys from England to America.
>
> I wouldn't like to go to any of those countries unless I bring back a sum about three to four thousand pounds nett. This will help you in knowing what to do. (30 March 1927)

> Let me first announce you my marriage to Dr José Carteado Mena which took place last Saturday the 27th of August, and tell you that I am tremendously happy. Happily too this won't mean that I have in any way to give up my carrière, rather the reverse for now I can consider the possibility of going to America as in that case my husband will accompany me. Now regards invitation for Norwich, I find it more convenient to me to stay at that nice hotel I stayed last time, as I shall come straight from Ayr and probably very tired after the tour in Scotland and not well prepared to be entertained by strangers. So please will you excuse me and thank Mr Gurney for his kindness and book me a good double room at the same hotel which name I forgot.
>
> I could make some concession to Sir Dan Godfrey if the concert could fit the dates in February without much trouble. I think I mentioned seventy guineas as a sharing base or eighty, fixed fee. We

might do seventy five guineas fixed fee or on sharing terms on sixty-five guineas basis. I think this is reasonable.

P.S. Please note that my name for the programme will still remain Madame Suggia or Guilhermina Suggia. (3 September 1927)

Ref: America. I am going to write to Mr Hudson about two recitals in New York, but to save time, will you start communicating with him on the subject. If he would be prepared to risk it in case of any loss. Now I note you are offering me four engagements, viz:

Woking January 22nd	£68.5.0	Leeds Symphony February 9th	£52.10.0
Bradford February 10th	£73.10.0	Cambridge Feb 15th	£73.10.10

In the case of my having to be in London for the Jan 22nd, Cambridge can either be Jan 30th or February 15th. This depends on whatever other engagements may come along. I don't wish to be more than four weeks away from Portugal in the New Year. What about November. Couldn't these engagements not fit on my return from America as I shall hope to be in England from the 10th of Nov till middle of Dec? Why not get as many engagements together, then in that case I shouldn't go in January or February and only visit England in the Spring, which was my intention?

Also may I suggest that you procure me a change of playing in England at the beginning of Sept next, previous to my American tour, as I shall be so many months away from the public and would like a little training. I don't know if places like Margate, Ramsgate, Eastbourne, Brighton or Bournemouth, where I could get a sixty guinea fee or sixty-five, but I should like to play somewhere. I could even start at the end of Aug. I know that Eastbourne would like to have me and probably Bournemouth too. I don't know yet what date I am leaving for America, it depends on the boats I suppose, as I want to go on the large ones, *Majestic* or *Berengaria* or something like that.

I am afraid my proposed visit to England in June has to fall through as there are no parties, and therefore no excuse to go. (17 May 1928)

I am sending you a wire saying that I can't accept New York concerts so late in November, as I want to be in England then. I wish Copley could fit some things in October with orchestra. I couldn't reply before as I was in Madrid since the beginning of June playing at the Societa de Cultura Musical and only just arrived at Oporto.

Regards the programme for Pittsfield [America], I am quite prepared to start with:

I C major Bach Suite

II the F major Brahms

III Malipiero Sonata a tre if I like the work and if I have time to study it, as I haven't got the work, and I must have it as soon as possible, please. In case I don't like it, I would play an old sonata, Valentini or Eccles or Sammartini (whichever she chooses) and as number

IV I propose

a) Kol nidrei	Bruch
b) Serenade espagnole	Glazounow
c) Humoreske	Sinigaglia
or	
Waldesruhe	Dvořák
Piece en forme de Habanera	Ravel
Spanish dance	Popper

There is nothing Portuguese written for cello nor anything else Spanish worth doing. Please let me know about other programmes I sent for Copley, if he has accepted them. (11 June 1928)

I have just sent a wire accepting Mrs Bossom's party for July 12th, but do try and get the hundred guineas fee exclusive <u>not</u> including pianist, as I have to make the special journey for it and now I am missing here an engagement. Do explain this to her but of course, if she doesn't want, then I will engage my own accompanist. Probably I will play with Miss Stern, who is coming with me to England on the *Arlanza* due Southampton on the 10th – but if she stand the accompanists fee, then let her engage whoever she wants, preferable Reeves or Craxton. It would be splendid if I could get another 'At home' or a concert somewhere, as it is terribly expensive to move like this only for one party. Still, I am glad to have an opportunity of visiting England again soon.

Regards the travelling for America, I heard from Mr Hudson that he has already booked definitely a cabin on the *Aquitania* for Sept the 12th. I wonder if this is the correct date, but as I asked you to communicate with him, I guess you are aware of everything. Please let me know. Thank you for the Bulletin, which is very good this year. (28 June 1928)

In answer to your letter regards America, I don't want to spend money on advertising, although I know this is the way every artist does, but I have waited so long to go there that I wish to be engaged at a fixed fee by some societies, and I think that the fact of being engaged to play at Mrs Coolidge's Festival at Washington is in itself the biggest reclame and best introduction. I shall have to travel with a companion friend and the expenses are too big as you know. If this can't be then I shall remain in Europe, but I should like to have more countries in Europe to go to apart from England and Spain. Please tell me if you can manage other countries for me or if I have to deal directly with some agent.

I am surprised to hear nothing yet regards Queen's Hall, Manchester, Liverpool, Scotland etc for next winter. My friends in England are quite astonished to know that I have so little work to do in February. I wonder if there has been offers that you have turned down, but I should like always to hear what and why you have refused. As I wrote some days ago, I don't mind playing for a lesser fee at places where they can't afford my fees. Also let me know if Bradford has accepted my programme. (15 September 1928)

On the matter of income tax, many a foreign artist was only too glad to leave such matters in the agency's hands. Casals was one of them. This group of letters covers his activities first as a conductor, and then as a cellist, the last pair concerning arrangements with a gramophone record company. Casals' first wife, the American soprano Susan Metcalfe-Casals, was represented by the agency for a few years:

As you have records of my earnings in England of this last season, I beg you to put the sum in the enclosed income tax form after a reasonable deduction of my expenses, including fares from Spain. As Mrs Casals has been in England for professional purposes, her expenses can also be deducted. I authorise you to sign for me that income tax form and send it to the Midland Bank. In regard to the London Symphony [Orchestra] concert, please propose the following program:

1) *Tragic* Overture	Brahms
2) G major Pianoforte Concerto [No.4]	Beethoven
3) Symphony [No.9] in C major	Schubert

Please tell Mr [Bertram] Jones [Secretary of the LSO Board] that I have received many requests to repeat the *Tragic* Overture. Miecio Horszowski will be the soloist for the Beethoven Concerto. (19 July 1928)

I note the 13th of March 1930 for the Royal Philharmonic Society. As you know my minimum fee is $1000 but I shall be very pleased to play for the RPS for a special fee of 100 guineas. Will you please communicate to the Committee that I would very much like to see my name on the list of Honorary Members of the Society. This would mark my 30th anniversary of my debut in England, and as I suppose this fact will find no interest in the official quarters, a new token of friendship from the RPS would give me great satisfaction. The Schumann concerto suits me perfectly. (15 July 1929)

Please forgive my delay in replying to your two letters. I have been in Vienna and elsewhere. Enclosed you will find a draft for the amount due you on the exchange of dollars. In reply to your enquiry re the Columbia Gramophone Company, I wish to say that I would be willing to play for them the eight Nocturnes of Chopin (four double-sided records), provided they would pay me the terms I got for my last records, a bonus of $1000 for each double-sided record and a royalty of 10% on all manufactured discs.

Kindly give me as soon as possible an answer, as I am intending to leave for the States very soon. We will discuss my future appearances in England on the next occasion. In the meantime I would like to have a statement of my last recitals at Queen's Hall for the purpose of writing to Mr Max Lindlar to thank him for his generous co-operation. (1 June 1928)

> I just wired you in reply to your letter which I received last night. I am willing to forego the bonus and reduce the royalty of 10% from the selling price to 10% of the wholesale price, which is a considerable reduction as you will realize, but the advance royalty sum should be at least equal to the bonus I expected. This arrangement is very much lower than my former contracts with disc recording firms. I am willing to make the afore-mentioned concessions owing to the fact that I am going to concertize part of next season in Constantinople, Athens, Cairo, Alexandria, Jerusalem, Sofia, Belgrade, Bucharest etc. and the records of the Graphophone would help the concerts as much as my playing there would help the sale of my records. I would also appear at Morocco, Algeria and Tunisia besides other countries. I hope you will succeed in persuading the Graphophone people to see the reasonableness of my demands. I must return to Paris before my departure for New York and will therefore expect the company to pay my transportation from Paris to London and return and my hotel expenses during the few days that I will be recording. I could come to London the evening of the 18th and do all my recording on the 19th and 20th and even 21st, should there be any necessity for adding another day. (15 June 1928)

Combining engagements with recording sessions was now becoming the aim of foreign artists visiting Britain. The German conductor Hans Knappertsbusch discussed such a possibility with the agency for a visit to Liverpool:

> I must reply in German as my knowledge of English is not so great to make myself clearly understood. First I thank you sincerely for your invitation which I would very much like to accept. Would a fee of 75 guineas be acceptable to you? The first-class journey from Munich to Liverpool and the stay itself will amount to so much that I must ask if you can arrange some recordings with Electrola so that I do not lose money on the trip. (20 April 1928, translation from German)

The Swedish soprano Göta Ljungberg was enjoying repeated success at Covent Garden during the mid-1920s, though she was not represented by the agency until the 1929–30 season; however they did arrange concerts for her before that season, including one in the unlikely venue of Burnley in Lancashire:

> I am just returning to Berlin and by looking through my papers I don't feel quite sure about my concert dates. I therefore will have to trouble you to send me these once more. As I recall it, I think it should be as follows: October 7th in Burnley, October 9th in Liverpool, October 13th in Glasgow. Did you receive my last letter concerning *Isoldes Liebestod* in Liverpool? (21 August 1928)

At 81 years of age, the composer/conductor Sir Alexander Mackenzie, former Principal of London's Royal Academy of Music, was nearing the end of an active musical life when approached by the agency to accept an invitation to conduct in the Kent seaside resort of Margate, but regrettably he felt unable to comply:

> I have to thank you for your letter of the 20th, which, as I am as yet unable to personally attend to anything, could not be dealt with by return. The effects of a street encounter (June 25th) with a taxi-cab do not allow me to walk unaided yet, and it may be sometime before I can leave my room. Nothing would have given me greater pleasure than to have accepted the engagement you offer me at Margate on the 11th or 12th September. In the circumstances, however, I feel that I dare not take the risk of conducting at so early a date. In fact I cannot say with any certainty when I may be able to resume my normal public life. Meanwhile I shall be glad to let you know when that (to me) agreeable moment arrives. (22 July 1928)

Following a tradition which went back to Vert's role in sending the score of Elgar's new *Enigma* variations on to Hans Richter in 1899, nearly 30 years later they were doing much the same for the Russian composer Nicolas Medtner:

> Gentlemen,
> Yesterday I sent you two piano scores of my second piano concerto. May I ask you to be so kind and to send one copy to Sir Landon Ronald and the other to Sir Hamilton Harty. The orchestra score will be sent to you as soon as it is ready. (3 August 1928)

It was at the end of the 1920s when the agency entered into a brief correspondence with Yehudi Menuhin's father Moshe, keen to extend the phenomenal success his son was enjoying in America and France to the UK, with a debut appearance in London. The fact that the agency turned the boy down may be considered an act of folly by some, matched 30 years later by the Decca recording company's refusal to take on the Beatles in the 1960s. In trying to look for an explanation, perhaps John Tillett was reminded of the tragic consequences to his uncle Narciso Vert, which followed the child violinist Vivien Chartres' unlicensed appearance, landing him in court and possibly causing his death. Maybe he simply faced up to the agency's inability to fulfil properly the specialist handling of so young a child as the 12-year-old boy. Whatever the reasons, years later Yehudi and his wife Diana became close friends with John Tillett's widow Emmie, and while the agency kept copies of their replies to Moshe Menuhin's two letters, the Menuhin family reputedly have the originals framed, trophy-like, on a wall. What this correspondence does reveal, however, is the view Ibbs and Tillett took of their own operations as those of an agent and not a personal manager nor impresario, an entrenched attitude which many years later would have serious consequences and cause problems as times changed:

> Gentlemen,
> We have practically decided that after our son Yehudi Menuhin, violinist, gets through with his engagements in San Francisco, Los Angeles, New York, Philadelphia, Chicago, Boston and Cleveland this coming January and February in symphonic and recital appearances, that he will cross the Atlantic to accept a few of the very many engagements offered him now in the capitals of Europe. In Berlin, Yehudi will appear once with the Philharmonic, and then in recital under Wolff/Sachs, then in Rome in the St Cecilia Academy with the Augusteo under Molinari, then in Paris with the Société Conservatoire orchestra, to be followed by recital in the Opéra. Similar invitations and engagements reached us from all over Europe, but all, with the possible exception of Moscow Soviet, will not be accepted.
>
> Now comes London. We shall take Yehudi to London. When we were in Paris last year, after Yehudi took Paris by storm, many engagements came to us from London, but, if you are at all acquainted with Yehudi's history, we refused flatly all offers everywhere in order to preserve Yehudi's future art and career, and above all his youth and health. He is growing big now and will welcome a few carefully selected, dignified and grand debuts in Europe. Now we have enquired about the proper persons into whose hands we can entrust Yehudi's interests. Your firm has been The One best recommended, and therefore, if we can arrange mutually satisfactory conditions, we shall indeed be glad to do business with you. This time we shall not allow Yehudi to take any more than two appearances in one country, one introductory appearance with the leading symphony orchestra, regular subscription concert preferred, and then a recital. There is no reason why Yehudi should not carry London as he carried Paris, and thus sell out Albert Hall right after his symphonic appearance. In this country Yehudi's standing, dignity and rating with the masses, managers, press and critics is second to none. To judge by the demands pouring in upon us from Europe, Asia and Africa, Yehudi's rating over there is not any less than in the US. Do you think you can undertake a dignified grand presentation of Yehudi in London? If so, on what terms? Please remember that once these appearances are honourably, dignifiedly and properly managed, as I have no doubt they can be, you may look forward to many contacts with Yehudi in the future in England and elsewhere.
>
> While I shall appreciate a telegraphed answer, in your correspondances following cablegrams, please state definitely (to save time) on what basis you intend to "play" Yehudi in London, guarantees, form of contract and other such details. I shall appreciate prompt acknowledging of this letter as we keep in suspense those from London who have approached us already. (29 August 1928)

Ibbs and Tillett replied:

> Dear Sir,
> We are in receipt of your letter and enclosures of the 28th ult., the contents of which we have studied

with much interest. Firstly we should wish to express our appreciation of the compliment you pay us in approaching us regarding your son's professional interests in this country. We heard from friends in Paris, and have seen from the American press of your son's amazing talents, and there can be little doubt he would create as great a sensation here in due course. In this country, however, it takes a longer time for even a sensation in the musical world to leap into fame, and the wonderful experiences you have had with your son in America and Paris would, we fear, not be experienced here after only one appearance in public.

We have given the matter our fullest consideration, and whilst we greatly regret not being able to avail ourselves of the opportunity of being associated with this great young artist, we are not in a position to offer any such contract as would naturally be expected by yourself. We have made it a rigid rule all through our business career not to speculate, or take any financial risk whatever with any artist, and are compelled to adhere to this rule.

We work solely on commission upon business we are able to secure for the artists. In our view you really require an Impressario [*sic*] and Manager (such as Mr Lionel Powell) rather than an Agent.

With reference to your suggested idea of an Orchestral appearance, there are now only three permanent Orchestras in London, the London Symphony, Royal Philharmonic Society and the British Broadcasting Corporation, and all their engagements for the Autumn–Winter Season 1928–29 are already made, although there is the possibility of a vacancy occurring with the London Symphony.

We fear you would be sadly disappointed with the financial results of a Recital at the Royal Albert Hall if given after only one Orchestral appearance. Of course we may be wrong as to this, but we certainly should not advocate it personally. Again thanking you for your courtesy, and expressing our sincere regret we are not able to avail ourselves of it. (14 September 1928)

Gentlemen,
I wish to thank you for your prompt cable as well as your letter in which you explain your principles and methods of doing business. Frankly speaking I am more interested in your 'negative' reply than in a good many of those dazzling offers made at home and abroad, with few proper due exceptions. This note is in the nature of an exchange of notes between us, if you care. I can anytime sign up with 'the others'.

Now what I am interested in is the BASIS on which you might do business with us. What would be your procedure, method, recommendations and steps? If you understand me, the material phase is not the first consideration, however important. It is the laying of Yehudi's foundation that I am interested in now, and TIME is on our side. For example, I have practically decided to accept no engagements for Yehudi in London at all during this coming season 1928–1929, and have him appear there only around November 1929 before sailing back for his following season's engagements in America. In other words, he will not go to London until he will have made his Berlin, Paris and other few engagements which we are arranging now for him. And even then, if Yehudi's appearances in London may not definitely be deemed advisable from the standpoint of CONQUEST, we have time, even though it seems to me that you are attributing too much Sang Froid to your dear old conservative Englishman.

Meanwhile we are proceeding with the engagements of Yehudi in the US and Europe; meanwhile your British Gramophone Society has accepted for England and Europe etc Yehudi's Victor records; meanwhile a good many things will be done, and while I shall put off the other gentlemen from London with any definite answers for a while, I shall appreciate a prompt reply to this letter of mine to you. From my standpoint, and in the final analysis, whether the agent or manager arrives at his remuneration through commission, arithmetic or percentage he is always entitled to Pay for Services, and from the standpoint of the popular artist it should spell very little difference how the arithmetic is done, as long as justice, fairness and confidence is practised with devotion. I am rather impressed favourably by you, gentlemen, sufficiently to desire another exchange of correspondence. May I expect to hear from you soon? In your reply will you be so kind to mention a few of the leading artists you act for as agents. (27 September 1928)

Ibbs and Tillett replied:

Dear Sir,
We duly received your letter of the 27th ult, and regret that owing to the absence of the writer from England, we were not able to reply by return mail. We very greatly appreciate the spirit in which you write us, and we have given your letter our full consideration.

> We still feel that you need the assistance here of an Impressario, rather than an Agent, to properly present your son to our Public; one who can devote full time and publicity to such a task, and we feel somewhat diffident as to our being in a position to give this necessary attention, in view of the fact that we are more than fully occupied with our general business, and we feel sure you will appreciate our position.
>
> In the ordinary way, for special artists, we manage their London Concerts at a fixed fee of £21 for the Queen's Hall and ten guineas at the smaller Halls. We take 15% commission upon engagements secured for them, beyond this there are no charges by us, but as we told you, the artist is responsible for all expenses incurred in the working of the Concerts, publicity etc.
>
> As you ask us the question, we are managers for this Country for Rachmaninoff, Hofmann, Cortot, Casals, Moiseiwitsch, Thibaud, Segovia, English Singers, Suggia, Myra Hess, Harold Samuel among others. (18 October 1928)

Alfred Cortot, one of the pianists on the list just mentioned, had views on the combined roles of pianist and conductor. This was something which would be quite different 50 years later in the careers of artists such as Vladimir Ashkenazy and Daniel Barenboim, while 50 years before Cortot's letter below, Hans von Bülow had combined both activities with ease:

> I apologise for not having replied sooner to your letter about the Birmingham concert, but I only received it a few days ago midway through my tour in the middle of France. I don't think I can accept playing and conducting in the same concert. The act of conducting induces a tiredness which then does my piano playing a disservice. I am happy to accept one or the other, but if I am to conduct it must be at a time when I have a period of purely conducting engagements. Moreover it might be possible to arrange a concert in London with the Royal Philharmonic Society or the London Symphony Orchestra in the same week. Would you send me the list of engagements for March with the terms for each concert so that I can propose the programmes to you? Send it to Paris please. (15 January 1929, translation from French)

Another of Cortot's letters illustrates not only that visiting artists travelled the length and breadth of the country on their tours to Britain, but also the remarkable venues at which they played. One wonders if such places as Woodford Green (Essex), Croydon and Woking could attract such eminence today, despite the concert hall and theatre which the last two possess. The second letter lists his current concerto repertoire which Ibbs and Tillett would then pass on to orchestras in London and around the country.

Dear Friends,

Passing through Paris for 2 days, I am keen to send you my programmes for March.

2 March: Hastings	1) Concerto Schumann
	2) a: *Children's Corner* Debussy
	b: Rapsodie Liszt or, if preferred, Sonate funèbre Chopin
4 March: Croydon	1) Andante spianato et Polonaise, Valse, Nocturne, 2 Etudes Chopin
	2) Etude en forme de Valse Saint Saëns
	Bourée pour la main gauche seule Saint Saëns
	La Cathédrale engloutie Debussy
	2me Rapsodie Liszt
7 March: Harrogate	Récital Chopin – Les 24 Préludes, Sonata funèbre, 12 Etudes
9 March: Bournemouth	(same programme as Harrogate)
12 March: London	Quintette Franck
	Concerto fa mineur Bach (string quintet)
14 March: Woodford Green	(same programme as Harrogate)
15 March: Eastbourne	(same programme as Harrogate)
18 March: [Shrewsbury]	Please ask Miss Pugh-Jones for the programme which we have fixed, and send it to me.
19 March: Woking	1) Concerto da camera Vivaldi
	2) Sonate funèbre Chopin

	3) *Etude symphonique* Schumann
	(if the programme is too serious, tell me)
21 March: London	*Variations symphonique* Franck
	Ballade Fauré

(29 January 1929, translation from French)

The following is a postscript to a letter sent six months later.

> To make it easier for the Committees to choose my orchestral repertoire, I have made you a list of works I can play, providing I am notified before 15 July.

Beethoven	the 5 concertos
Bach	Concerto in F minor, Concerto for flute [oboe] and violin in D minor
Schumann	Concerto
Chopin	Andante spianato et grande Polonaise
Liszt	Concerto in E flat [No.1]
Saint Saëns	Concertos Nos. 4 et 5
Rachmaninoff	Concerto No.3
Brahms	Concerto [No.1] in D minor
César Franck	*Variations symphonique*
Grieg	Concerto
Vincent d'Indy	*Symphonie cèvenole*
De Falla	*Nights in the Gardens of Spain*
Fauré	Ballade
Mozart	Concerto in E♭ (with a Menuet in the Finale) [No.22 K.482]

(16 June 1929)

Another pianist, Artur Schnabel, was also meticulous in making his own concert arrangements, especially on the subject of multiple-programming. The days of artists playing some solos (with piano if they were non-piano instrumentalists), or of appearing twice in the programme, were fast disappearing and Schnabel was very keen to encourage the change, especially as the massive Brahms D minor Concerto was his main contribution. Ironically, in this case, he is in dispute with Hamilton Harty, conductor of the Hallé Orchestra, whose predecessor Richter was an early exponent of the change of programming style, yet here Harty seems to be taking a step back:

> Sir Hamilton Harty's suggestion to play a short solo piece as well as the Brahms D minor concerto in Manchester sits uneasily with me. I feel that solo pieces always fail in symphony concerts and it is no longer usual almost anywhere to play them. I would be grateful if Manchester would make do with just the Brahms. Under no circumstances do I wish to play alone in the second half, if I must appear again after the Brahms, I could do Weber's *Konzertstück* which lasts 12 minutes, but I would most prefer to appear in the Brahms alone. (26 August 1929, translation from German)

Coincidentally the German singer Elena Gerhardt had decided to place her British engagements with Ibbs and Tillett, taking her leave of Lionel Powell as John Tillett was himself recommending Powell to Moshe Menuhin. Gerhardt was a lady who knew exactly what she wanted and what she expected from an agent:

> This is to confirm our agreement in writing that I would very much like to put my further concert work all over the British Isles under the guidance of your firm. I am writing my decisions by the same mail to Mr Lionel Powell. Should he, however, want me for one of his celebrity tours, he would naturally make arrangements through your firm. Will you please go right ahead now to get as many dates as possible for next winter, or even perhaps for the season, as I easily can come over for private engagements.
>
> As for fees, I would not like to go under 50 g[uinea]s, but of course would take in whatever you can get when I am in England anyway. Societies who can afford higher fees surely should pay it. I can easily be twice in England during the winter season, therefore will you be kind enough to book

two good nights at Wigmore Hall, one perhaps in November and one during the second part of the season, and try to get provincial dates around these concerts.

I cannot tell you how glad I am to be connected with your firm from now on. I hope it will proof a great success for all of us. (24 March 1929)

The violinist Joseph Szigeti was also intent on exacting correct fees and suitable venues:

I am waiting impatiently for news about the Eastbourne date at the end of November as this prevents me from fixing my dates in Budapest, Vienna etc., where I had originally planned to play between Nov. 26th and Dec. 9th.

Did you receive my letters of the 11th and 15th inst.? I am enclosing the contracts for Rochdale and Dublin.

I hope to be free for Bradford January 3rd but couldn't possibly come over extra for a fee of 50 guineas. The least I could do it for would be 60 guineas.

In Manchester I would accept 45 guineas but without broadcasting; the broadcasting people would have to complete my fee to 55 or 60 guineas. I explained to you my point of view in this matter last season. My connections with Sir Hamilton and the orchestra are so friendly and the records we made of the Brahms [concerto] are also a strong bond between us, so I hate to make difficulties, but you know that I don't accept 40 guineas in any other country and to have raised this initial fee by 5 guineas (!) is perhaps exaggerated.

I hope you will be able to fix a suitable date for the Chelsea concerts; I would have to ask Mr Piggott to raise the fee to 75 guineas on account of the heavy expenses my accompanists cause me.

Please ask Dublin to wait for my definite programmes for another few weeks (as my accompanist isn't decided on yet). Perhaps it will suffice them to know that the two programmes will include Tartini, Bach, Veracini, Francoeur, Paganini, Ernest Bloch, Debussy, Szymanowski, Dvořák, Bela Bartók etc.

Please let me know by wire: 'Szigeti, Kauserhof, Bad Gastein' as soon as you have been able to fix Eastbourne (what fee?) and the other date (perhaps London with one of the orchestras?). I hope that Oxford, Cambridge and Bournemouth will come through this time. May I have two copies of your Bulletin and the MS Press notices I sent you?

P.S. I just received your letter of the 22nd for which many thanks. I am afraid I can't take the risk of accepting dates so far apart as January 3rd, 14th, 16th, 20th without trying to better the fees somewhat as I have indicated in this letter. I hope you will do your best in the case of the Hallé fee as well. The societies must bear in mind that my 'territories' include the whole of Europe and that the time I spend in England restricts my tours elsewhere seriously. They seem to base their fees on artists 'running down from London' for one or two concerts, but in my case, especially with an accompanist, it is a different matter.

For Chelsea concert January 28th you seem to have overlooked the fact that I am on the Mossel tour, then; is Jan 29th Ayr definite? If not, I could get to Glasgow (Jan 30th) in good time. For Eastbourne I would like to have the earliest possible date: Nov 25th or 26th, as I am pressed for time for my tour in Hungary and Austria.

I keep the Manchester contracts pending your news concerning the fee.
(27 May 1929)

Five days later, during which the agency had replied by telegram, Szigeti was in fighting mood:

Thank you for your telegramme concerning Eastbourne Nov 26th and the probability of the Philharmonic on Nov 28th.

I am sorry to have to 'fight out' the fee in each case, but you don't seem to realise that a fee of 40 guineas is quite inadequate in such a case. If I take the risk of coming to England for two concerts at 110 or 120 guineas together, even then the final result would be far from brilliant. I play in Zurich on Nov 19th and in Budapest on Dec 1st or 2nd and I must calculate these long and expensive journeys and the loss of time. I am sure you wouldn't ask me to undertake such risky things. Will you please explain to the Eastbourne people that I wasn't consulted about the fee and I feel sure they will raise it to 50 guineas.

You can dispose of my time between Zurich and Budapest: 21st and 28th Nov inclusive, for Oxford, Cambridge or any other engagement. What fee are you negotiating for with the Royal

> Philharmonic? [pencilled annotation by John Tillett: 'Nov 29 Cambridge 55 with accp.'] (1 June 1929)

Two singers handled by the agency in the late 1920s were the contralto Marie Olczewska and the soprano Eva Turner. Olczewska's decisions whether or not to accept or reject engagements seem to have been made on the basis of the fee offered:

> Unfortunately I am so engaged with enquiries that I cannot undertake any concert under 100 guineas. Should this sum be paid, then kindly let me know. I travel middle of October to America and remain there until the beginning of April. (14 March 1928, translation from German)

Eva Turner, on the other hand, was intent on comparing the musical attractions of Douglas on the Isle of Man with the arena in Verona, in particular their respective audience sizes:

> Many thanks for your kind enquiry re the concert at Douglas on August 16th but I regret it will be impossible to entertain the matter as during the whole of the month of August I am singing Mascagni's *Isabeau* at the arena of Verona to audiences of 20,000. This has compelled me to rush away from London to make the necessary preparation for the event. They wanted me to break with Covent Garden last year, but of course I would not do that, so this year they were well ahead with their booking of me. (17 June 1929)

The composer and conductor Richard Strauss, like Saint Saëns before him, was, at the age of 65 and with another 20 years to live, heeding the advice of his doctors before accepting winter engagements:

> I regret that you evidently did not receive my telegram which I sent a week ago. I have to inform you with regret that it is impossible to accept the friendly invitation from the Royal Philharmonic Society as I am not permitted to undertake any more such journeys in the winter months. (18 July 1929, translation from German)

On the other hand the 70-year-old Siegfried Wagner had no such fears for his own health, and readily accepted an engagement with the BBC. Unfortunately he died less than a year later:

> Many thanks for your kind letter. Your proposition suits me quite well and I will come and conduct the concert for the B.B.C. on Wednesday February 5th in Queen's Hall for 150 guineas netto. Will you please write and tell me particulars concerning any special wishes for my programme. Will there be a soloist and who? Your answer will reach me via Bayreuth. (1 September 1929)

CHAPTER THIRTEEN

Letters from Conductors: 1930–39

In his memoirs (*Much besides Music*, 1951), the Australian writer and critic Thorold Waters provides a vivid picture of the sheer quantity, let alone quality, of London's music scene on a visit to England in 1930:

> London's demure illusion of a Silly Season and a sad grey Lent came to my mind on arrival again in 1930. 'Pity you've come just now', my old friend John Tillett, impresario of a host of notable artists, lamented. 'We've just begun Lent, so there's very little doing, you know!' Forthwith he committed me to concerts of Casals, Elena Gerhardt, and Lotte Lehmann in the ensuing week, and in the next morning's post sent me invitations for 22 others within the fortnight, including the two brilliant violinist sisters Jelly d'Aranyi and Adila Fachiri, Frank Merrick, an English pianist of long repute and beard almost as long, and other quality performers.

Many years before that, he wrote an interesting piece in the *British–Australasian* magazine (30 June 1910) on the subject of artists coming from Australia to try and make an impression in London, considered the capital of the music world. They were still doing so 50 years later in the 1960s, but by that time Nellie Melba and Florence Austral (note that these singers felt they had to change their surnames from Mitchell and Wilson respectively in order to publicize their origins) were succeeded by the Joans, Hammond and Sutherland. The article written by Thorold Waters (himself the founder of the Sun Aria competition which sent many fine singers to Europe from the Antipodes) was entitled 'Australian singers and English agents':

> As a rule, the Australian girl who comes to London to sing says she will be content if during her first six months here she has her chance at a couple of Ballad concerts, but she would also like an appearance at the Albert Hall with the Royal Choral Society. 'Of course', she adds, somewhat modestly, 'I haven't come here with the idea that I can get everything at once.'
>
> What can one say? There are probably 20,000 professional concert singers in England. Of that number some twenty are chosen by Messrs. Chappell and another twenty by Messrs. Boosey to sing at their Ballad Concerts in the course of a season. The Royal Choral Society has openings for, perhaps, 24 singers, and most of those who climb that pinnacle of greatness have a ten or twelve years struggle with the provincial work first. During the last eight or nine years, the influx of Australian singers to England has totalled at least 300, and of that number not more than twenty have sung in the Queen's Hall. There are many excellent artists with as much work as they can do in the Provinces who look upon the Queen's Hall as something quite beyond their reach.
>
> But it is no good telling the newly-arrived singer little home truths like that. It is no good recommending a wait of a few months to see how the land lies. The desire to be up and doing is a commendable Australian trait but most of us could unfold a tale of premature visits to agents, premature auditions and – if we were specially unlucky – premature appearances. Of the 300 or more singers to whom I have alluded, some came direct from their little towns of Tantanoola, Bunyip, Gerung-Gerung, or wherever they might be. They came direct to invade London and the majority felt that they were ready to go in and tackle the agents and get work. Remember, this is the London in which Kreisler, prince of all violinists, walked about for months awaiting the royal pleasure of agents who would not deign to hear him, although he had already played with distinction on the continent.
>
> 'Is she ready?' is the first thing an agent asks. 'Ready' may mean two things, either ready with musical knowledge or ready with cash. But we may proceed upon the extremely charitable assumption that the first of these qualifications is the one implied. Now, is the newcomer from Bunyip likely to be ready as the term is understood in a land where the thoroughly equipped singer is expected to have a nodding acquaintance with four languages, a sound familiarity with music, a lot of which has has never been heard yet in Australia, and some distinction of voice, at least?

The singer who has queened it in a big Australian capital is not necessarily in any better position than the young lady from Bunyip. She arrives feeling that she must make an immediate splash – and she does. It is a matter of knowledge in musical circles that two or three popular artists from Australia made such splashes when they were entrusted with roles in great orchestral works that you couldn't see the conductors for bubbles. When anyone misses twenty bars in (say) Elgar's *Apostles* the news travels as quickly as indignant conductors and amused bandsmen [i.e. orchestral players] can spread it.

The first person apprised by the conductor is the agent. The agent, it must be borne in mind, is a wily customer. He is a more or less useless individual, pampered out of all proportion to his value to the artist. I have not spent much time on the doormats of agencies since one of the biggest of the genus said: 'You know, it is necessary for the artist to make his own work up to a point, and we come in afterwards'. 'If that is the case,' I thought, 'the thing is to prevent the agents from coming in afterwards'. But the agent has a say in that matter also. His purpose in life – with one or two honourable exceptions – is to keep the new artist out as long as he can, and to come in on a 10% commission basis if the new artist proves too much for him.

Big fees mean big commission, only singers of years' standing get big fees, and the agent only gives an opportunity to a new artist when all other resources have failed. But the majority of concert agencies, if they depended upon commission alone, would have to seek the bankruptcy court. There are more ways to killing a cat than one, and the favourite way with all save half-a-dozen of the London agencies is to secure musical aspirants with money. So long as one has a long, strong purse, 'audition' as conducted by some agents, is a mere empty formula. The fraternal feeling that exists between them and some of the great conductors is too beautiful to behold and for £50 or more one can get a very nice appearance at a really big concert. Just imagine what a lot of fame one can buy for £1,000!

From the aspirant's point of view, this sort of thing is, however, eventually disastrous. The fame lasts, as a rule, just as long as the money lasts. When the money is done, the hands of the whole profession are lifted against the interloper. I remember in an artists' room once hearing a popular baritone asked by the conductor what a new soprano was like. 'Rotten', he said, with more simplicity than gallantry. When I asked him why he was so unkind to a fairly good singer, he retorted, 'My boy, when you have been as long at this game as I have, you will know that everyone who pays for appearances is "rotten" so far as the profession is concerned'.

There are exceptions. In my time, a couple of people have managed to buy their way in. But their purses were very long, and it is questionable whether the fruits the years will bring, will ever quite make up for the preliminary seed that had to be sown.

One need not spend many minutes with an agent to discover his voracity. My very first encounter with one of the kind made me open my eyes very widely indeed. He sent for me 'with a view to mutual business'. The proposition was that I should induce a moneyed friend to put £500 into a big concert venture in Covent Garden Theatre. The moneyed friend was to have a series of appearances at these concerts and I was to have three.

The next time I interviewed an agent, I was offered a tour with a great prima donna. I was to pay £100. A couple of days afterwards I met an Australian contralto reputed to have pots of money. She had been offered the same tour, price £200. Nearly every great instrumentalist who comes to England to make a tour relies for support, vocal and financial, upon two or three people who have been made to understand that fame is a thing to be bought like a ton of coal or a breakfast kipper. Even one or two of the big regular provincial tours – once the pride of their managements and their artists – are now practically financed by silly unknowns.

Fortunately, there are not quite so many blackleg agents as there were three or four years ago. I believe one or two of the agents of those days are now 'doing time' while others are keeping very religiously out of this country to avoid the same experience.

It would be fair to assume that Ibbs and Tillett's agency was not in Thorold Water's sights when he wrote this acerbic but interesting piece, and it is worth pointing out that so many elements of his observations are relevant today.

The Tillett archive is rich in letters from the decade of the 1930s, so much so that this chapter alone can be devoted to those from conductors (who were not officially on the books of the agency, their names absent from the artists' lists, but whose affairs were nevertheless handled by the firm on many occasions). Having secured concerts for themselves, their soloists would often be provided by Ibbs and Tillett, while those in posts throughout the land were equally sought after by the agency for the same purpose. Their listing in this chapter is alphabetical rather than chronological. Several artists became personal friends of John Tillett, such as John Barbirolli, whose appointment as Toscanini's successor to the post of conductor of the New York Philharmonic Orchestra from the 1936–37 season, prompted congratulations and this response:

> Thank you so much for your kind letter of congratulation. It was very good of you to write and it did give me the greatest pleasure. Kindest remembrances to you and Mrs Tillett. (27 April 1936)

Two years later Barbirolli was keen to help a colleague:

> This is to introduce Maestro [Alberto] Erede of the Glyndebourne Opera. He is a charming fellow and fine musician. If there is anything you could do for him I should be grateful. I shall hope to see you when I return to London before I leave for the States. All good wishes. (7 July 1938)

The irascible Beecham issued his demands for appearances in Liverpool, his pen thundering no less than his voice judging by these two letters:

> I enclose programme for Liverpool. If *Sea Drift* [by Delius] be given, it is necessary that Dennis Noble sing it. The Mozart double concerto [Sinfonia Concertante K.364] should be played by [Albert] Sammons and [Lionel] Tertis. Then it is a grand piece!!
> Please urge on them to let me do the Brahms *Requiem* – I will waken up their choir for them. (17 June 1930)

> I send you three programmes for the Liverpool Philharmonic Society's concerts. With respect to the second and third of these, I am quite willing to exchange views with the Committee of the Society; but I want to make it particularly clear that, having expended a good deal of time and painful thought on the subject of a desirable and fitting selection of pieces for the historic occasion on January 10th 1939, I have not the slightest intention of altering anything nor do I wish to be addressed by anybody on the subject. Therefore any communications touching upon this forbidden subject addressed to me will be returned forthwith in an unstamped envelope to the Society at large. (5 August 1938)

The contentious programme was the one proposed for the re-opening of Liverpool's Philharmonic Hall (destroyed by fire in 1933), although in the event the concert had to be postponed, still under Beecham's direction, until 20 June 1939. The works he performed were skilfully designed to show off the new hall's acoustics and its organ, with G.D. Cunningham playing the last two movements of Elgar's organ sonata, the city's Philharmonic Chorus in two choruses from Handel's *Solomon*, and the soprano Florence Austral in operatic arias by Beethoven, Weber and Wagner, these interspersed among orchestral items from Weber to Elgar. Another letter containing a Beecham programme was written from Berlin, where he was conducting and recording opera. It concerns a concert given on 2 April 1938 finishing with the first London performance of Rachmaninov's *Rhapsody on a Theme of Paganini*:

> I suggest the following programme for the Rachmaninoff concert.

Part I	
(24 min) Symphony in B flat major No.102 (short work lasting 24 minutes)	Haydn
(30 min) Pianoforte Concerto in C major No.1	Beethoven
Part II	
(17 min) Tapiola	Sibelius
(18 min) Rhapsody on a Paganini Theme	Rachmaninoff

> If Mr Rachmaninoff has a work of his own of similar length to *Tapiola* (i.e.17 minutes), I would include that, if he would like me to do so. At the same time, it may be borne in mind that Sibelius, at the moment, is the composer of the hour. You might discuss the matter with him. (20 February 1938)

Two further letters to Emmie Bass come from Grosvenor House in London's Park Lane in the spring of 1930. Judging by the absence of his name from either the audition books or later artist brochures, the tenor recommended by Beecham seems to have made no favourable impression upon the agency:

> The bearer of this note – Mr James Fyfe – has a pretty light tenor voice, well trained in Milan. I think he might please at a certain kind of concert, as '*hoc genus*' is rather uncommon. In any case you are the best person to send him too [*sic*] if there is any opening for him. He is a protégé of the Duchess of Montrose. (20 March 1930)

> I forget the exact amount due from the Royal Philharmonic Society to you – the gentleman in charge of this exasperating business has disappeared into the void. I enclose however a cheque for £100 (my accountants) and you can let me know if anything further is required. Just off to Cologne. (16 April 1930)

Another side to the usually formal and reserved Adrian Boult is revealed in part of a letter concerning his fee for a concert in New York in 1939. By November of that year war had been declared, and Boult had moved, together with the BBC Symphony Orchestra, to Bristol from where the letter was written to Emmie Bass:

> ...Will you please think it over and tell me honestly? I should hate the matter to be left over with a feeling in your mind, or the firm's, that my Scottish blood had got the better of my judgement over this. It is a big sum which both of us (I expect) would be glad to have! I haven't the faintest notion where my taxes are coming from next January, but that is my fault for not thinking sooner that the taxes were bound to be awful. I think my only hope is to let them put me in court, grow a beard and say engagingly "My lord, I have a scheme". Do you think I could pull it off? I fear I should make a much poorer show than my distinguished confrère! [Beecham] But seriously, do please honestly tell me your view, because here is much that I may have forgotten. (22 November 1939)

Like John Barbirolli, Albert Coates was moved to make a recommendation to the agency, and one which was to be of mutual benefit both to Ibbs and Tillett and to the artist, the pianist Eileen Joyce. The letter was, however, addressed to and forwarded by Pedro Tillett, still artists' bookings manager at the BBC:

> I would like you very much to hear Eileen Joyce, the pianist, a little Australian bush girl and a pupil of my old Professor in Leipzig. I consider you can make an awful lot of her. She is wonderfully talented and is a jolly bright little fellow. Do try your darndest! (9 May 1930)

Coates wrote an interesting letter regarding programming for a concert he was to give in Birmingham in the spring of 1931, but in the event neither the programme nor Coates materialized because he was ill:

> In confirmation of our telephone conversation I have great pleasure in accepting March 5th 1931, for Birmingham, for which many thanks.
>
> I met Leslie Heward [Music Director of the Birmingham City Orchestra] at the Queen's Hall and he begged me to do, as one of the principal items on the programme, the *Faust* symphony of Liszt with men's chorus and tenor solo at the end. I think this an excellent idea and I would very much like to keep it. It is much too early in the day to build a programme, but as we want the tenor solo, we might also use the same tenor for several items on the programme, like I did once here in London when we gave a whole Faust evening; i.e. different composers writing on Faust subjects. It was most entertaining and artistic. The programme ran:

Faust Overture : Wagner
Jardin de Marguerite : Roger-Ducasse
Invocation from Nature from *Faust* : Berlioz
Kermes, mixed chorus from *Faust* : Gounod
and the wonderful *Faust* symphony

I would very much like to do this; it is very 'stilvoll' [stylish], if it can only be rehearsed. (3 April 1930)

Hamilton Harty had concerns about advertising, and urged the agency to use its contacts with the print media and the gramophone companies to ensure the maximum publicity for concerts:

> I know that in a big organisation like yours things must be kept in more or less water-tight compartments and that the question of advertisement is probably one of them. But I wish you would be so kind as to say a kindly word on my behalf whenever it is necessary, and point out that the *Messe des Morts* of Berlioz is really a big and important work and worthy of being advertised in big type. In the *Telegraph* of today it is announced as if it were a twopenny-halfpenny Harvest Cantata instead of being the most important and biggest scale work that is being produced in London this season. It is necessary to start my concerts with a good house and a sense of importance, and I don't think this will be quite achieved if my concerts are advertised in such a diffident and apologetic way. I think too that any *Columbia* advertisements ought to follow my own advertisements, not tucked away in quite another corner of the page. Perhaps a little palaver with *Columbia* would be suitable and pleasant all round in this connection. I know you will appreciate and back up my wish that these concerts, which are very important to me and the orchestra, should be advertised in a more dignified and thinking manner. (8 November 1930)

A year later Harty was presented by the impresario Lionel Powell with an offer he could not refuse, and decided to sever his connection with Ibbs and Tillett but in the most amicable way:

> As you know, I have last year and the preceding year lost a good deal of my own money over the Orchestral Concerts at Queen's Hall. Though these concerts were artistically successful, and I believe promise well for the future, I am not really in a position to lose money over them. Powell has offered to take over these concerts for me, and I am sure you will understand that it is purely economic reasons that make me accept this offer – especially as it is more or less connected with proposed Sunday concerts in London, which might probably have the effect of lessening or entirely eliminating the loss which is suffered on the regular Symphony Concerts on Fridays.
>
> It is hardly necessary, in the case of friends like us, for me to add that there is no other possible reason in my mind for making this change, except the probability which exists of a more bearable financial position being established in regard to these concerts.
>
> Perhaps at your leisure you will send Powell the contract for the dates at Queen's Hall etc., and of course I have to thank you very warmly for all that you have done for me in the last two years. I feel sure that your friendly interest and influence will still be exercised, even if not professionally, in regard to these concerts. (16 April 1931)

Nevertheless, Harty was back in the hands of Ibbs and Tillett four years later:

> On looking closely at the Suite by Scarlatti *The Good Humoured Ladies*, I am not greatly impressed by its suitability for the Torquay Festival concert on Friday next. It is rather late in the day to make alterations, and perhaps the programmes are already printed. But if not, and perhaps even if it meant slipping a leaflet into the programmes on Friday, perhaps Mr Goss would consider allowing me to substitute something else for the Scarlatti. I should be happy to pay for the cost of doing this. Perhaps you would be kind enough to write to him on these lines and explain that if he considers it essential I will do the piece originally chosen, of course; but if he should agree to a change, the following would be more popular I think – Suite: Handel transcribed by Hamilton Harty – Introduction, Rigaudon, Polonaise, Arietta, Passacaglia. If he were to wire his decision, I would undertake to bring the orchestral material with me, to save all trouble. (5 October 1935)

Otto Klemperer never had any luck with the visits to Britain which he proposed to Ibbs and Tillett; one in 1926 had not materialised, as described in Chapter 12, but neither did these two in 1936 and 1937:

> Thank you so much for your kind offer to conduct November first a Studio Concert of B.B.C. in London. I don't know whether a Studio Concert means a concert in the studio without audience; that would not be acceptable for me. Please let me know and then the honorarium! I am so sorry that I cannot accept less than 500 dollars or 100 guineas. If B.B.C. will pay 75 guineas and 25 guineas travelling expenses, that would be all right with me. I would like to conduct two Beethoven symphonies (the third and the fifth).
>
> I come back to the record question. I just conducted the nine Beethoven symphonies in Strasbourg with such colossal success, that everybody asked for records. Would *Columbia* be interested in the Beethoven symphonies? Another suggestion: October 25th I conduct with the Vienna Philharmoniker in Vienna Alban Berg's new violin concerto (with Louis Krasner as soloist). What about records for this concerto? Please give me an answer about everything at your earliest convenience. (? July 1936)

> May I take the liberty to tell you that I have the intention to come to Europe in May, June, September and October 1937. I would be happy if you could offer me an English tour. Unfortunately our negotiations last Spring were not successful. Let me hope that in 1937 we will co-operate. Perhaps you could me offer also some recordings in England in the time of my staying in England. Please let me know at your earliest convenience your plans. With the best wishes for a Happy New Year. (24 December 1936)

Ibbs and Tillett had written to the BBC in March 1936 asking for a concert for Klemperer later that year in October, but the Corporation's selection panel decided on 7 April 1936, that 'perhaps a Sunday Symphony Concert, but not in public and not at [more than] £75 or so. In spite of the fact that he held an eminent position in the conducting world, the panel felt it doubtful whether he could materially add to the scope of next season's programme scheme'. One senses an excuse here, for it was more likely that Klemperer's erratic behaviour was beginning to put a wary BBC on their guard.

Neither Wilhelm Furtwängler nor Pierre Monteux, unlike Klemperer at this time, found themselves short of engagements. The archive contains just one letter from Furtwängler, securely wedded to his Berlin Philharmonic Orchestra in the 1930s, but with whom the agency would have a more productive relationship in the immediate post-war years:

> I am answering your enquiry regarding the possibility of my conducting any of the London Philharmonic Orchestra Concerts next season only to-day as I can only now see clearly about my next year's plans.
>
> I very much regret to have to inform you that I find myself unable to accept your kind invitation as my engagements abroad take up all the dates mentioned by you. But I do hope that another year will give me an opportunity again which I may then be able to seize. Thanking you again. (22 May 1935)

Another conductor firmly committed to his own orchestra and unable to appear in England was Serge Koussevitsky:

> Just a line to acknowledge receipt of your letter of July 19th and confirm that, to my sincere regret, it is impossible for me to consider the offer to conduct the Courtauld-Sargent Concerts at the Queen's Hall on October 16th and 17th, as I am leaving for Boston next month.
>
> I should like to add that for several coming seasons, while engaged with the Boston Symphony Orchestra, I shall not be able to consider European engagements outside the short period of time, following my season in Boston – from the middle of May to early June. (1 August 1933)

On the other hand negotiations were more productive with Pierre Monteux:

> Coming back from California, where I conducted in the Hollywood Bowl, I find your letter and telegram that has not been sent to me because I was scheduled to come back through the Panama Canal, a long journey where it was impossible to reach me. I am sorry that I could not answer, naturally, and you may have thought that I was not interested and even not polite. Please accept my deepest excuses. As it is now, you have probably chosen another conductor for those two concerts that you so kindly offered me and that I could not have accepted anyhow because, perhaps you know, I have been offered the position of conductor for the San Francisco Orchestra and I am going there from January to end of April. Prior to this engagement I accepted to start the season in Los Angeles in November when Klemperer opens the season in New York. So my whole winter time is taken, and I regret very much not to be able to go to Manchester this season, where I made many friends. But I hope you can get these concerts for me next year again. (27 September 1935)

The endless correspondence between Ibbs and Tillett and artists about broadcast fees (always lower than in Europe and America) paid by the BBC must have been the cause of frustration and extra work for the administrative staff of the agency. Monteux could never understand it and made his view known:

> I received your letter on the subject of BBC concerts for which I accepted by cable to conduct on November 13th & 18th at a fee of 100 guineas inclusive, and I still accept that fee for this time; but you must remember that my ordinary fee was always 60 guineas and only in Depression time the Hallé Orchestra asked me to reduce to 50. I certainly understood that they had [a] hard time and accepted, but it seems to me that an organisation such as the BBC should not be put in the same category as any symphony [orchestra] and that they really could pay the real fee.
>
> In New York the NBC pays me $1500 plus $150 for taxes (for one concert). I am not expecting anything like that in Europe, but my fee in Paris, which is my home, is ten thousand francs and Amsterdam, Brussels, Rome and formerly Berlin and Vienna always paid me 15,000ff. It does not seem logical that the BBC should pay less than Paris, where I have no expenses like travelling and hotel. I would be certainly very glad if you would take up that matter again with them and try at least to get my former fee of 60 guineas, but as I said before, in the end I will accept as my telegram said. However I am asking you to please make my fee in the future 65 guineas for symphony concerts and 80 guineas for radio. (15 August 1938)

> … I hope that the BBC will give me more rehearsals for the Ravel memorial concert. Did you ask them about making a few little cuts in *Daphnis & Chloë*? I would like to know. Would you also tell me what they will do about orchestra materials; I hope I will not have to supply them. (22 September 1938)

> … I am sending you under separate cover my own score of *Daphnis & Chloë* with the three cuts recommended by Ravel for concert performances. These cuts do not concern the chorus at all, so they can learn their part entirely as I intend to use them. Would you be kind enough to let me know if I must wear the full evening suit for these concerts, as I understand they are to take place in a studio, and to recommend me a hotel near that place? (24 October 1938)

> … I am sending back the proofs of programmes with additions of details for *Rhapsodie espagnole* and *Suite Provençale*. I think the timing is exact. As for orchestral material, in a former letter you told me that the BBC would supply them all. However, I have my own materials of Cesar Franck and *Tombeau de Couperin* that I can bring if necessary. But as I intend to come by air, I would prefer to bring as least baggage as possible.
>
> To answer your letter of the 27th, I am sailing for America the 13th of December, going to San Francisco for my fourth season there and will not be available until next year. (29 October 1938)

This letter from Ernest Ansermet refers to a BBC Symphony Orchestra concert on 24 February 1937, in which violist Lionel Tertis marked his sixtieth birthday by appearing twice as soloist in Walton's concerto and Berlioz's *Harold in Italy*, neither of which is among Ansermet's suggestions at this stage, although one work which was, Hindemith's *Mathis der Maler*, did appear on the programme:

> I thank you for your cable and I can accept the date of 24th Feb. in Queen's Hall ... About the programme, I generally follow the suggestions of the BBC as they have their plans and I don't know their other programmes. It depends also of if there is a soloist or not, and which. Anyhow, if they will – French music, I indicate:
>
> Debussy Three Images a) *Ronde de printemps* b) *Gigues* c) *Ibéria* or only the last one (*Ibéria*)
> Ravel *Daphnis and Chloé* 2nd Suite
> Berlioz Three movements from *Roméo and Julia*
>
> But I would be particularly pleased to conduct Alban Berg Suite of *Lulu* or Violin Concerto or Hindemith *Mathis the painter* or new Viola Concerto (*Schwanandreher*)
>
> In case of Berg and a full programme, I could propose
> 1) Bach Suite in B minor
> 2) Berg *Lulu*
> 3) Schubert C minor symphony [No.4] or Bruckner No.5 or Beethoven No.7
> I would also be pleased to conduct the last Walton symphony [No.1] either with classical works (Bach, Haydn) or with modern ones (Berg, Debussy).
> (dated 1 August, no year but 1936; from Cunard White Star RMS *Queen Mary*)

Near the end of his life, Landon Ronald wrote to his friend John Tillett with words of recommendation about the 28-year-old bass Norman Walker, who was destined for a great career both on the concert platform and in the opera house, and who appeared on Ibbs and Tillett's books from the 1935–36 season, perhaps as a result of Ronald's words of praise:

> Francis Russell tells me that he is very kindly arranging for you to meet Norman Walker. I want you to know that I hold the very highest opinion of Walker as an artist and consider that he has a great future before him. Anything you can do to help him will be deeply appreciated. (6 February 1935)

A postcard to Emmie Bass from Georg Szell refers to a performance in Manchester with the BBC Northern Orchestra:

> Please let me have immediately the scores of the Bliss and Ireland works Mr Johnstone is suggesting, and perhaps try to find out whether he would be agreeable to my performing *Tintagel* by Bax as the British work on June 22nd. I shall suggest the further items of the programme within the next few days. (29 April 1937)

Programming and instrumentation, which determined the organization of rehearsals, had to be handled by the agency on the conductor's behalf, and feature prominently in a series of letters from Bruno Walter:

> I am just beginning to prepare my American programs and to study also novelties for this purpose. It will take two or three weeks until I could make a proposition of performing one of these novelties in our concert of January 25th [1934] and I hope you can wait so long for my program.
>
> The first sentence of your letter of the 26th inst. was not clear to me: you wishes me to make my choice of the enclosed list and 'to avoid the works already down'. Which works are already down? This is not to be seen from your list. By the way, how would the Philharmonic Society think about a performance of Bruckner's fifth symphony? It would be expensive in so far as the Finale contains an extra brass band of 3 trumpets, 3 trombones, and 4 horns, but it is a monumental work, which perhaps not yet or very rarely has been done in London. It has a duration of about 67 minutes and we could begin the concert either with a Mozart or Haydn symphony, or with an interesting novelty if I find one. (29 May 1933)
>
> With pleasure I am willing to give an entire Beethoven program on January 25th, but I suggest instead

of the 1st or 4th or 5th symphony the following program, which seems to me the best possible and with which I shall begin my coming season in New York.

Overture: *Coriolanus*
Symphony No.6 *Pastoral*
Interval
Symphony No.7
(10 June 1933)

Your suggestion of playing the symphonies No.1 and No.5 has the great disadvantage to make the program far too short. The duration of the first symphony is 24 minutes, of the fifth 30 minutes, whereas the sixth takes 38 and the seventh 45 minutes. Here you see the very reason why I think a Beethoven program could not consist only of an overture, the first and fifth symphonies. (27 June 1933)

In case it would seem to the Committee very important to have the fifth symphony in C minor on the program of my concert, may I propose to drop the idea of an all-Beethoven program and to make a classic concert about in that way: 1) Handel Concerto grosso in G minor, 2) Mozart Symphony [No.40] in G minor or a Haydn symphony instead of Mozart, 3) Beethoven 5th symphony in C minor. This seems to me a very attractive program. (4 July 1933)

I shall be perfectly content to have only two rehearsals for the Beethoven program, i.e. January 24th at 10am and 25th at 10am. (1 September 1933)

I confirm receipt of your letter from January 16th and the labour permit. There is an error in it; I am Austrian and not German but I think this will not be of any importance. But it is of importance that the hour of my first rehearsal has been changed. I was glad to meet the wish of the Philharmonic Society to prepare the concert with only two rehearsals, but I counted on morning rehearsals, which are the more efficient ones. An afternoon rehearsal has not the same sense – no orchestra is as fresh and keen in the afternoon as in the morning. [Lower half of letter missing] I beg therefore to change that back and would be much obliged to hear on my arrival in London, Hotel Claridge on January 23rd, afternoon, that both of my rehearsals will take place in the morning. (18 January 1934)

Following your telegram I send you here two programmes for the concert with the Royal Philharmonic on January 19th 1939.

Weber: Overture *Euryanthe*
Strauss: *Death and Transfiguration*
Bruckner: 4th Symphony (*Romantic*) in the original version
or
Wagner: *Faust* Overture
Strauss: *Death and Transfiguration*
Schubert: Symphony in C major [No.9]

The second number (*Death and Transfiguration*) could be replaced by Beethoven's 8th Symphony but I very often feel two Symphonies in one programme, i.e. eight movements, too heavy for the public in general. About the Schubert C major Symphony I have to say that I believe I performed it in my last concert with the Vienna Philharmonic Orchestra in London. (10 June 1938)

Euryanthe Overture and *Death and Transfiguration* are alright. Mahler's 4th Symphony does not fit in. If Mahler, I would like to do the 1st Symphony in D major (a bigger orchestra but no soloist, whereas the 4th has a soprano solo). As to the rehearsals I agree with two, each at 3 hours on January 17th on condition that at least two hours interval can be made between them, e.g. 11.30–2.30 and 4.30–7.30 or still better 5–8. (18 June 1938)

With great regret I accept, in view of the difficulties you mentioned, the proposal to do the Mahler Symphony in two rehearsals on Tuesday afternoon and Thursday morning. I shall do Strauss and Weber on Tuesday morning and parts of the Mahler Symphony in spite of the missing instruments.

I assume that the rehearsals take place in Queen's Hall on Tuesday from 10am–1pm and from 3pm–6pm and on Thursday from 10am–1pm. (13 January 1939)

There is a misunderstanding. I agree to do my rehearsal on Tuesday morning without the extras in the brass necessary for the last movement of Mahler. But of course I must have the brass asked for in the first, second and third movements, i.e. 7 horns, 4 trumpets, 3 trombones, 1 tuba. The last movement asks for a fifth trumpet and a fourth trombone, who will be necessary only on Thursday morning. The full woodwind are necessary in all three rehearsals. With regard to the percussion, may I explain that a second drummer is necessary for the last movement, and it is sufficient to have him in the afternoon rehearsal of Tuesday and morning rehearsal of Thursday. The three other musicians necessary for the percussion are wanted for all three rehearsals. Will you kindly let me know the exact hour of my rehearsals.

I found here the enclosed permit which I suppose has to be sent back to the Home Office. Will you kindly take notice that my nationality is not German but French. (10 January 1939)

Felix Weingartner was no less demanding and attentive to detail in a series of letters concerning concerts in London and elsewhere during the decade of the 1930s:

I could conduct in Hastings on 20th February [1935] but not later. 75 guineas is not very much but I am ready to accept it if I need only stay two days in Hastings. (28 March 1934)

I just received your letter and beg you to tell the Royal Philharmonic Society that I am indeed very satisfied to conduct after a long time again this old and famous Musical Association. I only beg to consider that since 1923 my engagements in London are paid without any discussion with [one] hundred guineas and more without % to an agency because our correspondences go in a direct way. Therefore it would be against my interests to accept a lower fee from the Philharmonic Society than a hundred guineas. (It is understood that you will have 10% from this fee). Please write me so soon as possible to Basle, if this matter goes in order.

The *Choral* Symphony would be possible if I could have a rehearsal with the soloists and chorus on the evening of the 16th January. My train arrives 15hrs and some minutes. I propose then 1st and 9th Symphony or 8th and 9th Symphony or 2nd and 9th symphony. The wonderful 2nd Symphony is very seldom played. (13 July 1934)

It is alright, 1st and 9th symphony. I shall bring with me both materials [orchestral parts]. (postcard, 8 August 1934)

It is important that chorus and soloists sing the same translation. I shall bring with me the orchestral material. (postcard, 29 October 1934)

It is alright, I shall be January 16th, 6.30 in the Duke's Hall of the Royal Academy of Music. Thanks for the permit. (30 December 1934)

I beg to confirm my wire today and am indeed very sorry that I cannot come to London. Since some days I am not very well, and have now an attack of *Grippe* ['flu]. At my age, and at this time of the season, the voyage to England could be dangerous. I beg to enclose the medical certificate, and should be obliged if you would be kind enough to express my deepest apologies to the Hastings committee. (14 February 1935)

I am in receipt of your favour of the 7th inst. The first programme which you propose is much too long. I should be very glad to conduct the first symphony of Bruckner, however its duration is about an hour, and therefore it would be quite impossible to make before still two symphonies. I think it the best to make the *Unvollendete* [Unfinished] of Schubert and before it perhaps the Scherzo of the *Summernight's Dream* of Mendelssohn.

I fully agree with the second programme which you are proposing. I am a little astonished to hear nothing from Liverpool up to now. I am really anxious to know why this Society, who have invited me many times before, now do not give a reply. Up to now they were always too late with their invitation, so that I was not able to accept it.

As regards the invitation of Sir Hamilton Harty, I beg to remember that I myself am only a guest of the Vienna Philharmonic Society, and cannot decide myself anything in this matter. I shall not fail to speak with the heads of the Philharmonic Society with regards Sir Hamilton Harty, but I am not sure that they will agree to my proposal as he is not yet known in Vienna. You may rest assured that I should be only too glad if, nevertheless, my suggestion will be accepted. (13 April 1936)

You know that my agent for England, except the Royal Philharmonic Society, is Mr Harold Holt. Therefore I beg you kindly to go in relation with him about this engagement for the Eastbourne Music Festival. I write to Mr Holt at the same time. The fee of 100 guineas is all right. Concerning my two concerts with the Royal Philharmonic Society, I would like to do once the *Faust* Symphony by Liszt, a work I have never done in England. For the last movement of this symphony I need a chorus of men, at least 60, and a tenor solo. It must be a light and high tenor. The program for the 24th February could be:

Wagner: Prelude *Meistersinger*
Beethoven: Violin Concerto [Carl] (Flesch)
Liszt: *Faust* Symphony

For this program I ask 3 rehearsals on 22nd, 23rd and 24th February. For the first concert I propose:

Haydn: one of the *London* symphonies
Mozart: Symphony in G minor
Beethoven: 2nd Symphony
(16 June 1937)

Following some questions and requests, would it be possible to have double woodwinds for the great Schubert symphony [No.9]? It is very important for the impression of this grandiose work. I have this double winds (2 flutes, 2 oboes, 2 clarinets, 2 bassoons more) everywhere I make this symphony. I would need these 8 musicians only for the rehearsal on 24th February. From my fees (10.2.1938 cash, 24.2.1938 cheque) please take off your percentage. (4 February 1938)

Please reserve for the 24th February 3 good seats for me. If the concert is sold out, as the last one, I am ready to pay for them. I suppose that the rehearsal is on the morning of the concert, 10 o'clock Queen's Hall. I begin the rehearsal with the last movement of the Schubert symphony with the 8 extra players, which I need for the end of the *Freischütz* overture. You gave me the full honorar for my first concert, please take off from the next cheque your % for both concerts.

Will you be good enough to say Sir Beecham that I had the intention to visit him, but that I was on the country when I was not occupied with rehearsals and concerts, and give him my collegial and most friendly greetings. (14 February 1938)

Please notify my address above [Lausanne] indicated until I shall give you another. Therefore I ask you kindly not to send letters to Vienna. The 24th June you have written to me that the soloists for the 23rd February [1939] are:
Arthur Catterall (Violin), Bernard Shore (Viola), Thelma Reiss (Cello)
It will be necessary to secure the material of my work Sinfonietta in a good time and to give the solo parts to the soloists to study them before the first rehearsal. (7 September 1938)

Replaying your letter from the 8th November just received, I propose to the committee of the Royal Philharmonic Society to change the Symphony No.31 in D by Haydn with Haydn Symphony *Der Philosoph*. I cannot give you the number [No.22], but it is very easy to find. It is a very original and particular work for two horns, two English horns and strings, probably never played in London. It is everywhere nearly unknown. But I also have a consideration concerning the concert February 9th. I have heard in London some weeks ago the Bach Brandenburg Concertos wonderfully played by A[dolf] Busch and his small orchestra in the original form. I think it would not be very prudent to play now one of these concertos with the full orchestra, what could be judged against the style of such a work. What do you think to play instead of the *Brandenburg* Concerto one of the symphonies by [Carl] Philip Emmanuel Bach or one of the concertos by Vivaldi with soloists from the orchestra? (16 November 1938)

You remember that the program for my first concert with the Royal Philharmonic Society was

Bach: *Brandenburg* Concerto
[Brahms]: *Haydn* Variations
Beethoven: Symphony No.5

> For this program one rehearsal was enough and I have asked you therefore to cut out the rehearsal provided for Tuesday 7th February. But now, as you know, we have changed the program and added (instead of Bach) the Symphony in B flat by Johann Christian Bach (the *London* Bach) and the Symphony No.5 by Schubert. These two pieces must be studied very conscientiously because they are not so well known to the orchestra as Beethoven's 5th, and Brahms' Variations. I ask the Committee of the Royal Philharmonic Society to restore the rehearsal of the 7th February (or to put it on the 8th). I would rehearse at this rehearsal first the symphonies by Schubert and Joh. Chr. Bach and at the end the Brahms Variations, on the 9th February the whole program. I shall bring with me the material of the Schubert symphony with special indications. You will receive from Basle a score of *The Philosopher* by Haydn [Symphony No.22] with my indications and I beg the Committee of the Royal Philharmonic Society that the material of this little symphony may be arranged after these indications. (9 January 1939)

Finally Sir Henry Wood maintained a close and amicable, if rather stiff and formal association with Ibbs and Tillett:

> I have put Miss Eunice Norton's name down on my list for the Promenade Concerts, but as you know, the BBC have the final say in the choice of artists. (2 May 1931)

> Many thanks for your letter of yesterday. I am sorry about Buenos Aires, but not surprised after hearing various things about it from friends as regards the climate at that time of year. Anyhow I don't think it would have been possible for me to go this year. Will you please thank M. [Ernest] Ansermet for me. (23 September 1931)

> I shall be very glad if you can do anything for Miss Mabel Ritchie. I secured her engagements with the Liverpool Philharmonic Society and the Leicester Philharmonic Society and she gave great satisfaction in Dvořák's *Stabat Mater*, songs and the *Messiah*. Her refined soprano voice and quiet style made a deep impression. (14 December 1931)

> Will you kindly call and see the New Symphony Orchestra as I hear they are changing conductors, and if they care to make it worth my while, I would consider it. I leave the matter in your hands, knowing you will understand the situation. (22 February 1932)

> I have just heard that the Copenhagen people have reverted to their original idea of arranging a concert for November, and so I can go to Torquay on Saturday April 29th. I should very much prefer a pianist to a cellist, and hope it may be possible to engage Eileen Joyce to play perhaps the Prokofiev concerto. (25 March 1933)

> Last season Miss Myra Hess promised to give my amateur Orchestral Society in Hull a helping hand – we discussed it again in Boston and in New York and she is still inclined to help us by playing a concerto. Do you happen to know if Nov 22nd or 29th 1933 would suit her, or March 28th or April 4th 1934. Perhaps you can send me a line, as I can then book the Hall. (9 March 1934 – Wood must have been referring to November 1934 or March 1935, as his next letter is clearly type-dated 15 March 1934)

> Many thanks for your letter about Miss Hess and Hull. I am afraid it looks fairly hopeless and as though we should have to leave it for next season. It is kind of you to take so much trouble. (15 March 1934)

> Would you kindly ask Dorothy Silk, Astra Desmond, Eric Greene, Roy Henderson to attend Piano Rehearsal at the Royal Academy of Music on Thursday March 22nd for the performance in Sheffield on Tuesday March 27th at 7pm. Band rehearsal 1.45. If Mr Eric Greene cannot get to RAM until 4.30 it will do quite well. (15 March 1934)

Wood was an absolute stickler when it came to tuning, each orchestral player having to run the gauntlet of his tuning fork before being allowed on to the concert platform, and so his concern for unanimity of pitch between four pianos as expressed in the next two letters is not in the least surprising. This particular concert took place on 6 December 1934 with an all-Bach programme including the Concerto for Four Pianos in A minor with soloists Clifford Curzon, John Hunt, Cyril Smith and Kendall Taylor. According to a pencilled annotation in John Tillett's hand, the four pianos were made by Bechstein, Bösendorfer, Bluthner and Grotrian respectively:

> It must be the same piano on Dec 6, so will you very kindly arrange this? (17 September 1934)

> Dear Mr Keith Douglas, [Hon. Sec. to the Royal Philharmonic Society]
> Can you please settle this question of the four pianos for next Thursday's Philharmonic concert. It has really nothing to do with me; of course I think it a great musical error to have four different makes of pianos on the same platform as there will be no unity in the tone. What I am nervous about is the tuning; when will there be time for the separate tuners to work on the instruments. I shall go up to London early on Tuesday morning and leave a proper fork (A 439) upon Mr Legg the doorkeeper at Door 15, Queen's Hall, and tell him that all the tuners must tune strictly to this fork. Pianos must be ready and on the platform by 1.30 on Wednesday and at 9am on Thursday – I trust you will assist me in carrying this out. (2 December 1934)

> Will you do me the great favour of hearing Mrs Ruth Stephansen-Smith sing; she is a soprano of great distinction and my friend Mr Kielland of the Oslo Philharmonic Society has very strongly recommended her to me, also the Swedish Legation. Any favours you can extend to her or advice you can give her, I shall much appreciate. (27 April 1935)

> This change of Adolf Busch has caused me hours of work and I have had to get new proofs of Calendar; it has completely upset the order of works and the order of singers, but I have done it. I can ill spare 40 minutes on Monday October 19th at 12.20 for the Brahms but I have managed it. If Professor Adolf Busch will be called for Band rehearsal of Brahms violin concerto Monday October 19th, Duke's Hall, RAM at 12.20. (16 February 1936)

> Thanks for letter and sketch of Hastings programme. It is a terribly light affair, not one piece of real musical distinction but of course Mr [Julius] Harrison knows what his public wants on a Saturday night. Please ask him to change the final item as this piece *Fantasie on British Sea Songs* is never allowed to be played except on the last night of the Proms and at Queen's Hall. May I suggest *Military March* in D, Schubert-Wood, as a final item. It is very popular and I had to play it twice at Bournemouth last season. (21 July 1936)

> I have tried every means of finding your private address this evening, as I have just received confirmation from the R.A.M. [Royal Academy of Music] that my proposal to take my rehearsal at a later hour on March 19th met with general approval; in this way I can direct the Nottingham Concert the previous evening, and catch the 7am train, which gets me in in good time to get to Queen's Hall.
>
> As I could not find you, I have telegraphed the Secretary of the Sacred Harmonic Society that I can conduct on the 18th March, to avoid the necessary delay which must ensue before I can get you at your office in the morning.
>
> I am very glad to have arranged this, but I could not do so before waiting agreement and obtaining same from the R.A.M. I am sure you will agree that I have followed the only course to avoid waste of time, with first post letters tomorrow. (7 August 1936)

> I learn from Lady Wood that you very kindly undertook to represent me at poor Harold Samuel's Memorial Service. Very many thanks indeed.
>
> Thanks for copy of a letter from Dublin – methinks that I shall always be engaged when Dublin asks again, but I don't think they will.
>
> P.S. Have you heard that no call will have to be made on the guarantors for the Sheffield Musical Festival? (23 January 1937)

> Many thanks for your letter about Miss [Elena] Glazounoff. I shall certainly try and put her in for one of my Hull concerts in 1937 or 8 for her father's F minor concerto.

> The weather has changed and my wife and I are enjoying our holiday [in Grantown-on-Spey, Scotland] tremendously. Have not netted a "twenty-pounder" yet but have nearly completed a couple of sketches 24"x18", which is more in my line. (27 June 1937)

> I am in receipt of cheque for Stowe – less commission. I am sure that I shall be invited again to conduct at Stowe. May I therefore suggest that you put forward The Queen's Hall Orchestra when opportunity occurs, unless they are wedded to any other. (18 December 1937)

> Thank you for your letter of May 3rd. I have booked the Royal Philharmonic Society for January 26th 1939. Should they broadcast, of course there will be an extra fee. (6 May 1938)

On 5 October 1938, Sir Henry Wood celebrated his Golden Jubilee as a conductor with a concert at the Royal Albert Hall, which has since become a milestone in the history of music in Britain. Ibbs and Tillett were asked to manage the event, with John Tillett a member of the Choral and Orchestral Sub-Committee. All the performers gave of their services including Rachmaninov and the 16 singers, who took solo roles in Vaughan Williams' *Serenade to Music*, written especially for the occasion. They were all on the roster of Ibbs and Tillett, namely Isobel Baillie, Stiles-Allen, Elsie Suddaby, Eva Turner, Margaret Balfour, Muriel Brunskill, Astra Desmond, Mary Jarred, Parry Jones, Heddle Nash, Frank Titterton, Walter Widdop, Norman Allin, Robert Easton, Roy Henderson, and Harold Williams. On the following day Wood wrote a warm letter of thanks to Ibbs and Tillett:

> Do please accept my warmest and deepest thanks for all your wonderful work in connection with my Jubilee Concert last night. It certainly came off without a hitch and believe me I do know the mass of details in connection with such a concert. Bravo! Bravissimo! Also to all your staff who have worked so loyally and by the last of this month, through the splendid press, we should still get in many more donations. No artist in my memory has ever secured three quarters of a column in the *Times*. It was just wonderful. Many, many thanks. I never heard Rachmaninoff play more beautifully – I am eternally grateful to him for his wonderful help. (6 October 1938)

> HULL : NOVEMBER 24th
> Would you please advise Miss GLAZOUNOV, that if she comes by the 10 o'clock train in the morning, it will be in good time for my rehearsal, as I do not want her there earlier.
> I am very glad to learn that Mrs Tillett has been so much better of late, and sincerely hope that the present indisposition is only the result of doing too much in excess of her strength. You have our kindest thoughts, and believe me,
> Yours very sincerely
> Henry J. Wood
> (17 November 1938)

> I have just received the score of the Prokofieff 2nd violin concerto, which came as a great shock to me. When I undertook to do this date for the Liverpool Philharmonic Society the violin concerto was not named and I naturally considered it would be a standard work when decided upon, commensurate with the $2^3/_4$ hour rehearsal provided for. In thinking the matter over very seriously I shall be very grateful if the Society will release me from my date, December 12th, as such a programme as they have now chosen cannot give me or my public any musical satisfaction; and now, if ever, we need a public to come and enjoy what we present, and they cannot possibly do this if we are to have such inadequate rehearsal for such ambitious programmes. (5 November 1939)

> I don't believe in allowing the Royal College of Music to hold complete sway over the musical world of Great Britain, or in passing all their engagements on to their College pals – if in writing round in connection with your artistes, a word from you might do the trick – Liverpool started with one date, last week another came in and as Sargent is away until December there are bound to be changes. (undated)

> I am most upset and disappointed about Olga Haley not turning up to Sunday afternoon's piano rehearsal with the other two singers. It's not fair on the Society's concert nor on the work. It has nothing to do with her having sung it before or knowing her part – she should have more consideration for her colleagues. But I shall not be caught again with this lady over a choral work. (undated)

Some lower halves of letters have survived, which, though impossible to date and with little or no context, are intriguing enough to merit inclusion.

> … African tour) is at the City Hall on Thursday evening April 4th at eight o'clock. If Miss [Irene] Scharrer will leave by the 10.10 train from King's Cross due at Hull at 2.27 and come straight to the City Hall this will do nicely as I can take the concerto at about 3.30.

> … If I could some time combine a winter holiday with a concert or two in Buenos Aires I might try to fix up something, but I know nothing at all about it, and it is just a vague idea at present. (see also letter of 23 September 1931 above)

> … play the Haydn concerto. Of course I shall ask the BBC to engage him for the Proms, and naturally he will make his terms reasonable for the first season; this will give him the opportunity of playing a fine concerto to the London public.

> … and while he was in the military hospital near … [I gave] him a number of lessons throughout one summer and afterwards sent him for a year to the Academy. I would have kept him there three years, but for private reasons he went to Milan after one year. He came down and sang to me here quite recently, and he has wonderfully improved during the last years and sings with taste and expression. He has a pretty, light tenor voice and is a very decent linguist. I really think you might find it worthwhile to try him. I believe he does quite a lot of work in the provinces for the BBC. He seems to be very keen on getting up anything.

CHAPTER FOURTEEN

Letters from Pianists: 1930–39

The Tillett archive has a rich seam of letters written by eminent pianists in the 1930s, most of them already familiar agency names; again they are listed alphabetically beginning with Harold Bauer, the English-born pianist resident in America since 1900:

> I am very glad that you can see your way to assuring me a minimum total sum of five hundred pounds free of commission for ten or twelve engagements during the month of October 1931 and on this understanding I shall be happy to place myself at your disposal in England for the period in question. While I think of it, please let me say that this is not to include any engagement in Ireland, for the sea trip is liable to upset me too much. Also with regard to the Mossel tour, will you kindly bear in mind (unless you wish me to give solo recitals) that it would be highly agreeable to me to be associated with some artist with whom I could play one or two sonatas, as for example Hubermann, Szigeti, Kindler or Suggia. Any arrangements you make regarding the fees for the BBC or other societies will be acceptable to me, and I would like to give one recital at Wigmore Hall if this fits in with your other plans, i.e. this recital, which may yield very small returns, should not be allowed to interfere with the sum total of the minimum guarantee of £500 nett which you are willing to assume.
>
> May I correct you on one small detail? I did not assume, as you think, that the Mossel tour would be free of commission. On the contrary, my cable (of which I have not kept a copy) was intended to convey my understanding that the commission was deductible. Relying on memory, I believe I said something to this effect: 'presume your offer (i.e. Mossel tour) means 300 guineas less commission', and this was one reason why I could not accept it, for when we discussed the question of this tour last Spring, I still had the figures of my previous engagement in mind (I think it was 540 guineas for eleven concerts), and although you told me that there were no longer so many concerts, I formed the impression that the difference would be practically made up through increasing the fees.
>
> Now how about the piano? The piano business is so universally bad that I feel it necessary to enquire whether or not our friend Berridge is in a position to assure me exactly the same service as before, that is the best of concert grands with a tuner to accompany me in every place. Will you kindly make this enquiry on my behalf? (4 December 1930)

> I have your letter of January 12th and note that you have arranged for Mme Croiza [Claire Croiza, French mezzo-soprano 1882–1946] to be on the Mossel tour. She is a fine artist and if you think it would add to the interest of the concerts, I should be happy to play with her in one group to end the programme. It seems to me logical that two artists performing at the same concerts should show some reason for their association and there are so many splendid duets where the usual accompanist could be advantageously replaced by the piano soloist. For example the *Frauenliebe* by Schumann, the *Bonne Chanson* by Fauré or a group by Schubert or by Brahms. I enclose a recent programme showing how this works out. Please refer this matter to Mme Croiza. My sole stipulations are that (if she accepts) it must be the final number and a group or series of songs by one composer so as to give altogether the effect of a duet or ensemble number. (28 January 1931)

> ... In the event of your making an arrangement with Mr Michell for the Pianoforte Society, it must be understood that I should play on the Bösendorfer piano. I was extremely uncomfortable on a previous occasion with the Blüthner piano and do not care to renew this experience; besides I should consider it discourteous to Mr Berridge to use a different instrument. Will you kindly bear this in mind? (9 May 1931)

> Your letters of Feb 26th and March 9th have only now come to my attention as my correspondence was not forwarded during the last three weeks of a long tour.
>
> I am very glad to hear that Mme Croiza approves of my suggestion and shall be happy to play the piano part in the Fauré *Bonne Chanson*, for such numbers as she may select this joint performance to be the final piece on our programme.

Regarding Mr Michell's offer to engage me for the Pianoforte Society on October 31st in place of my own recital previously fixed for that date, I think this would be a good plan, provided that I am not required to play the Blüthner piano, as I did once before. Consequently, if you consider this substitution advisable, I leave it to you to settle the amount of the fee with Mr Michell (shall I add, confidentially, conditions for its prompt payment?)

I am sorry to say that there has been a slight misunderstanding with regard to the question of my playing in Holland. Following a joint recital here, Miss Hess and I agreed that it would be pleasant if we could arrange for a couple of recitals in Amsterdam and the Hague at the time of her Dutch tour, when I might be able to join her for two or three days before my return to America.

She wrote asking you to try to have this arrangement made through Mr Koning, and I only now realise that she had mistakenly assumed that I desired Mr Koning to take charge of my personal business in Holland, which, however, was in no sense my intention for the double reason that Messrs Kiesgen and Ysayë are my official representatives for that country and that time will not allow of my accepting any other engagements in Holland next autumn. In other words, I might possibly go for the two concerts in question with Miss Hess (these being outside of strictly personal business) if the dates would fit in with a close connection for a sailing on the French Line, but not otherwise.

In the meanwhile, Kiesgen and Ysaÿe are very much upset to learn, not only that I have apparently thrown them over without notice, but that Mr Koning has been offering my services, right and left, for a considerably lower fee than what I had authorised them to suggest, moreover a lower fee than I have ever accepted in Holland. I therefore cabled you on the matter and I now repeat that I could only accept the two joint engagements (with Miss Hess) as originally suggested, in Amsterdam and the Hague, provided that these could be fixed on dates closely corresponding with a departure on the French Line enabling me to reach New York not later than November 10th or 11th.

I am aware that large fees are not to be expected in Holland, but may I say that I fail to understand on what grounds you should say (your letter of March 9th) that Mr Koning's offer is very fair and that you hope I shall accept it? I do not consider his offer fair at all. Dr de Koos paid me more (as Mr Koning should certainly know) and I left him because I found that he was appropriating to himself an excessive proportion of the fees he was actually receiving from the various Societies. (24 March 1931)

I have your letter of April 28th with reference to the Philharmonic Society. I am sorry to say that I could not accept an engagement for November 5th as I must sail for New York on the French boat leaving November 4th.

I do not recall whether or not I asked you if, in the event of your making an arrangement with Mr Michell for the Piano Society, it must be understood that I should play on the Bösendorfer piano. I was extremely uncomfortable on a previous occasion with the Blüthner piano and do not care to renew this experience, besides I should consider it discourteous to Mr Berridge to use a different instrument. Will you kindly bear this in mind?

I am indeed sorry about the misunderstanding in Holland. The extract you sent me from Miss Hess' letter is quite in accordance with what I wished you to know, except that it should, for perfect clarity, have read as follows in the second sentence: 'If he goes, he wants (and so do I) us to play together and he says he might as well be with Koning if you can fit in with his engagements in England', meaning that Koning might as well arrange such joint performances, for I did not for a moment believe that he could obtain a fee which would be acceptable to Miss Hess and myself.

I trust that you duly received the photos which I had sent to you in accordance with your request some time ago. (9 May 1931)

I have apparently mislaid the programme of the last recital I gave in London, Wigmore Hall in May or June 1929, and I need to refer to it so as to avoid repetitions when I play in October next.

This programme started, to the best of my recollection, with a Mozart *Fantasia*. I do not know if it is possible for you to help me in tracing it, but if you can, will you kindly cable me to the above address at my expense, giving the date of the concert and (in condensed form) the remaining numbers of this programme? I have typewritten copies of the programme of two recitals on June 6th and June 12th 1929 at Wigmore Hall, but it seems to me that they cannot be correct, or else that there was one more recital. These programmes are as follows:

June 6	Brahms	Waltzes
	Schubert	Sonata
	Cesar Franck	Prelude, Choral and Fugue
	Mussourgsky	*Pictures at an Exhibition*
June 12	Bach	Chromatic Fantasy
	Schumann	*Fantasiestücke*
	Beethoven	Sonata Op.111
	Chopin	Prelude and Nocturne
	Debussy	*Children's Corner*

In the event that I am mistaken in my belief that there was another programme beginning with Mozart, please cable me as follows: 'Programme correct no other found', providing of course that you can get the information. (9 July 1931)

I have yours of July 3rd and am glad to know that you have booked me for an orchestral concert on October 28th. I should like to have this programme settled at once if possible, and I suggest either Beethoven Concerto in E flat or the Schumann Concerto.

I am aware that these works are constantly being played, but I have no novelties with orchestra, and as the concert comes early in the season, I hope that one or other of the above-mentioned works can be decided upon immediately, before they are announced by some other pianists. Kindly reply as soon as possible replying the other programme matter of which I wrote.

I note that you have booked me at a reduced fee in a girls' school at Bedford and I take this opportunity of saying that I am always glad to meet the budget of an educational institution, this being a practice I have consistently followed during my long career in this country. (11 July 1931)

I confirm my cable of yesterday in reply to your letter regarding Mr Mangeot's offer. He is a good friend of mine and a worthy artist and I wish to meet his views, but I must confess I do not understand why, under precisely the same conditions as when I played with his quartet before, he should want to reduce my fee. I leave the matter in your hands and whatever you decide will be satisfactory to me.

If this concert is arranged, I presume the programme will be of the same kind as before, i.e. with one piano solo between two concerted works and I suggest the following:

1. Quartet (with piano) in G minor Mozart
2. Prelude, Choral and Fugue (piano solo) Cesar Franck
3. Quintet (piano and strings) Brahms

I enclose programmes for London (Piano Society), Chelsea, Oxford and Bedford respectively. Of course I can feel assured that these programmes will not be confused with each other, as each place has been considered separately. I am assuming that Bedford, being a girls school, will desire a programme of lighter character. Oxford asked for a Beethoven Sonata, so, as my records show that I have already played five other Beethoven sonatas there, I am sending the *Appassionata*. This for your guidance in case any remark should be made regarding such a familiar work.

I was compelled to answer your cable the other day (regarding a possible change in the date of the Piano Society) to the effect that October 3rd would be decidedly unsafe for me to accept, as I cannot possibly leave before September 26th steamer *France*. Please let me hear about Mme Croiza's programme for the tour, also what is required from me, so that I can arrange my part of the programme accordingly.

This is to confirm my cable suggesting Beethoven Concerto No.4 in G in place of the *Emperor* Concerto for the BBC concert – answering your letter of August 13th.

I regret my inability to give a larger choice of concertos at the present time, having a great deal of new material to prepare for next season's concerts in America. I must therefore confine myself to works already scheduled and, as you tell me that the Concerto should only last 30 minutes, the two Brahms concertos are out of the question, leaving me only the two Beethovens and Schumann ready for performance. I trust therefore that I may now consider the G major Beethoven definite.

I am glad the Chelsea Music Club is pleased with the programme, and I await Mr Mangeot's decision regarding the replacement of the Ernest Bloch quintet for the Brahms quintet.

P.S. As my steamer (France) will be due not later than October 4th and you tell me that my first concert, so far arranged, will be on the 10th, I should be glad to know as soon as possible if you have any prospects for me between the 4th and 10th. If not, I shall probably arrange to go to Paris for a few days. (23 August 1931)

It has just occurred to me that as I am at present free from any contractual engagement for phonograph recording it might be possible for me to make some arrangement while in England with either His Master's Voice or Columbia. All my recording has heretofore been made with the Victor Company. Last year I had some negotiations with the Columbia people but for several reasons it was not possible at that time to settle the affair.

They might be willing to take this matter up again. Will you see if you can pave the way for negotiations with either of the two companies and, just as soon as I arrive in London, I shall be ready in that case to talk business. Any arrangement which you may be successful in bringing about would of course be subject to commission. (18 September 1931)

([Tillett's pencil annotations indicate the nature of his reply:] Phoned Columbia – cannot offer anything. Would like to do something but hands tied at the moment. Must live on their accumulated reserves at the moment. Cannot undertake new recording until they see the outcome of the political/commercial position. Have in mind for future project.)

The French pianist Alfred Cortot, and his two colleagues Pablo Casals and Jacques Thibaud, who had formed their famous and popular piano trio back in 1905, were regulars with the agency for many years (Harold Bauer also played with Casals and Thibaud). This group of letters concludes with one written a week after war with Germany was declared in September 1939:

I have received word from my wife asking on your behalf for my programme for the recital in London on 16 February. Here's what I propose: 1) Prélude, Choral et Fugue by César Franck 2) 4 Ballades by Chopin 3) 1st book of Préludes by Debussy. Is that alright with you?

Regarding the Trio – 9 March – we thought the following programme: 1) Beethoven Op.70 E♭ or Schumann G minor 2) Ravel or Saint Saëns in F major 3) Mendelssohn C minor. Would you ask [Lionel] Powell what he prefers and let me know so that I can write to Thibaud et Casals? I have just played the Schumann concerto here [Berlin] at the Philharmonic under Furtwängler, and had a success which Berliners describe as colossal! That gives me pleasure as I have not played in Berlin since the war!

... Don't forget to reserve a room with a bath for me at the Park Lane Hotel for the evening of 15 February. (20 January 1930, translation from French)

With reference to your letters of 16 September I note that I shall play on 8 March in Torquay, the 9th of the same month in Bath, and on the 14th in Chelsea. Concerning my programme for Bedford [pencilled correction by John Tillett to Bradford], ... I am prepared to replace the Preludes, which you say I have already played there, with the four Ballades by Chopin.

... P.S. One of my oldest pupils from the Conservatoire, who is actually, in my opinion, the greatest French pianist, if not the most remarkable of all female pianists, Miss Yvonne LEFEBURE, is anxious to be heard in London during the course of next season. Would you be kind enough to let me know the cost of putting on a recital at the Wigmore Hall? I can assure you that this young artist will create an extraordinary sensation in England, not only with her technical ability but also her prodigious musicality. I commit myself actively to bearing the costs of presenting her and count on you, dear friend, to try to secure them at a minimum for her. (23 September 1932, translation from French)

I imagine that all our fine projects of concerts for October cannot be realised at present. Moreover it would be difficult for me to fulfill my contracts having been given an important post at the Ministry of Education. So let us postpone our musical activities until after our two countries, fighting the noblest of wars side by side, have secured victory! ... Long live England! Long live France! Those are the truest and proudest words of friendship I can send you. (10 September 1939, translation from French)

These final words of Cortot have a hollow ring. He was always a Germanophile, serving as a musical assistant at Bayreuth from 1898–1901, after which, in 1902, he conducted the first Paris performance of Wagner's *Götterdämmerung* and a month later *Tristan und Isolde*. He accepted the German occupation of France from 1940–44 quite readily, and for many years after the war, until his death at 85 in 1962, he was *persona non grata* in France and elsewhere, though his obituary in *The Times* took a more lenient view: 'When he last played in London a year or two after the last war he was received with acclamation in total disregard of some political aspersions.'

Only one letter survives from the German pianist Edwin Fischer with its bizarre English:

> I am very, very sad about what I have to tell you and I will only hope that you are so kind to understand my situation. I think it will not be possible to play the 48 [Bach's 48 Preludes and Fugues] and the Chopin studies in the winter which is coming. The practising of the new concerto by Furtwängler, which has to be played this autumn, is so hard that the doctor will not allow to play more and, having pains in the arm (coming from the bile–gall) means he is right. So I propose to postpone the 48 for over next winter (36/37) and, naturally if you will give me the two dates in November [19]35 *malgré* the change of programme, to play on November 16th a Beethoven sonata recital: Opp.110, 10 No.3, 27 No.2 (*Moonlight*) and 111. On 23rd Reger, *Variations and fugue over theme of Telemann*, Mozart Sonata in D major (6/8), Chopin Ballade in A flat major, Nocturne G major, Polonaise A flat major, Schumann Op.9 *Carneval*. If you will give me the two dates I leave it to you if you will make these recitals half part with me or on my own risk.
>
> Could you ask Cambridge if they could take a date earlier, January 27, 29, February 5th. I am asked to play three pianoforte concert[o]s with the Berlin Philharmonics and I am very anxious [not] to loose this as it means a very big fee. I am sorry to make you troubles, but perhaps we have more public on this way and can do the 48 then in short intervals with subscription. I must care now my healthy and hope to hear from you. (19 August 1935)

The Scottish-born, but German-based, pianist Frederic Lamond held extremely distasteful anti-Semitic views, and while the agency would have nothing to do with them, it is surprising that he continued to receive engagements through them throughout the decade under discussion. It also calls into question his entry in *The New Grove Dictionary of Music and Musicians*, 6th edition (1980): 'He lived in Berlin from 1904 until his opposition to the Nazi regime caused him to make his home in Britain'.

> If you could arrange some engagements, say 4 or 5, to fit in with the Historical Series in London, I would now book dates definitely at the Wigmore Hall. The engagements would have to be booked on the understanding that I do not play for less than 40 guineas. The difficulty is that my business arrangements would have to be handled individually, and my name not sent out with a crowd of Jew pianists, Jew violinists and Jew singers, but Ibbs & Tillett have always steadily refused to accept my suggestions and here I am, dissatisfied with my work in England, which is not worthy of my reputation as an artist. Are you waiting for me to become circumcised, because it is rather late in the day and I am afraid I cannot oblige you? I don't wish in anyway to irritate you, but you must try and see my point of view. The old conservatoire ideas of waiting for engagements have gone to the wall, and at the present day you have got to hunt for them, otherwise there is nothing doing. What about the Mossel tour or the successors of Mossel? What about the Beecham Concerts in London? I read about a series of subscription pianoforte recitals in Glasgow, which you seem to be unaware of. I am going to South America in the course of the next few weeks, and would like to have your answer before setting out on my journey. (22 April 1935)

> Not hearing from you in reference to a studio engagement at the BBC in connection with the concert on January 11th 1936, I am afraid the management of the BBC do not encourage the idea of a studio concert on January 12th as suggested in my letter to Mr Tilbrook about three weeks ago. Let me recapitulate. A second class fare (return) Berlin–London in addition to first class cabin on the boat

costs £17.4.0. alone, so that by the time I have arrived at my London hotel I have spent £19.0.0. Now if you add £4.4.0. commission and another £5.0.0. for general expenses, I am out of pocket by £28.0.0., which leaves roughly £12.0.0. for the concert on 11th January. Even if the B.B.C. are willing to pay me 50 guineas, that would only leave me £22.0.0., which is about 240 German marks, which was equivalent to £14.0.0. before the pound fell. I am afraid unless the B.B.C. see their way to a studio engagement on the 12th January, as I suggested, I shall have to cancel the engagement at the Promenade on 11th January, which would be unfortunate for many reasons. I return to Berlin tomorrow. (10 December 1935)

I have received a letter from Sir Henry Wood that Messrs Chappell & Co have given over to Mr [Harold] Holt the management of their concerts at the Queen's Hall, and that "naturally" only the artists which Mr Holt offers Sir Henry Wood will receive preference. What does this mean? Am I to understand that Messrs Ibbs & Tillett have nothing to do with London orchestral engagements; that is the B.B.C. Symphony and Promenade Concerts, and all the concerts, orchestral and otherwise, including the Beecham, Hamilton Harty, Boult series at the Queen's Hall? I do not wish to write you anything disagreeable, but I must know how I stand and what the situation as far as London is concerned applies to me. Another matter which I permit myself to draw your attention to. In your bill you charge £19.0.0. commission for the Mossel tour. I am sorry, but I understood the tour to be <u>your own</u> concerts, and taking into account the heavy deficit of the London recitals, could you not see your way to make a reduction in this sum? It is a painful thing to ask you, but I have some severe losses to make up in my foreign concerts, and find it difficult to make two ends meet. (2 February 1937)

With regard to the New Symphony Concert in April, and in particular to concert engagements in London, I wish it to be made perfectly clear, I do not under any shape or circumstances accept any fees less than forty guineas. Last season a well-known conductor [Sir Henry Wood] begged me to accept 20 or 25 guineas as a special fee (Sunday concerts, Queen's Hall), which I did and promptly wrote me three weeks later [that] he regretted not to be able to offer me any future engagement as Mr Holt had taken over the management. The same thing happened under the same conductor in Hull three years ago, where I played for ten guineas. As I am on terms of friendship with this conductor, I beg you to note that what I write is *entre nous* and <u>strictly confidential</u>, and only meant for your eyes. I did not receive any thanks, on the contrary, it injured my reputation. The Winter series of symphony concerts at the B.B.C., the Beecham series, not to mention the societies in the large towns, seem to forget that I exist. It is false policy and inconceivable that you ignore [me]. I can draw £205 at the Palladium in the face of a Kreisler concert, and I would much prefer Ibbs & Tillett refused to manage my business altogether than offer me 'special fees'. I am determined to go without any engagements in Great Britain next season rather than accept these offers. This would open up a new situation, and I would naturally be obliged to be guided by circumstances.

In reference to Eastbourne and Bournemouth, I understand Bechstein charges me 6 guineas for the two concerts. Do the piano charges fall under my care? As I am leaving London soon, I would be much obliged to have the Palladium and Bournemouth cheques before my departure. (14 February 1938)

In my letter to Mr Tilbrook I meant Ibbs & Tillett to bear in mind that the fact of my domicile in London is only for <u>your own private information</u>, otherwise the British cormorants, i.e. the musical societies, very useful birds, will fall upon the poor helpless black swan, and my fee will irrecoverably sink to 20 guineas and less. And then I may as well look out for a suitable tombstone with the appropriate inscription "Departed never to return". For all official purposes my address is permanently Hardenbergstrasse 9, Berlin–Charlottenburg, Germany, or anywhere you like. Only for Heaven's sake keep my market price up, no special fees for decrepit orchestras, no concessions to frisky females in Womens' Clubs etc. (18 May 1938)

As you are aware, there is a Beethoven Festival on an extended scale in London in April. Might I suggest that Messrs Ibbs and Tillett bring forward my name to the Committee who are running this Festival. This would mean a special letter on my behalf, and <u>not</u> under a list of pianists. At all events, I would be glad to hear from you. (15 December 1938)

> I have added to my repertoire Mozart's so-called *Coronation* concerto, D major (K.537), for piano and orchestra, and I thought this work might be acceptable to the directors for a future Studio engagement with orchestra at the B.B.C. as it is not played to death like the majority of the well-known repertoire concertos. When I mention the *Coronation* concerto I do not propose it for performance at the Proms, in fact would certainly prefer something else for these concerts. Sir T[homas] Beecham is very partial to Mozart and is a splendid interpreter of this composer's music. There might be an opportunity to arrange something in his series of orchestral concerts with this concerto, not to mention some stray orchestral society in the provinces which might particularly wish to have Mozart. (2 June 1939)

> Mr Johan Koning of The Hague has enquired if I could change the date of the Newcastle-upon-Tyne recital, 17 January 1940, as he offers me an engagement in Holland for the 16 January, although I answered him, there would be but little hope of altering the date in Newcastle. About a fortnight ago, you desired some information for publicity purposes (BBC). In the month of July, I have had great success in several concerts in Utrecht, Amsterdam and Scheveningen: also at the Beethoven Festival in Freiburg in Breisgau. Owing to the political situation, it might be perhaps wisest to leave out Freiburg. I enclose newest photo. Might I suggest to the head of the publicity department to leave out 'veteran pianist' in his notice about me. This is about as bad as 'Scotch pianist', 'Scotch accent' – all words which give me the cold shivers. I would be much obliged if you would kindly transmit my wish to the BBC publicity department. (11 August 1939)

When Pedro Tillett retired as booking manager with the BBC in 1934, he received this letter from Adelina de Lara, pianist and former pupil of Clara Schumann:

> I have read with sorrow and surprise that you have retired from the BBC. In this case may I once again thank you for all you have done for me in connection with BBC engagements and for all your courtesy and patience. Whatever your future plans may be, I wish you the greatest luck and happiness. Your interview in the *Radio Times* brought a very pleasant memory to me of the dear old days when I had the honour of receiving engagements from your famous uncle N.Vert. I have never forgotten one occasion. I was asking his advice about solos for a certain provincial concert and he made me very proud by replying, 'You know what the public wants, Miss de Lara'. (26 April 1934)

By the 1930s a close friendship had developed between Benno Moiseiwitsch and 124 Wigmore Street, and a dozen letters to John Tillett, 'Bobbie' Ibbs or Emmie Bass, written between 1914 and 1937 are in the archive, primarily on financial matters or discussing programmes, plans or ideas about further tours, and usually written from faraway places or on board ships. Moiseiwitsch hated writing letters 'full of woe' or 'unpleasant epistles' as he called them, and in the 1930s he often lost heart when it came to managing his finances. It was not easy, because he received no cash advances to pay for the travel and accommodation expenses associated with his engagements, and these letters from the 1930s track the highs and lows of a hard-worked itinerant concert pianist of the day. The first came from his home in Maidenhead:

> This is yet one more unpleasant epistle, and I hope the last.
>
> In spite of very stringent economies right and left, I am unfortunately forced to ask you for a loan of £300. I am aware of what I owe you, and I know that you are neither a charitable institution or loan office, but I can only ask you, because my overdraft at the bank is 'complete' and there is not a private individual to whom I could turn. Things have been bad for some time and you know that my engagements for the last 12 months did not account to anything decent.
>
> Now that Australia is fixed, I hope to land on my feet during that tour. The securities I can offer you are these: I want to make arrangements before I leave that the two thirds of my earnings in Australia are sent to you weekly for the moneys that I shall be owing you until all is cleared, and then you could bank the rest here.
>
> In March there should be some Gramophone returns, which you could also keep and then I could leave with you security in 'kind', that is insured for £500 to £600. The latter not as a guarantee of good faith, but simply in case of flood, earthquake, war etc., [in case] something goes wrong with

Australia. I don't expect much from America, as you know the engagements would barely cover the expenses, and I owe Copley 500 dollars and promised to pay him from the first American engagements.

I might be able to borrow very privately in America 1500 dollars to tie me over till Australia, but the £300 are rather necessary to me before I leave for America. If you pay my one or return fares to America, my indebtedness to you would be in the neighbourhood of six to six hundred and fifty pounds. To be still more frank, I might have cabled to my in-laws to China for a loan, but after long deliberation I still decided to write to you first.

Talk it over with John, and if you want to see me, I can be in town on Wednesday at 11. (7 December 1931)

Your cheerless but welcome letter arrived just prior to my leaving for my last few concerts in Japan. Many thanks for it – also for your sympathetic reference to my losing my father.

I often meant to write to you, but I do hate writing letters full of woe, and knowing that you are not keen on reading woeful epistles, I waited for something cheerful to happen; that unknown sensation has not happened, so I must make the best. The only saving grace about the whole situation is that I am not losing heart entirely; it is true that I wobble sometimes, but somehow my optimism conquers. Every dog has his day of good luck, and I had many – now it is my turn to suffer for my sins and it's only fair. The fortunate part is that I find myself in the majority and quite good company at that, so I don't feel quite lonesome.

I was hoping when I left 18 months ago to come back being able to balance my budget, but it did not take long to find that everything was going wrong. It is too tedious here to go into details, but to put it in a nutshell I have just scraped up enough to make our fares home. It is true I managed to send a little money home, but it was a drop in the ocean. Just as I managed to see daylight, viz India or the Masterclasses, things cropped up to shatter my illusions.

News from your office were not encouraging, so I decided to make the best in the East especially since Anita and Baby [son Boris] could live in comfort with her people and thereby save me considerable expense.

America was a dead loss of time and probably money out of pocket; I realise the necessity of America and probably would have done it had I been able to afford it, but it was impossible. Having exhausted the East, I must turn back to England. Perhaps in my absence it will have found its equilibrium and I might strike oil again. Coming down to brass tacks I suggest the following plan. I don't know what arrangements you are making for me in Europe. If you can find work for me – good; if things look very uncertain, I thought of making a flying trip to India again. As you know my last trip there was a washout thanks to lack of arrangements, but Mr Warren of the New Empire, Calcutta, told me that whenever I want to come back, he would be glad to arrange the whole of India himself. He would probably guarantee the principal towns, about ten concerts in the vicinity of a hundred pounds per concert. If you have no tangible prospects, I could go to India in November, December and part January, to be back in England for the Mossel tour.

I shall write to him myself from Bombay, but if you think it is a good plan, you might send him a cable. I would go without a guarantee but would feel safer with a minimum guarantee. He is a very keen and decent man. Strok feels quite disgraced about his last India fiasco, so he need not be taken in consideration, although if the prospective tour proves a success I would not leave him entirely out of it. You should get this letter about the middle of July and we are due to arrive on the 30th by the *Hadone Maru*, so I hope you will have some news for me. I want one decent tour to put me and some of my friends straight before my insurance expires in February and then I could breathe again. I have been working well and hard, but it all seems so futile! I hope things will be improving by next autumn. You will probably be leaving on the 29th July for your holidays, so will hope to see you on your return.

Within this fortnight I will have played the Brahms B♭, *Emperor*, Rachmaninoff, Tschaikowsky, Schumann and the Liszt concertos! Not so bad for the East?! Well, well, I won't bore you any more. I am looking forward to being back and hope this sentiment is reciprocated in some quarters. With love to you and the Office. Yours Benno. (12 June 1933)

I sent you today a letter to the effect that I am arranging with Quesada [a South American agent] to go to South America beginning end of April, also promising to mail Radio items for Jan 3rd. Quesada was passing through Chicago to Mexico and came to see me last night, and also this morning. He wanted me to go to Mexico this December or January, but I told him I could not, so we arranged that I go to South America after Canary Islands, arriving Rio about April 24–27 and exploit the whole of South and Central America and finish in Mexico about end of September or beginning of October, then come to America. I tried to pin him down to a guarantee, but so far unsuccessful. I complained about the way the tour was being run last time, and he admitted that it was his fault by having too many artists at the same time and that he never made that mistake again, and told me conditions are much better there than before. He left today for Mexico and promised to write to me on arrival a letter in form of a contract outlining the conditions.

He was earnestly enthusiastic and I can trust him. He might be back here before I leave America. I told him I was wiring you that I am allotting these months to South America. You can fix Canary Islands from about April 1st and he is cabling to Spain if anything can be arranged for the last twelve days of March. I hope this will materialize, as I understand Cherniavsky has been speaking to Anita about South Africa. I would not decline Cherniavsky definitely just yet.

Meanwhile I am making successful progress through the USA. Everywhere I had genuinely very big successes with several important re-engagements, but unfortunately the notices of my New York recital, I understand, have not been good. It is a pity, but I truly never played better in New York, but there you are! Please, please arrange for the Rachmaninoff for January 3rd. I am playing it a lot and it is improving in every way. Sir Henry is also keen on my doing it again. Below are the items for January 3rd; I am not sending alternatives as most of those are seldom played.

Waldesrauchen	4'	Liszt
La Legerezza	3 1/2'	"
Liebestraum	4'	"
Gnomenreigen	3'	"
Hark, hark the lark	3'	Schubert–Liszt
Tannhäuser Overture	15'	Wagner–Liszt
	32 1/2' (!)	

Hope things are thriving in the Office, and that I shall find myself as busy as a bee on my return. Love to the Office. Benno (25 November 1934)

S.S. *City of Nangpur*
I shall be sending a cable to Strok today from Madeira approximately thus: 'Would like tour India, China, Japan end Dec to end February *en route* Australia, cable care agency Johannesburg or Benmoise London'. Java I would like to tour either in Dec or March. I would like Koening to have the option for Java as I promised, although I shall have to give Strok at least 10% com[mission] on it. Please get Koening to get a reply as soon as possible about Java if they can have me there either in Dec or March. If any cables arrive for me at your office, you can open them and deal with them if they require immediate reply. I hope Australia will materialise. Java in March would be the best as in case Strok fails, I could go to India beginning there early in January (arranging the concerts myself) and go on slowly to Java *en route* to Australia.

I hope this might be the beginning of a better era, so that that 'bit of sunshine' opposite you might buy me a few oysters next winter! We are having a nice and very quiet voyage. Love to the office. (9 April 1936)

21 The Vale, [London] SW3
I meant to come in and talk to you about our financial position, but on second thoughts decided that I could outline my plans clearer in writing. You probably guess that it is not possible for me to put down a lump sum in reduction of my indebtedness to you, but if it is agreeable to you, I hope to substantially reduce the outstanding account by the end of the season through the following scheme. After each sharing concert, you to receive half of my share plus the commission – the commission of all engagements to be paid to you immediately or at the end of the month. If I have between now and end of March anything like the usual number of engagements, there is a likelihood of the outstanding account being reduced by over £100.

At the end of this month, after the ends of engagements, I intend to settle the commission due to you on the two Proms and the five engagements next week. If at any time I find I can do more than that, I should be just as anxious to do so as you would be. I had to make certain arrangements with the bank, after a nasty shock when they returned a cheque in which I promised to pay at the end of the month a certain sum in reduction of the overdraft, and also undertook to pay Steinways after each concert for their charges of the pianos plus two guineas on account of the old debt.

I am earnestly trying to get clear of these worrying things, and I hope I may succeed through these means. Anita is getting the S American accounts and will come to see you next week, and when you have time and want to talk to me, let me know. Hope I make myself more or less clear. (6 October 1935)

Carlton Hotel, Johannesburg
Many thanks for your cheery letter received today. I think the prospects for England look a little rosier. I only hope that the different societies do not take it for granted that the small fees I am accepting now will become a permanency. As long as it is 'in confidence', I don't mind doing it.

You probably had my wire re-Strok and the Australian Broadcasting. We must know one way or the other, as I think a tour under Lottermuzer in South America should be quite good. He is anxious to do it and is very energetic. Meanwhile, if you can extend my season in England – perhaps something can be done in Holland or Portugal, Spain or Belgium to keep things going until the Spring. The East could be arranged after the summer possibly. Strok's actual cable was 'Anxious to arrange, but do not advise'. He may have referred to the time he was in a mess with Chaliapine in any case at the time, so could not have been in a good mood. I am writing to him from here.

Things here [South Africa] so far – touch wood – went very well. I played 16 concerts and the receipts in all of them were better than last time, although Cherniavsky prophesied that for a return visit it will be half. He is quite sick he did not take me! He has been a tremendous help in instructing my advance and company managers, and also arranged a tour of about 30 small towns! I arrived today from Durban and am going to L[orenzo] Marques tomorrow for two guaranteed recitals (£50 each). I was able to refund £450 (borrowed to finance this tour) and am beginning to extricate myself from a well of very uncomfortable debts.

I hope it won't be long before I reach Wigmore St! The small towns would mean heavy travelling and about 5 concerts a week, but I hope it will be for a good cause. Anita and I kept comparatively well, but poor Boris was down with pneumonia – he gave us a terrible fright, but is now convalescing. Well, John, I hope we shall be able to keep the flag flying for a long time. All the best and love to the Office. (8 June 1936)

S.S. *Moulton*
I hope it is not too hot in England yet for you to read these few lines, but I thought you might be interested to know my reactions after Palestine and Egypt. Palestine, Orchestra and success were quite a revelation. I played four times with Orchestra, fee for three £120, the fourth I presented to the Orchestra. Everybody did something the first season towards the Orchestra, so this was my contribution.

One Recital Haifa £60, (record), one Recital Tel Aviv £94, (record), one Recital Jerusalem £45, quite good, capacity £50, odd. They are small halls and the top prices are about 8/- [40p]. Believe it or not I still have not received the final settlement. For your edification and in order for you to settle the amount of commission due to you, I can give you the following facts, moneys I received from the Palestine Orchestra £117, £42, £80, and about £10 is still due to me. Egypt was a washout. I was surprised to get for four concerts just about £55. I am giving you these figures so that you can jot down in your books the commission due to you – details we can discuss anon. I certainly hope to visit these countries again and before very long. I am enjoying these few days of respite and hope to be in good fettle for Australia. London must be seething with humanity now, and I don't envy you too much, but hope you will come out victorious. (17 April 1937)

Dunedin [New Zealand]
I am on the edge of the world and nearing the end of the tour. I am separated – temporarily speaking – from Anita, so am not sure what correspondence goes on between you. I asked her to send you a few programmes I played in Melbourne as samples for prospective recitals, and now I am enclosing a few groups for 'second half's'. Thank you for your letter to me. I am so glad that you are hopeful for a good season for me. I am still unable to say whether I could do justice to Beethoven No.4 for the LSO, as I have few facilities for peaceful and concentrated work. I certainly could do it if absolutely necessary, but will have to slave in London during Oct. By the time we leave here on Aug 26th, I will have played 37–38 concerts. I am not quite sure whether I am happy with the tour or not.

The conditions I went out on were punishing: 3rd from 1st £150; 40% from the next £100 etc. None of the houses reached £200, so a fortune I could not make. If you begin to deduct fares, expenses, income tax etc., you will see that I could not reach the affluence of Croesus. However, the redeeming features were the Broadcasting engagements in Australia: 6 for £525; £240 Taits –£285 M. In New Zealand I have four B'casts £300 less 20% Taits [Australian agents, see Chapter 5]. On the whole the recitals were a little better financially than five years ago. I had better notices, a great deal more enthusiasm than last time, so came to the conclusion that these countries want new sensations.

However, I am not dissatisfied. Has anything transpired with your friend da Costa or Cid for Portugal? About Xmas time would be nice to have a glass of home made port! Next summer I might go to S. Africa or S. America, but if the English season is particularly good and can be extended to the summer, I might stay on in England and as a Britisher try and keep the European situation in order. On the back, [below] you'll find the '2nd half' groups. I hope you are bodily well and are not worried in business. Give my love to the 'heads' in the office. We are leaving on the *Rangitata* on Aug 26th, arriving London Sept 18th via Panama Canal. Now I will desist from boring you any further. Cheerio and Salams Brother Savage, and all the best.

I	(10 minutes)	
	La Maya e le Rossignol	Granados
	Presto : *Mouvement Pereretuel*	Poulenc
	Capriccio F minor	Dohnányi
II	(12 minutes)	
	Variations	Paganini–Brahms
	(rather piquant after R[achmaninoff]'s Rhapsodie	
III	(10 minutes)	
	Rondo E flat major	Hummel
	Prelude in G major	Rachmaninoff
	Rhapsodie No.6	Liszt
IV	*Jeux d'eau*	Ravel
	Hark, hark the lark	Schubert–Liszt
	La Campanella	Liszt
V	Chopin ad lib	

(4 August 1937)

Hotel St George, Wellington, New Zealand
I had a letter from Anita in which she mentions that the Prom wishes for items in the 2nd half. I enclosed a few 'second halfs' in my letter to John T., but in case you are still waiting for specific items – here they are:

La Maya e le Rossignol	Granados
Capriccio F minor	Dohnányi

I had a letter from Cid (Lisbon) dated June 22nd, saying that he made most arrangements for next season, but keeps date or dates for me and wants to know whether he can announce me in the preliminary circulars. It sounds good to me, especially if it can be combined with Oporto. I also had an enthusiastic letter from Valmalète dated April 21st. Gaveau communicated with him and they are anxious for me to make a re-appearance in Paris with a view of procuring me engagements later in France, Belgium, Switzerland etc. Gaveau is giving the hall free and Valmalète promises to manage the recital well on 4000 francs.

In view of the present exchange, I think it is worth having a go, on the way to Portugal, or after Holland. Would you please have a directors meeting and see what could be done?! I think I would like to stay in England till after Easter and possibly go later for a short trip to S Africa. I am plodding along merrily here, though a bit tired, but quite happy.

We are leaving on the 26th [August] arriving London 28th September. I hope you had more sunshine than we experienced. Looking forward to a restful journey back, and hope to reach the land of civilisation in good form. In case you want to get some urgent information, our only stop is Panama about middle of Sept on board *Rangitata*. Give my love to the office. (12 August 1937)

The German pianist Egon Petri set up many of his own engagements, before handing them on to Ibbs and Tillett to arrange the details or pursue any encouraging replies. In the 1930s he lived in Zakopane (Poland) but in 1939 he moved from Germany to America, where he died a fortnight before Cortot in May 1962. He developed a cordial relationship with Emmie Bass (by the end of the decade they were on Christian name terms), and carried a torch for his teacher Busoni.

> This was a terrible week. I have been wanting to write to you every day, but something always happened. I hope the Huddersfield programme is still in time. I may have to leave for Zakopane on August 1st. I have been working rather strenuously since the middle of September with no real rest in between, so that a complete holiday is indicated. And that I can get best at home, however I may remain here (Mills College, California).
>
> I was awfully glad about Manchester. Have they remembered me at last? It took them a good long time! I suppose they would not want the Busoni Concerto? (It could be done without the male choir at the end). Otherwise I would like to play the Brahms B flat. If not that, then one of the following:
>
> Bach–Busoni D minor
> Beethoven C minor G major or E♭ major
> Brahms D minor
> Chopin F minor
> Liszt A major (or E♭ major)
> Mozart C minor or E♭ major
> Schubert–Liszt *Wanderer* Fantasy
>
> The Busoni concerto for the BBC is fine. Who is conducting? Have they got a male choir? Have they got the parts?
> By the way, I may play Steinway in England. I will let you know as soon as I have talked to them in New York.
> I cannot quite remember what I played in Huddersfield last time. Let them try the enclosed programme and if they don't like it or some of it, let them substitute something from the printed programmes which I add. Many thanks for everything. I hope the recital at the Grotrian Hall will materialise. (22 July 1933)
>
> Hotel Great Northern, New York City
> I hope you will forgive me for answering your 5 letters so late, but I am incredibly busy, teaching every week in Boston and New York and broadcasting every Sunday. During this season I played 25 times – a record! Well, I trust that there is still plenty of time!
>
> 1 Birmingham. Would they do the Busoni Concerto? That would be fine. If not, then the Rachmaninoff concerto in D minor [No.3]. If not that either, they must choose something from the list of concertos. I don't play any other modern works – not liking any of them (except the 3rd Prokofieff) well enough to study them. The *Indian Fantasy* of Busoni I played already in Birmingham, if I remember right – also the Liszt E♭.
> 2 Norwich. If Birmingham wants the Rachmaninoff D minor, I should like to play it in Norwich too. Otherwise something from the list. Solos: any of the following 6 groups.
> 1) Chopin Ballade A♭ major (6)
> Nocturne D♭ major (5)
> Waltz A♭ major (3) or Polonaise A♭ major (7)
> 2 Brahms 3 Intermezzi Op.117 E♭ major, B♭ minor, C♯ Minor (10)
> Rhapsody G minor (5)
> 3) Medtner Two fairy tales Op.20 B♭ min – B minor (6)
> Prokofieff Prelude C major (5)
> Gavotte F♯ major
> March from *Love for Three Oranges*
> Rachmaninoff 2 Preludes G major – G minor (6)
> 4) Schubert–Tausig Andante and Variations B minor (7)
> *Marche militaire* (5)

5) Paganini–Liszt 3 Studies
Andante capriccioso La Chasse La Campanella
6) Liszt Spinning song from Wagner *The Flying Dutchman*
XII Rhapsody

3 Liverpool
A 1) Bach
a) Praeludium, Fugue and Allegro E♭ major
b) Capriccio on the departure of his beloved brother
c) Italian Concerto
2) Beethoven Sonata Op.111 C minor
3) Brahms Three Intermezzi Op.117 E♭ major B♭ minor C♯ minor
4) Chopin 12 Studies Op.25
B 1) Franck Prelude, Choral and Fugue
2) Bach *Goldberg* Variations
3) Beethoven Sonata Op.81a E♭ major (*Les Adieux*)
4) Liszt Six Paganini Studies
or Schubert–Liszt Six Lieder
Love's Message The Trout Margaret at the Spinning Wheel The Lime-tree Barcarolle Erlkönig
C 1) Mozart Sonata A major
2) Bach Chromatic Fantasy and Fugue or Bach-Busoni Chaconne
3) Schubert–Tausig Andante and Variations
4) Franck Prelude, Aria et Final
5) Medtner Two fairy Tales Op.20 B♭ minor – B minor
6) Prokofieff Prelude C major
Gavotte F♯ major
March from *Love for Three Oranges*
7) Liszt *Don Juan* Fantasy (or *Figaro* Fantasy)
D 1) Bach 4 Choral Preludes (arranged by Busoni)
a) *Awake, calls the voice* b) *In Thee is joy* c) *I call to Thee* d) *Rejoice Christians*
2) Beethoven Sonata Op.53 C major (*Waldstein*) or Sonata Op.57 F minor (*Appassionata*)
3) Brahms *Variations on a theme by Handel*
4) Chopin a) Nocturne C minor b) Ballad F minor
5) Liszt 2nd Legend *Saint Francis of Paolo walking on the waves*

4 List of Piano Concertos
Bach–Busoni D minor
Beethoven C minor; G major; E♭ major
Brahms D minor; B♭ major
Liszt E♭ major; A major
Mozart E♭ major; A major: C minor; D minor; F major
Saint Saëns No.5 F major
Schubert–Liszt *Wanderer* Fantasy
Schumann A minor
Tchaikovsky B♭ minor

5 I enclose the contracts signed

6 Dr Stiedry No, I cannot go to Russia. I have refused another offer. It is no use, as long as they do not pay in 'real' money. Besides, I have no time (Besides I don't want to!) Very sorry.

7 I am very sorry there were no later dates available for the Promenade concerts. But I am sorely in need of a rest and it would mean leaving Zakopane about three weeks earlier and not getting a proper holiday. Too bad.

8 Please accept Kingston[-on-Thames] on Nov 19th for a reduced fee of 20 guineas.

It is really a shame – this is the 18th of June! This letter has been weighing on my mind for weeks. Once I took it to Boston, but forgot my draft of the programmes! Am so busy that even now I write in a hurry. Hope everything is clear and satisfactory – and hope to be forgiven! (begun 5 June 1934)

Many thanks for the engagement in Glasgow, the contract for which I have signed and am enclosing herewith. I am perfectly willing to play the two concertos suggested by Mr Barbirolli (Brahms B flat major and Liszt E flat major) and note that the rehearsal will take place on Dec 30th at 10am. When I was in London last time I spoke to Mr Edward Clark about playing with the BBC Symphony Orchestra, and we even talked about the programme. Would you be so kind as to remind him of the project? I hope that something will materialise. I have written to Mr Forbes about playing with the Hallé Orchestra, possibly with Sir Thomas Beecham, but I think it would be a good thing if you got in touch with the Committee or Sir Thomas. I am sending you two programmes for the two London recitals and four for Huddersfield and Mr van Wyck to choose from. They can also pick out certain groups from the four programmes and let me know what they prefer – then I will put them together and arrange them into a new programme. How I hate making programmes – I never know what to play. (7 July 1935)

At last I am sending back the two contracts with my signature. Please forgive the delay – I had a severe attack of 'Noletterwritis'.

Will you send the list of concertos to Leeds and ask them to choose? I would love to play the Mozart *Coronation* if they agree to that. Or perhaps Brahms B flat?

A pupil of mine in Liverpool tried to get me an orchestral engagement there and was told 'that they keep me in mind for the Busoni concerto'. (I like being kept in mind, but it is not quite enough!) He thought it would be a good thing if my agents reminded them of me, as I was a great success in L'pool and had a good following there. Do you think you could do something about it? (Only don't 'keep me in mind').

I owe you 5 guineas – may I go on owing it until October? Am rather destitute at the moment – unless you would accept a draught on my Russian bank? Or will you take one of the silver foxes? (they are caged up in Moscow at present). I shall try to say goodbye before I leave for Paris on Friday. (8 June 1936)

I think the programme would be best if the Bach Capriccio were included – so let us decide on that. This then is the final shape:

1. Bach *Capriccio on the departure* etc
2. Beethoven *Hammerclavier* Sonata

Interval

3. Schubert *Wanderer* Fantasy
4. Schumann *Carneval*

The first half lasts 42, the second 43 minutes – that fits excellently.

Now comes trouble. I have been offered an interesting engagement in Schaffhausen (Switzerland) on Dec 9th. – Busoni Concerto and Liszt's E flat. Also possibly three recitals in other Swiss towns. Now the question is first: will Glasgow Dec 5th materialise? If so, the whole project must fall through. Then secondly: could Bromley Dec 10th be changed possibly? Only if it could be managed easily, without causing any inconvenience. Otherwise I shall write and tell them, that I cannot manage Dec 9th (which I fear is what is going to happen). Perhaps they can change the date (which I am sure they won't do).

Please be an angel and let me know as soon as you can. Here [Zakopane] it is heavenly, and so far there are no pupils – Paradise regained!

P.S. Could you let me know in good time what the Proms want me to play? What about the Busoni Concertstück (D minor) and the Liszt Malédiction for one of the dates? I did both with Sir Henry in Maida Vale. (13 June 1938)

Here is the contract for October 2nd signed. It seems to me that 50 minutes is allowing too much time for the *Hammerklavier* sonata. I play it in 33 minutes. I'll run through it again and tell you at the end of this letter. If it really takes no longer, I might play something else (6 Bagatelles Op.126, 13 mins. or 32 Variations C minor, 10 mins), or perhaps they can cut down the time to 40 mins. The programmes for September 18th (Alkan symphony) is quite in order.

So, I suppose, is the bill which I got from the office a few days ago. I hope you will be kind enough to wait until I get to London – it is rather complicated to send money from here [Poland].

I have been interrupted by pupils and visitors and have just finished timing the *Hammerklavier* sonata. In my mature age I seem to have acquired much more calm and repose, which accounts for the addition of one minute and a quarter to the timing of about 40 years ago. I leave it to you to calculate how many seconds of additional calm per year that comes to. Anyhow I take 34¼ minutes to play it, which, with two short breath-takings after the first and third movements comes to 35 minutes. The BBC must now decide whether to shorten the broadcast or with what to fill up the remaining 15 minutes.

Your letter of August 22nd came to hand this morning. Many thanks for the information about Leeds. I hope it Leeds (sorry!) to a definite engagement.

P.S. As my wife and our Polish maid are only coming to London at the end of Nov, I will give you all the details when I see you. (begun 23 August 1938, finished 25th)

Rachmaninov continued to put his British musical affairs through the agency and, on occasion, asked them to look after bills and subscriptions he had neglected to pay. His last surviving letter to the agency was written in October 1930, and is included with all the others in Appendix 14.

Moriz Rosenthal's voluminous correspondence continued, but in this decade he provided some interesting personal recollections of Brahms as well as further insights into his programming:

Enclosed the programme. Would it not be better policy to announce only the concert of March 18th (entirely made up from compositions by Chopin) and to advertise the second recital (Schumann/Liszt) after the first one? A week is quite sufficient to sell tickets for a much larger hall than Wigmore Hall. Of course I leave the decision to you. (undated, but answered 2 March 1932)

After our last recital at Queen's Hall 8 or 10 years ago, you never wrote me about some opportunity to play in London, still less about an engagement. When, after years and years of waiting in vain, I received a very tempting offer from Lionel Powell for two concerts (Sunday and Monday at Albert Hall and Queen's Hall), I could not resist and accepted. I had a huge success at both concerts, and press and public acted magnificently towards me. It was impossible for me to see you then. I arrived on Saturday and went off Tuesday morning, but had rehearsal and concert on Monday which gave me more to do than at former occasions, because I also had to arrange my concert grand with Mr Berridge. I hope you were not angry about my not seeing you, and knew my unalterable friendly feelings for you and Mr Ibbs.

I would like to come to London again. I would be delighted to give a recital at Queen's Hall between May 12th and say the 17th at my own risk if you could get me some engagement at a nice fee with Mr Adrian Boult, Sir Henry Wood or Sir Landon Ronald. Or if you could get me some provincial engagement or at homes in London like those when I played long ago in London. Please answer as soon as you can, give me a statement about the expenses at Queen's Hall and believe me your old friend. (8 April 1932)

It would be bad policy to arrange a costly recital against your advice, which is backed by a life long experience. Gladly will I therefore postpone my new appearance in London for autumn, say end of October around 25th. I have not the least objection to play at the Radio, as long as they offer substantial fees, only I and you will have to think over which space of time should lie between the Radio appearances and my own recital. You know that the late Mr Robert Newman paid me 100 guineas per concert, a fee which may be difficult to obtain just at present. Still I hope you will do your and Pedro's (many greetings to him) best to arrange the fee of those two Radio concerts most satisfactorily. I would love to perform with orchestra 1) the F minor concerto of Chopin and 2) by way of contrast and big climaxes my own Variations on an original theme for piano and orchestra, on which Felix v. Weingartner showered enthusiastic praise in a letter I keep for you. (14 April 1932)

Schnabel's feat to play all Sonatas by Beethoven has nothing new about it. It has been done by the following artists: Risler, Hoehn, Pauer, Backhouse, Katarina Bacon, Olga Samaroff. Only the others have done it in six recitals. I wonder how London will take to this scheme, which is very likely baked by the Grammophone industry. Can you give me the address of Mr Ernest Newman? (18 July 1932)

About the offer of the BBC, I have to refuse it most emphatically. There is not the least reason why I should satisfy myself with a fee which is lower than those offered to other pianists. I know, for instance that the BBC pays [Wilhelm] Backhouse (who, by the way, has only a small fraction of my name and fame in Germany, the whole European and American continent!) a fee of 125 guineas for one and 200 guineas for two consecutive performances. Why the BBC persists in trying to get me for a fee which is not customary to offer to great artists I cannot conceive. From the 75 guineas [a 'ridiculously small fee' of 60 guineas had been 'emphatically refused' in his last letter of 27 August] I would have at least to allow 10 guineas to the Manchester people, 7.5 for commission and about 15 to the income tax inspector. This means that I would play for about 35 to 40 guineas. I will therefore wait until they pay me 125 guineas for one or 200 for two performances at the Radio, and if they think they are not prepared for such a fee I will resign myself not to play at the Radio. (5 September 1932)

I always considered you not only as my musical Manager but as an old friend, therefore I accepted those two November dates endorsed by yourself. Yesterday I received letters from my London friends who are simply desperate about the change we effected. They say there is no possibility of a success with an audience if one plays on weekday afternoons. That no gentlemen, only ladies will be present and so on. They also dissuade me to play on Saturday November 5th, saying that Schnabel will have a big audience, which of course will harm my recital.

I am going to ask your advice. 1) Shall I return to my original dates? October 8th and 11th? or 2) Shall I postpone my recitals for a time where Saturday afternoons and weekday evenings are still to let? Let us say in March, where I am free? Or 3) Would it be possible or even advisable to create quite a new thing in giving my recitals November 1st and 5th but not at 3 o'clock but rather at 5 o'clock afternoon? There would be some better possibilities for gentlemen to attend to my recitals and would clash less with Schnabel. Let me hear from you by telegram. I am pretty upset about the situation which awaits me, as a success at London is a big thing, which should not be trifled at. (16 September 1932)

… Will you kindly enquire at once if they [Hallé Orchestra] possess the scores and parts of the E minor concerto by Chopin and also of the *Hungarian Fantasy* by Liszt. If not we must borrow them on my expenses. (27 October 1932)

I got a letter of the Income Tax Service. I should give them the figures of my recent receipts in England. It seems that the nett receipts of my two recitals at Wigmore Hall were £24.12s.9d [£24.63p] Kindly write me if this supposition is right, also how much I hold from the Manchester engagement after deducting your fee? I left some money to my pupil Miss Walton in order to pay you your fee for Manchester etc. Undoubtedly she has already spoken with you. Any monies I have to get from you, I beg you to send to my bank in Bern but not to Vienna! Kindly write me to Vienna as I will not keep waiting the income tax office.

P.S. Don't you think you could get some Manager to arrange a concert (recital) at Manchester at a gross percentage basis? The success and *Manchester Guardian* were colossal. Of course it should take place between or better after my London recitals. What are the costs for a good advertised Manchester recital? [Tillett pencilled annotation £90 to £100] (11 November 1932)

I select the 1st of December for my recital with Mr van Wyck. There are so many pieces I would like to play in London and would not give away the choice just now, more than a half year before the date. When would be the last time for giving the programm?

Mr G.C., who wrote the dirty criticism in the *Musical Times*, seems now to be at the staff of the *Daily Telegraph*. He seems to be in such love with Schnabel that he is armed against all other pianists. Who is now at the head of the *D.T.*? (Musical editor) Would you pay the lawyer (Rubinstein) one guinea, deducting it off my fee at London? There is great difficulty to send money from Vienna. (undated)

I note that my recital with Mr van Wyck will take place end of November 1934 and I would be thankful if he would fix the exact date as soon as possible. About the two alternativ programms, it would be more advantageous for us both if we would state some cardinal points before we fix the whole programm. 1) Would Mr van Wyck accept the Sonata in B flat Op.106 [Beethoven] for the beginning of the recital? It takes 40 minutes but is my special favourite which, however, I never played in England. 2) Would he prefer another Sonata, say Op.31 No.3 in E flat, and in this case would he rather advise to follow up with the *Paganini Variations* by Brahms, or by a Chopin number and after this one of my own Variations on an original theme? (More difficult than the Brahms/Paganini perhaps).

As soon as Mr van Wyck will decide about those cardinal points, I will send him my best programm and he can ask for changements. If I send two programms, one of them both will be necessarily more effectiv or attractiv as the other and it would be a pity I should not be judge of the selection to be made as I played every piece of them many many times. Still, I will abide if Mr van Wyck persists to have the final word.

The Palladium 13th January would suit me perfectly.

As to the libel case, your esteemed solicitors are themselves in grave doubts and will take an opinion of counsel for six guineas. They don't seem to be of any experience in such a case and I decided to ask my friend Herbert Hughes (formerly at the *Daily Telegraph*) what he thinks. For this purpose I beg you to send me two copies of the whole number [*Musical Times*, March 1934] where this criticism appeared. (28 April 1934)

[Rosenthal appears to have confined himself to a riposte in a letter to the editor of the *Musical Times* in the December 1934 issue]

Enclosed two programms from which Mr van Wyck may select No.1 or No.2, but shall not make a new one from both. They are made up with very much care. Will you give me the programm which Mr van Wyck has selected, the first or the second one? I think the first may make more impression. Am leaving soon for Buenos Aires, could you get me a good engagement for South Africa?

I

1) Three Sonatas	D. Scarlatti
2) *Kreisleriana*	Schumann
3) Variations on a theme by Paganini	Brahms
4) Fantasie impromptu/Scherzo E major/Two Etudes Op.25 Nos. 6 & 11	Chopin
5) Poeme F sharp major/Etude D flat	Scriabine
Miniatures (Serenade/*At the brook*/Valse)	Rubinstein
Tarantella (*Portici*)	Liszt

II

1) 32 variations [Diabelli]	Beethoven
2) Nocturne C sharp minor	Chopin
Impromptu A flat major	
Ballade G minor	
Valse in F major	
Mazurka	
Scherzo C sharp minor	
3) *Carnaval*	Schumann
4) *Orientale*	Albeniz
5) *Variations on an original theme*	Moriz Rosenthal

(5 June 1934)

My *Variations on an original theme* are of course in no way similar to a paraphrase. They are ten characteristic pieces built on the same theme. But if Mr van Wyck is particularly anxious for me to play the Brahms *Paganini Variations* I will gladly do it. Only it seems to me that I should play the first or the second, each one 14 variations (like for instance Horowitz did in Vienna), both sets growing monotonous for the public. Or I could play a long, but not overlong, selection of about 22–24 variations from the 28. My first selection made by myself with the approval of Brahms himself brought forth 18 variations. However all this is not so important as long as the great impression of a pianistically and musically heroic deed is evoked.

You are by the way mistaken if you think Mr van Wyck made it quite clear that he did not wish me to play any transcriptions. He only refused the Strauss *Fantasie* from my pen and sonatas by Beethoven. I included therefore a Tarantella by Liszt, where the melodic contents are derived from the opera *La Muette de Portici* [Auber]. Should Mr van Wyck be interested to banish this (very effectiv) piece from the programm I would substitute it by the 2nd *Hungarian Rhapsody* with my cadenza approved by Liszt himself. In no case should arise a quarrel about the programm! In searching through your correspondence with Mr van Wyck, you will find that he did not bar each transcription but especially those on Strauss works. If we arrange now definitely the programm I would suggest for the first number, instead of three pieces by Scarlatti to play:

a) Aria con variazione	Händel
b) Gavotte	Padre Martini
c) Sonata	Domenico Scarlatti

There are everywhere Händel celebrations this year and his piece would please very much. (25 October 1934)

Will you express my sympathies to Mr Evans and tell him the following: I will play by Chopin Three nouvelles Etudes in F minor, A flat major and D flat major, so-called because they were composed after his two sets op.10 and op.25 with the aim to be inserted in Moscheles and Fétis' *Méthode des Méthodes*. In grace and poetry they almost go beyond the famous 24.

Then Etude op.25 no.2 F minor, Etude op.10 no.1 C major. I will play furthermore: Valse in A minor, which Chopin himself considered as his best Valse he ever composed, as he told Stephen Heller, and Valse op.42 A flat. The conversation between Chopin and Stephen Heller about the Valses may be found in the biography of Chopin by [Frederick] Niecks. It is very interesting.

Poëme op.32 no.1 F sharp major [by Scriabin], a true poëme and wonderful in its harmonies. Variations by Brahms on a theme of Paganini.

I spoke of course frequently and at length with Brahms about this interesting composition. He was not very fond to perform them complete as the two finales make the work rather heavy. He told me humoristically that he played once the first set and was prepared to play the second one as a *bis* [an encore], if the public would applaud with full force; but (he said) there was no demand for it. He approved of a selection I made and played at my Viennese recital in 1884 and afterwards repeatedly, where he listened to them every time and even told: 'Nobody plays my Variations as this young man of 22 Moriz Rosenthal' (printed in *50 years of Vienna musical life* by Doctor Theodor Helm). In the last years, however, I enlarged the number of variations played to 24, 13 from the first set and 11 from the second. It seems to me diminishing the effect of the piece if each variation gets a comment, and I would propose to leave them to speak for themselves. (undated)

A touching letter to John Tillett and Robert Leigh Ibbs came at the end of 1936 from composer Howard Ferguson on behalf of his friend and mentor, Harold Samuel, who died a month later:

Harold asks me to write: Dear John or (on the other hand) Dear Bob,
I was so touched at receiving your gift that my lower lip is still quivering. Quite seriously, to be remembered and thought of by old friends is a really valuable condition. Thank you all most sincerely for thinking of me. There is a lot more that I could say, but one thing is (and I hope you will agree with me) that I hope I may soon be climbing up the stairs at No.124 grumbling and asking why there are not more engagements for me! (16 December 1936)

P.S. from Howard Ferguson
Harold is still continuing satisfactory and we hope to get him up to Hampstead just before Christmas.

John Tillett's personal humanity is revealed in letters from Irene Scharrer, who decided in 1935 to sever her association with the agency, but then changed her mind and was taken back with no fuss. Some 30 years later his widow Emmie treated John Ogdon in exactly the same fashion.

After all these years of unbroken friendship with your firm and every member of it, I could feel very sad at having to write this letter. In sheer desperation I have decided that I must change my arrangement. I know you have done your best for me and I appreciate your invaluable kindness, and I feel that you must know (and can only sympathise with me when I tell you) that now it is a matter of necessity. I shall only ever feel real affection and friendship for you all and can only hope you will consider that I deserve the same from you and that you will wish me God speed. (4 March 1935)

Even though I saw you yesterday, I feel that I must write a thank you for your letter. I was very deeply touched. (13 March 1935)

In all humility I write admitting that I made a grave mistake (at a time of acute anxiety) in ever leaving "the dear firm", and would now beg them to be magnanimous and take me back. (5 November 1935)

The kindness of your letter has moved me very deeply. I shall never forget it. (9 November 1935)

However much artists professed their distaste for discussing financial matters, before long they always seemed to get on to the subject. Finances worldwide were in a parlous state in the 1930s, particularly in America after the 1929 Wall Street crash and in inflation-ridden Germany from where Artur Schnabel wrote:

Mrs Courtauld's nervousness about my vaguely (and never without her consent) intended appearance in one of the LSO concerts next season is not easy to be understood. Her concerts have an audience different from the people frequenting other concerts, her concerts have been sold out always, and, as it seems to me, no reason exists to fear a decline in demand for the attractions she is offering next season. In biggest towns like London, New York, Paris, Berlin we musicians are never asked to play exclusively for one of the musical institutions of the town (not even in these times which are hard for everybody). Nobody cares how often we appear and what distances are between the several appearances (which is best proved just by Mr Powell's invitation to me). In small towns we are sometimes asked to limit our work in the interest of the local enterprise and in consideration that there one can only count with a certain number of always the same concert-goers.

But of course I shall not accept the invitation of the LSO. Please will you tell them that it would have been a pleasure to come, but playing already several times next season I would prefer an engagement for 1932/33. If Mrs Courtauld wants to announce my appearances in her concerts as my only ones in London next season, I also agree to this request, though I think that accent quite superfluous if I promise to play only for the Courtauld concerts. No condition was connected when Mrs Courtauld and I fixed our coming mutual activities, but she learned now that before accepting an invitation for some other London music place I first wanted to know whether she would like to see me there, so she might have been quite confident that I would not start anything which she considers to be harmful to her ambitions, even if I cannot share her opinion. (20 April 1931)

The problem of my next concerts in England begins to trouble me seriously. It was obvious that at the time when the engagements have been fixed, everybody on earth would have risked his life for the security of the pound. Therefore it was neither usual or necessary to make it a special point in contracts that the pound meant gold pound. Now we learned once more that no human institution is safe. But the change of the institution will of course be followed by a changed attitude of him who is affected by the new situation. That is my case. The new situation makes it very difficult, if not impossible, to decide now, whether I shall be able to come some weeks later to play my concerts. It could easily happen, theoretically, that just during the period of the concerts the pound would be so low that my expenses would surpass my earnings. Certainly nobody would expect me to work for nothing, We in Germany are most familiar with the painful surprises which are threatening every minute if the currency fluctuates. The artist's profession does not belong actually to the general commercial intercourse or to the exchange of goods. It is rather indifferent for the economical circulation (and speculation). But do you think that British musicians or writers performing or being published in foreign countries would now agree to or offer to get reduced fees and royalties, to receive perhaps the name instead of the substance?

I need not tell you how I detest to discuss such matters, but there is no alternative and first of all I feel obliged to announce already now (to avoid later disappointment about a cancellation at the last moment), that my appearances in England completely depend from the further development of that money – chaos, except the societies which invited me would be disposed to count the pound as it was counted the day of our stipulation or would suggest some other acceptable solution. I would be more upset than I can express if conditions would compel me to abandon my concerts in England, and hoping that it will not come to such a deplorable end. (6 October 1931)

At Christmas I shall be back in London, I think. It will be time then to discuss all we have to talk of. Musical activities in America are quite satisfactory (Beethoven, it seems, [is] at the start of a promising career). (3 December 1933)

I cabled yesterday my preparedness to accept the invitation to play at the Leeds Musical Festival and hope that my answer did not arrive too late for the decisions of the Festival Committee. Brahms B flat major, 100 guineas, if you think this sum the limit, are accepted. You are quite right about my antipathy against the performance of solo pieces at orchestral concerts, but I would not object to play another piano concerto, either one by Mozart or, should this be too long, the *Konzertstück* by Weber.

Palestine is most interesting. I shall be in London about April 17th and then report my impressions. The programme for the recital with Hubermann has been sent to you by his secretary. Please do alter the order of succession of the four works: 1) Beethoven, 2) Brahms, 3) Mozart, 4) Schubert. (26 March 1934)

At the Hallé Concert I propose to play a second work (with Beethoven's E flat) Mozart's Concerto in D minor.

I accept with pleasure the invitation to appear at the BBC Symphony – concerto in London on April 10th 1935, and should like best to perform at that occasion Beethoven's C minor concerto. Appearing next season only once with orchestra in London, I should appreciate very much if Dr Boult would agree to let me play two concertos; if the programme could be arranged in accordance to my request, I am suggesting Mozart's A major concerto.

For Glasgow I should prefer to stick to Beethoven E flat and Mozart D minor. (I am, as you know, a little tired of the Brahms concertos and think they ought to be reserved to younger colleagues).

I am enclosing the contract for Liverpool. The programmes in detail for my London recitals as well as for the Mossel tour I shall send in perhaps a fortnight or three weeks.

My son is very grateful to you for the endeavour to find him activities in England, and he hopes (as I do) that you may succeed in helping his career. He will write to you himself.

On the 18th I shall be back in Tremezzo after three weeks in the Dolomites, which unfortunately have been less enjoyable as usual, by depressing persistence of rain, rain, rain and winter temperature. (14 August 1934)

CHAPTER FIFTEEN

Letters from Instrumentalists, Singers and Composers: 1930–39

A selection of letters written in the 1930s from instrumentalists (other than pianists), singers and composers, begins with Casals, who starts with some sharp comments on the lack of financial benefits to be gained from performing in England, in particular when a BBC engagement was under discussion:

> I have received your letter regarding the BBC with their new proposition. Considering the actual value of the pound and the exaggerated high taxes in England, the offer of the BBC does not reach my minimum fee for an ordinary concert. I am very sorry to be obliged to decline the offer. (7 July 1933)

Casals was, for a time, a close friend of the eminent scholar, pianist and composer Donald Francis Tovey, who had founded the Reid Orchestra in Edinburgh in 1917 three years after taking the Chair of Music at the city's university, and with which he gradually built up a series of notable concerts over the years. During 1931, Tovey gave serious thought to composing a cello concerto for his friend and by the spring of 1934 (when Tovey visited Barcelona to play his Piano Concerto with Casals' Orquesta Pau Casals) the work was well advanced. A date, 22 November 1934, was set for the first performance to be given in Edinburgh and a series of letters trace the ebb and flow of plans. Unfortunately the proposed performance in London on 6 December did not take place.

> I have received your recent telegram. I accept the two concerts for March of next year for a fee of 400 guineas. At the same time I wish to give the première of Tovey's cello concerto in Edinburgh, in homage to the great master and would like to combine this concert with a similar occasion in London at one of concerts of the Philharmonic Society. I would be grateful for the name of the Society's secretary so that I may put this proposal to him. (27 January 1934, translation from Spanish)

Ibbs and Tillett replied:

> I am much obliged for your letter of the 27th ult., regarding the proposed engagement at the Courtauld–Sargent Concerts, which I note you would be prepared to entertain at a fee of four hundred guineas for the two consecutive concerts, and would prefer the month of March 1935. I will take the earliest opportunity of consulting Mr Courtauld, and will write you again in due course.
>
> In the event of this engagement materialising, I note it is your wish to give the premier performance of Professor Donald Tovey's concerto in Edinburgh, and also in London with the Royal Philharmonic Society, and I will take this matter up as soon as the question of the Courtauld-Sargent engagement is settled. The Secretary of the RPS is Mr Keith Douglas, RPS, 19 Berners Street, London W1. We know Mr Douglas very well, and in fact negotiate all the engagements for the RPS. (1 February 1934)
>
> Your letter of 29th May received. I am delighted to play and conduct for the BBC – will Dr Adrian Boult conduct the proposed concert of November 14th? I am sorry that the date of November 8th will be impossible for me. Will it be possible for the Reid Orchestra to place their concert on Thursday 22nd? Then the dates could be November 14th Queen's Hall (playing), November 18th Studio concert (conducting), November 22nd Reid Orchestra. This arrangement would give me the necessary time for rehearsals in Edinburgh. (3 June 1934)

Ibbs and Tillett replied:

Thank you for your letter of the 3rd inst., which came duly to hand. We have since been in communication with the BBC, who have just telephoned advising that we can regard as definite Wednesday November 14th next Queen's Hall Symphony (as soloist), and Sunday November 18th Studio Orchestral Concert (as conductor), so will you please book those dates, and we will send you the usual formal confirmation in due course. Thursday November 22nd is a convenient date for the Reid Orchestra, and we are therefore advising Miss Mary Grierson that you will be able to play for Professor Tovey on that date. By the way, Sir HENRY WOOD will be the Conductor at the BBC Concert on November 14th.

Now with regard to your kind offer to play Professor Tovey's concerto for the Royal Philharmonic Society in London, the only date that is possible is December 6th. Would that be convenient for you? As a matter of fact the Royal Philharmonic Society had arranged to give a Bach Concert on that date, but they would do everything possible to postpone this programme to a later Concert if December 6th happened to be convenient to you. Would you mind sending me a telegram at this point as the Committee will be meeting next week. (13 June 1934)

Prof. Tovey has accepted the date of November 22nd for Edinburgh. At that occasion I shall give the first performance of Prof. Tovey's cello concerto. Logically the second performance belongs to the Philharmonic Society and I hope that it will be so. The Hon. Secretary of the Ph. S. has not yet sent to me the announced letter regarding this question. Would you kindly speak to the Hon. Secretary? As my wish is to pay my homage of admiration to Prof. Tovey, I would not consider any fee for the two concerts. Please make this known to the Phil. S. and to Dr Mary Grierson, 12 Crawford Road, Edinburgh. (13 June 1934)

Ibbs and Tillett replied:

Thank you for your letter of the 13th. Inst., which has crossed my communication to you of the 14th inst. As you will learn from that letter, the Committee of the Royal Philharmonic Society would like you to play Professor TOVEY's cello concerto, and the date suggested is Thursday December 6th next, which I hope will be possible for you. The Committee of the Royal Philharmonic Society greatly appreciate your kindness in agreeing to play without a fee on this special occasion, and as desired I have advised Dr Mary Grierson of your generous decision as regards the Reid Symphony Concert on Thursday November 22nd. (19 June 1934)

BBC – It will be necessary to consider three rehearsals for the concert which I shall conduct:- Nov. Friday 16th afternoon, Saturday 17th morning, Sunday 18th morning. Possible concert in Haslemere on the afternoon of Saturday 17th (not the 24th). I do not wish to play the concerto by Monn (arranged by Schoenberg), but I propose *Don Quixote* by Strauss which I played long ago with Sir Henry Wood. (18 August 1934, translation from Spanish)

Ibbs and Tillett replied:

Many thanks for your letter of the 18th instant duly to hand, in accordance with which we advised the BBC that you would like to have three rehearsals for the concert which you are conducting on November 18th next. We have just heard from them that Saturday morning, November 17th and Sunday morning November 18th will certainly be available for you, and they hope also to arrange for you to have Friday afternoon, the 15th, although it might be a little easier to fix up from their point of view if the Friday morning suited you equally well. Presumably it would make no difference to you, but if you particularly prefer the afternoon perhaps you would let me know. We note that Haslemere must take place on Saturday afternoon, November 17th, and that November 24th is not possible for you. Miss Dakyns is just waiting to hear from HORSZOWSKI as to whether he can manage the 17th. We have also advised the BBC that you are not prepared to play the Monn Concerto (arr. Schoenberg) but suggest *Don Quixote* by Strauss. The BBC are very interested in your proposal, but it is just a question as to whether it will fit into their programme scheme. (28 August 1934)

Ibbs and Tillett replied:

... Unfortunately I shall not be able to meet you on your arrival at Victoria Station as I have to be in Gloucester on the 12th inst., but I shall be back in London the next day, and shall look forward to the pleasure of seeing you again. During my absence Miss Bass will, of course, be able to attend to any matters of importance. (2 November 1934)

Tovey's cello Concerto had its first London hearing in November 1935, but, unfortunately, it was both inadequately rehearsed and incompetently conducted by the composer. In June 1936 plans were made with Fred Gaisberg and the Gramophone Company to record it together with the concerto by Elgar, who had recently died, but they were scrapped at the last minute, much to Casals' irritation. Happily a year later the record was made and simultaneously broadcast across Europe, although the discs themselves were not issued until 1992, over half a century later.

I confirm my telegramm "Please send copy Elgar". It is a good idea the Elgar concerto for the BBC concert (18th November). Before my definite decision I must see the work again. I hope that I shall have to prepare it during the summer. (27 June 1936)

I accept the proposed programme for November 22nd.

Eine kleine Nachtmusik	Mozart
Symphony No.3	Schumann
Till Eulenspiegel	Strauss

I have sent a word to Mr Gaisberg regarding the recording from performances of the Tovey and Elgar concertos, which in principle I accept. I would propose that the fee of £150 be accepted [increased] to £200. It is my wish to be in London in time for the necessary rehearsals. (3 October 1936)

Another Spanish cellist, though a generation younger than Casals, was Gaspar Cassadó, who made a notable appearance in February 1933 at a Royal Philharmonic Society concert under Beecham to mark the centenary of the birth of Brahms. In it he played the composer's Double Concerto with the violinist Jelly d'Aranyi, an artist with Ibbs and Tillett. A letter survives from him, written a couple of years later:

... I therefore beg you, Miss Bass, to find me a pianist to accompany me at the concert at Wycombe Abbey school. You will well understand that for one concert, I would not wish to inconvenience Miss Mendelssohn who is in Florence, and would therefore have to make such a long journey. I willingly accept the little concert on 14 March at the Royal Academy. Perhaps the same pianist who accompanies me at Wycombe Abbey could also do so at the Royal Academy – do you understand? The programme could remain the same. If it were possible, I would very much like to have Mr Gerald Moore as my pianist. (24 February 1935, translation from Spanish)

A cellist who also had dealings with the agency was the Austrian Emanuel Feuermann, who died tragically early in 1942 at the age of 40. He fled Germany in 1939 and, for the last three years of his life, settled in America, where he played trios with Heifetz and Rubinstein, Schnabel and Huberman.

Dr Schiff asks me for you the concertos I play. Here please: Tartini, Boccherini, Monn, Ph. E. Bach, Haydn, Schumann, Dvořák, Volkmann, Lalo, d'Albert, Saint Saëns, Toch, Hindemith, Honegger, Schoenberg, Ibert, Beethoven triple concerto, Brahms double concerto, Tchaikovsky *Rococo* variations, Strauss *Don Quixote*, [Walter] Schulthess [1894–1971, Swiss composer and later a Zurich-based agent] Variations [Symphonic Variations Op.14 for cello and orchestra 1926].

I am in high spirits; Dr Schiff rang me up this morning and told me that in September and October I will play in Japan and, I think you know it, January and February I will be in America. Now travelling the whole time I think on the nice weeks in London with great pleasure. Having the security to have Ibbs & Tillett and you, I know, that for my future in England I need only one [thing] more, to play well. (27 February 1934)

It is only 2 months since we arrived in New York, and we are already living not only in our own

> house but even in our own furniture from Switzerland! We are happy not to be in Europe in these hectic months, people over here treat us very nicely, the house is situated in the most charming neighbourhood. Eva likes it here very much – to her own surprise – Monica is sweeter than ever. I myself had a few outdoor concerts with unbelievably big success – altogether we are grateful and very satisfied. On Wednesday we are expecting Mrs Reifenberg for a long visit and we are working very hard to have the house entirely finished til then.
>
> Enclosed you kindly find the paper for the Promenade Concerts. I even do not know the publishers of Strauss *Don Quixote*; and the Haydn concerto I am playing from the copy of the very first print. Mr Huberman and I never seem to agree at first about dates. I heard from Dr Schiff that he does not like me to play on Sept 26th, thinking that that would interfere to a high degree with our recordings. I just wrote him a line in which I tried to explain to him that he is mistaken. I am looking forward to Europe and I am more than sorry Eva cannot come with me this time.
>
> I remain with kindest regards, yours very sincerely
> Emanuel Feuermann
>
> [P.S.] I forgot to mention the most important question: my permit! I have to stay in England from Sept 25th to Oct 21st. I wrote to Mr Rex Palmer to get in touch with you. As I have to sail at the end of August, I simply must have the permit and contracts not later than middle of August!!! Many thanks! (22 July 1939)
>
> Will you try to insist that I shall play at both occasions with [Ernest] LUSH !!!!!!!!!! I like him best. Thanks for the permit. Everything was settled that Schnabel, Hubermann and I should meet at H's place in Switzerland on Sept. 8th, what does Good? Mr Schnabel changed his plans and shall go directly to London, but about 10 days later. I very gladly am following his footsteps and shall also come to London right away round the 10th of Sept. Mr Hubermann will feel like Napoleon after Waterloo, I am afraid. I never had a busier summer than this one, playing, recording, teaching, driving round etc. and the later I have to leave the better. When we have our luncheon at Bellini's I will start working to persuade you to come to America once. (15 August 1939)

Gregor Piatigorsky, the Russian cellist (but like Feuermann, a naturalized American) was just beginning his international career in 1930, when he wrote the letter below to the agency. In later years he formed a famous duo with the violinist Heifetz:

> As you no doubt know by this time, I have severed all connections with my former representative Mr Alexander Merovitch. I understand [he] has made some arrangements for Horowitz and myself to play in a joint recital known as the Aeolus Concert Series. I would appreciate knowing all the details of this concert as regards programme, date etc., and I would ask you therefore to kindly let me have this information … I also want to inform you that all matters will be handled by me direct in the future. (13 April 1933)

Guilhermina Suggia's prose style all but matches her haughty pose in Augustus John's portrait:

> … Regards recitals, I agree that they are an incentive for the Provinces and I am willing to give them but not this year on account of having no orchestral engagements, and the time I can spare to be in England will be too short to fit in serious recitals which need much rehearsing and preparation. I would like you to kindly find out for me as soon as possible if Dohnányi will be in England end March beginning April, and if so, if he could join me in a recital in which I would like to play his cello sonata. He may remember my having come to Budapest years ago to hear him play this sonata with Casals. Also if Lamond could give a joint recital playing all the five Beethoven sonatas and a third date for a recital with Gerald Moore or Harold Samuel … I guess Wigmore Hall is the best. (Oct/Nov 1934?)
>
> Will you suggest the Saint Saëns concerto for Belfast – it takes just 20 minutes – I take note of the date of my first recital with Gerald Moore. Am I playing Lalo in Bromley or do they want something else? (29 August 1935)

> … Also order from Toms, Wellington, Somerset three A, one D and one C [strings], the very best quality but the A string must be a little thinner than the last he sent me … they never received my order – the post is so irregular owing to Spain [civil war]. (27 July 1937)

The Spanish Civil War had more serious consequences than supplying cello strings for Suggia. Guitarist Andrès Segovia was an artist who also became a close friend of the agency, in particular with Emmie Bass, who seems to have handled his affairs from the start of his career in England, which began in 1936:

> … Before finishing this letter, which is the number one I write in English, ask Mrs Ibbs and Tillett to arrange some radio in order to endorse both my London recitals. It would be a pity to loose the profit of my first tour in England in repairing the deficit, if any, of those concerts. Naturally I do not believe such a lossing, but it is wiser not too much rely upon the volubility of the public. My best regards to Mrs Ibbs and Tillett. (23 March 1936)

Five months later Segovia was forced by the alarming events of the Spanish Civil War to flee Barcelona for Italy, from where he sent desperate letters to Ibbs and Tillett.

> My wife recently sent a letter to Miss Bass explaining to her a little of what has happened to us, and it's possible that she has already reported the sad news to you.
>
> In fact we have had to leave Barcelona for good to save ourselves from the horrors threatening the city by the criminal masses – our house with its considerable literary and musical library, pictures, carpets, table service, silverware, furs, jewelry, and several instruments. But that signifies nothing compared to another anxiety which I have – my children spent the summer not far from Madrid. I know nothing of them. I hope that the armies which passed there have respected their vulnerability. It is my only hope.
>
> Forgive me if I have said all this before, my wife having already written to Miss Bass, but I cannot take up my pen without my worries pouring forth. The point of my letter to you is to ask about a tour of Scotland, which I forgot to include in the letter from my wife. I have to work now more than ever. In the difficult circumstances in which we now find ourselves the victims, it is necessary to respond courageously by working.
>
> My friends, you must redouble your efforts on my part. I do not wish to offend you in any way if I suggest that I am disposed to give your firm 15% per engagement instead of the usual 10%. That allows you to spend a little more on correspondence, publicity and other similar expenses. Please do not read into this the slightest doubt about the efficiency of the work you do, nor any intention on my part to encourage you to give me any preferential treatment above the other artists on your lists. Nothing like that. I know, from long years' experience, that you always work for your artists with the utmost loyalty. I ask only that you might intensify your activities in my favour and obtain as many engagements as possible, so that, in some way, I may make up for the great losses this evil revolution has put me through. Since I am the only one as far as my instrument is concerned, the contracts you would get me would not be taken up by other virtuosi …!
>
> I hope that you are sympathetic to all this and that I can count upon your collaboration. Now I ask you to tell me how long the programmes for Scotland should be. I shall also send you very soon those which I am preparing for my recitals in London. Regarding these, I would like to cover the risks with a radio engagement. Is that possible? Propose either an all-classical programme or all-Spanish.
>
> I apologise for writing in long-hand, I have also left my typewriter in Barcelona. We are living in a little village near Geneva, my wife, her three children, and me. Do you know anything about Casals? (10 August 1936, translation from Spanish)

> We have been touched for your very sympathetic letter, which shows us how did you love also our poor Spain and the appreciation and friendship towards us. We feel awfully thankful for this on the meantime that we want you to be sure of our sincerely correspondence to your feelings.
>
> I am sending enclosed the programme for the Mossel tour, divided in two parts with an interval of two or three minutes, for it is forty minutes long. I think that may be too tiresome for the auditorium playing it entirely but if you wish you can make it straight. Also you will find the St Andrew's one. Those of my London recitals I will send them later. (23 August 1936)

An amusing telegram sent to Emmie (by now Tillett) seems a far cry from the bleak sentiments of his earlier correspondence.

> Telegram: to Emma Tillett
> Argentine Gentleman whose name I have forgotten asks me to introduce to you a feminine artist whose name I never knew STOP He may contact you If he does please be kind with him If he does not never mind STOP Love Andres (31 October, year unknown)

Turning to singers, letters from the 1930s include one from the Scottish-born American soprano Mary Garden, who created the role of Mélisande in Debussy's opera *Pelléas et Mélisande*, though in this instance the correspondence was unusually about acting in a play rather than singing in an opera:

> Many thanks for your most interesting and charming letter. I have never done a straight play, but I feel I should like to if I found the right one. For the moment I am not free as I leave for America to fill a five month engagement the end of October. I could come to London on my way back from America and I could come in and see you and talk things over if you cared to. (22 September 1934)

> Would you send me the libretto of the play *Viceroy Sarah*. I shall take great care of it and send it back to you at once after reading. If I like the play there might be a chance of talking business with you at once, but before anything said or done I want to read the play. (19 October 1934)

Elena Gerhardt ended her association with the agency in 1933, but once again this seems to have been handled by Ibbs and Tillett with remarkable equanimity and the friendship endured despite the break. Her reasons were rather misplaced considering that she was at that very moment being offered a tour with Max Mossel, but the final letter, with its reference to the current financial status of her late accompanist Nikisch, who had died back in 1922, reveals a dry sense of humour.

> I have just been thinking of my recitals for the season 1933–34, and I think to get good dates we should get them now. And I also thought again about your offer concerning the Mossel tour; of course I don't know if you already engaged some other artist in my place, but as the pound sterling seems to keep steady I would do this tour for you. And if you still can place me in it, we could arrange the recitals according to it. I would like to give one in November and one in February.
>
> How would you think about one for popular prices in Queen's Hall for a change? So many people cannot get in at Wigmore Hall on account of the high prices, and how much does one concert in Queen's Hall cost now? Of course we could have less expensive programmes etc. Do let me know about all this. And do you think it would be possible to get me a date at the BBC for May in a Brahms programme? I would so love to come over then with Dr Kohl. (4 March 1933)

> It is quite difficult for me to write to you today and tell you that I decided to put my business affairs in England again into the hands of my old friend Harold Holt. You will remember that I left the firm Powell & Holt when he left it, as I could not keep on working with Lionel Powell.
>
> I have been very happy during the years working with your firm, except that you could not get me sufficient provincial dates. Just the same, I know you tried to do your best for me and I want to thank you therefore very much, hoping that we may stay the same good friends we always have been. With kindest regards to all my friends in your office as well. (15 May 1933)

> Dear Ibbsey,
> Many thanks for your kind words in your letter of May 7th. I am very glad that I feel just the same about our friendship for the future.
>
> I am awfully sorry to hear that Mr Nikisch still owes you this big amount of money, but I am in no contact with him anymore and simply recommended your firm, as he asked me who I think are the best agents in London to give recitals with. I know nothing about his financial possibilities, therefore you will understand that I cannot do anything in the matter. (24 May 1933)

The bass Alexander Kipnis had double cause for concern when he wrote a terse note to the agency asking for redress:

> It has just come to my notice that the explanatory note on the first page of the program book speaks of me as a German baritone. May I ask you to correct this in your forthcoming programs to read Russian bass of American extraction if any biographical comments are to be made. (29 January 1934)

He wrote from Buenos Aires the following year:

> Thank you for your airmail letter of July 26th, offering me a return engagement in Burnley. Crowding this date between Glasgow and Edinburgh involves considerable fatigue, but I would endure that if my fee of fifty-five guineas is acceptable to them.
>
> The Belfast contract I have sent you a week ago as ordinary mail, and should reach you in a fortnight. (5 August 1935)

Kipnis was a member of the ensemble at the Vienna State Opera, and had to organize his schedule carefully when it came to asking for leave of absence.

> Thank you for your letter of the 7th inst. I am very pleased that you have secured a BBC engagement for January 25th, and I herewith enclose contract and my program.
>
> I regret not being able to change the Bristol date, January 14th, to February 10th, but my Leave of Absence as granted me by the Staatsoper, was based upon the dates of my English tour, and the repertory since then has been so arranged that my presence is imperative here at the conclusion of my tour. However any day of my present visit you can offer the Bristol people, if that will facilitate their plans any.
>
> P.S. If I am not mistake, Gerald Moore offered to play for me in a broadcast, should he be free. [pencilled annotation by John Tillett: No; engaged] This offer to entail no financial outlay. Kindly ask Mr Moore for his decision, and also request the BBC to let me know whether they accept the program I offer them, or make use of the ALTERNATIVES listed. I wish to avoid carrying more music than is essential. Thank you for your attention to these details. (10 December 1936)

> I delayed in answering your first letter offering me the Glasgow Choral Society engagement until I could overlook my arrangements for next season. As I am absent from the Staatsoper three months for my American tour starting in October, with an additional four months for the Australian tour, I am at the disposal of the Staatsoper for a bare three months, which I feel must not be further interrupted. It is with regret that I must decline your offer of an engagement, and I trust it will be possible to obtain a booking with them in the following season. I am sending you under separate cover the desired photographs and advertising material. As I have but few copies of my circulars, I hope I can have them copied should you require a number of them. My repertory consists of the following.
>
> ARIAS: From the operas and oratorios of:
> Bach, Mozart, Haydn, Handel, Wagner, Beethoven, Tschaikovsky, Moussorgsky, Verdi, Gounod, Meyerbeer, Lortzing, Halevy, Flotow, Nicolai, Mendelssohn.
>
> SONGS, LIEDER of:
> Schubert, Schumann, Brahms, Hugo Wolf, Richard Strauss, Tschaikovsky, Moussorgsky, Gretchaninow, Haydn, Beethoven, and Russian Folksongs.
>
> As an example of what my programs are like, I suggest you send the ABC [Australian Broadcasting Commission] copies of my last two concerts in London. So that I can avoid carrying along with me a needlessly large bulk of music, will you please ask them what they do not want.
>
> Regarding my operatic activities, I have appeared in the following principal capitals of Europe, North and South America: London, Glasgow, Edinburgh, New York, Chicago, Los Angeles, San Francisco, Boston, Montreal, Buenos Aires, Montevideo, Rio de Janeiro, Paris, Brussels, Antwerp, Amsterdam, Hague, Berlin, Munich, Dresden, Hamburg, Vienna, Prague, Geneva, Bern, Warsaw, Budapest, Belfast, Copenhagen, Oslo, Stockholm, Goteborg, etc etc.
>
> I have heard that such artists as Lehmann have been allowed the services of an accompanist taken along from Europe at the expense of the company [pencilled annotation by John Tillett: Yes, but

> she pays them]. Is it possible for you to obtain this privilege for me, for I need not tell you how important it is for me to have an accompanist thoroughly familiar with my requirements, and that I can find someone whose services are very moderate, I know without question?
>
> I forgot to mention the important Festival engagements in which I have participated in Bayreuth under Toscanini, Siegfried Wagner, Dr Karl Muck, Dr Richard Strauss, also the Salzburg Festival under Toscanini, and the Glyndebourne Festival.
>
> The enclosed biographical sketch is unfortunately in German, but I hope it will not entail too much trouble for you to have it translated. As regards my sailing to Australia, I am not insistent upon the use of any particular Line, merely desirous of travelling in the shortest possible length of time. If the Australian Line offers this advantage, I certainly prefer your booking with them. (4 May 1937)

Friedrich Schorr, a famous Wotan of the 1930s, could not accept an invitation to sing in Liverpool, but hoped for further opportunities.

> I regret it would be impossible for me to accept the offered engagement with the Liverpool Philharmonic Society as my duties with the Metropolitan Opera in New York, with the Opera Association in San Francisco and Los Angeles, and finally all my concert engagements in America require my presence there from September 1931 until the end of March 1932. As I am to be in London for the Opera season from April 23rd until May 22nd, singing the parts of Wotan and Wanderer in both of the [*Ring*] cycles, I hope there will be a good opportunity of having a talk at a mutually convenient time. I shall be staying at the Grosvenor Hotel, Park Lane and await your further communication. (18 April 1931)

Elisabeth Schumann also wrote in similar vein.

> I am very grateful for your kindness to release me from my engagement on the Max Mossel tour. I am awfully sorry not to be able to hold my promise, but be sure next season I will make good for it. Please give my love to all my English and Scotish audience and tell them to be patiente just a few month more. (25 June 1934)

The English tenor Steuart Wilson had a varied and chequered career, affected initially by injury to one lung in the First World War, then later by domestic and legal upheavals. He turned from singing to administration in his later years, rising to become Head of Music for the BBC. Wilson's wife Ann married Adrian Boult in 1933, and despite the understandably bitter tone of this letter to John Tillett, he remarried twice, Mary Goodchild in 1937 (who died in 1960) and Margaret Stewart in 1962:

> I'm sorry to have to trouble you with my personal affairs. My wife and I are parting company and she is taking divorce proceedings against me which will come up in May. I have written to the Dean of Worcester, who is of course a personal friend of mine, and told him the circumstances, and I am not accepting any invitation for Worcester [Three Choirs Festival] this year – or I suppose ever again! [It was to be another 25 years before he appeared at the Three Choirs Festival, as the narrator in Honegger's *King David* at Worcester in 1957]
>
> I have also written to [Ivor] Atkins because after all I have known him for nearly thirty years. Well there it is. You can guess that we haven't come to this decision without difficulty, and I don't want to bother you with a long story to which you are not a party except in so far as results go.
>
> I am hoping very much that an engagement at Worcester, Mass[achusetts, USA] will turn up for *Gerontius*, which they are doing there in October, and I have every reason to hope that it will. In that case I shall try and take from October to February in America.
>
> You will use your discretion about speaking of my personal affairs. I don't pretend it is a secret at all, but for the sake of the children at school, as well as my own business on which we still have to depend for a living, I don't want any more publicity and talk than is necessary. I am not contemplating another marriage – I'll tell you that. One life spoiled is enough for me. (5 March 1932)

Three composers feature in the files for the 1930s. The first, the Russian Alexander Glazunov died in 1936, five years after the only dated letter (the rest are either incomplete or undated).

In principle I am gladly prepared to conduct a concert of my works in Eastbourne on 26 November and a radio concert in London. As I have to depart England on the 27th it would be preferable if the latter could take place between the 20th and 22nd. In order to give you a definitive reply I need to know the nature of the programme, especially as I would like to introduce my second piano concerto into one of the concerts with my daughter Helene Tarnowska as soloist. Two rehearsals would be necessary for each concert. The cost of music hire must be borne by each organisation. (21 August 1931, translation from German)

There are also four undated and incomplete letters:

… programm with *Carneval.* Regarding the programm and details of the BBC concert in London, I shall expect your further information. I hope that BBC will engage my daughter Madame Tarnowska as exception in quality of pianist soloist for she has played under my direction my second piano concerto in first audition in Paris, Madrid and New York. My passport and the one of my wife were issued in Leningrad by the Soviet authorities on June 1st 1928 under the number $\frac{117402}{212332}$ and $\frac{117388}{212294}$.

We have used these passports already on our last trip to London when I gave in June a radio concert with the BBC and made recording for Columbia.

… or at his representative for England, Mr Hawkes. I cannot do it myself owing to an agreement with my Editor. Will you kindly let me know the hour of the beginning of the concert as well as the day and hour of the rehearsal.

Of course I am sorry that the Radio concert in London cannot take place on my coming trip to England. I understand the present circumstances but I hope that things will turn for the better in the future. Can you tell me what is the best way from France to Eastbourne? If I shall take the route from Dieppe to Newhaven, will I be able to go right away to Eastbourne not via London? I hope you will kindly take care of the visas for myself, my wife and my daughter.

… (without violin solo) will last 35 minutes. I do not conduct usually such a long program and I am willing to do it only as exception for you, but insist on my condition to have 2 rehearsals. The artistic success of the concert depends exclusively from quality of the preparing work and even the very best orchestras cannot obtain it [if] they do not rehearse enough. I have no objection to conduct myself my violin concerto, but I would like to clear out what shall be the pieces which will be performed by the violinist with the piano accompaniment.

… this engagement I enclose the programme which I should like to give on this occasion.

P.S. Considering the last events on the Stock Exchange and unstable value of the pound, I should prefer to receive the payment for my concerts in American or French money, so that amount should correspond to 150 guineas in gold. I am sorry to make this observation, but I hope you will understand that it is quite natural under the present circumstances.

Eastbourne programme:
A.Glazunow
1) 1er tableau du Ballet *Les Saisons* 'L'hiver' ('The Winter') (8½ mins.)
2) Symphonie No.4 ou No.7 (30–33 mins.)
3) 2nd concerto pour piano en si maj. (22 mins.) soliste Mme Tarnowska
4) 1er Valse de concert en ré maj. (12 mins.)

BBC programme (London)
1) *Ouverture solennelle* (11½ mins.)
2) Symphonie No.4 ou No.7 (30–33 mins.)
3) 2nd concerto pour piano en si maj. (22 mins.) soliste Mme Tarnowska
4) 1er Valse de concert (en ré maj.) (12 mins.)

The other two composers were both female, one of them Ethel Smyth, by now near the end of her life, but who had clearly lost none of her pugnacious style.

> I am going to call on you tomorrow about 5 to consult with you as to an arrangement I shd like to make with you. It is roughly this. I have been forced by deafness right out of the realm of music and I want to start a sort of agent. It may or may not be possible for you to act, but I won't go into details till I see you. I may be a few minutes after 5 (it depends on whether the doctor is punctual) but only a few. (24 March 1936)

Finally Nadia Boulanger wrote from her Paris home in the Rue Ballu:

> I acknowledge your letter of February the 9th. In principle I am still free in January and February, but would prefer the 13th of 10th [*sic*] in February.
>
> As far as fee is concerned, it is difficult to answer before knowing what the programme could be. But we could consider 80 guineas. Let me have informations about the musical side of the question – if I could have choir, soloists, or orchestra alone. In one word, give me necessary informations which can help me to take a decision. (14 February 1937)

CHAPTER SIXTEEN

Artists and Auditionees: 1930–39

At the beginning of Chapter 11, a statistical survey was set out of the artists listed in four of Ibbs and Tillett's brochures available to promoters during the ten years 1911–20. A decade further on in this history, and it is timely to view a sample of five of the years between 1921 and 1930 (two of these, 1924–25 and 1929–30, are reproduced in full in Appendix 3).

	Singers	**Pianists**	**Violinists**	**Cellists**	**String quartets**	**Reciters**	**Entertainers**
1921–22	288	56	53	39	13	26	71
1924–25	310	60	51	40	22	27	47
1927–28	308	70	55	45	21	20	50
1928–29	322	101	57	47	21	10	46
1929–30	359	111	61	47	28	8	52

The final two years of the 1920s saw a marked increase in the number of singers and almost double the number of pianists taken on, though with smaller increases in the number of violinists and cellists. There was a gradual rise in the number of string quartets, but a definite drop in recitation as a form of entertainment (the wireless a factor no doubt). This was accompanied by a slight revival in the number of entertainers after a big falling off midway through the decade. The increase in pianists was unequal between genders; in 1921–22 there were 25 women and 31 men on the books, and, although by 1928–29 a gradual increase to 34 women had taken place, the number of men had more than doubled to 67. Figures for singers also make interesting reading. In 1921–22 there was, as if reflecting company policy, an equal division of the 288 singers on the books into 72 each among the four voice groups of sopranos, contraltos, tenors, and baritones/basses. By the end of the decade, however, the larger total of 359 was divided into 109, 78, 76, and 96 respectively, reflecting a large rise in the numbers of sopranos and baritones/basses, many of them coming from Europe.

Before making a similar analysis of the audition books and brochures for the 1930s, some of the artists whose first associations with the agency began in the 1920s are now listed. If their careers were already established elsewhere, their names are prominent in the brochure; if, on the other hand, they were just beginning, then they might be buried lower in the lists. Even in the case of singers, not all have entries in the agency's audition books, whether this reflects a slackness in keeping them up to date, or whether the information was logged elsewhere is impossible to discover, or perhaps they were taken on reputation, recommendation or heard in performance. Among these artists who made their first appearances on the Ibbs and Tillett roster were the singers:

Years	Artists
1920–21	Joseph Hislop, Horace Stevens, Dinh Gilly, Peter Dawson, Harold Williams
1921–22	Florence Austral, Muriel Brunskill, Lauritz Melchior, Steuart Wilson, Walter Widdop, Parry Jones
1922–23	Noel Eadie, Elena Gerhardt, Tilly Koenen, Frank Titterton, Tudor Davies, Theo Lierhammer
1923–24	Eva Turner, Bella (Isobel) Baillie, Keith Falkner
1924–25	Stuart Robertson
1925–26	Elisabeth Schumann, Roy Henderson, Robert Easton
1926–27	Olive Groves, Dennis Noble, John Brownlee, Arthur Fear
1927–28	Percy Manchester
1928–29	Lotte Lehmann, Marie Olczewska, Leo Slezak, Heddle Nash, Webster Booth
1929–30	Göta Ljungberg, Frida Leider, Ninon Vallin, Ina Souez, Gladys Ripley, Alfred Piccaver, Eric Green (spelt Greene from 1934)

A similar table follows, which includes significant additions to the lists of pianists, string and wind instrumentalists (listed each year in that order) during the period 1920–30.

Years	Artists
1920–21	Rachmaninov, Moriz Rosenthal, Busoni, Siloti, Isolde Menges, Jacques Thibaud, Hubermann
1921–22	Josef Hofmann, William Murdoch, Arthur Rubinstein, Leff Pouishnoff, Egon Petri, Frank Merrick, Kreisler, Albert Spalding, César Thomson, Laurance Turner, Pablo Casals, Jean Gérardy
1922–23	Vivian Langrish, Carl Fuchs, Arnold Dolmetsch
1923–24	Eugen d'Albert, Serge Prokofiev, Sapellnikoff, Ernest Schelling, Nikisch, Marcel Ciampi, Dohnányi, Georges Enesco, William Primrose, Joseph Szigeti
1924–25	Emil Sauer, Solomon, Walter Gieseking, Maurice Cole, Angus Morrison, Evlyn Howard-Jones, Margaret Harrison, Léon Goossens, Sidonie Goossens
1925–26	Ethel Bartlett, Nikolai Orloff, José Iturbi, Max Pauer, Edwin Fischer, Sidney Harrison, Achille Rivarde, Antonio Brosa, Marie Goossens
1926–27	Betty Humby, Denise Lassimonne, Arthur Benjamin, Zino Francescatti, Jean Pougnet, Gaspar Cassadó
1927–28	Youra Guller, Wanda Landowska, Arthur Schnabel, Godowsky, Adolf Busch, Enrico Mainardi, Andrès Segovia
1928–29	Backhaus, Robert Casadesus, Jan Smeterlin, Medtner, Donald Francis Tovey, Yves Nat, Alexandre Borovsky, Maurice Dumesnil, Alexander Tcherepnine, Samuel Kutcher
1929–30	Elly Ney, Ignaz Friedmann, Josef Lhévinne, Horowitz, Friedrich Wührer, Rudolf Serkin, Marie Wilson

It can be seen that there was an increase in the number of soloists from Europe and America, taken on as the decade advanced, and other instrumentalists or groups were beginning to appear. Though Lionel Tertis uniquely continued to hold a torch for the viola from 1928 (violist William Primrose's appearance from 1923 was as a violinist), from 1924 he is joined by the oboist Léon Goossens and, by 1927, the guitarist Andrès Segovia. The interest in early music is reflected in Arnold Dolmetsch's inclusion in 1922, though by the end of the decade he is joined by members of his family, while harpsichordists become four in number (Landowska, Dolmetsch, Violet Gordon Woodhouse, and Gerald Cooper). By 1930 small choral groups proliferate (nine chamber choirs plus eight vocal quartets), and the more exotic offerings include a recital of American Red Indian songs. Notable also in the 1929–30 brochure are the black American singer Paul Robeson and, at the bottom of the list of entertainers, the comedian Tommy Handley, famous ten years later for his role in BBC Radio's comedy show *ITMA*.

During the 1920s, Ibbs and Tillett produced small seasonal brochures 'Of Special Interest to Chamber Music Societies', in which their chamber music groups, selected instrumentalists, singers, and duo recitalists, were listed together with forthcoming availability and previous press reports to encourage bookings. Nine pages of such advertisements in the 1922–23 brochure had increased to fifteen by 1929–30, although by then there were neither press reports nor dates of availability included. In other words, by this stage the booklet had effectively become a summary of the agency's best sellers, the *crème de la crème* of their artists' stable targeted at non-orchestral sources of hirers. Whereas solo artists and string quartets or trios are already found in the complete brochure, it is interesting to record instrumental partnerships sent out by the agency in 1930.

Two Pianos
Myra Hess & Irene Scharrer   Myra Hess & Harold Samuel   Ethel Bartlett and Rae Robertson
Two Violins
Jelly d'Aranyi & Adila Fachiri
Violin and Piano
Dohnányi & Emil Telmanyi   Myra Hess & Jelly d'Aranyi   Donald Francis Tovey & Adila Fachiri
William Murdoch & Albert Sammons   Rudolf Serkin & Adolf Busch
Viola and Piano
Howard-Jones & Lionel Tertis
Cello and Piano
Harold Samuel & Ivor James
[Miscellaneous]
Fanny Davies/Susan Metcalfe-Casals (soprano)/Casals
Recitals of the Compositions of Nicolas Medtner (piano) and Tatiana Makushina (soprano)
Bach Recitals : Dorothy Silk (vocalist)/Joseph Slater (flute) or
Léon Goossens (oboe)/George Reeves (piano)
Songs of the Hebrides collected and sung by Marjory and Patuffa Kennedy-Fraser with Margaret Kennedy
Sea Shanties and Sociable Songs : John Goss and the Cathedral Male Voice Quartet
Madrigals, Ayres, Folksongs etc : The English Singers (six)
Songs and Duets: Megan Foster and John Goss
The Old Time Singers : Margaret Stephen/Leslie Holmes/Gilbert Bailey. At the piano: Edith Ashby
Old Songs and Ballads : Jean Sterling MacKinlay
Recital of American-Indian Songs : Os-Ke-Non-Ton
Lecture Recitals
Plunket Greene : Interpretation in Song
Wanda Landowska : Harpsichord and Piano
Edward Mitchell : Lectures on Piano Music

A further advertisement appeared for the 1927–28 season; entitled 'Famous String Quartets', it listed four groups in chronological order of availability from autumn to spring, namely The Pro-Arte of Brussels, The Hungarian String Quartet, The Rosé String Quartet, and the Budapest String Quartet, each group accompanied by a paragraph or two of press reports from England and abroad. It carried the advice on the back 'In view of the short periods for which these Quartets will be available in this Country, early application for dates is advisable'. This publication was in a larger format than anything else produced by the agency (apart from *The Bulletin*), three extant later examples from the last years of the 1930s revert to the normal (A5) size of artists' brochures. It should be mentioned that (again apart from *The Bulletin*) no photographs were included in any Ibbs and Tillett brochure after the First World War. *The Bulletins* were certainly produced during the 1920s, the last known being 1929. They carried many photographs, dates of availability, and press reviews, some of the issues running to nearly 50 pages in length. Most artists had a page to themselves, but sometimes two shared a page, while not all were accompanied by a photograph. The front cover was obviously a prestigious location for a publicity photograph, and clearly showed the agency's preferred artist of the moment. For June 1925 Augustus John's famous portrait of the cellist Guilhermina Suggia was used, March 1927 carried a photograph of the singer Elisabeth Schumann, Rachmaninov gazed, rueful as ever, from the cover of the issue for April 1928, while April 1929 had a posed photograph of Myra Hess seated at a very prominently advertised Steinway grand piano accompanying the violinist Jelly d'Aranyi. One assumes that these publications, which carried the advice to Music Societies and Orchestras, 'Kindly file for future reference', were issued annually. As we have seen, the artists' brochures for the 1929–30 season saw a marked increase in the numbers of sopranos and baritones/basses. These numbers were maintained for a further year, but then cut back from two pages to one from 1931–32. So for another year, Ibbs and Tillett continued to take on more singers of those voice groups, though some became casualties of a policy change which evidently occurred in 1931.

Of the remaining 90 or so pages in the last of the audition books kept by Ibbs and Tillett, covering 1930 to the last recorded, in April 1950, 73 of them were heard during the decade 1930–39. First to succeed was soprano Bessie Davies (10 March 1930), a dramatic coloratura from South Wales, and a typewritten list of her engagements for the previous three months showed that the bulk of her singing was done in the Principality. She had 'an exceptionally fine voice, and with experience and culture ought to do well. Appearance not in her favour. Can sing almost anything.' She sang Violetta's aria from *La Traviata* and a sacred aria by Alberto Randegger, but her name appeared for one season only. The typed 'list of Miss Bessie Davies' engagements' presents an interesting snapshot of a busy schedule of 26 events, mainly 'Miscellaneous' (which probably meant song recitals shared with other artists) but also much of the standard oratorio fare of the day by Handel, Mendelssohn, and Spohr, including *Messiah*, *Joshua*, *Elijah*, *St Paul*, *Judas Maccabeus*, and *The Last Judgement* in places which varied considerably from large cities such as London and Birmingham, Swansea and Cardiff to small Welsh venues such as Tonypandy, Pencoed, and Maesteg. Another artist accepted was Harry (Henry) Gill, a bass-baritone gifted with 'a very fine voice, rich and noble in quality, good throughout, much impressed with him. Safely recommend him' and heard on 10 April 1930. Two north-country contraltos taken on later the same month were Elizabeth

Willan and Elsa Frood, who appear for 1931–32 but not thereafter (the archive does not have the brochure for 1932–33).

Despite a rather half-hearted response by John Tillett to the bass Tom Kinniburgh (30 October 1930) 'real bass voice, should be useful for Oratorio, small fees', he made it onto the books from 1931–32 and beyond. So, too, at the same session, did the dramatic coloratura soprano Francesca Duret, who had 'a very good and brilliant voice, full middle register, think highly of her, prepared to take anything'. Keith Falkner recommended the York Minster-based tenor George Armitage for audition; he was heard on 30 December 1930 in the 'Sanctus fortis' from Elgar's *Dream of Gerontius*, 'an old Handelian aria and a song by [York's organist Sir Edward] Bairstow'. Armitage was accepted, having impressed with his 'good, robust voice. Sings with great conviction after style of [John] Coates and [Gervase] Elwes. Very pleased with his singing of Gerontius'. On the same day a contralto called Meryl Myles Mitchell, having tried (and failed) to impress with the bizarre combination of Delilah's aria from Saint Saëns' opera and Hebridean songs, was 'advised to specialize in Hebridean songs in costume etc'. The costume theme continued three months later when an Indian contralto, Bina Addy, also auditioned unsuccessfully with Italian, English and Indian songs on 16 March 1931, but was nevertheless considered a 'very interesting artist, voice good, and sympathetic in quality. She sings in native Indian costume'. None of the seven singers auditioning in 1931 was taken on despite some positive comments such as the New Zealand baritone Lance Fairfax, whose Verdi and Wagner revealed 'a very good voice with dramatic style, ought to be most successful, quite individual in style'. Elizabeth Richards, a lyric soprano whose appearance was 'not good, has to wear very strong glasses but promises an excellent voice, big top range quite good but unfortunately not a prepossessing appearance for the concert platform' unsurprisingly did not make it through. Sir Edward Bairstow's recommendations were always taken seriously by Ibbs and Tillett and often led to the start of a career. One such success was Mary Worth (12 February 1932), a 'young, pleasant' lyric soprano from Yorkshire with a 'charming voice, bright and telling, [and] an engaging style'. Another successful applicant from Yorkshire, though not through Bairstow, was Norman Crabtree (7 April 1932), a 'robust tenor, short, age 22–23, winner of many prizes and championships in the North, excellent voice [Handel/Wagner], full quality, needs greater freedom otherwise quite good, sings with musical conviction and from memory'. This last comment is interesting in its implication that (contrary to today's convention) singers did not memorize their audition pieces.

When the contralto Linda Seymour auditioned on 9 June 1926 (see Chapter 11), she was accepted, although with reservation ('voice quite good but not big'), but managed to survive on the books. When she re-auditioned almost six years to the day on 14 June 1932 with Verdi's *Requiem* and Elgar's *Sea Pictures*, the comment was: 'has made great progress and can safely recommend her. Voice very good'. Also on 14 June 1932 they heard an 'exceptionally good voice, quality later reminded me of John McCormack in his early days. Should go far.' This was Webster Gibson, a tenor who had studied for four years in Italy and was recommended by Plunket Greene and Francis Harford. He only stayed with Ibbs and Tillett until the 1936–37 season, maybe because (according to the brochure for that season) another tenor with the Christian name of Webster, Webster Booth, had joined at the same time as Gibson. A week later (22 June) and a *basso cantante* from Bolton in Lancashire, Samuel Worthington (also with experience in Italy) did well in his renditions of Verdi and Rossini arias, having 'an exceedingly fine voice, full and musical in quality. Very impressed with him.' The contralto Mary Morris auditioned at the Grotrian Hall on 20 September 1932, but curiously does not appear on the books of the agency until the 1935–36 season, a full three years later, this after the comments 'good voice, deep contralto range, sings with conviction, pupil of Kennedy Scott, remember her specially for *Messiah*, *Mass of Life* (Delius), *Mass in B minor*, has sung for Philharmonic Choir on several occasions, recital work at Wigmore and Grotrian [Halls], appearance nothing striking'.

Of only two heard in 1933, Muriel Wilson, an Australian soprano joined after her audition at the Wigmore Hall in October, having a 'charming voice and refined style'. Only four are listed for 1934, of whom two were accepted, Emelie Hooke, another Australian lyric soprano sang on 18 January and had 'an exceptionally good voice, usual middle register for her type of voice', while the baritone Wilfrid Blunt, ('6 foot 5 inches tall and a gentleman') recommended by Keith Falkner and heard on 19 September, had 'an excellent voice, mellow, big head range, good production. Master at Haileybury [College] who wishes to take up singing as a profession.' The year 1935 began propitiously on 3 January with the engagement, upon the recommendation of Cyril Rootham, of the 'small, bright and pleasing lyric soprano Margaret Field-Hyde, an ideal Bach singer, having the requisite parity of voice and phrasing, diction excellent, a very bright and attractive young singer'. Elizabeth Barlow, 'unfortunately lame which will prove a handicap', also had 'a tendency to sing under the note', despite being a 'most intelligent singer, voice warm and expressive', so did not join the contraltos after her audition on 3 October 1935, unlike Margaret Pirie, an Australian recommended by Roger Quilter, who sang at the Grotrian Hall on 29 November. She had an 'excellent voice, dramatic bright quality, extensive range. Sympathetic artist'. It was to be more than a year (18 December 1936) before the next new names, the bass-baritone Philip Hattey ('good, young, tall, excellent sonorous and pleasing voice, good diction, well-trained throughout'), and (on 30 December) a soprano from Hull called Doris Wells, 'excellent voice youthful in quality and pur[ity], good legato, would compare her with Elsie Suddaby as an artist but possessing a better voice. Very pleased'. There were another couple exactly a year later, at the Grotrian Hall on 10 December 1937, both of whom were finds for the agency. First was the contralto Edith Coates, already experienced on London's opera stages, who auditioned with *Aida*, *Faust* and *Messiah*, and was perceived at once as an 'excellent contralto, voice big range, dramatic style. Can safely recommend her for any class of work'. She was followed later the same day by the tenor David Lloyd, sent by his teacher Walter Hyde, who elicited the comment 'a really excellent voice, pure and telling quality, good diction, delivery and deportment. Should have a splendid career'. Quite why the soprano Marjorie Gordon was accepted (20 April 1938) is hard to understand, given such observations as 'big dramatic voice inclined to give too great a volume, needs control, voice inclined to be strident, needs further study. Appearance stout, not good'. Not all those taken on were, as one might expect of newcomers, listed at the bottom of the page (the lists were never alphabetical); for example the Yorkshire contralto Maud Heaton (19 May 1938), experienced in German opera houses, had an 'exceptionally good voice, even throughout the register, sings with intelligence, think highly of her' and, like the tenor David Lloyd a few months before, shot straight to the top third of the names listed in the 1938–39 brochure.

A review of numbers of artists on Ibbs and Tillett's books during the 1930s follows with a sample of five from the years 1930–39 (those for 1934–35 and 1938–39 are fully laid out in Appendix 4).

	Singers	**Pianists**	**Violinists**	**Cellists**	**String Quartets**	**Entertainers**
1930–31	366	115	63	49	31	52
1933–34	220	68	50	36	29	34
1935–36	257	74	66	38	35	52
1937–38	256	77	61	39	33	54
1938–39	283	102	62	44	34	–

A close study of these figures sees the high numbers from the 1929–30 season persisting for a further year, before an evident rethink of policy cut numbers back in all areas, in some instances drastically so. In the first year the vocal proportions soprano, alto, tenor, bass (SATB) were still weighted in favour of sopranos and basses with the four voices respectively totalling 114, 80, 76, 96. In the next example selected, the balance was more even at 61, 53, 53, 53. The number of pianists, having risen slightly on the previous year, then settled back to a number nearer to that of 1927 (a change of practice occurred with the 1933–34 brochure, listing male instrumentalists before females). By 1938–39 figures were once again picking up (markedly so in the case of pianists, while SATB singers were 75, 68, 64, 76 respectively that year), before the advent of the Second World War put a stop to this boom. One final observation of Ibbs and Tillett's brochures from 1938–39 onwards is the absence of entertainers. The likes of Arthur Askey, Stanley Holloway, Tommy Handley, and Elsie and Doris Waters were no longer to be engaged through the agency. On the other hand some practices going back to Vert's firm in the latter decades of the previous century continued into the 1930s, such as the availability of artists for private functions. In April 1935, for example, Ibbs and Tillett distributed a card stating:

> Messrs. Ibbs & Tillett have pleasure in announcing that the following eminent Artists will be available for Private Concerts, At Homes, etc., during the coming season.
> M.M. Elisabeth Schumann, Alexander Kipnis, Herbert Janssen, Engel Lund, Szigeti, Orloff, Suggia, Jelly d'Aranyi, Andrès Segovia, Cortot.
> Messrs. Ibbs & Tillett are prepared to negotiate engagements for any artists desired.

Famous artists (and those considered to have an assured future), whose associations with Ibbs and Tillett began in the years 1930–39, but who did not in all instances appear in the audition books, were now listed, beginning with singers:

Years	Artists
1930–31	Mary Jarred, Conchita Supervia
1931–32	Oda Slobodskaya, Winifred Radford, Nora Gruhn, Sigrid Onegin, Herbert Janssen

1933–34	Maria Ivogun, Laelia Finneberg, Joan Cross, Jan van der Gucht
1934–35	Vladimir Rosing, Alexander Kipnis, Heinrich Schlusnus, Henry Cummings
1935–36	Margaret Field-Hyde, Gerhard Hüsch, John Kentish, Norman Walker
1936–37	Lisa Perli, Audrey Mildmay, Anne Ziegler
1937–38	Pierre Bernac, Peter Pears, Redvers Llewellyn
1939	Edith Coates, David Franklin, Bruce Boyce

It should be noted that in 1930 the soprano Eva Turner returned to the agency after her first appearance in 1923, which lasted only two years. Newcomers often displaced an earlier generation from the concert platform or opera stage. Among those who retired were the 53-year-old soprano Agnes Nicholls in 1930, the tenor Ben Davies in 1937 at the ripe old age of 79 (he lived on until 1943), while those who 'shed the mortal coil' included long-standing friends of the agency such as Kirkby Lunn, who died on 17 February 1930 aged 57, Robert Radford, who died aged 59 on 1 March 1933, three years after his name disappeared from the list, and Fanny Davies, whose name is no longer included from 1933, and who died a year later at the age of 73. Some artists made career moves by changing their names, including soprano Bella Baillie, known from 1930 as Isobel, tenor Eric Green, who added the extra 'e' to his surname from 1933, the pianist Louis Kentner, who was still Ludwig in 1931, and the 14-year-old cellist Zara Nelsova, who changed her Christian name to Sara in 1933. William Primrose changed from violin to viola in 1934, joining not only Tertis but also Bernard Shore.

Events taking place in Germany during Hitler's rise to power were beginning to make themselves felt in England, such as the immigration of many artists from that country and other parts of Europe. Some can be seen among the new singers, even more among the list of new instrumentalists below, whose work they placed with Ibbs and Tillett during the decade under discussion. The ranks of British pianist–composers, such as Alan Bush, York Bowen, Arthur Benjamin or foreigners such as Dohnányi, are now joined by Prokofiev, Casella, Bartók, Szymanowsky, and Poulenc, while Hindemith now appears as a violist. Again these musicians are listed below in the order of pianists, violinists, and cellists:

Years	Artists
1930–31	Kathleen Long, Hubermann, Peers Coetmore, Antonia Butler
1931–32	Béla Bartók, Alfredo Casella, Ludwig Kentner, Lili Kraus, Carl Friedberg, Gregor Piatigorsky
1933–34	Prokofiev, Abram Chasins, Rudolf Firkušný, Cyril Smith, Clifford Curzon, Frank Laffitte, Kendall Taylor, Eileen Joyce, Henri Temianka, Wolfgang (Wolfi) Schneiderhahn, Emmanuel Feuermann, Anthony Pini, Sara Nelson
1934–35	Stefan Askenase, Milstein, Zimbalist, Maurice Clare, Georg Kulenkampff, Henry Holst, William Primrose, Bernard Shore, Florence Hooton
1935–36	Szymanowsky, Carlo Zecchi, Iso Elinson, Heifetz, Simon Goldberg, Frederick Grinke, Paul Hindemith, Hermann Busch

Years	Artists
1936–37	Nikita Magaloff, Alfredo Campoli, Leonard Hirsch, Thomas Matthews
1937–38	Nina Milkina, Phyllis Sellick, Louis Krasner, Harry Blech
1938–39	Francis Poulenc, Julius Isserlis, Ernest Lush, Elena Glazounov, Max Rostal, Pierre Fournier

A big change took place at 124 Wigmore Street with the retirement in 1937 of Robert Leigh Ibbs, and the election of Emmie Bass to replace him as one of the four Directors, who were now John Tillett, William Tilbrook, Monica Nixon, and Emmie Bass. Three years earlier, in April 1934, Pedro Tillett also retired from his post as bookings manager at the BBC, to which he been appointed ten years before. In a farewell interview printed in the *Radio Times* (20 April 1934, p.178) under the title 'The Man who knows 2,000 Musicians', he recalled many of his early childhood musical experiences from the first days of the D'Oyly Carte Opera Company in a performance of Gilbert and Sullivan's *H.M.S. Pinafore* to the last recital given in London's St James's Hall by Anton Rubinstein ('I can remember how excited I was to be allowed to sit on the platform quite close to the piano throughout the recital'). He went on:

> Some years later I entered the office of my uncle, the late N.Vert, for many years the leading impresario and concert manager. Here I learnt the business in all its aspects and came into contact with the foremost artists of the day – Adelina Patti, Trebelli, Albani, Melba, Marie Rose, Lillian Nordica, Antoinette Sterling, Emma Eames, Calvé, Sims Reeves, Edward Lloyd, Santley, and Foli the famous bass. Sarasate, world-renowned violinist, Vladimir de Pachmann, Hans von Bülow, Carreño, Saint-Saëns, Bottesini, the famous double bass player, Sir Arthur Sullivan, Sir Charles Hallé, Augustus Manns of the Crystal Palace Concerts. Life then was full of interest.

He recalled that there had been many long-forgotten prodigies of the keyboard, but not Josef Hofmann, Mark Hambourg, or Gertrude Peppercorn, whose playing had since been heard by millions on air. He also recalled the Richter Concerts which launched the debuts of Moriz Rosenthal, Jan Kubelik, and Fritz Kreisler, as well as first performances of many works which, by the 1930s, were established classics. Over 40 years earlier, he had helped to arrange the first visits to England of Grieg, Albeniz, and Busoni, the first recitals of Clara Butt and Ruth Draper, the first English appearance of Yvette Guilbert, the first recital tours of George Grossmith (known as 'Piano and I' Grossmith), of Henry Irving, Ellen Terry, William Terriss, and Jessie Millward in the world of theatre. He went on to describe his years as an impresario after the death of Vert, and before his appointment to the BBC some 18 years later:

> I was drawn into the theatrical world and toured with Violet Vanbrugh, and in 1921 I managed Sir Harry Lauder's season at the Palace Theatre. In August of this year I went to America as General Manager for Marie Löhr and her company, returning the following March (1922) to manage another London season for Harry Lauder, whose success was so phenomenal at the Palace Theatre. On this occasion we were obliged to split the season between the Princes Theatre and the London Pavilion. Following this I became manager to Robert Loraine, who had a season at St James's Theatre followed by a tour. In December 1923 I was asked to undertake the management of the first series of Symphony Concerts to be given under the auspices of the British Broadcasting Company. These concerts took place at the Central Hall, Westminster in February, March, April, and May 1924. They were six in number, conducted by Percy Pitt, Sir Landon Ronald, Eugene Goossens, Sir Hamilton

> Harty, Stanton Jeffries, and Sir Edward Elgar. In July 1924 I joined the staff of the Company ... Among our many activities in those early days we toured popular artists around the various transmitting stations – Cardiff, Manchester, Belfast, Glasgow, Aberdeen, Newcastle, and Birmingham. It will be remembered that the BBC's first series of Symphony Concerts was succeeded by a second at Covent Garden, later at the Albert Hall, and of course last of all at the Queen's Hall.

Naturally the BBC became a new and constantly developing source of employment during the 1930s, and before long correspondence and contracts began to flow between Ibbs and Tillett and the Corporation, though none survives in the Tillett archives. The BBC's contracts manager, Arthur Wynn, who was promoted to the post from his position as Pedro Tillett's assistant, became an increasingly important figure. When the contralto Gladys Ripley was engaged for some provincial broadcast work, an issue arose concerning her name. An internal memo was sent by H. Foster Clarke to Wynn on Christmas Eve 1937:

> This artist wishes to sing with a light combination we are using, but she wants to use another name for this light music. I know there was a definite ruling against this, although one or two artists such as Esther Coleman have used other names. Will you let me know the present ruling, bearing in mind that it is even more dangerous for a serious artist to appear in very light programmes in the regions than it is in London. I have no doubt that "going gay" would seriously injure Gladys Ripley's oratorio and concert work in the north.

On 29 December Wynn replied that:

> it is not possible for artists to have two names. We always suggest to London artists that they should have the courage of their convictions, and we have never found that they have lost anything by retaining their own name.

From 24 June 1922, the beginning of regular music broadcasts on the BBC or 2LO as it then was, the relationship between agents and broadcasters was ambivalent and wary. On that day the baritone Charles Knowles and the cellist Beatrice Eveline (both artists managed by Ibbs and Tillett) were the performers. Concert promoters and agents suspected that broadcasting a live performance would provide no incentive for an audience to attend, therefore halls would take lower receipts. The British National Opera Company (BNOC) had a more positive attitude and allowed broadcasts during their 1922–23 season from Covent Garden, some of them involving Ibbs and Tillett artists. As a result the BNOC's Music Director, Percy Pitt, was lured away to become the BBC's first Music Adviser, then its first Music Director from 1924–30 under John (later Lord) Reith. The initial hostility of concert managers and agents towards the BBC is demonstrated by the attitude of Lionel Powell, who, in 1924, steered the LSO away from conductors who did broadcast, telling the Controller of Programmes, Roger Eckersley, that he had 'spent his life finding, publicising and building up these artists, who were his exclusive property in this country. Why should he let the Corporation use them unless we made it worth his while?' Sir Landon Ronald guarded his Hallé Orchestra players from being poached by the BBC for their new orchestra, planned for 1930 after negotiations with Beecham came to nothing. On 22 October that year, the BBC's newly appointed Music Director, Adrian Boult, walked on stage at the Queen's Hall to conduct the new orchestra, with an Ibbs and Tillett artist featured as soloist, this time Guilhermina Suggia in the first cello concerto by Saint Saëns. Artists in the agency's stable, such as Moiseiwitsch, Elisabeth Schumann, and Backhaus would continue to appear with the BBC from those early days, while it also negotiated engagements for conductors such as Ansermet, Strauss and Stravinsky.

The 1930s also saw the advent of television broadcasts, however rudimentary until after the Second World War, but nevertheless providing a taste of things to come. A curious choice for the first of its genre to be televised was Albert Coates's new opera *Pickwick*, transmitted on 13 November 1936, only 11 days after TV transmissions began, and a week before its Covent Garden premiere with Coates's new British Music Drama Company. In its initial stages, television transmissions ran for only about an hour from 3pm and again from 9pm (and not on Sundays at all), and for its first three months the transmission system itself changed weekly between Baird and EMI, so nothing too ambitious could be attempted. Excerpts from *Pickwick*, lasting 25 minutes were played by the newly formed BBC Television Orchestra (22 players), and sung by Ibbs and Tillett artists William Parsons (in the title role) and Dennis Noble (as Sam Weller). Another adventurous undertaking took place on 27 March 1937, when agency artists Janet Hamilton-Smith and John Goss provided early forms of 'voice-overs' for a documentary programme about Haydn's puppet operas.

In January 1932 Lionel Powell died, while former agency artists such as Melba, Destinn, Tivadar Nachèz, Sims Reeves, Albani, Ysaÿe, and Kirkby Lunn all died in either 1930 or 1931. Economic circumstances in Britain became straitened as the depression took hold, but despite such gloom, London was still the place for successful and vibrant musical occasions such as the Courtauld–Sargent concerts, where the likes of Ibbs and Tillett artists Paderewski, Kreisler, Rachmaninov, and Paul Robeson performed. Back in 1924 (and 12 years after the death of its composer Samuel Coleridge-Taylor) a dramatic version of *Hiawatha* was first staged in the Royal Albert Hall. It proved so popular that it became an annual event each June without a break (apart from during the General Strike of 1926) until 1939. The performers, including 800 members of the Royal Choral Society in full Red Indian costume had to sing from memory, and there was a ballet of 200 dancers, with the whole ensemble usually in the hands of Malcolm Sargent. As mentioned earlier, even the Mohawk chief Os-Ke-Non-Ton can be found on the roster of Ibbs and Tillett artists as available for a recital of American-Indian songs from 1929–30 to 1933–34 and again from 1936–38. Taking the year 1932 as an example of a *Hiawatha* season (Robin Legge calls it an opera in his foreword to the programme), the cast list was largely stocked by Ibbs and Tillett with Elsie Suddaby (Minnehaha), Stiles-Allen (Nokomis), Arthur Cox (Iagoo), Trefor Jones (The Monk), Francis Russell, Frank Titterton and Henry Wendon (Chibiabos), Horace Stevens and Harold Williams (Hiawatha), and William Parsons (Famine) for the 14 performances (including two matinees). The Director T.C. Fairbairn also staged Mendelssohn's *Elijah* to great effect, so for example in February 1936, there were 14 performances of this 'dramatised pageant' conducted by Albert Coates and, on one occasion, by the BBC conductor Joseph Lewis. Of the dozen soloists used (again on a rota basis) most came from the agency, Harold Williams, Henry Gill, and Joseph Farrington rotating the title role.

In 1932 Beecham formed the London Philharmonic Orchestra with Harold Holt, Powell's former agency partner. As well as putting on a regular Sunday series at the Queen's Hall, this became the orchestra for the Courtauld–Sargent concerts, and for those promoted by the Royal Philharmonic Society, who had now disbanded their former orchestra. Elsewhere there was still the LSO, with Harty directing their Monday night concert series. While it is true that the BBC's Symphony Concert series, like today, did not attract Prom-size audiences, nor were the *glitterati* present in the audience (Lady

Cunard and her fashionable friends saw to that by supporting Beecham), nevertheless it remains hard to understand that the likes of violinist Carl Flesch could only attract half a house for standard concerto repertoire. The BBC Symphony Orchestra under Boult presented highly imaginative and forward-thinking programmes at this period (Berg's *Wozzeck* on 14 March 1934 is a fine example, while the music of Bartók, Stravinsky and Hindemith, as well as the latest British music, was regular fare). Henry Wood also played a progressive role with, for example, the first performance in the UK of Mahler's Symphony No.8 (*Symphony of a Thousand*) on 15 April 1930, all but one of the eight soloists coming from Ibbs and Tillett (Elsie Suddaby, May Blyth, Muriel Brunskill, Clara Serena, Walter Widdop, Harold Williams, and Robert Easton). On Good Friday, Brunskill and Williams sang for Wood again in excerpts from Wagner's *Parsifal*, while on 23 May, Brunskill, Stiles-Allen, and Keith Falkner broadcast *Elijah* with the Wireless Symphony Orchestra under Stanford Robinson.

The list of soloists for the 1933–34 season of Wednesday orchestral concerts and Friday evening chamber music events promoted by the BBC reads like an Ibbs and Tillett artists' brochure for that season: Gieseking, Flesch, Bartók, Samuel, Piatigorsky, Busch String Quartet, Tertis, Solomon, Cortot, Hess, Prokofiev, Lamond, Kolisch String Quartet, Petri, Szigeti, Busch, Sammons, Miriam Licette, Bernard Shore, and the Brosa String Quartet. Of the choral works performed, Beethoven's *Missa Solemnis* featured Margaret Balfour, Parry Jones, and Keith Falkner (soprano Adelheid Armhold was not an Ibbs and Tillett artist). Similarly in Sir Henry Wood's Good Friday performance of Bach's *St John Passion*, only the maid, Margaret Godley, does not appear in their brochure, the rest being Elsie Suddaby, Astra Desmond, Eric Greene, Arthur Cranmer, Stuart Robertson, Roy Henderson, and James Topping. Even in the first British performance of *Wozzeck*, singers from Ibbs and Tillett dominate the cast list: Parry Jones, Tudor Davies, May Blyth, Mary Jarred, Percy Heming, Walter Widdop, and Philip Bertram, while baritone Richard Bitterauf was imported from the Stuttgart Opera to sing the title role. Having had a short series of six concerts devoted to British music in January 1934, which, mainly for reasons of music politics, had mediocre success, the BBC then added a short series of six concerts between 4 and 16 May at the Queen's Hall. Rather grandly named the London Music Festival, it persisted annually until the end of the decade, with the conducting shared between Boult, Bruno Walter and Felix Weingartner. Ibbs and Tillett once again acted for most of the participants, Flesch, Horowitz, Feuermann, Backhaus, with many familiar vocalists also among the soloists. The setting up and development of the BBC's music department and orchestra did Ibbs and Tillett no harm at all, and before long, and for many years thereafter, a member of the agency's staff (beginning with Audrey Hurst) was allocated purely BBC engagements.

The mid-1930s were eventful days for music throughout the country. Not only was broadcasting becoming a source of employment for musicians and entertainment for the public, concert life now seemed to be flourishing with the Queen's Hall host to almost daily evening events, festivals continued to attract audiences to choral, orchestral and chamber music, and opera added a new summer venture at Glyndebourne from 1934. The recording industry too was widening its horizons after the advance in recording techniques from acoustic to electrical during the mid-1920s. On the distaff side, the world of music lost three great British composers, Elgar, Delius, and Holst, in 1934, but on the other hand Rachmaninov and Strauss continued to appear in their own works as soloist and conductor respectively, while the hugely popular Sibelius was awarded the Royal Philharmonic Society's Gold Medal *in absentia* (1935).

Ibbs and Tillett continued to supply artists to festivals and music societies around the country. The Three Choirs Festival remained a favourite of the agency (and continued to do so for many years to come), and was considered a vitally important venue at which to place its singers and instrumentalists each year at the three venues, Hereford, Gloucester and Worcester. It was also the one event which could entice first John, and then Emmie, to leave London for a summer break, albeit still connected to work. The inter-war years up to his death in 1934 were the years of the Elgar Festivals, with agency artists such as Elsie Suddaby, Mary Jarred, Heddle Nash, Roy Henderson, Keith Falkner, Harold Williams and Steuart Wilson just some of the vocal soloists. Certain changes in programming were creeping in. *Elijah*, almost a compulsory work, was dropped in 1930, 1934 and 1936, Walton took part during the decade under discussion, although *Belshazzar's Feast* remained banned for another quarter century, Dyson and Vaughan Williams conducted their works, and Kodály appeared in 1937. By the following year, Thursday was becoming known as the 'modern' day, when such novelties would be performed.

In Birmingham, bereft of its Triennial Festival since 1912, the conductor Harold Gray, associated with the City of Birmingham Orchestra for 55 years from the late 1920s, was in charge of the Birmingham Festival Choral Society, who booked any soloists they needed through Ibbs and Tillett. Some letters from the Society's archive show the degree of attention to which John Tillett gave such organizations. He was always alert to the health of a society's budget, even if it meant that the artist, who was servant to the client, could be short-changed as a result. The following correspondence is between John Tillett and either Harold Gray or J Edward Stokes, an official on the Society's Committee:

> Thank you for your letter of the 21st inst. In accordance with your instructions we have much pleasure in definitely booking the services of the under-mentioned Artists for the dates, works and at special terms set forth herein:-
>
> BIRMINGHAM FESTIVAL CHORAL SOCIETY (Town Hall)
> Wednesday evening November 9th 1938
> *Creation* Haydn
>
> | | |
> |---|---|
> | NORA GRUHN | Ten guineas (£10.10.0.) |
> | WEBSTER BOOTH | Ten guineas (£10.10.0.) |
> | NORMAN WALKER | Ten guineas (£10.10.0.) |
>
> Wednesday evening December 14th 1938
> *Messiah* Handel
>
> | | |
> |---|---|
> | THEA PHILIPS | Ten guineas (£10.10.0.) |
> | ERIC GREENE | Twelve guineas (£12.12.0.) |
> | JOSEPH FARRINGTON | Ten guineas (£10.10.0.) |
>
> Saturday evening March 4th 1939
> *Chandos Anthem* Handel and *Stabat Mater* Dvořák
>
> | | |
> |---|---|
> | RUTH NAYLOR | Ten guineas (£10.10.0.) |
> | TREFOR JONES | Ten guineas (£10.10.0.) |
> | REDVERS LLEWELLYN | Ten guineas (£10.10.0.) |
>
> I am happy to say that RUTH NAYLOR and TREFOR JONES are available, and have agreed to meet you in regard to the question of fee. We are advising the Artists in question that there is a

possibility of this Concert being broadcast. By the way, which of the *Chandos Anthems* are you going to perform? No.5? (23 May 1938)

Thanks for your letter of the 23rd inst., by which I note it is the 6th *Chandos Anthem* of Handel that will be performed at your Concert taking place on Saturday evening March 4th 1939.

Regarding the question of broadcasting, Mr Harold Gray gave me to understand that this would only concern your March Concert, and in issuing our contracts to Miss RUTH NAYLOR, Mr TREFOR JONES and Mr REDVERS LLEWELLYN, we stated that you reserved the right to broadcast this Concert without extra remuneration.

You are doubtless aware of the arrangement between the BBC and the Incorporated Society of Musicians regarding the question of broadcasting, whereby the Artists receive an additional 25% of their respective fees for outside broadcasts. However, if there is any likelihood of your November and December Concerts being relayed, then we will certainly do our best to get the Artists concerned to make their fees inclusive. (24 June 1938)

BIRMINGHAM FESTIVAL CHORAL SOCIETY (Town Hall)
Wednesday evening November 9th 1938 at 7.30pm
Creation Haydn, Parts 1, 2 and 3
Thanks for your letter of the 2nd inst., enclosing announcements of the above concert, which we are forwarding to Miss NORA GRUHN, Mr WEBSTER BOOTH , and Mr NORMAN WALKER, at the same time advising them that the rehearsal will take place at the Town Hall, Birmingham at 10 o'clock on the morning of Wednesday next the 9th inst., and asking them to attend as near that time as possible.

We have also advised the above Artists that Mr Harold Gray is observing the same cuts as when he did the work at Derby last year, which are in the Air 'On Mighty Pens', and in the duet at the end of 'Graceful Consort'.

Trusting you will have a most successful Concert from every point of view. (3 November 1938)

BIRMINGHAM FESTIVAL CHORAL SOCIETY
Messiah December 14th 1938
Many thanks for your letter. We find Joan Coxon has now accepted an engagement in the North of England for the above date, but as far as we know both Janet Hamilton-Smith and Alice Moxon are still free. We would also recommend Mary Worth who is now quite well known for Choral work. We shall be glad to know your views in due course. (23 August 1938)

Messiah December 14th 1938
Since writing you about Miss Mary Worth we find she has accepted an engagement for the above date, but both Miss Alice Moxon and Miss Hamilton-Smith are still free and have promised to pencil the date for you. (30 August 1938)

Messiah December 14th 1938
With reference to your letter of August 26th last, we shall be glad to know whether your Committee has yet been able to come to a decision with regard to a Soprano for the above performance, we have still two Artists in pencil to you for this date, namely ALICE MOXON and MARY WORTH [*sic*]. (29 September 1938)

BIRMINGHAM FESTIVAL CHORAL SOCIETY
Thank you for your letter of the 3rd inst., which came duly to hand. If we could get in touch with Miss THEA PHILIPS, we would gladly convey to her your Committee's suggestion, but to be quite frank, we have no knowledge of the lady's actual whereabouts, beyond the fact that she sailed for Australia. Miss PHILIPS did not even advise us of her intended departure, and it was only through a friend that we learned she had left the country.

Now regarding the question of a substitute for your *Messiah* performance, ELSIE SUDDABY is quite out of the question, as she is already booked to sing in Lancaster on December 14th.

We cannot say offhand whether JO VINCENT is available, as this Artist resides in Holland, but in any case we are afraid she would require a minimum fee of 30 guineas if she had to make a special journey to England for one engagement.

We therefore again strongly advise your Committee to consider JANET HAMILTON-SMITH, who is one of the most successful sopranos now before the public.

At the moment the only other Artists we can suggest who might be prepared to accept a fee of 10 guineas are: MAY BLYTH, OLIVE GROVES, JEANNE DUSSEAU, RENEE FLYNN, GARDA HALL, MARGARET FIELD-HYDE and MARY HAMLIN For your information, we may mention that ISOBEL BAILLIE, STILES-ALLEN, ELENA DANIELI, and KATE WINTER are otherwise engaged. (4 October 1938)

BIRMINGHAM FESTIVAL CHORAL SOCIETY – *Messiah*

We thank you for your letter of the 8th instant and agree with you with regard to Miss Thea Philips and her treatment of everyone concerned. We need scarcely say how sorry we are for this unfortunate disappointment to you and acting upon your instructions we have pleasure in booking the services of Miss OLIVE GROVES to replace Miss Philips on Wednesday Evening, December 14th, 1938, at a special fee of Ten Guineas (£10.10.0.) inclusive of broadcasting rights. (10 October 1938)

BIRMINGHAM FESTIVAL CHORAL SOCIETY

Wednesday evening December 14th 1938

Messiah Handel

We thank you for your letter of the 5th inst., enclosing announcements of the above Concert, which we are to-day forwarding to Miss OLIVE GROVES, Mr ERIC GREENE, and Mr JOSEPH FARRINGTON, at the same time advising them that the rehearsal will commence at 10 o'clock on Wednesday morning next the 14th inst.

As desired, we have asked these Artists to be present at the Town Hall as soon after 10 o'clock as may be possible.

Trusting you will have a most successful performance from every point of view. (8 December 1938)

BIRMINGHAM FESTIVAL CHORAL SOCIETY

Saturday evening March 4th 1939

Mr REDVERS LLEWELLYN has just advised us that to his regret he finds the bass part in Dvořák's *Stabat Mater* lies too low for his voice, and rather than give an inadequate performance, he thinks it would be advisable to engage the services of another Artist for the above Concert.

Naturally Mr LLEWELLYN regrets having to forego the opportunity of singing for you, and at the same time asks us to apologise for this late notice, but he has been so fully occupied during the past few weeks with Concerts and Operatic work.

Unless there is any other Artist you may prefer, we can strongly recommend Mr DAVID FRANKLIN, who recently took part in a performance of Dvořák's *Stabat Mater* in Sheffield, see enclosed notice. (3 February 1939)

BIRMINGHAM FESTIVAL CHORAL SOCIETY

Saturday evening March 4th 1939

Thanks for your letter of the 6th inst. Undoubtedly an Artist is at fault in accepting an engagement without first ascertaining that the works are within his range of voice. Mr REDVERS LLEWELLYN admits this, and apologises for his negligence in this respect, that is to say, so far as the *Stabat Mater* Dvořák is concerned.

As explained in our letter to Mr Harold Gray, the Dvořák work requires a real bass, and Mr LLEWELLYN thinks it would be madness for him to undertake this work, as it would mar the performance, and certainly do him no good in the eyes of the public.

As a way out of the difficulty, Mr LLEWELLYN is prepared to make himself responsible for Mr DAVID FRANKLIN's fee, who in our opinion would be an excellent choice for the Dvořák work, and for him (Mr LLEWELLYN) to take part in the 6th *Chandos Anthem*, which would keep his name still in the bill.

We were unable to reply by return, owing to the fact that Mr LLEWELLYN was yesterday on his way to Dundee, and we were only able to get into telephonic communication with him last night. We trust your Committee will accept this proposal. (8 February 1939)

BIRMINGHAM FESTIVAL CHORAL SOCIETY

Thanks for your letter of the 16th inst. We are glad to learn from same that your Committee have decided to accept Mr REDVERS LLEWELLYN's proposal, and we are therefore arranging matters accordingly, it being understood that Mr DAVID FRANKLIN will sing the bass part in the performance of Dvořák's *Stabat Mater* to be given by the above Society at the Town Hall, Birmingham on Saturday evening March 4th next, and that Mr REDVERS LLEWELLYN sings the bass part in the 6th *Chandos Anthem* (Handel) on the same occasion, Mr LLEWELLYN making himself responsible for Mr FRANKLIN's fee.

The fee already agreed upon for the services of Mr LLEWELLYN, viz., Ten Guineas (£10.10.0), can either be handed to Mr LLEWELLYN on the night of the Concert, or forwarded to us.

BIRMINGHAM FESTIVAL CHORAL SOCIETY
Saturday evening March 4th 1939
6th *Chandos Anthem* Handel and *Stabat Mater* Dvořák

We thank you for your letter of the 23rd inst., enclosing announcements of the above Concert, which we are to-day forwarding to Miss RUTH NAYLOR, Miss FREDA TOWNSON, Mr TREFOR JONES, Mr REDVERS LLEWELLYN and Mr DAVID FRANKLIN, at the same time advising them that the rehearsal will take place at the Town Hall, Birmingham at 2.30pm on Saturday afternoon March 4th next. We have advised the Artists concerned that the Latin Text of the *Stabat Mater* will be used. (24 February 1939)

In Bournemouth in 1935, the municipal orchestra, now in its first season under Sir Dan Godfrey's successor Richard Austin, had artists of international celebrity provided by the agency, such as Moiseiwitsch, Szigeti, Cassadó, while Solomon, Horowitz, Medtner, Huberman, Noel Eadie and Harold Williams went to Glasgow or Edinburgh to work either with John Barbirolli and the Scottish Orchestra or, in the case of the last two singers, to sing with the Choral and Orchestral Union. Laelia Finneberg sang Isolde's *Liebestod* under Carl Schuricht with the Hallé in Manchester, Rispah Goodacre sang Brahms's *Alto Rhapsody* in Belfast (a BBC broadcast), while Eric Greene and Frank Phillips travelled to Barnsley to provide the male solos for Elgar's *The Kingdom*. Norwich heard Jelly d'Aranyi and Walter Glynne, and Henry Cummings sang with the Brentwood Choral and Orchestral Society in Essex. In Liverpool in 1934, W.J. Riley was celebrating his Golden Jubilee as an officer (Secretary from 1908) of the Liverpool Philharmonic Society, and a concert to mark the event was given on 9 October at St George's Hall. Boult, Harty and Beecham shared the conducting, Dora Labbette, Isolde Menges, Solomon, and Harold Williams were the soloists. Five years later the first concert at the city's new Philharmonic Hall took place on 20 June 1939. Riley was still Honorary Secretary, Beecham conducted, and Ibbs and Tillett supplied the soprano Florence Austral and organist G.D. Cunningham for the solo spots on the mixed programme, and for the choral concert two days later in this, the Philharmonic Society's centennial season, when Dennis Noble sang Delius's *Sea Drift* and Walton's *Belshazzar's Feast* under Albert Coates. The Philharmonic Hall was built after the disastrous fire, which destroyed its predecessor in 1933, and fortunately it went on to survive the numerous fires Liverpool would have to endure during the Second World War, which was destined to break out barely three months later. The mutually beneficial association between such clients as Liverpool Philharmonic Society or Birmingham Festival Choral Society and Ibbs and Tillett, which supplied soloists for their events between the two world wars, illustrates the agency's facility to provide out-of-London, high profile engagements for its artists.

Meanwhile, elsewhere in the Provinces, cellist Antonia Butler and soprano Dora

Labbette were accompanied by the ubiquitous George Reeves at a concert given by Bradford Music Club. This Club, by 1936 in its seventh season, was run by the efficient Keith Douglas (who was also President of the Royal Philharmonic Society from 1932), and its attractive and popular monthly Tuesday concerts were generally given by artists or chamber groups from the agency, such as Cyril Smith, the Brosa and Kolisch String Quartets, Adolf Busch, Rudolf Serkin, Thelma Reiss, Roy Henderson, and the Pougnet–Morrison–Pini Trio, who, in the 1936–37 season, shared a concert with the agency's sole saxophonist Sigurd Rascher.

Douglas was also Honorary Secretary of the Bradford Festival of Chamber Music, which took place in 1926, 1927, and 1930. For the first one, Ibbs and Tillett sent the Virtuoso String Quartet, William Murdoch (piano), Gwendolen Mason (harp), Léon Goossens (oboe), Haydn Draper (clarinet), Robert Murchie (flute), the Brosa Quartet, Kathleen Long (piano), Hubert Eisdell (tenor), James Lockyer (viola), Ambrose Gauntlett (cello), and Marie Korchinska (harp). The event took place on 5 and 6 October, each day had a morning and evening concert, and the programmes were exceedingly generous. The opening morning concert consisted of Brahms's sextet, Mozart's piano trio in E, Beethoven's string quartet Op.59 No.1, an interval of 'strictly one hour', followed by Schoenberg's sextet *Verklärte Nacht*, and Fauré's piano quartet Op.15. That evening the Virtuoso Quartet were joined by oboist Goossens; the concert began with César Franck's string quartet in D followed by Mozart's oboe quartet; the interval was followed by Bax's oboe quintet and the concert concluded with Dvořák's *Dumka* string quartet in E flat Op.51. The next morning's substantial programme was Elgar's piano quintet, Delius's violin sonata No.2, Debussy's string quartet, and, after the hour-long interval, Eugene Goossens' Phantasy string quartet Op.12 and César Franck's piano quintet. The festival concluded that evening with Brahms's string quintet Op.115, Bax's harp quintet, Mozart's flute quartet and Ravel's Introduction and Allegro for harp, flute, clarinet and string quartet.

The Festival for 1927 had much the same personnel as the year before, Charles Draper (clarinet) substituting for his nephew Haydn, Aubrey Brain (horn) and Claude Hobday (double bass) replacing Murchie, Lockyer, and Gauntlett while Arnold Bax was a second pianist. This time a much more enterprising repertoire consisted of Beethoven's septet, Schubert's octet, quartets by Brahms, Ravel, Dohnányi, J.B. McEwen, and Frank Bridge, quintets by Mozart, Schumann and Bax, trios by Mozart, Brahms, John Ireland, and Poulenc, *Prelude Music* for harp and strings by Julius Harrison, and *The Masque of the Red Death* (after Edgar Allan Poe) by André Caplet. By 1930, the Festival was described as triennial and remained a two-day event with the Brosa String Quartet pivotal to the programmes. The other participants were Hubert Eisdell, Kathleen Long, Ambrose Gauntlett, Marie Korchinska, Léon Goossens, James Lockyer, Victor Watson (double bass), Joseph Slater (flute), Ralph Clarke (clarinet), and Pierre Tas (violin). The composers Mozart, Brahms, Schubert, Bridge, Dohnányi, Dvořák, Handel, Beethoven, and Bax were familiar; Bliss, Chausson, Tchaikovsky, Medtner, Vaughan Williams, Quilter were newcomers. From the programme book it would appear that Ibbs and Tillett also supplied artists to the Bradford Philharmonic Sunday Concerts held at the Theatre Royal. The autumn season for 1927 had a strong Ibbs and Tillett presence with such names as the singers Norman Allin, Frank Mullings, Peter Dawson, Harold Williams, Constance Willis, John Goss and the Cathedral Male Voice Quartet (in Sea Shanties according to the agency brochure for 1927–28), and instrumentalists such as Arthur de Greef, Cortot and Segovia. Douglas also conducted the Bradford Philharmonic Orchestra, and for its autumn season of 1926 (shared with the Leeds Symphony Orchestra under Julius Harrison) he hired an array of the agency's talent from Isolde Menges and Peter Dawson to Cortot and Segovia for the Sunday concerts. Before leaving the Bradford Chamber Music Festival, the change in economic fortune of music over the four years from 1926 to 1930 is reflected by the quantity of advertising. By 1930 only the piano showroom Blüthner and Cortot's pupil Olwen Pughe-Jones each took a half-page, sharing the frontispiece of the programme, this after local businesses, and the record companies HMV and Columbia had all taken pages in 1927. On the other hand, advertisements in the 1926 programme, though far too numerous to list, are worthy of a mention because they reflect better economic times, including a mouth-watering fortnight of opera from the British National Opera Company at the Theatre Royal, Leeds during the first two weeks of November. In 13 days it gave 17 performances (matinees on Tuesdays, early closing day perhaps, and Saturdays), not one of which was a repeat, of *Romeo and Juliet*, *Hugh the Drover*, *Carmen*, *Tosca*, *Marriage of Figaro*, *Parsifal*, *Rigoletto*, *Aida*, *Mastersingers*, *Hansel and Gretel*, *La Bohème*, *Tristan*, *Tannhäuser*, a double bill of *Gianni Schicchi* and *Pagliacci*, *Madam Butterfly*, and *Othello*, all of which had casts packed with singers from Ibbs and Tillett.

Newcastle also had a flourishing Chamber Music Society (founded in 1884), with six monthly concerts on Thursdays from October to March. They were held in the Grand Assembly Rooms, Barras Bridge, and from the 212th concert which began the 1928–29 season, transferred to the Old Assembly Rooms, Westgate Road, which were built in 1774. From the 1920s to the mid-1930s, programmes tended to be focused around a string quartet or solo artist, with another artist (usually a singer) on the bill to provide some variety. The Flonzaley Quartet, for example, began the 1920–21 season and Herbert Heyner sang two groups of songs for baritone in each half, accompanied by Edgar Bainton. For other concerts that season Olga Haley provided similar respite for the Bohemian String Quartet, Dorothy Helmrich for Frederic Lamond, John Goss for the Philharmonic String Quartet, and Phyllis Lett for Moiseiwitsch. On the other hand Suggia and Orloff shared the concert on 17 November 1927 on an equal basis. By 1934, and no doubt for financial reasons, concerts tended to feature one group or one artist alone, but often with the accompanist contributing a short solo. In this same year they were celebrating their Silver Jubilee, despite persistent implied threats in the programmes that 'it has been decided to continue the Society's concerts another season'. Ibbs and Tillett continued to provide all the artists for the season and sent The Chamber Music Players (a piano quintet consisting of William Murdoch, Arthur Catterall, Laurance Turner, Bernard Shore, and Cedric Sharpe in quintets by Elgar, Dvořák, and Brahms), Le Quintette Instrumental de Paris, an octet based around the Griller Quartet, the Italian Trio, the Brosa Quartet (with the contralto Claire Croiza), and to crown this celebratory season, Rachmaninov. As the decade closed, the six concerts all featured artists from the agency, the Grinke Trio (Kendall Taylor, Frederick Grinke, and Florence Hooton), Arthur Rubinstein, the Pro Arte String Quartet, the Société des Instruments à Vent de Bruxelles, the Boyd Neel String Orchestra (18 players), and the violinist Antonio Brosa accompanied by Frank Mannheimer.

The Newcastle-based North of England Piano Society was founded in 1936 but, due to the war, had a brief existence. The impresario Wilfrid van Wyck was responsible for managing the four monthly recitals given each year at the City Hall between November and February, sometimes (as in the case of Moiseiwitsch and Schnabel in February and November 1937 respectively) by arrangement with Ibbs and Tillett. Perhaps this involvement was a reason why, by Hofmann's recital in April 1938, van Wyck's name had disappeared from the programmes. Instead there was an 'Important Notice', which stated:

> The Committee have pleasure in announcing to members and others that although Mr Wilfrid van Wyck is no longer interested in this Society, arrangements have been made whereby a well-known London Concert Agency has accepted responsibility for the presentation of next Season's Recitals, which will therefore be continued. The Agency in question represents Artistes of pre-eminent celebrity and ability, and a tentative selection for the Season 1938–9 has already been made by the Committee.

Although Ibbs and Tillett's name did not appear in the programmes for their first (and last) season, their input is clearly discernible in the four artists who took part, Solomon, Egon Petri, Moiseiwitsch, and the two-piano duo of Ethel Bartlett and Rae Robertson.

Norwich was also a city which was enjoying a long-standing relationship with Ibbs and Tillett, one which stretched back to the first decade of the century in supplying artists to the Triennial Norfolk and Norwich Music Festival under Henry Wood from 1908. By 1930, the year of the 33rd of these four-day festivals held at St Andrew's Hall, the likes of Agnes Nicholls, Kirkby Lunn, Gervase Elwes, and Thorpe Bates had been succeeded by Elsie Suddaby, Muriel Brunskill, Walter Widdop, and Roy Henderson as well as instrumentalists such as Myra Hess, Frederic Lamond, and Jelly d'Aranyi. Henry Wood, conducting the Queen's Hall Orchestra, was in charge for the fifth and last time.

There were also the Norwich Municipal Concerts, a series of popular Saturday concerts presented at St Andrew's Hall by the Norwich Municipal Orchestra under R.J. Maddern Williams on alternate Saturdays from October to March. During the decade of the 1930s, it featured such Ibbs and Tillett stalwarts as Irene Scharrer, Eric Greene, Albert Sammons, Nellie Palliser, Walter Widdop, Evelyn Scotney, Clara Serena, Edward Isaacs, Joseph Farrington, Roy Henderson, Trefor Jones, and the violinist Melsa. Interestingly some of these artists were paid for by private individuals, who were then duly credited in the programmes, for example with the words 'The Engagement of this Artist [Albert Sammons] is due to the kindness of Henry N. Holmes, Esq., J.P.' from the 1929–30 season, while in 1931 'it was learned that the distinguished Spanish cellist [Gaspar Cassadó] would be in England in February. Mr Arthur G. Howlett was approached and generously made an offer which enabled this artist to be engaged.' What is curious is that these soloists very rarely performed with the orchestra; there were no concertos but an occasional aria. Instead they had two or three solo spots in a programme which was interspersed with orchestral items. By 1931, radio entertainers were beginning to make an appearance, such as Stainless Stephen, Clapham and Dwyer, and Muriel George with Ernest Butcher in folksongs and comedy, sharing the platform with the orchestra and soloists such as Eileen Joyce, Phillipowsky, and Betty Bannerman. These programmes, with their cross-over style to Music Hall, were also beginning to take on the lengthy dimensions of those Victorian and Edwardian days, but by the mid-1930s, some radical changes had taken place, though programmes still persisted in averaging between six and eight items. The orchestra was briefly

(October to December 1937) restyled as the New Norwich Municipal Orchestra, 'constituted on the lines of Section C of the BBC Orchestras', which meant an orchestra of 36 players. Indeed there seems to have been a strong BBC influence afoot with the employment of three guest conductors with BBC connections, Clarence Raybould, Leslie Woodgate (for many years in charge of the BBC Chorus), and Joseph Lewis. With these guests, the soloists did play concertos, whereas Maddern Williams continued to avoid them. Meanwhile in January 1938, the orchestra dropped the 'New' from its title. For this season the agency supplied them with 'Leading London Artists' such as Phyllis Sellick, Muriel Brunskill, Dennis Noble, Walter Widdop, Dorothy Clark, Jan van der Gucht, Janet Hamilton-Smith, Harold Williams, violinist Lisa Minghetti, and the obligatory quartet of soloists for the *Messiah*, on this occasion (Good Friday 1938) Garda Hall, Anne Broadhurst, Arthur Jordan, and William Parsons. For the 1938–39 season two of the five guest conductors were Raybould and Woodgate once again, but there were also three others from towns of similar size to Norwich (perhaps with a negotiated reciprocal invitation to Maddern Williams), Eldridge Taylor, Musical Director of Folkestone Corporation, Julius Harrison, who held a similar post with Hastings Corporation, to both of which bodies due thanks had to be credited for allowing their employees to appear, and Maurice Miles, Conductor of the Pump Room Orchestra in Bath. These were heady days when such towns could afford to sustain a paid Musical Director. Unlike resorts such as Harrogate or Torquay which could rely upon holidaying professionals from London, Manchester, Birmingham and Liverpool to form small but high quality professional orchestras for the summer seasons, the likes of Norwich were largely dependent on local amateurs and teachers. Nevertheless, a live broadcast was taken of the first five items of the concert conducted by Maddern Williams on 25 February 1939, consisting of orchestral items and those for a male voice choir and the singer Harold Williams.

Another musical occasion which continued to be of immense significance for the agency was the Triennial Festival in Leeds, three of which took place during the 1930s, in 1931, 1934, and 1937. Beecham and Sargent shared the conducting at each of these October Festivals, which consisted of morning and evening concerts on each of four days in 1931 and 1934, a fifth day added for the 1937 event. All the soloists came through the agency, in 1931 they were the singers Stiles-Allen, Dora Labette, Elsie Suddaby, Muriel Brunskill, Astra Desmond, Hubert Eisdell, Francis Russell, Walter Widdop, Keith Falkner, Dennis Noble, and Horace Stevens, while the instrumentalists were Nicholas Orloff, Dorothy Hesse, Albert Sammons, Isolde Menges, Lionel Tertis, and Antonio Sala. The orchestra was the London Symphony Orchestra, and among standard choral and orchestral fare were first performances of new works, namely Frederic Austin's *Pervigilium veneris* conducted by Beecham, *The Seasons* conducted by its composer Eric Fogg (a Mancunian, then working at the BBC, but who was to die by falling in front of an Underground train in 1939 at the age of 36), and Walton's *Belshazzar's Feast* conducted by Sargent. In 1934 the orchestra was the new London Philharmonic Orchestra, the soloists included some from 1931 but also Isobel Baillie, Joan Cross, Ninon Vallin, Edith Furmedge, Olga Haley, Mary Jarred, Gladys Ripley, Constance Willis, Arthur Cox, Heddle Nash, Frank Titterton, Percy Heming, Hermann Nissen, Roy Henderson, William Parsons, and the instrumentalists Schnabel and Szigeti. On this occasion the new works were Cyril Scott's *La Belle Dame sans merci* and George

Dyson's *The Blacksmiths*. Finally in 1937 Ina Souez, Jan van der Gucht, Steuart Wilson, Robert Easton, Myra Hess, Louis Kentner, Egon Petri, and Adolf Busch were agency additions to other singers and instrumental soloists from 1931 and 1934, the new works for that year being Walton's *In Honour of the City of London*, and Lennox Berkeley's *Jonah*.

CHAPTER SEVENTEEN

The Politics of Music: 1930–39

The 1930s saw a plethora of visiting orchestras to Britain. The Vienna Philharmonic came with Furtwängler in 1930, again in 1934 and 1937 under Bruno Walter, and in 1935 under Walter and Felix Weingartner. In May 1937 Willem Mengelberg came with his Concertgebouw Orchestra from Amsterdam, and during the course of the decade Gabriel Pierné came with the Colonne Orchestra from Paris, so did the Finnish National Orchestra (which did much to increase Sibelius's popularity in Britain), the Prague Philharmonic Orchestra under Vaclav Talich (again in 1937 under Rafael Kubelik), the Vienna Symphony Orchestra and the Dresden State Opera Orchestra in 1936. Walter Damrosch had already been with the New York Philharmonic Orchestra in the 1920s, but Toscanini came with them for the first time in the early summer of 1930 to give four triumphant concerts at the conclusion of a European tour. Between 1927 and 1938, the Berlin Philharmonic Orchestra under Furtwängler visited not only London on several occasions, but also other principal cities of the UK, many of these events arranged for these foreigners at the London end by Lionel Powell.

It was therefore no wonder that such orchestras, and in particular those from Vienna, Berlin, and New York which gave such revelatory performances, put into perspective the relatively mediocre standards of many British orchestras of the day. It was not the quantity of music-making in Britain in the early 1930s which was striking, but its quality, which was frankly spurious, and there was much in British orchestral playing which justifiably depressed the discerning music critic. Frank Howes worried about 'easy-going performances', Ernest Newman, impressed by American standards after a visit there, wrote of his relief that the LSO at least 'ranks as our premier orchestra', while the *Musical Times* of May 1935 mused that Hamilton Harty had 'caused the LSO to recover its lost prestige, among musicians at least, if not yet among concert-goers in the mass'. In an introductory retrospective of the decade, the handbook of the 1939 London Music Festival containing its magnificent programmes, admitted that:

> the visit of the New York Philharmonic Orchestra to this country in 1930, under the direction of its famous maestro Arturo Toscanini, emphasised in the minds of many musical people that all was not well with our resident orchestras ... and the playing of his orchestra appeared to audiences in this country as almost magical.

Several factors seem to have contributed to the wave of xenophobia and protectionism, which dominated the pages of newspapers and journals within and without the musical profession during the early 1930s. This was a period of economic stagnation and hardship, so serious that a National Government was formed in 1931. Looking beyond the problems of social welfare and employment that the people of Britain, Europe and America were encountering during the ten years 1929–39, in the performing arts generally and in music particularly, the impact of the improved technical developments in radio, sound cinema and gramophone records during the 1920s were now beginning to be reflected in the job market. Home music-making was substituted by the radio and the gramophone, sales in pianos slumped, numbers of teachers (particularly of the piano and of singing) fell in due proportion to fewer numbers of pupils. The standard of orchestral playing dropped, the deputy system became as bad as it had been at the turn of the century, concerts were put on with one rehearsal to save costs, the only standard which rose seemed to be that of sight-reading. In the *Daily Telegraph* (31 October 1931) Herbert Hughes, in an article entitled 'Protection for the British Musician', called for a 'need for drastic action, plain thinking, plain speaking and abnormal remedies in these abnormal times'. It stirred up a hornet's nest, and was immediately followed by a pronouncement from the Incorporated Society of Musicians (ISM), whose past and present presidents were Directors of two of London's music colleges, Sir John McEwen (Royal Academy of Music) and Sir Hugh Allen (Royal College of Music). The ISM's manifesto, calling for the urgent need for protection and published in the *Daily Telegraph* (4 November 1931), was by no means wholly supported by its members, from whose ranks Harold Samuel, Myra Hess, Isolde Menges and Donald Francis Tovey promptly resigned. On the other hand, both it and Hughes's article together were strongly supported by pianist William Murdoch, singer Harry Plunket Greene, and a host of others, many of whom attended a dinner at the Musicians' Club at the Hotel Great Central on 2 November, and, judging by the guest list, many were Ibbs and Tillett artists. Despite the fact that not all its artists would agree, the agency took a strong stand against these developments which sought to exclude foreign artists from performing in Britain. Hughes interviewed Elgar (*Daily Telegraph*, 5 November 1931) on the subject of 'The Music Crisis' three years before his death. The composer had read the ISM's manifesto but took a more sanguine, tactful view, broadening his carefully chosen comments to include the current fall in attendances by concert audiences:

> 'You cannot blame the BBC for a decline in concert-going that began before the radio had come into existence' … Sir Edward's sympathies are naturally with the practising musician, and he brought the vast experience of English conditions to bear in discussing a highly involved situation. He noted the adverse effect of celebrity tours upon the activities of local societies, many of which have lost their audiences in consequence. He noted that the public is attracted by the names of artists of international reputation, that often enough there is a strong element of snobbery in the adulation of the foreign artist to the exclusion of artists of equal, and even greater ability at home. While we must admit the Kreislers and the Paderewskis of our time, history is only repeating itself, for there was precisely the same snobbery forty and fifty years ago as there is today.
>
> And for a moment the Master of the King's Musick relapsed into a reminiscent mood. He talked of his own early struggles of days when English music was practically non-existent … of the old Philharmonic Concerts (the audiences for which never went to any other concerts), of days when Sir Frederic Cowen was their conductor, a conductor, he said, whose work was greatly undervalued by the present generation … Sir Edward went on to talk of the forgotten Promenade Concerts at Covent Garden, of the Saturday Concerts at the Crystal Palace under August Manns, of the vogue of Joachim, and of many other persons and things. But there was a moral to all this, as I soon discovered, for he drove home instance after instance as an example of a movement or a revival of which no trace remains today.
>
> There were great singers in those days, he remarked incidentally, Albani, Edward Lloyd, Santley, Sims Reeves, and then he proceeded to speak kindly of the artists of our own times, of Beatrice Harrison, Albert Sammons, Horace Stevens 'the finest Elijah I have ever heard', he said, 'not even excepting Santley'.
>
> 'Reconstruction', said Sir Edward, as we walked in the garden, 'is the vital necessity of the moment. You must create new audiences'. Sir Edward spoke with reserve. 'You mustn't say you have seen me', he said. 'But I have seen you', I replied, 'and I shall say you are looking very well'. And as we said goodbye he smiled a little quizzically, for he was just off to the Worcester Races, and the sun was shining like mad after the rain.

The *Musical Times* also took the protectionist view, though some its tabloid-style outbursts on the standing of some foreign artists were outlandishly ill-considered, such as one in the issue for March 1932:

> … this country is not in a state of barbarism so far as orchestral music is concerned, and all the works given by the Berlin Philharmonic Orchestra can be heard many times in a season played by English orchestras very little, if at all inferior to the visitors, under conductors certainly far superior to Furtwängler.

While it is true that Beecham did good works in forming the London Philharmonic Orchestra in 1932, it is also hard to imagine who, among British conductors of the day, could have put Furtwängler in the shade. The December 1931 issue of the same journal carried a review of recitals at London's Wigmore Hall entitled 'Singers of the Month'. It included the names of several distinguished foreign artists damned with faint praise, including Elena Gerhardt ('one recital is very much like another'), the Greek mezzo-soprano Alexandra Trianti ('it took [her] the whole course of a song to make exact vocal adjustments at her first Wigmore Hall recital'), Elisabeth Schumann ('[she] sang in English, and it was at least distinct'), and poor Ganna Walska, who was dismissed in three sentences:

> Ganna Walska dressed up to sing at the Wigmore Hall. Her costumes were becoming but not becoming enough to distract one's attention from her indifferent singing. She made a hash of Schubert.

To counteract all this intemperate invective or considered criticism, the agency joined the fray, and in December 1931 began a correspondence with the Ministry of Labour. In view of the public uproar over the seeming neglect of British artists at the expense of foreigners (and the influx would grow considerably larger two years later when Hitler's Nazi party came to power in Germany), the UK Government decided to invoke the Aliens Order of 1920 and prohibit the entry of certain musicians during 1932. Ibbs and Tillett wrote to protest:

> On behalf of certain Concert Societies and Music Clubs of Great Britain and Ireland, we as Agents have entered into definite contracts with Artists of international repute to appear during the earlier part of the coming year, 1932, including the following:

Rachmaninov

Cortot	Ravel
Bela Bartók	Elisabeth Schumann
Artur Schnabel	Dohnányi
Hubermann	Adolf Busch
Guilhermina Suggia	Joseph Szigeti
Alfredo Casella	Poltronieri
Arturo Bonucci	Robert Heger
Carl Schuricht	Gaspar Cassadó
Renée Chemet	Rudolf Serkin
Alexandra Trianti	Emmy Heim

The Roth String Quartet of Budapest
The Prague String Quartet
The Hungarian String Quartet
The Stradivarius String Quartet of New York
The Busch String Quartet

> In view of the fact that permission has been refused to allow the Quintette Instrumental de Paris to enter this country to fulfil a series of engagements we had contracted for them during this month, we are compelled to ask for a ruling regarding the existing contracts for the above-mentioned artists.

> We would emphasise the fact that should such permission be refused, the Societies concerned will be involved in serious difficulties with their subscribers, the majority of their tickets being already sold for their whole season which lasts until April next.
>
> May we beg the favour of a reply at your earliest convenience, the matter being so urgent. (2 December 1931)

In their reply the Ministry of Labour wrote that they had no objection to 14 of the 21 soloists listed by John Tillett but:

> ... in regard to the other artists mentioned in your letter [Casella, Bonucci, Schuricht, Renée Chemet, Trianti, Poltronieri, Serkin and the five string quartets] I am to say that the Department is in some doubt whether the issue of permits would be justified, having regard to the present circumstances and to the general policy of which you have been made aware. The question will be further considered if you can furnish further particulars as to the engagements of the artists and the fees to be paid together with any other information to assist the Department in arriving at a decision. (18 December 1931)

A conference was convened by the Ministry of Labour on 7 January 1932 'to discuss the admission of foreign artists who desire to fulfil professional engagements', and John Tillett attended on behalf of the agency. Meanwhile he not only responded to the Ministry's letter with brief career details of the seven soloists, five string quartets and the fees already negotiated with them, but also collected the unanimously protesting views of the various music society committees threatened with cancellations because of Government policy. He sent selected extracts for consideration by the Department officials. In the file on the subject are typewritten thoughts, probably John Tillett's because of his handwritten pencilled 'orchestras', which he felt should be included in point two of the list, and his colourful language which, though destined for an unsympathetic reception by bureaucratic civil servants, typified his trenchant views:

> Although fully in sympathy with anything that will better the position of British artists and remove the unjust prejudice under which they have laboured for many years (since 1714 in fact), yet we must lodge a protest against the methods that are being employed for the betterment of the present state of affairs.
>
> 1. It is unfair and un-English to force an artist to hand over a definite contract to another, thereby dislocating all the arrangements the injured party may have had to make.
> 2. It is bad business to exclude those who would spend their money in recital-giving, thereby hurting the business of concert halls, orchestras, managers, printers, newspaper advertisers, over here.
> 3. It will be another millstone round the neck of those concert clubs and musical societies, who already have difficulty in providing entertainment, to hold the interest of their members. This does not imply that we consider the British artist is not good enough to do that, but that while one is persuading subscribers against their century-old-prejudices, the coffers will have emptied and the societies will be dead.
> 4. It will, in all probability, have a boomerang-effect on those who derive some of their livelihood from abroad, and do not forget that this is a rapidly increasing body which helps to build up a better respect for British music abroad than has been the case in the past. It does not follow that other countries will be in agreement as to our methods of selection, and [they] might decide on our wholesale exclusion. The resulting congestion of British artists over here would be something that the imagination would boggle at.
>
> Surely it would be better to prevent by discouraging the engagement of foreign mediocrities than to snatch their engagements from them like disgruntled children, and it will be all to the good to allow only good artists in, but that implies hearing them first in many cases. After all we have not been without our own bad artists who have tried it on abroad. (undated)

John Tillett also had an ally in Samuel Courtauld, whose wife Elizabeth (of Courtauld–Sargent Concerts fame) died on Christmas Day 1931, yet just a week after becoming a widower, he rallied to the call with a letter to *The Times* on the subject of 'Foreign Musicians'.

> Sir, – The most welcome note yet heard in this controversy has been struck by Mr. Harold Samuel in resigning his membership of the Incorporated Society of Musicians.
>
> It is intolerable that in a so-called civilized country, music, or ideas in any form, should be classed with material imports and subjected to restrictions impeding their untrammelled flow. England makes herself a laughing-stock by such measures, which could not be bettered if they were expressly designed to advertise that 'inferiority complex' of which Sir John McEwen spoke at the meeting of the Incorporated Society of Musicians last night.
>
> Moreover, British musicians who support these restrictions are merely pathetically engaged in trying to cut their own throats, for nothing is better calculated to lessen their chances of steady employment than a course of action tending to stifle the growing and deep-seated interest in the best music which is becoming increasingly manifest in this country.
>
> I remain, Sir your obedient servant, SAMUEL COURTAULD, 20 Portman Square, W.1. Dec. 31. 1931

Ironically for a country which virtually invented the word 'Protectionism', these events were viewed from America with similar scepticism in the magazine *Musical Courier* on 20 February 1932:

> Musical 'Protection'
>
> The British Government's policy to keep out foreign musical artists of a certain category, which is due to the action of a disgruntled section of the musical fraternity, has entered upon a new stage. Finding it very difficult to distinguish between first-rate artists (who are to be admitted) and 'mediocrities' (who are to be kept out), the Ministry of Labor has acted with liberality and issued permits to the great majority of applicants thus far. Also, very wisely, it has relaxed its ruling in favor of all artists who go to England in order to give recitals at their own risk (which, as every musician knows, mostly result in deficits), and such artists are permitted to accept a maximum of two paid engagements each.
>
> Nevertheless, the campaign continues, especially in certain sections of the press, and other countries are cited as taking measures to protect their own artists, including the United States. These statements are misleading, for no European country thus far has taken similar official action, nor would they find it as easy as Great Britain, an island, to keep artists out.
>
> The *Musical Courier* has been quoted in England as favoring a similar 'protective' policy for the United States. Nothing could be further from the truth. If we were to keep out 'mediocrities', applying similar standards as have already been applied in England (a contralto of the Staatsoper with a national reputation in Germany having been refused admittance), it is obvious which countries would suffer most. The United States, which has been the world's greatest playground for foreign musical talent of all kinds and grades, is not going to cut its nose to spite its very handsome musical face. What we did protest against is people evading the immigration laws under false pretences, but everybody knows that even these stringent laws provide for exceptions in favour of real artists and other professionals. Why England, which has set so splendid an example to the world in free trade, should be the one country to favor a narrow-minded policy in music, is indeed a riddle. Such a policy, if carried to its logical conclusion, would destroy the musical profession, which is, and must be, essentially international.
>
> Vaudeville artists, who have been hit by similar exclusionist measures, have recognised this danger and shown a professional solidarity which puts the 'legitimate' musicians to shame. Both in England and France they have already protested, and in England have petitioned the Ministry of Labor on behalf of their foreign colleagues. Why have the musicians remained so silent? Are they more afraid of the 'competition' – a word which ought to belong to the vocabulary of commerce and not of art – than their brethren of the lighter muse?

The *Musical Courier* seems to have been selective in its implication that 'serious' musicians, or those connected to the performance of 'serious' music, were silent, leaving the protests to those in the field of lighter music. Ibbs and Tillett went further and drew up a series of arguments for their view. The agency was becoming increasingly concerned, not only that a panel of civil servants would be responsible for determining who should or who should not be permitted to perform in Britain, but also alarmed at the lack of any defined criteria as to how such judgements would or could be reached.

> Internationalism in the Arts, especially music, is an absolute necessity to our national life, and it is a stronger force for world peace and understanding than we can ever measure.
>
> It is not possible to conceive any sort of Advisory Committee who would come to any kind of agreement on such a difficult problem, for the reputation and standing of great artists, foreign or otherwise, is a matter entirely in the hands of the general public who go to hear them at Concerts or Opera and it is not a matter for individual opinion.
>
> Only those foreign artists will make any headway in England whose artistic gifts are such that we should be definitely poorer without them.
>
> None of the really first class British performers has ever raised any sort of objection to the engagement of foreign artists, because they well know that real talent need have no fear of competition.
>
> Can it truly be said that any authority is capable of deciding whether a foreign artist is or is not better than a native one?
>
> It is contrary to all British traditions to break contracts made in good faith. Whatever means may have to be taken to safeguard the interest of British musicians these should not affect contracts already made. Any audience expects variety and to be kept acquainted with the best Continental representations and that without any intended slight to British musicians it will not be seriously disputed that in respect of quartets and quintets of string and wind instruments several of the Continental groups have international reputation and are admittedly pre-eminent.
>
> Regarding the qualifications of foreign artists, it is extremely difficult to make a definition that would be just and satisfactory. Nothing could be more productive of ill feeling among musicians here and abroad.
>
> It is very difficult to see what good such steps can do, except to create a lot of bad feeling which must eventually react against our own artists travelling abroad to fulfil engagements.
>
> The exclusion of foreign artists would not lead to more British artists being employed in the long run, but would result in great lack of interest among the audience and the ultimate death of any Societies whose aim is the promotion of good music.
>
> The exclusion of foreign quartets of the first rank would inevitably entail a serious check to the cause of chamber music in this country, and would be prejudicial to the best interests of British music and British musicians, both of which in recent years have been winning increased recognition abroad.
>
> How is one to decide which is and which is not an artist of sufficient importance for admittance into this country?
>
> UNIMPORTANT ALIEN ARTISTS
>
> A means by which the Ministry might determine, without outside advice, the question of the unimportant alien artists, would be to fix a minimum fee (25 [guineas]?), and possibly a minimum number (3?) of engagements, which should prevent the smaller artist being brought in for such engagements as an isolated 'At Home' arrangement.
>
> Surely the Ministry would prefer a method such as this so that they could decide the question for themselves, rather than have to resort to outside advice which cannot be unprejudiced? It is common knowledge that certain members of the Incorporated Society of Musicians are making it public that they have been consulted by the Ministry in regard to the admittance of foreign artists and are flaunting their power in the matter.
>
> If there is to be an Advisory Board then surely it must consist of disinterested parties and not disgruntled musicians.
>
> INCOME TAX
>
> A flat rate of, say, 10% on the gross fee of each engagement to be paid before leaving the country.
>
> That this condition be stated on the contract and the agent to collect it and become responsible to the Inland Revenue Authorities.

This procedure would ensure the immediate payment of tax by every artist, whereas under present conditions the artist has left the country before he is assessed, and we know by experience the endless difficulties in collecting the tax.

RECITALS BY FOREIGN ARTISTS

Foreign artists should be allowed to give recitals at their own risk without the condition that they do not accept engagements, otherwise it is a one-sided bargain and when once this limitation becomes common knowledge is sure to have a prejudicial effect, causing serious loss to the concert halls, concert managers, the printing and advertising trade.

The artists are called upon to deposit a sum for the rental of the hall and to cover the working expenses, and in the event of a permit not being granted, what redress is there for the artist not being allowed to give the concert after all or practically all the expenses have been incurred? The manager could not be held responsible. Such a position might arise unless there is a definite understanding in regard to the granting of unconditional permission for the artist to enter this country.

Dates are usually booked at least six months ahead.

A very large percentage of concert givers are of foreign birth, in fact it is doubtful if the halls could carry on without them.

Most of the great celebrities first came to this country unknown and were introduced to the British public by means of recitals; to cite a few instances – Paderewski, Busoni, Cortot, Elena Gerhardt, Schnabel.

GRANTING OF PERMITS

The present procedure is for application to be made a month in advance, whereas engagements are made six to eight months beforehand.

A review of the engagements made during the past five years, by those Societies who engage foreign as well as British artists, shows an average of 85% British or resident artists. As regards vocalists, with a few exceptions, the artists are all British. The exceptions being an occasional Lieder singer or an outstanding Operatic artist.

All our instrumental ensembles of any note are engaged from time to time, and the periodical visits of such String Quartets as the Lener, Hungarian, Budapest, Roth, Pro Arte, Busch, Stradivarius, do not cause any hardship to British artists in the same category. Certain British String Ensembles including the London, Brosa are engaged on the Continent and in America and have become international.

British solo artists are also welcomed in America and on the continent, such as Myra Hess, Katharine Goodson, Harold Samuel, Harriet Cohen, Bartlett and Robertson, Beatrice Harrison, The English Singers, Florence Austral, Eva Turner, John Goss. A perusal of the annals of the Cincinnati Festival, one of the greatest musical festivals in the world, will find the names of some of our greatest singers from Edward Lloyd down to our present day singers, Austral, Brunskill, Widdop, Horace Stevens. British Conductors are to be found either domiciled or visiting the States: Stokowski, Eugene Goossens, Sir Thomas Beecham, Sir Hamilton Harty, Basil Cameron.

I was recently asked by an American manager to approach Albert Sammons with a view to his visiting the States but he was not interested.

ISSUE OF PERMITS FOR SEASON 1932–33

As the Societies will shortly be making their arrangements, naturally they will want to know how they stand in regard to foreign artists. It will be useless their booking such artists unless we can give them the assurance that they will be allowed to fulfil their engagements. To this end it will be essential to obtain the necessary permission at the time the engagement is negotiated, which in most cases is anything from six months to ten months ahead, to avoid such a contingency again arising as in the case of Quintet of Paris when permission was withheld until the eleventh hour causing serious inconvenience to the societies concerned.

Under the present policy we cannot take it as definite that artists who have appeared here in the past will again be admitted. In the case of Renée Chemet and the Quintet of Paris who have recently been refused, are we to take it that they will never be allowed here again?

If the Ministry has not a definite mind on this point then the situation becomes impossible.

To strengthen their case, Ibbs and Tillett also produced a number of statistics comparing the employment of British and foreign artists during the five seasons covering the years 1927–32 (except for the Bradford Philharmonic Concerts which produced figures for just four years 1927–31), and recitals given during 1931 at the Wigmore Hall in London.

Wigmore Hall : Recitals during 1931

	British	Foreign
January	12	10
February	15	14
March	19	13
April	12	4
May	16	11
June	21	8
July	11	1
August	–	–
September	1	–
October	20	9
November	15	12
December	17	3
TOTAL	159	85

Liverpool Philharmonic Society (1927–1932)
Conductors 31 (British 19) : Singers 48 (British 45) : Instrumentalists 25 (British 11)
Hallé Concerts Society, Manchester (1927–1932) Permanent Conductor (British)
Singers 84 (British 84) : Instrumentalists 52 (British 22)
Choral and Orchestral Union of Glasgow (1927–1932)
Conductors 25 (British 11) : Singers 74 (British 69) : Instrumentalists 54 (British 20)
Royal Philharmonic Society, London (1927–1932)
Conductors 41 (British 31) : Singers 34 (British 32) : Instrumentalists 34 (British 17)
Woking Music Club (1927–1932)
4 String Quartets (3 British) : 5 String Ensembles (4 British) : 2 Instrumental Ensembles (foreign)
1 Wind Quintet (British) : 16 Solo Instrumentalists (11 British) : 20 Vocalists (19 British)
Dorking Music Club (1927–1932)
5 String Quartets (2 British) : 18 Solo Instrumentalists (12 British) : 10 Vocalists (8 British)
The Bouverie Society, Folkestone (1927–1932)
1 String Quartet (British) : 13 Solo Instrumentalists (8 British) : 17 Vocalists (16 British)
Woodford Green Subscription Concerts (1927–1932)
2 String Ensembles (British) : 9 Instrumental Ensembles (8 British)
23 Solo Instrumentalists (15 British) : 20 Vocalists (British)
Chelsea Music Club (1927–1932)
3 String Quartets (2 British) : 13 Instrumental Ensembles (9 British)
25 Solo Instrumentalists (19 British) : 11 Vocalists (4 British)
Oxford Subscription Concerts (1927–1932)
1 String Quartet (British) : 14 String Ensembles (11 British)
13 Solo Instrumentalists (4 British) : 8 Vocalists (4 British)
Banbury & District Musical Society (1927–1932)
2 String Quartets (1 British) : 4 Instrumental Ensembles (3 British)
11 Solo Instrumentalists (7 British) : 9 Vocalists (8 British)
Huddersfield Music Club (1927–1932)
11 Instrumental Ensembles (5 British) : 11 Solo Instrumentalists (4 British) : 11 Vocalists (6 British)
Newcastle Chamber Music Society (1927–1932)
17 String Quartets (6 British) : 2 Wind Quintets (1 British)
16 Solo Instrumentalists (12 British) : 16 Vocalists (14 British)

Bowden Chamber Concerts (1927–1932)
4 String Quartets (3 British) : 1 String Trio (British)
16 Solo Instrumentalists (12 British) : 18 Vocalists (16 British)
Derby Municipal & County Chamber Concerts (1927–1932)
2 String Quartets (British) : 11 String Ensembles (8 British)
16 Solo Instrumentalists (7 British) : 9 Vocalists (8 British)
Blackpool Chamber Concerts (1927–1932)
6 String Quartets (3 British) : 8 Instrumental Ensembles (4 British) : 11 Solo Instrumentalists (9 British)
Bradford Philharmonic Concerts (1927–1931)
2 String Quartets (British) : 1 Instrumental Ensemble (British)
37 Solo Instrumentalists (24 British) : 28 Vocalists (British)

The societies were also asked by Ibbs and Tillett to describe in detail any objections they might have to the Government's proposals, which the agency would then summarize and forward to the Ministry of Labour. Among them was this colourful mix of publishable and non-publishable contributions from the conductor of the Bradford Philharmonic Concerts, Keith Douglas, a future concert promoter himself:

Dear Emmie
Here is a formal letter which you can use. You know my views on this stupid situation: apply my ideas as you like. As ever, K.D. (Tuesday night)

Dear Miss Bass
The Embargo upon foreign artists
(What is an embargo Mr Justice Darling?)
You have already received a lengthy letter from me on this subject, in which I stated that I strongly disapproved of the present attitude of the Incorporated Society of Musicians, and in which I propounded a very practicable proposition as far as foreign musicians are concerned.

My suggestion was that any foreigner who had the audacity to charge a fee of twenty-five or thirty guineas, should be automatically allowed to enter the country, but that he should not leave it before paying a tax upon his musical earnings equal to the tax that the average English citizen has to pay on his income – five bob in the pound [25p in the £ or 25%]. My extended views on this subject were expressed in a previous letter.

May I add that my opinions on this matter are endorsed by the Committee of the Bradford Music Club, by Mrs Eaglefield-Hull of Huddersfield, who has written to me about this silly nonsense, and by the Entertainments Committee of the Hastings Corporation, in which place I am acting as Musical Director until Julius Harrison is better. Furthermore I represent the future interests of the Bradford Philharmonic Concerts – if any. Sincerely yours, Keith Douglas (5 January 1932)

My dear Emmie
You have set me rather a hard problem, but one which is not insoluble I think.

In this craze for "Buying British", it is only natural that the Ministry of Labour and the Incompetent Society of Musicians, which I joined two years ago because I was told that it was going to do great things for music, and that my name in the North would be a valuable asset, and which I left a year ago because it had fulfilled none of its promises, should have lost their befuddled heads. In the first place, the Ministry of Labour ought to be closed down, it serves no useful purpose. In the second, if this Utopia cannot be achieved, it might pay attention to banning some of the things that we can make or grow in this country, instead of banning people that we cannot do without. As for the ISM, one might as well advocate the Channel Tunnel as hold any brief for them. I am fully aware of the disgruntled maniacs who started this ramp. And the ramp would have been quite all right if we could have replaced the foreigners by our own noise-makers. But we cannot. So, as a conclusion and summing up of this paragraph, let us say that the idea is praiseworthy, but owing to England's inability to provide adequate substitutes, misguided.

Now as to your suggestion that it is concert promoters who are the people to make the next move, I quite agree. And I am willing to get in touch with Newcastle, Nether Wallop, Wantage, Woking, Poking, Dorking, Little Belching or Kettering (without trying to be funny or crude at the same time), if we can get a full-fronted support, and if you think that this will do any good. First of all I must call my Committee together, which I must do as soon after Christmas as possible, and then I have not the slightest objection to heading the whole crowd, if it is going to come to a rumpus with the Ministry of Labour. The Hallé Society will, I think, come in. I have a potential ally in Sir Thomas Robinson, Vice-Chairman of the BDA and late Chairman of Committees in the House of Commons, whose advice I would take at any moment, and who would be able to give me details of the right procedure, to say nothing of doing things behind the scenes. If you will put me in touch with the other people who are affected or likely to be interested, I will try to put the wheels in motion.

I have turned over the obvious points in my mind, Emmie. I think that, for the time being, if I do make such a move I can afford to neglect the cries of the Albert Sammonses (and to pay for them when I require their services), and, as I am not overkeen on conducting in London, I can probably afford to neglect the Norman O'Neills and the [William] Murdochs. But not altogether. One has, in this unstable state of England to consider the future.

I would suggest a scheme, the tenor of which I wired to you this morning. Allow any foreigner to come in, if he or she is prepared to accept a fee of not less than thirty guineas. Before leaving the country any such artist would be required to pay tax on this fee to the British Government at the full rate of Income Tax as applied to any unfortunate inmate of this country – i.e. 5/- in the £.

Under this system there could be no grouse on the part of British artists, because the fee would act like a tariff, and would keep out those who would lose their heads (like Suggia) and the tax would act as a further deterrent. As a matter of fact, what would happen is that all those artists who had any knowledge of giving shows in America would realise that England was only following suit, and they would readily undertake any contract, given a sufficient number of contracts, in which they could get three quarters of the fee charged to the concert societies, minus your own ten per cent. BUT artists with low fees wouldn't think the game worth the while. So you would automatically get only the big people and at the same time, benefit the British Exchequer and reduce the English 'hostiles' to silence, because they couldn't very well damn something which would tend to keep alien artists out of the country while admitting them on conditions, and at the same time benefiting the British Treasury.

Here is an essential point for you. And it is this point that I shall push if you want me to take the matter up to headquarters. Let these ladies and gentlemen from the Continent come in by all means, but make them pay for it. The ones that we want will come, and the creatures that will be about as much use as a sick headache will get wind-up, and stay away. And then Mr Sammons may be invited to take the place of Thibaud. The result of the invitation will be that Thibaud will come and leave a spot of money in this country when he goes back across the Channel. But Fraulein Crxzchyxz from Prague will think twice about giving a recital in the Wigmore Hall with a view to bamboozling Henry [Wood] into a Prom next August, and therefore Mr Sammons will have a chance of a Prom. If Fraulein Crxzchyxz still chooses to come and perform in that place that looks like a mixture between a urinal and an Anglo-Catholic Altar-piece, she will leave a spot of money behind her. Add this to what Thibaud leaves behind him, and then Mr Sammons may get his Income Tax reduced.

In any case Emmie, it is absurd to suggest that if foreigners are not allowed to play, they will be replaced by exactly the same combination, consisting entirely of Englishmen. They will not. The duds will still remain out of work because they are duds, and the well-paid and over-worked people will be better off and completely over-worked.

So here is your four-page answer. You deserve it because, although it costs you sevenpence-halfpenny, you were rather gassy yourself. I think that I have put a constructive suggestion before you. If not, write again and I will try to think of something better. Remember that I am with you in this affair, and that I will do whatever I can to help. But we must contrive something diabolically clever, so as to be able to refute any super-patriotic argument that may pop out from the Incompetent Society of Musicians. My scheme, I think, would work. What about it?

All good wishes to you and Gran [Florence Bass, Emmie's mother], and John, if his liver is working sufficiently to recognise politeness! As ever, Keith (Tuesday evening)

In response to canvassing support from the various clients of the agency, that is, music clubs and choral societies throughout the land, Ibbs and Tillett received replies from Cambridge, Ipswich, Derby, Newcastle, Westminster, Glasgow, Banbury, Tunbridge Wells, Kendal, Llandudno, Oxford, Bangor, Bowdon, and Huddersfield, and John Tillett selected salient points from their letters to put to the Government. The cancellation of concerts given by foreign artists meant lost work for accompanists such as Gerald Moore. Cambridge used the financial rewards of the full houses often achieved by foreign artists of repute to fund concerts for British artists. Ipswich was concerned that a lot of bad feeling would arise and affect British artists travelling abroad. Concerns were raised by several about who would decide which artists were deemed worthy or unworthy of entry into Britain. Newcastle's audiences expected to be kept acquainted with the best continental groups. The Government felt that talented British artists were not raising objections to the employment of foreign artists in the UK (at least not openly), and that such protests were only emanating 'from the less successful British artists'. Glasgow considered that, however well-meaning to the interests of British musicians, these developments were against the spirit of 'British Sportsmanship'. All agreed that internationalism in the Arts could only benefit from the awareness and understanding between countries, which would ensue from visits by foreign artists to Britain and by British artists abroad.

The creation of the first fully salaried orchestras by the BBC in London and around the country was certainly spurred on by the opportunities to hear visiting foreign orchestras. Yet even in Britain there were exceptions. Hamilton Harty's Symphony Concerts, this time using his Hallé Orchestra, were inaugurated in the 1929–30 season. There were six on Fridays at Queen's Hall between November and February which Ibbs and Tillett managed, and, of them, Harvey Grace wrote in glowing terms, 'if (as the Jeremiahs affirm) an occasional visit by a crack orchestra is necessary in order that London may not forget what high-grade playing is like, there is no need to send to the Continent. Manchester is good enough.' Regrettably, finances proved to be a stumbling block and the series did not survive beyond the following 1930–31 season (Harty bore the £3000 deficit himself). This was despite the fact that the programmes were attractively constructed, and the agency's soloists popular and of the highest calibre, Backhaus, Moiseiwitsch, d'Aranyi, and the singers, Florence Austral, Muriel Brunskill, Oda Slobodskaya, Parry Jones, Francis Russell, Norman Allin, and Robert Parker. Two of the concerts were for orchestra alone, one was entirely devoted to Berlioz (a Harty favourite), while two others, in true Richter style, consisted of extracts from Wagner's *Ring* cycle.

The agency's work was increased further by other ventures at this time. Where the collaboration with Harty had lasted a mere two years at the beginning of the decade, it was the Second World War which curtailed another scheme after two seasons, this time the London Theatre Concerts, managed by Ibbs and Tillett and which took place on Sunday nights at the Cambridge Theatre. The first season of nine concerts in 1937–38 was entirely devoted to the music of Mozart, of whom Beecham, as President of the organization, wrote in the foreword to the programme: 'if I were a dictator, I should make it compulsory for every member of the population between the ages of four and eighty to listen to [Mozart] for at least one quarter of an hour daily for the coming five years'. The orchestra was the Haigh Marshall Orchestra led by George Stratton throughout, but with different conductors, Haigh Marshall himself, Reginald Goodall, Bernhard (later Boris) Ord, Jack Westrup, Beecham (but conducting his London Philharmonic Orchestra), and Mosco Carner. There were also two chamber music concerts with each based around a string quartet, the Stratton Quartet and the Griller

Quartet. The orchestral concerts often had more than one concerto, even for the same instrument, and therefore more soloists than usual were billed. Both the pianists Cyril Smith and Betty Humby together with the soprano Nan Maryska opened the first series; the second had a similar combination in Guy Jonson, Karl Ulrich Schnabel (son of Artur) and Joan Cross; the third not only had the pianists Hilda Bor and Kurt Appelbaum, but also the violinist Jean Pougnet and soprano Isobel Baillie. Heddle Nash, Betty Humby and William Glock, Nina Milkina, Clifford Curzon and David Franklin, Denise Lassimonne, John Hunt and Pougnet completed the line up for the rest of the concerts. Beecham made do with just one soloist, the violinist Henry Holst, while the two chamber concerts featured Reginald Kell, Maryska, Lassimonne, Max Gilbert, Bor, Jonson, Hunt, Edward Walker, Evelyn Rothwell, Watson Forbes, and various other members of the orchestra around which the concerts were built. For the second season the orchestra was renamed the London Theatre Concert Orchestra with conductors Stanley Chapple, Anthony Collins, Fritz Heinig, Georg Szell, Goodall (twice), and Carner, and all the music was devoted to Mozart, Haydn or Schubert. The soloists were very much the same, the chamber concerts were given by the Stratton and Budapest Quartets, but an extra concert was a Schubert piano recital by Schnabel on 15 January 1939.

Schnabel's association with the agency had only begun comparatively recently with the 1927–28 season. His manager from the start of his career was the German Hermann Wolff, and his first appearance in England was back in 1904 at a Richter concert, followed by another visit the following year. There was a gap of twenty years, before he came again in 1925 for two recitals arranged by the piano firm Bechstein, after which he returned each year. He became very friendly with the Courtauld family, and was deeply involved in establishing the Courtauld–Sargent concerts in London. Schnabel was also a prolific editor of music, including the complete Beethoven sonatas in the late 1920s, which in turn led to a series of seven matinee recitals in Berlin in 1927, at which he performed them all for the first time. Having constantly resisted invitations to record, he finally agreed to do so with the complete Beethoven sonatas in London, the discs being made available only to a list of subscribers called the Beethoven Sonata Society. His relationship with HMV was to last until the outbreak of the Second World War, when he emigrated to America. In his memoirs (in which his memory for dates is often unreliable), Schnabel relates in detail his experiences of touring England, where the concert halls provided 'a very special type of experience' in many cases and usually bad ones. Bristol, for example, had constant draughts despite a £40 000 renovation, a hall in Oxford (also used as a gymnasium) was on the third floor above a police station, opposite dog kennels and within earshot of Great Tom, the bell of Christ Church which struck 101 times during one of his recitals. The audience in Folkestone was lifeless, while the one in Glasgow was shrouded in fog.

> My manager, Mr Tillett, never tried to persuade me. He immediately agreed with me when I told him that I did not want to play under certain circumstances or in certain places. He accepted my reasons and would never recommend me for such places. If they asked for me, he would say, 'Mr Schnabel does not want to accept. He is nervous about his health' or something similar.

Between 1933, when the Nazis came to power in Germany, and February 1939 when he moved to America, Schnabel divided his time between living in Italy and spending the winters in London. During these months in the English capital, Ibbs and Tillett arranged piano recitals at the Queen's Hall including all Beethoven's piano sonatas in seven autumn recitals in 1932 (the only time in Britain when Schnabel undertook the complete cycle, but he also did it twice in Berlin and once in New York). In 1934 another autumn series of seven recitals of the music of Mozart, Schubert and Schumann was arranged, 'I have never repeated this anywhere else', he wrote.

The Wigmore Hall, a stone's throw from Ibbs and Tillett's premises at 124 Wigmore Street, was not only a frequent venue for their auditions, but also for a new series of concerts managed by them from the autumn of 1929 until the spring of 1931. Four series of fortnightly chamber concerts took place on Wednesday evenings organized by a committee of six agency artists, Dorothy Silk, Isolde Menges, Myra Hess, Ivor James, Harold Samuel, and William Murdoch, with 20 concerts having been promoted by the spring of 1931. Silk, Menges, Hess, and James, with Orrea Pernal, Lionel Tertis, Aubrey Thonger, and George Reeves accompanying where required, opened the series at 8.30pm on 9 October 1929 in works by Mozart, Brahms and César Franck. The concerts were notable for their sheer variety of performers and diversity of works, for example the 17th concert on 4 February 1931 featured Albert Sammons and John Coates (accompanied by Gerald Moore), while Harold Samuel, Howard Ferguson, The London String Players under Herbert Menges, and Isolde Menges were among those taking part two weeks later in an all-Bach programme, and the final one on 18 March 1931 was given by Ethel Bartlett and Rae Robertson, and the English Singers (a group of six vocalists) in music ranging from madrigals and folksong to contemporary music for two pianos.

In London there were also the South Place concerts of chamber music (dating back to 1887), which the agency supplied with instrumentalists and singers for their regular series (still going strong as the London Chamber Music Society on Sundays at the Conway Hall), but the agency also had to continue supplying the music clubs and concert societies of Britain's provincial towns and cities. One of the most important of these became, over the years, the Max Mossel Concerts. Mossel was Dutch, born in Rotterdam in 1871, who trained as a violinist under Willy Hess and Sarasate, and enjoyed a short career as a recitalist and orchestral leader (including the Concertgebouw Orchestra for a brief period). On 5 July 1892 he appeared as soloist in a Saturday Concert at the Crystal Palace, and two years later moved to England with his cellist brother and singer sister-in-law, and settled in Birmingham. There he turned his hand to teaching (at London's Guildhall School of Music from 1910 and at the Midland Institute in Birmingham) and concert organization. The programmes for his Drawing Room Concerts in Birmingham's Grand Hotel were focused around his own Max Mossel String Quartet, but also provided a platform for many established soloists; for example in their first season (four concerts in 1896) Ysaÿe, de Greef, Kleeberg, and the Henschels appeared, while in November 1900 Moriz Rosenthal first played in the city. At this time it would have been Vert who supplied Mossel with celebrities from London, while Mossel himself supplemented the programmes with newcomers or local musicians (his own brother and sister-in-law included). Mossel died at The Hague in the summer of 1929; the previous season Ibbs and Tillett had added the likes of Dora Labbette, Isolde Menges and Betty Humby (Ayr, 31 January 1928) to the starry pairing of Elisabeth Schumann and Artur Schnabel. On 25 January 1929, as if in anticipation of his own death later that year, Mossel drew up an agreement with Ibbs and Tillett whereby the agency took over the management of the concerts from the start of the 1929–30 season in October. The agreement stated that, for an initial three years (with an option for a further three if Mossel were no longer alive), the agency would have sole control, that the concerts would continue to be called Max Mossel Subscription Concerts, and that profits or losses would be shared by the parties, 60 per cent by Mossel and 40 per cent by the agency, and that Mossel would not lend his name to any other similar enterprise during the period of the contract. These concerts became a vital part of the agency's work until 1940.

In conclusion, it is worth noting some of the many events which occurred during the 1930s, and with which Ibbs and Tillett either became involved or actually managed themselves. Muriel Brunskill and Walter Widdop were sent out to Cincinnati for the 1931 May Music Festival (conducted by Eugene Goossens), and for their 1938–39 season of subscription concerts, Myra Hess, Ethel Bartlett and Rae Robertson were supplied. In London, the centenary of the birth of Brahms was celebrated in 1933 with a series of eight concerts at which his complete chamber music was played. Under the management of the agency, they took place at the Wigmore Hall between 25 April and 6 May and were given by the Isolde Menges String Quartet, Alfred de Reyghere, Helen Just, Frederick Thurston, Aubrey Brain, and Harold Samuel. On 6 December 1933 the Royal Choral Society put on *Messiah* at the Royal Albert Hall for the sick Malcolm Sargent. Beecham conducted, Baillie, Brunskill, Widdop and Williams were the Ibbs and Tillett quartet of soloists for this and also for *Elijah* under Geoffrey Toye a month later on 6 January 1934. The first season of the Royal Philharmonic Society's Chamber Concerts took place at the Aeolian Hall from January to March 1934, largely based around the Brosa String Quartet. Cortot came to London in 1935 under the agency's sole management, and among the many vocal recitals arranged at the Wigmore Hall were those by Tatiana Makushina (accompanied by Gretchaninoff), and Joan Cross (with Lawrance Collingwood). Elena Gerhardt came regularly throughout the decade accompanied by Conraad von Bos, Ivor Newton, and, by 1938 when she was living and teaching in London, Gerald Moore. It was he who accompanied Astra Desmond there in September 1937, while two months later Cortot returned to accompany Maggie Teyte in a Debussy recital.

While Szigeti undertook a tour of South Africa in 1938, Moiseiwitsch went annually to America and many other countries throughout the 1930s, both of them represented by Ibbs and Tillett. Meanwhile Rachmaninov returned to Britain for a series of piano recitals and concerto appearances in 1935. Empire Day was marked on 24 May 1938 by a concert at the Royal Albert Hall, beginning with three eminent organists playing for half an hour, followed by a long mixed programme of choral and orchestral items by British composers from the 13th century to Dyson and Howells. The concert was under Sargent and Wood, with familiar Ibbs and Tillett artists taking solo parts ('No encores whatever can be given. Applause may well be STRONG but not LONG', was the written command in the programme). To mark the death of King George V a couple of years earlier, a memorial concert was given on 4 February 1936 under Harold Holt's direction, but with soloists Astra Desmond and Eva Turner from Ibbs and Tillett (and once again solo organ music preceded the concert for 15 minutes).

Like Brahms, Bach was another composer celebrated in the decade, for the year 1935 was the 250th anniversary of his birth, and so the agency managed the Bach Choir's concert at the Queen's Hall on 7 April to mark the occasion. Reginald Jacques conducted the *St Matthew Passion* (traditionally an annual event for the choir each Passion Sunday) with Suddaby, Bannerman, Nash, Wilson, Parsons, and Falkner, while the Royal Choral Society under Sargent celebrated the same anniversary with the *St John Passion* sung by Suddaby, Cranmer, Manchester, Falkner, and Wilson. Adolf Busch celebrated the Bach year by performing all six Brandenburg Concertos at the Queen's Hall on two days in October, with an eminent team of musicians including the pianist Rudolf Serkin (who became a close friend of the Tilletts), flautist Marcel Moyse, and oboist Evelyn Rothwell (Lady Barbirolli). Back in February 1932 the Busch Quartet and Serkin were, according to the publicity, 'persuaded to give a series of [six] concerts' of music from Bach to Reger at the Wigmore Hall. The Royal Philharmonic Society's 1937–38 season of concerts was stocked with agency artists such as Eda Kersey, Myra Hess, Louis Kentner, and Clifford Curzon, as were Henry Wood's Promenade Concerts in 1938. This was his Jubilee season (and a punishing one of 49 consecutive concerts), with the agency represented by the soloists at virtually all the events over the eight week season from 6 August to 1 October.

The London Music Festival, held from 23 April to 28 May 1939, was to become a final outburst of artistic merry-making before war, for the second time in the century, effectively shut the country down for nearly six years. 'Never before', wrote Sir Walford Davies, Master of the King's Musick, in his foreword to the prospectus, 'has a musical event of such scope and comprehensive importance been planned for London, and indeed, for the whole cause of British music and music-making'. It was also designed 'to make apparent, not only to our own people, but to Europe, what we are doing as a nation, and where we stand musically'. Conductors included Toscanini, Wood, Beecham, Sargent, Boult, Bruno Walter, Boyd Neel, Constant Lambert, Anthony Collins, Ernest Read, and Reginald Jacques. Ibbs and Tillett provided the Lener, Griller and New Hungarian String Quartets (supplemented by father and son horn duo Aubrey and Dennis Brain), oboist Léon Goossens, singers Suddaby, Jarred, Wilson, Walker, and Parsons for the *St John Passion*, Ripley, Nash, and Williams for *Dream of Gerontius*, pianists Myra Hess, Solomon, Backhaus, Moiseiwitsch, Betty Humby, Ethel Bartlett and Rae Robertson, violinist Szigeti, and for an informal Ayres and Ale outdoor concert, John Goss and the London Singers. The last two events of the festival were the opening two nights (1 and 2 June) of the Glyndebourne Festival, now in its sixth season, and added on after the official closing date. The Prom season began as planned on 12 August, but with the outbreak of war, was curtailed on 1 September; new works performed included Arthur Bliss's Piano Concerto played by Solomon, and two songs from Britten's yet unfinished Rimbaud cycle (*Les Illuminations*) sung by the soprano Sophie Wyss, one of those 'culled' from the list in the agency's purge of 1931.

Before leaving the bright days of the 1920s and 1930s for the darkness of the Second World War years, it would be as well to look at the recording industry, which took off in terms of scientific advance and public popularity during those two decades. Earlier in this chapter, the conductor Albert Coates was identified as a pioneer television conductor, and so he was with the recording industry, though regrettably he did not work long enough to record long-playing records (LPs), unwisely moving to the high altitude of Johannesburg in South Africa in 1943 and dying there from a heart condition in 1953. Coates was renowned for his conducting of Wagner, and of the Russian operatic and orchestral repertoire, and much of his large recorded legacy focuses on both. Though he recorded between the years 1919 and 1945, the bulk of his work in the studio was between 1923 and 1937, and of the singers he worked with, Ibbs and Tillett were agents for all but a handful including Elisabeth Schumann, Elsie Suddaby, Florence Austral, Margaret Balfour, Edna Thornton, Tudor Davies, Walter Widdop, Percy Heming, and Robert Radford to name but a few. The best source of tracing the recording activities of artists is often found in the recital and concert programmes of the period, in which advertisements for records (often of the music being played that afternoon or evening) are placed either by the record companies themselves or by local retailers.

CHAPTER EIGHTEEN

A Conductor in 1933

As has been noted before, the relationship between Ibbs and Tillett and conductors was generally speaking not a formal one, at least not before the Second World War. On the other hand, the agency run from Steinway Hall by Frank L. Cooper (who was joined by the former tenor John McCormack early in 1939), listed 27 conductors, including Beecham, Barbirolli, Coates, Furtwängler, Sargent, Toscanini, Walter and Wood (and a host of other singers and instrumentalists also to be found on Ibbs and Tillett's lists). They were evidently not exclusive; indeed that word does not appear anywhere in Cooper's brochure, while Ibbs and Tillett's first pages are devoted to artists for whom they are sole representatives. It is worth pausing to consider the career conductor between the two world wars, using Albert Coates as an example. Among his papers, not located in the Ibbs and Tillett archive but in the author's possession, there are two typewritten undated lists evidently made during the summer of 1933, relating to the period from September to November that year. They are entitled 'Secretary's General Instructions', and 'Secretary's Instructions, Concert after Concert' respectively, and were probably drawn up by his permanent secretary and intended to help a temporary replacement. Ibbs and Tillett and its competitor Harold Holt are mentioned at various points and the document provides a detailed description of Coates's routine. The notes are very specific and not only reveal the punishing schedule this conductor undertook, but also follow the complex infrastructure of his and many another musician's life, which such an agency would have to coordinate.

It also probably accounts for Ibbs and Tillett's wary approach to operatic work for its artists. Companies between the two world wars were forever in financial trouble and at risk of dissolution, particularly, though not exclusively, if Beecham was involved. Covent Garden, the BNOC, and a new venture in the autumn of 1933, the Metropolitan Opera Company (MOC) encountered considerable problems. This last company was the brainchild of the bass-baritone Robert Parker, who had been an Ibbs and Tillett artist until the season of 1930–31, and was coming to the end of a successful singing career, though with a Wotan yet to sing in *Siegfried* under Coates at Covent Garden in 1935. Parker put together a company of 30 singers and an orchestra of 50, mainly members of the defunct BNOC, opening with a week of Wagner at Streatham Hill Theatre in south London before undertaking a national tour. It was an exceedingly ambitious venture, including as it did a complete *Ring* cycle, *Die Meistersinger*, *Flying Dutchman*, *Lohengrin*, *Tristan*, and *Tannhäuser*. Agency singers Florence Austral, Walter Widdop, and Horace Stevens were among those who took major roles.

A few observations on the list of instructions reproduced below are worth making. MOC business heads the anonymous secretary's instructions to her substitute entitled 'Concert after Concert', which show how remarkably late the basics, let alone the details of engagements were decided, such as dates, availability, rehearsal schedules, venues (even in which towns or cities performances were to take place), programmes, and access to scores. It should also be made clear that Coates, who was a giant of a man, conducted with great vigour and energy, and was renowned for the amount of sweat he produced both at rehearsals and concerts. Evidently some of the outstanding questions were answered before this missive was completed and so handwritten margin annotations were added, and both are incorporated here (described as 'scored through' and 'added'). Much of what is asked would have been done by Ibbs and Tillett had Coates been a singer or instrumentalist, or even a foreign conductor but, for this evidently totally disorganized and absent-minded man, there is necessary 'nannying' for which a personal manager or secretary would have had to take responsibility.

Secretary's instructions, concert after concert.

Mr Coates arrives August 31st. He must arrange with Mr Parker of Opera Co his rehearsals with piano and singers. Also what performances he can do in the provinces after October 7th, at what theatres these are and at what time. Write these in Mr Coates' diary and make a list for yourself. Also get from Mr Parker a list of where the Company plays each week so you always have an address in case Mr Coates should be ill and you have to notify him [scored through, 'list enclosed' added in margin, though this is not extant]. Remind Mr Coates, when making arrangements, to be careful not to accept provincial performances when there is a rehearsal in London early the next morning. Mr Coates promised the librarian two guineas for making cuts in the orchestral parts, remind him to pay the man.

Pack up at once four orchestral scores of *Taming of the Shrew* [Coates' own composition and part of his concert programme in Liverpool on 17 October 1933] and send these to W Riley Esq, Liverpool Philharmonic Society, Bluecoat Chambers, 20 School Lane, Church Street, Liverpool. Write note that you have sent them.

Friday Sept 1st Orchestral rehearsal *Götterdämmerung* 10 o'clock to 1 at *Helvetia*, Gerrard Place (opposite Shaftesbury Theatre stage door). Find out how best to get there. [scored through]
Saturday Sept 2nd Orchestral rehearsal *Götterdämmerung* & *Meistersinger* 10 o'clock to 1 at *Helvetia.*
Friday Sept 8th Dress rehearsal, 10-1 *Meistersinger* at ?
Saturday Sept 9th Dress rehearsal, 10-1 *Götterdämmerung* at ?
Mon Sept 11th Performance *Meistersinger* at Streatham Hill Theatre. Find out what time it begins.
Remind Mr C. to take a double lot of clothes as [he] may wish to change in the middle of performance.
Tuesday [Sept 12th] Lunch 1pm *Elijah* Park Lane.
Friday Sept 15th Performance *Götterdämmerung.* Same instructions as for *Meistersinger.*
Subsequent performances are at Golders Green *Hippodrome* on Sept 18th, 22nd, 25th, 29th.
Oct 2nd and 6th are at Bradford. See list. Money!

Sat Oct 7th Dinner at London Musical Club, 22 Holland Park, Time 7.30. He must go to this. If by chance he should be ill, then telephone Mr Armstrong (Park 7094).
Sometime during these weeks, when there are only performances, Mr Coates must see Cyril Scott about the tone poem *Disaster at Sea*, of which the first rehearsal will be on Oct 13th. Scott's address is 37, Ladbroke Grove, W2. Phone him up and arrange for him to come and demonstrate his work to Mr Coates. During these weeks Mr Coates must also see Mr Clive Carey of the Old Vic in order to go through the opera *Tsar Sultan* with him. Carey's private telephone is Park 2730, if not there phone the Old Vic.

Sometime between Sept 11th and Oct 5th (except Mondays & Fridays when Mr C is conducting) the choir master of Huddersfield Choral Society [Herbert Bardgett] is coming to see Mr Coates re *Elijah.* He must come before Oct 5th so as to give him time to rehearse with the choir after he has seen Mr Coates. Tell Mr Coates this when arranging appointment. Choir master will probably write; if he doesn't, then telephone Messrs Ibbs and Tillett, concert agents, Welbeck 2325 (address 124, Wigmore Street, W1) and ask them to arrange it, providing Mr Coates still wishes it. Remind Mr C to be at home when choir master comes.

Oct 9th Performance *Meistersinger* in Birmingham, Find out name of theatre. [scored through : 'Prince of Wales theatre' added]
See beforehand that Mr Coates has sufficient money for expenses. Find out time of train, station he leaves from and name of good hotel. Also return train from Birmingham after performance in case

Mr C wishes to return same night. If he does, see that he takes latchkeys with him. Same for all provincial engagements, especially that he always has enough money.

Oct 13th Two rehearsals for the Royal Philharmonic concert, at 10 and at 2.30. One of these may be changed to another day. [sentence scored through] Telephone beforehand to the Royal Philharmonic Society of 19, Berners Street, W1. Telephone Museum 7877. Ask where these rehearsals will be, when and what time. A week before Oct 13th ask Philharmonic Society to send Mr Coates the orchestral scores of *Burleske* by Strauss and *Concertino* by Honegger. These scores must be in the house by Saturday 7th [last three sentences scored through, 'has these' added]. Ask Mr Coates before you telephone whether he would like any of the other scores as well and make them send all he asks for. See that he takes all the scores he has at home to rehearsal with him. Verify by programme. Remind him to pack sufficient clothing for both rehearsals as [he] will not have time to come home in between. Pack his programme.

Monday Oct. 16th Leaves for Liverpool. Find out on Saturday previous time of train, station. Go into the money question on Friday as banks close early on Saturday. Also that [he] has sufficient money. Inquire if lunch possible on train. If not, take earlier train. Week beforehand ask Mr Coates whether he would like to have a look at the score of Symphony No.2 Borodin. If yes, telephone Goodwin and Tabb or Boosey and Hawkes, or Chester & Co and ask them to let Mr C have this score for a couple of days. Mr Coates does not take this score to Liverpool (they have their own), you return it after he has left. If by any chance the scores of the *Taming of the Shrew* suite have not been sent to Liverpool in September as per instructions, see that Mr Coates packs these four scores and takes them with him. Ask Mr Coates. Pack his programme. See that he takes his diary.

Wednesday Oct 18th Mr C returns to London and must have a piano rehearsal with Gieseking. Arrange this before he leaves for Liverpool so he knows what time he must be back. Telephone Ibbs and Tillett about it. Also phone Mrs Lindars, Primrose 0932 and ask her if this rehearsal can take place at her house, since she has two pianos. He must take the scores of the *Burleske* and Honegger.

Thursday Oct 19th Ten o'clock rehearsal Royal Philharmonic concert at Queen's Hall. Must take all scores needed. Evening, concert Royal Philharmonic, Queen's Hall. Begins at 8.15.

Friday Oct 20th Choral rehearsal in Huddersfield in the evening. Inquire beforehand from Ibbs and Tillett what time it begins and at what hall it takes place [scored through: 7.30 at High Street Sunday School added]. Sufficient money, time of train, station as before. Also return trains as [he] will return the same night. Ask Tillett about how long rehearsal lasts. See takes latchkeys since will be back late.

Monday Oct 23rd *Meistersinger* somewhere in the provinces. Money, time of train, station, latchkeys.

Friday Oct 27th Performance *Tsar Sultan* at Sadler's Wells. He has two orchestral rehearsals for this. Phone beforehand to Miss [Lilian]Bayliss (Old Vic. Hop. 6837) or Mr [Lawrance] Collingwood (Willesden 0918) and ask which days and what times these are. Also arrange for any piano rehearsals with singers Mr C may want. Do all this well beforehand as opera performances in provinces with Metropolitan Opera Company will depend on what days Mr C has free. Do not think he can do rehearsal Sadler's Wells on Oct 24th as he has *Meistersinger* in the provinces evening of 23rd. Remember this. Ask what time Sadler's Wells performance starts and remind him to take a double set of clothing so as to change in the middle.

Saturday Oct 28th Two rehearsals for BBC concert morning and afternoon. These are not yet fixed. Telephone BBC, ask for Mr Kenneth Wright and ask what time these rehearsals are and where they will take place. They will probably be at 10 and 2.30 but make sure. Mr C is bringing the scores of suite [by] Shostakovich and Symphony No.1 [by] Borodin with him. These he must take with him to rehearsal. The orchestral parts of the Shostakovich are either at the BBC or at Mrs Lindars. Find out and see that if necessary, these parts are sent to the BBC in plenty of time. Ask Mr C a week beforehand if he wants any other scores to study, and if so ask Mr Wright to have them sent. All scores to be taken to rehearsal. Give Mr C his programme.

Sunday Oct 29th Rehearsal BBC probably at 10. Find out, also where it takes place.

Sunday evening Oct 29th BBC concert. Probably at 9.15 pm but make sure. Also at which studio takes place and in what building.

With regard to this BBC concert, the programme is not yet decided upon definitely. If the BBC want something different to suggested programme, see that Mr Coates decides this and lets them know. For suggested programme three rehearsals are necessary (they gave him three last time). Make sure that there will be three rehearsals before this programme is definitely decided upon. If different numbers are wanted, tell Mr Coates first how many rehearsals he will have before he makes up a new programme. Mr C would of course like three rehearsals if he can get them. There may be a soloist at this concert. If there is, ask Mr C what time he would like the soloist to come to rehearsal on the Sunday morning, and let Mr Wright know. All this should be done well in advance.

Monday Oct 30th *Meistersinger* in the provinces providing Mr Coates can get there in time. Money, time of train etc.

Wednesday Nov 1st. Second choral rehearsal in Huddersfield, evening. Same instructions as for first choral rehearsal. If by any chance this choral rehearsal should HAVE to be on Oct 31st, which date Mr C has free, then look up trains from whichever town *Meistersinger* was in the night before to Huddersfield and give him the whole route and where he has to change. Try to arrange with Ibbs and Tillett that this rehearsal should be on Nov 2nd since Mr Coates can then stay on over for the concert instead of having to come back to town. If 2nd impossible, then Nov 1st, but do your best to avoid Oct 31st as fear this may cause a muddle on account of *Meistersinger* the night before. [Scored through after first sentence, 'Thursday Nov 2nd' deleted, '7.30 at High Street Sunday School' added]

Friday Nov 3rd Orchestral rehearsal Huddersfield in the afternoon. Find out from Ibbs and Tillett what time and in what hall [scored through, '2.30 at Town Hall' added]. Also time of concert and ask name of good hotel. Time of train, money etc.

Friday Nov 3rd evening. Concert, Huddersfield.

Monday Nov 6th *Meistersinger* in provinces. Usual instructions.

Thursday Nov 6th PERHAPS performance *Tsar Sultan* at the Old Vic. Either this date or on Nov 18th. See general instructions and instructions for first performance of *Sultan.*

Monday Nov 13th *Meistersinger* in provinces. Trains etc.

Saturday Nov 18th PERHAPS *Tsar Sultan* at Old Vic. If not on Nov. 9th.

Monday Nov 20th *Meistersinger* somewhere.

Thursday Nov 23rd or Friday Nov 24th Or perhaps on both days, rehearsals for the Beecham concert in London on Sunday 26th. Two rehearsals for this concert. Since Mr C will be conducting in Eastbourne evening of Saturday 25th and will get back late, he has asked the manager Harold Holt to try to arrange one rehearsal on Thursday and one on Friday (for the Beecham concert) so as to avoid the necessity of rehearsing Sunday morning. If this cannot be done, then there will probably be one rehearsal Friday and one on Sunday morning or else two on Friday. If there is any choice ask Mr C which he would prefer. Find out as early as possible when rehearsals can be, what time and at which Hall. When phoning Holt's office, ask for Miss Hampshire. [All but last sentence scored through. 'Wed Nov 22nd 1st rehearsal for Beecham concert, afternoon, at Stoll Picture House rehearsal rooms' (probably with regard to the Hall) '2nd rehearsal Sunday morning Nov 26th, Queens Hall' added].

Ask Mr C what scores he wants to study a week before first rehearsal and ask Holt's office to send them. Must have them several days before first rehearsal. Also ask Mr C beforehand if he wants a private rehearsal with Horowitz, who is soloist at this concert. If yes, arrange it through Holt's office. Also ask Mr C what time he wants Horowitz to come to the last orchestral rehearsal and tell this to Holt's office.

Saturday Nov 25th At 10am rehearsal Eastbourne, evening concert.
With regard to this Eastbourne concert, since Mr C has to get back to London the same night, remind him to telephone Mrs Lindars and to ask her if she could possibly fetch him back from Eastbourne in her car. He will probably miss the last train as he has to cool down before travelling. If she cannot, then see to it that Mr C makes some arrangement re a car to come back in. Remind him. Warn the housekeeper that he will be back very late.

Sunday Nov 26th Morning. Second rehearsal for Beecham concert. Take all necessary music.

Sunday Nov 26th Afternoon. Beecham Concert. Queen's Hall.
If the second rehearsal has to be on Sunday morning, I beg you to be with Mr C in spite of its being Sunday, if he wishes it. He will be tired after the rush back from Eastbourne and may need your help. The following is necessary anyway: Ask the housekeeper on Saturday to prepare a cold lunch, enough for two, and pack it up in a parcel on Sunday morning and give it to Mr C to take with him to the hall. Coffee and milk in a thermos flask (buy a Thermos). Coffee must not be too strong. There is no time to come home between rehearsal and concert. Remind Mr Coates by telephone on Sunday morning at nine o'clock to pack not merely what he needs for rehearsal but also what he needs for the afternoon concert. Also remind him re taking music he needs. Ask him if he wishes you to come to rehearsal and stay over concert. Consult with him about all these details before he goes to Eastbourne so you get his wishes exactly.

Monday Nov 27th *Meistersinger* somewhere. Instructions as usual.

Thursday Nov 30th Rehearsal and concert in Manchester. Inquire of Ibbs and Tillett times of same. If the rehearsal is at 10am, Mr C will have to leave London the night before. [scored through, 'Rehearsal at 1.30, concert at 7.30. Free Trade Hall' added]. Pack his programme. Train, money etc. Find out name of hotel in Manchester. Arrange a private rehearsal in London with Madame Slobodskaya if Mr C wishes it (through Ibbs and Tillett). This should be arranged for either Tuesday afternoon Nov 28th or on morning of 29th or before 23rd. Anyway, sometime when Mr C is not so rushed. Also find out at what time Madame Slobodskaya will be at the orchestral rehearsal in Manchester, so that Mr C knows how to arrange his rehearsing. She has been asked to come for the beginning of the rehearsal but she may not be able to do so. (If the private rehearsal in London with Slobodskaya is on Tuesday 28th, make sure that Mr C will get back from the *Meistersinger* performance in time!)

Secretary's General Instructions. Please read through as there are many additions.

First day give Mr Coates's address and telephone number to:
Harold Holt Concert Management, 3 Clifford Street, New Bond Street, W1
Ibbs and Tillett, 124 Wigmore Street, W1
Robert Parker, Director Metropolitan Opera Company, Bechstein Hall, Brook Street, W1
BBC Mr Kenneth Wright, Broadcasting House, W1
Royal Philharmonic Society, 19 Berners Street, W1
W J Riley Esq., Liverpool Philharmonic Society, Bluecoat Chambers, 20 School Lane, Church Street, Liverpool.
Miss Lilian Bayliss, The Old Vic, Royal Victoria Hall, Waterloo Road, SE1
Lawrance Collingwood, 1a, Stonebridge Park, NW10
Mrs Hilda Lindars, Duff House, 43a Acacia Road, St John's Wood NW8, asking her to give it also to her husband's office.
Talbot Holland Esq., Messrs Williams, Stoker, Worssam and Holland, 9 Bedford Row, WC1
Fred Gaisberg, His Master's Voice Gramophone Company, Hayes, Middlesex

Remind Mr Coates to pay his weekly rent in advance, five guineas a week. This should be sent to the agents Messrs Warmington & Co, 19 Berkeley Street, Piccadilly, W1. Also must pay his food and laundry bill week by week to the housekeeper. Check all bills and see that Mr C does not get overcharged. At the end of stay must pay agents for making inventory, cleaning certain curtains, light and heat bill. From these last bills is to be deducted £5 which was paid as deposit on entry. Look at agreement and see that all is correct. If Mr C wishes to leave and go elsewhere, he must give a week's notice. If he stays the whole time, give agents a week's notice anyway before the last week. Notice to be given in writing.

See to it that all concert and opera fees due are paid. You will find fees due on programmes. Put cheques in bank.

After each concert, when clothes are dried, look if they are very creased. If not too bad, then hang trousers in wardrobe trunk over bars where they press themselves. Coat to be hung in cupboard on hanger. If they are too bad, take coat and trousers to nearest valeting place and have them pressed. Do not have suits pressed unless necessary, as too much pressing ruins suits. Pressing is chiefly necessary after a provincial performance when suit has been packed wet.

Always keep an eye on Mr Coates' linen and make sure beforehand that he always has enough shirts, collars, vests, pants, handkerchiefs, white waistcoats etc for whatever concerts and rehearsals are coming up. For rehearsal Mr C wears tennis shirts. Please do his laundry list week by week so that you have full control. Always see that he has glycerine and blackcurrant lozenges for his throat and eau de Cologne toilet water to rub himself down after rehearsals and concerts.

Always give Mr Coates a copy of his programme when he goes to rehearsal, especially when concerts are in the provinces.

On concert days Mr C likes, instead of dinner, just a light meal (a couple of eggs or some fish and salad). Ask him about it in the morning and arrange with the housekeeper. See that she is punctual on concert days so Mr C does not get rushed before a concert. Housekeeper should count these two light meals as the equivalent of one dinner and not charge extra. Try to arrange this.

Make a note of Mr Coates' social engagements and see that he keeps them. Write them in his diary but also remind him.

Settle as soon as possible which date, November 9th or 18th, he will do a second performance of *Tsar Sultan* at the Old Vic. Remind Mr C that space for a conductor is very small at Old Vic and to ask Mr Collingwood whether there will be enough room for him.

Fill in on programmes where missing, times of rehearsals, times of concerts, name of hall, name of hotel if any, times of trains, name of station leaving from and all information as per detailed instructions.

Agents fees are due for the following concerts to: Ibbs and Tillett for Liverpool, Huddersfield and Manchester. Harold Holt for Liverpool, Royal Philharmonic, London, Eastbourne and Beecham concert. See that Mr Coates sends the necessary cheque after each concert. Agents fees in both cases are 10%. No agents fees are due for the opera engagement nor for the BBC. Performance at Sadler's Wells Mr C does free of charge but they have offered him ten guineas for his expenses.

You will find in file address for cheque to be sent to composer Shostakovich plus directions. This is for BBC to pay. Give it to Mr Wright. Mr Coates must also send cheques to Russia on his own as follows:

1) Tongsin, Leningrad. For Shostakovich for having music copied
2) Tongsin, Moscow. For translation of *Pepys* [Coates's opera *Samuel Pepys*]. All information necessary in Katja's German letter to me, which is clipped to group of papers marked 're Shostakovich'. Also read instructions on title page 're Shostakovich'.

Sometime Mr Coates must see Sir Thomas Beecham and speak to him about Minolfi and Lanskroy. Lanskroy's repertoire is in file if needed.

Remind Mr C that he wants a full score of *Rosenkavalier*. Get this for him (hire) and return when he has finished with it.

At anytime that Mr C leaves London, see that you have his address in case anything urgent crops up.

In all things you must be Mr Coates' memory. He is too busy with his music to think of details.

If Mr Coates conducts any extra concerts, find out whether these are to be broadcast. If yes, then write at once to the Gramophone Company for the necessary permission re broadcasting (see letter to Fred Gaisberg in file). I was not able, in my letter about this to Gaisberg, to give him definite dates of opera performances in the provinces, nor the second performance of *Tsar Sultan.* If these definite dates should be required for broadcasting permission, send the exact list of dates immediately to Gramophone Company and ask for permission. If I get answer from Gaisberg re this permission for the concerts Mr C has at present, I will clip it to my letter to Gaisberg in file. If therefore you do not find this answer, it means that none has been received. Get in touch with Gramophone Company at once and ask them to send it to you. If Mr C should have any performance of his broadcast without permission, he loses his royalties from the Company.

Ask for all letters received during the day as Mr Coates may forget to tell you about them.

Mr Coates must sometime see Thomas Fairbairn re performances of *Elijah* two weeks in February. Address of Fairbairn is 51 Queen's Road, St John's Wood. Telephone Princess 2141.

Mr C must try to arrange BBC concert for Italian conductor Maestro Rito Selvaggi, address Signor Direttore Rito Selvaggi, Istituto Musicale Pergolesi, Varese, Provinzia di Varese, Italy

Mr Coates should see Mr Arthur Mason, the London representative of the Australian Broadcasting Commission, address 7 Morshead Mansions, Maida Vale. Telephone Abercorn 4457. Mason offered Mr C a two-month engagement of radio concerts in Australia for October and November. Mr C had to refuse as already engaged. He should, however, see Mason with a view to future times and to keep up friendly relations. Mason is a great admirer of Mr C, suggest Mr C asks him to lunch.

List of works for making programmes is in big envelope in trunk. Also driving licence. If Mr C drives a car, see that he has his licence with him. When Mr C returns to Italy, please pack all the papers I have sent as I need these for my files.

CHAPTER NINETEEN

Concerts, Artists and Auditionees: 1940–49

As Malcolm Sargent wrote in his foreword to Robert Elkin's wartime book tracing the history of the Queen's Hall, 'London, and music, and England are still with us, flourishing far more than we could have imagined or dared to hope'. The major casualty in London's musical life was this very hall, destroyed by German bombers on 10 May 1941, and a venue which had been popular with audiences and familiar to musicians since its opening on 25 November 1893. When war was declared at the beginning of September 1939, the Prom season was curtailed, the BBC Symphony Orchestra left London for Bristol (and later Bedford when Bristol proved equally vulnerable to bombing raids), and all public music-making ground to a halt. But after a month, as far as music was concerned, the phoney war came to an end when two Ibbs and Tillett artists gave concerts, Lamond in a recital at the Wigmore Hall (7 October) and Myra Hess as soloist in Beethoven's Fourth Piano Concerto with the LSO the following day. Two days later, on 10 October 1939, Hess launched her series of National Gallery Concerts which became not only a morale booster for performers and audience alike, but virtually the mainstay of wartime-London's musical life. The haste with which Hess undertook this project meant that she had to cancel an American tour, which left her agent there, Annie Friedberg, most displeased. The help of Ibbs and Tillett was enlisted and the following lengthy telegram sent, probably by Emmie, in two parts (British Library Cup.404.c.1 to 1/11).

> MYRA DEEPLY DISTRESSED YOUR ATTITUDE IN PRESENT SITUATION STOP BEG YOU REALISE HER PRESENT WORK OF NATIONAL IMPORTANCE PRESSURE BEING BROUGHT BEAR FROM HIGHER QUARTERS FOR HER REMAIN HERE AS NO ONE CAN TAKE HER PLACE STOP SUGGEST YOU COMMUNICATE SOCIETIES GIVING THEM OPTION CANCELLING NEW YEAR DATES OR WAITING EARLY DECEMBER MYRAS FINAL DECISION STOP PLEASE HANDLE MATTER YOUR USUAL DIPLOMACY STRESSING MYRAS UNIQUE POSITION HERE AND TREMENDOUS NEED FOR MUSIC SHE IS SATISFYING IN COUNTRYS EMERGENCY STOP IN ANY CASE MYRA PREPARED COMPENSATE YOUR LOSS IBBS AND TILLETT

As the *Times* reported on the day of the 1000th concert in July 1943,

> The concerts were born of a combination of ideas in the minds of several persons who were anxious to restart the musical life of the country, which had been brought to a complete standstill by the near approach of war … The persons met, the ideas were pooled, the authorities were approached, and from a room in Wigmore Street, well known to musicians, the plan was launched … Miss Emmie Bass dealt with the details of organisation from the room in Wigmore Street … And so the concerts began which have done for chamber music what the Proms have done for orchestral music.

It took only two months for the *Musical Times* to end its first report about them with the words 'these concerts have already become an institution'. Crucially they were held daily at lunchtime (some of them repeated later in the afternoon but these were rarely as full), attracting many working people and serving men and women on leave, soon becoming both popular and renowned. A key player in their organization was the composer and musicologist Howard Ferguson (a near neighbour to Hess in Hampstead), but Emmie Bass from Ibbs and Tillett was also seconded to the Executive Committee.

According to Ferguson, 'Programmes were planned about a month in advance by Myra and myself … They were then passed to Messrs Ibbs and Tillett, the concerts agents, who booked the artists for us and made all the arrangements for printing and advertising'. A review of the concerts was printed in 1944 to mark their fifth anniversary, including a description of the agency's involvement.

> When programmes have been planned, they are handed to Messrs Ibbs & Tillett, the concert agents, who book all the artists and make arrangements for the printing and advertising. This side of the organization entails an enormous amount of detailed work; and a very real debt of gratitude is owed to Messrs Ibbs & Tillett – and in particular to Miss Bass, who looks after the Gallery work – for the faithful and patient care they have devoted to carrying out the minutest wishes of the organizers since the concerts began. Their representative, Mr Worman, has been a tower of strength at each day's performance at the Gallery, where his quiet efficiency and devotion have made him invaluable to performers and organizers alike.

According to Hess's biographer Marian McKenna, the agency received a weekly fee of ten guineas for its work on the National Gallery Concerts. Promising young performers were given the opportunity to appear alongside established musicians, initially for no fee but after a while all received a standard 'expense fee' of five guineas regardless of musical standing, with the exception of Myra Hess, who never took a fee for any of her 146 appearances. Ticket prices were affordable to the audiences, which, says Ferguson, varied in number between 200 and 1750 according to 'war news, the weather, the type of programmes offered (a solo pianist drew more than a string quartet, and a singer less than either), the eminence of the performer, and even the day of the week'. Not all the events were infected by the gloomy mood of wartime, for early in 1940 the Director of the National Gallery, Kenneth Clark, directed a performance of Haydn's *Toy Symphony*. Based around the Griller String Quartet (now officially the RAF's own string quartet), the other performers included Hess and Irene Scharrer playing the cuckoos 'in widely differing interpretations' (*Picture Post*, 20 January 1940). Benno Moiseiwitsch playing the triangle ('and put so much vigour into his part that he dropped his stick'), Denise Lassimonne and William Murdoch the drums, Elena Gerhardt the tambourine ('they played where they could, laughed where they couldn't'), and the three pianists Eileen Joyce, Kathleen Long, and Cyril Smith the toy trumpets ('they started off in deadly earnest, but they got breathless, began to laugh, and so did the audience'). By the time the concerts ended on 10 April 1946 they numbered 1698 with an even division among pianists and string players (238 and 236 respectively), 64 wind players, 157 singers, 24 string quartets and 56 other groups, 13 orchestras, 15 choirs, 24 conductors, while audience numbers, which totalled 824,152, produced an acceptable average of 485 for each concert. Over £10000 from the proceeds was paid to the Musicians' Benevolent Fund, who duly honoured Hess with a 'Tribute of Gratitude' at a dinner held on 14 June 1945 at the Savoy Hotel. She was made a Dame of the British Empire (DBE) in the 1941 Birthday Honours List for her services to British music (Queen Elizabeth had been an early supporter of the concerts). As a token of her gratitude, Myra Hess presented John and Emmie (now Tillett since their marriage on 10 April 1941) with a small album of photographs taken by Ronald Procter at the 500th concert on 14 August 1941, a recital she gave herself. The pictures appear to trace the eventual successful outcome of an incident involving running repairs to the strings of the Steinway piano, with a little help from a member of the audience. The extent of the support, which Hess received from the Tilletts in keeping the concerts going, is clear from her handwritten inscription on the flyleaf which reads:

> National Gallery August 14th 1941 500th concert: To my very dear John and Emmie, to whom I owe a very, very great deal for the success of our historical adventure; in fact I couldn't have realised this dream without you. These concerts have made my whole career worthwhile, and I don't even mind being a pianist as long as you both look after me. Your devoted Myra.

As for the Proms, after abandoning the end of the 1939 season, the BBC prevaricated about promoting the next one until it was too late to book the Queen's Hall from its owners Chappells. Instead, Henry Wood entered into an uneasy business relationship with the impresario Keith Douglas (a man of wealth who could afford to indulge his passion for music, even to the extent of conducting the LSO on its wartime tours of the provinces – see Appendix 6) and Owen Mase, formerly of the BBC's Music Department. Douglas was also Honorary Secretary of the Royal Philharmonic Society (and promoted the Proms through this Society to avoid entertainments tax), and organizer of the hospital concerts of the ISM. John Tillett's help was sought largely in the matter of soloists for the Proms. The 1940 season was billed as 'Sir Henry Wood's 46th and Farewell Season', which transpired to be a premature description. Douglas also ran them for the 1941 season, when they transferred to the Royal Albert Hall, but a year later the BBC had resumed its responsibility, much to Henry Wood's relief. For two seasons Douglas had done everything he could to keep costs to a minimum, including a reduction in fees for soloists (which in turn must have had repercussions for Ibbs and Tillett), introducing only a few new works in 1940, while none at all in 1941. A further change took place in 1941 when, for the first time in the history of the Proms, Wood agreed to share the conducting, directing one half himself and giving the other to Basil Cameron. On the occasion of Wood's 75th birthday (3 March 1944) a celebratory concert was organized at the Royal Albert Hall (25 March). It was followed by what proved to be his last season, and even that had to be abandoned after three weeks due to attacks by flying bombs. The concerts were transferred to Bedford Corn Exchange, from where many were broadcast by the BBC Symphony Orchestra, but Wood did not see out this Golden Jubilee season, for he died on 19 August 1944. On 15 March 1944, Wood posted one of his last letters to John Tillett.

> I am sure you will appreciate how the delay in acknowledgement of your kind birthday greetings has vexed us, but at the same time I know you will understand how hard-pressed we have been, and still are, with the extraordinary avalanche of expressions of kind wishes on the occasion of my birthday, so please accept my warm thanks for your remembrances of me.
>
> I need not tell you how sorry I am that, so far, you do not appear in connection with Management or arranging concerts and so on in connection with my Jubilee Promenade Concerts year, but you will see only too well that the *Daily Telegraph* Concert [25 March] has not been in my hands, and that the Promenade Concerts take their place, as they should do, under the management of the BBC.
>
> I would at this time, like to tell you how much I appreciate the happy association which goes back to the early days of Festivals, and that during the many years of Promenade Concerts, during which we have been so closely associated in connection with the engagements of artists, I shall always remember with gratitude your ready response and help to any suggestion I may have offered – indeed to sum it all up, I value our long association, not only on the business side, but for the years of friendship and kindness it has established between us.
>
> Believe me, with love (from Jessie as well),
> yours affectionately
> Henry J Wood

Music was also sustained during the war by the Carnegie Trust and by the creation of CEMA (Council for the Encouragement of Music and the Arts). This not only organized concerts (often in factory canteens) but also, for two years through the Pilgrim Trust and then through the Treasury, gave financial support to orchestras and music clubs around the country, and proved to be the forerunner of the post-war Arts Council of Great Britain. Ibbs and Tillett worked with the Carnegie Trust and Pilgrim Trust/CEMA when managing tours by the LSO under the auspices of both bodies, and used their own solo artists whenever possible. The orchestra's programmes between December 1940 and May 1944 (see Appendix 6) reveal a gruelling touring schedule of virtually daily concerts, which, given wartime travelling conditions, must have taxed the players' strengths. Another organization was ENSA (Entertainments National Service Association), which had a classical music division and, from 1943, a symphony orchestra with soloists' fees set at a standard three guineas. Solo recitals were also managed by Ibbs and Tillett, with Moiseiwitsch and Solomon being frequent favourites at the National Sunday League recitals on Sunday afternoons at the Palladium in Argyll Street in London's West End. The proceeds of such events were frequently donated to wartime charities, such as Clementine Churchill's Red Cross 'Aid to Russia' Fund and the Duke of Gloucester's Red Cross and St John Appeal. The same charities were beneficiaries of the proceeds of a concert managed by Ibbs and Tillett and given at the Royal Albert Hall on 7 June 1943 as a tribute to Rachmaninov, who had died three months earlier. Henry Wood conducted the LSO, and Moiseiwitsch played an excessively taxing programme of both the Second and Third Piano Concertos and the *Paganini Variations.*

Sadler's Wells was the first to resume operatic performances with *Faust* on 30 September 1939 with a half-sized orchestra but a full cast of principals. Initially performances were restricted to Saturday afternoons (*Cavalleria rusticana*, *Marriage of Figaro*, *Madam Butterfly*, and *Il trovatore* followed *Faust*) but then Owen Mase, under whose management the season was given, added a second one during the week (on Thursdays), and a further one on Saturday evenings by November of that year.

The BBC had a dreadful breakdown in public relations in their efforts to provide music at the start of the war. It was 'as if a few harassed officials had fled to the country, snatching up a box or two of records and the band parts of the first dozen light orchestral pieces that came to hand … Needing the refreshment of fine music, we found a cinema organist fixed in his everlasting seat,' wrote W.R. Anderson. The BBC was further embarrassed by having already announced that 'arrangements for meeting a state of emergency had been made far ahead', but it certainly did not seem that way for a month or two. By the beginning of November 1939, the BBC had mended its ways and public concerts began in Bristol, though only the second half (an hour's duration) was broadcast. Travel restrictions were preventing the appearances of foreign artists as soloists in concerts, except for those who had fled to the UK before the outbreak of war. Appropriately enough, therefore, it was Myra Hess who was the choice of solo pianist for the occasion of this first concert, for which the BBC Symphony Orchestra (initially decimated by the loss to war of 40 players) was now settled at a playing strength of 90. Through the darkest years of 1940 and 1941, Bristol remained their home, but in July 1941 the orchestra moved to Bedford. The working relationship between Ibbs and Tillett and the BBC in Bristol, and the *modus operandi* in the music profession brought about by the uncertainty of the times, is illustrated by two letters from Emmie Bass to Arthur Wynn. The roots of Emmie's legendary watchful attitude throughout her working life to the costs of communication on behalf of the firm, by whatever means, may well lie here:

> Since the increase in postage, all the letters from the BBC have been coming to us under one cover. That is quite in order so far as letters addressed to this firm are concerned, and we are returning the compliment, but in the case of letters addressed to artists care of us for forwarding (particularly when they are artists whose business we do not look after), while we admire the BBC's National Economy Campaign, we feel it is not quite right that it should be at our expense at 2½d a time!! Perhaps, therefore, you would be so kind as to ask your Post Department to stamp the envelopes as heretofore, when letters are addressed personally to artists care of this firm for forwarding. (4 May 1940)

> Herewith we are sending you a list of artists who can be called upon at short notice for BBC engagements at the London Studio, together with a supplementary list giving those who are not available from tomorrow, Thursday, until Monday next inclusive. On Saturday next we will send you a further list of artists not available on Tuesday, Wednesday and Thursday of next week, and shall continue to send you this information twice a week for as long as may require it. When communicating with us in regard to fixing artists at an hour or two's notice, it would be a great help if you could give us the option of two names in the order in which you would prefer they are used. Presumably in the case of Singers and Instrumentalists where an Accompanist is required, you will wish the artists to supply their own. You may like to keep in mind that both the Fleet Street Choir and the London Madrigal Group can be mustered in an hour or two. (19 June 1940)

Exactly like insurance companies, the contractual relationship between agents and artists were changed upon the outbreak of war, so Ibbs and Tillett promptly sent a letter to all its artists under contract advising them of how the changed circumstances of the international situation would affect work generally. There was also the curious fact that they should 'please note that until further notice these offices will be closed between 1 and 2pm', apparently a state of war meant that lunch hours were now official. The rest of their letter, as in this example addressed to the baritone Roy Henderson, ran as follows:

> As you are doubtless aware, an outbreak of war automatically cancels all existing contracts between Concert promoters and Artists.
>
> Although we feel sure it will be the desire of many Concert Societies to carry on as soon as the Government raises the embargo on public entertainments, we are now writing to ask you to regard as cancelled any engagements made through this Agency for the present and approaching season, and we will advise you later if it is found possible to reinstate any bookings whatsoever.
>
> Hoping that the time may not be far distant when Concert activities can resume their normal course,
> We remain,
> Yours sincerely
> Ibbs and Tillett
> (6 September 1939)

Choral music was an instant casualty of wartime circumstances, because their infrastructure was rendered unbalanced by the conscription of male singers, their concerts incurred the loss of large performing venues, and soloists encountered difficulty travelling out of London. Orchestral concerts, on the other hand, fared better. The Courtauld–Sargent and Royal Philharmonic Society concerts were soon resumed by the London Philharmonic Orchestra during the late autumn (Brosa and Cassadó played the Brahms double concerto under Sargent at a Courtauld–Sargent concert on 9 December

1940), and this orchestra toured to various provincial towns and cities The LSO was booked by Jay Pomeroy for Sunday afternoon concerts at his Cambridge Theatre, and the Stoll Theatre (now demolished) was the venue for popular mass concerts of so-called Music for the People.

Throughout the war, Hess produced irresistible attractions at the National Gallery with agency soloists and ensembles, some of them especially put together for the occasion. A new venue for orchestral concerts became Sadler's Wells on Sunday afternoons, while the Wigmore Hall continued its recital programmes. New works from Tippett (Concerto for Double String Orchestra), Berkeley (Divertimento), and Britten (Serenade for Tenor, Horn, and Strings) were heard in 1943, and an example of an Ibbs and Tillett promotion was a Schubert recital on 30 April 1944, with Clifford Curzon playing piano solos in the first half, and Britten accompanying Pears singing *Die Schöne Müllerin* in the second. In the early days of the war, Betty Humby and Marjorie Glock were the prime movers of a scheme designed to bring music to evacuees, predominantly by performing at afternoon tea-time in cathedrals in the south and west of the country, with extra morning concerts for children. Harrow Philharmonic Society managed Haydn's *Creation* in February 1940 (with Ibbs and Tillett soloists Elsie Suddaby, Jan van der Gucht, and Norman Walker). Meanwhile, in order to perform Brahms's *Requiem*, the Surbiton and District Co-operative Musical Society advertised desperately for choral singers to come to their Friday night rehearsals, conducted by Michael Tippett, in the Tolworth Branch Hall. What seemed to become a fairly regular event (at least in London), was the precursor of today's scratch performances of familiar choral works. Harold Darke often arranged these communal sing-alongs with Handel's *Messiah* or (on 4 May 1940 at Central Hall, Westminster) a 'drop in and sing' *Mass in B Minor* by Bach (with the LSO and soloists Suddaby, Greene, and Walker from the agency). The struggle to keep choral singing going was, in one instance at least, imaginatively solved when the Chislehurst Caves Choral Society gave their first subterranean concert on 20 December 1941. Shortly before the Queen's Hall was destroyed in May 1941 the Bach Choir held its annual *St Matthew Passion* (morning and afternoon of Sunday 30 March) with Suddaby, Jarred, Greene, Henderson, Jones, and Parsons, conducted by Reginald Jacques.

Despite constant problems Ibbs and Tillett continued, where possible, to supply artists throughout the country. The Liverpool Philharmonic Society kept their Thursday and Sunday evening series alive during the war years, with such agency artists as Moiseiwitsch, Solomon, Louis Kentner, Colin Horsley, Joan Cross, Mary Jarred, Parry Jones, Heddle Nash, Peter Pears, Isobel Baillie, Clifford Curzon, Roy Henderson, Eileen Joyce, Moura Lympany, Noel Mewton-Wood, Albert Sammons, Denis Matthews, Max Rostal, Linda Parker, Dino Borgioli, Gladys Ripley, Norman Walker, and Cyril Smith. In Birmingham, the dramatic renaming of the City of Birmingham (Emergency) Orchestra produced Saturday afternoon concerts at the Midland Institute. Elsewhere the Hallé Orchestra gave Sunday afternoon concerts in the Paramount cinema in Manchester, the Free Trade Hall having first been taken over by the Government and used as a store, then gutted by fire during an air raid on 22 December 1940. Wood, Beecham, and Sargent conducted, and the orchestra continued to travel to their usual haunts, such as Bradford and Blackpool, usually thanks to financial subsidy from CEMA. When the City Council permitted cinemas to open on Sundays in 1941, the concerts were moved to the Opera House, and later in the war (1944–45 season), when Wednesday evening subscription concerts were added to the Sunday afternoon popular concerts, two venues were used, the King's Hall in Belle Vue and the Albert Hall in Peter Street. For these 24 concerts the agency acted for pianists Curzon, Smith, Matthews, Solomon, Iso Elinson, and Margaret Maddison, violinists Albert Sammons and Henry Holst, and for singers Baillie, Jarred, Ripley, Pears, Olive Groves, Parry Jones, Victoria Sladen, Marjorie Thomas, Norman Walker, and Tom Williams. By now Barbirolli, returned for good from New York, was in his second season as principal conductor but Coates, Sargent, and Constant Lambert also appeared. The seasonal prospectuses for the Choral and Orchestral Union of Glasgow show an average of 26 concerts for the three seasons between 1943 and 1946, doubling the length of the concert season from 1942, and reflecting the defiantly optimistic view of the committee. To mark the 1844 centenary of the Choral Union, a four-day choral festival (consisting of *Elijah*, *Creation*, *Gerontius*, and *Messiah*) was planned for the last week of the first of these seasons. Ibbs and Tillett were much in demand for this organization's musical activities. For the 1943–44 season alone, they represented pianists Curzon, Elinson, Joyce, Lympany, Moiseiwitsch, Irene Kohler, Lamond, Solomon, Kentner, violinists Jean Pougnet, Ida Haendel, Kersey, and singers Joan Cross, Eva Turner, Ripley, Widdop, Lumsden, Suddaby, Parsons, and Borgioli.

Seaside resorts such as Torquay, Bournemouth and other towns on the south coast issued statements, that it was 'business as usual', while the Municipal Concerts in Burnley were resumed on a trial basis. On behalf of the Torquay Musical Festival, the agency wrote to one of their harpists, Gwendolen Mason. Once again, the letter illustrates how late (just nine days before the first concert) such approaches were made, though judging by pencilled annotations in the margin, telephone attempts were being made to contact others ('away till Sunday', 'no reply'), so perhaps the booked harpist (presumably for the orchestra and not as soloist) had withdrawn:

> May we ask you to kindly let us know by return whether you are free to take part in two Orchestral Concerts at the above Festival on Friday afternoon October 27th and Saturday evening October 28th, and in which case what inclusive fee you would like us to quote. The concert on October 27th will be conducted by [Anatole] Fistoulari and on the 28th by Stanford Robinson. (18 October 1944)

Of letters written to Ibbs and Tillett during the war years, only those from three artists have survived, from the composer Frank Bridge, pianist Artur Schnabel, and conductor Sir Henry Wood. The Reid Orchestra in Edinburgh soldiered on during these difficult times, and evidently Frank Bridge was invited by the agency to conduct a concert. Negotiations must have come to nothing as the concert under discussion was eventually conducted by Leslie Heward, though more significantly Bridge may have decided against the idea for health reasons, as his death took place barely three months later in January 1941 at the age of 61:

> I have an Ibbs & T.[illett] communication this morning (of Oct. 16) respecting the Reid Symphony Orchestra, Edinburgh, Sat[urday] aft[ernoon] November 30th. Please help me. If this is not your department, forgive me. I don't know what the Edinburgh Fares are, nor what time is involved for rehearsals etc. I only know the RSO is, or was an amateur organization which Donald Tovey ran. To get to concrete matters, I want a sum of Twenty five Guineas clear of all expenses. Perhaps you would very kindly work this out for me & if this eng'[agemen]t is or is not in your hands to ask for information as to size of orchestra & kind of programme.
>
> You see, nothing being known of the position, whether Mr X is not now available (probably interned!!) & preliminary programme already announced (perhaps). Present conditions may deem it

necessary to have only an orch. of strings. Only one wants to know! In any case, as will be noted by this reply, I am "disposed to entertain" etc. All best wishes. (18 October 1940)

This error has crept in on many previous occasions, but kindly note I am Frank Bridge and not Dr Frank Bridge. As you know, evil report is difficult to catch up with, but a completely harmless one takes almost as much effort. It does indeed. No reply needed, thank you. (23 October 1940)

Schnabel's two letters from his exile in America, the first written before that country entered the war, the second two years after, give a fascinating view of events seen from afar and reveal his humanity, helplessness, and his genuine concern for his fellow artists.

Dearest Mr Tillett,
It is long, too long, since my last letter to you was written. My long silence will, I am certain, not lead you to wrong conclusions about my attitude to dear friends. They are always in my mind, my thoughts and wishes are always addressed to them, and I am quite confident that they never doubt the character and stability of my feelings towards them. I am of course just as confident that they have not forgotten their old friends.

It is not too easy here to imagine a mode of existence created by terror and horror, an adjustment to incessant dangers, difficulties and sufferings never before divined, a pursuit of one's work inmidst of a general struggle to resist a general attack on values that made life worth living. It does, on the other hand, not demand much imagination to presume that the comfort and satisfaction produced by successful resistance to the aggressive and destructive forces must be something absolutely different from the automatic, the routine "comfort" of a society not exposed to such tasks and tests as you have got to conquer. I don't mean to criticise people living in ordinary conditions for not developing or showing exceptional qualities. It might, however, be expected that the display of such exceptional qualities elsewhere would inspire the well-protected people to think a bit more and more seriously about some defects in ordinary conditions. There are still too many who conceive that everything is alright as long as they personally are not in trouble and their own affairs not chaotic. How to convince them without coercion that their conception is a primitive fallacy as well as a sign of hopeless confusion is, to be true, a complex, crucial problem.

We live here [New York] as quiet as possible and keep aloof from the exhibits of a mongrelised civilisation. I don't perform in public this season. I am composing and giving a few lessons. The sons are married, one has a sweet little girl, both are just sufficiently active, though not always in adequate jobs, to afford a very modest living. My European colleagues, who formerly loved to come to USA for short tours, are now, as permanent residents for obvious reasons, not quite so happy. Music and musicians have been spoilt in Europe; here they get a more robust treatment.

Our hopes, yours and mine and those of multitudes, are surely identical, and in the spirit of these hopes Thérèse and I are sending you and all connected with you our warmest greetings. (19 December 1940)

My dear Mr Tillett,
I ought to have written this letter long, long ago. My keen desire and intention to write you has always been, and will always be, present. I myself feel therefore somewhat astonished that I did not write you sooner than today. Looking for the true reason why I did not, I find still the same old one, either too lazy or too busy. Pardon for the delay.

I was very happy with your letter, bringing me good news about yourself and Mrs Tillett and was very interested in your report of the adjustment of public musical life to the truly unusual conditions created by the war (where it is physically as close as to England). I think it absolutely admirable how it is done. That much of it does not compare with the 'perfection' of pre-war days is perhaps only wholesome. This (alleged) 'perfection' has been overemphasised – and overrated too – probably to the detriment of music itself, which is always in danger if musicians count more than music. If now one learns that this is by no means true, it might be a gain which, somehow, expresses the same spirit that appears in actually everything done in your country. Thanks to that spirit we can in future hope for a period in which men may try to see in other men friends, partners, collaborators rather than enemies, accomplices, customers, suckers, or slaves. Lack of confidence, moderation and discipline – lack created by almost total subordination to utilitarianism – was, I think, the principal cause of the horrible destruction we have got to suffer and, worse still, also to execute.

> Reconstruction will be our next task. Without having liberated ourselves of distrust, violence and inconstancy, we shall hardly have a good chance towards the desired change.
>
> We have been quite well and active here, for now already four years. Our mode of existence, in a hotel, with none of our belongings around us, is still rather provisional. I have been playing, teaching, composing (the most cherished pastime) and even lecturing. The outcome of this last named attempt was a little book, *Music and the line of most resistance*, which, I believe, is also circulated in Britain. I have done also some recording which, as you certainly know, is now stopped by a ban decreed by the organisation I had to join in order to be allowed the making of records. Curious!! Music here has a wide market, too wide probably for some of its more sensitive products.
>
> I have not seen Sir Thomas [Beecham] and our old (and now titled) friend Betty [Humby] since the early summer. At that time they seemed thoroughly happy, capricious and enterprising as ever. Sir Robert (Mayer) is now back in London and has, I am sure, already given you details in telling of the glint as well as the gloom of conditions here in regard to music. The news of Carl Flesch's lucky escape to Switzerland has presumably reached you months ago. It was a real relief when I learned of it. [Georg] Szell has arrived at the Metropolitan [Opera], where, in co-operation with Beecham and [Bruno] Walter, he is already acknowledged to have miraculously drawn some attention of the operagoers to the music of the show, a development proudly hailed as a revolution, and, greater miracle even, the voice stars, formerly the sole centre of attention, do not complain at all. Szell has, in spite of his very remarkable success, not yet been offered any of the several worthy conductor positions open in the last two years. Reasons for the preference of admittedly less good men are not obscure to the initiated ones. Quality is apparently not the most important requirement.
>
> I was very sorry to hear of the loss you have suffered by the passing away of your old comrade Mr Ibbs. I can imagine how you must feel everywhere in your work the absence of his kind personality. It is now almost five years since I have been last in London. I am absolutely confident that it will not take another five years until I shall be there again. I need not tell you how impatiently I am looking forward to that day. I anticipate the joy and satisfaction of my return to values for which I feel as much love as respect. Please remember me to all our mutual friends. I am thinking of them with the old attachment. (24 November 1943)

Meanwhile Sir Henry Wood, in a letter before his death three months later, was still recommending young artists to Ibbs and Tillett:

> My wife has just told me that Janet Howe has become one of your artists. I am glad and delighted for she has the makings, in my opinion, of becoming a very distinguished vocalist. Combined with a very musical mezzo-soprano voice, of great compass and evenness, she looks so well on the platform and has dramatic emotional feeling. We are both deeply interested in her career and at anytime I can help her, musically, don't be afraid to write and ask me. I don't want her to go in for grand opera yet, as the conditions are so bad for a refined vocalist – five or ten years solid concert work should be her goal, after that she can sing anything. I am really delighted that you have taken her up, for she is a delightful person to work with and I shall do all in my power to help her on every and all occasions. (23 May 1944)

Familiar names from the agency's list over the years were continuing to disappear. During the war years death claimed the singers John Coates and Dorothy Silk, pianist William Murdoch, and violinist Eda Kersey, while those from its early days such as the Czech violinist Jan Kubelik, singers Blanche Marchesi and Luisa Tetrazzini, and pianists Ernest Schelling, Paderewski and Rachmaninov were also no more. Meanwhile the wartime deaths of such influential conductors as Felix Weingartner, Hamilton Harty and Sir Henry Wood would impact on the activities of the company. Only one agency brochure has survived from the war years, the one for 1940–41; some pages have been added with handwritten names while other printed names are scored through. Due to paper shortages it is probable that this brochure, Emmie Tillett's own copy judging by the evidence of her initials on its front cover, was used for further years (exactly how many is hard to define), and it is reproduced in Appendix 5. Auditions were necessarily fewer because of the war, so this explains why there are barely a dozen names recorded in the last pages of this, the third and last of the audition books. One of those auditionees went on to enjoy a glittering career, another became one of the most memorable artists the agency ever had on its books.

Two contraltos had auditions on 12 April 1940 at Wigmore Hall, Winifred Ingham a singer with 'a promisingly fine voice, big and rich in quality but in need of more finesse', the other Ruth Freeman, 'well taught' by Blanche Marchesi and Miriam Licette, who had an 'excellent voice, rich and powerful'. Strangely it was Ingham's name pencilled into the brochure rather than that of the more refined Freeman. At Queen's Hall on 26 March 1941 John Tillett heard a 'tall [tenor] of good appearance, extensive compass, dramatic and lyric quality with experience in Lancashire and Yorkshire, a pupil of Norman Allin'. He sang an aria by Bach and the opening aria from Handel's *Messiah*. Tillett thought 'highly of his abilities, excellent voice, easy production, good head and middle registers, diction good, Handelian runs quite good'. His name was Thomas Thomas, but this was soon changed to Richard Lewis, for the entry in the brochure has the change pencilled in brackets. This was at about the same time that the soprano Mabel Ritchie changed her Christian name to Margaret, and Lisa Perli gave up further thoughts of opera, and reverted once again to her oratorio name of Dora Labbette. John Tillett did not hang around in promoting Lewis, who went on to make his debut later that same year with the Carl Rosa Opera Company as Count Almaviva in Rossini's *Barber of Seville* and Lieutenant Pinkerton in *Madam Butterfly*. The accompanist at the audition also made a good impression, Albert Knowles, who had, with Lewis, come down to London from Manchester for the occasion. He then played for another Allin pupil, the soprano Edna Hobson, also taken on by Tillett. Her voice had 'dramatic quality, extensive compass', she was 'a big woman' and sang Purcell and Mendelssohn with 'an excellent dramatic voice, vibrant and full of colour, equally good in lyric and dramatic music'. Both singers and their accompanist could be 'safely recommended' by Ibbs and Tillett. On 19 May 1941, the mezzo-soprano Enid Garden (currently appearing in Lehar's *Land of Smiles*) was heard ('tall, young, and charming') and considered suited for miscellaneous concerts after her renditions of songs by Gretchaninov, Sibelius, Delilah's aria from Saint Saëns's opera (a surprising choice for a light voice), and a light song. It was another year before the next singer was heard, Joan Fullerton, a lyric soprano from North Wales, 'short but attractive', recommended by her teacher Isobel Baillie, 'whom she resembles greatly in parity of voice and style. Charming voice, easily produced, think highly of her abilities and can safely recommend her.' She sang Handel, Bridge, and Gluck at Wigmore Hall on 9 June 1942 and was duly taken on.

Only a month later, John Tillett arranged another audition, on 9 July 1942, the venue was, as usual, the Wigmore Hall. This time it was a contralto, who had also come down from the north-west to be heard. Her appearance was described as 'attractive', she sang 'Hark the echoing air', 'Then shall the eyes' and 'Come unto Him' (*Messiah*), and a song by Hugo Wolf. She had 'an excellent voice, even throughout, very good head register, warm and vibrant, good diction'. The compass of the voice was described as 'extensive'. Her teacher was Dr J.E. Hutchinson of Newcastle, whom she called 'Hutchy', and her name was Kathleen Ferrier. She had already begun to make a name for herself in and around her native town of Blackburn, and it was Malcolm Sargent who, having heard her in his Manchester hotel at 3 o'clock on the afternoon of 21 May 1942, advised her that she would need to move south to London in order to further her career, and, on

29 May, he followed up this advice with a promise that he would send a letter of recommendation to Ibbs and Tillett. Her diary entry for 9 July 1942 reads as follows: 'Wigmore Hall 2pm. Audition went off well. Decided to live in London! Phew!' After her encounter with John Tillett, she was offered engagements through the agency, and for the rest of her tragically short life, just over ten years more, she was never without work at the highest level. Emmie Tillett became a close friend, both professionally and socially (both women were talented water-colourists and formed a small, closely knit circle of painters). She was already busy with many dates arranged for her by CEMA before her Wigmore Hall audition, but her first engagement through Ibbs and Tillett was to sing in *Elijah* at Runcorn, Cheshire, on 23 December 1942 ('Engagement from Ibbs and Tillett – Whoopee!!', she wrote in her diary). The title role was sung by Roy Henderson, who was asked by John Tillett to report back to him on Ferrier's performance. Henderson, who subsequently became a close friend as well as her teacher and mentor, thought she had 'a good voice, but it was too dark, and she kept her nose buried in the score the whole time, terrified to look up. I told her she should learn her words and throw away the book'. She was also given a National Gallery concert, which turned out to be her only appearance in the series run by Myra Hess. It took place on 28 December 1942 and she was accompanied by Maurice Jacobson. Pianist Maria Donska began the concert with a March and an Impromptu by Schubert, Ferrier then gave her programme of songs by Brahms, Wolf, and an English group by Ivor Gurney, Stanford, Parry and Armstrong Gibbs, and to conclude Donska played Beethoven's Sonata Op.111. According to the concerts' archive held at the British Library (Cup.404.c.1 to 1/11), £21.8s.0d was received at a shilling a head from the audience of 428, among whom was the composer Lennox Berkeley, there at the request of Arthur Wynn of the BBC to make a report on Ferrier. He wrote:

> I heard the above at the National Gallery on December 28th. She has a fine and powerful voice of real contralto quality, and seemed to me an accomplished singer. Her intonation was on the whole very accurate and her diction was good. On the other hand I found her rather dull; her tone was monotonous. I cannot imagine that she could ever move one, though there is no doubt about her competence or the good quality of her voice. (28 December 1942)

Less than a month later, on 20 January 1943, Kathleen Ferrier did a Prom audition for the BBC, 'Letter re audition in Albert Hall. Gosh!', she wrote enthusiastically in her diary on 7 January. She sang Handel's 'Where'er you walk' and the aria 'Softly awakes my heart' from *Samson and Delilah* by Saint Saëns. The panel's report on her was even more qualified, not to say damning, and unsurprisingly she was turned down:

> Rich, clarinet-like quality voice, limited in range and technique at the moment. Good diction. A promising singer, but only suitable at present for small works such as Bach's songs from Schemelli's *Gesangbuch*. Sang the Saint Saëns completely without passion.

Ferrier's career, brief though it may have been, was nevertheless blessed by contact with a remarkable number of important musicians (particularly conductors and composers), artists, and managers. Whether by accident or design, she always seemed to be at the right place at the right time, and with people who, like a chain-link fence, passed her on to their colleagues. Fortunately the agency and its advisers also had more faith in her than others, and, as a result of a meeting with John Tillett on Wednesday 12 May 1943, she became a sole artist for Ibbs and Tillett. Chapter 21 is devoted to the career of this artist and her relationship with Ibbs and Tillett, while all surviving personal and business correspondence between them is located in Appendices 16–18. During the following winter season, the agency substituted Ferrier for the sick Astra Desmond in several concerts, and after one of them (a radio broadcast) the older singer wrote to congratulate her replacement, but not without the hint of a warning that, though down, she was by no means out:

> Dear Kathleen Ferrier
> I hear you deputised for me in Manchester this week, so it was with special interest that I listened to you this afternoon. After hearing your lovely voice and beautifully clear diction, I know that you will have compensated easily for any disappointment they may have felt in Manchester over my non-appearance.
>
> All good luck to you and if a greatly senior singer may be allowed a liberty! don't let the success you are having and will, I hope, have yet more abundantly, ever let you cease from studying. I have seen so many resting on their laurels and then fall by the wayside when youth begins to fade – the perpetual student lasts ever so much longer! Forgive this sermon! With my best wishes, Yours sincerely (16 February 1944)

Only two other auditions are recorded in the agency's record books as having taken place during the war, on 10 and 11 August 1943 when four singers were heard, sopranos Sylvia Petriss (also heard back in 1935) and Doreen Parry, together with contraltos Jeannie Mordue and Kathleen Kay, but, despite a variety of positive comments on each of them, only the last named found her way on to the books of the agency. Scraps of paper, which imply additions to the artists' prospectus for 1940 and beyond, include the names of the bass Hervey Alan as 'exceptionally good, a magnificent, virile voice and fine artist', but there is no date recording when he was heard. The name of the accompanist Viola Tunnard also appears, described as a pupil of Kathleen Long but with no further comment. Both Alan and Tunnard went on to enjoy illustrious careers as agency artists. John Tillett recorded only one other auditionee, the lyric soprano Rita Lynch, on 20 March 1947 at the Wigmore Hall, after which Emmie Tillett heard six singers in 1950, listed in Chapter 22.

A singer who spent 30 years on the books of Ibbs and Tillett was the Chesterfield-based bass-baritone John Dethick, who, after a brief time with Sadler's Wells, spent virtually his entire career on the northern circuit of choral societies and music clubs, with occasional forays down south or abroad. In a letter to the author (28 September 2002), his daughter Janet described John Dethick's dealings with Ibbs and Tillett:

> My father began his singing career when he was working in a railway wagon repair shop at Staveley near Chesterfield. As this was classed as a reserve occupation during the war, he was not called up to fight, and hence had many opportunities to stand in for full-time professionals. During the early 1940s my father had an audition with Sir Henry Wood with a view to finding out whether or not he should take up singing professionally. The audition was at the Blüthner Studios in Wigmore Street and, shortly before his death my father recalled that Wood said, 'You can congratulate yourself my boy, you've the best baritone voice I've heard since before the war', and immediately after I left him he called Ibbs and Tillett and told them about me.
>
> They were at that time the main concert agents in London. In 1943 they were sending me to deputise for singers who were in the Army. One weekend John Tillett rang Staveley works and asked me to go to Liverpool to sing in two performances of the *Messiah* with the Liverpool Philharmonic, conducted by Malcolm Sargent. The following weekend he phoned again asking me if I would go to Bolton on Saturday night to sing the *Messiah*, and to the King's Hall, Bellevue, Manchester on the Sunday afternoon, again with Sargent, and then on the Monday night up to Barrow-in-Furness for another performance of the *Messiah*. I was late for the rehearsal both at Liverpool and Manchester because during the war there were very few trains, and taxis were only allowed to travel so far beyond the city boundary. Isobel Baillie, who was the soprano soloist at

> Manchester and was concerned about my lateness, said to me, 'I told Dr Sargent that during the week you worked as a railway wagon repairer – Did I do right?' I sang for Dr Sargent on many occasions afterwards.
>
> In the 1970s I was still with Ibbs and Tillett, and they sent me to sing in Watford Town Hall with a choir from Ambassador College, and through them I was invited to sing both *Messiah* and *Elijah* in four cities in California on two separate occasions.

Britain's music-making emerged battered and bruised from the Second World War. Hess's National Gallery Concerts may not have attracted the critics, the programmes may have been very familiar, a few careers were made as a result of them, but the public turned out, and its response to chamber music was changed forever and for the better. As she herself said: 'The experience of war sharpened all of our faculties. It led to a re-evaluation of everything.' With peace restored to Europe and America by the summer of 1945, Myra Hess could travel to Holland, and Casals could return to England for a countrywide tour (joining Hess in London's Cambridge Theatre on 3 November). It turned out to be one of his last recitals in England, for he was soon to become disillusioned by the country's refusal to condemn or isolate his native Spain, still in the hands of the Fascist Franco. Repeated efforts were made to make him change his mind, the agency behind many of them, but to no avail. This reply (in a translation made by Ibbs and Tillett) was received from him to one such entreaty from John Tillett, the second, and last, letter received by the agency from Casals was written three years later to Emmie.

> Dear Friend,
> I hope you and Mrs Tillett are well and in good form for the coming season's work. It is sad that the matter which is so close to my heart has not yet been resolved – the cause of my separation from England! You can imagine with what impatience we await what UNO [United Nations Organisation] will have to say on Spain in the near future. Will they get us out of this terrible suspense which is wearing us down? For a matter which I have asked Milly to look after I should be grateful if you will transfer to her the sum of £1500 from the money which you are holding for me. I shall need it shortly. Thank you. I should like to say '*à bientôt*' but unfortunately this does not depend on me. With affectionate greetings to Mrs Tillett and yourself, dear Friend. (26 September 1947)

> Dear Friend,
> I thank you and Lady Wood for their renewed affectionate request on behalf of the Sir Henry Wood Society. Unfortunately I still cannot have the pleasure of saying 'yes'. Circumstances have regrettably not yet changed. Please convey my regrets and affectionate greetings to Lady Wood. Yes, dear friend, the Bach Festival [the first Prades Festival held in June 1950] was something of unique emotion. You would have been happy to have been here, and pleased me! (17 August 1950)

Solomon was once again on the touring road, and wrote to Emmie (calling her Miss Bass rather than Mrs Tillett) on 30 March 1946 'to acknowledge receipt of cheque for £126 re Kirkcaldy. And very many thanks for all your good wishes for my forthcoming tour.' Scotland was also the venue for the post-war renaissance of the music festivals, namely the first Edinburgh Festival in the autumn of 1947 under the stewardship of Rudolf Bing (covered in more detail later). Artur Schnabel, who had already made a triumphant return to London in 1946 with six Royal Albert Hall concerts followed by another tour in the spring of 1947, was one of the international artists to take part. For the purposes of the festival, he formed the Festival Piano Quartet with Szigeti, Primrose, and Fournier to celebrate anniversaries of the respective births or deaths of Schubert, Mendelssohn, and Brahms with programmes of their piano trios and quartets. It was such a success, that they thereupon gave the recitals in London and broadcast parts of them. Ibbs and Tillett were then involved in Schnabel's re-engagement as a concerto soloist in the 1948 festival when he played five Mozart piano concertos with three different orchestras. This proved to be his last appearance in public in Britain, for he died in 1951.

> Thanks for your report of the preparations for the second Edinburgh 'fair'. [Rudolf] Bing's suggestion does not quite correspond to what I had in mind; maybe I have been rather vague when I spoke to you about my work there. This is what I hoped for, three appearances at which six concertos would be presented, if possible all of them with the same orchestra and conductor, preferably one with whom I had collaborated before, otherwise with two or even three orchestras and their respective maestri. To provide sufficient time for rehearsals will, I think, be a minor problem. In case we must adhere to the schemes listed in your letter I would choose September 1, 3, 6. The conductor, or conductors, can be expected to protest against two concertos on one programme. Lasting approximately (maximum) one hour, they would reduce the time left for purely orchestral works to less than is customary, though at a Festival the fare is always usually copious and two hours of music easily consumed. The best solution would be to present three Mozart programmes: one symphony, one serenade or divertimento or overture and two concertos. Mozart's concertos, by the way, are real ones, orchestra and soloist equally endowed with music. My appearance in Edinburgh will, for 1948, be my only one in Europe. The fee ought to be one thousand pounds, not including broadcasts.
>
> Our passage home was very pleasant. We are, however, after six months in calm, balanced, grown up Europe (all this by comparison) not yet fully adjusted to the fear, noise, dope and dupe factory here [New York], now up to full capacity. (9 November 1947)

> Elaborating my cable message of today, I shall now inform you of the content of my letter to Bing. I agreed to play with the three different orchestras, to a first rehearsal with [Malcolm] Sargent to be held in Liverpool, and to rehearsals in Glasgow. I suggested that before going to Liverpool, a rehearsal with the BBC or at least a so-called piano rehearsal with Sir Adrian [Boult] ought to be arranged in London. I insisted on playing only Mozart, recommended to make one section of the total Edinburgh programme a sort of Mozart Festival. I, in any case, wish to perform just his music, two concertos with the Liverpool, two with the Scottish, and, if two are not acceptable to them, one with the BBC. I did not discuss the fee; they will grant it. (22 November 1947)

Bing stayed at Edinburgh (and at Glyndebourne where he was also General Manager) for only three Festivals, for, on a fund-raising trip to America in 1949 on behalf of both organisations, he secured for himself the post of running the New York Metropolitan Opera House. Edinburgh agreed reluctantly to let him go, John Christie the founder of Glyndebourne was far less willing and much bitterness ensued as a result. One letter of farewell from Bing to the agency survives.

> Thank you very much indeed for your nice letter. As you can imagine, I too am laughing with one eye and crying with the other at the prospect of leaving here. I have enjoyed working with you and hope that in my new job I need not entirely forego that pleasure. (3 June 1949)

Ibbs and Tillett's archive has two post-war letters from pianist Alfred Cortot, arranging an afternoon recital at the second Edinburgh Festival in the Usher Hall on the 4 September 1948 to mark the centenary of Chopin's concert in the Hopetown Rooms in the city on 4 October 1848. Chopin was desperately ill (a year from death) but managed to play a long programme, which Cortot did his best to reproduce after much research, and then adapted in his follow-up letter:

> Edinburgh Festival agreed, and the 4 Sept, as well as the terms which you describe, suits me, though there would need to be a supplement to cover any broadcast. Here is the programme which Chopin played on 4 Oct 1848:

1 Andante and Impromptu
2 Selection of Etudes
3 Nocturne and Berceuse
4 Andante, preceded by a Largo? (identification impossible)
5 Preludes, Ballade, Mazurkas and Waltzes
(translation from French)

Cortot went on to suggest in this letter of 20 November 1947 that it was difficult to establish the exact details of the composer's original programme, and felt that, in any event, the *Sonata funèbre* and the Polonaise in A flat should be included. John Tillett evidently agreed, and Cortot outlined his revised programme as follows:

1 *Sonata funèbre*
2 Selection of items played by Chopin at the concert on 4 Oct 1848:
  A 2 Etudes
  B Nocturne
  C Impromptu
  D Berceuse
  E Grande Valse brillante
3 A Preludes (3 or 4)
  B Ballade
  C 2 Mazurkas
  D Polonaise in A flat
What do you think?
(25 November 1947)

Three other letters from the 1940s are of interest, the first from the outstanding young French violinist Ginette Neveu, whose name appears all too briefly in the artists' brochures of the late 1940s, because tragically she was killed in an air crash on 28 October 1949. She was just thirty years old.

Dear Miss Bass
I have promised to help a friend who wants to spend his holidays in London. Would you be kind enough to make fifty pounds available to him with a mandate from my account, and address it to M. Alberto Fruzza, 83 Gordon Road, Ealing, London W5. M.Kiesgen will be writing to you with regard to the matter of my concerts in England. Everything is going well in America; my success is very great, so is the amount of work, sixty concerts in four months. Too much work!!! (8 December 1948, translation from French)

The other is a considerate and confidential letter from the composer Vaughan Williams to Emmie Tillett about the pianist Michael Mullinar, together with her reply:

I hope you will forgive my taking the liberty of asking you for some advice, which I know you are able and, I hope, willing to give. I am writing a piece for pianoforte and orchestra which will probably be done at one of the provincial Festivals, and I want Michael Mullinar to play the pianoforte solo part; but it occurs to me that it might damage his chances as an accompanist if it was supposed that he had set up as a solo pianist, and it is as an accompanist that he has to earn his living, since as you know better than I do, only a few people like Myra Hess or Solomon can make their living as solo pianists. I shall be very grateful for your opinion on this problem. (14 September 1949)

Dear Dr Vaughan Williams,
Thank you so much for your letter of the 14th instant. Quite frankly I don't think for one moment that the fact of MICHAEL MULLINAR playing a solo work with orchestra can in any way affect his chances of obtaining work as an accompanist, in fact in my opinion it is likely to enhance his reputation as such. There are several artists I can mention who combine solo work with accompanying and in my experience it has never had any adverse effect on the latter. (16 September 1949)

Another composer, Arnold Bax, wrote to Emmie recommending an Irish singer. Bax did not put the year in which he wrote it, and, without the envelope, it is hard to date but clearly has to be between 1945, when the BBC Home Service was created, and his death in 1953:

> This is to introduce a friend of mine from Co. Waterford, Maura O'Connor, who at the present moment is giving a BBC recital of Irish songs on the Home Service. I believe she has been in correspondence with you already and wishes to see you with a view to being included in your agency list. She is an intelligent singer with a particularly fresh mezzo soprano voice and an excellent linguist. (19 October)

CHAPTER TWENTY

Agency Changes: 1940–49

The dark days of the Second World War and the immediate aftermath of rationing, stringent controls, and austere living were not the only shadows to be cast across the agency in the 1940s. There were many changes, largely brought about by retirements or deaths, not only among artists but also the among the management itself. As noted, Rachmaninov and Wood died within a year of one another (1943 and 1944 respectively), so did the stalwart Welsh tenor Ben Davies, who lived to the ripe old age of 85, having been associated with the agency since the days of Vert. He was in touch with John Tillett during his last years and, before retiring to Bath, wrote from his West Hampstead home, thanking him for organizing a dinner to celebrate his 50th anniversary as a professional singer:

> My dear Johnny,
> My most grateful thanks to you for all the trouble you took over Saturday's dinner – it was a splendid evening and one that I shall always remember with the greatest pleasure and gratitude. Kindly convey to the Committee my deepest sense of the obligation which I feel, and give them my heartfelt thanks. Our love to you and Hetty, ever yours, Ben
> (19 May 1930)

> My dear Johnny,
> Accept my warmest thanks for the lovely book of names, with which I am charmed. It will always be to me a most delightful reminder of a very memorable evening, which will ever lie enshrined in the inmost recesses of my heart. And now also please accept our united thanks for the Stilton you and Hetty have so kindly sent us. It's very kind of you to treat us so generously. I like the conjunction of those two gifts, one so spiritually uplifting in memories, the other so pleasant to the taste. Well, a truce to all this, and expressing again our best thanks and wishing you and Hetty with all our hearts the best of everything for Xmas and the New Year. (21 December 1930)

By the outbreak of war Davies had moved to Bath, where he died on 28 March 1943. Three more letters survive from the old man, by now increasingly sad, his wife growing more senile, the last written just four months before his death. John Tillett kept all five of these letters in his personal leather-bound file, so clearly Ben Davies meant more to him on a personal basis than just having a business relationship with this eminent singer on the roster of the agency.

> My dear John,
> Although I've not written you for a long time, I would not have you think that I've been unmindful of you. I often wonder how you are getting on in these terrible days. I trust your health is good and that you are as happy as one can be under the awful circumstances. What a horrid world it has become!, and all thro' a few devils let loose to work destruction – no punishment will be too heavy for them when we win this war, (which we shall do).
> I learn that 'Biz' is not very good with you, but I hope it has not entirely vanished. Glad to say we are well. My dear wife's memory is not getting any better, but she is very happy and is spared the horrors of the world. Derek and Kitty are in Bermuda, they were asked to go there in the censorship. Derek could not pass the M.O. and had to return from Aldershot, he was earnestly disappointed as he wanted to fight. His chief was very pleased with what he was doing (training cadet officers) and wrote very highly of his work, however the M.O. said he had blood pressure. I hope his visit to Bermuda will put him right.
> I wonder if you can help me to help a man who had some lessons with me – he was in the

Admiralty at Bath – and used to cycle over to see us sometimes. Well, his wife would not leave her home in Carshalton, Surrey, so he had to return home. He is a very nice chap, has a very good voice, and wants to use it, not for earning money, but to be of some use. He would like to sing in these parties that entertain the forces. Could you let me know who manages these things? Perhaps you could spare a moment to see him?? He is really a good chap. If you'll send me a line I'll tell him to call on you (cussed nuisance), his name is J King-Currie. Gwen is in London and hard at work. She writes very bravely. Well my dear John, I've bothered you enough. God bless and keep you safely. Yours ever, Ben. P.S. Oh for the days that are no more.
(10 December 1940)

My dear John
Just a line to let you and Emmie know that you are in our thoughts and prayers. We send you our love and every good wish for as happy a Xmas as these dire days will allow, and may the New Year bring us all a just and righteous peace. I hope you are both well. My dear wife has not been so well lately, her memory has completely gone, she eats and sleeps very well and seems happy. We thought that she had another stroke but the Dr. said it was a spasm. However she's got over it thank God. Excuse this writing and paper, this is a one-horse place, excuse also a short note. Accept our fond love.
May God bless and keep you. Yours ever, Ben
(20 December 1941)

My dear John,
I am ashamed of myself for not having written you 'ere this, forgive my neglect. I cry '*mea culpa*', I fear that I am getting very lazy, but two things have thrust your dear old 'Phiz' prominently before me this week. One was the death of Bobbie Ibbs, which I was sorry to read of, I hope he did not suffer much. R.I.P. Although he had quitted the firm some time ago, it's the last snapping of a long and successful association, and I daresay you feel it muchly. The other was a letter from Gwen saying you had very kindly sent her tickets for Benno's [Moiseiwitsch] concert, which she much enjoyed. She said he was magnificent.

I hope you and Emmie are in good health. I see with pleasure the old firm's name every Saturday in the *Telegraph*, which gives me great joy. You will be sorry to hear that I am not very happy about my dear Clara. Her health is A1, but her mental condition is much worse, she cannot converse with us, in fact her speech is very difficult and we cannot make out what she wants to say. So you can imagine what it is like for us all. I only pray she may not get worse. I am sure you will understand that I would rather she died than be worse than she is, however she is no trouble except in the evening when her mind wanders and she talks of going home. It's very sad after such a happy life as we've had. Excuse more dear John. My love to you both. God bless you.
Ever yours, Ben
[second half of November 1942]

In this last letter Ben Davies alluded to the death of Robert Leigh Ibbs, which took place on 17 November 1942 at Instow, North Devon. It was reported in the press as follows:

A well-known cricketer and member for many years of the Hampstead and Middlesex Clubs and of the Nondescripts, Mr Robert Leigh Ibbs died on Tuesday at Instow. He was in his 74th year. Senior partner in the firm of Messrs Ibbs and Tillett of Wigmore Street until he retired five years ago, Mr Leigh Ibbs took an active part in concert organisation and management for over 50 years, and had travelled throughout the world with Madame Albani, Dame Nellie Melba, Dame Clara Butt, and other famous artists. He was also a personal friend of M. Rachmaninoff.

Three letters from Ibbs (who remained unmarried at his death) and the newspaper clipping above were, like the Ben Davies letters, also kept by John Tillett in his personal file. Evidently the two friends and business partners had remained in touch, and the first two replies date from the summer of 1942:

My dear Jack
Very glad to hear from you, and that Emmy and yourself are keeping fit notwithstanding your hard work and worry. It is good to hear you have got some business to somewhat repay you for all your slavery, but it's rotten to feel that others are benefiting by it, who apparently do so little of the hard work! I suppose the lordly "Bill" [William Tilbrook] has gone off for five or six weeks as usual! Has Maurice N. dropped out altogether? But I imagine so. I hope Worman is still with you. Give him my salaams. It is useless to say you should sack Roy P[embridge] as we've been saying that for years, but it really seems to have got to an absolute block, and I'm afraid you'll get into severe trouble with the I[ncome] T[ax] people. It seems incredible he can ignore things and people as he does, and I don't see how you can possibly let him go on in his own sweet way. I suppose I cannot do the Joint a/c books for you, if you were to send me all the necessary here? I don't want 'em for myself, and please don't think of sending me any money, as I cannot think there can be any profit to come, unless you have got all the premises well let!! Yes, I heard about Rumford's marriage. He wrote me that I mustn't think badly of him for doing so, but he was so utterly lonely and wanted companionship and a home again. From rumours I've heard (this keep to yourself) I'm terribly afraid it is not a success, but I do hope the old boy is not too miserable over it. I had a letter from him last week and he never mentioned 'her' or what is happening as regards his house. He wants me to go and see him for a day or two, but I've so rooted myself down here that I don't feel inclined to move at all.

It would be just grand if Emmie and yourself could get down here, but I'm afraid it is almost impossible to find a corner vacant. I think I told you the Admiralty have turned out all the houses on the front including the two small hotels, so that the only place now is the Marine Hotel, half of which has been collared by the military, leaving only a few rooms, which are chock-a-block always. There is the Royal Hotel at Bideford (3 miles off) or the Imperial at Barnstaple (6 miles off), where it might be possible to get in. If you want an absolute laze in the quietest of quiet country surroundings, there is a wonderfully well run hotel in a tiny village, Lifton, 3 miles from Launceston. Arundell Arms Hotel. Unlimited food, well furnished and comfy rooms, and really well run. It belongs to a Major Morris and is always full of people wanting a real rest. Trout fishing is the only other attraction. I went for a week with the Beresfords last May, but it is too relaxing for me and I wasn't able to walk much, which is what you could do to your heart's content! Just a one-street village and so restful. The Beresfords have taken refuge there, having been turned out of their beautiful house here. It may interest you to know I am gradually 'breaking up'! I've had acute lumbago all this week, the result of overdoing amateur gardening and too much stooping, so now I've got to keep quiet for a time. Tennis and golf are things of the past, and we have no cricket now. Well old boy, it would be lovely to see you both again, and I still hope to before I pass out, so shall live in hope. My love to you both and God bless.
Yours Bob. [P.S.] The Arundell Arms charge 18/- a day all in but it's worth it.
(29 July 1942)

My dear Jack
Many thanks for your letter and the cheque! Are you quite sure this can be spared? At any rate it is good to know you are not losing money over the premises, and that you have a prospective new tenant, whom I hope you'll secure. The news you give me of Pedro [Tillett] is what I have been expecting to hear for sometime, as I could not picture him a lonely bachelor for long! I do hope he has been drawn a prize as he had a long spell of unhappiness, I'm afraid. As you say, it is 'secret'. I cannot send him a line but when it is made public give him my love and the best of good wishes. Emmie and yourself must get away for a bit, business or no business, or you'll both crack up, so just see about it. I really would take a strong line about Roy P[embridge] and cut him out altogether. Probably Stanley R[ubinstein, the firm's lawyer] could put you onto someone who could pick up the threads of your complicated business, and it would be a load off your mind. I'm amused to hear of Dennis Noble and Lord's. He was always touting round people there likely to be of use, but membership of MCC has fallen from its high estate, I fear, from the weird creatures I have seen elected in the past few years. 'Scuse a scrawl and scrappy letter, but I'm not at my best just now as my doctor tells me I have got a light 'bladder' trouble (this to yourself) which worries me a lot. Added to the lumbago I feel not less than 95 ! Much love to you both. God bless.
Bob
(13 August 1942)

Ibbs's last letter, written to Emmie in pencil seventeen days before his death and signed 'Padre', is dated 31 October with no year, but it has to be 1942 for several reasons. Beecham's divorce had taken place earlier that month, the reference to Menuhin may well be the violinist's attempts at that time to get back to Europe from America in order to make a musical contribution to the war effort, while the Ibbs and Tillett artist, pianist William Murdoch, had died on 9 September 1942 at the early age of 54.

> How nice of you to have written, and our dear John also, but you really should not bother to as you can't have much time for private letters. Will you thank John for me, and say I won't add to his pile as I am writing to you. I saw the doctor again yesterday and he at once accused me of skipping about the room etc (true!!) and that if I was so insensate as not to really keep the leg up, I could never expect to get rid of the trouble, so now I am back tight in bed again and suppose I really must stay there, but it's very 'ard Mum!
>
> Whatever has brought back Monica [Nixon] again? I thought she had retired for good. I only hope she is a real help to you both and will pull her weight for you. Does she go back to her old room, and if so what do you do? I had forgotten W.L.T[illbrook] is a Councillor! He does not seem to have been very successful with the new clerk he got in!! I am so truly sorry about poor K.D. I am not at all surprised to hear about T.B., as I always suspected it, but the other part I know nothing of. I only hope he will be able to pull himself round now that conditions are so altered. He's too good a chap to be wasted! I'm relieved that the advert was a wrong one!
>
> I had not seen about Beecham. Poor Dora [Labbette], I'm so sorry for her but how does B get the divorce? I was delighted to see about Menuhin, then thought it was only a publicity stunt on his behalf. What a thrill about Myra [Hess]. Give her my dear love and wish her the bestest of good luck all through. You must be proud of your brother and I can only think he must have got a large part of his brains from you!! Will you give my love to your mother. I'm so glad she is in such splendid health and spirits. Long may it be so. Was Billy Murdoch's death unexpected? Sad at his age. I'm glad to hear the other flat is let, not from the pecuniary point but I know it will relieve John. Tell him he has got to sack Pembridge or you'll get awfully tied up with the I.R. Well my dear, I won't worry you with more. Forgive pencil and scrawl. I hope the day is not too far distant when we may meet again. It will be great. Love to you both as always. Your affect. Padre
> (31 Oct)

Material in the Ibbs and Tillett archive relating to the running of the agency is, perhaps unsurprisingly, weighted towards John Tillett and, after him, Emmie. Over the years there has had to be a disposal of papers, contracts and letters, either because of limited capacity to house them or through two moves of premises in the last decade of the agency's existence. Material would be thrown away upon the departure of members of the firm, and whenever artists were lost either to other agents or died. In researching this book, the uniqueness of the archive became clear, for no other agency today has anything like such material, regrettably not even Harold Holt (now Askonas-Holt). It is ironic that, over the years, the shorthand reference to Ibbs and Tillett among musicians and managements has been simply 'Ibbs' rather than 'Tillett', calling it after the man who nobody knows now, rather than after the two personalities who dominated its activities for so long, John and Emmie Tillett.

Robert Leigh Ibbs remained a background figure throughout his 31 years with the firm, and after reporting from Australia and New Zealand on that initial tour in 1907, which the agency managed for Clara Butt, his name rarely features. Research has found Ibbs's name on the passenger list of the *Mauretania*, which sailed from Southampton and arrived in the USA on 25 November 1919, his occupation then given as 'Agent'. A bizarre slip occurs on the manifest when, perhaps because the passenger lining up ahead of him at immigration control was Scandinavian, Ibbs is described as from 'Denmark, Scandinavia', his residence as 'London, Denmark'. It stated he had been to America before and to 'various' places, and that his destination was the 'Wolfsohn Bureau. West 34th Street, New York City'. In compliance with strict immigration laws, he did not 'intend to seek American citizenship, had no criminal record, was not a polygamist or an anarchist, and did not intend to overthrow the US government'. His mental health was good and he was not a cripple, his height was given as five feet eight inches, eye colour as blue, hair as fair.

Rather like Emmie Tillett in the post-Second World War years, Ibbs had his favourites such as Rachmaninov but, judging from what evidence remains today, he did not run auditions or sign contracts, neither did he get involved in the minutiae of agency business, although, when not in the MCC members' stand at Lords or out on the golf links with his regular partners, the three baritones Roy Henderson, Keith Falkner and Harold Williams, he was clearly hard at work at 124 Wigmore Street. Robert Leigh Ibbs appears to have been a well-built man with close-set eyes, ruddy complexion and a benign gaze. A photograph of him, taken in 1938, has been supplied to the author by its owner, Reginald Franks, whose name appears in Ibbs's will as the recipient of a small legacy. One of Ibbs's godchildren, Haydon Leigh Bradshaw, in a letter to the author, recalls:

> Bob's beaming face and his monocle, though it is clear in the enlarged print that he carries a pipe, not a monocle, which made some impression on a four year-old. Clearly he was close friends with my father, a tea broker in the City, played rugby for Richmond, captained squash for England, not musical. (8 August 2003)

However Reginald Franks, at 83, has more detailed memories of Robert Leigh Ibbs, whom he remembers as Leigh (indeed the photograph is signed 'Leigh 1938').

> Leigh was a very special, beloved and unforgettable person, very well known in certain circles in his time. The photograph is a good likeness, though somewhat serious. Normally there was a twinkle in his eye, but I would say it would do very well for a book about his business.
>
> He was a very big man, not so much in height, but in size. He must have weighed sixteen stone plus, but he was immensely powerful and could carry it. A very handsome face, large again, and always a high colour, and the whole seemed to glow! My mother and sister always said he was so wonderfully clean to kiss!! He could look extremely smart, but the picture that I conjure up most is of him dressed in an old casual grey suit, white shirt with MCC tie, and a brown trilby turned up all round, wandering off to Lords to watch his beloved cricket. His looks demonstrated the lovely character that he was.
>
> Concerning his life (naturally I only knew it between the wars), why he never married I could not say but although he got on wonderfully with the opposite sex, I cannot imagine him other than a bachelor. Of course he lived in the days when to be a bachelor was easy. He had a housekeeper called Kate for many years, who looked after him in every way, and when she sadly died he was truly upset, but a successor was very quickly installed!
>
> A different world, it was a remarkably small house at 102 Eaton Terrace SW1, near Sloane Square. Housekeeper in the basement for cooking and her sitting room, lounge/dining room on ground floor, and I think two more storeys but only three bedrooms, and every inch covered in signed photographs of friends and artists – quite extraordinary! It was a quite unique and I suppose typical bachelor establishment of those days. When, as a young man, I wanted a bed in town, he put me up. He loved sport and in particular cricket. He was a member of MCC and was a very well-known figure in the Pavilion at Lords. He loved his golf, though dreadfully slow on the course, and played garden party tennis to everyone's delight. From this and from his work he had an enormous circle of friends, and in his younger days with his connection with the entertainment world, I am sure he had a very gay life indeed, and that his evening clothes were very well used. How many times he was a best man and a Godfather I simply cannot imagine!
>
> He also had his special friends, especially in his later years, where he was a very special weekend guest, and I cannot think he ever spent many weekends in London. He was a real Londoner, never

had a car or a driving licence to my knowledge. There were always cabs, porters at the station, and buses. Why worry? He spent his summer holidays at Instow in Devon. How this started I have no idea, but he took the whole of August and a bit more down there, and there again he was much loved. They said that when he arrived, they knew the season had started.

I have been to his office in Wigmore Street and loved the anecdotes of his clients. Rachmaninoff would not move in this country without him, and there was Moiseiwitsch and Clara Butt among others. I imagine he started up through sheer character, and the wish by the artists to be represented by no other. Whilst I am sure he was a brilliant musical agent, he was not a financier, was not particularly well off, and had to watch his pennies at one time.

Many years ago he took Clara Butt to Australia. He also went to America, which he hated, and to the Continent several times. On the Australian tour they stopped in Cairo, and by various means of transport were meant to visit the Pyramids. Leigh was on a camel which took off into the desert and eventually landed him in some British regimental camp. This story, told by him, has had dinner parties in a complete state of collapse!

Leigh was my father's best man and was his greatest friend to the day he died. My mother loved him dearly, as I am sure did all his special hostesses, and my sister and I adored him. Uncle Leigh, though no blood relation, was very special. He spent many weekends with us [at Warwick's Bench, Guildford] and always one in the school holidays, which we looked forward to enormously. He was my sister's Godfather and made a speech at her wedding, 'if brevity is the source of wit, I am going to be damned funny'. I remember that to this day. In the day of servants, they looked forward to his visits just as much. He took an enormous interest in his friends' children, and became their friend too. Such was the man.

The end, when it came, was very sad. At the beginning of the war he decamped from London, feeling as an old man that he would be in the way, and went to his beloved Instow, where he found rooms. He became ill with some wasting disease and simply fell to pieces. My father played a big part then, continually travelling down from Guildford, a good effort in the war, and apart from friends in Instow, was the one old friend with him throughout and to the end. A much loved man, a great character, and a raconteur with no equal. (3 September 2002)

Evidently John Tillett's own health was not so robust at the end of the war. Even Ibbs had been giving him advice from North Devon which implied that overwork, aggravated by weak links in the already reduced numbers of staff, was beginning to take its toll. Fortunately he now had the much younger Emmie by his side to take more responsibility and more control of running the agency, but John did not really ever relax his grip. In a letter dated 10 September 1945 replying to a telephone call from Mexborough, Yorkshire, he listed singers (with their fees in guineas) available for a concert planned for that autumn:

Sopranos			
Isobel Baillie (30)	Margaret Eaves (25)	Ceinwen Rowlands (20)	Joan Taylor (18)
Elsie Suddaby (25)	Sylvia Welling (25)	Edna Hobson (20)	Nora Gruhn (18)
Noel Eadie (25)	Olive Groves (25)	Ruth Packer (20)	Patricia Davies (18)
Elena Danieli (25)	Laelia Finneberg (25)	Ada Alsop (18)	
Contraltos			
Mary Jarred (25)	Essie Ackland (20)	Valetta Iacopi (20)	Muriel Gale (18)
Muriel Brunskill (25)	Janet Howe (20)	Freda Townson (20)	Constance Shacklock (18)
Gladys Ripley (25)	Nancy Evans (20)		
Tenors			
Frank Titterton (35)	Parry Jones (25)	Tudor Davies (20)	Bradbridge White (18)
David Lloyd (30)	Robert Naylor (25)	Eric Greene (20)	Walter Glynne (18)
Walter Widdop (25)	Jan van der Gucht (20)	Stephen Manton (20)	John Myrddin (18)
Francis Russell (25)	Trefor Jones (20)		
Basses			
Norman Allin (30)	Redvers Llewellyn (25)	William Parsons (20)	Joseph Farrington (20)
Robert Easton (30)	Henry Cummings (25)	Bruce Dargavel (20)	David Franklin (18)

Nowakowski (30)	Tom Williams (20)	Ronald Stear (20)	Stanley Pope (18)
Roy Henderson (25)	Henry Gill (20)	Norman Lumsden (20)	George Pizzey (18)
Arthur Fear (25)			

The firm was restructured in these immediate post-war days. In the Spring of 1945 John Tillett wrote to both of his fellow Directors, William Tilbrook and Monica Nixon, insisting on a dissolution of their partnerships in the agency from the end of the calendar year. To Tilbrook he wrote:

> Dear Bill
> For some considerable time I have been very worried as to the future of the Business and not only the future but the present situation causes me great concern, and I am sure that you will be the first to agree that it cannot continue.
>
> Your inability, owing to the unfortunate state of your health to carry a Partner's responsibility, has thrown a heavier burden on the shoulders of my Wife and myself. We have therefore been forced to the conclusion that only by a re-arrangement in the Office is it possible for us to carry on.
>
> You have only to examine the Balance Sheets of the past few years to realise that Emmie and I by our joint efforts have made practically the entire income of the Firm, and your acceptance of the yield of our work as a matter of course, not to mention your disinclination to encourage any fresh enterprise, has convinced me that you are no longer interested in the active side of the Business.
>
> Briefly, we are not prepared to continue our Partnership on the present basis and we intend to seek additional properly qualified assistance for the added work, and the responsibility in which your attitude for some long time past, has involved us.
>
> I shall be glad to hear whether you have any suggestions to make before we proceed to consider more judicially, the position into which you have forced us. After so many years association, it is with regret that I am obliged to write this letter, but I can only reiterate that the position compels me to do so.

When the war was intensified by the Blitz on London, Monica Nixon refused to remain in the capital. She moved to the country until 1942, after which she returned.

> Dear Monica
> You will doubtless remember the conversation I had with you in 1942, when I explained that at the end of the War it would be necessary to re-organise the administration of the Firm, and in consequence of this I proposed that your return to the Business should be for a term of three years, which will expire at the end of the present year.
>
> The march of time is a cruel reminder that none of us is getting younger, and makes it essential that new blood must be brought into the Firm in order to carry on its tradition, and to meet the exacting demands which are now made upon the personnel. I therefore propose to dissolve our Partnership and in order to make things as easy for you as possible I am writing to advise you, that I do not propose to renew our agreement which expires on December 31st next, so that our Partnership will be dissolved as from that date.
>
> Our association has been a long and pleasant one, but you cannot have failed to realise that Emmie and I, by our joint efforts, are making practically the entire income of the Firm in which you are participating without sharing any of our burdens. Your voluntary absence from the Business for a matter of three years caused you to lose touch with the work, which has certainly become more exacting and calls for greater and youthful enterprise. If, therefore, you compare the value of the work you are doing with our success during the past few years, you must realise that, but for our efforts, such results could not have been achieved.
>
> The Deed of Partnership of the 17th April 1937 lays down the procedure to be followed and I am, of course, exercising my option to purchase the Business.

William Tilbrook had been with Ibbs and Tillett from the start in 1906 (see Chapter 4), whereas Monica Nixon, though in the agency business from the same time, was clearly still working then for Pedro Tillett at N. Vert's agency. A letter dated 17 July 1907 was written to her at 6 Cork Street, in which Ibbs and Tillett confirmed a telephone call with her to book singer Perceval Allen for a Postmen's Concert in

Manchester on 19 February 1908. Both Nixon and Tilbrook agreed to Tillett's proposal and left the firm at the end of 1945.

At this time, the flute player John Francis was putting together an ensemble based around himself and his wife, harpsichordist Millicent Silver, plus violinist Jack Kessler and cellist George Roth. Called the London Harpsichord Ensemble, Francis was evidently under instructions from the agency to cost a tour with various groupings of players and singers, before it would consider placing them on their artists' list, which, however, it subsequently did:

> I have worked out a scale of fees for large and small LONDON HARPSICHORD ENSEMBLE, which I think explains itself. I have worked on the basis that fares would be in the region of £2.10s and we would have to stay a night for each day away. I think I have made them as low as possible, but we are anxious to make it a success and are open to suggestions. We might be able to reduce a little, especially the larger ensemble, if it were not far from London and did not mean staying the night.
>
> I think we could get Margaret Field-Hyde or Ena Mitchell or Veronica Mansfield with the small ensemble for a proportionate increase in fee, e.g. 25%. We hope to arrange for the singer to be (as it were) a part of the ensemble, as we can then present a much more coherent programme. I have talked to the singers mentioned and they are all interested in the idea. (13 June 1945)

Within a year of the end of the war in Europe (May 1945), despite continuing stringent controls, there were developments in the musical life of Britain. Though Britten's opera *Peter Grimes* made its now historic impact at Sadler's Wells, London on 7 June 1945, Covent Garden was still a Mecca dance hall, and Glyndebourne's reopening only at the planning stage. However in 1946, and largely because Britten had been so disillusioned by his treatment at the hands of the Sadler's Wells management after the success of his opera, it was decided to stage *Rape of Lucretia* with Kathleen Ferrier at the Sussex opera house, followed a year later by *Albert Herring*. By the summer of 1948, however, Britten, together with his newly created English Opera Group created the first Aldeburgh Festival, which opened in June that year with a repeat of *Albert Herring*.

In the autumn of 1946, the BBC launched its Third Programme, which was to provide another highly important outlet for music as well as the other performing arts. There was of course the continuing season of Henry Wood Promenade Concerts, and the list of artists required of the agency for 1945 and 1947 is listed in Appendix 7 (together with works they played). The Three Choirs Festival resumed at Hereford in 1946, with Ibbs and Tillett once again providing many of the soloists and favourite artists, such as Isobel Baillie, Elsie Suddaby, Astra Desmond, Gladys Ripley, Heddle Nash, Eric Greene, Tom Williams, Phyllis Sellick, Jelly d'Aranyi, and Lionel Tertis. There at least, it was matter of picking up where the agency had left off before the war. Kathleen Ferrier, however, was now the name on everyone's lips, and her career, entirely in the hands of Ibbs and Tillett and, from the summer of 1948, under Emmie's personal watch, tended to dominate much of the agency's activities. As already mentioned in the previous chapter, the first Edinburgh Festival took place in the summer of 1947 under the artistic direction of Bruno Walter with the Vienna Philharmonic Orchestra, and Ferrier was booked to appear there. It was to prove to be a monumental step in her singing career, especially as Walter had earmarked her for Mahler's *Das Lied von der Erde*, a work virtually unknown in Britain. Already by the summer of 1945, Ibbs and Tillett were writing to Arthur Wynn at the BBC on the matter of fees paid to Ferrier and Peter Pears, both of whom were making their Proms debuts that summer:

> Kathleen Ferrier and Peter Pears have both asked us to advise you that they feel they cannot continue to broadcast at the fee they at present are receiving. Their minimum concert fee is Twenty Guineas and for all future broadcasts they wish to regard Fifteen Guineas as their minimum. (29 June 1945)

In Manchester, the Tuesday Midday Concerts, then in their 25th year under the artistic direction of the pianist Edward Isaacs and healthily supported by an ever-swelling number of subscribers, were packed with artists from the agency, among them Isobel Baillie, Gerald Moore, Benjamin Britten, Louis Kentner, Cyril Smith, Phyllis Sellick, Max Rostal, Kendall Taylor, Frederick Grinke, the Philharmonia Quartet, and the Boyd Neel Orchestra. Elsewhere two triennial festivals resumed normal operations in the autumn of 1947. They were the Norfolk and Norwich, where seven concerts were given over five days (23–27 September) and two weeks later at Leeds, where eight concerts were given over five days from 7–11 October. Ibbs and Tillett supplied all but two of the soloists for Norwich, the singers Victoria Sladen, Gladys Ripley, Kathleen Ferrier (wrongly billed as a soprano in her role as the Angel in *Dream of Gerontius*), Peter Pears, Heddle Nash, Roy Henderson, Norman Walker, and Dennis Noble, violinists Ida Haendel and Max Rostal, pianists Solomon and Louis Kentner, and horn player Dennis Brain. The agency provided all the solo artists for Leeds, namely singers Elsie Suddaby, Victoria Sladen, Ena Mitchell, Ljuba Welitsch, Kathleen Ferrier, Gladys Ripley, Janet Howe, Eric Greene, James Johnston, Parry Jones, Ronald Hill, Trevor Anthony, Dennis Noble, Norman Walker, Harold Williams, and Tom Williams, pianists Moiseiwitsch and Denis Matthews, violinist Maurice Raskin, violist William Primrose, and cellist Pierre Fournier.

The first Edinburgh Festival began on 24 August 1947. In the post-war absence of international festivals such as those at Salzburg and Munich, it was Rudolf Bing and Audrey Mildmay (Mrs John Christie) who conceived the idea, allegedly during a wartime tour of a small-scale Glyndebourne production of the *Beggar's Opera*. In 1946, an approach by Bing to the Lord Provost of the city (Sir John Falconer) was favourably received, and the first event a year later set the highest standards, and was characterized by a spirit of excitement, adventure and enterprise. Bruno Walter and the Vienna Philharmonic were not the only conductor and orchestra to participate, there was also the Orchestre de Colonne from Paris under Paul Paray, the Hallé conducted by Barbirolli, the Royal Liverpool Philharmonic with Sargent, the Scottish Orchestra with Walter Susskind, and the BBC Scottish Orchestra conducted by Ian Whyte. Solo artists managed by Ibbs and Tillett included Elisabeth Schumann, Schnabel, Isolde Menges, Leon Goossens, Szigeti, Roy Henderson, Casadesus, Ferrier, Pears, Nancy Evans, Margaret Field-Hyde, Ena Mitchell, Fournier, William Primrose, Marie Korchinska, and Cyril Smith. Glyndebourne was invited to stage operas at the King's Theatre, Verdi's *Macbeth* and Mozart's *Marriage of Figaro*, revivals from the last pre-war season in 1939 and both with singers from the agency such as John Brownlee and Margherita Grandi. The inaugural festival, with 180,000 tickets sold, was justifiably deemed a success.

London orchestral concerts were now regular weekly events. The BBC and Royal Philharmonic Society shared alternate Wednesday evenings for symphony concerts with programmes of a fairly eclectic nature, the London Philharmonic Orchestra (now self-governing and unshackled from Beecham, who, from 1946, had spawned yet another orchestral creation, the Royal Philharmonic Orchestra) took Thursdays and Sundays for more popular and conventional programmes. Ibbs and Tillett provided two vocal quartets for the London Philharmonic Orchestra's two Royal Albert Hall concerts in May 1949 under Victor de Sabata, Sylvia Fisher, Nancy Evans, William Herbert, and William Parsons (Beethoven's *Missa solemnis*), Joan Hammond, Constance Shacklock, and Richard Lewis (Verdi's *Requiem*), with the conductor bringing his own Italian bass soloist Gianpiero Malaspina, while Moura Lympany and Clifford Curzon were solo pianists with the orchestra in June that year. Meanwhile Walter Legge's Philharmonia Orchestra (founded in 1945), as well as making superb gramophone recordings of opera for EMI where he was a senior executive and record producer, also performed for the new non-profit making New Era Concert Society. This existed from 1948–55, and was in effect a reconstituted Courtauld–Sargent Society from pre-war days. Sargent himself was still at the helm of the Royal Choral Society, whose final concert of the season at the Royal Albert Hall on Saturday 18 May 1946 at 2.30 in the afternoon featured agency artists Joan Taylor, Astra Desmond, Jan van der Gucht, Dennis Noble, and Norman Walker for a double-bill of Walton's *Belshazzar's Feast* and Mozart's *Requiem*. The Royal Choral Society's season in those days was an extremely full and active one. As an example, and to illustrate the rich source of work for the agency which it represented, its 76th season between November 1946 and May 1947 consisted of eight concerts, *Elijah*, *Aida*, a carol concert, a performance of *Messiah* in January and on Good Friday, *The Apostles*, *Dream of Gerontius*, and Holst's *Choral* Symphony.

Outside London the orchestral scene was less rosy and only thriving in patches. The Scottish Orchestra had emerged very uncertainly from the war, and its management committee (rather than its highly talented new conductor Walter Susskind) wasted a golden opportunity to put things right when the Edinburgh Festival invited them to become the resident orchestra for the inaugural event in 1947. An ill-conceived plan of an experimental summer season (for which too many experienced players proved unavailable), together with an earlier two-month hiatus of inactivity produced very sub-standard playing, and the invitation was not renewed in 1948.

Prospects were much happier in Liverpool, where concerts were abundant and attractive in the immediate post-war years, so it is worth considering two of these seasons in detail, remembering that this was just one city in the UK which the agency supplied with artists. Liverpool had been dogged by ill-luck regarding its Philharmonic Hall, for, immediately after the rebuild in 1939 (six years after the fire which destroyed its predecessor), war broke out. By this time the debts were mounting, but fortunately a solution of sorts was found when the Corporation bought the Hall from the Philharmonic Society for the cost of its debts (£33000) and a £4000 annual subsidy, providing that the programmes were up to the old standard, more popular in content, and that educational concerts were given. A further perk was the free use of the hall for rehearsals and concerts by the orchestra, which, from 1942, was in the hands of Sargent, who had just had three unhappy years with the Hallé before Barbirolli took over. In 1945–46 there were three concerts given each week, 16 Saturday subscription concerts, 20 Sunday afternoon Popular Concerts, and another 20 Popular Concerts on Thursday evenings, which, from 1946–47, switched to Tuesdays. Besides the ubiquitous four Englishmen Sargent, Boult, Beecham, and Barbirolli (who came once with the Hallé Orchestra), Karl Rankl, Charles Munch and Roger Désormière were also conductors. Neveu, Solomon, Moiseiwitsch, Curzon, Kentner, Smith, Lympany, Casals, Rostal, Campoli, Haendel, Brain, and Goossens were among the instrumental soloists from the agency, while the vocalists numbered Baillie, Jarred, Henderson, Nash, Ferrier, Field-Hyde, Turner, Pears, and Walker among their ranks.

The season 1948–49 saw a fine tuning of the Liverpool Philharmonic's schedule, still 16 subscription concerts (but now on Tuesdays), 16 Sunday afternoon Popular Concerts, and another 16 Popular concerts on Saturday evenings. To these were added three Orchestral Concerts for Youth (15–21 years) introduced and conducted by Dr Reginald Jacques. The agency supplied 47 soloists to the orchestra during that season:

Gina Bachauer	Marjorie Blackburn	Gioconda de Vito	Mary Jarred	Kathleen Long
Phyllis Sellick	Antonio Brosa	Valentine Dyall	Lance Dossor	Reginald Gibbs
Joseph Greene	Richard Lewis	Mantle Childe	Denis Matthews	Moiseiwitsch
Dennis Noble	Manoug Parikian	Max Rostal	Bernard Shore	Solomon
Emil Telmanyi	Themeli	John Vallier	Elisabeth Schumann	Monique Haas
Joan Hammond	Eileen Joyce	Lilian Niblette	Shulamith Shafir	Olive Zorian
Clifford Curzon	Jean Françaix	Leon Goossens	John Kennedy	Alan Loveday
John Mason	Mewton-Wood	Navarra	Raymond O'Connell	William Parsons
Cyril Preedy	Karl Schnabel	Cyril Smith	Kendall Taylor	Paul Tortelier
Stephen Wearing	Joseph Weingarten			

There were also the Rushworth Saturday afternoon recital concerts, four in all that year given by Myra Hess, Isobel Baillie (with Colin Horsley), Pouishnoff, and Max Rostal (with Nina Milkina) respectively. The Rodewald Concert Society promoted six chamber music concerts that season, using the Griller, New Italian, Hungarian, London, and Paganini String Quartets, and the London Czech Trio, while in the field of choral music there were also six concerts put on by the Liverpool Welsh Choral Union, each having anything from two to six vocal soloists. Not to be outdone, the North Liverpool Union of Church Choirs also seems to have called upon the agency for Baillie, Ripley, van der Gucht, Parsons (*Messiah*), and Doris Gambell, Ethel Davies, Rene Soames, and Trevor Anthony (*Samson*), while the Liverpool Cymric Vocal Union (Male Voices) needed Elsie Suddaby and Bruce Dargavel for its 53rd annual concert. A healthy list of music societies and clubs including Aigburth Boulevard Club, Garston Woodcutters' Male Voice Choir, and Warrington Music Club all needed servicing, so too did the outlying areas of Cheshire, with the Chester and District Music Society leading the way with agency artists of the calibre of pianist Iris Loveridge, singer Kathleen Ferrier (with Phyllis Spurr), violinist Alan Loveday, the Rubbra–Brainin–Pleeth Trio, violinist Max Rostal (with John Wills), and pianist Barbara Hill for their season.

Over in Manchester, Barbirolli's Hallé Orchestra gave 52 concerts in the city between October 1945 and May 1946 at the Albert Hall on Tuesdays (repeated the next day), and Popular Concerts on Sunday afternoons at Belle Vue. Ibbs and Tillett provided Thibaud, Milkina, Curzon, Rostal, Kentner, Taylor, Sammons, Shulamith Shafir, Casals, Matthews, Haendel, Moiseiwitsch, Smith, Solomon, Grumiaux, and Neveu as instrumentalist soloists, with singers Marjorie Thomas, Parry Jones, Nora Gruhn, Joan Hammond, Tom Williams, Henry Cummings, Isobel Baillie, Peter Pears, Kathleen Ferrier, Norman Walker, Edna Hobson, Walter Widdop, Janet Howe, Dennis Noble, Booth Unwin, and Gladys Ripley. Some of the programmes were taken to Sheffield, alternating Fridays with Saturdays. For the four concerts promoted by the Sheffield Philharmonic Chamber Music Club in the first half of the season, Ibbs and Tillett suggested the Griller String Quartet (twice), the Budapest Trio, and the duo of Max Rostal and Franz Osborn in a violin and piano recital.

In Chapter 16, correspondence from 1938 and 1939 was reproduced between Ibbs and Tillett and the Birmingham Festival Choral Society, and a few letters are extant a decade later, this time with the agency's replies written by Kathleen Cheselden rather than John Tillett.

BIRMINGHAM FESTIVAL CHORAL SOCIETY
We are in receipt of your favour of the 23rd inst., by which we note you propose giving a Concert in the Large Lecture Theatre of the Midland Institute, Birmingham, on Monday evening April 26th next, for which occasion you require a soprano and contralto vocalist.

Unfortunately we have to disappoint you regarding the Artists mentioned, as ISOBEL BAILLIE will be abroad at the time and KATHLEEN FERRIER is already booked on the date in question.

We therefore suggest the following sopranos and contraltos for your consideration, who appear to be free, together with their fees, and from which we hope you will be able to make a choice.

Sopranos:
Gwen Catley 40 guineas
Elsie Suddaby 30 guineas
Laelia Finneberg, Elena Danieli, Olive Groves, Ceinwen Rowlands, Edna Hobson, Ada Alsop, Emelie Hooke 25 guineas
Ena Mitchell, Ingrid Hageman, Linda Parker, Joan Taylor 20 guineas
Patricia Davies 18 guineas

Contraltos:
Gladys Ripley 35 guineas
Mary Jarred 30 guineas
Muriel Brunskill, Valetta Iacopi, Nancy Evans, Janet Howe 25 guineas
Freda Townson, Muriel Gale 20 guineas
May Pearson 18 guineas
Veronica Mansfield 15 guineas
Awaiting your further communication.
(24 January 1948)

BIRMINGHAM FESTIVAL CHORAL SOCIETY
Thank you for your letter of the 12th inst. We are glad to advise you that Miss MARY JARRED is still available, and in accordance with your instructions we therefore have pleasure in definitely booking this Artist for the performance of Pergolesi's *Stabat Mater*, and a group of songs, to be given in the Large Lecture Theatre, Midland Institute, Birmingham, on Monday evening April 26th 1948, at a fee of Thirty guineas (£31.10.0).

Unfortunately we have to disappoint you in regard to Miss ADA ALSOP, who is now not available for April 26th, and we will therefore await your further choice of soprano, when we hope to be more successful.
(16 February 1948)

The Henry Wood Concert Society was founded in August 1946 on a non-profit making basis. Its main activity is to sponsor concerts of the highest class throughout the country and to devote itself to causes and services which advance the Art of Music and extend its appreciation – especially to those causes and services which Sir Henry Wood had most at heart.

Thus ran the Society's description of itself in the foreword to its programmes of concerts promoted under the management of Ibbs and Tillett. There was always an annual concert to celebrate Wood's birthday as near as possible to 3 March each year, and generally four or five other promotions besides. The season 1948–49, for example, began with a performance of *Messiah* given by eight massed choirs under Sargent on 3 November 1948. On 13 December, he conducted the LSO in an orchestral concert which, as well as works by Beethoven, Mozart and Stravinsky, also included the first performance of Lennox Berkeley's Double Piano Concerto (Cyril Smith and Phyllis

Sellick). On 12 February 1949, Rafael Kubelik conducted Janacek's Sinfonietta and Dvořák's *Stabat Mater* with Gabriella Gatti, Kathleen Ferrier, Heddle Nash and Harold Williams as soloists. The birthday concert in 1949, as well as using the baritone Redvers Llewellyn and violinist Ida Haendel, also included Bach's Concerto for Four Harpsichords (but pianos were used) with young soloists who had not long left the Royal Academy of Music, where Wood taught conducting. They were now on the agency's register, namely sisters Eleanor and Christine Pembridge, Violet Graham, and Ruth Harte. According to Ruth Harte in an interview with the author, each was carefully instructed by Sargent not only in the colour of their dress, but also in how they were to stand around him as a group while acknowledging the audience's applause, the idea being to present a tableau for the audience of the dapper conductor surrounded by four attractive young ladies. On 13 April, Boult conducted a concert performance of Wagner's opera *Parsifal*, all 12 singers in the cast coming from the agency, with the tenor Franz Vroons in the title role. The season concluded at the Royal Albert Hall with an Elgar Festival of nine concerts between 30 May and 15 June 1949. These were either orchestral or choral events, as well as a chamber music concert held at the Concert Hall in Broadcasting House.

The following season, 1949–50, began with a Mahler concert on 1 October 1949 consisting of *Kindertotenlieder* and the *Resurrection* Symphony (No.2), with Dora van Doorn and Kathleen Ferrier as soloists with the BBC Symphony Orchestra under Bruno Walter. Sargent again conducted *Messiah* on 2 November 1949 (Jo Vincent, Kathleen Ferrier, Heddle Nash, Harry Shaw and 'One Thousand Voices' drawn from eight choirs from the London area). The Birthday Prom on 3 March 1950 featured Solomon and the soprano Elena Daniela in music by Mozart and Beethoven (LSO and Sargent), and Kubelik conducted the LSO with Menuhin (neither of them Ibbs and Tillett artists but appearing by arrangement with Harold Holt) playing Brahms's Violin Concerto on 10 May. The following year the birthday concert on 3 March 1951 featured solo cellist Vera Canning playing the first performance of Herbert Murrill's Cello Concerto and Moiseiwitsch in the more familiar Second Piano Concerto of Rachmaninov.

That London Elgar Festival of 1949 had filled a place in the two quiescent years of the Triennial Malvern Elgar Festival, which itself began in 1947 and was very much the brainchild of one of its four conductors, Julius Harrison, but managed by Ibbs and Tillett. In 1950 the Liverpool Philharmonic Orchestra was used, with agency soloists Astra Desmond, Parry Jones, Henry Cummings as vocalists and Thomas Matthews (violin) and Anthony Pini (cello) as instrumentalists. The next festival took place in September 1950 when the London Philharmonic Orchestra, Boult, violinist Jean Pougnet, cellist Thelma Reiss, and contralto Mary Jarred were resident for the four-day event, in programmes which were by no means confined to the music of Elgar. Meanwhile Delius also had a festival of his music in the immediate post-war years, when the tireless Beecham (assisted by Richard Austin) put a series of events together under the auspices of the Delius Trust and the BBC, but managed by Ibbs and Tillett. There were seven concerts between 26 October and 11 December 1946, at either the Royal Albert Hall or Central Hall, Westminster, using many choral societies and, from the agency, solo vocalists such as Redvers Llewellyn, Marjorie Thomas, Gordon Clinton, John Kentish, Victoria Sladen, Heddle Nash, Oda Slobodskaya, Nancy Evans, and Elsie Suddaby, and violinist Jean Pougnet.

Ibbs and Tillett also managed the Gerald Cooper Concerts in aid of the Musicians' Benevolent Fund, which in seventeen concerts throughout 1946, performed Mozart's chamber music at the Wigmore Hall. The participants in the six performed in the early summer of that year were the Harry Isaacs Piano Trio, Marie Wilson String Quartet, Zorian String Quartet, the Pougnet–Morrison–Pini Trio, Griller String Quartet, and the Aeolian String Quartet. But in the field of chamber music, there was no group which approached anywhere near the popularity for the public and the significance to the agency of the Amadeus String Quartet, for it was from this time that the two organizations became and remained wedded together in personal and professional partnership for the next 42 years. It was Imogen Holst who initiated and (with £100 to underwrite it) funded their Wigmore Hall debut on 10 January 1948, a Saturday afternoon and with every seat sold, for which their programme was Mozart, Verdi, and Beethoven, and the event was placed in the hands of Ibbs and Tillett. It was not long before their reputation had spread beyond London, because the agency was immediately able to substitute them for the Hungarian String Quartet in Bradford (March 1948), for Poulenc and Bernac (the latter sick) in Birmingham, and for the Busch Quartet in Cornwall, while it did them no harm that the BBC had taken them up in a big way. Though the agency scheduled their dates and negotiated their fees, they always deferred to the quartet at every stage, in particular to Siegmund Nissel, the quartet's second violinist, who, given his natural bent for such managerial matters, became business spokesman for the group. To quote Daniel Snowman's portrait of the quartet: 'The Amadeus have never had to hunt for work. From the earliest years offers regularly poured in and life was, and has ever been since, an almost uninterrupted whirl of concerts, broadcasts, foreign tours, recording sessions, festival appearances, and various summer and winter schools.' Ibbs and Tillett were loyal partners throughout.

The years immediately following the arrival of peace in 1945 were notable for the return of many artists, who were unable for a variety of reasons to perform in Britain, but were now joining those from other countries who had been resident in the UK. There was once again, therefore, a more international flavour to the performers who were appearing in London and elsewhere, many of them managed by the agency. Elisabeth Schumann, accompanied by Gerald Moore, came to the Wigmore Hall on 29 October 1949, pianist Lili Kraus gave a solo recital at the same venue on 5 December 1948, and appeared as soloist with the Hallé in Manchester. Jascha Heifetz performed at the Royal Albert Hall on 4 November 1947 with the Royal Philharmonic Orchestra. Edwin Fischer and Ginette Neveu went to Scotland and Manchester, while Cortot travelled to Liverpool and Brighton. Schnabel gave solo recitals in Birmingham, Liverpool and Newcastle (May 1946), and, with Szigeti, Primrose and Fournier, performed chamber music on the BBC in September 1947. Rudolf Serkin, Gina Bachauer, and Wolfgang Schneiderhahn also went to Manchester during the 1947–48 season, while the city's Hallé Orchestra went to Austria in the spring of 1948. Travelling in the opposite direction from Germany to Britain in November 1948 came the Berlin Philharmonic Orchestra, and Ibbs and Tillett managed their tour which had the following itinerary:

- Wednesday 3 November, Empress Hall, Earl's Court, London
- Thursday 4 November, Philharmonic Hall, Liverpool

- Friday 5 November, Town Hall, Birmingham
- Sunday 7 November, Town Hall, Oxford
- Monday 8 November, Civic Hall, Wolverhampton
- Tuesday 9 November, De Montfort Hall, Leicester
- Wednesday 10 November, Town Hall, Huddersfield
- Friday 12 November, King's Hall, Belle Vue, Manchester
- Sunday 14 November, City Hall, Newcastle
- Tuesday 16 November, Usher Hall, Edinburgh
- Wednesday 17 November, St Andrew's Hall, Glasgow
- Thursday 18 November, Albert Hall, Nottingham
- Saturday 20 November, Royal Albert Hall, London
- Sunday 21 November, Empire Theatre, Cardiff
- Monday 22 November, Central Hall, Bristol

The founder of Christian Action, Canon John Collins of St Paul's Cathedral in London, was a friend of Emmie Tillett and, finding it impossible to interest London agents or impresarios in his organization's plan to sponsor and bring the orchestra to Britain 'in pursuance of its work for reconciliation in the international field and for promoting friendship and understanding in Europe', he took the idea to her. She embraced the project at once. Of the 15 concerts, its newly de-Nazified and reinstated conductor, Wilhelm Furtwängler, conducted the first four, and the only soloist to appear was Myra Hess playing Beethoven's Fourth Piano Concerto at the first concert only. In the vast Empress Hall at Earls' Court, an audience of 6000 witnessed this Jewish pianist playing with a German orchestra and conductor, so soon after the end of the war. To some it was seen as a gesture of reconciliation, though there were also many dissenters to that view. The remaining concerts were conducted by Sergiu Celibidache, recently displaced as Music Director after just two years.

In Yorkshire, a brave new venture was begun with the creation of the Yorkshire Symphony Orchestra, which gave its first concert in Leeds on 3 September 1947. Regrettably, after only eight years, the enterprise foundered in its dealings with councils and bureaucrats, despite its high-quality playing and top rank soloists. Ibbs and Tillett were asked to supply them with their solo artists, in the first season pianists Clifford Curzon, Lance Dossor, John Hunt, Irene Kohler, Phyllis Sellick, Cyril Smith, and Kendall Taylor, singers Doris Gambell, Trefor Jones, Marjorie Thomas, and William Parsons, violinists Frederick Grinke, Jean Pougnet, Henry Holst, and Maurice Raskin, violist Keith Cummings, and clarinettist Frederick Thurston. Whereas in their first season, 19 artists had come from Ibbs and Tillett's roster, by the orchestra's final season in 1954–55 this number had risen to 46.

The consequences of Kathleen Ferrier's successes in 1946 and 1947 brought an immediate deluge of offers for her to sing in Italy, France, Scandinavia, and, after Bruno Walter met her in the summer of 1947, a hastily arranged tour of America in 1948. So Ibbs and Tillett were forced to rearrange her schedule, adding further stress to John Tillett's already declining health. Nevertheless he insisted upon accompanying her to America, and together they set sail on the *Mauretania* on New Year's Day, 1948, leaving Emmie behind to manage the agency. The passage was stormy, though there were breaks in the weather during which the singer and her manager were able to promenade on the sun deck, and then indulge themselves in the good food and luxurious benefits of ship-board life. At the Hotel Weylin in New York, they were pleased to find that Moiseiwitsch was a fellow guest. The weather was cold yet they strolled down Broadway on their first night, though at John Tillett's slow pace rather than Ferrier's brisker one (she was soon to suffer from a severe cold as a result).

Ferrier was on the books of the Columbia Concerts agency, and John Tillett was with her, acting as her adviser and manager, just as, when the agency was first formed 40 years earlier, Leigh Ibbs had accompanied Clara Butt and her concert party around Australia. Before she had even sung a note, Columbia booked her for the following year, a contract she signed on John Tillett's advice, despite her own reservations as to its terms (she was already having to pay her own travel, subsistence and publicity costs and would have to do so again in 1949, as well as forfeit any fee if she cancelled for any reason). To add to her problems, post-war restrictions on currency meant that she had limited funds with her, and Tillett not only appeared confused by America, its pace of life, customs, even its traffic, but also suffered because he was now eating so much rich food after the rigours of wartime dietary limitations at home. This inevitably frustrated Ferrier, who was younger, healthy, energetic and in a new land for the first time, but little did she realise the cruel irony that she was nursing a man who was dying from the disease which, just five years hence, would also strike her down. From New York (where she had repeated her earlier Mahler collaboration at Edinburgh with Bruno Walter), the pair travelled on to Illinois for concerts in Ottawa and Chicago. She told her sister Winifred of her concerns for him (see her letters in Appendix 18), and did her best to look after him while curbing her impatience. Among letters of condolence Emmie received after John's death later that year was one from the New York agent Annie Friedberg, who recalled that 'he was not feeling well at all, in fact I thought he looked quite bad. Perhaps the trip and all the excitement here was not good for him.' Clearly John could have done with Emmie's presence on the tour.

Once back in London, his health went into a further downward spiral. After commiserating with the New York agent Andre Mertens on being laid low with a cold, he went on to describe his own ailments in a letter dated 16 March 1948: 'Like yourself, I have been obliged to stay away from business, in fact I returned from America feeling anything but well, and have since been in the hands of the doctor and had three weeks at home on a milk diet.' Six weeks later and just over a month before his death, he wrote a letter to the singer Keith Falkner (always a close friend as well as an agency artist), in which their mutual love for cricket still managed to find a place amidst the gloomy report of his ill health:

> I guess Emmie has told you of my illness which has left me with anaemia, a recurrence of cystitis and sundry other ailments. Here I am, a weary and listless person with scarcely any appetite, in fact I hate the sight of food. I was off colour the whole time in America and since my return on Feb 10th have been in the doctor's hands. I had planned to see MCC v Yorks and Surrey, but it is much too cold to be sitting about out of doors. I too spent last Wednesday and Thursday listening to the Radio commentary from Worcester and am most anxious to see [Charles] Palmer in the flesh. Yorkshire's display at Bradford is most deplorable, especially Hutton's effort with the bat. I am just longing to see Keith Miller, and if it is warm enough to venture out, I shall hire a car and go to the Oval on Saturday, Surrey v Australia, but as I have to drink five pints of fluid every day, this may prove an obstacle. We shall see!

Lord's Test : I do hope you have been lucky and drawn a box. Upon my return from America I made application for a seat in the grandstand (uncovered part) and got them by return, so all that is necessary is fair weather and my complete recovery.

Kathleen Ferrier made a very big success and will be returning to the States for a three month tour next February. She has also had a triumph in Holland with two sold-out recitals in Amsterdam.

Holidays : provided we can find suitable hotel accommodation, we have decided to try Alassio where I believe the bathing is so good and we will travel by the Blue Train to Vertimiglia. I shall certainly have to pull myself together otherwise I shall sink instead of swimming. How unfortunate that you feel obliged to leave your lovely villa, but I can appreciate the difficulties with which you are faced. It is very kind of you to make the suggestion but I am afraid we should be lost taking on a flat, not to mention the shopping. You'll hardly believe it but this is the first I have heard of the best team between the Wars. My brain is somewhat weary, but I think you have chosen well, especially as only one player can [be] selected from each county. At the rate time is flying, you will soon be here and I need hardly say with what delight we shall welcome you here. All good wishes. Yours ever, John (5 May 1948)

John Tillett died from cancer at The Clinic in Devonshire Place on 20 June 1948, but was 'spared the worst ravages' according to his physician Lionel Grunbaum. His memorial service, which Emmie did not attend, took place on 24 June at St Marylebone Church. Elgar's Serenade for Strings and the first movement of Tchaikovsky's work bearing the same title were played by Boyd Neel's orchestra, Freddie Grisewood read from the Bible, and mid-way through the service Myra Hess delivered the following address:

John Tillett was a most remarkable and unusual character. I don't think any of us have ever known anyone quite like him. From his unassuming manner, no one meeting him for the first time could have realized that, for nearly half a century, he had held one of the most prominent positions in the musical world.

The foundations on which his life was built were an unassailable integrity and an unfailing sense of values and loyalty, both in his work and in his human relationships. He was unaffected by these days of excessive speed, and behind his leisured manner that we all knew so well, lay a profundity of wisdom and quiet consideration that gave dignity to all he said and did.

He achieved his unique position largely by his intuitive understanding of the nature of our musical life. He knew the tempo of the British people, and above all he had a profound distaste of anything meretricious or superficial. John Tillett's honesty and long-sighted judgement never allowed him to raise false hopes or to make hasty promises, and it was from him I learned that the road must be long, if a musical career were to have a solid foundation. There must be many of us here today who have felt his pride and happiness, when we made good.

His whole life was centered in his work; the work that identified him with every traditional musical activity in Great Britain. Perhaps people knew him best as a guiding spirit of the Three Choirs Festival, but there can be hardly a single concert society that has not relied on and benefited by his counsel. I know he had looked forward to a few years of leisure, but when the war, the third in his career, broke out in 1939, he re-dedicated himself to his work, in order to help keep alive the continuity of British traditions.

He was fortunate in having a wonderful partner in his wife, known to us for many years as Emmie Bass. Together they worked almost to breaking point, throughout the war, their staff being reduced to a minimum. I often found them both doing office boy's work late in the evening, before trundling home with cases full of papers that had to be dealt with before the following morning. Those of the staff who remained, worked under the same pressure and with equally high endeavour, and this devotion was deeply appreciated by them both.

In spite of his unbroken record of work for music, John Tillett was a man of wide interests. His fastidious taste and appreciation of beauty permeated his home, where he surrounded himself with rare and exquisite things; books, furniture and pictures. Many will remember what a perfect host he was and also his knowledge of good wines, but with all his love of the best things of this world, his poise and moderation kept a perfect balance.

It is impossible in this short time to touch on all the facets of his personality, but there are two

> I must mention – his genius for wit and humour, a kind humour that laughed with and not at people; and his love of cricket. Whenever he did desert his office, you could be sure that he had gone to Lord's, and it was characteristic that this should be his favourite game, for it exemplifies all that he held in high esteem – sound sportsmanship and team work, with no thought of personal display.
> His friends were legion, in many countries besides our own, and I speak for us all in saying that although his presence has gone from us, his warm friendship will live for ever in our hearts. (London 24 June 1948)

In some ways John Tillett was a shadowy figure (though far less so than Robert Leigh Ibbs), and ironically it took his death, which produced a flood of tributes, to reveal his character and personality. He was evidently a man of principle, who inspired affection and friendship from many people, but if there was one word which was frequently used about him, it was 'gentleman'. His brother Pedro, still alive at 76 and living in Highgate in London was, according to his wife Mary, 'feeling the loss of his brother – his last remaining link'.

The Times (3 July 1948) published a letter from J. Mewburn Levien of the Royal Philharmonic Society:

> It is not too much to say that all those whose calling lay in the world of music in London during the last half century will wish to join in the deserved tribute Dame Myra Hess has so admirably paid to the memory of John Tillett. As the oldest of those left who were concerned in days gone by with and were responsible for the arrangements of the concerts of the Royal Philharmonic Society, I can testify to the value of his assistance, the soundness of his artistic judgement, and the *con amore* spirit in which he joined in the work of the old society, of which he was a Fellow. In a charitable cause, too, nobody ever asked John Tillett's help in vain. His passing will be widely and long regretted.

Messages of condolence (the archive contains just under 500 letters and telegrams addressed to Emmie or to the firm) flooded in to Ibbs and Tillett from all areas of the music profession. They came from music societies throughout the land, colleges of music, other agencies and concert managements in Britain and elsewhere, and from many artists and friends. They ranged from the Education Secretary of the Banbury Co-operative Industrial Society Ltd to the Secretary of the Savage Club. Many came from people who had only met John once, some had never done so, and had only communicated with him by telephone, yet they felt compelled to write, drawn by the warmth and kindness of his personality despite the limited contact they might have had with him. A humble note penned by three employees from Ibbs and Tillett's Box Office was touchingly genuine:

> We, the members of the Box Office respectfully tender our deepest sympathies at your great loss. The firm has lost not only a great gentleman, but also a man loved and respected by all who knew him and sought his advice on all matters musical.

Members of the office also wrote, curiously still addressing Emmie as 'Miss Bass' seven years after she had become Mrs Tillett. Kathleen Cheselden, pledging her support for the future of the firm, noted in her letter, that:

> it will be so hard for you at No.124 as everything there <u>is</u> Mr Tillett, but I will help you all I can and in any way possible. The messages and telegrams which have come during the day are wonderful and you must be so proud to know the esteem in which he was held ... I think you understand that I have always loved dear Mr Tillett for the wonderful and sweet person he was, and I shall more than miss him.

Sadie Lereculey expressed her 'pleasure to know that, in addition to his thoughtful generosity, Mr Tillett considered me worthy of holding such a position in his business. That is something which it will always make me proud to remember.'

Audrey Hurst would 'always be proud of having known Mr Tillett', while Edwin Worman had 'known Mr Tillett since 1920 and all this time he has been a true friend and guide to me at the office, with his unique and great knowledge of the musical world. I feel that it is like losing one's father.' There was also a former employee, Marjorie Taylor, who wrote from retirement in Taunton:

> It's such a long time since I worked for you as 'Miss Cole', you will probably hardly remember me, but I shall always think of my time with you with great pleasure and remember how very kind both you and Mr Tillett were to me.

Clifford Curzon, abroad in Switzerland with his wife (the American harpsichordist, and fellow Ibbs and Tillett artist, Lucille Wallace), wrote that 'he really had something of the *grand seigneur* about him' and 'it always seems a privilege to know an ideally matched couple, and that's how we thought of you and John'. Another pianist abroad was Moiseiwitsch, who cabled from Australia: 'Deepest and sincerest sympathy, Emmie dear. Will sorely miss dear old and best friend and benefactor.' Elisabeth Schumann, now living in London, wrote that 'all his friends are mourning with you, and nobody who had the great privilege of knowing him will forget this wonderful man, his noble character, his true friendship'. Maurice Johnstone of the BBC in Manchester described him as 'one of the few straight ones in a rather crooked profession', while his London-based superior, Steuart Wilson (former tenor and now Head of Music) bemoaned the fact that: 'all the music profession has lost a friend and we have lost a colleague whose connection goes right back to the beginning of our history, and I in person made my first approach to N Vert [that is, the agency] in 1914'. Other singers included Elsie Suddaby, who wrote that 'John was one of the nicest men I have ever known, always considerate and helpful … I cannot imagine that anyone could have done so difficult a job as his and remain so beloved by so many'.

Gwen Catley recalled:

> for over 25 years dear John has been there as loved friend and adviser all through my career. He was always there as the last word in any difficulty to advise and help. He always so steadfastly held up the dignity of our profession, in these days when singers especially are less and less esteemed.

Kathleen Ferrier:

> [could] only feel that you must know in your own mind that no-one can have had such care, devotion and loving kindness bestowed upon them in their last illness as that with which you surrounded your beloved John, and I know that he has been one of the most fortunate of men, as well as the most loved.

Fellow agent Harold Holt telegraphed 'his deepest regret. The loss will be deeply felt amongst those who appreciate a man who throughout his career carried on the faithful tradition of straightforwardness and respected the decencies of our profession'; other agents to do so included Joan Ingpen of Ingpen and Williams, Wilfrid van Wyck, E.A. Michell, Nicholas Choveaux, Alan Priestley (in Birmingham), Ivor Dargavel (the Principality Concert Agency of Briton Ferry in Wales), and many in Australia, Holland, France, South Africa, and America. C.S. Taylor, General Manager of the Royal Albert Hall wrote, so did Jay Pomeroy, owner of the Cambridge Theatre, and, of course, members of staff at the Wigmore Hall. W.A.K. Murray of the Glasgow firm Paterson (primarily a piano dealer but which also ran a concert and entertainment bureau) wrote:

> ever since I joined this firm, just on thirty years ago [1918], we have had many dealings with your husband and Mr Ibbs. It was always a great pleasure to meet them when they came with visiting artists and to realise when we had problems we could rely on receiving immediate answers to all our queries.

Other piano firms who wrote were Chappell ('His name will long be remembered by all those engaged in the musical profession – loved and respected by all') and Pleyel ('it will be a great grief to Cortot. Your dear husband was one of the very kindest of men'). From the music publishers Curwen, Maurice Jacobson, also a pianist and composer, thought that 'it seems impossible to think of musical life in England without him; that his name will remain time-honoured as long as music lives here is the only comfort I, a comparative stranger, can offer you'. In these days of Entertainment Departments in County or Town Boroughs it was no surprise that business relationships had evolved, if only by letter or telephone, between their officers and Ibbs and Tillett, hence letters of condolence from Dover, Hastings and Colwyn Bay. Chancellor of the Exchequer, Sir Stafford Cripps and his wife, Isobel, lovers of music and friends of the Tilletts, wrote from 11 Downing Street, while the music critic of *The Times*, Frank Howes, recalled:

> The last time I saw him was at the Gloucester [Three Choirs] Festival when he entertained my breakfasts with conversation at once shrewd and kindly. My association with you and him in our various National Gallery celebrations remains a valued memory, in which again that wisdom and tolerance is outstanding.

Other newspaper music critics to write were Richard Capell of the *Daily Telegraph*, who mourned 'a man of such judgement and integrity, much thought of by all', and Neville Cardus of the *Manchester Guardian*:

> I have waited until the passing of time shall have quietened the general voice. It is very hard to write to friends in their moments of loss – very hard to avoid platitudes. I didn't meet John many times; but it was not necessary for routine to make links with him. The spirit of friendship flowed out of him. And he was, using the word in a sense almost obsolete nowadays, a gentleman.

Among the choirs and orchestras who sent tributes were the Bach Choir, Alexandra Choir, Fleet Street Choir, LSO, London Philharmonic Orchestra, Yorkshire Symphony Orchestra, and Boyd Neel Orchestra. It was, however, from the country's music clubs and choral societies, with whom the agency had such strong ties, that a genuine groundswell feeling of sadness emerged in their letters. They came from as far apart as Milngavie in Scotland and Tunbridge Wells in Kent, with Bradford Music Club's letter summing them all up by typically describing John Tillett as 'one who for many years has been a trusted and reliable adviser in musical matters. Confidence in the ability and integrity of one's business associates is a precious thing, and this we are fortunate to have had always in our dealings with Mr Tillett'. Many societies had Honorary Secretaries or Conductors who had dealt with John for many years (40 in the case of the conductor Arnold Barter, writing on behalf of the Bristol Philharmonic Society) and most mentioned his professional expertise and friendly, helpful manner. 'We as a Society', wrote C.D. Pilcher of the Brighton Philharmonic Society (of which Herbert Menges was conductor), 'are, and always will be, conscious of the debt which we owed to Mr John Tillett for his invaluable support, consideration and encouragement over so many years, and if we know that the loss will be irreplaceable for ourselves, how much greater it must be for you'. From Lincoln, Gordon Slater wrote to Kathleen Cheselden, 'on the rare occasions when in town I had the time to visit him, he always received me as if I was the only person in whose affairs he was interested, and devoted all his attention to matters which, by comparison with the numerous and important concerts and musical events he managed, must have appeared very small and unimportant'. Sheffield Philharmonic Society's Kenneth Crickmore (from 1951 destined to run the Hallé and become Barbirolli's personal manager) owed 'a debt of gratitude for the kind help and guidance he has given'. Cheltenham Philharmonic Society's conductor Eric Woodward 'first got to know him during the running of the old Max Mossel concerts here and he was always a great help and inspiration', while Croydon Philharmonic Society was sure 'he will be missed by choral societies throughout the country'. Blackburn Music Society could not resist combining its message of condolence with confirmation of a booking for the bass Gordon Clinton later that year for 15 guineas. Clinton himself was among the many singers who wrote:

> Words cannot express my feelings because you more than anyone know my debt of gratitude to him. At home, if I was worried over anything it was 'ask Mr Tillett', and at my first appearances at the Albert Hall and the Three Choirs he was there to help one through. I shall never forget him. Curiously enough I never felt he was my business manager, as I suppose officially he was, because, in company with you, an atmosphere of personal friendship was always the chief thing. There must be many of us feeling this pretty deeply … If it is given to me to have a successful career, the foundation of it will have been his interest, shrewd knowledge, and his encouragement.

The soprano Elena Danieli gave Emmie a fairly detailed, if somewhat rambling, account of the memorial service before including some of her reminiscences of John:

> I feel I must write and say how beautiful the memorial service was for dear Mr Tillett. The music was divine, the orchestra so wonderful in tone, and it sounded particularly beautiful in that lovely old church. The hymns sung by so many fine voices were an inspiration to hear. Freddie Grisewood read so beautifully from the Bible. You perhaps know his father was a vicar. Myra Hess read the most moving and beautiful tribute to you both. In fact I felt better in every way after the service, and I'm sure you would have been pleased with everything.
>
> I must tell you what Melba said when she took me to your office twenty years ago this very summer. 'I'm taking you to the only honest agents I know in the profession – Mr Ibbs and Mr Tillett are both gentlemen'. When Mr Tillett used to telephone and, in his beautiful speaking voice, say 'Elena, are you free to go etc?', it was always a very special engagement to me, and more important just because he had telephoned.

Szigeti, living in California, wrote:

> I can't tell you how grieved we are to hear of the blow which struck you just as both you and John were about to reap the many satisfactions that your unremitting work entitled you to. I know how much the successes of some of his artists always meant to John, thus the recent American successes of some of his friends and his renewing of contacts during his last trip must have promised both of you many more satisfactions.
>
> I have always had a warm personal regard and sympathy for him and I owe him many an insight into some of the more tragic aspects of an artist's career. It was he who told me about Josef Hofmann's fabulous successes as a boy prodigy and of his half-empty Wigmore recitals when he returned to London as a world-famous master of his art.
>
> But I mustn't go on and only want to wish you that you conserve the strength and the quiet determination characteristic of you, so you can carry on the work in John's name and spirit. I am sure you will find solutions for all the problems of reorganisation, but you must take care not to overwork yourself in the difficult times ahead of you.

Schnabel was in London with his wife Thérèse, and wrote from his Knightsbridge Hotel:

> We loved John; to be with him, to think of him was always pure joy. He was so gentle, so delicate and loyal. He was wise, warm and brave, a noble man, a solid and subtle friend, with an irresistible charm and a precious sense of humour and proportion. Our great affection for him goes on, as a treasure cherished in our memory.

Violinist Renée Chemet first appeared in an Ibbs and Tillett artists brochure way back in 1910, and was a longstanding friend to both Emmie and John. She had heard of his death from the singer Miriam Licette, who herself recalled that she had 'known him since 1915 and always admired him so much', and Chemet wrote to Emmie:

> I wish, my dear, I could write to you in French, so as to express you how much I share your sorrow, but I do not find the words in my very limited vocabulary to tell you that I can hardly believe that "my dear Tillett" as I used to call him, is no more, and it seems to me that he took with him in the grave all my youth, and all the so marvellous memories of the numberous years passed in your country and my happy hours spent at Wigmore Street. All my heart is near you, my Bassy, and I ask you to allow me to kiss you very affectionately.

A musician whose name had appeared in a brochure even earlier than Renée Chemet's was the cellist W.H. Squire, whose association with Ibbs and Tillett went back to 1908. Already four years older than John and destined to live another 15 to the age of 92, he sent a card on behalf of himself and his wife, commenting 'your late husband's gentle manner endeared him to everybody in the musical profession and he will be sorely missed'.

Guitarist Segovia had known John for over 20 years and was charmingly honest, and, like so many correspondents, sensed and encouraged Emmie's ability and determination to carry on running the agency in a manner of which John would both have approved and been proud. Recalling Hans von Bülow's telegram to his ex-wife Cosima on her husband Wagner's death, '*Soeur, il faut vivre*', Segovia's letter must also have been a great source of strength and inspiration to Emmie at this difficult time, and his words would, over the next 30 years, be fully vindicated:

> Unfortunately life did not offer us, outside of our respective activities, an occasion for unfolding the affection we felt for each other to the point of changing it into real friendship. But the seed of it was in our souls and only time and intimacy was missing for its full development. I regret that I did not approach him more, but I find consolation when I think that since 1925, when I entered to your organisation up to now, I never failed to show my sincere consideration and deepest sympathie to your husband.
>
> I understand your sorrow and I participate in it, exhorting you however to win it with courage and adhering to your decision of honouring his memory by continuing the work to which he devoted so many years of his life. I sincerely believe that you can take over the activities of your late husband, and you may be sure he will approve your decision, and that all of us, the artists that worked with him, will be grateful to you.

Sir Percy Hull in Hereford agreed: 'How wise of you to carry on his great work. This is a great relief to so many of his old friends who had the privilege of his fine advice and same outlook.' Hull's Three Choir Festival colleagues also wrote – Sir Ivor Atkins from Worcester (he was a 'a wise counsellor and a good friend'), and Herbert Sumsion from Gloucester ('John was such a tower of strength to people like myself, living away from the centre of things, and we got to count on his help as a matter of course'). Adrian Boult recalled 'that delightful humorous wisdom and breadth of judgement, and wonderful sense of service and helpfulness'. Fellow conductor George Weldon of the City of Birmingham Symphony Orchestra had, he felt, 'lost a good friend both musically and personally. I always found John so helpful and patient however much trouble I gave him over artists'. Siegmund Nissel of the Amadeus Quartet considered John 'a great man and a great and wise influence in the shaping of music in England. I think all true British musicians will feel that they share with you your loss.' Violinist Alfredo Campoli reflected 'how much I shall miss the deep and friendly voice on the telephone, usually asking what free dates I have for the Liverpool Philharmonic'.

Myra Hess, after the tribute she wrote for the memorial service, continued to be a pillar of support. On a train journey she wrote a letter which had a clever mix of sensitivity and a (typically) wickedly suggestive sense of humour:

> My darling Emmie, I have just had a cup of hot coffee to try and keep warm. We are now at Bath and it has rained since we left London. Oh, to be in England – but I wouldn't be anywhere else! It was no use. I couldn't get the lovely Riley up me passage, in fact I had to tell the nice Mr Bacon it was no use trying!! In the end I have bought a second hand Austin 10, which I like much better than the Morrises we saw. It is said to be in very good condition and is nicer than the models they are making now – so that's that, and unless I move, or have me passage enlarged (which isn't humanly possible apparently!!) I can never have a slap up car. I expect I'd loathe to look opulent too?!
>
> I hate coming away and leaving you, my darling, although I know that I, or anyone, can do so little for you just now. You must let me say how deeply I feel about your magnificent courage and indomitable spirit. I would like to use a capital S for you have reached something higher than the word spirit as we use it every day. You and John are in my thoughts and my heart constantly. Ever your Myra

Benjamin Britten and Peter Pears, shortly off to the Holland Festival with their English Opera Group, both wrote:

> Only a line to say that I know you realise that you are as much in our thoughts in your great loneliness as you were in the terrible days of worry. It would be lovely to see you whenever you feel able to see friends. We will telephone you when we are back in London in July. It would be impossible to begin to say how much we valued John's work and friendship. Alas, he will be irreplaceable. This brings, dear Emmie, our best love and deepest sympathy, Your devoted Ben

> Emmie my dear, I want to give you all my sympathy and loving thoughts in these sad days and to say that Ben and I are with you very much in spirit, as indeed I am sure are all your friends and John's. It must help you to remember what a valuable full life his was, how much he helped people like us and what he contributed to musical life in this country. We are grateful to him, thankful and proud of having known him. John won't be forgotten by us, Emmie dear. We shall be at the church tomorrow. Very much love to you, Peter.

From within the profession, however, it was the singers who felt the loss most keenly. Many sent just short notes but all expressed sincere regret at the passing of a man who had taken such encouraging interest in their careers, and continued to make them feel special once they were established and in regular work. The tenor Frederick Steger remembered:

> with gratitude his kindly letter to me when I joined the army, and his readiness to see me when I was demobilised last August. He was full of enthusiasm at our interview, giving me much shrewd advice on how to rehabilitate myself after my long absence in the service. As usual he was humorous, which happy characteristic I note he retained to the end. I shall retain a vivid recollection of him, and he will be greatly missed in our music world.

The bass Norman Lumsden reflected:

> to artists like myself, who saw him not often, he was the spirit of kindliness and good humour, and always ready in the midst of work to listen to our troubles. And I well remember that when I first met him I was really afraid of him. I left him on that occasion full of respect for him, his good humour and in the knowledge that I was safe in the hands of a gentleman.

Younger talents who had not known John long nevertheless had cause to be grateful to him, such as the bass Owen Brannigan, whose career was now beginning to blossom:

> I am sure that younger members of the profession like myself feel as I do, the loss of one whom we looked upon as a parent, a father, whose advice and guidance we often sought and [which] was granted so readily, and in my case always proving to be the right course to follow in all I asked of him. My lifelong respect for his name will be the only way I can now hope to honour or faintly repay such a personality – this I pledge myself to do.

Winifred Radford remembered '"Uncle John" with deep affection from the days of my early childhood, he has always been greatly loved and esteemed by all those who have had the privilege of knowing him'.

A final tribute came from an old friend, Rae Robertson, writing on behalf of himself and his wife Ethel Bartlett. They operated a popular piano duo who had been with Ibbs and Tillett for 20 years since 1928:

> I think you do know how sincerely we treasured John's friendship and of course our long association in business is something that we shall never cease to be grateful for. In a world where the fine things of life are not too easy to find, to be associated in business with a real gentleman, whose integrity and straight-dealing could never be questioned, has been a rare privilege.

As noted earlier, the word 'gentleman' continues to feature throughout the letters from every branch of the profession, and the sadness felt by so many comes across in all the messages of support as totally genuine. An era had come to an end, the original Ibbs and Tillett were no more, but in Emmie Tillett both men had a worthy successor to carry on the work of the agency, and she would be supported by an enormous feeling of goodwill from every quarter of the music profession, and from the clubs and music societies which it provided with artists.

CHAPTER TWENTY-ONE

Kathleen Ferrier

The new decade of the 1950s, and the decision to re-enact the Great Exhibition of 1851 a century later as the Festival of Britain, epitomized the post-war euphoria of the period. The nation was both willing and able to re-invent itself, with much of the focus on London, though by no means exclusively so. In the field of music, each city planned its own programmes and events while London witnessed the opening of the Royal Festival Hall. Barely a year later King George VI died and a new Elizabethan age began. While these occasions generated more work than ever for Ibbs and Tillett, there was an air of sadness which overshadowed its work between the spring of 1951 and the autumn of 1953, two and a half years during which Kathleen Ferrier battled against the cancer to which she eventually succumbed. Although the disease may have begun as much as 15 years earlier, more definite signs seem to have appeared in June 1949, followed by rheumatic discomfort in October, and neck and shoulder pains two months later in December, yet it was only in March 1951 that the disease was finally diagnosed. These were difficult times for Emmie Tillett, for death had already claimed her husband in 1948 after only brief years of marriage. Now it took her mother (to whom she was extremely close) at the end of 1950. Ferrier's courageous fight against her insidious disease has been documented elsewhere in memories penned by professional colleagues, her sister Winifred, and by her biographers, but Emmie Tillett kept material about the singer, for they had become close friends after her husband's companionship during the singer's first American tour in 1948. Letters written by Kathleen Ferrier (to family, colleagues and friends as well as to Ibbs and Tillett) can be found in the author's *Letters and Diaries of Kathleen Ferrier* (2003), but Appendices 16–18 here contain both sides of the correspondence between the singer and her agent.

Once Ferrier's career was launched as a fully fledged professional from 1943 and even more so once peace was re-established in 1945, it initially focused on the towns and cities of Britain, with London, Manchester (she was close to Barbirolli), and the Edinburgh Festival as favourite venues. She sang at the first six Edinburgh Festivals where she met Bruno Walter, and (thanks to Britten) at Aldeburgh after Glyndebourne. Here and at Covent Garden, New York and in Holland, she sang only two operas, Britten's *Rape of Lucretia* and Gluck's *Orfeo*, because she never saw herself as an opera singer. She gave concerts and recitals overseas in America, Holland, Austria, France, Switzerland, Italy, Denmark, Norway, and Sweden between September 1946 and May 1952. She became part of Emmie's inner circle of friends which included Myra Hess, Roy Henderson, Gerald Moore, Keith Falkner, and John Barbirolli. Her initial correspondence was with John Tillett and duly deferential, but gradually, as she became more experienced and therefore self-confident, her letters become more assertive and direct, even quite 'matey'. Apart from their confirmation of taking on her sole representation (12 May 1943), the earliest letter to have survived from Ibbs and Tillett to Kathleen Ferrier was written at the end of 1944, in response to an undated one from the singer to John Tillett. This is a letter of an *ingénue*, an untried artist, whose repertoire is still severely limited, but who has a burning to desire to seize every opportunity to perform, to learn, and to give only her best. It also shows a singer, hitherto either used to finding her own engagements on a local basis and with small fees or being fed by CEMA with recitals in the North and Midlands, now having to cope with a far higher profile and the promise of not only a burgeoning career, but also more lucrative rewards.

The Tillett archive contains many letters to and from Ferrier, most of them sorting out programme details, accepting or refusing engagements, or reporting news from tours to America and Europe. Clearly there are none to the agency from her first American tour because John Tillett was with her, and after their return to Britain it was not long before Emmie took over responsibility for the singer's work from her ailing husband. The tone of the letters changed immediately, and their greetings 'Dearest Emmie' and 'My dear Kathleen' emphasized the personal as well as business nature of the relationship. Ferrier comes across as a serious artist with a bubbling, direct personality, full of fun despite her ever-increasing health problems. She can be 'bawling mi eyes out' during *Das Lied von der Erde* one minute and be 'Klever Kaff' the next. Emmie brought Ferrier into the bosom of her family. During her last years, Emmie's mother was cared for at Elm Tree Road by a New Zealand nurse called Bernadine Hammond known as 'Bernie'. In December 1950 Bernie was no longer needed by Emmie, so she introduced her to Ferrier, whom she was supposed to assist with secretarial duties, but after only a matter of days it was clear that she would have to resume the profession from which she was seeking an escape, and for the next three years she never left Kathleen's side.

The extant letters were written between the years 1944 and 1953, and include many from abroad covering her touring plans, travel arrangements, programmes and personal matters between friends. Some of these overseas agents also became friends, though enjoying nothing like the closeness of the relationship that Ferrier had either with Emmie or the office at Ibbs and Tillett, with whose staff she was very friendly, affectionate and considerate. In America there was Andre Mertens, a Vice-President and also the Director of the Foreign Division of Columbia Concerts Incorporated, a vast organization which, over the years, had subsumed several smaller or defunct agencies such as the Wolfsohn Musical Bureau of New York. This was the firm with which John (on his uncle Vert's behalf) had dealings back in 1902 (see Chapter 2). Ferrier undertook three tours to America, the first in January and February 1948, the second from February to the end of May 1949, and the third from December 1949 to the end of March 1950. Plans for further tours had to be abandoned as her illness took hold. Details of her third tour were laid out in a letter from Mertens, in which he also significantly alludes to signs of her failing health:

> I have now definitely set aside for Kathleen's tour of the United States the period from January 1 to and including about March 25th 1950. I will bear in mind that she must be back in England before Good Friday, April 2nd. I am glad that Kathleen received her itinerary. I only hope that she will not be too tired and that you will not let her sing too many concerts in Scandinavia, Holland, and England since her health does not seem to be the best after all that you have gone through. (14 December 1948)

Apart from a free week at the beginning of February, Ferrier's schedule was very full with concerts given to Music Clubs, Colleges, the Community Concert Service (CCS), and with the San Antonio, San Francisco and Chicago Symphony Orchestras. Her fees varied from a minimum $250 (New Friends of Music, New York) to $1500 with the

San Francisco Symphony Orchestra, at an average of $750 for each of her 32 engagements. She had signed a two-year contract with Columbia Artists (from June 1949), the second year of which, due to Kathleen's parlous state of health, was never fulfilled. Certain minimum fees were stipulated, such as $1000 for Regular Concerts and Symphony Orchestra appearances, while Civic, Community and similarly organized concerts had a net fee of $700. The agency took not more than 20 per cent commission for the former and 15 per cent for the latter, while their deduction for radio appearances and engagements, including electrical transcriptions, for phonograph records and for operatic engagements was a maximum of 10 per cent. Community Concerts, a uniquely American feature for half a century from 1921, were conceived by the Chicago-based concert agents Dema Harshbarger and Harry Harrison, who noted that firms such as theirs were being denied expected revenue from out-of-town recitals, because of inadequate audience numbers. Instead, and in order to eliminate any financial risk, clubs and societies were expected to pay fees up-front, by forming themselves into Civic Music Associations run by dedicated enthusiasts to raise the full booking fee from advance ticket sales. The idea caught on and larger agencies, including Columbia Artists, used it to disperse their artists throughout the continent, proudly proclaiming in its 'Artists' Almanac' that it could 'supply all concert demands, however great or modest, of every club, school or college, organisation or individual entrepreneur'. In complete contrast, Ibbs and Tillett's business relationships with music societies in Britain were based on a gentleman's agreement, and the agency would never have contemplated demanding money before the event. Neither would their artists' annual booklets have deemed it necessary, as Columbia Artists clearly did, to use such excessive hyperbole to sell their musicians as the following:

> In the task of recovery, the solace and inspiration of music will play its accustomed part, and the artists listed in this book, couriers of that lovely muse, are ready and eager to spread the message of cheer and joy to the four corners of this great land

The role of Ibbs and Tillett in Kathleen Ferrier's American affairs was purely advisory, and, to that end, Emmie took care in 1950 to see that her artist was getting the best deal possible for herself, especially in view of the less than generous treatment she had received on her two previous visits. In the archive, there is the draft of a letter Ferrier wrote to Mertens during her second tour in the spring of 1949. Evidently provoked by a thoughtless letter from him, which proved to be the last straw, it was written while she was staying at the Colonial Hotel in Florence, South Carolina, on Thursday 28 April 1949. This was late in a tour, which had involved a change of accompanist as it became increasingly clear that the one she had, Sandor Arpad, was having a nervous breakdown ('Arpad about as helpful as a can of beans. How I loathe his playing', she wrote in her diary on 9 March), and so he was replaced by the highly satisfactory John Newmark. She had written of her unhappiness to Emmie from Kentucky (27 April 1949 in Appendix 18), though at that point she had not written to Mertens, but wished to see how much money would be left over by the end of her tour, which was proving very expensive. A day later she had evidently decided to put pen to paper in the following *cri de coeur*, although even its darkest moments are lit by flashes of her gritty humour. It is probable that the letter was never sent; words or sentences in square brackets are scored through in the original draft.

My dear Andre

Thank you for your letter. It seems hardly worth going out of the USA in the middle of a tour, with all the bother of Income Tax clearances etc. I will ask for Mr Meyer's letter at Macon (I have already sent him all my accounts to date) and do as he says.

Mr Newmark is absolutely first rate, the difference to my own performance is unbelievable, and he also helps enormously with the travelling, tipping and general looking after. I should like to have him for next year, and would be glad of a list of engagements – with fees – so that I know how I stand and what I can afford to pay him.

I spoke to Mr Wisner because it is never very possible with you in the office with numerous telephones ringing and interruptions, and I hadn't had much experience of touring when I last saw you. I told him I was disappointed and amazed that I should come here as an established European artist and receive the lowest possible fees. Committees told me of this in good time, though I didn't need to be told, as I have been eating in drugstores and taking the cheapest rooms in hotel[s] to save money, and I didn't think this was usual unless one was a local beginner.

The halls are terrifyingly large for recital – oh I can fill them – but only by bawling all night, so that they have been a worry and an effort instead of a great pleasure. The Evanston concert particularly was miserable. The piano was shocking, the stage was unlit and it was in a high school gymnasium where the people at the back couldn't see me at all, and yet they were receptive. For work like this I should receive a double fee and some recompense for wear and tear!

I am becoming very American and speaking straight out, but there won't be time after the tour. I am completely ignorant of this commercial way of using artists and of all other business regarding visas, income tax etc., and that is why I have <u>you</u> to guide me.

I told you about the customs form when I was in your office one day. They told me <u>you</u> were responsible for my appearance here and would have to claim an extra week. It's nothing, just a formality, and considering I'm supposed to be a musician I think my organisation is surprisingly good!

I tried to get the Income Tax clearance for Cuba from Mr Meyer, but it was only possible to get the two Canadian ones, as I couldn't let them know what my expenses were a month or two ahead. I think the organisation has been lacking at your end, Andre, not mine. I am trying to cope with you, Holland, Salzburg, London, Edinburgh, Scandinavia, and so far have managed it as well as coping with these long journeys and singing at the end of them.

I want to sing only if I am wanted. I have only a short time to spare here and I want to sing not more than twice a week if there are long journeys and get a top-rate fee. I have turned down lovely work in Europe at the highest fees to people who have been trying to get me for three years – this is the honest truth. My war work was singing to village and factory audiences and now I must pick and choose. If I have any money left out of this tour, it will be because I have scrimped and saved, and that for $3^1/_2$ months work is just plain silly.

[There is so much work in Europe that I am not interested in coming here unless I can make a lot of money.]

I am getting this off my chest, what with Sandor and everything else, I have been [going about in a] most harassed [state], and I want you to know, because after all your endeavours on my behalf, [and not just say to you] I don't want to disappoint you at the end of my two year contract by saying "Sorry, I've had enough". I want you too to advertise as little as possible. I can <u>not</u> afford 480 dollars for *Musical America* and 500 dollars a time for leaflets. I need that money to pay my rent in England.

I am very tired after three nights and a whole day in the train [including a bilious attack], and am also recovering from [succumbing to] a bad bilious attack, and your letter saying I needed better organisation was just too much for me, so I hope you will forgive me for talking straight out to you in this fashion. (28 April 1949)

At the beginning of August, Emmie wrote a thoughtful and touching letter to Mertens, in which she sought not only to protect Kathleen from overwork, but also to emphasize her protegée's artistic status and quality. Ferrier was already a woman of 37 at this time. Having been a late starter, she leap-frogged the stage of being a young rising star, so she was not that easy to sell to the American public. The letter's concluding paragraph has an eerie sense of foreboding and uncomfortable prescience regarding Kathleen's fragile health, for the hoped-for career of 'some years to come' would soon be denied her:

> … Concerning Kathleen, I have been on the point of writing you for some little time, but I have not been able to get down to it as we are so frantically busy, and it was a matter to which I wanted to give some considerable thought.
>
> When she arrived back from America there is no doubt she was terribly tired and overworked, and consequently very dispirited, not with all your arrangements and the way you had looked after her, but by the type of work she had been doing and the very little financial gain at the end of it. I am sure you have gathered that Kathleen is not the person who is only out after the money – very far from it – but she is terribly unhappy with what we call here 'hack-work', and it is something for which she is not fitted at all! By hack work I mean the type of concert she was doing here before John found her and was able to set her on her artistic feet – hacking round the country for ENSA, singing the same programme day after day. She has outgrown all that and now occupies about the most envied position in Europe that any Singer has been fortunate enough to attain this decade. So far as England and the Continent are concerned, I very carefully pick and choose the work that she should do – her favourite oratorios – *St Matthew Passion* and other Bach works – *The Dream of Gerontius*, Mahler, Recitals with her own Accompanist, usually Gerald Moore, and programmes entirely of her own choosing. Miscellaneous programmes or with other artists I have cut out entirely, and even then we have more offers for her than she can possibly hope to fulfil! You, of course, know your own field much better than I do, but I just want you to know that Kathleen will be far happier if she does fewer dates at better fees, so may I beg of you not to think that she wants to sing every day and all day just for the sake of dollars. If necessary cut down her time in America and just let her come for say six weeks, and in that time say twelve or certainly not more than fifteen dates, consisting of oratorios, recitals for the really important Societies, and Orchestral concerts.
>
> You know me well enough to realize that the last thing I want to do is in any way interfere with your most admirable management, but I do so want you to understand that with Kathleen we are not dealing with the ordinary type of artist, but one that must be looked after most carefully and nursed in such a way that her art, which is so very exceptional, will last for some years to come and not show signs of wear, not only through overwork but by having to do the things she isn't happy about. (2 August 1949)

Although Andre Mertens' reply is not extant, he evidently took Emmie's wise words and underlying message to heart, for Ferrier's third (and last) tour of America (during the first three months of 1950) was more sensitively handled, and brought her even greater success. While she was in Canada he wrote to her:

> I am really delighted about your great San Francisco success, and that the reviewers there recognised you as a really outstanding artist and paid you full tribute. San Francisco notices are just as important as New York notices and I think with this material in hand, I can go to town and get better terms for you in the future than I hoped for. When you are in New York, we can sit down quietly and then make our plans for the future so that I am fully acquainted with what you have in mind and what I would like to suggest to you.
>
> It gives me great pleasure to learn from you that the tour went smoothly and that you are in a happier frame of mind than before. I know now what you want and it is my sincere desire to arrange for you in the future a tour that will give you financial and artistic reward. (1 March 1950)

A month earlier he had written to Emmie, giving a detailed explanation of the problems local promoters were having in America, but that Kathleen's visits to America were probably unaffected:

> Kathleen seems to be pleased with the results of this season since we have all done our very best to accommodate her. We are all deeply interested in Kathleen's career and it is our sincere wish to make her happy here. If we draw up a new contract, the fee for the 1951–52 season can be left open for the time being and settled on mutual agreement at a later date. At that time we will have a better picture of the economic situation in the United States. The Local Managers have definitely been suffering because of the exorbitant fees a number of artists have been demanding. It is essential for an artist to understand the many problems faced by these Local Managers. In addition to the artist's fee, the manager must pay for the hall, the promotion of the concert which includes publicity, salaries etc, which amounts to at least $1500. When these expenses are balanced against the capacity of the

> hall, there is a very slim chance for profit. Indeed, the manager counts himself fortunate if he meets his expenses.
>
> If the Local Managers could count on capacity audiences for all of their concerts, their position would be stronger. While this country is not in a depression at this moment, there is a marked reluctance on the part of the people to spend money on luxuries. This is not only felt in the entertainment world, but also in luxury clothing, jewelry, furs etc. People are becoming careful with their money. Another factor which seriously hurt many concert managers was the widespread strikes which not only paralysed the striking area but also many industrial areas. When industry slows down, money becomes very scarce. When the Local Managers had their annual meeting in December, all of these issues were discussed at length. They came to a unanimous decision that they could not continue to lose money when presenting artists, and called for a 25% reduction of fees. I do not believe that this will be necessary in the case of Kathleen, because I am extremely optimistic about the future of this country. I am sure that her fee can be maintained and possibly set a little higher, if there is no drastic change in the market. However, we can discuss this later and set the fee in mutual agreement.
>
> Kathleen asked me to forward her a contract which she wanted to look over with the lawyer. I advised her to look it over with you because it was your husband who first examined our contract form, and, after my explanation, accepted the terms. We can only sign a standard form printed contract which has been approved by the Artists' Union (AGMA) [American Guild of Musical Artists]. As soon as I have a little more time, I shall write to Kathleen and explain everything in detail. She will then have time to think about it and discuss it with you. (1 February 1950)

With Kathleen away in Holland at the time, Emmie responded:

> [while I can] fully appreciate all the difficulties with which you are meeting over the question of fees, as we are similarly placed, although on a smaller scale, but nevertheless the position is just as acute, particularly in regard to the artists who only understand American fees, which are, of course, quite beyond the Societies in this country, particularly in the present economic situation. However, I suppose all these troubles will solve themselves. (13 February 1950)

Although Ferrier was fully booked in Britain and Europe for the 1950–51 season and could not undertake a trip to America, she did make plans for a visit there from October to December 1951, with a maximum 22 performances to be scheduled during these ten weeks. A minimum fee of $1000 was envisaged and Mertens, Ferrier and Emmie Tillett met at Wigmore Street on 27 April 1950 to make plans for a tour, which, as events unfolded, never took place. One can feel sorry for Mertens, who, by the autumn of 1950 was being pressed by organizations as diverse as the Ladies Morning Music Club in Montreal or the Chicago Symphony Orchestra for confirmation that Ferrier would sing for them in the following season, for which programmes were having to be planned and artists booked. It took until October 1950 before Emmie sent the signed contract to Mertens, who in turn requested updated publicity material, because it only described her career to 1949. Ferrier went ahead and booked her passage on the *Queen Elizabeth*, leaving Southampton on 21 September and arriving in New York five days later. Mertens was also worried about the effect the Korean War was having on audiences in America, and dissuaded Ferrier from giving a recital at Carnegie Hall:

> I want you to know that very few artists can sell out this big hall, perhaps Lily Pons and the pianist Horowitz … in view of the fact that all recitals in New York are half empty and most of the artists are losing money because of the terrific war scare. (December 1950)

He wanted her to opt instead for Hunter College and an outright fee of $1000. By January 1951 her forthcoming tour was virtually full with engagements from Miami to Montreal, and by February all the concerts were, with one exception, sold out.

After much prevarication, Emmie was eventually forced to break the catastrophic news to managements abroad of Kathleen Ferrier's illness, of its diagnosis on 24 March 1951 (without revealing any medical details), of the operation which followed on 10 April, and the anticipated period of convalescence. Whereas for Europe some managements had necessarily to hear the news as soon as possible because of imminent engagements, in the case of Mertens she delayed until the beginning of May, when she wrote:

> I am afraid this letter brings you some bad news. I have specially refrained from cabling you as I felt it better for you to have all the facts rather than the bald announcement.
>
> KATHLEEN FERRIER recently had to undergo rather a serious operation, but I am very happy to say that she is making wonderful progress and her doctors are very pleased indeed with her. It has meant, however the cancellation of the whole of her Scandinavian tour in April and engagements in England in May, and at present up to June 19th, but we are hoping that she will be able to undertake a performance of the *B Minor Mass* (Bach) in the Albert Hall on that date, and from thence to continue her work, although it will have to be curtailed for some time to come and made as easy as possible for her.
>
> Now comes the question of America. I had a long consultation with her doctors yesterday, and they told me it is essential that for some time to come Kathleen must not be out of touch with them for more than two months at a time on account of certain treatment which she must have under their supervision as they understand her particular case.
>
> I am afraid this means that part of her American tour must be cancelled, very much to Kathleen's regret as you can well imagine, but as her future health depends upon it you will understand the absolute necessity of abiding by her doctors' decision. We shall have to ask you, therefore, to cancel certain of Kathleen's work so that she begins not before October 25th in Montreal and terminates not later than December 17th. Having been into the question of sailings, I find that the "Queen Mary" will sail on October 16th , due New York October 21st , and on the return journey the "Queen Mary" leaves New York December 22nd. This exceeds the two months by two weeks or so, but the doctors are agreeable to this little additional time as she will at least be resting on the journeys.
>
> In her itinerary there is an engagement booked at Hamilton, Ontario, on November 14th and at Miami on 17th. This will necessitate a very long journey which may prove too tiring for her, so perhaps it would be possible to cancel one or the other. Incidentally it is very important that no further engagements are interpolated between October 25th and December 17th, and everything must be made as easy as possible for her. I cannot tell you how deeply sorry I am to have to write to you in this strain, but at the same time I am thankful that Kathleen can at least fulfil part of her tour. (3 May 1951)

For the next few months, from spring into summer, Emmie was clearly trying her best to send as much optimistic news as she could from London, while between them she and Mertens attempted to salvage what they could of a shortened tour. A medical certificate was obtained from Ferrier's doctor, Reginald Hilton, and its contents distributed to those concert promoters from whom she was forced to withdraw her services.

> To whom it may concern
>
> This is to certify that Kathleen Ferrier is under my medical care for a serious illness which has involved a major operation, from which she is now making a good recovery. I expect her to be able to travel to America by mid-October. She will, however, need medical supervision for some time, and it is essential that she should not be absent from this country for longer than two months. (21 May 1951)

In July Emmie told Mertens:

> Kathleen returned to the concert platform in a performance of the *B minor Mass* on June 19th, when she thrilled a very large audience at the Albert Hall by her really wonderful singing, which is completely unimpaired by her recent illness, in fact it is more beautiful than ever. (13 July 1951)

But in less than a month, she was forced to send him a cable which read:

> DEEPLY REGRET FERRIER MUST CANCEL ENTIRE TOUR STOP WAIT MY LETTER STOP TILLETT. (2 August 1951)

This next letter was sent the same day, although only Emmie's handwritten draft has survived. It must have been hard for her to write.

> It was with a heavy heart I had to send you a cable to say about our Kathleen – cancelling the remainder of her American tour, but things are not going as well with her as we had all hoped. I am writing you this personal and private letter as I feel it is only right that you should know everything, and then you will know better what steps to take when cancelling her engagements.
>
> The operation Kathleen had in April last was for a malignant growth and the entire left breast was removed. I was there at the nursing home and saw the surgeon immediately afterwards. The spine was also affected but immediately following the operation she was also given [X] ray treatment and very miraculously it cleared up. Following a holiday by the sea, she looked more fit and well than I have seen her for years but her doctors – I can assure you they are the finest possible – warned us that the next year would be extremely critical and at all costs she must be guarded against extreme fatigue, catching cold etc. She started work, as you know, on June 19th and following several engagements here, went off to Holland where she had a very strenuous fortnight during the Festival with rehearsals and performances of *Orpheus* and several concerts.
>
> She looked very fatigued when she came back, when she was at once examined again and X ray photos taken only to reveal that a secondary growth had started in her spine. One small comfort – it is in a different spot, the first place having healed wonderfully and the bone actually grown again. She takes the rays extraordinarily well and is of course now in the midst of further treatment to which we can only hope and pray this horrible thing will yield.
>
> She has no further engagements now until the Edinburgh Festival in September and the complete rest and treatment over the next five or six weeks should be effective, but in any case, in view of this further recurrence I know you will understand that it is impossible for her to undertake her American tour, and her doctors have told me that it is out of the question.
>
> It does not seem possible that such a thing could happen to our wonderful Kathleen, does it? She is so courageous about the whole thing and her sense of humour never leaves her for a moment. Miracles do happen sometimes – one has got to happen now.
>
> Do you think you can make the cancellations without revealing the nature of her illness? You will know the best course to take of course.
>
> I am just on the eve of leaving for a short holiday – my first for four years but I feel most unhappy about going away and leaving Kathleen, although she is in wonderful hands and everything that is humanly possible is being done for her. (2 August 1951)

Mertens was genuinely concerned for Ferrier, who by now was a good friend both to him and to his wife Klara. Kathleen made a recovery that summer which enabled her to appear at the 1951 Edinburgh Festival in September, but Mertens felt compelled to hold back the public announcement of the cancellation of her tour to America until she had sung in the Scottish capital because, as he wrote to her directly:

> it would be very difficult for me to explain to the people why you are singing in England [*sic*] and are not able to come to the United States. (24 August 1951)

The public announcement of her withdrawal was made the following month, and, as he told Emmie:

> Everyone who knows Kathleen as a most responsible person realises that only an illness of a very serious nature could have prevented her from coming. Rumours are spreading all over the country and unfortunately they are worse than what I believe her state of health actually is. (13 September 1951)

In October, Mertens issued the following press release to try to dispel these alarming rumours, and he also began to advertise Ferrier for the following season in an effort to keep her name before the public:

> Columbia Artists Management Inc. is happy to report that good news has been received from England concerning KATHLEEN FERRIER, whose American tour for this season had to be cancelled because of illness. Mrs Emmie Tillett, the contralto's British manager, writes that Miss Ferrier has made 'quite a wonderful recovery', and will spend the three months she was to be in America in further rest and recuperation. This gives us hope that Miss Ferrier will be able to return to us during the 1952–1953 season.

Later in 1951, Ferrier's condition seemed to improve with secondary tumours evidently responding well to radiotherapy. Tentative plans were made. Bruno Walter asked her to sing *Das Lied von der Erde* with the New York Philharmonic Orchestra in January 1953 but Emmie cautioned against making any plans:

> I must stress the fact that so much will depend upon the next year or two; if she can get over that without recurrence, we can breathe again. (3 December 1951)

The Walter engagement was declined ten days later. In March 1952 Ferrier was asked to sign a new contract with Columbia Artists Management Inc. for three years from April 1952 to April 1955, although, as Emmie wrote to Mertens:

> there is no question of talking about a visit in 1953/54 at present. Strictly between ourselves I think the chances of her making anything of a tour that season are very remote, although we might contemplate a flying visit for perhaps a New York recital and one or two other things, but we cannot think of discussing it until, say, the end of this year. (7 March 1952)

Her proposed fees were $1300 for 'Regular Concerts' and 'Symphony Orchestra Appearances' (at 20 per cent commission) and for 'Civic, Community and Similarly Organized Concerts', $1000 for budgets up to $5000 and $1200 for budgets over $5000 (both at 15 per cent commission). Radio, opera appearances and phonograph recordings would be charged 10 per cent commission. Two months later Mertens had not yet received the signed contract and it took a further month for Emmie to explain why.

> Quite frankly and confidentially, I have not discussed the matter with Kathleen, as, on account of the question of her health, one keeps off such subjects as the future as far as it is possible to do so. However I have had a little chat with her about signing the contract, and while she understands your reasons, she says that she would rather leave it over for the time being, as the chances of her going over for the next year or two are most unlikely.
>
> Just between ourselves I think she feels a little twinge of superstition that if she does not sign it, she is much more likely to go back later on, so may we leave it over for the time being? (30 May 1952)

No further letters survive between Ibbs and Tillett and Mertens in America, but for the countries of Scandinavia, Kathleen Ferrier was represented from the end of 1948 by Einer Gylling of Wilhelm Hansen, a firm in Copenhagen whose activities combined music publishing with that of a concert agency. By December 1949, he was addressing her as 'Klewer Kaff' and signing himself 'Einer kleiner' (her nickname for him derived from Mozart's famous Serenade *Eine kleine Nachtmusik*) in letters written in quaint English.

> I know quite well what a busy artist you are, no wonder that all countries want to hear you … I am looking forward to hear from you, when you once upon the time will have one minute left to drop me some lines. (3 December 1949)

She made two visits, in September 1948 and October 1949, but a visit planned for April

1951 consisting of a dozen engagements accompanied by Ernest Lush as well as orchestral concerts, had to be cancelled after her cancer was diagnosed on 24 March, five days before her departure. Just three weeks earlier, Gylling had written to confirm programme details, a letter to which Kathleen had added some handwritten comments before sending it on to Emmie:

> … A last question: The Royal Theatre has now got *Orpheus and Eurydike* on the repertoire, and it would indeed be very amusing if you would sing in this opera here in Copenhagen. The Theatre is most enthusiastic about the idea, and I expect to be able to obtain a fee of 2,500 Danish Kroner.

To which Kathleen added, 'Impossible, nicht wahr? No time for rehearsal and must be home to rehearse my Rape! Would like to sometime – in Italian!' There was no hint of impending disaster in Emmie's reply of 16 March to Gylling, in which she gave detailed confirmation of Kathleen's programmes, but she was compelled to send a telegram cancelling the tour with a follow-up letter written on the day the singer should have been giving her first recital in Aarhus. It was no doubt one of many letters Emmie forced herself to write, as it meant that Ferrier made no further appearances for the next two months, among which was a scheduled concert with Toscanini to open the Festival of Britain with Beethoven's Ninth Symphony.

> You cannot imagine with what regret I was obliged to telegraph you concerning Kathleen and the necessary cancellation of her tour, but it was entirely upon doctor's orders, as immediate medical treatment was necessary, in fact you will be sorry to hear that she has to have an operation next week. However I have good reports from the doctors, so there is no need for alarm, but of course it will mean that she may be out of action for about two months, which means an enormous amount of cancellation for us as well as for yourselves.
>
> I have talked the matter over with Kathleen, but I see no possibility of transferring her Scandinavian tour to a period in the immediate future, as we cannot say at this juncture as to when she will commence singing again, and therefore, very regretfully, it must wait until 1952. I won't discuss the actual period at the moment until I know how things go with her and how much more will have to be cancelled, but all the same I have every hope that by the beginning of June she will be well enough to sing again. I shall keep in touch with you and let you know how she progresses. (31 March 1951)

Einer Gylling was deeply shocked, both personally and professionally:

> It was really the worst news I have received in my time as a concert manager that Kathleen Ferrier had to cancel her tour. We have never had an artiste who, in so short time and so totally, has impressed the big audience, and people has been waiting all the night at the box offices in order to secure tickets for the concerts. We have done everything in order to make this tour pleasant for Kathleen, so imagine our very big disappointment. Of course the whole thing is worst for Kathleen, and we sincerely hope that she will soon recover again. Will you, please, give her our very best regards and wishes for a soon recovery. (3 April 1951)

Gylling hoped for a postponement only till the autumn, but Ibbs and Tillett had already committed her to a three-month tour of America (which was already sold out at the time of this correspondence) but, as has already been related, at the beginning of August this too would be cancelled. Gylling kept up a constant stream of requests stretching into 1952, to all of which Emmie could only reply in the following vein:

> Just as soon as I am able to let you have a period I will write to you again, but I know you will appreciate that we have got to treat our Kathleen very gently for some time to come, as although she has made a wonderful recovery and the doctors are delighted with her, she has got to guard against fatigue and all possible infections, so that we must cut her work down to the minimum. (6 June 1951)

By February 1952, it was the doctors and not the agents or managements who were making the decisions, and they were advising her not accept work outside the country, though they did not stand in her way for the long-awaited and subsequently legendary recording of Mahler's *Das Lied von der Erde*, which she made in Vienna with Bruno Walter in May, her last trip abroad. Poor Gylling, when he heard that she was going there, begged for even a single concert in Copenhagen, even offering an unprecedented high fee of 10000 Danish Kroner. Emmie annotated his letter (1 April 1952): 'Get through May and then see!!! Just for Bruno Walter.' A vague promise was intimated for the end of September 1952, but then the file goes silent.

In France, Ibbs and Tillett established a business relationship on behalf of Kathleen Ferrier with the Bureau International de Concerts run by Charles Kiesgen from his Paris office on the Faubourg Saint Honoré. Emmie made an initial approach in October 1948, offering her French management to Kiesgen on the strength of Kathleen's recent successes in America and Scandinavia, as well as her impending appearance (the first by a British singer) at the Salzburg Festival in August 1949. Kiesgen accepted, recognizing her as 'a very exceptional artist', but he also drew attention to the problems encountered by artists appearing in Paris for the first time because of the French capital's highly conservative public. Her fee would have to be modest as 'her appearance will not bring in any receipts for this concert' (under the auspices of the Philharmonic Society of Paris), and the programme would have to be selected with care. Of course her success was immediate when she gave her debut recital in the French capital on 8 November at the Salle Gaveau, singing her typical German Classical-Romantic repertoire of Schubert, Schumann, and Brahms. Thereafter most of the correspondence between the London and Paris agencies is a matter of Ibbs and Tillett turning down offer after offer, including some from the North African countries occupied by France such as Morocco and Algeria. Ferrier could not return to Paris until she gave another recital (this time accompanied by Gerald Moore) at the same venue on 23 January 1951. She then travelled to Zurich and Rome, where she learned of her father's death.

> My poppy died peacefully after flu and slight stroke. Rang up home and decided to carry on with tour. Had all my Swiss francs stolen, £40. Rather bleak day. (Ferrier's diary 30 January 1951)

Then it was on to Milan, Florence, and Turin, before returning to Paris for a further concert on 18 February, where Emmie and her sister Winifred joined her. By May 1951 Kiesgen was pleading with Emmie for dates of Kathleen's availability, 'Please have pity on me, dear Madam, and give me the desired periods', but by now he too had heard news of her illness, although Emmie was compelled to inform him that it was more serious than he had been led to believe:

> … Miss Ferrier has been very seriously ill and had to undergo a major operation, but I am thankful to be able to say, however, that she has made a wonderful recovery and her doctors are delighted with her progress. She says herself that she feels better than she has for a very long time, but we must face the fact that for some considerable time to come we have to take the greatest care of her and guard against all possible fatigue and the risk of infection such as colds etc. This illness has meant the cancellation of the whole of her Scandinavian tour in April and engagements in England right up to June 19th, but we are hoping that she will be able to undertake a performance of the *B minor Mass* (Bach) at the Albert Hall on that date, and from then to continue her work, although it will have to be curtailed for some time to come and made as easy as possible for her. Miss Ferrier was due to leave for America in September, but after consultation with her doctors they told me it is essential that for some time to come she must not be out of touch with them for more than two

months at a time on account of a certain treatment which she must have under their supervision, as they understand her particular case.

You can quite understand the consternation Miss Ferrier's illness has caused, not to mention the difficulties with which we are faced in trying to replace all these cancelled commitments, which has meant a complete recasting of all her work for the next year or more. I fear, therefore, that we have no course open but to postpone her visit to France in March, although she would like to retain her Paris recital on February 15th. As to whether you wish this concert to be her own recital under your management or for the Philharmonic Society, I leave in your hands to make the best arrangement. Meanwhile would you please convey to the various Societies Miss Ferrier's deep regret that during the coming season she will not have the pleasure of appearing for them, but you can rest assured that as soon as we possibly can do so, we shall give you a period during which to reinstate these various bookings. (5 June 1951)

On 19 December 1951, Emmie was forced to cancel Kathleen's recital proposed for the following February (it was meant to be at the start of a European tour), once again on doctors' orders. A similar cancellation followed at the end of April 1952, just days before she was to fly to Paris to sing in a broadcast of *Das Lied von der Erde* on 5 May with Bruno Walter. Two weeks later she did fly to Vienna to record it with him. One last attempt was made for an appearance at the Besançon Festival in September 1953, but earlier in the year Emmie was once again warning Kiesgen that the prospects were not looking good:

I must send you all my apologies for not having written you concerning Kathleen Ferrier in reply to your various letters, but her health has not been too good of late and although she gave two performances of *Orpheus* at Covent Garden, which were really wonderful, the other two have had to be cancelled and she is going to hospital for a course of intensive treatment. We have to cancel everything for the next six weeks but towards the end of March I shall be in a better position to tell you what the chances are of her fulfilling the proposed engagement in Besançon in September. I know you will appreciate that under the particular circumstances it is quite impossible to sign their contract, which includes the clause concerning the 'non-fulfilment' of engagement, and if they insist upon that remaining in, then I fear it will be a question of their making other arrangements. I am so sorry I cannot send you more favourable news, but I know you understand the problem. (9 February 1953)

The Besançon Festival Committee issued what was tantamount to an ultimatum, demanding the return of a signed contract by the end of March, but, judging by Emmie's last letter to Kiesgen, she had already intimated to him the true prognosis of Kathleen's illness, whose withdrawal was announced instead:

We note that the Besançon Festival Committee are not prepared to wait beyond March 31st for Miss Ferrier's acceptance, but in any case I am afraid there would be no question of her appearing at the Festival, for reasons of which you are already aware. However if you would just refuse on Miss Ferrier's behalf, and let us leave it at that so far as they are concerned. (30 March 1953)

In Switzerland her manager was the Zurich-based Walter Schulthess, who proposed Kathleen for *Das Lied von der Erde* conducted by Paul Kletzki at the August 1949 Lucerne Festival, but in the end it was almost a year later before she sang in Switzerland in June 1950, at the Zurich Festival while journeying back from Vienna. She was initially asked to sing Brahms's *Alto Rhapsody* and Mahler's *Kindertotenlieder* under Erich Kleiber on 27 June, though in fact it was only the latter which she performed. As part of her big European tour in the New Year of 1951, she sang *Kindertotenlieder* in St Gallen on 25 January and gave a Lieder recital in Zurich three days later. Plans were then made for an extensive return visit to the country in February and March 1952 to sing in Basle, Zurich, Winterthur, Geneva, Berne, Neuchatel, Fribourg, La Chaux de Fonds, and

Lausanne. This was to be a mix of orchestral concerts (some conducted by Ernest Ansermet), and recitals in which Gerald Moore was to accompany her. All concerts were cancelled by a telegram from Emmie on 21 December 1951, and Schulthess made a couple more enquiries after Kathleen's health and possible future engagements in the spring of 1952 and 1953, the latter for a concert in Zurich with Barbirolli planned for March 1954.

Ferrier did not sing in Germany, although plans were made for a two-week tour to Düsseldorf, Cologne, Leverkusen, Baden-Baden and Frankfurt in March 1952 but then cancelled on 21 December 1951 by telegram to the Westdeutsche Konzertdirektion in Cologne, whose manager Gustaf Fineman was her representative in the country. He did not take kindly to the 'really not very happy news' which put him 'in a quite difficult position'. Kathleen was to be the main artist in their Master Concert Cycle, while the radio station had acceded to her special request for a performance of *Orfeo* in Italian, and Baden-Baden had only included *Das Lied von der Erde* because she would be singing. While fully understanding the serious nature of the operation Kathleen had undergone, Fineman pleaded for a reconsideration of the decision to cancel, by arguing that London was only a few hours away by plane if she had need of her doctors. Emmie replied that they were 'quite adamant and [therefore] cannot give permission for her to leave the country', and insisted that the singer 'must come first'. Later (12 August 1952) Fineman suggested a concert in March 1953, which would have included 'a new work from Stravinsky, that is a Cantata for mezzo-soprano, tenor, small chorus of female voices and chamber orchestra'. Emmie 'at once had a word with Miss Kathleen Ferrier. She is interested to hear about the new work of Stravinsky but unfortunately neither date is possible, that is to say March 18th or 25th, as she is already booked for this country. Miss Ferrier is so sorry as she would have liked to have considered taking part in the performance of this work.' In fact the work is scored for a soprano, and the scoring hardly that of a chamber orchestra at two flutes, two oboes and cello, but despite the performance being brought forward to 28 November 1952, Emmie continued to reject it for the same reason. On 16 December 1952, Fineman offered *Das Lied von der Erde* in Berlin in September 1953 conducted by Barbirolli, which was accepted 'in principle', though on behalf of Ferrier, Emmie reminded him of 'the difficulties of committing herself so far ahead in view of the state of her health'. On 1 April a last attempt was made to secure Ferrier for *Das Lied von der Erde* in Düsseldorf in May 1954, but by now Fineman himself was anticipating at best non-commitment, at worst rejection by Emmie in his letter containing the offer.

In Italy, Keith Falkner was the British Council's Music Officer in Rome and wrote (7 November 1949) of 'a general demand for Kathleen Ferrier' and asked for three weeks of the 1950–51 season. Emmie acknowledged that 'there is certainly a general demand for Kathleen Ferrier, in fact I don't know how to cope with it as offers are coming in from all over the world'. She made two trips, in June 1950 and February 1951. As far as the second trip was concerned, Falkner was asked to keep 'a fatherly eye on the whole thing to see that the dates are arranged so as to make it as easy as possible for Kathleen'. The first visit appears to have been a last-minute substitution, as Ferrier was already in Zurich when letters were exchanged between Emmie and La Scala on 19 June 1950. She was asked to sing just ten days later in two performances each of Beethoven's *Missa Solemnis* and Bach's *Mass in B minor* at La Scala, Milan, with

Elisabeth Schwarzkopf as her fellow soloist, and the two performances conducted by Herbert von Karajan. Her Swiss commitments precluded her arrival in time to sing in Beethoven's work, but she did sing in the Mass. The second visit, during the first two weeks of February 1951, consisted of Lieder recitals in Rome, Perugia, and Milan, an orchestral concert (*Kindertotenlieder* conducted by Ermanno Wolf-Ferrari) in Turin and one in Florence. The possibility of staged performances of *Orfeo* at La Scala foundered when dates could not be agreed, and an offer (see letter of 29 August 1950 in Appendix 18) to sing two performances of Verdi's *Requiem* under Victor de Sabata during the 1951 Festival celebrating the 50th anniversary of the composer's death, was rejected by Ferrier. After she cabled from Edinburgh on 31 August 1950 'Have restudied Verdi *Requiem* and regretfully feel it still unsuitable', Emmie wrote to La Scala's Director Antonio Ghiringhelli.

> Up to the present Miss Kathleen Ferrier has not sung the Verdi *Requiem* as she has always found it a little too high for her, but in view of the importance of the occasion for which you wish to book her services on January 21st and February 1st, we again put the matter to Miss Ferrier. We have just received a telegram from Edinburgh where she is at present, to say that she has restudied the work but very regretfully must refuse the offer for the two dates in question, as she still feels it is unsuitable to her voice. I am more than sorry that it is not possible for Miss Ferrier to be included in the Verdi Celebrations, but I am sure you will understand the situation. (31 August 1950)

It was while she was in Florence singing Mahler that her father died, but she was reassured by both Emmie and Win that there was no reason to return home. Apart from a further attempt by La Scala to attract Ferrier with an operatic role other than Gluck's *Orfeo* (an offer that had to be refused because, as Emmie pointed out on 22 February 1951, 'we must advise you that the only opera which Miss Ferrier sings is *Orfeo* by Gluck'), there were no engagements under discussion thereafter.

Myra Hess had always had much of her continental European work from Holland, and Kathleen Ferrier also visited that country fairly regularly during her career, namely in April 1948, June 1949, April and November 1950, January and July 1951, six trips in all, the last of them an appearance at the Holland Festival. In fact it was earlier, with the cast of Glyndebourne's production of Britten's *Rape of Lucretia* which toured to Holland in October 1946, that she first went there, and also met the Dutch impresario Peter Diamand. He persuaded her to give recitals there in April 1948, and she immediately established a rapport with the Dutch public, who took her to their hearts. The archive contains several exchanges of letters between Diamand and Ibbs and Tillett, mostly finalizing the usual details of such visits by Ferrier to foreign countries. The last extant letter was written after the revelations of her serious medical condition. After thanking Emmie for introducing him to the pleasures of painting, Diamand continued:

> May I take the opportunity to resume the point of our conversation last week which, as I gather, causes concern to you and me. Since I am back from England I noticed that the rumours about Kathleen's illness and its grim outlook for the future increase constantly. Not only American friends whom I saw or who wrote to me refer to it. Even here, I was approached by the Secretary of the Bach Society who, after having heard from various sides that Kathleen had to undergo a second operation and would therefore be prevented from appearing in public at least for a long time to come, planned to send her flowers with an accompanying note referring to that sad state of affairs. Of course I could prevent her from this well-meant plan. But I know that you agree that these rumours are harmful; they cannot fail to reach Kathleen earlier or later and are bound to worry her. How could this possibility be helped?

I was thinking whether it might not be possible that one of those illustrated newspapers, such as *Life* or *Picture Post*, always in search of Glamour Girls, could publish a story about her which would deny the rumours. In view of the wide circulation of these papers it might serve the purpose. There will be surely other, and perhaps better ways and I guess you know them better than I do. But it is my impression that the question should be tackled, in some way or other before Kathleen's career and, still more important, her moral conditions could be endangered. You know how devoted I am to Kathleen, and I think therefore that you will not disapprove of me expressing my thoughts in this question. (12 November 1951)

The mere mention of cancer was taboo at the time. It was the disease that dare not speak its name, neither in Charles Rigby's unauthorized biography of the singer published two years after her death, nor in the collection of short memoirs penned by Barbirolli, Britten, Moore, Cardus, Walter and Henderson a year earlier. Joan Hammond, remembering Ferrier in her autobiography *A Voice, A Life* (1970), refers to it as 'the cursed illness which took her from us', and concludes her memories of that other short-lived and fine British contralto Gladys Ripley with the words, 'she died soon after Kathleen with the same tragic illness'. Emmie, whose draft letter to Andre Mertens reproduced earlier in this chapter was more candid because it was confidential, did her best to assuage Peter Diamand's fears, and adopted the same optimistic approach she pursued in all her dealings with her fellow agents at home and abroad, when it came to the question of Kathleen's recovery:

It is extremely difficult to know just how to cope with the Kathleen situation and the only thing that will really set people's minds at rest is for her to sing in public. You may be interested to know that Mertens has released a paragraph which has already appeared in the *New York Herald Tribune*, which reads as follows:

'Kathleen Ferrier has made "quite a wonderful recovery" from the illness which caused the cancellation of her American tour for this season, according to her British manager, and will spend three months in rest and recuperation before resuming her artistic activities. She is expected to make an American tour next season'.

I do not think we need worry unduly about these rumours reaching Kathleen as she is already aware of a great deal that has been said but takes it all in her stride. You probably know that she is going to sing *Land of Hope and Glory* at the official opening by the Queen of the new Free Trade Hall in Manchester on Friday [16 November], which will certainly mean a considerable amount of publicity throughout this country. I will in any case send you some of the cuttings which you may like to circulate the press in Holland. As she is so popular there, they would undoubtedly give a little space. (14 November 1951)

In Austria, Kathleen's business affairs were put in the hands of the Austria Concert Agentur, who also managed the Gesellschaft der Musikfreunde. She made three visits to Austria, in August 1949 (Salzburg Festival followed by Vienna, for *Das Lied von der Erde* under Bruno Walter), June 1950 (to Vienna for the Bach Festival to sing *St Matthew Passion*), and May 1952 (to Vienna once again to record *Das Lied von der Erde* with Bruno Walter for Decca). A misunderstanding arose in the summer of 1950 when Dr Rudolf Gamsjäger, Secretary of the Gesellschaft der Musikfreunde, personally asked Ferrier in Milan to sing in Beethoven's Ninth Symphony and Mahler's Second Symphony with the Vienna Philharmonic Orchestra under Paul Kleztki in May 1951, with the added possibility of giving two Lieder recitals. Evidently Kathleen had made encouraging noises, but remained non-committal, which was duly misinterpreted as a firm acceptance (this despite the qualification that she must first defer to Emmie in London). At the time she was committed to the probability of two performances of Beethoven's *Choral* Symphony with Toscanini to open the Festival of Britain, an offer she could not (and did not want to) refuse. This London engagement was then confirmed in the middle of August 1950, and the news caused complete pandemonium in Vienna, where the Society had jumped the gun by announcing her for the forthcoming season.

> [It has] plunged us into great difficulties … we are now in the unfortunate position that we have told our subscribers that Miss Ferrier will be appearing in Mahler's Second Symphony at the period reserved for her in Vienna and also in her song recital on May 3rd. Of course I can understand that it is a very tempting offer for Miss Ferrier to sing in Beethoven's Ninth Symphony under Toscanini, and from my heart, I wish her to have this important artistic experience in her life. However in Milan I gave Miss Ferrier the dates of the Vienna rehearsals and performances and she assured me, as far as her calendar of engagements was concerned, she would do everything possible to accept them … It is naturally of great importance for us that Miss Ferrier should come to Vienna and I am accordingly asking you about the possibility of combining the London and Vienna concerts. It is conceivable if Miss Ferrier were to sing the Ninth in London during the first days of May, for her then to fly to Vienna in time to sing it here, meaning that only the first recital would be postponed. In any case Miss Ferrier must be in Vienna to sing Mahler's Second as she herself asked for it to be on this date. (20 September 1950)

Emmie's reply is not extant in the file, but it can be imagined. Despite this, Vienna was still trying to get her to agree to accept them in January 1951, when Walter Legge (on HMV notepaper) begged Emmie on the Gesellschaft der Musikfreunde's behalf, 'Director Gamsjäger tells me that Miss Ferrier promised him these dates when she was in Italy with Herr von Karajan'. Emmie put him right:

> … we informed Dr Gamsjäger as far back as August 18th last year that it was impossible for Miss Ferrier to undertake the proposed engagements early in May. When she was in Vienna last June, Dr Gamsjäger mentioned the proposed engagements to her, but she did not give him any promise that she could undertake them, and I think she told him at the time that it would be necessary to communicate with us as her sole representatives. As you know Miss Ferrier is singing with Toscanini at the Festival Hall on May 4th and 8th. (27 January 1951)

Events, as has already been mentioned, turned out quite differently, for Kathleen was prevented by illness from appearing (Gladys Ripley sang instead), and Sargent took the date instead of Toscanini. In June 1951 another offer was made to Kathleen, this time to sing in three performances of the *St Matthew Passion* to be conducted by Furtwängler in April 1952, but her 1951–52 season was by then already fully booked, and the offer had to be declined. Apart from her final collaboration with Bruno Walter in the city during May 1952, Ferrier did not appear in Vienna again. As her fame grew, so did the number of offers from other organizations in other countries, but they had to take their place in the queue. The Israel Philharmonic Orchestra wrote to Ibbs and Tillett on three occasions during 1952 in an attempt to secure Kathleen for the three seasons 1952 to 1955. Requests were also received from Yugoslavia, Egypt (the Cairo Society of Music), and from Iceland (Musical Society of Reykjavík) who pleaded 'Iceland also has its culture, the people are music interested in spite of their small number, and it only takes four hours to fly from England to here in a first class airplane', but Emmie could do nothing other than make vague promises for a future which Kathleen did not have.

Her penultimate performance of Elgar's *Dream of Gerontius* was at Hereford Cathedral on 11 September 1952. The conductor was the cathedral organist Meredith Davies who, in 1988, wrote to the tenor Charles Corp:

> When Mrs Tillett suggested that Kathleen Ferrier might be able to sing *Gerontius* at the 1952 Three Choirs Festival, she warned me that rehearsal time would have to be limited, but of course I gladly accepted, even though I had not conducted the work before – or very much else for that matter! In the event there was no rehearsal at all, not even with a piano: Kathleen had not sung a note to me before the performance. We had met a week or so before [in fact it was a month earlier on 8 August], over a cup of tea in Emmie Tillett's house, and she simply filled me with confidence that it was all going to be alright, and that I could manage. She was so friendly, kind and calm that it would have been churlish to have misgivings. I remember two points she made – that she would like enough time to sing 'beasts' in the phrase 'like beasts of prey' [Part 2, one bar before fig 42], and that the phrase 'cherish a wish which ought not to be wished' [Part 2, three bars before fig.20] was not the easiest to sing musically! I may have asked her about one or two other places, but certainly our conversation about the music was brief. I think she knew (as I have learned since) that discussing details of performance intentions can be dangerously misleading. Her approach was entirely right; at the performance she radiated calm assurance, and with relief I realised that so unwavering and certain was her sense of direction that I could relax and follow instinctively. From the moment she came onstage (dressed in white) she held the packed Cathedral spellbound – including me. I am sorry I can't give a more detailed account musically. I don't think we realised quite how ill she was (and certainly she concealed it), but we knew we should spare her as much as possible, so that my actual contact with her was minimal, but unforgettable.

Her last public appearance took place at the beginning of February 1953 at London's Royal Opera House, where Barbirolli, helped by David Webster, Covent Garden's General Administrator, had instigated a new production of *Orpheus* in a production sung in a fresh English translation the conductor had made with Ferrier. Four performances were planned but only two took place, on 3 and 6 February. At the second, her femur partially disintegrated and a portion of bone came away while she was on stage. With superhuman effort she made it through to the end of the performance, standing motionless. An injection of morphine saw her through the curtain calls and Green Room visits from friends and admirers, after which she was taken home on a stretcher. Emmie kept Myra Hess informed in America where she was on tour. Hess replied from New York:

> … The news of Kathy is utterly heartbreaking. We had read in the *Times* of the second performance of *Orpheus*, and you told me all that I had feared. What a triumph of spirit those two performances have shown, but isn't it unbearable. I wish I were at home and that we could be together, for I know how deeply this tragedy affects you, my darling. You have had too much to bear these last years. I went to see Bruno Walter in the interval of his concert here on Friday [13 February 1953]. He had already heard about Kath from the Hamish Hamiltons. I was deeply moved when he said 'it is not well with our friend' and then continued to say that he considers her one of the greatest people of our century. Bless her, it is absolutely true. Your letter took nearly a week to arrive, and as I cannot get K out of my mind, I cabled asking Beryl [Ball, Emmie's secretary] to let me have regular news, also by cable. But I know you will make time to tell me all you can … Oh how I wish I were at home. You will keep me posted with news of our beloved K? (15 February 1953)

Kathleen was taken from her flat in Frognal back to hospital, where she remained until 4 April, and, after only six weeks at a new home (40 Hamilton Terrace), was taken in again for the last time on 22 May ('must have mi ovaries removed', she confided to her diary that day). In June, Emmie suggested to the Royal Philharmonic Society that Kathleen be awarded its prestigious Gold Medal and this proposal was unanimously adopted by its Committee. She had a final operation on 27 July in an attempt to put off the inevitable, and to ease her pain. She lived through the summer, but died peacefully in University College Hospital on 8 October 1953. Britain had lost its finest lyric contralto, Ibbs and Tillett its finest artist, and Emmie her closest friend. She was never forgotten, neither by Emmie nor by many others whose lives she had touched. A quarter of a century later, Emmie (and by its implication, Kathleen's surviving sister Winifred) received this brief but poetic note from the French composer Nadia Boulanger:

> Dear Mrs Tillett
> Once more October 8th … Everything remains, the sorrow and the privilege, and I need to say to her sister and to her friend, my most faithful thoughts. (6 October 1978)

CHAPTER TWENTY-TWO

Artists and Agents: 1950–59

In these immediate post-war years, after the deaths of the two founders and the retirement of some of the Directors, Emmie Tillett increasingly assumed sole responsibility for running the agency. Before the war, the dissolution of the partnership with Robert Leigh Ibbs took effect from 31 December 1936, when Ibbs retired and Emmie was appointed as a Director. At the same time, Ibbs's goodwill was purchased by John Tillett and his fellow Directors, W.L. Tilbrook and Monica Nixon and now Emmie. Following Ibbs's death, his share of the lease of 124 Wigmore St was bought from his estate for £725 on 6 September 1944 by John Tillett, followed by W.L. Tilbrook's interest when he retired from the agency on 31 December 1945. John and Hetty Tillett lived at 1 Fellows Road, NW3, where Hetty died on 21 February 1939. On 29 June 1943, while retaining the maisonette for letting purposes (and also the studio flat at 1 Belsize Studios, Glenilla Road, NW3 which was let to a Major Clémençon in May 1941), John moved to 87 Belsize Park Gardens, NW3, which initially he rented, then bought in April 1943, and where he died. In his will, made the year before his death, he left sums to Emmie's mother Florence, his fellow Directors, his staff Sadie Lereculey, Edwin Worman, Frank Turpin, and his secretary Kathleen Cheselden. The rest, including the house, was left to Emmie, although, as it happens, they had decided to move to 11 Elm Tree Road, in St John's Wood and behind Lord's cricket ground. Sadly John, a lover of cricket and a member of MCC, did not live to make the move, but Emmie, together with her mother Florence and two German housekeepers Mona Werner and Erica (in order of seniority), had done so by the beginning of 1949. When Florence Bass died at the end of 1950, Emmie received letters of sympathy not only from close friends such as Hess and Ferrier, but also from Cortot:

> Very dear Friend, I learn of your sad loss and the cruel gap it has left. Allow me, at this sad time, to take part in your grief and to say that all our sincere and affectionate thoughts are with you. I was very struck on the occasion of my visit to your house by the vital intelligence of your Mother. I like to think she retained her astonishing facilities until the end and that she was spared any prolonged suffering. Allow me, dear Emmie, to embrace you very affectionately. Your Alfred Cortot (20 January 1951)

Walter Legge also sent a kind letter of condolence:

> Please accept my heartfelt sympathy on the death of your mother. Having been privileged to see in these last months the wonderful relation of friendship and comradeship which existed between you, a richer and deeper bond than the usual one between elderly parents and children in the prime of life, I can appreciate the extent of your loss. On the other hand you have every reason for inner peace. Your mother enjoyed good health and the full force of her keen mind and delight in life to a great age, and watched and shared with you the success of your career. That must be a great consolation for you. (30 November 1950)

Another came (as a postscript) from Benjamin Britten:

> My dear Emmie, So sorry to have left your letter so long unanswered but I have been away. Thank you for the nice suggestion that I should do a talk for WQXB in New York, but I am afraid this is not possible at the moment. Perhaps when this great strain of work is over I might be able to undertake such a thing, but I frankly do not see how it is possible until at least early next Spring.

Perhaps you will let me know how you feel about this. With lots of love and good wishes for 1951, Ben

[Handwritten postscript] My dear Emmie, I have only recently heard the most sad news of the death of your mother. I do send my deepest sympathies to you on this great loss. I have an idea of how much your sweet mother meant to you. Your life at home must seem terribly empty to you, but I know that your resources are numerous, and that you will find a way of filling it. Anyhow, Kath tells me that you are starting painting! Is that so? And how does it go?
Lots of love and deep sympathies. Yours ever, Ben
(11 January 1951)

Emmie was now alone, though she had her cat (Miss Tillett), a love she shared with Ferrier, whose kitten was called Rosie, and after Kathleen's death, she threw herself into her work. Judging by the amount of time and work devoted to running Kathleen Ferrier's career alone, it seems inconceivable that Ibbs and Tillett also had a vast amount of work for many artists, whose careers were in their hands. Myra Hess was kept active with work, which both she and the agency sourced. She wrote while on tour to America in the middle of February 1953, after receiving news of Ferrier's Covent Garden ordeal (that part of her letter is quoted in Chapter 21). For many years, Hess had had an American manager, Annie Friedberg, who by this time had become ill and senile, but fortunately she could turn for help to an old friend, the German musicologist and critic César Searchinger, who had a hand in her first tour there back in 1922. The 'music factories' to which she refers were the large agencies, such as Columbia Artists or one run by the impresario Sol Hurok.

My very darling Emmie
… I was nearly too overcome to get through my work this weekend. Poor Gina [the pianist Gina Bachauer] has the most frightful neuralgia, and a swollen face and couldn't play last night with Alec [Bachauer's husband, the conductor Alec Sherman]. I was so sorry for them, and as Gina had stood by for me last year when I wasn't sure that I could play at a Phil[harmonic] concert, I offered to play for her, and DID play the *Emperor* again, last night. It was a concert for a Greek charity. The Phil orchestra like Alec very much and played beautifully for us both. We had to postpone going to Chicago for a day and I shall have a close call for my four Mozart concertos. Gina was hoping to fly to Holland today, but I begged and begged her not to run such an insane risk, so her doctor was thankful that she has cancelled her concerts. It would have been sheer madness. They are giving her Penicillin, which sounds to me very much like an infection in the head. We'll keep that to ourselves, and it may be just nervous exhaustion.

Thank Heaven I am not with these 'music factories' who send their artists North, South, East and West, and that brings me to César. Touching wood, we think it is going to work out well. He is going to use the Friedberg Management title which pleases me very much, and he is joining with David Rubin, who is CHARMING, and I think and hope quite capable from a business point of view. César will not have many artists, and their respective lists will be separate. So it looks as if I can finish my days here as I began in 1922. César will keep Annie's very efficient secretary who knows our ways. It is an awful business having to plan dates for 1954 now, and poor Saz [her secretary Anita Gunn] is kept busy with telephones from coast to coast.

You will not be surprised to hear that I have promised to go to Prades again, but only to play one concerto (Beethoven 4) and one sonata with Pau [Casals]. My dates are July 5 and 7, unless everything is changed????? It is disturbing that you have so many 'inquiries', as Annie called them, for next season, but I still feel I MUST call a halt.

The BOYS [the Griller Quartet to whom she was 'Auntie' while they were her 'nephews'] are playing here this afternoon, and I expect I shall have to see them this evening. You probably heard that Philip [the Quartet's cellist Philip Burton] had his PILES removed, poor dear, but he is much better. He looked pretty frightful when we arrived a few days after the event. Howardie's [Howard Ferguson] concerto had a success beyond my wildest expectations in spite of the DDDDDDDDDDDD critics. If they hear a new work that gives pleasure and is easily understood

> and enjoyed by everyone, it must be BAD. Everyone has been quite furious with the papers, but Howardie, always the philosopher, and, after all, the appreciation of four thousand people (on the two days) is far more important. It is horrid that we won't see him again when we leave here tomorrow. I am sure he will give you all our news when he gets home about March 16th.
>
> And now my darling, I must stop talking to you and pack and practise at the same time. Oh how I wish I were at home. You will keep me posted with news of our beloved K[athleen]? I have given you Bismarck Hotel, Chicago and Beryl [Ball] or Marj[orie] Gunn [Anita's sister] have the intermediary addresses, from day to day. Saz send her very best love and you know you have my deep devotion. Y[ou]r Myra
> (15 February 1953)

Having arrived in Chicago from New York, Hess promptly fell ill and had to have her gall bladder removed, an operation which had been threatening for some years, and which she had been constantly putting off through pressure of work. She played once in the city, on 16 March, after which the operation was successfully performed on 25 March (apparently just in time to avoid the more serious possibility of peritonitis setting in). Two days earlier she had written to Emmie:

> My darling You really are an angel, making time to write regularly (when you haven't any time at all!) and I am so happy that Alec's flat is free for Kathie. Did he murder the would-be lessees??? Do give her my love always – I hope she had my letter from New York after I had seen Bruno Walter?
>
> And now you will have heard of my B….. G. B. and its mean behaviour. I wish I had been sufficiently warned of such a possible infection, but as Beecham would say, 'it is luck out of muck' that it didn't catch me in Kalamazoo or Cedar Rapids!!!! This is supposed to be one of the finest medical centres in the country, and the doctors couldn't have been kinder. They are looking forward to the Op enormously!!! And I only wish they'd take the D….. thing out this afternoon instead of waiting with tiresome caution until Friday or so. If you hear an explosion it'll only be me, and it will be lovely when my tummie doesn't resemble the dome of St Paul's anymore. César has taken the blow wonderfully, as although I shall be able to play quite soon, the doctors won't let me do the necessary travelling for the rest of my tour. I got a bit further this time than the Hippopotamus season, but it is damnable to have to cancel, and who knows that better than my Emmie? (23 March 1953)

The piano duo of Ethel Bartlett and Rae Robertson were frequent visitors to America, and evidently they too enjoyed a personal friendship with Emmie and her mother ('Auntie Flo'). From New York they wrote:

> … We finished the first part of our tour yesterday, and when I tell you that we've been playing 4 or 5 concerts every week since early October, you will know that we have been working!! I think we can now say that our new venture is a success. We've travelled fully 7,000 miles with our pianos and I'm real proud of my brother who manages the car and trailer wonderfully. Pictures will follow! I cannot tell you what a joy it is to always have our own beautiful pianos with us – a dream come true. Now we have almost a month to rest before the second half follows. We shall be thinking of you this Christmas [the first since John's death] – not much joy in it for you, and we shall be with you in our thoughts so very much. Our warmest love to you and Auntie Flo, Your old friends Ethel and Rae (19 December 1948)

Myra Hess's reference to the 'music factories' is an interesting observation, for in some ways Ibbs and Tillett was also something of a production line, sending individual soloists or combinations thereof hither and thither around the country every week. The image of these artists meeting up at Crewe station on a Friday night or Saturday morning, alluded to at the start of this book, may be an apocryphal tale, but its underlying point is a serious one. By 1955, Narciso Vert had been dead for half a century, but his legacy lived on and the argument persisted about whether an agent should act as an impresario or (as John Tillett strongly believed) as a service industry for the benefit of music clubs, choral societies, orchestras, and festivals. Vert had promoted the likes of Sarasate, Hans Richter, and the child prodigies of his day (one of them, Vivien Chartres, possibly hastening his own death), and in that respect it was Lionel Powell, not Ibbs and Tillett, who proved to be his natural successor. Emmie Tillett now had to decide how she was going to run the agency on her own. According to an article about Powell, written a month after his death and printed in *The Monthly Musical Record* (February 1932):

> devotion to music was the mainspring of his activities, and that if mere lucre was his only end, he could any day choose among a dozen other callings that would be more advantageous than the uncertain one of introducing musical lions to a fickle public … Powell was genuinely proud of his 'circus' – his celebrities, his virtuosos, his prodigies – and no doubt made what for a man of business were real sacrifices for its sake.

Powell was a real showman (in the mould of the nineteenth-century Barnum), but he was also a genuine lover of music as well as a very astute businessman. He was, however, very conservative in his taste, eschewing not only contemporary music, but also the recent past such as Bruckner or Mahler. A regular diet of Beethoven and Tchaikovsky's symphonies had been the time honoured formula of Hermann Franke, Narciso Vert, and Hans Richter, and it was then taken up by Powell. It persists today at London's Royal Albert Hall and the Barbican, espoused first by Victor Hochauser and then by Raymond Gubbay. Powell was wedded to the Royal Albert Hall, believing in attracting large numbers of the public to his events, even though it was a highly unsuitable venue if the event was a solo recital and the audience exceeded four thousand (his break-even figure). He also had to cope with the advent of broadcasting and recording. He feared the former more than the latter, because he sensed that a member of the audience, who was listening from the upper reaches of the Royal Albert Hall, would have felt nearer to the performer if he had his ear glued to the radio at home. Menuhin was Powell's last triumph, for when Ibbs and Tillett turned him down they did so knowing the boy would be better off in his hands. Unfortunately for Powell, death intervened before the young boy's famous association with Elgar, and although Powell still has his successors, Emmie Tillett was not one of them.

It is appropriate at this point to survey the nature of the competition facing Emmie in the 1950s. The 1953–54 *Concert Artists (Classical Music) Directory* (with the majority of its artists pictured) begins with a listing of agencies and their exclusive artists. Ibbs and Tillett tops the list with 13 pianists, two each of violinists, violists, and cellists, three string quartets, a piano quartet, an ensemble, six sopranos, four contraltos, seven tenors, and four baritones or basses, whose names are familiar and to be found in brochures of these years listed in Appendix 8. The other agents listed, all based in London, are as follows:

- Harold Holt of 3 Clifford Street, New Bond Street, W1 had pianists Claudio Arrau, Wilhelm Backhaus, and Artur Rubinstein, violinists Jascha Heifetz, Yehudi Menuhin and Isaac Stern, cellist Gregor Piatigorsky, soprano Jennie Tourel, and conductor Rafael Kubelik.
- Wilfrid van Wyk of 80 Wigmore Street, W1 had pianists Robert Casadesus, Joseph Cooper, Irene Kohler, and Witold Malcuzynski, sopranos Victoria de los Angeles and Kirsten Flagstad, cellist André Navarra, and conductor Eugene Goossens.

- Ingpen and Williams (a mythical partnership, for Joan Ingpen was working alone and Williams was her dog) of 31 Clarges Street, W1 had sopranos Erna Berger, Suzanne Danco, Sena Jurinac, Irmgard Seefried, and Ljuba Welitsch, baritone Hans Hotter, conductors Vittorio Gui, Erich Kleiber, and Clemens Krauss, and the Vegh String Quartet.
- Nicholas Choveaux (founded in 1948) of 28 Bury Walk, Chelsea, SW3 had the pianist Eric Hope and the tenor William McAlpine.
- Mark Lynford of 17 Cavendish Square, London W1 had the baritone Paolo Silveri.
- John Joel of 5 Hamilton Close, London NW8 had the baritone Tito Gobbi.
- S.A. Gorlinsky of 123 Pall Mall, SW1 had the soprano Maria Callas and the tenor Luigi Infantino.
- Richard Heller of 77 Dean Street, W1 had the soprano Elena Liarosa and the pianist Arthur Thomson.
- W.H. Barrington-Coupe of 40 Goodge Street, W1 had the pianist Martin Fogell and the baritone Montague Zolowsky.
- The Imperial Concert Agency of 20 Kingly Street, Regent Street, W1 had no exclusive artists. Established back in 1905, the year of Vert's death, and now operated by Gladys Crook and Tilly Connely they promoted themselves thus:

> The Imperial Concert Agency have long experience in recommending artists for special works and programmes; a brochure giving representative lists and suggestions will be sent post free on application. The Agency can obtain the services of any artist whom clients wish to engage, and as booked dates of leading artists are entered regularly, they can frequently offer their services at 'en route' fees. The Agency are always glad of the opportunity to suggest outstanding young artists at moderate introductory fees: none are recommended without personal knowledge of their work.

The brochure consists of 182 pages, divided into sections according to instrument or voice, and is a gallery of publicity photographs of 200 artists, taking a whole, half or quarter page, listing their agent if they have one, the phrase 'all leading agents' commonly appears with or without personal contact addresses or telephone numbers, though not for exclusive or well-established artists. Conductors appear for the first time, and those with exclusive representation are already listed above. On the other hand, Adrian Boult and Hugo Rignold were available *via* their orchestras (the London and Liverpool Philharmonics respectively), Sargent could be contacted by 'all leading agents', and Clarence Raybould, George Stratton, and Aylmer Buesst could be reached at their homes.

Ibbs and Tillett acted as agents for the 1950 Bath Bach Festival, a week in October packed with concerts to celebrate the bicentenary of the composer's death. For the four choral concerts, three orchestral concerts (with a section of the LSO), two chamber music concerts, four organ recitals and a harpsichord recital, they supplied the singers Isobel Baillie, Elsie Suddaby, Astra Desmond, Kathleen Ferrier, Eric Greene, Alfred Hepworth, David Lloyd, Henry Cummings, William Parsons, and Norman Walker, as well as many of the instrumental soloists for the remaining events. The following year, as part of the Festival of Britain, the same city contributed to the celebrations with two weeks of concerts at the end of May. It would appear that, according to some commentators, the festival was a timely shot in the musical arm of Britain.

A retrospective survey of the year 1950, contributed by Geoffrey Sharp to Ralph Hill's edition of *Music 1951*, took a very pessimistic and jaundiced view of London's musical scene, noting some names which have little resonance 50 years later:

> London's orchestral music in 1950 will not bear any kind of detailed comparison with what was provided in the middle and late thirties ... Among conductors Greenbaum, Harty, Heward, Kabasta, Weingartner, and Wood are dead, Mengelberg has retired, and Beecham, Toscanini and Walter are all past their prime. One might be excused for thinking the same of Furtwängler if his recent English performances [the Christian Action/Ibbs and Tillett tour of 1948] represented his greatest achievements since the war ... Is there one horn player in the country [Dennis Brain unaccountably overlooked] who can be relied on not to make a fool of himself and shatter the ensemble at any point where his instrument is called in to play? Why do our [orchestral] violinists plague us with a scraping noise, as of ten fiddles with wire strings being tortured with abrasive bow? ... On the whole foreign conductors are better at their job; who is there among our own younger men to compare with Erich Leinsdorf, Ferenç Fricsay, Rudolf Schwarz and Joseph Post?

Reports of music-making in Liverpool and Manchester were far more positive, but programme planning in Birmingham was considered as 'played for safety'. There, George Thalben-Ball had succeeded the late G.D. Cunningham as city organist (both players managed by Ibbs and Tillett), while the name of David Willcocks was beginning to impress when he exchanged the post of organist at Salisbury Cathedral for that of Worcester, succeeding Sir Ivor Atkins. He took over the Birmingham City Choir from the Birmingham Symphony Orchestra's conductor George Weldon. Later, Emmie Tillett would have a role to play in Willcock's career.

As noted in Chapter 19, Ibbs and Tillett lost the violinist Ginette Neveu, killed in an aeroplane crash on 28 October 1949, sixteen days after she appeared with the Hallé under Barbirolli in Sibelius's Concerto. Though Barbirolli (Sir John from June that year) was a close personal friend of Emmie and though his wife Evelyn Rothwell's solo career as an oboist was managed by the agency, the conductor had, from 1947, put his affairs in the hands of Kenneth Crickmore. As well as managing Barbirolli, he also became the Hallé Orchestra's manager succeeding T.E. Bean, who left to run the new Royal Festival Hall in London. Nevertheless, Barbirolli did use many artists from the agency. Apart from Ferrier, whom he alone called 'Katie' and with whom he forged a close personal friendship, Segovia, Navarra, Brosa, Lili Kraus, Gina Bachauer, Eileen Joyce, Serkin, Curzon, Schneiderhahn, Solomon, and Fischer were among many who appeared in the late 1940s and early 1950s. Manchester also had its new Free Trade Hall, opened on 16 November 1951 by Queen Elizabeth with Emmie in attendance, and the following night William Primrose played Walton's Viola Concerto in the first of eight festive concerts, the last of which featured a quartet of agency soloists, Isobel Baillie, Marjorie Thomas, Richard Lewis, and Norman Walker, four Lancastrians singing Beethoven's *Choral* Symphony under Sargent.

Wilhelm Kempff gave his belated debut recital at the Wigmore Hall under Ibbs and Tillett's management on 27 October 1951. So too, in that year and at that hall, did Elisabeth Schwarzkopf (although she was known to operatic audiences, because she was just completing a three-year guest contract at Covent Garden). Emmie appears to have had a particularly soft spot for singers, and frequently formed deep friendships with them. At this time, the baritone Pierre Bernac and his accompanist, the composer Francis Poulenc, renewed a close association begun shortly before the war, and both men featured predominantly in the artists' brochures of the 1950s. Immediately war was declared, Bernac was conscripted into the French army and in another example of quaint English, wrote to Emmie:

> Thank you so much for your charming letter. Poulenc send it to me but the letters are still very slow in the army. I am somewhere on the front and simple soldier. Certainly it is hard, but I am happy enough to have to drive a truck (I mean what we call *camion*). It is certainly much better than to walk in the mud. The idea of singing again in some years seems to me perfectly phantastic for the time being.
>
> A letter of [Charles] Kiesgen tells me that Cortot is now the head of the *Propaganda françois*, and that he thinks to Poulenc and myself for concerts in foreign countries, but I don't know if I shall accept these propositions if they are true. I cannot imagine my feelings as a civil[ian], leaving my comrades on the front. Well for the moment I must not think to that and do my simple duty unending hours after hours, days after days, and also perhaps years after years, [until] our undoubtless victory ... For the time being I think that the dear Francis is not mobilised and always [i.e. still] in Noizay.
>
> Dear Miss Bass, all my visits in London are very soft souvenirs, let us hope and pray that all this will be again, not too far. Very faithfully and affectionately yours.
> (5 September 1939)

Poulenc himself wrote three letters which have survived in the archive, only one of them dated (at the end of 1950 and a further condolence for her mother's death), but the others obviously written during the war with Bernac at the front while he himself is at home, though too troubled to be able to compose.

> Dear, dear friend, I can't tell you just how much your letter moved me. I am still a civilian for the moment. I expect to leave any minute. Pierre has left for the war three days now. I haven't had any news but I'm not too worried as I don't think he'll be in danger, at least for the present. I can't tell you what comfort I feel to know that our countries are so solidly united, I who have so many friends in England. It must be stopped, you'll admit and it's the opinion of all in France that it can't last. There's no other defence against bad faith but still, it's all profoundly sad, so much blood shed, so much youth cut down. Even for me at home, I can't work anymore. One's thoughts are elsewhere. I am forwarding your letter to Pierre. Like me, he'll be very grateful. It was delightful working with you, for you have become our friend. Let us hope for a glorious peace, which will spare the young the horrors we are seeing for a second time. Affectionate kisses, Francis Poulenc
> (Thursday, translation from French)

> Dear friend, I am sorry to be so slow in replying but I have been ill for three weeks. I had to do six concerts with Bernac!!! I am back at Noizay, where I am well again. I am on a diet which is very sad. It was a great joy to know my Mass was so well sung. Alas it is impossible to go and hear it as six concerts in a month have left me impoverished. I shall think about them all tomorrow. I did so enjoy my winter in London. We laughed a lot, didn't we? A thousand greetings from your faithful Poulenc
> (Sunday, translation from French)

> Dear Emmie, I have just met up with Pierre in the Hague after playing the concerto with Klemperer in Amsterdam. I heard of your poor mother's death and want to tell you that you have all my sympathy.
>
> Even when we have our loved ones with us for a long time, it's always a terrible wrench. Fortunately you have your work to keep you going. Dear Emmie, alone this Christmas. I embrace you very, very affectionately, Francis
> (17 December 1950, translation from French)

The death of Kathleen Ferrier on 8 October 1953 was not the only loss the agency suffered that year, for just two months later the brilliantly gifted Australian pianist, Noel Mewton-Wood, committed suicide at the tragically young age of 31, his career having lasted only two years more than Ferrier's. There was no short supply of new, young, up-and-coming artists to replace those who died or retired. The brochure for 1951–52 (see Appendix 8) is covered with handwritten additions of British names in Emmie's handwriting, such as the singers Geraint Evans, and Norma Procter, instrumentalists Julian Bream, Hugh Bean, Janet Craxton, Georgina Dobrée, and Bram Gay, while from abroad there came far more, among them Dietrich Fischer-Dieskau, Clara Haskil, Wolfgang Schneiderhahn, Tibor Varga, Bronislav Gimpel, Gustav Leonhardt, Leonard Pennario, Bela Siki, and Jorg Demus. The young New Zealand pianist, Colin Horsley, was among those young players taken on during the war and whose careers were now beginning to take flight. In a telephone interview with the author (3 November 2001) from his home on the Isle of Man, the 81-year-old pianist recalled the staff of Ibbs and Tillett and their various responsibilities. Sadie Lereculey handled music societies, Audrey Hurst the BBC engagements, while Emmie herself dealt with the engagements with orchestras as well as overseeing the whole apparatus. The always sober-suited Edwin Worman stage-managed Wigmore Hall recitals, often so vital to solo debutant pianists. Worman's name appears elsewhere, for in her contribution to a memoir of Myra Hess, the comedienne and *raconteuse* Joyce Grenfell recalled how:

> Mr Worman of Ibbs and Tillett, who for many years stage-managed so many of her concerts, kept a firm hand on the door of the artists room after a performance. Crowds rushed there to pay homage and they had to be controlled … Mr Worman, one of her most devoted admirers, was a controlled man used to concerts and artists, but he was often visibly moved by Myra's playing and would shake his head in wonder as if to say, 'I don't know how she does it'. (Denise Lassimonne, *Myra Hess by her Friends*, 1966)

Two fine pianists whose careers were in the hands of the agency were Solomon and Cyril Smith, both of whom suffered cruel blows to their health in the 1950s. During 1956, Solomon gradually lost the use of his hands before, in December, suffering a massive stroke, as a result of which he never played the piano again. His agent had been E.A. Michell since his first appearance as a nine-year-old prodigy back in 1911. Michell had an ambivalent attitude to securing foreign engagements for his artists, as it meant that he would receive only a part-fee, and although he did sterling work for Solomon in the years between the wars, his ability to manage his own financial affairs proved lamentable, and, after the Second World War, he was twice declared bankrupt. Solomon, unlike all Michell's other artists, could not bring himself to desert his agent, and bailed him out on more than one occasion. Despite having been a friend, and, together with Myra Hess and Benno Moiseiwitsch, a bridge partner of John Tillett for years, it was only when Michell died in 1951 that Solomon decided to place his career in Emmie's hands for what was to be a brief five years. Bryan Crimp, Solomon's biographer, relates how:

> British engagements now had to be 'selected' before being slotted into his diary, which was now being managed with characteristic efficiency and understanding by none other than Emmie Tillett, queen of the Ibbs and Tillett agency. E A Michell had died and Solomon was, at long last, free of his obsessive obligation. Emmie Tillett's long-standing secretary, Beryl Ball, confided to Solomon many years later that, on hearing of Michell's death, Emmie had declared herself to be the happiest woman in London.
>
> The new partnership and subsequent close friendship was secured over lunch at the then highly fashionable *Pastoria* restaurant. Emmie arrived feigning puzzlement as to what the occasion could be about, but as both parties placed their cards on the table there was no disguising Emmie Tillett's jubilation upon the realisation that she had at last captured the one artist who had for so long eluded her.

> … Furthermore international recognition had come comparatively late and this prompted him to embrace just about everything that came his way. He must, at this time, have rued the many unproductive years so loyally spent with E A Michell. Since being with Emmie Tillett, who worked so harmoniously with overseas agents, new horizons were continually opening up before him.

Solomon (or 'Solo' as he was known to his friends) retired to his house in Blenheim Road, St John's Wood. Emmie Tillett kept in constant touch with him and his partner (later his wife) Gwen, providing tickets and transport to concerts, so that he could keep abreast of musical events, the seats always having easy access for the disabled pianist. As the years passed, his condition deteriorated and he suffered not only physically but also from dark moods and bouts of depression. His fellow artists such as Hess, Moiseiwitsch, Gerald Moore, all close friends, were no more by the end of the 1980s and he mourned them all. Emmie's death in May 1982 was a particularly heavy loss. If she was not prevented from doing so by concerts or recitals, at which her presence was essential, she was a regular visitor to Blenheim Road every Sunday evening, when, according to Crimp, she would 'over a drink or two, bring Gwen and Solo up to date with all the latest happenings in the musical world. Her concern and fondness for the couple became apparent from her will which left them her house [in Elm Tree Road] for the rest of their lives.' This was a wonderful gesture, but Solomon would not consider leaving his beloved Blenheim Road and its garden, and so the legacy was politely refused. Solomon died on 22 February 1988 at the age of 86, 32 years after his massive stroke in 1956.

In an interview with the author on 19 January 2000, Gwen, then 93 years of age (she died a year later) related her memories of Emmie:

> Emmie was a strange mixture. When my husband had his stroke, she was so good and kind right up to the time he died. It was really like Emmie, she took enormous trouble over him, drove us to concerts and took us everywhere, she couldn't have been nicer. She used to come in every Sunday evening. He had very little speech after his massive stroke, and he lived for [a further] 30 years. She was incredibly kind to him, took enormous trouble. People used to laugh at her and say she had no time for her other artists, but she wasn't working for Solo as an agent, but as a friend.
>
> Emmie was a great driver. She had a big car and drove quite fast but extremely well, though she took no interest in anybody else on the road. She used to drive us to the Festival Hall for concerts, we'd come down Park Lane and she'd always drive on the outside [lane] and come round Hyde Park Corner in the wrong lane for going into the park. I used to sit in the back, Solo in the front, and there was a poor young man in a sports car in the correct lane who was forced to struggle up onto the pavement by Emmie, who was quite unaware of what she had done. She never had an accident, but she used to terrify me.
>
> She was a strange person; she valued every penny she came into contact with, she was tremendously conscious of money and very careful with it, especially about herself. She would not take a bypass if it was a mile longer. I think she must have been very poor when she was younger. She was not mean, but she could not bear spending money. Mona was the famous German maid who Emmie had for ages and ages and was even more of an economist.
>
> She had a reputation for being completely honest, which is very rare, and she would not do what so many [agents] would do, and say 'give me a couple of hundred pounds and I'll launch you'. She did not really know anything about music, but she had an unfailing instinct if she heard somebody young for whether they were going to be a success or not. She felt it with the audience. She never had to get work for Solo, all she had to do was to write down the requests that came in. All the other agents called her Queen Emmie. She was fundamentally very shy, hated going to meetings and parties but it did not show. She was a workaholic but she was not very interested in anything much except her work, but then she took a house in the country [Bungay, Suffolk] and that was rather good for her. She paid her staff below the average.

It is hard not to compare Emmie's driving with that of Toad of Toad Hall in Kenneth Graeme's *Wind in the Willows*, not only after reading Gwen Cutner's hair-raising ride around Hyde Park Corner, but also this brief and somewhat sheepish entry from Emmie's diary on 29 May 1965:

> Met Gérard Souzay, tried to make 5.45pm [train] from Victoria but got chased by police for speeding. Said I nearly caused an accident. Absolute rot! Was travelling pretty fast all the same (82mph).

It was a cruel coincidence that, earlier in that same year 1956, another pianist, Cyril Smith, was also felled by a stroke, although happily his career, though drastically changed, was not cut short, as it has been in Solomon's case. Smith, with his wife Phyllis Sellick (another Ibbs and Tillett artist), went on a tour to Russia in the Spring with a delegation of concert artists consisting of Sir Arthur Bliss, Léon Goossens, Jennifer Vyvyan, and Clarence Raybould. In Kharkov on 3 May, Smith suffered a stroke, but having been transferred to Moscow, both he and Phyllis were stranded there until 8 June before he was deemed fit enough (though still as a stretcher case) to make the journey back to England. This had to be done by train, and once again Emmie was involved behind the scenes to ensure a safe journey. From Moscow's Institute of Neurology, Phyllis wrote to her:

> How excited we were to have the thrilling news that you will come to Paris to meet us. I have a lovely little bubbly feeling inside at the thought of it! Cyril has made wonderful progress, but it will be necessary for him to have an ambulance, as they have not taught him to walk yet. The Embassy is making all the arrangements. Thank you very much indeed for keeping an eye on affairs at home – the news from there keeps us happy.
>
> What a wonderful anonymous friend we have. Perhaps one day we may know who it is? In the meantime, please, our heartfelt thanks. All our love, Phyllis
> (1 June 1956)

In an interview with the author (11 November 1996), Phyllis Sellick related that many years later Emmie Tillett identified the anonymous donor as Sir Adrian Boult, and the money was used to pay the rail fare for the British Embassy doctor, Dr Humphreys, to accompany them from Moscow as far as Paris. Cyril, in his memoirs *Duet for Three Hands* (1958), described Emmie as:

> a tall, grey-haired, handsome woman, a very important figure behind the scenes of English music and a dear friend of ours. As managing director of Ibbs and Tillett, the concert agents, she handles the bookings of leading concert artists and often decides who shall conduct which orchestra. In the musical world she has immense power and is much loved.

Extensive references to agents are hard to find in published memoirs, biographies or in music history books, but John Joel in his autobiography *I Paid the Piper* (1970) is a rare exception, as he was himself an agent. He and Mark Lynford set up an agency called Lynford–Joel Promotions Ltd at 17 Cavendish Square, soon after both were de-mobbed at the end of the Second World War. In effect they were impresarios, but it was to prove a short-lived business, lasting only about seven years after an uneasy start. Like many ambitious young men, they assumed the world was their oyster and held trenchant views on all the established agents, who they simply dismissed as 'old-fashioned':

> We were not worried about competition from Harold Holt or Ibbs and Tillett. We thought them old-fashioned. Holt's business we regarded as a sort of artistic labour exchange. He was tied up with all the leading Americans of pre-war days; great names like Schnabel, Heifetz and Horowitz. When they came to England, they belonged to him, we knew we could never get them away from him, and

> we didn't intend to try. They would not go on for ever. We were going to seek out and sign the next generation of American artistes. We felt it an impresario's function to build new stars. We expected to spend a lot of money on publicity for them, and we did not believe that Harold Holt was prepared to do this.
>
> We thought even less of Ibbs and Tillett as rivals. To us they were simply agents working on commission. Their office was a central registry for artistes who wanted to perform for music societies, civic authorities or anyone else who was promoting in Britain. The big orchestras submitted lists of dates on which soloists were required, and Ibbs and Tillett nominated the top names on their lists. Meanwhile, I'm afraid, quite talented artistes often regarded themselves as lost until somebody higher on the list ceased to work. I have had one of those candidates for dead men's shoes come to me and declare: 'When Pouishnoff dies, I'll be all right. Until then I've got to keep well in with Emmie and hope for a break'.
>
> Emmie Bass was a woman of great talent and perception, and she was responsible for much of the inside workings of Ibbs and Tillett. She always knew who was exactly right for whatever solo spot had to be filled. If some civic promotion needed a soprano, Emmie might nominate Eva Turner because she recognised that Eva was a great socialite as well as a competent singer. She would charm the Lord Mayor and the councillors on the entertainment committee, and this would be good for Ibbs and Tillett. ... The known opposition could be ignored; it controlled fields we did not wish to enter. We had no need of Harold Holt's stars, and we knew that any Ibbs and Tillett [non-exclusive] artiste could be ours for the usual fee. Inevitably Lynford–Joel must succeed.

The two young men, despite their cynicism, not to say arrogance, had to swallow their words when promotion costs were studied and budgets formulated. They decided on piano recitals at the Wigmore Hall and selected Cyril Smith, Phyllis Sellick, Iso Elinson, and Marguerite Wolff, with all but the last-named Ibbs and Tillett artists. They had to go cap in hand to Emmie:

> We told her where we wanted them to play and she said we had better come round to see her. So Mark and I appeared before Emmie, and she gave us a long, searching look. We were both fairly dressed in our demob suits and apparently she thought we must have enough money to pay her artistes' fees, but we had the feeling she did not think we were sane. 'I suppose you two know what you are doing?', she said. We were sure that we did, and were equally certain that Ibbs and Tillett didn't, so we replied: 'Yes, thank you'. 'All right', said Emmie, and agreed that we could have the pianists.
>
> ... The first Wigmore Hall recital was a sensation. All the critics behaved as if they were writing for the tabloid press. Their theme was 'Amazing Scene at the Wigmore Hall'. And what was the amazing scene? Why, people! For just about the first time in living memory the place was full of them. Every one of our piano series was sold out. The pianists were delighted. It is always pleasant to play before a good house and to have good reviews, and they were really happy when they phoned Emmie Bass about their fees and she told them everything had been settled. 'Good God,' said one, 'I didn't think I'd ever get paid for playing at the Wigmore Hall!' And I suppose Emmie must have had doubts herself. Certainly that accounted for the strange looks we got when we booked established pianists for the Wigmore Hall, because it is not an ordinary concert hall at all. Its principal use is for debut recitals. Novices pay impresarios something like £150 for the privilege of appearing there. In our innocence we had given our pianists their normal fees and we had sold about 500 tickets at the usual prices of 3/-, 6/-, and 9/-, and they and the usual complimentaries for the press had given us full houses. And when we had paid for the hire of the hall and the printing charges, and for bill posting, we were left with about £5 each from each concert.

John Joel's agency had a roller coaster existence. It passed up the opportunity to present the Bulgarian bass Boris Christoff, because Joel believed that 'all the most popular and financially rewarding singers of both sexes have had high voices', and then promoted some bizarre productions such as *Hiawatha* on ice. His book makes some highly contentious statements, especially about singers, who 'do not need to understand music; indeed some can barely read it. Their instrument, the voice, can be made adequate for operatic performances with the thinnest veneer of musical appreciation'. From the 1953–54 *Concert Artists (Classical Music) Directory*, detailed earlier in this chapter, it would appear that Lynford, acting for Silveri, and Joel for Gobbi (both blessed with rather more than 'adequate voices') had gone their separate ways.

The year 1953 had further significance for Ibbs and Tillett, with the death that year of Harold Holt. His agency had been founded in 1876 by Alfred Schulz-Curtius, primarily to promote Wagner's music in England, and it continued in business until the First World War when, as an 'enemy' alien, he was interned. He took Lionel Powell into partnership (Schulz-Curtius and Powell, 44 Regent Street, London W1), and after Schulz-Curtius's death, Powell joined up with Harold Holt, a South African Jew, whose father was a diamond merchant. Holt junior trained as a barrister, but did not practise. He was, according to the late Sir Ian Hunter in an interview with the author in 1996, 'the greatest raconteur in London, who wasted away his fortune'. When Powell died in 1931, the agency became known as Harold Holt Ltd. Holt died in 1953, at which point Hunter was running the Edinburgh Festival. He was approached by Leslie Boosey (Chairman of Harold Holt) and offered the running of the business, but he also continued for two more years with the Edinburgh Festival. Meanwhile Emmie Tillett, as a member of the Board of Directors of Harold Holt, subsumed the agency into Ibbs and Tillett at the end of 1953. Malcolm Sargent wrote to congratulate her:

> I ought to have written to you long ago to congratulate you on your enterprise in taking over the Holt organisation. I feel it was a very noble and praiseworthy thing to do, and am very happy in the outlook for the future. I believe you have chosen the right man in Ian Hunter. May I wish you all possible happiness in the future. (30 November 1953)

As in the years before and after the First World War, Ibbs and Tillett began another magazine for their clients, the music clubs, choral societies, orchestras, and festivals. *The Bulletin* and *The Review* had been devoted purely to extracts from press reports of the artist featured, whereas although *Prelude* (begun in January 1958) was more varied in its information, it only advertised its artists' activities in London, alerting societies thereby that their foreign artists would be 'in town' and thus available for further engagements. This bulletin was 'edited and produced on behalf of Ibbs and Tillett Ltd, and Harold Holt Ltd, by Wilfred C. Stiff, International Artists Publicity', whose name would feature more and more significantly in the affairs of the agency over the next 32 years. The first issue of *Prelude* had a brief introduction printed above facsimiles of the signatures of Emmie Tillett and Ian Hunter.

> ... introducing *Prelude*
>
> It is with great pleasure that we introduce to you the first edition of 'PRELUDE', a publication which will be issued monthly to provide advance information of the concerts presented under the management of Ibbs and Tillett Ltd and Harold Holt Ltd. In addition details will be given of the London concerts promoted by the London Philharmonic Orchestra.
>
> It is not intended that 'PRELUDE' should in any way enter into competition with existing musical publications, but rather that it should provide a supplementary service for those interested in London's musical life. We hope that you will like it.

A brief essay follows, entitled 'Half a Century of Music' (actually 52 years since the founding of the agency in 1906):

> Clara Butt, Kennerley Rumford, Rachmaninoff, the great Cortot–Casals–Thibaud Trio, all legendary names in the music of this century, are just a few of the many great artists, who have appeared on the books of Ibbs and Tillett since it was first formed in 1906.

When John H. Tillett and Robert Leigh Ibbs went into partnership they little realised that within a few years they would be representing in this country several hundred artists ranging from Busoni to Olly Oakley, a well known virtuoso banjoist of the early part of the century. In 1942 Robert Ibbs died and the business continued and prospered under the direction of John Tillett. By then, however, a new partnership had been formed when Miss Emmie Bass, who had been associated with the firm for 20 years, had become Mrs Emmie Tillett, and soon after she became a co-director in the new limited company. The loss of John Tillett in 1948 was felt by artists all over the world.

Today, under the direction of Mrs Tillett, the prestige and influence of Ibbs and Tillett Ltd in the musical world stand higher than ever before, and with their associated company of Harold Holt Ltd they are proud of their reputation for integrity and enterprise.

It was in 1924 that Harold Holt went into partnership with Lionel Powell, who earlier had taken over the business of Schultz Curtis [*sic*], founded in 1876. It is fascinating to glance through some of the famous names contained in their artists list of the twenties, to find Kreisler, Heifetz, Tetrazzini and Galli-Curci rubbing shoulders with Norman Long and Chief Os Ke-Non-Ton ('Running Deer' of the Mohawk tribe), a Canadian Red Indian who appeared in tribal costume. 'Never a dull moment' could well have been the motto of the business which Harold Holt took over on the death of Powell in 1931.

Now with Ian Hunter as Managing Director, for six years Artistic Director of the Edinburgh Festival, the motto could well be the same, if we stop to think of such events as the European tour of the Boston Symphony Orchestra in 1956 or the more recent Middle East tour of the Minneapolis Symphony Orchestra running concurrently with the management of *Son et Lumière* at Greenwich, and the Harold Holt International Celebrity Concerts.

And now we look to 1958 and it will bring forth in exciting events and the discovery of the great artists of tomorrow. 'PRELUDE', as its name implies, will provide advance information and in addition, a permanent record of the activities of London's largest concert agents and promoters.

And so, for the next sixteen years, Ian Hunter ran the Harold Holt side of Tillett and Holt under Emmie's watchful gaze. In 1969, the firm of Harold Holt was sold to him by Emmie for a nominal few pounds, and for a while the two continued their side-by-side, literally next-door relationship, with Holt's business upstairs at No.122 linked to No.124 by a connecting door. As a business, Harold Holt was more of the glamorous impresario style, and when Hunter suggested fairly seriously to Emmie many years later that she should hand over Ibbs and Tillett to him upon her retirement, she refused point blank. For her, Hunter was the Spender, while she was the Saver. She never considered him to be an agent if only because, unlike her, he would never go to the office on a Saturday morning, a vital part of her working week. In Emmie's view, it was essential to be by the telephone during these three or four hours, in case an emergency arose. She wanted to be on hand to deal with any cancellation through illness or other mishap which may have befallen a soloist due to perform that evening, and therefore requiring replacement, and she also took pride in the knowledge that all her clients knew she would be there if they needed her. A further development was the establishment of the International Artists Management called Strok, Tillett and Holt Limited to work for artists abroad or for foreign artists to work in Britain, Emmie and Ian Hunter being listed as its managers (for the 1957–58 artists' list see Appendix 8). The broader international flavour of the list was a sign of change at Ibbs and Tillett, as was the inclusion of conductors at this time, both nationally and further afield.

The agency's influence on the Three Choirs' Festivals of the 1950s (the event had resumed immediately after the Second World War in 1946) was as strong as ever. It had always been a particular favourite with John Tillett, and Emmie ensured the strength of the connection with the firm by continuing to supply significant numbers of soloists. In 1953 they included Ena Mitchell, Joan Fullerton, Nancy Evans, Eric Greene, David

Galliver, Thomas Hemsley (although he withdrew), Campoli, Dennis Brain, Gervase de Peyer, the Amadeus Quartet, while the following year they included Isobel Baillie, Eileen Ralf, Norma Procter, Wilfred Brown, Gordon Clinton, Norman Walker, Roderick Jones, John Carol Case, Joan Alexander, Grace Bodey, Eric Greene. In 1955 they sent Amy Shuard, Constance Shacklock, Rowland Jones, and Owen Brannigan (replacing an indisposed Norman Walker) for Verdi's *Requiem*, in 1956 Elsie Morison, Hervey Alan, Marjorie Thomas, William Herbert, Pamela Bowden, Eric Greene, and John Carol Case, while in 1958 Britten, Pears, Jennifer Vyvyan, Ilse Wolf, David Galliver, Richard Standen, Colin Horsley, and Manoug Parikian were provided.

Emmie herself relates much of what was happening to the agency in a series of letters written in the 1950s to her close friends, the baritone Keith Falkner and his wife Christabel, who had moved to Ithaca, New York, where he was on the staff of Cornell University. He still had a singing career with appearances at the Three Choirs Festival, but by the end of the decade he was appointed Principal of the Royal College of Music in London, an appointment in which Emmie evidently had a role to play.

> I was delighted to have your letter of the 13th instant, confirming that you can arrive here about May 20th 1955 and remain until September. On the strength of this we are sending out a special letter to all the Societies – Orchestral, Choral and Chamber Music – announcing your availability for certain choral works and also in conjunction with John Hunt in recitals, and I hope we shall be able to collect enough to keep you going fairly comfortably through the summer. You ought to be able just to manage the Hereford Festival, and I have sent a line to Meredith Davies [then organist at Hereford Cathedral] to tell him that you will be here. John Denison [Music Director of the Arts Council] mentioned to me the possibility of two Wigmore Hall recitals, which will be very useful. The holiday season is on (and the weather is appalling!!) and the poor so-and-so's left in the office are grappling with three peoples' work at once! (26 July 1954)

> … I knew you had been extremely busy with Vaughan Williams, and although I have not seen him and Mrs since their return, I understand he enjoyed his visit enormously and had a whale of a time! It is quite true nothing is yet settled in regard to Edinburgh, although I believe they intend coming to a definite decision next week, and also via the grapevine I believe they are probably going to appoint Ian Hunter's assistant, a man named Robert Ponsonby, who has been working with him for some years.
>
> Just about the coming summer, about which we have sent out something between three and four hundred letters. The response at the moment is extremely small, but I think that is only because very few plans seem to have been made between May and September … Hereford Festival: Three Choirs would like to have you for two dates, namely Tuesday evening September 6th for the *Mass in B minor*, and Thursday afternoon September 8th, a chamber music concert in conjunction with Julian Bream the fine young lute and guitar player. I think I can get eighty guineas for the two dates, although it is somewhat more than they usually pay as a rule … I think there is no doubt that you would be able to do some teaching here as well and a little later on I would suggest putting a note in the *Daily Telegraph* one Saturday morning to say that you will take a few special pupils whilst you are here. I am keeping well in mind the fact that you have done *Façade* a number of times recently as well as the Bach cantata No.82 [*Ich habe genug*].
>
> Uproariously busy! A new company has come into being since I saw you last. Strok, Tillett and Holt – International Concert Bureau specialising in world tours. Strok is the uncrowned Mikado of Japan, so we are pooling our resources, so to speak … Good [cricket] news from Australia isn't it; John would have approved!! (24 January 1955)]

> … So thrilling to think that by the time cricket is a'cummin in, you'll soon be on the way! Not that I look at cricket much these days without John, but it's nice to know it's there. (7 February 1955)

> … I know it is a nuisance having to fly here, but you will save a lot of time and be able to spend more happy hours at Lords. Don't forget how close I live to it, and you know how welcome you

will be if you would like to stay at No.11 [Elm Tree Road, St John's Wood, London NW8]. Whilst you are in South Africa would you like to do some concerts, as I think we can fix a date with the Cape Town orchestra and perhaps two or three broadcasts? Philip Tongue, who is the Associated Board representative in South Africa and also runs a concert agency with whom we are in association, is at present in London and I had a talk with him about it ... I think we ought to be able to get £50 apiece. (17 February 1955)

... I only have to introduce you to my friend Dr [Reginald] Hilton over the road and you will be able to go in and out of Lords over his wall quite easily! (16 March 1955)

... The new Travel Bureau comes into being on January 1st and we are going to make a special feature of the European Festivals with expert musical advice laid on as well. It's going to be a bit of fun I think.

... A funny sort of Christmas. Benno [Moiseiwitsch] has been in and out of here; Anita [his second wife] is just lingering on, she is now completely paralysed and can scarcely speak. I do so hope it will not go on for long, it is just too cruel for words. Today I have been to Bognor to Gladys Ripley's funeral; she died last Wednesday, only 47, same disease [cancer], sorry to be so depressing. (11 December 1955)

... It was terribly sad news about little Anita Moiseiwitsch. Benno has been wonderful but it was a terrible time for him. I'm just getting him ready to go off to India and Australia. He's going to take Boris (his son) with him ... Oooh! nearly forgot to say thank you for the maple syrup, which arrived in an exquisitely non-sticky state. It's just heaven – specially with Mona's special pancakes! (19 January 1956)

... I've just returned from the airport meeting Lotte Lehmann, who starts her Master Classes on Monday. She was in great form. (18 September 1957)

... I am in awful trouble over PETER PEARS and JULIAN BREAM. Peter is most anxious to visit Cornell but we have booked JULIAN BREAM for an engagement in Bristol on February 14th ... [and] he is announced and tickets are already selling. I also have Bermuda lined up for them and it really is a shame that we may have to miss these two dates ... Peter and Ben [Britten] are at present in Madeira having a well-earned holiday. (24 October 1958)

... Actually I've got a Sunday off ... We've been having three to four concerts every Sunday as well as every weekday and I've been to quite a few of them!! ... I think it won't be long, Keith, before there'll be news from the College [Royal College of Music]. They have their next meeting within the next few weeks when their final decision is made. I don't think there is any doubt about it as far as you are concerned and I believe the financial conditions are not too bad! Here's hoping! You cannot imagine what tremendous pleasure it will be to have you both back here for keeps.

Cyril Smith has just written an awfully good autobiography (actually done by a ghost extremely well). I got Jimmie Smith [no relation to Cyril] to get his firm [W.H. Smith, Lord Hambledon, was Jimmie Smith's brother] to interest themselves in it and they have done a wonderful job with a special display in every one of the shops and stalls. It is very readable and most interesting, so I think it will have a very good sale. Poor old Jimmie goes into Middlesex Hospital tomorrow to have his gall bladder removed. I hope he will be alright!

Our printing works is in full swing and we're turning out very good work! They have not yet absorbed all the work we, the Holt firm and London Philharmonic Orchestra, have. There's a heck of a lot of it but we're gradually increasing the staff to be able to compete. I've got to think soon of enlarging the works and building on. Nothing ever stands still does it!!

We've just done (Holt office) two hilarious concerts at the [Royal] Festival Hall – the Hoffnung Interplanetary Festival. We sold two houses right bang out in three hours – a record I think! It's useless to try to describe it, you've got to see for yourself. In any case I'll [send] you a copy of the programme, which is quite illuminating.

... Paul Robeson is making a fantastic success with his recitals (Holt office) all over the country. It is extraordinary, the drawing power of that man. Sold out houses everywhere, including the Albert Hall next Sunday. He will insist on using a microphone, but it doesn't seem to make any difference from the public's point of view. (2 February 1959)

Thank you for the book [*Lolita* by Vladimir Nabokov]. It seems (unbeknown to me) that there has been quite a lot of letters in the press about its possible publication over here. In possessing a copy I seem to be the envy of all. Ian Hunter asked me to lend it to him but to be sure and carry it down well wrapped up otherwise the police would be on me!! Thank you too for the Christmas book [*I was Monty's double*] which I thoroughly enjoyed; it is enthralling. We once put a recital on for Clifton James at the Wigmore Hall, which I think would have been the book in potted form – it was most interesting, and there is no doubt he is Monty's double. Solo, Gwen and I had a heavenly holiday in Cannes … Solo walked about a mile every morning and is progressing, although very slowly. 4pm sharp every day we were in the casino and how we enjoyed it. They are both great gamblers and I can do my bit too. We didn't fare very well I regret to say, but it was such fun. Left the casino at 6pm and was in the bar at 7.15pm to the dot. It was a very regular life!! I painted quite a lot and have a few masterpieces to show you … Can't remember whether I told you I am having the garden redesigned by Percy Cane, who recently did the Emperor of Abyssinia's in Addis Ababa!!

The weather has been too dreadful and the amount of flu about simply appalling. You can guess what we have had to contend with at the office with every other artist dropping down with it, not to mention losing the others in the fog!! I went to the first night of *Rusalka* at the Wells last Wednesday with Joan Hammond singing the name part, and very beautifully she did it too, but at 5.15pm, when she left home to go to the Wells, she did not know whether she would be singing Russalka or Butterfly! The tenor went down with flu, but the throat specialist managed to patch him up for the performance.

When I emerged from the theatre, the fog was so thick that I wondered how on earth I was going to get home. I had Jennifer Vyvyan with me, and for most of the time she could just see the kerb. I seemed to be the only thing moving in the whole of London as visibility was really nil, but when I got to St John's Wood in my endeavour to get her home I met my Waterloo and had to abandon the car, and both of us went our respective ways. I've never been in quite such a pea-souper! I went to collect the car next morning and there were literally hundreds of cars everywhere strewn all over the place … I popped round to see Jessie Wood [widow of Sir Henry]. She is not in very good shape poor old darling with this awful muscular dystrophy which is slowly creeping on, but she is making a wonderful fight and actually holding it at bay. Adrian [Boult] and Ann have a lovely new flat in Whitehall Court with a wonderful view of the river and London generally from their 5th floor windows. (22 February 1959)

Loving hurrahs!!! I hope this will fetch up with you at the same moment as "the" letter. Adrian [Boult] called me last evening (it was his 70th birthday yesterday by the way) to tell me the result of the RCM meeting [appointing Falkner its new Principal] which thrilled and cheered me more than anything has done lately. Ernie Bullock [Sir Ernest Bullock, the retiring Principal] phoned to ask when you were coming … and ask you to get in touch with him as soon as you arrived … I did not tell him that probably much would depend on what was on at Lords as to when you would find time to contact him. Anyway I expect you will want to see him to find out what his filing system is and if you will get elevenses as well as tea at 4! … *Lolita* is in great demand! (9 April 1959)

The expansion of activities by Ibbs and Tillett included the Travel Agency based at its premises, which had begun as a service for its artists but was now open to the public. As the advertisement in its magazine *Prelude* stated: 'The Travel service for Artists at Ibbs and Tillett is also available for you and an expert is present at 124 Wigmore Street on Mondays to Fridays from 10am to 5pm'. Its letter heading described its proprietors as Pall Mall Safe Deposit Travel Bureau Ltd, and its activities as 'Agents for all British and Foreign Railways, Steamships, and Airlines'. Besides planning artists' itineraries once engagements were contracted, it also had to deal with emergencies; for example a surviving letter, written by R.J. Crafter on behalf of soprano Elizabeth Harwood, was addressed to the Seat Reservation Attendant at Paddington Station as follows.

Re: Miss E Harwood

The above named client booked through us to travel on the 3.55pm departure to Cardiff on Saturday 20th April. The tickets, together with the seat reservation tickets were posted to her, but these have been lost in the post. Seat reservation ticket number 165515 was issued, and the allocation given to us by Paddington Seat Reservations was B.17 facing 1x second class non-smoker.

The counterfoil of this seat reservation ticket was sent to Paddington on the 8th April, and as Miss Harwood will not have the top copy of this counterfoil in her possession, we would be grateful if you would avail her every assistance in obtaining her reservation seat. Thank you in anticipation of your kind co-operation in this matter. (18 April 1963)

Before long (February 1959), the firm had also taken over a firm of printers, E. Jones and Woolverton Ltd, based off the Old Kent Road in London SE15, while Emmie's nephew, Fred Bass, was given premises in the basement of 124 for his Allegro Photographic Studios.

There was, however, a further expansion involving the agency and that took place in 1957. The London Philharmonic Orchestra was, along with other British orchestras during the 1950s, in particular financial trouble and tried all sorts of ways to cut costs, such as slimming down the administrative staff, transferring the contents of pension and sick-pay funds to run the orchestra on a short-term basis, and, more significantly, abandoning the principle of salaried players so that they would be paid engagement by engagement instead. What with helping Cyril Smith and Phyllis Sellick a year earlier in anonymous fashion, it will be seen that Sir Adrian Boult was once again showing what an extraordinarily kind and generous man he was. As Edmund Pirouet relates in his history of the LPO (*Heard Melodies are Sweet*, 1998):

The solution to their problems came through the good offices of Ibbs and Tillett, an anonymous donor, widely believed to be Sir Adrian Boult, offering an interest-free loan sufficient to meet the demands of the creditors. Together with the generous stance taken by Boult in respect of outstanding conducting fees, and assurances from the Arts Council about further losses that might arise before the new scheme came into force on 1 April 1957, this timely injection of cash ensured the LPO's survival. The relationship with Ibbs and Tillett, who were working in close alliance with Harold Holt Limited, was to bear considerable fruit, and a Board of Trustees was set up to co-ordinate future activities. Chaired by Sir Adrian Boult, this comprised Eric Bravington and Samuel Lovett from the LPO, with Mrs Emmie Tillett and Major Denzil Walker representing Ibbs and Tillett.

... Sunday evenings were given over to popular concerts under the title 'Masterworks'. Advertised as being 'in association with Ibbs and Tillett and Harold Holt Limited', the LPO agreed that in return for financial backing from the agents they would share any profit from these concerts with them.

... Thursdays were given over to 'International Celebrity Concerts', promoted by Harold Holt, the cover of each programme bearing the logo of that company rather than that of the LPO

... The partnership with the agents heralded the formation in 1959 of the London Philharmonic Society, under whose auspices the concerts were now given. Modelled on the Royal Philharmonic Society, this was the brainchild of Eric Bravington, its formation, in association with its new allies, a bid to restore the LPO to the front rank of London's orchestras ... [By the end of the decade there] was evidence of the LPO's improved standing and the benefits derived from the link with Ibbs and Tillett and Harold Holt.

The audition books used by the agency over the years were only briefly part of Emmie's operations after a gap of three years since John's last entry in 1947. Just seven singers were entered in January, February and April of 1950. Thereafter, the system seems to have been abandoned. The supply of extant letters from artists to Ibbs and Tillett virtually dries up by the 1950s. A couple of last glimpses of a bygone age do occur, however. One is this letter from the eccentric Dame Edith Sitwell, who wrote from Florence:

> Dear Mrs Tillett, It was a great pleasure to hear from you. I never got your previous letter. My former secretary has fled to Sweden, luckily for her, otherwise I should have killed her owing to her multitudinous mistakes.
>
> Alas I cannot recite *Façade* in Milan owing to great pressure of work, but I have written to Messrs Ricordi and have suggested Mr Peter Pears and Miss Irene Worth. They must have a curtain. As there is probably not time for an elaborate curtain to be painted, they could use a white sheet painted with two Roman masks (a tragic mask and a comedy mask).
>
> I do hope you are very well. I have had a terrible summer, really dreadful overwork, eye strain and acute migraine, and am only just beginning to recover. When I return to London in the Spring I do hope you will find time to come and lunch with me. (7 November 1958)

The other comes from Lotte Lehmann, who gave masterclasses at the Wigmore Hall in September 1957, in which the young Grace Bumbry took part. Lehmann and Emmie were old friends, and, like Ferrier, she hated the taxman. '… My Lord, your accountant is a wizzard!!! I am quite overwhelmed. Thank you! Thank him!', she wrote on 20 December 1959, as the decade came to a close.

CHAPTER TWENTY-THREE

The Winds of Change: 1960–69

The 1960s may have been the 'swinging sixties' for popular music, but for Ibbs and Tillett the decade would prove to be full of changes, not all of them wished for, and many of them of more significance than might have appeared to Emmie and her fellow Directors at the time. Because of the proliferation of agencies, Ibbs and Tillett was no longer quite the power it once was in the musical landscape. This despite the fact that, as a personality, Emmie was still held in awe by many artists beginning their careers, and it was still an agency on whose books most aspiring musicians wished to be included. Despite the ever-growing number of agencies, ironically brought about largely by the intransigence of Ibbs and Tillett, the agency was still the giant among them. The year 1956 had been its Golden Jubilee year and the pianist Gina Bachauer and her husband, the conductor Alec Sherman, organized a party for Emmie and the agency's staff on Saturday 2 June. As the firm's long-standing solicitor, Stanley Rubinstein, wrote to thank the Shermans, 'it was a charming gesture for I & T, and at the same time as one thought affectionately of Emmie, one also remembered John and Bobby with gratitude'. Telegrams of congratulation were received from Nancy Evans, Cyril Smith, Phyllis Sellick, and Ilona Kabos, while Lady Jessie Wood cabled her 'congratulations on keeping the flag flying in traditional manner'. With the best of intentions, the Honorary Secretary of the Edinburgh Choral Union seems to have got his facts wrong, when he wrote to Emmie on behalf of the choir to congratulate her (rather than the agency) on 'some fifty years' business life with the firm so very closely associated with your name, a very great achievement indeed, and one of which you must be very proud', whereas Emmie had been a young girl of 10 when it was formed back in 1906.

An artist whose career burgeoned during the early 1960s was the pianist John Ogdon, and Emmie featured in no small measure here and there. Ogdon had come second in the Liverpool piano competition held in May 1959, and on the jury were Ibbs and Tillett stalwarts Cyril Smith and Solomon, both of whom would have had Emmie's ear in recommending the young man. The relationship between Ogdon and Emmie was a somewhat turbulent one (and a clue to why this was the case could well have been that there was seemingly no love lost between her and his wife, Brenda Lucas). As events turned out, Emmie proved to have unlimited faith in his great talent, particularly after 1962, when he and Vladimir Ashkenazy jointly won the Moscow International Tchaikovsky piano competition. Then, after two years, Ogdon became restless and made the crucial decision to sever his connection with the agency for Basil Horsfield, but as it happened matters did not improve, while Elsie Illingworth, who worked for the American impresario Sol Hurok, also told him that he would have to look elsewhere for the management of his American career. After a year or so, it became apparent to Ogdon and his wife that the number of concert dates he was receiving had dropped considerably, so there was only one course of action to take, even if it meant eating humble pie, but Emmie accepted Ogdon back with good grace

Among several former employees of Ibbs and Tillett interviewed for this book by the author was Terry Palmer. In January 1957, he came over from his native Australia, where he had been working in the publicity and record department of the Australian Broadcasting Corporation and joined Ibbs and Tillett in August that year. A new General Manager, Major Denzil Walker, had recently been appointed by Emmie, and he in turn interviewed and then appointed Palmer to the concerts department. He worked there for five years and recalled that he hardly saw Emmie:

> who sat in the grand office and did the big business with the conductors and saw any famous artists who came in. I saw Joan Hammond in the waiting room before being ushered up into Emmie's presence, striving to adjust her hat in a mirror placed too high on the wall for her short frame. There was also the composer Kodály with his young wife.

In Palmer's last year (1962), he took over the department when Edwin Worman died. These were the years in which the London debuts of many talented young musicians took place in recitals, often given as part of the London Pianoforte Series put on in association with Harold Holt Ltd. There was also the 16-year-old cellist Jacqueline du Pré. As in the past, it would have been recommendation rather than audition which counted for so much with Ibbs and Tillett, and in this case it would have been William Pleeth who brought Emmie's attention to his talented pupil. As Elizabeth Wilson wrote in her biography of the cellist (1998):

> For the evening of 1 March 1961 the Wigmore Hall was sold out and even the gallery, normally closed off to the public, was chock-a-block full. Jackie's reputation had preceded her and Mrs Tillett, the doyenne of London concert agents, saw to it that the audience included many influential names, representatives of London orchestras and concert societies, BBC producers and a bevy of critics … Word had got around in London that this would be an exceptional event … [Its] enormous success had been the logical outcome of a singular investment of time and energy in her talent. Emmie Tillett, with her long experience in concert management, recognised the unique nature of Jackie's critical success and lost no time in inviting her on to the Ibbs and Tillett roster. 'Ibbs' was something of an institution and in those days was at the height of its fame. As the longest established concert agency in London, it practically controlled the national music club circuit within Britain. Mrs Tillett, the director of Ibbs and herself something of a legend in London musical circles, was quick to realise that Jackie could become one of the brightest stars on her lists.

Letters to the agency during its last three decades of existence are very few indeed, barely a dozen or so. Some of them came from the record producer Walter Legge, who, on hearing of Gerald Moore's intention to retire from the concert platform as a renowned Lieder accompanist, set his heart on organizing a farewell concert in which Moore would accompany Dietrich Fischer-Dieskau, Victoria de los Angeles, and Legge's wife, Elisabeth Schwarzkopf. It took place on 12 February 1967, and Ibbs and Tillett were involved from the very start, about a year and half earlier, when Legge wrote to Emmie:

> … As soon as Gerald Moore told me that he was retiring (from the profession, not by nature) I felt that it was my duty to give him 'the works' in the form of a prima donna's Farewell Concert at the R[oyal] F[estival] H[all] under the auspices of the Philharmonia Concert Society. Will you, as an old friend of his and mine, manage it for me? My idea is for a joint recital by Fischer-Dieskau, Los Angeles and Schwarzkopf, the three artists with whom he is most closely associated in the public mind. F-D., E.S. and I have already drafted the programme, the immediate problem is date … The artists have agreed to accept the gross profit equally shared as fees. What prices do you think we can charge for this fantastic triple bill; 1, 2 & 3 guineas? The public will never get such a Holy Trinity again. (? September 1965)

Emmie Tillett replied:

> … Your plan for a concert for Gerald with such a wonderful cast is certainly a great idea and I am

> at once going into the question of available dates at the Festival Hall after November 7th. For such a programme I think one could aim at a 4 guinea top; I understand that the Stravinsky concert last night, where the actual prices were 4, 3, 2, and 1 guinea, was practically sold out … Surely with such names we should be able to get these prices without the slightest difficulty. (15 September 1965)

Legge continued to fire off a series of similar letters, funny if stretching the boundaries of civility.

> … Now that I have recharged my batteries and had time dispassionately to see the reasons for my past successes and mistakes, I am, I hope, a wiser person. (8 November 1965)

> … Please investigate insurance to cover the normal fees of two of the artists if the third should drop out, or cover in case Gerald (God forbid) should die and make the concert unnecessary. (8 September 1966)

> … If Mr D[enison, General Manager of the South Bank Concert Halls] had stopped for one moment to consider the girth of each of the four artists, it would dawn even on his modicum of intelligence that the problem will be rather not to have them seen, but to get them all on the platform. (29 November 1966)

> … It would be nice to know that the Parson's Nose [the accompanist Geoffrey Parsons] had been engaged for this date [Schwarzkopf's recital 6 May 1967]. (29 November 1966)

> … The whole point of my requesting the Festival Hall for November 30th 1968 is that it will be the centenary of Ernest Newman's birth, and since I learnt almost everything I know from him and since he was also a wise counsellor to my wife – he was witness at our wedding – in addition to being the greatest critic in the world for over sixty years, he deserves a concert of particular distinction. (15 February 1968)

> Secretary Bird is nesting, hence my scrawl. Between 20 Oct and 10 Nov for R.F.H., please ask your Reverend Mother (E.M.T.) [Emmie Tillett] to build in a few concerts in this period if, and only if, the Parson's Nose is not occupied elsewhere. E.S. [Elisabeth Schwarzkopf] would like to do a TV recital of popular Lieder with G.P., introducing the songs herself. Please get your colleagues on the tips of their toes for this. N.B. [The] R.F.H. should be the start of the trip when she is daisy fresh. (3 May 1968)

But it was not musicians from the past like Lotte Lehmann nor, more recently, Gerald Moore, who would propel Ibbs and Tillett into a new era, but rather the up and coming talents of du Pré, Ashkenazy, and even Barenboim, whose affairs had been handled by the Harold Holt agency since 1956. There was also Janet Baker, a mezzo-soprano whose career was beginning to take off some four years after she came second in the Kathleen Ferrier Competition in 1956. She was to become a close friend, loyally staying with the agency until Emmie's death, followed by several years in the care of Emmie's Personal Assistant, Beryl Ball.

Ibbs and Tillett were still at the heart of British music, their presence felt not only at all the regular series of concerts in London, the provinces, the festivals, and in opera houses and on radio, but also at special events. One such occasion was at Coventry Cathedral on 30 May 1962, the first performance of the *War Requiem* by Benjamin Britten. Ibbs and Tillett not only supplied the artists, but had to deal with the sudden emergency caused by the refusal by the Soviet authorities to allow the soprano Galina Vishnevskaya to leave the country and sing at the premiere. At ten days notice Heather Harper was her last-minute replacement. After the performance Britten wrote revealingly to Emmie:

I was so touched by your sweet note. I am still a bit overwhelmed myself by the occasion and by the immensity of the subject (I have never felt greater doubts or more inadequate over a piece). But it is lovely that so many people have understood what I wanted to say. And didn't they all do well? – [Dietrich] Fischer Dieskau and Peter [Pears] of course, but Meredith [Davies] and our dear Heather [Harper] – how clever you were to get her. I was so sorry you had such anxiety over that wretched situation, and do thank you warmly for your superhuman and noble (and thank God, entirely successful!) efforts.
Much love, dear Emmie, and warm thanks again,
Ben
P.S. I'm so sorry to be causing everyone such trouble over my wretched shoulder.
[undated]

The agency also took a lively interest in the activities of the Bach Choir, and in 1960 the post of conductor fell vacant with the resignation of Dr Reginald Jacques. David Willcocks, already known to Ibbs and Tillett through his work with the Three Choirs Festival when he was in charge of the music at Worcester Cathedral between 1950 and 1957, was appointed, and Emmie had clearly played her part in bringing him to the attention of the selection committee. Willcocks wrote from his base at King's College, Cambridge:

Now that my first concert with the BACH CHOIR is over, I want to send you my sincere thanks for being one of those who initially suggested to the Committee that I be given the opportunity to work with the Choir (for I imagine I have you and Dr Jacques to thank for that!). I shall try to uphold the great traditions of the Choir during the coming years and I know that my association with the Choir will bring me great joy.

It was so kind of you to bring Mr and Mrs Keith Falkner round to see me yesterday evening. (22 June 1960)

Ibbs and Tillett's powerful influence and enduring reputation throughout the music profession continued to draw aspiring musicians during the 1960s, but it was also becoming clear that the agency's infrastructure was beginning to creak. Yehudi Menuhin, who as a child prodigy back in 1928 had been deflected by John Tillett to Holt's partner Lionel Powell, described Powell's office as 'a sort of terrestrial microcosm, each continent assigned a different room', a marked contrast to Ibbs and Tillett with its preoccupation with the national, rather than the international music scene, and with each room and its occupant assigned to different performing contexts. Menuhin became a close friend of Emmie and their paths were crossing more because Holt was now owned by Ibbs and Tillett, and particularly because of Emmie's work servicing Britain's many annual festivals. In this case it was Bath, founded by the ubiquitous Ian Hunter in 1948, and of which Menuhin was Artistic Director for ten years from 1959:

I would so liked to have seen your good and cheerful face among the happy ones that shared the Bath Festival with me. I know how busy you are, but hope that perhaps next year you too will be with us for at least a few days in Bath.

As I owe so much to Harold Holt Ltd for the success of this venture I feel that it is indirectly also to you that I must acknowledge part of this gratitude. The office has in fact been admirable. Apart from the vision and initiative of Ian Hunter who sets the grand lines in motion, I would like first of all to commend Mr Jack Phipps: he has really done the major part of organisation and administration, especially in view of Ian's long absence in the Far East. He has carried out the incredibly intricate functions as well as the diplomatic handling of artistic temperaments – in fact he has always been available to do whatever job had to be done, from the making of a stool for Segovia of just the right height to the concert arrangements, artists' billeting, artistic perception essential for programmes, letters and all human contacts which are such an important part of a 'local' effort. There is not one of the people in Bath, from the Chairman – Ted Leather – to the porters at the Guildhall, who are not on good terms with him and charmed by his easy and completely spontaneous manner; he is enthusiastic, his integrity and loyalty unquestionable and his ability flexible and manifold.

Miss Lachmann too is a sweet person, who was on her feet a good part of the day and night – to very good effect, I might add. My best wishes to you, hoping I shall come and see you in the near future. (15 June 1961)

Emmie's status as a *grande dame* in the music profession was beginning to be recognized and rewarded, although she was a very reluctant recipient of any accolade (her diary entry for 4 January 1968 records 'Dinner with Gina [Bachauer] and Alec [Sherman] at Brompton Grill. [They] think I should have some recognition for 'services to music'. Begged them to lay off it!!'). The Royal Academy of Music Club, however, had awarded her honorary membership in the autumn of 1961 and its secretary, Leslie Regan, wrote to her both formally and informally to convey the news:

Dear Mrs Tillett
It gives me great pleasure to tell you that at the Annual General Meeting last Thursday you were elected an honorary member of the club. It is the one way in which we can show our appreciation of your great kindness to us in the past, and we hope, the future. (23 October 1961)

My dear Emmie,
I am v[ery] glad that this has happened while I am secretary: so that I can write the letter.
Sempre con amore, Your ever faithful foghusband
(23 October 1961)

The greatest accolade she received came on 18 November 1970. It was a letter on headed notepaper from 10 Downing Street signed by Sir Robert Armstrong, the Cabinet Secretary, and informing her:

The Prime Minister [Edward Heath] has asked me to inform you, in strict confidence, that he has it in mind, on the occasion of the forthcoming list of New Year Honours, to submit your name to The Queen with a recommendation that Her Majesty may be graciously pleased to approve that you be appointed a Commander of the Order of the British Empire.

Before doing so, the Prime Minister would be glad to be assured that this would be agreeable to you.

It took no time at all for Emmie to respond, though she took advice from Jimmie Smith on exactly how to couch it:

Will you please convey to the Prime Minister my gratitude for the very great honour he has bestowed on me in considering me for recommendation to Her Majesty for admission to the Order of the British Empire.

It was the wish of my late husband, who founded Ibbs and Tillett at the beginning of this century, that no personal recognition for their work should be sought or expected by any individual member of our company and, though the passage of time may put this sentiment into oblivion, I personally would like to respect his wish.

I trust, therefore, that the Prime Minister will appreciate this reason for my preferring to ask him to withdraw my name from his list. (21 November 1970)

As her diary for the period reveals (see Appendix 12), Emmie moved in the circle of the musical greats, whether or not they were artists on the agency's books, and many of them were personal friends. On 13 December 1962, the 87-year-old French conductor Pierre Monteux collapsed while conducting a concert at the Royal Festival Hall and had to be helped offstage to recover. He completed the concert with the LSO, and the front page of the *Daily Mail* had a photograph of him leaving the hall, its caption being, 'A woman admirer kisses Monteux as he leaves after the concert'. That 'woman admirer' was none other than Emmie Tillett. Many of her friends and professional colleagues (including members of the office) were entertained by her at 11 Elm Tree Road, where her German cook Mona would prepare after-concert suppers, lunches or dinner parties. According to one former employee, who was invited to eat there on occasion, the food was plain and not especially good, while Emmie made her own bad wine from a kit. Mona kept a diary of menus from September 1951 until just five months before her death on 4 August 1978, and notes of the favourite foods or breakfast preferences of overnight-guests, as well as menus, are scattered throughout the notebook:

> Mr K[eith Falkner] Bran for breakfast. T[oast] with apricot, pineapple jam. Marmalade.
>
> Clara Haskil, very light food, no salt.
>
> Mr [Shura] Cherkassky loves ice-creams, plenty.
>
> Mr Solomon no pork!!!
>
> Mrs Cyril Smith [Phyllis Sellick] likes coffee for breakfast, toast, soft-boiled eggs, apricot jam and fruit.

Emmie is always referred to as 'Madame', 'Miss Ferrier' is frequently accompanied by 'Nurse', that is, Bernie Hammond, and the many guests include:

> Dame Myra, Madame Bachauer, Lady J Wood, Mr Legge, Mr Szigeti, Lady and Sir John Barbirolli, Sir Steuart Wilson, Miss Isobel Baillie, Dr Rankl, Mr and Mrs Gerald Moore, Mr Kubelik, Madame Lympany, Mr Solomon, Sir [*sic*] B Britten, P Pears, Mr Pedro and Mrs Mary Tillett, Mr Segovia, Lady and Sir A Bliss, Mr Moiseiwitsch, Mr Hunter, Miss Joan Cross, Miss Jennifer Vyvyan, Miss Pamela Bowden, Sir Adrian Boult, Mr Fournier, Dr Malko, Miss Joan Hammond, Mr and Mrs Clifford Curzon, Rosalyn Tureck, Mr P Monteux, Sir Thomas Beecham, Mr Gérard Souzay, Mr and Mrs John Ogdon, Mr Howard Ferguson, Mr Herbert Menges, Mr Ivor Newton, Miss Janet Baker, Miss Elizabeth Harwood, Mr John Pritchard, Mr and Mrs Ashkenazy, Mr Sol Hurok, Miss Valda Aveling, and Miss Norma Procter.

Back at 124 Wigmore Street there was more than a fair share of eccentric characters, such as Mr Nolan, who handled the mail, wrote artists' names on the back of their photographs, and dealt with their biographies. The long-serving telephonist Edna Walters sometimes became so bored at the switchboard, that she would relieve the monotony and answer 'Tillett and Ibbs' to incoming calls. She often complained vociferously about wrong numbers received in her cubicle where she worked, in the corner of the common room. On the former dialling mechanism on receivers, with its combination of letters and numbers, the telephone number for Ibbs and Tillett spelt WELBECK and, according to her, many wrong numbers came through because people simply dialled all the letters instead of just WEL. One of Emmie's sherry parties was dedicated to Edna Walters in March 1972, to celebrate her 25 years as the agency's telephonist since 1947. Sherry tended to feature fairly regularly in the office (such as on Saturday mornings) and it was even donated by Clifford Curzon for the annual Christmas party.

The 1960s are usually credited with a variety of changes in the fabric and *mores* of society, and while this may not be the book to explore that area in any detail, it is relevant to study its impact on the fortunes of Ibbs and Tillett. The next three decades witnessed both the decline of the agency's influence and its status in the music profession. There was a change beginning to take hold in the perception of management and manipulation in the media and communications industries. New agencies for advertising, architecture and design began to appear. Celebrities were beginning to dominate television, films, theatre, the pop music world and in the print media, while through technological developments in travel and telecommunication, a new feeling of internationalism was beginning to take hold. Revolution was in the air. It had already been attempted in Hungary and was yet to happen in Czechoslovakia. The dismantling of the British Empire, begun in India after the Second World War, continued in Africa, while unrest among students in America and Europe was leading to confrontation on the streets, often with violent results. It was now a questioning world, eager to shake off the gloom and austerity of the 1950s, and with a growing technological ability to do so. A desire to 'get away from it all' was taken to its ultimate limits, for the exploration of outer space was now within reach.

In 1961 Emmie Tillett was 65 years old, and at the age at which most people would either choose to, or be compelled to retire, but not only had she every intention of carrying on doing the work she loved, she also had no plans to change with the times. The infrastructure of the agency remained the same, with its various departments headed almost entirely by increasingly elderly women like a girls' school run by a formidable headmistress. At the sound of her voice, and invariably with the words, 'Can you spare me a moment?', her employees would run for cover, but while the communal staff-room enjoyed a fairly jolly atmosphere, it did so largely because Emmie generally stayed away from it. Sue Price worked there in 1962 and 1963 for nine pounds a week, and was one of the secretaries in the top-floor offices, which were nothing like as grand as Emmie's. She and Carol Borg worked for Sadie Lereculey on music society dates, with Price dealing with those south of Birmingham while Borg covered those north of the city: 'We had to liaise with the societies, plan their concerts, engage the musicians, draw up the contracts and programmes, and organise travel arrangements and hospitality for them.' There were perks; Emmie's industrialist friend Sir Leon Bagrit had stall seats in row J at Covent Garden which he invariably passed on to her for use by the staff. Sue Price recalls attending Tippett's *King Priam* in 1962 with three colleagues, all of them deciding to stay put in their seats during the interval as, having come straight from Wigmore Street, none of them had dressed appropriately for what transpired to be a black-tie gala performance. She assisted Sadie Lereculey with Jacqueline du Pré's first tour, when she was accompanied by Paul Tortelier's pianist daughter Maria de la Pau. One enduring memory she has of Emmie is her unfailing habit of sending a telegram to any member of the music profession who had won an award in the Honours Lists; whoever the recipient, it always read 'congratulations on an honour richly deserved'. Of her immediate boss, Sadie Lereculey, she remembers, 'a sweet, kind person, erudite and with a good sense of humour. I recall her telling me of her embarrassment when she accidentally emptied a cup of tea into the lap of the composer Poulenc.'

There were many major agencies around the world run, like Ibbs and Tillett, by women 'of a certain age' such as Frau Adler in Germany, Marie-Anne de Valmalète in France, Emy Erede-Moresco in Italy, Felicitas Keller in Spain, Hannah Wilhelm Hansen in Denmark, Ann Colbert, Thea Dispeker, and Mariedi Anders in America, and Regina Ridge in Australia. At a time when women were only just beginning to rise to the top in the business world, this was a remarkable statistic. Furthermore, a large number of these women (including Emmie) had, when young, married the owner of the agency and outlived them to run their inheritances single-handed. Although they may not have had anything similar to the British music club or choral society to provide a primary source of work for their business in their respective countries, they nevertheless exercised an enormous influence over opera houses and concert halls throughout their long working lives. But in the view of most people at the time, Emmie Tillett had a much stronger grip on the music scene in Britain than her continental counterparts had on theirs.

In 1961, however, a seismic change occurred when Ibbs and Tillett decided to employ a young man called Christopher Hunt. Having left Cambridge (where he read Anglo-Saxon) in 1961, and after considering a career in music as an oboist, Hunt looked instead for a job in music management. First he worked in the record department at Harrods (an excellent grounding for acquiring knowledge both of the repertoire and of performers), but he chanced to meet the organist of St Paul's Cathedral, John Dykes-Bower, who gave him an introduction to Emmie Tillett. He started work at Ibbs and Tillett in November 1961 at a salary of seven pounds a week, with an extra 10/6d (52½p) to attend concerts managed by the agency. Employees were expected to be present at such events, but encouraged to leave the office early in the afternoon to go home and change. According to Hunt (interviewed in August 2002), Emmie was very helpful and kind, and, because she scorned gramophone records, passed on to him what had been sent to her. He was put in charge of the debut recitals department and given a good deal of leeway, such as designing publicity materials (his first leaflet was for a recital by the singer Kerstin Meyer). He found the music world very old-fashioned and set in its ways, with poster layouts for Wigmore Hall recitals, whether issued by Wilfrid van Wyck or Ibbs and Tillett, unchanging in their typeface, colour, uniformity of size and placing of photograph. Simply put, they looked like handouts from an estate agent's office. Hunt's leaflet, produced by the printers Vail and Co. and in creative consultation with Gosden's advertising agency, was different, with the publicity for Kerstin Meyer down one side reversed out of a colour block, the remaining half totally blank. When Emmie asked 'So what's going in this section?', she raised no objection when he replied 'Nothing'.

Hunt received no initiation into the agency business from his female colleagues, so he literally learned his trade as he went along. He worked at Ibbs and Tillett for two years, during which time he organized the management of Alfred Brendel's recitals covering all the Beethoven sonatas at the Wigmore Hall in 1962. When new artists or beginners asked Emmie to be taken on by the agency, she would inform them that they had to have press notices, and in order to get those, they would have to give a recital at the Wigmore Hall, which Ibbs and Tillett would manage for them. The total cost, including the hire charge for the Hall was £166. Hunt would fix a date and an accompanist (for which the aspiring singer or instrumentalist would have to pay), work out programme content and design, and organize press reviews (generally three critics would attend). There were about four such debutant recitals a week from mid-September to May. In the two summers of his employment, he was seconded to Harold Holt to work on the City of London, Bath and Coventry Festivals with Jack Phipps, which proved to be a good preparation for his next job, running the English Bach Festival for Lina Lalandi. By then Hunt was becoming impatient with operating methods at Ibbs and Tillett, and also needed a salary increase to support his wife and child. He wanted £4 a week more, taking his salary to £11, but Emmie would only offer him £2 (Segovia once tipped him £5, almost a week's wages, for meeting him at London

Airport, carrying his guitar, and going with him by car to the Connaught Hotel). Hunt left Ibbs and Tillett in May 1963, setting a pattern from now on, for many similarly placed young men would average only two or three years employment at the agency. It was usually as much as they could bear.

At this time, there appeared to be many young British artists who needed help in getting underway in the profession, and although Emmie told them that good press notices were essential to the start of a career, even if they succeeded in getting them, it was by no means an assured entry on to the roster of the agency. Hunt and his friend Richard Gaddis would talk endlessly in the Green Room at the Wigmore Hall during recitals (Gaddis provided page-turners from Trinity College of Music where he worked), and gather young musicians together on Sunday evenings for parties, where they would discuss the state of the music profession in general and Ibbs and Tillett in particular. While it was possible to achieve a career with another agent, it was far harder, for they were generally considered inferior unless they were Gorlinsky or Hochauser dealing on a very special level with certain types of musicians. The route for British artists who wanted a livelihood out of music clubs and choral societies was to go through Ibbs and Tillett, as it was with Robert Schulz in Germany for singers trying to get into that country's opera houses, or with Ronald Wilford at Columbia Artists Management Incorporated (CAMI) in America for conductors.

Hunt and Gaddis wanted to help young British singers avoid having to self-finance a Wigmore Hall recital. After they both left their respective jobs and were thrown together in Oxford for the first English Bach Festival, they decided to start lunchtime concerts at the Hall, persuade the press to come, and attempt to break the monopoly held by Ibbs and Tillett. This attracted a lot of press attention in the process, and they followed it up with a similar event in Newcastle. In trying to set up an organization to run the careers of a small number of people in whom they believed, and to whom they could give real personal management, they approached all the firms in and around Wigmore Street (with the obvious exception of the occupant of No.124) for a contribution of £5. They thought themselves lucky if they could get £1, although Sir Robert Mayer later proved to be a great supporter. Once up and running, they failed to keep below an optimum maximum number of artists on their books. This was not only because there were so many who were eager for their management, but also because the demands of opera require just such singers for smaller roles, understudies, and emergency replacements due to illness or cancellations. It proved vital to enjoy close, trusting terms and good relationships with the opera houses in order to be able to fill such small roles with new young singers. Glyndebourne proved the perfect example, where in one season more than half the singers (even if they were not generally in the principal roles) came from Hunt and Gaddis.

The two men then went anywhere and everywhere throughout Britain looking for good players, which at the time was an unprecedented operation. Fortunately for them, there were no other young agents around looking for the best young artists, though both men perceived themselves as promoters rather than agents. The consequence was that clients who wanted young musicians to play for them suddenly began to turn to Hunt and Gaddis. They in turn soon realized that they would run out, because at the rate of one a week it would take just 18 months to present all the artists they had. They also realized that, despite the good notices, their protegées' careers were not changing to any significant degree. Instead they found that matters improved if they spent more time dealing with the people who were asking for recommendations of a young artist for engagements. In other words they were in danger of becoming a cloned version of Ibbs and Tillett.

If Ibbs and Tillett did not send staff out and about to look for new singers and instrumentalists, neither did they network the musical organizations and associations. This was a task which was soon proving to be an essential part of Hunt and Gaddis's operation when they set up their agency. The two men toured all the British music clubs and choral societies for three years, trying to persuade them to use their artists as well as (or instead of) those from Ibbs and Tillett. Emmie was heard to dismiss the threat of competition with the comment, 'they won't last a year'. At first they could not earn a living, but after a while they were able to take a commission of any fees they secured, so that they could be paid for doing the work. In order to take such a commission, they had to set themselves up as agents (which they did from their own homes) and then register with the local council. While finding it relatively straightforward to place instrumentalists with concert work, they also discovered that choral societies generally refused to break their traditional ties to Ibbs and Tillett. These organizations would not abandon the security of knowing that, if something untoward occurred before a concert, they could rely on the agency to find a substitute artist immediately, so long was their general list of singers. Hunt and Gaddis also sensed the intimidating presence of Emmie, when they were offering their services to the secretaries or chairmen of these choral societies, however far away from London they happened to be located.

Gaddis soon left the partnership to work for Basil Horsfield, and it took Hunt two or three years to secure sufficient opportunities to gain experience for his young singers, and the difficulty he had placing them with choral societies was proving far worse than his efforts on behalf of young instrumentalists with music clubs. As it happened, many of these clubs were not very happy in their dealings with Ibbs and Tillett, and were ready for change. They thought that a lot of the fees were high and were looking for a mix of cheap, young, good talent. To test his theory, Hunt used the new Gabrieli String Quartet and secured 36 concerts with music clubs for its first season, which shook the idea that there was an unalterable routine in the way in which music was run. Each member of the quartet talked in turn to their friends and colleagues, which brought the partnership even more work. This included a TV programme, followed by a series of four in 1963, directed by Herbert Chappell, about young musicians, including singers Margaret Price, Anne Howells, Yvonne Minton, Sheila Armstrong, Maureen Morelle, and Ryland Davies. Yet despite his success with instrumentalists, Hunt was now discovering that a management that did not want to be just an agency carrying many artists, had to roster mainly singers to cover the more lucrative field of opera and its more plentiful openings and opportunities. Neither was there any real rival in the field of opera management as far as Ibbs and Tillett was concerned, thanks to Emmie's relative indifference to it. She often used to give Hunt tickets she had received, preferring to attend rehearsals instead. For Emmie, opera was not a financial resource and barely featured in the agency's business affairs.

It seems hard to believe now, but for 20 years after the Second World War, choral societies still maintained their well-defined tradition of singing, and there was still an absolute and unbroken divide between the opera singer and the oratorio singer (almost inconceivable today), which probably explains why Emmie worked tirelessly for the latter and hardly dealt with opera. Tenors such as Philip Langridge, Ian Partridge and Robert Tear credit Christopher Hunt with getting opera work for them, which Ibbs and Tillett did not do, because of the public and commercial perception of the agency as a source of booking concert singers. Times were changing, and the opera and concert activities of the profession gradually fusing. An example was the perception in the profession of the counter tenor, who, as well as recital and some oratorio work, was now being required for operas such as Britten's *A Midsummer Night's Dream*, and by composers such as Monteverdi and Cavalli as part of the discovery or revival of seventeenth-century Italian opera, but while Emmie may not have been entirely inflexible, she had nevertheless been around too long to take a real revisionist view.

In 1974, Hunt, by then somewhat disillusioned, closed his agency business. At the time, there were just 3000 telephone lines from Britain to the Continent of which 1500 were kept open by the major City firms, so the chances of operating as an international agent based in Britain were virtually nil, and for opera, almost non-existent because vital, instant communication to deal with crises was impossible to achieve. The reasons he gave to his artists for ending his business were that he did not want to be just a booking agent, neither did he want to act as their psychiatrist or accountant, continually arguing on their behalf for higher fees than they deserved (which was what they almost all wanted). Most were placed with the American Tom Graham working at HarrisonParrott, while the rest went to other agencies. Hunt went on to enjoy a successful career at the topmost level in festival direction and opera house management in America, Australia and Europe. He has fond memories of and the highest regard for Emmie Tillett, and, despite her resistance to them, credits her with more awareness of the changes taking place in the music profession than distance of memory may allow. To him, she remains a courteous, if remote figure, old-fashioned in her perceptions with a business philosophy belonging to pre-war years. She never acknowledged how significant the changes that were taking place during the 1960s were, while Ibbs and Tillett was still a household name in the musical world. After Hunt's departure, there was a period of about two years at Ibbs and Tillett which might be described as the lull before the storm. The Kraken was about to wake, and after 1965 things would never be the same again.

The next man to join Ibbs and Tillett was Terry Harrison. The son of a Sheffield bus driver, he left school at 15, completed his National Service at the end of the 1950s and then moved to London. He loved music, particularly opera, and, because vacancies were rarely advertised, he took the initiative and wrote to companies, agencies, and orchestras in an attempt to enter the profession. Having failed to get any positive response, he was forced to join a bank to make ends meet. One of the customers he got to know at the branch in Swiss Cottage where he worked was Griselda Kentner, wife of the pianist Louis Kentner, who was on the books of Ibbs and Tillett, and she gave him a personal introduction to Emmie Tillett. He was interviewed and told that not only was there currently no vacancy, but that, if one were to arise, only a woman would be taken on. Nevertheless, he was told that the situation might change, and his name would be kept on file. Shortly thereafter, he was head-hunted by a Middle Eastern merchant bank at a considerably better salary than he received at the high street branch and after a year, was offered promotion. It was at this point that Ibbs and Tillett wrote to say that they wanted to fill two posts (and Christopher Hunt remains convinced that Emmie did this because of his growing success as an agent). Harrison was interviewed, as was customary, first by Major Walker, then (on 22 June 1965 according to her diary, see Appendix 12) by Emmie with Walker in attendance, and finally by Emmie alone at her home in Elm Tree Road (on 26 June for drinks and, as it turned out, the only occasion Harrison was invited there). He was told that two young men were to be taken on to replace Christine Sunderland, who was leaving the agency's foreign department, and that it needed both reorganization and development. The other new employee would be Jasper Parrott, who was on the point of coming down from Cambridge University.

Harrison's salary at the merchant bank was £1500 per annum, with the promotion offer of a raise to £2200 available. Emmie Tillett's initial offer of £500 per annum was rejected at once, so she then suggested £750, increasing by £50 per annum over the next five years, plus 10 per cent of the foreign department's profits above its estimated annual expenditure of £10000. Harrison accepted and started in the summer of 1965. The only men working there at the time were not directly involved in booking artists, namely Major Walker, the General Office Manager, Emmie's nephew photographer, Fred Bass, accountant Denys Rowlands, and Mr Nolan, the firm's general *factotum* and messenger. Completing the work force of about 20 employees were the secretaries, all young ladies from good families, some of them debutantes. Jasper Parrott joined in the autumn of 1965, and as the two men were chalk and cheese in terms of background and education, they were, unsurprisingly, wary of each other at first. They worked in adjacent offices, and Emmie gave each of them a group of artists of varying talents and with careers at various stages, with Parrott getting more of the agency's top artists than Harrison. Only gradually did the two men become friends.

Jasper Parrott was the son of Sir Cecil Parrott, First Minister at the Embassy in Moscow when Cyril Smith, Phyllis Sellick, Bliss, Campoli, Jennifer Vyvyan, Clarence Raybould, Léon Goossens, and Emmie Tillett toured Russia in April 1956. It was on this occasion that Smith had his serious stroke and lost the use of his left arm. Sir Cecil and Ellen Parrott became friends with Emmie, and when he later became ambassador in Prague, she visited the couple in the summer of 1962. She and the Parrott family were also invited to stay the night with Clifford Curzon in Salzburg. Like Christopher Hunt, Jasper Parrott became an oboist but went to Cambridge to read history. In 1965, not wanting to follow in his father's footsteps as a diplomat, he wrote to Emmie to ask for her advice on how he might enter the music business. She had invited him to concerts from time to time, including hearing Ashkenazy play a Mozart concerto in 1964. She offered him a job at the agency starting in the autumn of 1965 at a salary of £520 per year (note the starting salary was lower than the hard-bargaining demands of Harrison). Emmie returned from her annual trip to the Three Choirs Festival (at Gloucester that year) on the day before Parrott started work on Tuesday 14 September. Short-staffed because Harrison was away and Beryl Ball leaving for her holiday the next day, the new employee was thrown in at the deep end, with the rest of the staff hardly aware of his presence. He started with Tillett and Holt, 'the export division of Ibbs and Tillett' arranging foreign contracts for artists, and was allocated some of Emmie's artists, including the Amadeus String Quartet, Clifford Curzon, Sir Adrian Boult, Janet Baker, John Shirley-Quirk, Robert Tear, and Helen Watts.

Harrison only learned of Parrott's appointment when he returned from his own holiday the following week, and was none too pleased. Emmie had given Harrison a similar position to Parrott within the firm, but without informing either of the other's appointment, a case of playing one off against the other. She openly showed her unbridled distaste for Harrison's working-class background to the preferred one of Parrott, even addressing the former as 'Mr Harrison' but the latter as 'Jasper'. In fact, though she did not realize it at the time, both men complemented one another. Harrison was good at figures, had unstoppable energy, an incredible intuition for quality, and a tireless ambition to network, while Parrott was good at languages, knowledgeable about music and at ease in the company of artists, but what they both shared was a love of music and a hunger to be part of the music business. Parrott learned much from watching Harrison and a healthy spirit of competition was engendered between them, which Emmie had unwittingly created in the manner of their respective appointments and in the way she treated them.

Their arrival was received with despair and frustration by the senior ladies Sadie Lereculey and Kathleen Cheselden, particularly the former who seemed to resent them. Lereculey was a prouder, more self-contained person than Cheselden, who by nature was more maternal and friendly. In fact both women should have been reassured that their 'patches' (the music clubs and choral societies respectively) were relatively safe, as neither was part of the young men's brief. But they seemed put out by the confidence of both men, in particular by the ease with which each established cordial relationships with the artists, and they found it hard to accept that such informality was very much a sign of the times. The two ladies were also nonplussed by the newcomers' self-confidence in handling Emmie, by whom they, on the other hand, were treated almost as house servants and to whom they were clearly deferential despite being Directors of the firm in their own right. On the other hand Beryl Ball, another employee seemingly kept in her place by Emmie, was someone with more personality and a sense of humour, who liked a good gossip and welcomed the novelty of the presence in the firm of two good-looking young men. In Major Walker, however, Harrison and Parrott both saw someone of limited imagination, loyal to Emmie, and clearly an ex-Army officer who liked to keep a clean mess.

All communications had to pass across Emmie's desk, though the Misses Lereculey and Cheselden were generally exempt from this rule, and she herself took responsibility for singers who had big careers, everything to do with professional music-making in London, and all recordings. Parrott was given singers' foreign work but only in partnership with Emmie, who therefore remained firmly in control. With an eye on finances, she did not want the men to travel abroad to find business, nor even to do so by telephone, insisting 'We don't telephone Paris, we write letters to Paris'. For the first year they had to type their own letters, then, when Emmie saw that the department was beginning to be turned around (by 1966 it was beginning to show a small profit), they were allowed to share a secretary. This foreign department was also linked to Tillett and Holt (originally run by Audrey Hurst and Susan Pears, the latter married to Jack Phipps of Harold Holt), but in essence this partnership did not really work out and the two agencies tended to run their own artists separately.

One of two significant events initiated by Emmie occurred in the autumn of 1965, when she introduced Jasper Parrott to the pianist Vladimir Ashkenazy. He had arrived in London from Russia in July 1963 and was under the management of the impresario Sol Hurok for his American career, but he was with Ibbs and Tillett for the rest of the world. In his book *Beyond Frontiers*, written with Jasper Parrott in 1984, Ashkenazy writes of agents in general and Hurok and Emmie Tillett in particular. Defecting as he did from the Soviet Union, where there was only one state-operated agency, Gosconcert, his remarks become very revealing. Whereas his relationship with Sol Hurok lacked affection, it had a certain degree of respect but remained essentially commercial. Hurok had a nose for talent and unlike Emmie, relied solely on his own instincts. She, on the other hand, relied on a combination of instinct and the recommendation of others:

> Now with Mrs Tillett it was certainly different. When it was arranged that she would represent me, I had no clear idea as to what I could or should expect from her or from the agency. This was not only because I was completely new in the music business of the West but also, being still very young, I had no real concept as to how my life should be. I had no basis for making relative judgements of people. My reaction was quite irrelevant – I liked her as an individual and felt comfortable in her presence. She seemed a solid person, with nothing contrived about her, and she genuinely tried to do the best in her relationships with the artists in order to support them. But she didn't have any very clear idea what to do with me or my career. She just followed up all the leads from where I had played before, or from people who were interested in having me. There was no question of a plan for, say the next three years.

Ashkenazy was a formal and very polite man, punctilious in attention to detail, very clear in what he wanted regarding his career, all of which began to produce an uneasy relationship with Emmie. She had never really come across an artist like him and neither did she know how to handle him. He was only on the books of Ibbs and Tillett due to a somewhat unseemly deal made with Victor Hochauser, who, because he did not want to damage his relationship with the Soviet authorities by representing an artist who had defected, passed him on to Ibbs and Tillett subject to a percentage from all commissions earned from engagements the agency secured for him over the next five years or so. When Ashkenazy discovered this arrangement, he was furious and flatly refused to let it continue. Given Parrott's cosmopolitan background and his experience of living in Russia as a child, it was rather an astute move on Emmie's part to bring the two of them together, and, eager to extricate herself from the awkward encounters she was having with the pianist, she gradually let go of all Ashkenazy's affairs, even his British contracts, and placed them in Parrott's hands. This was in stark contrast to all Harrison and Parrott's other activities, over which she continued to keep a watchful eye.

The second event in which Emmie took a hand was in the summer of 1966, when she instructed Parrott to accompany Sir Adrian Boult to America, sailing out on the *France*, and back on the *Queen Mary*. Boult, who refused to fly, had been invited to conduct and give master classes at Tanglewood, the summer home of the Boston Symphony Orchestra, and Parrott went because Lady Boult had to remain behind to organize a house move. While there, the young man forged connections with musicians such as conductor Erich Leinsdorf, singer Simon Estes and pianist Malcolm Frager. Back in London, artists such as the members of the Amadeus Quartet, or pianists Cherkassky and Curzon would come regularly to 124 Wigmore Street for a conference with Emmie to discuss their availability for the forthcoming season, and for part of these planning meetings Parrott would join to discuss their foreign work. Because phone calls overseas were discouraged, everything had to be done by letter, (telex was then only in its early stages of development), and progress was becoming frustratingly slow.

Parrott also ran the foreign work for Ibbs and Tillett's singers list, including Sheila Armstrong, Benjamin Luxon, and Gerald English, developing personal contact with them and then following up directly with managements, especially concerning the possibility of return engagements. In the mid-1960s, such British singers as these were much in demand in Germany, Austria, Holland, Belgium and, to a certain extent, Scandinavia, because they were cheaper, extremely professional, highly dependable, and (contrary to many singers at German opera houses) wide-ranging in their Lieder and oratorio repertoire.

Gradually, as the pressure of these frustrations began to build up, it was dawning on both Harrison and Parrott that they were working in a passive organization with extremely little pro-activity. Generating business was based solely on supplying artists in response to written or telephoned approaches from managements. In such a way, and it was probably unintentional, Emmie sustained a dominating and ruthless control of much of the British music scene. While she would never let anyone else book Ibbs and Tillett artists, it was quite different when the boot was on the other foot. There were many areas of the choral society and music club network, which put all of their business through Ibbs and Tillett, even for artists who were not on the agency's list, so the firm would think nothing of demanding a split commission with the artist's agent. As to the fees themselves and taking a random sample, when Harrison and Parrott joined the agency in 1965, fees for work in Britain were respectively: Ashkenazy £350, Curzon £300, Cherkassky £200, Janet Baker £200. By 1967 Ashkenazy's fee had gone up to £500, Curzon's remained at about £300, and Cherkassky's had risen to about £250. Fees abroad were largely higher, the pecking order remaining much the same. Ashkenazy also earned more because, being in such huge demand, he played much more than say Curzon or Cherkassky, with as many as one hundred concerts a year, with his overseas fee somewhere between 20 per cent and 70 per cent higher than his British fee. Emmie did not believe in pushing up artists' fees in Britain, where traditionally there has never been a lot of money for classical music. Because it was in control of so many artists, the agency was able to set the rate of fees with orchestral managements, festivals, music clubs and choral societies, very often according to their individual budgetary limitations. It was therefore a philosophy of benign pragmatism on Emmie's part.

When Terry Harrison joined the agency, he looked after about ten to a dozen artists including André Tchaikovsky, Antal Dorati, Shura Cherkassky, Alfredo Campoli, and John Ogdon after he was taken back by Emmie. Although technically all Ibbs and Tillett artists were eligible for work abroad, and from time to time Emmie would ask for more foreign dates for an artist because they had requested them, in practice it was not cost effective to push the middle-ranked bread and butter artists for the sake of one or two dates. Good though they may have been, if they had not made it to the higher echelons after a few years, then trying to open up a career overseas proved very hard to achieve. To make life harder for some (but not all) British artists, in the first few years of the 1960s there was a sudden increase in the numbers of pianists of the younger generation coming from Eastern Europe and elsewhere through international piano competitions such as the Chopin competition in Warsaw, the Tchaikovsky competition in Moscow and the Queen Elisabeth of the Belgians competition in Brussels, which produced pianists of the calibre of Ashkenazy, André Tchaikovsky, Malcolm Frager, John Browning, John Ogdon and Martha Argerich.

Ibbs and Tillett may have had one of the greatest artists list in the world, but its financial strength and artistic potential lay in the British-based general management list. This built itself up from the conveyor belt of performers which, over the years, flowed naturally into the agency each season, drawing them like a magnet (particularly from the music colleges) simply because of its reputation as the dominant place in the British music profession. For those on the list, there was work and a modest income, and within a couple of years a good young singer could be getting 50 to 60 concerts a year from clubs and choral societies through the agency. Between 1930 and 1970 inflation was generally stable and at a low level, so there was no pressing need to push the clubs and societies for higher fees, but although it was not an instrument of policy to resist any attempt to raise them, neither was Emmie unaware of her customers' budgets, despite the agency's low salaries and relatively low overheads. But if the system was passive – indeed for some artists it proved stifling – the alternatives were very limited. Emmie sailed this ship of state and, pursuing the analogy, for anyone who bucked the system, it meant transferring to a much smaller ship with far fewer ports of call, but in any case she always held the view that staff and artists were replaceable. Ibbs and Tillett's reputation in Europe and elsewhere was sufficiently large, that foreign agencies looked to it to organize British appearances for their artists. Meanwhile, there were also historical connections and long associations abroad, personified by such conductors as Szell and Dorati, artists of the calibre of Segovia and Casals, and, in the 1960s, new ones represented by Fischer-Dieskau and many others. On the other hand, in post-war years, the agency also managed to lose some significant artists, because it never really synchronized with the developing nexus of the Salzburg and Vienna Festivals. There were two other important spheres in which Emmie's direction of Ibbs and Tillett was weak. She did not really understand how the record business operated, nor, as Christopher Hunt had discovered, did she have either sympathy for or patience with the world of opera, and many singers either did not join the agency or simply left it when they realised she was not a 'Green Room person'.

Harrison and Parrott soon built up the foreign department, feeding ideas and suggestions to artists, while at the same time increasing their incomes. These musicians also began to enjoy the interest evidently being shown by the two young agents, for instead of receiving just a brief phone call to offer a date, they went on to discuss repertoire or a personal career plan. In Britain, the two men also attended many more of their artists' concerts, went to their rehearsals, or accompanied them to dinner after engagements. This proved to be in stark contrast to their predecessors or indeed to Emmie, who had a habit of either taking office work with her to recitals, or making a token appearance towards the end. In short, the artists were beginning to like the attention they were now beginning to receive. This was personal management.

After six months, Parrott nearly quit through the sheer exasperation of being 'an ignominious, miserably paid clerk', when his salary was increased to £12 a week. Like Hunt before him, but now for £1 extra, he was obliged to undertake page-turning duties at debut recitals at the Wigmore Hall, 'some of them unspeakably boring and low grade, paid-for events'. There were also occasions which provided an insight into how others perceived Ibbs and Tillett, one of them unwelcome when Stockhausen visited London and the agency undertook some practical arrangements for his concerts. According to his interview with the author, Parrott went unofficially to a rehearsal at Cecil Sharp

House and, when he introduced himself as a representative of the agency, was met with a torrent of abuse from the composer about the arrangements for his visit. Both Harrison and Parrott were very proud of the firm, and they were convinced that they could not only consolidate its activities and reputation, but also help to make it the greatest international music agency in the world, but at a price.

After consultations with Major Walker, an incentive scheme was agreed, whereby the two men would receive 10 per cent of the profits of their department once all its running costs had been taken care of. Within 15 months, they had already exceeded the projected calculation of what they were expected to have achieved after five years. A bigger bonus followed in 1967, but significantly the year 1968 was even better, and gave rise to problems when Walker realized that they were going to earn too much money compared to other more senior employees, such as the Directors Kathleen Chelselden and Sadie Lereculey. Emmie would not concede that the earning capacity of Harrison and Parrott was in the best interests of the company; she was irritated by it all and delegated Walker to put a stop to it. The firm's solicitor Paul Strang was brought in as a mediator, but even that seemed to harden Emmie's line. Major Walker allegedly tried to play Parrott off against Harrison, by suggesting that his future was more or less secure because in due course he would be asked to take the firm over, and even going on to suggest that the source of all the current problems might be his colleague. However the two men sustained a united front, and presented an ultimatum agreeing to void the incentive scheme, but only if they were guaranteed a salary structure which would reflect what they would have expected to earn. The result was stalemate when Emmie summoned them, rejected their proposal and told them they would have to go if her terms were not accepted. She accused them of unacceptable arrogance, even taking the opportunity to complain to Parrott about his 'completely illegible' signature on letters.

Both men rejected Emmie's final proposal, and so she promptly fired them, and as soon as she was told that they intended to start up their own agency, she wanted them out of the building as soon as possible. Denzil Walker then intervened to warn her that she might be liable to a charge of unfair dismissal, so a compromise was reached for them to take those artists who wanted to join them, and the commission on any dates which were currently in their diaries. They included Ashkenazy, who went personally to explain to Emmie why he wanted to go with Parrott, reminding her that it was she who had brought the two men together in the first place. There was also the American conductor Lawrence Foster (an artist relatively new to the agency), and the singer Anna Reynolds. It was in 1962, that this mezzo-soprano was singing Geneviève in Debussy's opera *Pelléas et Mélisande* at Glyndebourne, and met Beryl Ball, who offered her representation by Ibbs and Tillett. She told the author in the summer of 2003:

> Then came my first meeting with Emmie, who reminded me forcibly of the Headmistress of Cheltenham Ladies College, who interviewed me when I was 13, terrifying, very grand, and remote. I took up Emmie's offer and we discussed my concert fee. I told her I had done my apprenticeship in Italy and was not prepared to sing for peanuts in England. She quite agreed with me, to my surprise, and we fixed the fee at £50. The average fee then was half that. I stayed with them till 1968, when Jasper Parrott and Terry Harrison left to form their own agency and they asked me to join them along with Sheila Armstrong, Gerald English, and later, John Shirley-Quirk. My work had already begun to improve since the arrival of Jasper. I was beginning to get work abroad, which Emmie did little to encourage, and after 1968 it went ahead by leaps and bounds. Emmie rang me

> up very rarely, and if she did it was always extremely polite but never, as far as I know, did she use anyone's first name. I suppose I felt a little guilty at leaving Ibbs.

Both Harrison and Parrott were careful not to lure any artist away from Ibbs and Tillett to their agency, which began operations as HarrisonParrott in October 1969, with Radu Lupu, Kyung Wha Chung and André Previn joining soon afterwards.

Parrott acknowledges that from the moment he began to behave 'awkwardly' Emmie felt betrayed, and that had he stayed the course (which would have been 15 years), he would probably have succeeded her. Emmie stood by her views on personal management. It was a working method which she felt was not in the interests of the company, and totally contrary to the way in which she carried out her business, because it made the company too dependent upon the artist. She was not comfortable with the concept, nor, despite a fairly good grasp of the repertoire, did she know about music in enough detail when it came to career direction. She did not 'talk music' to musicians, other than to those of her own generation such as Curzon or Cherkassky, whom she tended to mother. Younger artists were generally uncomfortable in her presence, because she could not bridge the generation gap, slip into a relaxed informality, or open up to them. There was some degree of unpleasantness after Parrott's departure; Emmie was very cool towards him and, in his view, pressured artists not to leave Ibbs and Tillett for theirs. She felt that the two men were undermining the agency business from beneath her, resented their style and approach, but above all she abhorred the extensive publicity and high public profile, which the new agency attracted from the moment it was formed. According to Parrott, she was ruthless for a while and tried to freeze them out of international contacts, which only made them realize how vulnerable they were. Instead they changed their tactics when it came to business abroad, and made direct approaches to orchestras and festivals, rather than go through local foreign agents. On the other hand, in Britain they refused to allow music clubs or choral societies to go through Ibbs and Tillett if they wanted a HarrisonParrott artist. It was a monopoly which Emmie had always insisted upon, but now it was broken.

The original concept of HarrisonParrott was to form an agency consisting of about 12 to 15 artists between them, whose careers they would be able to control and personally manage. This they achieved for about three or four years, but because of its success it inevitably became too large. Commissions during the 1970s remained static, while fees, salaries, overheads and inflation rose. By this time, agents were not only incurring higher telephone bills (particularly with more accessible but still expensive overseas calls), but were also expected to travel more to attend artists' concerts or to hear new people. Then there was also the growing problem of 'split commissions'. As a general manager for an artist, if deals were direct with managements, then commission could be charged directly, even though the cost of doing so was necessarily higher and more time-consuming. If, however, other agents were involved (such as those abroad), then the commission would have to be split with the local agent taking 10 per cent and the British agent 5 per cent.

Viewed from Terry Harrison's perspective, a brief recapitulation of these events provides further insight into the reasons for the schism, because Emmie's approach to both men was very different. In the Spring of 1969, Emmie came to Harrison saying that she had received a letter from Daniel Barenboim, which she apparently found very insulting, and as a result she had decided to remove him and his wife Jacqueline du Pré from the agency's lists. Barenboim had apparently asked her to instruct Harrison to handle not only his engagements but also any joint work he could obtain for him and du Pré. Although the bulk of Barenboim's work was done by Harold Holt and other managers elsewhere, Harrison protested to Emmie that he too had already been doing much on the pianist's behalf for engagements abroad and his career was now taking off. Far from reassured, Emmie was now convinced that Harrison was conspiring with the couple, and neither did she want to be 'told what to do by some upstart, so I've told him to go and take Jacqueline with him'. Harrison reminded her that both musicians probably accounted for 5 per cent to 10 per cent of their department's turnover for Ibbs and Tillett, but Emmie forbade him to seek any new work for them, and only to service contracts which were already in place. Some days later, Emmie called in her two male employees and announced the new contract of employment designed to protect the company's interests. They received it a few days later, valid for two or three years complete with restriction clauses, including one which stated that if they left the company, they were not allowed to go into another management for a further two years. All decisions made either by her or by any other Director must in future be accepted without question, and they would not be allowed any input into the agency's policy. Their current salary with its bonus arrangement was to be reviewed, because she was not happy with its levels. Both men expressed their deep unhappiness with the new proposals, and warned of the agency's headlong rush to ignore changes which were fast occurring in the musical world, losing touch with new artists, and of the competitive threats from other agencies such as those run by Christopher Hunt and Ian Hunter.

Events took a further twist when, in the summer of 1969, Harrison was alerted by the pianist John Bingham (then studying in Moscow) to the hugely talented Rumanian pianist Radu Lupu, already a prize-winner but at the time still studying at the Moscow Conservatoire, and who now intended to enter the 1969 Leeds Piano Competition in the autumn. Instinctively Harrison signed him up, even though Emmie was away on holiday. When she returned, she discovered a letter from Lupu's Russian management confirming the negotiations which Harrison had been undertaking in her absence. She immediately informed him that he had no authority to act unilaterally, and that it was her intention to cancel any agreements he had made. She was not interested in Lupu, and Harrison was furious, for although he had not yet heard him, he sensed the artist's worth. Not only was he the first pianist of note to emerge from the Eastern bloc since Ashkenazy, he was also unusual in being able to play the classical repertoire, like Sviatoslav Richter and Gilels before him, and significantly all three had been taught by the great pedagogue Heinrich Neuhaus. Harrison had also heard a tape of the young Korean violinist Kyung Wha Chung and was keen to sign her up, but Emmie was unaware of his attempts to bring this about.

Harrison told Parrott that he would not sign the proposed new contract, and that he wanted to leave Ibbs and Tillett. The two men were summoned by Emmie once again and, when pressed, repeatedly denied any intention of planning a takeover of Ibbs and Tillett, stating that they simply wanted to rebuild and modernize the agency. They refused to sign the contract and were dismissed on 18 September 1969, at first with immediate effect (told to clear their desks within a couple of hours), then extended to a couple of days, but finally to a month as this was the start of the season and, as

Harrison pointed out, artists (Cherkassky was one) were on the point of starting tours and could not be let down. Lupu duly fulfilled all Harrison's expectations, won at Leeds in November 1969 and was taken on by HarrisonParrott. Emmie never spoke to either of them again, her last comment on the affair being that, while she would have 'expected such behaviour from Harrison, who is from Yorkshire, she did not expect it from Jasper with his family background'. There is another strange twist to the Harrison and Parrott affair, for what Emmie, nor any other employee at the agency, did not know was that in 1968 Walter Legge flew Harrison and Parrott out to his home in Switzerland for a weekend to discuss the formation of a new agency, but because he insisted on owning 51 per cent of the shares and would therefore have been in overall control, the two men turned him down. Unlike Emmie, Legge had recognized their talent for far-sightedness, but, like her, he tried to clip their wings and failed.

There was a third young man who was employed by Ibbs and Tillett at the time of these turbulent events. From New Year's Day 1966, Martin Campbell-White began work in the broadcasting department at a starting salary of £15 a week. The BBC was one of the best clients for Ibbs and Tillett at the time, with not only the Promenade Concerts and Winter Seasons, but also the expanding television service providing opportunities for musicians. Campbell-White, in an interview with the author in 1997, recalled the booking procedures which Emmie insisted had to be followed to the letter:

> If the BBC Proms rang up with an enquiry to engage the tenor Robert Tear, you had to traipse upstairs to her office to look at the Diaries which were always kept outside her office on a ledge. You pencilled the date in her diary and rang back to confirm availability. Only then was I allowed to approach Tear to ask if he was interested. If he was, you marked in the rehearsals as well as the date itself, and the contract was then sent to me c/o Ibbs and Tillett. When it came to senior artists such as Curzon, Segovia, Szell, or Dorati, I would have to ask Emmie to approach the artist about the engagement. Only Emmie was allowed to ink in the artist's name when an engagement was confirmed.

Campbell-White (unlike with Harrison or Parrott, Emmie could not quite decide whether to call him 'Martin' or 'Campbell-White') trained as a singer, but was advised by his teacher to enter the profession in another capacity. He and others basically ran the artists for Tillett and Holt, which looked after Ibbs and Tillett artists for their overseas work, and as Emmie spoke no foreign languages, travelled very little, and, in his view, 'didn't really trust foreigners', she was happy to let them get on with it. During Campbell-White's six years at Ibbs and Tillett (1966–72), he observed how, with its nation-wide predominance over choral societies, singers who wanted to join that circuit had to be on their books. As an artist's fame grew and societies began asking for them, so it would not be long before, alerted to their success, Emmie would take over their management (Janet Baker being a typical example). They then immediately graduated from the smaller provincial choral society circuit to the major ones in London, in the provinces, and at the major festivals. Meanwhile, although opera was not a significant part of the agency's work, there were opera singers whose oratorio work they handled, such as that of Forbes Robinson, Owen Brannigan, and Benjamin Luxon.

Campbell-White too observed how younger artists were handled by younger members of staff, highlighting a generation gap and rift with senior management. Emmie was thought to have lost touch, for while the employees complained that there was no after-work socializing with her, the artists were resigned to the prospect of not seeing her at their concerts. When Harrison and Parrott were fired in the autumn of 1969, Campbell-White was promoted *faute de mieux* and given the overseas department at Harold Holt. Emmie continued to resist delegating any of the decision-making process, but he could tolerate her interference. He was offered a Directorship in 1970, and it seemed to him that he was being groomed to succeed her. But the gulf between them began to widen, with the frustrations, the old-fashioned, unyielding approach (such as the *Buckingham* code), and the resistance to any attempt to modernize the agency. In 1972 she announced that Wilfred Stiff was being brought in as her eventual successor. Stiff already had a room in the building for his own public relations company and, as related in Chapter 22, had edited the agency's bulletin *Prelude* in 1958. It looked as if another collision between the generations, and further disagreement about running the business, was unavoidable.

In a memorandum written at the start of 1972, Campbell-White put forward various proposals 'for the good of Ibbs and Tillett', although feeding and clothing a growing family meant that he was having to consider his own longer-term prospects with the firm. He proposed setting up a new group of artists within the agency, which he suggested might be called 'Ibbs and Tillett International', and which he and Andrew Rosner might run. Rosner had joined Ibbs and Tillett in 1970, taking over the broadcasting department from Campbell-White. After a year or so, Rosner in turn proposed the idea of an opera department, which after some persuasion, Emmie agreed to try. Rosner, who ran it in addition to his broadcasting department responsibilities, was particularly successful in establishing a link with Peter Hemmings at Scottish Opera. Hemmings was very supportive and gave work to the young British artists proposed to him by the agency. But, like Harrison and Parrott before them, Campbell-White and Rosner were now beginning to suffer the frustrations of the slow-pace of response they were encountering. Campbell-White's memo of 27 January 1972 began by outlining three main reasons for discontent among the agency's artists. An increasing number were:

> unhappy with our system of working and would much prefer one person in the firm to be responsible for all their work. We are not attracting enough young artists, and, thirdly, I find that too much of my time is taken up with non-productive work for artists, who are unsuccessful for whatever reasons.

He was asked to elaborate on certain proposals, and specifically to answer two questions, namely: 'Which artists he proposed should be managed personally within the firm and by whom', and 'How liaison within the firm could be achieved.' In his response a month later on 25 February 1972, Campbell-White acknowledged the basic difference of view between him and Emmie, that she felt that the agency's policy must be 'biased in favour of the societies' whereas he preferred it to be 'weighted more towards the needs of the artists on our list'. In his view, four deficient areas required urgent attention. The first was that young artists were going elsewhere (to Christopher Hunt or HarrisonParrott), or, worse still, they were not even considering Ibbs and Tillett as a first option when starting their careers. The second area drew attention to underproductive departments within the agency, such as the box office and concert management, requiring five full-time salaries between them. The third focused on a more efficient use of personnel resources within the agency to avoid frustrations among a number of young members of staff, who were eager for more responsibility. There were petty rivalries which needed to be eliminated, and too rapid a turnover of secretaries engaged at low salaries and producing a poor standard of work. The problem of low pay was producing a low return at all levels. His fourth and final area of concern would prove the most contentious, because it struck at the heart of Emmie's business philosophy, which she had inherited from her husband and Robert Leigh Ibbs, and that was the way in which artists were booked as well as 'the co-ordination and rationalisation of an artist's career'. Too much time was being wasted when co-ordinating an artist's availability each time a request for his or her services came to the agency, especially when it came by telephone and callers were either asked to hang on or await a return call. In an undisguised attempt to introduce the concept of personal management, Campbell-White took the bold step of suggesting to Emmie:

> you must admit that you do in fact already 'manage' the careers of quite a few artists, such as Janet [Baker], Clifford [Curzon] and Segovia, and these artists would not expect otherwise.

On the other hand, 'younger artists' such as John Lill, Stephen Bishop, John Williams, and Andrew Davis 'would prefer to be looked after by Andrew [Rosner] and me'. He was even bolder to confront her with the assertion that:

> many of the younger artists find you rather unapproachable. This is not surprising; there is a generation gap. A number of artists would like to see younger, more active people working for them. By the same token we find it more difficult to talk to the senior artists.

Denzil Walker, who had originally asked Campbell-White to put his thoughts in writing, responded with a substantive, if fence-sitting memorandum. He acknowledged that the proposals should 'receive deep consideration', and was already perfectly aware that artists wanted 'to get the best of both worlds by having personal management, while still retaining the advantages of our unique position with Societies at home and abroad'. In his view, however, if it was personal management they wanted, then they should go elsewhere to further their careers (citing John Ogdon as an example of an artist who had already made that mistake). On the other hand, he cautioned against dismissing the idea out of hand and 'running the risk of not attracting the right kind of young artist'. Having already lost Hunt in 1963 followed by Harrison and Parrott in 1969, Walker was reluctant to see a further haemorrhage with the possible loss of Campbell-White and Rosner with him, and furthermore he was aware of the negative signal it would send to the profession if more young men of ideas were seen to walk away after only a handful of years in post. As a compromise, he suggested that to resolve the dispute it should now undergo three stages:

> Stage 1. I should like to suggest that Mrs Tillett (with Beryl Ball), Miss Cheselden, and Martin Campbell-White indicate with a tick on our current List, independently and without collusion, who they think could be considered for preferential treatment and be managed by 'one person in the firm'. With that information collated, it will give us an idea of the number of Artists involved and also enable us to obtain an estimate of the total revenue brought in by those Artists during the past year. As I see it, increased expenditure will arise with personal service, and it may well be that we shall have to consider a service charge or an increase to 15% commission (Inland) and 20% (Abroad).
>
> Stage 2. Having drawn up a potential List, it will then be possible to consider revising the format of our present printed List of Artists under Sole Management. It might be possible to consider carrying these Artists under a special heading of world representation (or some other phrase) and continue to carry the other names under a heading of Artists with whom we are in a position to negotiate (or some other phrase). To that latter List could be added many other names such as Heather Harper and others who have no Sole Management, and for whom we do a lot of work, together with the

names of many of the singers dealt with by Miss Cheselden, and who do not appear on the printed List [the so-called General List] at the present time.

Stage 3. Always supposing we have got as far as this in this exercise, we must then consider the following. Which Artist is to be managed 'personally' within the firm and by whom, and how can liaison within the firm be achieved? Both these will present difficulties but of the two, the second will, in my opinion, be more difficult. The first will not be easy!

Anyone offering Artists engagements either at home or abroad will expect to deal with one person at Ibbs and Tillett, and cannot be expected to be passed from one person to another when booking a number of Artists at the same time, for that matter at any time! An Artist given personal representation will expect the person with whom they deal at Ibbs and Tillett to be fully conversant with all possible engagements at home or abroad and the sources thereof. Both these points and many others strike me as presenting initial difficulties, and at this stage should the plan be considered further, I think Martin Campbell-White should be given the opportunity of making suggestions for solving them, and so I suggest that the ball be returned in his court for further points.

In response to what was now asked of him, Campbell-White proposed two lists of artists, one for Emmie and Beryl Ball (though 'we would still look after the foreign work of your artists'), the other for himself but supported by Andrew Rosner and a team of three secretaries, though he felt that even more help would be necessary. The two lists were as follows:

Mrs Tillett
Gina Bachauer
Shura Cherkassky
Aldo Ciccolini
Clifford Curzon
Alicia De Larrocha
Jorg Demus
Annie Fischer
Wilhelm Kempff
Moura Lympany
Nikita Magaloff
George Malcolm
Rudolf Serkin
Rosalyn Tureck
Malcolm Williamson
Christian Ferras
Arthur Grumiaux
Paul Tortelier
Andrès Segovia
Sir Adrian Boult
Antal Dorati
Elisabeth Schwarzkopf
Jennifer Vyvyan
Janet Baker
Richard Lewis
Dietrich Fischer-Dieskau

Martin Campbell-White
Malcolm Binns
Stephen Bishop
Anthony Goldstone
John Lill
John Ogdon
Garrick Ohlsson
Maurizio Pollini
Janos Solyom
Szymon Goldberg
Erich Gruenberg
Josef Suk
Zara Nelsova
Arto Noras
Thomas Igloi
Aeolian String Quartet
Amadeus String Quartet
Lindsay String Quartet
Tel Aviv String Quartet
John Williams
Andrew Davis
Meredith Davies
Raymond Leppard
Eduardo Mata
Elizabeth Harwood
Maureen Forrester
Norma Procter
Helen Watts
John Mitchinson
Robert Tear
Simon Estes
Benjamin Luxon
Brian Rayner Cook
John Shirley-Quirk

He continued:

> There are a number of ways we could divide up responsibility for my group; I could look after the orchestras and festivals, Andrew could look after the opera and recording contracts. We could divide up the foreign work. This is only one solution. If any artist objects to dealing with so many people, then one person only is designated to speak to him and other members of staff must also work through that one person. Naturally certain societies such as the Three Choirs, Brighton Philharmonic, Bach Choir etc would want to continue to deal with you such as before. I do not think this is going to upset the societies in general, on the contrary I think we must go out and meet [them] more than we have done in the past.

As Campbell-White himself admitted, 'all this is pretty revolutionary', but he was genuinely keen to streamline the running of Ibbs and Tillett and to increase its prospects. As a Director, he wanted monthly Board meetings ('When was the last?') and more open discussion of new ideas.

To protect anonymity, typewritten, unsigned responses to his proposals varied between the patronizingly uncharitable to the sympathetically considered. His harshest critics accused him of personal ambition in the pursuit of his career and domestic needs, an obsession with the glamour of the music industry, inexperience and ignorance of the profession, and of being too 'prepared to listen to tittle tattle to which we have all had to listen for many years'. On the other hand, there was general agreement that his letter should be taken seriously and its suggestions explored and costed:

> We can't stand more changes. If there is any way in which we can improve the image of Ibbs and Tillett conducive with modern times, we must do so, but we must not destroy the unique position Ibbs and Tillett holds with the sources of employment for the Artists we look after. They would be nowhere without that. We all know there are faults, but these must be balanced overall. We must investigate the strength of this idea of personal treatment for Artists, and if it is in anyway feasible within the framework of the firm as it now is, we shall have to settle numerous administrative and financial details.

The phrase, 'feasible within the framework of the firm as it now is', doomed Campbell-White's ideas, for there was clearly no desire to change the *status quo*. Walker found Campbell-White's proposals 'admirable in their concept [but they] were only ones which had already been considered by Mrs Tillett and were not new', while some of his 'suggestions about the staff and their rates of pay together with other administrative details about temporary staff were far from the reality or truth'. The proposed list of artists to be divided between Emmie and himself numbered 58, 32 of which were based in Britain, 26 abroad. Of those in Britain, 23 were to be his, nine to be allocated to Emmie and, of this already small number, seven of them were 'already established'. Walker noted that to go along with the plan, both Emmie Tillett and Beryl Ball would be 'left with very little to do', and furthermore he had little good to say about the team Campbell-White proposed to put together to run the 'firm within the firm'. Words such as 'slapdash', phrases such as 'efficient but slow', 'no idea of economy' or 'an enthusiastic amateur' abound in his memo, and he concluded that his 'previous estimation' of Campbell-White had been 'completely wrong'.

Not surprisingly, Martin Campbell-White left Ibbs and Tillett's employment later in 1972 and, freed of any constraints imposed by Emmie on Ian Hunter in the matter of poaching staff, he joined Harold Holt next door taking Robert Tear, Benjamin Luxon, Andrew Davis, Helen Watts, John Williams, and John Lill with him. This represented a far more serious loss of artists from the books than that which had occurred three years

1 Robert Leigh Ibbs

2 John Tillett

3 Emmie Tillett

4 Clara Butt and Kennerley Rumford

5 Rachmaninov (photograph signed and dated London, 3rd November 1911)

6 Joseph Szigeti

7 Harold Bauer

8 Rosé Quartet (photograph signed and dated London, February 1926)
l. to r. Paul Fischer, violin; Arnold Rosé, violin; Anton Ruzitska, viola; Anton Walter, cello

9 Muriel Brunskill

10 Walter Widdop

11 Dora Labbette

12 Elsie Suddaby

13 Harold Williams

14 Roy Henderson

15 Bella (Isobel) Baillie

16 Heddle Nash

17 Norman Allin

18 Undated postcard to John Tillett from Robert Radford

19 Sir Henry Wood
'To my dear old friend John Tillett. June 1938'

20 Pierre Monteux
'To John H. Tillett, most sincerely. 27th January 1927'

21 Harold Samuel

22 Artur Schnabel

23 Harriet Cohen

24 Alfred Cortot

25 Beatrice Harrison

26 Guilhermina Suggia

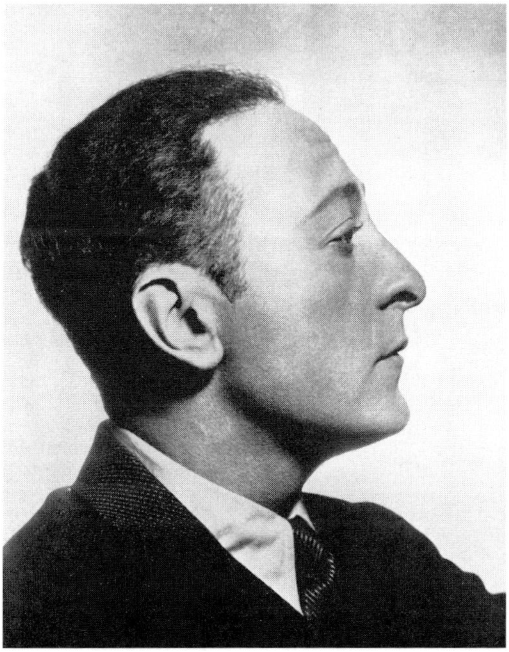

27 Jascha Heifetz

28 Lionel Tertis

29 Myra Hess (piano) and Jelly d'Aranyi (violin)

30 Jelly d'Aranyi (piano) and Myra Hess (violin)

31 Rudolf Serkin

32 Irene Scharrer

33 Benno Moiseiwitsch

34 Solomon

35 Cyril Smith and Phyllis Sellick

36 Elisabeth Schumann

37 Gladys Ripley

38 Peter Pears

39 Emmie Tillett with Kathleen Ferrier, Paris 17th February 1951

40 Emmie Tillett with Sergiu Celibidache and Wilhelm Furtwängler London, November 1948

41 Amadeus String Quartet

42 Francis Poulenc and Pierre Bernac

43 Richard Lewis

44 Elisabeth Schwarzkopf 'would like to know:
what would British musical life be without Emmie?? October 1971'

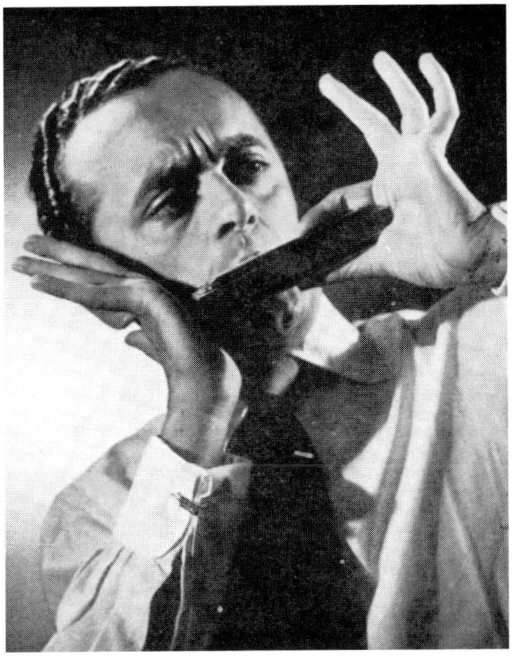

45 Larry Adler

46 Andrès Segovia

47 Julian Bream

48 Moura Lympany

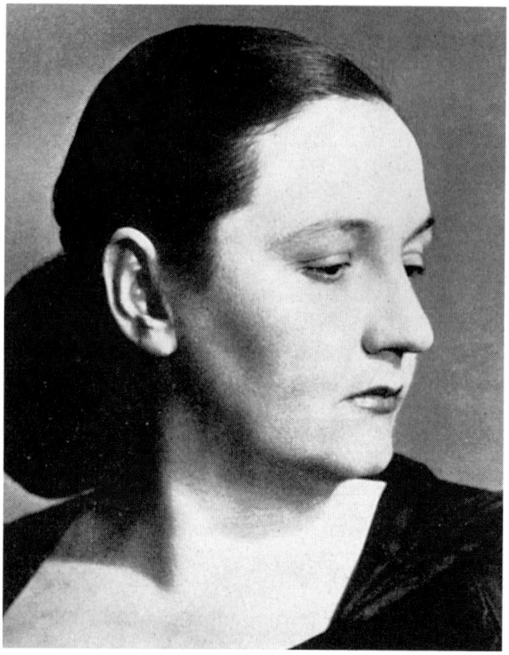

49 Gina Bachauer

50 Wilhelm Kempff

51 Shura Cherkassky

52 Clifford Curzon

53 Stephen [Bishop] Kovacevich

54 Vladimir Ashkenazy

55 John Ogdon

56 Emil Gilels

57 Sir Adrian Boult

58 Paul Tortelier with Wilfred Stiff at the cellist's post-concert 70th birthday party

59 Janet Baker

60 Jacqueline du Pré

61 Felicity Lott

62 Anthony Rolfe Johnson

63 Robert Tear

64 John Shirley-Quirk

65 Julian Lloyd Webber

66 Lesley Garrett

67 Elizabeth Harwood

68 Dietrich Fischer-Dieskau

69 Peter Donohoe

70 Richard Hickox

71 Alicia de Larrocha

72 Mitsuko Uchida

73 The memorial lunch for Norman Allin held at the Royal College of Music
standing l. to r. Geraint Evans, Ivor Newton, Robert Easton, Sir Thomas Armstrong, Richard Lewis, Redvers Llewellyn, Roy Henderson, Keith Falkner
seated l. to r. Kathleen Cheselden, Mary Jarred, Isabel Baillie, Eva Turner, Muriel Brunskill, Carrie Tubb, Emmie Tillett

74 Emmie Tillett painting

75 John Tillett with the 'Buckingham' ledger

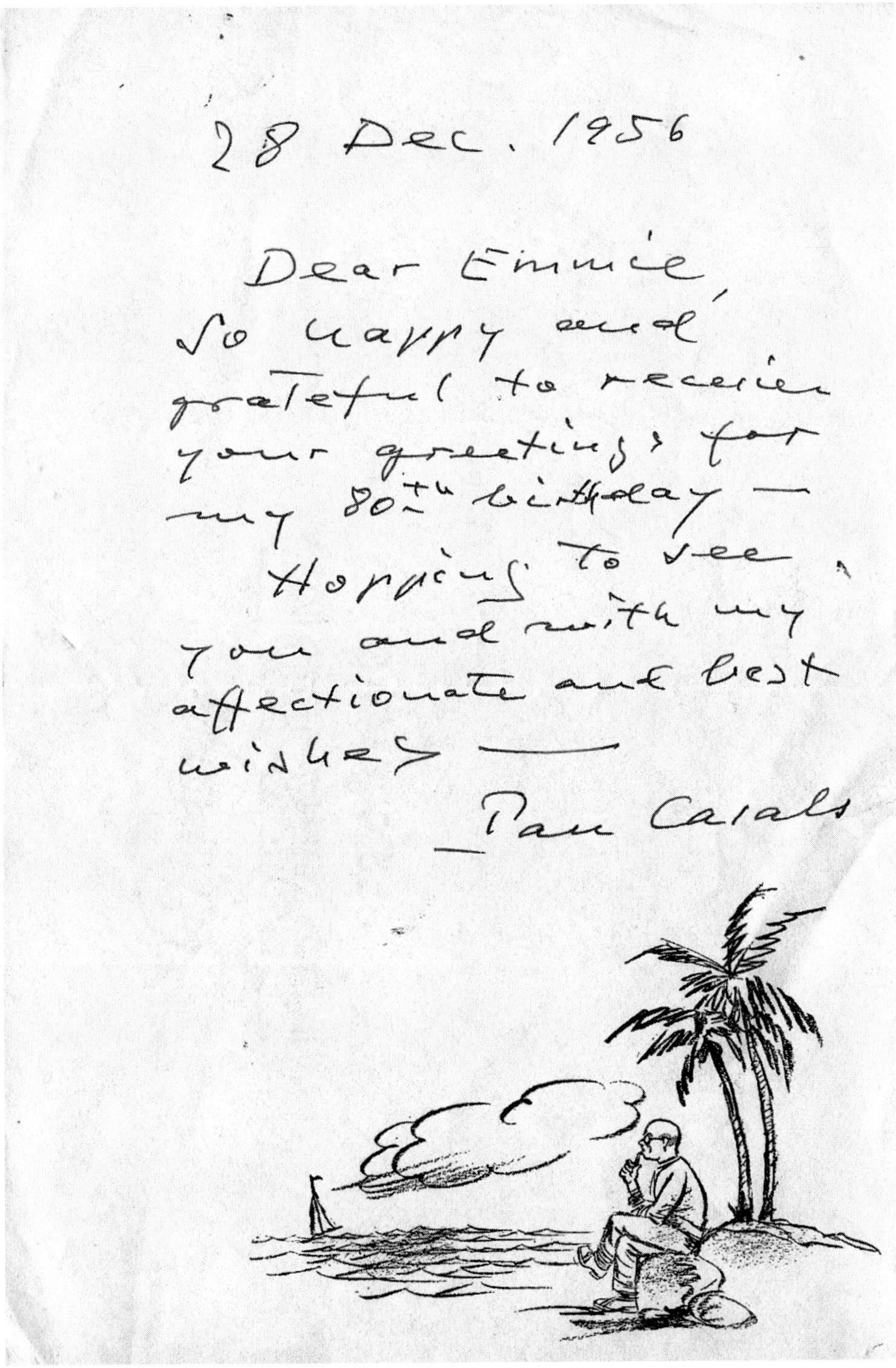

28 Dec. 1956

Dear Emmie,
So happy and grateful to receive your greetings for my 80th birthday —
Hoping to see you and with my affectionate and best wishes —
Pau Casals

76 Letter from Pablo Casals to Emmie Tillett

77 John Tillett caricature

earlier. Like Hunt, Harrison, and Parrott, Campbell-White went on to enjoy a highly successful career. As joint Managing Director of AskonasHolt (his co-Director another future Ibbs and Tillett employee, Robert Rattray), he is a significant player in the artists' management profession. Once again it seemed that Ibbs and Tillett had miscalculated, and brought upon themselves the loss of one of their most talented assets.

As Emmie had done with Harrison and Parrott before him, Campbell-White was now cut off from one day to the next (not helped by frequent encounters between them, because he worked next door), although in his words, she was 'noble' about it. In his view, Emmie had no strategy or vision for the future, but he also sensed that she herself had a gut feeling that she could not come to terms with these so-called young Turks. What they wanted was personal management, though with the *caveat* of being neither management in a vacuum, nor agency work. Ironically it had been Denzil Walker who alerted her to the danger of not employing young people, and that she should take on young men who were long-term prospects, rather than young women who tended to leave after a year or two. As it happens Walker's assumptions in his memo were misplaced, but overriding everything was Emmie's constant concern that the firm would be taken over by one of the ambitious young men she employed.

CHAPTER TWENTY-FOUR

End of an Era: 1970–82

By the mid-1960s, the leases of the two Wigmore Street properties needed attention. The rent was something like £100 a year and the leases, which were due to expire in 1995, were worth a fortune as commercial rents were now beginning to rise alarmingly. As far as Emmie was concerned, when it came to paying death duties, the business would be worth very little, for though the name of Ibbs and Tillett was of some value, the assets came to nothing at all, so the business would have to be sold. For many years the agency had not been realizing its full earning potential, part of the reason being the low fees charged for the artists. For most of her working life, Emmie operated a monopoly and could tell artists what they were worth and what they could be sold for. Ibbs and Tillett was therefore like a musical *Exchange and Mart* acting for both parties, a clearing house marrying promoters to artists. To the question, 'who are your clients?', she would answer, 'everybody', for she owed a duty both to the artist and to the client, regarding herself as a servant of the profession, never earning big sums of money. In her eyes, her role was to feed the profession and concert promoters with artists at an affordable fee, not to promote their careers. In fact she believed that she did promote artists' careers and in a totally fair way, but realistically she had always had her favourites, and they were generally the cream of the artists who were also her close friends. So while there was an element of truth in the fact that artists were leaving because of low fees, it was more a case of the lack of career promotion which other agents were now doing, which made them go. Generous and altruistic as she was as a person, Emmie was also economical with the handbag.

As a result of his warning to Emmie about the leases and assets, the firm's solicitor Paul Strang reorganized the company completely. In about 1963, and with a view to mitigating taxation, the shares were held by members of staff, and each signed a covenant with the newly formed Tillett Trust that, if they left, they would sell their shares back to the Trust. Towards the end of the decade, this scheme was disbanded, for, with the property removed from the equation the shares were worth virtually nothing, and the firm reconstructed, which was common practice. The properties were taken out of the company and a separate company called Ibbs and Tillett Properties Ltd formed, which held the properties while the Tillett Trust held the shares in the properties, so effectively the value of the company was taken out and put into the Trust. As a result, Emmie was able to carry on and the properties preserved with money in the Trust, a situation which pertained for some while. The interiors of both 122 and 124 Wigmore Street were modernized and sold back to Great Portland Estates, who owned the freehold, while Ibbs and Tillett Properties Ltd owned the long leasehold, worth something like £350000–£400000. This came into the Trust when it sold the company, not the lease. The three original trustees were Paul Strang, Jimmie Smith and Keith Falkner. In October 1968 a public statement was issued by the agency about these structural changes in the organization:

> Certain changes in our organisation took place at the beginning of this month. Some five years ago [1963] a Trust was created called the Tillett Trust. The intention was to perpetuate the name

> of the late John Tillett by creating a charitable trust whose objects would be the advancement of music.
>
> Our business, together with Tillett & Holt Records and our interest in Tillett & Holt, is now being carried on by and for the benefit of the Trust.
>
> There are, however, no administrative changes: Mrs Tillett continues as before, but with the title of Managing Trustee, and the previous Directors remain as such. Dealings with neither artists nor management are in any was affected, but we feel that it should be known that this business, the oldest established in its field, is now carried on not for profit, but for the benefit of music in this country generally.

In 1969 Ian Hunter bought Harold Holt Ltd from Emmie Tillett, putting into practice his philosophy of being the instigator of events rather than the middle man. Hunter also continued to use his previous experience as a Festival Director by running those at Bath, Brighton, Windsor, the City of London, Hong Kong, and, in 1965, the Commonwealth Arts Festival. Harold Holt Ltd celebrated its centenary in 1976, taking its starting date as Alfred Schultz-Curtius's activities in London a century earlier. The increase in competition, caused by general revivals throughout the agency and management business during the 1960s, now forced Ibbs and Tillett to preface their artists' list brochures with the following paragraph, its language and presentation typically a throwback to earlier in the century and somewhat cumbersome for the decade of the Beatles:

> Notwithstanding the fact that the names of some of the Artists shown herein may appear in lists emanating from other sources, whilst these ARTISTS remain under SOLE MANAGEMENT for Great Britain and – in many cases – abroad, this is the ONLY OFFICE from which complete and up-to-date information regarding Terms and Availability can be obtained. A comprehensive List of all Artists with whom engagements can be negotiated is available, on request.

Gramophone records were sold in Tillett and Holt's shop situated in the neighbouring premises of 122 Wigmore Street, where 'a warm welcome is always assured' from the 'specialist staff', while Fred Bass, Emmie's nephew, still ran his business making publicity shots of artists from the basement. While Martin Campbell-White was working for her, Emmie told him that John Tillett had the chance, back in 1946, to buy the freehold of 122 and 124 Wigmore Street for £1100, but decided against it because it was £100 too much. 'Oh I do regret that he didn't buy them', she said.

Meanwhile changes of personnel were taking place as the 1960s gave way to the 1970s. Not only had the talented Harrison and Parrott left in the autumn of 1969 followed by Martin Campbell-White in 1972, but now the agency was witnessing the departure of the ever-faithful and long-serving ladies when Sadie Lereculey retired in 1972 and Kathleen Cheselden died in November 1975. In her reply to the tenor Charles Corp, who had written with condolences on hearing the news of Miss Cheselden's death, Emmie wrote:

> We shall all miss her sadly, as she was a great and gallant person, but we are determined to carry on her fine work in her memory and as she would have wished. Meanwhile the work goes on just as usual.

Corp, like many other young hopefuls, had developed a genuine affection for Kathleen Cheselden and noted her natural role as a mother hen to him and others. In August 2002, he penned some memories of her and the agency for this book:

> In the Spring of 1966 I was invited to an interview with Kathleen Cheselden, who presided over a large desk (seemingly covered with letters from choral societies) in a rather gloomy office at the back of the building on the first floor. She stressed that Ibbs and Tillett were not impresarios and could not give me work, I had to be asked for. If they were ever holding auditions she would contact me,

possibly by telegram. We would have to see what would happen. In her view one did not have to sing opera to make a living, and cited her husband (she was Eric Greene's third wife) who had made a living from singing Bach [in particular the Evangelist in the Passions]. If one was to sing opera, it was best to have established a concert career first.

In February 1969 I sang in Handel's *Susannah* at the Victoria & Albert Museum with the Handel Opera Society, and informed Ibbs and Tillett of the concert. I spotted Mrs Tillett in the audience and hoped to hear something, but nothing happened, although I realised sometime later that I should have written again after the concert. In July that year I won the Gold Medal at the Guildhall School of Music, and the adjudicator was Dame Eva Turner. That did the trick. I had a most courteous letter from Beryl Ball saying that they had indeed heard me at the V & A Museum and would I phone for an appointment with Mrs Tillett. It was an exceedingly hot July afternoon, and I had on my best and only dark lounge suit. I had to wait in the front office for what seemed a long time, and then was taken up to Mrs Tillett's office on the first floor, overlooking the street. She was sitting behind an elegant desk, beautifully dressed and immaculately coiffured. She motioned me to sit down and remarked that 'it was very hot for telephoning'. Tactfully I agreed, and then we sat looking at one another for what seemed an eternity. She then indicated that I should start the conversation, so I thanked her for agreeing to see me and asked if her firm could help me find concert work. I described my modest engagements so far and that I had been asked back quite a few times; she agreed that it was always nice and good too, to be asked back, and that she would take me through to Miss Cheselden, who dealt with choral society bookings.

Nothing had changed since 1966. The room was still gloomy, despite the summer sunshine, the desk still covered in letters. Kathleen Cheselden remembered we had met before, bade me sit down, and after Mrs Tillett had left, some time was spent discussing what my quoted fee should be, 25 or 30 guineas. Eventually she opted for 30 and offered me a job on the spot, the *St John* [Bach's Passion] arias with the Northampton Bach Choir, saying that I would not have to sing the 'nasty long one' ['Erwäge wie sein blutgefärbter Rücken'], which I thought was a nice, sympathetic approach to a new singer. For some reason I turned the engagement down, but she did not seem to mind, and asked for a biography, which in due course was printed in a brochure.

Nothing happened for two months until the phone rang one morning. The operator at Ibbs and Tillett [Edna Walters] had a rather distinctive voice and novel way of dealing with calls leaving the office. When answering a call from the agency there would first be a silence, then she would say your name and after you had confirmed it, 'good … (long pause) … I have Miss X', or 'I have a call for you'. After a further silence Miss Cheselden's gravelly voice, or Mrs Tillett's pleasant but business-like voice, would come on the line and launch into whatever was on offer. Miss Cheselden's first words were invariably 'Now are you free on' such and such a date? For the next six years I found her pleasant and kindly, clearly very conscientious. I was told she always took the Diary home with her at weekends so that in case of illness, she knew where all her singers were and who would be available to step in. I remember her phoning one Saturday morning to see if I would like to sing *Gerontius* that night in Hertford with Alfreda Hodgson and John Carol Case. I hesitated, for though I knew the music very well I had not yet sung it and the first part sat high for me. She sensed my hesitation and said 'don't do it if you are not entirely happy about it'. I did refuse and she found someone well-suited to the part. On another occasion, returning from a concert performance of Handel's *Samson* in Harlow about midnight, the phone was ringing. It was Miss Cheselden. 'I thought you'd be back about now. Can you go to Oxford tomorrow to sing the arias in the *St Matthew Passion* in German? There's a 10 o'clock rehearsal at the Sheldonian Theatre'. I said I did not own a copy in German, not ever having sung it in the language. She assured me someone would lend me a copy. I agreed and sensed her relief. If I had not been before to the Sheldonian Theatre, she went on, I should have a good look at the beautiful ceiling.

By 1982 things were very different if one fell ill at the last moment. I woke up one Saturday in May that year, more or less voiceless and with a Verdi *Requiem* to be sung that night. I phoned Ibbs and Tillett and spoke to the only person in the office, the accountant. Having explained the situation, I suggested one or two names of singers who would sing the part well, but I subsequently surmised that he got hold of an alphabetical list of tenors and started working his way down, finding an excellent Bach singer among the Bs who manfully took on the job, which was in Bath Abbey, quite a building and with a big orchestra. I don't think that would have happened in Kathleen Cheselden's time. A final memory of her; when she offered me that first job, *Elijah* in Harlow, she said 'we have broken the ice'.

> The Three Choirs was for years Mrs Tillett's festival. Just about all the singers were booked through Ibbs and Tillett, and she would go for the week, purchasing a Steward's ticket. The fees were not astronomical. In 1951 Isobel Baillie received 90 guineas for four sessions in the Cathedral and one in the Odeon cinema, while no doubt some of the lesser singers would have been lucky to get much more than 20 or 25 guineas. I saw an Ibbs and Tillett list of fees for 1958. Joan Hammond was at the top with 100 guineas, Richard Lewis was next at 75, Baillie, Elsie Morison, Norma Procter, Constance Shacklock and Jennifer Vyvyan were all at 40, Marjorie Thomas 35. Pears was 40, Greene and William Herbert 35. The choral societies were the clients and if they could only afford 25 when your fee was 40, bad luck. Doubtless the sole artists had to take it, while the freelance could refuse it, but at the risk of not being offered anything ever again.
>
> A Special Fee might be as little as 15 guineas – 'it will only cost you a few pence to get there on the tube' – and a reduced fee might be 20 or 25 guineas instead of 30, the plea usually being 'they haven't got much money'. I remember a Special Fee at Banbury for Haydn's *Creation*, and at the bottom of the contract it was noted 'Our clients usually provide a nice meal after the rehearsal'. The meal was a dubious pie and a pint in the pub behind the parish church, though to be fair I was given hospitality (this was generally free bed and breakfast and a lift to the station the next morning) so that I could travel on to Dudley in Gloucestershire for an engagement the next evening. With the change to decimal currency [in 1972], fees to guineas were rounded DOWN to pounds.

With the advent of the new decade of the 1970s and Emmie now approaching the age of 75, Paul Strang, not only in his capacity as the firm's solicitor but also as a close friend, suggested that she should think of appointing a successor to run the business. She responded by saying that the obvious person to take over was Ian Hunter, but 'quite frankly I think he'll turn the business into what I do not want it to become, which is another Harold Holt'. She wanted Ibbs and Tillett to continue to represent both promoter and artist. Ian Hunter regretted that Emmie had decided not to let Harold Holt take over Ibbs and Tillett at this time. In his view it was a decision which would reap havoc with the firm's name over the next two decades. With the benefit of hindsight it might have proved a wise suggestion, but Emmie never thought of Hunter as an agent.

Strang then suggested the name of Wilfred Stiff, already known to her not only through his work as a publicist in London, but earlier in the agency's dealings with the Royal Liverpool Philharmonic Orchestra of which Stiff was General Manager from 1946 to 1956. There he had performed excellent work, steering the orchestra from its base at Philharmonic Hall through major financial crises and battles with the city's council, inaugurating Industrial Concerts, relocating Promenade concerts to a boxing stadium, raising the orchestra's profile by seeking royal status (which happened just a year after his departure), involving himself in the creation of the Merseyside Youth Orchestra, and bringing Glyndebourne to Liverpool (which was a catalyst in the concept of Glyndebourne Touring Opera). In 1956 he left to set up his public relations business in London, and was given a couple of rooms in 122 Wigmore Street, before taking offices on the corner of James and Wigmore Streets. He realized the vital importance of PR at a time when the impact of communication through broadening technology was growing fast, and expanded the work of a wide range of artists from Gina Bachauer to Tom Lehrer, as well as the LSO. He then became Administrator to London Festival Ballet (later English National Ballet) with offices in Welbeck Street, but having decided that dance held less appeal for him than music, he left to create a classical music wing within the firm of London Management. When the dust had settled after Campbell-White's departure for Harold Holt, Wilfred Stiff was appointed Executive Director of the agency from 1 October 1972. Stiff was to play a pivotal role in the agency's fortunes over the next 12 years until he retired in 1984 (he died in 1996). Dapper in appearance with his daily, fresh-picked button-hole rose, and ever the diplomat, he was very popular with artists, while some employees at Ibbs and Tillett, especially those with radical views on reforming the business and who then went on to develop their own careers as agents, had a wider range of views. When an amalgamation with a particular car hire company was mooted, some wag pointed out that it could result in the firm's renaming as Stiff, Tillett, Hertz. Wilfred Stiff was a man of ideas and enthusiasms, though not all of them either achieved success or even made it to the starting blocks. What none deny was his ability for spotting genuine talent among young musicians, many of whom still speak warmly of his personal interest in their professional careers and his concern for their personal welfare. He was a realist, 'dates do not grow on trees' being a frequent riposte to impatient artists, though one singer whom he was said to have reassured with the words 'you are our busiest contralto', came back with 'well if that's so Wilfred, God help the others'. On the other hand the up-and-coming accompanist Graham Johnson, when forming his Songmakers' Almanac concerts in the mid-1970s, had considerable cause to be grateful to Wilfred Stiff, who 'allowed me to plan a whole series of concerts without the money to pay for them: *autre temps, autre moeurs*, thank heavens', while former agency employee Callum Ross remembers Stiff's unflagging support for his Young Artists Platform scheme.

This further upheaval in the history of Ibbs and Tillett, and from now such disturbances appear fairly regularly, occurred in the summer of 1972. To trace its course we have to go back a couple of years and bring Michael Emmerson into the narrative. He created and ran the Belfast Festival from 1962, and first contacted Ibbs and Tillett in order to book artists such as guitarists Segovia and Julian Bream. Having made a success at Belfast, he took on the Newcastle Festival in 1968, Wavendon in 1970, and Westminster in 1972, at which point he decided on a career change and moved to London. In an interview with the author, he described events as he perceived them from the sidelines, and which led to the next set of changes at Ibbs and Tillett:

> About 1970 Wilfred Stiff (then a publicist) went to a dinner given by EMI and sat next to Dennis van Thal, who had been a movie casting director and had formed London Management with Lew Grade. Van Thal was a successful theatrical manager who looked after such actors as Alec Guinness and Dirk Bogarde, and he told Stiff how much he loved music and wanted to get into the music business. Stiff suggested he add a musical dimension to London Management and buy Wilfrid van Wyck Ltd, which was up for sale. Van Wyck had managed Arthur Rubinstein since the early 1930s in Wigmore Street, and his firm was based either on such major artists or on the own-risk business (debut recitals paid for by the artist including a management fee, similar to Ibbs and Tillett's system). Van Wyck's business was going downhill. He himself had had a bad road accident, and another of his big money earners, pianist Julius Katchen, had died the year before. Stiff and van Thal negotiated with van Wyck who sold the business for £19000 though he kept himself employed as joint Managing Director at Wilfred Stiff's side for four years. They moved from Wigmore Street to the offices of London Management at 235–241 Regent Street where the business (still called Wilfrid van Wyck Ltd) continued to go downhill and lose money.
>
> After about two years (in 1972) Stiff conceived a scheme to stop the firm losing money. In his view the answer lay in buying another agency, namely Ibbs and Tillett, and because he did not get on personally with van Wyck, he had already moved his office into 124 Wigmore Street. He proposed a buy out of Ibbs and Tillett to Emmie. The weekend it was all due to happen two incidents occurred, Martin Campbell-White left the firm for Harold Holt and Emmie decided she would not go ahead with the sale. She nevertheless proposed that Wilfred Stiff join the firm as a Director, which he did, at the same time resigning from van Wyck.

Ibbs and Tillett employee Helen Fraser, who was there in a secretarial and administrative capacity from March 1971 to May 1974, kept a diary at the time and recalled these events of 1972. As a lowly member of staff, she was told nothing of the amalgamation with van Wyck, but like many others, she heard the rumours. 'Nobody knows anything about it and Major Walker does not keep the staff informed', she wrote. Others were also concerned, such as Carol Borg, who compiled a ten-point memorandum dated 7 June 1972:

> Why has the merger come about? From what date does the merger take effect? What will be the title of the Firm?
>
> Some members of the staff have still not been told officially, and are worried as to how they will be affected. Will there be any redundancy?
>
> Does Ibbs and Tillett come under the control of London Management? May I please have a list of the Directors of London Management? Does Ibbs and Tillett's Board of Directors remain as at present, and do they have any control in the running of Ibbs and Tillett, or will they be under the direction of London Management?
>
> Is London Management under the control of the Grade Organisation, or is it run completely separately and merely has some Directors who are connected with both concerns? What size is London Management as regards numbers of staff and artists. Are copies of London Management lists available to us?
>
> What position does Wilfred Stiff hold as regards Ibbs and Tillett?
>
> Is the Tillett Trust to be disbanded? Do the Tillett Trust Trustees retain any say in the running of Ibbs and Tillett, or is their connection with the Firm finished?
>
> Are the staff of Wilfrid van Wyck Ltd moving into our premises, and if so when and where? Are the two firms to be merged completely or to remain separate but using consistency of methods?
>
> Will salaries be paid by Ibbs and Tillett as a separate entity or by London Management? What is the situation regarding the Pension Scheme?
>
> Does all London Management business operate on $12^1/_2\%$ commission, or only the 'classical' side? Are van Wyck artists to be incorporated into the Ibbs and Tillett list? Are we likely to have sufficient information on this for preparing our new lists in late August/early September, and will my Department still be responsible for preparing the lists?

Helen Fraser noted that 'new contracts would be drawn up effective from 1 October 1972 and Carol Borg says that the staff are agitating for higher salaries'. Her diary recorded:

> Friday 29 September 1972: Amalgamation in place, this was the last day of I&T, and everything was now set for takeover as from Monday 2 October. Major Walker retired and the staff would be invited to a party at his house. They were told that nothing would change and that they were being taken over by London Management.

When the amalgamation went into effect on 2 October, all staff were instructed not to use Ibbs and Tillett headed notepaper, only the new one with the Directors listed as: Wilfred Stiff, Dennis van Thal, Ronald Ricardo from Wilfrid van Wyck, Emmie Tillett, Beryl Ball, Kathleen Cheselden, and Denys Rowlands, but this order was rescinded without explanation on Thursday 5 October, though apparently because a legal complication had arisen. Emmie took Helen Fraser to Denzil Walker's retirement party ('a strained journey'), and held her own cocktail party for the agency staff on Sunday 15 October 1972 at Elm Tree Road to celebrate her half century with Ibbs and Tillett, but all was still unclear regarding what was actually going on. The notepaper was now back to Ibbs and Tillett but 'in association with the Tillett Trust' rather than Ibbs and Tillett Ltd, while the Directors' names were listed as only those belonging to Ibbs and

Tillett. Paul Strang had warned Emmie of the choices she faced, and put forward a proposal based on a three-part premise, that:

> the basic philosophy of the business remains unchanged (i.e. the concept of a dual responsibility not only to artist but also to promoter), continuity of and security for executive staff, and the necessity to vacate the Wigmore Street premises in March 1976 at the latest.

Despite the fact that this represented a structure which appeared acceptable to all parties, Emmie included, and that the option of a merger with van Wyck was attractive to her because Wilfred Stiff was part of it, she eventually decided against it because she did not want to lose the identity of the business. Nevertheless she was happy to bring Stiff into the firm in the autumn of 1972.

According to Michael Emmerson, agents of his generation went to the two great training schools, either Ibbs and Tillett or Victor Hochauser, to learn about the music business. To start a festival, all it seemed to involve was a 'cosy chat' at the Arts Council, and a letter rather than protracted negotiations over periods of months to get a project off the ground. This lasted through the heady days of the 1960s, in retrospect, golden years under the Labour government's Arts Minister Jennie Lee, until the early 1970s. Harrison, Parrott, and Emmerson were part of a new culture not interested in being agents and just booking dates, but who wanted to make things happen by managing. Emmie did not manage, but booked artists on request, except for some personal friends whom she handled in what, by the 1970s was fast becoming a very old-fashioned way. The new breed of artist wanted personal management and they found it in a similar new breed of go-ahead young men. Emmerson felt that a lot of artists were held back, because Ibbs and Tillett was servicing a lot of institutions, which it had been doing for 50 years. Musicians of quality did not stay with Ibbs and Tillett, or did not go to them in the first place, because of low fees and resistance to the concept of personal management. In the old days, there had been few alternatives to whom they could turn, but by the 1970s the situation had changed, while only a handful of clubs or societies could afford £350 for an artist or a chamber group. In Emmerson's opinion (and it is a widely held one), a booking agency such as Ibbs and Tillett would hold no place today in a music business which is much tougher than it was 30 years ago.

By 1970 Denys Rowlands, the accountant at Ibbs & Tillett from 1956 to 1978, had also become Company Secretary. In his view, the Box Office managed by the German Eva Metzler, may not have made much profit but did at least have a degree of prestige. The London Glyndebourne Box Office was also run from 124 Wigmore Street, while the travel agency, brainchild of the agency's administrator Denzil Walker, in conjunction with the Pall Mall Company, linked its activities to musical events, particularly national and international festivals. Besides those already mentioned, Tom Ponsonby, Andrew Green, Robert Rattray and Robert Birley were all young men who now passed through the employ of Ibbs and Tillett during the 1970s, though any bright ideas they might have had still needed approval from Emmie, ensconced on high in her first-floor office. Carol Borg was first Walker's secretary, then worked for Sadie Lereculey. Annabel Whitestone (later Lady Weidenfeld) became Lereculey's secretary, while Jane Gray (dubbed 'Lady Jane' by Elisabeth Schwarzkopf) was now on the staff and in charge of London concert promotions. Trained as a pianist and cellist, Gray became particularly adept at concert management, and many artists have fond memories of her, following her death in 1994. While in the employ of Ibbs and Tillett, she had a particularly close working relationship with the Amadeus Quartet, Schwarzkopf, Fischer-Dieskau, and Gerald Moore. Robin Coulson, Jane Gray's assistant, took over concert promotion from 1974 until 1977. According to the writer of Gray's obituary in *The Times*, Tim Bullamore:

> her formidable boss Emmie Tillett would rarely allow her near the concerts themselves, preferring to go herself or to send a man. On one occasion Mrs Tillett told her to promote a new show as a favour for the son of a client. In so doing Jane Gray spent considerable energy persuading the young man that, by paying for a second colour on his posters, his production stood a better chance of being noticed. Great was her amusement, therefore, when the show, *Joseph and his Amazing Technicolour Dreamcoat*, was revived with a somewhat more substantial budget by the same young man, Andrew Lloyd Webber, in the West End show almost 25 years later.

The late pianist, radio personality and quiz master Joseph Cooper began his career as organ scholar at Keble College, Oxford (1931–34). The post carried with it the responsibility of running the Music Club as its Secretary, so he had to book the artists for each season, inevitably with Ibbs and Tillett. Miss Bass (as she then was) proposed a whole package of artists, and, as she knew the society's budget, duly organized the programme for the year. Cooper studied with Egon Petri after Oxford, but was forced to cancel his first Wigmore Hall appearance due to the war, and remained a soldier until 1946. He then gave several Wigmore Hall recitals, paying Ibbs and Tillett £100 for the hall hire, which also included a rehearsal, some publicity, and the programme, as well as agency commission. He auditioned successfully for the BBC in 1952, played five times at the Proms during the 1950s, making an unwanted speciality of Tchaikovsky's Piano Concerto No.2, and became an Ibbs and Tillett artist. Emmie Tillett was described to the author by Cooper as:

> a smiley, helpful person, who had an agent's instinct for a marketable artist, and responded to advice about the latest discoveries. She was in no way a musician (she loathed cadenzas), and tended to take work to do at the back of halls during her artists' concerts. Though devoted to her artists, she was also a shrewd, if extremely fair business woman.

When Cooper retired from the concert platform (he could not memorize concertos) and went on to develop a career in television, Emmie refused any commission for the show which made him famous, *Face the Music*. Similarly when, during his playing days, he went to Wilfrid van Wyck for foreign tours, she was supportive despite her personal dislike of van Wyck, and said that he could always come back. Some years after the death of his first wife, Cooper married Carol Borg, who mostly handled dates for music clubs. Emmie reacted 'rather crossly' when Miss Borg now left the firm to become Cooper's wife, but a few years later the relationship was patched up at a Steinway concert. Emmie, Cooper recalled:

> liked having good-looking young men around her. She also enjoyed playing bridge with Solomon, Moiseiwitsch and Hess. Hess could speak but wouldn't, poor Solomon couldn't speak but tried, and Moiseiwitsch never said anything anyway, so everything was conducted in silence!

Another pianist, Peter Katin, whose career also began in the post-war years has:

> general recollections of Emmie. In 1948 and for several years afterwards it was a question of Emmie or nobody and, apart from her few 'favourites', one was put on a particular shelf and expected to stay there. Maybe, with an eventual roster of 350 pianists, that was the way it had to be, but there was no exit door except by taking a big risk. Neither did she necessarily have a lot of influence in other countries. I, for instance, had a very fine agent in Holland, but enquiries from Germany and

> Austria came to me and I passed them on to Emmie. An example of this is Myra Hess, who of course had a great career here and in the USA, where she had a different agent, likewise in Holland, but elsewhere in Europe she had very little success, and Emmie either could not help her or possibly did not like the idea of another agent taking the credit.

A feature of the agency's brochures from the 1970s was the regular, if belated inclusion of conductors, who, if it had been realised earlier, could provide a source of engagements for artists within the agency, especially if they were contracted to an orchestra. Evelyn Barbirolli (interviewed 14 October 1996) recalled that her husband Sir John had a personal manager in England (though the experience was far from a happy one), while Sandor Gorlinsky looked after him in Italy. Barbirolli had been with Ibbs and Tillett, but as a cellist not as a conductor. 'They did not do conductors', said Lady Barbirolli, 'for though they did foreign conductors, home-grown ones tended to be approached directly.' As to her own career as a solo oboist, at first it was Sadie Lereculey, then Carol Borg who looked after her dates. Emmie was a personal friend of the couple, but never telephoned on a professional basis 'unless an unpaid date came in, such as one for a prestigious charity, at which point she would say 'I've got a nothing date for you, dear'. According to the broadcaster John Amis, telephone calls from Emmie would invariably sign off with the single word 'Rightie'.

Further recollections of working for Ibbs and Tillett in the 1970s come from Helen Fraser's diary. She started by working for Beryl Ball, typing and preparing *pro forma* contracts (the artist was sent two copies, two were retained in the office, the booker received a letter of confirmation). Three weeks after starting, she became assistant to Carol Borg to service the music clubs, and kept a record of the artists' programmes, which she first offered to the clubs and then discussed with the artists. There was one occasion when oboist Léon Goossens was asked for by a Scottish music club, and in particular for Mozart's oboe quartet K370, but with piano accompaniment substituting for the three string instruments. Goossens naturally refused the request but offered instead the oboe part of Beethoven's Fifth Symphony. Helen Fraser maintained a card index of programme material containing all the chamber music repertoire with descriptions of each work's movements, a file which was continually in need of updating. When she started in 1971, there was still no central heating at 124 Wigmore Street, only small electric fires, and in the subsequent politically turbulent winters with their three-day weeks, the staff were forced to sit in unheated offices on the two days when the power supply was turned off. Page-turning at lunchtime or evening recitals at the Wigmore Hall, Bishopsgate Institute, or for BBC auditions was still considered part and parcel of a member of the staff's duties, and whereas work for sole artists had to be cleared with Emmie, that for the general freelance list could be handed out by others. Helen Fraser recalls another couple of her employer's catchphrases: to artists in the Green Room after a concert or recital she would invariably give a non-committal 'What a performance!' whether or not she had actually been present for part or all of it.

The other was her cheery cry, by way of greeting to one and all, of 'Ready for the orf?' when she arrived for work each morning. This may well have had the following origin. Many years earlier, Emmie's circle of four water colourists, the Elm Tree Road Group of herself, Kathleen and Winifred Ferrier and Bernadine Hammond, met on Sunday mornings at 11 Elm Tree Road for a painting session followed by a roast for Sunday lunch. When Kathleen sailed for America on 18 February 1949, she happened to glance that morning at her luggage, which stood ready in the hallway of her flat in Hampstead. Two teddy bears were perched on top of the substantial pile of trunks and cases (this was to be a trip of more than three months), and when she returned to Britain, she painted the scene from recall as a still-life, calling it her 'Opus One: Ready for the Off'. It can still be seen amongst the Ferrier material housed at the Museum and Art Gallery in Kathleen's home town of Blackburn in Lancashire. Who originated the catchphrase, whether Emmie or Kathleen, we shall never know.

In April 1977 a new venue became available in London for musical events or auditions, and Ibbs and Tillett had a hand in its restoration. This was the New Gallery in Regent Street, and its opening was announced in the agency's brochure for the 1977–78 season.

> The establishment of the New Gallery as an important concert venue has been brought about by Ibbs and Tillett, who have made arrangements with the owners to provide management and music advisory services. This will enable musical events to be held in the hall from Mondays to Thursdays of each week. The New Gallery, situated in Regent Street just two minutes walk north of Piccadilly Circus, has a seating capacity of over 1300. Originally built as an Art Gallery in 1887, it later became a cinema and now is preserved as a building of historic interest.
>
> The New Gallery, whose ceiling has recently been restored, will become available for musical events as from the beginning of April 1977. Any enquiries regarding the use of the main hall for concerts or the small hall for rehearsal purposes should be addressed to Ibbs and Tillett, 124 Wigmore Street, W1H 0AX Tel. 486 4021.

The project was, according to agency staff of the 1970s such as Robert Rattray and Tom Ponsonby, very much the brainchild of Wilfred Stiff, but its wisdom was highly questionable. Audiences proved very reluctant to attend, and the venture, despite the programming of some highly respected performers, could never compete with either the South Bank concert halls or the Wigmore Hall. According to Emmerson, the New Gallery Concerts were a disaster waiting to happen, because there was too little of the promotion and publicity vital to such new ventures, which somewhat contradicts Stiff's background in public relations. New employees were now staying on average for three to five years, producing a sense of unrest as new agencies mushroomed and others merged. Careers in arts management were now becoming more readily available at college and university level, while more music students than ever were leaving music colleges, taking any available opportunity to get into the Arts, especially if the competitive life of a practical musician either no longer appealed or proved unattainable.

As a student, Robert Rattray was spotted in 1972 by Wilfred Stiff, who was visiting and addressing the Arts Council Management course he was on. Rattray was invited to develop the opera department of Ibbs and Tillett from the summer of 1973. When recruited, such young men tended to be given the foreign department, stayed for just a few years, then left. Rattray observed how, as an older man, Stiff may have enjoyed Emmie's confidence, but his presence was resented by the ladies, who regarded him as an ambitious interloper seeking the succession. All changes were now viewed with suspicion, especially since the upheavals caused by the departures of artists and managers in the late-1960s. In Rattray's view, Stiff wanted to compete with the operatic activities of Christopher Hunt and HarrisonParrott, who now had the cream of British singers. Using his considerable skills as a talent spotter, Stiff took on such gifted singers as Ann Murray, Linda Esther Gray, and Anthony Rolfe-Johnson, placing them in Rattray's hands as well as others already with the agency, such as Philip Langridge and

Michael Rippon. Rattray soon discovered that the level of fees demanded by Ibbs and Tillett for artists was far too low. Emmie had never really grasped the fact that a fee of 40 or 50 guineas was inadequate, while HarrisonParrott were dramatically raising the worth of their artists.

Tom Ponsonby was working at the Barga Opera Festival in 1973, when he heard that Emmie was looking for someone with languages to work in the foreign department. He started in October 1974, and worked for the agency's instrumentalists at 122 Wigmore Street until 1978, being directly responsible to her. Telephoning abroad was forbidden unless an emergency arose, but there was a telex machine. All letters had to be acknowledged immediately (even if no action was taken) using the same formula 'we beg to acknowledge receipt of your letter *xxth* inst or ult, which has come duly to hand'. Ponsonby holds the commonly held view that the decline of Ibbs and Tillett began with the departure of Harrison and Parrott, whose innovations were far ahead of their time. He describes the artists who went with them as the 'filling in the sandwich', and so the agency was left with either young unknown musicians (some of whom went on to enjoy good careers) or the 60- to 85-year-olds who were long established artists. As a result, the finances of the agency were inevitably affected by the low earnings of the former and the waning incomes of the latter. His starting salary in 1974 was £1500 per year, and four years later it had risen by only £150 to £1650. One of Wilfred Stiff's schemes was to take on Richard Hickox and his orchestra (the Richard Hickox Orchestra later renamed City of London Sinfonia), and he wanted Ponsonby to manage it from within Ibbs and Tillett, even though he was totally inexperienced in such matters. He was also expected to do so without relinquishing any of the work he was already doing, was given no extra salary for doing so, and had to be available at weekends if the orchestra required him, and this without either days off or extra money in lieu. Ponsonby considered this 'almost a case of constructive dismissal'. During his four years with the agency, he recalls 32 changes among the 28-strong staff. Emmie, in his view, seemed unaware of what was going on, but though she depended very much on Wilfred Stiff, she was still very much at the helm. Like so many ideas launched at this time, the Hickox scheme did not last much longer.

Ponsonby remembers Emmie as a shrewd operator. By dividing the company up into departments, it meant that no artist developed a one-to-one relationship with any employee, which might have led them to leave and take the artist to another agency. She also actively discouraged any touting for work from organizations on behalf of artists, believing that the long-standing reputation and the good name of Ibbs and Tillett itself attracted both clients and artists, and she would not concede that change was in the air – a serious blind spot. At HarrisonParrott, on the other hand, the whole range of an artist's diary was looked after by one person, who negotiated fees and travelled to drum up new business, a system which prevails to this day. Concert promotion is another area which has been developed today, where an agent will put together a package of artists (soloists, conductors) and an orchestra and send them on a national or international tour, or organise a series of recitals and concerts. Ibbs and Tillett, though basically booking agents rather than concert promoters, did go part-way down the concert promotion route with the International Piano Series in the late 1950s and early 1960s, and with the New Gallery Concerts in the 1970s, although these failed to compete with London's South Bank. The agency's list of artists by no means reflected the amount of work offered, for although many names appeared, few were or could be in regular work, not least because costs and fees were rising while grants were dwindling. Music clubs and choral societies could afford less, and many of them were closing down.

Andrew Rosner joined Ibbs and Tillett in 1970, taking over from Campbell-White to run the broadcasting department. He too recalls the girls' school atmosphere and its several departments run by middle-aged ladies, with Emmie, its presiding headmistress, seemingly determined to divide and rule. Nevertheless, Rosner concedes that he learned much during these two years about the diary system, and made many contacts in the broadcasting industry. He was keen to sell the agency's artists to radio producers and each year went to discuss fees with them, although everything had to be sanctioned by Emmie and no dates confirmed without her approval. One of Rosner's enduring memories of her is that she would never renege on agreements. In 1971, as well as continuing to run the broadcasting department, he proposed the idea of servicing British opera with agency singers, as many of them were missing out through the lack of an opera department (this was a revival of Christopher Hunt's thinking a decade earlier). It took some persuasion, but Emmie agreed to a pilot scheme. Rosner went to see Peter Hemmings at Scottish Opera, who expressed his enthusiasm and proceeded to give work to the young British artists recommended by the agency, as did Glyndebourne's General Administrator Brian Dickie. Like Terry Harrison before him, Rosner had recognized that opera would prove very lucrative for the agency because several performances could be generated from one contract, something that, by definition, one-off concerts could not do.

Rosner made his decision to leave in 1972, when Emmie refused to agree to the rationalization which would allow one person to manage one artist's affairs, which he and Campbell-White proposed for new British artists. When an artist came to 124 Wigmore Street to discuss career matters, they were having to make separate appointments with the head of each department, so it was impossible to achieve an overview of future plans and avoid clashes or conflict of dates. Without exception, young artists found a departmentalized career very confusing, seeing opportunities slip past at the expense of an occasional single, less lucrative choral society or music club date. Major Walker happened to agree with both men. He tried unsuccessfully to persuade Emmie to go along with the proposal, recognizing that this would be a way not only of modernizing the firm, but also of keeping in touch with the new generation of artists and agents, and thus avoid people leaving. It was impossible for managers to build an artist's career and have the freedom to place them in opportunities as they arose. At the same time, artists disliked management in a vacuum. Rosner went to seek advice from Howard Hartog, whom he described as the Godfather of agents (Emmie was the Headmistress), and found him encouraging of the new generation. Rosner respected Emmie despite her narrow views, but he could also understand why young people found her distant and difficult to communicate with. When Rosner left together with Campbell-White in 1972, he joined with Robert Slotover to form Allied Artists, a partnership which still endures.

Whatever persuasion Wilfred Stiff may have brought to bear on Emmie throughout the 1970s, it seems to have borne fruit only by the autumn of 1978, and by then, after ten years of her resistance to the kind of changes first mooted by Harrison and Parrott, it was probably too late. Both Stiff and Emmie signed a memorandum to all staff members, dated 1 September 1978, in an attempt to reassure them of the firm's future and the change of direction which it would now be taking. Even the dread words 'personal management' were finally permitted to appear on Ibbs and Tillett headed notepaper:

> Everyone is aware that discussions have been proceeding with regard to the future of Ibbs and Tillett. At a meeting of the Tillett Trust earlier this week various matters were resolved which are summarised below.
>
> It is proposed that the emphasis of the business will become that of personal management of artists. Within the new framework we shall endeavour to provide some continuing service to music clubs and choral societies, but the extent of this has yet to be fully determined. A list of the artists to be retained will be drawn up as soon as possible.
>
> The new concept will mean some degree of internal reorganisation of staff and of office systems, and all members of the staff are asked to bear with us until these can be communicated in more detail.
>
> Mrs Tillett becomes the Chairman of the Company and Mr Stiff the Managing Director. We regret that Mr Denys Rowlands will be leaving the Company to take up a position as Accountant to Trinity College of Music and he will therefore cease to be a Director.
>
> The Concert Management Department will continue as hitherto.
>
> The Tillett Trust proposes to dispose of the leases of 122 and 124 Wigmore Street in order to capitalise on their present market value and Ibbs and Tillett will move to new premises.
>
> The change of emphasis of the business and the move can only be effected over a transitional period, which we hope to achieve within the next six months, and we will advise everyone as soon as possible about the various steps to be taken.

To put her name to such a document, which only promised to 'endeavour to provide some continuing service to music clubs and choral societies', the lifeblood and *raison d'être* of Ibbs and Tillett since 1906, and the inclusion of the two words she had always resisted as the new concept of the firm, must have been a bitter pill to swallow.

After the death of her housekeeper Mona, Emmie was looked after by Barbara Gould, a friend of Bernie Hammond, followed by a young actor, Godfrey Hamilton, who became her housekeeper. As for Emmie herself, she was in good health until Christmas Day 1978, when she had the first of a series of strokes. She more or less gave up the day-to-day running of Ibbs and Tillett, with *de facto* control passing to Wilfred Stiff. As the business continued to shrink, and with the decision taken by the Tillett Trust to move from 124 Wigmore Street, she withdrew more and more. When Stiff selected 450–452 Edgware Rd as the new home of the agency, Emmie took one look at the premises situated above a plumbing merchants and below an office cleaning company, and promptly voiced her disapproval. She took no office space, and it was only with great reluctance that she occasionally appeared there during the few years remaining to her.

The musical world continued to honour her for the Royal Academy of Music appointed her an Honorary Fellow in April 1975, and clearly no royal displeasure had been incurred at Court when she refused her CBE in 1970, as 'The Lord Chamberlain' was 'commanded by Her Majesty to invite Mrs Emmie Tillett to a Garden Party at Buckingham Palace on Tuesday 10 July 1979 from 4 to 6pm'. By the 1970s there are very few letters from artists in the archive. Early in the decade, another special concert organized by the agency was given at the Wigmore Hall to mark the 80th birthday of the Master of the Queen's Musick, Arthur Bliss on 30 June 1971, at which his song cycle *Angels of the Mind* Op.118 was performed. Three months earlier, he sent programme notes to Ibbs and Tillett:

> As promised, here are the programme notes and text of the song cycle as I wish them printed in the programme for 30th June. It is a long way off, but it is a good thing to get them out of my cluttered room. I hope you do not feel embarrassed by them being on the Soviet paper I was given for a Moscow Tchaikovsky Competition! I want a proof of all these papers please. I should like after my name the words – born August 2nd 1891. As this is rather a souvenir occasion I enclose a photograph that you might like to reproduce in the programme. (16 March 1971)

Walter Legge, who died in 1979, had continued to send missives containing typically pithy language:

> Geoffrey Parsons, that son of a seacook's wetnurse, has let us down for October 1973. He is away in foreign parts ... playing with kangaroos? (2 February 1972)

> ... I am sick of making artists' careers and then being milked for my kindness. (12 February 1973)

> ... I appreciate that for the general public Schwarzkopf's farewell recital will not have the same drawing power as the Callas-di Stefano-Methuselah jamboree. Last Saturday she, Menuhin and [Nikita] Magaloff gave a charity concert here [Geneva] in the Opera House (1800 seats). A dull programme, a Bach–Lipatti transcription, a shortish group of Wolf songs, Bach Chaconne, Enesco Sonata No.1, Liszt's 'Die drei Zigeuner', Strauss' 'Morgen'. The receipts, including programmes, were (at today's rate of exchange) £23,620. That's money! (31 August 1973)

> ... We couldn't ask a reasonable price for a programme with [William] Mann's wisps of notes – one of them incidentally proclaiming (contrary to fact) Dr Franz Strauss still alive and combative, a bastard, which might well have cost Mann, Tibbletts and me fortunes for libel! (19 October 1973)

The Australian soprano Joan Hammond was a long-standing personal friend, and described Emmie as 'one of those few people who can be completely businesslike while giving advice and comfort to her artists. An agent among and above all agents'. She had a similarly high opinion of John Tillett, whom she first met just before the outbreak of the Second World War, and whose 'advice was invaluable at that time and served me well in years to come'. From retirement in Geelong, Australia, she wrote:

> We were shattered by your news. We had no idea of your stroke on Christmas Day 1978, nor about dear Mona. That must have given you an immense shock. It is wonderful to know what a splendid recovery you have made after being paralysed down one side of your body. You deserved the very best nursing and you got it with dear Beryl and the New Zealand lass. I remember Bernie Hammond well – an exceptionally nice person.
>
> I cannot imagine Ibbs and Tillett without you at the helm! And at a new address! I am so glad I am not there to see the change. It is splendid to know that you are enjoying gardening and excavating old ruins! (7 April 1980)

From Nice, Paul Tortelier wrote that 'Ibbs and Tillett is still going strong with a nice spirit in its teamship' and that he imagined 'Emmie with a straw hat on, painting some charming landscape in its most beautiful spring dress'. Her friends still kept in touch and she still looked after the engagements of Cherkassky, Curzon, Segovia, Janet Baker, the Amadeus Quartet and a few other intimate friends, but she was clearly winding down her activities in spite of a fairly full diary of appointments seeing new artists (including the author) and old friends. She appears only three times on the Concert Duty Roster for November 1975, attending recitals by Kempff, the Bliss Memorial concert on 12 November, and Tortelier's recital accompanied by his daughter Maria de la Pau. Her name does not feature at all in the following month. She was losing many friends and colleagues as artists died during the 1970s. In one ten-day period alone, in May 1975, she attended memorial services for Muriel Kerr, Arthur Bliss and Lionel

Tertis. After Pierre Bernac died on 17 October 1979 at the age of 80, the singer and teacher Winifred Radford hoped for Emmie's support by agreeing to allow her name to appear on the *Comité de l'Honneur* set up to promote a reissue of his records. From America, Rudolf Serkin wrote in 1979 with Christmas greetings from Vermont to express his concern for her health as well as undying affection based upon years of friendship, so too did Dohnányi's widow in Florida and the New York agent Harry Beall, who wrote, 'I know your office has moved to Edgware Road and I doubt you stir up quite so much dust as was your habit'.

On 16 May 1982 Emmie Tillett died from a stroke while gardening at Elm Tree Road; she was 85. Her obituary appeared in *The Times* five days later, headlined 'Notable figure in concert artist management':

> Mrs Emmie Tillett, who died on May 16 at the age of 85, was, for a major part of her life, one of the most remarkable and important figures among concert artist managers in the world of music and her regal presence in London's concert halls was a familiar sight. She started her working life in the box office of Chappells and joined the firm of Ibbs and Tillett in 1922.
>
> By then Ibbs and Tillett, originally founded in 1906, had become a major force among artists agencies, and it brought Emmie Bass, as she then was, into immediate contact with such eminent figures as Rachmaninoff, Clara Butt, Busoni, Suggia and Casals, to name only a few. Prior to the second world war, she became a director of the firm following the death of Leigh Ibbs, and in 1941 she married John Tillett, a joint founder of the business. On his death in 1948, she became Managing Director, a position she continued to hold until her retirement in 1978.
>
> In the course of her highly disciplined working life, she involved herself in many enterprises, some significant, but none of which was ever less than interesting. These included a close association with Dame Myra Hess in the organisation of the now legendary National Gallery Concerts and various ventures with Ian Hunter, which included the revival of the Watergate Theatre, where they presented John Cranko's review *Cranks*. Also she was responsible for negotiating the first visit of the Berlin Philharmonic Orchestra to England after the war when it played in Coventry Cathedral and for Pablo Casal's last concert in England when he conducted his own oratorio *El Pessebre*.
>
> She played a significant part in the careers of a great many international artists, one in particular being Segovia, with whom she was associated from the time of his first London concert in 1924. It is perhaps not invidious to mention some of the British artists who also occupied a special place in her life, such as the Amadeus Quartet, who she managed from their first appearance 34 years ago, Sir Adrian Boult, Dame Janet Baker, Sir Clifford Curzon, Kathleen Ferrier, Elizabeth Harwood and Solomon, but there are many more who have cause to remember her with gratitude and affection.
>
> In her lifetime Emmie Tillett watched over many young musicians as they grew and blossomed into fine artists. She died as she would have liked, tending her garden.

On 17 November 1982, a memorial concert for her took place at London's Wigmore Hall, barely yards from 124 Wigmore Street. The artists were to have included her great friend Clifford Curzon as pianist with the Amadeus Quartet, but he died as suddenly as Emmie on 1 September. The programme for the concert was as follows:

String Quartet in E flat Op.64 No.6 : Haydn
Amadeus Quartet

Ballade No.4 in F minor Op.52 : Chopin
Liebestraum No.3 in A flat : Liszt
Tarantella *Venezia e Napoli* : Liszt
Shura Cherkassky : piano

Liebeslieder Waltzes Nos.1–6 : Brahms
Elizabeth Harwood : soprano
Norma Procter : contralto
Richard Lewis : tenor

Derek Hammond-Stroud : baritone
Valda Aveling and Geoffrey Parsons : piano

Fancy; 1904; La Grenouillère; Avant le Cinéma; Toréador : Poulenc
Richard Jackson : baritone
Graham Johnson : piano

Let Beauty Awake; Tired; Silent Noon : Vaughan Williams
Who is Sylvia?; It was a Lover and his Lass : Finzi
Dame Janet Baker : mezzo-soprano
Geoffrey Pratley : piano

The programme also carried the following tribute:

It is impossible to express adequately by either the spoken or written word the influence which Emmie Tillett had upon those for whom and with whom she worked, in a lifetime of service to the music profession. The initial contact which most would have made with her was probably by telephone and the first impression would have been that of a soft-toned and sympathetic voice, anxious to help, giving a feeling of reassurance and efficiency. This and more was confirmed on meeting her, although anyone entering her office for the first time would certainly have been struck by her handsome features, dignity, and regal bearing. Whether it was a young artist taking his or her first steps into the professional world, or the secretary of a music society seeking help on the booking of artists, she created an atmosphere of confidence and reliability that put everyone at their ease.

As Emmie Bass, she joined Ibbs and Tillett in 1922 from Chappells, where she had been working in the box office. She became a director of the firm following the death [retirement] of Leigh Ibbs, and in 1941 married John Tillett whom she succeeded as Managing Director upon his death in 1948. She remained as such for the next thirty years until her own retirement. Thus it was that for fifty-six years she worked closely with a large number of the world's great musicians, many of whom are now legendary in musical history.

Emmie's strength lay in her personality, her self-discipline, her tireless energy and remarkable instinct for recognising talent. Until the last few years of her working life, her day would start and end with the walk between St John's Wood and the office. There would be a brief respite for a sandwich at lunchtime and most evenings she was to be seen at one (sometimes two!) of our concert halls, supporting her artists. She travelled relatively little, believing firmly that she could accomplish more by being at her desk and telephone. She always felt strongly that she would best serve her artists by creating a close bond with music societies and, in those days when the agency field was less competitive, she was able to establish strong links with music-making organisations throughout the country. One of those most dear to her heart was the Three Choirs Festival, for which she annually allowed herself one of her rare excursions away from the office in Wigmore Street.

Behind her outward image of formality there was always a twinkle in her eye which would become even brighter at the prospect of some new enterprise. So it was that she involved herself in such ventures as the Watergate Theatre Club, a gramophone record shop and a printing business, remaining a director of the latter until her death.

Emmie would have been the first person to have acknowledged her own indebtedness to Mona, her loyal and devoted housekeeper for nearly 30 years, and by virtue of whose help she was able to relax in, and enjoy, her house and garden. She had many interests, was more than a competent water-colourist, took great pride in her wine making and few would have realised that many of the clothes she wore were the result of her own skill with the needle.

There are today many established artists who feel indebted to her for the support which she gave at the outset of her careers, support which was often not just moral but tangible, and it was her interest in helping young musicians which led to the formation of the Tillett Trust, in aid of which this concert is being given. The Trust is therefore grateful to the distinguished artists who have come together tonight to pay tribute to Emmie Tillett, artists who all remember her with affection and gratitude, and who, through their music, make this a joyous way of remembering her.

CHAPTER TWENTY-FIVE

The Final Decade: 1980–90

During the 1980s, Ibbs and Tillett, the flagship of British music agencies, but with Emmie no longer at the helm, steamed on inexorably towards its appointment with fate and finally sank in 1990. It could be said that, like the *Titanic*, the agency struck its iceberg back in the 1960s, and, having been holed below the water line, took another 25 years to sink. During the six or seven years that Hunt, Harrison, Parrott, and Campbell-White were employees, opportunities had presented themselves for the agency to keep up with and even get ahead of the times, but Emmie kept faith with her memories of her husband and would change neither her ways nor the agency's methods of operation. After her departure in 1979 and death in 1982, Ibbs and Tillett needed a generation jump at the head of management, but what it got instead was Wilfred Stiff, a gentleman of the old school, courteous, enthusiastic and experienced, but, in the view of his younger employees, 25 years behind the times. He took over at a point when what the agency urgently needed was the right sort of infusion of energy, competitiveness, and capacity to deal with new ideas. It also required rationalization by someone in mid-career, rather than leadership from a man who was approaching the age of retirement. History was repeating itself, for ten years earlier Emmie was at a similar point in her life at the time of the rise and fall of Harrison and Parrott.

Wilfred Stiff gave an interview for Norman Lebrecht's book *When the music stops*, in which he said that 'Emmie's kind of business was bound to have problems unless it changed philosophy and took on fewer artists. No one realised how near she came to insolvency.' He also recalled that 'Ibbs and Tillett never had a written contract with an artist. If a relationship didn't work, the artist was free to get up and go somewhere else'. By the 1980s, the music business had no respect for such etiquette. It was more competitive than ever, and had no time for the niceties of gentlemanly negotiations, which hitherto had been conducted at a leisurely pace and were invariably free of unseemly pushiness or fierce ambition on behalf of the artist. Meanwhile, the control of cash flow and turnover could never be relaxed for one moment, particularly in a music agency with a narrow profit margin. Keeping an eye on the ball, being alert to short-, medium- and long-term perspectives were now vital ingredients in business operations. Perhaps to the detriment of the agency, Wilfred Stiff possessed an unselfish willingness to take on a heavy workload, for not only did he run Ibbs and Tillett, he also managed a substantial list of its artists himself to whom he gave loyal devotion and unstinting commitment. Of those who to this day speak most highly of him are the artists themselves, among them such singers as Ann Murray, Philip Langridge, Anthony Rolfe-Johnson, Kate Flowers and Glenville Hargreaves, all of whom were encouraged by him in their early days. Yet still, the managers who worked for the firm in the final decade (like their predecessors over the previous decade or so), rarely stayed for more than five years, because they continued to experience the frustrations of being locked into old-fashioned ways. Nevertheless, his successor as Managing Director, Richard Apley, would write when Stiff finally withdrew in the autumn of 1986:

> Your huge general experience, your sharp business mind, your very great kindness and human understanding, to say nothing of your very large numbers of specific contacts, are all things on which we have come to rely, and we would feel lost without you there.

When Emmie died in 1982, of those employees at Ibbs and Tillett whose memories could have gone back 35 years to the days of John Tillett, only Beryl Ball now remained, but she only stayed for a further year as a consultant. She undertook the management of a very small number of artists, with most of her work focused on the diaries of two, both inherited from Emmie and to whom she was devoted, singer Janet Baker and guitarist Segovia. The other Directors of the agency at this time, under Managing Director Wilfred Stiff, were Richard Apley, Richard Grace, Andrew Green, and Andrew Parkinson, and all had a part to play in the final twists and turns in fortune which lay ahead. Apley joined the agency in the late 1970s as general administrator of the Richard Hickox Orchestra, which Ibbs and Tillett took on its books in 1977, and which, despite being a bold if not unprecedented undertaking, soon became fraught with problems. While it was true that, during the 1950s, Ibbs and Tillett had worked for several orchestras, such as the Philharmonia, Haydn Orchestra, London Mozart Players, Arnold Goldsbrough Orchestra, Kalmar Orchestra, and numerous string groups such as the Jacques, Kathleen Merritt, Boyd Neel, Harvey Phillips and Kathleen Riddick orchestras, they were not being administered within the agency, as was now the case with the Richard Hickox Orchestra. Neither did these groups place work exclusively with Ibbs and Tillett in the way that the Philharmonia had in its earlier close association with Ingpen and Williams.

When he arrived, Apley was also assigned to assist Robert Rattray in the department for opera and singers abroad and which, despite his inexperience, he then had to take over within a few months when Rattray left for Lies Askonas' agency. According to an interview with Apley (*Classical Music*, September 1990), Ibbs and Tillett was already a derelict and moribund business by the end of the 1970s, and many of his observations, made to the author during an interview in July 2002, could be those described ten years earlier by Harrison, Parrott or Campbell-White. *Plus ça change* indeed.

> [It was] like a pre-war solicitors. All the artist diaries were kept in Mrs Tillett's room, so if a manager phoned from Buenos Aires you had to ask them to hang on and then hope for the best as you sprinted up the stairs. The business was essentially geared to promoters rather than artist management, so the list was huge. I remember saying to Mrs Tillett that I only felt comfortable selling an artist if I believed in him or her. 'Oh no, you don't do things like that', she said. 'It's a question of making available what the promoters want'. Emmie fascinated me immensely; her mind was so sharp and you just marvelled at how this spare woman had played such a huge part in the music profession for over forty years.

As well as running her small coterie of artists, she was also responsible for negotiating all dealings with recording companies, and Apley recalled that many of her senior artists were not on royalty contracts. With Emmie now gone and the move made to the cramped quarters at 452 Edgware Road, Wilfred Stiff made the young men Directors of the business, and gave them the chance to practise personal management with their sole artists, who were now openly saying that this was what they wanted. He was generous to a fault in letting these young men have their way, and should perhaps have questioned their judgement much more; nevertheless 'it was a marvellous opportunity to create something from scratch', said Apley, 'yet it still took far longer than expected to build a reputation, even when many artists were moved on very fast in their careers'.

Although the keeping of diaries was still done in the old-fashioned way, the departmental structure was dismantled, so that the firm became artist-led rather than presenter-led, and they managed to preserve the traditional links with promoters, which Ibbs and Tillett had built over many years. Artists and presenters alike preferred this, and furthermore the old agency maxim to promoters that 'we sell a lot of it' or 'it's very popular' had now been dropped. Under the watchful eye of accountant and Company Secretary Richard Grace, who worked at the agency from 1978 to 1983, the financial administration and contract systems were tightened up, while managers themselves became more involved in their artists' work, having gone out to hear them much more than had been agency practice over the previous ten years.

Grace described to the author the accounting methods in practice during his five years at Ibbs and Tillett. In 1978 he reported directly to Wilfred Stiff from his office on the top floor at 124 Wigmore Street, his initial task being to win the confidence of the artists. The accounts were run on a huge manual system with each artist allocated his or her own account, and on the date of the engagement its commission charge was posted to the particular artist's account. In some cases, fees were paid to Ibbs and Tillett on behalf of the artist, but more usually they were paid direct to the artist (particularly the 'smaller' artist). Commission had to be reclaimed by the agency, but there was no hard and fast rule, so the ledger would reflect money either owed to or owed by the firm. There was also money coming in from royalties of old recording contracts which accumulated, but there were no resources to monitor such sums, which might not have been paid to artists. Grace noted that there were many people working at Wigmore Street, all of them very busy but not necessarily very profitable. Wilfred Stiff therefore looked to him to make economies, not necessarily by a cull, but by trying to assess the likely anticipated income in the year ahead. This was an attempt to budget overheads within the firm, although when it moved from Wigmore Street, the number of employees was indeed slashed. The decision was taken to move to Edgware Road as part of the downsizing process, while a 20-year lease still remained on the two adjacent properties at Wigmore Street, which the Tillett Trust maximized by refurbishing and then renting out at a profit to a firm of solicitors.

In an effort to improve matters, the accounts were computerized, with monthly reconciliations, but the firm was constantly dealing with the problem of an income base which was both small and took a lot of hard work to achieve. With commission at 12.5 per cent of an average fee set at a modest £250–£300, and with the amount of associated contract paperwork (each one had five parts), typing, and manual labour involved, the return was very small, so large numbers of engagements had to be generated to make the firm pay its way. The profile of the firm's income was missing the top heavyweight band of people at four-figure fees, where the work was much the same but the return much bigger, and so the quality of the business relied on many small transactions with music clubs and choral societies. Grace noted the success of HarrisonParrott, whose operation was more tightly focused on a smaller roster of artists with bigger fees and a more proactive management. He compared it unfavourably to Ibbs and Tillett, where eager young men may have been working hard to keep the firm afloat, but were not making much impact, because it was substantially living on past glories and producing a slowly declining revenue stream.

Ibbs and Tillett bought the employment firm of Gordon Yates in February 1981, and sold it to Grace when he left in 1983. Now from the sidelines, he observed that those in charge at Ibbs and Tillett were clearly best at finding new, exciting talent, and new deals to generate future income, but securing the accuracy of the detail and making sure it all added up did not necessarily follow. Financial management of a company is not something which comes naturally to most people, and, while in good times this would not have been a problem because revenue can be generated to keep income ahead of expenditure, in a downturn or when the unexpected happened, then a close eye had to be kept on monthly figures to ensure that there were sufficient funds to cover the bills. Many a view has been taken of exactly when the 'rot set in', and how that 'rot' should be described, but Grace's opinion is that Ibbs and Tillett collapsed sometime before Emmie left the business. It had already lost its way, and, from the time of the creation of HarrisonParrott and other such agencies, kept losing its next generations of potential leadership. By the time it moved into Edgware Road, it was a pale shadow of its former glory, no longer a unique institution but a low-grade booking agency, and no longer respected by a shrinking market.

Andrew Green joined the agency in February 1978 to manage the Richard Hickox Orchestra, while Apley moved to replace Rattray in the singers' department. Apley was required to train Green into his post, while Green himself was also having to deal with artists' foreign work, yet another example of young, inexperienced men thrown in at the deep end with barely adequate training for their work. At the time of his appointment, Green was working at a record shop. At his interview, he recalls that he was shown into Emmie's room and was immediately struck by its faded gentility, plush purple carpet, smell of oak varnish, and large window overlooking Wigmore Street. The interview panel (Wilfred Stiff, Beryl Ball, Denys Rowlands, and Mr Nolan) flanked her desk on either side like courtiers, and she opened proceedings with the words: 'Well Mr Green, tell us about yourself.' When he had finished, she then turned to her panel and put the question, 'Has anyone anything else they wish to ask Mr Green?' and, as no-one had, that was the end of the interview. In his view, it had clearly been a case of being vetted to see if he 'sounded like a decent chap'. This bizarre first impression was made even more bewildering later that day, when Stiff telephoned him at the shop to offer him the job, and they were accidentally cut off. During the time it took to be reconnected, Stiff had been talking, clearly unaware that he was not being heard. Green remembers that he was a great talker, and was convinced that the agency's fortunes would be revived under his leadership when he took it over in 1979. In Green's opinion (given in an interview by the author in June 2003), Stiff did not always realize that the core business of an agency was focused on conductors, singers, pianists, violinists and cellists, and that to venture further presupposed very special reasons. Even the marketing of string quartets was, in financial terms, not very profitable.

According to Green, Wilfred Stiff's agreement to take on the Hickox orchestra lost Ibbs and Tillett a lot of money and was, from the agency's point of view, an unwise idea, even if it was just what the orchestra needed at that particular stage of its development. This very fine young orchestra (competing at the time with the English Chamber Orchestra and the London Mozart Players, among others) was still at the stage where it had to be flexible about fees in order to get work, and therefore could not command top fees. Meanwhile, on its behalf, the agency was cutting its margins to the absolute minimum, spending too much on administration, and inevitably losing money as a result. Stiff was a man whose heart was always in the right place, and he never curbed his enthusiasm for ideas which appealed to him or caught his imagination. To Green's recall, he would go to a concert and hear superb playing from an individual orchestral player, and then suggest to his managers that the horn player, trumpeter or whoever it might be, should be taken on. This he did without a moment's thought about the difficulties involved in creating a solo career for such an instrumentalist, or its cost in time and money to the agency. When the decision was finally taken at the end of 1978 to drop the in-house management of the orchestra, Green was sacked by association but, in response to protests from certain key artists, reinstated during December. In Green's opinion, a failing of the agency was to consider itself bigger than its artists; that was the basis of the diary system, and was why, with few exceptions, managers were rarely sent along with artists on tours at home or abroad, or even met at stations or seen off at airports. One such exception was Clifford Curzon, who always paid £50 directly to a travelling companion supplied from among the agency staff, money which Stiff insisted was always accepted by whoever had been allocated the task. Green recalls that promoters still came to Ibbs and Tillett; the agency did not go to them other than to send out the annual artist list. He also observed that the move from Wigmore Street was symptomatic of the state of the agency at the time, and could only damage its reputation. From central, prestigious W1, with its offices of spacious proportions, it may have relocated just one postcode to W2, but the rooms were too small, tramps were seen urinating on the doorstep of the building, and there was no decent restaurant within 500 yards where clients or artists could be wined and dined.

Despite all its apparent problems, Andrew Green holds the view that Ibbs and Tillett was beginning to turn a corner during the course of 1983. Apley and Andrew Parkinson were working hard to galvanize the singers' department The agency was attracting artists, reviving the British appearances of some foreigners who had been neglected, such as pianist Alicia de Larrocha, while the young managers were beginning to travel the world using the *cachet* of the name of Ibbs and Tillett as a means of obtaining new business. The agency took on Caroline Baird, who became Green's hard-working and energetic assistant, and she managed Howard Shelley's hugely successful Rachmaninov series at the Wigmore Hall in September 1983. Like so many agents still very active in this new twenty-first century, some in the trade call them 'Ibblets', Baird began her career with Ibbs and Tillett (having been recruited as a non-musician through the Gordon Yates agency). Green regretted the departure of Richard Grace (who had a falling-out with Wilfred Stiff) and, with the benefit of hindsight from his new career as a broadcaster and music journalist, came to consider it a critical factor in the firm's fortunes, for without Grace's watchful eye over the finances, later ventures of a more reckless nature might have been vetoed.

Green left in the autumn of 1983, for a combination of domestic reasons and the repetitiveness of his work. Although, during his five years at Ibbs and Tillett, the Endellion Quartet joined the list as winners of the Portsmouth competition for string quartets, and he himself brought the Alban Berg Quartet to the agency, it was not generally common practice to take people on by going out to look for them. He was now aware that in order for the job to become more attractive, he would have to go out on the road more in order to take the artists he already handled a further rung up their respective career ladders. Beryl Ball tended to keep an eye on the general list, and, because she still practised the old system, would frequently pose the question 'can't we find some work for X?' which frustrated some younger managers. They would respond that investing in people like X was a total distraction from what would make the firm's future, namely working intensively for very particular people and not being side-tracked by finding a couple of dates here and there for artists who were never going to make it as top performers. Some artists, having found themselves lingering inertly on the agency's books, managed to progress their careers through their own initiative. Having come second in the Leeds International Piano Competition back in 1971, the Japanese pianist Mitsuko Uchida languished for several years on the Ibbs and Tillett list before putting on her own South Bank recital. She ensured that it was expertly recorded, and followed it with a hugely successful Mozart piano series at the Wigmore Hall. Green gave a cassette of the recital to Erik Smith at Phillips, who was so impressed that he signed her up to record Mozart's solo piano music followed by the complete concertos. This somewhat belatedly provided the impetus for Ibbs and Tillett to progress her career to the top, but it was she alone, and not the agency, who had activated her European career.

The company was in trouble and a remedy had to be found. It took the unprecedented move of producing a one-off *Promoters' Handbook* in September 1982, which listed some 3000 artists available from 76 agents for UK performances. All artists from Ibbs and Tillett were printed in bold type, and its 80 photographs were only of Ibbs and Tillett artists (among whom mezzo-soprano Margaret Cable must have been irritated to find her picture lacking any identifying caption). Ibbs and Tillett clearly realized the controversy its publication might cause among fellow agents, so all copies were stored in the flat of the office cleaner opposite the Edgware Road premises to avoid any seizure resulting from possible injunctions taken out to prevent distribution. Its foreword included these two paragraphs, and it is not hard to imagine what either John or Emmie Tillett would have made of its style.

> This handbook has been prepared by Ibbs and Tillett with the co-operation of the British Music Yearbook specifically to aid you, the music promoter. In addition to giving details of some 3000 artists available for United Kingdom performance, it contains on its latter pages diary/calendar information for 1982 to 1986. We hope you will find the format useful.
>
> The handbook appears at a time when the promotion and presentation of live music has never been more difficult. Declining attendances, escalating costs, and increasingly restricted grant support have already meant the loss of very many concerts and other musical events throughout the UK. Yet music needs its live performances, and nowhere more so than in the heart of each individual community.
>
> We cannot do your job for you, but we can at least recognise the difficulties and constraints under which you work. This handbook comes with our sincere compliments. The fact that it contains artists other than our own may, on occasion, lead you into contacting other agents. *C'est la vie*! If in service of live music it makes your life a little easier, then it will have done its job.

Callum Ross worked for two years at Ibbs and Tillett from January 1982, assisting Andrew Green in work for instrumental artists for the music club circuit. When Green resigned, Ross was appointed a Director, which meant not only receiving a pay rise but also having more control over the artists' lists, and a little more freedom to select those he could represent. In an interview with the author (June 2003), Ross recalled that by the time he joined the agency, its activities were no longer reactive but fully proactive in seeking work for artists, and that the days of waiting for the telephone to ring were past. Like Tom Ponsonby before him, Ross remembered two distinct 'levels' in the artist hierarchy; top-level artists generated work and income because of their well-established and deserved reputations, while newcomers starting out in the profession were happy to gain valuable opportunities and experience through music clubs and choral societies.

However, Ross soon recognized a problem facing the agency, in that once the newcomers became more established – often when the agency had invested a fair amount of time and money before reaping any worthwhile return, (as any company would do when launching a new 'product') – many of them became aware that they were growing out of Ibbs and Tillett and would move elsewhere. He felt that matters were not helped by the agency having a relatively weak roster of conductors, people who, besides their own work, could often generate solo opportunities for their instrumental and vocal colleagues within the agency. Unlike Andrew Green, Ross felt that a certain demoralizing air began to infect the company, particularly during 1983. The list of artists was too large, unwieldy and unmanageable and needed to be reduced. On the matter of fees, Ross remembers that most of the clubs and societies were extremely reasonable, despite working within very tight budgets, but there was one club which in its first call to him declared 'we never pay full fees', even before artists or figures had been discussed. Another requested that, because it had spent virtually all of its budget by engaging a very distinguished group of musicians, a young quartet which it wished to engage should have to reduce its fee accordingly. In other words, the very artists who could ill-afford to reduce fees were being pressed to do so.

Speaking to other Ibbs employees at that time, it was clear to Ross that some of the clubs, and even some of the more senior and established societies, still needed encouragement to seek local sponsorship for their activities, a concept which many of their committees frowned upon as an undignified use of the begging bowl. Their view of such operations was that hall hire, publicity, flowers and programmes constituted the expenditure, while subscriptions and tickets produced the income, so whatever profit was generated as a result provided the means to pay the performers, and if they happened to be a singer with accompanist or a string quartet, so be it and the fee would have to be shared among each performer, leaving only the solo pianist at a distinct advantage.

During these years of the 1980s, Wilfred Stiff began to take the agency down the Victor Hochauser path, which led to business dealings with countries behind the iron curtain, importing Russian singers and instrumentalists, and exporting Western artists. One such deal occurred in the autumn of 1984, when he visited Gosconcert in Moscow for discussions relating to the following season and beyond:

> Talks were held from 12th–20th September 1984 between Wilfred Stiff and officials from Gosconcert consisting of the Director, his Deputy, the Deputy Head of Planning, Senior Consultant, Editor, and an interpreter. The minutes were recorded on 20 September as follows:
>
>> During these talks the sides taking part discussed questions relating to the organisation of tours by the Soviet musicians in Britain and of British musicians in the USSR in 1984–1985. Among those under discussion were:
>>
>> Pianist Emil Gilels to give two concerts between 26 February–3 March, at a fee of £2400 nett per concert and with fares paid by Gosconcert or £1700 nett per concert if Ibbs and Tillett paid first class fares for two from London to Moscow.
>>
>> Singer Paata Burchuladze (with accompanist) to give at least four concerts between 7–21 July

> 1985, both sides to consider not less than four concerts at a fee of £1000 nett per concert, Gosconcert to pay travel to and from for singer and accompanist. Both sides also agreed that for a fifth concert (a BBC studio broadcast recital 'which would serve as an advertisement'), Ibbs and Tillett would pay 50% of the concert fee. Gosconcert proposed that any opera appearances would command a fee of £1500 nett.
>
> Ibbs and Tillett undertook to consider the possibility of concerts for the Vilnius String Quartet, Komitas String Quartet, singers Gleb Nikolsky, Bulat Menzhilkiyev, Mati Palm, and pianists Mikhail Pletnev and Nikolai Demidenko. They also proposed representation for Paata Burchuladze in several European countries, and concluded that 'Gosconcert USSR, taking into account the Firm's [Ibbs and Tillett] efforts to further the singer's career, will consider this proposal and inform the Firm of its decision'.
>
> Regarding artists from Ibbs and Tillett, discussions took place about visits to the USSR by cellist Stephen Isserlis and accompanist Peter Evans ('the contract has been signed' was recorded), and pianist Shura Cherkassky (4–15 March 1985). The financial terms were recorded as 'a fee of 400 American dollars plus 200 roubles per concert, Gosconcert paying travel from Moscow to London, and singer Linda Esther Gray for whom four to six concerts would be arranged between 1–15 March 1986 at £600 plus 200 roubles (the fee to include the piano accompanist) and Ibbs and Tillett to pay the fares London–Moscow–London.
>
> Both sides agreed to consider tours in 1987–1988 for the Amadeus and Endellion String Quartets and guitarist Paul Galbraith.

Another newcomer to the agency was Christa Phelps, who joined in the spring of 1981 as secretary to Beryl Ball. As so many good or potentially good earners had left Ibbs and Tillett during the past dozen years, Phelps was charged with bringing in new, young artists. This ongoing rebuilding process then had to survive a sequence of fast-moving events and several upheavals during the two years 1983 and 1984, when Andrew Green and Andrew Parkinson both left, the agency dropped the Hickox orchestra, and Callum Ross resigned. When Beryl Ball retired in 1983, Phelps became Apley's assistant, and during the course of 1984 Wilfred Stiff retired as General Manager, though, like Emmie and Beryl Ball before him, he remained in the shadows as Consultant for a further two years. When Richard Apley took over as Managing Director, he immediately took the opportunity to prune the secretarial staff and the non-exclusive general list of artists to whom the agency had no obligation and little allegiance, replacing some of them by 'demoting' artists hitherto exclusively represented. With Apley's elevation, Phelps became a director and was given her own artists' list of string quartets. Mark Hildrew was appointed a director from 1986 and established a link with Russian artists, particularly from Georgia, while a fourth, Dan Quinton was brought in and appointed a director from 1988, specializing in Russian events such as ballet companies and orchestras. Meanwhile the agency had made another move at the end of 1987, this time to 18b Pindock Mews, off Warwick Avenue in Little Venice.

The stage was now set for the last act two years later, the final ventures born of travels by Apley and Hildrew, this time to Georgia. If all had gone well, they might have been praised for their imagination, but instead it went badly wrong. Stiff had already expressed concerns about the firm's finances in a memo to Apley and Phelps dated 17 June 1986, which, having proposed Hildrew's appointment as a Director, went on: 'I am concerned about the deficit forecast for next year in the projection sent by [the company's auditors]. How soon are we likely to have figures anticipating the result for this year, and is it possible to see the draft accounts for 1985 please?'

Apley's analysis of the final problems at Ibbs and Tillett focuses essentially on its cash flow. In his view (given to the author in a taped interview on 24 July 2002), as long as most of the money was coming in and accounted to the artist, the balance could then be transferred into the office account. On the other hand, if most of the money was going directly to the artist, statements needed to be sent out, and control of the money was lost. When he first went there in 1977, most of the income for a performer went to Ibbs and Tillett from the concert organization, music club, choral society, or festival, and at the end of the month, the agency accounted to the performer, sending them their fees less commission, travel expenses, and accommodation on what was essentially a steam-age accounting system. However, over the course of the next ten years, quite a small proportion of the money came straight to the firm, and went instead to the artist, because more of them were insisting on receiving payment from the organizer on the night, some even making it a condition of staying with the agency. This meant that the working artist was always owing money to Ibbs and Tillett, who had done the work but had not been paid, whereas the artist had fulfilled the engagement and had been paid. Therefore, every now and again, money had to be transferred from the artists' account into the office account in anticipation of money from the artist.

In Emmie's day, 70 per cent of the business was UK-based for which the firm got paid and then accounted to its artists, but by the time Apley left in the summer of 1990, and shortly thereafter when the agency folded, the percentages were probably reversed, leaving about 30 per cent of the business generated in the UK. Over the course of these 13 years, therefore, it became increasingly more common practice to transfer money from artists' accounts to office accounts. The rules governing financial practice then were quite different from today. What Apley and others did at Ibbs and Tillett, and, according to him, was the practice in other agencies too, was to guess what needed to be transferred across from the artists' account to service the office account. On the whole it was a pretty accurate, even if not a precise reconciliation, but it was essential that the artists' money should not be used, but instead only the agency's rightful proportion, which it was entitled to take.

The reason that the agency ran out of cash was unwise investment. Apley had more experience than the other three Directors Phelps, Hildrew, and Quinton in coping with difficult financial situations, and compared their response to the fast-moving events of the last four months of 1990 to water-skiing. As long as he was with the firm, matters moved fast enough to keep it afloat and no one had time to look down, but after he left, someone did, and fell in. According to Apley's interview, exactly what happened in those last few months and where the money went he does not know. At the time of the crash the agency still had a healthy artists' list, including cellist Tortelier, singers Fischer-Dieskau, Burchuladze, and Hvorostovsky, pianists Cherkassky, Serkin, and Pletnev, clarinettist Emma Johnson, and many top flight string quartets such as the Takacs. According to Apley, over the course of the next two or three years revenue generated by these names should have seen off the debt. The firm had spent an enormous amount in creating this list; for example Hildrew undertook as many as ten trips in one year to the USSR to sign up Russian artists (and spotted Hvorostovsky before he won the 'Singer of the World' competition in Cardiff), Quinton spent two months out of six there, while Apley went to Japan twice, to Texas and New York, and two or three times to Russia.

Several plans were afoot, some of which did not work out, such as a big Georgian scheme. Apley had three meetings with the management of a big Georgian dancing troupe, and tried to set up a state agency to avoid deals going through Moscow's Gosconcert. Sol Hurok had also managed to do so at the end of the 1950s, but he dealt directly with the formidable Minister of Culture, Yekaterina Furtseva. Another mooted scheme was the sponsorship of the All-Russia Violin Competition in 1989, a fairly hare-brained idea, according to Apley, but nevertheless one in which the agency secured Maxim Vengerov and Vadim Repin as a result. They came out to the West under Ibbs and Tillett's management, were presented in one or two venues, and then taken on with a value which was probably worth more than all the agency's turnover in its last year of existence. The scheme nearly worked but cost a lot money trying to get established, and the agency simply ran out of cash. They were trying to establish a Western equivalent of Gosconcert, not only in Russia but also in Poland and Czechoslovakia where they were in competition with IMG. Owned and staffed locally by the Georgians, but run by Ibbs and Tillett's expertise and consultants, they took on the representation of Georgian artists world-wide. Any Russian artist who worked anywhere in the West had hitherto had their contracts serviced by Gosconcert, with similar organizations in other Soviet satellite states. The booking was done through them, the entire administration was done by them, they decided whether or not the artist could take the date or not, and they took a huge percentage of the fee, up to 50 per cent in some cases. Ibbs and Tillett tried to set up a similar agency in Tsiblisi, through which all Georgian artists would put their contracts; they chose dance and theatre companies, an opera company and orchestra (of only reasonable quality), and some outstanding singers. While these negotiations were taking place, they were introduced to some wine-growers, Russian tea-makers, and to some art dealers, while a little later Quinton met a Russian football agent and talks were held about the possibility of representing players. According to Apley, these peripheral schemes, had they come to fruition, would have been 'terrific', but they took longer to get off the ground than was bargained for, and the firm could not sustain the delays.

A view was held at this time that British artists were not the key to the business. A singer such as Hvorostovsky required all Hildrew's time and attention once he had won the Cardiff 'Singer of the World' competition and his career took off. He needed to initiate him into Western ways, fend off predatory managements and get the right people to hear him, which was all very expensive, including spending weeks in America, and the firm was not able to sustain that kind of budget, so rather than being a matter of neglecting British artists, it became one of focusing on the real money-earners.

According to Apley, at some point after his departure the Directors held a meeting with solicitors, who looked at an account, said the firm was insolvent and that they must cease trading forthwith. Apley considered this a hasty decision because the firm's accountant happened by chance to be away and had not updated the ledgers, and therefore at that point it was true that they were technically inaccurate. It had taken two years to get the ledgers in order, undoing a clever scheme which was perfectly correct and not fraudulent, but inappropriate for the firm, but due to the Directors' inexperience had been allowed to run. Every concert fee on the monthly statement would be shown for each artist, whether the artist or the firm had received it, or even if neither had. It would appear with an amendment in pen at the bottom of the computerized system, which would state either 'not yet received' or 'artist paid direct', or left as it was. Because it was not always known whether they had or had not been paid, (due to the combination of accounting and a manual system), it became inaccurate, and was extremely hard to correct. Apley considered this the cause of much of the trouble. While an attempt was currently underway to sort out the accounts, they were possibly not all reconciled by the time of the meeting with the solicitors. To make matters worse, Apley went on, the liquidator was given a state-of-the-client ledger which was wrong, and his first letter to most of the artists (the creditors) gave a hugely inaccurate figure for the deficit, at least by a factor of ten, as was the figure that Christa Phelps and Mark Hildrew took to the solicitors. In Apley's view they acted prematurely and had they waited for the accounts to be accurately reconciled, the resources or potential resources of the firm would have been perceived to be sufficient to remain solvent. Naturally the bank withdrew its support at the first sign of insolvency, all creditors called for their money at once, and the firm fell flat. Apley characterized the fall of Ibbs and Tillett as a tragedy in which a snapshot view of the firm was taken, but one which, in his opinion, gave a false picture.

On the day of his departure from Ibbs and Tillett (24 August 1990), to begin studies leading to a new career in law, Apley wrote to a friend who worked at a well-known international firm of accountants. It is part of a file of letters he gave to the author at the time of his interview for the purposes of this book:

> Things here at Ibbs have worked out well in the ways that matter to me, even though there have been quite heavy problems. We have ended up agreeing the auditors' figures, for various reasons, and that means that although [19]89 itself came in with a small profit as projected, for the third year, there is a prior year adjustment of £28k debit relating to years before '86. We simply do not have the time, resources or understanding (nor probably the documentation since it was bad here then) to challenge or prove this, and just have to pass it. But it does make our accumulated deficit £28k worse than we had expected at the end of '89.
>
> Furthermore there is a certain number of bad-ish and bad debts, and some 'completed' investments, which I was sitting on quietly, waiting for a sunny day before I wrote them off; my rather differently minded successors have decided (perhaps quite rightly, but very bravely) to write them all off right away, also at the end of '89. That leaves us at the end of '89, with an accumulated deficit of somewhere around £80,000, despite demonstrating control of expenditure, predictability of earnings, and steady trading profit. Not good at all.
>
> The first problem has been to convince the chaps that they are not trading fraudulently. I think I have demonstrated to them, with the auditors, that the fact that we have been able to meet our bills for the last several years, means that they are acting in good faith continuing to try to trade into profitability – the record of the last few years shows it to be real. There is also the point that our work-in-progress is only valued at 33%, but would certainly fetch very much more in a wind-up, which helps the asset position.
>
> The second problem will be the bank. The chaps have not been able to find anyone to take over my personal guarantee of the overdraft, on the basis of this deficit. Rather than allow the bank to call in the overdraft and precipitate bankruptcy, (though it would probably be worth much more to me to wind it up!), I have agreed to keep guaranteeing for the moment, and we are working out some safeguards on both sides. For them, removing my majority shareholding so they don't find they've traded into profit and then I kick them out; for me very regular and detailed cash and creditor information, some time-limits, and a continuing minority shareholding which I had not intended to keep. We've stayed friends, for which I am glad above all else. I must say though that I would love to get rid of the guarantee if I could find a way.
>
> As for the value of my shares, we discovered that the share-holders' agreement appointed the auditors as experts. They feel that the very high accumulated deficit makes my shares effectively valueless. I am therefore having to accept zero value, which is a pig.
>
> What I am getting is a good feeling that comes from knowing that the company I ran for several years is going to do well in the immediate future. I still have no doubts about that, and despite the immediate financial pressures, neither the auditors nor the chaps do either. It has also been interesting

> to see how peoples' reactions to my news [of his departure] has shown us just how well the company's profile is standing at the moment, and I am sure that the guys can make it fly very high. It is also, I guess, no bad thing to be keeping some shares in case they do succeed – if the new agreement binds them in to buy me out in three or five years, it might be worth something.

Apley remained the firm's majority shareholder but his optimism that the company would do well in the immediate future proved misplaced, for just over three months later, on 3 December 1990, Ibbs and Tillett went into voluntary liquidation and ceased trading. When the storm broke, accusations were levelled against the agency's management of plundering artists' accounts in order to pay its operational debts, and that these same artists were being fobbed off with reasons such as cash-flow problems caused by delays in payments from concert promoters. On 17 December a meeting between creditors and management was held at an hotel in the north London suburb of Hendon, an event which unsurprisingly became acrimonious as evidence emerged of diverting resources into areas other than music. Hildrew reported that for the four years from 1987 to the end of August 1990, Ibbs and Tillett produced an average turnover of £240 000 with its profit after tax falling annually over the same period from £21 871, £12 790, and £9226 to a loss of £2322. The net position given for 1987–89 revealed losses of £41 676, £28 886 and £48 217 respectively. The rent for the premises at Pindock Mews was £25 000 for 1990, with anticipated annual increases of £2000. Hildrew continued:

> The 1989 accounts are unaudited and previous audit reports included a qualification assuming the continued support of the Directors and the Company's bankers.
>
> The accounts were subject to certain adjustments, most notably as a result of a fundamental accounting error which was discovered following the implementation of a new double entry computerised accounting system in 1989. This discrepancy resulted in a difference on the client ledger control account totalling £28,557, which was written off in the 1989 accounts as a prior year adjustment.

Creditors then heard the reasons for the firm's failure:

> The Company's financial controls were historically very poor and particular problems were encountered with regard to funds held in the client account. The Company's accounts show overall net liabilities in the mid-1980s and in the course of the preparation of the 1989 accounts it transpired that the position had been understated. Therefore it became clear that whilst more recently the Company had traded moderately profitably, it would not be able to clear the balance of accumulated losses brought forward without further injections of capital.
>
> During 1989, despite strong opposition by Ms Phelps, the Company entered into a number of new projects mainly in Russia. This involved activities, not only relating to music but also wine and tea importation, touring of Soviet football teams world-wide [one was rumoured to be Spartak Moscow] dance tours, and the importation of contemporary Soviet art. Key partners to these new activities did not perform as expected; in addition Soviet red tape effectively slowed down the process to such an extent that many of the projects became unprofitable. Costs accelerated well beyond expectation and in the Directors' opinion, total losses associated with this venture exceeded £100,000.
>
> Detailed investigations into the client account have indicated that there are insufficient funds to meet liabilities in respect of fees received by the Company, and due to be paid over to the artists. Faced with this situation and increasing pressure from trade creditors, the Directors considered that there was no alternative to placing the Company into voluntary liquidation.

Although Phelps and Hildrew were both absolved of the prime responsibility for the company's collapse by creditors, but 'as directors they had been at the very least naïve' (*Classical Music*, 12 January 1991), Phelps was quoted in the same report as saying that 'the very day we took over on Richard [Apley]'s departure, we realised there were problems and we went straight to the auditor and sought other financial advice'. The sub-editors of Sunday broadsheets and music magazines had a field day with headlines such as 'The agents of doom play musical chairs' and 'Soviet maestros lose out to a capitalist fiddle', but Andrew Green's article in *The Independent* (22 December 1990) carried the appropriately sober 'End of an era'. Creditors included 40 trade suppliers such as printers, hotels, travel and advertising agencies, piano tuners, and publicists as well as musicians. According to the 'Report of the Liquidator' dated 3 September 1993:

> Total preferential claims of £33,587 have been paid in full and a dividend of 26.37 pence in the pound has been paid to other unsecured creditors whose claims amount to £212,493.

Another section, entitled 'Sale of work in progress, goodwill and contracts', reported:

> work in progress, pencillings and the name 'Ibbs and Tillett' were sold to [Andrew Lloyd Webber's] Really Useful Group [RUG] and Transart (UK) Limited in January 1991.

Phelps and Hildrew joined RUG in a new company trading as Artist Management International, while another Ibbs and Tillett employee, Fiona Blyth, joined the newly formed UK branch of the French company Transart. As a result, some Ibbs and Tillett artists were allegedly cherry-picked, compensating them their losses to the tune of £32,000 as a *quid pro quo*, to the displeasure of those creditors who were left out. As the liquidator reported it:

> as part of the agreement with the Really Useful Group PLC the claims in the liquidation of over twenty artist creditors totalling approximately £95,000 have been waived ... As a result total claims have been reduced and now total approximately £63,000.

Meanwhile, Ibbs and Tillett had been the subject of an investigation by the liquidator to:

> investigate the possibility of bringing an action against a former director for wrongful trading ... a case was prepared and action commenced as a result of which the former director offered to make a payment in the sum of £16,000 to the company. This was accepted by the liquidation committee who agreed that no further action should be taken, given the likely costs involved and the personal financial situation of the former director.

Many believed that the manner of the collapse of Ibbs and Tillett had called the name of music agents into disrepute and that, like solicitors and accountants, the profession should in future adopt stricter rules in order to police its financial operations. The British Association of Concert Agents (BACA) was shocked by these unprecedented events, and, when they met on 30 January 1991, promised stringent action to prevent such a situation ever recurring, but as far as Ibbs and Tillett was concerned, the stable door had been shut long after the horse had bolted.

Joeske van Walsum (Chairman of BACA at the time) is a Dutch agent who has been in business in London for 30 years, and is one among a handful of agents who did not start his career with an apprenticeship at Ibbs and Tillett. Instead he built up his successful business from his own humble one-man operation, though his two senior artists, pianists Stephen Kovacevich and Mitsuko Uchida, were originally with Ibbs and Tillett. In an interview with the author (20 June 2003), van Walsum described the current function of an agent and reflected on events of the past decade, taking into account the lessons learned by the profession from what happened to Ibbs and Tillett:

In the normal course of events an agent acts on an artist's behalf, and for his services takes a commission, which is anything between 10 and 20% of the artist's earnings. There is another riskier, but perfectly legal way to do business, and that is to act as a principal which means that the agency becomes involved in buying and selling, with the artist as the commodity. For example, when dealing with artists from the Soviet Union the agent was acting as a principal rather than as an agent, and a fee was paid to the State agency Gosconcert, who then decided what proportion of that money would be passed on to the artist, keeping the rest for itself. Meanwhile the principal had sold the artist on to a Western orchestra, and from that fee paid travel, accommodation, publicity, an interpreter's services and other expenses, but also had to build in a profit margin. So it was perfectly possible for the agency to make more money than the artist. As the middleman, the principal was legally responsible to pay Gosconcert for the artist, even if the UK promoter to whom the artist was then to be sold on might in turn become insolvent. A long-proven method, practised by Ibbs and Tillett but of which Victor Hochauser was probably the most successful exponent with his concerts at the Royal Albert Hall followed by UK tours, was for the principal to promote events himself rather than to sell the artist on, which increased the profit margin and minimised the risk. During the 1980s, Russian and other Eastern European artists were increasingly suggesting direct deals with Western agencies which bypassed Gosconcert.

At the time of its insolvency, Ibbs and Tillett should have been operating three accounts, a promotions or projects account for buying and selling, a clients' account, and an office account. In order to receive a licence to practise under the Employment Agency's Act 1973, there were certain obligations made of agents, such as the legal requirement to keep the clients' money in a current account, though at the time of the firm's problems such practice was not policed by the Department of Employment. After the liquidation, BACA (now superseded by International Artists' Managers Association (IAMA)) decided to self-regulate, and all its members now have to produce annual certification of audited accounts showing that all monies due to clients are lodged securely in the clients' account. It made all agencies tighten up their act and put their house in order, indeed several were also found to have contravened the system, and one or two resigned from the Association or were expelled.

In the 1980s Ibbs and Tillett, despite its methods of operation and the steady decline it was undergoing, was still a magnet to young artists beginning in the profession. Today there is less work for the artist in the middle, the sort of comfortable life that was available to those who never achieved the pinnacle of the profession but whose diaries were somehow always filled with recital work throughout the country. It is relatively easy to get work for talented beginners, who are expected to and want to get experience even if it means doing so for small fees (an irony because of all musicians, those starting out need the money most). Today the recording industry is not investing or making so much profit, so recording contracts are no longer a vital element in developing an artist's career. In former days record companies would invest in an artist for five or six years, and the artist benefited from all sorts of spin-offs, such as advertising and exposure in broadcasting and the media. Even if artists were not making money from recordings, it increased their status and got them a better name at least by keeping their names before the public. This is now replaced by the development of website technology, the potential to download music and information, and the access to music by video and DVD, while artists are also now turning to making and marketing their own records. Competitions today have less impact on a career than in the past, some agents do not even attend them because so often they are won by people who may be at home in that particular competitive environment which is hardly typical of the profession, and many winners cannot cope with the sudden onrush of engagements which invariably arise thereafter.

Today there are more agents than there were when Ibbs and Tillett collapsed but each works for fewer artists, and some of them are single-person operations. Somehow, despite the competition and almost non-existent profit margins, they are managing to survive. Fees are effectively reducing, an average fee for a reasonably well-known person who is not a star in any sense might be £2000–£3000, and they may well play no more than 30 concerto dates per year. Others may stipulate only capital cities and a limit of say 45 concerts per year. Recitals are not as popular as they used to be, there are fewer music clubs, and those that still exist cannot afford the fees that generate a profit to the agency. Nevertheless they can be useful testing grounds for young artists with more prestigious dates in prospect. Sometimes a six-week tour for a young artist loses money for the agency. Broadcasting is a shrinking market, the BBC seems to have less money to spend on artists, while in the USA there are some broadcasting stations to which an artist and even an orchestra has to pay for the opportunity to perform.

The opportunity to hire a hall and pay for a recital is now less common practice, because, for example, the Wigmore Hall now has a fully active calendar with recitals given by established artists and its own promotions. Occasionally recitals are given in private houses to which an agent might invite influential people from the music profession such as orchestral managers or festival directors. Decisions are hardly ever taken on the strength of press reviews, which in any case are given far less space in newspapers and magazines than twenty years ago. Promoting an artist is more dependent on strategic placement and tactical moves rather than a blanket harassment of outlets for performances. Reliance is placed more on word of mouth and spreading the news of a new talent in a targeted way.

Projects are an innovation and an agency employee has that responsibility. Events can be spread over one or two seasons, linked in to festivals, a concert series and/or recordings. They tend to be hard to sell as enterprising outlets are reluctant to promote a project which they have not themselves originated.

Today van Walsum, who acts as a consultant to his firm, manages 45 artists with a staff of 27, 11 of whom sell and manage, another 11 administrate (contracts, itineraries, schedules, publicity, biographies, collection of fees), the rest comprise three accounts staff, a projects manager, and a general administrator. Following Ibbs and Tillett's practice, new artists are often taken on by recommendations from people in the music world, whose opinions are trusted, such as teachers, festival directors, or record producers. Letters written by aspiring artists to his agency are mostly ignored, and competitions avoided.

An unscientific survey, using information taken from websites of some agencies in 2003, produced some interesting statistics, which highlight changes since the demise of Ibbs and Tillett at the end of 1990. Emmie's remark to Evelyn Barbirolli that 'we don't do conductors' would be quite out of place today, for now they usually form the backbone of an agency's list. String quartets have almost disappeared, requiring four times the amount of work with a poor return from a fee equivalent to a solo artist but divided into four. Solo instrumentalists no longer dominate the roster; there are usually single-figure numbers of pianists and violinists, sometimes no cellists, and barely a handful of guitarists, wind and brass instrumentalists. A small number of opera directors and composers now appear, while, with large agencies, projects now constitute a core activity and a separate department, highly labour-intensive and always requiring a constant flow of new ideas.

AskonasHolt lists 41 orchestras and 11 dance companies, while IMG, with over 40 orchestral tours per season, have 68 orchestras on their projects lists. Such departments provide extensive areas of expertise to developing arts organizations, festivals or one-off events, including, in the case of IMG, 'strategic planning, technical operations, artistic planning, marketing, business development, box office and event management'. Diversification by an agency into the audio/visual field of marketing the arts is exemplified by IMG, who, in a pioneering operation during the course of the 1990s, ventured into sourcing, producing, promoting and marketing an archival operation of video programmes such as 'The Art of' (conducting, piano, violin and singing) series, and, on more than one hundred compact discs so far, the BBC Legends label of historical live recordings. Such has been the success of these two projects, that a collaboration was subsequently forged with EMI Classics to produce a series entitled 'Great conductors of the 20th century', another on DVD of live broadcast performances made in the 20 years 1950–70 and drawn from British and French TV archives, while similar projects are now underway with the Italian State broadcasting service RAI and the Royal Stockholm Philharmonic Orchestra.

Both AskonasHolt and IMG have singers' lists of three figures which recall any average year one cares to select from the heyday of Ibbs and Tillett (of the 207 singers listed below with IMG, 111 are UK based). On the other hand, managing tiny lists, which became the watchword of the young managers at Ibbs and Tillett during the 1980s, is fairly commonplace today. Operations such as those run by Caroline Baird, Terry Harrison and Christa Phelps could be called micro-management, where one person might handle no more than half a dozen artists from their own home.

Agency	Conductors	Singers	Instrumentalists	Chamber	Other
Allied Artists	15	26	4(p) 1(ww)	1(sq)	2(dir) 4(comp)
Askonas Holt	40	122	20(p) 12(v) 6(vc)	1(sq)	6(dir) 4(comp)
Caroline Baird	–	–	1(p/conductor) 1(v) 1(vc)	1(sq)	–
Christa Phelps	–	–	2(p) horn	2(sq) 1(we)	–
Connaught Artists	10	19	6(p) 2(v) 2(vc) 1(ww)	2(sq)	1(dir)
HarrisonParrott	32	14	12(p) 7(v) 1(va) 3(vc)	1(sq)	1(dir) 2(comp)
IMG (Europe division)	56	207	14(p) 13(v) 5(vc) 3(ww)	1(sq) 3(e) 3(o)	7(dir)
Ingpen & Williams	21	56	7(p) – 2(vc) 3(ww)	4(sq)	2(o) 3(dir)
Intermusica	17	–	4(p) 3(v) 1(va) 2(vc)	4(sq)	1(dir)
Terry Harrison	3	–	3(p)	–	–
Van Walsum	19	16	4(p) 2(v) 1(ww)	1(sq) 1(we)	2(dir) 4(comp)

p = piano, v = violin, va = viola, vc = cello, ww = woodwind, sq = string quartet, we = wind ensemble, e = ensemble, dir = opera director, comp = composer, o = orchestra

The violinist Henri Temianka (born in Scotland of Polish parentage) mentioned Ibbs and Tillett in his autobiography *Facing the Music* (1973):

> During all the years I knew them, Ibbs and Tillett, the biggest English agents, who are more a clearing house than a management, did all their business by surface mail, considering airmail an extravagance to be resorted to only in dire emergencies ... One has the distinct impression that a firm like Ibbs and Tillett deliberately refrains from promoting its artists as an ungentlemanly pursuit, alien to the British concept of good sportsmanship. They are confident that concert societies all over the British Isles will keep coming back year after year, as they have for the past seventy or eighty years, and in subdued tones make their decisions known. No contract is ever necessary. I never signed one with Ibbs and Tillett because their word was as good as a contract.

He went on, 'Sometimes, in moments of euphoria, I try to imagine what the ideal manager would be like', and described the strengths and virtues of various examples located around the world, concluding that 'he would be gentlemanly, with the most scrupulous sense of integrity, like Ibbs and Tillett in London'.

A decade and more after the demise of Ibbs and Tillett, those who remember it speak less of its sad end and more of its golden heyday, and when they do, it is invariably with a mixture of admiration and respect. It was an institution which survived two world wars, many economic crises, and the huge changes in the technology by which music reached its listeners and affected their concert-going habits. It fed and thrived on the life-support machinery of music clubs and choral societies, which in turn could not function without Ibbs and Tillett. The very nature of its invaluable archive of letters from musicians during the nineteenth and twentieth centuries reflects its pre-eminence in the music profession. Having learned their craft from Narciso Vert, Robert Leigh

Ibbs and John Tillett were succeeded by Emmie. She learned her craft from her hugely experienced and well-respected husband, and for thirty years from his death to her retirement, loyally carried his torch whatever the cost. In the words of Joan Ingpen to the author: 'Emmie was very correct, and known in the trade as the Duchess of Wigmore Street'.

Ibbs and Tillett: Artists' Brochures 1907–8, 1908–9

(Author's note: names appear in their original listed order, and as spelt by Ibbs and Tillett; [ ] indicates Christian names added).

1907–8

Singers

Clara Butt and Kennerley Rumford
Agnes Nicholls
Esta d'Argo
Kirkby Lunn
Mrs George Swinton
William Green
Plunket Greene
Charles Knowles
Dalton Baker

Pianist

Leopold Godowsky

Violinists

Johannes Wolff
Tivadar Nachèz

Violincellist

Joseph Hollman

1908–9

Sole representation continued for the artists as in the 1907–8 brochure, plus the American bass Herbert Witherspoon and the Capet String Quartet. Then follow 444 artists or ensembles.

Mesdames

Sopranos (51)

[Nellie] Melba
[Emma] Albani
Agnes Nicholls
Pauline Donalda
Ella Russell
Suzanne Adams
Antonia Dolores
Evangeline Florence
Mary Münchhoff
Fanny Moody
Zélie de Lussan
Clementine de Vere
Alice Esty
Blanche Marchesi
Susan Strong
Gleeson-White
Amy Castles
Perceval Allen
Esta d'Argo
Louise Sobrino
[Mrs] Henry J Wood
Louise Dale
Emily Squire
Helen Jaxon
Mary Conly
Hilda Foster
Lilian Coomber
Edith Evans
Elizabeth Parkina
Jenny Taggart
Ada Forrest
Lillie Wormald
Zara Minadieu
Ethel Wood
Mary McDiarmid
Bertha Rossow
Eleanor Felix
Euneta Truscott
Lenora Sparkes
Hilda de Angelis
Caroline Hatchard
Mabel Manson
Ethel Lister
Violette Londa
Nora Long
Nora Newport
Amy Evans
Pauline Hook
Fanny Wood
Edith Kirkwood
Florence Macnaughton

Contraltos (36)

Clara Butt

Kirkby Lunn
Ada Crossley
Marie Brema
Camilla Landhi
Rosa Olitzka
Edna Thornton
[Mrs] George Swinton
Theodora Salicath
Gertrude Lonsdale
Alice Lakin
Carmen Hill
Marie Stuart
Edith Clegg
Gwladys Roberts
Edith J. Miller
Mildred Jones
Phyllis Lett
Violet Elliott
Dilys Jones
Maria Yelland
Grainger Kerr
Mabel Braine
Verena Fancourt
May Peddle
Marie Stiven
Belle Thynne
Maud Wright
Joan Ashley
Frederica Richardson
Amy Dewhurst
Sylvia Blackston
Palgrave Turner
Clare Hamilton
May Currie
Povla Frijsh, the Danish contralto

MM

Tenors (45)

Ben Davies
William Green
John Coates
Gervase Elwes
Harold Wilde
Henry Beaumont
Robert Cunningham
Hirwen Jones
Anderson Nicol
Ernest Pike
Harry Stubbs
Furness Williams

Evan Williams
Lloyd Chandos
Gregory Hast
John McCormack
Joseph O'Mara
Herbert Grover
John Harrison
Philip Newbury
Webster Millar
Charles Saunders
Henry Brearley
Henry Turnpenney
Samuel Masters
Alfred Heather
Philip Simmons
Spencer Thomas
James Davis
Fred Fallas
Walter Kirby
John Bardsley
William Maxwell
Roland Jackson
Noel Fleming
Ager Grover
Haigh Jackson
Gwilym Richards
Dennis Creedon
Whitworth Mitton
Bertram Binyon
Walter Hyde
Albert Watson
Paul Reimers
Paul Schmedes

Baritones and Basses (45)
Charles Santley

———

Plunket Greene
Kennerley Rumford
Ffrangcon-Davies
Dalton Baker
Herbert Witherspoon
Charles Knowles
Robert Radford
Reginald Gooud
Watkin Mills
Charles Clark
Theodor Lierhammer
H. Lane Wilson
Frederic Austin
Ivor Foster
Herbert Brown
Robert Burnett
Charles Tree
Denis O'Sullivan
Charles Manners
Hamilton Earle
Harry Dearth
Charles Copland
Albert Archdeacon
Charles Magrath
Charles Bennett
Francis Braun
Dan Price
David Hughes
Francis Harford
Horatio Connell
Reginald Davidson
Thorpe Bates
Albert Garcia
W.A. Peterkin
Frederick Ranalow
Campbell McInnes
Stewart Gardner
Thomas Meux
Aubrey Dean Paul
Pedro de Zulueta
David Evans
William Higley
Hugh Peyton
[Raimund] von zur Mühlen

Mesdames

Violinists (53)
Lady Hallé [Wilhelmine Norman-Neruda]
Marie Hall
Vivien Chartres
Beatrice Langley
Nora Clench
Dorothy Bridson
Ivy Angove
Ethel Barns
Inez Jolivet
Elsie Playfair
Edie Reynolds
Gwendoline Pelly
Jessie Morris
Ethel Marsh
Irene Penso
Nora Thomson
Grace Triggs
Elsie Southgate
Maude Meldrum
May Harrison
Louise Ferraris

MM

[Pablo de] Sarasate
[Eugène] Ysaÿe
[Fritz] Kreisler
Tivadar Nachèz
Jacques Thibaud
Max Mossel
[Enrique] Arbos
[Franz von]Vecsey
Arthur Catterall
Harold Ketélby
Adolf Rebner
Carl Barré

Johannes Wolff
[Michael] Zacharewitsch
Carl Halir
Emile Sauret
Mischa Elman
Willy Hess
César Thomson
Johann Kruse
Achille Rivarde
Aldo Antonietti
John Dunn
Louis Pecskai
William Henley
Dettmar Dressel
Haydn Wood
José Gomez
Jan Hambourg
Willy Woltman
Jóska Szigeti
Bromley Booth

Violoncellists (24)
[Joseph] Hollman
Robert Hausmann
Hugo Becker
W.H. Squire
Jean Gérardy
Pablo Casals
Herbert Withers
Boris Hambourg
Alfred Gallrein
Herman Sandby
W.E. Whitehouse
Herbert Walenn
Dezso Kordy
Sydney Brooks
Jacques Rénard
Carl Fuchs
Alexander Blaess

Mesdames
Elsa Ruegger
Warwara Irmanoff
May Mukle
Ethel Beningfield
Maye Gray
Beatrice Harrison
Beatrice Eveline

Pianists (52)
[Teresa] Carreño
Fanny Davies
[Cécile] Chaminade
Gertrude Peppercorn
Mathilde Verne
Adela Verne
Katharine Goodson
Evelyn Suart
Johanne Stockmarr
Ella Správká
Amina Goodwin
Auriol Jones
Madeline Payne
Alma Stenzel
Marguerite Elzy
Adelina de Lara
Rosamond Ley
Vera Margolies
Ethel Leginska
Gertrude Meller
Marie Novello
Mania Seguel
Else Gipser
Jeanne Blancard

MM
[Leopold] Godowsky
Moriz Rosenthal
Eugen d'Albert
Vladimir de Pachmann
[Ferruccio] Busoni
Raoul Pugno
[Ernst von] Dohnányi
Leonard Borwick
Emil Sauer
Frederick Lamond
Ernst Denhof
Benno Schönberger
Alexander Siloti
Archy Rosenthal
[Ossip] Gabrilowitsch
Harold Bauer
Mark Hambourg
Wilhelm Backhaus
Frederick Dawson
Gottfried Galston
Herbert Fryer
Percy Grainger
Frank Merrick
Willibald Richter
Edouard Risler
Edward Isaacs
Arthur Newstead
James Friskin

Vocal Duets, Quartets etc. (16)

Herr and Frau Franz von Dulong
Misses Pauline and Ethel Hook
Misses Sassard
Misses Carbone
Meister Glee-Singers
The New Meister Singers
Westminster Singers
The Royal Welsh Male Choir
The Cambrian National Glee-Singers (comprising twelve Vocalists and Accompanist)
The Glasgow Select Choir
Clara Novello-Davies Partsingers
'The Folksong' Quartet
The Alexandra (Ladies) Quartet
St George's Glee Singers
The Alexandra Part-Singers
Royal Windsor Glee Singers

String Quartets etc. (15)

Bohemian Quartet
Capet Quartet
Rosé Quartet
Brussels Quartet
Brodsky Quartet
Kruse Quartet
Hambourg Quartet
Mossel Quartet
Wesseley Quartet
Chaplin Trio
New Trio
Grimson Trio
London Trio
Fransella Wind Quintet
London Chamber Musicians (Wind and Strings)

MM

Accompanists (45)

Henry R. Bird
S[amuel] Liddle
Hamilton Harty
F.A. Sewell
Conraad van Bos
Wilhelm Ganz
Ernest Walker
Stanley Hawley
Frederick B. Kiddle
Herbert L. Cooke
Richard Epstein
Theodore Flint
R.J. Forbes
Harold Garstin
Arthur E. Godfrey
P. Mavon Ibbs
Charlton Keith
Edward Croager
Frank Mummery
Algernon Lindo
Harold Samuel
Frederick W. Sparrow
Haddon Squire
Walter Wiltshire
George F. Boyle
C.H. Kempling
Howard Hadley
Victor Marmont
Herman Grünebaum
Giles Higgins
Percy B. Kahn
Albert Ketelby
Harold Scott
Arthur Thompson
Cyril Towsey
Harold L. Brooke

Mesdames

Kate Eadie
Marguerite Swale
May Christie
Fraser Henry
Constance Stockbridge
Nellie Viveash
Marguerite Tilleard
Hilda Meiggs
Louie Heath

Entertainers (30)

Yvette Guilbert

———

Margaret Cooper

———

Helen Mar
Fanny Wentworth
Nellie Ganthony
Nora and Frederica Conway
Clara Alexander
Kitty Cheatham
Kathleen Mayer

MM

George Grossmith	The Follies	Byrd Page
Rutland Barrington	Fred Upton	The Gems
George Grossmith Jr.	Nelson Jackson	Griffith Humphries
Maurice Farka	Huntley-Wright	Robert Ganthony
Harrison Hill	Walter Churcher	Ulph Smith
Barclay Gammon	Earle Douglas	Arthur George
Douglas Beaufort	Frank Lincoln	Tom Clare

Mesdames

Elocutionists (12)

[Mrs] Beerbohm Tree	Ellen Bowick	Iona Robertson
Evelyn Millard	Nora Conway	Maggie Neill
Lena Ashwell	Gertrude Tomalin	

MM

Lewis Waller	Ernest Meads	Richard Temple
Charles Fry		

Bands (15)

1st Life Guards	Grenadier Guards	Royal Marines
2nd Life Guards	Coldstream Guards	Lieut. James's Forest Light Infantry
Royal Horse Guards	Scots Guards	
Royal Artillery	Irish Guards	Rauscher's Austro-Hungarian

Red Viennese Band	Blue Hungarian Band	Empress Orchestra
White Viennese Band		

Song-Lectures (4)

Miss Madeleine O'Connor	Mme Annie Grey	Mme Bertha Moore

Mr Charles Saunders

Piano recital-lectures (1)

Dr Otto Neitzel

Madame Clara Butt and Mr Kennerley Rumford's Tours
Miss Agnes Nicholls' Song Recitals
Madame Kirkby Lunn's Song Recitals
Mr Plunket Greene's Song Recitals
Mr Kennerley Rumford's Song Recitals
Mr Herbert Witherspoon's Song Recitals
Herr Godowsky's Pianoforte Recitals
Mons. Tivadar Nachèz's Violin Recitals
The Capet String Quartet Concerts
The Brussels String Quartet Concerts

Under the Management of Messrs. Ibbs & Tillett

Ibbs and Tillett: Artists' Brochures 1911–12, 1914–15, 1915–16, 1919–20, Agency Bulletin 1913

1911–12

Sole representatives for
Madame Clara Butt and Mr Kennerley Rumford

Miss Agnes Nicholls
Miss Louise Dale
Miss Esta d'Argo

Madame Kirkby Lunn
Mrs Elsie [George] Swinton
Mr Ben Davies
Mr William Green
Mr Plunket Greene
Mr Dalton Baker
Mr Robert Burnett
Mr Robert Radford

Herr Leopold Godowsky
Herr Ernst von Lengyel
Herr Edward Goll
Herr Moriz Rosenthal

Herr Rachmaninoff

Mons. Tivadar Nachèz

Mons. Joseph Hollman
Mons. Jean Gérardy

Mesdames
Sopranos (41)

Agnes Nicholls
Pauline Donalda
Antonia Dolores
Blanche Marchesi
Evangeline Florence
Susan Strong
Clementine de Vere
Amy Castles
Emily Squire
Mary Conly
Louise Sobrino
Lenora Sparkes
Jenny Taggart
Ada Forrest
Jean Waterston
Laura Evans-Williams
Helen Henschel
Eve Simony
Beatrice La Palme
Helen Le Mar
Hilda Foster

Perceval Allen
Gleeson-White
Esta d'Argo
Louise Dale
Maggie Teyte
Edith Evans
Mary Münchhoff
Lilian Coomber
Lillie Wormald
Caroline Hatchard
Mabel Manson
Amy Evans
Pauline Hook
Edith Kirkwood
Gladys Honey
Alice Baxter
Dorothy Silk
Carrie Lanceley
Carrie Tubb
Kaloola Atherton

Contraltos (42)
Clara Butt

———

Kirkby Lunn
Ada Crossley
Marie Brema
Edna Thornton
Tillie Koenen
Phyllis Lett
Elsie Swinton
Gertrude Lonsdale
Muriel Terry
Lucy Nuttall
Alice Lakin
Carmen Hill
Marie Stuart
Dilys Jones
Mildred Jones
Gwladys Roberts
Maria Yelland
Katherine Jones
Edith Clegg
Mabel Braine
Grainger Kerr
Ethel Hook
Violet Elliott
Verena Fancourt
Marie Alexander
Joan Ashley
Palgrave Turner
Maud Wright
Dorothy Wiley
Alice Mandeville
Amy Dewhurst
Belle Thynne
Marie Stiven
May Currie
Irene Ainsley
Aimée Parkerson
Violet Oppenshaw
Kate Rooney
Hazel Gray
Sara Silvers
Phyllis Archibald

MM
Tenors (46)
Ben Davies
William Green
John Coates
Gervase Elwes
John McCormack
Walter Hyde
Lloyd Chandos
Gregory Hast
Joseph O'Mara
Lawrence Kellie
John Harrison
Maurice d'Oisly
Paul Reimers
Paul Schmedes
Webster Millar
Charles Saunders
Harold Wilde
Alfred Heather
Cynlais Gibbs
Anderson Nichol
Morgan Kingston
Henry Turnpenney
Samuel Masters
Henry Brearley
Albert Watson
Ernest Pike
James Davis
William Maxwell
Bertram Binyon
Gwilym Richards
Haigh Jackson
Whitworth Mitton
Philip Ritte
Hubert Eisdell
Roland Jackson
Dennis Creedon
Fred Fallas
Joseph Cheetham
Philip Simmons
Frank Tebbutt
Joseph Reed
Frank Mullings
John Booth
Thomas Meux
William Foxon
James Hay

Baritones and Basses (45)
Sir Charles Santley

Plunket Greene
Kennerley Rumford
Robert Radford
Dalton Baker
Frederic Austin
Herbert Brown
Harry Dearth
Watkin Mills
Charles Clark
H. Lane Wilson
Theodor Lierhammer
George Henschel
Thorpe Bates
Charles Knowles
Ivor Foster
Robert Burnett
Campbell McInnes
Charles Tree
Francis Harford
Frederick Ranalow
David Hughes
Dan Price
Albert Archdeacon
Lewys James
Peter Dawson
Marcus Thomson
William Higley
Stewart Gardner
Albert Garcia
Charles Magrath
Joseph Lycett
Robert Charlesworth
Jamieson Dodds
Pedro de Zulueta
Hamilton Harris
Robert Maitland
Humphrey Bishop
David Brazell
Edmund Burke
Norman Allin
Fraser Gange
Wilfred Douthitt
Dillon Shallard
Julien Henry

Pianists (52)
Mesdames
Carreño
Fanny Davies
Adela Verne
Katharine Goodson
Irene Scharrer
Johanne Stockmarr
Gertrude Peppercorn
Evelyn Suart
Ella Správkà
Auriol Jones
Marguerite Elzy
Rosamond Ley
Vera Margolies
Ethel Leginska
Gertrude Meller
Marie Novello
Tora Hwass
Else Gipser
Mildred Pritchard
Myra Hess
Tosta de Benici
Myrtle Meggy
Edith Walton

MM
Moriz Rosenthal
Godowsky
Vladimir de Pachmann
Busoni
Raoul Pugno
Emil Sauer
Ernst von Lengyel
Sapellnikoff
Dohnányi
Leonard Borwick
Frederick Lamond
Alfred Cortot
Alexander Siloti
Mark Hambourg
Wilhelm Backhaus
Edward Goll
Harold Bauer
Gottfried Galston
Gabrilowitsch
Benno Schönberger
Edouard Risler
Percy Grainger
Egon Petri
Archy Rosenthal
Harold Brewerton
Frank Merrick
Ernst Denhof
Herbert Fryer

M. Rachmaninoff

Violinists (46)
Lady Hallé

Mesdames
Marie Hall
Viven Chartres
Renée Chemet
May Harrison
Marjorie Hayward
Beatrice Langley
Marie du Chastain
Nora Clench
Dorothy Bridson
Evangeline Anthony
Audrey Richardson
Ivy Angove
Valerie Knoll
Jessie Morris
Grace Triggs
Bessie Spence
Hilda Lett
Ethel Marsh

MM
Ysaÿe
Kreisler
Tivadar Nachèz
Jacques Thibaud
Mischa Elman
Franz von Vecsey
Sigmund Feuermann
Zacharewitsch
Johannes Wolff
Johann Kruse
Achille Rivarde
Max Mossel
Sasha Culbertson
Arrigo Serato
Aldo Antonietti
Jóska Szigeti
Josè Gomez
Hans Neumann
Louis Pecskai
John Dunn
Arthur Catterall
Charles Barré
Haydn Wood
Bromley Booth
William Henley
Dettmar Dressel
Alessandro Certani

Cellists (26)

MM
Hollman
Jean Gérardy
Hugo Becker
Julius Klengel
Pablo Casals
W.H. Squire
Herbert Withers
W.E. Whitehouse
Carl Fuchs
Boris Hambourg
Arnold Trowell
Ivan Mossel
Herbert Walenn
Jacques Rénard
Felix Salmond
Johan C. Hock
John Linden
Dezso Kordy
Sydney Brooks
Darbishire Jones
Abbas

Mesdames
May Mukle
Warwara Irmanoff
Beatrice Harrison
Beatrice Eveline
Evelyn Seth-Smith

Cello and harp duets (1)
Mesdames Beatrice Eveline and Josephine Sullivan

String quartets, trios etc. (15)
Brussels Quartet
Bohemian Quartet
Capet Quartet
Rosé Quartet
Brodsky Quartet
Max Mossel Quartet
Wesseley Quartet
Munich Quartet
Walenn Quartet
Triester Quartet
New Trio
Chaplin Trio
Grimson Trio
London Trio
Cherniavski Trio

Hamilton Harty Chamber Music Union (Piano, Wind, Strings)
London Chamber Musicians (Wind and String)
La Société des Instruments Anciens de Paris
La Société Moderne d' Instruments à Vent

Sonata recitals
Jacques Thibaud (Violin)
Alfred Cortot (Piano)

Le Double Quintet de Paris

Bulletin issued by Messrs. Ibbs & Tillett, Musical Agents, 19 Hanover Square, W.

No.1 January 1913

Artists featured in this publication (with photograph unless stated otherwise)
Madame Clara Butt & Mr Kennerley Rumford (photo only) World's Tour, 1913–14. Opening at New York, January 7th 1913

Miss Agnes Nicholls	singer
Mme Renée Chemet (no photograph)	violinist
Miss Esta d'Argo	singer
Mrs Fannie Bloomfield-Zeisler (no photograph)	pianist
Madame Kirkby Lunn	singer
Miss Phyllis Lett	singer
Madame Saima Neovi and Miss Ellen Beck	singer duettists
Mr Ben Davies	singer
Mr Maurice d'Oisly	singer
Mr Robert Radford	singer
Mr Herbert Brown	singer
Miss Daisy Kennedy	violinist
Sigmund Feuermann	violinist
Rachmaninoff	pianist, composer, conductor
Ernst von Lengyel	pianist

1914–15

Sole representatives for
Madame Clara Butt and Mr Kennerley Rumford

Mesdames
Agnes Nicholls
Louise Dale
Esta d'Argo
Evans-Williams

Kirkby Lunn
Phyllis Lett
Dilys Jones

MM
Ben Davies
John Coates
John Booth

Plunket Greene
Robert Radford
Herbert Brown

Rachmaninoff
and
Scriabine

Moriz Rosenthal
Ernst von Lengyel

Tivadar Nachèz
Sigmund Feuermann
Daisy Kennedy

Hollman

Brussels String Quartet
Geloso String Quartet
Fransella Trios
Hamilton Harty Chamber Music Union
London Wind Sextet

Sopranos (47)

Mesdames

Agnes Nicholls   Louise Dale   Carrie Tubb   Esta d'Argo   Evans-Williams

Ruth Vincent
Aïno Ackté
Mignon Nevada
[Pauline] Donalda
Maggie Teyte
Blanche Marchesi
Lucy Gates
Elsie Cochrane
Gleeson-White
Perceval Allen
Evangeline Florence
Eve Simony
[Alice] Wilna
Ellen Beck
Saima Neovi
Helga Petri
Edith Evans
Amy Castles
Amy Evans
Mabel Manson
Ada Forrest
Caroline Hatchard
Rosina Buckman
Jean Waterston
Emily Breare
Jenny Taggart
Dorothy Silk
Alice Baxter
Kitty Ryan
Clara Butterworth
Marie Houghton
Mary Leighton
Lilian Dillingham
May Huxley
Bettina Freeman
Mary Sykes
Gladys Moger
Emily Shepherd
Eva Rich
Dora Gibson
Leah Felissa
Noordewier-Reddingius

Contraltos (46)

Mesdames

Clara Butt   Kirkby Lunn   Ada Crossley   Phyllis Lett   Dilys Jones

Muriel Foster
Julia Culp
Edna Thornton
Tilly Koenen
Doris Woodall
Elsie Swinton
Lucy Nuttall
Gertrude Lonsdale
Alice Lakin
Carmen Hill
Margaret Balfour
Maud Santley
Mabel Mann
Gwladys Roberts
Marion Beeley
Maud Wright
Mildred Jones
Maria Yelland
Edith Clegg
Mabel Braine
Ethel Hook
Violet Elliott
Joan Ashley
Irene Ainsley
Violet Oppenshaw
Sara Silvers
Winifred Lewis
Ella Caspers
Florence Taylor
Lysette Mostyn
Megan Jones
Hilda Cragg-James
Alys Gear
Dorothy Webster
Ethel Wynne-Jones
Helen Blain
Lily Crawforth
Annie Johnson
Evelyn Althaus
Lily Fairney
de Haan-Manifarges

Tenors (46)

MM

Ben Davies   Maurice d'Oisly   John Coates   John Booth

John McCormack
Gervase Elwes
[Giuseppe] Lenghi-Cellini
[Elvino] Ventura
Walter Hyde
Frank Mullings
Ivor Walters
Webster Millar
John Adams
Edward Davies
Gwynne Davies
Charles Saunders
Philip Ritte
Hubert Eisdell
Roland Jackson
Joseph Cheetham
James Hay
Frank Webster

Lloyd Chandos
John Harrison
Paul Reimers
Morgan Kingston
Alfred Heather
José de Moraes
Burke-Leigh
Joseph O'Mara
Harold Wilde
Cynlais Gibbs
Anderson Nicol
Henry Turnpenney
Henry Brearley
Albert Watson
Ernest Pike
Bertram Binyon
Wilson Thornton
Frank Foster
Hardy Williamson
John Watkyn
Walter Glynne
J. Hughes Macklin
Joseph Reed
John Perry

Baritones and basses (45)

MM

Plunket Greene
Robert Radford
Kennerley Rumford
Herbert Brown

Frederic Austin
Harry Dearth
Watkin Mills
Charles Clark
Thorpe Bates
Edmund Burke
Ivor Foster
Charles Tree
Robert Burnett
Julien Henry
Frederick Ranalow
Wilfred Douthitt
Robert Maitland
Peter Dawson
H. Lane Wilson
Charles Knowles
Campbell McInnes
Norman Williams
Charles Mott
David Hughes
Lewys James
Marcus Thomson
Stewart Gardner
Herbert Heyner
Albert Garcia
Joseph Lycett
Robert Charlesworth
Jamieson Dodds
Hamilton Harris
David Brazell
Norman Allin
Fraser Gange
George Parker
Herbert Parker
Reginald Herbert
Robert Pitt
George Baker
Bridge Peters
Montague Borwell
David Evans
Dawson Freer

Pianists (61)

Moriz Rosenthal
Busoni
Frederic Lamond
Irene Scharrer

Rachmaninoff
Scriabine

Carreño
Fanny Davies
Adela Verne
Tina Lerner
Johanne Stockmarr
Katharine Goodson
Maria Levinskaja
Suzanne Morvay
Winifred Christie
Antonie Geiger
Marguerite Melville
Gertrude Peppercorn
Auriol Jones
Marguerite Elzy
Vera Margolies
Marie Novello
Tora Hwass
Myra Hess
Tosta de Benici
Myrtle Meggy
Florence Smith
Mildred Pritchard
Lucy Polgreen
Lonie Basche
Adelina de Lara

Godowsky
Ernst von Lengyel
Mark Hambourg
Emil Sauer
Alexander Siloti
Max Pauer
Edouard Risler
Alexander Raab
Cernikoff
Archy Rosenthal
Herbert Fryer
Frank Merrick

Wilhelm Backhaus
Alfred Cortot
Sapellnikoff
Leonard Borwick
Dohnányi
Harold Bauer
Egon Petri
Benno Moiseiwitsch
Percy Grainger
Solomon
Max Darewski
Norman Wilks
Louis Edger
Harold Brewerton
Leopold Schultz
Cecil Baumer
Lloyd Powell
Walter Morse Rummell

Violinists (48)

Tivadar Nachèz
Daisy Kennedy
Renée Chemet
Sigmund Feuermann

Mesdames

Marie Hall
May Harrison
Isolde Menges
Marjorie Hayward
Rosa Ehrlich
Beatrice Langley
Dorothy Bridson
Ivy Angove
Valerie Knoll
Bessie Spence
Joyce Brown
Hilda Lett
Isabel Leatham
Erna Schultz
Muriel Pickupp

MM

Ysaÿe
Kreisler
Jacques Thibaud
Mischa Elman
[Efrem] Zimbalist
Zacharewitsch
Kocian
Henri Marteau
Joan Manen
[Daniel] Melsa
Achille Rivarde
Joska Szigeti
Geloso
Georges Enesco
Nandor Zsolt
Aldo Antonietti
Jose Gomez
Max Mossel
Renee Bohet
Louis Pecskai
John Dunn
Arthur Catterall
Charles Barré
Haydn Wood
Bromley Booth
Godfrey Ludlow
Maurice Warner
Vivian Burrows
Thomas Fussell

Cellists (34)

MM

Pablo Casals
Hollman
Jean Gérardy
W.H. Squire
Joseph Malkin
Paul Grummer
Belooussoff
Henry Bramsen
Carl Fuchs
Herbert Withers
Georges Pitsch
W.E. Whitehouse
Boris Hambourg
Arnold Trowell
Ivan Mossel
Herbert Walenn
Jacques Renard
Felix Salmond
Johan C. Hock
Darbishire Jones
Warwick Evans
Jacques Gaillard
Luigi Gasparini
Don Luiz Figueras
Ivor James

Mesdames

Beatrice Harrison
May Mukle
Vera Poppe
Beatrice Eveline
Evelyn Seth-Smith
Adelina Leon
Helen Mott
Eileen Craig
Gwenhilda Birkett

String quartets, trios etc. (14)

Brussels Quartet
Geloso Quartet
Rosé Quartet
Bohemian Quartet
St Petersburg Quartet
Arthur Catterall Quartet
Brodsky Quartet
Max Mossel Quartet
Wesseley Quartet
London Quartet
The Henkel Piano Quartet
Chaplin Trio
London Trio
Fransella Trios
Hamilton Harty Chamber Music Union
London Wind Sextet

Piano and cello sonata recitals
Wassili Safonoff and M.E. Belooussoff

Bach, Beethoven, Brahms recitals
Joska Szigeti (Violin) and Ernst von Lengyel (Piano)

Harp and flute duets
Miriam Timothy and Victor Borlee
Alfred Kastner and Albert Fransella

Nellie Chaplin's ancient dances and music

Plunket Greene's recital lectures on interpretation in song with vocal illustrations

Vocal duets (4)
Madame Noordewier-Reddingius and Madame de Haan-Manifarges
Madame Saima Neovi and Miss Ellen Beck
Mary and Ethel Williams
Flora Mann and Lilian Berger

Vocal quartets etc. (6)
The Westminster Singers
The Meister Glee-Singers
The Royal Windsor Glee Singers
St George's Glee-Singers
The Folk-Song Quartet
The Alexandra Ladies' Quartet

Mr Clive Carey and Miss Beatrice Dunn (Country Songs and Duets in Costume)
Mr Denis O'Niel – Irish Songs

Reciters (22)
Lady Beerbohm Tree

Constance Collier
Evelyn Millard
Phyllis Neilson Terry
Marie Lohr
Lena Ashwell
Esme Beringer
Kate Phillips
Beryl Faber
Ellen Bowick
Gertrude Tomalin
Nora Conway
Iona Robertson
Grace Jean Crocker
Clara Hubbard
Comtesse de Armil

Henry Ainley
Basil Gill
Matheson Lang
Charles Fry
Paul Leyssac
Ernest Meads

Frank Speaight's Dickens recitals

Entertainers (10)

Yvette Guilbert
Helen Mar
Marie Dainton
Kitty Cheatham
Marguerite Scialtiel
Jean Sterling Mackinlay
Nora and Frederica Conway
Decima Moore
Clara Alexander
Greta Wood

Entertainers at the piano (36)

Margaret Cooper

Barclay Gammon
Nelson Jackson
Harold Montague
Cooper Mitchell
Ernest Hastings
Harrison Hill
Selwyn Driver
Astley Weaver
T. Sterndale Bennett
H.M. Tennant
Frederick Chester
Dorothy Varick
Nina Gordon
Josephine La Barte
Olive Turner
Ivy St Helier
Griffith Humphreys
Tom Clare
Archie Naish
Leslie Harris
J. Foster Kershaw
Frank Leedham

Helen Henschel

Maurice Farkoa
Albert Whelan
Stacey Aumonier
Thornley Dodge
Walter Churcher
Charles Wreford
Fred Upton
Dr. Byrd Page
Douglas Beaufort
Leslie Lambert
Herbert Collings
Edward Victor

1915–16

Sole representatives for
Madame Clara Butt and Mr Kennerley Rumford

Mesdames
Agnes Nicholls
Carrie Tubb
Alice Wilna
Louise Dale
Esta d'Argo
Elsie Cochrane
Evans-Williams

Kirkby Lunn
Phyllis Lett
Dilys Jones

MM
Ben Davies
John Coates
John Booth

Plunket Greene
Robert Radford
Herbert Brown

Renée Chemet
Daisy Kennedy

Hollman

Geloso String Quaetrt
Philharmonic Quartet
Belgian Piano Quartet

Hamilton Harty Chamber Music Union
Fransella Trios (flute, violin, piano [or] flute, cello, piano)

Frank Speaight
Selwyn Driver

Sopranos (32)

Mesdames

Agnes Nicholls

Carrie Tubb
Esta d'Argo

Elsie Cochrane
Alice Wilna

Louise Dale
Evans-Williams

Ruth Vincent
Mignon Nevada
Tamaki Miura
Blanche Marchesi
Gleeson-White
Perceval Allen
Amy Evans
Caroline Hatchard
Rosina Buckman

Ada Forrest
Mabel Manson
Jean Waterston
Edith Evans
May Huxley
Emily Breare
Dorothy Silk
Clara Butterworth

Lilian Dillingham
Emily Shepherd
Eva Rich
Dora Gibson
Lilian Stiles-Allen
Phyllis Lansdell
Gertrude Blomfield
Aileen d'Orme

Contraltos (34)

Mesdames

Clara Butt

Kirkby Lunn
Ada Crossley

Phyllis Lett

Dilys Jones

Muriel Foster
Marguerite d'Alvarez
Edna Thornton
Doris Woodall
Alice Lakin
Lucy Nuttall
Camen Hill
Margaret Balfour
Gertrude Lonsdale
Mabel Mann

Gwladys Roberts
Marion Beeley
Maud Wright
Mabel Corran
Phyllis Archibald
Violet Oppenshaw
Doris Manuelle
Ethel Grow
Hayward Webb
Etty Ferguson

Edith Clegg
Ethel Hook
Winifred Lewis
Florence Taylor
Hilda Cragg-James
Dorothy Webster
Helen Blain
Annie Johnson
Lily Fairney

Tenors (35)

MM

Ben Davies
Maurice d'Oisly

John Coates

John Booth

Gervase Elwes
Walter Hyde
Lenghi-Cellini
Frank Mullings
Lloyd Chandos
John Harrison
Alfred Heather
Burke-Leigh

John Adams
Edward Davies
Gwynne Davies
Harold Wilde
José de Moraes
Cynlais Gibbs
Frederick Blamey
Anderson Nicol

Philip Ritte
Hubert Eisdell
Roland Jackson
Joseph Cheetham
Frank Webster
Frank Foster
John Watkyn
Walter Glynne

Ivor Walters
Webster Millar
Octave Dua
Henry Brearley
Bertram Binyon
J. Hughes Macklin
Joseph Reed

Baritones and basses (36)

MM

Plunket Greene
Robert Radford
Kennerley Rumford
Herbert Brown

Frederic Austin
Harry Dearth
Thorpe Bates
Herbert Heyner
Ivor Foster
Charles Tree
Robert Burnett
Julien Henry
Frederick Ranalow
Peter Dawson
Campbell McInnes
Norman Williams
Charles Mott
Lewys James
Stewart Gardiner
William Samuell
Robert Charlesworth
Hamilton Harris
Norman Allin
Fraser Gange
Harry Reynolds
William Hayle
Thornley Gibson
Percy Heming
Pitt Chatham
Herbert Parker
Robert Pitt
George Baker
Bridge Peters
Jamieson Dodds
David Evans
Dawson Freer

Violinists (36)

Renée Chemet
Daisy Kennedy

Marie Hall
May Harrison
Isolde Menges
Marjorie Hayward
Beatrice Langley
Dorothy Bridson
Ivy Angove
Ethel Barns
Bessie Spence
Leila Doubleday
Winifred Smith
Joyce Brown
Hilda Lett
Mary Law
Muriel Pickupp

Ysaÿe
Zacharewitsch
Melsa
Achille Rivarde
Albert Sammons
Geloso
Aldo Antonietti
Max Mossel
Désiré de Fauw
Louis Pecskai
John Dunn
Arthur Catterall
José Gomez
Samuel Dushkin
Charles Barré
Haydn Wood
Bromley Booth
Vivian Burows
Thomas Fussell

Pianists (34)

Irene Scharrer
Benno Moiseiwitsch

Fanny Davies
Adela Verne
Gertrude Peppercorn
Myra Hess
Maria Levinskaja
Winifred Christie
Tosta de Benici
Myrtle Meggy
Auriol Jones
Marguerite Elzy
Dorothy Martin
Marie Antoinette Aussenac
Marie Novello
Tora Hwass
Florence Smith
Lucy Polgreen
Lonie Basche
Adelina de Lara

Mark Hambourg
Sapellnikoff
Leonard Borwick
Arthur de Greef
Solomon
William Murdoch
Cernikoff
Archy Rosenthal
Frank Merrick
Cyril Scott
Cecil Baumer
Lloyd Powell
Victor Buesst
Walter Morse Rummell

Violoncellists (25)

Hollman
W.H. Squire
Maurice Dambois
Emile Doerhaerd
Emile de Vlieger
Arnold Trowell
Jacques van Lier
Warwick Evans
Herbert Withers
Felix Salmond
Johan C. Hock
Darbishire Jones
Luigi Gasparini
Don Luiz Figueras
Ivor James
Cedric Sharpe

Guilhermina Suggia
May Mukle
Vera Poppe
Beatrice Eveline
Evelyn Seth-Smith
Adelina Leon
Helen Mott
Eileen Craig
Gwenhilda Birkett

String quartets, trios etc. (14)

Geloso Quartet (of Paris)
London Quartet
Philharmonic Quartet
English Quartet
Arthur Catterall Quartet
Max Mossel Quartet

The Belgian Piano Quartet
The Henkel Piano Quartet

Chaigneau Trio (of Paris)
Chaplin Trio
London Trio

Fransella Trios (Flute Violin/Cello Piano)

Hamilton Harty Chamber Music Union (Piano Wind Strings)

The Queen's Hall Wind Sextet

Harp and flute duets

Miriam Timothy & Victor Borlee
Alfred Kastner & Albert Fransella
Jeanne Chevreau & Edith Penville

Nellie Chaplin's ancient dances and music

Plunket Greene's recital-lectures on interpretation in song with vocal illustrations

Vocal Duets: Mary & Ethel Williams
Flora Mann & Lilian Berger

Vocal quartets etc.

The Westminster Singers
St George's Glee-Singers
The Meister Glee-Singers
The Folk-Song Quartet
The Royal Windsor Glee-Singers
The Alexandra Ladies' Quartet

Reciters (23)
Lady Beerbohm Tree

Constance Collier
Evelyn Millard
Marie Lohr
Lena Ashwell
Esme Beringer
Tita Brand-Cammaerts
Beryl Faber
Ellen Bowick
Gertrude Tomalin
Lilian Braithwaite
Marguerite Scialtiel
Nora Conway
Grace Jean Crocker
Clara Hubbard

Henry Ainley
Basil Gill
Matheson Lang
Charles Fry
Paul Leyssac
Ernest Meads
Mollison Kidd
Carlo Liten

Frank Speaight's Dickens Recitals

Entertainers (10)
Yvette Guilbert
Helen Mar
Marie Dainton
Marguerite Scialtiel
Jean Sterling Mackinlay
Gertrude Tomalin
Clara Alexander
Greta Wood
Nora & Frederica Conway

Entertainers at the piano (37)
Margaret Cooper

Selwyn Driver
Nelson Jackson
Harold Montague
Cooper Mitchell
Ernest Hastings
Harrison Hill
Astley Weaver
T. Sterndale Bennett
H.M. Tennant
Frederick Chester
Tom Clare
Archie Naish
Rupert Hazell
J. Foster Kershaw
Dorothy Varick
Nina Gordon
Josephine La Barte
Olive Turner
Ivy St Helier
Norah Blaney
Helen Henschel

Maurice Farkoa
Bransby Williams
Albert Whelan
Stacey Aumonier
Thornley Dodge
Walter Churcher
Charles Wreford
Fred Upton
Dr Byrd Page
Douglas Beaufort
Leslie Lambert
Herbert Collings
Edward Victor
Henry Hull
Leslie Harris

1919–20

Sole representatives for

Agnes Nicholls
Carrie Tubb
Donalda
Esta d'Argo
Zoia Rosowsky
Elsie Cochrane
Madeline Collins
Dora Labbette
Rene Maxwell

Kirkby Lunn
Margaret Balfour
Dilys Jones

Ben Davies
John Coates
Frank Mullings
John Booth

Robert Radford
Herbert Brown
Norman Allin
Plunket Greene
Thorpe Bates
Herbert Heyner

Rachmaninoff

Moiseiwitsch
Irene Scharrer
Myra Hess
William Murdoch

Renée Chemet
Daisy Kennedy
Sybil Eaton
Margaret Fairless

Guilhermina Suggia
Hollman
Felix Salmond

Philharmonic String Quartet
Selwyn Driver
Margaret Cooper's Recitals

Mesdames
Sopranos (54)

Agnes Nicholls
Madeline Collins
Mignon Nevada
Dora Labette
Carrie Tubb
Donalda
Esta d'Argo
Zoia Rosowsky

Ruth Vincent
Flora Woodman
Rosina Buckman
Evans-Williams
Elsie Cochrane
Elsa Stralia
Miriam Licette
Margaret Sheridan
Desiree Ellinger
Mabel Manson
Florence Mellors
Gladys Ancrum
Helen Henschel
Ada Forrest
Clara Butterworth
Dorothy Silk
Minnie Searle
Lilian Dillingham
Eva Hunsdon Brown
Olive Sturgess
Helen Gilliland
Doris Vane
Elsie Suddaby
Dorothy Robson

Amy Evans
Caroline Hatchard
Louise Dale
Jeanne Brola
Rene Maxwell
Perceval Allen
Lilian Stiles-Allen
Alice Wilma
Dorothy Moulton
Eva Rich
Gladys Moger
Emily Breare
May Huxley
Emilia Conti
Kate Campion
Katherine Arkandy
Annie Rees
Sophie Rowlands
Megan Foster
Lily Paikin
Jeanne L'Hommedieu
Ida Cooper

Mesdames

Contraltos (49)

Clara Butt
Kirkby Lunn
Marguerite d'Alvarez
Dilys Jones
Phyllis Lett
Edna Thornton
Margaret Balfour
Astra Desmond

Muriel Foster
Doris Woodall
Leila Megane
Carmen Hill
Olga Haley
Lucy Nuttall
Ethel Peake
Dorothy Webster
Marion Beeley
Mabel Corran
Phyllis Archibald
Ethel Hook
Violet Oppenshaw
Doris Manuelle
Etty Ferguson
Edith Clegg
Winifred Lewis
Florence Taylor
Hilda Cragg-Lewis
Helen Blain
Annie Johnson
Lily Fairney
Ethel Toms
Ida Kiddier
Maud Murray
Gertrude Higgs
Ethel Fenton
Nellie Walker
Helen Anderton
Phyllis Evennett
Evelyn Arden
Vera Horton
Margaret Norton
Elsie Chambers
Paula St Clair
Rispah Goodacre
Norah Scott
Irene Flanders
Carrie Hirwen
Una Austin
Elsa Cameron

MM

Tenors (53)

Ben Davies
Frank Mullings
Walter Hyde
John Booth
John Coates
Gervase Elwes
Maurice d'Oisly
Arthur Jordan

Thomas Burke
Mischa-Léon
Webster Millar
Vladimir Rosing
Lenghi-Cellini
John Harrison
Alfred Heather
Hubert Eisdell
Frederick Blamey
Yves Tinayre
Sidney Coltham
Boris Lensky
Edward Davies
Gwynne Davies
Harold Wilde
José de Moraes
Henry Brearley
Bertram Binyon
Philip Ritte
Roland Jackson
Frank Webster
Joseph Reed
Herbert Cave
Cynlais Gibbs
Herbert Teale
Sidney Pointer
Ivor Thomas
Herbert Thorpe
David Ellis
Walter Glynne
John Collett
Sam Hempsall
John Clarke
Thomas Watson
Richard Ripley
Alfred O'Shea

J. Hughes Macklin
William Boland
John Adams
Horace Binks
Spencer Thomas
Constantin Stroesco
Gabriel Chamlys
William Heseltine
Lovat Crosley

Baritones and basses (51)

Robert Radford
Herbert Brown
Norman Allin
Herbert Heyner
Plunket Greene
Thorpe Bates
Fraser Gange
Frederick Ranalow

Kennerley Rumford
Harry Dearth
Frederic Austin
Ivor Foster
Charles Tree
Campbell McInnes
Murray Davey
Foster Richardson
Robert Parker
Charles Knowles
George Ferguson
Norman Williams
George Baker
Frederick Taylor
Robert Burnett
Lewys James
Percy Heming
Edward Dykes
Topliss Green
Hamilton Harris
William Hayle
Robert Pitt
Bridge Peters
David Evans
Dawson Freer
George Parker
John Buckley
Bernard Manning
Joseph Farrington
David Brazell
John Huntington
Charles Till
Kenneth Ellis
Powell Edwards
Arnold Stoker
Klinton Shepherd
Aubrey Millward
Stewart Gardner
Kingsley Lark
James Howell
Sidney Stoddard
Vivian Gosnell
Norman Notley

Pianists (53)

Moiseiwitsch
Myra Hess
William Murdoch
Irene Scharrer

Fanny Davies
Isabel Gray
Amy Hare
Evangeline Livens
Gertrude Peppercorn
Amina Goodwin
Jessie Bristol
Harriet Cohen
Maria Levinskaja
Beatrice Bellini
Auriol Jones
Katharine Goodson
Winifred MacBride
Rosamond Ley
Chilton Griffin
Lilia Kanevskaya
Agnes Maud Winter
Katharine Hogg
Berthe Bernard
Eurydice Draconi
Lonie Basche
Adela Verne
Ethel Hobday
Kathleen Long
Katherine Doubleday
Tosta de Benici
Gertrud Hopkins
Winifred Purnell

Frederic Lamond
Alfred Cortot
Mark Hambourg
Leonard Borwick
Arthur de Greef
Frederick Dawson
Herbert Fryer
Cyril Scott
York Bowen
Norman Wilks
Archy Rosenthal
Harold Samuel
Vivian Langrish
Frank Merrick
Lloyd Powell
Sidney Rosenbloom
Cecil Baumer
Edward Isaacs
Harold Craxton
Claud Biggs
Arthur Alexander

Violinists (40)

Renée Chemet
Margaret Fairless
Daisy Kennedy
Sybil Eaton

Kathleen Parlow
Nancy Phillips
Constance Izard
Rhoda Backhouse
Marjorie Hayward
Marian Jay
Ethel Barns
Nanette Evans
Tessie Thomas
Marie Hall
Maud Delstanche
Evelyn Cooke
Edith Abraham
Murray Lambert
Adila d'Aranyi
Winifred Smith
Marjorie Gunn
Marjory Bentwich
May Harrison
Muriel Hay
Dora Garland
Winifred Small
Lena Kontorovitch
Jelly d'Aranyi

Albert Sammons
Anton Maaskoff
John Dunn
Zacharewitsch
Jaroslav Kocian
Horace Ayckbourn
Michael Doré
Aldo Antonietti
Arthur Beckwith
Désiré Defauw
Arthur Catterall
Max Mossel
Joseph Coleman
Melsa
Philip Cathie
Louis Pecskai

Viola (4)

Lionel Tertis
Frank Bridge
Alfred Hobday
Raymond Jeremy

Violoncellists (29)

Guilhermina Suggia
Beatrice Eveline
Adelina Leon
Valerie Valenson
Thelma Bentwich
Beatrice Harrison
Eileen Craig
Maud Bell
Helen Mott
Fernande Kufferath
May Mukle
Marie Dare

Hollman
Walter Hatton
Ivor James
Warwick-Evans
Emile Doehaerd
James Richardson
Cedric Sharpe
W.H. Squire
Arthur Williams
Herbert Walenn
Herbert Withers
Emile de Vlieger
Johan C. Hock
Arnold Trowell
Felix Salmond
Purcell Jones
Giovanni Barbirolli

Recitals of music for two pianofortes

Irene Scharrer and Myra Hess

Violin and pianoforte recitals (3)

Daisy Kennedy & Moiseiwitsch
Albert Sammons & William Murdoch
Sybil Eaton & Harold Samuel

Violin, cello and pianoforte recitals

Albert Sammons
Felix Salmond
William Murdoch

String quartets, trios etc (8)

London String Quartet
Philharmonic String Quartet
Bohemian String Quartet
Catterall String Quartet
English String Quartet
Allied String Quartet

London Trio
Fransella Trios (Flute–Violin–Piano Flute–Cello–Piano)

Harp and flute duets

Miriam Timothy & Albert Fransella
Gwendoline Mason & Victor Borlée

New Queen's Hall Light Orchestra
Gwynne Kimpton's Ladies Orchestra
Philip Lewis Octette
Rene Ortman's Orchestra
Lotus Ladies Orchestra

Plunket Greene's recital-lectures on interpretation in song with vocal illustrations
Jean Sterling Mackay in old songs & ballads
Helen Henschel in folk songs at the piano

Vocal quartets (4)

The Westminster Singers
The Meister Glee-Singers
The Gresham Singers
The Folk-Song Quartet

Reciters (27)

Lady Tree

Lena Ashwell
Vera Beringer
Hutin Britton
Lilian Braithwaite
Constance Collier
Madge Titheradge
Esme Beringer
Lillah MacCarthy

Tita Brand-Cammaerts
Cordelia Coe
Edythe Wattson
Nora Conway
Ellen Bowick
Margaret Halstan
Annie Tribrick
Agnes Bartholomew
Clara Hubbard
Gertrude Tomalin
Marguerite Scialtel

Henry Ainley
Mollison Kidd
Ernest Meads
Matheson Lang
Basil Gill
Bassett Roe
Fisher White

Duologues (2)

Matheson Lang & Hutin Britton
Basil Gill & Fisher White

Frank Speaight's Dickens recitals
Entertainers at the piano (30)
Margaret Cooper
Selwyn Driver
Melville Gideon
Astley Weaver
Dr Collisson
Nelson Jackson
Harry Ivimey
Tom Clare
Rupert Hazell
Ernest Hastings
Archie Naish
T. Sterndale Bennett
J. Foster Kershaw
Finlay Dunn
Bertram Brennan
H.M. Tennant
Leslie Harris
Harold Montague
George Bolton
Frederick Chester
Harrison Hill

Dorothy Varick
Georgia Drayson
Olive Fox
Ivy St Helier
Olive Turner
Alma Goatley
Joan Fowler

Clara Evelyn & Ivy St Helier
Norah Blaney & Gwendoline Farrar

Entertainers (33)
Marie Dainton
Edward Victor
Henry Hull
Douglas Beaufort
Charles Wreford
Albert Whelan
Ernest Sewell
George Ellis
Thornley Dodge
Helen Mar
Melani Castelle
Arthur Brough
Leslie Lambert
Walter Churcher
Stacey Aumonier
Fred Wildon
Walter Montagu
Foden Williams
Ernest Wellbeloved
Bransby Williams
Douglas Dexter
Herbert Collings
Fred Upton
W.V. Robinson

Wilson James & Ruby Wilson
Ben Osborne & Nellie Perryer
Percy Kahn & Lilian Hoare
Fred Romeo & Gertie Vincent

Denis O'Neil
Henri Leoni
Jerome Murphy

Muriel George & Ernest Butcher in old English folk songs and duets
Jessie Broughton & Dennis Creedon

APPENDIX 3

Ibbs and Tillett: Artists' Brochures 1923–24 (for Chamber Music Societies), 1924–25, 1929–30

1923–24

Of special interest to Chamber Music Societies

[The following group included personnel, months of availability and some reviews.]

The Flonzaley String Quartet
The Chamber Music Trio
The Bohemian String Quartet
The Trio Belge
The Hungarian String Quartet
The Chamber Music Players
The Rosé String Quartet
The Harrison Trio
The Dutch String Quartet
The London Wind Quintet
The Lener String Quartet
The English Trio
The Copenhagen String Quartet
The Fransella Trio

[The following gave no further details beyond names of the group.]

Philharmonic String Quartet
Edith Robinson String Quartet
The Marguerite Meredyll Piano Quartet
Birmingham String Quartet
Catterall String Quartet
The Beatrice Hewitt Piano Quartet
English String Quartet
McCullagh String Quartet
Spencer Dyke String Quartet
Kendall String Quartet

Pianists

Busoni
Moiseiwitsch
Myra Hess
Dohnányi
Marcel Ciampi
Leonard Borwick
Fanny Davies
William Murdoch
Egon Petri
Irene Scharrer
Ivan Phillipowsky
Adolphe Hallis
Harold Craxton
Harold Samuel
Cyril Scott

Violinists

Jelly d'Aranyi
Daisy Kennedy
Lydie Demirgian
Margaret Fairless
Sybil Eaton

Viola

Lionel Tertis

Cellists

Pablo Casals
Joseph Salmon
Ivor James
Beatrice Harrison
Guilhermina Suggia
Maurice Dambois
May Mukle

Vocalists

Plunket Greene's recital lectures	Anne Thursfield	Dorothy Silk
Olga Haley	Cedar Paul (Singer and Diseuse – folksongs, tales and sagas)	Marcia Van Dresser
Megan Foster	Roland Hayes (The Negro tenor)	Jean Sterling Mackinlay in old songs and ballads
Tatiana Makushina		Vladimir Rosing
Mischa-Léon		Helen Henschel

Recitals by the following combination of artists

Dorothy Silk's recitals of old music with the assistance of John Goss (vocalist), the Birmingham String Quartet and flute and piano

Bach Recitals – Dorothy Silk (vocalist) Albert Fransella (flute) George Reeves (piano)

Recitals of old and modern music – Dorothy Helmrich (vocalist) Joseph Slater (flute) Gerald Cooper (harpsichord and piano)

Recitals of compositions of Cyril Scott – Astra Desmond (vocalist) Cyril Scott (piano)

Trio recitals – Myra Hess, Marjorie Hayward, May Mukle

Pianoforte and cello recitals – Harold Samuel and Ivor James

For Harpsichord and cello – Violet Gordon Woodhouse and Beatrice Harrison in Bach's compositions

The English Singers – Madrigals, ayres and folksongs etc.

The Agnes Nicholls and Hamilton Harty recitals

Violin and piano recitals – Daisy Kennedy and Moiseiwitsch
Albert Sammons and William Murdoch
Jelly d'Aranyi and Myra Hess

Recitals of compositions for two pianos – Irene Scharrer and Myra Hess

1924–25

Sole representatives for

Agnes Nicholls	Carrie Tubb	Kirkby Lunn
Olga Haley	Florence Austral	Dora Labbette
Astra Desmond	Dilys Jones	Dorothy Silk
Elsie Suddaby	Margaret Balfour	Clara Serena
Miriam Licette	Marcia van Dresser	Esta d'Argo
Noel Eadie		
Ben Davies	Vladimir Rosing	Robert Radford
Norman Allin	Frank Mullings	Lauritz Melchior
Herbert Heyner	Thorpe Bates	Walter Hyde
Tudor Davies	Herbert Brown	Harold Williams
William Boland	Hubert Eisdell	Horace Stevens
George Baker	Webster Millar	John Booth
Arthur Jordan	Walter Widdop	Roland Hayes
Moiseiwitsch	Busoni	Harold Samuel
Myra Hess	Moriz Rosenthal	William Murdoch
Irene Scharrer	Dohnányi	Rachmaninoff
Renée Chemet	Toscha Seidel	Daisy Kennedy
Jelly d'Aranyi	Albert Spalding	Margaret Fairless
Pablo Casals	Guilhermina Suggia	Maurice Dambois
Beatrice Harrison		
Flonzaley String Quartet	Rosé String Quartet	Bohemian String Quartet
Copenhagen String Quartet		

Sopranos (79)

Agnes Nicholls	Carrie Tubb	Maggie Teyte
Dorothy Silk	Esta d'Argo	Donalda
Florence Austral	Elsie Suddaby	Mignon Nevada
Miriam Licette	Megan Foster	Flora Woodman
Dora Labbette	Noel Eadie	Marcia van Dresser
Caroline Hatchard	Desirée Ellinger	Rosina Buckman
Rene Maxwell	Stiles-Allen	Sarah Fischer
Ruth Vincent	Rosa Alba	Elsie Cochrane
Sylvia Nelis	Birgit Engell	Eva Turner
Doris Vane	Gertrude Johnson	Susan Metcalfe-Casals
Annie Rees	Evans-Williams	May Huxley
Beatrice Miranda	Ida Cooper	Hilda Blake
Maryan Elmar	Gladys Ancrum	Dorothy Robson
Florence Mellors	Louise Trenton	Mair Jones
Bella Baillie	Winifred Lawson	Dorothy Moulton

Olive Sturgess
Nora Delmarr
Rosa Rubery
Helen Henschel
Marie Williams
Hilda Searle
Marion Browne
Marjorie Ffrangcon-Davies
Hylda Whipp
Phyllis Denmead
Leonie Zifado
Madeline Hylton
Beatrice Sirette
Agnes Treacy
Cecilia Farrar
Elsa Murray-Aynsley
Alice Moxon
Mary Congreve
Lily Meagher
Gwladys Roberts
Olivia Hilder
Evelyn Tierney
Norah Pasley
Gwladys Naish
Flora Mann
Tatiana Makushina
Lillian Davies
Margaret Stephen
Gladys Verona
Megan Thomas
Garda Hall
Lucy Goodwin
Gladys Moger
Mary Hamlin

Contraltos (81)

Kirkby Lunn
Edna Thornton
Phyllis Lett
Olga Haley
Margaret Balfour
Astra Desmond
Carmen Hill
Dilys Jones
Muriel Brunskill
Clara Serena
Marguerite d'Alvarez
Elena Gerhardt
Anne Thursfield
Leila Megane
Dorothy Helmrich

Doris Woodall
Marie Cartwright
Lula Mysz-Gmeiner
Dorothy Webster
Ivy Philips
Constance Willis
Juliette Autran
Elsie Chambers
Lily Fairney
Nellie Walker
Gladys Parr
Margaret Lewys
Norah Scott
Margaret Champneys
Ada Mylchreest
Catherine Mentiplay
Phyllis Evennett
Kathleen Harding
Catherine Stewart
Winifred Lewis
Elsie Fisher
Annie Hughes
Dorothy Clark
Lucy Nuttall
Evelyn Arden
Jeanne Jouve
Helen Anderton
Mary Foster
Etty Ferguson
Phyllis Archibald
Ethel Hook
Rose Myrtil
Stella Murray
Gladys Palmer
Dorothy d'Orsay
Muriel Hughes
Bessie Kerr
Violet Roberts
April Pendarvis
Virginia Perry
Dorothy Ledsome
Monica Scott
Tessa Richardson
Ina Janssen
Elizabeth Munthe-Kaas
Lilian Berger
Isobel McLaren
Enid Cruikshank
Dorothea Webb
Ethel Fenton
Molly O'Callaghan
Violet Openshaw
Edith Furmedge
Blodwen Caerleon
Gertrude Entwistle
Elsa Cameron
Alice Mandeville
Cynthia Davril
Winifred Fisher
Mary Ogden
Gladys Divas
Rispah Goodacre
Millicent Russell
Ethel Barker
Jessie McLennan
Esther Coleman

Tenors (70)

Ben Davies
Hubert Eisdell
Vladimir Rosing
William Boland
Arthur Jordan
Frank Titterton
Roland Hayes
Frank Mullings
John Booth
Joseph Hislop
Tudor Davies
John Coates
Walter Hyde
Webster Millar
Walter Widdop
Mischa-Léon

Steuart Wilson
Lauritz Melchior
Archibald Winter
William Heseltine
John Perry
Lenghi-Cellini
Frederick Blamey
John Adams
Maurice d'Oisly
Sidney Pointer
Cecil Sherwood
Frank Webster
Sydney Coltham
Gwynne Davies
Alfred O'Shea
John Collett

J. Hughes Macklin
Philip Wilson
Ivor Walters
David Ellis
Browning Mummery
Spencer Thomas
Lloyd Chandos
Henry Brearley
Glyn Dowell
Ifor Thomas
Bertram Binyon
Walter Glynne
Hardy Williamson
Herbert Thorpe
Parry Jones
Yves Tinayre
Sam Hempsall
Herbert Cave
Furness Williams
Roland Jackson
Richard Ripley
Ernest Hargreaves
Barrington Hooper
John Turner

Ben Williams
Manuel Jones
Leonard Lovesey
Joseph Reed
Cynlais Gibbs
Ben Morgan
Oswald Rippon
Wilfred Temple
David Hutchison
Frederick Steger
Frank Taylor
José de Moraes
Edward Roberts
Seymour Dossor

Baritones and basses (80)

Robert Radford
Frederick Ranalow
Reinald Werrenrath
Mostyn Thomas
Horace Stevens
Robert Parker
Norman Allin
Herbert Heyner
Robert Maitland
Dinh Gilly
Harold Williams
Plunket Greene
Thorpe Bates
Herbert Brown
Harry Dearth
Peter Dawson

George Parker
Edward Dykes
Douglas Marshall
Andrew Shanks
Charles Tree
Dr Theo Lierhammer
Foster Richardson
George Baker
Howard Fry
Joseph Farrington
Percy Heming
Arthur Cranmer
Norman Williams
Ivor Foster
John Goss
Topliss Green

Malcolm McEachern
Herbert Stancliffe
Raymond Ellis
Reginald Herbert
Robert Burnett
Roy Russell
Augustus Milner
Frederic Collier
Powell Edwards

Eric Marshall
Hamilton Harris
Samuel Mann
Charles Knowles
Hebden Foster
Frederick Taylor
Walter Saull
William Hayle

Mirsky
David Brazell
Harry Brindle
Gilbert Bailey
Kenneth Ellis
Booth Hitchen
John Huntington
Bertram Ayrton

Keith Falkner
Ugo Donarelli
Lewys James
John Buckley
Tom Kinniburgh
David Evans
William Anderson

Earle Spicer
Kingsley Lark
Kennedy Arundel
Dawson Freer
Lee Thistlethwaite
Arthur Evans

Clive Carey
Charles Till
Stuart Robertson
Arthur Broadbent
Ernest Groom

William Michael
Norman Notley
Robert Watson
Lawrence Folker
Alfred Benham

Pianists (60)

Irene Scharrer
Belinda Heather
Isabel Gray
Gertrude Peppercorn
Katharine Goodson
Martha Baird

Adela Verne
Myra Hess
Desiree MacEwan
Dorothy Hess
Harriet Cohen

Winifred MacBride
Marie Antoinette Aussenac
Fanny Davies
Helena Morsztyn
Hetty Bolton

Moiseiwitsch
Harold Samuel
Walter Rummel
Leff Pouishnoff
Frederic Lamond
York Bowen
Francesco Ticciati
Richard Buhlig
Sapellnikoff
Adolphe Hallis
Anderson Tyrer
Walter Gieseking
Arthur de Greef
Rae Robertson
Vivian Langrish

Rachmaninoff
Busoni
Cyril Scott
Dirk Schafer
Mark Hambourg
Emil Sauer
Ivan Phillipowsky
Victor Schioler
Solomon
Ernest Schelling
Herbert Fryer
Reginald Paul
Marcel Ciampi
William Murdoch
Angus Morrison

Dohnányi
Moriz Rosenthal
Alfred Cortot
Backer Grondhal
Evlyn Howard-Jones
Nikisch
Serge Prokofieff
Edward Isaacs
Harold Craxton
Frederick Dawson
Leonard Borwick
Lloyd Powell
Maurice Cole
Egon Petri

Violinists (51)

Renée Chemet
Margaret Fairless
Kathleen Parlow
Adila Fachiri
Marjorie Hayward
Bessie Rawlins
Constance Izard
Elsie Owen
Katie Goldsmith
Daisy Kennedy
Marie Hall
Lydie Demirgian
Lena Kontorovitch
Murray Lambert
Rhoda Backhouse
Evelyn Cooke
Editha Braham
Dorothy Brook
Jelly d'Aranyi
Isolde Menges
May Harrison
Sybil Eaton
Amy Neill
Winifred Small
Sylvia de Gay
Phyllis Allan
Margaret Harrison

Toscha Seidel
Manuel Quiroga
Aldo Antonietti
Melsa
Anton Maaskoff
William Primrose
John Dunn
Laurance Turner
Albert Sammons
Jacques Thibaud
Albert Spalding
Balokovic
Jaroslav Kocian
Joseph Szigeti
Desiré Defauw
Harold Fairhurst
Georges Enesco
Joan Manen
Zacharewitsch
Bratza
Arthur Catterall
Max Mossel
Louis Pecskai
Alfred Barker

Viola (4)

Lionel Tertis
Frank Bridge
Alfred Hobday
Raymond Jeremy

Violoncellists (40)

Guilhermina Suggia
Judith Bokor
Hildegard Arnold
Marie Dare
Alison Dalrymple
Beatrice Harrison
Kathleen Moorhouse
Beatrice Eveline
Rita Sharpe
Vyvyan Lewis
May Mukle
Helen Mott
Eileen Craig
Bessie Griffiths
Adelina Leon

Pablo Casals
Hollman
Ivor James
Emile Doehaerd
Luigi Gasparini
Johan C. Hock
Purcell Jones
Mischel Cherniavsky
Seth Lancaster
Maurice Dambois
W.H. Squire
Arnold Trowell
Cedric Sharpe
Warwick-Evans
Walter Hatton
James Richardson
Livio Manucci
Joseph Salmon
Carl Fuchs
Jacques van Lier
John Barbirolli
Herbert Withers
Arthur Williams
John Snowden
Lauri Kennedy

Recitals of music for two pianofortes: Irene Scharrer and Myra Hess
Pianoforte and violin recitals: Myra Hess and Jelly d'Aranyi
William Murdoch and Albert Sammons
The Chamber Music Players: William Murdoch Albert Sammons Lionel Tertis Cedric Sharpe
The Chamber Music Trio: William Murdoch Albert Sammons Cedric Sharpe
The English Trio: Ethel Hobday Marjorie Hayward Cedric Sharpe
May, Margaret and Beatrice Harrison

String quartets, trios etc. (29)
Flonzaley String Quartet
Rosé String Quartet
Bohemian String Quartet
Lener String Quartet
Hungarian String Quartet
Copenhagen String Quartet
Dutch String Quartet
London String Quartet
Capet String Quartet and Trio
Philharmonic String Quartet
Catterall String Quartet
English String Quartet
British String Quartet
Spencer Dyke String Quartet
Kinsey String Quartet
Pennington String Quartet
Kendall String Quartet
Snow String Quartet
Birmingham String Quartet
Edith Robinson String Quartet
McCullagh String Quartet
Backhaus String Quartet
Philharmonic Piano Quartet
Margaret Meredyll Piano Quartet

The London Trio
The Russian Trio
The Dorian Trio
The Fransella Trio
The London Wind Quartet

Landon Ronald Recitals
Plunket Greene's Recital-Lectures
The English Singers
The Oriana Singers (Kennedy Scott: Conductor)
Marcel Dupré and Joseph Bonnet: The famous French organists
The Kennedy Fraser Combination (Hebridean folksongs with piano and harp accompaniment)

Harpsichord (4)
Violet Gordon Woodhouse
Arnold Dolmetsch
Gerald Cooper
Marguerite Delcourt

Harp (4)
Gwendolen Mason
Astrid Yden
Jeanne Chevreau
Sidonie Goossens

Flute (4)
Albert Fransella
John Amadio
Robert Murchie
Joseph Slater

Oboe (1)
Léon Goossens

Vocal quartets (9)
Gresham Singers
de Reszke Singers
Ensemble Singers
Westminster Singers
Aeolian Singers
Windsor Castle Quartet
Windsor Castle Royal Harmonists
Border Mixed Voice Quartet
Templars Quartet

Reciters (27)

Lady Tree	Lillah MacCarthy	Henry Ainley
Milton Rosmer	Lilian Braithwaite	Constance Collier
Maurice Moscovitch	Harcourt Williams	Esme Beringer
Madge Titheradge	Matheson Lang	Utt Ridge
Vera Beringer	Sybil Thorndike	Basil Gill
Cyril Lidington	Ellen Bowick	Katrina Lund
Ruth Draper	Melville Gideon	Gertrude Tomalin
Marguerite Scialtiel	Yvette Guilbert	Cordelia Coe
Clara Hubbard	Agnes Bartholomew	Tita Brand-Cammaerts

Entertainers at the piano (23)

Selwyn Driver	Ernest Hastings	Harold Montague
Morland Hay	Norman Long	T. Sterndale Bennett
Warwick Pryce	Finlay Dunn	Nelson Jackson
Robert Murray	J. Foster Kershaw	Frederick Chester
Hubert Leslie	Astley Weaver	

Dorothy Varick	Alma Goatley	Ivy St Helier
Olive Turner	Mary Mackie	Hilda Bertram
Phyllis Bateman	Joan Fowler	Doris Grover

Entertainers (24)

Bransby Williams	Albert Whelan	Stacey Aumonier
Will Kings	Thornley Dodge	T.W. Cunningham
Foden Williams	Jock Walker	Bret Hayden
Walter Churcher	Walter Montagu	W.V. Robinson
Rupert Hazell	Leslie Lambert	Herbert J. Collings
Edward Victor	Arthur Brough	Douglas Dexter
Ernest Sewell	Fred Wildon	

Norah Blaney and Gwendoline Farrar	Mary Barton and Marjorie Slaughter
Grace Ivell and Vivian Worth	Robert Pitt and Langton Marks

Muriel George and Ernest Butcher in old English folksongs and duets
Jean Sterling Mackinlay in old songs and ballads
Poet Reciter and Singer: John Drinkwater and Carmen Hill
Cedar Paul Recitals

1929–30

Sole representatives for

Elisabeth Schumann	Elsie Suddaby	Bella Baillie
Miriam Licette	Carrie Tubb	Maggie Teyte
Mavis Bennett	Dora Labbette	

Astra Desmond	Margaret Balfour	Olga Haley
Muriel Brunskill		

Frank Mullings	Tudor Davies	Roland Hayes
Hubert Eisdell	Walter Widdop	Arthur Jordan
Steuart Wilson	Parry Jones	

Robert Radford	Horace Stevens	Norman Allin
George Baker	Herbert Heyner	Harold Williams
Roy Henderson	Dennis Noble	

Rachmaninoff	Josef Hofmann	Egon Petri
Lamond	Artur Schnabel	Harold Bauer
Cortot	Dohnányi	Moiseiwitsch
Harold Samuel	Godowsky	Orloff
Medtner	William Murdoch	Myra Hess
Irene Scharrer	Katharine Goodson	

Jelly d'Aranyi	Isolde Menges	Thibaud
Joseph Szigeti	Renée Chemet	Adila Fachiri
Toscha Seidel	Lionel Tertis	

Pablo Casals	Gaspar Cassadó	Ivor James
Guilhermina Suggia	Beatrice Harrison	Raya Garbousova

Rosé, Budapest, Hungarian, Pro Arte String Quartets; The English Singers; Segovia; The London String Players (Conductor: Herbert Menges)

Sopranos (109)

Elisabeth Schumann	Lotte Lehmann	Maggie Teyte
Rosina Buckman	Agnes Nicholls	Florence Austral
Mignon Nevada	Caroline Hatchard	Carrie Tubb
Flora Woodman	Evelyn Scotney	Noel Eadie
Dorothy Silk	Stiles-Allen	Anne Thursfield
Doris Vane	Miriam Licette	Elsie Suddaby
Tatiana Makushina	Hilda Blake	Dora Labbette
Bella Baillie	Megan Foster	Megan Thomas

Gertrude Johnson	Dorothy Moulton	May Blyth
Olive Sturgess	Joan Elwes	Marcia van Dresser
Eda Bennie	Kate Winter	Mavis Bennett

Luella Paikin
Garda Hall
Ida Cooper
May Huxley
Elena Danieli

Evans-Williams
Helen Henschel
Kathlyn Hilliard
Gwladys Naish
Rosa Alba

Ethel Osborn
Mair Jones
Valentina Aksarova
Alice Moxon
Lucy Goodwin

Mary Hamlin
Gladys Ancrum
Rachelle Maragliano-Mori
Elisabeth Ohms
Sybil Scanes
Eleanor Toye
Delia Rheinhardt
Sara Fischer
Anita Desmond
Margaret Valdi Mellor

Göta Ljungberg
Leonie Zifado
Winifred Lawson
Ninon Vallin
Ursula van Diemen
Dorothy Robson
Louise Trenton
Susan Metcalfe-Casals
Eveline Stevenson

Violetta Pampanini
Frida Leider
Bessie Jones
Elsa Murray-Aynsley
Vera Janacopulos
Greta Stückgold
Margaret Stephen
Joan Sheppard
Ida Bloor

Elsie Cochrane
Winifred Comstock
Dorothy Tillett
Beatrice Sirette
Dorothy Bennett
Mabel Ritchie
Mary Bonn
Jennie Bleasdale
Sophie Wyss
Gertrude Concannon
Joan Hordern

Violette Browne
Flora Mann
Cecilia Farrar
Annie Rees
Dorothy Stanton
Bertha Steventon
Dorothy Astra
Phyllis James
Maud Bostock
Ida Cowey
Nellie Palliser

Sybil Crawley
Maryan Elmair
May Busby
Hilda Searle
Helen Ogilvie
Ina Souez
Bertha Whitaker
Elsie Griffin
Sophie Rowlands
Frances Allsom
Gretta Don

Contraltos (78)

Kirkby Lunn
Margaret Balfour
Muriel Brunskill
Phyllis Archibald
Elena Gerhardt
Claire Croiza
Constance Willis
Ethel Barker
Gladys Palmer
Rispah Goodacre
Lily Fairney
Dorothea Webb
Doris Dutson
Sybil Cropper
Rose Myrtil
Blodwen Caerleon
Gwladys Garside
Thelma Peterson

Edna Thornton
Leila Megane
Astra Desmond
Carmen Hill
Marguerite d'Alvarez
Dorothy Helmrich
Enid Cruikshank
Gladys Parr
Lillian Berger
Isobel McClaren
Helen Anderton
Denne Parker
Muriel Hughes
Ethel Fenton
Molly O'Callaghan
Elsie Chambers
Norah Scott
Norah Dahl

Olga Haley
Clara Serena
Edith Furmedge
Dilys Jones
Marie Olczewska
Isobel Lamond
Catherine Stewart
Millicent Russell
Joan Muirella
Mary Foster
Betty Bannerman
Myra Mortimer
Marie Cartwright
Stella Murray
Muriel Koolhoven
Margaret Lewys
Lillie Mitchell
Olive Kavann

Essie Ackland
Tessa Richardson
Mary Ogden
Millicent Knight
Winifred Osborne
Dorothy Gerard
Dorothy Purvis
Annie Pimblott
Dorothy Smithard
Dorothy d'Orsay
Doris Cowen
Cathcart Lynn
Betsy de la Porte
Dorothy Reid
Rachel Hunt
Margaret Bissett
Linda Seymour
Anne Liddell
Elsie Boardman
Vera Wright
Annie Hughes
Annie Broadhurst
Gladys Ripley
Elsie Black

Tenors (76)

Ben Davies
Arthur Jordan
Walter Widdop
Parry Jones
Joseph Hislop
William Boland
John Adams
Percy Manchester
Hughes Macklin
William Heseltine
Tom Burke
Roland Jackson
Furness Williams
Robert Naylor
Norman Stone
Ivor Walters
Charles Hedges
David Hutchinson
John Armstrong
Bruce Flegg
Webster Booth
Eric Green
Osmond Davis
Glyn Hopkin
Edgar Williams
Frank Mullings
Hubert Eisdell
Tudor Davies
Roland Hayes
Alfred Piccaver
Frank Titterton
Walter Glynne
Heddle Nash
Sydney Coltham
Barrington Hooper
Maurice d'Oisly
Gwynne Davies
Herbert Thorpe
John Collett
Ernest Hargreaves
Bell Walker
Herbert Teale
Ali Khan
Henry Wendon
Arthur Cox
Percy Bilsbury
Helmar Fernback
George Turner
Frederick Steger
Bertram Davis
Walter Hyde
John Coates
Steuart Wilson
Leo Slezak
Morgan Kingston
John Booth
Leonard Gowings
Francis Russell
Trefor Jones
Archibald Winter
Lenghi-Cellini
Ben Williams
John Turner
David Ellis
Tom Pickering
Kennedy McKenna
Murray Stewart
Vittorio Orsini
Seymour Dossor
John Collinson
Joseph Green
Dennis Butterworth
Horace Vincent
Sydney Northcote

Baritones and basses (96)

Robert Radford
Roy Henderson
George Baker
John Goss
Reinhold von Warlich
Reinhold Gerhardt
Arthur Cranmer
Stuart Robertson
Robert Easton
Leslie Holmes
John Thorne
Horace Stevens
Norman Allin
Dennis Noble
Harold Dahlquist
Charles Panzera
Peter Dawson
Mostyn Thomas
Dale Smith
Topliss Green
Watcyn Watcyns
Harry Brindle
Harold Williams
Herbert Heyner
Plunket Greene
Augustus Milner
Keith Falkner
Percy Heming
Arthur Fear
Joseph Farrington
Howard Fry
Lee Thistlethwaite
Frederick Taylor

Hamilton Harris
William Anderson
Leyland White
Gilbert Bailey
Rex Palmer
Flintoff Moore
Powell Edwards
David Brazell
John Brownlee
Mark Raphael
Harry Dearth
W.R. Allen
Sumner Austin
Herbert Brown
John Buckley
Booth Unwin
Richard Watson
Tom Kinniburgh
Arthur Evans
Sydney Shepherd
Ivan Mellodew
Foster Richardson
Frank Phillips
Raymond Ellis
Norman Notley
Booth Hitchen
William Michael
Franklyn Kelsey
Frederick Woodhouse
Robert Parker
Eric Marshall
Thorpe Bates
Brabazon Lowther
Robert Burnett
Bertram Ayrton
Bruce Anderson
Herbert Simmonds
Reginald Whitehead
Arthur Broadbent
William Evans
Stanley Beckett
Stanley Pope
Norman Williams
Owen Bryngwyn
Clive Carey
Kenneth Ellis
David Evans
Edward Dykes
Percy Underwood
Armand Crabbé
Robert Maitland
Andrew Shanks
George Parker
Malcolm Davidson
Anlon Young
Charles Knowles
Glyn Eastman
Leonard Salisbury
Charles Harrison
Richard Ford
Paul Mortimer
J. Challoner Heaton
Robert Algar

Pianists (111)

Myra Hess
Wanda Landowska
Guiomar Novaes
Elly Ney
Johanne Stockmarr
Gertrude Peppercorn
Betty Humby
Dorothy Hesse
Yanesse d'Alexandrowska
Juliette Wihl
Dai Buell
Belinda Heather
Hetty Bolton
Irene Scharrer
Fanny Davies
Youra Guller
Marcelle Meyer
Lubka Kolessa
Effie Kalisz
Lucie Caffaret
Marguerite Morgan
Vera Moore
Esther Fisher
Una Bourne
Pia Damerini
Jessie Bristol
Katharine Goodson
Harriet Cohen
Yolando Mero
Marie Antoinette Aussenac
Elsa Karen
Isabel Gray
Irene de Marik
Denise Lassimonne
Ethel Bartlett
Ruth Gourlay
Desiree MacEwan
Kathleen Frise-Smith
Hilda Bor

Rachmaninoff
Josef Hofmann
Godowsky
Dohnányi
Egon Petri
Moriz Rosenthal
Walter Gieseking
Robert Casadesus
Chavchavadze
Josef Lhevinne
Donald Francis Tovey
Moseiwitsch
Cortot
Harold Samuel
Medtner
William Murdoch
Mark Hambourg
Sapellnikoff
Franciszek Goldenberg
Ignaz Friedmann
Horowitz
Solomon
Artur Schnabel
Lamond
Harold Bauer
Orloff
Backhaus
Arthur Rubinstein
Edwin Fischer
Pouishnoff
Jan Smeterlin
José Iturbi
Brailowsky

Meecio Horszowsky
Walter Rummel
Friederich Wührer
John Powell
Maurice Cole
York Bowen
Edward Isaacs
Leslie England
Ivan Phillipowsky
Vivian Langrish
Sidney Harrison
Claud Biggs
Harold Rutland
Alexandre Borovsky
Paul Weingarten
Rudolf Serkin
Beveridge Webster
v. Ernst Wolff
Harold Craxton
Rae Robertson
Arthur Benjamin
Edward Mitchell
Angus Morrison
Harry Isaacs
Thomas Marshall
Daniel Ericourt
Howard-Jones
Arthur de Greef
Yves Nat
Stephan Bergmann
Marcel Ciampi
Herbert Fryer
Ernest Hutcheson
Adolphe Hallis
Francesco Ticciati
Frank Merrick
Reginald Paul
Charles Kelly
Geoffrey Tancred

Violinists (61)
Jelly d'Aranyi
May Harrison
Cecilia Hansen
Sybil Eaton
Murray Lambert
Eileen Andjelkovitch
Bessie Rawlins
Rhoda Backhouse
Seymour Whinyates
Marie Wilson
Isolde Menges
Renée Chemet
Daisy Kennedy
Marjorie Hayward
Eda Kersey
Maude Gold
Margaret Harrison
Winifred Small
Jean Robley
Phyllis Allan
Alma Moodie
Adila Fachiri
Marie Hall
Leila Doubleday
Orrea Pernel
Sonia Moldawsky
Ruth Kemper
Elsie Playfair
Mercia Stotesbury
Florence Lockwood

Jacques Thibaud
Arthur Catterall
Emil Telmanyi
Paul Kochanski
Bratza
Antonio Brosa
Loris Blofield
Samuel Kutcher
Laurance Turner
Alfred Barker
Paul Belinfante
Joseph Szigeti
Mischa Elman
Albert Spalding
Zino Francescatti
Melsa
Zacharewitsch
Solloway
John Dunn
Harold Fairhurst
Robert Silvester
Albert Sammons
Adolf Busch
Georges Enesco
Samuel Dushkin
William Primrose
Balokovic
Cyril Towbin
Louis Pecskai
Louis Godowsky
Sidney Bowman

Viola (1)
Lionel Tertis

Cellists (47)
Guilhermina Suggia
May Mukle
Kathleen Moorhouse
Valentine Orde
Marie Dare
Vyvyan Lewis
Beatrice Harrison
Judith Bokor
Joan Willis
Hildegarde Arnold
Rita Sharpe
Ruth Tvermoes
Raya Garbousova
Juliette Alvin
Adelina Leon
Beatrice Evelin
Alison Dalrymple
Margaret Sampson

Casals
Arturo Bonucci
Gerard Hekking
Herman Sandby
Ivor James
Carl Fuchs
Emile Doehaerd
Sheridan Russell
Charles Hambourg
Howard Bliss
Gaspar Cassadó
W.H. Squire
Maurice Dambois
Maurice Marechal
Maurice Eisenberg
Cedric Sharpe
Luigi Gasparini
Herbert Withers
John Snowden
Bohus Heran
Antoni Sala
Enrico Mainardi
Paul Hermann
Arnold Trowell
Lauri Kennedy
Jacques Serres
Livio Manucci
John Gabalfa
Walter Hatton

Recitals of music for two pianofortes
Irene Scharrer and Myra Hess
Ethel Bartlett and Rae Robertson
Myra Hess and Harold Samuel

Pianoforte and violin recitals
Myra Hess and Jelly d'Aranyi
William Murdoch and Albert Sammons
Rudolf Serkin and Adolf Busch

The Chamber Music Players
William Murdoch, Albert Sammons, Lionel Tertis, Cedric Sharpe

Guitar
Andrès Segovia

The Aguilar Lute Quartet

String quartets (28)
Rosé
Bohemian
Busch
Brosa
International
Hewitt
Dutch
Birmingham
Marie Wilson
Yorkshire
Lener
Hungarian
London
Catterall
Guarneri
Entente
Hirsch
Backhouse
Altra
Budapest
Pro Arte
Virtuoso
Roth
Venetian
Zimmer
Spencer Dyke
Robinson
Stratton

Piano quartets (4)
English Ensemble (Piano Quartet)
Kinsey Piano Quartet
English Piano Quartet
Philharmonic Piano Quartet

Trios (8)
Chamber Music Trio
Pirani Trio
Beatrice Hewitt Trio
Budapest Trio
Modern Trio
Philharmonic Trio (Flute/Oboe/Piano)
English Trio
Dorian Trio

The London Wind Quintet
The Aeolian Players
The Harp Ensemble
Arnold Dolmetsch and Family
London Chamber Orchestra (Anthony Bernard, Conductor)
London String Players (Herbert Menges, Conductor)
Modern Chamber Orchestra (Stanley Chapple, Conductor)

Harpsichord (4)
Wanda Landowska
Violet Gordon Woodhouse
Arnold Dolmetsch
Gerald Cooper

Harp (6)
Mildred Dilling
Gwendolen Mason
Marie Korchinska
Jeanne Chevreau
Marie Goossens
Sidonie Goossens

Flute (6)
René Le Roy
John Amadio
Robert Murchie
Joseph Slater
Joseph Ridgway
Edith Penville

Oboe (1)
Léon Goossens

The Famous French Organists
Marcel Dupré and Joseph Bonnet

The English Singers
The Elizabethan Singers
John Goss and The Cathedral Male Voice Quartet
London Select Choir (Arnold Fulton, Conductor)
The Chelsea Singers
The Tudor Singers (13 voices) (Cuthbert Bates, Conductor)
The Oriana Singers (Kennedy Scott, Conductor)
The Wireless Singers (Stanford Robinson, Conductor)
The London Male Voice Octet

Vocal quartets (8)
Kedroff Quartet
Gresham Singers
Temple Quartet
Eton Singers
Westminster Singers
Windsor Castle Royal Harmonists
Chilworth Singers
Concord Singers

Paul Robeson
Beatrice Beaufort and Janet Christopher
Jean Sterling Mackinlay
Ita Cope and Jean Duncan

The Kennedy Fraser Combination (Hebridean folksongs with piano and harp accompaniment)
The Old Time Singers (Margaret Stephen, Leslie Holmes, Gilbert Bailey)
Os-Ke-Non-Ton (Recital of American-Indian songs)

Entertainers at the piano (20)

Ernest Hastings
Selwyn Driver
Finlay Dunn
Cecil Harrington
Clara Evelyn
Dorothy Varick
Phyllis Bateman
Norman Long
Morland Hay
Nelson Jackson
Dick Henty
Norah Blaney
Alma Goatley
Helen Alston
T. Sterndale Bennett
Vernon Lee
Joe Pearson
Thomas Sidney
Ivy St Helier
Hilda Bertram

Entertainers (32)

Will Kings
Wilby Lunn
Charles Hayes
Bret Hayden
Barclay Powell
John Henry
Foster Kershaw
A.C. Astor
Douglas Dexter
Tommy Handley
Thornley Dodge
Emil Clare
Foden Williams
Harry Hemsley
Will Gardner
Vivian Foster
Middleton Woods
Herbert Collings
Ernest Sewell
Wallace Cunningham
Fred Gibson
Jock Walker
Kit Keen
George Ellis
Rex Harold
Rupert Howard
Cyril Shields
Bransby Williams

Mona Grey
Edith Faulkner
Ann Penn
Mabel Constanduros

Ruth Draper
Flotsam and Jetsam
The Maestros Quintet

Grace Ivell and Vivian Worth
Clapham and Dwyer
Robert Pitt and Langton Marks
Dorothy Hogben and Arthur Jay

Muriel George and Ernest Butcher

Reciters (8)

Esmé Beringer
Agnes Bartholomew
Cyril Lidington
Katrina Lund
Harcourt Williams
Adrian Harley
Clara Hubbard
Utt Ridge

Ibbs and Tillett: Artists' Brochures 1934–35, Chamber Music 1935–36, Artists' Brochures 1938–39

1934–35

Sole representatives for

Elisabeth Schumann
Elsie Suddaby
Dora Labbette
Mary Hamlin
Florence Easton
Greta Stückgold
Thea Philips
Maggie Teyte
Isobel Baillie
Dorothy Silk

Muriel Brunskill
Mary Jarred
Margaret Balfour
Olga Haley

Roland Hayes
Hubert Eisdell
Heddle Nash
Steuart Wilson
Walter Widdop
Arthur Jordan

Norman Allin
Alexander Kipnis
Roy Henderson
Heinrich Schlusnus
Keith Falkner
Henry Gill
Harold Williams
Herbert Janssen

The New English Singers

Busch, Budapest, Griller, Kolisch, London, Menges, Prague, Pro Arte, Roth, and Stradivarius String Quartets

The Chamber Music Players

Le Quintette Instrumental de Paris

Rachmaninoff
Myra Hess
Moriz Rosenthal
Rudolf Serkin
Moiseiwitsch
Howard-Jones
Smeterlin
Cyril Smith
Schnabel
Josef Hofmann
Irene Scharrer
Dohnányi
William Murdoch
Edwin Fischer
John Hunt
Cortot
Harold Samuel
Lamond
Alexander Borovsky
Orloff
Harriet Cohen
Egon Petri

Ethel Bartlett and Rae Robertson

Adolf Busch
Adila Fachiri
Milstein
Alma Moodie
Jelly d'Aranyi
Zimbalist
Isolde Menges
Szigeti
Renée Chemet
Lionel Tertis

Casals
Beatrice Harrison
Antoni Sala
Suggia
Arturo Bonucci
Maurice Eisenberg
Gaspar Cassadó
Emanuel Feuermann

Goldberg-Hindemith-Feuermann Trio
Andrès Segovia (Guitar)
Casella-Poltronieri-Bonucci (The Italian Trio)
The Nelson Trio
The London String Players

Sopranos (61)

Elisabeth Schumann
Lotte Lehmann
Florence Easton
Povla Frijsh
Dora Labbette
Oda Slobodskaya
Noël Eadie
Tatiana Makushina
Alexandra Trianti
Stiles-Allen
Elena Danieli
Garda Hall
May Blyth
Joan Coxon
Mabel Ritchie
Dorothy Stanton
Gertrude Johnson
Flora Mann
Dorothy Bennett
Mary Worth
Frances Morris
Eva Turner
Maggie Teyte
Göta Ljungberg
Miriam Licette
Jo Vincent
Isobel Baillie
Adelheid Armhold
Mary Hamlin
Evelyn Scotney
Megan Foster
Ina Souez
Sarah Fischer
Marjorie Parry
Nora Gruhn
Megan Thomas
Mavis Bennett
Hilda Blake
Olive Groves
Dorothy Tillett
Eveline Stevenson
Florence Austral
Greta Stückgold
Dorothy Silk
Soffi Schonning
Elsie Suddaby
Laelia Finneberg
Thea Philips
Ria Ginster
Odette de Foras
Flora Woodman
Sybil Crawley
Joan Cross
Doris Vane
Kate Winter
Joan Elwes
Alice Moxon
Gladys Cole
Monica Warner
Hilda Searle
Muriel Wilson

Contraltos (54)

Elena Gerhardt
Olga Haley
Conchita Supervia
Mary Jarred
Leila Megane
Emmy Heim
Isobel Lamond
Gladys Ripley
Joan Muirella
Rispah Goodacre
Ethel Barker
Muriel Brunskill
Sigrid Onegin
Astra Desmond
Hedda Kux
Gabriele Joachim
Dorothy Helmrich
Betty Bannerman
Edith Furmedge
Lillian Berger
Catherine Stewart
Anne Wood
Marie Olczewska
Margaret Balfour
Claire Croiza
Clara Serena
Enid Cruickshank
Constance Willis
Flora Collins
Vera de Villiers
Gladys Parr
Dorothy Clark
Gladys Palmer

Blodwen Caerleon
Linda Seymour
Ethel Davies
Betsy de la Porte
Freda Townson
Maud Nelson
Joyce Newton
Tessa Richardson
Stella Murray
Isobel McLaren
Gladys Knight
Jessie King
Muriel Gale
Margaret McArthur
Esther Coleman
Essie Ackland
Doris Cowen
Gwladys Garside
Constance Stocker
Edith Bartlett
Anne Liddell

Tenors (52)

Roland Hayes
Walter Widdop
Tudor Davies
Hubert Eisdell
Joseph Hislop
Parry Jones
Robert Naylor
Percy Manchester
Arthur Cox
Edward Reach
Leonard Gowings
Archibald Winter
Norman Stone
Tom Pickering
Sydney Northcote
Bell Walker
James Topping
Joseph Congdon
Ben Davies
Steuart Wilson
Francis Russell
Arthur Jordan
Frank Mullings
Browning Mummery
Trefor Jones
Henry Wendon
Bruce Flegg
Walter Glynne
Barrington Hooper
John Armstrong
Frank Webster
Ernest Hargreaves
George Armitage
Alec John
Norman Crabtree
Rosing
Heddle Nash
Frank Titterton
John Coates
Yves Tinayre
Hughes Macklin
Ben Williams
Lenghi-Cellini
Eric Greene
Jan van der Gucht
William Heseltine
Ronald Murgatroyd
Horace Vincent
Andrew Clayton
Frederick Steger
Helmar Fernback
Webster Gibson

Baritones and basses (57)

Norman Allin
Harold Williams
Heinrich Schlusnus
Horace Stevens
Henry Gill
Percy Heming
Thorpe Bates
Herbert Heyner
Joseph Farrington
Howard Fry
Clive Carey
Watcyn Watcyns
Kenneth Ellis
Gilbert Bailey
Philip Bertram
Owen Bryngwyn
Tom Kinniburgh
Ellis Keeler
Henry Cummings
Peter Dawson
Herbert Janssen
Roy Henderson
William Parsons
Charles Panzera
Dennis Noble
Arthur Cranmer
John Morel
Frank Phillips
Laurence Holmes
George Baker
Lee Thistlethwaite
Charles Mayhew
Sumner Austin
Stanley Pope
Bertram Ayrton
Gabriel Lavelle
Victor Harding
Victor Evans
Alexander Kipnis
Keith Falkner
Stuart Robertson
Arthur Fear
Jorgen Bendix
Eric Marshall
Robert Easton
Dale Smith
Samuel Worthington
Topliss Green
Harry Brindle
Foster Richardson
Norman Williams
Norman Notley
William Michael
Leyland White
Arthur Broadbent
Walter Delmar
Booth Unwin

Pianists (72)

Rachmaninoff
Schnabel
Moiseiwitsch
Egon Petri
Dohnányi
Edwin Fischer
Gieseking
Robert Casadesus
Horszowski
Pouishnoff
Arthur de Greef
Ruda Firkusny
Beveridge Webster
Stefan Askenase
Leslie England
Angus Morrison
Kendall Taylor
Israel Hoffman

Backhaus
Josef Hofmann
Harold Samuel
Orloff
Rudolf Serkin
Horowitz
Harold Bauer
Donald Francis Tovey
Solomon
Prokofieff
William Murdoch
Howard-Jones
Cyril Smith
Karl Ulrich Schnabel
Francesco Ticciati
Reginald Paul
Anderson Tyrer

Cortot
Moriz Rosenthal
Lamond
Alexander Borovsky
Smeterlin
Arthur Rubinstein
Alfred Casella
Iturbi
Brailowsky
Medtner
Henri Deering
Chavchavadze
John Hunt
Maurice Cole
Frank Laffitte
Harry Isaacs
Eric Brough

Irene Scharrer
Elly Ney
Lili Kraus
Yvonne Lefébure
Vera Moore
Dorothy Hesse

Myra Hess
Katharine Goodson
Ania Dorfmann
Isabel Gray
Eileen Joyce
Hilda Bor

Harriet Cohen
Kathleen Long
Lubka Kolessa
Esther Fisher
Denise Lassimonne

Violinists (54)

Adolf Busch
Szigeti
Arthur Catterall
Georges Enesco
Juan Manen
Bratza
Emil Telmanyi
Samuel Kutcher
Harold Fairhurst
Alfred Barker

Huberman
Zimbalist
Mischa Elman
Albert Sammons
Georg Kulenkampff
Melsa
Robert Soëtens
Boris Schwarz
Anatole Melzak
Laurance Turner

Thibaud
Milstein
Carl Flesch
Samuel Dushkin
Henry Holst
Henri Temianka
Antonio Brosa
Jean Pougnet
Louis Godowsky
Maurice Clare

Jelly d'Aranyi
Adila Fachiri
Erna Rubinstein
May Harrison
Viola Mitchell
Marjorie Hayward
Seymour Whinyates
Violet Pusey

Renée Chemet
Alma Moore
Marie Hall
Orrea Pernel
Sybil Eaton
Winifred Small
Murray Lambert
Editha Braham

Isolde Menges
Erica Morini
Daisy Kennedy
Eda Kersey
Sonia Moldawsky
Maude Gold
Rhoda Backhouse
Esmé Haynes

Jelly d'Aranyi and Adila Fachiri in works for two violins
Goldberg-Hindemith-Feuermann Trio (violin-viola-violoncello)

Viola (3)
Lionel Tertis
Bernard Shore
William Primrose

Violoncellists (36)
Casals
Piatigorsky
Cassadó
Arturo Bonucci
Antonio Sala
Maurice Eisenberg
W.H. Squire
Maurice Maréchal
Arnold Trowell
Ivor James
Sheridan Russell
Lauri Kennedy
Carl Fuchs
Cedric Sharpe
Luigi Gasparini
Livio Manucci
John Gabalfa
John Snowden
Anthony Pini

Suggia
Beatrice Harrison
Antonia Butler
Thelma Reiss
Raya Garbousova
May Mukle
Judith Bokor
Juliette Alvin
Sara Nelson
Rita Sharpe
Peers Coetmore
Yvonne Morris
Joan Bonner
Audrey Pigott
Helen Just
Florence Hooton

Casella-Poltronieri-Bonucci (The Italian Trio)
Harold Samuel, Isolde Menges and Ivor James

Andrès Segovia – Guitar

Recitals of music for two pianofortes
Ethel Bartlett and Rae Robertson
Isabel Gray and Claude Pollard
Vitya Vronsky and Victor Babin
Mary and Geraldine Peppin
Esther Fisher and Cyril Scott
Hilda Bor and Eric Brough

Pianoforte and violin recitals
Myra Hess and Jelly d'Aranyi
Rudolf Serkin and Adolf Busch
Harold Samuel and Isolde Menges
William Murdoch and Arthur Catterall
Kathleen Long and Adila Fachiri

Violin and viola recitals
Albert Sammons and Lionel Tertis

String quartets (30)
Busch String Quartet
Pro Arte String Quartet
London String Quartet
Lener String Quartet
Kolisch String Quartet
Budapest String Quartet
Stradivarius String Quartet
Roth String Quartet
Hungarian String Quartet
Poltronieri String Quartet
Prague String Quartet
Weiss String Quartet
Isolde Menges String Quartet
Brosa String Quartet
Kutcher String Quartet
Griller String Quartet
Brussels String Quartet
Amar String Quartet

Rothschild String Quartet
Virtuoso String Quartet
British String Quartet
Whinyates String Quartet
Hart House String Quartet
Spencer Dyke String Quartet
English String Quartet
Beredin String Quartet
International String Quartet
Stratton String Quartet
Hirsch String Quartet
Deira String Quartet

The Chamber Music Players
William Murdoch, Arthur Catterall, Laurance Turner, Bernard Shore, Cedric Sharpe

The English Ensemble (piano quartet)

Pianoforte trios etc. (8)
The Italian Trio
The Pirani Trio
The Nelson Trio
The Elly Ney Trio
The Trio Players
The Amati Trio
The Grinke Trio
The New London Trio

The Philharmonic Trio (flute-oboe-piano)
The English Wind Players
The New Aeolian Players
The Harp Ensemble
Arnold Dolmetsch and His Family
Le Quintette Instrumental de Paris
The London Chamber Orchestra (Anthony Bernard, Conductor)
The London String Players (Herbert Menges, Conductor)
The Barbirolli Chamber Orchestra (John Barbirolli, Conductor)
The Boyd Neel String Orchestra (Boyd Neel, Conductor)
The Birmingham Phiharmonic String Orchestra (Johan C. Hock, Conductor)

Harpsichord (4)
Wanda Landowska
Alice Ehlers
Violet Gordon Woodhouse
Rudolph Dolmetsch

Harp (5)
Gwendolen Mason
Marie Goossens
Marie Korchinska
Sidonie Goossens
Jeanne Chevreau

Flute (5)
René Le Roy
Joseph Slater
John Amadio
Edith Penville
Robert Murchie

Oboe (1)
Léon Goossens

Saxophone (1)
Sigurd Rascher

Marcel Dupré and Joseph Bonnet (The Famous French Organists)

The New English Singers
The St George's Singers
The English Singers Quartet
The Elizabethan Singers
The Chelsea Singers
The Round Table Singers
The Tudor Singers (12 voices) (Cuthbert Bates, Conductor)

The Oriana Singers (Kennedy Scott, Conductor)
The London Madrigal Group (T.B. Lawrence, Conductor)
The London Select Choir (Arnold Fulton, Conductor)
The Chanticleer Opera Company in *Così fan tutte* and *Hansel and Gretel*
The London Male Voice Octet

Vocal quartets
Gresham Singers
Concord Singers
Windsor Castle Royal Harmonists
Westminster Singers
Chilworth Singers
Temple Quartet
Salisbury Singers

Yvette Guilbert
Beatrice Beaufort and Janet Christopher
Engel Lund
Roy Henderson's Lecture Recitals
Jean Sterling Mackinlay
The Old Time Singers
Basil Maine

Entertainers at the piano (8)
Selwyn Driver
Norman Long
Nelson Jackson
Ernest Hastings
T. Sterndale Bennett
Cecil Harrington
Ronald Gourley
Finlay Dunn

Sterndale Bennett and Fred Gregory
Cecil Harrington and Noreena Feist
Phyllis Pearson and Lawson Reece

Entertainers (24)
Will Kings
Vivian Foster
Charles Hayes
Herbert Collings
Naunton Wayne
Ernest Sewell
Fred Priddoe
Giovanni
Will Gardner
Wallace Cunningham
Ronald Frankau
Leslie Sarony
Douglas Dexter
Bret Hayden
Cardini
Richard Harbin
Leonard Henry
Arthur Askey
Stainless Stephen
Cyril Shields
Harry Hemsley
Lionel King
Middleton Woods
Fred Gwyn

Ruth Draper
Flotsam & Jetsam
The Western Brothers
Muriel George and Ernest Butcher
Ann Penn
Gillie Potter
Clapham & Dwyer
Mabel Constanduros and Michael Hogan
Layton & Johnstone
Bransby Williams
Albert Whelan and Billy Bennett
Elsie and Doris Waters

Chamber Music 1935–36

[No title or date but calendar for 1935–36 at the rear flyleaf.]
Statement on first page reads: 'In issuing this Brochure Messrs. Ibbs and Tillett hope that the contents will be of interest and service to Concert Societies and Music Clubs'.

[Personnel of all groups are listed, some groups are followed by one or two press comments.]

String quartets

Busch String Quartet	Stradivarius String Quartet	Virtuoso String Quartet
Pro Arte String Quartet	Hart House String Quartet	Spencer Dyke String Quartet
Lener String Quartet	Weiss String Quartet	Stratton String Quartet
Budapest String Quartet	Rothschild String Quartet	Whinyates String Quartet
Roth String Quartet	Calvet String Quartet	British String Quartet
Poltronieri String Quartet	Pro Musica String Quartet	Hungarian String Quartet
English String Quartet	Prague String Quartet	Hirsch String Quartet
Brussels String Quartet	Isolde Menges String Quartet	Zagreb String Quartet
Griller String Quartet	Kolisch String Quartet	Catterall String Quartet
Brosa String Quartet	International String Quartet	Kutcher String Quartet

Unnamed trios

Myra Hess/Jelly d'Aranyi/Gaspar Cassadó	Harold Samuel/Isolde Menges/Ivor James	Pougnet/Morrison/Pini

Named trios

The Busch Serkin Trio	The Italian Trio	The Pasquier Trio

Piano trios

The Budapest Trio	The Trio Players	The New London Trio
The Elly Ney Trio	The Dorian Trio	The Pirani Trio
The Belgian Trio	The Grinke Trio	The Nelson Trio

The Chamber Music Players	The English Ensemble	Arnold Dolmetsch and Family
Le Quintette Instrumental de Paris	The Harp Ensemble	The Philharmonic Trio
The English Wind Players	Harry Isaacs and The Griller String Quartet	The New Aeolian Players
		The Sylvan Trio

Chamber Orchestra (14 players), conductor: Hamilton Harty
The London String Players, conductor: Herbert Menges
The Boyd Neel String Orchestra, conductor: Boyd Neel
The Birmingham Philharmonic String Orchestra, conductor: Johan C. Hock

René Le Roy (flute) Joseph Slater (flute) Léon Goossens (oboe) Sigurd Rascher (saxophone)

Piano and violin recitals

Myra Hess/Jelly d'Aranyi	Rudolf Serkin/Adolf Busch	Harold Samuel/Isolde Menges
Alma Moodie/Eduard Erdmann	William Murdoch/Albert Sammons	Frank Mannheimer/Antonio Brosa
Kathleen Long/Adila Fachiri		

Duos

Jelly d'Aranyi/Adila Fachiri
Albert Sammons/Lionel Tertis
William Murdoch/William Primrose
Solomon/Lionel Tertis
Harriet Cohen/Thelma Reiss
The Griller String Quartet and Harry Isaacs (piano)

Duo pianists

Ethel Bartlett/Rae Robertson
Hilda Bor/Eric Brough
Vitya Vronsky/Victor Babin
Mary and Geraldine Peppin
Isabel Gray/Claude Pollard

Andrès Segovia – A genius on the guitar
Harold Samuel – Lecture recitals on Bach
Roy Henderson – Lecture recitals
Basil Maine – Lectures on the life and works of Sir Edward Elgar
Composer Pianists: Prokofieff, Szymanowsky, Béla Bartók

Pianists

Rachmaninoff
Moriz Rosenthal
Josef Hofmann
Orloff
Arthur Rubinstein
Egon Petri
Horszowski
Cortot
Moiseiwitsch
Lamond
Harold Bauer
Gieseking
Rudolf Serkin
Karl Ulrich Schnabel
Schnabel
Backhaus
Edwin Fischer
Dohnányi
Smeterlin
Alexander Borovsky

Myra Hess
Solomon
Pouishnoff
Howard-Jones
John Hunt
Eileen Joyce
Kendall Taylor
Harold Samuel
Irene Scharrer
Harriet Cohen
Kathleen Long
Cyril Smith
Frank Mannheimer
Israel Hoffman
Donald Francis Tovey
Katharine Goodson
William Murdoch
Clifford Curzon
Isabel Gray
Kurt Applebaum

Violinists

Hubermann
Szigeti
Jelly d'Aranyi
Isolde Menges
Georg Kulenkampff
Antonio Brosa
Murray Lambert
Mischa Elman
Carl Flesch
Adila Fachiri
Alma Moodie
Roman Totenberg
Orrea Pernel
Beatrix Marr
Adolf Busch
Georges Enesco
Renée Chemet
Albert Sammons
Arthur Catterall
Eda Kersey

Violists

Lionel Tertis
Paul Hindemith
William Primrose

Cellists

Pablo Casals	Suggia	Gaspar Cassadó
Emanuel Feuermann	Antoni Sala	Arturo Bonucci
Maurice Eisenberg	Hermann Busch	Ivor James
Raya Garbousova	Beatrice Harrison	Antonia Butler
Thelma Reiss	Florence Hooton	

Alice Ehlers: Harpsichord Recitals (Bach/Handel/Scarlatti 250th anniversary and J.C. Bach 200th)

The New English Singers	The English Singers Quartet	The Tudor Singers
The Oriana Singers	The London Madrigal Group	The Round Table Singers
The St George's Singers	The Chelsea Singers	The Old Time Singers
'Intimate Opera'		

Lieder recitals

Elisabeth Schumann	Claire Croiza	Olga Haley
Muriel Brunskill	Mary Jarred	Alexander Kipnis
Keith Falkner	Hermann Schey	

Engel Lund – Folksongs of many lands
Liesbet Sanders – International folksongs
Naima Wifstrand – The Swedish actress in her character songs

Songs and duets

Nellie Carson/Cuthbert Kelly   Norman Notley/David Brynley

1938–39

Sole representatives for

Elisabeth Schumann
Thea Philips
Nan Maryska
Elsie Suddaby
Amy Evans
Isobel Baillie
Laelia Finneberg

Elena Gerhardt
Muriel Brunskill
Margaret Balfour
Mary Jarred
Olga Haley

Roland Hayes
Eric Greene
Edward Reach
Heddle Nash
Arthur Carron
Steuart Wilson
Jan van der Gucht

Alexander Kipnis
William Parsons
Harold Williams
Norman Allin
Ronald Stear
Roy Henderson
Keith Falkner
Henry Gill
Redvers Llewellyn

Rachmaninoff
Lamond
Moiseiwitsch
Smeterlin
Louis Kentner
Myra Hess
Lili Kraus
Helen Perkin
John Hunt
Karl Ulrich Schnabel
Cortot
Schnabel
Friedrich Wührer
Rudolf Serkin
Brailowsky
Irene Scharrer
Eileen Joyce
William Murdoch
Cyril Smith
Chavchavadze
Egon Petri
Dohnányi
Edwin Fischer
Orloff
Horszowski
Harriet Cohen
Ray Lev
Clifford Curzon
Frank Mannheimer

Ethel Bartlett and Rae Robertson
Lucille Wallace

Adolf Busch
Szigeti
Milstein
Alma Moodie
Jelly d'Aranyi
Renée Chemet
Telmanyi
Isolde Menges
Adila Fachiri
Temianka

Casals
Emanuel Feuermann
The Italian Trio
Gaspar Cassadó
Antoni Sala
The Pasquier Trio
Suggia
Thelma Reiss
Segovia

Sopranos (74)

Elisabeth Schumann
Florence Austral
Miriam Licette
Isobel Baillie
Eva Turner
Audrey Mildmay
Megan Foster
Lotte Lehmann
Noel Eadie
Elsie Suddaby
Ninon Vallin
Lisa Perli
Laelia Finneberg
Elena Danieli
Maggie Teyte
Dorothy Silk
Tatiana Makushina
Jo Vincent
Joan Cross
Ina Souez
Thea Philips

Amy Evans
Anna El Tour
Dorothy Moulton
May Blyth
Maria Morova
Janet Hamilton-Smith
Mabel Ritchie
Margaret Elwes
Megan Thomas
Monica Warner
Margaret Field-Hyde
Léonie Zifado
Marguerite Natalia
Mae Craven
Doris Wells
Marjorie Gordon
Vera Burton
Ria Ginster
Soffi Schonning
Nan Maryska
Stiles-Allen
Luella Paikin
Joan Coxon
Cecilia Wessels
Jeanne Dusseau
Alice Moxon
Renée Flynn
Dorothy Bennett
Hilda Searle
Lettice Walsh
Nellie Carson
Ceinwen Rowlands
May Bartlett
Margaret Brown
Irene Holt
Anne Ziegler
Olive Groves
Oda Slobodskaya
Garda Hall
Ruth Naylor
Kate Winter
Nora Gruhn
Dorothy Stanton
Mavis Bennett
Mary Hamlin
Winifred Radford
Mary Worth
Frances Morris
Catherine Wendol
Meta Murray
Millicent Ward
Mary McDougall
Myra O'Neill

Contraltos (68)

Elena Gerhardt
Margaret Balfour
Mary Jarred
Catherine Stewart
Enid Cruikshank
Vera de Villiers
Essie Ackland
Flora Neilsen
Dorothy Humphreys
Diane van Dommelen
Anne Wood
Muriel Gale
Doris Cowen
Gwladys Garside
Margaret Tann-Williams
Esmé Webb
Grace Batchelor
Joyce Sutton
Anne Broadhurst
Mary Morris
Etta Harry
Kathleen Willson
Sylvia Brendt
Muriel Brunskill
Clara Serena
Claire Croiza
Dorothy Helmrich
Edith Coates
Constance Willis
Edith Furmedge
Rispah Goodacre
Dorothy Clark
Maud Heaton
Gladys Palmer
Ethel Davies
Jessie King
Gladys Knight
Linda Seymour
Winifred Osborne
Joyce Newton
Norah Scott-Turner
Winifred White
Emylon Biedenharn
Jean Laird Bruce
Janet Howe
Katharine Miller Jones
Olga Haley
Astra Desmond
Gladys Ripley
Betty Bannerman
Else Rykens
Herta Glückmann
Gladys Parr
Freda Townson
Miette Muthesius
Jenny Sonnenberg
Grace Bodey
Ethel Barker
Dorothy d'Orsay
Marjorie Ffrangcon-Davies
Tessa Richardson
Mary Davies
Eileen Pilcher
Constance Stocker
Mary Bruce
Anne Liddell
Molly Mitchell
Mary McNally

Tenors (64)

Heddle Nash
Pierre Bernac
Eric Greene
Roland Hayes
Steuart Wilson
Frank Titterton
Walter Widdop
Arthur Carron
Jan van der Gucht

Tudor Davies
Edward Reach
Frank Mullings
Robert Naylor
Ben Williams
Bruce Flegg
David Lloyd
Franks Sale
Ronald Murgatroyd
Norman Stone
George Armitage
Geoffrey Dunn
Hubert Carta
Joseph Congdon
Ian Glennie
William Booth
Frederick Steger
Peter Pears
Ailwyn Best
Trefor Jones
Henry Wendon
Arthur Jordan
Derek Oldham
Percy Manchester
Eric Starling
Alec John
Leonard Gowings
Spencer Thomas
Andrew Clayton
David Brynley
Howard Hemming
James Topping
John Wright
Charles Hedges
Helmar Fernback
John Lewis
Edward Ransome
Francis Russell
Joseph Hislop
Parry Jones
Webster Booth
John McKenna
John Fullard
Walter Glynne
John Armstrong
Hindley Taylor
Sydney Northcote
Ernest Hargreaves
Richard Kyle
Alfred O'Shea
John Dudley
Martin Boddy
Mervyn Saunders
Colin Cunningham
Robert Wilson

Baritones and basses (76)
Norman Allin
Herbert Janssen
Charles Panzera
Yves Tinayre
John Goss
Redvers Llewellyn
Robert Easton
David Franklin
Stuart Robertson
Thorpe Bates
George Baker
Dale Smith
Arnold Matters
Raymond Newell
George Hancock
Richard Watson
Watcyn Watcyns
Kenneth Ellis
Sumner Austin
Owen Bryngwyn
Alan Greig
John Hargreaves
Roland Robson
Alexander Henderson
John Bradley
Frederick Sharp
Alexander Kipnis
Harold Williams
Gerhard Hüsch
Arthur Fear
Peter Dawson
Henry Gill
Ronald Stear
John Brownlee
Malcolm McEachern
Arthur Cranmer
Mark Raphael
Joseph Farrington
Howard Fry
Samuel Worthington
Frederick Woodhouse
Michael Head
Lee Thistlethwaite
Henry Cummings
Norman Notley
Leyland White
Tom Williams
Ellis Keeler
Gerald Cassen
Philip Hattey
Trefor Anthony
Keith Falkner
Roy Henderson
Dennis Noble
Hermann Schey
William Parsons
Bruce Boyce
Norman Walker
Percy Heming
William Brownlow
Herbert Heyner
John Morel
Frank Phillips
Laurence Holmes
Stanley Pope
Topliss Green
Roderick Lloyd
Foster Richardson
Bernard Ross
Broomfield Robertson
Tom Kinniburgh
Richard Ford
Booth Unwin
George Pizzey
Norman Menzies
Harold Child

Pianists (102)

Rachmaninoff
Cortot
Medtner
William Murdoch
Arthur Rubinstein
Edwin Fischer
Smeterlin
Prokofieff
Solomon
Arthur de Greef
Clifford Curzon
Cyril Smith
Iso Elinson
Lance Dossor
Aleksandr Helmann
Julius Isserlis
Claud Biggs
Vivian Langrish
Ernest Lush
Israel Hoffman
Robert Collett
Francis Cassel
Louis Kentner
Moiseiwitsch
Lamond
Orloff
Backhaus
Gieseking
Pouishnoff
Chavchavadze
Josef Hofmann
Horszowski
Rudolf Serkin
Frank Mannheimer
Francis Poulenc
François Lang
Karl Ulrich Schnabel
Ivan Phillipowsky
Eduardo del Pueyo
Etienne Amyot
Leslie England
Reginald Paul
Kendall Taylor
Thomas Marshall
Guy Jonson
Schnabel
Dohnányi
Egon Petri
Moriz Rosenthal
Brailowsky
Robert Casadesus
Ignaz Friedmann
Donald Francis Tovey
Alexander Borovsky
Friedrich Wührer
John Hunt
Alexandre Uninsky
Nikita Magaloff
Peter Stadlen
Georg van Harten
Franz Osborn
Maurice Cole
Angus Morrison
Harry Isaacs
Adolph Hallis
Norman Tucker
Frank Britton

Myra Hess
Harriet Cohen
Ray Lev
Helen Perkin
Elena Glazounov
Reine Gianoli
Merete Söderhielm
Stell Andersen
Phyllis Sellick
Vera Moore
Tessa Bloom
Eileen Ralph
Irene Scharrer
Lili Kraus
Kathleen Long
Nina Milkina
Ireen Maclaren
Yvonne Lefébure
Dorothea Braus
Denise Lassimonne
Barbara Smyth
Dorothy Hesse
Pamela Norris
Guirne Creith
Katharine Goodson
Eileen Joyce
Betty Humby
Ania Dorfmann
Lubka Kolessa
Marika Papaianou
Irene Kohler
Isabel Gray
Bertha Hagart
Dorothy Manley
Jean Norris

Recitals of works for two pianofortes

Ethel Bartlett and Rae Robertson
Heinz and Robert Scholz
Vitya Vronsky and Victor Babin
Mary and Geraldine Peppin

Pianoforte and violin recitals

Myra Hess and Jelly d'Aranyi
Lili Kraus and Simon Goldberg
Rudolf Serkin and Adolf Busch
Georg Szell and Henri Temianka
William Murdoch and Albert Sammons
Adolph Hallis and Lisa Minghetti

Harpsichord (6)

Wanda Landowska	Lucille Wallace	Alice Ehlers
Ernest Lush	Rudolph Dolmetsch	John Ticehurst

Violinists (62)

Adolf Busch	Szigeti	Carl Flesch
Milstein	Telmanyi	Temianka
Heifetz	Huberman	Thibaud
Albert Sammons	Mischa Elman	Georges Enesco
Zino Francescatti	Samuel Dushkin	Georg Kulenkampf
Arthur Catterall	Bratza	Melsa
Loris Blofeld	Samuel Kutcher	Harold Fairhurst
Henry Holst	Robert Soëtens	Louis Krasner
Antonio Brosa	Simon Goldberg	Max Rostal
Paul Makanowitsky	Peter Bornstein	Alfredo Campoli
Jean Pougnet	Frederick Grinke	Thomas Matthews
Maurice Clare	Leonard Hirsch	Harry Blech
Anthony English		

Jelly d'Aranyi	Isolde Menges	Alma Moodie
Lisa Minghetti	Renée Chemet	Adila Fachiri
Erica Morini	Cecilia Hansen	Guila Bustabo
Yvonne Astruc	Daisy Kennedy	May Harrison
Orrea Pernel	Eda Kersey	Sybil Eaton
Beatrix Marr	Beatrice Carrelle	Sheila Collins
Margaret Fairless	Leila Pirani	Winifred Small
Seymour Whinyates	Rhoda Backhouse	Maude Gold
Irene Richards		

Jelly d'Aranyi and Adila Fachiri in works for two violins
Myra Hess, Jelly d'Aranyi and Gaspar Cassadó
Adolf Busch, Hermann Busch and Rudolf Serkin (The Busch-Serkin Trio)

Viola (4)

William Primrose	Bernard Shore	Keith Cummings
John Yewe Dyer		

Cellists (44)

Casals	Piatigorsky	Gaspar Cassadó
Emanuel Feuermann	Antoni Sala	Arturo Bonucci
W.H. Squire	Enrico Mainardi	Hermann Busch
Maurice Eisenberg	Paul Hermann	Pierre Fournier
Maurice Maréchal	Arnold Trowell	Ivor James
Anthony Pini	Mischel Cherniavsky	Cedric Sharpe
Luigi Gasparini	Livio Mannucci	John Gabalfa
John Snowden	David Ffrangcon-Thomas	

Suggia
Beatrice Harrison
Juliette Alvin
Audrey Piggott
Marie Dare
Eleanor Warren
Joan Bonner
Marjorie Edes
Thelma Reiss
Raya Garbousova
Florence Hooton
Peggie Sampson
Rita Sharpe
Zara Nelson
Peers Coetmore
Antonia Butler
May Mukle
Leily Howell
Onorina Semino
Vera Canning
Helen Just
Rita Sharpe

Casella-Poltronieri-Bonucci (The Italian Trio)
The Pasquier Trio
Segovia (Guitar)

String quartets (34)

Busch
Kolisch
Brosa
International
Kutcher
Hirsch
Catterall
Zagreb
Gertler
Spencer Dyke
MacNaghten
Amar
Lener
New Hungarian
Catterall
Poltronieri
Griller
Hart House
Rothschild
Zepparoni
Virtuoso
Stratton
British
Budapest
Pro Arte
Roth
Prague
Weiss
Manhattan
Brussels
Calvet
Pro Musica
Whinyates
Blech

Piano trios (11)

Grinke
Belgian
New London
Dorian
Pirani
Kamaran
Maurice Cole
The Pougnet-Morrison-Pini Trio
Kutcher
The Trio Players
Canadian

Instrumental ensembles

English Ensemble (Piano Quartet)
Reginald Paul Piano Quartet
The Léon Goossens Ensemble (flute–oboe–clarinet–bassoon–horn)
Philharmonic String Trio
Philharmonic Ensemble (harp–flute–violin–viola–cello)
The Sylvan Trio (flute–oboe–piano)
The Lyra Quartet (flute–violin–viola–harp)
The Cembalo Trio (two violins–harpsichord)
The New Aeolian Players (piano–violin–viola–flute)

Arnold Dolmetsch and Family
Le Quintette Instrumental de Paris
Société des instruments à vent de Bruxelles
Quintet à vent de Paris
The London String Players (Herbert Menges, Conductor)

The Boyd Neel String Orchestra (Boyd Neel, Conductor)
The Jacques String Orchestra (Reginald Jacques, Conductor)
The Edric Cundell Chamber Orchestra (Edric Cundell, Conductor)
The Birmingham Philharmonic String Orchestra (Johan C. Hock, Conductor)
The Haigh Marshall Chamber Orchestra (Haigh Marshall, Conductor)
The Dorothy Erhart Chamber Orchestra (Dorothy Erhart, Conductor)
The Mannucci Chamber Orchestra (Livio Mannucci, Conductor)
The Manchester Women's String Orchestra (Claire Dunington, Conductor)
The Cedric Sharpe Sextet

Harp (5)
Gwendolen Mason
Marie Korchinska
Jeanne Chevreau
Marie Goossens
Sidonie Goossens

Flute (5)
René Le Roy
John Amadio
Marcel Moyse
Joseph Slater
Johann Feltkamp

Oboe (1)
Léon Goossens

Saxophone (1)
Sigurd Rascher

Organists (7)
Marcel Dupré
Joseph Bonnet
G. Thalben-Ball
Fernando Germani
G.D. Cunningham
Harold Darke
R. Arnold Greir

The New English Singers
The English Singers Quartet
The Kedroff Vocal Quartet
The Chelsea Singers
The Old Time Singers
The Tudor Singers (12 voices) (Cuthbert Bates, Conductor)
The A Cappella Singers (Charles Kennedy Scott, Conductor)
The London Madrigal Group (T.B. Lawrence, Conductor)
The Fleet Street Choir (T.B. Lawrence, Conductor)
Intimate Opera (Presented by Frederick Woodhouse)
The Chanticleer Opera Company
The One-Act Opera Company
John Goss and The London Singers
Engel Lund
Jean Sterling MacKinlay
Eve Maxwell-Lyte
Scotia (Celtic folksingers – Harpiste)

Vocal Duets (11)

Nellie Carson and Cuthbert Kelly
Norman Notley and David Brynley
Olive Groves and George Baker
Janet Hamilton-Smith and Gilbert Bailey
Anne Ziegler and Webster Booth
Dorothy Bennett and Edward Reach
Anita Oberländer and Gabriele Joachim
Beatrice Beaufort and Janet Christopher
Viola Morris and Victoria Anderson
Guelda Waller and Vera Maconochie
Mary Worth and Mary Davies

Vocal quartets (8)

Gresham Singers
Temple Quartet
Westminster Singers
Concord Singers
Chilworth Singers
Windsor Singers
Chantry Singers
Ludgate Singers

Northern Concert Tours 1939–40, Chamber Music 1939–41, 1946–48, Artists' Brochures 1940–41, 1948–49

Northern Concert Tours 1939–40 by Artists of International Reputation

Under the direction of Ibbs & Tillett, 124, Wigmore Street, LONDON W1 in association with J. Howroyd

Northern Concert Tours have been promoted with the object of enabling schools and musical societies with limited funds at their disposal to enjoy a series of recitals by front-rank artists at an exceptionally moderate cost.

Terms: Three solo recitals 38 guineas
Two solo recitals and one ensemble recital 43 guineas

Not less than three recitals may be taken. Any additional number over three, however, or two artists for one concert, may be booked at an extra proportionate cost. Fees payable in three parts, after each concert respectively. Cheques should be made payable to 'Ibbs & Tillett'.

Artists Available for 1939–40

Pianists: Eileen Joyce John Hunt Lance Dossor
Violinist: Antonio Brosa
Harpist: Gwendolen Mason
Recorder and harpsichord recital: Carl Dolmetsch and Joseph Saxby
Singer: Olive Groves
Lecture recital (illustrated): Roy Henderson
Ensembles: The Kutcher String Quartet The Pirani Trio The Carl Dolmetsch Trio
Guelda Waller and Vera Maconochie in Old Song Pictures

Artists for Chamber Music May 1939–April 1941

String quartets

Busch
Kolisch
Poltronieri
Hart House
Roth
Corda
Gertler
Griller
Blech
Macnaghten
Lener
Weiss
Zagreb
Budapest
Prague
International
Stratton
Calvet
Spencer Dyke
British
Pro Arte
Brussels
Manhattan
New Hungarian
Kutcher
Holst
Menges
Catterall
Whinyates
Nancy Phillips

Piano trios

Busch–Serkin
Murdoch–Brosa–Sala Trio
Borovsky–Roth–Boomkamp Trio
Trio Players
Canadian Trio
New English Trio
Trio Horszowski–d'Aranyi–Cassadó Trio
Grinke Trio
Pirani Trio
New London Trio
Dorian Trio
Italian Trio
Pasquier Trio
Pougnet-Morrison-Pini Trio
Kutcher Trio
Maurice Cole Trio
Kamaran Trio

English Ensemble
Société des Instruments à Vent de Bruxelles
Marcel Moyse Trio
Lyra Quartet
London Symphonic Players
Edric Cundell Chamber Orchestra
Merseyside Chamber Orchestra
Reginald Paul Piano Quartet
Quintette à Vent de Paris
Virtuoso Wind Quintet
Sylvan Trio
Philharmonic Ensemble
Boyd Neel String Orchestra
Birmingham Philharmonic String Orchestra
Le Quintette Instrumental de Paris
Léon Goossens Ensemble
New Aeolian Players
Philharmonic String Trio
Jacques String Orchestra
Mannucci Chamber Orchestra
Dorothy Erhart Chamber Orchestra

Piano and violin recitals

Myra Hess and Jelly d'Aranyi
William Murdoch and Albert Sammons
Frank Mannheimer and Antonio Brosa
Rudolf Serkin and Adolf Busch
Georg Szell and Henri Temianka
Egon Petri and Joseph Szigeti
Lili Kraus and Simon Goldberg
Kathleen Long and Adila Fachiri

Recitals of works for two violins: Jelly d'Aranyi and Adila Fachiri
Piano and viola recitals: Clifford Curzon and Bernard Shore
Piano and cello recitals: John Hunt and Thelma Reiss George Reeves and Antonia Butler
Piano and flute recitals: Kathleen Long and René Le Roy Ivor Newton and John Amadio
Piano and oboe recitals: Cyril Smith and Léon Goossens

Recitals of works for two pianos: Ethel Bartlett and Rae Robertson Heinz and Robert Scholz Vronsky and Babin Dorothy Manley and Myers Foggin Wiener and Doucet Mary and Geraldine Peppin

Arnold Dolmetsch and Family

Guitar: Segovia

Viola: Bernard Shore Frederick Riddle Keith Cummings John Yewe Dyer

Flute: René Le Roy Marcel Moyse Joseph Slater John Amadio

Oboe: Léon Goossens

Saxophone: Sigurd Rascher

Harp: Gwendolen Mason Marie Korchinska Sidonie Goossens

Pianists

Rachmaninoff	Cortot	Schnabel
Backhaus	Moiseiwitsch	Dohnányi
Lamond	Egon Petri	Arthur Rubinstein
Edwin Fischer	Orloff	Gieseking
Smeterlin	Brailowsky	Medtner
Rudolf Serkin	Louis Kentner	Friedrich Wührer
Horszowski	Eduardo del Pueyo	Chavchavadze
Karl Ulrich Schnabel	Peter Stadlen	George van Renesse
Adrian Aeschbacher	Myra Hess	Solomon
Irene Scharrer	Harriet Cohen	Clifford Curzon
William Murdoch	John Hunt	Kathleen Long
Eileen Joyce	Lili Kraus	Cyril Smith
Franz Osborn	Frank Mannheimer	Betty Humby
Helen Perkin	Ray Lev	Etienne Amyot
Kendall Taylor	Lance Dossor	Moura Lympany
Ireen Maclaren	Nina Milkina	Israel Hoffman
Dorothy Manley	Maria Curcio	Frank Laffitte
James Ching		

Violinists

Adolf Busch	Szigeti	Carl Flesch
Milstein	Jelly d'Aranyi	Telmanyi
Robert Virovai	Adila Fachiri	Renée Chemet
Isolde Menges	Zino Francescatti	Yvonne Astruc
Albert Sammons	Arthur Catterall	Henry Holst
Lisa Minghetti	Ruth Posselt	Temianka
Antonio Brosa	Simon Goldberg	Robert Soëtens
Paul Makanowitzky	Orrea Pernel	Eda Kersey
Thomas Matthews	Jean Pougnet	Frederick Grinke

Cellists

Casals
Gaspar Cassadó
Arturo Bonucci
Maurice Eisenberg
Raya Garbousova
Antonia Butler
Peggie Sampson
Zara Nelson
Peers Coetmore
Suggia
Emanuel Feuermann
Enrico Mainardi
Hermann Busch
Thelma Reiss
Leily Howell
Florence Hooton
Onorina Semino
Piatigorsky
Antoni Sala
Pierre Fournier
Attilio Ranzato
Beatrice Harrison
Anthony Pini
Joan Bonner
Vera Canning

Harpsichord

Lucille Wallace

Harpsichord and piano recitals

Wanda Landowska

Harpsichord and Gamba recitals

Alice Ehlers and Eva Heinitz

Carl Dolmetsch (Recorder–violin–viol)
Tudor Singers
Old Time Singers
Round Table Singers
The One-Act Opera Company
The Carl Dolmetsch Trio
The Cembalo Trio
London Madrigal Group
English Singers Quartet
John Goss and The London Singers
Arte Antica
New English Singers
Fleet Street Choir
Chelsea Singers
Chanticleer Opera Company
Intimate Opera

Song recitals

Elisabeth Schumann
Jo Vincent
Alexander Kipnis
Keith Falkner
John Goss
Elena Gerhardt
Anna El Tour
Herbert Janssen
Yves Tinayre
Mark Raphael
Maggie Teyte
Megan Foster
Gerhard Hüsch
Hermann Schey

Vocal and piano recitals: Pierre Bernac and Francis Poulenc
Folksongs of many lands: Engel Lund
Recitals of works by Nicolas Medtner: Tatiana Makushina and Nicolas Medtner
Songs and duets from the 16th century: Eric Greene and Keith Falkner (Michael Mullinar at the piano)
Recital of songs by Grieg: Astra Desmond
Songs and duets: Nellie Carson and Cuthbert Kelly   Anita Oberländer and Gabriele Joachim
Traditional songs: Eve Maxwell-Lyte
Song-pictures: Guelda Waller and Vera Maconochie
Lecture recital (The Singer's Art): Roy Henderson

Artists for Chamber Music May 1946–April 1948

String quartets

Hungarian	Calvet	Gertler
Prague	Loewenguth	Griller
Menges	Hirsch	Blech
Philharmonia	Zorian	Aeolian
Marjorie Hayward	Ebsworth	

Piano trios

Pougnet–Morrison–Pini Trio	Budapest Trio	Czech Trio
Harry Isaacs Trio	Cecilia Hansen Trio	Kamaran Trio
New English Trio	Pasquier Trio	Carter Trio
Philharmonic Trio	London Belgian Piano Quartet	London Pianoforte Quartet
English Ensemble	Sylvan Trio	Dennis Brain Quintet
Ars Rediviva Ensemble	Philharmonic Ensemble	London Harpsichord Ensemble
Carl Dolmetsch (recorder) and Joseph Saxby (harpsichord)	London Baroque Ensemble	

Kathleen Merritt String Orchestra	Jacques String Orchestra	New London Orchestra
	Boyd Neel String Orchestra	London Wind Players

Violin and piano recitals

Ginette Neveu and Jean Neveu	Adolf Busch and Rudolf Serkin	Max Rostal and Franz Osborn
Maurice Raskin and Marcel Gazelle	Arthur Grumiaux and Gerald Moore	Jelly d'Aranyi and James Sherrin
Yfrah Neaman and Howard Ferguson	Marie Wilson and Maria Donska	Frederick Grinke and Kendall Taylor
Thomas Matthews and Eileen Ralf	David Martin and Iris Loveridge	Maria Lidka and Franz Reizenstein
Telmanyi and Dohnányi		

Cello and piano recitals

Maurice Gendron and Ivor Newton	Anthony Pini and Gerald Moore	Florence Hooton and Kendall Taylor
James Whitehead and Kathleen Long	Thelma Reiss and Edgar Knight	William Pleeth and Margaret Good
Wykeham George and Veronica Parker	Douglas Cameron and Eric Harrison	

Recitals of works for two pianos

Ethel Bartlett and Rae Robertson	Cyril Smith and Phyllis Sellick	Hilda Dederich and Ethel de Gomez
Joan and Valerie Trimble	Mary and Geraldine Peppin	Eileen and Joan Lovell
Harry Isaacs and York Bowen	John Tobin and Tilly Connelly	Tom Bromley and Mantle Childe

Recitals of works for two violins
Jelly d'Aranyi and Adila Fachiri

Guitar: Segovia
Harpsichord: Lucille Wallace
Viola: Lionel Tertis Bernard Shore Watson Forbes Keith Cummings Max Gilbert
Flute: John Amadio Joseph Slater John Francis
Oboe: Léon Goossens Evelyn Rothwell John Wolf
Clarinet: Pauline Juler Reginald Kell Frederick Thurston
Horn: Dennis Brain
Harp: Marie Korchinska Gwendolen Mason Sidonie Goossens

Pianists

Cortot
Dohnányi
Solomon
Cyril Smith
Pouishnoff
Rudolf Serkin
Iso Elinson
John Hunt
Joseph Weingarten
Franz Reizenstein
Angus Morrison
Mantle Childe
Harriet Cohen
Kathleen Long
Nina Milkina
Maria Donska
Valda Aveling
Margaret Maddison
Adelina de Lara
Cherry Isherwood
Schnabel
Lamond
Louis Kentner
Orloff
Chavchavadze
Denis Matthews
Colin Horsley
Mewton Wood
John Simons
Maurice Cole
Myra Hess
Moura Lympany
Phyllis Sellick
Ilona Kabos
Eileen Ralf
Denise Lassimonne
Dorothea Braus
Jean Mackie
Margerie Few
Moiseiwitsch
Egon Petri
Clifford Curzon
Smeterlin
Franz Osborn
Julius Isserlis
Kendall Taylor
Lance Dossor
Leslie England
Eric Harrison
Irene Scharrer
Monique de la Bruchollerie
Irene Kohler
Michal Hambourg
Iris Loveridge
Kyla Greenbaum
Natasha Litvin
Ruth Gipps
Gina Bachauer
Yvonne Lefebure

Violinists

Adolf Busch
Jelly d'Aranyi
Henry Holst
Yfrah Neaman
Alfredo Campoli
Thomas Matthews
Ivry Gitlis
Frederick Grinke
Alan Loveday
Szigeti
Ginette Neveu
Albert Sammons
Telmanyi
Cecilia Hansen
Simon Goldberg
Marie Wilson
May Harrison
Harold Fairhurst
Winifred Roberts
Ida Haendel
Max Rostal
Arthur Grumiaux
Maurice Raskin
Bratza
Melsa
Elizabeth Lockhart
Olive Zorian
Audrey Catterall

Cellists

Casals	Suggia	Gaspar Cassadó
Piatigorsky	Maurice Gendron	Felix Salmond
Anthony Pini	Andre Navarra	Thelma Reiss
Beatrice Harrison	Antonia Butler	Florence Hooton
James Whitehead	Douglas Cameron	Wykeham George
Harvey Phillips	Eleanor Warren	Vivian Joseph
Leily Howell	Norina Semino	Peers Coetmore
Helen Just	Audrey Piggott	Kathleen Moorhouse
Gwendolin McGill	Marie Earnshaw	Eileen Croxford

New English Singers	London Madrigal Group	Fleet Street Choir
English Singers Quartet	Intimate Opera	

Song recitals

Elisabeth Schumann	Frieda Hempel	Elena Gerhardt
Maggie Teyte	Isobel Baillie	Oda Slobodskaya
Jo Vincent	Alexandre Trianti	Elsie Suddaby
Megan Foster	Flora Nielsen	Else Rykens
Astra Desmond	Kathleen Ferrier	Mary Jarred
Muriel Brunskill	Janet Howe	Noel Eadie
Nancy Evans	Sophie Wyss	Margaret Field-Hyde
Betty Bannerman	Emilie Hooke	

Dino Borgioli	Keith Falkner	Aksel Schiøtz
Heddle Nash	Harold Williams	Roy Henderson
Bruce Boyce	Jan van der Gucht	Robert Irwin
Frederick Fuller	Mark Raphael	Henry Cummings
Dale Smith	Eric Greene	David Franklin
Frederick Grisewood	Alvar Lidell	John Morel
Bruce Flegg	Frederic Sharp	Rudolf Comacho

Vocal recitals: Pierre Bernac and Francis Poulenc   Peter Pears and Benjamin Britten

Folksongs of many lands: Engel Lund

Recitals of songs and duets: Kathleen Ferrier and Roy Henderson   Mary Linde and Eric Greene

Songs and duets from the French operas: Joan Cross and Peter Pears with Benjamin Britten at the piano

Ibbs and Tillett: Artists' Brochures 1940, 1948

[Author's note: The brochure for 1940–41 is heavily annotated, with extra pages interleaved and many names added or crossed out in the handwriting of Emmie Bass, or EMT[illett] as she doodled her initials on the cover. Probably due to the wartime paper shortage and the assumption that musical activity would be curtailed, this brochure would have had extended validity, at least until 1942 given Kathleen Ferrier's inclusion. For 1940-1941 the artists are not listed in any order of prestige, instrumentalists are no longer separated by gender, and no artist was given sole representation, but in brochures thereafter the earlier format was used once again.]

1940–41

Sopranos

Maggie Teyte
Noel Eadie
Irene Eisinger
Megan Foster
Joan Cross
Garda Hall
Nora Gruhn
Jeanne Dusseau
Anne Ziegler
Mary Hamlin
Doris Wells
Keturah Sorrell
Ruth Packer
Ada Alsop
Elisabeth Parry
Elsie Morison
Beryl Hatt
Carmen del Rio
Rose Alper
Joan Butler
Christina Barry
Desiree Ellinger
Patricia Davies
Gladys Lorimer
Dorothy Stanton
Joan Fullerton
Estelle Aplin
Emilie Hooke
Helen Hill
Irene Baker
Florence Austral
Oda Slobodskaya
Tatiana Makushina
Isobel Baillie
Luella Paikin
Olive Groves
Mabel (Margaret) Ritchie
Laelia Finneberg
Molly de Gunst
Mary Worth
Mary Bonin
Joan Collier
Audrey Strange
Audrey Langford
Phyllis Mander
Margarete Krauss
Norah Moore
Gita de la Fuente
Winifred Radford
Grace Powell
Muriel Rae
Audrey Strange
Vera Benton
Joan Taylor
Myra O'Neill
Ceinwen Rowlands
Elizabeth Abercrombie
Lorely Dyer
Margaret Eaves
Doris Doré
Miriam Licette
Stiles-Allen
Dorothy Silk
Lisa Perli (altered by hand to Dora Labbette)
Kate Winter
Janet Hamilton-Smith
Joan Hammond
Hella Toros
Margaret Field-Hyde
Ruth Naylor
Leonie Zifado
Edna Hobson
Ena Mitchell
Dorothy Bond
Hilda Zweig
Edith Lewin
Estelle Canliss
Sophie Wyss
Elizabeth Doll
Joy McArden
Linda Parker
Joan Tribe
Rose Hill
Evelyn Campbell
Soffi Schonning
Elena Danieli
Gwen Catley
Celia Sturt

Contraltos

Elena Gerhardt
Constance Willis
Betty Bannerman
Gladys Ripley
Muriel Brunskill
Margaret Balfour
Essie Ackland
Edith Coates
Flora Nielsen
Enid Cruickshank
Astra Desmond
Nancy Evans

Doris Cowen
Ethel Davies
Freda Townson
Muriel Gale
Joyce Newton
Winifred Ingham
Margaret Boys
Janet Howe
Joyce Sutton
Marian Severn
Constance Shacklock
Esther Salamon
Elsa Cavelti
Ruth Bowman
Molly Leaper
Geneviève Touraine
Catherine Stewart
Eileen Pilcher
Grace Bodey
Anne Wood
Anne Broadhurst
Else Rykens
Janet Fraser
Ethel Barker
Sybil Evers
Linda Gray
Catherine Lawson
Margaret McArthur
Diana Lake
Kathleen Kay
Christine Chesters
Gwladys Garside
Olga Haley
Maud Heaton
Margaret Tann-Williams
Mary Jarred
Tessa Richardson
Joan Gray
Sheila Melville
Sabine Kaeter
Betty St Leger
Kathleen Ferrier
Veronica Mansfield
Janet Smith-Miller
Betty Sagon
Norah Meagher

Tenors

Walter Widdop
Derek Oldham
Tudor Davies
Parry Jones
Frank Sale
Eric Starling
Henry Wendon
John Wright
George Armitage
Max Meili
Max Lichtegg
Alfred Deller (counter tenor)
James Johnston
Alfred Hepworth
W.T. Goy (RCM)
Tom Purvis
Roy Ashton
Ronald Hill
Aksel Schiøtz
Dino Borgioli
Francis Russell
Trefor Jones
Jan van der Gucht
John McKenna
George Chitty
Edward Reach
Hindley Taylor
Harold Bradbury
Cyril Tucker
Stephen Manton
David Lloyd
Arthur Servent
Bradbridge White
Peter Pears
Stanley Wheatley
Michael Pearce
René Boria
John Caunce
Frank Titterton
Webster Booth
Heddle Nash
Bruce Flegg
Leonard Gowings
John Dudley
Ronald Murgatroyd
Howard Hemming
Edgar Evans
John Kentish
Arthur Carron
Eric Greene
Rene Soames
Thomas Thomas
(Richard Lewis)
Joseph Dollinger
Roy Sheldon
Ronald Bristol
John Lewis

Baritones and basses

Arthur Fear
Robert Easton
Arthur Cranmer
Dale Smith
Redvers Llewellyn
Frederick Woodhouse
Frederick Sharp
Keith Falkner
Booth Hitchin
Dennis Noble
John Goss
Henry Cummings
Norman Allin
Ronald Stear
Stanley Pope
Roderick Lloyd
William Parsons
Samuel Worthington
Percy Heming
Joseph Farrington
George Baker
Norman Walker
Tom Williams
George Hancock
Trefor Anthony
Henry Gill
Laurence Holmes

Leyland White
John Hargreaves
Frederick Grisewood
Donald Munro
Richard Wood
Otakar Kraus
Bruce Boyce
Hervey Alan
Malcolm Davidson
Randell Stevens
Frank Vaughan
Howard Fry
Alfred Orda
John Steabben
A. Kiriloff
Henry Costigan
Ellis Keeler
Swales Atkinson
Erin Tosi
Ifor Hughes
Arthur Reckless
George James
Harry Wallington
Philip Hattey
George Pizzey
Arthur Copley
Frederick Fuller
Michael Head
Clement Hardman
John Morel
Graham Clifford
Edmond Donlevy
Scott Joynt
Gordon Clinton
Charles True
Malcolm McEachern
Owen Brannigan
David Franklin
Robert Irwin
Roy Henderson
Fabian Smith
Stanley Mason
Robert Rowell
Norman Lumsden
Mark Raphael
Harold Williams
Salisbury Baker
Reginald Gibbs
Watkin Watkins
Ernst Mubach
Waldemar Johnsen
Murray Davies
Anton Young
Nowakowski
Kingsley Lark
Roderick Jones

Pianists

Medtner
Harriet Cohen
Mark Hambourg
William Murdoch
Moura Lympany
Frank Merrick
Eileen Ralph
Etienne Amyot
Jean Norris
Isabel Gray
Kendall Taylor
Dorothy Manley
Tessa Bloom
John Simons
Denise Lassimonne
Daisy Guth
Robert Collet
Geoffrey Philippe
Myers Foggin
Frank Mannheimer
Norman Tucker
Chavchavadze
Adela Verne
Gina Bachauer
Frank Britton
Edna Iles
Cyril Preedy
Irene Scharrer
Pouishnoff
Myra Hess
Eileen Joyce
Franz Osborn
Irene Kohler
Jean du Chastain
Pamela Norris
Lamond
Leslie England
Nina Milkina
Louis Kentner
Vivian Langrish
Dorothy Hesse
Clifford Curzon
Stephen Wearing
Valda Aveling
Israel Hoffmann
Jessie Hall
Jacques Fevrier
Shepherd Munn
Susan Slivko
Terence Beccles
Paul Baumgartner
Eric Hope
Peter Cooper
Jean Merlow
Solomon
Lubka Kolessa
Kathleen Long
Lance Dossor
Phyllis Sellick
John Hunt
Ireen Maclaren
Frank Lafitte
Maurice Cole
Michal Hambourg
James Ching
Geoffrey Tankard
Helen Perkin
Angus Morrison
Reginald Paul
Bertha Hagart
Cyril Smith
Eduard del Puego
Lillian Niblett
Anthony Baldwin
Molly Garwood
Anita Harrison
Smeterlin
Renata Bongatti
Charles Ellam
Severin Turel
Lucy McLaren

Muriel Dickson
Ruth Brudburg
Meyer Rosenstein
Olga Carmine
Ronald Smith
Vera Henderson
Julius Isserlis
Colin Horsley
Franz Wagner
Jean Hamilton
Shulamith Shafir
Henry Bronkhurst
Natasha Litvin
Franz Reizenstein
Roy Ellett
Gerald Moore
Joan Mackie
Alexis Kligeman
Kyla Greenbaum
Eiluned Davies
Monique Haas
Barbara Kerslake
Wilfred Maggiar
Ruth Dyson
Eric Harrison
Barbara Hill
Ella Pounder
Rosalie Inskip
Yvonne Catterall
Ilona Kabos
Raymond O'Connell
Emilie Boettcher
Ethel de Gomez
Margaret Maddison
Vera Benenson
Kathleen Cooper
Dennis Murdoch
Noel Mewton-Wood
Iso Elinson
Dorothy Howell
Joan Burns
Cherry Isherwood
Henry Mierowski
Alfred Kitchen
Edith Vogel
Georgette Petit
Gerald Gover
Yvonne Lefebure
Sheila Mossman
Lionel Bowman
Margory Few
Peter Stadlen
Anthony Hopkins
Maria Donska
Joan Baker
Hilda Bor
Dorothea Braus
Harry Isaacs
Joseph Weingarten
Ivor Newton
Iris Loveridge
Ruth Gipps
Rose Symondson
Hetty Bolton
Lisa Fuchsova
Ada Vera Kluger
Robert Schmitz

Violinists

Albert Sammons
Paul Beard
Thomas Matthews
Bratza
Brosa
Frederick Grinke
Winifred Small
Beatrice Carrelle
Alfred Cave
Yfrah Neaman
Arthur Grumiaux
Raymond Cohen
Olive Zorian
Gloria Pashley
Cecilia Hansen
Susan Davies
Maria Lidka
Felix Kok
Edith Eysler
Maurice Clare
Michele Carte
Anne Warden
Norbert Brainin
May Harrison
Henry Holst
Josef Hassid
Eda Kersey
Melsa
Isolde Menges
Samuel Kutcher
Alfred Barker
Irene Richards
Marie Wilson
Ginette Neveu
Robert Masters
Ealasard Robay
Ivry Gitlis
Marjorie Lavers
Audrey Catterall
Winifred Roberts
Raymond Mosley
Harold Fairhurst
Sheila Vine
Colin Sauer
Theo Olof
Arthur Catterall
Ida Haendel
Jelly d'Aranyi
Alfredo Campoli
Maurice Raskin
Peter Bornstein
Alan Loveday
Beatrix Marr
Adila Fachiri
Jean Pougnet
Symon Goldberg
Max Rostal
Nancy Phillips
Dea Gombrich
David Martin
Maria Lonova
Joan Spencer
Jozef Cetner
Elizabeth Lockhart
Cecilia Keating
Vera Kantrovitch
David Wise

Violas

Lionel Tertis
Frederick Riddle
Keith Cummings
Watson Forbes
John Yewe Dyer
Max Gilbert
Winifred Copperwheat
Bernard Shore

Cellists

Beatrice Harrison
Peggie Sampson
Charles Hambourg
Ivor James
Livio Mannucci
Antoni Sala
Vera Canning
Leily Howell
Peers Coetmore
Antonia Butler
Audrey Piggott
Norina Semino
Joan Bonner
Thelma Reiss
Marjorie Edes
Marie Dare
Gaspar Cassadó
Louis Poulet
Piatigorsky
Maurice Dambois
Joseph Schuster
Alfred de Bryghere
Kathleen Moorhouse
Maurice Gendron
Penelope Sims
Henri Honegger
André Navarra
Gwendolen McGill
Eleanor Warren
Joy Hall
Alexander Kok
William Pleeth
Helen Just
Olga Hegedus
James Whitehead
Vivian Joseph
James Phillips
Douglas Cameron
Anthony Pini
Marie Earnshaw
Karel Horitz
John Shinebourne
Eileen Croxford
Gethyn Wykeham-George
Beatrice Clare
Joyce Cordell
Florence Hooton
Penelope Simms
Mischel Cherniavsky

Harpsichord

Lucille Wallace
Susi Jeans
Luise Minden

Two pianofortes

Kentner and Kabos
Smith and Sellick
Bartlett and Robertson
Howard Ferguson and Denis Matthews
Tom Bromley and Mantle Childe
Eileen and Joan Lovell
Cecily Hoye and Veronica Parker
Joan and Valerie Trimble
Mary and Geraldine Peppin
Alec Rowley and Edgar Moy

Two violins

Jelly d'Aranyi and Adila Fachiri
Olive Zorian and Ealasard Robay
Winifred Small and Nancy Phillips

Viola and piano

Tertis and Curzon

Pianoforte trios

Albert Sammons, Thelma Reiss, Geoffrey Tankard
Eda Kersey, James Whitehead, Kathleen Long
Frederick Grinke, Florence Hooton, Kendall Taylor

Recorder

Carl Dolmetsch

Flute
John Amadio
Noreen Mason
Joseph Slater
Wilfred Smith
Marcel Moyse

Harp
Gwendolen Mason
Marie Korchinska
Carlos Ames

Oboe
Léon Goossens
Joy Boughton
John Wolf

Horn
Dennis Brain

Clarinet
Reginald Kell
Olive Wright
Pauline Juler
Frederick Thurston

Bassoon
Archie Camden

Double bass
Victor Watson
James Merritt
George Hatton

Organists
Fernando Germani
Ralph Downes
G.D. Cunningham
George Thalben Ball

Piano and cello
Wykeham George and Una Parkin
Helen Just and Arthur Alexander
Karel Neumann and Barbara Kerslake
Penelope Simms and Margery Field
Cedric Sharpe and Gerald Moore
Joyce Cordell and Mary/Geraldine Peppin
Oliver Vella and Gerald Gover

Piano and violin
Maria Lidka and Leonard Isaacs
Alfred Cave and Reginald Pane
Olive Zorian and Michael Maclean
Colin Sauer and Ronald Smith
Harold Fairhurst and Eric Harrison
David Martin and Iris Loveridge
Cecilia Keating and Alan Richardson
Max Rostal and Franz Osborn
Marie Wilson and Maria Donska
Audrey and Yvonne Catterall
Samuel Kutcher and Cherry Isherwood

Piano, clarinet, cello
Mantle Childe, Pauline Julier, Helen Just

Piano trios

Holst Trio
New London Trio
New English Trio
Harry Isaacs Trio
London International Trio
Fairhurst Trio
Merrick-Catterall-Moorhouse
Czech Trio
Maurice Cole Trio
Dorian Trio
Lyric Trio
Pougnet, Morrison, Pini Trio
Kutcher, Joseph, Bronkhurst Trio
Kutcher Trio
Kamaran Trio
Lydian Trio
Blech Trio
Czech Trio
Budapest Trio

Piano quartets

English Ensemble
Silverman Piano Quartet
London Piano Quartet

String trios

Grinke, Forbes, Phillips
Carter String Trio
London String Trio
Philharmonic String Trio

String quartets

Menges
Kutcher
Rosé
Blech
Whinyates
Macnaghten
Ebsworth
Aeolian
Griller
Holst
International
New English
Leighton
British
Zorian
Mannucci
Catterall
Stratton
Hirsch
Spencer Dyke
Laurance Turner
Nancy Phillips
Philharmonic
Marie Wilson

Miscellaneous

Sylvan Trio
Chamber Music Players
New English Singers
London Madrigal Group
London Song-Men
Intimate Opera (Humorous dialogues presented by Frederick Woodhouse, Winifred Radford, and Geoffrey Dunn)
Philharmonic Ensemble
London Wind Quintet
Tudor Singers
Fleet Street Choir
St David's Singers
Anne Ziegler and Webster Booth
Olive Groves and George Baker
Victoria Kingsley
New Aeolian Players
Engel Lund (Folksongs of many lands)
Old Time Singers
Mayre Lawson (Character sketches)
Yorkshire String Players
Kathleen Merritt Orchestra (14 players)
London Music Group

Lecture recitals

Maurice Jacobson
Harold Craxton
Bernard Shore
Boyd Neel
Ruth Dyson (with Mollie Sands)
Roy Henderson
Engel Lund
Frederick Fuller
Dorothy Hogben
Janet and Norman Fraser
Gerald Moore
John Francis
Bail Maine
Kenneth Adams
Sidney Harrison

1948–49

Sole representatives for the following artists

Cortot
Moiseiwitsch
Smeterlin
Cyril Smith
Mewton Wood
Julius Isserlis
Irene Scharrer
Renata Borgatti
Colin Horsley
Lance Dossor
Chavchavadze
Nikita Magaloff
Lucille Wallace
Adolf Busch
Telmanyi
Adila Fachiri
Arthur Grumiaux
Maurice Raskin
Alan Loveday
Casals
Pierre Fournier
Enrico Mainardi
Maurice Marechal
Schnabel
Louis Kentner
Orloff
Denis Matthews
Franz Osborn
John Hunt
Harriet Cohen
Yvonne Lefebure
Irene Kohler
Joseph Weingarten
Frank Mannheimer
Monique de la Bruchollerie
Ralph Kirkpatrick
Ginette Neveu
Jelly d'Aranyi
Marie Wilson
Szymon Goldberg
Yfrah Neaman
Lionel Tertis
Suggia
Maurice Gendron
André Navarra
Segovia
Dohnányi
Rudolf Serkin
Clifford Curzon
Francis Poulenc
Kendall Taylor
Myra Hess
Gina Bachauer
Phyllis Sellick
Nina Milkina
Michal Hambourg
Eileen Ralf
Ethel Bartlett and Rae Robertson
Max Rostal
Thomas Matthews
Szigeti
Antonio Brosa
Christian Ferras
William Primrose
Gaspar Cassadó
Paul Tortelier
Joseph Schuster

Sopranos

Isobel Baillie
Lotte Lehmann
Gwen Catley
Oda Slobodskaya
Ceinwen Rowlands
Joan Hammond
Elena Danieli
Megan Foster
Victoria Sladen
Soffi Schonning
Desi Halben
Linda Parker
Margaret Eaves
Mary Hamlin
Ingrid Hageman
Joan Butler
Sylvia Patriss
Winifred Radford
Janette Sclanders
Elisabeth Schumann
Joan Cross
Jo Vincent
Edna Hobson
Alexandra Trianti
Joan Taylor
Dora van Doorn
Eva Turner
Miriam Licette
Helen Hill
Ljuba Welitsch
Cecilia Wessels
Nora Gruhn
Hella Toros
Mary Linde
Emelie Hooke
Monica Warner
Vera Terry
Joan Coxon
Elsie Suddaby
Maggie Teyte
Ada Alsop
Margherita Grandi
Ena Mitchell
Doris Doree
Ruth Packer
Ruth Naylor
Laelia Finneberg
Olive Groves
Margaret Field-Hyde
Lorely Dyer
Margaret Ritchie
Patricia Davies
Kate Winter
Joan Stirrup
Joan Fullerton
Estelle Applin
Leonie Zifado

Sylvia Welling
Elizabeth Darbishire
Elisabeth Parry
Elizabeth Green
Marian Davies
Phyllis Mander
Sylvia Fisher
Helen Roberts
Sophie Wyss
Mary Lake
Rose Hill
Olwen Davies
Susanna Thackeray
Margery Field
Bettine Young
Margaret Roux
Mary Worth
Minnia Bower
Dorothy Bond
Jennifer Vyvyan
Gita de la Fuente
Elsie Morison
Norah Moore
Doris Gambell

Contraltos

Kathleen Ferrier
Muriel Brunskill
Astra Desmond
Flora Neilsen
Marjorie Thomas
Grace Bodey
Flora Collins
Sara Buckley
Gladys Parr
Gladys Palmer
Maud Heaton
Bessie Collins
Joyce Newton
Margaret Boys
Mary Davies
Beatrice Gibson
Monica Sinclair
Norma Procter
Mary Peters
Geneviève Touraine
Kathleen Willson
Gladys Ripley
Elena Gerhardt
Janet Fraser
Janet Howe
Margaret McArthur
Else Rykens
Freda Townson
Constance Shacklock
Betty Bannerman
Anne Wood
Doris Cowen
Veronica Mansfield
Kathleen Kay
Margaret Tann-Williams
Joan Gray
Joyce Sutton
Betty Sagon
Anna Pollak
Maude Baker
Margaret Bissett
Winefride Ingham
Mary Jarred
Valetta Iacopi
Nancy Evans
Edith Coates
Muriel Gale
Rosina Raisbeck
Catherine Lawson
Edith Furmedge
Eileen Pilcher
Ethel Davies
May Pearson
Constance Stocker
Winifred White
Ruth Bowman
Kathleen Coxon
Molly Leaper
Frances Gorick
Gertrude Holt
Ethel Bird
Lily Kettlewell

Tenors

Heddle Nash
Dino Borgioli
Eric Greene
Walter Widdop
Jan van der Gucht
Richard Lewis
Francis Russell
Robert Naylor
Tudor Davies
Andrew Macpherson
Alfred Hepworth
Stephen Manton
John Kentish
Bruce Flegg
Tom Culbert
Roland Hayes
Henry Wendon
Frank Titterton
David Lloyd
William Herbert
Webster Booth
Trefor Jones
Arthur Servent
Bradbridge White
Walter Midgley
James Etherington
Rowland Jones
Gerald Davies
Kenneth Neate
John Myrddin
Peter Pears
Aksel Schiøtz
Arthur Carron
James Johnston
Edward Reach
Parry Jones
Franz Vroons
John McHugh
Frank Sale
Rene Soames
Ronald Bristol
Edgar Evans
Ronald Hill
Ronald Murgatroyd
Walter Glynne

John Caunce
John Duncan
Bradshaw Macmillan
George Armitage
Edward Boleslawski
George Chitty
Murray Dickie
Alfred Deller
Roy Ashton
John Tainsh
John Turner
Frank Davey
Lloyd Strauss-Smith
Joseph Dollinger
John Lewis
Raymond Nilssen
Hindley Taylor
Howard Hemming
Cyril Tucker
Bryn Jones
John Searl
Ivan Dixon
John Wright

Basses and baritones

Harold Williams
Norman Allin
Owen Brannigan
Dennis Noble
Trevor Anthony
Gerard Souzay
George Pizzey
Peter Dawson
William Parsons
Roderick Jones
Arnold Matters
George Hancock
Kenneth Ellis
Joseph Farrington
Arthur Copley
Edmond Donlevy
Booth Unwin
John Dethick
Leyland White
Ivor Evans
Henryd Jones
Frederick Fuller
Richard Wood
David Carver
Donald Munro
Stanley Mason
Keith Falkner
Norman Walker
Nowakowski
Henry Cummings
David Franklin
Robert Irwin
Stanley Clarkson
Oscar Natzke
Tom Williams
George Baker
Henry Gill
Raymond Newell
Dale Smith
Frederick Harvey
Scott Joynt
Howell Glynne
Clement Hardman
George James
Robert Rowell
Harding Jenkins
Clifford Deri
Philip Hattey
Kenneth Adams
Ellis Keeler
Fabian Smith
George Allen
Roy Henderson
Pierre Bernac
Redvers Llewellyn
Robert Easton
Gordon Clinton
Hermann Schey
John Brownlee
Arthur Fear
Arthur Cranmer
Otakar Kraus
Bruce Dargavel
Ronald Stear
Norman Lumsden
Laurence Holmes
Arthur Reckless
Frederick Sharp
Hervey Alan
Frederick Woodhouse
Bruce Clark
Tudor Evans
Reginald Gibbs
William Dickie
Dennis Dowling
Stanley Pearson
Alfred Swain
Frank Keyte

Pianists

Cortot
Dohnányi
Clifford Curzon
Smeterlin
Kendall Taylor
Franz Osborn
John Hunt
Chavchavadze
Solomon
Robert Casadesus
Schnabel
Louis Kentner
Edwin Fischer
Denis Matthews
Francis Poulenc
Colin Horsley
Julius Isserlis
Robert Riefling
Mark Hambourg
Iso Elinson
Moiseiwitsch
Rudolf Serkin
Cyril Smith
Orloff
Mewton Wood
Joseph Weingarten
Lance Dossor
Varella Cid
Pouishnoff
Medtner

Peter Stadlen
Franz Reizenstein
Maurice Cole
Marcel Gazelle
Leslie England
Sidney Harrison
Gerald Gover
Geoffrey Tankard
Ronald Smith
Blaszczynski
Meyer Rosenstein
Alfred Blumen
Ross Pratt
Dennis Murdoch
Eduardo del Pueyo
Aleksandre Helmann
Alexis Kligermann
Frank Mannheimer
Herbert Fryer
Eric Harrison
Harry Isaacs
Stephen Wearing
Peter Cooper
Aronowitz
Raymond O'Connell
Rolf Langnese
Geoffrey Philippe
Frank Britton
Nikita Magaloff
Karl Ulrich Schnabel
Franz Wagner
Angus Morrison
John Simons
Mantle Childe
Eric Hope
Reginald Paul
Cyril Preedy
Charles Ellam
Isador Goodman
Lionel Bowman
Myers Foggin
Terence Beckles

Myra Hess
Michal Hambourg
Monique de la Bruchollerie
Irene Kohler
Renata Borgatti
Kathleen Long
Ilona Kabos
Dorothea Braus
Denise Lassimonne
Ruth Gipps
Eiluned Davies
Jean Mackie
Joan Baker
Edna Iles
Maria Donska
Yvonne Catterall
Nicole Henriot
Irene Scharrer
Gina Bachauer
Eileen Ralf
Nina Milkina
Rena Kyriakou
Eileen Joyce
Shulamith Shafir
Liza Fuchsova
Kyla Greenbaum
Dorothy Hesse
Agnes Walker
Margerie Few
Barbara Hill
Cherry Isherwood
Susan Slivko
Jean Merlow
Muriel Kerr
Harriet Cohen
Yvonne Lefébure
Phyllis Sellick
Marika Papaioanou
Adela Verne
Moura Lympany
Adelina de Lara
Iris Loveridge
Valda Aveling
Natasha Litvin
Daisy Guth
Ivey Dickson
Ella Pounder
Margaret Maddison
Sheila Mossman
Monique Haas

Two piano ensembles
Ethel Bartlett and Rae Robertson
Hilda Dederich and Ethel de Gomez
Cyril Smith and Phyllis Sellick
Mary and Geraldine Peppin
Eileen and Joan Lovell
Joan and Valerie Trimble
Harry Isaacs and York Bowen
Rawicz and Landauer

Harpsichord
Lucille Wallace
Millicent Silver
Dr Thornton Lofthouse
Raymond Russell
Ralph Kirkpatrick

Violinists
Adolf Busch
Telmanyi
Max Rostal
Adila Fachiri
Szigeti
Erica Morini
Marie Wilson
Arthur Grumiaux
Ginette Neveu
Jelly d'Aranyi
Szymon Goldberg
Yfrah Neaman

Maurice Raskin
Alan Loveday
Henry Holst
Bratza
Melsa
Samuel Kutcher
Alfred Cave
Ivry Gitlis
Maurice Clare
David Wise
John Creichton Murray
Thomas Matthews
Thibaud
Campoli
Frederick Grinke
Jean Pougnet
Colin Sauer
Harry Blech
Peter Bornstein
Christian Ferras
Robert Masters
Antonio Brosa
Albert Sammons
Theo Olof
Robert Soëtens
Harold Fairhurst
David Martin
Leonard Hirsch
Felix Kok
Ede Zathureczky
Raymond Mosley

Ida Haendel
Elizabeth Lockhart
Olive Zorian
Michelle Carte
Joan Spencer
Isolde Menges
May Harrison
Vera Kantrovitch
Maria Lidka
Cecilia Hansen
Winifred Roberts
Maria Lonova
Audrey Catterall

Violas

Lionel Tertis
Watson Forbes
Winifred Copperwheat
William Primrose
Keith Cummings
Bernard Shore
Max Gilbert

Cellists

Casals
Enrico Mainardi
Pierre Fournier
Thelma Reiss
Anthony Pini
Maurice Eisenberg
Mischel Cherniavsky
James Whitehead
Vivian Joseph
Harvey Phillips
Alexander Kok
Suggia
Gaspar Cassadó
Paul Tortelier
Joseph Schuster
Maurice Marechal
Maurice Dambois
Luigi Gasparini
Wykeham George
Douglas Cameron
David Ffrangcon-Davies
Piatigorsky
André Navarra
Maurice Gendron
Felix Salmond
Henri Honegger
Livio Mannucci
Karel Horitz
William Pleeth
Ivor James
John Shinebourne

Beatrice Harrison
Leily Howell
Norina Semino
Marie Earnshaw
Marie Dare
Antonia Butler
Eleanor Warren
Peggy Sampson
Eileen Croxford
Kathleen Moorhouse
Florence Hooton
Peers Coetmore
Helen Just
Gwendolen McGill
Beatrix Clare

Harpists

Marie Korchinska
Marie Goossens
Gwendolen Mason
Lily Laskine
Sidonie Goossens
Carlos Ames

Flute

Rene Le Roy
John Francis
Marcel Moyse
John Amadio
Geoffrey Gilbert
Russell King
Joseph Slater
Arthur Cleghorn
Gareth Morris

Oboe

Léon Goossens
David Tucker
Evelyn Rothwell
Leonard Brain
John Wolf

Guitar

Segovia

Clarinet

Benny Goodman
Pierre de Bavier
Frederick Thurston
Pauline Juler
Reginald Kell
Gervase de Peyer

Bassoon

Archie Camden
Cecil James

Horn

Dennis Brain
Charles Gregory

Trumpet

George Eskdale
Harold Jackson
Harry Mortimer
Jack Mackintosh

Saxophone

Sigurd Rascher

Organists

Fernando Germani
G.D. Cunningham
G. Thalben-Ball
R. Arnold Grier
Geraint Jones
Harold Darke
Arnold Richardson
Sandy Macpherson
Reginald Foort
Reginald New
Charles Smart
Charles Saxby

The Boyd Neel String Orchestra
The Arnold Goldsbrough Orchestra
The Jacques String Orchestra
The London String Orchestra
The Kathleen Riddick String Orchestra
The New London Orchestra
The Kathleen Merritt String Orchestra
The Alexandra Orchestra

The Leslie Bridgewater Quintet
The Leslie Jeffries Trio
Charles Enesco Quintet
Jan Berenska Ensemble

New English Singers
Fleet Street Choir
Intimate Opera
Hedli Anderson
English Singers Quartet
Tudor Singers
Singers in Consort
Eve Maxwell-Lyte
London Madrigal Group
London Singers
Engel Lund
Peggy Stack

Pierre Bernac and Francis Poulenc

Peter Pears and Benjamin Britten

Anne Ziegler and Webster Booth

Janet Hamilton-Smith and John Hargreaves

Olive Groves and George Baker

Sylvia Welling and Mervyn Saunders

Hella Toros and Edward Reach

Victoria Anderson and Viola Morris

APPENDIX 6

LSO-CEMA 1940–44

Ibbs and Tillett Management of Concerts given by the London Symphony Orchestra for Carnegie Trust/Pilgrim Trust, later CEMA (Council for the Encouragement of Music and the Arts)/Music, Art, and Drama Society (Jay Pomeroy) between 1940–1944

Date	Venue	Conductor	Soloist	Programme
28 December 1940	London RAH	Keith Douglas	Moiseiwitsch	Smetana/Debussy/ Rachmaninov/ Tchaikovsky
29 December 1940	Leicester	all details as 28 December		

February 1941 (known venues: Watford, Newcastle, Hull, Barnsley, Bath, Malvern, Stratford-upon-Avon)

Nine programme variations

A	Keith Douglas	Moiseiwitsch	Beethoven/Debussy/Rachmaninov/Tchaikovsky
B	Douglas	Hess	Weber/Delius/Grieg/Tchaikovsky
C	Douglas	Hess	Beethoven/Debussy/Tchaikovsky
D	Douglas	Moiseiwitsch	Smetana/Beethoven/Tchaikovsky
E	Douglas	Hess	Smetana/Beethoven/Tchaikovsky
F	Weldon	Moiseiwitsch	Beethoven/Debussy/Rachmaninov
G	Douglas	Hess	Weber/Delius/Grieg/Beethoven
H	Cameron	Hess	Weber/Beethoven/Schubert
I	Douglas	Hess	Weber/Delius/Grieg/Schubert

April–May 1941 Three programme variations

1	Wood	no soloist	Wagner/Elgar/Brahms/Tchaikovsky/Mendelssohn/Liszt
2	Wood	Lympany	Weber/Elgar/Brahms/Liszt/Wagner/Mendelssohn
3	Wood	Lympany	Brahms/Vaughan Williams/Beethoven/Grieg/ Tchaikovsky/Liszt

29 April 1941	High Wycombe	programme 1
30 April 1941 afternoon	Bath	programme 2
30 April 1941 evening	Bath	programme 3
1 May 1941 afternoon	Cheltenham	programme 2
1 May 1941 evening	Cheltenham	programme 3
2 May 1941 afternoon	Reading	programme 1

May 1941 Six programme variations

A	Cameron	Hess	Weber/Beethoven/Schubert
AA	Cameron	Moiseiwitsch	Weber/Beethoven/Schubert
B	Cameron	Moiseiwitsch	Glinka/Wagner/Schumann/Beethoven
C	Douglas	Hess	Nicolai/Beethoven/Franck/Dvořák
D	Douglas	Moiseiwitsch	Glinka/Wagner/Rachmaninov/Dvořák
E	Cameron	Moiseiwitsch	Glinka/Wagner/Schumann/Brahms

5 May 1941 Watford programme A
6 May 1941 Hull programme A
7 May 1941 Huddersfield programme AA
8 May 1941 Newcastle programme A
9 May 1941 Sunderland Cameron Hess Glinka/Mendelssohn/Schumann/Beethoven
10 May 1941 Edinburgh Douglas other details as 9 May
12 May 1941 Aberdeen programme C
13 May 1941 Dundee programme C
14 May 1941 Glasgow programme C
15 May 1941 Middlesbrough programme B with Douglas
16 May 1941 Sheffield as 15 May
17 May 1941 Bradford programme B
18 May 1941 Harrogate programme B
19 May 1941 Southport programme D
20 May 1941 Buxton programme D
21 May 1941 Blackpool programme D
22 May 1941 Blackburn some of programme D; also Coleridge-Taylor/Mendelssohn/ Blackburn Music Society/conductor Harold Briggs
23 May 1941 Hanley programme D
24 May 1941 Nottingham programme B
25 May 1941 Leicester programme B
26 May 1941 Wolverhampton programme AA
27 May 1941 Bedford afternoon programme E
27 May 1941 Bedford evening Cameron Moiseiwitsch Nicolai/Schubert/Rachmaninov/ Dvořák

October–November 1941 Eight programme variations

A	Cameron	Sammons	Mendelssohn/Arensky/Beethoven/Dvořák
B	Cameron	Sammons	Mendelssohn/Arensky/Beethoven/Brahms
C	Douglas	Sammons	Borodin/Schubert/Brahms/Dvořák
D	Cameron	Scharrer	Glinka/Handel-Harty/Schumann/Brahms
E	Douglas	Scharrer	Wagner/Grainger/Douglas/Schumann/Grieg/Dvořák
F	Douglas	no soloist	Glinka/Delius/Borodin/Arensky/Grieg/Elgar
G	Douglas	Scharrer	Wagner/Douglas/Schumann/Dvořák
H	Douglas	Kersey/Reiss	Wagner/Grainger/Douglas/Brahms/Tchaikovsky
I	Cameron	Moiseiwitsch	Sullivan/Handel-Harty/Schumann/Dvořák

28 October 1941 Wolverhampton programme A
29 October 1941 Malvern programme A
30 October 1941 Huddersfield programme B
31 October 1941 Harrogate programme C
1 November 1941 Middlesbrough programme C
2 November 1941 Newcastle programme C
11 November 1941 Reading programme I
12 November 1941 afternoon Bath programme A
12 November 1941 evening Bath programme D
13 November 1941 afternoon Cheltenham programme B
13 November 1941 evening Cheltenham Cameron Scharrer programme E

14 November 1941 afternoon Bristol Weldon programme F
14 November 1941 evening Bristol Weldon programme G
24 November 1941 Rhyl programme A
25 November 1941 Bolton programme A
26 November 1941 Blackpool programme A
27 November 1941 Blackburn with Blackburn Music Society Cameron/Briggs Sammons Weber/Handel-Harty/Elgar/Bruch/Dvořák
28 November 1941 Hanley programme H
29 November 1941 Nottingham programme H
30 November 1941 Leicester programme H

January 1942 Six programme variations

A	Cameron	Sammons	Weber/Arensky/Elgar/Dvořák
B	Cameron	Moiseiwitsch	Elgar/Tchaikovsky/Beethoven
C	Cameron	Sammons	Weber/Elgar/Tchaikovsky
D	Douglas	Moiseiwitsch	Mendelssohn/Butterworth/Rossini-Respighi/Grieg/Dvořák
E	Douglas	Moiseiwitsch	Glinka/Grainger/Douglas/Rossini-Respighi/ Rachmaninov/Dvořák
F	Cameron	Sammons	Weber/Beethoven/Schubert

12 January 1942 Bedford afternoon programme A (without Arensky)
12 January 1942 Bedford evening programme B
13 January 1942 Newcastle programme C
14 January 1942 Dundee programme D
16 January 1942 Glasgow programme E
17 January 1942 Edinburgh programme D
18 January 1942 Newcastle programme B
19 January 1942 Grimsby programme E
20 January 1942 Grimsby programme F
21 January 1942 Grimsby programme B Cameron Curzon
22 January 1942 Halifax programme D
3 February 1942 Watford Douglas Moiseiwitsch Beethoven/Debussy/Rachmaninov/Tchaikovsky
4 February 1942 Bolton Douglas Hess Beethoven/Debussy/Tchaikovsky
5 February 1942 Wigan all details as 4 February
6 February 1942 Huddersfield Douglas Hess Berlioz/Beethoven/Tchaikovsky
7 February 1942 Rochdale all details as 4 February
8 February 1942 Bradford all details as 4 February
9 February 1942 Harrogate all details as 4 February
10 February 1942 Sunderland Douglas Moiseiwitsch programme as 4 February
11 February 1942 Newcastle all details as 3 February
12 February 1942 Hull all details as 3 February
13 February 1942 Barnsley all details as 3 February
17 February 1942 Weston-super-Mare afternoon Weldon Moiseiwitsch Beethoven/Rachmaninov
17 February 1942 Weston-super-Mare evening Douglas Moiseiwitsch Beethoven/Tchaikovsky
19 February 1942 Bath all details as 3 February

20 February 1942 afternoon Cheltenham all details as 17 February afternoon
20 February 1942 evening Cheltenham all details as 17 February evening
21 February 1942 Malvern all details as 3 February
22 February 1942 Stratford-upon-Avon all details as 3 February
23 February 1942 Wolverhampton all details as 4 February
26 February 1942 afternoon Bedford Weldon all details as 6 February
26 February 1942 evening Bedford Douglas Hess Grieg/Schubert
27 February 1942 Cambridge Douglas Hess Weber/Delius/Grieg/Beethoven
28 February 1942 Ipswich Weldon Hess Smetana/Beethoven/Tchaikovsky
1 March 1942 Nottingham Cameron Hess Weber/Beethoven/Schubert
2 March 1942 Leicester all details as 1 March

May–June 1942 Two programme variations

A	Barbirolli	no soloist	Elgar/Bach–Barbirolli/Tchaikovsky/Brahms
B	Barbirolli	no soloist	Beethoven/Wagner

26 May 1942 Dundee programme A
27 May 1942 Aberdeen programme A
28 May 1942 Glasgow programme A
29 May 1942 Edinburgh programme A
30 May 1942 Newcastle programme A
31 May 1942 Newcastle programme B
1 June 1942 Middlesbrough programme B
2 June 1942 Bradford programme B
3 June 1942 Huddersfield programme B
4 June 1942 Leicester programme B
5 June 1942 Wolverhampton programme B

31 August 1942 Town Hall, Watford Douglas Kersey/Reiss Humperdinck/Franck/Brahms/Dvořák

September–October 1942 Nine programme variations

A Weldon Kentner Mendelssohn/Fauré/Schumann/Beethoven
B Mathieson Joyce Rossini/Wagner/Mozart/Addinsell/Beethoven
C Weldon/Claud Powell d'Aranyi Mendelssohn/Fauré/Beethoven
D Mathieson Moiseiwitsch Handel–Harty/Mendelssohn/Beethoven/Dvořák
E Weldon Moiseiwitsch Humperdinck/Svendsen/Tchaikovsky/Brahms
F Mathieson d'Aranyi Brahms/Wagner/Beethoven
G Weldon Kentner Humperdinck/Svendsen/Schumann/Brahms
H Mathieson Mewton-Wood Rossini/Wagner/Beethoven/Addinsell
I Mathieson Joyce Addinsell/Wagner/Mozart/Rossini

7 October 1942 afternoon Bristol programme B
7 October 1942 evening Bristol programme E

2 December 1942 Exeter Weldon Moiseiwitsch all-Beethoven programme
3–5 December 1942 Bristol (five concerts at Colston Hall):
3 December evening Weldon Moiseiwitsch all-Beethoven programme

4 December afternoon Weldon Purcell–Wood/Nicolai/Rossini–Respighi/J. Strauss/ V. Williams/Weber/Elgar
4 December evening Cameron Hess/Scharrer Mozart/Bach/Mozart/Mendelssohn/Brahms
5 December afternoon Harrison Scharrer Beethoven/Schumann/Holst–Jacob/Dvořák
5 December evening Weldon Joyce Tchaikovsky/Grieg/Debussy/Addinsell/Elgar

4 January 1943 Watford Fistoulari Joyce Rossini/Grieg/Addinsell/Tchaikovsky
6 January 1943 People's Palace Fistoulari Moiseiwitsch all-Beethoven
16 January 1943 Tooting Broadway all details as 4 January
19 February 1943 Tooting Broadway Fistoulari Lympany Rossini/Schubert/Schumann/ Tchaikovsky
20 February 1943 People's Palace Fistoulari Joyce Rossini/Schubert/Grieg/Tchaikovsky
4 May 1943 afternoon Cheltenham Fistoulari Kentner Rossini/Schubert/Schuman/ Brahms
4 May 1943 evening Cheltenham Mathieson Joyce Mozart/Rachmaninov/Elgar
7 May 1943 Winchester Fistoulari Moiseiwitsch Mozart/Rachmaninov/Brahms
8 May 1943 Southampton Weldon Moiseiwitsch Berlioz/Elgar/Tchaikovsky/Beethoven
9 May 1943 afternoon Bournemouth Cameron Moiseiwitsch Berlioz/Elgar/Tchaikovsky/ Beethoven
10 May 1943 Watford Weldon Moiseiwitsch Mozart/Rachmaninov/Elgar
12 May 1943 Exeter Cameron no soloist Berlioz/Elgar/Mozart/Beethoven
13 May 1943 Newport Mathieson Moiseiwitsch Berlioz/Elgar/Rachmaninov/Beethoven
14 May 1943 lunchtime Bristol Mathieson George Stratton Mendelssohn/Sibelius/ Bruch/Liszt/Rossini
14 May 1943 evening Bristol Weldon Moiseiwitsch Mozart/Rachmaninov/Elgar
15 May 1943 afternoon Bristol Cameron Smith Berlioz/Lalo/Brahms/Beethoven
15 May 1943 evening Bristol Mathieson Mewton-Wood Verdi/Schumann/Beethoven/ Film Music (Vaughan Williams/Walton/Addinsell/Bliss)
18 May 1943 Rugby (School) Cameron Smith Berlioz/Mozart/Rachmaninov/Elgar
19 May 1943 Hull Cameron Smith Mozart/Rachmaninov/Elgar
20 May 1943 Halifax Weldon Smith Mozart/Tchaikovsky/Elgar
21 May 1943 Sheffield Cameron Moiseiwitsch Mozart/Rachmaninov/Elgar
22 May 1943 Middlesbrough Weldon Moiseiwitsch Berlioz/Elgar/Tchaikovsky/ Beethoven
23 May 1943 Newcastle Cameron Moiseiwitsch Berlioz/Mozart/Rachmaninov/Beethoven
24 May 1943 Edinburgh Cameron Moiseiwitsch Berlioz/Mozart/Rachmaninov/ Beethoven
25 May 1943 Glasgow Cameron Kentner Mozart/Rachmaninov/Elgar
26 May 1943 afternoon Aberdeen Weldon Mewton-Wood Mozart/Tchaikovsky/Elgar
26 May 1943 evening Aberdeen Cameron Moiseiwitsch Berlioz/Mozart/Rachmaninov/ Beethoven
27 May 1943 Dundee Cameron no soloist Berlioz/Mozart/Grieg/Beethoven
28 May 1943 Sheffield Weldon Moiseiwitsch Svendsen/Wagner/Rachmaninov/Brahms
23 June 1943 Oxford Weldon Curzon Brahms/Elgar/Tchaikovsky/Dvořák
24 June 1943 afternoon Cheltenham Weldon Curzon Brahms/Elgar/Tchaikovsky/ Dvořák
24 June 1943 evening Cheltenham Weldon Stratton/Walker/Whittaker/Eskdale Wagner/Prokofiev/Bach/Tchaikovsky

25 June 1943 Exeter Weldon Kentner Brahms/Elgar/Tchaikovsky/Dvořák
26 June 1943 afternoon Exeter Weldon Stratton/Walker/Whittaker/Eskdale
Wagner/Prokofiev/Bach/Tchaikovsky
26 July 1943 Bradford Mathieson Lympany/Stratton/Walker/Whittaker/Eskdale
Berlioz/Bach Beethoven/Sibelius
27 July 1943 Leeds Mathieson Lympany/Stratton/Walker/Whittaker/Eskdale
Berlioz/Bach Beethoven/Sibelius
28 July 1943 Hull Mathieson Kentner/Stratton/Walker/Whittaker/Eskdale
Berlioz/Bach Beethoven/Dvořák
29 July 1943 Halifax Mathieson Lympany/Stratton/Walker/Whittaker/Eskdale
Berlioz/Bach Beethoven/Dvořák
30 July 1943 Lincoln Mathieson Lympany/Stratton/Walker/Whittaker/Eskdale
Berlioz/Bach Schumann/Dvořák
31 July 1943 Highgate Mathieson Joyce/Stratton/Walker/Whittaker/Eskdale
Berlioz/Bach Schumann/Dvořák

Tour of Wales 6–18 September 1943

6 September Blackwood Irwyn Walters no soloist Glinka/Rimsky-Korsakov/Borodin/Mussorgsky/Tchaikovsky
7 September Treorchy Cameron no soloist Berlioz/Prokofiev/Wagner/Liszt/Dvořák
8 September Ferndale Cameron no soloist Weber/Svendsen/Debussy/Elgar/Beethoven
9 September Pontypridd all details as 6 September
10 September Maesteg all details as 8 September
11 September Porthcawl all details as 7 September
12 September Cardiff Cameron Moiseiwitsch Berlioz/Prokofiev/Rachmaninov/Dvořák
13 September Neath all details as 8 September
14 September Carmarthen all details as 7 September
15 September Garnant all details as 6 September
16 September Swansea Walters Moiseiwitsch Glinka/Rimsky-Korsakov/Rachmaninov/Borodin
17 September Aberdare Weldon no soloist Weber/Svendsen/Debussy/Elgar/Beethoven
18 September Cardiff Cameron Moiseiwitsch Berlioz/Prokofiev/Rachmaninov/Dvořák
29 September 1943 afternoon Winchester Weldon Kentner Mendelssohn/Fauré/Rimsky-Korsakov/Schumann/Beethoven
29 September 1943 evening Winchester Mathieson Joyce Rossini/Mozart/Wagner/Addinsell/Beethoven
30 September 1943 afternoon Basingstoke all details as 29 September afternoon
30 September 1943 evening Basingstoke all details as 29 September evening
1 October 1943 Reading all details as 29 September afternoon
2 October 1943 afternoon Petersfield all details as 29 September afternoon
2 October 1943 evening Petersfield all details as 29 September evening
3 October 1943 Guildford Weldon/Powell d'Aranyi Mendelssohn/Fauré/Beethoven
4 October 1943 Southampton Mathieson Moiseiwitsch Handel–Harty/Mendelssohn/Beethoven/Dvořák
5 October 1943 Tiverton Weldon Kentner Mendelssohn/Fauré/Schumann/Beethoven
6 October 1943 Taunton Weldon d'Aranyi Mendelssohn/Fauré/Beethoven
8 October 1943 afternoon Cheltenham Mathieson d'Aranyi Brahms/Wagner/Beethoven

8 October 1943 evening Cheltenham Weldon Kentner Humperdinck/Svendsen/Schumann/Brahms
27 November 1943 afternoon Derby Cameron no soloist Weber/Arensky/Svendsen/Brahms
30 November 1943 Tiverton Weldon no soloist Berlioz/Elgar/Mozart/Brahms
November–December 1943 Exeter all details as 30 November
4 December afternoon Newport Weldon Lympany all-Beethoven
4 December evening Newport Weldon no soloist Berlioz/Elgar/Tchaikovsky/Brahms
1 May 1944 Oldham Mathieson Smith Nicolai/Alwyn/Grieg/Tchaikovsky
2 May 1944 Glasgow Mathieson Smith Nicolai/Alwyn/Rachmaninov/Tchaikovsky
3 May 1944 Aberdeen all details as 1 May
4 May 1944 Dundee all details as 2 May
5 May 1944 Newcastle all details as 2 May
6 May 1944 Middlesbrough all details as 2 May
7 May 1944 Newcastle Braithwaite Curzon Berlioz/R. Strauss/Rachmaninov/Elgar
8 May 1944 Oldham all details as 7 May
9 May 1944 Hull all details as 7 May
10 May 1944 Lincoln all details as 7 May
11 May 1944 Halifax all details as 7 May

Promenade Concerts 1945, 1947

Ibbs and Tillett Artists appearing at the BBC Promenade Concerts 1945

(* first appearance)

July 21	Benno Moiseiwitsch	Rachmaninov	*Paganini* Variations
23	Cyril Smith	Tchaikovsky	Piano concerto No.1
25	Elsie Suddaby	Handel	Aria
26	Louis Kentner	Liszt	Piano concerto No.1
27	Redvers Llewellyn	Verdi	Cortigiani (*Rigoletto*)
27	Irene Scharrer	Beethoven	Piano concerto No.4
28	Heddle Nash	Mozart	Un aura amorosa (*Cosi fan tutte*)
30	Clifford Curzon	Brahms	Piano concerto No.1
August 1	Noel Eadie	Mozart	Dove sono (*Marriage of Figaro*)
2	Gladys Ripley	Dvořák	Inflammatus (*Stabat Mater*)
3	Angus Morrison	Beethoven	Piano concerto No.2
4	Margaret McArthur	Saint Saëns	*Samson et Delilah* (aria)
4	David Lloyd	Mozart	*Die Zauberflöte* (aria)
6	Dino Borgioli	Massenet/Puccini	*Manon*/*Tosca* (arias)
7	Louis Kentner	Liszt/Schubert	*Wanderer* Fantasy
7	Oda Slobodskaya	Liszt	Die Lorelei
8	Isobel Baillie	Handel/Patrick Hadley	*Semele*/Travellers (arias)
11	Owen Brannigan	Mozart	Catalogue aria (*Don Giovanni*)
11	Mary and Geraldine Peppin	Saint Saëns	Carnival of the Animals
13	Moiseiwitsch	Tchaikovsky	Piano concerto No.1
15	Elene Danieli	Mozart	Non mi dir (*Don Giovanni*)
15	Denis Matthews	Mozart	Piano concerto No.20 (K.466)
16	Clifford Curzon	Ireland/de Falla	Piano concerto/*Nights in the garden of Spain*
21	Norman Walker		aria to be announced
22	Mary Jarred	Mahler	*Das Lied von der Erde*
22	Max Rostal	Bach	Violin concerto in A minor
28	Oda Slobodskaya	Tchaikovsky	Letter scene (*Eugen Onegin*)
29	Kathleen Long	Mozart	Piano concerto No.24 (K.491)
30	Roy Henderson	Delius/Vaughan Williams	*Sea Drift*/Five Tudor Portraits
30	Astra Desmond	Grieg/Vaughan Williams	A Dream/A Swan/ Five Tudor Portraits
31	Frederic Lamond	Beethoven	Piano concerto No.5

September 1	Colin Horsley	Rachmaninov	Piano concerto No.3
1	Isobel Baillie		aria to be announced
5	Harriet Cohen	Bach	Piano concerto in F minor/ Brandenburg Concerto No.5
6	Tom Williams	Wagner	Wotan's farewell (*Die Walküre*)
6	Henry Wendon	Liszt	Faust Symphony
7	Kyla Greenbaum	Schoenberg	Piano concerto
7	Trefor Jones	Beethoven/Busoni	Adelaide/Rondo (*Arlecchino*)
8	Myra Hess	Beethoven	Piano concerto No.4
8	Laelia Finneberg	Verdi	*Nabucco* (Scena)
10	Cyril Smith	Brahms	Piano concerto No.2
11	Peter Pears*	Britten	*Les Illuminations*
11	Moiseiwitsch	Rachmaninov	Piano concerto No.1
12	Myra Hess	Mozart	Piano concerto No.9 (K.271)
12	Elisabeth Schumann	Mozart/Schubert	*Il re pastore*/Shepherd on the Rock
13	Oda Slobodskaya	Borodin	Jaroslavna's aria (*Prince Igor*)
13	Kendall Taylor	Prokofiev	Piano concerto No.3
14	Elsie Suddaby	Vaughan Williams	Thanksgiving for Victory
15	Phyllis Sellick	Rawsthorne	Piano concerto
15	Kathleen Ferrier*	Tchaikovsky	Air des adieux (*The Maid of Orleans*)
15	Norman Allin	Handel	*Partenope* (aria)

Ibbs and Tillett Artists appearing at the BBC Promenade Concerts 1947

July	19	Elena Danieli	Handel	aria
	22	Redvers Llewellyn	Delius	*Sea Drift*/Mass of Life (arias)
	23	Kyla Greenbaum	Lambert	*Rio Grande*
	24	Kyla Greenbaum	Liszt	Piano concerto No.2
	25	Phyllis Sellick	Beethoven	Piano concerto No.3
	26	Henry Wendon		aria
	29	Kendall Taylor	Ireland	Piano concerto
	30	Mary Jarred	Elgar	*Music Makers*
	30	Alexander Choir	Handel/Elgar	The King shall rejoice/*Israel in Egypt* (choruses)/*Music Makers*
August	2	Janet Howe	Wagner	Adriano's aria (*Rienzi*)
	4	Michal Hambourg	Chopin	Piano concerto No.2
	6	Maurice Raskin	Brahms	Violin concerto
	11	Max Rostal	Tchaikovsky	Violin concerto
	12	Elsie Suddaby/ Astra Desmond/ Roy Henderson	Vaughan Williams	*Benedicite*
	13	Norman Walker	Handel	aria
	13	Harriet Cohen	Bach/Bax	Piano concerto in D minor/ Morning Song
	15	Irene Kohler	Moeran	Rhapsody
	16	Jo Vincent		aria

	16	Cyril Smith	Franck	Symphonic variations
	18	Arthur Carron	Wagner	*Götterdämmerung* (excerpts)
	19	William Primrose	Berlioz	*Harold in Italy*
	19	Isobel Baillie	Mozart	aria (*La finta gardiniera*)
	21	Laelia Finneberg	Verdi	Scena/Cavatina (*Macbeth*)
	23	Gladys Ripley	Elgar/Lambert	*Sea Pictures*/*Rio Grande*
	27	Kathleen Ferrier	Mozart/Brahms	aria (*Clemenza di Tito*)/ Alto Rhapsody
	27	Denis Matthews	Brahms	Piano concerto No.2
	28	Louis Kentner	Bartók	Piano concerto No.3
	29	Marie Wilson	Bax	Violin concerto
	30	Muriel Brunskill	Purcell/Harrison	Mad Bess/Song
	30	Lance Dossor	Grieg	Piano concerto
September	1	Janet Howe/Tom Williams/David Lloyd	Wagner	*Die Meistersinger* (excerpts)
	3	Elisabeth Schumann	Bach/Mahler	arias/Symphony No.4
	3	Winifred Roberts	Bach	Violin concerto in A minor
	4	Edna Hobson	Tchaikovsky	Joan of Arc's farewell (*Maid of Orleans*)
	4	Clifford Curzon	Mozart	Piano concerto No.23 (K.488)
	5	Myra Hess	Beethoven	Piano concerto No.5
	6	Cyril Smith	Rachmaninov	Piano concerto No.3
	9	Oda Slobodskaya	Liszt	Lorelei's song
	9	Denis Matthews	Liszt arr.Busoni	Spanish Rhapsody
	10	Iris Loveridge	William Schuman	Piano concerto
	11	Noel Mewton-Wood	Humphrey Searle	Piano concerto
	12	Gladys Ripley/ Harold Williams	Beethoven	Symphony No.9
	13	Natasha Litvin	Mendelssohn	Piano concerto No.1

APPENDIX 8

Chamber Music 1949–51, Artists' Brochures 1951–52, Strok, Tillett and Holt 1957–58

Chamber Music May 1949–April 1951

String quartets

Hungarian
Prague
Paganini
Barylli
Latvian
Blech
Philharmonia
Laurence Turner
Peter Gibbs
Marie Wilson
Calvet
Loewenguth
New Italian
Sweelinck
Griller
Amadeus
Aeolian
Hirsch
McGibbon
English
Gertler
Busch
Poltronieri
Pascal
Menges
Martin
Marjorie Hayward
Hurwitz
Sturdy
Zorian

Piano trios

Trio di Trieste
London International Trio
Harry Isaacs Trio
Rubbra–Brainin–Pleeth Trio
Pasquier Trio
London Czech Trio
London Piano Trio
Kamaran Trio
Alan Loveday Trio
Carter Trio
Cecilia Hansen Trio
New English Trio
Prague Trio
Dorian Trio
Philharmonic Trio

Piano quartets

London Belgian Piano Quartet
London Pianoforte Quartet
Robert Masters Piano Quartet
English Ensemble

Piano quintet

Quintette de l'atelier

Dennis Brain Ensemble
Alma Musica
Zephyr Trio
Pro Musica Antiqua
Musica Antica
London Baroque Ensemble
Chamber Music Ensemble of the Berlin Philharmonic Orchestra
Moyse Trio
London Harpsichord Ensemble
Philharmonic Ensemble
Kammer Quintet
Sylvan Trio
Wigmore Ensemble
Quintette Instrumental Pierre Jamet

The Boyd Neel String Orchestra (Conductor: Boyd Neel)
The Jacques String Orchestra (Conductor: Reginald Jacques)
The New London Orchestra (Conductor: Alec Sherman)
The London String Orchestra (Conductor: Alan Bush)
The Kathleen Merritt String Orchestra (Conductor: Kathleen Merritt)
The Kathleen Riddick String Orchestra (Conductor: Kathleen Riddick)

Violin and piano recitals: Ginette Neveu and Jean Neveu Adolf Busch and Rudolf Serkin Max Rostal and Franz Osborn Arthur Grumiaux and Leon Degraux Brosa and Kathleen Long Maurice Raskin and Marcel Gazelle Jelly d'Aranyi and James Sherrin Yfrah Neaman and Howard Ferguson Frederick Grinke and Kendall Taylor Marie Wilson and Liza Fuchsova Szymon Goldberg and Gerald Moore Jean Pougnet and Wilfrid Parry David Martin and Iris Loveridge Thomas Matthews and Eileen Ralf

Violin and harpsichord recitals: Winifred Roberts and Geraint Jones
Recitals of works for two violins: Jelly d'Aranyi and Adila Fachiri Alan Loveday and Neville Marriner
Piano and viola recitals: Max Gilbert and John Hunt
Recitals of works for two cellos: Maud Martin and Paul Tortelier

Cello and piano recitals
Pierre Fournier and Ernest Lush
James Whitehead and Harry Isaacs
William Pleeth and Margaret Good
David Ffrangcon-Thomas and Myers Foggin
Maurice Gendron and Ivor Newton
Eleanor Warren and Walter Susskind
Marie Earnshaw and Joan Vernon
Anthony Pini and Gerald Moore
Antonia Butler and Norman Greenwood
Douglas Cameron and Eric Harrison

Recitals of works for two pianos
Ethel Bartlett and Rae Robertson
Harry Isaacs and York Bowen
Cyril Smith and Phyllis Sellick
Mary and Geraldine Peppin
Hilda Dederich and Ethel de Gomez
Joan and Valerie Trimble
Eileen and Joan Lovell
Olive Rees and Mary Madden

Guitar: Segovia
Flute: Rene Le Roy John Amadio Joseph Slater John Francis Geoffrey Gilbert Gareth Morris Arthur Cleghorn Marcel Moyse Russell King
Oboe: Léon Goossens Evelyn Rothwell John Wolf David Tucker Leonard Brain
Clarinet: Frederick Thurston Reginald Kell Pierre de Bavier Pauline Juler
Bassoon: Archie Camden Cecil James
Horn: Dennis Brain
Trumpet: George Eskdale Harold Jackson
Harp: Marie Korchinska Gwendolen Mason Sidonie Goossens Marie Goossens Lily Laskine

Carl Dolmetsch (recorder) and Joseph Saxby (harpsichord)

Pianists

Cortot
Pouishnoff
Iso Elinson
Alexander Uninsky
Edwin Fischer
Clifford Curzon
Franz Reizenstein
Karl Ulrich Schnabel
Jean Francaix
Spivakowsky
Frank Mannheimer
Francis Poulenc
John Simons
Eric Harrison
Eric Hope
John Hunt
Chavchavadze
Geoffrey Tankard
Peter Cooper
Ross Pratt
Frank Britton
Tom Bromley

Solomon
Rudolf Serkin
Medtner
Louis Kentner
Julius Katchen
Paul Baumgartner
Wilhelm Kempff
Smeterlin
Denis Matthews
Orloff
Kendall Taylor
Angus Morrison
Mewton Wood
Mantle Childe
Colin Horsley
Julius Isserlis
Cyril Preedy
Joseph Cooper
Robert Collet
Leonard Cassini
Terence Beckles
Ronald Smith

Schnabel
Moiseiwitsch
Dohnányi
Peter Stadlen
Eduardo del Pueyo
Nikita Magaloff
Cyril Smith
Jacques Février
Pierre Sancan
Maurice Cole
Robert Riefling
Leslie England
Sidney Harrison
Aronowitz
Joseph Weingarten
Lance Dossor
Varella Cid
Stephen Wearing
Raymond O'Connell
Dennis Murdoch
Peter Katin
Franz Osborn

Myra Hess
Lili Kraus
Monique de la Bruchollerie
Eileen Ralf
Renata Borgatti
Kathleen Long
Shulamith Shafir
Lisa Fuchsova
Kyla Greenbaum
Dorothy Hesse
Agnes Walker
Ivey Dickson
Ella Pounder
Susan Slivko
Yvonne Catterall
Nicole Henriot
Desiree MacEwan

Irene Scharrer
Gina Bachauer
Yvonne Lefébure
Nina Milkina
Rena Kyriakou
Moura Lympany
Adelina de Lara
Iris Loveridge
Valda Aveling
Natasha Litvin
Jean Mackie
Joan Baker
Edna Iles
Marika Papaioanou
Jean Merlow
Muriel Kerr
Rucky van Mill

Harriet Cohen
Michal Hambourg
Phyllis Sellick
Irene Kohler
Adela Verne
Ilona Kabos
Dorothea Braus
Denise Lassimonne
Ruth Gipps
Eiluned Davies
Margerie Few
Barbara Hill
Maria Donska
Sheila Mossman
Monique Haas
Ingebjorg Gresvik
Muriel Dixon

Harpsichord

Lucille Wallace
Millicent Silver

Dr Thornton Lofthouse
Raymond Russell

Ralph Kirkpatrick

Violinists

Adolf Busch
Thibaud
Szigeti
Henry Holst
Campoli
Albert Sammons
Telmanyi
Devy Erlih
Ginette Neveu
Max Rostal
Jelly d'Aranyi
Bratza
Marie Wilson
Arthur Grumiaux
Szymon Goldberg
Antonio Brosa
Yfrah Neaman
Adila Fachiri
Theo Olof
Thomas Matthews
Ida Haendel
Cecilia Hansen
Maurice Raskin
Isolde Menges
Frederick Grinke
Robert Soëtens
Alan Loveday
Jean Pougnet
Harold Fairhurst
Melsa
Colin Sauer
Ivry Gitlis
Samuel Kutcher
Felix Kok
Christian Ferras
Peter Bornstein
Raymond Mosley
Hannah Wishart
Ede Zathureczky
Winifred Roberts
Olive Zorian
May Harrison
Maria Lonova
Michelle Carte
Vera Kantrovitch
Audrey Catterall
Joan Spencer
Maria Lidka

Viola

Lionel Tertis
William Primrose
Bernard Shore
Watson Forbes
Max Gilbert
Winifred Copperwheat

Cellists

Casals
Suggia
Piatigorsky
Gaspar Cassadó
Enrico Mainardi
André Navarra
Pierre Fournier
Paul Tortelier
Maurice Gendron
Thelma Reiss
Felix Salmond
Anthony Pini
Maurice Marechal
Henri Honegger
Maurice Eisenberg
Maurice Dambois
Livio Mannucci
Mischel Cherniavsky
Luigi Gasparini
Karel Horitz
James Whitehead
Wykeham George
William Pleeth
Vivian Joseph
Douglas Cameron
Ivor James
Harvey Phillips
David Ffrangcon-Thomas
John Shinebourne
Alexander Kok
Beatrice Harrison
Antonia Butler
Florence Hooton
Leily Howell
Eleanor Warren
Peers Coetmore
Norina Semino
Peggie Sampson
Helen Just
Marie Earnshaw
Eileen Croxford
Gwendolen McGill
Marie Dare
Kathleen Moorhouse
Beatrix Clare
Malka Cossack
Amaryllis Fleming

New English Singers
London Madrigal Group
Fleet Street Choir
Tudor Singers
London Singers
English Singers Quartet
Intimate Opera

Song recitals

Elisabeth Schumann	Isobel Baillie	Kathleen Ferrier
Oda Slobodskaya	Jo Vincent	Alexandre Trianti
Gabriella Gatti	Joan Hammond	Eugenia Zareska
Elsie Suddaby	Megan Foster	Astra Desmond
Joan Cross	Ena Mitchell	Mary Jarred
Muriel Brunskill	Janine Micheau	Flore Wend
Flora Nielsen	Dora van Doorn	Marjorie Thomas
Soffi Schonning	Nancy Evans	Desi Halban
Geneviève Touraine	Emelie Hooke	Sophie Wyss
Margaret Field-Hyde	Betty Bannerman	Audrey Strange
Dino Borgioli	Keith Falkner	Aksel Schiøtz
Heddle Nash	Harold Williams	Roy Henderson
Bruce Boyce	Gerard Souzay	Hermann Schey
Marko Rothmuller	Jan van der Gucht	Robert Irwin
Frederick Fuller	Eric Greene	Richard Lewis
William Herbert	Rene Soames	David Franklin
Alvar Lidell	Laurence Holmes	John Kentish
Henry Cummings	Dale Smith	Gordon Clinton
Scott Joynt	Hervey Alan	Philip Hattey
Alfred Hepworth		

Vocal recitals: Pierre Bernac and Francis Poulenc Peter Pears and Benjamin Britten
Viorica Ursuleac and Clemens Krauss Janet Fraser and Norman Fraser
Recitals of songs and duets: Kathleen Ferrier and Roy Henderson
Folksongs of many lands: Engel Lund
Recitals of folksongs: Eve Maxwell-Lyte Frederick Grisewood Hedli Anderson Peggy Stack
Songs and duets from the French operas: Joan Cross and Peter Pears with Benjamin Britten
Diversity of song: Mary Linde and Eric Greene
Recitals of songs and partsongs, madrigals etc: Roy Henderson and Nottingham Oriana Choir
Music through the centuries: Ivey Dickson and Hervey Alan
Songs with guitar accompaniment: Olga Goelho

Ibbs and Tillett Artists' Brochures 1951–52

Sole representatives for the following Artists

Elisabeth Schumann
Elsie Suddaby
Oda Slobodskaya
Joan Taylor
Mascia Predit
Blanche Turner
Flore Wend
Adrienne Cole
Eleanor Houston
Anny Konetzni
Isobel Baillie
Margherita Grandi
Ena Mitchell
Laelia Finneberg
Emelie Hooke
Gabriella Gatti
Mary Linde
Dorothy Bond
Ingrid Hageman
Elisabeth Schwarzkopf
Joan Cross
Alexandra Trianti
Jennifer Vyvyan
Dora van Doorn
Margery Field
Janine Micheau
Elsie Morison
Ruth Packer

Kathleen Ferrier
Muriel Brunskill
Marjorie Thomas
Flora Nielsen
Constance Shacklock
Mary Jarred
Astra Desmond
Anne Wood
Nancy Evans
Norma Procter
Gladys Ripley
Nancy Thomas
Valetta Iacopi
Janet Howe

Heddle Nash
William Herbert
Rene Soames
Jan van der Gucht
Ronald Hill
Stephen Manton
Peter Pears
Eric Greene
Trefor Jones
Aksel Schiøtz
David Galliver
Richard Lewis
David Lloyd
Bradbridge White
Lloyd Strauss-Smith
John Kentish

Harold Williams
Roy Henderson
Dennis Noble
Nowakowski
Robert Irwin
Trevor Anthony
John Dethick
Richard Standen
Keith Falkner
Dietrich Fischer-Dieskau
Norman Walker
Owen Brannigan
Gordon Clinton
Hervey Alan
Scott Joynt
Pierre Bernac
Mack Harrell
Redvers Llewellyn
Henry Cummings
Gerard Souzay
Stanley Clarkson
Norman Tattersall

Cortot
Schnabel
Lili Kraus
Dohnányi
Louis Kentner
Nina Milkina
Friedrich Wührer
Cyril Smith
Michal Hambourg
Gonzalo Soriano
Chavchavadze
Nikita Magaloff
Solomon
Irene Scharrer
Edwin Fischer
Gina Bachauer
Phyllis Sellick
Smeterlin
Orloff
Colin Horsley
Francis Poulenc
Yvonne Lefébure
Wilhelm Kempff
John Hunt
Myra Hess
Moiseiwitsch
Themeli
Harriet Cohen
Clifford Curzon
Irene Kohler
Shulamith Shafir
Denis Matthews
Lance Dossor
Cherkassky
Reine Gianoli
Anatole Kitain

Frank Mannheimer
Franz Osborn
Cyril Preedy
Weingarten
Sheila Randell
Clara Haskil
Prina Salsman
Ethel Bartlett and Rae Robertson
Mewton-Wood
Eric Harrison
Lyell Barbour
Peter Katin
Monique Haas
Germaine Leroux
Moura Lympany
Lucille Wallace
Valda Aveling
Liza Fuchsova
Kendall Taylor
Iris Loveridge
Monique de la Bruchollerie
Arnaldo Estrella
Jacqueline Potier
Angelica von Sauer Morales
Ralph Kirkpatrick

Adolf Busch
Szymon Goldberg
Jelly d'Aranyi
Maurice Raskin
Betty-Jean Hagen
Igor Ozim
Lionel Tertis
Szigeti
Telmányi
Antonio Brosa
Nadia Koutzen
Marta Eitler
Eugene Prokop
William Primrose
Max Rostal
Arthur Grumiaux
Adila Fachiri
Johanna Martzy
Theo Olof
Robert Soëtens

Casals
Joseph Schuster
Pierre Fournier
Enrico Mainardi
Paul Tortelier
Zara Nelsova

Segovia
Engel Lund
Mildred Dilling
Olga Coehlo
Larry Adler
Julian Bream
The Fleet Street Choir
Germani

String Quartets
Griller
Budapest
Vienna Konzerthaus
New Italian
Amadeus
Paganini
Hirsch
Peter Gibbs
Hungarian
Loewenguth
Rome

London Belgian Piano Quartet
Loveridge–Martin–Hooton Trio
Quintette instrumental Pierre Jamet
Quintetto Boccherini
Robert Masters Piano Quartet
Trio di Trieste
Alma Musica
Quintetto Chigiano
Salzburg Menuetto
Pasquier String Trio
Février–Le Roy–Albin Trio
Quintette de l'atelier
London Harpsichord Ensemble

The Philharmonia Orchestra

Sopranos
Elisabeth Schumann
Joan Hammond
Margherita Grandi
Maggie Teyte
Arda Mandikian
Isobel Baillie
Gwen Catley
Elisabeth Schwarzkopf
Mascia Predit
Alexandra Trianti
Dora van Doorn
Gabriella Gatti
Elsie Suddaby
Ena Mitchell
Irmgard Seefried
Jo Vincent
Oda Slobodskaya
Janine Micheau
Sena Jurinac
Joan Cross
Ada Alsop

Laelia Finneberg
Joan Taylor
Ruth Naylor
Megan Foster
Isabelita Alonso
Minnia Bower
Priscilla Childs
Elena Danieli
Olwen Davies
Mirimi del Pozo
Lorely Dyer
Margaret Field-Hyde
Sylvia Fisher
Joyce Goodwin
Nora Gruhn
Mary Hamlin
Helen Hill
Betty Huntley-Wright
Marian Lowe
Christine Orr
Elisabeth Parry
Winifred Radford
Glenda Raymond
Edwina Savage
Soffi Schonning
Victoria Sladen
Louise Stranzinger
Vera Terry
Olive Turner
Maria Walkowsky
Flore Wend
Sophie Wyss
Lily Windsor
Elizabeth Grümmer
Marian Hughes
Eleanor Houston
Adrienne Cole
Linda Parker
Muriel Rae
Elsie Morison
Jennifer Vyvyan
Margery Field
Ingrid Hageman
Nancy Bateman
Phyllis Brooks
Mary Collier
Elizabeth Darbishire
Patricia Davies
Diana de Rosso
Martha Dyson
Joan Fullerton
Elizabeth Green
Rosanna Giancola
Bertha Hann
Janys Holm
Mary Lake
Phyllis Mander
Ruth Packer
Sylvia Patriss
Rosina Raisbeck
Olivia Rossi
Emerentia Scheepers
Maria Scotti
Joan Stirrup
Joan Stuart
Susanna Thackeray
Myra Verney
Ljuba Welitsch
Kate Winter
Bettine Young
Jean Austin-Dobson
Rose Hill
Rita McKerrow
Barbara Brutton
Janet Hamilton-Smith
Stella Hitchens
Maureen Springer
Emelie Hooke
Margaret Ritchie
Blanche Turner
Joan Alexander
Dorothy Bond
Joan Butler
Joan Coxon
Marian Davies
Gita de la Fuente
Dora Drake
Margaret Eaves
Doris Gambell
Olive Groves
Una Hale
Beryl Hatt
Zuilmah Hopkins
Mary Linde
Karin Monk
Dorothy Parfitt
Pamela Petts
Dorea Raye
Ceinwen Rowlands
Janette Sclanders
Amy Schuard
Audrey Strange
Marion Studholme
Hella Toros
Diana Vernon
Sylvia Welling
Mary Worth
Leonie Zifado
Edna Hobson
Dora Drake
Patricia Howard
Anny Kunetzni
Thelma Godfrey
Isabell Sage
Veronica Dunne

Contraltos

Kathleen Ferrier
Astra Desmond
Marjorie Thomas
Edith Coates
Valetta Iacopi
Constance Shacklock
Maud Baker
Gladys Ripley
Janet Howe
Nancy Thomas
Eugenia Zareska
Anne Wood
Margaret McArthur
Betty Bannerman
Mary Jarred
Muriel Brunskill
Flora Nielsen
Nancy Evans
Grace Bodey
Irene Baker
Norah Beaves

Ethel Bird
Ruth Bowman
Irene Byatt
Doris Cowen
Myfanwy Evans
Edith Furmedge
Frances Gorick
Maud Heaton
Dora Jones
Patricia Kern
Molly Leaper
Jennie Mordue
Gladys Parr
Eileen Pilcher
Betty Sagon
Constance Stocker
Freda Townson
Winifred White
Rose Boelsma
Eva Gustavson
Elisabeth Robinson
Margaret Bissett
Margaret Boys
Nora Carstairs
Kathleen Coxon
Winifred Ewer
Ruby Fotheringham
Joan Gray
Gertrude Holt
Kathleen Joyce
Lily Kettlewell
Bruna MacLean
Joyce Newton
May Pearson
Anna Pollak
Monica Sinclair
Anne Storry
Madge Warner
Sybil Willey
Kathleen Willson
Esther Salamon
Patricia Black
Sara Buckley
Bessie Collins
Ethel Davies
Janet Fraser
Muriel Gale
Vera Healy
Winefride Ingham
Kathleen Kay
Catherine Lawson
Veronica Mansfield
Gladys Palmer
Mary Peters
Norma Procter
Muriel Smith
Joyce Sutton
Monica Warner
Mona Benson
Jean Austin-Dobson
Audrey Brice

Tenors

Heddle Nash
Richard Lewis
Webster Booth
James Johnston
Trefor Jones
Jan van der Gucht
Leslie Andrews
Arthur Ayton
John Caunce
Tom Culbert
Tudor Davies
Ivan Dixon
Edgar Evans
Walter Glynne
Herbert Hainsworth
Cyril Hornby
Rowland Jones
Gwent Lewis
Bradshaw MacMillan
John McHugh
Ronald Murgatroyd
Robert Naylor
Mervyn Saunders
Cragg Sinkinson
Anthony Strange
Peter Pears
Rene Soames
Franz Vroons
Aksel Schiøtz
Parry Jones
Frank Sale
George Armitage
Ronald Bristol
George Chitty
Colin Cunningham
Alfred Deller
Joseph Dollinger
Bruce Flegg
Andrew Gold
Howard Hemming
Llewellyn John
John Kentish
John Lewis
Andrew Macpherson
Clifford Mills
John Myrddin
Kenneth Neate
John Searl
Frederick Steger
Lloyd Strauss-Smith
Eric Greene
William Herbert
Walter Midgley
David Lloyd
Bradbridge White
Ronald Hill
Roy Ashton
Arthur Carron
Joseph Congden
Gerald Davies
Murray Dickie
John Duncan
David Galliver
Alfred Hallett
Alfred Hepworth
Bryn Jones
Patrick Largey
Norman Lilly
Stephen Manton
Hubert Milverton Carta
Raymond Nilssen
Ereach Riley
Arthur Servent
Dennis Stephenson
John Tainsh

Hindley Taylor
Robert Thomas
Frank Titterton
John Torney
Cyril Tucker
John Turner
Laurence Watts
Henry Wendon
Cecil Wigley
Max Worthley
John Wright
Alexander Young
David Price
William McAlpine
Helmut Krebs
Richard Langdon
Ernst Wolff
Tom Round
Wilfrid Brown
Laurens Bogtman

Baritones [and basses]

Pierre Bernac
Owen Brannigan
Dennis Noble
Harold Williams
Roy Henderson
Keith Falkner
Norman Walker
Redvers Llewellyn
Henry Cummings
Norman Allin
Dietrich Fischer-Dieskau
Robert Irwin
Gordon Clinton
Mack Harrell
Bruce Boyce
Gerard Souzay
Tom Williams
Nowakowski
Frederick Fuller
Trevor Anthony
William Parsons
Robert Easton
Norman Lumsden
Hervey Alan
Marko Rothmuller
Pierre Mollet
Hermann Schey
Scott Joynt
John Dethick
Richard Standen
Stanley Clarkson
Kenneth Adams
George Allen
George Baker
Maurice Bevan
Ian Blair
James Bond
Richard Bowen
John Brownlee
Henry Bush
David Carver
Denis Catlin
Bruce Clark
Arthur Copley
Arthur Cranmer
Bruce Dargavel
George Delderfield
Clifford Deri
William Dickie
Edmond Donlevy
Denis Dowling
Kenneth Ellis
Ivor Evans
Tudor Evans
Joseph Farrington
Arthur Fear
David Franklin
Reginald Gibbs
Henry Gill
Howell Glynne
George Hancock
Clement Hardman
Frederick Harvey
Philip Hattey
Thomas Hemsley
Laurence Holmes
Roy Hickman
George James
Herbert Janssen
Harding Jenkins
Roderick Jones
Ellis Keeler
Otakar Kraus
Martin Lawrence
Emrys Lloyd
Stanley Mason
Arnold Matters
Norman Miller
Fisher Morgan
Donald Munro
Oscar Natzke
Raymond Newell
Gordon Parfitt
Stanley Pearson
George Pizzey
Stanley Pine
David Perrin
Norman Platt
George Prangnell
Arthur Reckless
Robert Rowell
Frederick Sharp
Harry Shaw
Eric Shilling
Dale Smith
Fabian Smith
Sydney Smith
Bernhard Sonnerstedt
Ronald Stear
Jack Townend
Booth Unwin
Ian Wallace
Denis Weatherley
Leyland White
Richard Wood
Frederick Woodhouse
Fraser Gange
Jess Walters
Joseph Leader
John Heddle Nash
Doda Conrad
Reginald Hipperson
Gwyn Griffith
Gerhard Gröschel
Lawrence Lott
Norman Tattersall
Geoffrey Colely

John Cameron
James Atkins
Claude May
Kenneth Stevenson
Albert Balaam
Frederick Calvert
Aubrey Pankey
Laurence Edwards
David Allen
Roger Stalman
Arthur Wallington
Geraint Evans
Inia te Wiata
John Hargreaves
Geoffrey Walls
Bryan Drake

Pianists

Moiseiwitsch
Edwin Fischer
Clifford Curzon
Cyril Smith
Wilhelm Kempff
Orloff
Kendall Taylor
Anatole Kitain
Lyell Barbour
John Hunt
Weingarten
Eduardo Del Pueyo
Baumgartner
Frank Britton
Leonard Cassini
Mantle Childe
Joseph Cooper
Leslie England
Albert Ferber
James Gibb
Mark Hambourg
Eric Hope
Clive Lythgoe
Loudon Merry
Dennis Murdoch
Ross Pratt
Pierre Sancan
John Simons
Geoffrey Tankard
Stephen Wearing
Greer Holesch
Frank Lafitte
Jorg Demus
Ivo Macek
Thomas Rajna
Christopher Wood
William Glock
James Ching
Robert Weisz
Frank Pilleg
Schnabel
Louis Kentner
Magaloff
Cherkassky
Smeterlin
Gonzalo Soriano
Franz Osborn
Colin Horsley
Iso Elinson
Lance Dossor
Eric Harrison
Geza Anda
Terence Beckles
Tom Bromley
Aldo Ciccolini
Maurice Cole
Peter Cooper
Arnaldo Estrella
Jacques Février
Richard Glas
Conrad Hansen
Julius Katchen
Malcuzynski
John Moores
Raymond O'Connell
Franz Reizenstein
Rudolf Serkin
Ronald Smith
Uninsky
Friedrich Wührer
Horszowski
Hans Alexander Kaul
Rodolfo Caporali
Annarosa Taddei
Anderson Tyker
Leon Fleischer
John Brennan
Yuri Boukoff
Hubert Harry
Wilhelm Backhaus
Cortot
Dohnányi
Denis Matthews
Solomon
Themeli
Francis Poulenc
Mewton-Wood
Isserlis
Chavchavadze
Cyril Preedy
Peter Katin
Aronowitz
Lionel Bowman
Murray Brown
Varella Cid
Robert Collet
Sequiera Costa
Richard Farrell
Jean Francaix
Reginald Godden
Sidney Harrison
Colin Kingsley
Frank Mannheimer
Angus Morrison
Pouishnoff
Robert Riefling
Karl Ulrich Schnabel
Peter Stadlen
Gordon Watson
Rudolf am Bach
Gordon McLean
Bela Siki
Dorel Handeman
Leonard Pennario
Harold Rubens
Robin Wood
Gerard Hengeveld
Tonis Giorgiou
David Stimer
John Rauck

Myra Hess
Lili Kraus
Phyllis Sellick
Irene Kohler
Yvonne Lefébure
Liza Fuchsova
Celia Arieli
Marcella Barzetti
Dorothea Braus
Joan Davies
Ivey Dickson
Edith Farnadi
Virginia Fortescue
Violet Graham
Monique Haas
Barbara Hill
Ilona Kabos
Germaine Leroux
Jean Mackie
Diana Merrien
Marika Papaioanou
Eileen Ralf
Mary Syme
Elsie Jacobs
Magda Tagliaferro
Melinée Peris
Angelica von Sauer Morales
Patricia Carroll
Joyce Riddell
Thorunn Trygvason
Gina Bachauer
Harriet Cohen
Kathleen Long
Monique de la Bruchollerie
Reine Gianoli
Valda Aveling
Joan Baker
Marjorie Blackburn
Yvonne Catterall
Adelina de Lara
Muriel Dixon
Henriette Faure
Ruth Gipps
Kyla Greenbaum
Nicole Henriot
Barbara Holt
Muriel Kerr
Natasha Litvin
Desiree McEwan
Joan Moore
Christine Pembridge
Sheila Randell
Agnes Walker
Bronwen Jones
Janine da Costa
Dorothy Roberts
Jean Harvey
Daphne Spottiswoode
Lois Phillips
Clara Haskil
Irene Scharrer
Nina Milkina
Michal Hambourg
Shulamith Shafir
Iris Loveridge
Fiona Addie
Philippa Barnes
Anthea Bowring
Eiluned Davies
Rosa Dennis
Maria Donska
Margerie Few
Katharine Goodson
Ingejorg Gresvik
Dorothy Hesse
Edna Iles
Denise Lassimonne
Moura Lympany
Jean Merlow
Sheila Mossman
Ella Pounder
Susan Slivko
Fanny Waterman
Melita Lorkovic
Bertha Hogart
Grete Scheizer
Susan Tunnell
Ruth Harte
Margaret Vogel

Two-piano ensembles

Ethel Bartlett and Rae Robertson
Mary and Geraldine Peppin
Olive Rees and Mary Madden
Sheila Randell and Philippa Barnes
Cyril Smith and Phyllis Sellick
Joan and Valerie Trimble
Tony Lowry and Clive Richardson
David Rance and Philip Crocker
Luboschutz and Nemenoff
Eileen and Joan Lovell
Rawicz and Landauer
Harry Isaacs and York Bowen

Harpsichord

Ralph Kirkpatrick
Raymond Russell
John Ticehurst
Arnold Goldsborough
Thurston Dart
Gustav Leonhardt
Sylvia Marlowe
Dr Thornton Lofthouse
Millicent Silver
Aimee van de Weill
John Churchill
Susi Jeans
Lucille Wallace
Boris Ord
Geraint Jones
Hubert Dawkes
John Wills
Frank Pillig

Organ

G. Thalben Ball
Sandy Macpherson
Harold Darke
Charles Amart
Flor Peeters
Claire Coci
Fernando Germani
Geraint Jones
Reginald New
Virgil Fox
Jean Trevelyan
R. Arnold Grier
Reginald Foort
Arnold Richardson
Hugh Giles
Margaret Cobb

Violin

Szigeti
Brosa
Theo Olof
Frederick Grinke
Adila Fachiri
Manoug Parikian
Peter Bornstein
Campoli
Gioconda de Vito
Devy Erlih
Ivry Gitlis
Ida Haendel
Jurgen Hess
Tom Jenkins
Louis Kaufman
Nona Lidell
Thomas Matthews
Raymond Mosley
Eugene Prokop
Winifred Roberts
Jan Sedivka
Thibaud
Hannah Wishart
Marta Eitler
Wolfgang Schneiderhahn
Betty-Jean Hagen
Elise Csafalvi
Roland Stanbridge
Gerald Briscor
Adolf Busch
Arthur Grumiaux
Telmányi
Jean Pougnet
Johanna Martzy
Raymond Cohen
Bratza
Michelle Carte
Nico Dikeos
Harold Fairhurst
John Glickman
Cecilia Hansen
Ralph Hollander
Granville Jones
Felix Kok
Maria Lidka
Melsa
Yfrah Neaman
Maurice Raskin
Suzanne Rozsa
Robert Soëtens
Alfredo Wang
Olive Zorian
Roman Totenberg
David Montagu
Igor Ozim
Bronislav Gimpel
Endre Wolff
Max Rostal
Szymon Goldberg
Jelly d'Aranyi
Alan Loveday
Nadia Koutzen
Beryl Kimber
Ricardo Brengola
Audrey Catterall
Denis East
Christian Ferras
Erich Gruenberg
May Harrison
Henry Holst
Vera Kantrovitch
Samuel Kutcher
Maria Lonova
Isolde Menges
Ruth Pearl
Tessa Robbins
Colin Sauer
Joan Spencer
Marie Wilson
Elizabeth Lockhart
Tibor Varga
Henriette Canter
Hugh Bean
Jean Harvey
Mischa Elman

Two violins

Sybil Copeland and John Glickman

Viola

Lionel Tertis
Max Gilbert
Watson Forbes
Hubert Downes
Bernard Shore
Winifred Copperwheat
Anatole Mines
William Primrose
Frederick Riddle
Harry Danks

Violoncello

Casals
Paul Tortelier
Pierre Fournier
Gaspar Cassadó
Joseph Schuster
Zara Nelsova
Thelma Reiss
Henri Honegger
Enrico Mainardi
Anthony Pine
Mischel Cherniavsky
Juliette Alvin
Joan Bonner
Antonia Butler
Douglas Cameron
Vera Canning
Beatrix Clare
Peers Coetmore
Malka Cossack
Eileen Croxford
Maurice Dambois
Marie Dare
Marie Earnshaw
Maurice Eisenberg
Amaryllis Fleming
David Ffrangcon-Thomas
Francisco Gabarro
Luigi Gasparini
Wykeham George
Beatrice Harrison
Florence Hooton
Karel Horitz
Leily Howell
Ivor James
Vivian Joseph
Helen Just
Alexander Kok
Livio Mannucci
Maurice Marechal
Gwendolen McGill
Kathleen Moorhouse
André Navarra
Harvey Phillips
Piatigorsky
Anthony Pini
William Pleeth
Felix Salmond
Peggie Sampson
Janos Scholz
Norina Semino
John Shinebourne
Atis Teichmanis
Eleanor Warren
James Whitehead
Antonio Janigro

Piano and cello

Margaret Moncrieff and Robert Keys

Guitar

Segovia
Julian Bream (and lute)

Harmonica

Larry Adler

Harp

Marie Korchinska
Marie Goossens
Sidonie Goossens
Gwendolen Mason
Lily Laskine
Carlos Ames
Mildred Dilling

Flute

Rene Le Roy
John Amadio
Joseph Slater
John Francis
Arthur Hedges
Lambert Fleck
Geoffrey Gilbert
Gareth Morris
Arthur Gleghorn
Marcel Moyse
Russell King

Oboe

Léon Goossens
Evelyn Rothwell
Elizabeth Hawkins
John Wolf
David Tucker
Leonard Brain
Janet Craxton
Mary Murdoch

Clarinet
Pierre de Bavier
Frederick Thurston
Reginald Kell
Gervase de Peyer
Georgina Dobrée

Bassoon
Archie Camden
Cecil James

Horn
Dennis Brain
Charles Gregory

Trumpet
George Eskdale
Harry Mortimer
Bram Gay
Jack Mackintosh
Harold Jackson

Saxophone
Sigurd Rascher

Songs/guitar
Olga Coehlo
John Gavall

The Philharmonia Orchestra
The New London Orchestra
The London String Orchestra
The Arnold Goldsbrough Orchestra
Max Rostal Chamber Orchestra
The Boyd Neel String Orchestra
The Kathleen Merritt String Orchestra
The Alexandra Orchestra
Harvey Phillips String Orchestra
The Jacques String Orchestra
The London Mozart Players
The Kathleen Riddick String Orchestra
The Kalmar Orchestra
The Haydn Orchestra

The Leslie Bridgewater Quintet
Charles Enesco Quintet
The Leslie Jeffries Trio
Jan Berenska Ensemble
Michael Krem Saxophone Quartet

New English Singers
Fleet Street Choir
The Golden Age Singers
London Bach Group
Renaissance Singers
Hedli Anderson
Winifred Radford
English Singers Quartet
Tudor Singers
Intimate Opera
Lydian Singers
Victoria Kingsley
Eve Maxwell-Lyte
Emlyn Williams
London Madrigal Group
London Singers
Singers in Consort
Kenneth Ellis Singers
Engel Lund
Peggy Stack
The Opera Players
Scenes from the Operas (Directed by Hervey Alan)

Pierre Bernac and Francis Poulenc
Peter Pears and Benjamin Britten

Vocal duets
Anne Ziegler and Webster Booth
Sylvia Welling and Mervyn Saunders
Olive Groves and George Baker
Victoria Anderson and Viola Morris
Janet Hamilton-Smith and John Hargreaves

Strok, Tillett and Holt Ltd: International Artists' Management

Artists' List 1957–58

Sopranos

Jacqueline Delman	Elizabeth Grümmer	Hilde Güden
Joan Hammond	Pilar Lorengar	Elsie Morison
Amy Shuard	Blanche Thebom	Jennifer Vyvyan

Contraltos

Marian Anderson	Pamela Bowden	Nancy Evans
Norma Procter	Constance Shacklock	Muriel Smith

Tenors

Jussi Björling	William Herbert	Richard Lewis
Jan Peerce	Peter Pears	

Baritones

Bruce Boyce	Owen Brannigan	Dietrich Fischer-Dieskau
Gerhard Hüsch	Heinz Rehfuss	Gerard Souzay

Groups

The Deller Consort	The Golden Age Singers	

Pianists

Geza Anda	Gina Bachauer	Daniel Barenboim
Shura Cherkassky	Richard Farrell	Annie Fischer
Ingrid Haebler	Eugene Istomin	Louis Kentner
Denis Matthews	Benno Moiseiwitsch	Jan Smeterlin
Claudio Arrau	William Backhaus	Alexander Brailowsky
Clifford Curzon	Emil Gilels	Myra Hess
Peter Katin	Moura Lympany	Arturo Benedetti Michelangeli
Abbey Simon	Rosalyn Tureck	

Violinists

Campoli	Zino Francescatti	Heifetz
David Oistrakh	Ruggiero Ricci	Max Rostal
Gioconda de Vito	Ida Haendel	Yehudi Menuhin
Michael Rabin	Isaac Stern	Bronislav Gimpel

Cellists

Pierre Fournier	Gregor Piatigorsky	Zara Nelsova
Paul Tortelier		

String quartets

The Amadeus Quartet	The Griller Quartet	The New Lener Quartet
The Paganini Quartet	The Robert Masters Quartet	The Smetana Quartet

Guitar
Julian Bream

Flute
Elaine Schaffer

Harmonica
Larry Adler

Horn
Dennis Brain

Tenor and piano
Peter Pears and Benjamin Britten

Conductors
Sir John Barbirolli
Leonard Bernstein
Sir Arthur Bliss
Sir Adrian Boult
André Cluytens
Alberto Erede
Alexander Gibson
Josef Krips
Rafael Kubelik
Efrem Kurtz
Nicolai Malko
Dimitri Mitropoulos
Eugene Ormandy
Karl Rankl
Arthur Rodzinski
Sir Malcolm Sargent
Thomas Schippers
William Steinberg

Orchestras
London Philharmonic Orchestra (exclusive management)
Boston Symphony Orchestra
Minneapolis Symphony Orchestra

Ballet dancers
Beryl Grey – Oleg Briansky
Nadia Nerina – Alexis Rassine
The Beryl Grey Ballet Group
Soloists from the Royal Danish Ballet

Pipes and drums
Regimental Band, Pipes, Drums and Dancers – The Black Watch
Regimental Band, Pipes and Drums – The Cameron Highlanders

Outstanding attraction
Hoffnung Music Festival

Artists' Brochures 1962–63, 1964–65, 1968–69

Tillett and Holt Artists' List: 1962–63

(*exclusive representation)

Pianists

Geza Anda
Claudio Arrau
Gina Bachauer*
Wilhelm Backhaus
Daniel Barenboim
Alfred Brendel
Idil Biret
Alexander Brailowsky
Shura Cherkassky*
Varella Cid
Clifford Curzon*
Phillipe Entremont
Annie Fischer
Leon Fleisher
Andor Foldes
Emil Gilels
Glenn Gould
Ingrid Haebler
Myra Hess*
Eugene Istomin
Peter Katin*
Louis Kentner
Moura Lympany*
Hephzibah Menuhin
Michelangeli
Denis Matthews*
Moiseiwitsch*
John Ogdon*
Bela Siki
Rudolf Serkin
Abbey Simon
Ann Schein
Smeterlin
Rosalyn Tureck*
Friedrich Wührer

One piano – four hands (or two pianos)

Ingrid Haebler : Ludwig Hoffman
Yaltah Menuhin : Joel Ryce*

Two pianos – three hands

Cyril Smith : Phyllis Sellick*

Violinists

Alfred Campoli
Zino Francescatti
Bronislav Gimpel
Artur Grumiaux
Heifetz
Ralph Holmes*
Beryl Kimber*
Leonid Kogan
Alberto Lysy
Wolfgang Marschner
Johanna Martzy
Yehudi Menuhin
David Oistrakh
Igor Oistrakh
Igor Ozim
Manoug Parikian*
Michael Rabin
Ruggiero Ricci
Max Rostal
Wolfgang Schneiderhan
Isaac Stern
Tibor Varga
Endre Wolf

Cellists

Gaspar Cassadó
Pierre Fournier
Zara Nelsova
Leonard Rose
Rostropovitch
Rohan de Saram*
Paul Tortelier

Sopranos

Ingrid Bjoner
Joan Hammond*
Heather Harper
Elizabeth Harwood*
Pilar Lorengar
Elsie Morison*
Maria Stader
Jennifer Vyvyan*

Mezzo-sopranos and contraltos

Janet Baker*
Pamela Bowden*
Grace Hoffman
Irma Kolassi
Kerstin Meyer
Louise Parker
Norma Procter*
Nell Rankin
Marjorie Thomas*
Helen Watts*

Tenors

Wilfred Brown*
Ronald Dowd
Gerald English
David Galliver*
Richard Lewis
John Mitchinson*
Peter Pears*
John Wakefield*

Baritones and basses

Hervey Alan*
Donald Bell*
Owen Brannigan*
Dietrich Fischer-Dieskau
Thomas Hemsley*
Hermann Prey
Heinz Rehfuss
Forbes Robinson*
Gerard Souzay
Richard Standen*

Tenor and piano

Peter Pears and Benjamin Britten*

Oboe

Léon Goossens
Evelyn Rothwell*

Harpsichord

George Malcolm*
Fernando Valenti

Harp

Nicanor Zabaleta
Osian Ellis*

Guitar

Segovia
John Williams*
William Gomez

Harmonica

Larry Adler*

Recorder and harpsichord

Carl Dolmetsch and Joseph Saxby

Conductors

Leonard Bernstein
Sir Arthur Bliss*
Sir Adrian Boult*
Meredith Davies
Colin Davis*
Antal Dorati
Alberto Erede
Massimo Freccia
Ferenc Fricsay
Alceo Galliera
Pierino Gamba
Alexander Gibson
Bernard Haitink
George Hurst*
Josef Krips
Jaroslav Krombholc
Rafael Kubelik
Enrique Jorda
Erich Leinsdorf
Lawrence Leonard*
Jean Martinon
Pierre Monteux
Charles Munch
Harry Newstone
Eugene Ormandy
Karl Rankl
Thomas Schippers
William Steinberg

Orchestras

London Philharmonic Orchestra*
Bath Festival Chamber Orchestra* (with Yehudi Menuhin)
English Chamber Orchestra* (conductors Colin Davis and Raymond Leppard)
Netherlands Chamber Orchestra (with Szymon Goldberg)
Tureck Bach Players (with Rosalyn Tureck)
Varga Kammer Orchester (with Tibor Varga)

String ensembles

Allegri String Quartet*
Amici String Quartet*
Amadeus String Quartet*
Carmirelli String Quartet
Griller String Quartet*
Smetana String Quartet
Quintetto Chigiano

Ballet

Beryl Grey*

Regimental bands

Regimental Band – Coldstream Guards
Regimental Band, Pipes and Drums – The Black Watch
Regimental Band, Pipes and Drums – The Cameron Highlanders
and other Regiments

Outstanding attractions

Emlyn Williams in readings from Dickens, Dylan Thomas etc.
Joyce Grenfell entertains
Marta Schlamme (folksongs etc.)
Shirley Abicair (folksongs with zither)

Artists represented exclusively by Ibbs and Tillett Ltd: 1964–65

Pianoforte

Vladimir Ashkenazy
Gina Bachauer
Stephen Bishop
Brailowsky
Alfred Brendel
Monique de la Bruchollerie
Thierry de Brunhoff
Chieko Cassadó
Cherkassky
Joseph Cooper
Sequeira Costa
Clifford Curzon
Karl Engel
Annie Fischer
Andor Foldes
Malcolm Frager
James Friskin
Alasdair Graham
Eric Harrison
Eric Heidsieck
Eric Hope
Colin Horsley
Horszowski
Maureen Jones
Peter Katin
Wilhelm Kempff
Louis Kentner
Jacques Klein
Yoko Kono
Lili Kraus
Yvonne Lefébure
Ray Lev
Moura Lympany
George Malcolm
Denis Matthews
Yaltah Menuhin
Nina Milkina
John Ogdon
Hans-Erich Riebensahm
Jerome Rose
Joel Ryce
Ann Schein
Karl Ulrich Schnabel
Phyllis Sellick
Rudolf Serkin
Shulamith Shafir
Allan Schiller
Bela Siki
Smeterlin
André Tchaikowsky
Toh Yi-Lung
Valerie Tryon
Rosalyn Tureck
Sergio Varella-Cid
Weingarten
David Wilde
Friedrich Wührer
Anna Xydis

Two pianofortes and piano duets

John and Richard Contiguglia
Maureen Jones and Dario de Rosa
Denis Matthews and Howard Ferguson
Yaltah Menuhin and Joel Ryce
Cyril Smith and Phyllis Sellick (three hands)

Harpsichord

Thurston Dart
Ralph Kirkpatrick
George Malcolm
Zuzana Ruzickova
Rosalyn Tureck

Harp

Osian Ellis
Marisa Robles

Violin

Salvatore Accardo
Norbert Brainin
Pina Carmirelli
Devy Erlih
Lorand Fenyves
Christian Ferras
José Luis Garcia
Robert Gerle
Bronislav Gimpel
Szymon Goldberg
Arthur Grumiaux
Betty-Jean Hagen
Ralph Holmes
Brenton Langbein
Wolfgang Marschner
Johanna Martzy
Igor Ozim
Yan Pascal
Max Rostal
Gillian Sansom
Michel Schwalbe
Szigeti
Tibor Varga
Endre Wolf

Viola

Lina Lama
Peter Schidlof
Ernst Wallfisch

Violoncello

Senta Benesch
Christopher Bunting
Gaspar Cassadó
Rohan de Saram
Jacqueline du Pré
Maurice Eisenberg
Pierre Fournier
Enrico Mainardi
Bernard Michelin
Zara Nelsova
Joseph Schuster
Paul Tortelier

Violin and pianoforte

Lorand Fenyves and Bela Siki
Frederick Grinke and Joseph Weingarten
Alan Grishman and Joel Ryce
Langbein-Jones Duo
Alfred Loewenguth and Françoise Doreau
Rostal-Horsley Duo
Gillian Sansom and Alasdair Graham

Viola and piano

Milton Thomas and Georgia Akst
Ernst and Lory Wallfisch

Violoncello and pianoforte

Gaspar and Chieko Cassadó
Jacqueline du Pré and Stephen Bishop

Pianoforte trios

Alberneri Trio
Dumka Trio
Martin–Hooton–Coxe
Rostal–Cassadó–Schröter
Trio Tcheque
Trio di Trieste

Pianoforte quartet

Quartetto di Roma

Pianoforte quintets

Quintetto Chigiano
Warsaw Piano Quintet

String quartets

Alberni String Quartet
Allegri String Quartet
Amadeus String Quartet
Amici String Quartet
Bastiaan String Quartet
Benthien String Quartet
Budapest String Quartet
Carmirelli String Quartet
Heutling String Quartet
Hungarian String Quartet
Juilliard String Quartet
Loewenguth String Quartet
Prague City String Quartet
Quartetto Italiano
Roth String Quartet
Smetana String Quartet
Strauss String Quartet
Stross String Quartet
Tel-Aviv String Quartet
Vlach String Quartet
Weller String Quartet

String quintet

Quintetto Boccherini

Ensembles

Kammer Trio Köln (flute, harp, gamba)
Vienna Octet

Orchestras

Berlin Philharmonic Orchestra
Israel Philharmonic Orchestra

Chamber orchestras
I Solisti Veneti
London Baroque Ensemble directed by Karl Haas
Tureck Bach Players directed by Rosalyn Tureck

Guitar
Presti-Lagoya Duo
Segovia
John Williams

Flute
Claude Monteux
Elaine Schaffer

Oboe
Evelyn Rothwell

Harmonica
Larry Adler

Accordion
Toralf Tollefsen

Conductors
George Barati
Dietfried Bernet
Sir Arthur Bliss
Sir Adrian Boult
Antal Dorati
Alceo Galliera
Pierino Gamba
Walter Hendl
Paul Hindemith
George Hurst
Eugene Jochum
Enrique Jorda
Jaroslav Krombholc
George Malcolm
Jean Martinon
Pierre Monteux
Charles Munch
Harry Newstone
Paul Paray
Tibor Paul
Stanley Pope
Karl Rankl
James Robertson
George Szell
David Tidboald
Heinz Unger
Alfred Wallenstein

Organists
Catherine Crozier
Kamiel d'Hooghe
Ralph Downes
Fernando Germani
Piet Kee
Jean Langlais
George Markey
Marilyn Mason
Flor Peeters
Jiri Ropek
John Sanderson
Arno Schonstedt

Sopranos
April Cantelo
Jacqueline Delman
Dorothy Dorow
Agnes Giebel
Hilde Gueden
Margaret Hallin
Joan Hammond
Elizabeth Harwood
Emilie Hooke
Elsie Morison
Eileen Poulter
Ana Raquel Satre
Honor Sheppard
Oda Slobodskaya
Jennifer Vyvyan
Ilse Wolf
Rae Woodland

Mezzo-sopranos and contraltos
Janet Baker
Pamela Bowden
Janet Fraser
Marina de Gabarain
Maureen Guy
Grace Hoffman
Irma Kolassi
Maureen Lehane
Kerstin Meyer
Louise Parker
Norma Procter
Nell Rankin
Barbara Robotham
Constance Shacklock
Marjorie Thomas
Nancy Thomas
Helen Watts

Tenors
Kenneth Bowen
Wilfred Brown
Gerald English
Edgar Fleet
David Galliver
Richard Lewis
John Mitchinson
Peter Pears
Duncan Robertson
Robert Tear
Philip Todd
John Wakefield

Baritones and basses
Hervey Alan
Maurice Bevan
Owen Brannigan
John Cameron
John Carol Case
John Dethick
Dietrich Fischer-Dieskau
John Lawrenson
Nowakowski
John Shirley-Quirk
Gerard Souzay
Roger Stalman
Richard Standen
Norman Tattersall

Voice and guitar
Wilfred Brown and John Williams

Voice and pianoforte
Peter Pears and Benjamin Britten

Songs of many lands
Martha Schlamme

Vocal groups
Cornell University Glee Club
Sestetto Italiano Luca Marenzio

Tillett and Holt Artists (supplementary) List: 1964–65

Violinist
Willy Boskowsky

Sopranos
Jutta Meyfarth
Anneliese Rothenberger
Erika Schmidt
Felicia Weathers
Ruth-Margret Pütz
Leonie Rysanek
Hanny Steffek
Hilde Güden
Eva Maria Rogner
Gerda Scheyrer
Rita Streich

Contraltos
Ursula Boese
Sandra Warfield
Marga Hoeffgen
Hertha Töpper

Tenors
Hans Hopf
Arturo Sergi
Wolfgang Windgassen
Peter Klein
Gerhard Stolze
Fritz Wunderlich
James McCracken
Fritz Uhl

Baritones
Carlos Alexander
Kostas Paskalis
Otto Wiener
Benno Kusche
Paul Schöffler
Raymond Wolansky
Gustav Neidlinger
Eberhard Wächter

Basses
Kurt Böhme
Gottlob Frick
Oscar Czerwenka
Ludwig Welter
Otto Edelmann
Fernando Corena

Conductors
Karl Böhm
Willy Boskowsky
Nello Santi

Artists represented exclusively by Ibbs and Tillett Ltd: 1968–69

Pianoforte

Vladimir Ashkenazy
Gina Bachauer
Stephanie Bamford
John Bingham
Malcolm Binns
Stephen Bishop
Brailowsky
Chieko Cassadó
Cherkassky
Aldo Ciccolini
Clifford Curzon
Monique de la Bruchollerie
Jörg Demus
Annie Fischer
Norma Fisher
Andor Foldes
Malcolm Frager
Liza Fuchsova
Gabor Gabos
Ruth Geiger
Youra Guller
Eric Harrison
Eric Heidsieck
Colin Horsley
Horszowski
Byron Janis
Grant Johannsen
Kathleen Jones
Constance Keene
Wilhelm Kempff
Louis Kentner
Yoko Kono
Lili Kraus
Yvonne Lefébure
Ray Lev
John Lill
Iris Loveridge
Brenda Lucas
Moura Lympany
Anthony Mott
Nikita Magaloff
George Malcolm
Denis Matthews
Yaltah Menuhin
Nina Milkina
Ruth Nye
John Ogdon
Rafael Orozco
Maurizio Pollini
Jerome Rose
Joel Ryce
Ilan Rogoff
Pnina Salzman
Ann Schein
Karl Ulrich Schnabel
Phyllis Sellick
Peter Serkin
Rudolf Serkin
Alice Shapiro
Bela Siki
Abbey Simon
Gabriel Tacchino
André Tchaikowsky
Toh Yi-Lung
Valerie Tryon
Rosalyn Tureck
Balint Vazsonyi
Bryan Vickers
Weingarten
David Wilde
Malcolm Williamson
Katherina Wolpe
Helen Wong
Friedrich Wührer

Two pianofortes and piano duets

John and Richard Contiguglia
Gold and Fizdale
Denis Matthews and Brenda McDermott
Yaltah Menuhin and Joel Ryce
John Ogdon and Brenda Lucas
Cyril Smith and Phyllis Sellick (Three hands)

Harpsichord

Thurston Dart
Ralph Kirkpatrick
Philip Ledger
Raymond Leppard
George Malcolm
Frank Pelleg
Zuzana Ruzickova
Rosalyn Tureck

Harp

Osian Ellis
Marisa Robles

Violin

Salvatore Accardo
Eszter Boda
Norbert Brainin
Pina Carmirelli
Raymond Cohen
Devy Erlih
Lorand Fenyves
Christian Ferras
Charmian Gadd
José Luis Garcia
Robert Gerle
Bronislav Gimpel
Esther Glazer
Szymon Goldberg
Arthur Grumiaux

Betty-Jean Hagen
Jean-Jacques Kantorow
Dennis Kovacs
Wolfgang Marschner
Johanna Martzy
Igor Ozim
Manoug Parikian
Yan Pascal
Edith Peinemann
Austin Reller
Sylvia Rosenberg
Max Rostal
Gillian Sansom
Michel Schwalbe
Maureen Smith
Josef Suk
Tibor Varga
George Whitman
Camilla Wicks
Yoshio Unno

Viola

Lina Lama
Peter Schidlof
Ernst Wallfisch

Violoncello

Christopher Bunting
Rohan de Saram
Jacqueline du Pré
Maurice Eisenberg
Maud Martin-Tortelier
Zara Nelsova
Leslie Parnas
Joseph Schuster
Paul Tortelier

Violin and pianoforte

Norbert Brainin and Lili Kraus
Alfredo Campoli and Valerie Tryon
Raymond Cohen and Anthya Rael
Lorand Fenyves and Bela Siki
Frederick Grinke and Joseph Weingarten
The Heutling Duo
Edith Peinemann and Jorg Demus
Rostal-Horsley Duo
Ralph Holmes and Denis Matthews
Josef Suk and Jan Panenka

Violin and harpsichord

Josef Suk and Zuzana Ruzickova

Viola and pianoforte

Ernst and Lory Wallfisch

Violoncello and pianoforte

Rohan de Saram and Bryan Vickers
André Navarra and Pierre Sancan

Pianoforte trios

Budapest Trio
Dumka Trio
Ebert Trio
Göbel Trio
Martin Trio
Oromonte Trio
Reizenstein Trio
Rostal–Palm–Schröter Trio
Suk Trio
Tagore Trio
Trio di Trieste

Pianoforte quartets

London Belgian Quartet
Quartetto di Roma

Pianoforte quintet

Warsaw Quintet

String quartets

Alberni String Quartet
Allegri String Quartet
Amadeus String Quartet
Amici String Quartet
Amsterdam String Quartet
Benthien String Quartet

Budapest String Quartet
Delmé String Quartet
Drolc String Quartet
Heutling String Quartet
Hungarian String Quartet
Juilliard String Quartet
Loewenguth String Quartet
Prague String Quartet
Quartetto Italiano
Reger String Quartet
Smetana String Quartet
Strauss String Quartet
Tel-Aviv String Quartet
Vlach String Quartet
Weller String Quartet

String quintet
Quintetto Boccherini

String sextet
Sestetto Chigiano

Octet
Vienna Octet

Orchestras
Berlin Philharmonic Orchestra
Israel Philharmonic Orchestra

Chamber orchestras
London Baroque Ensemble directed by Karl Haas
London Mozart Players directed by Harry Blech
Tureck Bach Players directed by Rosalyn Tureck

Guitar
Alexandre Lagoya
Segovia
John Williams

Flute
Elaine Schaffer

Oboe
Evelyn Rothwell

Organists
Melville Cook
Catherine Crozier
Kamiel d'Hooghe
Fernando Germani
Piet Kee
Jean Langlais
George Markey
Marilyn Mason
Flor Peeters
Jiří Ropek
Arno Schonstedt
Malcolm Williamson

Lecture
Gerald Moore

Conductors
Dalia Atlas
Karsten Andersen
Harry Blech
Sir Arthur Bliss
Sir Adrian Boult
Robert Bronstein
Boris Brott
Arthur Davison
Antal Dorati
Lawrence Foster
Alceo Galliera
Pierino Gamba
Enrique Garcia-Asensio
Arthur Hammond (opera)
Maurice Handford
Hans Heimler
Walter Hendl
George Hurst
Hiroyuki Iwaki
Eugene Jochum
Donal Johanos

Enrique Jorda
Hans Jordans
Efrem Kurtz
Philip Ledger
Raymond Leppard
David Lloyd-Jones
Fritz Mahler
George Malcolm
Jean Martinon
Wyn Morris
Charles Munch
Paul Paray
Stanley Pope
Karl Rankl
James Robertson
Redentor Romero
Hans-Hubert Schönzeler
Elyakum Shapirra
Frank Shipway
Adrian Sunshine
George Szell
David Tidboald
Paul Tortelier
Günter Wand
David Zinman

Sopranos

Sheila Armstrong
April Cantelo
Agnes Giebel
Hilde Gueden
Margaret Hallin
Elizabeth Harwood
Margheretta Kalmus
Malvina Major
Elsie Morison
Eileen Poulter
Janet Price
Ana Raquel Satre
Elizabeth Schwarzkopf
Honor Sheppard
Elizabeth Simon
Oda Slobodskaya
Rita Streich
Jennifer Vyvyan
Mary Wells
Ilse Wolf
Rae Woodland

Mezzo-sopranos and contraltos

Janet Baker
Birgit Finnilä
Janet Fraser
Marina de Gabarain
Maureen Forrester
Maureen Guy
Grace Hoffman
Elizabeth Holden
Irma Kolassi
Norma Procter
Nell Rankin
Barbara Robotham
Marjorie Thomas
Helen Watts

Tenors

Peter Bamber
Helge Brilioth
Kenneth Bowen
Wilfred Brown
Adrian de Peyer
Bernard Dickerson
Gerald English
Edgar Fleet
David Johnston
Richard Lewis
John Mitchinson
Ian Partridge
Donald Pilling
Duncan Robertson
Robert Tear
John Wakefield

Baritones and basses

John Barrow
Donald Bell
Maurice Bevan
Owen Brannigan
John Cameron
Geoffrey Chard
John Carol Case
John Dethick
Bryan Drake
Simon Estes
Dietrich Fischer-Dieskau
Josef Greindl
Raimund Herincx
Eishi Kawamura
John Lawrenson
John Shirley-Quirk
Gerard Souzay
Yi-Kwe Sze
Norman Tattersall
Nigel Wickens

Voice and guitar

Wilfred Brown and John Williams

Vocal groups

Cornell University Glee Club
Sestetto Italiano Luca Marenzio

Artists' Brochures 1973–74, 1977–78, 1982–83, 1989–90

Artists represented exclusively by Ibbs & Tillett: 1973–74

Pianists

Gina Bachauer
Malcolm Binns
Idil Biret
Shura Cherkassky
Aldo Ciccolini
Clifford Curzon
Maria de la Pau
Alicia de Larrocha
Jörg Demus
Annie Fischer
Andor Foldes
Anthony Goldstone
Andrew Haigh
Eric Heidsieck
Colin Horsley
Grant Johannesen
Wilhelm Kempff
Leonidas Lipovetsky
Brenda Lucas
Moura Lympany
Brenda McDermott
Nikita Magaloff
George Malcolm
Israela Margalit
Denis Matthews
Yaltah Menuhin
Nina Milkina
Barbara Nissman
Ruth Nye
John Ogdon
Garrick Ohlsson
Geoffrey Parsons
Maurizio Pollini
Pnina Salzman
Ann Schein
Karl Ulrich Schnabel
Phyllis Sellick
Peter Serkin
Rudolf Serkin
Howard Shelley
Bela Siki
Abbey Simon
Janos Solyom
Gabriel Tacchino
Alexander Tcherepnin
Valerie Tryon
Martino Tirimo
Rosalyn Tureck
Ilse von Alpenheim
Weingarten
Frank Wibaut
Malcolm Williamson

Two pianofortes and piano duets

Garth Beckett and Boyd McDonald
John and Richard Contiguglia
Denis Matthews and Brenda McDermott
John Ogdon and Brenda Lucas
Cyril Smith and Phyllis Sellick (three hands)

Harpsichord

Ralph Kirkpatrick
Raymond Leppard
George Malcolm
Geoffrey Parsons
Zuzana Ruzickova
Rosalyn Tureck

Harp

Osian Ellis
Marisa Robles

Flute and harp

Christopher Hyde-Smith and Marisa Robles

Violinists

Salvatore Accardo
Eszter Boda
Norbert Brainin
Christian Ferris
Bronislav Gimpel
Esther Glazer

Szymon Goldberg
Eric Gruenberg
Artur Grumiaux
Ralph Holmes
Jean-Jacques Kantorow
Wolfgang Marschner
Johanna Martzy
Theo Olof
Igor Ozim
Manoug Parikian
Max Rostal
Maureen Smith
Joseph Suk
Yan Pascal Tortelier
Uto Ughi
Takayoshi Wanami
Ruth Waterman

Violin and piano

Alfredo Campoli and Valerie Tryon
Ralph Holmes and Anthony Goldstone
Manoug Parikian and Malcolm Binns
Max Rostal and Colin Horsley
Yan Pascal Tortelier and Maria de la Pau

Violin and harpsichord

Joseph Suk and Zuzana Ruzickova

Viola

Lina Lima
Peter Schidlof
Ernst Wallfisch

Cello

Lawrence Foster
Thomas Igloi
Maud Martin-Tortelier
Zara Nelsova
Arto Noras
Leslie Parnas
Paul Tortelier
Victor Yoran

Cello and piano

Zara Nelsova and Grant Johannesen
Paul Tortelier and Maria de la Pau

Guitar

Carlos Barbosa-Lima
William Gomez
Michael Lorimer
Segovia

Flute

Christopher Hyde-Smith
Elaine Schaffer

Oboe

Evelyn Barbirolli

Clarinet

Yona Ettlinger

Organists

Catharine Crozier
Kamiel d'Hooghe
Ralph Downes
Fernando Germani
Anton Heiller
Piet Kee
Jean Langlais
George Markey
Marilyn Mason
Flor Peeters
Jirí Ropek
Arno Schonstadt
Alena Vesela
Malcolm Williamson

Conductors

Karsten Andersen
Dalia Atlas
Sir Arthur Bliss
Sir Adrian Boult
Boris Brott
Meredith Davies
Arthur Davison
Antal Dorati
Sixten Ehrling
Jean Fournet
Alceo Galliera
Irwin Hoffman
George Hurst
Hiroyuki Iwaki
Raymond Leppard
George Malcolm
Stanley Pope
James Robertson
David Tidboald
Paul Tortelier
Akeo Watanabe
David Zinman

Orchestras

Berlin Philharmonic
Israel Philharmonic
Stockholm Philharmonic

Pianoforte trios

Göbel
Holmes
Rostal–Palm–Schröter
Tortelier
Trieste

Clarinet trio

The Israeli Trio

Harp trio

The Robles Trio (flute, viola, harp)

String quartets

Aeolian
Alberni
Allegri
Amadeus
Assman
Benthein
Czech
Heutling
Italiano
Juilliard
Lindsay
Loewenguth
New Hungarian
Prague
Reger
Sinnhoffer
Slovak
Smetana
Tel-Aviv
Vlach

Pianoforte quartets

Brahms
Martinu
Roma

String quintet

Boccherini

Pianoforte quintet

Warsaw

String sextet

Chigiano

Octet

Vienna

Ensembles
Berlin Philharmonic Soloists
The Music Group of London

Lecture recital
Gerald Moore

Sopranos
April Cantelo
Wendy Eathorne
Christianne Eda-Pierre
Caroline Friend
Agnes Giebel
Elizabeth Harwood
Elsie Morison
Eileen Poulter
Janet Price
Elisabeth Schwarzkopf
Honor Sheppard
Elizabeth Simon
Rita Streich
Jennifer Vyvyan
Rae Woodland

Mezzos and contraltos
Janet Baker
Astra Blair
Margaret Duckworth
Maureen Forrester
Grace Hoffman
Elisabeth Holden
Elizabeth Muir
Norma Procter
Barbara Rowbotham
Marjorie Thomas

Tenors
Peter Bamber
Kenneth Bowen
Wynford Evans
David Galliver
Neil Jenkins
David Johnston
Phillip Langridge
Richard Lewis
John Mitchinson
Ian Partridge
Donald Pilley

Baritones and basses
Maurice Bevan
Owen Brannigan
John Cameron
John Carol Case
John Dethick
Simon Estes
Dietrich Fischer-Dieskau
Josef Greindl
Raimund Herincx
John Lawrenson
Benjamin Luxon
Bryan Rayner Cook
Yi-Kwei Sze

Vocal groups
Cornell University Glee Club
The Scholars

[Amendments to this 1973 brochure included violinists Ralph Holmes and Szymon Goldberg, and pianist Anthony Goldstone who 'have left our sole management', while soprano Eiddwen Harrhy and cellist Raphael Sommer joined.]

Booking arrangements for the undermentioned artists should also be made through this office.

Piano
Michael Studer

Dancer
Miguel Godreau

Sopranos

Linda Esther Gray	Anne Conoley	Wendy Pashley

Mezzo

Anne Wilkens

Tenors

Anthony Rolfe Johnson	Stuart Kale

Baritones and basses

Glyn Davenport	Michael Follis	Derek Hammond-Stroud
Anthony Ransome		

Ensemble

The New London Consort (Mediaeval and Renaissance music)

Artists represented exclusively by Ibbs and Tillett: 1977–78

Sopranos
Ann-Marie Connors
Anne Conoley
Meryl Drower
Wendy Eathorne
Christiane Eda-Pierre
Kate Flowers
Linda Esther Gray
Elizabeth Harwood
Patricia Hay
Kathleen Livingstone
Felicity Lott
Rosalind Plowright
Janet Price
Rita Streich

Mezzos and contraltos
Janet Baker
Anne Collins
Linda Finnie
Grace Hoffman
Elisabeth Holden
Ann Murray
Patricia Price
Barbara Robotham
Elizabeth Stokes
Anne Wilkens

Counter tenor
Paul Esswood

Tenors
Peter Bamber
David Galliver
Martyn Hill
Stuart Kale
Neil Jenkins
Anthony Rolfe Johnson
David Johnston
Philip Langridge
Keith Lewis
Richard Lewis
Neil Mackie
Ian Partridge

Baritones and basses
John Barrow
Ian Comboy
Brian Rayner Cook
Glyn Davenport
Dietrich Fischer-Dieskau
Michael Follis
Derek Hammond-Stroud
Jorma Hynninen
Eishi Kawamura
Richard Jackson
John Lawrenson
Rodney Macann
Michael Rippon
Malcolm Singer
Russell Smythe
Graham Titus
John Tranter
Norman Welsby
David Wilson-Johnson
Yi-Kwei Sze
Jacek Strauch

Conductors
Karsten Andersen
Dalia Atlas
Sir Adrian Boult
Daniel Chorzempa
Meredith Davies
Arthur Davison
Antal Dorati
Sixten Ehrling
Charles Farncombe
Dietrich Fischer-Dieskau
Jean Fournet
Massimo Freccia
Piero Gamba
George Hurst
Hiroyuki Iwaki
Isaac Karabtchevsky
Raymond Leppard
George Malcolm
John Poole
Stanley Pope
James Robertson
William Rutledge
Hans-Hubert Schönzeler
Frank Shipway
Paul Tortelier
Yan Pascal Tortelier
Akeo Watanabe
Gerard Akoka

Pianoforte

Joaquin Achucarro
Paul Badura-Skoda
Malcolm Binns
Idil Biret
Christian Blackshaw
Shura Cherkassy
Daniel Chorzempa
Aldo Ciccolini
Clifford Curzon
Maria de la Pau
Adam Fellegi
Alicia de Larrocha
Jorg Demus
Misha Dichter
Annie Fischer
Andor Foldes
Emil Gilels
Andrew Haigh
Eric Heidsieck
Colin Horsley
Byron Janis
Grant Johannesen
Mindru Katz
Wilhelm Kempff
Leonidas Lipovetsky
Iris Loveridge
Brenda McDermott
Nikita Magaloff
George Malcolm
Denis Matthews
Heinz Medjimorec
Yaltah Menuhin
John Ogdon
Jan Panenka
Eric Parkin
Pnina Salzman
Ann Schein
Karl Ulrich Schnabel
Peter Serkin
Rudolf Serkin
Howard Shelley
Bela Siki
Janos Solyom
Michael Studer
Alexander Tcherepnin
Martino Tirimo
Dubravka Tomsic
Valerie Tryon
Rosalyn Tureck
Mitsuko Uchida
Ilse von Alpenheim
Weingarten

Two pianofortes and pianoforte duets

Garth Beckett and Boyd McDonald
John and Richard Continguglia
Denis Matthews and Brenda McDermott
John Ogdon and Brenda Lucas
Phyllis Sellick and Terence Beccles

Harpsichord

Raymond Leppard
George Malcolm
Zuzana Ruzickova
Rosalyn Tureck
Fernando Valenti

Organ

Daniel Chorzempa
Melville Cook
Kamiel d'Hooghe
Ralph Dowmes
Fernando Germani
Anton Heiller
Piet Kee
Jean Langlais
Marilyn Mason
Flor Peeters
Michael Radulescu
Jirí Ropek
Arno Schonstedt
Alena Vesela

Violin

Norbert Brainin
Christian Ferras
Robert Gerle
Arthur Grumiaux
Erich Gruenberg
Daniel Heifetz
Leonid Kogan
Wolfgang Marschner
Johanna Martzy
Yfrah Neaman
Theo Olof
Eugen Prokop
Manoug Parikian
Max Rostal
Michel Schwalbe
Berl Senovsky
Maureen Smith
Josef Suk
Yan Pascal Tortelier
Takayoshi Wanami
Ruth Waterman
Wanda Wilkomirska

Viola
Stefan Kamase
Lina Lama
Peter Schidlof

Cello
Boris Heller
Mirel Iancovici
Aurora Natola-Ginastera
Zara Nelsova
Leslie Parnas
Raphael Sommer
Paul Tortelier
Julian Lloyd Webber

Flute
Christopher Hyde-Smith
John Solum

Oboe
Evelyn Rothwell

Clarinet
Yona Ettlinger

Guitar
Segovia
Carlos Barbosa-Lima
Guilliermo Fierens
William Gomez
Juan Martin

Violin and piano
Erich Gruenberg and Valerie Tryon
Robert Gerle and Marilyn Neeley
Yfrah Neaman and Mindru Katz
Manoug Parikian and Malcolm Binns
Max Rostal and Colin Horsley
Yan Pascal Tortelier and Maria de la Pau

Violin and harpsichord
Josef Suk and Zuzana Ruzickova

Cello and piano
Paul Tortelier and Maria de la Pau

Flute and piano
John Solum and Ann Schein

Flute and harp
Christopher Hyde-Smith and Marisa Robles

Piano trios
Dumka
London
Göbel
Haydn of Vienna
Tortelier
Trieste
Suk
Yuval

Harp trio
The Robles Trio

String quartets

Allegri String Quartet
Amadeus String Quartet
Benthien String Quartet
Brandis String Quartet
Caecilia String Quartet
Heutling String Quartet
Italiano String Quartet
Loewenguth String Quartet
New Hungarian String Quartet
Orford String Quartet
Prague String Quartet
Salzburg Mozarteum String Quartet
Sinnhoffer String Quartet
Slovak String Quartet
Smetana String Quartet
Tel Aviv String Quartet
Vlach String Quartet

Pianoforte quartets

Brahms
Israel
Roma

Extended ensembles

Allegri-Robles Ensemble
Berlin Philharmonic Soloists
Quintetto Boccherini
Richard Lewis Ensemble
New London Consort
Vienna Octet
Warsaw Piano Quintet

Orchestras

Cologne Chamber Orchestra
Israel Philharmonic
Stockholm Philharmonic

Ibbs and Tillett Artists' List: 1982–83

Sopranos

Wendy Eathorne
Christiane Eda-Pierre
Lesley Garrett
Linda Esther Gray
Elizabeth Harwood
Kathleen Livingstone
Jane Manning
Janet Price
Mitsuko Shirai
Helen Walker

Mezzos and contraltos

Dame Janet Baker
Margaret Cable
Ameral Gunson
Mary King
Elizabeth Stokes
Anne Wilkens

Countertenor

Paul Esswood
John York Skinner

Tenors

Martyn Hill
Neil Jenkins
Stuart Kale
Keith Lewis
Richard Lewis
Neil Mackie
Adrian Thompson
Kenneth Woollam

Baritones and basses

Richard Angas
Ian Caddy
Brian Rayner Cook
Dietrich Fischer-Dieskau
Philip Gelling
Derek Hammond-Stroud
Richard Jackson
Laszlo Polgar
Michael Rippon
William Shimell
Stephen Varcoe
David Wilson-Johnson

Conductors

Roberto Abbado
Karsten Andersen
Serge Baudo
Sir Adrian Boult
Meredith Davies
Antal Dorati
Sixten Ehrling
Richard Hickox
George Hurst
George Malcolm
Woldemar Nelsson
James Robertson
Paul Tortelier
Yan Pascal Tortelier
Akeo Watanabe

Pianoforte

Joaquin Achucarro
Malcolm Binns
Idil Biret
Christian Blackshaw
Shura Cherkassy
Clifford Curzon
Alicia de Larrocha
Maria de la Pau
Emil Gilels
Colin Horsley
Grant Johannesen
Diana Kacso
Peter Katin
Wilhelm Kempff
George Malcolm
Allan Schiller
Rudolf Serkin
Howard Shelley
Bela Siki
Valerie Tryon
Rosalyn Tureck
Mitsuko Uchida
Ilse von Alpenheim

Violin

Norbert Brainin
Christian Ferras
Arthur Grumiaux
Leonid Kogan
Pavel Kogan
Yfrah Neaman
Max Rostal
Eugene Sarbu
Josef Suk
Yan Pascal Tortelier
Uto Ughi
Takayoshi Wanami
Wanda Wilkomirska
Yossi Zivoni

Viola
Csaba Erdelyi
Peter Schidlof

Cello
Robert Cohen
Julian Lloyd Webber
Janos Starker
Paul Tortelier

Guitar
Julian Byzantine
Guillermo Fierens
Segovia

Harp
Osian Ellis
Nicanor Zabaleta

Harpsichord
Christopher Hogwood
George Malcolm
Rosalyn Tureck

Piano trios
Dumka Piano Trio
Suk Piano Trio
Tortelier Piano Trio

String quartets
Alban Berg Quartet
Endellion String Quartet
Smetana Quartet
Amadeus Quartet
Orford String Quartet
Tel Aviv Quartet
Brandis Quartet of Berlin
Prague Quartet

Ensembles
The Academy of Ancient Music
Philip Jones Brass Ensemble
La Grande Ecurie et La Chambre du Roy
Myrha Saxophone Quartet
The Fires of London
Nash Ensemble

Orchestras
Symphonisches Orchester Berlin
Stockholm Philharmonic Orchestra
Camerata Bern
City of London Sinfonia
Stuttgart Chamber Orchestra
Israel Philharmonic Orchestra
Netherlands Radio Chamber Orchestra

Ibbs and Tillett International Artist Management: Artists' List 1989–90

Piano

Boris Beresovsky	Ronald Brautigam	Malcolm Binns
Shura Cherkassky	Peter Frankl	Horatio Gutierrez
Ingrid Haebler	Zoltan Kocsis	Alicia de Larrocha
Ivan Moravec	Tatyana Nikolaeva	Vladimir Ovchinnikov
Mikhail Pletnev	Rudolf Serkin	Alexsei Sultanov
Vladimir Viardo		

Violin

Olivier Charlier	Norbert Brainin	Augustin Dumay
Hrachya Harutunyan	Nikolay Madoyev	Gyorgy Pauk
Natalia Prishepienko	Vadim Repin	Oscar Shumsky
Josef Suk	Vilmos Szabadi	Maxim Vengerov
Alexander Vinnitsky		

Viola

Tabea Zimmermann

Cello

Caroline Dale	Ivan Monighetti	Zara Nelsova
Alexander Rudin	Janos Starker	Paul Tortelier

String quartets

Allegri Quartet	Brandis Quartet of Berlin	Emerson Quartet
Endellion String Quartet	Enesco Quartet	Keller Quartet
Prague Quartet	Schoenberg Quartet	Sine Nomine Quartet
Smetana Quartet	Takacs Quartet	Vogler Quartet
Ysaÿe Quartet		

Piano trios

Amadeus Piano Trio	Frankl–Pauk–Kirschbaum Suk Trio	Ovchinnikov–Vinnitsky–Rudin Trio Trio

Harp

Nicanor Zabaleta

Recorder

Frans Brüggen

Clarinet

Emma Johnson

Orchestras/ensembles

Amsterdam Loeki Stardust Quartet
Entr'acte
Georgian State Symphony Orchestra
Minsk Ballet
Orchestra of the 18th Century
Suk Chamber Orchestra
Amsterdam Guitar Trio
Budapest Wind Ensemble
Franz Liszt Chamber Orchestra
London Chamber Players
Nash Ensemble
Schoenberg Ensemble
Young Georgian Dancers
Armenian State Chamber Orchestra
Georgian State Opera
London Brass
London Mozart Players
Orchestra of the Age of Enlightment

Conductors

Serge Baudo
Janos Fürst
Hiroyuki Iwaki
Woldemar Nelsson
Karl Anton Rickenbacher
Takuo Yuasa
Frans Brüggen
Hartmut Haenchen
Jansug Kahidze
James de Priest
Gerard Schwarz
Jean Fournet
George Hurst
Alexander Myrat
Alexander Rahbari
Hiroshi Wakasugi

Sopranos

Iano Alibedashvili
Teresa Cahill
Susan Dunn
Eileen Hulse
Ann Monoyios
Carol Vaness
Maureen Brathwaite
Janice Cairns
Gillian Fisher
Emma Kirkby
Catherine Pierard
Julia Varady
Susan Burghardt
Arax Davtian
Maria Gulegina
Patrizia Kwella
Olga Romanko

Mezzo/contralto

Dame Janet Baker
Cynthia Clarey
Bernadette Greevy
Elizabeth McCormack
Janice Taylor
Cecilia Bartoli
Catherine Denley
Ameral Gunson
Jard van Nes
Catherine Wyn-Rogers
Margaret Cable
Sandra Graham
Jadranka Jovanovic
Mitsuko Shirai

Countertenor

Paul Esswood
Timothy Wilson

Tenor

John Mark Ainsley
Howard Crook
Ralph Eschrig
Alberto Remedios CBE
Jeffrey Talbot
Paul Charles Clarke
Ryland Davies
Ghegam Grigoryan
Markus Schäfer
Enrique Viana
Vinson Cole
Kurt Equiluz
William Kendall
Peter Schreier
Kenneth Woollam

Baritone/bass

Paata Burchuladze
Simon Keenlyside
Mikhail Rysov
Dietrich Fischer-Dieskau
Jean-Philippe Lafont
Barseg Tumanyan
Dmitri Hvorostovsky
Brian Rayner Cook
Laszlo Polgar

APPENDIX 11

Contracts with Julius Isserlis 1938–62

Contract No. 11565 Ref: EMB/SEL Dated 15 June 1938

To Julius Isserlis, 23 Royal Avenue, LONDON SW3
We have pleasure in offering you the following engagement. Please sign one of these forms and forward it to us by return of post, retaining the other for your guidance.
Town: Bramshaw, Lyndhurst, Hants
Society: Bramshaw Music Club
Hall: The Warrens, Bramshaw, Lyndhurst, Hants.
Date: Monday afternoon, November 7th 1938 @ 5 o'clock
Work: Recital
Special Fee: Fifteen Guineas (£15.15.0) subject to 10% commission.
Yours faithfully,
Ibbs & Tillett

To Messrs Ibbs & Tillett, 124 Wigmore Street, London W1
I accept the Terms and conditions of the above-mentioned engagement and undertake to attend rehearsal if called upon to do so. Signed..

Ref: EMB/SEL Dated 8 January 1943

To Julius Isserlis, 60 Parkhill Road, LONDON NW3

Dear Mr Isserlis
We have pleasure in offering you the following engagements. Please sign one of these letters and forward it to us by return of post, retaining the other for your guidance.
Towns: a) WAKEFIELD b) HUDDERSFIELD c) HARROGATE d) OLDHAM e) BLACKBURN f) BOLTON g) PRESTON h) ROCHDALE i) DEWSBURY j) HALIFAX
Society: Bournemouth Philharmonic Orchestra
Halls: a) Unity Hall, Wakefield b) Town Hall, Huddersfield c) Royal Hall, Harrogate d) Equitable Co-operative Society Hall, Oldham e) King George's Hall, Blackburn f) Royal Victoria Hall, Bolton g) Queen's Hall, Preston h) Champness Hall, Rochdale i) Victoria Hall, Dewsbury j) Victoria Hall, Halifax
Dates:
a) Thursday evening, January 14th 1943 @ 6.30
b) Friday evening, January 15th 1943 @ 6.30
c) Sunday afternoon, January 17th 1943 @ 2.30
d) Monday evening, January 18th 1943 @ 6.30
e) Tuesday evening, January 19th 1943 @ 6.30
f) Friday evening, January 22nd 1943 @ 6.30
g) Monday evening, January 25th 1943 @ 6.30
h) Tuesday evening, January 26th 1943 @ 6.30
i) Wednesday evening, January 27th 1943 @ 6.30
j) Thursday evening, January 28th 1943 @ 6.30

Work: Tchaikovsky Concerto in each case.
Fee: Ten Guineas (£10.10.0) for each concert (subject to 10% commission).
Rehearsals: Particulars later.
Yours sincerely,
Ibbs & Tillett

To Messrs Ibbs & Tillett, 124 Wigmore Street, London W1
I accept the Terms and conditions of the above-mentioned engagement and undertake to attend rehearsal if called upon to do so. Signed..

Contract No. E 7278 Dated 24 May 1944

To Julius Isserlis, 60, Parkhill Road, LONDON NW3
We have pleasure in offering you the following engagement. Please sign one of these forms and forward it to us by return of post, retaining the other for your guidance.
Town: LONDON – HOME SERVICE
Society: British Broadcasting Corporation
Hall: London Studio
Date: Wednesday 31st May 1944 at 11.30–12.00 midnight
Work: Recital. To include works by Scarlatti and Brahms as arranged with Mr Val Drewry
Special Fee: Fifteen Guineas (£15.15.0) subject to 10% commission.
Remarks : Mechanical reproduction fees at usual rate
Yours faithfully,
Ibbs & Tillett

To Messrs Ibbs & Tillett, 124 Wigmore Street, London W1
I accept the Terms and conditions of the above-mentioned engagement and undertake to attend rehearsal if called upon to do so. Signed..

Contract No. E 7143 Dated 25 May 1944

To Julius Isserlis, 60, Parkhill Road, LONDON NW3
We have pleasure in offering you the following engagement. Please sign one of these forms and forward it to us by return of post, retaining the other for your guidance.
Town: LONDON
Society: British Broadcasting Corporation (European)
Hall: Maida Vale Studio No.2
Pre-recording date: Saturday afternoon June 10th 1944, 5 to 6pm
Transmission date: Friday morning June 16th 1944, 10.30 to 11am
Work: Taneiev Piano Quartet with the Grinke, Forbes, Phillips Trio
Special Fee: Fifteen Guineas (£15.15.0) subject to 10% commission.
Remarks: Rehearsal Saturday afternoon June 10th at 3.15pm
Mechanical reproduction fees at usual rate
Yours faithfully,
Ibbs & Tillett

To Messrs Ibbs & Tillett, 124 Wigmore Street, London W1
I accept the Terms and conditions of the above-mentioned engagement and undertake to attend rehearsal if called upon to do so. Signed..

Contract No. 8214 Ref: EMT/SEL Dated 11 August 1944

To Julius Isserlis, 60, Parkhill Road, LONDON NW3
We have pleasure in offering you the following engagement. Please sign one of these forms and forward it to us by return of post, retaining the other for your guidance.
Town: LONDON – EUROPEAN TRANSMISSION
Society: British Broadcasting Corporation
Hall: No. 25a Marylebone Road
Pre-recording date: Tuesday afternoon August 8th 1944 @ 2.15–3.15pm
Transmission date: Wednesday morning August 16th 1944 @ 10.30–11.00am
Work: Sonata Recital with James Harvey-Phillips to play cello sonata (Rachmaninoff) as arranged with European Music Supervisor
Special Fee: Fifteen Guineas (£15.15.0) subject to 10% commission.
Mechanical reproduction fees at usual rate
Remarks: Rehearsal 1.45–2.15pm August 8th
Yours faithfully,
Ibbs & Tillett

To Messrs Ibbs & Tillett, 124 Wigmore Street, London W1
I accept the Terms and conditions of the above-mentioned engagement and undertake to attend rehearsal if called upon to do so. Signed..

Contract No. 9891 Ref: EMT/SEL Dated 9 October 1944

To Julius Isserlis, 60, Parkhill Road, LONDON NW3
We have pleasure in offering you the following engagement. Please sign one of these forms and forward it to us by return of post, retaining the other for your guidance.
Town: LONDON – HOME SERVICE
Society: British Broadcasting Corporation
Hall: London Studio
Date: Sunday morning October 29th 1944 @ 11.20–11.50am
Work: Recital. Medtner Sonata in G minor, as arranged with Mr Val Drewry
Special Fee: Fifteen Guineas (£15.15.0) subject to 10% commission.
Mechanical reproduction fees at usual rate
Yours faithfully,
Ibbs & Tillett

To Messrs Ibbs & Tillett, 124 Wigmore Street, London W1
I accept the Terms and conditions of the above-mentioned engagement and undertake to attend rehearsal if called upon to do so. Signed..

Contract No. E14818 Dated 18 August 1945

To Julius Isserlis, 60, Parkhill Road, LONDON NW3
We have pleasure in offering you the following engagement. Please sign one of these forms and forward it to us by return of post, retaining the other for your guidance.
Town: GLASGOW
Society: Choral & Orchestral Union of Glasgow
Hall: St Andrew's Hall and Green's Playhouse, Glasgow

Date: Saturday evening February 16th 1946 (St Andrew's Hall)
Sunday afternoon February 17th 1946 (Green's Playhouse)
Work: Concerto and group of solos to be decided
Inclusive Fee: Fifty Guineas (£52.10.0) subject to 10% commission.
Remarks: Time of rehearsal to be advised
Yours faithfully,
Ibbs & Tillett

To Messrs Ibbs & Tillett, 124 Wigmore Street, London W1
I accept the Terms and conditions of the above-mentioned engagement and undertake to attend rehearsal if called upon to do so. Signed...

Contract No. E17288 Ref: EMT/JMcF Dated 18 October 1945

To Julius Isserlis, 60, Parkhill Road, LONDON NW3
We have pleasure in offering you the following engagement. Please sign one of these forms and forward it to us by return of post, retaining the other for your guidance.
Town: ST ANDREWS
Society: St Leonard's School
Hall: School Hall
Date: Monday afternoon or evening February 18th 1946
Work: Recital
Fee: Twenty-five Guineas (£26.5.0) subject to 10% commission.
Yours faithfully,
Ibbs & Tillett

To Messrs Ibbs & Tillett, 124 Wigmore Street, London W1
I accept the Terms and conditions of the above-mentioned engagement and undertake to attend rehearsal if called upon to do so. Signed...

Contract No. E20590 Ref: EMT/SEL Dated 8 March 1946

To Julius Isserlis, 60, Parkhill Road, LONDON NW3
We have pleasure in offering you the following engagement. Please sign one of these forms and forward it to us by return of post, retaining the other for your guidance.
Town: LONDON
Society: National Symphony Orchestra
Hall: Royal Albert Hall
Date: Tuesday evening March 26th 1946 @ 7 o'clock
Work: Concerto No.1 in B flat minor (Tchaikovsky) with the National Symphony Orchestra.
Conductor: Sidney Beer
Fee: Twenty-five Guineas (£26.5.0) subject to 10% commission.
Remarks: Particulars of rehearsal to follow
Yours faithfully,
Ibbs & Tillett

To Messrs Ibbs & Tillett, 124 Wigmore Street, London W1
I accept the Terms and conditions of the above-mentioned engagement and undertake to attend rehearsal if called upon to do so. Signed...

Contract No. E44623 Ref: EMT/SEL Dated 3 September 1946

To Julius Isserlis, Mill Race Hotel, SALISBURY, Wilts
We have pleasure in offering you the following engagement. Please sign one of these forms and forward it to us by return of post, retaining the other for your guidance.
Town: SWANSEA
Society: Universal Concerts
Hall: To be advised
Date: Tuesday evening October 1st 1946 (Time to be advised)
Work: 'Emperor' Concerto (Beethoven) with the MIDLAND SYMPHONY ORCHESTRA
Special Fee: Twenty Guineas (£21.0.0) subject to 10% commission.
Yours faithfully,
Ibbs & Tillett

To Messrs Ibbs & Tillett, 124 Wigmore Street, London W1
I accept the Terms and conditions of the above-mentioned engagement and undertake to attend rehearsal if called upon to do so. Signed……………………………………

Contract No. E 51577 Ref: SEL/RB Dated 4 June 1947

To Julius Isserlis, 99b, Addison Road, LONDON W14
We have pleasure in offering you the following engagement. Please sign one of these forms and forward it to us by return of post, retaining the other for your guidance.
Town: LONDON – LATIN AMERICA
Society: British Broadcasting Corporation
Hall: London Studio
Date: Saturday/Sunday 5th/6th July 1947: 2.30–3.00am
Work: Recital – please send suggested programme as soon as possible to Mr Norman Fulton, P.O.Box 4, Boreham Wood, Herts or Elstree 1621
Fee: Fifteen Guineas (£15.15.0) inclusive subject to 10% commission plus one pound (£1.0.0.) subsistence. Mechanical reproduction fees at revised rate
Yours faithfully,
Ibbs & Tillett

To Messrs Ibbs & Tillett, 124 Wigmore Street, London W1
I accept the Terms and conditions of the above-mentioned engagement and undertake to attend rehearsal if called upon to do so. Signed……………………………………

Contract No. G 8418 Ref: SEL/ES Dated 29 May 1957

To Julius Isserlis, 99b, Addison Road, LONDON W14
We have pleasure in confirming the following engagement. Please sign one of these forms and forward it to us by return of post, retaining the other for your guidance.

Town:	LONDON
Society:	The Institution of Civil Engineers
Hall:	Institution of Civil Engineers, Great George Street, Westminster, SW1
Date:	Wednesday evening June 19th 1957 at 8.45 to 9.30pm
Work:	Programme of 45 minutes duration
Special Fee:	Thirty Guineas (£31.10.0) subject to 10 per cent. commission
Remarks:	Please let us have your programme suggestions as quickly as possible, including a good group of Chopin. The programme is to be given complete in one appearance of 45 minutes.

Yours faithfully,
Ibbs & Tillett

I accept the Terms and conditions of the above-mentioned engagement and undertake to attend rehearsal if called upon to do so.
Date...................... Signed..

Contract No. I 7612 Ref: AH/HE Dated 16 January 1962

To Julius Isserlis, 99b, Addison Road, LONDON W14
We have pleasure in confirming the following engagement. Please sign one of these forms and forward it to us by return of post, retaining the other for your guidance.

Town:	CARDIFF – NETWORK THREE
Society:	British Broadcasting Corporation
Hall:	Charles Street, Cardiff
Date:	Saturday 20th January 1962, 2.30–4.30 pm
Work:	SATURDAY PROM – to play the piano as arranged
Fee:	Thirty-three Guineas (£34.13.0) subject to 10 per cent. commission inclusive. Plus fare London/Cardiff £3.7.0. and one night's subsistence £2.10.0. Mechanical reproduction fees at usual rate
Rehearsal:	Saturday 20th January, 10.30 am at Charles Street Studio

Yours faithfully,
Ibbs & Tillett

I accept the Terms and conditions of the above-mentioned engagement and undertake to attend rehearsal if called upon to do so.
Date...................... Signed..

Emmie Tillett's Five-Year Diary 1965–69

The following are extracts from Emmie Tillett's only extant personal diary, her five-year diary for the years 1965–69. It provides an insight into her busy life as well as revealing some of her more private thoughts.

16 January 1965 Saw [Vladimir] Ashkenazy afternoon [to] discuss future plans.

1 March 1965 Worked till 10.30pm. Horrifying amount to cope with. Oh for some more good typists!

4 March 1965 Blizzard, bitterly cold. Couldn't get car out of garage, so went straight to Albert Hall. Mahler 8, Henry Wood Society, four Colleges [of Music]. Malcolm hung his coat in conductor's room much to Adrian's annoyance. Saw M, gave cold shoulder.

8 March 1965 Terrible day in office. Left at 7pm. Signed over 100 letters, can't think where it will all end, staff shortage acute.

9 March 1965 Festival Hall, LPO Cherkassky, Svetlanov. Khachaturian, superb playing, pedal stuck. Shura dived under and released it.

30 March 1965 Lunch with Daniel Barenboim. Wants us to try to get work, but doesn't want to upset Ian [Hunter] and Jack [Phipps]. Promised for music clubs, will speak to Ian. Festival Hall to hear [conductor Eliahu] Inbal. Very nice looking but not very effective.

31 March 1965 Took Jacqueline du Pré to lunch. [She] broke news, going to Russia, study with Rostropovich, a year. Clifford [Curzon] from 4.30–6.30, walked three quarters round park to get his car! Drove me home, collected my car, straight back to office. Festival Hall saw Dorati. Affectionate greeting from Geza Anda, back to office.

28 April 1965 Shocking day office. Row over Anna Reynolds' rehearsal. Barbirolli forgotten she would not be at piano rehearsal then [Elizabeth] Vaughan fell out. Verdi Requiem Hallé wanted Mary Wells. Vanished, found her at Norwich.

18 May 1965 Harold Shaw phoned from New York. Trouble in Hurok office! Festival Hall Bach Choir, Walton programme. WW conducted, Amaryllis Fleming played [cello] concerto, looked lovely, beautiful dress. John Ogdon and B[renda] appeared in artists' room. Shook hands with him, ignored her.

29 May 1965 Left for airport 3.15, met Gérard Souzay, tried to make 5.45pm from Victoria but got chased by police for speeding, said I nearly caused accident. Absolute rot!! Was travelling pretty fast all the same (82mph).

30 May 1965 Stephen Bishop RFH recital, took Solo and Gwen. Surprised to find Jacqueline du Pré there with Stephen. Is she the cause of Stephen's separation with wife?

31 May 1965 Called on Jessie Wood 8pm, getting very frail. On to RAM to hear Olive Groves' pupil Richard Angas in Lieder recital, good bass-baritone, excellent interpretation, promises well.

11 June 1965 Sandwich at home, *Boheme* at Covent Garden, Freni as Mimi, pretty corny performance altogether, left before last act. Searched for parked car, ended in Dover Street and went to Vendome, shocking service, forgot melon and salad we had ordered, left in a huff.

12 June 1965 Matinée 3pm, John Osborne, awful, incomprehensible, rushed home, changed in ten minutes, collected Solo and Gwen for dinner, Keith and Christabel, played bridge, lost four shillings.

18 June 1965 Theatre with Jimmie 'Present Laughter' at Queen's, deliciously refreshing, clever and witty, such a change from present day plays and how we laughed.

22 June 1965 Seen two young men to replace Sunderland [who gave notice on 12 June]. Quite possible. Alarmed by amount of work. Festival Hall, Cleveland Orchestra and Georg Szell, out of this world. Took Szell to supper Savoy after, he said he would always remember how kind and helpful John and I were to him in his early days.
26 June 1965 Worked till 4pm, [Saturday] Harrison and his wife came at 8.30 to talk about his joining us. I think he may fit in, I like them both, not modern type at all. Very keen on business and I think would be a good worker. Not quite same type as Jasper, but seems to have good business head.
2 July 1965 AGM of Holt firm, warned about future and specially extravagances re 'expenses'. Didn't get much help from Leslie (Boosey), Ian co-operative. Making plan re cutting down which they will submit to me.
21 July 1965 Camden. Benjamin Luxon singing *[Die] Schöne Müllerin* – very promising! Miss Hadfield left for her holiday. Harrison spent the day with Sunderland preparing to take over.
29 July 1965 Harrison's first day. Certainly intelligent. Think he will be thorough and attentive to detail.
21 August 1965 [Saturday] Office morning. Golders Green Hippodrome 6pm Marlene Dietrich. Wonderful artist, exquisite figure – youth personified but over 60?
31 August 1965 Not too bad in office. Harrison will do I think! Went to see Hurok 5pm. Ian & Jack there. Left them to it!
14 September 1965 Jasper Parrott arrived for his first day
15 September 1965 Beryl left for three weeks holiday. Heaven help me! Jasper struggling on. Took him to Festival Hall, first concert RPS–LPO Adrian. Saw him and Ann in the interval, introduced Jasper.
25 September 1965 Office till 5.15pm. Lost without Beryl. Only that stupid idiot D! Trying to cope with everything is getting me down. Teaching Jasper. Harrison away, back on Monday thank God.
10 October 1965 John Williams first RFH recital. Good house. Beautiful artist.
11 October 1965 Heard Swedish girl, Birgit Finnila at Wigmore. Pupil of Roy. Lovely voice.
21 October 1965 Shocking day. Meeting LPO 5pm, left at 7pm for office. Signed letters and cleared up. Went to Wigmore to see Geraint Jones about Malcolm Binns. He didn't turn up. Stephen Bishop playing. Jacqueline there also! Very obvious, walking out of artists' room as he starts to play.
22 October 1965 Ralph Holmes decided to go to Basil Horsfield!!! Hair cut.
26 October 1965 Called for Segovias at Francis Hotel [Bath] at 10.30. Foggy ride back to London, took three hours to Westbury. Home by 2, in office at 3. More trouble! Miss Clark gone to pieces. Unable to cope with BBC, got beyond her, nervous breakdown obviously.
27 October 1965 Hauled Jasper in to help out with BBC and get it in order. Very valuable.
17 November 1965 Engaged young man for BBC department. Liked him very much. Hope I'm right!! [Martin] Campbell-White.
21 November 1965 RFH afternoon, du Pré and Bishop recital. Good house. Naughty children changed programme at last moment. Myra sinking, end might be very soon.
24 November 1965 Bad news about Myra, the end very near, now unconscious but without pain. Laid on everything with papers, BBC etc. Dinner with Alec and Gina at Highgate. Talked business but lovely evening all the same. Very loyal, wonderful couple.
25 November 1965 Ian Hunter called for me at 7.30pm and we went to a buffet supper with Czech Ambassador. Shocked to hear his wife had committed suicide (or so it was thought) a few weeks ago. Mme Svetlikova, Secretary to the [Czech] Philharmonic Orchestra, a charming woman. We have much in common. I like the Czechs.

26 November 1965 Saz [Anita Gunn] phoned 8.30am. Darling Myra died last night at 11pm. Great deal of phoning all day. Hoping to arrange memorial service at St Paul's on December 13th through Canon Collins. Henry Wood Society *Messiah* Albert Hall. Malcolm very nice about Myra, otherwise his heavenly snobbish self!

27 November 1965 Went to see Jessie Wood. Getting very frail but mind quite wonderful. Wants me to have power of attorney. She thought Myra's memorial service should be at St Sepulchre's!!

13 December 1965 Memorial service to darling Myra in St Paul's Cathedral. Everyone of importance there, Sir Edward Boyle, Edward Heath, representative of the Prime Minister, Jennie Lee, all famous musicians. Canon Collins made lovely address. Allegri Quartet and Gervase de Peyer played.

21 December 1965 Jacqueline du Pré and Stephen Bishop came to dinner. He is extremely nice and very amusing. J not feeling well, very overtired. Left soon after 10pm.

13 January 1966 Took Jacqueline du Pré to lunch. Talked about future following her return from Russia in the summer. Went to St Paul's Cathedral for memorial service for [Albert] Schweitzer.

19 January 1966 Festival Hall BBC concert. 1st performance Tippett's new work [*The Vision of St Augustine*] with Fischer-Dieskau. Mrs [Joan] Ingpen and Mrs Blech both 'tremendously moved' by it. I told F-D I was moved out of the hall!

25 January 1966 Blow up over Clifford [Curzon] and BBC. Arranged [to] record programme tonight, LSO Festival Hall without telling him. Lunch House of Lords with Lord and Lady Lucas. Went wrong day. Should be tomorrow!! Met them again and had coffee during concert. Like them both!! Clifford played Liszt A major [Piano concerto No.2] magnificently.

15 February 1966 Audition Wigmore. Royal Academy evening. Lili Kraus played Mozart quite lovely. Don't like her chats in between. Lots of old acquaintances. Shocked to see how they have all aged. Megan Foster, Garda Hall. Suppose I have too!

16 February 1966 Wigmore Hall – Alfred Brendel. Very fine. Hope we can build him. Festival Hall to see Toni Dorati in interval, back to Wigmore, wonderful Liszt playing.

9 March 1966 Arrived home 7pm. Great excitement. Elm Tree Road. BBC filming episode 'Dixon of Dock Green'. Girl supposed to commit suicide from top floor flats next door. Real fire engine, ambulance, police cars. Fred [Bass, nephew] and I got ourselves into a crowd scene, we hope.

12 March 1966 Ashkenazy and Dodie until 1.45pm in office. All well and Jasper a great success with them.

5 May 1966 Visit from Basil Douglas and Wilfrid van Wyck on question of commission. Want to put up to 12½% or 15%. I won't hear of it. Must find some other way to meet 'service' tax. Will cost us about £1,000 per year.

23 May 1966 Lunch with Segovia at Westbury. Royal Academy of Music evening to see opera class do Verdi's *Joan of Arc* in Italian. Girl [Donna Faye-Carr] aged 21 sang Joan, wonderful voice but all over the place at times. Pupil of Roy Henderson. Told her shouldn't be singing role like that yet. Didn't like it.

25 May 1966 Andrès [Segovia] robbed at Westbury. Two suitcases broken open, his insignia stolen while having dinner on Tuesday night [24th May] then someone tried to enter his room at 2am. Festival Hall, his recital. He hadn't slept but played marvellously. Took him to supper at Genevieve, managed to get rid of the entourage.

26 May 1966 Spanish Embassy party as 'black tie' decided on short dress – all wrong!! Princess

Margaret and Tony there, very distinguished gathering, lovely dresses. Arrived home 1.45am, before that went to Festival Hall, Annie Fischer played Bartók 3, magnificent.

27 May 1966 Took Annie Fischer to lunch at Genevieve, joined by Maria Curcio. Dinner with Gina and Alec in evening, laughed a lot. Dose of good smutty jokes from USA. Home 10.45, slightly tired.

31 May 1966 Beryl in Newcastle with Segovia, ton of work, did some typing myself, simply cannot manage without her, she's wonderful, the amount she does.

2 July 1966 [Saturday] Sandwich with Beryl, home by 3pm, Started to redecorate Mona's sitting room. Donald Bell called from Holt's about 4.30pm. Could I find someone to sing *War Requiem* that night. He had bad throat, said impossible.

5 July 1966 Sandwich lunch and AGM of Harold Holt Ltd. Leslie B, Ian, [Tom] Hazlem [accountant], Jack [Phipps]. A small profit but not enough. Difficult to know how to step it up. Started papering Mona's sitting room in the evening.

7 July 1966 Dinner with Win Ferrier. Home at midnight. Blown silencer on car – makes a gorgeous noise.

11 July 1966 Took Solo and Gwen to Southwark Cathedral. First night *[Burning] Fiery Furnace* – Britten's new opera (Church). Ben and Rostropovich there, introduced them to Solo. Very impressed with play.

30 August 1966 First day at office, Good to be back. Kathleen Cheselden, Harrison, Denzil away. Ghastly day, poured solidly.

18 September 1966 Gardened. Schnabel – Wigmore. Rang Annie Fischer and Gérard Souzay during morning. Solo and Gwen. Arthur Bliss called in and had three drinks, left slightly bottled!!

7 October 1966 Took Annie Fischer to lunch Genevieve. Terrific tales of Leeds [international piano] competition. [William] Glock and [Hans] Keller impossible. Annie no idea 'English gentlemans' could behave like it. Took her till 3.30pm to tell me about it.

11 October 1966 Audition Wigmore, no one worth while. Dinner Worshipful Company of Musicians. Dreary music after. Man asleep, fell off chair.

19 October 1966 Had dinner with John and Brenda Ogdon night before [18th]. Not happy with management! Wonder whether they will ask to come back?? St Mary's evening. Sheila Armstrong gave recital, enchanting singer. Accompanied by Steuart Bedford, grandson Liza Lehmann, excellent.

21 October 1966 First night of [Britten's] *Gloriana* at Sadler's Wells. Outstanding production. Always thought it was a great opera, now convinced. Ending still debatable. Congratulated Stephen Arlen on *Gloriana* and baby!! Party for cast, took Jasper, met Colin Graham.

11 November 1966 Lunch with Shura at White House. Shocking afternoon capped by Miss Concannon demanding a room to herself (a new typist coming in to help Kathleen, only place to put her). Miss C will probably give notice.

22 November 1966 Lunch with Forbes Robinson at Genevieve. Wants us to do more abroad. Royal Concert Albert Hall evening. Elizabeth Harwood sang Glière most beautifully. It's a lovely voice, great acclaim. John Ogdon played. He and Brenda came and spoke to me, all very friendly, a real rapprochement.

30 November 1966 Four conductors out of action this week! Malcolm Sargent in hospital. 'Lumbago', but personally think it's more serious. Sylvia Darley told Jessie 'jaundice had set in'. Been through it all with darling John.

6 December 1966 Grim day. Eric Greene sinking, end imminent. Frightfully busy in office with many troubles. Ben Britten furious about Lisbon moving date. 10pm John Shirley-Quirk phoned, cannot sing tomorrow, bad cold. Tried to get Beryl talking on phone for one hour. At last went down to office and fixed John Cameron.

7 December 1966 Eric Greene died last night. My 70th birthday, wonderful telegrams and flowers – unbelievable. Will take a long time to acknowledge!!

14 December 1966 Cracked my back in bed, felt it go. Very painful. Lunch (birthday) at Festival Hall. John Denison, David Webster, William Glock, Ernest Bean, John Culshaw, Peter Andrey, Wilfred Stiff. Enjoyed enormously having all my business associates 40 years or more!

8 January 1967 Worked morning & afternoon. Went to see Jessie [Wood] 5.30pm, fell down outside, tripped over paving stone, picked up by two Beatniks. On to Solo and Gwen.

16 January 1967 Back at office. New York has assumed a dream-like quality [Emmie was there with Janet Baker 10–14 January]. All quiet at 124. Fire alarm exercise a few days ago. Lereculey refused to budge.

4 February 1967 Brenda Ogdon made ghastly mistake. Take John back. Motored down to Arundel Castle for gala performance of *Let's make an opera* in Barons Hall. Supper after (sit down for 300). Dress affair. Champagne galore, freezing cold, huge log fires. Left at 11pm, home by one

6 February 1967 Told office my interview with Brenda Ogdon on Saturday morning. She was evidently very distressed. Admitted to them making ghastly mistake and would I take John back!! Told her [she] has had courage to admit; would not say no.

9 February 1967 Spoke to John Ogdon on phone from New York. Sounded just the same as if nothing has happened.

12 February 1967 Gerald [Moore's] Farewell Concert RFH evening. Marvellous occasion, all went well.

13 February 1967 Airport to see Ashkenazy off. Disgraceful scenes with teenagers meeting a member of the Monkees group. Scene at office while I was away. Trevor Barnard slapped Miss Lereculey's face then went straight to GLC and reported assault!? Denzil broke news retiring September.

16 February 1967 Festival Hall evening. LSO–Kempff. Took Solo and Gwen. Quite lovely but feel he has aged and lost his vitality.

1 March 1967 Opening of new Queen Elizabeth Hall by the Queen. Memorable evening. Britten conducted interesting little programme. Jimmie and Dedie there. Dedie fainted at reception, very quietly behind a buffet. St. Johns ambulance people coped.

12 March 1967 Peter Pears [has a] cold. Unable to sing Evangelist. Didn't let anyone know until 10am. Robert Tear took over in morning. Located Gerald English, sang arias afternoon.

14 April 1967 Jacqueline du Pré phoned from Manchester to tell me she and Daniel Barenboim were to be married in September.

25 May 1967 Jacqueline du Pré, Daniel Barenboim and Ronald Kinloch Anderson came to dinner. Daniel has strained wrist badly. Can't play Saddleworth.

31 May 1967 Jacqueline du Pré cabled from Israel, renouncing engagements, her duty to be there with 'her' people etc. Cabled impossible.

14 June 1967 Lunch with Ian down the road, wants to get rid of lots of artists who are not money-making. Might take over some of them

3 July 1967 Lunch with Hazlem (he with me! I paid!) To discuss HH business, on to see Paul. Decided on plan, Ian has separate business, I&T run HH.

19 July 1967 Lunch with Ian (sandwiches in office) to discuss future in view of disturbing balance sheet. Made suggestion we to take over agency. Ian has own company for festivals etc.

20 July 1967 AGM Holt. Serious discussion as to future. Leslie Boosey suggests amalgamation. I don't think so but did not say so. Decided all to think about it and have another meeting in near future.

30 July 1967 Went to see Jessie Wood. She is in quite good spirits. News of Malcolm [Sargent] (operated on last week) not very good.

3 August 1967 Sandwich lunch with Ian. He has decided to accept my suggestion of his own company and I will take over Holt office.

15 August 1967 Walter Legge playing up like the B- he is! Shan't forget Hong Kong and Fordingbridge in a hurry.

16 August 1967 Legge refusing to accept calls from London, leaving his secretary to deal. Still an impasse. Dinner with Ashkenazys at Hendon. Vodka, caviar, bortsch. André Previn and Jasper there also. J tells me AP may want to come to us!

17 August 1967 Still terribly worried by Legge affair. Fordingbridge being very difficult about changing date. Hong Kong claiming $10,000 compensation.

21 August 1967 Not a sound from Walter Legge, cannot move till he deigns to communicate. I went to see 'Day in the death of Joe Egg'. Wonderful acting but did not like it. Funny but harrowing.

17 September 1967 Very worried about Malcolm. Had made appearance at Prom night before and obviously very ill.

20 September 1967 Ian gave lunch at Garrick for Barenboims, father, son, mother, Jacqueline, Sandy Goehrs, Hurok. Jessie phoned; Malcolm has stomach cancer – no hope.

27 September 1967 Called for Arthur and Daphne Judson, Dorchester Hotel at 9.45. To Clifford's at Highgate for lunch. AJ more unbending than I have ever known him. Delicious lunch.

3 October 1967 Malcolm Sargent died afternoon. Jessie phoned to tell me 3pm. News released 7pm. Wilhelm Kempff recital QEH. John Denison announced Malcolm's death to audience after interval. Audience stood in silence. Terrible night, pouring rain.

9 October 1967 Paul called for me at 6.30pm for dinner at home with Ian Hunter and Hazlem to discuss future of Harold Holt Ltd. Four possibilities, only one feasible and acceptable to me. Ian to have own business, we to take over HH and clients who want to come to us.

21 October 1967 Came on to pour with rain, no windscreen wipers! Dinner with Jacqueline and Daniel Barenboim at their flat. [William] Pleeth and wife also there. Melon, stew and rice. Not quite done and rice soggy!

24 October 1967 Lunch in office. Miss Lereculey to dinner in evening to do [artists'] lists for 1968–1969. Drove her home at 10pm.

29 October 1967 Wigmore Hall afternoon – David Wilde, very promising. Liszt excellent. Solo and Gwen. Home for evening. No TV or radio, both packed up. Getting a new Decca TV.

14 November 1967 Took Paul to lunch to discuss HH Ltd. Serious position. RFH Bach *B minor Mass* with Klemperer, [Agnes] Giebel, Janet Baker, [Nicolai] Gedda, [Hermann] Prey, [Franz] Crass. 7.15pm!! Finished 10.15pm. Very slow tempi. Supper at the Savoy with Peter Andrey, [Robert] Kinloch Anderson and Janet. Home 1am.

17 November 1967 Audition Wigmore to hear Early Music Consort. Very good.

7 December 1967 Birthday – busy day! Telegrams from Gina, Alec, and Shura. Called on Dorati at RFH. LPO and Rubinstein, three Beethoven concertos, then to QEH for Barrow Poets. Delightful.

8 December 1967 Terrific snowstorm, traffic and trains chaotic. Was going to Croydon, Bournemouth Symphony Orchestra with David Tidboald (his concert). Orchestra failed to arrive, instruments showed up somewhere, concert cancelled. Beryl came home to dinner instead.

24 December 1967 Had drinks with Herbert Menges. Caroline Hatchard (84) there, looks wonderful.

12 January 1968 Trouble over [Nikita] Magaloff's concerto for Tuesday, announced for Rach[maninov] 2, booked for 3.
13 January 1968 Talk with Jasper [Parrott] – wants three weeks holiday! Told him doesn't know a thing about running a business! Thinks he's hard worked.
24 February 1968 Trouble over Clifford's pianoforte. RFH for tomorrow. Smooth it down somehow!!
12 March 1968 Lunch with Wyn Morris at White Elephant club to celebrate his appointment as conductor Royal Choral Society. Seemed to be well known at the club. Dinner with Janet Baker and Keith [Shelley, her husband] to discuss all business. Just back from USA.
9 April 1968 RFH [Hugo] Rignold and Ashkenazy last of the Rachmaninovs. 10.30pm, Ian gave a party for Sol Hurok – his 80th birthday. Margot Fonteyn, Nureyev, Barenboim, du Pré, Ashkenazy, Frederick Ashton, David Webster, Frederick Lloyd (D'Oyly Carte). Cake with one candle.
20 August 1968 Went to Lady Lamington to hear quite remarkable Hungarian boy pianist (14 years).
30 September 1968 Ibbs and Tillett Ltd gone up the spout again. From 1 October (tomorrow) Ibbs and Tillett is under the TILLETT Trust.
1 October 1968 Beryl arrived back evening, had long chat on phone. Trouble (more) over Richter – has cancelled rest of tour. Arranged Ogdon for Chichester, Tortelier for SNO, Bachauer for Northern Sinfonia.
8 October 1968 Bristol and Bournemouth in trouble over Richter. Got them Schwarzkopf and Segovia.
7 November 1968 Lunch with Sheila Armstrong, Copper Grill. QEH evening, Cherkassky recital. Magnificent. Solo very pleased with his 'pupil'. I was between halls. Szell and Clifford with NPO in RFH.
28 November 1968 Bad day. Clifford Curzon ill. Cancelled Germany. Janet Baker throat infection, cancel everything till end of December! RFH LSO David Oistrakh conducting Mahler 4 with Elizabeth Harwood.

8 February 1969 Lunch with Beryl. Discussed Lereculey affair. Decided I would enlist help of Dr. Bott to order her to take things much more easily or retire??
20 February 1969 Slight brush with Jasper over Alicia de Larrocha and Hartog whom he seems to admire! Eve of J's departure for five-week tour of South America. Never met anyone so argumentative.
6 June 1969 Took von Stresemann, wife and Ian to lunch at Café Royal, prices gone up tremendously. Bill nearly £12 for grilled sole, veg, sweet and coffee. No wine!
10 June 1969 Long interviews with Paul and Denzil over future of Tillett and Holt, Jasper, Harrison. Talked to Miss Lereculey re unloading her work, did not meet with much success. Wigmore Hall evening, Stephen Bishop. Took Solo, Gwen and Mona.
18 June 1969 Terribly busy day, Clifford Curzon came 4.30, very bothered about Dorati affair. RCM for opera *Full Circle* (Robin Orr) and *The Bear* (Walton) both excellently performed, Della Jones (*The Bear*) very promising.
6 July 1969 [Sunday] Office in morning to make up for Friday. Souzay there, warming up his voice in the office!!
24 July 1969 Difficulties over contract with Jasper and Harrison. They want to dictate re policy etc. Don't know what to do for best. Must talk to Paul.
3 September 1969 Paul saw Jasper and Harrison.

4 September 1969 Received Paul's letter about interview. Jasper intolerable over Gerald English engagement Rome December 28th – Liverpool 29th!!
5 September 1969 Lunch with Paul. He says only one solution to 'Jasper and Harrison' – they must go!!
10 September 1969 Talk with Denzil. Agreed intolerable re Jasper and Harrison. Prepared excellent memoranda.
13 September 1969 Impertinent and insolent letter from Jasper to Denzil. Their demands conveyed to Paul were their minimum requirements, certainly not maximum!!
15 September 1969 Beryl off for three weeks holiday and Lereculey one week.
17 September 1969 Campbell-White and wife came up after RFH Elgar concert. Arrived at 9.50pm to talk about taking over foreign department. I like him and am sure I can work with him. Like her too. Left at 11.50pm.
18 September 1969 Interviewed Harrison and Jasper to discuss!!
19 September 1969 Harrison and Jasper went to see Campbell-White last night. Both appalled at turning events as did not expect anything to happen at the moment, and wanted to lay their own plans. Told J I would speak to EMI as they want a recording manage[ment].
25 September 1969 Saw Ashkenazy. Fear we shall lose him to Jasper!! Very friendly meeting, may keep [him for] England. RFH evening. LSO Barbirolli and Schwarzkopf. Lovely singing but age showing in voice.
26 September 1969 Took Elizabeth Harwood and Julian to dinner at Festival Hall. Told them about Jasper and Harrison. I think E feels her work may suffer but assured her not the case. Everyone seems satisfied that C-W is taking over.
29 September 1969 Campbell-White broke news on arrival. Jasper and Harrison opening their own agency taking with them Ashkenazy, Orozco, Tchaikovsky, Lawrence Foster!!
1 October 1969 Lunch with Peter Andrey at Oriental Club. Told him all about P & H. He feels a pity losing Ashkenazy but must find someone else.
2 October 1969 Lunch with John Shirley-Quirk. Very friendly with Jasper but very loyal to Ibbs and Tillett. Must give him more attention. RFH evening Clifford with RPO and Dutoit.
13 October 1969 First day without Jasper and Harrison – heaven! So quiet and dignified again along our corridor! Campbell-White efficient and business like.
18 October 1969 Should have left for Bath Festival but too much doing. Been a wonderfully peaceful week without J and Harrison. Good shopping in market. Excellent card table for ten shillings. Painted green bottles.
19 October 1969 Went to Albert Hall for Elgar cello concerto (du Pré – gestures impossible). Beautiful performance of *Gerontius*. Janet Baker, Bob Tear, John Shirley-Quirk. John Pritchard conducted instead of Barenboim – ill.
5 November 1969 Barenboim told Ian he has <u>not</u> made any arrangement with H & P re representation. Ian saw Harrison at RFH and cut him.
8 December 1969 RCM afternoon. Concert for centenary of birth of Sir Hugh Allen. All the 'old sweats' there, Brunskill, Suddaby, Isobel Baillie, Eugene Cruft, Lionel Tertis, Maurice Jacobson.
24 December 1969 Lunch with Shura. Daniel Barenboim came in to the restaurant to wish Shura Happy Christmas on the way to get his hair cut. Drink with the Staff. Home early.

Letters from Edward Elgar 1899–1932

Craeg Lea, Wells Road, Malvern
March 30 [1899]
Dear Mr Vert
I hear from Novello that the score has not yet arrived; it will take some time to produce the copies & I hope the score has started – cd. you find out if Dr Richter has despatched it & if it is delayed on the way.
Yrs v. truly
Edward Elgar

[On Worcestershire Philharmonic Society paper]
Malvern
Oct 13 1901
I had hoped to have seen you before you left Leeds only to say this. The Variations went well &, as you have perhaps seen, were a great triumph for the orchestra & for me: I have to thank you for the introduction to Richter which led to the first performance of the work – you may have forgotten this – but I have not & shd. like you to understand that I am very grateful to you for your kindness when I much needed it.
Kind regards
Yours sincerely
Edward Elgar
Plenty of people are kind to me now!

Craeg Lea, Wells Road, Malvern
Nov 6 1901
Dear Mr Vert,
I have acknowledged the enclosed & have said I have sent it on to you to answer. I am disengaged but I don't see why I shd. go without a fee; if you can arrange anything please do – if not I won't go. You can say I am disengaged.
Kind regards
Sincerely yours
Edward Elgar
I ought not to go for less than ten guineas.
Copy: This is what I have said: 'Many thanks for your letter; I have sent it to my agent, Mr Vert, who will tell you of my engagements &c. Yrs v try E.E.'

Craeg Lea, Wells Road, Malvern.
Nov 13: 1901
Dear Mr Vert,
Many thanks: of course I cannot go about the world for nothing. I return the Bristol letter.
Yours sincerely
Ed: Elgar

Craeg Lea, Wells Road, Malvern
Ap 30 [date of receipt is 1/5/1902]
My dear Mr Vert:
Many thanks for your letter: I shall be at the Langham on Thursday for a few days: will you kindly send a line there & I will take an early opportunity to see you. I am not quite sure as to my engagements until I arrive in town (Thursday p.m.) but I have promised to attend rehearsals at Q's Hall.
Very kind regards
Yours sincerely
Edward Elgar

[on mourning stationery]
Malvern
Sep 19 02
My dear Mr Vert:
You were kind enough to write to Mr [George] Riseley about my conducting [at Bristol on 7 October, his *Coronation Ode*, *Cockaigne* overture and a new orchestration of his song *The Pipes of Pan* sung by Andrew Black] – I refused at first but since have accepted & he offers 20 guis: – so this will please go thro' your hands – or if they send direct to me I will of course gladly settle the commission &c when we meet.
Mr [Archibald] Ramsden is here to-day & sends his love
Kindest regards
Yours sincerely
Edward Elgar

Plas Gwyn
Hereford
Dec 19 1905
Dear Mr Tillett
Russell in Baker St has the latest & probably the best photo of me – Window & Grove have also some good ones. I much prefer that my photo should not appear but as it seems to be a fashion now that cannot be changed, I suppose it cannot be helped.
As to the photographs of my family & my house, will you please say, as kindly & firmly as you can, that on no account are any of them to appear: the idea is too dreadful.
The biographical nonsense is also too much overdone. It should be quite sufficient to say whence I come & how old I am: if the Cincinatti gentleman insists, please ask Messrs Novello for further information.
Believe in
Yours v try
Edward Elgar

Ullswater Hotel, Patterdale.
8 Augt 1916 (in the hand of Elgar's wife but signed by Elgar)
Dear Sirs
I am sorry there has been any delay in replying to your letter – I see you say the Committee had their final meeting on Monday, will you kindly let me know if the question of my conducting a Concert is still open?
Yours very truly
Edward Elgar

Ullswater Hotel, Patterdale.
Augt 11: 1916
Dear Sirs

Liverpool Phil

Many thanks for your letter: the Society must offer me what terms they can afford to pay: they know my pre-war term: it is the duty of the Society, not the musician, to suggest new terms. If the terms proposed by the Society are possible I will accept them. If they are too low I will refuse. It must be understood that I can suggest no terms.
Yours very truly
Edward Elgar

Brinkwells, Fittleworth, Sussex
Oct 7 : 1918
Dear Sirs:
Many thanks for your letter. I shall be pleased to conduct the L'pool Philharmonic on March 15th for fifty guineas [*Dream of Gerontius*].
Yours very try
Edward Elgar
I shall be home in a few days

Brinkwells, Fittleworth
Oct 8 [1918]
Dear Sirs:
I am sorry for the delay but you will have had my note by this time. We have been at the cottage all the summer but shall be at Hampstead – temporarily – at the end of this week.
Yours very truly
Edward Elgar
Messrs Ibbs & Tillett

Severn House, 42 Netherhall Gardens, Hampstead, N.W.3
March 8 : 1919
Dear Sirs:

Liverpool

The interval should be at the end of P.I. [of *Dream of Gerontius*]
Eleven o'c will do perfectly for the soloists on Saturday morn. I have made a note of the Friday evening rehearsal at 7.30 & that the concert commences at 2.30.
Yours very try
Edward Elgar
Messrs Ibbs & Tillett

Severn House, 42 Netherhall Gardens, Hampstead, N.W.
[Postcard with red date stamp] 17 MAR 1919
Dr. Sirs:
The L'pool Philharmonic gave me a cheque on Saturday.
Yrs v try
Ed: Elgar

Brinkwells, Fittleworth, Sussex.
July 27 1919
Dear Sirs:
I recd. the enclosed some days ago: have you heard anything more from Amsterdam? You see what the writer says. I shall be at home Hampstead
[incomplete: the top half of a torn letter]
[Ibbs & Tillett pencilling: Telephoned Michell & Sir Ed. 28/7/19]

Severn House, 42 Netherhall Gardens, Hampstead, N.W.3
Sep 12 1919
Messrs Ibbs & Tillett
Dear Sirs:
Many thanks for your letter of the 10th inst: I accept the terms for Amsterdam £125 – date Novr. 20.
Yours very truly
Edward Elgar

Severn House, 42 Netherhall Gardens, Hampstead, N.W.
Oct 22 1919
Dear Mr Tillett:
As I said over the telephone, I have heard nothing from Amsterdam. Would you write and suggest the programme given on the other side; also recommend from me that Mr Felix Salmond shd. be engaged for the new Concerto.
Yrs try
Ed/ Elgar
Suggested programme:
Overture *Cockaigne*
Symphonic study *Falstaff*
Concerto Violoncello
Variations for orchestra

Severn House, 42 Netherhall Gardens, Hampstead, N.W.3
Oct 30 1919
Dear Mr Tillett
I shall be away at
The Elms
Stoke Prior
Bromsgrove
Worcs:
for about a week. Address telegrams
Elgar,
The Elms,
Stoke Works.
Stoke Works is a telegraph office. I write this in case anything comes from Holland as to the programme.
I am quite willing to include the Violin concerto if they prefer it – but it takes 50 mins: if it is included the programme might be 1. *Falstaff*
2. Violin concetro
3. Introdn & Allegro for String orchestra

I think this wd. be long enough. In place of No.3 the overture 'In the South' might be substituted. It may save time if you know this.
Yrs sincy
Edward Elgar

Severn House, 42 Netherhall Gardens, Hampstead, N.W.
June 13 1921
Dear Sirs:
I enclose a letter: will you see what is wanted & what can be done? I have heard nothing of suggested terms.
I have telephoned to Mr Oppenheimer asking him to communicate with you etc.
Yours very try
Edward Elgar
Messrs Ibbs & Tillett P.T.O.
P.S. – I also enclose Miss B[eatrice] Harrison's letter: kindly return this. EE

37, St James's Place, S.W.1.
Oct 20 1922
Dear Sirs:
Thank you for your letters about Southsea. I shall be quite willing to go but it wd. be a question of terms. I suppose there wd. be a rehearsal either on the day of the concerts or the day before. Will you propose a fee?
In haste – I am only this moment back
Yrs faithfully
Edward Elgar
Messrs Ibbs & Tillett
[Notated by Ibbs & Tillett: 2 perfs. Mr Story 50gs.]

37, St James's Place, S.W.1.
Oct 25 1922
Dear Sirs:
I could go to Southsea for Sixty guineas & wd. be glad to see Mr Story if he agrees to this fee.
Yrs v try
Edward Elgar
(In greatest haste)
Messrs Ibbs & Tillett

Brooks's, St James's Street, S.W.1.
June 18 1923
Dear Sirs:

L'pool Philc.

I could go to L'pool on the dates named but the fee proposed is low: can you propose something better? Fifty guineas clear wd. be more in order.
Yrs v siy
Edward Elgar

37, St James's Place, S.W.1.
Oct 10 1923
Dear Sirs:

Liverpool.

Will you kindly suggest the programme as follows: Mr Riley will see that the concerts cannot begin with the Symph. – two or three, or four movements from the 'Wand of Youth' cd. be selected, the number of movemts depending upon the length of the vocal items in Pt II.
Yrs sncly
Edward Elgar
Messrs Ibbs & Tillett P.T.O. P.S. As to soloists either Miss [Astra] Desmond or Miss [Olga] Haley

Pt I

Overture D minor Handel (arrgd. by E.E.)	4 min
Sea pictures	12 min
Symphony No.2	45

Pt II

Apollo (Austin)	30
Songs?	
Wand of Youth selected	

37, St James's Place, S.W.1.
Oct 20 1923
Dear Sirs:

Liverpool

Yes: the Symphony II takes 50–55 minutes. – I had forgotten this. So that 3 numbers from the *Wand of Youth* will be enough – I give these on the other side.
You may ask what Songs will be in the Second Part –
Yrs vy try
Edward Elgar
Wand of Youth Suite I
Nos. 1 Overture
2. Serenade
3. Sun Dance
4. Fairies & Giants

Napleton Grange, Kempsey, Worcester.
July 11th. 1925
Dear Sirs:

Margate

I find I recd. sixty guineas for a concert at a Margate festival: I am disengaged on Sept 15th. – will you find out if the above named terms will be agreeable?
Kind regards
Yours sincy
Edward Elgar

Napleton Grange, Kempsey, Worcester.
Augt 9th. 1925
Dear Sirs:

Margate. Sept 15th.

I have booked the above date.
Will you let me know if the Directors wish a programme of my own compositions only or a varied programme. Would they consider the Violoncello Concerto (Miss Beatrice Harrison) – I should like to include this.
Yours very try
Edward Elgar
Messrs Ibbs & Tillett

Napleton Grange, Kempsey, Worcester.
Augt 17th 1925
Messrs Ibbs & Tillett
Dear Sirs:

Margate

Thank you for your letter. I suppose Mr. Bainbridge [Robinson] is still Musical Director: would he arrange the programme to include my version of the

Handel Overture in D minor for 1st item
Overture *Polonia* (Elkin)
Variations
Sea pictures (?the whole – in 2 pts)
Wand of Youth Suite No.2
& anything else he wishes

Yours sincy
Edward Elgar
Meditation. 'Light of Life'
Imperial March or
Pomp & Circumstance Nos. 2 & 1

[Typewritten on notepaper headed: Memorandum from Sir Edward Elgar, Master of the King's Musick, Lord Chamberlain's Office, St James's Palace, S.W.1.]
Napleton Grange, Kempsey, Worcester.
26th August 1927
Dear Sirs:
I believe that Sir Henry Coward is performing *The Apostles* this season. I shall be obliged if you will strongly recommend Miss Joan Elwes for the soprano part.
As to the notes for the Margate programme, I have none and suggest that the authorities should ask Mrs Newmarch to allow the use of her annotation.
Yours faithfully
Edward Elgar
Messrs Ibbs & Tillett

Brooks's, St. James's Street, S.W.1

X Country address Battenhall Manor, Worcester. Kindly correct this

Jany 17th. 1928

X Here till Friday a.m.

Dear Sirs:

Brand Lane, Manchester

Many thanks for your letter of the 14th. – I forget what fee I had for the former concert: if this is adequate (please let me know what it was) & a date can be arranged I shall be pleased to conduct *Gerontius*.
Kind rgrds
Yrs sic
Edward Elgar

Battenhall Manor, Worcester.
Jany 27th. 1928
Dear Sirs:

Brand Lane, Manchester

I cannot think why I went to Manchester for the fee you name, there must have been some 'extenuating' circumstances. I will go next season for seventy-five guineas: will you let me hear as soon as possible.
Kind regards
Yours sny
Edward Elgar

[Written on notepaper headed: Memorandum from Sir Edward Elgar, Master of the King's Musick, Lord Chamberlain's Office, St James's Palace, S.W.1.]
Battenhall Manor, Worcester.
8 FEB. 1928
Dear Sirs:

Brand Lane Concerts

Many thanks; I have pencilled Jany 26th 1929 for Mr Newton Lane & await his decision.
Yrs sincerely
Edward Elgar

Tiddington House near Stratford-upon-Avon.
21 JAN 1929
Dear Sirs:
Will you please ask Mr Newton Lane if [he] will kindly send three tickets to the enclosed address.
Yours very try
Edward Elgar

Marl Bank, Rainbow Hill, Worcester Telephone: Worcester 924. Telegraph: Elgar, Worcester.
23rd June 1930
Dear Sirs:
The above is now my address.
I shall be delighted to sign the Souvenir book: as I shall not be in London probably for some time perhaps it would be convenient for you to send the volume here?
Yours very truly
Edward Elgar
Messrs Ibbs & Tillett

[Postcard] Marl Bank, Rainbow Hill, Worcester
15th Ap: 1931
Dear Sir:
I have sent to your address a letter to Melsa: I shall be greatly obliged if you will forward it to him.
Yrs v try
Ed. Elgar

Langham Hotel, Portland Place, London W.1.
15th Decr 1931
Dear Tillett
Here are the two letters from which you will see how matters stand.
Yours sincy
Edward Elgar

Marl Bank, Worcester
10th Sept: 1932
My dear Tillett:
Thank you for yours of the 9th. – under the circumstances I wd. accept the small fee & have (as you kindly suggest) passed on the 'idea' to Novello with whom the affair originated.
Kind rgrds
Yrs sny
Edward Elgar

[Written on notepaper headed: Memorandum from Sir Edward Elgar, Master of the King's Musick, Lord Chamberlain's Office, St James's Palace, S.W.1.]
Marl Bank, Worcester
3 OCT. 1932
Dear Tillett:

<u>South Africa</u>

There have been a letter or two & newspaper pars: in relation to a suggested visit. If Messrs. Novello have any letter or anything I have asked them to send direct to you.
Will you kindly take the matter (which arose during Mr G.B.Shaw's visit) up &, if possible, straighten things out.
The enclosed letter came on Thursday: I have not replied & shall be glad if you will find out anything you can.
I have only said, generally, that I wd. consider anything if matters cd. be arranged.
Kind rgrds
Yours sincly
Edward Elgar

Brooks's, St. James's Street, S.W.1.
Saturday morning [this may be before 1930, when the St. James's Place flat was given up]
My dear Tillett:
Thank you for your note. I expect you [are] away today <u>but</u> in case you are disengaged, will you come <u>here</u> to lunch say at one – I am passing through.
Yr sny
Edward Elgar
My valet will bring word, just yes or no.

Letters from Sergei Rachmaninov 1911–30

Letters after 1918 are written in English, those prior to that year (complete with their alternative dates according to the Russian calendar) are in German, reproduced here in my translation. Those prior to 1928 are handwritten, but not by Rachmaninov, though he did sign them 'Sergei Rachmaninoff'. Letters written between 1928 and 1930 are typed and signed 'S. Rachmaninoff'.

3/16 January 1911
Regarding the letter from M[essrs] N Vert, please will you answer it.
I remain
Yours sincerely
Sergei Rachmaninoff

4/17 February 1911
I have received your letter and contract (Liverpool). Meanwhile there are some details I wish to clarify in the contract. How big and how good is the orchestra in Liverpool? How much time do the choral numbers need? How long are the rehearsals? Are there only two or can there be a third? Who [conductor] will accompany the concerto? Perhaps matters can be arranged as follows: I play the 3rd concerto (length about 40 minutes), and conduct the tone poem *Isle of the Dead*, and perhaps the rest of the programme can consist of an overture and choral items, which the conductor who accompanies me can conduct. After I have received your confirmation and news of who shall conduct, I will send the signed contract.
On 18 October Middlesbrough – I assume. Programme as follows: 1) Adagio and finale from the [first] piano sonata (D minor), 2) Élégie, Prélude, Mélodie, Polichinelle [Fantasy Pieces] Op.3, Barcarolle, Humoresque Op.10. To this I can add the second sonata [in B flat minor] and 6 Preludes from Opp.23 and 32. This programme is for all piano recitals. I agree to a fee of 60 guineas, however only for an appearance as soloist, but this depends upon the number of engagements that you procure me.
I can come to England on 15th October and stay for three weeks, that is till 6–7 November but not later because on 11th November my tour of Russia begins.
Sincerely
Sergei Rachmaninoff

2/15 March 1911
I am in receipt of your letter of 7 March. I have taken note of the concerts on 19 October and 7 November.
About the concert in Liverpool, I fear very much that two rehearsals will be too few, and this complicates the choice of programme. Let us assume the following programme.
1 *Night on the bare mountain* (20 minutes long) Mussorgsky
2 the singer
3 the chorus (I do not conduct)
4 Concerto No.3 Op.30

II Part
1 the singer
2 the chorus
3 2nd symphony of Tchaikovsky (40 minutes long)
I will sign the contract after further concerts have been fixed. With reference to our previous verbal conversation and agreement, I would like during the three weeks I shall stay in England to have not less than 7 or 8 concerts.
Sincerely
Sergei Rachmaninoff

21 March/3 April 1911
The programme sent to me from Liverpool is unacceptable.
1 I cannot accept two rehearsals for two overtures, my symphony which lasts about an hour, and the new piano concerto (lasts about 40 minutes)
2 I cannot play solos, nor such a difficult and long concerto and also conduct the whole programme
Under such circumstances, I would prefer to refuse the concerts completely.

Dear Sirs 4 July 1911
Unfortunately I could not reply to your three letters until now, because they have only just reached me in the country having been sent on from Moscow. You have probably forgotten that my summer address is as follows: c/o Music Shop A. Gutheil, Moscow, Schmiedebrücke 16
1 I can only send the [orchestral] parts of my concerto (for Liverpool) on 10 October
2 I agree to the concerts on 21 October (Dundee) and 1 November (Hull)
3 I shall send you the contract at once.
Sincerely
Sergei Rachmaninoff

Dear Sirs 29 January 1912
I much regret that at present I am unable to give you dates for my concerts next season. I fear above all, that it will be impossible for me to come to England in the 1912–1913 season. As I already told you personally, I would like to limit my next season to two or three, but already for Russia alone I have more engagements than time will allow. I apologise and ask you not to expect a definite answer at present.
Yours sincerely
Sergei Rachmaninoff

Dear Sirs 9 April 1913
In haste I reply to your questions.

1) I accept the piano recitals in Sheffield and Nottingham, but not for less than 70 guineas per concert. Nowhere do I wish to accept less than that sum for piano recitals, which are very strenuous for me.
2) Please let Mr Bechstein know about Messrs Paterson's refusal (which I find incomprehensible). If Bechstein also refuses to provide grand pianos in these cities, I cannot play in them and must sort the matter out personally with Bechstein in Berlin.
3) There's one other matter to clarify. I can no longer undertake engagements where I play and conduct during the same evening. That is beyond my powers, therefore the engagement in Liverpool must be changed. I can either only play or only conduct,

preferably play. But I'd like to know immediately who will accompany me in Liverpool. I hope not the same conductor with whom I had to play last year. That would be impossible.

4) I agree to play my cello sonata in Bradford.
5) I cannot leave England later than February 15th as I have a 9am rehearsal in Moscow on the 19th.

[Only the bottom half of this next letter, dated 5/18 December 1913, has survived. Originally with four 'bullet' points, the third of them seems to end with a blistering attack on 'the dreadful Royal Albert Hall'. It concludes:]
4) I cannot accept the London recital under the terms offered. Please send me all the dates of my English concerts. I shall remain in Moscow for the whole of December.
Sergei Rachmaninoff

Dear Mr Ibbs 2 July 1914

1) I am returning the signed contract for Liverpool. I shall play the 3rd Concerto, two solo pieces; if the Committee can make a selection, I shall naturally play them if possible. There are things I cannot stand and never play anywhere.
2) In Manchester – the 3rd Concerto, Solo: two arrangements a) Romance *Flieder* b) *Polka de W.R.* [the French title transliterates the initials of Wladimir Rachmaninoff, the composer's father, whom his son mistakenly thought had composed the polka on which he based his concert arrangement. It was in fact by Franz Behr (1837–98)]
3) Norwich – the 2nd Concerto, Solo: three Preludes, which I ask to be copied from the programmes of last season.
4) London – the 2nd Concerto. I won't refuse the *Capriccio* (I cannot stand it!) I agree to perform the *Isle of the Dead* (20 Minutes) but will Sir Henry Wood prepare the orchestra? If not, how many rehearsals can I have? I ask for news of this.
5) As far as the Albert Hall, London is concerned, I urgently ask to be released from this. In case you are going to remind me that I promised to play there again one last time, then this one time should preferably be with orchestra. The 2nd Concerto again (the 3rd is too hard for them) and Solos – two arrangements (as in Manchester).

With hearty greetings
Sergei Rachmaninoff

[From Copenhagen] 13 June 1918
Dear Sir
I rather think that my visit to America will be put off till the next season, but I should be glad to come to England for as many concerts as you are able to arrange now. The time that suits me best is after the first of December. Will you be so kind as to write to me here. I'll stay here the whole summer. Thank you so much for your kind letter which I was glad to receive.
With kindest regards
Yours sincerely
Sergei Rachmaninoff

12 July 1918

Dear Sir

I send you a telegram today to which I have to add what follows: I'm playing on the 23rd November for the last time in Norway, so that I can leave for England in the morning of the 24th. All depends on the English Consulate's permission and my getting a steamer leaving at this time. I ask you to undertake all you can to help me to get the permission in question at the Consulate in Copenhagen. I on the other side will also try to get it.

Now what concerns the honorary. I have not touched this subject because I believe you see by yourself the necessity of raising it, with regard to the dearth and the most expensive travel. Our conditions remain as they have been – 10% from my honorary – so you see it is also in your interest to raise it. I also want to say some words about my program. I'm able to play 2 piano concert[o]s in each symphony concert. My program contains three of my own concert[o]s (the first in a new edition) and three of other composers – Liszt E flat major, Tchaikovsky C minor [B♭ minor] and Rubinstein D minor.

Yours sincerely

Sergei Rachmaninoff

31 July 1918

Dear Sir

I wired to you saying that I cannot fix exactly the day of my arrival to England. I can leave Christiana in the morning of the 24th November, and I ask you to help me on your side to get the permission from the English and the Russian Consulates and to help me to get a place on a nice and rapid steamer. What concerns the Albert Hall concerts, so wired I that I'm ready to play there on the condition that my first appearance in London will be in a symphonic concert as we have talked about. You say in your letter of the 28th June that the fees are not so high as they have been before the war. I think that this does not concern foreigner artists and I insist on getting the highest fees.

With kindest regards

Yours truly

Sergei Rachmaninoff

P.S. Wouldn't you have the kindness to inform yourself if the concert[o] material to my second and to my third concert[o] is to be found at Chester's? The material to my first concert[o] will be with me.

[Note by Robert Leigh Ibbs] This can wait as it is answered by our last letter. Will you ask Chester's if they have the band parts of the 1st and 2nd concertos, and we can let him know later.

[Pencilled annotations 'No' and 'Yes' respectively confirm that Chester's had only the 2nd concerto]

'Les Pelouses', Villers sur Mer, Calvados, France September 7th 1928

Dear Mr Ibbs,

The following are the full particulars regarding our passports:

Sergei Rachmaninoff born April 2, 1873 in Novgorod, Russia

Natalie Rachmaninoff née Satine born May 26, 1877 in Tambov, Russia.

Both are Nansen passports. The permanent residence is 505 West End Ave., New York City, U.S.A.

I have sent a copy of this to Dr De Koos and have also asked him to reserve rooms at the Hotel des Indes, in the Hague for the whole time that I will be in Holland.
With kind regards
Sincerely yours
S. Rachmaninoff

'Le Pavillon', Clairefontaine par Rambouillet, S[eine] et O[ise] July 11th 1929
Dear Mr Ibbs
I remember that your holiday usually lasts about a month, and as you expect to leave about July 22nd, that means that you will be back by Sept 1st. Please allow me to send you the programmes for that date. I hate even to think about my concerts while I am having my vacation.
Could you be kind enough to write to Mr De Koos that I am counting on his help in obtaining the Dutch visas for Mrs Rachmaninoff and myself. Maybe he could have them sent to the Consulate in Paris.
Hoping that you will enjoy your holiday, and with kindest regards
Sincerely yours
S. Rachmaninoff

[Telegram dated 20 September 1929 from De Rambouillet, France to Ibbs and Tillett]
SURPRISED POWELLS ACCEPTING TWO CONCERTS WITHOUT MY AGREEMENT. WILL NOT PLAY THERE. GREETINGS = RACHMANINOFF =

[Telegram dated 21 September 1929 from De Rambouillet, France to Ibbs and Tillett]
TOO TIRED ACCEPT EXTRA CONCERTS. KINDLY CANCEL. GREETINGS – RACHMANINOFF –

'Le Pavillon', Clairefontaine par Rambouillet, S[eine] et O[ise] September 22nd 1929
Dear Mr Ibbs
I am very sorry indeed to cause you so much displeasure, but I really can not accept those two concerts in Ireland. It makes me nervous just to think that I have seventy concerts ahead of me and I am really too tired to accept any more.
When I was in London last Spring, you told me that if I would agree to play a third time in London, it was not worth while to make such a long trip and go to Ireland just for two concerts. I thought that this was settled, and therefore your cable was a great surprise to me. I do think that having a month and a half of time ahead of us, it will be quite easy to cancel these performances.
With kind regards
Sincerely yours
S. Rachmaninoff

505 West End Ave., New York City, U.S.A. January 2nd 1930
Dear Mr Ibbs
Let us begin with business.

1. After my conversation with Mr Sachs we decided that in future they will communicate directly with me. Thus regarding Germany everything will be as before, and they will communicate with you about the dates of their concerts only.
2. I met on the steamer Mr De Koos and told him that if he decides to make symphony concerts, only I would like to play not less than three times, and if possible on three

consecutive dates. In case if it would be my Fourth Concerto, I would insist that they give me a two hours rehearsal.

In case if instead of symphony concerts I were to give recitals, Mr De Koos offers me $1000.00 guarantry for each recital in Amsterdam and Haag, but I would like to get in addition 50% of extra net receipts. Mr De Koos has agreed to receive the following fees: 5% in case of symphony concerts and 10% in case of recitals.

3. Regarding Belgium. I have promised the Zerbason Agency to manage my Brussels concerts if I would ever play there next season.
4. Now I wish dear Mr Ibbs, to clear up our financial affaires with you. For instance: last year when you were travelling on account of my ten recitals in Scandinavia and Holland, you have charged me a little more than $50.00 per recital, while this year, when you have travelled in Holland only, you have charged me with 10% on net proceeds from my five concerts, or in total 834 Gulden, that is a little more than $60.00 per concert.

   As per our former agreement with you, your fees for all my concerts which you would organize yourself in England should be 10% of net receipts. But we never discussed the question of your fees for concerts organized by other managers under your supervision only. This question not being quite clear to me, I would appreciate your opinion thereon.

   All my European concerts were very good. The only thing which bothered me quite a bit was my back. Everybody says this is a lumbago but if this lumbago would stick to me all the rest of my life – it would not be very pleasant!

With season greetings and best wishes to you and Mr Tillett, I am
Sincerely yours
S. Rachmaninoff
[Pencilled annotation by Ibbs: Ring. 5% 417 Gulden]

[Telegram dated 25 January 1930 from New York to Ibbs and Tillett]
LETTER RECEIVED ANSWER FOLLOWS PLEASE CONTINUE NEGOTIATIONS YSAYE STOP WRITING ZERBASON ACCORDINGLY. RACHMANINOFF.

505 West End Avenue, New York City January 24th 1930
Dear Mr Ibbs

Your letter of 14th inst. gives me an impression that you are somewhat angry with me. If so – I am very sorry because when I wanted to bring a little more clarity in our financial relations with you (and you would agree that they never were very definite!) I had no intention to hurt you in any way. My feelings for you always were and are now of sincere friendliness and esteem. To show me that you are not angry with me – please do not refuse to accept the check which you have sent with your letter and which I return herewith.

In order to settle once for ever the question of your fees for management and supervision of my European concerts, I am glad to confirm that it is satisfactory to me if you charge me for your services ten percentum of the net proceeds from my concerts organized entirely by you in England, and five percentum of the net proceeds from my concerts in other European countries organized by other managers but under your supervision.

This settles one delicate question and now comes another one regarding my concert in Belgium. Frankly speaking, I have entirely forgotten that I have asked you to negotiate with Mr Ysaÿe regarding my eventual appearance in Brussels, and that is why I promised to Zerbason to arrange my Belgian concerts. This, however, could be easily changed and I am writing today to Zerbason

asking them to stop their negotiations in that respect as you are going to take care of same. This will explain my cablegram to you of today which reads:
LETTER RECEIVED ANSWER FOLLOWS PLEASE CONTINUE NEGOTIATIONS YSAYE STOP WRITING ZERBASON ACCORDINGLY.
Regarding my Belgian concerts, I would like to receive a guarantee of $2000.00 for a recital in Brussels and, if possible, $1500.00 per recital in Antwerpen and Liege. My Belgian concerts should be as near as possible to my recital in Paris (before it or after).
Regarding my Paris recital, I think it would be advisable to make it on November 23rd instead of November 30th. If I have to play in Belgium, I could do it immediately after Paris on my way to Germany and start my German concerts a little earlier, that is during the last week of November.
This is all at present time about our business questions.
Please let me hear from you that you have no angry feeling for me and believe me
Sincerely yours
S. Rachmaninoff
Encl. Check

505 West End Avenue, New York City March 5th 1930
My dear Mr Ibbs
On March 22nd, on S.S. *Lancastria*, I will ship my new Lincoln car to Le Havre, France. I would appreciate it if you call on the Secretary of the AA Association and ask him to instruct their agent at Le Havre to take care of my car upon its arrival at Le Havre. As I am sailing on S.S. *Mauretania* on April 9th to Cherbourg, I could come from Paris to Le Havre on April 17–18 only and take delivery of my car. Therefore I would prefer that my car should be in care of the Automobile Association's agent from the time of its arrival up to the day when I will take it. You know what means to me a car, and especially a new car, and you will understand that I could not sleep quietly if I would not know that my car is in a safe place. Kindly let me know the name and address of the agent at Le Havre, as I shall communicate with him immediately upon my arrival in Paris.
[signature cut out]

505 West End Avenue, New York City March 6th 1930
My dear Mr Ibbs
Referring to my letter mailed to you yesterday, I forgot to tell you that I overlooked to pay my membership fees in the Automobile Association. Will you so kind as to pay it for me and charge my account with you? One more request: kindly ring up Mayfair 3119, Pharmacy Nelson & Co., 73 Duke Street, and find out if there is any outstanding bill for me. If so, kindly pay that bill too.
Sincerely yours
S. Rachmaninoff

505 West End Avenue, New York City March 20th 1930
My dear Mr Ibbs
I have received your letter of 11th inst. regarding my English taxes. I was surprised to see how much I have to pay! Thank you anyhow for your endeavour to reduce them and to protect my interests. I have instructed the National City Bank of New York to pay you the sum of £470 and would appreciate if you pay my tax for me.
Very sincerely yours
S. Rachmaninoff
P.S. Don't you think it would be much better if I take to recitals in Holland instead of concerts with orchestra, especially as Mr De Koos is willing to give a guaranty for recitals?

[Telegram dated 1 April 1930 from New York to Ibbs and Tillett]
HAVE YOU ARRANGED AUTOMOBILE ASSOCIATION REGARDING MY CAR SHIPPED MARCH TWENTYSECOND TO HAVRE. RACHMANINOFF.

[Telegram dated 3 April 1930 from New York to Ibbs and Tillett]
LONDON BRISTOL ACCEPTABLE PREFER PLAY BELGIUM BEFORE PARIS IF LAUSANNE NOT BOOKED OTHERWISE TRY INCLUDE ZURICH ONE TRIP WITH LAUSANNE. RACHMANINOFF.

[Telegram dated 9 April 1930 from New York to Ibbs and Tillett]
WOLFFSACHS CONCERTS ACCEPTED HOW IS MR IBBS GREETINGS RACHMANINOFF.

[Telegram dated 18 April 1930 from Paris to Ibbs and Tillett]
THANKS YOUR PRESENCE PARIS UNNECESSARY BELGIUM HOLLAND ALLRIGHT LETTER FOLLOWS ABOUT SCANDINAVIA RACHMANINOFF.

24 rue Desbordes Valmore, Paris 16 April 23rd 1930
My dear Mr Tillett
In every city of my European tour I have one concert, and to prepare a second programme for Stockholm only does not seem worthwhile. Therefore it would be necessary either to arrange a second recital in Oslo or to cancel one in Stockholm. In the last case I would prefer to begin my tour a little later, for instance Oslo on the 25th and Stockholm on the 28th.
May I ask you to see the secretary of the A.A. Club again and to tell him that I got my car in perfect order, but was surprised to see that the plates were given out by France instead of Gr. Britain, which I do not like for many reasons. (F. No...... instead of G.B. No......) Could these be changed for G.B. ones or have the French plates already been registered?
I am enclosing a letter, which I would like you to answer for me. If they expect me to pay them for the article, they are mistaken.
How is Mr Ibbs? I do hope he is better.
With kindest regards to you both
[signature cut out]

Le Pavillon, Clairefontaine par Rambouillet, S[eine] et O[ise] May 16th 1930

Dear Mr Ibbs

It gave me great pleasure to hear that from May 14th you are back at your office. Please do not play again that awful game [cricket] which was so bad for you. I cannot tell you anything positively now about the Leeds Musical Festival in 1931. The only thing I know is that I never play solos in symphony concerts. It seems to me that I could take part in one of these concerts if the whole programme would be composed out of my works, for instance *The Bells*, Russian songs and in the second half my second concerto. Please find out if the choir and orchestra are good, and tell me if you think it worthwhile. Concerning my fee, please decide yourself. Better ask more.

With kindest regards

S. Rachmaninoff

Le Pavillon, Clairefontaine par Rambouillet, S[eine] et O[ise] May 20th 1930

Dear Mr Ibbs

Has my income tax been paid? I am positive that I sent you money for that purpose, though I do not remember exactly the sum and the date when it was done. You never acknowledged receipt of that money, and in the meantime, a few days ago, to my address here, came another notice of assessment.

Please inquire what is the matter and let me know as soon as possible, as I am greatly worried. I am sure that the money was sent not later than in March.

Thanking you in advance and with kindest regards,

Yours sincerely,

[signature cut out]

Le Pavillon, Clairefontaine par Rambouillet, S[eine] et O[ise] May 29th 1930

Dear Mr Tillett

I would be glad if you could arrange a few Provincial Recitals instead of Bristol. I think that the very great defect in my coming season is that I have such long pauses between my concerts, which disturb me in my work. The tour in Germany is the only one that has been well planned. For instance, between my London and Paris recitals I have a pause of 15 days. Of course, as I already told to Mr Ibbs, I would have preferred to give all my concerts in one month.

If you would be able to arrange a few concerts to fill in that empty space of 15 days before Paris, I would be most grateful to you.

With kind regards

[signature cut out]

Le Pavillon, Clairefontaine par Rambouillet, S[eine] et O[ise] June 3rd 1930

My dear Mr Tillett

It was my new 4th piano concerto that I expected to play with the Concertgebouw Orchestra on November 1st and 2nd. Please, when writing this to them, don't forget to say that I insist on a two hour rehearsal for this concerto. But if they want me to, I could play my 3rd concerto instead.

With kind regards

Sincerely yours

[signature cut out]

P.S. Please do not ask me now about my programmes, which will not be ready before October.

S.R.

Le Pavillon, Clairefontaine par Rambouillet, S[eine] et O[ise] June 10th 1930
My dear Mr Tillett
Your offer to play at the concert of the British Broadcasting Corporation surprised me, as did the sum of the fee proposed by them. No doubt this company knows how little I think of a broadcasted performance, and therefore their offer seems quite inopportune to me. Of course I will not accept it.
With kind regards
Sincerely yours
[signature cut out]

Le Pavillon, Clairefontaine par Rambouillet, S[eine] et O[ise] July 1st 1930
My dear Mr Tillett
I regret to say that the proposition of Captain Amers, the Director of Music for the Eastbourne Corporation, seems absolutely unacceptable to me. As concerns the fee for Manchester, I leave it to your judgement. If you consider the fee of two hundred guineas a right one, I will accept the engagement. So far I have noted the following dates: November 8th – London, November 12th – Liverpool, November 15th – Manchester, November 18th – Bristol, and November 20th – Torquay. I regret that I could not answer your letter before. How is Mr Ibbs? Please remember me to him.
Yours very sincerely
S. Rachmaninoff

[Telegram dated 10 July 1930 from Rambouillet to Ibbs and Tillett]
CANCEL LIÈGE = RACHMANINOFF =

Le Pavillon, Clairefontaine par Rambouillet, S[eine] et O[ise] August 12th 1930
My dear Mr Tillett
May I ask you the following. Instead of my forty proposed concerts in the coming season, I have again almost sixty. Looking over my list I found two which could be easily cancelled. They are in Oslo and Stockholm, on October 21st and 23rd respectively. Will you be kind enough to write there, giving whatever explanation you think necessary, that I will play in each town only once, on Oct. 25th and 28th. These dates were reserved for my second recitals.
Will you also please ask the managers of those two cities to obtain visas for my wife and for myself. They should be sent to the Paris Consulates here. I will also need visas for Great Britain and Holland. It is so hard to get them that I think it wiser to start already now.
Thanking you in advance and with kindest regards to Mr Ibbs and to yourself,
Sincerely yours
S. Rachmaninoff

Le Pavillon, Clairefontaine par Rambouillet, S[eine] et O[ise] September 9th 1930
My dear Mr Tillett
Will you kindly let me know if you have been able to cancel my two first recitals in Stockholm and Oslo respectively. I also do not know if you have heard from Amsterdam which of my two concertos they would like me to play with the Concertgebouw Orchestra.
Hoping to hear from you soon, and with kind regards
Sincerely yours
S. Rachmaninoff

Villa Majestic, rue Laperouse, Paris 8 October 12th 1930
Dear Mr Ibbs
I note that you changed my concert in Torquay to Wednesday November 19th. I expect to leave Paris on October 22nd, and to arrive in Oslo on the 24th. Please reserve Hotel accommodation there for that date, and likewise in Stockholm, which I expect to reach on the morning of October 27th.
It gave me great pleasure to hear that you are feeling better. Nevertheless I do not want to see you in Oslo. You have to be very careful now, and it will be much wiser to remain in London.
With kindest regards
Sincerely yours
S. Rachmaninoff
P.S. Please reserve my usual suite at the Piccadilly for November 7th, as I will probably leave Holland on the 6th.

Hotel Majestic, Avenue Kléber, Place de l'Etoile, Paris October 19th 1930
My dear Mr Ibbs
Will you be so kind as to forward to Messrs Herm. Wolff & Jules Sachs, Berlin, the detailed programms in your possession. I have gotten all the visas and am starting on the 22nd.
Yours sincerely
S. Rachmaninoff
P.S. Kindly forward the programms likewise to Zerbason, Paris

11 East 92nd Street [New York] [undated]
My dear Mr Tillett
I am in receipt of your letter and in reply to your questions, would say that I cannot accept your proposal to play in England next winter as I intend to remain here.
With my best wishes to you and thanks for your interest, I remain
Very sincerely yours
Sergei Rachmaninoff

Letters from Myra Hess 1922–49

Hotel Wellington, Seventh Avenue, New York April 2nd 1922

My dear Mr Tillett

Thank you so much for your lovely letter. It was worth waiting for and I do appreciate it enormously, knowing how precious your spare moments are. There is no time for a long letter, life in New York being a degree more hectic if possible than in London. At the rate I am going at present, it is just as well that I am sailing on a slow boat on the 15th! I shall see you very soon after this reaches you, and will come and waste some of your idle hours, telling you all about everything. I really am feeling enormously encouraged. I didn't for a moment anticipate having such a success, and shall soon have to buy some new hats!!!

I was nearly overwhelmed last Sunday at the Mengelberg concert, with Carnegie Hall packed, no standing room left even. Next Sunday I am playing the Grieg concerto at the Metropolitan Opera House. I am not very much looking forward to playing there, it is too large for a piano, in fact the orchestra (when on the stage for concerts) doesn't sound well even. However it is my last concert, also the last concert of the season by the Philharmonic so it will be in the nature of a romp home! I have just about cleared expenses, but things are already shaping for next season when I shall hope to start a banking account!!!

This has been an exciting week, have heard Rachmaninoff play his 2 concertos and have heard Harold Bauer for the first time since about 1913! Rachmaninoff is terrific. I also heard Lhévinne a little while ago. The 'techniques' over here are enough to make you give up playing! The only thing which is clouding the horizon is that Max [Mossel] has not engaged me for his tour next season …! (Between you and me, Bauer is not quite certain of being able to get over yet, so he may have to rearrange things for a change). *O Lovely Night*'s title seems to have been too much for him??

Many thanks for the nice printed press notices and card. I was very amused at the latter. It has a distinctly American flavour! I am still planning to be here at the beginning of January 1923, Mengelberg wants me to play with him in Amsterdam in the autumn, but we shall see!! Damrosch has discussed a concerto for next year, Coates arranged his, and Mengelberg wants me with him again, so between them all I probably shan't play with orchestra at all!!

I could write 20 pages but I won't take up your time now, when I shall be seeing you and repeating it all very soon. To be sure of sending you a line, I am writing before breakfast before the telephone begins! I do hope you and Mrs Tillett are well. Perhaps you will be away for an Easter holiday when I first get back about 25th.

With all best wishes and it will be very nice to see you again.

Yours always sincerely

Myra Hess

P.S. I forgot to mention Oxford to you!

Felix Salmond has had splendid press notices!

Please remember me to all in the office!

8 Carlton Hill, St John's Wood, N.W. [postmarked 14 June 1922]

Dear "John"

I have been meaning to remind you that I have not had an "Account" for ages and ages! I presume that it was not presented to me before I went to America in case it would have meant my going "steerage"! When it is sent to me, I do feel that all the help you gave me for America – correspondence, advice, time etc – ought to be accounted for. Hoping that the accounts may grow larger as my years become fewer.

Yours very sincerely

Myra

8 Carlton Hill, St John's Wood, N.W. Train – Tuesday [17 October 1922, postmarked Folkestone]

Dear John (no inverted commas)

If you are mentioning my concerts in Holland in Saturday's *Telegraph* – please don't omit to mention that I shall be playing on a BECHSTEIN piano (by the way, it was quite a beautiful piano last night – I meant to ring up Mr 'urton to ask which one it was. It would be good for a London recital!)

Am enclosing my grossly unmerited criticisms – I haven't any duplicates, so will you kindly keep them in your safe? (I would like them back when you are tired of reading them!) My love to you and Mrs Tillett and I'll bring you back some Bols.

Myra

8 Carlton Hill, St John's Wood, N.W. November 8th 1922

'Lest we forget'. Again so many thanks for arranging my journey so satisfactorily!

Myra

S.S.Adriatic

Dec. 23rd 1922 (It seems so long since I left that I nearly wrote January!)

Dear John

Thank you so very much for your lovely wire. I know you will be pleased to hear that Mr Fothergill (didn't we see him at the White Star office?) has given me a most luxurious cabin with bathroom, so, weather permitting (!?) I shall have a very comfortable journey. Am already looking forward to coming home! It was very wet and miserable at Liverpool. Thank you again for my lovely bag, and all the best wishes I can think of.

Your friend ever

Myra

[P.S.] The boat is very empty.

Hotel Laurelton, 147–149 West 55th Street, New York Jan 3rd 1923

Dear John

There is no doubt about it, I am in New York (although as a matter of fact I feel today as if I am still on the Ocean!) You will not be surprised to hear that I have decided not to come back in the Spring! Three more journeys this year, like this last one, do not appeal to me!! With the exception of one fine day, I leave you to find the adjective to describe the weather!

The actual arrival however was very much more pleasant than last year, and I was met by nice friends, and feel more or less at home?? This is quite a comparatively quiet hotel, and very clean,

just round the corner from the Wellington, so I can run round and see my friends when I want to! I have just had to change my rooms, luggage and piano though, so thought I would calm my nerves by writing you a line!
… I have just been down to choose a piano for Friday. What instruments! I could have "purred" like a cat!"
Mayfair 3940 did you say?
Well, I must do some work. Don't forget to write sometimes. Give my love to Mrs Tillett and keep some for yourself.
Yours always
Myra

Train Jan 18th 1923
Dear John
Your lovely cable for my recital was more comforting than I can say. I was still feeling pretty "rocky" from the journey, and it put some courage into me! Personally I don't think I was in good form until nearly the end of my recital, but everybody seemed to think I had "grown" since last year (I am dieting strictly!!!).
I played 6 encores, and the critics weren't too bored, so altogether it was considered a success. I played far better at the Philharmonic last week. Mr [Henry Kimball] Hadley, who was conductor (I was spared from [Josef] "Stransky") had never done the 4th concerto of Beethoven before!!!! and the rehearsal was most disconcerting. (This diabolically dull journey today is making me mentally feeble!) However he allowed me to teach him the concerto bar by bar and it didn't go badly "on the night" considering all things. If I can find some criticisms, I will send them! Mother has probably sent you the recital ones by now.
I forgot to warn you that I should be sending you affectionate cables to your office again. Many thanks for 'phoning them to Mother.
I have just done 6 concerts in 8 days with some awful cross-country journeys. I am now in the train for 2 days and 3 nights. I have succeeded in making them turn the heating off, but it is appallingly stuffy and I wish the men wouldn't snore <u>and</u> spit. Am sorry to be so graphic! I must say that Englishmen are more pleasant to travel with.
I see that Charlton, Daniel Meyer, and Hansel and Jones have amalgamated. It would be unfortunate if Irene [Scharrer] got in to D.M.'s hands again I should think? The L.S.Q. [London String Quartet] have cabled for Beckwith, who is going to take Levey's place [as first violin]. I was going to try to fit in some dates and play 4tets with them otherwise.
I have met and heard my beloved Bauer and went to a Beethoven Association concert and supper. Bauer, Thibaud and Casals – it was supposed to be an "ensemble" concert, but it was a revelation of what can be done by three artists playing the same work quite differently at the same time! The great "Willem" [Mengelberg] arrives at the end of the month, and am curious to see if I shall play with him. I expect it is highly improbable as I have already appeared with the Philharmonic. Coates was gushingly friendly when I met him. I have been told that he probably will not be invited to come next year, but that may not be true. This is a land of gossip; I was told that I was <u>23</u> the other day!!
Well, this is not a very interesting letter, but what can you expect in a train. Hope to hear from you soon and that all is going well.
Love to you both
Myra

Hotel Laurelton, 147–149 West 55th Street, New York February 19th 1923

Dear John

I can't let this mail go without sending you a line to say that I shall write you a really long letter by the next mail!! I was so glad to have your lovely letters, and I have been trying in vain to answer them. Now I am in New York for a few weeks, I hope to have time to breathe. I have a lot to tell you and to ask you!!!

Am giving another recital on March 10th and 'Benno' [Moiseiwitsch] has one at Carnegie the same afternoon! The only alternative was to give one the same day as Rachmaninoff!

Have just written the usual 'budget' to Mother, (who seems to have had a very enjoyable afternoon with you!) and that is all there has been time for. (I was in Montreal yesterday!)

Love to you and Mrs Tillett to go on with, and I am looking forward to writing a real letter.

Yours always

Myra

Hotel Laurelton, 147–149 West 55th Street, New York February 20th 1923

Dear John

I sent you a hurried line last night by the *Berengaria*, now I am going to write you all the news, and break some news!! (No, I haven't married a coal-king or a movie star). I think I had better begin with it and get it over!

As you know, an old friend has come over, partly to keep me company, but also she has promised her husband, who is an engineer in Egypt, that she will go to California and British Columbia to see if there is any engineering to be done there! She has decided to go at the end of April, when all my concerts are over (Queensboro', North Carolina has been changed to April 20th) and I think it would be a wonderful opportunity to go too!! It will be the best time of year, and going for a holiday, I could really see something of the country. (It is just possible that my British Columbia dates could be fitted in then). But now I am coming to the point, which, with your quick experienced perception, you have no doubt guessed at?

IF I take a holiday from the end of April to end of May, it would be quite impossible to give a Queen's Hall recital on June 7th!! I can hear all your arguments against it, but it really is a chance of a lifetime to have a friend to go to California and B.C. with – for a holiday! Unfortunately the tour in Cal. in March has definitely fallen through. It is no use taking that time for a holiday, because it was going to be a terrible rush anyhow, and I can't travel for 3 weeks without working, and then come back and play immediately.

I will not decide anything though until I hear from you. It would be useless for my friend Mrs Newhouse to rush to the coast and back, so if you think I really must play in London [in] June, I shall give up the idea of going and come back at the end of April. As it would be my "only appearance", and so late in the season, do you think that June concert would be so vital?? If it weren't so expensive, I should telephone to you to talk it over. Could you let me have a cable – 'YES' or 'NO', as we ought to be booking our passages as soon as possible.

I have been interrupted umpteen times including a visit from Mrs America, which resulted in my consenting to spend $1047! Must now dress for a dinner party at Steinways (your friend [Frederic] Lamond is to be there). I believe there is another mail out tomorrow, so I'll post this and continue the letter later.

Give my love to all in the office and keep some for yourself.

Yours always

Myra

Hotel Laurelton, 147–149 West 55th Street, New York March 9th 1923
Dear John
I wanted to write you a long letter by this mail but my B- recital is tomorrow, and I have worked for 8 hours today! So this is just to thank you for yours, and again for cable (hope you had mine) and I will write you a real letter on Sunday. I think the Press Notices are "beautiful", most tastefully arranged!!
Am enclosing a more mundane looking page from Mrs A[merica].
Love to all
Myra

Hotel Laurelton, 147–149 West 55th Street, New York March 19th 1923
Dear John
Come what may, I must send you a letter by tomorrow's mail. The telephone has been going all day and within the last 1/4 of an hour, Bauer has phoned to say that he, Dohnányi and I are to play a three-piano concerto at the Beethoven Association on April 16th (very nice?), and our friend (???)Bottenheim has phoned to say that Mengelberg wants me to play with him next year on February 3rd, 6th & 7th. What am I to do? He is a "big wig" here of course – came to my recital – wants to help me – knows it would do so if I play with him etc etc etc etc. I could sail on Feb. 8th perhaps and be back by 14th or so, what do you think? I wish you were here to talk everything over!
There will be a Committee meeting of the Philharmonic within the next month, and I suppose I shall have to decide, especially as it will make a difference of course to Miss F's [Friedberg's] arrangements, giving me an extra month to play, or waste as the case may be!!!
Meng[elberg] can do a lot for me if he likes, here, in Holland, and he murmured something about England! Once more, I wish we could discuss it instead of scribbling hectic letters.
My recital seems to have made a good impression, also the Mozart with Damrosch. Have you had time to see Mrs America?
I haven't had time to thank you properly for your sympathetic cable. (I really don't think I could have faced a Queen's H recital with a new programme on June 7th after this tumultuous existence!) Our present plan is to set forth on April 23rd for California, return by Canadian Rockies, and sail from Quebec on May 26th, arriving England June 2nd (Oxford is June 22nd I think) It sounds pretty good doesn't it? It is a thoroughly extravagant thing to do, but that will probably make it all the more enjoyable!
We have just heard that it will be too late for the concerts in B[ritish].C[olumbia], so that's that. In ten minutes we have to go out to dinner, and I haven't even washed my face!! It is marvellous having Mrs Newhouse with me and makes everything so much easier and more enjoyable. I should like to write a lot more but I ought to have stopped 10 minutes ago. My love to all and I suppose it is useless to hope you are not over-working? Do let me know what you think about the Phil. concerts here next year.
Yours ever
Myra

C/o Miss Friedberg, 1425 Broadway, New York City March 28th 1923
Dear John
It seems that I do nothing but write about going or coming or staying in this blessed country. While I am waiting for your answer about my accepting the Phil. concerts here in February, I am coming to the conclusion that, provided things look hopeful in England, it would be unwise and a risk to be away so long. (I can see you smiling!!!) I don't want another few weeks like

these again, living in New York and not earning any money. It has made a big hole in my finances, added to the loss of the 7 concerts, that is why I have decided to be consistently (?) reckless and "blow" another few hundred dollars on a holiday (but what a holiday!!!)

And now apart from all these arrangements for 1924, I am afraid I shall have to worry you about September 1923. It has just occurred to me that the boats are full in Sept months ahead and it would probably be advisable to book a cabin?? How diabolical it sounds. Mrs Coolidge's concerts are Sept 28th and 29th and I suppose I had better be here a full week before (especially as I may have to study Rebecca Clarke's Sonata after I arrive!) Could you whisper in the friendly ears of the White Star Co? (although I shan't expect such luxury in Sept as I had in December, except better weather D.V!!)

Things are coming along for next season. Chicago (orchestra), Cleveland, Minneapolis, Damrosch called me "darling" the other day, so I hope that will produce a re-engagement!!? Miss F says she has numerous inquiries. (She still talks of taking me round the world. She hasn't suggested managing me in England yet – so there is still hope!!!) She is very attentive and energetic, but exceedingly exhausting!

Between ourselves, I am feeling a little dubious about Irene's tour next season? Excepting a reproduction of your cable about her last recital in a Chicago paper, I haven't seen a single announcement. Of course you know that Charlton wanted to postpone having her? I hope it will be all right. It will be just as well if I get out of the way before she comes, I expect. I am doing some records for the D[uo] Art [piano rolls], and Schaad suggests my finishing my London contract here, and is giving me a new one to begin here in the Autumn. I have just had an interview with *The Musical Digest* (another 300 dollars). I wonder if I shall ever really make any money?? Anyhow I shall expect you to drive me to the workhouse in your CAR!!! Have you had any exciting expeditions lately or are you glued to that beastly office? I must stop writing and do some work for a change. Do write again soon.

Love to all

Yours f'rever

Myra

P.S. We sail from Quebec May 26th, Southampton June 2nd. Oxford Ladies Musical Club is June 22nd.

I feel very morbid today, so am sending you the £50 I owe you (and more I believe?) in case you never see me again! Have dated it April 20th by which date said sum should be in my Bank!!

Hotel Laurelton, 147-149 West 55th Street, New York Sunday April 15th 1923

Dear John

A hurried scribble to thank you 10000000000 times for your cable and letter which came yesterday.

You have said everything I wanted you to say! And I agree with all you wrote about the great "Willem"!! I dined with them last night and told them definitely that it was imposs. for me to stay. He is now anxious that I should play with him in Holland, and I said I could probably do so early in January before he leaves for USA. When they get back to Holland in a few weeks time, they will see about it and write directly to you (unless they forget all about it, which is the most likely!!). It would be about Jan 7th.

I was amused about the [pianist Ernest] Schelling–Liverpool business. He promises everything to every soloist he meets, like someone else we know!

Once more, ever so many thanks for cabling and writing. You can't think what a relief it is to be able to decide not to stay here from September till February!!! I am just about "all in", as they say here, and more than ready for a holiday.

I played Rachmaninoff's concerto yesterday with him at 2nd piano – very thrilling and he was so nice. He spoke very affectionately of you. Tomorrow I have to do income tax and two rehearsals with Bauer and Dohnányi, and concert in the evening! On Wednesday we leave. I play in North Carolina on Thursday and then goodbye to work! This writing shows you that I am in rather a hurry, and you won't have time to decipher any more!!
Love to all, and I'll write from the trip.
Yours aye
Myra.
P.S. Miss F will always know our whereabouts!

Empress Hotel, Victoria, British Columbia May 11th 1923
Dear John
I have been meaning to write ever since we left New York, but one doesn't do anything one expects to do in California!! It is the most marvellous country, and I have quite decided to spend the summer of 1925 there!!??
I shall probably arrive almost as soon as this letter will, so won't waste your valuable time with a long account of our doings. I will show you some lovely pictures, including one of me on a mule!!! We have bathed in the Pacific (d------y cold!!), climbed 4,000 feet (partly on mules and partly in snow nearly to our waists) and seen the coast from San Diego to Seattle from "whence" we took a steamer this morning, arriving here this afternoon.
A statue of the dear late Queen [Alexandra] greeted us, and the hotel is full of dilapidated old retired colonels and their wives. I was sorry to bother you with boats, engagements in Holland etc, and hope it wasn't the last straw.
The slight stickyness of this paper is caused by a liqueur we have been indulging in!! (too freely you might say). I am obviously not in a serious writing mood. All being well, I shall be home 3 weeks from tomorrow, June 2nd, and hope to find something left of you.
Love to all
Myra

The Old Cottage, Shooters Way, Berkhamstead, Herts Friday [postmarked 20 July 1923]
Dear John
Thank you so much for your contribution for my old lady. I am so grateful.
The peace here is indescribable. Once more, best wishes for a real holiday, also once more, thank you. Yours always
Myra
Actually only one post a day here!

[Germany] Im Zug [in a train] Thursday [no date]
Dear John
We seem to have been wiring to each other furiously, and I received yours and Organol's [Ibbs and Tillett's telegraphic address] yesterday, also your nice one on Tuesday. I think you would have been very pleased if you had been there on Tuesday night, and I wish I could have ten minutes' talk with you about my complicated future.
I didn't wire again yesterday, because I know Lütgert will say that a fortnight is not long enough, and I spoke to Mr Trautwetter again, and he says the same. I saw de Koos, and he says that he can condense my concerts into a fortnight, but my feeling about it all is______________ i.e. 1) that if I begin the season with that strenuous week in Scotland 2) go straight on to Holland and play almost every day for a fortnight 3) to Germany to do the same (probably travelling

most nights) 4) America, where Miss Friedberg seems to be booking a strenuous programme including Texas, California, B.C., that I shall be an absolute wreck, if I can even get through it!!

If you don't think I can give up England (with the exception of the September Queen's H. recital and possibly one (at Steinway Hall????) between Germany and America, then I think, if de Koos will allow it, that we had better postpone Holland, or perhaps just play at a few concerts there on my way to America.

Perhaps Germany could be arranged in three weeks, but they all seem so convinced that it must be a month! I expect Lütgert will have written to you again by now, and Trautw is also going to. So you will be thoroughly bombarded with letters from or concerning me and will begin to wish that I had signed a contract with Lionel Powell!!

De K asked me to go to the Hague to see him. I can easily do so if necessary, but am not too keen. I am not very much attracted by his manners and personality. I hope this is all clear – I am too tired to think very coherently! Miss Moore, Mr Kern, Cesar [Saerchinger], Carey and Cooper had supper on Tuesday night. I saw Frau Wolff in the distance and she told C Saerch. that she was coming to see me yesterday, but needless to say she didn't.

A Mr Simon (?), W&S's representative in America I believe, came to the concert on Tuesday and was very friendly and nice. The Hall was about 3/4 full and I am quite interested to know if they were all 'frei Karten' [free tickets]. They didn't sound like it! I had another very good criticism from Weissman, and the Hamburg ones are wonderful. I do hope W & S will send them all to you. I suppose I ought to send you the ones I have, but I'll wait and see if you get them!

You will be amused to hear that I pretended to have a violent headache on Monday evening as the Saerch's thought it absolutely wrong that I should dine alone with Traut, Weiss, and de K. I certainly agreed that another lady should have been asked, and I was thankful to get out of it. They say it is an awful place for gossip, and if Frau W had seen me, I should never have heard the end of it. Traut told me that Weiss turned up in a dinner jacket, which was an epoch-making occurrence, but he bears me no malice apparently, and they all believed implicitly in my indisposition. So, I think that's all that, and I think I shall now have 10 days or so of peace and quiet in Holland, and then come home.

Tertis wants to begin rehearsing between May 1st and 10th, so I am afraid I shall not be able to meet Benno in Paris! I think I shall go later in May, when Mengelberg is going to the Passion music.

Miss Moore sends her kindest regards, and wants to know when she may come and see Mr Ibbs!!!

Love to you both, and I hope you will enjoy the Easter holiday.

Myra

c/o Miss Gertrude Watson, Pittsfield, Mass. October 12th 1923

Dear John

I hear from Mother that you don't look too well, so presume that you are still insisting upon over-working, or perhaps going to too many dinner parties??

The Festival here [Boston] was great fun and Tertis and I made quite a "HIT"! Between you, me and the wastepaper basket poor Katharine G[oodson] didn't have a very good time. It was really rather uncomfortable and a stupid thing anyhow to put two pianists even in the same programme! Half the unmusical world was – were – here and you will see by enclosed programme that England was well enough represented.

...To finish the gossip in this letter, you will also be amused to hear that Felix's lawyer ... came

up to me after the Brahms Sonata with Tertis and (I thought very generously) said that it was the finest chamber music he had ever heard!!!
I sent [Richard] Aldrich's (*N. Y. Times*) notice to Mother and asked her to send it on to you. Perhaps Mr [Robin] Legge [*Daily Telegraph*] would like to quote some of it? Tertis made a great impression and he has been tremendously enjoyable to work with, and altogether has only shown his most charming side. I always hear he can be otherwise, but have never seen it.
I have been here all the time, staying in a lovely house with lovely people! The country is glorious and it was quite a new experience to drive through the woods to the concert hall! I have promised to give one or two lessons, so am going to New York on Monday. My list of concerts isn't very long, as you will see [below], but Miss F has managed to keep my fee up, and I am sure it is wisest even if I lose things for the moment. However I will have to "chat" with her before leaving?!!!
I had a very happy letter from Irene on her way home from Norway, but I have already heard from Mother that she wasn't happy with her piano at Q.H. [Queen's Hall] Oh – dear!
I wonder if you have had time to write to de Koos for me? Do try and make "Willem" and his handsome friend fix dates for me next Autumn!
The enclosed letter from Penarth has just reached me. Have I any free dates between January and March???? As you will see, it was answered from Carlton Hill, merely saying I was away, so I will leave you to do the rest.
Do send me a line soon.
Give my love to Mrs Tillett, and I should like to hear that you are not quite killing yourself.
Yours always
Myra

Sept $28^{th}/29^{th}$	Pittsfield
Oct 24th	N.Y. recital
31st	Boston, own recital
Nov 6th	Rochester
$9^{th}/10^{th}$	Columbus (Ohio)
19th	Lincoln (Nebraska)
$22^{nd}/23^{rd}$	Minneapolis
	St Paul
25th	Milwaukee
29th	Montreal
Dec 7th	New Haven (Yale University)

Amounting to about $5000. Today a wire came from Vassar College. Hope it will be fixed.

Hotel Laurelton, 147–149 West 55th Street, New York [postmarked 29 October 1923]
No time for letter. Steinways financing a recital for me November 17th. Shall probably cancel my tour in England!
!!!
Myra

1800 Asbury Avenue, Evanston, Illinois Nov 26th 1923
Dear John
I was so glad to have A LETTER from you. Am scribbling this between a lunch and a tea party, and as I shall arrive soon after this will, I will save all the news until then.
(Criticisms of last recital have been very useful again!) Mrs Coolidge has engaged me, and one or two other things are coming along, I believe, before I sail on 15th *Majestic*. Am enclosing Q.H. contracts and Yellow Perils.
Love to all
Myra
Please tell Miss Nixon, Mr Tilbrook and Miss Bass that I would have written if I ever had a moment to breathe, but that I love them all as much as ever! You forgot to enclose de Koos' letter! Had a letter from [Cesar] Saerchinger wanting me to go to Hamburg etc in the Spring!

Hotel Laurelton, 147–149 West 55th Street, New York December 27th 1924
Dear John
Ever so many thanks for your lovely cable. I am afraid this will be a little late to wish you all good wishes for the New Year, but you know what they are.
I have lunched with the Saerchingers, and they are sailing on the *Olympic* tonight. They will post ('mail') this in London.
The latter part of our journey was quite pleasant, but we will draw a veil over the first few days. Miss Hare is an immaculate sailor, and we will leave it at that! Anyhow being a DRY ship, we were able to obtain champagne!
This week has been one mass of rehearsals for the orchestral concert tomorrow, the Bach concerto with Bauer on Monday, and the 'circus' on Tuesday. They have already sold £6000 of tickets for it!
Miss F has written to you, I believe, saying that she wants me to come back next season. I hope Lütgert will soon be definite so that we can make plans. I am still against coming here if I am going to Germany for as much as two months, but if Germany should fall through, or I only go for a week or two, perhaps it would be foolish to refuse work here?
Do send me a word sometimes, and I do hope you will get away and take care of yourself for a bit. The 'bananas' are <u>still</u> being enjoyed! We had a very gay Xmas, and our rooms are full of flowers and presents. This is the country for 'turning the head' as they say. However Max [Mossel] will always keep me in my place!!!
Love to all, and again thank you for the cheery cable
Myra

Hotel Laurelton, 147–149 West 55th Street, New York January 6th 1925
Dear John
You may be pleased to hear that all is going well. My four appearances in N.Y. last week made a very good beginning – the criticisms are lovely (even Newman gave me a good one when I played with Bauer!!) and in spite of a terrible snowstorm and several counter-attractions, including Rachmaninoff (who, however, did not appear, being ill at the last moment) we took just on $900 at my recital.
I had a long talk with Miss Friedberg yesterday, and it looks as if it will be worth my while to come back next season after all! Carl Friedberg thinks that four weeks would be the most I should need in Germany for a first tour, especially as everything is so uncertain there.

Even if Lütgert does guarantee, he (Carl Friedberg) isn't very hopeful about my making much, or any money there. There are several engagements here already which are certain, and Miss F feels confident of getting me at least 15–20 concerts, and wants me to decide to come for January and February. She thinks that I can easily do one more season, and that it is too soon to stop coming. I had a talk with Mr Schaad yesterday too, and he is inclined to respect A.F's judgement. If we decide on this, then Max must have me in the Autumn or not all!

Furtwängler conducted here on Saturday; Carl Friedberg has talked to him about me, and when I was introduced to him after the concert he immediately talked about my playing with him in Berlin. If he is coming to London again and you have anything to do with him, perhaps you could put a word in about it?

The two-piano concerto with Bauer was very thrilling, and I think we shall do it again here. I am afraid California will fall through. Miss F has had an awful time about it. I may have two concerts in Winnipeg during that time, in which case we shall only (try to!!) make the Cal. agents pay up for three concerts instead of the five.

No time for more now. I shall hope to hear from you by the time I get back from the south, saying that you agree to my coming back for Jan and Feb 1926.

Love to all, and I hope you are going to have your prescribed holiday.

Myra

Hotel Statler, Buffalo February 18th 1925

Dear John

So very many thanks (bother this narrow note-paper!) for your marvellously businesslike and nice letter. I had better try to answer it methodically, i.e. e.g.:-

I am glad you have made it possible for me to come back here [USA] next year as everyone seems to think it is too soon for me to miss a season. Miss Friedberg is quite reconciled to my missing the following season. After that, this between you and me, she "hopes" to be able to ask, and actually get, $1000. She would probably be furious if she knew I had mentioned it, as it will depend how things go, and are by 1927 or 8 (whichever it will be?)

Anyhow, that is how things are progressing, and what she is hopefully looking forward to. The earlier I can get here in February (1926) the better because of the long journeys and the time it takes to play half as many concerts in twice the time as it does to do twice the number of concerts in a quarter of the time in England! I hope that is quite clear????? So much for America.

Germany. Lütgert's letter is most consistently inconsistent isn't it? And how about the guarantee he promised, in spite of my not going this last Autumn?? However, I agree that we must trust him to do his best, at the same time making sure that I am not going to "blow" more money than really necessary on recitals. I don't see how it is going to be possible for me to spend more than a month there.

Holland. First of all, I am terribly sorry but I can't play on August 12th at Scheveningen. I particularly told de Koos anytime in June or July but NOT August. It is the only month in the whole year that I can really shut the piano, or forget about music and the whole 'delightful' profession. Although I don't want to play in London when I get back, I am going to work pretty strenuously until the end of July or August, and then old clothes and oblivion, or I shall die and need a Chappell Coffin!!

I hope de K can give me a date in June or July. I quite see the whole position, and much as I dislike him, I agree that we must give him another chance. But the number of concerts AND FEES must be in the contract.

I am afraid that I shall miss Mengelberg there and here, as he is coming to New York in

October. If I play with his orchestra in Holland though, and should happen to play with Furtwängler or Toscanini here, I shouldn't be too unhappy!!
Spain!! You say: 'Of course, if these recitals could have taken place next May, Daniels would most probably have been able to secure engagements in 1926–27 etc'. If it only means giving two recitals in Madrid, and if it isn't too late to arrange now, why shouldn't I go in this next May??? As long as I don't play in London, I don't mind what I do, and should certainly feel equal to two recitals in a new country!
I have just met Casals and he said!! 'If you ever come to Spain tell your managers to be sure and let me know'. I believe he is in Barcelona in May or June, at any rate his orchestra is still having concerts then.
We are sailing on April 30th, on the *Ohio* (R.M.S.P.). I believe she is a very good boat and much more modest in price than the *Majestic*. We shall arrive at S'hampton on May 9th. So I shall be on time for Sutton on the 16th, unless you tell me that you have arranged for me to start then for Spain!
I mean it quite seriously, if it is a possibility (presuming that I need only be away for a week or two?) in fact, I should be quite thrilled to hear that you had fixed it!!!
I presume that I shall be back again by May 1926 unless I go on to Honolulu and Australia?????
I really am sorry that I was the cause of one of your delightful Max conferences!! When he has made up his mind how many extra concerts he won't give, perhaps we can let Miss Friedberg know when I can get here. She is very anxious to know as soon as possible.
It is being rumoured that I am going to 'vanish' before my next recital, also that I am going on the 'movies'. I regret to say that there is very little hope of either!
Did you say that [Mark] Hambourg's audience was taken out on a stretcher, oh no, I misread it!!? Why did he need a bath-chair, too much poker with Max at the Savage Club???
It is nice to hear [Harold] Samuel so well spoken of, and I am glad he is coming back.
As I have been called Miss S – why not an **S** – two-piano recital?? Is that still going to come off??
I couldn't tell you for certain about Bauer, but I think it is most unlikely that he will be playing in England next season. He will probably be there during the summer, but not to play, I believe. I am afraid he is 'off' Europe altogether.
Well, this letter will probably take you two days to get through. I was so glad to hear that you did get away, and that it has done you good. Do let [Dr Yarrow] Eccles keep an eye on you, and don't let yourself get overworked again. It isn't worth it in the long run!
Give my love to the Padre [Robert Leigh Ibbs], Monica, Emmy, Tilbrook, everybody else you think I might send my love to. Once more take care of yourself, and I shall look forward to hearing from you again and to know if I am going to Spain!! We are travelling for five weeks, but letters are forwarded. Am giving a N.Y. recital April 1st !!! and another in Boston April 4th and another engagement has come along for the 22nd, so that's all that.
Yours ever
Myra

Hotel Muehlebach, Kansas City, Montana March 2nd 1925
Dear John
I have just received a birthday cable from 'John'. Was it my brother John, or was it not my brother John???? Anyway, I will be on the safe side and thank you!! I dreamt last night that you made me come to England in the middle of an American tour to play at one Promenade concert!!! Please promise not to!

I expect you have received my letter by now, saying that I am quite ready to go to Spain in May!! However, I imagine that it is too late to arrange it now, even if you approved of the idea. If I am not going, couldn't old 'James' at Sutton give me a little later date? But don't trouble about it if it would be an awful nuisance.
The *Ohio* is cancelled, so we have finally decided to sail on the *Majestic* on May 2nd. I have an engagement near Boston on April 22nd, and then must do some Duo Art records, so I can't very well leave any earlier. We are gradually working our way west, and are going to spend nearly two days at the Grand Canyon, Arizona, on our way to Los Angeles. We shall be back in New York on March 23rd.
Maggie van Riemsdijk tells me that she had a letter from you, and that you will probably see her in Holland at the end of this month! She also says what she thinks about my going back to de Koos! But I am going to leave the whole thing in your hands now, and know you will do what is advisable. I wonder if he has given me another date for Scheveningen?
I hope you are still feeling better, and that you are letting Yarrow Eccles look after you. It will be nice to see you all again. It seems at least a century since I left! I must enclose you my picture as it appeared in the paper here yesterday!
My love to all, and so very very, many thanks for the cable, which I think you sent?!
Myra

New York April 10th 1925
Dear John
I wanted to write you a nice letter by this mail, but now all my important concerts are over, there is no time to breathe!!! I am already late for a party, so this must be a scribble. Am enclosing a few notices and have asked Mother to send you some N.Y. ones. In spite of a mild attack of 'flu, my recital here and the Boston Symph! and recital, were the biggest successes I have had here I think. People were 'turned away' at Boston and we took $1200 !!!
I envy you going to Spain, am glad you are going, and that you managed to get away to Holland (Mother told me you were just going off when she saw you). It will do you good.
Shall be home on May 9th. Suppose you won't be back by then? Am going to thank the Padre for his nice letter by next boat. Must go and dress for party.
Love to all
Myra

Hotel Laurelton, 147–149 West 55th Street, New York February 12th 1926
Dear John
I am waiting for Benno to fetch me for lunch, so there will probably be time to write you a long letter!!!
We arrived on the 10th, and considering what the weather might have been, we were very lucky, and were a very happy little party.
At that 'juncture' his Lordship arrived, and I must 'mail' this now or it will lose the 'steamer'.
Steinways are being so marvellously hospitable and attentive, that I am finding it very difficult to 'keep my head'. I wish I knew what to do. I think I shall try and see W.B., if he comes over, and talk the whole thing out and risk the consequences. If you happen to know when he is coming, could you let me know, and if necessary, and possible, I would make a point of being here. It really is a problem. It is so wonderful to have superlative pianos to play on again, and if they (Steinways) will do for me in England what they do for me here, what in the ---- would you do in my place???

There are rumours that my N.Y. and Boston recitals are going to be 'sold out' – I wonder!
Love to all and do tell me your views about this ---- piano business.
Yours always
Myra
P.S. Miss Bass mentioned that Mr Hurton was sending some flowers to the boat. They didn't turn up, so if he mentions, by any chance, that he hasn't heard from me, perhaps she would say why?!!

Hotel Laurelton, 147–149 West 55th Street, New York March 12th 1926
My dear John
There simply isn't time to breathe, and still less to write a letter!!
It was marvellous of you to remember my birthday, and I was so pleased and 'touched' with your cable. Also many thanks for cable re W.B.! He must be here by now, but haven't heard from him, and don't know how to get hold of him. Anyhow, I still feel between the D and the Deep Sea, and don't know what to do !!!
You will probably be pleased to hear that all is going well, and after giving me $1000 and all the expenses of my Boston recital, Mrs Chase (the manager-ess there) made something herself. I believe tomorrow is going to be alright too.
Everybody thinks I play about 1,000,000 times better than I do – Gawd 'elp and bless 'em!
I leave on April 9th for California and sail for home on June 2nd!! Irene [Scharrer] has had a splendid success. Benno seems to be working quite a lot!!! and looks and seems more cheerful than I have ever seen him.
Must work, dress and go to Providence !!!
Love to all, and do tell Monica and Emmy that I hope to write one day.
Yours aye
Myra

Norddeutscher [North German] Lloyd Bremen. Am Bord des D. [on board the steamer] *Columbus*
November 1st 1930
My dear John
I was very touched by your lovely letter before I left. I was sorry you had such a wretched cold at Norwich, and hope by now you have forgotten all about it.
It must be at least six months since I left?? Thank goodness we are due to arrive this evening, although I wish it were going to be Southampton! Don't forget to miss me, and I am already looking forward to the Spring!
Love to (all?)
Yours aye
Myra

8 Carlton Hill, St John's Wood, N.W. Friday [27 December 1935]
My dear John
Thank you so very, very, VERY much for this wonderful book. It will be a treasured possession. Also I have never seen a more beautiful Azalea plant, and it is a joy to look at while I am hobbling about!! [Hess had just had her appendix removed]
I do hope your cold is quite better, and that you may find a moment to pop in soon. My chief pastime at the moment is Jigsaw puzzles. How the unmighty fall!
Thank you again for your lovely presents.
Yrs ever
Myra

Hotel Laurelton, 147–149 West 55th Street, New York
February 29th [1936], and I haven't found anyone to propose to …
My dear John
I found your letter here yesterday, when we got back from Georgia. A week ago we were in 25 below zero weather, and summer in Atlanta the day before yesterday.
You can imagine how pleased I am that I am at last going to Scandinavia, and I am 'tickled pink' that you have prevented my going with A.S [the conductor, Alec Sherman]. Really I can't think of anything more boring than going to Scandinavia with him. I suppose I ought to feel a pig for doing him out of it, but I presume he will be given another chance (with any other pianist??? H.C. [Harriet Cohen])
Annie is already in trouble with dates for next season and apparently I am already booked for the Washington orchestra on the 3rd and 5th of January. I shall therefore have to sail from home before Xmas. As I must also have time to breathe before I sail, and am ready to plunge into another tour here, we really shall have to restrict the English engagements (if they are offered???) to a very limited number. Do promise me not to book more than one (at the most?!!!) between my October London recitals. Surely it wouldn't hurt if I just play at Hereford (and Norwich?????) festivals, Proms, my recitals, and then any other orchestras or important occasions??
I am going to get through this tour I know (although I have insisted upon cancelling at least three concerts) but it was pretty mad to attempt it so soon after my Opus ???????? Appendix, and I do feel that next winter must not be so terrifically strenuous, either in England or here. I am going to manage to talk to Annie's secretary to make sure that she does not book me eight times a week. Scandinavia in November is a real reason for saying that my time in 'the old country' will be limited.
We have just heard that King Edward VIII is going to speak on the 'Radio' on Sunday, and we hope to hear him. I spoke to Keith on the phone yesterday evening (he is in this hotel) and hope to see him soon.
Now thank you for the letter you wrote me just after I sailed, and do write me the news from time to time, whether you have time or not!!!, and please thank Mrs Tillett for her nice letter.
Just off to Princeton!
Much love
Yrs as ever
Myra
Love to the Padre, and I hope he is enjoying have [*sic*] Rach !!!!!
Have written other news interesting or otherwise to E[mmie]

Rock House, Thurlestone Sands nr Kingsbridge, Devon June 25th 1936

Dear John

Your, or rather Riley's [W J Riley, Secretary of the Liverpool Philharmonic Society] substitute for *Punch* cheered my breakfast this morning! (Not wishing to be disrespectful to M. Vincent d'Indy).

I am very loathe-loath-lothe-loth??? to suggest a Brahms concerto, as I shall be 'up to my eyes' in work just then. The only doubt in my mind about the Mozart is that I have an idea that I played Mozart for my last two appearances in L'pool (about 7 and 10 years ago??) Sazzie could look it up if someone would 'phone her. Let us persist in suggesting Beethoven No.4 as an alternative, and keep the Brahms B♭ (not D minor) well up our sleeves!!

I lunched with Hay [Hamilton Harty] to discuss the programme, and he has probably 'built' a programme around the Mozart, if at all!!

It would be cruel to tell you how heavenly it is here! Am just watching the sunset across the sea!

Much love

Myra

Shall be home on Monday night.

[Incomplete and undated third and final page of a typed letter]

Hotel Laurelton, 147–149 West 55th Street, New York

What beautiful players they are. I played Mozart with them, and I think we all enjoyed it. Harold Bauer could not be present, but he actually sent me a nice telegram. Perhaps the stupid hatchet will be buried. There is enough misery in the world without quarrelling with one's friends???

Would you like me to fill the rest of this page with accounts of my triumphs or shall I send for H.C. and let her tell you what a riot I am?

I will leave you in peace, and send you my love instead.

Yours ever devotedly

Myra

Am so delighted to hear about Hay.

Hotel Laurelton, 147–149 West 55th Street, New York January 7th 1937

Dear John

I am in a 'divil' of an awkward position, and I have used your name, perhaps not in vain, to ease the situation for the moment. Heifetz called on me almost as soon as I had landed, to tell me about an American Musicians' Guild, which he is helping to organise. He and Lawrence Tibbett seem to be the prime agitators and they have roped in a considerable number of artists already (incidentally only one or two pianists of not particularly outstanding importance). It is the same old story, a Union to fight for musicians' rights, and of course they mean to deal with the international situation.

Heifetz assured me that they were going to work for the freedom of artists all over the world, but now I have learnt that they are backing, in fact seem to have originated, a bill which is to come before the Senate, and which if passed will tighten up the restrictions considerably for all musicians wanting to come over here. It is called the Dickstein Bill !!! and you may have heard of it by now??

Whether they think that reprisals will frighten Europe into waiving Labour Permits etc., I don't know, but it is a most complicated business at the moment, and all the concert managers are getting together to form an Association of their own, so that they and the artists can negotiate

(or fight ????) with each other. The managers are trying to prevent the Dickstein Bill being passed as far as we can make out.
Heifetz hoped that I would 'sign on' then and there, but in spite of a splitting headache I thought I had better 'watch my step'. To gain time, I said I would have to write to you and ask if it would be politic for me to join anything of the kind over here, having resigned from the ISM [Incorporated Society of Musicians], which in a smaller way has similar ideals. I told him my reason for resigning from the ISM and that I had intended never to belong again to any such Association. This could be one of my reasons for refusing to join this American Guild. There are so many contradictory reports as to what their policies are to be, that I do not feel at all inclined to tie myself to a Society from which it would be impossible to resign if I disagreed with them, and most important of all, in which I should have no vote. Heifetz said I could attend meetings, and say anything I liked, but what would be the use of that when no one except Americans have votes?
Heifetz said I COULD resign if I disapproved, but on reading through their 'booklet' after his visit, I found one rule saying definitely that resignation is impossible. He also rather held a pistol to my head by saying that later on it might become compulsory for all artists to join (it smacks somewhat of the Soviet ?????). He telephoned the next day for my answer, and I repeated that I must discuss it with you before coming to any decision. He is hoping to get Benno to join when he goes to England next month. Incidentally it is 75 dollars for the first year, and 25 per annum afterwards! I shall continue to get all the information I can, but at the moment I feel my answer is NO, and anyhow Mr Heifetz will have to wait! I hope you will hear about it again via Benno, but do send me a line as soon as you can, after reading this lengthy epistle. Meanwhile, if I hear anything which makes me decide that it would be definitely wrong for international artists to join, I will let you know.
So much for a restful afternoon, and I am sorry to add to your correspondence! It would be terrible if H.C. were forced to play the virginals to the Immigration Officers, to pay or pave her way into the United States?!
I have just enjoyed playing with Hans Kindler again in Washington. I wish he could get some concerts in England; he would love to conduct there.
Much love to all
Yrs
Myra

[From 'Sazzie' (Anita) Gunn]
Hotel Laurelton, 147–149 West 55th Street, New York January 12th 1937
Dear Mr Tillett
Myra asked me to drop you a line to ask you not to take what she wrote you about the American Musicians Guild as final, so not to pass it on, till you hear from her again. We have heard yet more conflicting rumours about it and also Sir Gerald Campbell has arranged to meet Myra, Ethel [Bartlett] and Rae [Robertson] and talk to them about it. Myra does not know what his opinion is, but it must be very definite, as he took the initiative over discussing it with them. They meet on the 25th of this month and Myra will write to you immediately afterwards.
She sends her love to you and Emmie
With kindest regards
Yours sincerely
Sazzie Gunn

Hotel Laurelton, 147–149 West 55th Street, New York February 22nd 1937

Dear John

There seems to be so much to say that I had better begin on this infernal machine before going to the 2nd and 3rd acts of *Siegfried*, and I want this to catch the *Queen Mary* tomorrow. (By the way, don't advise any of your friends to travel on her. You know I am not given to superstition, but I have had queer prognostications, which I hope and pray are NOT true).

GLOUCESTER. Oh dear. Of course I am very flattered that they can't give a Festival without 'dear old Myra' (H.C.'s title for me), but between you and me and the stuffed birds …, I wonder if they will want me to play a Hummel concerto???? Brosa???? Why not dear Albert?????

SCHEVENINGEN No, I am going to be lazy as a toad this summer. Tell Koning that I am sorry to disappoint him ???? but I hope to be in Holland in the Autumn or Winter???

COLUMBIA As I ain't got no tuppeny [*sic*] stamp, can you endorse this mighty cheque for me and pay into Barclay's 42 High Road, Kilburn, or if that is not possible, it can wait until I get home, can't it? [Gaspar] Cassadó and Jelly [d'Aranyi] had better have their dues ???? Perhaps you can pay this cheque into <u>your</u> account, and give us all our share of the buns and milk ??? (Cassadó has had a great success here). The Columbia people want me to make some more records over here. I believe one of the managers is coming to see me, this week. I will let you know what they suggest, as Emmie told me that His Master's Voice had thought of being interested in the 'old lady'. If Columbia's offer is more 'propitious', I don't think I have any obligations in England ?????

And now about this 'infernal international artists' business, as you so aptly put it. I have still refused to join, in spite of more entreaties form the 'hyphenated Heifetz' (thank you for the marvellous title). There is a terrific hooroosh about it all here and in Washington, and in every paper, and Heifetz was obviously very anxious to get a (prominent ?????) British artist's name. I can't go into it all now (and I am sure you don't want me to), but Sir Gerald Campbell is on the warpath, and as far as England is concerned, the statistics are going to make those look very foolish, who are saying that we are so nasty about letting foreigners in !!!

In 1935 there were 907 applications from professionals of various kinds (for England). All but eleven were admitted, and no musician was refused. Sir G is now trying to get the figures for 1936, and then hopes to get them published. This is between us, of course. I have told Heifetz (in case you should see him via Benno???) that I cannot join their Guild unless I rejoin the Society in England, which I don't want to do, and that until the general issue becomes more urgent (I was rather pleased with that), I cannot make a decision. If we all HAVE to join, it will be time enough, but many people think this Dickstein Bill will not be passed. So that's enough of that.

The day after

And in the meantime I have met Mr Meckel, Segovia's manager, whom I believe you must know? He was at the concert last Saturday, at which I played two concertos, and he seems to want me to go to Paris and other European cities where he has connections. I like him (and hope you do?) and as he is sailing for England this week, I hope he will come and talk things over with you. As you probably know, he actually discovered Argentina [the Spanish dancer Antonia Mercè (1888–1936), stage name La Argentina and known as 'Queen of the Castanets'], and for 7 years devoted himself almost entirely to her affairs. Apparently he rather neglected the rest of his business, but everyone presumes he will be more "on the spot" now. He is heartbroken about Argentina, it is quite pathetic. He is taking the Indian dancer Shankar to London, and we met them all last night. They are wonderful I believe. Meckel is coming to see me before he sails, and I have told him already that everything would have to be discussed with you. It would be very nice if he can add to the fun and games next season, when I would like to play in different places. He has also suggested Vienna, Budapest, Prague etc.

Here endeth the 'business section'. By the way, I had a cable from the R.A.M. [Royal Academy of Music] and had to agree to playing at their Coronation concert on May 21st. Have just had a charming letter from Marchant. One of the first things he has done as Principal is to bring Mr Matthay 'back into the fold'. You can imagine how happy we all are.

PERSONAL !

And now I will add a line in my own 'fair hand' (although I cannot compete with yours!!) Thank you for your very lovely letter. You can imagine how happy I was to hear THE NEWS [? Emmie Bass to become a Director of Ibbs and Tillett on Leigh Ibbs' retirement]. You will feel the breaking of a long association, changes always have their melancholy aspect, but I know this is going to be a 'good thing', as they say in 1066! [Hess is referring to *1066 And All That* by W.C. Sellar and R.J. Yeatman, published in 1930], and as you say, the new appointment is a well-deserved reward for invaluable services rendered!

Thank you so very much for thinking of sending some flowers for me to our beloved Harold [Bauer]. It is selfish to wish him back, in the circumstances, but I cannot get used to the thought of never seeing him again. I had so looked forward to being near him at Hampstead, and enjoying many more years of his great friendship, musical and otherwise. I shall miss the inspiration of his incomparable playing. Everyone has been deeply moved here.

And now I must leave you in peace. Do tell Emmie that I am writing to her later in the week.

With my love

Yrs aye

Myra

[written during her British Council tour of the Balkans]

British Legation, Sofia December 3rd (probably) [*sic*] 1937

My dear John

Time means nothing at all to Roumanians and Bulgarians, and I never know which day of the week it is. I wish you could have seen and heard our arrival this morning. We were met by one Bert Andrews! a touching old chap, who spends his life persuading the Bulgars that they love music, and especially British?! Mr Kramona, who speaks German, Christo Petkoff!! gabbling in French, all this at 7.30 A.M. with snow on the ground, and fog in the air!! I had a charming letter from the Minister, Maurice Peterson, inviting us to stay here, and it is a delightful change after the very interesting, but screeching Roumanivlatperkaliescus?? and their overpowering aroma of garlic. My hand will be too stiff to play tonight if I begin to tell you everything, or a quarter of the amazing things of the last week.

The Anglo-Roumanian Society entertained? us at tea soon after we arrived at Bucharest, and there is much to tell you about Dr Meteescu when we meet. We dined at the Legation (although they forgot to invite us until nearly 7, the dinner at 8.30!) The next evening I played to Queen Marie ! (Lady Hoare drove me to the Palace). She is still ill in bed, but I played in an ante-room, and she received me 'before and after'. She was absolutely charming. The concert was a scream. It was supposed to begin at 9, and the audience was finally seated about 9.30. By the end of the evening, they became wildly excited and crowded round the platform, yelling and screeching until it sounded like feeding time in the monkey house.

Yesterday, we were motored to the Danube (which we had to cross) by Dr Meteescu and a steward of the Queen. We swerved through an unending procession of double or treble horse vehicles driven by innumerable fur-hatted ruffians. The surface of the road would have been

quite good, if there had been less mud, and when there wasn't enough, they were throwing it all over the place from the ditches! It was appallingly cold waiting for the ferry and we were thankful to get into the Wagon-lits after an endless, and again smelly business of passports and luggage. I wish the British Council would give their artists a diplomatic Pass. I wonder if it could be done??
It is all tremendously interesting and so far the audiences have been 'most cordial'! Prague was the most beautiful city, although Budapest is marvellously situated. We spent two nights at Dresden on the way, and Cassadó and Wührer gave a most enjoyable concert, and we supped together. The next day I met Segovia in the train! but we have just missed each other in Prague and Buda.
We must have a pow-pow, and I would like to talk to the British Council (if they care to listen?!!) I have the same impression as in Scandinavia, that there should be much more organisation.
The Britishers are treating me royally!! and we had a lovely time in Budapest. I also lunched with Dohnányi. In each place so far, they want me to come back and play with orchestra, but???? Apparently part of my concert is to be broadcast tonight, and I believe they want me to do an extra broadcast in Belgrade.
No more now. Will you show this to Emmie, and tell her re Eastbourne SCHUMANN!!! unless it is being broadcast? I played Beethoven No.4 last time. If it is to be BBC-ed, I don't mind if they would like the GRIEG!! (I mean it!) Am enclosing some killing criticisms from Budapest!
Much love, and I am sorry you are having such vile fogs!
Yrs
Myra

48 Wildwood Road, N.W.11 Thursday [envelope postmarked 12 May 1938]
My dear John
I am thinking of you so much knowing so well what a hard time you are having to face. If I were not rehearsing morning, noon, and night, I would have popped in to see you.
With my love
Myra

Hotel Laurelton, 147–149 West 55th Street, New York December 7th 1938
My dear John
Before I start off 'on the road', I want to send you my affectionate thoughts for Xmas.
I am afraid it cannot be a very happy one for you, but I hope all will be as comfortable as possible. I may send a more or less formal cable to you both when I get back here on Xmas Eve, but this short line assures you of my special thoughts.
With my love
Yours as always
Myra
I am still wondering when I will come back here next season, and would like to know if Hereford is to be or not to be?

National Gallery Concerts April 10th 1946
My dear John and Emmie
Instead of sending you an official letter, which our Committee asked me to do, I would prefer to send these few personal lines.
We all of us want to thank not only yourselves, but every member of the Firm for their

wonderful help throughout the National Gallery Concerts. Your never failing enthusiasm has been one of our greatest supports, and so too has been the knowledge that we could always count on you in every conceivable emergency.
We thank you with all our hearts and ask you to include in our thanks especially Miss Lereculey and Mr Worman, who have helped us so faithfully throughout these long years.
As for myself, I shall never forget this wonderful experience that you have shared with me.
Ever devotedly
Myra

[To the Griller Quartet]
48 Wildwood Road, N.W.11
For NOVEMBER 8TH 1949
Dearest Sidney, Jack, Philip, and Colin
I feel I must send you all a little present to celebrate your united 21st birthday.
I know this is a great day in your lives, but it is a still more important event in the world of music. It is a celebration of 21 years of selfless dedication and you can hardly measure yourselves the wealth of beauty that you have given to people all over the world.
You are not only carrying on the tradition of the great quartets, but setting the standard of all that is finest in chamber music today.
All my love and congratulations, and both for your sakes and ours, may you have many, many more years of ever-increasing achievement.
Yours, to the last Beethoven quartet!
Myra

APPENDIX 16

Correspondence with Kathleen Ferrier 1943–46

[*letter located in Blackburn Museum and Art Gallery]

12 May 1943
Dear Miss Ferrier
We hereby undertake to act as your sole representatives for all your professional engagements in Great Britain and Ireland, commencing from the above date. It is understood that we will use our best endeavours on your behalf, it being agreed that all letters and applications that may be addressed to you shall be referred to us; in fact that the control of your business in Great Britain and Ireland shall be left in our hands.
Our remuneration is to be Ten percent (10%) of the terms you receive on all engagements during the continuance of this Contract. Yours sincerely.

[undated but 1944] Thorn Hotel, Burnley
Dear Mr Tillett
Could you answer the enclosed for me? I would rather like to do the Pergolesi, though I know you will think the fee small. I don't know Miss Jaco, only that she is a friend of Maurice Jacobson [chairman of the music publishers J. Curwen], who will have told her about me probably. So I will leave it to you to do as you think best. Mr Lingard wants me back at Hebden Bridge, but I was engaged for the date they wanted in Feb. but you will probably be hearing from them for a date in Oct. I warned them that my fee had rocketed skywards!
Re Cradley Heath 20th Oct., I shall be most happy to have hospitality, only thought if it were possible to get back to Birmingham t'would be more convenient, especially if the others were going. Hope it will be with Miss Lawley of Sunnyside as formerly.
Here are two programmes.

Newcastle under Lyme Nov. 15th:
1 With string orchestra (I will provide the parts for this first group)
   a. Where'er you walk – Handel b. Cradle song – Wm Byrd c. The Arch Denial – Arne
2 With piano accomp.
   a. Love is a bable – Parry b. Sweet chance that led my steps abroad – M. Head
   c. Come, let's be merry – [Lane] Wilson

Yours sincerely
Kathleen Ferrier

[undated but 1944] 2 Frognal Mansions Hampstead NW3
Dear Mr Tillett
I received a contract from you today for Pontardulais on December 30th, but I have to be in Bournemouth that night for a rehearsal in the morning and two performances of the *Messiah* on the 31st. The man from Pontardulais asked me if I could do it when I was in S.Wales last week and I said quite impossible and explained in detail about the Bournemouth concerts.

Would you be so kind as to keep the 22nd–25th Dec. incl. free so that I shall be in good form for the broadcast from Manchester on the 27th Dec. Must do that well.
Kind greetings and best wishes,
Yours sincerely
Kathleen Ferrier
P.S. For the Hereford concert on 26th Oct. I shall be leaving Crewe that morning on the 10.38, arriving Hereford 1.18. For Merthyr Tydfil on Nov. 2nd I cannot get in at the guest house, and the New Inn there is dire! Could the promoters be asked if it's possible to get to Pontypridd after the concert, if so can they book me a room there.
Yours sincerely
Kathleen Ferrier

29th Nov. [1944] 2 Frognal Mansions Hampstead NW3
Dear Mr Tillett
I enclose a letter from Warrington which arrived yesterday, and here are two programmes you are wanting.

<u>Shaw – Jan. 27th 1945</u> Ref. K.C.
1 What is life to me without thee? (*Orfeo*) – Gluck
2a Love song – Brahms
 b Why go barefoot my pretty one? – Brahms
3a Sweet chance that led my steps abroad – Michael Head
 b The bold unbiddable child – Stanford
Duet suggestions with Mr Lloyd [tenor David Lloyd]
It was a lover – Walthew

I don't know any other 4tettes and will fall in (!) with the others, but I should have thought one quartette was enough – it means six appearances otherwise – a continual shooting on and off stage. It is going to be endless if we all do as many.

<u>Witney 7th March 1945</u>
1 What is life to me without thee? (*Orfeo*) – Gluck
 b Pack clouds away – Handel
 c The Erl King – Schubert
2a Love song – Brahms
 b A May night – Brahms
 c Why go barefoot my pretty one? – Brahms
3a Sweet chance that led my steps abroad – M Head
 b A Piper – Michael Head
 c Down by the Salley Gardens – Gurney
 d Pretty ring time – Peter Warlock
(Four songs in last group)

I think that is all – I hope you can read it – I am in a train.
Yours sincerely
Kathleen Ferrier

In train. Friday. [? December 1944] 2 Frognal Mansions Hampstead NW3

Dear Mr Tillett

Looking through my contracts again just before I came away, I noticed that the rehearsal for the *St Matthew Passion* for Dr Jacques on the 16th March starts at 10am. I have signed a contract for Pontypridd the day before (15th), and even if I get up for the first train, cannot be in London before about 12.15. I don't want to miss any of the rehearsal as I am not so well acquainted with this work. I have also been told by one or two people that I am doing the Southwark *Passion* on 17th March, but I haven't had a contract as yet for it. If this is so I would be grateful if I didn't have to go to Pontypridd, and if you could keep the 14th and 15th March free, as there is a lot of exacting singing for me and I want to make a good job of it. Could you possibly?

Mr Nicholson of B[lack]pool wants me again the day I am doing the Manchester Midday, 27th Feb for a Miscellaneous Concert. He wants me to do some operatic and old ballads (e.g. *Angus Macdonald* and *Promise of Life* etc!!) with orchestra without rehearsal, but I said I would only do it with pianist and my choice of songs, as I have so much to learn and very little time for learning, and I think I told him my fee had gone up too! He is a very persistent Lancastrian, but then so am I, and I couldn't possibly go straight on to sing with an amateur orchestra without rehearsal, could I? Thank you very much for the Bradford contract – that's lovely.

Yours sincerely

Kathleen Ferrier

18 December 1944

Dear Miss Ferrier

It is certainly a bit of a mystery why you never received a contract for the performance of *St Matthew Passion* to be given in Southwark Cathedral on March 17th 1945, especially as the other artists engaged for that date received their contracts. The engagements are always entered in our Diary from the actual contracts, and the booking was duly registered, which somewhat adds to the mystery. We are now enclosing the necessary contract which should have reached your hands last April.

[1945]

Dear Mr Tillett

Enclosed please find some contracts and also a letter from Nelson. Would you be good enough to answer it for me. I shan't be able to do it as I am in the Albert Hall the day before singing in *Gerontius*. Definite dates for CEMA now are 4th–8th June (Stoke area) and 30th May (Crane Hall, Liverpool, lunch hour).

Yours sincerely

Kathleen Ferrier

In train. [Jan. 1945] 2 Frognal Mansions Hampstead NW3

Dear Mr Tillett

Enclosed please find contract for Reading. Also returned cheque for Ferry Hill as I was paid on the night of the concert by cheque and was given Miss Baillie's cheque too to give to her the following morning on the train. (I won't refuse it if they think I was worth double!)

I wonder if you could tell me who the other principals are for Glasgow, Beethoven Mass on Feb. 3rd, because if they are willing I should be so grateful if they would rehearse before going to Glasgow. Would you keep the 28th Jan.–3rd Feb. free, as this is the only time I have to really get down to learning it.

My sister and I are trying to arrange a holiday at Whitsun and in the summer, so would you also

keep free 15th–24th May and 25th July–11th August. We hope to go to Fleetwood the latter period, during which I shall be singing there.
For the Huddersfield broadcast on Dec. 27th I received £14. 7. 4. which was 10gns and expenses. Should I get 25% for public performance? I am told I should by various people, so thought I would ask you.
With sincere good wishes for 1945 to you all
Most sincerely
Kathleen Ferrier

5th January 1945
Dear Miss Ferrier
Thank you for your letter returning the signed contract for Reading, also the cheque for Ferryhill. Evidently the Secretary of the Society in question was not aware that you and Miss Baillie were paid on the night of the performance.
Miss Janet Hamilton-Smith, Mr Eric Greene, and Mr William Parsons are the other Artists taking part in the performance of the Beethoven Mass in Glasgow on February 3rd.
As desired we will keep the following periods free from any engagements:-
January 28th to February 3rd, May 15th to 24th, July 15th to August 11th.
Now regarding the broadcast performance of *Messiah* in Huddersfield on December 27th, as the audience present was entirely by invitation, the performance in question is not regarded in the nature of a public Concert, and consequently the soloists are not entitled to any extra remuneration – so sorry.
Heartily reciprocating your good wishes for 1945.
Yours sincerely

[January 1945] 2 Frognal Mansions Hampstead NW3
Dear Mr Tillett
I enclose 5 contracts and a cheque for £76. 6. 3., also my programme for Blackpool on Feb.27th. I hear Mr Nicholson at B'pool is hurt because I won't sing with his orchestra, but I explained when I saw him that I wouldn't be able to rehearse because of the Manchester Midday concert, and therefore would prefer piano accompaniments. I am away from home at the moment, but I don't think I have had a contract for this concert.
Here are my suggestions with alternative items:

1 What is life to me without thee (*Orfeo*) Gluck
or *Joan of Arc* Farewell Tschaikowsky
2 Art thou troubled? Handel
or Verdant meadows Handel
3 Sigh no more Aikin
or How lovely are thy dwellings Liddle?
4a Ca' the Yowes (Bevins) Scots folksong arr. Maurice Jacobson
b The Spanish Lady (Irish) Hbt. Hughes or
4a Water boy (Negro) arr Robinson
b The stuttering lovers arr Hughes

Duet with Mr Francis Russell

It is the merry month of May (*Merrie England*) German
or Home to our mountains (*Il Trovatore*) Verdi

I enclose a letter from Miss Cullen of Leith Hill Festival Choirs which I have answered, as it had been delayed a bit thro' being forwarded, and I saw that I was already engaged.
In reference to your letter of the 26th inst re Bargoed – I would be grateful if I could have those days free 13th, 14th, 15th. I also mentioned to Mr Walter Legge that I was free on the 13th and 14th if he wanted me for recording, as he had asked for free dates.
I also enclose a letter from Devizes which I have not answered, as I thought you would deal with the fee problem, but I shouldn't be able to do it as I am in the Liverpool area. Hope you can make this muddle out.
Yours sincerely
Kathleen Ferrier

25th January 1945
Dear Miss Ferrier
Some little while back we promised Mr Kenneth Stubbs, the Music Master at Rugby School, that you would give a Recital at the School, also one for the Rugby Musical Society, consisting of 40 to 50 members, at a special fee of 25 guineas.
The dates finally decided upon for this engagement is [*sic*] Saturday evening June 30th for the Musical Society, and Sunday evening July 1st at Rugby School, for which we have pleasure in enclosing our usual forms of contract.
Yours sincerely

31st January 1945
Dear Miss Ferrier
We are much obliged for your letter returning the several signed contracts, also enclosing cheque for £76. 6. 3d, in settlement of our commission account.
You are quite right, a contract has never been sent you for the Blackpool concert on February 27th. On referring to our correspondence we find that the Secretary has not confirmed your engagement, which is the reason for the absence of a contract, which we now have pleasure in enclosing. In returning the programme to the Secretary we are reminding him of this omission and formally confirming the engagement.
We are sorry that Mr Nicholson feels hurt, but he has been advised by you and ourselves the reason why you are obliged to sing all your items with pianoforte accompaniment on this occasion.
We are replying to the letter from Devizes and note you have advised Miss Cullen that you are already booked on April 28th. You are not much of a loser as both Devizes and the Leith Hill Societies pay small fees as a rule. We note you are not disposed to consider the Bargoed engagement, also that you have given March 13th and 14th as free dates to Mr Walter Legge.
With kind regards

12th February 1945
Dear Miss Ferrier Hexham & District Choral Society Thursday evening December 6th 1945
With reference to your engagement on the above occasion, will you please note that it has been decided to perform Mendelssohn's *Elijah*, and we shall be glad if you will kindly add this to your contract.
Yours sincerely

[received 28 February 1945] 2 Frognal Mansions, Hampstead NW3

Dear Mr Tillett

I enclose a letter from Bishop Auckland and would be grateful if you would deal with it. I shan't be able to do it as I am in Swansea the day before (Landore).

Will it be alright for me to sing for Harry Vincent at the opening of a new hall in which they hope to do recitals in the future? It is in Etruria I think. It is in the nature of an opening ceremony – Maurice Jacobson is going – and the date is Friday 23rd March. He only wants a couple of songs and I would like very much to oblige him. Do hope this is alright.

With best wishes

Yours sincerely

Kathleen Ferrier

[received 29 February 1945] Midland Hotel, Manchester Friday

Dear Mr Tillett

I saw Mr Hutchinson (Newcastle), my old teacher, yesterday and he wants me to do the Bach *Mass* for him in March next year, but unfortunately can't give a date just yet as the secretary is ill. Would you let me know if you pencil anything in for any Sunday in March 1946 so that I can let him know? He will get in touch with you as soon as ever it is possible, but would be grateful if you would keep him a Sunday meanwhile.

I would be grateful too if you wouldn't book anything else in July and August as arranged, unless it were a broadcast or a London job, or something extra special. I do need some time off for learning all the things I don't know! I enclose three signed contracts.

With best wishes

Yours sincerely

Kathleen Ferrier

February 28th 1945

Dear Miss Ferrier

Thank you for your letter with enclosure from Bishop Auckland which is receiving immediate attention. Of course it will not be possible for you to entertain the proposed engagement but in any case you may be interested to hear that this is the fourth letter of the kind to which we have had to reply.

Friday March 23rd is a free date and we have no objection to your obliging Harry Vincent, but the date strikes us as being very near to your engagement with the Ceramic City Choir on April 5th – unless I am mistaken Etruscan and Hanley are only about a mile apart. Perhaps you will telephone me on your return to town when we can discuss this matter further, and settle on the fee, which must be more than you received last time.

I also received your note asking me not to book any further engagements for you during July and August. At the moment we have July 3rd pencilled for Bargoed, July 5th booked to Cambridge, July 15th pencilled for Hampton Court, 18th pencilled for Dartford, Kent, and that is all.

Now regarding Dr Hutchinson at Newcastle who I note wants you for a performance of the Bach *Mass* in March 1946. As you already know the 24th is booked for the *Apostles* at Bournemouth, but at the moment all the other Sundays are free.

With kind regards

Yours sincerely

14th March 1945
Dear Miss Ferrier
With reference to the enclosed engagement at Llanelly, as you will remember, Mr Thomas asked you to reserve February 5th and 6th in addition to the 7th, but as it has now been decided to perform *King Olaf* on the 5th and 6th, in which there is no contralto part, you will only be required for the *Messiah* performance on February 7th.
Yours sincerely

[received March 22nd 1945]
In train. 2 Frognal Mansions, Hampstead, NW3
Dear Mr Tillett
Would you please answer the Haltwhistle letter for me. I had a card from Dr Hutchinson asking me to fix Sunday 31st March 1946 for the *B minor Mass* at Newcastle (YMCA). Do hope this is alright. I will ask him to write to you.
Best wishes
Yours sincerely
Kathleen Ferrier

March 22nd 1945
Dear Miss Ferrier
Thank you for your note with various enclosures.
I am glad to say that Sunday 31st March 1946 is quite free and we will therefore reserve that date to Dr Hutchinson for the performance of the *B Minor Mass* to be given by the YMCA Choir in Newcastle. What fee would you like us to quote? Personally I think it ought to be 25 guineas, but certainly not less than 20 guineas.
We are acknowledging the letter from Haltwhistle telling them that you are already engaged on April 18th and 25th, in fact we are pointing out that your first free Wednesday is August 15th. It will be interesting to see if they 'grab' that date.
With kind regards

[received 27 March 1945] Liverpool
Dear Mr Tillett
Enclosed pse. find several contracts.
You mention Aug. 15th for Haltwhistle, but that is the date I was asked to keep for Wells Cathedral for Dr Rickett of Sherborne. Do you remember?
Please don't book me anything else in July and August – I must learn the *Apostles* sometime!
Kind greetings
Sincerely
Kathleen Ferrier

March 27th 1945
Dear Miss Ferrier
Thank you for your letter enclosing the signed contracts.
Yes I do remember your speaking to me about Wells Cathedral, but to be quite frank I quite forgot the suggested date, namely August 15th. There has been no reply from Haltwhistle so we shall have to tell them that August 15th is bespoken elsewhere, should they wish to engage you.
I note you do not wish us to accept any further engagements for you during the months of July and August, unless of course it should be something tempting in the nature of a Promenade Concert at the Royal Albert Hall!
Yours sincerely

April 13th 1945
Dear Miss Ferrier
Southwark Cathedral. Saturday afternoon February 23rd 1946
Will you please note that the work to be performed on the above occasion will be the *Messiah* and not the Bach *Mass* as stated on the contract. May we ask you to kindly make the necessary alteration in your Diary and contract.
Yours sincerely

April 16th 1945
Dear Miss Ferrier
Thank you for your letter of the 13th inst. giving your programme items for the Concert at Darlington, June 27th.
I note you have promised to sing for Mr Edward Isaacs at the Manchester Mid-Day Recital on December 11th, which date we have entered in our Diary. As you say, it will fit in quite well with the Derby *Messiah.*
With kind regards
Yours sincerely

17th April 1945 EMT/SEL
Dear Miss Ferrier
Would you please note we are pencilling your services to sing the Brahms Serious Songs at one of the BBC Public Symphony Concerts at the City Hall, Newcastle-upon-Tyne on Sunday afternoon, May 6th next at 2.30–4.30pm, with a rehearsal the same morning at 10 o'clock. This programme will be broadcast in the Home Service. We understand the BBC have already mentioned this to you and that you have agreed, but may we remind you that it will be necessary for you to make a night journey following your engagement at Croydon on the 5th?
Yours sincerely

24th April 1945 EMT/SEL Miss Kathleen Ferrier, Adelphi Hotel, Liverpool
Dear Miss Ferrier BBC – April 26 and 27
We have just heard from the BBC that owing to the fact that they have been unable to get all the programme material together for the recording of the *Sunday Rhapsody* Victory programme on the above dates, they greatly regret they must ask you to cancel this engagement. They hope, however, that it will only be a postponement and will be getting into touch with us a little later in regard to this matter.
Yours sincerely

In train [undated but 1945]
Dear Mr Tillett
I would be grateful if you would answer the enclosed letters for me, from Battey and Chelmsford respectively. Would you not engage me anywhere before the Birmingham *Gerontius* concerts (Oct 7th and 8th) so that I can have [a] day off before them please? Also 29th, 30th, 31st Oct if possible so that I can recover!
Yours sincerely
Kathleen Ferrier

3rd May 1945 EMT/SEL
Dear Miss Ferrier BBC – June 2
Owing to the fact that the programme period for which your services were required on the above date has had to be cancelled, the BBC greatly regret that they must ask you to erase the pencilling for June 2 for the performance of Vaughan Williams' *Tudor Portraits*. They hope, however, to reinstate this broadcast a little later on.
BBC – May 27
Would you please contact Mrs Titchener at WELbeck 5577 as soon as possible concerning your programme for this date, which is now urgent.
Yours sincerely

17th May 1945 Miss Kathleen Ferrier, Westover Gardens Hotel, Bournemouth
Dear Miss Ferrier
Here is the cheque (8 guineas) in part payment of the fee for your engagement in Liverpool on April 25th–26th. This leaves a balance of 22 guineas from Messrs Bibbys, which you shall have as soon as it comes to hand. For the Concert in Manchester on June 11th our Clients would like you to submit an entirely different programme to the one which you gave in Liverpool.
Bournemouth must be ideal in such lovely weather, and we hope it may continue during your holiday.
Yours sincerely

May 30th 1945
Dear Miss Ferrier Cambridge Philharmonic Society
Owing to the forthcoming General Election the Guild Hall has been requisitioned, and in consequence it will be necessary to postpone the date of the performance of the *Dream of Gerontius*, which will now take place in the King College Chapel on Thursday July 12th with rehearsal the same afternoon at 2.15. Will you, therefore, book the date in place of July 5th and alter your contract accordingly.
May we remind you of the necessity to make early application for hotel accommodation.
Yours sincerely

June 14th [1945] 2 Frognal Mansions, Hampstead NW3
Dear Mr Tillett
I enclose the letter I spoke to you about from Leicester, also contract for Oxford. Please would you ask Miss Bass not to book any more engagements for me in July or August unless they are 'home' ones. I am staying in Sherborne for Wells Cathedral on Aug 15th and had said I would stay on for a little rest, and it will be rather an awkward journey, Sherborne to Oxford, but will do it now it is all arranged, and with my 'Prof'! [Roy Henderson]
I should like to do the Leicester *St Matthew* [*Passion*] if it is at all possible – it's such a lovely performance.
Yours sincerely
Kathleen Ferrier

July 23rd 1945
Dear Miss Ferrier Croydon Philharmonic Society *The Dream of Gerontius*
We have been asked to inform you that it has been decided to hold the performance of *The Dream of Gerontius* in the Civic Hall, Croydon on Saturday May 11th 1946 in the EVENING and not in the afternoon as previously arranged. May we ask you to make the necessary alteration on your contract and in your diary.
Yours sincerely

Aug 6th [1945]
Dear Mr Tillett
Would you be so good as to reply to the two enclosed letters for me? I am unable to do either of them.
Yours sincerely
Kathleen Ferrier
P.S. I am very sorry I had mixed up two dates. I've got it right now I think – 23rd Jan Witney, 24th Derby
I enclose the contract for Derby and Aldenham. I have sent the programme for the latter to Mr Maurice Miles.

11th August 1945
Dear Miss Ferrier
Herewith we have pleasure in sending you our contract for a further engagement in the West which fits in with Trowbridge and Bridgwater. By the way, we notice on the contract for the latter that through a typographical error 1945 was stated instead of 1946. Perhaps you would be so kind as to rectify this on your part. Both recitals at Bridgwater and Stroud will be in conjunction with Watson Forbes (Viola), so you will be able to include the Brahms Viola Songs if you so wish.
Yours sincerely

11th August 1945
Dear Miss Ferrier Sheffield Philharmonic Society: Friday evening April 26th 1946
Dream of Gerontius : Elgar
In the rush of things yesterday we notice that the wrong fee was stated on your contract for the above occasion – this should be twenty-five guineas (£26.5.0.), so perhaps you will make the necessary amendment.
Yours sincerely

Aug 17th [1945]
Dear Mr Tillett
Would you reply to the enclosed for me please? I have received a contract for Blackpool on March 8th 1946.
I am in Crookhill, Co. Durham on the 9th, and can say only arrive in Newcastle (if I catch all connections) at 1/4 to 4pm. Is this soon enough for rehearsal and shall I be met in Newcastle by car? Otherwise it is going to be an awful struggle to get there in time.
In haste
Yours sincerely
Kathleen Ferrier

Sep.12th [1945]
Dear Mr Tillett
I am so very sorry to have caused an upheaval, and to have had to cancel two concerts. I tried all Sunday morning to get a deputy, but was unsuccessful, but by having my throat painted I managed to do 3 groups of 2 songs (instead of the printed 5) and the rest as printed. I wonder if I ought to offer some rebate of fee as they didn't get the full programme? Actually they said it was much too long for the Sunday afternoon. They were all most kind and understanding.
Stroud March 28th 1946 Quite willing to do the children's programme in the afternoon.
South Shields Oct 24th and 25th
Wed[nesday]:
1 What is life to me without thee? (*Orfeo*) – Gluck
2a Fairest Isle – Purcell
b Hark the echoing air – Purcell
3a Have you seen but a whyte lily grow? anon arr. Grew
b Come, let's be merry – anon arr. Lane Wilson

10th December 1945 Miss Kathleen Ferrier, Palatine Hotel, Blackpool
Dear Miss Ferrier
I am afraid we have to trouble you again regarding the programme items for the orchestral concert in Glasgow on January 1st, as the items you have suggested are not considered sufficiently popular and the Conductor Mr Warwick Braithwaite suggests your singing 'Softly awakes my heart' and 'O don fatale' as bracketed arias for your first appearance which, no doubt you will decide is asking too much, then he wants more popular songs in place of the Elgar *Sea Pictures*. Last week we were advised by Mr Barnes that they wanted you and Miss Elsie Suddaby to sing the duet from the second act *Lohengrin*, but we turned this down flat without consulting you.
By the way, Mr Barnes asks us to tell you that you are assured of sleeping accommodation for your return journey to London in a Cabin for two, and there is the possibility of your being allowed a separate cabin.
Regarding your engagement with Mr Moodie in Dunfermline on December 30th, he is anxious to include a duet in the programme and Miss Suddaby has suggested the following optional duets:
'O lovely Peace' (*Judas Maccabeus*), 'Sound the trumpet' (Purcell) or Barcarolle (*Tales of Hoffmann*). We take it you would be willing to fall in line with whichever Mr Moodie selects. Mr Moodie also asks us to say that he will so arrange the programme to enable you to catch the 8.46pm to Glasgow.

The more I think about that Opera proposal the less enthusiastic I feel, for many reasons which perhaps Roy Henderson will have explained to you, that is in the event of your having seen him in Manchester last weekend. I wish I could see you personally to explain my views, otherwise matters will have to remain in abeyance until your return to London.
Meanwhile Buxton want to book you for June 8th and 9th at 35 guineas, the fee quoted, but these dates unfortunately clash with the proposed performances of the Beethoven *Mass in D.* Which engagement would you prefer in the event of your being free at the time?
With all good wishes
Yours sincerely

In train 28th Dec. [1945]
Dear Mr Tillett
I should have mentioned on the telephone the other night that Maurice Johnstone had asked me to do broadcast with Northern Orchestra on March 11th (Monday) and I said I thought I was free. Would you pencil it until you hear from him please?
I'm sorry about the reversed charges on 'phone call, but it was callbox and I couldn't get change. Will settle my debts when I see you!
Best wishes for the New Year
Very sincerely
Kathleen Ferrier

13th March [1946]
Dear Mr Tillett
Enclosed please find signed contracts.
Would you be good enough to reply to the enquiry here enclosed. Also Mr Edward Isaacs wants to know if I will keep March 11th 1947 for him, as it will not be such a busy month as December. I would like to do this for him – it always means an enlargement of repertoire for me, and is good for me!
Yours sincerely
Kathleen Ferrier

21st March 1946
Dear Miss Ferrier
We have received a letter from Mr Thompson of the Memorial Methodist Church, North Shields, who is prepared to release you from your engagement on October 2nd on the condition that you will sing for them at their next concert, taking place on Wednesday March 12th 1947. Fortunately you are disengaged and we are therefore transferring your engagement with these people from October 2nd to March 12th.
Yours sincerely

29th March 1946
Dear Mr Tillett
Re Liverpool May 1st – here is suggested programme:

Dearest consort – Handel
Come to me soothing sleep – Handel
Ombra mai fu – Handel
Pack clouds away – Handel

The Blacksmith – Brahms
Roses three – Brahms
The swallow – Brahms
Why go barefoot, my pretty one? – arr. Brahms

I enclose several contracts. Would you please in future cut out all church weekends and the like? I am getting more work than I can cope with, and I would be grateful if you would only book me for large towns, choral societies, and music clubs. The large fees only go in Income Tax, and in your case in excess profits! And the smaller places book up so far in advance, that worthwhile jobs are crowded out.
I should be grateful, too, if my broadcasting fee were to be put up to 25 gns. if you are agreeable.
Yours sincerely
Kathleen Ferrier

8th April [1946]
Dear Mr Tillett
Enclosed please find signed contract and enquiry from Ossett – would you be good enough to reply to this for me? Just to confirm my fortnight off – Jan 4th to Jan 18th inclusive 1947! Seems kinda long way away!
Yours sincerely
Kathleen Ferrier

13th May [1946]
Dear Mr Tillett
Can you keep May and June 1947 and the summer months free for the moment, until I see how I am fixed for holidays? There is plenty of time to book yet for that period, and I don't want to find myself without any free period.
Yours very sincerely
Kathleen Ferrier

16th May 1946
We have received a letter from Mr H. Vincent asking us to book you for a concert to be given by the Etruscan Choral Society in the Philharmonic Hall, Etruria, Stoke-on-Trent on Thursday evening March 27th 1947, but before confirming we would be glad to know if you have undertaken to accept a special fee for this occasion.
We duly received your letter of the 13th instant in which you ask us to keep May and June 1947 free for the moment. We presume you have not overlooked the following engagements already booked:
May 3rd Southwark and May 24th Romford
Yours sincerely

17th May 1946
Dear Mr Tillett
Thank you very much for cheque for £68. 5. [0d] from Cambridge duly received. Re Reading May 29th – I am in Oxford the next day. So would be grateful if accommodation could be arranged for me in Reading. Re Harry Vincent March 27th 1947. This concert is in the Victoria Hall, Hanley, so will be a proper fee as far as I know. I haven't overlooked May 3rd and May 24th 1947, but would like the summer months kept free at the moment.
Mr [Herbert] Sumsion of Gloucester [Cathedral] has written mentioning Three Choirs in Sept next year, and Leeds want me for their Festival in Oct – 1st week or thereabouts. Thought I would mention it, and perhaps you will keep it in mind if they don't write immediately.
Yours sincerely
Kathleen Ferrier

[?June 1946 – initial page(s) missing]
… It's quite all right about the Liverpool cancellation. I would prefer not to take another job on that day. Please would you ask me before booking any more engagements in March next year, and I'll do the same!, as I think I have as much as I can do well now. Also if possible I would like to have Easter, April 2nd–9th at home, as I shall be in Croydon and Wimbledon on the 2nd and 4th, would accept a London engagement, but would be glad to be free of travelling.
And would you also keep from the 10th Feb to the end of that month free of any more work, unless it is the Dublin recital after Belfast that Miss Bass mentioned might materialise. My address from Monday onwards until about July 22nd will be: Glyndebourne, nr Lewes, Sussex.
With best wishes
Yours sincerely
Kathleen Ferrier

29th June 1946 Miss Kathleen Ferrier c/o Glyndebourne, nr Lewes, Sussex
Dear Miss Ferrier

City of Birmingham Choir

You will doubtless remember our having advised you that the Birmingham Town Hall had been requisitioned for a Nursing Exhibition during the week of April 28th 1947, and in consequence the performance of Beethoven's *Mass in D* arranged to take place on Tuesday April 29th would have to be moved to another date. Unfortunately the date now definitely decided upon is Monday April 21st, when you are booked to sing in Stourbridge. We are therefore obliged to ask you to be good enough to cancel your engagement for the occasion in question.
Kind regards
Yours sincerely

1st July 1946 Miss Kathleen Ferrier c/o Glyndebourne, nr Lewes, Sussex
Dear Miss Ferrier
As perhaps you remember, the Newcastle-on-Tyne Bach Choir Society is to give a performance of the *St Matthew Passion* in the City Hall, Newcastle, on Sunday afternoon March 9th 1947, and we have promised Mr Chalmers Burns to ask you to be good enough to accept a fee of 25 guineas in this instance, although it will mean your having to attend a rehearsal on the previous day, Saturday afternoon March 8th. I am enclosing our usual forms of contract in anticipation that you will be prepared to help Mr Burns.
I understand that Mr Byng [*sic*] is already approaching some of the artists in order to obtain the option of their services for next summer and early autumn. If you have been approached will

you please bear in mind that there will be a Gloucester and Norwich Festival during the month of September and Leeds in the early part of October, which you must not miss.
Yours sincerely

2nd July [1946] Glyndebourne, Lewes, Sussex
Dear Mr Tillett
Re Leeds University recital, I should be willing to sing for them on Feb 7th for a fee of 30 gns to include accompanist's fee. Apart from any other Irish dates at the end of the month, would you not book any more dates now in February – also all March and Easter week in April. I inadvertently signed the Bournemouth contract for Easter Saturday, but already dread the journey at that time!
I shall be quite willing to sing the *St Matthew Passion* in Newcastle for 25 gns on March 9th. We have all been approached here re next season, and I have mentioned already to Mr Bing that the Three Choirs Festival will be in September. He can let us know something definite in a month's time. Meanwhile I have neither promised nor signed anything!
Shall you be able to come to Glyndebourne? I do hope you can. I am doing the first night here [Britten's *Rape of Lucretia*] with Joan Cross and Peter Pears, so Nancy Evans will be doing the London first night. Am enjoying it tremendously and I should think it's the most marvellous part one could possibly have. Joan Cross has helped me very much and we're a very happy band so far! Touching wood!
With best wishes
Sincerely
Kathleen Ferrier

5th July 1946 Miss Kathleen Ferrier c/o Glyndebourne, nr Lewes, Sussex
Dear Miss Ferrier
Thank you for your letter of the 2nd instant duly to hand. I note you are prepared to give a recital at Leeds University on February 7th at a fee of 30 guineas to include Accompanist. I have had a visit from Mr Bimrose of Cambridge, and he particularly wants you to give a recital at the Technical College next Season. The date I have suggested, Saturday January 25th, is free and does not conflict with other engagements, so may we definitely book?
I note you do not wish to entertain any further engagements for the month of February, March and during Easter week.
Much as I would like to be present at the first night of the new Opera, I am afraid I shall have to deny myself that pleasure as I see little chance of leaving London, as we are simply up to our eyes with important work, in fact we have now had to postpone our long-anticipated holiday until the end of August.
Kind regards and all good wishes
Yours sincerely

10th July 1946 EMT/SEL Miss Kathleen Ferrier c/o Glyndebourne Opera Company, nr Lewes, Sussex
Dear Miss Ferrier

Orpington Concerts Society

Our clients are organising a Children's Concert to take place at 5 o'clock on February 13th next, and in the hope that you will be prepared to undertake it in addition to the evening programme, we have pleasure in sending you an amended contract herewith. Only a short concert will be required.
Yours sincerely

11th July [1946] Glyndebourne, Lewes

Dear Mr Tillett

Sat Jan 25th will be all right for Cambridge – and also Jan 29th for Mr Sumsion – Gloucester – at the fee you mention. I think that must be all for January now, as they are all heavy recitals.

In haste

Yours sincerely

Kathleen Ferrier

P.S. Re broadcast on 23rd Jan, that is the date I promised Nicholas Choveaux (St Bartholomew's) and it is at 6.15. What a nuisance – I'm so sorry.

19th July 1946 Miss Kathleen Ferrier c/o Glyndebourne, nr Lewes, Sussex

Dear Miss Ferrier

We have two engagements in view, one with the Watford and District Philharmonic Society for a performance of the *Messiah* on Monday evening March 24th 1947 (Conductor: Leslie Regan), and the other for a concert to be given in the Royal Albert Hall on Friday May 30th 1947. The latter is with the London Junior and Senior Orchestras conducted by Ernest Read, and you would be required to sing the 'Angel's Song' from the *Dream of Gerontius* only. Will you please let us know if you are prepared to consider these two engagements?

Yours sincerely

Tuesday [July 23rd 1946] Glyndebourne, Lewes

Dear Mr Tillett

Thank you for your letter. I would rather not accept the engagements you mention, March 24th and May 30th. Three concerts in a row are too much when the first two are *St Matthew Passions*, and May 30th is Whit week, and I would prefer to leave it free at the moment. It's old age creeping on, I fear!

Herewith programme for Leeds Feb 7th 1947:

How changed the vision	Handel
Lascio ch'io pianga	Handel
Have you seen but a whyte lily grow?	anon arr. Grew
Willow song	anon arr. Jacobson
Flocks are sporting	Clarey
Four Serious Songs	Brahms

Love is a bable	Parry
The fairy lough	Stanford
The bold unbiddable child	Stanford
Down by the Salley Gardens	arr. Hughes
The Spanish lady	arr. Hughes

Hope all is well with you and your holiday materialises.

Yours sincerely

Kathleen Ferrier

[undated but early August 1946] All next week c/o 11 Oxford Drive, Waterloo, Liverpool 22
Dear Mr Tillett
I could do the Aberystwyth concerts Apr. 15, 16, 17, but I believe John Francis has asked Miss Bass for Apr. 15 for either a Wigmore Hall or Chelsea Town Hall recital, and I believe it is the only date we could fix. I will be seeing him today and will ask what he has done about it.
Would you not definitely book Gloucester (Sept 1947) for the moment until we see how the Edinburgh Festival fits in. I would like to do Gloucester, but don't want to spoil a season for one date.
Am still enjoying being raped three and four times a week! Only Holland as far as we know is materialising for the European tour, with a possibility of Denmark, but I shall be going to Denmark in any case after Holland for a fortnight's holiday with Mr & Mrs Aksel Schiøtz. Peter Diamand, Amsterdam, wants me to do a broadcast while I'm in Holland. Is this all right to you?
Best wishes
Sincerely
Kathleen Ferrier

6th August [1946] c/o 11 Oxford Drive, Waterloo, Liverpool 22
Dear Miss Ferrier
Thank you for your letter duly to hand regarding the proposed performances of the *B minor Mass* at Aberystwyth. Yes, I had overlooked the fact that Tuesday April 15th is in pencil to John Francis for a recital in the Chelsea Town Hall, and if this materialises it will of course put Aberystwyth out of count.
You mention that you will be seeing John Francis to find out exactly how matters stand, as the opportunity presents itself. Peter Pears has also been approached for the Aberystwyth performances and is willing to take them on.
Of course we shall not commit you for the Gloucester Festival without first consulting you. You may, however, take it that you would be wanted for more than one performance at this Festival.
I am glad to hear that Holland is a certainty with a possibility of Denmark, either professionally or *en vacance*.
Kind regards
Yours sincerely

9th August 1946 EMT/JMcF Miss Kathleen Ferrier, c/o The Glyndebourne Opera Coy.
Royal Court Theatre, Liverpool

Dear Miss Ferrier

City of Bath Bach Choir

The above choir, which has recently been formed by Mr Cuthbert Bates, is hoping to give a performance of Bach's *B minor Mass* in Bath Abbey on June 7th 1947, and we should be so glad if you will let us know as soon as possible as to whether you will be able to manage this date. It is of course dependent upon your arrangements with Glyndebourne.
We have also had an enquiry for your services for a concert at the Royal Albert Hall on Sunday November 3rd next, which is being sponsored by the *Daily Herald*, and is likely to be a very important affair with an orchestra of 100. There is a rehearsal on November 1st, and at the moment you are quite free on these two dates. Perhaps you would let us know whether you would like to undertake this booking.
Yours sincerely

[Undated and initial page(s) missing but probably early autumn 1946]
… work I have been doing, I just cannot learn new things.
Can I ask you again to try and keep the number of concerts down to ten a month, and to restrict these to recitals, oratorios and orchestral concerts, and to cut out all miscellaneous concerts? I will do the same and not promise to do them in a weak moment!
Also will you keep May, June, July and August completely clear at the moment – (excepting the ones I have already signed for in May) and not book anything definite after that time. I have heard vague rumours of a possible first performance of a new work in America next Autumn (very confidential) and if it materialises would not like to miss it, or have to ask you again to get me out of a hole!
Mr [Roy] Henderson will be sending the Elland programme [11 April 1947] in, as it is a joint one.
With best wishes and many regrets for putting you to extra trouble.
Yours sincerely
Kathleen Ferrier
P.S. I am sorry to have to go to Huddersfield in a rush in November [26th 1946] and feel that as they hadn't confirmed it, it is their own lookout, but as you are so keen that I should do it, I will of course.

26th September 1946 Miss Kathleen Ferrier 2 Frognal Mansions, NW3
Dear Miss Ferrier
The Glasgow Committee have decided to invite you to sing at the evening orchestral concert on New Year's Day at an additional fee of 20 guineas, making the total fee 55 guineas for the *Messiah* and orchestral concerts. We are enclosing our contract.
Yours sincerely

28th October 1946
Dear Miss Bass
Thank you for your letter. I would prefer not to sing at Saddleworth on April 13th or 20th if you don't mind.
Re Chester on Nov 20th, they ask me to sing 'The Fairy Lough' which I have already put down in the programme, also a song by Elizabeth Hughes, which they say I have sung many times. It is a new one to me, and I haven't ever sung it, but if I can learn it in time with all the other things to do, I will sing it as an encore (if I get one!) and the programme can stand as it is.
I had a press cutting today which says I am singing in the Albert Hall on Nov 20th in the *Messiah* with Dr Sargent, but this is a mistake isn't it? Thought I would mention it to avoid any misunderstandings.
If I can keep my engagements down to about ten a month, then without being completely worn out, I shall still be able to do a few broadcasts and enjoy it all, but otherwise I don't give my money's worth as [my] voice is tired and I go about in a dirty state because I haven't time to wash my smalls!!
Hope you are getting a little more time off now, and that you had a good holiday.
With best wishes
Yours sincerely
Kathleen Ferrier

31st October [1946] 2 Frognal Mansions, NW3

Dear Mr Tillett

Enclosed please find cheque for stationery account. Also I believe Anthony Lewis wants me to do some Bach Cantatas with John Francis on 17th March and 28th April on the Third Programme. Could you pencil in these dates for me please? I haven't been asked for programme for Brecon on the 8th Nov and as it is getting near here are some items:

1	Art thou troubled?	Handel
	Pack, clouds, away	Handel
2	Have you seen but a whyte lily grow?	arr. Grew
	Willow song	arr. Jacobson
	Come let's be merry	arr. Lane Wilson
3	Sigh no more	Aikin
	Star candles	Michael Head
	The bold unbiddable child	Stanford

Hope this will be in time for Brecon

Sincerely

Kathleen Ferrier

1st November [1946]

Dear Miss Ferrier

Thank you for you're your letter of the 31st *ultimo* enclosing cheque in settlement of the stationery account. We have already in pencil the dates in question for the Bach Cantatas on the BBC Third Programme, namely Tuesday March 17 and Monday April 28 1947. We will let you know the moment we are in a position to formally confirm these dates. Miss Cheselden has since been in telephonic conversation with you regarding the programme for Brecon, November 8, so everything is in order.

Yours sincerely

14th November 1946

Dear Miss Bass

Re New Concerts Assoc: Edinburgh – I am unable to accept any other engagement in May just yet, as I don't know what is happening about Glyndebourne. I probably shall do in a fortnight or so, and will let you know immediately.

Yours sincerely

Kathleen Ferrier

P.S. Herewith programme for Glasgow Jan 1st evening – nearly forgot!

1	How changed the vision	Handel		
	Watts Cradle Song	Sumsion	Hark the ech'ing air	Purcell

(the first and last orch parts obtainable from Novellos, have my own parts of the Sumsion)

2 (with piano)

A New Year Carol	Helen Pyke
Star candles	Michael Head
A piper	Michael Head
Pretty ring time	Peter Warlock

Hope those are all right.

15th November 1946
Dear Miss Ferrier
Just to let you know that we have definitely engaged Mr Herbert Sumsion to act as your accompanist at Melksham on Thursday January 30th, fee Ten guineas.
Kind regards
Yours sincerely

16th December 1946
Dear Mr Tillett
Thank you for your letter. I'm sorry but I would rather you kept July free as well as June and August for the present anyhow. I don't think I'm a very good 'Sea Pictures-ite' and have been wondering if for Brighton – May 10th – they would let me off with the middle three – 'In Haven', 'Where corals lie', and 'Sabbath morning' – and let me push in something else in which I'm happier! ('Che faro' or any of the Handel arias or Purcell)
I think I would like to give Liverpool a rest as I have been so much and have run out of a change of frock! (not to mention repertoire!) I would like to do *Gerontius* in Manchester Cathedral. I'll leave the fee to you.
'How changed the vision' I think it is from *Admeto* by Handel – parts procurable in D major at either Novellos or Goodwin & Tabbs.
Re Glasgow and Milngavie. Travelling by sleeper 31st Dec from Liverpool – staying Central Hotel 1st and 2nd and sleeper back to London on the 3rd (10.35pm).
I'm very sorry but I shall have to return this contract for Twickenham. I can't possibly do five recitals running, especially with the Third Programme at the end of the five with eight new songs which I haven't seen yet! Please, please ask me before booking any more dates. Having just done seven concerts in six days in six different towns, am feeling more than usually weary, not having recovered from travelling from Stoke to Bradford in five different trains, starting at 9.26am, catching all the right connections and arriving late for rehearsal with Dr Sargent (1/4 to 3) and still lunch-less! It isn't possible to sing well at this rate.
I hear (not officially) that *Orfeo* is not materialising, I wonder if you have heard?
I wonder too if, at my own expense, Cambridge would mind if I took my own accompanist on Jan 25th. I will write to Mr Bimrose myself to plead, but one has to rehearse so much with him, voice is a mere croon by 4.15!!
Sorry to be a nuisance. If you think I should write, could you let me have his address please.
Best wishes
Sincerely
Kathleen Ferrier

19th December 1946 Miss Kathleen Ferrier c/o Adelphi Hotel, Liverpool, Lancs
Thank you for your letter. I note you would rather not break your rest in order to sing at the proposed Elgar Festival in Malvern; also that you are not prepared to take on the Twickenham engagement. As a matter of fact I did not wish that contract to be sent without first obtaining your acceptance.
I can well appreciate your wish to avoid having to undergo a long rehearsal for the Cambridge recital on January 25th, and as I know how successfully you plead, I think it would be better for you to send a personal line to Mr Eric Bimrose, 'White Gates', Harston, Cambs., as suggested. I think you have a very good excuse. All the other matters referred to in your letter shall receive immediate attention.

It is bad enough sitting indoors in this Arctic weather, and I can fully sympathise with the suffering you have been undergoing, fulfilling all your *Messiah* engagements. We must do our best to make things easier for you in future.

Kindest regards

Yours sincerely

Correspondence with Kathleen Ferrier 1947

[*denotes letter is located in Blackburn Museum and Art Gallery]

1st January 1947 Miss Kathleen Ferrier, Central Station Hotel, Glasgow, Scotland
Dear Miss Ferrier
We have been trying to contact you by telephone the last two days, to break the news that no orchestral parts are available of 'How changed the vision', and we therefore fear you will be obliged to sing this aria with piano accompaniment at tonight's concert.
There are two matters we wish to consult you about. On May 20th the Liverpool Philharmonic Society propose giving a performance of the *Choral* symphony and would like you to undertake the contralto part. Does this work appeal to you?
Mrs Carter, the conductor of the Horsham Orchestral Society, has been in touch with us with a view to your singing at their concert taking place on Wednesday evening May 21st. Owing to the limited seating capacity of the hall, they are unable to exceed Twenty Guineas, and we promised we would see if you could be persuaded to help them. It would be possible for you to return to London by the train leaving Horsham at 8.22pm.
We presume your final decision will be dependent upon Glyndebourne. Kind regards and all good wishes for the New Year.
Yours sincerely

1st January 1947
Dear Miss Ferrier
Many thanks for your letter of the 26th December addressed to Mr Tillett, giving various programmes.
We note your suggestions for Ilkley on February 26th and are sending same on to our clients.
With regards to Leeds University on February 7th, the Accompanist is Mr Frederick Allam and we are afraid there is no chance of your taking your own on that occasion. We shall be dealing with the same question for Bolton on the 8th in a separate letter.
Melksham: January 30th: Our clients are now pressing us for your programme suggestions for January 30th, and as time is getting short we shall be glad if you will let us have your proposals by return. As you know the Accompanist there will be Herbert Sumsion.
Yours sincerely

January 9th 1947
Dear Miss Ferrier Blackpool Philharmonic Society : Handel's *Messiah*
It has been found necessary for the above Society to alter the date of their *Messiah* performance from Wednesday December 10th to Thursday December 11th, and we shall be glad if you will kindly make the necessary alteration in your diary and on our form of contract for this engagement.
Yours sincerely

15th January 1947
Dear Miss Ferrier
Thank you for your letter of the 12th instant enclosing the communication from Rudolf Bing, which I have read, and I am wondering whether it is to be returned to you or posted on to

Peter Pears, who is in Switzerland. As a matter of fact we have already pencilled in our diary the period in question for rehearsals in Edinburgh.
I am afraid the period suggested by Peter Diamand for Holland is not possible, seeing that it clashes with the Norwich Festival, which will take place during the week commencing September 22nd, and we have you provisionally reserved for the *Gerontius* performance which takes place on Wednesday September 24th.
We are also hoping that you will be engaged for the Leeds Festival, which will commence on October 7th, with rehearsals during the previous week. You certainly must not be absent from these two important Festivals.
With kind regards
Yours sincerely

6th February 1947
Dear Miss Ferrier North Road Methodist Church Choir, Darlington
We understand from Mr Edmund Hall that you have asked him to be good enough to alter the date of your engagement in order to avoid a tiresome journey to Keighley on Sunday October 26th. The alternative date which you have suggested to Mr Hall, namely Saturday evening November 1st, is quite free, so will you please transfer your engagement from Saturday October 25th to that date, and oblige us with a line of confirmation?
Yours sincerely

10th February 1947
Dear Miss Ferrier
Owing to the Government's present lighting restrictions, the committee of the Wrexham Clef Society have no alternative but to alter the time of the concert on Sunday next, the 16th instant, which will now commence at 7.45pm.
Yours sincerely

17th February EMT/SEL
Dear Miss Ferrier The British Music Society of Northern Ireland
This is just to confirm formally that we have definitely booked the services of Gerald Moore to play for you in Belfast on Saturday afternoon and evening next, 22nd instant, at a fee of Fifty Guineas (£52.10.0) for the double engagement.
Yours sincerely

24th February 1947
Dear Miss Ferrier
Mr Bing has been in touch with us regarding the question of terms for the performances of Gluck's *Orpheus* at Glyndebourne. There will be nine performances of this opera, and it is proposed to offer you the sum of Thirty pounds per performance, and the period it will cover for rehearsals and performances is from May 12th to July 5th, during which time you will stay at Glyndebourne as a guest. Will you please let us know if you are prepared to consider this offer?
We notice in our diary that we have you pencilled to the BBC on Tuesday May 13th for a Schubert recital, which we will try and get altered to another date; otherwise we will see whether Mr Bing would agree to your fulfilling this engagement.
Yours sincerely

18th March 1947
Dear Miss Ferrier

Hannah Memorial Church, Lincoln

We are glad to tell you that the date suggested, Wednesday evening April 23rd, is suitable for your postponed recital at the Hannah Memorial Church, Lincoln, so will you please definitely book that date in place of March 19th. We are enclosing a fresh contract with the altered date.
Yours sincerely

26th March 1947
Dear Miss Ferrier
We have pleasure in sending you herewith the contract for your engagement with the Glyndebourne Productions Ltd., for the nine performances of Gluck's *Orpheus*, the counterpart of which you have signed and has now been returned to Mr Bing.
Yours sincerely

27th March 1947
Dear Miss Ferrier
We cannot do better than quote from the letter which we have just received from Peter Diamand, which is disappointing so far as the postponement of the proposed performances of Mahler's *Song of the Earth* is concerned, but it is a pleasant prospect that the Concertgebouw are prepared to invite you to sing at one of their future concerts, and with this end in view will you please let us have the desired repertoire of arias with orchestral accompaniment.

> 'Bruno Walter wanted for the performances of Mahler's *Song of the Earth* in Amsterdam both Miss Ferrier and Peter Pears. As Pears will not be available, the Concertgebouw is afraid Walter will refrain from doing the Mahler work altogether and feels under these circumstances not justified in suggesting to Miss Ferrier to cancel the dates she had already accepted in England on October 15th, 16th, 18th, and possibly 19th. However the Concertgebouw would like to invite Miss Ferrier as a soloist for another occasion, and I hope to let you know more about it within a short time. You would oblige me by letting me have Miss Ferrier's orchestra repertoire'.

Yours sincerely

27th March 1947 Telegram Kathleen Ferrier 11 Oxford Drive, Waterloo, Liverpool
Lincoln transferred to April twenty-five stop. Would you sing Wakefield April twenty-three stop Please phone urgent Organol Wesdo London

28th March 1947 Telegram 9.15am Stoke-on-Trent to Organol Wesdo London
Lincoln OK 25th but please leave 23rd free if humanly possible Kathleen

29th March 1947 EMT/EB
Dear Miss Ferrier Brighton Philharmonic Society
It is with great regret we have to advise you that the Committee of the above Society are reluctantly obliged to cancel certain of their concerts owing to the Brighton Corporation having withdrawn part of their Grant. This effects the concert at which you were to have appeared on Saturday evening May 10th next, but Mr [Herbert] Menges asks us to tell you that he has every hope that he will be able to make this engagement good next season.
Yours sincerely

31st March 1947
Dear Miss Ferrier The Liverpool Philharmonic Society Ltd
As you are aware, you are booked to the above Society for a *Messiah* performance in Liverpool on Sunday afternoon December 28th, but it has now been decided to give the performance in the Opera House, Blackpool on the evening of that date instead of in Liverpool. We are therefore enclosing a fresh contract and will ask you to kindly make the necessary alteration in your diary.
Yours sincerely

2nd April [1947]
Dear Mr Tillett
Re Manchester April 12th – I have applied for a sleeper to get back to town, so will be unable to accept Mr Gregson's hospitality.
I have altered the date on my Lincoln contract to Friday 25th April. I enclose the signed contract.
Re Elland April 11th – I shall be arriving about 3.30 in Huddersfield from Stoke-on-Trent, staying at Queen's Hotel, Huddersfield. I don't know Mr Henderson's items, but mine are as follows:

How changed the vision – Handel
Come to me soothing sleep – Handel
Sweet rose and lily – Handel

Silent noon – Vaughan Williams
A piper – Michael Head
Sleep – Peter Warlock
Pretty ring time – Peter Warlock

And a joint group with Mr Henderson [all by Purcell]

Let us wander – duet
Fairest Isle – K.F.
Hark the ech'ing air – K.F.
Music for a while – R.H.
The knotting song – R.H.
Sound the trumpet – duet

Re Bournemouth 5th April – we are travelling on the 12.30, arriving Central 2.35 and hope to catch the 7.25 back to town. Would you corroborate the Elland programme with Mr Henderson to see that we agree!?
With best wishes
Yours sincerely
Kathleen Ferrier

3rd April 1947
Dear Miss Ferrier
This letter is to formally confirm the further alteration in the date of your recital in Lincoln, which it is understood now takes place on Friday evening April 25th next.
Yours sincerely

3rd April [1947]
Dear Miss Bass
Herewith the madrigals which you asked me to return to you – with grateful thanks for intervening (is that the right word?) on my behalf!
Might I remind you again of Romford on the 24th May? Now that Brighton has been cancelled on the 10th, do you think Romford might be transferred to that date, so as not to interfere with Glyndebourne rehearsals? I have been released for broadcast of the *St Matthew Passion* on the 22nd and don't like to ask for the 24th as well.
With best wishes and many thanks for all your kindness
Kathleen Ferrier

12th April 1947 SEL/AK
Dear Miss Ferrier Romford Music and Arts Society
Many thanks for your letter of the 3rd instant. We have had a word with the secretary of the above Society, who is quite prepared to accede to your request to transfer your engagement arranged for May 24th. He was, however, on the point of telephoning us to ask if it could be postponed until the Autumn as they have been suffering rather heavy losses lately, and in the circumstances do not feel they are in a position to proceed with this concert, particularly in view of the fact that it falls on Whit Saturday, which they had previously overlooked.
If therefore you are prepared to accept this arrangement, would you delete May 24th and we will leave the matter in abeyance until such time as our clients are in a position to draw up their plans for next season, in the hope that you will be able to offer them a date then.
Yours sincerely

[? June 1947] Glyndebourne, Lewes
Dear Mr Tillett
Thank you for your letter. I had hardly a minute when I was in town for [*St Matthew*] *Passion* with rehearsal and long performance. I am probably up this weekend for orchestral rehearsals, and will come in to see you if I may. You can always throw me out if you are too busy.
Eric Crozier wants me to do some Lucretias in Oct. Here are the dates: 1st Bournemouth, 4th Bournemouth (matinee), 8th, 14th, 16th Covent Garden, 21st and 23rd Newcastle, 29th and 31st Oxford. The last one I can't do because of Darlington on the 1st Nov. This would rule out BBC pencilling on 29th Oct but I could do 17th Nov. Would you be good enough to pass this on to Miss Hurst.
All fairly serene here. Please, please, please will you do your very best to come? Will arrange seats and everything if you will. Shall be cut to the quick if you miss it. If only to see me singing my way thro' Hell fire wiv me 'arp in mi 'and!! Please try.
Yrs
Kathleen F.

[? June 1947] Glyndebourne, Lewes

Dear Mr Tillett

I couldn't get in to see you on Sat as the rehearsal was from 10–1 and 2–5, and now it doesn't look as though I shall be up in town again before the first night. All *Orfeo* is being recorded by Decca and also the *St Matthew Passion.* Isn't that lovely! Both in June and July.

I have at last managed to get a copy of the Mozart aria for my Prom and it is completely hopeless for me. Tessitura is round about Es and Fs and finishes on top A. It is a soprano aria and says so in the score. I am looking out some Italian arias here from Mr Christie's library and will let you know if I find a suitable one.

I shall be able to sing in Romford on Nov 15th 1947. My Lucretia dates have been altered to fit my plans better. Here they are: Oct 1st & 4th Bournemouth, 8th, 14th, 17th Covent Garden, 21st & 23rd, Newcastle, 28th & 30th Oxford.

Dr [Fritz] Stiedry, our conductor here, tells me he has had some enquiries about me from the New York Metropolitan, but they seem to want me to do Amneris in *Aida*, and I think it's much too much of a scream. I am very willing to let Columbia Concerts, New York, have an option on my services.

With best wishes

Sincerely

Kathleen Ferrier

16th June 1947 Miss Kathleen Ferrier c/o Glyndebourne Opera Coy., Glyndebourne, Lewes, Sussex

Dear Miss Ferrier

With so many away on holiday I have been more than rushed during the past two weeks, and this is the first opportunity I have had to acknowledge your letters.

I have taken note of the opera dates which you have undertaken to do in Bournemouth, Newcastle, Oxford, and at Covent Garden. It is unfortunate that one of the Covent Garden dates should fall on October 8th as Sir Malcolm Sargent has called the artists to attend a rehearsal in Leeds at 12 noon on October 9th, which I am afraid will mean a bit of a rush for you.

The BBC have been duly advised that the Mozart aria is out of the question for you to undertake, and Mr Julian Herbage is now puzzling his brain to find another and more suitable aria for the Prom.

I have told Miss Lereculey that you will be able to do the engagement at Romford on November 15th.

I note you are prepared to let Columbia Concerts, New York, have the first option of your services, but we shall have to warn them that you are not an opera singer in the line of [Margaret] Matzenauer, Louise Homer etc, in fact in due course it will be advisable to let them have your concert repertoire. I wonder who was responsible for suggesting that you should do Amneris in *Aida*?

I only wish I could be present to witness your triumph in *Orfeo*, but alas there isn't the slightest chance of my leaving London, in fact I am wondering how on earth we are going to cope with the mountains of work in front of us, in time to leave for our holiday on Saturday next. I shall, however, be thinking of you on Thursday evening.

Kindest regards and good wishes

Yours sincerely

20th June 1947 Miss Kathleen Ferrier c/o English Opera Group, Glyndebourne, Lewes, Sussex

Dear Miss Ferrier Grimsby Philharmonic Society

Owing to unforeseen circumstances the committee of the above Society are obliged to cancel the *Messiah* performance on Wednesday December 3rd 1947, which means that only two performances of that work will be given, namely on Thursday and Friday evenings December 4th and 5th, and for these two performances we have arranged for you to receive an inclusive fee of Sixty-five guineas

Yours sincerely

2nd July 1947 SEL/AK

Dear Miss Ferrier

We have just been advised by the London Philharmonic Orchestra that the *Song of the Earth* (Mahler) has been deleted from the Bruno Walter programme on November 6th next, and they greatly regret, therefore, that they must ask you to cancel your engagement for this date.

Yours sincerely

11th July 1947

Dear Miss Hurst

This is a joint letter to all and sundry about many matters to which I have not had time to reply.

BBC Tuesday 5th August: shall be sunbathing (ever hopeful) in Devonshire! I shall be on holiday from Monday 14th inst to about the 12th August.

Leonard Isaacs: BBC overseas has asked for a recital. I think it is the 27th September but am not very sure. Would you corroborate (?) this date with him and let me know? This is for Rubbra songs, so perhaps I could do the same programme for Basil Douglas on the 28th.

London Phil[harmonic]: Nov 14th repeat concert of Bruckner *Te Deum.* OK

Romford Nov 15th: Please may I take my own accompanist as I am so busy round that time. I shall need to save my voice – Phyllis Spurr would go for 10 gns and I will lower mine if necessary. What about 35gns for the whole lot?

Woking: I would rather not accept any more engagements this year and September 29th I shall be rehearsing *Lucretia.*

Bath May 29th 1948: There is a suggestion that *Orfeo* will be done next year at Glyndebourne, and if so I shall be busy in May. I will try to find out as soon as possible, but would rather you did not accept at the moment.

Archway Choral Society: As far as I know I could sing for Mr Crellin on Sat 14th Feb.

Farnham Music Club want me sometime and I have suggested Sat 21st Feb with Phyllis Spurr as accompanist. Could you do something about this for me please?

Would somebody reply to the enclosed for me please, and all accept my apologies for having kept you waiting for my replies!

Yours sincerely

Kathleen Ferrier

7th August 1947 Miss Kathleen Ferrier, Saunton Sands Hotel, Saunton, N Devon
Dear Miss Ferrier
We have just had a visit from Miss Anne Wood, who asks us to inform you that it has been found necessary for the Opera Group to visit Newcastle on October 1st and 4th, instead of Bournemouth, which town will be visited at the end of that month. At present you are booked to appear with the Opera Company on October 21st and 23rd, but they would like to make the dates either October 21st and 22nd or October 21st and 24th, whichever you find the more convenient. Will you kindly let us know your wishes.
Yours sincerely

12th August 1947 EMT/BB Miss Kathleen Ferrier, Saunton Sands Hotel, Saunton, N Devon
Dear Miss Ferrier
Herewith we are sending you the Declaration Form which it is necessary for you to complete in respect of the passage provisionally reserved on the *Mauretania* sailing from Southampton on January 2nd next. We have been able to reserve for you M94, which is an inside single Cabin with Shower and Toilet, and is well situated in the ship; the rate is £90.0s.0d. The Cunard people will require a deposit of 25%, so perhaps you would like to let us have a cheque when returning this Form.
With kind regards
Yours sincerely

26th August [1947]
Dear Mr Tillett
Enclosed please find cuttings, photographs and repertoire for America. I leave the biography to you as we arranged. I will just corroborate the dates for Miss Anne Wood:

Oct 1st & 4th Newcastle, 8th, 14th & 17th Covent Garden, 21st & 22nd Bournemouth, 28th & 30th Oxford (with a possibility of one of the Covent Garden dates being altered from the 8th to the 7th).

Yours sincerely
Kathleen Ferrier

4th September [1947]
Dear Mr Tillett
Could you please reply to the enclosed letter from Whitehaven for me? My sister tells me she's booked for my carol concert on December 19th in the Albert Hall – but my contract says Central Hall, and I'm wondering if there is an alteration in arrangements?
With best wishes
Yours sincerely
Kathleen Ferrier

5th September 1947 JHT/RB

Miss Kathleen Ferrier c/o Mrs Maitland
6 Heriot Road, Edinburgh

Dear Miss Ferrier

I am writing to thank you for your letter addressed to my wife in which you enclosed a cheque for the balance of your passage to New York.

So far as I am aware, nothing further has transpired regarding the proposed performance or performances of *Lucretia* in New York, but I do agree with Bruno Walter that it will be necessary to obtain some further information before definitely committing yourself. In any case I mentioned at the time that it would be necessary for Mr Ralph Hawkes to get into touch with Columbia Concerts Incorporated who are your representatives in America.

I have just received word from your sister that Bruno Walter recommends you to stay at the Dorset Hotel, so I will act accordingly.

I am leaving for the Gloucester Festival on Monday and shall be thinking of you on Thursday 11th, when, as I believe you know, the *Song of the Earth* is to be performed in Edinburgh. My very best wishes for your triumph on that occasion.

Don't forget that the Worcester Festival will take place during the week commencing September 6th 1948 and that your appearance at a Three Choirs Festival is long overdue. I have a nice engagement waiting for you.

Yours sincerely

16th September [1947]

Dear Mr Tillett

I enclose a contract for Cardiff. With reference to piano rehearsal at Norwich on the 22nd inst. I am sorry I shall be unable to be there as I have a rehearsal in London in the morning (*Lucretia*!) I have noted the piano rehearsals with Dr Bruno Walter and will wait instructions as to where they are to be held. There were not very many press cuttings for the Mahler but I enclose all I have. Looking forward very much to seeing you in Norwich.

Yours sincerely
Kathleen Ferrier

[undated]

Dear Miss Bass

Thank you very much for my sailing ticket. I enclose here the cheque for the remaining amount. Mr Tillett mentioned a possibility of some *Lucretias* in New York whilst I am there. I mentioned it to Bruno Walter and he says I must be very careful as it may be some inferior opera group, and it would only do me harm. I thought I would mention it as I was keen to do it when Mr Tillett told me of the possibility.

With best wishes
Yours sincerely
Kathleen Ferrier

[undated]
Dear Mr Tillett
Would you please reply to the enclosed for me?
I have to tell you from Dr Hutchinson (N'castle) that he has a pupil (baritone) who is going to be a world shatterer! And is there any chance of your hearing him?
Léon Goossens has asked me to sing for him at Lewes for the Musicians' Benevolent Fund on November 28th and I have said I would. There will be Carter String Trio, Léon G and myself – all giving services. OK?
Have a lovely photograph of you at Norwich – am getting it enlarged and will send it to you.
Yours sincerely
Kathleen Ferrier
Enclosed cheque for Mr Hawkes for 6 tickets for November 13th Albert Hall

14th October 1947 JHT/SB
Dear Miss Ferrier
Thank you for your note enclosing the letter from Mr Pattinson of Whitehaven, which has been duly attended to. I imagine you have no special desire to visit Whitehaven at any rate during the present Season.
The concert for which you are engaged on Friday December 19th certainly takes place in the Central Hall, Westminster, in accordance with your contract. There is, however, a Carol Concert with the Royal Choral Society at the Royal Albert Hall on Saturday December 20th, and perhaps your sister has confused that event with the other one, in which case she will be listening to Dennis Noble.
Kindest regards
Yours sincerely

22nd October 1947 JHT/SB
Dear Miss Ferrier
I have just discovered that the concert on Friday December 19th will actually be held in the Royal Albert Hall, and not the Central Hall Westminster as inadvertently stated on your contract.
Your sister was therefore right and I can only hope that she has not exchanged the tickets she had purchased for the Royal Albert Hall, as there is actually a concert taking place in the Central Hall on December 19th – at which you will not be present.
Kind regards
Yours sincerely

1st December 1947 EMT/BB Iden R Reed Esq., Cunard White Star Limited, 26–27 Cockspur St SW1

Dear Mr Reed Kathleen Ferrier
Many thanks for your letter of the 28th ultimo enclosing Miss Kathleen Ferrier's steamer ticket duly completed, together with a supply of Baggage Labels.

Szigeti and Party. May we assume you have been so kind as to secure four reservations on the 10.38am train to Southampton on Tuesday December 9th?
With kind regards
Yours sincerely

4th December 1947 CW/VR

Dear Miss Ferrier Ernest Read Concerts, December 19th

Further to our recent letter, we are now enclosing final details of the programme items for the above concert, which includes taking part in the carol 'Lullay my liking', which is additional to the items previously requested. A copy of this carol is enclosed herewith for your use.

Yours sincerely

5th December EMT/BB

Dear Miss Ferrier

With regard to your Decca recording on December 18th, this is to confirm that the rehearsal with the London Philharmonic Choir will take place in the Guildhall School of Music on Monday next, 8th instant, at 5pm.

Yours sincerely

6th December EMT/BB

Dear Miss Ferrier

With regard to your Decca recording on December 18th, this is to confirm that the rehearsal with the London Philharmonic Choir will take place in the West London Synagogue, 33 Seymour Place, W1 on Monday next, the 8th instant, at 5.45pm.

Yours sincerely

Correspondence with Kathleen Ferrier 1948–53

[*denotes letter is located in Blackburn Museum and Art Gallery]

*7th January 1948 124 Wigmore Street London W1

KATHLEEN FERRIER

Continent – 1948–49

[from Emmie, possibly to John Tillett, who was en route to the USA with Kathleen Ferrier]

I am writing Hansen, Copenhagen, to say we accept in principle on Kathleen's behalf the offer of engagement for September 20th at Kr.1200 (Danish Kronen are 19.32 to the £, so this is a fee of £60), and are discussing with her the question of fee for recitals, about which I will write to him further as soon as I hear from you. I think his suggestion is quite good of £40 guarantee for Copenhagen and £40 flat fee for the others.

In regard to period, I have two pencillings for recitals in September which can easily be scrapped, so what I propose is as follows: Denmark–September 13 to 22 or 23. Hansen can arrange the Copenhagen recitals a day or two after the orchestral concert. It is all to the good to have it fairly adjacent, don't you think so? Then I will give Envall September 24 to October 2. It is not very long for the latter, but it should suffice for a first visit.

The Hallé haven't yet decided whether they want October or November, so I have dropped them a line, as we really must know with several things pending. I don't know whether you have Kathleen's list with you, but here's a copy of it so that you can decide the best thing to do. I am acknowledging Envall's letters to say he will hear from us very shortly.

By the way, Dr Kalmus for the Anglo-Austrian Society rang up to say Kathleen had told Mosco Carner she would do a Schubert recital for them. He now wants us to try to get a date for the Wigmore Hall in either May or June. As you know, it is now fully booked, so the only hope is if something comes available, and then it would depend upon whether she is free. Meanwhile I have quoted 40 guineas to Kalmus. Failing the Wigmore, he might go to the Chelsea Town Hall. Presumably it will be alright to fix this.

City of Cardiff Philharmonic Orchestra : Sunday afternoon February 29th 1948

Please let me have suggestions for two groups with orchestra including 'Ombra mai fu', nothing too heavy, and also items for which band parts are easily obtained.

*2nd June [1948] 2 Frognal Mansions, London NW3

Dear Miss Lereculey

I should be very glad to rehearse with Mr Szell for the Amsterdam performance of the Mahler and here is a list of my free times: Sunday 13th anytime until 3.30, Monday 14th 10am–11.30 or 2pm–4.30 Tuesday 15th anytime morning, Monday 21st afternoon or evening, though I am recording on the 22nd and would rather not sing too much on this day. I shall be free to record on the evening of June 10th for Decca. Here are some suggestions for Denmark for items with orchestra.

Che faro (*Orfeo*)	Gluck (my own parts)
Deh placatevi con me	ditto
Cara Sposa (*Rinaldo*)	Handel E minor
Ombra mai fu (*Xerxes*)	Handel
Schlage doch Contralto cantata	Bach 6 mins
Prepare thyself Zion *Xmas Oratorio*	Bach
Watts Cradle Song	Herbert Sumsion (my own parts)
Evening Hymn	Purcell E major
Hark the ech'ing air (*Fairie Queen*)	Purcell G major
Songs with double string quartet accomp.	(I have my own parts for the following)
Cradle Song	Wm Byrd
Art thou troubled (*Rodelinda*)	Handel
My boy Willie	folksong
I have a bonnet trimmed with blue	folk song

You say in your letter this concert in Copenhagen is November 20th but I take it you mean September!?
Here are the words to Rahoon.

> Rain on Rahoon falls softly, softly falling where my dark lover lies
> Sad is his voice that calls me, sadly calling at grey moon rise.
> Love, hear thou how soft, how sad his voice is ever calling
> Ever unanswered and the dark rain falling, then as now.
> Dark too our hearts O love, shall lie, and cold as his sad heart has lain
> Under the moon-grey nettles, the black mould and muttering rain.

If the programme for Edinburgh has not been printed could you ask for the order of the last group to be altered? I would like it to be: Parry, Stanford, two Moerans and the Warlock last. I found this worked better in Holland!
Yours sincerely
Kathleen Ferrier

6th January 1949 Mr Stokes, Thos. Cook & Son c/o Selfridges Ltd, Oxford St, London W1
Dear Mr Stokes Miss Kathleen Ferrier
Would you be so kind as to arrange the following reservations and tickets for Miss Kathleen Ferrier: Two First Class tickets with Sleepers: London to Wengen (Switzerland) leave at the end of July

i.e. July 30th or 31st or August 1st or 2nd.
Wengen to Salzburg – arrive August 17th
Salzburg to London – leaving August 24th or 25th.

One First Class berth: London to Copenhagen – leaving October 4th.
We should, by the way, be glad to know the amount for Miss Ferrier's tickets to Holland and back, so that we can collect them.
Yours sincerely

7th January 1949 From Thos. Cook & Son to Mrs E Tillett 124, Wigmore St, London W1
Dear Mrs Tillett Miss Kathleen Ferrier
Many thanks for your letter and confirming our telephonic conversation of this morning, I have registered Miss Ferrier and yourself for one compartment, two berths, in the 2nd class sleeper leaving Calais for Interlaken in connection with the train leaving London, Victoria station, at 1.30pm on July 30th or 31st or August 1st or 2nd, and have applied to our Zurich office for two single rooms at the *Baur au Lac* Hotel for the night of August 16th at the same time requesting them to register Miss Ferrier and yourself for one compartment, two berths, second class sleeper in the train leaving Zurich for Salzburg at 10.10am on August 17th, and have applied to Salzburg for two first class single compartments or failing that, one compartment, two berths, 2nd class in the sleeper leaving Salzburg for Calais at 7.45am on August 24th or 25th. Travelling by that train, you would arrive London 3.20pm on August 25th or 26th.
I have requested telegraphic replies immediately allotments are open and will advise you accordingly. With regard to the latter paragraph of your letter, I have registered Miss Ferrier for one 1st class single berth cabin in the steamer leaving Harwich for Esbjerg on Tuesday October 4th and have requested a first class seat in the train leaving Esbjerg to Copenhagen in connection. We attach hereto statement of account for Miss Ferrier's tickets to Holland and back leaving London, Liverpool Street Station at 8pm on January 13th.
I understand that Miss Ferrier and yourself are in possession of valid passports and that you will be applying for the necessary military permits and Austrian visas, in which case will you kindly let me know the number of days you will be remaining in Austria in order that I may issue the necessary tourist card which must be obtained before applying for the visas for Austria.
Yours faithfully

*25th March 1949 AH/SG c/o Columbia Artists Management, 113 West 57th St, New York
Dear Miss Ferrier
The BBC have implored us to write to you to know if you could be persuaded to sing in the Proms this year! We have told them that it is very unlikely you could accept but they ask us to try to persuade you, so perhaps you would let us know what you think about it! The only possible time would appear to be the first week of the Prom season – i.e. 23rd to 30th July. The BBC are quite prepared to accept any date and you can choose your own programme (*Four Serious Songs* or *Alto Rhapsody*?)
Yours sincerely
pp Ibbs & Tillett
Audrey Hurst

4th April 1949 From Thos. Cook & Son to Mrs E Tillett 124, Wigmore St, London W1
Dear Madam Miss K. Ferrier
Confirming telephonic conversation, we understand that you are contacting Miss Ferrier on the subject of obtaining the necessary Swiss currency authorisation direct from the Authorisation Office at 11c Lower Regent Street. We enclose the necessary forms which must be completed in detail and, as already pointed out, must be sent direct.
The schedule has just been announced in connection with the journey from Zurich to Salzburg, from which we understand there will be a 2nd class Pullman coach attached to the Arlberg Express leaving Zurich at 7.12am on August 17th, and we have therefore cancelled the registration for a sleeping compartment and have registered Miss Ferrier for two seats in the 2nd class Pullman. We trust this will be satisfactory.
Yours faithfully

12th April 1949 S.A. Stokes Esq, Thos. Cook & Son, Selfridges Ltd, Oxford St, W1
Dear Mr Stokes Miss Kathleen Ferrier
Many thanks for your letter of the 4th instant. Miss Ferrier's Sister, who will be travelling with her, is obtaining the necessary currency.
We note the reservation you have made on the Arlberg Express, leaving Zurich at 7.12am on August 17th. Can you please let us know what time this will arrive in Salzburg?
We now wait to hear from you as to the date of the reservation for Miss Ferrier and her Sister, from London to Interlaken, at the end of July or early August.
Yours sincerely

27th April [1949] The Gilcher Hotel, Danville, Kentucky
Dearest Emmie
I have a feeling you may have written me, but my letters don't get forwarded, or have missed me, so I thought I would write and let you know where I am in case you need me in a hurry.

Florence, South Carolina (Hotel Colonial)	April 28th, 29th
Macon, Georgia (Hotel Dempsey)	April 30th, May 1st & 2nd and probably 3rd
Havana, Cuba (I don't know where!)	May 4th–7th
Miami Beach, Florida (Coronado Hotel)	May 8th–about 20th

All goes fairly well. Sandor [Arpad] (accompanist) turned out to have been mentally ill for 12 months. I didn't find out for some time until his wife told me after the New York recital!, and a fortnight ago I asked for a new accomp[anist] – one John Newmark from Montreal. He's played for Simon Goldberg and Aksel Schiøtz and he's excellent, so life has taken on a rosier hue! Sandor had acute melancholia and nearly drove me nuts too, and his playing to me was unbearable as well, so the change to someone normal, who plays beautifully too is just heaven!
I believe I am completely booked up for next year here too, at slightly increased fees. I have been so hard up and have been eating in drugstores (very nice too!) and taking the cheapest rooms etc, and to me this seems crackers! The fees seem good – 600, 700 & 800 dollars – but I had to pay Sandor 105 and all his travelling, 20% to Mr Mertens, my own travelling and expenses, all cabs and tips, income tax, and accountant's fees, and learned on arrival that I was hundreds of dollars in debt despite the 800 dollars I left last year for advertising! I have no money except what I earn, so I borrow in advance all the time. It's a miserable feeling and I loathe it.

I have been singing to audiences of 2,500 & 3,000 regularly at these Community Concerts, and I couldn't help wondering where the rest of the money went! They are supposed to be non-profit making. I tackled Mr Wisner (Columbia – Chicago) and for $1^1/_2$ hours told him how good I was (I'm getting very American!) I even managed not to cry, which is a triumph for me! – but his only answer was that Chicago was a young city. I don't get it!

Two ladies from one of the Concerts who are on their committee, travelled 200 miles to hear me again, and to tell me that I ought to have a lawyer, and that I was being exploited, which just capped all I was thinking in my own suspicious way. In a way these committees have, they discussed fees and I am getting just about the lowest fee paid.

I am rambling on like this, Emmie dear, because if Mr Mertens writes you for 1951 my fees must be at least doubled or I don't want to go. I told Mr Wisner I hated singing in such bad conditions, huge halls and bad acoustics and oh! this travelling, and that if I were not enjoying the job I wanted a lot of money recompense. I can't talk to Mr Mertens, he talks all the time and his phone rings constantly on which he has longer talks than to me.

I seem to be 'sold' to places by glib-mouthed salesmen like a bloody vacuum cleaner, and I arrive in some of the queerest places you ever did see. This is not what I want of foreign appearances – I only want to go where I'm wanted. I suppose it's different here in such a big country and I'm not known, but I'd rather sing less at a bigger fee where I'm wanted. I know Toronto have tried to get me two or three times this trip, but I was booked up. The concerts have gone very well and I've met some lovely people, but I don't think my programmes are right for the sort of concerts I'm doing.

Forgive this long screed, love, but I did want you to know something of conditions before Mr Mertens wrote you. I had to sign a contract before I started on the tour and it is for two years and a year's option (this year and next – and then a year's option I suppose – I'm not very clear). I haven't written to Mr Mertens because I want to see how much money I have left at the end of it all! I hate myself for counting every nickel, but I just have to.

I hope all is well with you, love, and your sweet Momma – my fondest love to you both, and again apologies for this grouse! Look after yourself! – if I can't get nylon tricot, would you like me to get you either night-gown, pants or petti's, because I'm told there isn't much sold by the yard. I've bought a nightie and it's marvellous. Wash it in the morning, it's dry for mi afternoon nap! (No ironing!) Shall have lots of time to shop in Miami – let me know love

Fondest love

Kathleen

2nd May 1949 EMT/BB — Coronado Hotel Miami Beach, Florida, USA

My dear Kathleen

I have just received your letter of the 27th ultimo, which causes me very great concern from the financial point of view. There is no question of your being grasping, as now that you have served your apprenticeship in the USA, you must have fees that are commensurate with your position, especially as you have to pay your own Accompanist which is a terrible drain. As I have had some little experience of dealing with American Impresarios of the Mertens type, would you like to say to him that you can settle nothing of yourself, and that you must consult me? It is no use wearing yourself out, especially in that country, unless you are going to get something really worthwhile out of it. I am hoping that you have not definitely closed for 1950, in which case I can step in and put my foot down, but in any case, just pretend you don't know what money is and that I won't allow you to answer any questions yourself about such horrible stuff!

I am rather afraid that there some of my letters which you have not had, so to save time I am enclosing copies as some of them are a bit urgent. A further letter from Gylling saying that although they would so much have liked to have organised a tour for Gerald with you, the fee he wants is much higher than the organisations are prepared to pay, and the principal difficulty is that they cannot possibly arrange all your recitals together, owing to the fact that they have booked you in Sweden, Norway and Denmark, and that you will have to do orchestral concerts and recitals in each place, as you cannot possibly go running backwards and forwards between the three countries in order to accommodate Gerald. Of course it would be possible for you to pay the difference in his fee yourself and I am just waiting to hear from Gylling how much they could contribute towards it so as to give you some idea of what you might be let in for. On the other hand they hope that it will be possible to arrange for Gerald next year, when you are already known in Norway and Sweden and can command a bigger fee. Mr Gylling in any [case] says that you can rest assured that he can arrange for you to have a first class Accompanist, and if you do not want Olsson again, will try to get either Folmer Jensen of the Broadcast or Eyvind Møller, who was also the Accompanist of Aksel Schiøtz.

3rd May 1949 S.A. Stokes Esq, Thos. Cook & Son, Selfridges Ltd, Oxford St, W1
Dear Mr Stokes Miss Kathleen Ferrier
You will remember that some time ago you reserved a passage by sea, London – Copenhagen, for Miss Kathleen Ferrier on October 3rd or 4th. Owing to a change in her plans, Miss Ferrier will now have to fly, by the first plane on the morning of Wednesday October 5th, so would you cancel the sea passage and make instead a reservation on the first plane on the Wednesday morning.
By the way, have you any further news about Miss Ferrier's reservations in Switzerland, Salzburg – London?
Yours sincerely

6th May 1949 From Thos. Cook & Son to Mrs E Tillett 124, Wigmore St, London W1
Dear Madam Kathleen Ferrier
We are in receipt of your letter and as requested we have cancelled our registration in favour of the above for one single cabin Harwich–Esbjerg, October 3rd or 4th, and have applied for one seat in the plane leaving London for Copenhagen on Wednesday October 5th. We will advise you later immediately we receive confirmation.
At the time of writing we have no definite news regarding Miss Ferrier's reservations to Switzerland and Austria. Again we assure you that immediately confirmation is received the undersigned will advise you.
Yours faithfully

17th May 1949 Hotel Weylin, New York City
Dearest Emmie
I have just returned from Miami to talk business with Andre Mertens, and found waiting for me here 56 letters from 28th March onwards!! Some ass at Columbia hadn't bothered to look up my itinerary, and had just sent everything here – and I've been enquiring for 2 months where all my letters were! So I have a whole batch from you, love, requiring answers, and I'm terribly sorry to have kept you waiting.
I'll try and work 'em out! chronologically. (What lovely contracts!)
In reply to 25th March. BBC Proms. I would like to do the *4 Serious Songs* the week 23rd–30th July. OK? 31st March : letter. I have had a letter from Decca saying they won't release me to Columbia unless Columbia loan them Bruno Walter, and as Columbia won't do this, things are at a deadlock I'm afraid. They say they have lent artists before and never can they get one out

of HMV or Columbia. But the flying can still remain the morning of the rehearsal in Copenhagen, just in case it works out with Columbia.
I thought the 13th was a good date for Edward Isaacs as I am already in Manchester, that is why I agreed so readily, but abide by your final decision. I always love to sing there. I do hope Central Hall is all right with Bruno Walter – don't like the sound of the Dorchester. But shall see!
11th April: I refused Knokke as I must be at home sometime, and will do the Prom instead. Poor Peter [Diamand], I'm refusing everything!
I am booked in Chicago March 23rd/24th. Oh dear! I hadn't known Passion Sunday was on the 26th – I am sorry about that. I would have loved to have done it, but I'm even advertised already. I couldn't do it now if I flew. Tell Dr [Reginald] Jacques I'm terribly sorry, will you love?
14th April letter : I think to do the *Passion* in Holland is too complicated as we can't know how the boats sail, and I don't want to fly, 'cos I'll be ready for a rest. I'll write to P.D. and explain. Oh! good! I see in this letter the Central Hall is straightening out. Hurrah! I don't know anything about broadcasting rights, but will do what you suggest.
I note I fly now to Denmark on Oct 5th. O.K.
I'm sorry about Gerald as he has probably kept this time free, and if I wouldn't be completely out of pocket by taking him, will gladly pay something out of my fees.
22nd April letter : I think the 8th Nov is impossible for the Central Hall, especially as I shall have already been there, and the thickness of my bookings just then. Will you refuse firmly but kindly for me, love? Ta ever so!
I could do the 13th in Edinburgh but not the 11th. Think I'd be better not doing either as I've been there so much a few weeks previously?
2nd May : Well I lunched with Mr Mertens today and dined with him and the big white chief Ward French. They tell me a sob story of managers going broke here because of a depression (he took me to the Waldorf Astoria!), and that I would never get any work if my fee were put up. I pointed out the success I'd had and that my fees, if anything for 1950 were down, not up, and he immediately put my lowest fee up from [$] 700 to 750, which is better than a kick in mi new nylon pants!
They were very nice and I've got things off my chest that have been smouldering there for 2 months, and didn't wrap it up, and they seemed to like me for it. My contract, which I have only read today, tho' I signed it before I left on the tour, is for 1949 & 1950 with an option for '51, but Mr Mertens says if I'm unhappy he wouldn't bind me.
There's so much to tell you, I'll save it up for a great fat dinner (on me!) when I get home, if you'll do me the honour, love?
Miami and Havana were wonderful, and I'm peeling off in large chunks all in mi exposed parts! I was sick at having to come back to New York, but feel, after today, that it was worth it! If you have written me again in Miami it will be forwarded to me at the Brown Hotel, Louisville, Kentucky (22nd–25th) as I left a forwarding address.
Much love to you, dear Emmie, and a 1000 apologies for not replying – but it really wasn't me this time. See you soon – whoopee!
Love
Kathleen

16th June [1949]
Dear Miss Lereculey
Herewith my programme for Hull Nov 16th and York Nov 17th

Spring (*Ottone*) Handel
Like as the lovelorn turtle (*Atalanta*) Handel
Hark the ech'ing air (*Fairy Queen*) Purcell
Mad Bess Purcell arr. Britten

Gretchen am Spinnrade Schubert
Tod und das Mädchen Schubert
Heidenröslein Schubert
Erlkönig Schubert
Wir wandelten Brahms
Botschaft Brahms
Sonntag Brahms
Von ewiger Liebe Brahms

The Ash Grove Welsh folksong arr Britten
Ca' the Yowes Scottish arr Jacobson
Spanish Lady Irish arr Hughes
Shenandoah American
Bobby Shaftoe English arr Whittaker

Here also is my Scandinavian programme for recitals: No! As you were! If you don't think it is too late, I'll send it after July 16th when I can see my last year's diary! OK? Will send other programmes soon.
Best wishes
Kathleen Ferrier

27th June 1949 EMT/BB
My dear Kathleen
At last we have the Cunard sailings for December next, and here they are. *Queen Elizabeth* – December 21st. The *Queen Mary* goes on January 4th, which of course is too late as your first date is January 4th, but there is the *Medea* (an eight-day boat) from Liverpool on December 24th. It would seem that December 21st will be the best for you, although it will mean spending Christmas on board, but I have an idea that Myra Hess may be with you, as she will probably go on the same ship. As you were hoping to sail after Christmas however, I am endeavouring to find out whether there is a French or Dutch boat leaving about December 26th, and shall hope to add a note to this letter.
Meanwhile we have one or two dates held up, as you know: December 17th and 18th *Messiah* [in] Liverpool, and December 19th Albert Hall *Messiah* for the London Philharmonic Orchestra. If you sail on December 21st will this make it too much of a rush for you, or would you like to do these dates?
As you will see from the enclosed, I have at last fixed up a satisfactory appearance for you in Paris on November 8th. There is not a great deal of money in it when you boil it down to pounds, shillings and pence, but it is a better fee than they pay in the ordinary way. I shall hope to be there with you.

We are now receiving enquiries for you for the Festival taking place in 1951, and a letter from York this morning, wants you for a performance of the *Dream of Gerontius* in the Minster between June 2nd and 16th. As you know, the big International Festival which is being planned for this country will take place between May and September, and there are sure to be some important appearances for you. I am just wondering what we shall do about the question of fee, as with the enormous demand for your services, it will certainly have to go up. I think for works it should be 50–60 guineas and for recitals a minimum of 75 guineas for your personal services. What do you think?

Incidentally the York contribution to the Festival will be with Sir John Barbirolli and the Hallé Orchestra.

Scottish Orchestra: It is now practically certain that they will decide to do a performance of the *Dream of Gerontius* in Edinburgh on November 11th. It is a tight fit with Paris, but you could come back by the day service on November 9th (flying might be a bit uncertain at that time) and then go up to Edinburgh on the night of the 10th. Is this alright by you or do you feel it is going to be too much?

Tuesday [June 28th? 1949] American Hotel, Amsterdam

My dear Emmie

Thank you for your letter re Denmark. I do not want to do another concert either 25th or 27th as it will be strenuous enough, and the 2nd Copenhagen recital is too important. I'm sorry about Gerald – I only hope there is time to rehearse, but will leave the choice to Mr Gylling.

All goes wonderfully well here, and *Orfeo* has been a great success and I'm surrounded by Dutch flowers and roses as I write! I'm very spoiled! An American friend sent me the enclosed article, and as it is very true I thought you would be interested to read it before you write [to] Mr Mertens.

Hope all is well with you, Emmie dear, and love to your Momma.

Just off to Hades and Elysium again with mi flamin' 'arp! *Quel vie*! Mr [Pierre] Monteux is a poppet, and so is the producer, so life is most pleasant. The Maitlands are here, absolutely adoring it all – Win too for the weekend.

See you soon, love, I hope.

Much love

Kathleen

4th July 1949 EMT/BB American Hotel, Amsterdam

My dear Kathleen

Thank you so much for your letter concerning Denmark.

By the way, I have written [to] my Oslo friends Clive and Vera Robinson, that you would stay with them and they have written to say how delighted they are. They seem to know a bit about your fixtures, as you are due in Oslo on the morning of October 12th for rehearsal, and 13th and 14th with the Oslo Society.

There is also a small tour of other towns in Norway I understand, but they expect you to stay with them in Oslo just as long as you are there, and I know they will look after you the whole time. Clive and Vera are due in England on July 13th, and are coming to London before the end of the month, I hope before you leave for Switzerland, so I shall arrange for you to meet them. By the way all is fixed for your journey to Switzerland, and you and your Sister leave on July 30th.

Please give my warmest greetings to Pierre Monteux, whom I have known for many years, and if you have the chance, put in a word with the Maitlands for Ian Hunter as successor to Rudolf Bing, as in my humble opinion, and having dealt with him a good deal, he is by far the best bet as Bing's successor.
Looking forward to seeing you next week
Always yours

4th July 1949 EMT/BB American Hotel, Amsterdam
My dear Kathleen Bach Festival – Vienna
I think I have come to a satisfactory arrangement in regard to the question of terms for your appearance at the Vienna Festival in June 1950, and hope you will agree with what I have done. You are wanted for the undermentioned dates:-

Sunday June 4th 1950 *B minor Mass* – Bach
Thursday June 8th *St Matthew Passion* – Bach
Thursday June 15th *B minor Mass* – Bach

and the Gesellschaft der Musikfreunde in Vienna have agreed to pay you £150 in sterling and 1000 Austrian schillings. As you know, this has been fixed up through Mr Walter Legge.

25th July [1949] [incomplete]
My dear Emmie
I am enclosing a letter from Mr Mertens [of 21 June but not extant], which I received some time ago, and also my itinerary so far for next year. It is not so busy as I thought it was because two of the orchestral concerts have been cancelled. I don't know a Welsh Choir for the Bible Belt, do you duckie? I could sing many praises miself about mi Nylon Belt!
I talked to my Prof [Roy Henderson] on Saturday, as I always do when puzzled, and he says I must have first a rest and then some study on my vocal chords, which are showing signs of wear and tear, so I have decided, apart from Vienna, not to accept anything after May 15th next year, and have refused both Holland and Glyndebourne. It seems an awful shame to miss them and to miss Italy too, but I think it is only sense, especially if the 1951 Festival is going to spread over the summer months of the following year. The Brighton contract for May 14th 1950 I thought was going to be for *Das Lied von der Erde*. The *Lieder eines Fahrendengesellen* are too high for me. I have written to Sir J.B. about them too, and we have changed them to the Lennox Berkeley *Poems of St Teresa*. Do you think the Brighton one can be changed too? I could do the *Kindertotenlieder* if he particularly wants Mahler.
I enclose a cheque for 12/- for Prom tickets – thank you very much indeed.

[undated but mid-August 1949] Hotel Alpenrose, Wengen, Nr Interlaken
My dear Emmie
Here is my Reading programme [29 November 1949] but I think I sent it in already as I have it all marked down in my diary – but perhaps I am mistaken.

Spring (*Ottone*) Handel
Come to me soothing sleep – Handel
Hark the ech'ing air (*Fairie Queen*) Purcell
Mad Bess Purcell arr. Britten

Die junge Nonne Schubert
Du bist die Ruh Schubert
Romance from Rosamunde Schubert
Der Musensohn Schubert

Wir wandelten Brahms
Botschaft Brahms
Sonntag Brahms
Von ewiger Liebe Brahms

The Ash Grove Welsh folksong arr Britten
Ca' the Yowes Scottish arr Jacobson
The Spanish Lady Irish arr Hughes
Shenandoah American
Bobby Shaftoe English arr Whittaker

Do you want to buy any masterpieces in oils, love? Win and I have been painting madly and she has one, supposed to be of a hillside that is the perfect reproduction of stewed tired lettuce! And I have some pine trees that look like Holland bulb fields in flower!! So speak quickly 'cos I know there'll be great bargaining for them! It so lovely here and the weather has been perfect – we're both bright puce, sore and itching, but it's worth it! We have to watch our pennies 'cos everything's very expensive but think we will just last out until Salzburg.
If you have any news from Salzburg of where we are staying or who we can rustle for a little ready cash, t'would be a great help. We leave here for Zurich on the 16th, arr Salzburg 17th. Hope you are well, mi darlint – wish you were having a holiday. I feel re-born for the rest and the good air.
Much love and God Bless you and your Momma!
Kathleen

[undated and incomplete]
Re Wimbledon April 25th. Phew! That's a long time ahead! Same programme as Oxford Nov 6th

Spring
Soothing Sleep
Ech'ing air
Mad Bess

Wir wandelten
Botschaft
Sonntag
Von ewiger Liebe

Suleika
Wanderers Nachtlied
Musensohn
Erlkönig

Ash Grove
Ca' the Yowes
Spanish Lady
Shenandoah
Bobby Shaftoe

also for Dorchester May 5th
I am a bit worried about Highgate, as I am in Kings Lynn the day before with two recitals – could it possibly be altered do you think? Here are the words of 'Du liebst mich nicht'. I will call in with the *Frauenliebe.*

Mein Herz ist zerrissen, du liebst mich nicht!
du liessest mich's wissen, du liebst mich nicht!
Wiewohl ich dir flehend und werbend erschien,
und Liebe beflissen, du liebst mich nicht!
Du hast es gesprochen, mit Worten gesagt
mit allzu gewissen, du liebst mich nicht!

So soll ich die Sterne, so soll ich den Mond,
Die Sonne vermissen? du liebst mich nicht!
Was blüht mir die Rose? Was blüht der Jasmin
Was blühn die Narzissen? du liebst mich nicht!

I haven't got a poetic translation, but here is a literal one: My heart is broken, you do not love me. You want me to know that, although I have implored you, you even said it in words, with complete certainty that you loved me not. Am I to miss the stars, the sun and the moon? Why do the roses, the jasmin, and the narcissi bloom for me when thou lovest me not? (She's in a bad way, poor lass!)
Hope this is all right.
Love
Kathleen

15th August 1949 EMT/BB c/o Baron Puthan, General Intendanz der Salzburger Festspiele, Salzburg

My dear Kathleen
Thank you so much for your recent letter and card. It is a nuisance about Edinburgh and Glasgow, but as it is only *Gerontius*, perhaps it won't be too trying, so I am now telling the Glasgow people that you are prepared at a great deal of personal inconvenience, to accept their (blank) engagement! I will save the contract against the time you get home again. Miss Hurst is coping with Sleepers to Edinburgh on August 31st and from on September 11th.
Miss Lereculey was in Salzburg about ten days ago, and called on Baron Puthan to find out what arrangements he had made for you in regard to hotel. He promised to telegraph us, but not a sound, so I have been rather at a loss to know what to do. However, I hope that by the time you receive this letter you are safely installed in a comfortable spot, and that he met you as we asked him to do.
Worcester want a programme for November 4th for the Grammar School for Girls. Shall we give them the Oxford one?
Re Scandinavia: I think I asked you in one of my letters as to whether you would feel inclined to accept a broadcast engagement with the Norwegian Radio at a fee of 500 Norwegian Kroner, which is the equivalent of about £25. I don't know whether you have your Scandinavian dates with you, but I think it can be fitted in quite comfortably unless you feel you have enough already. You are in any case, doing two orchestral dates in Oslo. If you could let me have a note about this I should be glad, as Gylling has asked me again about it.

Postcard to Emmie
22.8.1949 Salzburg
Furtwängler enquiring about my services for 29th Sept for Brahms *Alto Rhapsody* in London. Original date 28th but have told him impossible, but if 29th then should be very happy to do it. So you will know what it's all about when you hear! Am willing to do Norwegian radio date if possible at all. Have already sent programmes to Mr Gylling. Will send prog for Worcester tomorrow. First perf here just over and a colossal success. Whoopee. Luv. Kathleen.

23rd August 1949 EMT/BB
My dear Kathleen
When you have time, would you mind sitting down and composing a new biography as the enclosed appears to be rather out of date – or you can paint me one if you prefer!

*29th August 1949 2 Frognal Mansions. London NW3
My dear Emmie
Here's mi life story love! I thought if I painted it I should use too much scarlet!! I have used all your exaggerated sentences about mi gracious appearance etc., and just brought the other bits up to date.
I was asked by a Mr Saab in Salzburg to contact Mr Carl Schuricht, Fontanirent, Montreux, Switzerland about singing under his direction in the Bach Mass in Paris next year with the Orchestre des Concerts du Conservatoire. He thought it was probably about the 30th May and if so, it would be lovely to break my journey to Vienna – what do you think – and will you write to him for me luv? I will put in his card. Okeydoke?
What shall I do about an accompanist for Paris, and are you coming too love? I do hope so. Mr Gylling wrote saying he hadn't accomp[anist] yet and who did I want, so I have suggested taking Phyllis [Spurr] as our time is going to be so short for rehearsal and they are long programmes.
I shall be at Mrs Maitland's, 6 Heriot Row, Edinburgh until the 11th Sept., if you want me for anything.
I'm still thrilled with your house [11, Elm Tree Road, London N.W.8] – I think it is gorgeous, and it will be a wonderful surrounding for all your lovely furniture. Klever Emmie!
With love
Kathleen
PS I'll enclose the snap in case you can use it. The negative is away at the moment but if you need that I shall have it in two weeks time.
Just realised I never answered the questions in your other letter!

1. I don't know about certificate but I don't see it will make much difference, they can easily get one, and we are the easiest people to trace, speshally me!
2. Didn't receive form for Swiss currency. I did write to the bank two months ago about it and haven't heard.
3. B. Walter – Central Hall – Sept. 28th. It won't be publicised until after Edinburgh because it's being put on by Glyndebourne, and they don't want to detract from Edinburgh. But three weeks will be plenty of time.
4. Tentative bookings for Holland June 24th (Friday) First night *Orfeo*, 27th The Hague, 28th Amsterdam

The Maitlands are flying on the 24th so as not to miss the first night!! Aren't they poppets? Clever our Winnie – you'll be a ruddy MP before we know where we are – but then politics goes mit painting, don't it? Tarawell!

2nd September 1949 EMT/BB Miss Kathleen Ferrier, 6 Heriot Row, Edinburgh
My dear Kathleen
A note this morning from Mr Gylling to say that the Philharmonic Orchestra (I think he must mean in Oslo, although he does not say so) would like you to do the *Four Songs of St Teresa* by Lennox Berkeley. Presumably you will take the orchestral material with you?

11th September [1949]
My dear Emmie
I think it is too much of a rush from Bideford to Manchester and Birmingham. They are all recitals and a bit too strenuous I think, to do all well! I'm very sorry for Edward [Isaacs] – it is just bad luck, but I'll go another time.
Am enquiring about the orchestral material for the Lennox Berkeley and will send on a score when I get home. Herewith Cambridge programme November 27th:

Spring : Come to me soothing sleep – Handel
Ech'ing air : Mad Bess – Purcell
Die junge Nonne : Suleika : Musensohn : Romance (*Rosamunde*) : Erlkönig – Schubert
Wir wandelten : Botschaft : Am Sonntag Morgen : Von ewiger Liebe – Brahms
Sleep : Pretty Ringtime – Peter Warlock
Rahoon : Merry Green Wood – Moeran
Ash Grove : Oliver Cromwell – arr Britten

I have had a strong week with both Holland and Glyndebourne chasing me for next year, but you will [be] surprised and pleased to know that I was firm – just for once! Klever Kaff!
Wish you had been here – I missed you because I felt the recital with Bruno Walter was a peak to which I had been groping for the last three years! He was pleased and so were the critics, so everybody's happy. I hope you enjoyed your change at Hereford and feel refreshed for it – am home tomorrow – in fact, I'm just rushing for the train now! See you soon I hope.
Yours
Kathleen

27th September [1949]
Dear Emmie
I am sorry Decca worried you with details of rehearsals and recording sessions, because usually they contact me direct. I am not happy about the fee on your contract, as I should be paid in royalties (for my old age!), and I have spoken to Mr Sarton and this is going to be arranged. Hoped you liked the photies of your Momma, but I shall be seeing you tomorrow?? I have the negatives if you would like them. Herewith programme for Ministry of Supply Nov 30th:

Spring : Come to me soothing sleep – Handel
Hark the ech'ing air – Purcell
Mad Bess – Purcell arr Britten

Have you seen but a whyte lily grow? – arr Grew
Willow, willow – Eliz[abethan]: arr Warlock
Pur dicesti – Lotti
Che faro (*Orfeo*) – Gluck

Gretchen am Spinnrade : Romance : Der Musensohn – Schubert
Wir wandelten : Botschaft : – Brahms

The Ash Grove – arr Britten
The Spanish Lady – arr Hughes
Ca' the Yowes – arr Jacobson
Bobby Shaftoe – arr Whittaker

Keep your fingers crossed for me love!
Yours sincerely
Kathleen Ferrier

27th September 1949 EMT/BB
Herewith your (and Phyllis Spurr) return ticket for Copenhagen on Wednesday October 5th next. You have to report at Kensington Air Station at 10.40am. We have left you to contact the Copenhagen office of the British Airways in order to arrange the date of your return passage.

7th October [1949]
My dear Emmie
I'm sorry I didn't get in to see you before I left – I was recording with Bruno Walter until the last minute, and had a ruddy blush, love!
I enclose the Paris contract. What am I to do about an accompanist? I think I'd better have a French one because the fee won't cover expenses and fees for two.
I think it would be a good idea to do a similar programme to Edinburgh – all Lieder – with a slight change in the Schubert:

Die junge Nonne/Suleika/Romance/Musensohn/Tod und das Mädchen/Du bist die Ruh
Frauenliebe und Leben – Schumann
Six songs (as Edinburgh) – Brahms

Re Oxford : Nov 6th Brahms *Serious Songs* OK and English Songs. I haven't last year's diary with me, so don't know what I sang but here are two alternative groups:

Silent Noon – Vaughan Williams : Merry Green Wood/Rahoon – Moeran
A soft Day/The bold unbiddable child – Stanford
or
Love is a bable – Parry : The Fairy Lough – Stanford : Sleep/Pretty Ringtime – Warlock

I could have done the Rubbra *Psalms*, but they won't go with the Brahms *Serious Songs* – much too much gloom!
Our plane was an hour late leaving! You should have seen us skid through the Customs and the traffic to the Radio for immediate rehearsal! Being very well looked after – but nearly dead! Fly to Stockholm today. Hope all is well with you.
Love to you and your Momma.
Kathleen
P.S. I hate being called Katleen! (see contract!)

30th October 1949
My dear Emmie
I would love to sing the *Alto Rhapsody* on Aug 31st or Sept 1st 1950 at Edinburgh – then please can I have the rest of the ten days off to hear the other concerts there? I've heard so little in my time and it is such a wonderful opportunity. I would prefer not to sing at the morning concerts this time, but just do the one appearance and really do it well.
How wonderful if 1951 with Bruno Walter comes off!! (Fingers crossed!).

Haslingden : Shall be happy to accept same hospitality.
Herewith Chelsea : How changed the vision/Like as the lovelorn turtle – Handel
Hark the ech'ing air/There's not a swain on the plain/Mad Bess – Purcell
Frauenliebe und Leben – Schumann
Immer leise wird mein Schlummer/Wir wandelten/Am Sonntag Morgen/
Botschaft/Von ewiger Liebe – Brahms

Will speak to you tomorrow about Worcester and Oxford. Hope your home is looking beautiful, I'm sure it is.
Affectionately
Kathleen

23rd December 1949 To Miss Kathleen Ferrier c/o Hotel Weylin, Madison Ave, 54th St, NY22 NYC
My dear Kathleen
I am so sorry I forgot to send you the translations of the French Press notices, but here are two sets which you may like to have by you in America.
One other small point, I don't think you made any comment on the question of the broadcasting fee for the Edinburgh Festival. You will no doubt remember that I sent you a line about it and suggested that they should pay you 100 guineas if the concert is relayed. If this is all right by you, then I will inform Ian Hunter accordingly.
Don't forget to let me have the suggested items with orchestral accompaniment to send to Zurich. The original suggestion was the *Alto Rhapsody* and the *Kindertotenlieder*, but they now say it might be necessary to alter the programme. Enclosed is a list that I have in the office – could you add to it?

15th January 1950 Hotel Phillips 12th and Baltimore Kansas City-6-Missouri USA
Dearest Emmie
I am a diva of the deepest dye for not writing e'er this, and I'm very sorry. All is very well now, but I was met with the news that my pianist, John Newmark, being Canadian, would not be allowed to enter the US to play for me, so I had to contact Canadian and British Embassies and a Washington lawyer, and, finally, at the 11th hour he was allowed to come! *Quel* greeting! But it was worth all the cafuffle, because he is superb. But it did make me neglect all else meanwhile. Our concerts have gone well, and I've got the New Friends of Music off my chest, which was worrying me frightfully because of the fuss I had had over programme. I thought I dithered my way through like an un-set jelly, but the critics were good. Paddy has the *Tribune* and *Times*, and I will enclose the afternoon papers.
I do hope your back is really better now, love, and that Momma is blooming as usual, bless her. John N and I went to dinner with Andre Mertens the other night and the next day, when I was starting off for the rest of the tour, he rang me to say that if I didn't sing in the US until Oct

'51, my year's option would be out of date, as the contract ends in May '51. It would mean signing another one, and he wasn't allowed to get jobs for me without a signed and sealed contract, and as it was just like the last, he'd put it in post and would I sign it? So I said I had promised you I wouldn't sign anything, and that these matters were beyond me and distasteful to me (!), and that I would either have to send it to you or take it to a lawyer. Strangely enough, two nights before I had been with the Simon Goldbergs and he is with Schang of Columbia, and was urging me to take any contract to his lawyer, as he says they know exactly what fees one should get and will fight for orchestral dates and straight sales and keep the Community down etc; and keep an eye all the time to see that one isn't overworked. So I thought I would put this all down and see what you think? Andre flared up for a minute when I said I needed a lawyer, and asked if I had had such bad treatment under his care? All frightfully difficult, having just had a smashing great dinner!
Otherwise I am enjoying every minute, and am looking forward to some hot sun in Santa Fe and Phoenix, Arizona in a fortnight's time and then a fortnight's holiday in Beverly Hills. Lucky me! What'll you say if I get signed up with Bing Crosby for a musical? Would be able to afford two bags of white flour then!
I had some money to my credit when I arrived, so all's very well this time. Prices are exorbitant of course at the new devaluation, but I still divide by 4, and it's much less startling! Shall be coming back on 30th March with Mr & Mrs Benno M[oiseiwitsch], also the Goldbergs, so have a stretcher ready love!
If you would write me direct, I shall be at La Fonda Hotel, Santa Fe, New Mexico on the 24th Jan and c/o Dr Walter, 608 North Bedford Drive, Beverley Hills, California from 31st Jan to 6th Feb. But my letters seem to be arriving also thro' Columbia this year. Do hope you're really better – much love to you and Momma and all my buddies in the office and your two German girls.
God bless
Love
Kathleen
Today's funny story
After the New Friends Concert where I sang Bach in German and Brahms in English, a German came up to someone and said – of course I was German, because my German pronunciation was perfect and I sang in English with a marked accent. (it's true, honest!) I didn't know my Lancashire came thro' quite so strongly!

*16th January 1950 To Miss Kathleen Ferrier c/o Hotel Weylin, Madison Ave, 54th St, NY22 NYC

My dear Kathleen
When you have a moment to write to me, there are a few things I want to know. Firstly, you will remember that you are booked to sing *Das Lied von der Erde* at the Albert Hall on the afternoon of Sunday April 23rd next. Now the BBC want to repeat this work with the same cast and orchestra, but the only time that they can do it is the same evening at 9 o'clock, and it is just a question as to whether you will find it too heavy going.
Gloucester Festival. Dr Sumsion wants me particularly to ask you whether you would just pop down for the Friday Chamber Concert, which is given in the Shire Hall, and for which the Boyd Neel Orchestra have been engaged. I told him that the chances were very remote, but that I would let him know when I had had a word with you.
Scandinavia. You will remember that we discussed the possibility of your giving Gylling part of March as well as the whole of April, as he suggested, so that he could arrange for you to take

part in some works, and you were inclined to agree to this proposition. Fortunately I had not written to Gylling as, according to Roy [Henderson], you promised to sing for him at Bournemouth on Good Friday 1951, which falls on March 23rd. Would you therefore like to remain on here until that date, and then we can give Gylling from say March 27th to the end of April?

Sagra Musicale de Perouse – Italy. They want to engage you for this Festival to take part in 'a big religious oratorio', and they are most anxious to know whether there is any possibility of your considering it. The Festival is from 18 September to 4 October, but they could arrange for your appearance to take place within three or four days. Our Italian Correspondent is most pressing that you should undertake this as it would be such excellent propaganda for your February tour, but I do not know whether you will feel inclined to go over to Italy just for this one thing. They have asked us to let them know what fee you would want, and they would arrange matters. What do you think?

I know you will be more than sorry to know that our Keith [Falkner] will have left Italy by the time you, or we, get there, as his job comes to an end on August 31st next. I have one or two things in view for him, however, which I hope will keep him a little nearer to us, but this is very private at present.

I think this is all for the moment, and a little short note about these various items will be very helpful.

24th January 1950 c/o Dr Bruno Walter 608 North Bedford Drive, Beverley Hills, California, USA

My dear Kathleen

I was so glad to have your letter of the 15th, which will have crossed one of mine with several queries in it. What a worry about your accompanist when you arrived, but I am thankful you got him into the country. We are always coming up against little problems like that with our foreign visitors, so I know how trying it can be. All the same, I don't see why you should have been worried with it as Mertens should have looked after it. However, as he got there, all is well.

I am thankful you have not signed the contract. I am always a little scared of lawyers, as they have a habit of stirring up trouble between a manager and an artist, but if the man that Goldberg recommends is really good and understands the position, then I would suggest you go to him, but at the same time I would like you to let me have a copy of the contract as well, so that between us and the lawyer you will have a square deal.

Now the Edinburgh Festival 1951. Hunter has just telephoned to say they are contemplating doing *Orpheus* (Gluck) with the Glyndebourne Opera, Bruno Walter conducting, Ebert producing, and yourself, and they want to know what you think about it. Rehearsals would commence on approximately July 20, which will mean cutting your holidays short by about ten days, but I am sure you will want to do it, so it will only remain for me to arrange that you have a good fat fee. I am still in trouble between settling the Hallé, and arranging for Holland to Diamand's satisfaction, but I expect it will sort itself out. I do hope you are having a real rest and a lovely holiday.

30th January 1950 EMT/RB Miss Kathleen Ferrier c/o Hotel Weylin, Madison Ave, 54th St, NY22 NYC

My dear Kathleen

There are several things to ask you about next season, on which I want to have your ideas.

Bach Choir: *St Matthew Passion*, Sunday March 11th 1950 : Dr Jacques asked me to pencil your services for this date (and Dr Cook of Southwark wanted you for March 18th, but that is just an aside)

The Hallé are now settling their dates and they are to be as follows:

February 27 Rehearsals, February 28 Manchester *Das Lied von der Erde*
March 1 Manchester *Das Lied von der Erde*, March 3 Rehearsals *Orfeo*, March 4 Manchester *Orfeo*, March 7 Hanley *Orfeo*, March 10 Sheffield *Orfeo*

I tried to get the Hallé to move the Sheffield performance to a date between March 12 and 21, as I felt you would like to do the *St Matthew* for Jacques, but this morning we have had a letter from [T.E.] Bean to say there is no other date possible, and they will have to cut this work out at Sheffield if you cannot do it. Having prepared *Orfeo*, John [Barbirolli] wants to give it in at least three towns, in fact he would have liked to play it more often, but it does not look very possible. It is, however, for you to decide whether you do the additional performance of *Orfeo* or the *St Matthew* for Jacques. (Bach Choir rehearsal might be arranged for Friday March 9th, but then of course it would mean a night journey for you from Sheffield on the night of the 10th, which would be terribly tiring).

Now that we know that the Hallé performances are all to fall in the New Year, I have given Peter Diamand the period from November 20th to December 10th, which I hope will satisfy him. He must get the best fees possible for you, by the way. Have you any arrangements with him in this respect?

This is how next Season works out:-

August 27 to September Edinburgh
September 12 to November 19 England
(September 22 to 27 – query Perugia Festival)
November 20 to December 10 Holland
December 12 to 31 England
January 1 to 31, 1951 Holiday
February 1 to 15 Italy
February 17 to 24 France
February 27 to March 23 England (assuming you do Bournemouth on Good Friday)
March 27 to April 30 Scandinavia
May 1 to June 30 England (Festival of Britain)

Ceramic Choir, Hanley are doing a performance of *Apostles* on November 8th and would very much like to book you. I cannot quite remember whether you are happy about this work. So far we have not encountered any difficulty about your fee, that is to say 50 guineas for choral works, and 75 for recitals.

Royal Choral Society. We are pencilling your services for their Festival performance of the *Dream of Gerontius* on May 24th 1951.

I am afraid there are rather a lot of queries for you to answer (my letters of December 23, January 16, 24, and this one). I do hope you have received them all by the way, but if not, let me know and I will send you copies at once.

*3rd February 1950 c/o Dr Walter, 608 North Bedford Drive, Beverley Hills, California
My dear Emmie
Thank you so much for your letters love, but I have only had two of them – 24th and 30th January. What a nuisance, and I thought they were coming through well this time, but perhaps they have been forwarded too late somewhere. I am so sorry to cause you extra work. Anyhow I will answer the questions you ask in these two letters, and write to Columbia to check up on them.
I am so glad your back is better again, and your Momma well – much love to her, and I am looking forward to seeing her when I get back. I heard Dame Myra is ill and has cancelled her tour here. I do hope it isn't serious.
Ooooooooo, boy….*Orpheus* with Dr Bruno?????? YES PLEASE—-would forgo all my holiday for that.
The Hallé and *Orpheus*? I think as it was my suggestion that they do it, I must do the Sheffield date, tho' I feel rather badly about the *Passion* if Dr Jacques has asked for me – but I couldn't travel overnight to do it, as you say.
I have no arrangement with Peter Diamand over fees, but have always been well in pocket from previous visits. What shall I do about an accompanist there? I wish I could take John Newmark – he's absolutely superb, but he'd be out of pocket to come to Europe, even if I paid his fare … ach well, we'll see.
Gee whiz//// all this work// aren't I a lucky ole twerp/ (I have no exclam[ation] marks on this machine – it does limit me).
Yes, I can do the *Apostles* for Hanley – it is the *Music Makers* that gets me doon. Lovely to do *Gerontius* for the Royal Choral on May 24th – whooppee.
All is going so well here. The concerts have been a great success – we've been to some lovely places – and now I am installed here, and have the house to myself with man and wife to look after me. It is just wonderful. Dr Bruno and his daughter and husband are in New York, so I shan't see them until March. The sun is shining – this place is just amazing – the palms and the houses and the glamour pussies, and the luxury of it all. I am being ruined here – I have the use of two superb cars at any time – my bathroom plumbing is an hourly – well nearly – delight, and oh it's so warm. I have so many dates with new found friends that it is almost embarrassing, but today I have started on my real holiday – ten days before going to North California, so I am as happy as a lark, and feel very grateful for this wonderful opportunity to see so much.
Mr Mertens has not sent on my contract yet – and I am being pressed all the time not to delay until the Autumn of '51 to come back, but of course it is all arranged. I have said I will come Oct 1st to Dec 15th 1951, and I STILL HAVEN'T SIGNED ANYTHING. Even *Musical America* wrote to me saying it was a bad policy not to return next Jan. What the heck … it's only 6 months later.
The concerts are much better this year, smaller halls and altogether different, and I should say I have one of the best accompanists in the world...honest...so we enjoy our music making and make the most of opportunities to study new things, so it is grand for me.
Here is where I am going to be, so that you can write me direct? I'll give the day of the concert, then you can make that day the latest for letters.
Leave here Mon 13th
Feb 14th Hotel Senator, Sacramento, Calif.
16th, 17th, 18th, 19th Hotel Whitcomb, San Francisco
21st Hotel Morek, ABERDEEN, Washington
24th, 25th c/o Mrs Cress, 2005 King St, La Crosse, Wisconsin
27th Hotel Tivoli, DOWNERS GROVE, Illinois

I think that is all love – I hope I have not forgotten anything. Much love to you and thank you for all your endeavours on my behalf – I am a lucky twerp – love too to Miss Lereculey and Miss Cheselden.
Look after yourself.
Love
Kathleen

*20 February 1950 EMT/RB c/o Hotel Weylin, Madison Ave, 54th St, NY22 NYC
My dear Kathleen
Just one or two points about programmes when you have a moment to think of them.
Firstly Highgate, April 29. I should like to have your programme for this date as soon as possible.
Next, Brighton, May 14. This is HERBERT MENGES' birthday party (his 25th anniversary as conductor of this Society) and he feels that *Kindertotenlieder* is hardly a suitable work to include on such a festive occasion, so in the circumstances, could you make one or two other suggestions; for instance he thinks the aria from the *St Matthew Passion* with violin obbligato and 'Che faro' would be suitable. (I do not altogether agree with him as both these are a bit subdued). Perhaps, however, you will have some other ideas.
I do so hope you have received all my letters by now, as there are quite a few things about which I am waiting your reply.

*3 March 1950 c/o Columbia Concerts 113 W 57th St. N.Y.C
My dear Emmie
I am a diva of the deepest and dirtiest dye for not having written e'er this. My only excuse is that I have a been a darn' industrious diva for the last two weeks, and I hope you'll forgive me. I will take your questions in turn and see what happens!

1. Me in a film? 'Pon mi soul! I don't know the part, or if it is suitable – and could the cameraman remove my curves? – but I couldn't give a definite answer just now until I know more about it. It would be interesting if it were rewarding, musically and financially!
2. If it is possible to do some Holland Festival 1951 I would like to, having missed this year. We will see what our programme looks like when I get home?
3. *Das Lied* April 23rd. I think I can stagger through the BBC if it's the only time it can be done. Wonder why they don't broadcast it from the hall?
4. Gloucester. I would like to stay on in Edinburgh. I would do Gloucester for Dr Sumsion with pleasure, but this is such a wonderful chance to hear some music, and Edinburgh and Gloucester are such miles away.
5. I don't remember promising to sing for Roy on Good Friday, but I've got a good 'forgettery'. All right Scandinavia March 27th onwards.
6. Would like to do Sagra Musicale de Perouse if it's something I can do well. Ask as big a fee as you like, and can. I'm awfully sorry Keith has left Italy. Whattashame!
7. Zurich. I wonder if they would be interested in Lennox Berkeley *Four Hymns of St Teresa*. I am awfully short of orchestral things. Am just learning Chausson *Poème de l'Amour et la Mer*, but would rather not do a first performance there – but if you are stuck, then I could manage it. What about Brahms *Serious Songs* – they are orchestrated, but I suppose I would have to do them in German there, and that's an awfie sweat!

I think that is all your questions, love. I saw Bruno Walter in Chicago. He asked me to do a recital with him in Salzburg this year, but I'm afraid t'will clash with Edinburgh – whattapity! He wasn't at all sure about *Orfeo* in 1951 – it's rather far ahead for him, but I'll keep the dates just the same, eh? All still goes well and San Francisco was a wow – everybody thrilled, and want

me next year – whoopee! Mrs Monteux gave me a lovely black fox stole, a pearl ring and the manager a lovely necklace, and Mr Monteux a kiss on each cheek with his walrus mustache! Mm! Mm! Ain't I spoiled!! Just off to see Niagra Falls before going to Toronto. Shall be at Hotel Weylin, New York 15, 16, 17, 18, 19, 20 and c/o Mrs Cardelli, 1130 Lake Shore Drive, Chicago 23, 24, and 25 March if you need me.
Hope all is well with you and your sweet Momma.
Much love to you both
Kathleen

*12th March [1950] The Admiral Beatty, Saint John, New Brunswick, Canada
My dear Emmie
I am enclosing a few criticisms I have collected on my travels, Los Angeles, San Francisco, New York and Montreal, and I would like – if you agree – to have an insertion in the *Times* and *Telegraph* with a few quotations, just to let people know I've been working hard and not disappeared for three months! Aren't they lovely ones? I'm being very spoiled and just lapping it up!
The two poppets in Montreal – Mrs Langdon and Mrs Russell-Smith – send kind greetings to you.
Just shooting off for yet another train! but wanted you to see that I've been behaving myself! All goes well here – it's been a lovely tour – and I still haven't signed owt! Klever Kaff!
Hope you are well, darling, and your Momma too. Won't be long now until I arrive in my new hat and the white flour under mi arm! O boy! Tell Miss Lereculey my French grows apace – I'm learning some Chausson – and she'll have to look out for competition! I can say 'Darling, *je vous aime beaucoup*', *passepartout*, *cul-de-sac*, '*voulez-vous couchez avec moi?*' – oh no! that's the rude one!! Heigh ho *quelle vie*! Ain't I a lucky ole budder! Much love to you all, Kathleen

*23rd March 1950 SEL/JA 2 Frognal Mansions, NW3
Dear Miss Ferrier
Just with regard to programmes for your forthcoming concerts.
April 25th Wimbledon. Here is a copy of the complete draft which has been agreed by our clients.
April 28th King's Lynn. We should be glad to receive your proposals as soon as possible. You may remember that there are two recitals of about 45 to 50 minutes duration, one at 1pm for adults and the other at 3.30pm for children. Phyllis Spurr has raised the question as to whether you want her to play solos on this occasion, in order to give you a short break.
May 5th Dorchester. We should also be glad to receive your suggested programme for this concert as soon as possible.
May 7th Bideford. Here again we want your suggested programme and there has been a special request for you to include the song cycle *Frauenliebe und Leben*.
May 8th Birmingham. We wrote you to America concerning the programme for this concert, and as already mentioned Professor Lewis would like you to include a song cycle possibly *Frauenliebe und Leben*.
Yours sincerely,
Ibbs & Tillett Ltd [Sadie Lereculey]

*1st April [1950] RMS *Queen Elizabeth*

Dear Miss Lereculey

Herewith my suggestions for B'ham programme – May 8th.

Bist du bei mir Bach
Like as the lovelorn turtle Handel
Have you seen but a whyte lily grow? arr. Grew
There's not a swain of the plain Purcell arr. Britten
Mad Bess Purcell arr. Britten

Frauenliebe und Leben Schumann

Silent Noon Vaughan Williams
Rahoon Moeran
The Merry Green Wood Moeran
Flower song (*Rape of Lucretia*) Britten
Down by the Salley Gardens arr. Britten
Oliver Cromwell arr. Britten

Howzat?

Here also Highgate April 29th.

Bist du bei mir Bach
Turtle Handel
Hark the ech'ing air Purcell
Che faro senz' Euridice (*Orfeo*) Gluck

An die Musik Schubert
Du liebst mich nicht Schubert
Suleika Schubert
Der Musensohn Schubert

Botschaft Brahms
Wir wandelten Brahms
Sonntag Brahms
Von ewiger Liebe Brahms

Down by the Salley Gardens arr. Britten
The Spanish Lady arr. Hughes
Blow the Wind Southerly arr. Whittaker
The Keel Row arr. Whittaker

'Che faro' and 'Have Mercy Lord' OK for Brighton. Sorry to have kept you waiting so long – just haven't had a minute.

See you soon – whoopee!

Affectionately

Kathleen F.

*10th April 1950 2 Frognal Mansions, NW3

Dear Miss Lereculey

Here, I hope, are the missing programmes:

King's Lynn [April 28]

Bist du bei mir Bach
Like as the lovelorn turtle Handel
Hark the ech'ing air Purcell

Suleika Schubert
Wanderers Nachtlied Schubert
Musensohn Schubert
Sonntag Brahms
Botschaft Brahms

Down by the Salley Gardens arr. Britten
The Spanish Lady arr. Hughes
Blow the Wind Southerly arr. Whittaker
The Keel Row arr. Whittaker

I will change the middle group for the children to:

Who is Sylvia? Schubert
Heiden Röslein Schubert
Musensohn Schubert
Sonntag arr. Brahms
The Vain Suit Brahms

Howzat? I don't think Phyllis needs to suffer and play solos – I'll stagger through – but it was a kind thought, *n'est pas*?

Dorchester and Bideford May 5th and 7th

Bist du bei mir Bach
Like as the lovelorn turtle Handel
Hark the ech'ing air Purcell
Che faro senz' Euridice (*Orfeo*) Gluck

Frauenliebe und Leben Schumann

Wir wandelten Brahms
Sonntag Brahms
Botschaft Brahms

Love is a bable Parry
A soft day Stanford
Blow the Wind Southerly arr. Whittaker
The Keel Row arr. Whittaker

I have sent Birmingham haven't I? I enclose a letter from Mr [Alan] Kirby, Croydon, and if Mrs Tillett agrees, I should like to sing for him – he's a sweet poppet! And also – if you can read it! – a letter from Dr Cook, Southwark – I leave them both in your hands – lucky me!
Best wishes
Sincerely
Kathleen Ferrier

*2nd May 1950 SEL/JAH 2 Frognal Mansions, NW3
Dear Miss Ferrier
Bridge of Allan & District Music Club
Here is our contract for the recital you are giving for the above Club on Monday, October 30th next. Mrs Tillett and I have decided to accept the very special en route fee of 80 Guineas to include your Accompanist on this occasion, but have asked our clients to treat it with the very strictest confidence!
We have offered November 2nd to Dundee as agreed by telephone and are just waiting to hear from them.
Here is the confirmation of the Royal Clarence Hotel, Exeter for next Sunday night. Would you, by the way, be sure and check the trains we gave you as you go along, as it may be there will be some alterations, although we do not anticipate any.
Yours sincerely
Ibbs & Tillett Ltd [Sadie Lereculey]

*2nd May 1950 EMT/RB 2 Frognal Mansions, London NW3
My dear Kathleen
We now have pleasure in sending you your return air ticket for Amsterdam, leaving Kensington Air Station at 13.15 on Wednesday, May 10th next and returning on May 13th, leaving Amsterdam at 13.15.

*24th May 1950 From Thos. Cook & Son to Ibbs & Tillett
Dear Sirs
With reference to Miss Kathleen Ferrier and Mr and Mrs Matthews, we have pleasure in enclosing their air tickets as follows:-

> 1 1st and 2 2nd class return tickets to Zurich, with a double 2nd class and a single 1st class sleeper Calais to Zurich on June 4th, 3 air tickets (return) Zurich to Vienna June 5th and Vienna – Zurich June 17th, and a double second class sleeper from Zurich to Calais on the 17th June.

For Miss Ferrier we have no homeward reservations yet as we have not received a definite date from you. We have reserved accommodation at the Hotel Astoria, Vienna for this lady, and the full charges must be paid here and they come to £13.0.0., and we therefore attach the necessary forms for the basic allowance with this £13.0.0. endorsed. If we do the travellers cheques, these forms are all that will be required, but if Miss Ferrier does her cheques through a Bank, we shall require a "V" form from her bank for the £13.0.0.

*26th May 1950 EMT/RB 2 Frognal Mansions, London NW3
My dear Kathleen
We have pleasure in sending you your tickets for the journey to Vienna as follows:

1 1st class return ticket London – Zurich – London
1 1st sleeper Calais – Zurich on June 4
1 Return air ticket Zurich – Vienna on June 5, Vienna – Zurich on June 17

Accommodation has been reserved for you at the Hotel Astoria, Vienna, from June 5 to 17

*12th June 1950 EMT/BB 2 Frognal Mansions, London NW3
My dear Kathleen
Just to let you know that I have booked hotel accommodation for you, and incidentally, myself, as under

Queen's Hotel, Leeds: October 2nd – 7th, 1950
Fernley Hotel, Bath : October 13th – 20th, 1950

By the way, can you let us have your programme for Rhyl on October 22nd as soon as you return, or at least some of the main items, as our clients are anxious to issue some advance publicity.

*13th June 1950 SEL/PAS 2 Frognal Mansions, London NW3
Dear Miss Ferrier Bromley Orchestral Concerts
On looking through your contracts we think perhaps the one for Bromley is not quite clear and, so that all shall be in order, would you kindly make a note that the date for this engagement is Saturday May 26th 1951.
Yours sincerely
Ibbs & Tillett Ltd

*15th June [19]50 Vienna
Dearest Emmie
I have neglected you because dates were still being altered when I received your wire. Now we're back to where we were and it's two concerts in Milan. Are they willing to pay the £175 – oh boy! I don't need to leave Zurich until the 29th and hope I can get back in time to get a sleeper home as originally arranged. But there isn't one booked on any special day, is there? So I'll go to Cooks in Zurich on Saturday.
I think the last performance in Milan is the 2nd, but I'll find out tonight. It's only 4½ hours train journey Milan to Zurich, and the easiest way home I'm told. MUST be home in time for G[lynde]bourne with you and the Prof and Profess.
All's gone well here and my crits have been wonderful, and they want me to do a recital here next year. Klever Kaff! Last concert tonight, so fingers still crossed!
If Scala comes off, could you ask them to arrange hotel with bath (oh! the agony here!) and that I shall be met in Milan as I shall have no money. I'll let you know train and date.
Victor Olof (Decca) is here recording and met me in, and has been an absolute pet – otherwise it would have been 'O sole mio!' Denis [Matthews – pianist] had good success too, so we haven't let you down, love!
Why I say 'the agony here'. The food is frrrrrightfully rich – too rich for my ole liver, and the pongy lav is a mile down the corridor – oh! the exercise I've had!

Am full of beans once more and back to my Wiener Schnitzels!
Shall be at Dolder Grand Hotel, Zurich until the 28th or 29th if you want me. Could you let me know who to contact for some of my earnings in Switz[erland] in advance? Am doing myself proud at the Dolder – shall enjoy having dearmaria with me own lav! Hope all is well darling – much love to you and your Momma.
Love
Kathleen

*23rd June [19]50 Miss Kathleen Ferrier, Dolder Grand Hotel, Zurich, Switzerland
My dear Kathleen
I was so happy to have your letter of the 15th yesterday, although it has taken a week to get here from Vienna. By now you will have had my telegram and letter of the 19th, I hope, and you may even have heard direct from the Scala, to whom I gave your address in Zurich.
This is just to let you know that we left the date of your return open, so did not make any sleeping car reservations back from Zurich. However, I hope Cook's will be able to fix you up. I hope that they will let you or me know about a hotel in Milan, and I will certainly write and tell them to meet you when I know the time of your arrival and the date.
Sorry about the hotel in Vienna. Perhaps you might have been better off in some ways at the Pension.
I had a little note from Mr Schulthess to say he was contacting you, so I hope you have heard from him by now. Of course you must be back by July 6, as I should not dream of going to Glyndebourne without you.

*10th July [19]50 EMT/RB 2 Frognal Mansions, London NW3
My dear Kathleen
Just to add to the things we have got to talk about, Vienna want you for Good Friday, March 23, and Munich for Sunday, the 25th, with a date in Paris afterwards. I have an idea this is for a Bach work with KARAJAN, and you may know something about it.
Peter and Ben want to know if there is any hope of your doing two or three performances of *Lucretia* in London during the first three weeks of May 1951. The producer will be Basil Coleman and it will probably be conducted by Ben.

*10th July [19]50 2 Frognal Mansions, London NW3
Dear Mrs Tillett
Here are a few replies to your queries

Rhyl programme Oct 22.

Spring is coming Handel
Come to me soothing sleep Handel
Hark the ech'ing air Purcell
Mad Bess Purcell

An die Musik Schubert
Lachen und Weinen Schubert
Du liebst mich nicht Schubert
Der Musensohn Schubert

Wir wandelten Brahms
Botschaft Brahms

Sonntag Brahms
Von ewiger Liebe Brahms

Love is a bable Parry
The fairy lough Stanford
A soft day Stanford
The bold unbiddable Child Stanford

Cambridge May 17th – OK for Brahms Viola Songs
Bolton 14th Nov Phyllis Spurr will accompany
Highgate May 5th No to recital here as I may go to Vienna, will come in and see you about this?
Bryanston May '51 I thought I could perhaps go the weekend May 19th, but perhaps you have something booked there? I would like to go as she is an old school friend, and leave it to you to fix.
Edinburgh '51 Ian Hunter tells me there is still a possibility of *Orfeo*, so would you keep all the time free from July 20th onwards until we hear definitely – I shall have to ask off to go to King's Lynn if it does materialise – I do want it to.
No Television *Bitte* – no time and too fat!!
Hindemith *Requiem* – still in Holland and can't do rehearsals
Will speak to Basil Douglas about concert in Wigmore Hall – want to know what he wants me to do – am I free on the 11th?
Mr Karajan wants me to sing in the Bach *B minor* [*Mass*] in Munich on Easter Sunday, and I said I would ask you, but I think it is pretty hopeless don't you? 25th March '51. Gamsjäger wants me in January but I am hoping I shall go to the Scala, then for *Orfeo* – and if I don't, I want a rest – but I said I might go in May for the Beethoven 9th and two recitals 8th and 10th? But I will come and see you about all these bits and bobs. Thank you so much for booking Leeds and Bath. What fun!
Hope your back is much better now, love.
Love
Kathleen

*12th July [19]50 EMT/RB
My dear Kathleen
Italy for February 1951 is coming along quite nicely, and we have got them up to scratch in regard to the money. The following have so far been fixed:-

February 2	Rome	No particulars as yet
February 4	Florence	Contract for 150,000 lire enclosed. On this occasion they want you to take part in a performance of *Das Lied von der Erde* – Mahler
February 9	Turin (Radio)	*Kindertotenlieder* – Mahler Conductor Wolf-Ferrari Waiting particulars of fee
Date to be fixed	Milan	Recital 150,000 lire to include your accompanist

I think we shall have to wait and see what else is forthcoming before you make any decision in regard to accompanist. Keith Falkner can advise us as to who would be good to have, as with only one or two dates it would not be worth while taking someone from this country. According to the rate of exchange, this fee represents nearly £100 a performance.

19th July [19]50 EMT/RB 2 Frognal Mansions, London NW3
My dear Kathleen
I have had a note from GYLLING in answer to ours asking him to terminate your tour by April 28 to give you good time to get back for the TOSCANINI concerts, and he says that he is awfully sorry that they cannot reckon upon the full month of April, as it is very difficult for them to arrange all the dates for you inside this period. However, here is the list as it stands so far:

April 1, 1951 Copenhagen recital
April 3, 4, 5, 6, 1951 4 South Jutland concerts at a total fee of d.kr 6,000 (including accompanist)
April 8, 1951 Silkeborg d.kr. 2,000 (including accompanist)
April 10, 1951 Gothenburg orchestral concert, s.kr 1,000
April 12, 1951 Copenhagen 2nd recital
April 15 or 16, 1951 Stockholm recital
April 18, 1951 Oslo orchestral concert
April 20, 1951 Sarpsborg
April 21, 1951 Oslo recital
April 24, 1951 Copenhagen radio concert
April 26, 1951 Copenhagen 3rd recital

Regarding the provincial concerts, they have obtained four dates with four societies in South Jutland in cities quite close to each other. When they book artists with these Societies they usually make their concerts on four consecutive days, and he hopes that in this case you will not mind, as you can make an easier programme than usual as you will be singing four days running. This is a provisional list pending your confirmation. What do you think about it?

*26th July [19]50 EMT/RB
My dear Kathleen OSLO PHILHARMONIC SOCIETY
The above are very anxious to leave the choice of the programme entirely to you, so would you let us have some suggestions which I can give to Clive when he arrives on the 5th, and he will then send them on to Miss Ovstaas. Alternatively I can use the list of arias etc with Orchestra that I have in the office.

26th July [19]50 EMT/RB 2 Frognal Mansions, London NW3
My dear Kathleen
ITALY
For some reason the concert at Florence has had to be transferred from February 4 to Sunday, February 11, 1951, so would you kindly alter the date on the part of the contract you hold. Your engagements for Italy for February so far, therefore, are as follows:

Rome recital February 2, 1951
Turin Radio February 9, 1951 (Orchestral)
Florence February 11, 1951 (Orchestral)
Milan recital February 15, 1951

Before the orchestral concert in Turin on February 9, they are hoping to arrange for a broadcast recital, and also other engagements.

You will, by the way, be able to leave Turin at 9.15am on February 10 arriving Florence at 4.42 that afternoon, and the first rehearsal will commence at 6 o'clock, and the second rehearsal will take place on the morning of February 11.

In regard to the question of accompanist for the recitals in Rome and Milan, GIORGIO FAVORETTO is recommended. He always plays for ELISABETH SCHWARZKOPF, VICTORIA DE LOS ANGELES etc., and as a matter of fact I know of him through WILLIAM PRIMROSE, who wants him for his recitals in Italy in November next, as he says he is fine. We understand, however, that he would require a fee of at least 50,000 lire for Milan, which seems pretty high, and at least as much as our Gerald requires for this country, but of course you could not possibly take anyone from here for that amount. So far as Rome is concerned, they make themselves responsible for the accompanist's fee, so you will only have the one to pay, so far. What do you think?

31st July [19]50 EMT/RB — 2 Frognal Mansions, London NW3

My dear Kathleen

We have just had a further letter from GYLLING to say that of course the South Jutland Societies are very disappointed [Gylling's letter of 29 July actually says 'the societies in question feel terribly depressed'] that you will not be singing for them, and that the schedule for your tour has accordingly been changed to the following:

April 2 Aarhus recital
April 4 Odense recital
April 6 Copenhagen, concert with chamber orchestra Collegium Musicum, 3 or 4 arias, and about 2 folksongs
April 8 Silkeborg recital
April 10 Gothenburg orchestral concert
April 12 Copenhagen 1st recital
April 15 Oslo orchestral concert
April 15 Stockholm recital
April 18 Oslo orchestral concert
April 20 Sarpsborg recital
April 21 Oslo recital
April 23 Copenhagen 2nd recital
April 24 Copenhagen radio concert

They are now waiting for us to confirm the above, and add that they will do everything to see that your travelling is as comfortable as possible.

*25th August [19]50 EMT/RB — c/o Mrs Maitland, 6 Heriot Row, Edinburgh

My dear Kathleen

Gylling of Copenhagen has sent a complete list of engagements to date, together with the fees. He is particularly pleased with the fee he has obtained for the Copenhagen broadcast engagement, namely 2000 Kr which he says is the highest fee ever paid to an artist at a Tuesday concert.

Out of the broadcast fees you will have to pay your own accompanist, so now it is a question as to what we can arrange with Ernest Lush. Gylling asks as to whether you would like to have Kjell Olsson as accompanist for the tour. Meanwhile I will find out from Lush what he would consider for the eight recitals.

You may be approached by a little American named Waxman, who incidentally wrote the music for *Sunset Boulevard.* He came to see me and wants you to do the Mahler Symphony No.3 in Los Angeles next April or May. I told him it was quite out of the question and he would have to approach Mr Mertens if he can postpone the performances to the autumn. Incidentally he brought all sorts of messages from Bruno Walter for me, and said that you were to ask him about Mr Waxman.

One last thing. Lord Dudley Gordon's daughter-in-law, Mrs June Gordon, gives a performance of the *St Matthew Passion* every year at her residence, Haddo House, Aberdeen, and next year it will take place on Sunday May 20th. They are awfully anxious for you to take part, but I said it was very doubtful indeed as you were so heavily committed. However, I thought I had better mention it as I thought you might like to visit Scotland, particularly as they have a very lovely house, I believe, and secondly somebody in Edinburgh might ask you about it, and if you didn't know anything, you might wonder what I was up to.

29th August [19]50 EMT/BB 2 Frognal Mansions, London NW3

My dear Kathleen

I have just had a cablegram from Ghiringhelli of The Scala. He is sorry about *Orpheus* but would we please ask you to accept Scala on January 21st and February 1st to sing the Verdi *Requiem* conducted by DE SABATA. These two concerts take place during the Verdi celebrations. I am not telegraphing him until I hear from you, as in view of the important engagements I am just wondering whether you would want to stretch a point and sing the Verdi.

There is now the question of a second engagement in Paris, which we can arrange on January 22nd, which you would take on your way out to Switzerland, for which Kiesgen can get 50,000 francs. I believe it is orchestral. Of course you could not do it if, by any chance, you have a shot at the Verdi. Would you be a dear and send me a telegram 'yes' or 'no' on receipt of this letter, and I will then cable Ghiringelli as he wants an answer. In any case he is coming over for the Festival and arrives at the North British Hotel early in September, in case you want to see him.

*3rd September [19]50 2 Frognal Mansions, London NW3

My dear Emmie

Here are a few answers to your queries luv:

Worthing : Brahms *Rhapsody* in English (Novello)

English group with Arthur Wayne

Love is a bable Parry
A soft day Stanford
The Fidgety Bairn arr Robertson
Ca' the Yowes arr Jacobson
The Spanish Lady arr Hughes

I could rehearse Fri or Sat 22nd or 23rd. If they want something more solid – e.g. Lieder – will change, but thought this might cheer things up!

May 28th Elgar *Sea Pictures*

Only sheer love for you Emmie makes me acquiesce, as the Bishop said to the actress!

Bridge of Allan etc. Gerald will be playing for me. (Miss Lereculey wanted to know – and will you say 'thank you', 'bless you' to her for her postscript – it did mi heart good!)

I have already given my prog: for Perth to David Yacamini – here is the prog: for the other two: Bridge of Allan Oct. 30th Dundee Nov. 2nd

Spring Handel
Come to me soothing sleep Handel
Have you seen but a whyte lily grow arr. Grew
Che faro senza Euridice Gluck

An die Musik Schubert
Musensohn "
Lachen und Weinen "
Erlkönig "

Wir wandelten Brahms
Botschaft "
Sonntag "
Von ewiger Liebe "

Ca' the Yowes arr. Jacobson
The Fidgety Bairn arr. Robertson
Blow the Wind southerly arr. Whittaker
The Keel Row arr. Whittaker

If only three groups are needed, will you cut out the Brahms?
I'm sorry about the Verdi *Requiem.* It breaks mi bloomin' heart, but it's no good, it's too high. The more I see of opera, the less I want to take part in it, except *Orfeo.* I think I'll have a rest in May. Am seeing Ben and Peter tomorrow and will let you know if any persuasions corrupt me! Would love to take Ernest Lush with me to Scandinavia and agree to his fee, I don't want him to reduce it. [Ibbs and Tillett's pencilling: Lush advised by phone]
Would prefer not to go to Aberdeen May 20th, too big a jump in between Cambridge and Peterborough.
Think that's all for the moment.
Much love
Kathleen

*6th September [19]50 EMT/BB c/o Mrs Maitland, 6 Heriot Row, Edinburgh
Dear Miss Ferrier
As you know, Mrs Tillett is at the Gloucester Festival this week, and so I am writing in her absence to thank you very much for your letter of the 3rd instant, which I am dealing with. Thank you too for the information concerning the Scottish Recitals and the programme. It is certainly nice to have it so well in advance.
Mr Kiesgen has just written enclosing the contracts for the Paris concert on February 18th, which will require your signature, so would you sign all three copies and return to us as soon as possible? You will see the fee is 45,000 francs and as you will notice in the additional clauses, there will be a private rehearsal on February 16th at 9 o'clock and a public rehearsal the following day at 10 o'clock, which we believe is usual.
If there are any other matters to tie up in regard to this engagement, Mrs Tillett will do so on her return to the Office next Monday, but I thought you ought to have this in the meantime.
Yours sincerely
Ibbs and Tillett Ltd [Beryl Ball]

*15th September [1950] 2 Frognal Mansions, London NW3

My dear Emmie

Re Worthing Sept. 24th. Will use the Simrock edition of the Brahms, and can rehearse with Mr Wayne at his pleasure Saturday afternoon – 23rd. Will you ask him to bring a copy with him, *s'il vous plait?* Shouldn't I wear gloves if it were Kirkby Lunn's copy?!

Will you tell Einer Kleine Gylling I can't do three recitals in a row. I would rather arrive on the 29th and perhaps sing on the 31st – if it's orchestral it's a different matter, but recitals are too hard work. It's no good working so hard – Chenhalls tell me I'm going to be highly taxed on my American dollars – and I just get tired into the bargain!

Haven't raped Ben and Peter yet, but shall be seeing them this week – don't really want to do *Lucretia* – would much rather have the time off – middle age creeping on!

Hope to have a drop of fizz on the twenty-tooth with Momma!

Please can you book hotels for Bridge of Allan, Perth and Dundee for Gerald and me. Just shooting off to rehearsal.

In haste

Love

Kathleen

*[December 1950] American Hotel, Amsterdam

Dearest Emmie

You must come to Holland just once, if only to let me see your eyes light up at the sight of the food here. Gerald and I still expand daily, but our morale is high, so what the heck!

I have written answering all Mr Mertens' questions, so you don't have to worry, at least until the next batch descend!

I tried to phone you from the airport and waited, because you were engaged, then had to join the plane and couldn't wait any longer.

Now to biz:

Lucretia's Rape. Can you get me out of this, sweetie? The thought of it worries me enormously, my big feet and all that, I don't want to go careering off to Wiesbaden when I'm only just back from Europe. I'm only going to have a few days to rehearse and re-learn the whole bluidy thing, and I certainly don't want to work any more in July. Can you talk me out of it, do you think? I would be relieved.

Italy. I'll take the material (orch) for 'Cara Sposa' and 'Ombra mai fu'.

Paris. I think I'll have my little handkissing Parisian again – because I want to study some French pronunciation with him. (*Voulez-vous coucher avec moi?* and all that!!)

Bournemouth. OK for Roy and *Gerontius* Sept. 15th

Gylling. Am in communication with Ernest Lush and have altered original arrangements to weekly payment – my responsibility – because of time-waster of orchestral concerts – but he has asked off from the 30th March, which means that he would fly that day. Could he make Silkeborg – where is it I wonder? Perhaps he could leave 29th night, depends on him entirely.

Will think out Paris popular programme and let you know.

In a rush

Much love

Kathleen

*4th December [19]50 EMT/EW
My dear Kathleen
Thank you so much for your letter to hand this morning. I will certainly try and get you out of the *Lucretia* performances.
Scandinavia. I have had a word with Ernest Lush, and he can arrange to fly over on March 29th, so now have written to Gylling to say that he can shift Silkeborg to March 30th.
Edinburgh Festival. I wrote Ian Hunter quoting a fee of 250 guineas, as you know. He writes pointing out that this is more than they paid you in 1949, which was the equivalent of 140 guineas. They now want us to suggest to you that they pay you a total and inclusive fee of 200 guineas for the double engagement. In the event of either or both concerts being broadcast, he suggests that they pay an additional 25% of 100 guineas. I am all for holding out for the 250 guineas, however. What do you think?
Yours sincerely
P.S. Herewith the contract for the Copenhagen broadcast on April 21st at a fee of 2,000 Danish Kroner. Would you please sign this and let us have it back.
Zurich recital, January 28th – presumably you would like Schulthess to engage a good accompanist for you, unless you are considering taking your own, and then on to Italy.

*5th December 1950 American Hotel, Amsterdam
Dearest Emmie
Enclosed the Scandinavian contract duly signed. Good that Ernest Lush can fly on the 29th – we can go together, can't we?
Edinburgh. I'm happy with 200 gns and 25% for broadcasts. I haven't a lot to do in the Chausson, but I leave it to you, luv.
Wired you tonight because Peter Diamand wants me to do my 3rd *Orfeo* on the 16th Jan and I just wanted to make sure that I don't have to leave for anything before the 17th. Okeydoke? I take it my 1st engagement after that is Paris 23rd Jan?
BBC North Region. OK for broadcast with Gerald 29th December – 'spleasure.
All goes well here – lovely concerts and a day off in between. Weather unpronounceable!!
Hope your Momma is better, love.
Love from us both,
Kaff

*Monday [December 1950] American Hotel, Amsterdam
My dear Emmie
I keep wondering how your Momma is, but haven't heard a word. I hope no news is good news, love.
Enclosed two letters with which, perhaps, you will deal, eh!
All is grand here, except the fog, Gerald and I getting more rotund with every meal! Four concerts safely over, and all gone well, praise be. Home on the 14th and look forward to seeing you.
Much love
K.K.

P.S. What do we do with Netherwood and his intimate association with me for 20 years? I'll sue 'im! Don't mind doing it for him at a proper fee, but perhaps he's mistaking me for Clara Butt or Muriel Foster??

P.S.S. Would be glad if Mr Reed will book an inside single first mit bath – what the heck! It comes off mi Income Tax. I'm glad he's interested in my passage!!

P.S.S.S. Will write to Bruno Walter myself re programme and his suggestions. OK?
TTFN

*5th January 1951 American Hotel, Amsterdam
Dearest Emmie
I don't mind the words of folk songs being printed – they like to have them when they're in another language (I'm talking about Zurich!)
I've just rung Paddy and she says 'Bernie' called round to see Pop – how terribly kind of her – I do appreciate it. Paddy says he's a lot better the last two days so that's a relief.
The flight was all right after the take off – though a young man in front lost all his Christmas cheer for the whole journey! But I'd had mi 'Quells' and I tucked in – I was so glad to be up and on an even keel! You're bound to come down once you're up, as the actress said to the bishop!
Emmie love, has your accountant made a mistake with Milan commission, £17.10.0. I think he's charging me 10%, and unless I am mistaken we arranged 5% for Europe, as most of the fee goes on accompanist, fares and hotels. It's so much more than Edinburgh, where I had a good fee and few expenses – thought I would ask before sending cheque.
All goes well here – working hard but treated with great care and all the others look as daft as I feel, so guess it's all right!
Yearning to see Op.4, 5 and 6 – look after yourself and much love to you and Bernie.
Kaff

*21 January 1951 Hotel Roblin, 6 Rue Chauveau-Lagarde, Paris 8
Dearest Emmie
I'm afraid 'Remanren' haven't got together after all, as I have just rung home, and it sounds as though Win is in bed with flu. She will be furious and disappointed. I hope you are keeping free from these so-and-so germs, the little budders are rampant, aren't they?
I rang home for all the things I might need, as the orchestral concert here isn't decided yet and I haven't had a word from Schuricht. So Gerald will bring everything I possess, including 'Che faro' and Lennox Berkeley and *Frauenliebe* etc.
I'm THRILLED with my French lessons with Pierre B[ernac]. He roared with mirth at first – but in the nicest way! – but now he's getting quite excited, and even I, by a series of lip contortions that might prove serious if indulged in too long, can hear an improvement. I would love a lesson a day for twelve months, then I would feel I was really getting somewhere! I passed on your message and he purred with pleasure – tell Miss Lereculey to look out! I'm after her! I don't really mind losing money here, it's such a gorgeous city! Why not pop over for Feb 16–18th????? Be a devil – I shall have found all the good eating places by then!
Now here is a programme for Italy – I honestly don't know where that programme came from – and I will stick to this for all the recitals unless they decree otherwise. I shall have everything with me if they insist.

1 Where'er you walk – Handel (*Semele*)
Like as the lovelorn turtle – Handel (*Atalanta*)
Hark the ech'ing air – Purcell (*Fairie Queene*)
Mad Bess – Purcell arr. Britten

2 Pur dicesti – Lotti
Lasciatemi morire – Monteverdi
Che farò – Gluck (*Orfeo*)

3 Gretchen am Spinnrade – Schubert
Lachen und Weinen "
Der Musensohn "
Sonntag – Brahms
Botschaft "

4 Love is a bable – Parry
The fairy lough – Stanford
Ca' the Yowes – arr. Jacobson
The Spanish lady – arr Hughes

That should keep 'em going a bit, shouldn't it? Realised I couldn't stay in Zurich as I have rehearsal.
Hating the thought of catching a 7.30 train!! Middle of the *nuit*!
I think that's all for the moment, love. All going beautifully so far – wish you were here.
Much love
Kathleen

*28th January 1951 Dolder Grand Hotel, Zurich
Dearest Emmie
I KNEW you wouldn't let me have all my own way with Pierre Bernac!!! Oh! clever Emmie! T'will be lovely to see you. wish you could have been there for the recital – it did go with a wow – I think it was my new Maitland frock wot done it! – but I'll have to put my best foot forward for the 18th, so's not to let you down. OH! BOY! (Programme still not settled!!)
Oh! I've kept forgetting in all the excitement – it's not going to be possible for me to do Cheltenham July 3rd with Sir John. They have tried all ways to make it possible, but I'd just be worn out with rushing around madly. I am sorry, I've kept forgetting to tell you. Peter D[iamand] told me just before I left Holland. It will be nice in Holland in July – just *Orfeos* and oratorios and orchestral – no recitals.
Gerald played like an angel in Paris, and was a source of confidence and inspiration as ever! I could murder the man here in Zurich and he's not really bad – just dumb! and no soul to boot! O sole mio!
All tickets and arrangements doing fine and managed to change money, languages and trains twice from Paris to St Gallen, and still have 5 bags at the end of it. I think I'm a ruddy wizard! What I would do if everybody didn't speak English, I can't think!
I'm afraid I shall have as near-bunk-mate tomorrow to Rome Herr Klemperer!! And as he sets everything on fire by putting his cigs all over the place, anything may happen! But at least it may melt some of the avalanches!
God bless, love, and see you soon – whoopee!
Kaff

4 February 1951 Florence [postcard to Emmie Tillett]
Thank you so much for your lovely letter, darling. Win says you have been an absolute angel and I can't thank you enough ever, bless you, bless you. Can only feel deep gratitude that it was all so peaceful for our sweet 'Pop'. Apart from his anaemia, he had never really had an illness in his life – wasn't it amazing! Just hope I did the right thing by staying and didn't leave too much responsibility to Win.
All goes fairly well here tho' I think the Rome audience were rude and fairly ignorant! Started $^1/_4$ hour late, then still $^1/_3$ empty but filled up by the end. Critics raving but I couldn't get over the way the people talked and wandered about. Have never used my compelling eye so much!! Am ready for anything today with Mahler in Florence!! The Maitlands here and in Rome – absolute poppets.
Much, much love
Kaff

*6th February 1951 Grand Hotel Duomo, Milan
Dearest Emmie
Arrived safely here all by miself and still with five bags, and now know the Italian for porter, hurry up and go to blazes!, so I am managing fine.
To answer some of your queries, love:
Salzburg. No, because I will need both holiday and time to learn Edinburgh programme, so must keep August free, but thank you very much all the same ([*Lieder eines*] *fahrenden Gesellen* still too high).
Holland fee. If you could just send it home or give it to Win, she will keep it for me. I think there is some difficulty of sending it straight to [the] bank.
Sir John rehearsal. I would much prefer to leave the next day (19th); it's such a rush to get out of evening things and pack and catch a train, but if you feel I should, then of course I will. I think Win should get Monday off too. Tell her not to be so blooming conscientious!
I can rehearse all the 20th, 21st, 22nd and 23rd with JB and will travel to him if it helps.
OSLO Filharmonik programme. This is what I could do and provide my own parts (all strings).

Where'er you walk Handel 4 min
Cradle Song Wm Byrd $2^1/_2$ min
Dearest Consort Handel 6 min
Hark the Ech'ing Air Purcell 4 min

Water Boy Negro song 3 min
I have a bonnet Irish arr. Hughes $1^1/_2$ min
My Boy Willie arr. Sharp 3 min

Otherwise the Brahms *Serious Songs* take 23 minutes and I haven't my own parts, or for any other Purcell.
Would you say a big and sincere thank you to Miss Lereculey for her most lovely letter. I was most moved to receive it and to know she had taken time out of her busy life to write to me. It was kind of her – thank you very much.
Mr Gylling. I could do a radio $^1/_2$hr on the 16th April if that would be any good.
Ripley Choir. (Miss Lereculey). Would you tell her I can provide all my own parts for May 26th and that if it's all the same to Miss Whyte, I feel it would be a better programme to sing 'Where'er you walk', Cradle Song, and then 'Hark the Ech'ing Air' (Purcell), it being a lively end. But if she prefers 'Art thou troubled', it's all right because all the orchestrations are together. I will post them to her the end of April.

I think that's all, love – business at least.
The weather's just like Manchester here today, cold, raining, and terribly slushy. I hope there isn't too much sickness that you must cope with, and that you are keeping fit. Bless you again for everything and I look forward to Paris.
Much love, darling,
Kathleen
P.S. Rome a great success – also Florence. Critics in ecstasies, so that's summut!

*2 March [1951] [on tour in North of England]
Dearest Emmie
Herewith suggestion for Newcastle – June 7th. He's awful highbrow, ain't he?
The Lennox Berkeley are only for strings and not suitable with piano. I could do the Bliss if that would please him, but I've forgotten its proper title [*The Enchantress*], but Bernie would tell you. It's in a brown-backed manuscript copy with either a Novello or Boosey & Hawkes label, and it's something about frying mi lover in hot oil!
I would prefer to do that with the Brahms *Serious Songs*, but the Rubbra would be all too much religious.
Will you suggest this:

An die Leyer	Schubert	
Suleika	"	
Gretchen am Spinnrade	"	
Wanderers Nachtlied	"	
Der Musensohn	"	22 mins
Bliss		18 mins
Pauze		
Four Serious Songs	Brahms	23 mins

Or if he prefers a mixed group instead of the Serious Songs I could do

Ich ging mit Lust	Mahler	
Ich atmet einen Linden duft	Mahler	
Liebestreu	Brahms	
Dein blaues Auge	"	
Sonntag	"	
Botschaft	"	
Von ewiger Liebe	"	about 25 mins

If either of these are suitable will you send me a copy and I'll pop it, for posterity, in mi pocket book!
It's lovely to think Bernie is at home – a strong rock! – I hope she's happy and getting enough to eat!
All well here – it's gorgeous to be with Sir John – but he's shrunk inches!
I suppose it's not possible to fly direct to Cologne on the 15th? I seem to remember it isn't. Could you be an angel and let Mr Fineman know my time of arrival wherever and whenever it may be so that I may be met?
Much love
Kaff

*9 March 1951 [on tour in North of England]

Dear Miss Hurst

Thank you for your letter. I shall be happy to sing the *Alto Rhapsody* on the 23rd June for Mr Isaacs.

Would you please pass on this group for Mrs Tillett for the Danish broadcast.

Gretchen am Spinnrade	Schubert
Lachen und Weinen	"
Sonntag	Brahms
Botschaft	"

This is with piano to go alongside 'Inflammatus' and 'O Rust in the Lard'!

In haste

Sincerely

Kathleen Ferrier

*21 May 1951 2 Frognal Mansions, London NW3

Dear Miss Lereculey

Here is a programme – baht 'at – for Ilkley, September 12th. Phyllis Spurr is already booked for it, so that's fine.

Where'er you walk	Handel
Come to me soothing sleep	Handel
Hark the ech'ing air	Purcell
Mad Bess	Purcell
Frauenliebe und Leben	Schumann
Pauze!	
Après un rêve	Fauré
Lydia	"
Nell	"
Silent Noon	Vaughan Williams
Go not happy day	Frank Bridge
The little road to Bethlehem	Michael Head
Pretty ring time	Peter Warlock

I think that will be all right for Scarborough too, don't you? Goody, goody! Oh no! Gerald plays group at Scarborough so I'll leave out the Fauré there.

22nd June 1951

Dearest Emmie

I am so bad at saying 'thank you' in 'poisson', love, so I just wanted to write and say how your simply lovely party the other night just made my day and completed my cure! It was just right and so lovely and oh! so delicious. Thank you, dear Emmie, so very much – not only for this, but for our lovely weekends, for your care and concern, – and I shall never forget how you and Myra waited for me to come round from the anaesthetic.

Bless you for everything – I only wish I could take a little of the burden of your work from your shoulders, but August will come and I sincerely hope you will holiday then. I know you have a fantastico 'panel' doctor who works miracles, but I don't want him to have to resort to his magic for you. That is another thing I have to thank you for (it is unending!), and that is for the most wonderful doctoring it is possible for anyone to have, and for the friendship of such rare people.

Thank you, love, for everything and look after yourself, and as Bernie said to me in a letter she wrote to Holland 'for goodness sake don't mention this or I shall fall down the lavatory in embarrassment!'

God bless, love, and much, much love

Kaff

*9th July 1951 American Hotel, Amsterdam

Dearest Emmie

Thank you for your letters love, and here are a few replies first. I haven't heard direct from New York about the Little Orchestra Concert. I can still do the 20th, because if I'm in N.Y. I can pay my Income Tax in advance – that's the only real rush – but if you are writing to Mr Mertens it would perhaps be a good thing to mention it. Ta ever so for booking our singles – why not come too, love? Oooo! I would have you merry on champagne cocktails, and Miami and San Fran – two of the loveliest, hottest, sunniest places. Eh? Eh?!

OK for car from Liverpool to Kings Lynn

OK Bliss October 2nd

Alternative programme for Kings Lynn.

Where'er you walk	Handel
Like as the lovelorn turtle	Handel
Dido's Lament	Purcell
Mad Bess	Purcell
Pur dicesti	Lotti
Lasciatemi morire	Monteverdi
Che faro	Gluck
Ganymed	Schubert
Ich ging mit Lust	Mahler
Dein blaues Auge	Brahms
Botschaft	Brahms
Down by the Salley Gardens	Gurney
Go not happy day	Frank Bridge
Sleep	Peter Warlock
Pretty ring time	Peter Warlock

Sorry to have caused such a cafuffle here!

I'm going on my holidays on the 30th July. I'm going to Sussex for a few days with the whole Barbirolli family! But I don't think I should be much good for John Lowe on a Monday morning after these four days!! I don't mind keeping Kings Lynn especially as I have so little to sing in the Krips concert – I leave it to you.

All well here – still hoping you might just pop over tomorrow – but it really is a pretty awful production, so p'raps it's just as well if you don't.

I spend most of my time in bed in between whiles being thoroughly lazy. It's so tiring here,

being below sea level I suppose. Oh! so looking forward to coming home on Saturday – can I paint on Sunday? Is it a date, or is it awkward? Dying to see your masterpieces!
Been rehearsing with Klemperer this morning – took Bernie for safety and she hasn't yet regained her natural colour! He terrified her!!
Hope work is easing up a little bit for you now – thought and talked about you such a lot.
God bless, love
Much love
Kaff

*2nd August 1951 2 Frognal Mansions, London NW3
Dear Miss Lereculey
Herewith some programmes
Marple and Southall

Where'er you walk	Handel – *Semele*
Like as the lovelorn turtle	Handel – *Atalanta*
Dido's Lament	Purcell
Hark the ech'ing air	Purcell – *The Fairie Queene*
Frauenliebe und Leben	Schumann
Love is a bable	Parry
The Fairy lough	Stanford
Down by the Salley Gardens	Gurney
Pretty ring time	Warlock
Ca' the Yowes	arr. Jacobson
Kitty my love	arr. Hughes

Some more following, but I know you are waiting for these. In a rush!
Sincerely
Kathleen Ferrier

4th August [19]51 EMT/BB
Dear Miss Ferrier
We have received the enclosed contract from the Westdeutsche Konzertdirektion of Köln in respect of your engagement at Leverkusen on March 11th next, and we should be so glad if you will kindly sign the blue copy and return to us as soon as possible.
Mr Schulthess has also written asking for your recital programme for Fribourg and La Chaux-de-fonds, so perhaps you could let us have these, as the Societies wish to go ahead with their printing.
We have had a letter from the Secretary of the Swansea Festival, which reads as follows:-

> 'The Town Clerk has received a letter from various citizens in America who are coming to some of our Festival concerts. They pay a very high tribute to Kathleen Ferrier, and the Town Clerk thought it might be a good plan if we were to try and arrange to present one of them with her signed autograph'.

They enclose a copy of last year's programme, and ask if you would be so kind as to autograph your photograph, which we are sending you herewith.
Yours sincerely,
Ibbs and Tillett Ltd

7th August [1951] [letter from, first Bernie Holland, then Kathleen Ferrier]
Dear Emmie
Ta everso for votre grande carde de poste, prego! Hope you are having a wonderful time. I am expecting great things of your canals. At least I won't have to spend me hard earned pennies on bus fares to the Wallace Collection when I can see the Tilletts at Elm Tree Road.
Have had conversations slightly one-sided with Mona and Erica and all is well. I had Erica laughing 'cause I rang and asked her if she was cleaning the windows when it never ceased raining yesterday.
Kath spent the weekend at Seaford and had a wonderful time. Everything settled there most favourably. Will talk to you about it when you come back. She is sparking on all plugs and doing a good hour with Phyllis daily singing now, and I just cannot concentrate. The treatment isn't making her feel too poorly and everything is going along well. Your pan-doc left today.
My best love
Bernie

Hello love!
Ta ever so for the Van Gogh-like pitcher – hope the weather's cheered up for you now. It's leeeousy here, pouring and hailing.
Had a lovely weekend with the whole Barbirolli family and have never seen John and Evelyn happier. Ethel B[artlett]'s talking through her bleedin' hat or I'm a Dutchman. Your pan-doc was invited to supper there before bringing me home on Sunday and it was a riot. He talked French to Mrs B, Italian to an aunt, set puzzles for two kid relatives, offered to make reeds for Evelyn and talked fiddles and *Turandot* with John. It was a riotous success.
<u>Do</u> hope you are having a gorgeous time and thinking of you so much and so relieved you really managed to get away. I'm fine – just can't touch mi toes mitout bellowing, but guess that's just old age! Bernie's a jewel, a jewel, a jewel.
Bless you and much love
Kaff

13th August 1951 SEL/BB
Dear Miss Ferrier
Further to our conversation over the telephone when you agreed to the recital in Düsseldorf on March 10th, we cabled Mr Fineman to this effect, but in case you want a list of the engagements he has planned for you, they are as follows:-

<u>March 10th – Düsseldorf</u>
Recital Fee: awaiting Mr Fineman's confirmation
<u>March 11th – Leverkusen</u>
Lieder Abend DM1500 to include accompanist
<u>March 13th – Cologne</u>
Lieder Abend DM1500 to include accompanist
<u>March 14th–17th – Cologne</u>
Broadcast recording of Gluck's *Orpheus* sung in Italian DM2500
<u>March 19th & 20th – Baden-Baden</u>
Broadcast – Lieder Fee not yet fixed
<u>March 23rd – Baden-Baden</u>
Rehearsal March 21st & 22nd
Mahler's *Das Lied von der Erde* DM1500

March 24th – Frankfurt-on-Main
Brahms *Alto Rhapsody* and arias by Handel, Byrd and Purcell DM1500

Mr Fineman tells us that you can stay in Cologne, go by car to Düsseldorf and that Leverkusen is a suburb of Cologne, which will not involve any travelling, and according to the itinerary, you will stay there up to March 17th.
With regard to Income Tax, Mr Fineman tells us that unfortunately he has no influence in this matter, as they take 25% everywhere, and for this reason they have fixed your fee so that you get the most possible.
Yours sincerely
Ibbs and Tillett Ltd

*14th August 1951 — 2 Frognal Mansions, London NW3
Dear Miss Lereculey

Dorchester September 18th

Where'er you walk	Handel – *Semele*
Like as the lovelorn turtle	Handel – *Atalanta* (by special request)
Dido's Lament	Purcell
Mad Bess	Purcell
Die junge Nonne	Schubert (by special request)
Lachen und Weinen	"
Suleika's zweiter Gesang	"
Ganymed	"
Der Musensohn	"
Silent Noon	Vaughan Williams
Pretty ring time	Peter Warlock
Down by the Salley Gardens	Ivor Gurney
Ca' the Yowes	Scottish
Kitty my love	Irish
Bobby Shaftoe	Northumbrian

It would be nice to stay with Mrs Higginson, but Bernie will probably be with me too, aussi Phyllis. If she can cope with us all that'll be fine. Will travel down the day of the concert.

Skipton January 27th 1952, and Belfast February 8th 1952
Where'er – in fact as for Dorchester

Fribourg and La Chaux de Fonds February 21st and 29th

Spring	Handel (*Ottone*)
Come to me soothing sleep	Handel (*Ottone*)
Dido's Lament	Purcell
Mad Bess	Purcell
Die junge Nonne	Schubert
Lachen und Weinen	"
Suleika's zweiter Gesang	"
Ganymed	"
Der Musensohn	"

Après un rêve	Fauré
Lydia	"
Nell	"
Silent Noon	Vaughan Williams
Go not happy day	Frank Bridge
Down by the Salley Gardens	Ivor Gurney
Pretty ring time	Peter Warlock

Klever Kaff!! I'm feeling very virtuous, having got these off mi chest, but fingers slightly crossed in lieu of objections! This'll do for Zurich too I think, and will you ask Gerald if he can do these dates with me – I don't mind the expense, but I should strangle Walter Lang – and though it would be good publicity, it's not good for me blood pressure! He (Gerald) is already reserved for the German tour.
TTFN
Yours sincerely
Kathleen

*3rd September 1951 6 Heriot Row, Edinburgh
Dear Miss Lereculey
Herewith Croydon. I haven't seen Gerald, but I'm sure he'd hate to play solos, don't you think?

Prepare thyself Zion	*Xmas Oratorio*	Bach
Like as the lovelorn Turtle	*Atalanta*	Handel
Hark the ech'ing Air	*Fairie Queene*	Purcell
Frauenliebe und Leben		Schumann
She walked thro' the fair		Irish arr. Hughes
I once loved a boy		"
The Spanish Lady		"

Carnforth as for Croydon
Carlisle Have seen Gerald and I believe he has already wired you, so I will do the date that is convenient for him. Okeydoke?
Best wishes to you
Very sincerely
Kathleen Ferrier

*21st September 1951 SEL/NH
Dear Miss Ferrier British Music Society of Northern Ireland
With reference to your engagement with the above society in Belfast on Friday February 8th, our clients have written to say they are a little disappointed with the programme you submitted, as it is very similar to the one which you gave them two years ago. They do not feel particularly happy about your last group (folksongs), which they do not think suitable for their purpose, and they ask if you would change Dido's Lament, which was included with your previous programme, also if you would substitute for your third group a group of songs by Mahler or Brahms, as they feel one of these composers is much more worthy of your art than the items which you suggested.

Our clients are having a committee meeting on the 27th instant (next Thursday) and would like to have some news before then, so would you be good enough to give the matter your early attention.

Newcastle January 17th

Would you kindly bear in mind that for this engagement the committee would like you to give a Lieder recital including a cycle not disconnected songs, and if you would be good enough to let us have suggestions we should be grateful.
Yours sincerely
[Sadie Lereculey]

*24th September 1951 2 Frognal Mansions, London NW3
My dear Emmie
I signed the enclosed cheque by mistake when it was given to me at the BBC in Edinburgh, so could I pass it on to you to cope mit, love?

Belfast 8th February 1952

OH! for ever more!! I have not sung Dido before in Belfast, and if they look at their programmes they wouldn't get their facts wrong. I have sung Mad Bess – probably the first time they ever heard it, and it's worth hearing twice, otherwise there is no resemblance to the 1949 programme. Anyhow let's see if this will be Third Programme enough for them.

Die junge Nonne	Schubert
Lachen und Weinen	"
Suleika	"
Ganymed	"
Der Musensohn	"
Poème de l'Amour et la Mer	Chausson
Four Serious Songs	Brahms

Gerald suggested we do the Chausson sometime – it was originally piano, and it will be a lovely rest for me 'cos it's nearly all piano – only don't tell them!!

Newcastle January 17th

Die junge Nonne	Schubert
Lachen und Weinen	"
Suleika	"
Ganymed	"
Der Musensohn	"
Frauenliebe und Leben	Schumann
Four Serious Songs	Brahms

Skipton January 27th

Would you ask them if they would like *Frauenliebe und Leben*, Schumann, which is eight songs. Would have to shorten the other groups or it really would go on all night!

Where'er you walk (*Semele*)	Handel
Like as the lovelorn Turtle (*Atalanta*)	Handel

Dido's Lament (*Dido and Aeneas*)	Purcell
Mad Bess	Purcell
Ganymed	Schubert
Lachen und Weinen	"
Suleika's zweiter Gesang	"
Der Musensohn	"
Frauenliebe und Leben	Schumann
Silent Noon	Vaughan Williams
The Fairy Lough	Stanford
Love is a bable	Parry
Kitty my love	arr. Hughes

Hope these several programmes straighten things out a bit.
Sincerely
Kathleen Ferrier

*25th September 1951 2 Frognal Mansions, London NW3
Dearest Emmie
Could you cope with the enclosed for me, love? And I have found a letter from Victor Olof in Vienna: quote:! "I have fixed the recording of *Das Lied* for May 12th–18th next year with the VPO. The Committee are delighted of the opportunity for a concert on the 18th with the general rehearsal on the 17th. Orchestral rehearsals will begin on the 12th so it will not be necessary, I don't suppose, for you to be there until the 14th. However Mr Hanyl (?) will discuss the details with Bruno in Lugano as he is going there to see him for his 75th birthday" – end quote.
Orl-rite love? Victor should be home tomorrow for just ten days, if you need to contact him.
I am up-to-date with my letters – it's the first time I ever remember it in the last ten years! It mikes yer fink!
Much love, sweetie pie!
Kaff

*13th November 1951 SEL/NH
Dear Miss Ferrier Cleethorpes String Orchestral Society
We should like to have your suggested programme for the recital you are giving for the above society with Gerald Moore on Monday January 14th next, so would you be good enough to let us have this information as soon as possible? At the same time perhaps you could put down on a piece of paper the details, if any, of the *Poème de l'Amour et de la Mer* by Chausson which you are singing in Belfast on February 8th.
You are, of course, singing in Carlisle on January 19th with Gerald Moore, so perhaps you would let us know what programme you would like us to send to Miss Simpson.
Yours sincerely
Ibbs & Tillett Ltd [Sadie Lereculey]

*24th November 1951 2 Frognal Mansions, London NW3

Dear Mrs Tillett

Re your letter of the 25th Oct., asking me to include another aria for Frankfurt. I could finish the group with 'Che faro senza Euridice' (*Orfeo* by Gluck), which would bring it up to the time required.

Here are some programmes.

Cleethorpes January 14th 1952

Where'er you walk	*Semele*	Handel
Come to me soothing sleep	*Atalanta*	Handel
Hark the ech'ing Air	*Fairie Queene*	Purcell
Mad Bess		Purcell arr. Britten
Gretchen am Spinnrade		Schubert
Heidenröslein		"
Suleika		"
Der Musensohn		"
Four Serious Songs		Brahms
Silent Noon		Vaughan Williams
The little road to Bethlehem		Michael Head
Pretty ring time		Peter Warlock
Kitty my love, will you marry me?		Irish arr. Hughes

Carlisle January 19th 1952

Bist du bei mir		Bach
Like as the lovelorn turtle	*Atalanta*	Handel
Hark the ech'ing Air	*Fairie Queene*	Purcell
Mad Bess		Purcell arr. Britten
Frauenliebe und Leben		Schumann
Gretchen am Spinnrade		Schubert
Lachen und Weinen		"
Der Musensohn		"
Sonntag		Brahms
Botschaft		"
Ca' the Yowes		Scottish arr. Jacobson
Blow the wind southerly		Northumbrian arr. Whittaker
The Keel Row		"
Kitty my love, will you marry me?		Irish arr. Hughes

If the Brahms *Serious Songs* are preferred, I can easily change the programme. I will pass on a copy of the Chausson *Poème* today to Miss Hurst, who will be visiting us to see our offspring, one Miss Rose Ferramond!

Sincerely

Kathleen Ferrier

*31st December 1951 2 Frognal Mansions, London NW3

My dear Emmie

Can you have a look at the Promotion of New Music letter for me and advise me as to reply thereto???? Ta ever so! Also this letter from Vienna is just a corroboration of the arrangements made with Bruno Walter. I haven't replied yet, as I thought you would want to see it first as no fee is mentioned, but I suppose it is all right?

Have replied to Mr Sykes saying you arrange all my work and that you will contact him. OK?

Yours etc

Kathleen Ferrier

[undated]

Would you pass on a message to Mrs Tillett re Berne 23 Feb 1952. Here is programme I suggest: 'Dearest consort' (Handel), 'Hark the ech'ing air' (Purcell), 'Che faro' (Gluck) Brahms *Alto Rhapsody*

I have my own parts for the first group. If they insist on two Handels instead of Handel and Purcell, I can sing 'Where'er you walk' and then 'Dearest consort' and 'Che faro', but the first is more varied.

I think that is all, isn't it? It was grand to see you all today – bless you for everything!

Love

Kathleen

22 April 1952 2 Frognal Mansions, London NW3

Dear Miss Ferrier

Would you just be so kind as to let us know what you feel about the following proposal:

We have been asked to pencil your services for a performance of *Messiah* which will take place at the request of Queen Elizabeth, the Queen Mother in the Little Chapel in Windsor Park on Sunday afternoon November 2nd next and Mr Laurence West, who is arranging this performance, would very much like you to take part. There is of course no fee attached as this is almost by way of a command performance. You may care to know that Isobel Baillie, William Herbert and Owen Brannigan have all expressed a wish to give this performance, but we have told Mr West that we must consult you before giving him a definite reply.

Queen Elizabeth, the Queen Mother will of course be present, but it is not known at this stage whether any other members of the Royal Family will also attend.

Yours sincerely

Ibbs and Tillett Ltd

S E Lereculey (Director)

*22 July 1952 2 Frognal Mansions, London NW3

My dear Emmie

Here are a whole lot of bad-to-decipher letters. The ones with 'write Ibbs and Tillett' on have been answered by Bernie. Could you make excuses for me on grounds of not accepting recitals at the moment or sump'n? And if you could have the Hanzl letter deciphered, that would be a help. It might contain a most interesting proposal – I should hate to miss that!!

The rest are signed contracts, and I am working on programmes at the moment and will let you have them in a day or two. Okeydoke?

Luv

Kaff

P.S. Re my relations – see United Appeal – no Mildreds in our family – only Fannys and Nancys!

*14th October 1952

Dearest Emmie

Herewith some programmes

Highgate November 15th

Where'er you walk	Handel
Come to me soothing sleep	Handel
Hark the ech'ing air	Purcell
Mad Bess	Purcell
Frauenliebe und Leben	Schumann
Après un rêve	Fauré
Lydia	"
Nell	"
Love is a bable	Parry
October Valley	Michael Head
Go not happy day	Frank Bridge
Pretty ring time	Peter Warlock

Carlisle December 11th

Prepare thyself Zion *Xmas Oratorio*	Bach
Come to me soothing sleep	Handel
Pur dicesti	Lotti
Che faro (*Orfeo*)	Gluck
An die Musik	Schubert
Die junge Nonne	Schubert
Wanderers Nachtlied	Schubert
Erlkönig	Schubert
Four Serious Songs	Brahms
Love is a bable	Parry
Go not happy day	Frank Bridge
The Little Road to Bethlehem	Michael Head
Pretty ring time	Peter Warlock

Leigh November 30th

Bist du bei mir	Bach
Like as the lovelorn turtle	Handel
Hark the ech'ing Air	Purcell
Pur dicesti	Lotti
Che faro (*Orfeo*)	Gluck
Frauenliebe und Leben	Schumann
or	
Four Serious Songs	Brahms
or	
Love is a bable	Parry
October Valley	Michael Head
Go not happy day	Frank Bridge
The Fairy Lough	Stanford
Pretty ring time	Peter Warlock

Now that's a good job done, ain't it, except that I haven't mentioned any duets – perhaps Richard [? Lewis – tenor] has some ideas?
Could you answer the enclosed for me please?
Did we tell you that Hilda Gélis-Didot died a few days ago? We had a letter from a friend. She had a heart attack and a stroke. Won't she be missed? I think she was the loveliest, warmest person.
Much love, sweetie
Kaff

*14th January 1953
My dear Emmie
Could you answer these enclosed letters for me, please?
I have had a letter from Bernard Miles asking me to sing in the City in May, June or July, but have said I haven't a Friday in May and will be in Rhodesia in June. Okeydoke luv?
In haste
Love
Kaff
PS Shan't be able to go to Aldeburgh if I go to Rhodesia, eh?

Select Bibliography

Arditi, Luigi, *My Reminiscences* (Skeffington and Son, London, 1896)

Aronson, Rudolph, *Theatrical and Musical Memoirs* (McBride, Nast and Co., New York, 1913)

Baillie, Isobel, *Never Sing Louder than Lovely* (Hutchinson, London, 1982)

Baker, Janet, *Full Circle* (Julian McRae, London, 1982)

Boughton, Rutland, *Death and Resurrection of the Musical Festival* (William Reeves, London, 1913)

Button, Stuart W., *Julian Bream: The Foundations of a Musical Career* (Scolar Press, London, 1997)

Buttrose, Charles, *Playing for Australia* (Australian Broadcasting Company/Macmillan, Sydney, 1982)

Cardus, Neville (ed.), *Kathleen Ferrier: A Memoir* (Hamish Hamilton, London, 1954)

Cohen, Harriet, *A Bundle of Time* (Faber, London, 1969)

Conway, Helen, *Sir John Pritchard: His Life in Music* (London, 1993)

Cooper, Joseph, *Facing the Music* (Weidenfeld and Nicolson, London, 1979)

Coward, Henry, *Reminiscences of Henry Coward* (Curwen, London, 1919)

Cox, David, *The Henry Wood Proms* (BBC, London, 1980)

Crimp, Bryan, *Solo: The Biography of Solomon* (Appian Publications and Recordings, Hexham, 1994)

D'Alvarez, Marguerite, *Forsaken Altars* (Rupert Hart-Davis, London, 1954)

Davison, James W., *From Mendelssohn to Wagner* (William Reeves, London, 1912)

Dawson, Peter, *Fifty Years of Song* (Hutchinson, London, 1951)

Diehl, Alice M., *Musical Memories* (Macmillan, London, 1897)

Diehl, Alice M., *The True Story of my Life* (Bodley Head, London, 1908)

Dressel, Dettmar, *Up and Down the Scale* (Selwyn and Blount, London, 1937)

Easton, Carol, *Jacqueline du Pré* (Summit Books, London, 1989)

Eckersley, Roger, *BBC and All That* (Sampson Low, London, 1945)

Edwards, R.A., *And the Glory: The Huddersfield Choral Society 1836–1986* (Maney, Leeds, 1985)

Ehrlich, Cyril, *The Music Profession in Britain Since the Eighteenth Century* (OUP, Oxford, 1985)

Ehrlich, Cyril, *First Philharmonic* (OUP, Oxford, 1995)

Elkin, Robert, *Queen's Hall: 1893–1941* (Rider, London, 1944)

Falkner, Julia, *Keith Falkner* (Thames Publishing, London, 1998)

Ferguson, Howard, *Music, Friends and Places* (Thames Publishing, London, 1997)

Ferrier, Winifred, *The Life of Kathleen Ferrier* (Hamish Hamilton, London, 1955)

Fifield, Christopher, *True Artist and True Friend: A Biography of Hans Richter* (Clarendon Press, Oxford, 1993)

Fifield, Christopher, *Letters and Diaries of Kathleen Ferrier* (Boydell and Brewer, Woodbridge, 2003)

Finck, Henry T., *Success in Music and How it is Won* (Scribner, New York, 1909)

Foreman, Lewis, *Music in England 1885–1920* (Thames Publishing, London, 1994)
Foster, Roland, *Come Listen to my Song* (Collins, London, 1949)
Hambourg, Mark, *From Piano to Forte* (Cassell, London, 1931)
Hammond, Joan, *A Voice, A Life* (Gollancz, London, 1970)
Hill, Ralph (ed.), *Music 1951* (Penguin, London, 1951)
Hurok, Sol, *Impresario* (Macdonald, London, 1947)
Jefferson, Alan, *Lotte Lehmann* (Julia Macrae, London, 1988)
Joel, John, *I Paid the Piper* (Howard Baker, London, 1970)
Kuhe, Wilhelm, *My Musical Recollections* (Bentley, London, 1896)
Lara, Adelina de, *Finale* (Burke, London, 1955)
Lassimonne, Denise (ed.), *Myra Hess by her Friends* (Vanguard Press, New York, 1966)
Lebrecht, Norman, *When the Music Stops* (Simon and Schuster, London, 1996)
Leonard, Maurice, *Kathleen: The Life of Kathleen Ferrier (1912–1953)* (Hutchinson, London, 1988)
Lucas Ogdon, Brenda and Kerr, Michael, *Virtuoso, the Story of John Ogdon* (Hamish Hamilton, London, 1981)
Lympany, Moura, *Moura, Her Autobiography* (Peter Owen, London, 1991)
Macleod, Joseph, *The Sisters D'Aranyi* (Allen and Unwin, London, 1969)
Mackerness, E.D., *A Social History of English Music* (Routledge, London, 1964)
Mapleson, J.H., *The Mapleson Memoirs* (Remington, London, 1888)
Maretzek, Max, *Crotchets and Quavers* (S. French, New York, 1855)
McKenna, Marian, *Myra Hess: A Portrait* (Hamish Hamilton, London, 1976)
Moiseiwitsch, Maurice, *Moiseiwitsch* (Muller, London, 1965)
The Monthly Musical Record (London, February 1932)
Moore, Gerald, *Am I Too Loud?* (Hamish Hamilton, London, 1962)
Moore, Gerald, *Farewell Recital* (Hamish Hamilton, London, 1978)
Moore, Gerald, *Furthermoore* (Hamish Hamilton, London, 1983)
Moore, Jerrold Northrop (ed.), *Music and Friends: Letters to Adrian Boult* (Hamish Hamilton, London, 1979)
Newton, Ivor, *At the Piano* (Hamish Hamilton, London, 1966)
O'Connor, Garry, *The Pursuit of Perfection. A Life of Maggie Teyte* (Gollancz, London, 1979)
Orchard, William Arundel, *The Distant View* (Currawong, Sydney, 1943)
Parrott, Jasper with Ashkenazy, Vladimir, *Beyond Frontiers* (Collins, London, 1984)
Pirouet, Edmund, *Heard Melodies are Sweet* (The Book Guild, Lewes, 1998)
Ponder, Winifred, *Clara Butt: Her Life Story* (Harrap, London, 1928)
du Pré, Hilary and du Pré, Piers, *Jacqueline de Pré: A Genius in the Family* (Chatto and Windus, London, 1997)
Primrose, William, *Walk on the North Side* (Brigham Young University Press, Provo, 1978)
Rigby, Charles, *Kathleen Ferrier: A Biography* (Robert Hale, London, 1955)
Rivière, Jules, *My Musical Life and Recollections* (Sampson Low, London, 1893)
Ronald, Landon, *Myself and Others* (Sampson Low, London, 1931)
Rosen, Carole, *The Goossens: A Musical Century* (André Deutsch, London, 1993)
Saerchinger, César, *Artur Schnabel: A Biography* (Cassell, London, 1957)
Santley, Charles, *Student and Singer* (Arnold, London, 1892)
Santley, Charles, *Reminiscences of my Life* (Pitman, London, 1909)
Sewell, G.F., *History of the Bradford Festival Choral Society* (Sewell, Bradford, 1907)

Slasberg, Terry, *The Pleasure was Mine … 40 Years a Concert Agent* (Thames Publishing, London, 1993)
Smith, Cyril, *Duet for Three Hands* (Angus and Robertson, London, 1958)
Snowman, Daniel, *The Amadeus Quartet: The Men and their Music* (Robson Books, London, 1981)
Spark, Frederick and Bennett, Joseph, *History of Leeds Musical Festivals 1858–1889* (Spark, Leeds, 1892)
Strutt, William Maitland, *Reminiscences of a Musical Amateur* (Macmillan, London, 1915)
Temianka, Henri, *Facing the Music* (David McKay, New York, 1973)
Tertis, Lionel, *My Viola and I* (Paul Elek, London, 1974)
Teyte, Maggie, *Star on the Door* (Puttnam, London, 1958)
Tortelier, Paul and Blum, David, *Paul Tortelier: A Self-portrait* (Heinemann, London, 1984)
Venables, L.C., *Choral and Orchestral Societies* (Curwen, London, 1886)
Waters, Thorold, *Much Besides Music* (Georgian House, Melbourne, 1951)
Who's Who in Music, ed. H. Saxe Wyndham (Pitman, London, 1915)
Who's Who in Music, ed. Landon Ronald (Shaw, London, 1935)
Who's Who in Music, ed. L.G. Pine (Shaw, London, 1949–50)
Wilson, Elizabeth, *Jacqueline du Pré* (Weidenfeld and Nicolson, London, 1998)
Wyndham, H. Saxe, *August Manns and the Saturday Concerts* (Walter Scott Publishing, London, 1909)
Young, Percy M., *The Concert Tradition* (Routledge and Keegan Paul, London, 1965)

General Index

Author's note: With the exception of Appendix 7 (pages 465–7), this index does not include the names of artists listed in the selection of Ibbs and Tillett's brochures to be found between pages 373 and 509, i.e. Appendices 1–6 and 8–10, neither does it include composers unless they are also performers. Consistency of spelling of names has not always been easy to achieve, as either the agency or the artists themselves sometimes changed or varied them.